Can we be controlled by subliminal messages? p. 125

What happens when we occasionally give in to children's tantrums for the sake of peace and quiet? p. 164

Why do we remember some things easily and others only if we study hard? p. 183

Why don't we have one big ear—perhaps above our one nose? p. 141

Should we physically punish children to change their behavior? p. 166

Can a good night's sleep improve test grades? p. 185

How do we experience pain, and how might we control it? p. 143

Why are some memories so much more crisp and clear than others? p. 189

What would it be like to live without being able to sense the positions of your limbs when you wake during the night? p. 147

Does the frequent pairing of red and sex—with Valentine's hearts, red-light districts, and red lipstick— naturally enhance men's attraction to women? p. 170

What causes déjà vu? p. 191

Why are habits so hard to break? p. 156

Can objects, sights, and smells associated with sexual pleasure become conditioned stimuli for sexual arousal? p. 159

Continued inside back cover.

PSYCHOLOGY
in everyday life
SECOND EDITION

David G. Myers

Hope College
Holland, Michigan

WORTH PUBLISHERS

Senior Publisher: Catherine Woods
Executive Editor: Kevin Feyen
Executive Marketing Manager: Katherine Nurre
Development Editors: Christine Brune, Nancy Fleming
Media Editor: Sharon Prevost
Supplements Editor: Betty Probert
Photo Editor: Bianca Moscatelli
Photo Researcher: Donna Ranieri
Art Director: Babs Reingold
Cover Designers: Lyndall Culbertson and Babs Reingold
Interior Designers: Lissi Sigillo, Lyndall Culbertson, and
    Babs Reingold
Interior Layout Designer: Lee Ann McKevitt
Chapter Opener Designer: Lyndall Culbertson
Associate Managing Editor: Tracey Kuehn
Project Editor: Dana Kasowitz
Illustration Coordinator: Bill Page
Illustrations: TSI Graphics, Keith Kasnot, Don Stewart
Production Manager: Sarah Segal
Composition: TSI Graphics
Printing and Binding: RR Donnelley

Credits for the cover, endpages, chapter beginnings, and
page 287 appear on p. xxxix, which constitutes an extension
of this copyright page.

Library of Congress Control Number: 2010942207

ISBN-13: 978-1-4292-6394-8
ISBN-10: 1-4292-6394-6

Printed in the United States of America

All royalties from the sale of this book are assigned to the David
and Carol Myers Foundation, which exists to receive and distribute
funds to other charitable organizations.

Worth Publishers
41 Madison Avenue
New York, NY 10010
www.worthpublishers.com

for Kevin Feyen, with gratitude for a decade
of superb support and faithful friendship

about the author

David Myers received his psychology Ph.D. from the University of Iowa. He has spent his career at Hope College, Michigan, where he has taught dozens of introductory psychology sections. Hope College students have invited him to be their commencement speaker and voted him "outstanding professor." In 2010, Myers was named to the FABBS (Federation of Associations in Behavioral and Brain Sciences) Foundation's Gallery of Scientists—a program that recognizes "scientists who have made important and lasting contributions to the sciences of mind, brain, and behavior." In 2011, he received the Society for Personality and Social Psychology's Award for Distinguished Service on Behalf of Social-Personality Psychology.

With support from National Science Foundation grants, Myers' scientific articles have appeared in more than two dozen scientific periodicals, including *Science, American Scientist, Psychological Science,* and the *American Psychologist.* In addition to his scholarly writing and his textbooks for introductory and social psychology, he also digests psychological science for the general public. His writings have appeared in three dozen magazines, from *Today's Education* to *Scientific American.* He also has authored five general audience books, including *The Pursuit of Happiness* and *Intuition: Its Powers and Perils.*

David Myers has chaired his city's Human Relations Commission, helped found a thriving assistance center for families in poverty, and spoken to hundreds of college and community groups. Drawing on his experience, he also has written articles and a book *(A Quiet World)* about hearing loss, and he is advocating a transformation in American assistive listening technology (see www.hearingloop.org).

He bikes to work year-round and plays daily pick-up basketball. David and Carol Myers have raised two sons and a daughter. In 2009, he and three of his family hiked Scotland's 95-mile West Highland Way.

brief contents

contents

CHAPTER 3
Developing Through the Life Span 62

CHAPTER 4
Gender and Sexuality 100

CHAPTER 5
Sensation and Perception 122

CHAPTER 6
Learning 154

CHAPTER 7
Memory 180

CHAPTER 8
Thinking, Language, and Intelligence 204

CHAPTER 9

Motivation and Emotion 236

CHAPTER 10

Stress, Health, and Human Flourishing 272

CHAPTER 11

Personality 292

CHAPTER 12
Psychological Disorders 316

CHAPTER 13
Therapy 350

CHAPTER 14
Social Psychology 376

APPENDIX A
Psychology at Work 411

APPENDIX B
Answers to "The Big Picture" Questions 421

preface

"THERE ARE STILL two sorts of jobs," wrote C. S. Lewis in *The World's Last Night*. "Of one sort, a [person] can truly say, 'I am doing work which is worth doing. It would still be worth doing if nobody paid for it. But as I have no private means, and need to be fed and housed and clothed, I must be paid while I do it.' The other kind of job is that in which people do work whose sole purpose is that of the earning of money; work which need not be, ought not be, or would not be, done by anyone in the whole world unless it were paid."

We who teach psychology are blessed to have the first sort of job. We are called to study the most fascinating subject on Earth and to discern and communicate its wisdom. By so doing, we also aim to expand minds, provoke thought, deepen understanding, increase compassion, excite curiosity, and supplement intuition with critical thinking. To assist teachers of psychology in this endeavor is, for me, a great privilege.

Psychology is indeed fascinating, and so relevant to our everyday lives. Psychology's insights can help us to be better students, more tuned-in friends, more effective co-workers, and wiser parents. With this new edition, I hope to captivate students with what psychologists are learning about our human nature, to help them think more like psychological scientists, and, as the title implies, to help them relate psychology to their own lives—their thoughts, feelings, and behaviors.

For those of you familiar with my other introductory psychology texts, you may be surprised at how very different this text is. I have created this uniquely student-friendly book with the help of input from thousands of instructors and students (by way of surveys, focus groups, content and design reviews, and class testing).

What's New in the Second Edition?

In addition to the long, chapter-by-chapter list of Content Changes that follows this preface, other significant changes have been made to the overall format and presentation of this new second edition.

Inquiry-Based Study Aids Revised to Reflect Research on Effectiveness

My inquiry-based narrative style, now organized by more numerous and specific learning objective questions, is also now supported by new *In Your Everyday Life* questions and *The Big Picture* questions. The Everyday Life questions are designed to help students make the con-

cepts more personally meaningful, and therefore more memorable. These questions are also designed to function as excellent *discussion forum prompts* for online course components. The Big Picture questions offer the kind of self-testing shown by cognitive psychology research to improve retention—short-answer reviews of key concepts from each section, with answers included in Appendix B. In addition, to help students see just how applicable psychology's concepts are to everyday life, we have highlighted (in orange) many of the *application questions* that occur naturally in each chapter's narrative. Our student reviewers helped us select 50 of the most interesting applications for inclusion in the front and back endpapers of the text.

These new features enhance the survey-question-read-rehearse-review (SQ3R) format. Chapter outlines allow students to *survey* what's to come. Main sections begin with a learning objective *question* (now more carefully directed and appearing more frequently) that encourages students to *read* actively. Periodic Practice Tests (now with three different, pedagogically effective types of questions) and chapter-ending *Key Terms* lists encourage students to test themselves—*rehearsing* their understanding. Chapter-ending visual concept maps *review* the material and help students make meaningful connections to reinforce what they have learned. (See **FIGURES 1** and **2** for Practice Test and Concept Map samples.)

> Scattered throughout this book, students will find interesting and informative notes and quotes from researchers and others that will encourage them to be active learners and to apply their new knowledge to everyday life.

> key terms Look for complete definitions of each important term in a page corner near the term's introduction in the narrative.

b. biological
c. behavioral
d. social-cognitive

THE BIG PICTURE
12G. What does it mean to say that "depression is a whole-body disorder"?

IN YOUR EVERYDAY LIFE
- Can you think of a time when being in a sad mood has actually helped you in some ways? Did you reevaluate your situation or make new plans for the future?
- How has student life affected your moods?

FIGURE 1 • Sample of our Practice Test feature

Reorganized Chapters and 600 New Research Citations

Thousands of instructors and students have helped guide my creation of *Psychology in Everyday Life,* as have my own wide reading and daily correspondence. The result is a unique text, now thoroughly revised in this second edition, which includes 600 new research citations. Chapter 3, Developing Through the Life Span, has been heavily revised, with added emphasis on Adolescence and Emerging Adulthood. Chapter 5, Sensation and Perception, has been reorganized with the concepts fully integrated rather than presented as sensation followed by perception. Chapter 6, Learning, now includes a new section, Biology, Cognition, and Learning. Chapter 7, Memory, has been reorganized, and the memory models have been clarified. For a chapter-by-chapter list of significant content changes, see the **List of Changes** on page xxvii.

Coordinated and Improved Learning Objectives in the Text and Supplements

Learning objectives, in a student-friendly question format, appear at the beginning of main text sections and now more care-

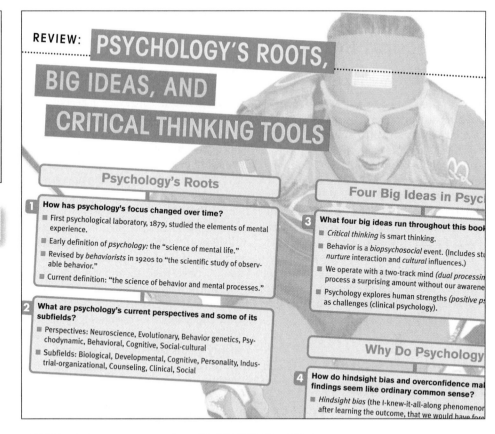

REVIEW: **PSYCHOLOGY'S ROOTS, BIG IDEAS, AND CRITICAL THINKING TOOLS**

Psychology's Roots

1 **How has psychology's focus changed over time?**
- First psychological laboratory, 1879, studied the elements of mental experience.
- Early definition of *psychology:* the "science of mental life."
- Revised by *behaviorists* in 1920s to "the scientific study of observable behavior."
- Current definition: "the science of behavior and mental processes."

2 **What are psychology's current perspectives and some of its subfields?**
- Perspectives: Neuroscience, Evolutionary, Behavior genetics, Psychodynamic, Behavioral, Cognitive, Social-cultural
- Subfields: Biological, Developmental, Cognitive, Personality, Industrial-organizational, Counseling, Clinical, Social

Four Big Ideas in Psyc

3 **What four big ideas run throughout this book**
- *Critical thinking* is smart thinking.
- Behavior is a *biopsychosocial* event. (Includes st nurture interaction and *cultural* influences.)
- We operate with a two-track mind (*dual processin* process a surprising amount without our awarene
- Psychology explores human strengths (*positive ps* as challenges (clinical psychology).

Why Do Psycholog

4 **How do hindsight bias and overconfidence ma findings seem like ordinary common sense?**
- *Hindsight bias* (the I-knew-it-all-along phenomeno after learning the outcome, that we would have fore

FIGURE 2 • Sample of our concept map Review feature

fully direct students to the key concepts and ideas they need to glean from each section. (These questions are repeated and answered in the concept map-style Review at the end of each chapter.) Those same learning objectives appear in *statement* format in the Test Bank, Study Guide, Instructor's Resources, and Lecture Guides so that instructors may organize their courses more easily.

More Design Innovations

With help from student and instructor design reviewers, the new second edition retains the best of the easy-to-read three-column design but with a new look that makes navigation easier, calls attention to each page's most important features, ties images and figures more closely to the associated narrative, and

integrates a sea-change of contemporary new photos.

Our three-column format is rich with visual support. It responds to students' expectations, based on what they have told us about their reading, both online and in print. The narrow column width eliminates the strain of reading across a wide textbook page. Illustrations often appear within the pertinent text column, which helps students see them in the appropriate context. Key terms are defined in page corners near where they are introduced.

In written reviews, students compared our three-column design with a traditional one-column design (without knowing which was ours). They unanimously preferred the three-column design. It was, they said, "less intimidating" and "less overwhelming" and it "motivated" them to read on.

What Continues in the Second Edition?

Writing

As with the first edition, I've written this book to be optimally accessible. The vocabulary is sensitive to students' widely varying reading levels and backgrounds. And this book is much briefer than many texts on the market, making it easier to fit into one-term courses. With only 14 chapters and 429 pages, this is not the book for those wanting encyclopedic coverage. Rather, my goal was to select the most humanly significant topics. I continually asked myself while working, "Would an educated person need to know this? Would this help students live better lives?"

Culture and Gender— No Assumptions

Even more than in my other texts, I have written *Psychology in Everyday Life* with the diversity of my student readers in mind.

- *Gender:* Extensive coverage of gender roles and the increasing diversity of choices men and women can make.
- *Culture:* No assumptions about readers' cultural backgrounds or experiences.
- *Economics:* No references to back yards, summer camp, vacation cruises.
- *Education:* No assumptions about past or current learning environments; writing is accessible for all.
- *Physical Abilities:* No assumptions about full vision, hearing, movement.
- *Life Experiences:* Examples are included from urban, suburban, and rural/outdoors settings.
- *Family Status:* Examples and ideas are made relevant for all students, whether they have children or are still living at home, are married or cohabiting or single; no assumptions about sexual orientation.

Four Big Ideas

I've often heard from instructors struggling to weave psychology's disparate parts into a cohesive whole for students, and from students struggling to make sense of all the pieces. In *Psychology in Everyday Life,* I have introduced four of psychology's big ideas as one possible way to make connections among all the concepts. These ideas are presented in Chapter 1 and gently integrated throughout the text.

1. Critical Thinking Is Smart Thinking

I love to write in a way that gets students thinking and keeps them active as they read. I have tried to show students not just the outcome of research, but how the research process works. Students will see how the science of psychology can help them evaluate competing ideas and highly publicized claims—ranging from intuition, subliminal persuasion, and ESP, to astrology, alternative therapies, and repressed and recovered memories.

In *Psychology in Everyday Life,* students have many opportunities to learn or practice their critical thinking skills:

- *Chapter 1 takes a unique, critical thinking approach to introducing students to psychology's research methods.* Understanding the weak points of our everyday intuition and common sense helps students see the need for psychological science. *Critical thinking* is introduced as a key term in this chapter (page 5).
- *"Thinking Critically About . . ." boxes* are found throughout the book. This feature models for students a critical approach to some key issues in psychology. For example, see "Thinking Critically About: How Much Credit (or Blame) Do Parents Deserve?" (Chapter 3) or "Thinking Critically About: Do Video Games Teach, or Release, Violence?" (Chapter 14). "Close-Up" boxes encourage application of the new concepts. For example, see "Close-Up: Some Weight-Loss Tips" in Chapter 9, or "Close-Up: Pets Are Friends, Too" in Chapter 10.

- *Detective-style stories* throughout the text get students thinking critically about psychology's key research questions. In Chapter 2, for example, I present as a puzzle the history of discoveries about where and how language happens in the brain. I guide students through the puzzle, showing them how researchers put all the pieces together.

- *"Try this" and "Think about it"* style discussions and side notes keep students active in their study of each chapter. I often encourage students to imagine themselves as participants in experiments. In Chapter 14, for example, students take the perspective of participants in a Solomon Asch conformity experiment, and later in one of Stanley Milgram's obedience experiments. I've also asked students to join the fun by taking part in activities they can try along the way. Here are a few examples: In Chapter 5, they try out a quick sensory adaptation activity. In Chapter 9, they try matching expressions to faces and test the effects of different facial expressions on themselves. In Chapter 11, students are asked to consider how they would construct a questionnaire for an Internet dating service.

- *Critical examinations of pop psychology* spark interest and provide important lessons in thinking critically about everyday topics. For example, Chapter 5 includes a close examination of ESP, and Chapter 7 addresses the controversial topic of repression of painful memories.

See **TABLE 1** for a complete list of this text's coverage of critical thinking topics.

2. Behavior Is a Biopsychosocial Event

Students will learn that we can best understand human behavior if we view it from three levels—the biological, psychological, and social-cultural. This concept is introduced in Chapter 1 and revisited throughout the text. Readers will see evidence of our human kinship—our shared biological heritage, our common mechanisms of seeing and learning, hungering and feeling, loving and hating. Yet they will also better understand the dimensions of our diversity—our *individual* diversity (in development and ability, temperament and personality, and disorders and health), our *gender* diversity (in emotions, abilities, and health), and our *cultural* diversity (in attitudes and expressive styles, child-rearing, and life priorities). **TABLE 2** on page xviii provides a list of integrated coverage of the cross-cultural perspective on psychology. **TABLE 3** on page xix lists the coverage of the psychology of women and men. Significant gender and cross-cultural examples and research are presented within the narrative. In addition, an abundance of photos, especially in the *Diverse Yet Alike* photo feature, showcases the diversity of cultures within North America and across the globe. These photos and their informative captions bring the pages to life, broadening students' perspectives in applying psychological science to their own world and to the worlds across the globe.

3. We Operate With a Two-Track Mind (Dual Processing)

Today's psychological science explores our *dual-processing* capacity. Our perception, thinking, memory, and attitudes all operate on two levels: the level of fully aware, conscious processing, and the behind-the-scenes level

TABLE 1	Critical Thinking

Critical thinking coverage may be found on the following pages:

A scientific model for studying psychology, p. 160
Are intelligence tests biased?, pp. 231–233
Are people who use antidepressants more likely to commit suicide?, p. 368
Are personality tests able to predict behavior?, p. 307
Are there parts of the brain we don't use?, p. 43
Attachment style, development of, pp. 75–78
Attention-deficit hyperactivity disorder (ADHD), p. 318
Causation and the violence-viewing effect, pp. 176–177
Classifying psychological disorders, p. 321
Confirmation bias, p. 209
Continuity vs. stage theories of development, pp. 87–88
Correlation and causation, pp. 14–15, 79, 85–86
Critical thinking, defined, p. 5
Critiquing the evolutionary perspective on sexuality, pp. 117–118
Discovery of hypothalamus reward centers, pp. 38–39
Do animals think and have language?, pp. 216–218
Do lie detectors lie?, p. 257
Do video games teach, or release, violence?, p. 396
Does catharsis relieve, or worsen, anger?, pp. 263, 396
Does meditation enhance immunity?, pp. 286–287
Effectiveness of "alternative" therapies, p. 363
Emotion and the brain, pp. 37–38
Emotional intelligence, pp. 222–223
Evolutionary science and human origins, p. 119

Extrasensory perception, pp. 150–151
Fear of flying vs. probabilities, p. 208
Freud's contributions, pp. 299–300
Genetic and environmental influences on schizophrenia, pp. 344–347
Group differences in intelligence, pp. 228–231
Heritability and weight, p. 247
Hindsight bias, p. 9
Hindsight explanations, pp. 117–118
How do nature and nurture shape prenatal development?, pp. 64–67
How do twin and adoption studies help us understand the effects of nature and nurture?, p. 69
How does the brain process language?, pp. 44–45
How much is gender socially constructed vs. biologically influenced?, pp. 103–106
How to be a "successful" astrologer, p. 306
How valid is the Rorschach inkblot test?, p. 298
Human curiosity, p. 1
Humanistic perspective, pp. 302–303
Hypnosis: dissociation or social influence?, p. 145
Illusory correlations, p. 15
Importance of checking fears against facts, p. 208
Influence of cognitive processes on behavior, pp. 169–173
Interaction of nature and nurture in overall development, pp. 80, 86
Is dissociative identity disorder a real disorder?, pp. 326–327
Is psychotherapy effective?, pp. 361–362
Is repression a myth?, p. 299

Limits of case studies, surveys, and naturalistic observation, pp. 12–13
Limits of intuition, p. 8
Nature and nurture's shared influence on gender and sexuality, p. 119
Nature, nurture, and perceptual ability, p. 138
Overconfidence, pp. 9–10, 209
Post-traumatic stress disorder (PTSD), p. 324
Powers and perils of intuition, pp. 210–212
Problem-solving strategies, p. 206
Psychic phenomena, p. 10
Psychology: a discipline for critical thought, pp. 3, 8–9
Religious involvement and longevity, pp. 287–288
Scientific method, pp. 11–12
Sex and human values, p. 111
Sexual desire and ovulation, p. 107
Similarities and differences between men and women, pp. 102–103
Stress and cancer, p. 278
Suggestive powers of subliminal messages, pp. 125–126
The divided brain, pp. 46–48
The powers and limits of parental involvement on development, p. 87
Using psychology to debunk popular beliefs, pp. 5, 7, 10
Values and psychology, pp. 20–21
What does selective attention teach us about consciousness?, p. 49
What factors influence sexual orientation?, pp. 112–115
What is the connection between the brain and the mind?, p. 34
Wording effects, pp. 12, 21

TABLE 2   Culture and Multicultural Experience

Coverage of *culture and multicultural experience* may be found on the following pages:

Academic achievement, pp. 229–230, 283
Achievement motivation, p. 414
Adolescence, onset and end of, pp. 85–86
Aggression, pp. 393–395
Anger, p. 263
Animal learning, p. 216
Animal research, views on, p. 19
Beauty ideals, p. 400
Biopsychosocial approach, pp. 5–6, 80, 103–106, 107–112, 263, 319–320, 336, 373, 397
Body image, p. 243
Cluster migration, p. 249
Cognitive development of children, p. 75
Collectivism, pp. 312, 378, 383
Contraceptive use among teens, p. 109
Crime and stress hormone levels, p. 328
Cultural values
  child-rearing and, pp. 79–80
  morality and, pp. 82–83
  psychotherapy and, p. 364
Culture
  defined, pp. 6, 79, 105
  emotional expression and, pp. 261–262
  intelligence test bias and, pp. 231–232
  the self and, pp. 312–313
Deindividuation, p. 388
Depression
  and heart disease, p. 280
  risk of, p. 340
  and suicide, p. 339
Developmental similarities across cultures, p. 80
Deviant behavior definitions, p. 318
Discrimination, p. 390
Dissociative identity disorder, pp. 326–327
Division of labor, p. 105
Divorce rate, p. 93
Dreams, p. 58
Enemy perceptions, pp. 404–405
Exercise, p. 246
Expressions of grief, pp. 94–95
Family environment, pp. 85–86
Family self, sense of, pp. 82–83
Father care, p. 77

Father's presence
  pregnancy and, p. 110
  violence and, p. 395
Flow, p. 411
Foot-in-the-door phenomenon, p. 380
Framing, and organ donation, p. 210
Fundamental attribution error, pp. 378–379
Gender
  aggression and, p. 102
  phone communication and, p. 103
  sex drive and, pp. 116–117
Gender roles, pp. 105–106, 118
General adaptation syndrome, p. 276
Happiness, pp. 266, 268
HIV/AIDS, pp. 109, 278
Homosexuality, attitudes toward, p. 107
Hunger, p. 240
Identity formation, p. 84
Individualism, pp. 312, 378, 383
  moral development and, p. 83
Ingroup bias, p. 392
Intelligence, p. 219
  group differences in, pp. 228–233
Intelligence testing, p. 223
Job satisfaction, p. 414
Just-world phenomenon, pp. 303, 392
Language development, pp. 214–215
Leadership, pp. 416–417
Learning, p. 172
Life satisfaction, p. 96
Mating preferences, pp. 116–117, 118
Meditation, p. 287
Mental disorders and stress, p. 319
Mere exposure effect, p. 397
Motivation, pp. 238–239
Naturalistic observation, p. 13
Need to belong, p. 249
Obedience, pp. 384–385
Obesity and sleep loss, p. 246
Optimism, p. 282
Ostracism, p. 249
Parent-teen relations, pp. 85–86
Partner selection, p. 401
Peer influence, p. 80
  on language development, p. 85
Personal control, p. 282
Personality traits, pp. 303–305

Phobias, p. 326
Physical attractiveness, pp. 399–400
Poverty, explanations of, p. 379
Power differences between men and women, pp. 102–103
Prejudice, pp. 392, 398
  automatic, pp. 392–393
  cooperative contact and, pp. 405–406
  group polarization and, p. 388
  racial, p. 380
  subtle versus overt, p. 391
Prosocial behavior, p. 174
Psychoactive drugs, p. 329
Psychological disorders, pp. 316, 320
Racial similarities, pp. 229–230
Religious involvement and longevity, pp. 287–288
Resilience, p. 377
Risk assessment, p. 208
Scapegoat theory, p. 392
Schizophrenia, pp. 344–345
Self-esteem, p. 310
Self-serving bias, p. 311
Separation anxiety, p. 77
Serial position effect, p. 184
Shaping behavior of rats, p. 163
Situational influence, pp. 380–381
Sleep patterns, p. 55
Social clock variation, p. 94
Social influence, pp. 383, 386
Social loafing, p. 387
Social networking, pp. 250–251
Social trust, p. 79
Social-cultural psychology, pp. 3–4, 6, 336–337
Stereotype threat, p. 232
Stereotypes, pp. 390, 392
Stranger anxiety, p. 76
Substance abuse, p. 337
Survivor resiliency, p. 324
Susto, p. 319
Taijin-kyofusho, p. 319
Taste preference, pp. 242–243, 244
Terminal decline, p. 92
Terrorism, pp. 208, 303, 379, 392, 395
Trauma, pp. 299, 361
Universal expressions, p. 6
Weight, p. 246

of unconscious processing. Students may be surprised to learn how much information we process outside of our awareness! Discussions of sleep (Chapter 2), perception (Chapter 5), cog-

nition and emotion (Chapter 9), and attitudes and prejudice (Chapter 14) provide some particularly compelling examples of what goes on in our mind's downstairs.

4. Psychology Explores Human Strengths as Well as Challenges

Students will learn about the many troublesome behaviors and emotions psychologists study, as well as the ways in which

TABLE 3 Psychology of Women and Men

Coverage of the *psychology of women and men* may be found on the following pages:

Abusive relationships, p. 249
Age and decreased fertility, p. 90
Aggression, pp. 102, 393–397
  testosterone and, p. 394
Alcohol dependence, pp. 330–331
Alcohol use and sexual assault, p. 330
Attraction, pp. 397–402
Beauty ideals, p. 400
Bipolar disorder, p. 339
Body image, p. 243
Depression, pp. 340–341
  among girls, p. 85
  heart disease and, p. 280
Eating disorders, p. 243
Emotional expressiveness, p. 260
Emotion-detecting ability, pp. 260–261
Empathy, p. 260
Father's presence, pregnancy rates and,
  p. 110
Freud's views on personality development,
  pp. 295–296, 298
Gender, pp. 6, 109
  anxiety and, p. 322
  biological influences on, pp. 103–105
  changes in society's thinking about,
    pp. 100, 105, 106–107, 118, 390–391
  social–cultural influences on, pp. 6,
    105–106
  weight discrimination and, p. 245
  widowhood and, p. 94
Gender differences, p. 6, 102–105, 113
  emotional memory and, p. 342
  evolutionary perspectives on,
    pp. 116–118

intelligence and, pp. 230–231
  sexuality and, pp. 116–117
Gender discrimination, p. 390
Gender identity, development of,
  pp. 105–106
  mismatch in transgendered individuals,
    pp. 104–105
Gender roles, p. 105
Gender schema theory, p. 106
Gender similarities, pp. 102–105
Gender typing, p. 106
HIV/AIDS, women's vulnerability to, p. 108
Homosexuality, attitudes toward, p. 107
Hormones and sexual behavior, pp. 107–108
Human sexuality, pp. 106–112
Leadership styles, pp. 102–103
Learned helplessness, p. 342
Life expectancy, p. 102
Marriage, pp. 93, 401–402
Mating preferences, pp. 117–118
Maturation, pp. 81–82, 89
Menarche, pp. 81, 88
Menopause, p. 90
Obedience, p. 384
Obesity and heredity, p. 246
Partner selection, p. 401
Physical attractiveness, pp. 399–401
Post-traumatic stress disorder, p. 324
Puberty, p. 81
  early onset of, p. 86
Relationship equity, pp. 401–402
Religion and longevity, p. 287
Responses to stress, pp. 276–277
Romantic love, pp. 401–402

Schizophrenia, p. 344
Seasonal affective disorder, p. 338
Sex, pp. 6, 107
Sex and gender, p. 104
Sex chromosomes, p. 104
Sex drive, p. 116
Sex hormones, p. 104
Sex-reassignment, p. 104
Sexual abuse, p. 79
Sexual activity and aging, p. 91
Sexual intercourse among teens, p. 108
Sexual orientation, pp. 112–115
Sexual response, alcohol-related expectation
  and, p. 331
Sexual response cycle, p. 108
Sexual scripts, p. 395
Sexuality, natural selection and,
  pp. 116–118
Sexually explicit media, pp. 109–111, 395
Sexually transmitted infections, pp. 108–109
Similarities and differences between men and
  women, pp. 102–105
Social connectedness, p. 103
Social power, pp. 102–103
Stress and heart disease, p. 279
Substance abuse and addiction, p. 331
Teen pregnancy, pp. 109–110
Violent crime, p. 102
Vulnerability to psychological disorders,
  p. 102
Weight loss, p. 246
Women and work, p. 94
Women in psychology, p. 2

psychologists work with those who need help. Yet students will also learn about the *beneficial* emotions and traits that psychologists study, and the ways psychologists (some as part of the new *positive psychology* movement) attempt to nurture those traits in others. After studying with this text, students may find themselves living improved day-to-day lives. See, for example, tips for better sleep in Chapter 2, parenting suggestions throughout Chapter 3, information to help with romantic relationships in Chapters 3, 4, 14, and elsewhere, and "Close-Up: Want to Be Happier?" in Chapter 9. Students may also find themselves doing better in their courses. See, for example, following this preface,

"Time Management: Or, How to Be a Great Student and Still Have a Life!"; "How to Be a Better Student" at the end of Chapter 1; and "Improving Memory" in Chapter 7.

Enhanced Clinical Coverage

Compared with my other texts, *Psychology in Everyday Life* has proportionately more coverage of clinical topics and a greater sensitivity to clinical issues throughout the text. For example, Chapter 12, Psychological Disorders, includes lengthy coverage of substance-related disorders, with guidelines for determining substance abuse

and substance dependence. The discussion of psychoactive drugs includes a special focus on alcohol and nicotine dependence. Chapter 12 also includes a more general table outlining the process clinicians use to diagnose disorders with the DSM-IV-TR. See **Table 4** on the next page for a listing of coverage of clinical psychology concepts and issues throughout the text.

Currency and Everyday Life Applications

Few things dampen students' interest as quickly as the sense that they are reading stale news. While retaining psychology's

TABLE 4	Clinical Psychology

Coverage of *clinical psychology* may be found on the following pages:

Abused children, risk of psychological disorder among, p. 160
Aggression, p. 393
Alcohol use and aggression, pp. 394–397
Alzheimer's disease, 185
Anxiety disorders, pp. 322–326
Autism, p. 219
Aversive conditioning, p. 357
Behavior modification, pp. 357–358
Behavior therapies, pp. 355–358
Bipolar disorder, p. 339
Brain damage and memory loss, pp. 184–185
Brain scans, p. 35
Brain stimulation therapies, pp. 368–370
Childhood trauma, effect on mental health, p. 78
Client-centered therapy, pp. 354–355
Client-therapist relationship, pp. 302, 327, 352–355
Clinical psychologists, p. 4
Cognitive therapies, pp. 343, 358–359
  eating disorders and, p. 358
Culture and values in psychotherapy, pp. 364–365
Depression:
  adolescence and, p. 85
  heart disease and, p. 280
  homosexuality and, p. 112
  mood-memory connection and, pp. 190–191
  outlook and, pp. 341–343
  self-esteem and, pp. 11, 14
  sexualization of girls and, p. 110
  social exclusion and, p. 86
  unexpected loss and, p. 94

Dissociative and personality disorders, pp. 326–329
Dissociative identity disorder, p. 320
Drug and alcohol treatment, p. 161
Drug therapies, pp. 16, 365–368
Eating disorders, p. 243
Emotional intelligence, pp. 222–223
Evidence-based clinical decision making, p. 363
Exercise, therapeutic effects of, pp. 285–286, 371
Exposure therapies, pp. 356–357
Generalized anxiety disorder, p. 322
Grief therapy, pp. 94–95
Group and family therapies, pp. 359–360
Historical treatment of mental illness, pp. 318–319, 352
Humanistic therapies, pp. 354–355
Hypnosis and pain relief, pp. 144–145
Intelligence scales and stroke rehabilitation, p. 224
Lifestyle change, therapeutic effects of, p. 371
Loss of a child, psychiatric hospitalization and, p. 94
Major depressive disorder, pp. 338–339
Medical model of mental disorders, p. 319
Mood disorders, pp. 338–343
Neurotransmitter imbalances and related disorders, p. 30
Nurturing strengths, pp. 301–302
Obsessive-compulsive disorder, pp. 323–324
Operant conditioning in learned disordered behavior, pp. 357–358

Ostracism, pp. 249–250
Panic disorder, p. 323
Personality inventories, pp. 303–305
Personality testing, p. 298
Phobias, p. 323
Physical and psychological treatment of pain, pp. 143–144
Post-traumatic stress disorder, p. 324
Psychiatric labels and bias, pp. 320–321
Psychoactive drugs, types of, p. 330
Psychoanalysis, pp. 352–353
Psychodynamic theory, p. 297
Psychodynamic therapy, pp. 353–354
Psychological disorders, pp. 316–349
  classification of, pp. 320–321, 392
  gender differences in, p. 102
  preventing, and building resilience, pp. 371–373
Psychotherapy, pp. 352–365
  effectiveness of, pp. 361–364
Rorschach inkblot test, p. 298
Savant syndrome, pp. 219–220
Schizophrenia, pp. 343–347
  parent-blaming and, p. 87
  risk of, pp. 344–347
Self-actualization, p. 301
Sex reassignment therapy, p. 104
Sleep disorders, pp. 55–56
Spanked children, risk for aggression and depression among, p. 166
Substance-related disorders, pp. 329–338
Suicide, pp. 339–340
Testosterone replacement therapy, p. 107
Tolerance, addiction, and dependence, pp. 329–330

classic studies and concepts, I also present the discipline's most important recent developments. In this text, 442 references (18 percent) are dated 2007 or later. Some of the most exciting recent research has happened in the area of neuroscience, especially cognitive neuroscience and dual processing.

Throughout this text, as its title suggests, I relate the findings of psychology's research to the real world, using stories, case histories, and hypothetical situations. (See inside the front and back covers for a listing of students' favorite 50 of this text's applications to everyday life.) Where psychology can illuminate press-

ing human issues—bias and prejudice, health and happiness, violence and war—I have not hesitated to shine its light.

APA Guidelines for the Undergraduate Psychology Major

In 2002, an American Psychological Association (APA) Task Force released a set of Guidelines for the Undergraduate Psychology Major, which contained Learn-

See www.worthpublishers.com/myers for a detailed guide to how *Psychology in Everyday Life,* Second Edition, corresponds to the APA Guidelines for the Undergraduate Psychology Major.

ing Goals and Outcomes for students graduating with psychology majors. These guidelines were extensively reviewed, modified a bit, and then adopted by the APA Council of Representatives in 2006 (www.apa.org/ed/precollege/about/psymajor-guidelines.pdf).

Psychology departments in many schools have since used these goals and outcomes to help them establish their own benchmarks for departmental assessment purposes. To assist your efforts, an APA task force came out with an excellent Assessment CyberGuide for Learning Goals and Outcomes in 2009 (www.apa.org/ed/governance/bea/assess.aspx).

Some instructors are eager to know whether a given text for the introductory course helps students get a good start at achieving these goals. **TABLE 5** on page xxii outlines the way *Psychology in Everyday Life,* Second Edition, and its supplements package could help you to address these goals in your department.

Innovative Multimedia Supplements Package

Psychology in Everyday Life, Second Edition, boasts impressive electronic and print supplements titles. For more information about any of these media and supplements titles, visit Worth Publishers' online catalog at www.worthpublishers.com.

PsychPortal

Integrating our top-quality online material, PsychPortal is an innovative course space that combines a powerful quizzing engine with unparalleled media resources. PsychPortal conveniently offers all the functionality, flexibility, and customizing you need to support the presentation, grading, and other needs of your course. The following learning materials contained within PsychPortal make it truly unique:

- **Learning Curve (NEW for 2012!)** allows students to focus their studying where it's needed the most. The Learning Curve quizzing engine produces a series of unique, adaptive quizzes for students. Based on their performance, students receive individualized study recommendations in the form of a Personalized Study Plan. Students then have a

rich variety of activities to build their comprehension of the chapter.

- **An enhanced eBook** allows students to highlight, bookmark, and make their own notes just as they would with a printed textbook.

- A suite of new materials from Thomas Ludwig (Hope College) brings key topics to life.

- **The Student Video Tool Kit for Introductory Psychology** allows instructors to assign videos for students to interact with outside of class, in an interactive assessible shell (**Figure 3**). Videos include classic experiments, current news footage, and cutting-edge research.

- *Scientific American's* news tidbits are updated regularly. This newsfeed also includes *Scientific American's* 60-Second Mind podcasts.

PsychInvestigator: Laboratory Learning in Introductory Psychology

Produced in association with Arthur Kohn, Ph.D., of Dark Blue Morning Productions, this series of activities models a virtual laboratory. After being introduced to core psychological concepts by a video host, students participate in activities that generate real data and lead to some startling conclusions! Like all activities in PsychPortal, PsychInvestigator activities may be assigned and automatically graded. *PsychInvestigator may also be purchased online by visiting www.worthpi.com.*

Additional Student Media

- Student Center Web Site (includes Careers in Psychology supplement)
- Psych2Go (audio review downloads)

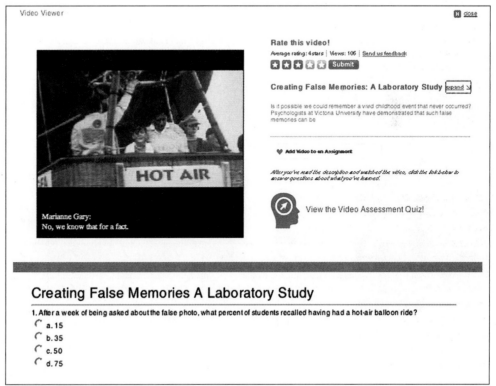

FIGURE 3 • **Sample of our Student Video Tool Kit**

TABLE 5 Psychology in *Everyday Life*, Second Edition, Corresponds to APA Guidelines

Relevant Feature from *Psychology in Everyday Life*, Second Edition	Knowledge Base of Psychology	Research Methods in Psychology	Critical Thinking Skills in Psychology	Application of Psychology	Values in Psychology	Information and Technological Literacy	Communication Skills	Sociocultural and International Awareness	Personal Development	Career Planning and Development
Text content	✓	✓	✓	✓	✓	✓	✓	✓	✓	
Four Big Ideas in Psychology as integrating themes	✓	✓	✓	✓	✓		✓	✓		
Thinking Critically boxes	✓	✓	✓	✓	✓		✓	✓		
Close-Up boxes	✓			✓	✓		✓	✓		
Learning Objective Questions previewing main sections	✓		✓	✓		✓				
Practice Tests	✓	✓	✓	✓	✓	✓	✓	✓	✓	
Visual, concept map-style chapter reviews	✓					✓	✓			
"Try This"-style activities integrated throughout	✓		✓	✓			✓	✓	✓	
Diverse Yet Alike photo feature	✓		✓	✓	✓		✓	✓	✓	
Psychology at Work text appendix	✓		✓	✓			✓	✓	✓	✓
PsychPortal media resources	✓	✓	✓	✓	✓	✓	✓	✓	✓	✓
Student Center Web site	✓	✓	✓	✓	✓	✓	✓	✓	✓	✓
PsychInvestigator activities	✓	✓	✓	✓	✓	✓	✓	✓	✓	✓
Psych2Go (audio review and self-test files)	✓	✓	✓	✓	✓	✓	✓	✓	✓	

APA Learning Goals

- PsychSim 5.0 (on CD)
- Student Video Tool Kit for Introductory Psychology (on DVD)

Course Management

- Enhanced Course Management Solutions

Assessment

- Printed Test Bank, Volumes 1 and 2
- Diploma Computerized Test Bank
- i>clicker Radio Frequency Classroom Response System

Presentation

- ActivePsych: Classroom Activities, Projects, and Video Teaching Modules (including Worth Digital Media Archive and *Scientific American Frontiers* Teaching Modules, Third Edition)
- Panopto Lecture Capture
- PowerPoint Slides (Art, Enhanced)
- Interactive PowerPoints
- Worth Image and Lecture Gallery at www.worthpublishers.com/ilg

Video and DVD

- Instructor Video Tool Kit
- Worth Digital Media Archive, Second Edition (available on DVD with closed captions; CD without closed captions may be found in ActivePsych package)
- Psychology: The Human Experience Teaching Modules
- The Many Faces of Psychology Video
- *Scientific American* Frontiers Video Collection, Third Edition (DVD with closed captions; CD without closed captions may be found in ActivePsych package)

Print Resources

- Instructor's Resources and Lecture Guides
- Instructor's Media Guide
- Study Guide
- *Pursuing Human Strengths: A Positive Psychology Guide*
- *Critical Thinking Companion,* Second Edition
- *Psychology and the Real World: Essays Illustrating Fundamental Contributions to Society* (An engaging collection of essays contributed by major researchers who volunteered the time to describe their landmark studies. Published in association with the not-for-profit FABBS Foundation, with a portion of all proceeds donated to The FABBS Foundation to support societies of cognitive, psychological, behavioral, and brain sciences.)

Scientific American Resources

- *Scientific American Mind*
- *Scientific American Reader to Accompany Myers*
- *Improving the Mind and Brain: A Scientific American Special Issue*
- *Scientific American Explores the Hidden Mind: A Collector's Edition*

In Appreciation

Aided by input from thousands of instructors and students, this has become a better, more effective, more accurate book than one author alone (this author, at least) could write. For this edition, I am especially thankful for the assistance of Amy Himsel (El Camino College) for helping craft the "In Your Everyday Life" study questions.

I greatly appreciate the colleagues who contributed criticism, corrections, and creative ideas related to the content, pedagogy, and format of this text in its first and second editions. They remind me of the wisdom of Woodrow Wilson: "I not only use all the brains I have, but all I can borrow." For their expertise and encouragement, and the gifts of their time to the teaching of psychology, I thank the reviewers listed below.

Tricia Alexander, *Long Beach City College*

Pamela Ansburg, *Metropolitan State College of Denver*

Randy Arnau, *University of Southern Mississippi*

Stacy Bacigalupi, *Mount San Antonio College*

Kimberly Bays-Brown, *Ball State University*

Alan Beauchamp, *Northern Michigan University*

Richard Bernstein, *Broward Community College—South*

Diane Bogdan, *CUNY: Hunter College*

Robert Boroff, *Modesto Junior College*

Christia Brown, *University of Kentucky*

Alison Buchanan, *Henry Ford Community College*

Norma Caltagirone, *Hillsborough Community College—Ybor City*

Nicole Judice Campbell, *University of Oklahoma*

David Carlston, *Midwestern State University*

Kimberly Christopherson, *Morningside College*

Diana Ciesko, *Valencia Community College*

TaMetryce Collins, *Hillsborough Community College*

Patricia Crowe, *Hawkeye College*

Jennifer Dale, *Community College of Aurora*

David Devonis, *Graceland University*

George Diekhoff, *Midwestern State University*

Michael Drissman, *Macomb Community College*

Laura Duvall, *Heartland Community College*

Jennifer Dyck, *SUNY College at Fredonia*

Laura Engleman, *Pikes Peak Community College*

Warren Fass, *University of Pittsburgh*

Vivian Ferry, *Community College of Rhode Island*

Elizabeth Freeman-Young, *Bentley College*

Ann Fresoli, *Lehigh Carbon Community College*

Ruth Frickle, *Highline Community College*

Lenore Frigo, *Shasta College*

Gary Gargano, *Merced College*

Jo Anne Geron, *Antioch University*

Stephanie Grant, *Southern Nazarene University*

Raymond Green, *The Honors College of Texas*

Sandy Grossman, *Clackamas Community College*

Lisa Gunderson, *Sacramento City College*

Rob Guttentag, *University of North Carolina—Greensboro*

Gordon Hammerle, *Adrian College*

Mark Hartlaub, *Texas A&M University*

Sheryl Hartman, *Miami Dade College*

Brett Heintz, *Delgado Community College*

Suzy Horton, *Mesa Community College*

Alishia Huntoon, *Oregon Institute of Technology*

Cindy Hutman, *Elgin Community College*

Laurene Jones, *Mercer County Community College*

Charles "Ed" Joubert, *University of North Alabama*

Deana Julka, *University of Portland*

Richard Kandus, *Mount San Jacinto College, Menifree*

Elizabeth Kennedy, *University of Akron*

Norm Kinney, *Southeast Missouri University*

Gary Klatsky, *SUNY Oswego State University*

Dan Klaus, *Community College of Beaver County*

Laurel Krautwurst, *Blue Ridge Community College*

Juliana Leding, *University of North Florida*

Gary Lewandowski, *Monmouth University*

Alicia Limke, *University of Central Oklahoma*

Leslie Linder, *Bridgewater State College*

Chris Long, *Ouachita Baptist University*

Martha Low, *Winston-Salem State University*

Mark Ludorf, *Stephen F. Austin State University*

Brian MacKenna-Rice, *Middlesex Community College*

Vince Markowski, *University of Southern Maine*

Dawn McBride, *Illinois State University*

Marcia McKinley, *Mt. St. Mary's University*

Tammy Menzel, *Mott Community College*

Leslie Minor-Evans, *Central Oregon Community College*

Ronald Mossler, *Los Angeles Valley College*

Maria Navarro, *Valencia Community College*

Daniel Nelson, *North Central University*

David Neufeldt, *Hutchinson Community College*

Peggy Norwood, *Community College of Aurora*

Fabian Novello, *Clark State Community College*

Fawn Oates, *Red Rocks Community College*

Ginger Osborne, *Santa Ana College*

Randall Osborne, *Texas State University—San Marcos*

Carola Pedreschi, *Miami-Dade College, North Campus*

Jim Previte, *Victor Valley College*

Sean Reilley, *Morehead State University*

Tanya Renner, *Kapi'olani Community College*

Vicki Ritts, *St. Louis Community College—Meramec*

Dave Rudek, *Aurora University*

R. Steven Schiavo, *Wellesley College*

Cynthia Selby, *California State University—Chico*

Jennifer Siciliani, *University of Missouri—St. Louis*

Barry Silber, *Hillsborough Community College*

Madhu Singh, *Tougaloo College*

Alice Skeens, *University of Toledo*

Jason Spiegelman, *Towson University & Community College of Baltimore County*

Anna-Marie Spinos, *Aurora University*

Betsy Stern, *Milwaukee Area Technical College*

Ruth Thibodeau, *Fitchburg State College*

Eloise Thomas, *Ozarks Technical Community College*

Susan Troy, *Northeast Iowa Community College*

Michael Verro, *Empire State College*

Jacqueline Wall, *University of Indianapolis*

Marc Wayner, *Hocking College*

Diane Webber, *Curry College*

Richard Wedemeyer, *Rose State College*

Peter Wooldridge, *Durham Technical Community College*

John Wright, *Washington State University*

Gabriel Ybarra, *University of North Florida*

I am also thankful to the 794 instructors who took the time to respond to our surveys. Their helpful and timely input was essential in the early formative stages of this text.

Several students provided more detailed feedback on pedagogy, design, and overall effectiveness. For their thoughtful input I thank:

Gregory Alleyne Jr., *Kingsborough Community College*

Ariadne Baker-Dunn, *Fordham University*

Heather Bates, *Marymount Manhattan College*

Jennifer C. Brad, *Pace University*

Gabriella Brune, *Robert Service High School*

Ryan Davenport, *Baruch College*

Patrick Joseph Giambelluca, *Hillsborough Community College, Ybor City*

Olivia Hazel, *SUNY New Paltz*

Angelika Jarosz, *The City College of New York*

Mayya Kats, *Baruch College*

Mark Kopernacki, *Baruch College*

Shannon Elaine McDowell, *Community College of Aurora*

Anthony Muller, *Florida State University*

Sarah Pumarejo, *Stony Brook University*

Maria Salazar, *CUNY Queens College*

Laura Shapiro, *University of Florida*

Nick Ungerson, *University of Delaware*

Barrett J. Viator, *CUNY Hunter College*

Xiu Qing Wu, *Syracuse University*

Julie Zeng, *CUNY Brooklyn College*

Sixty-two brave instructors agreed to class-test a chapter of this text in advance of its first edition publication. For their interest and enthusiasm, and for their helpful feedback, I thank the following instructors and their students:

David Alfano, *Community College of Rhode Island*

Harold Arnold, *Judson College*

Stacy Bacigalupi, *Mt. San Antonio College*

Emily Balcetis, *Ohio University*

David Carlston, *Midwestern State University*

Richard Catrambone, *Georgia Institute of Technology*

Kathy Coiner, *Scott Community College*

TaMetryce Collins, *Hillsborough Community College*

Victoria Cooke, *Erie Community College*

Stephanie Deturk, *University of Kansas*

Mark Eastman, *Diablo Valley College*

Michael Feiler, *Merritt College*

Lenore Frigo, *Shasta College*

William Rick Fry, *Youngstown State University*

William Goggin, *University of Southern Mississippi*

Gary Grady, *Connors State College*

Jerry Green, *Tarrant County College, Northwest Campus*

Stephen Guerin, *Motlow State Community College*

Chuck Hallock, *Pima County Community College*

Lori Harris, *Southeastern Iowa Community College*

Catherine Hawkins, *North Hennepin Community College*

Ann Hennessey, *Pierce College*

Richard Kandus, *Mt. San Jacinto College, Menifree Campus*

Jason Kaufman, *Inver Hills Community College*

Kevin Keating, *Broward Community College*

Betsy Klopcic, *Illinois Valley Community College*

Ken Koenigshofer, *Chaffey College*

Larry Kollman, *North Iowa Area Community College*

Cindy Lahar, *York County Community College*

Mary Lofgren, *Imperial Valley Community College*

Brian MacKenna-Rice, *Middlesex Community College*

David Malcolm, *Fordham University*

John Mavromatis, *St. John Fisher College*

Christopher Mayhorn, *North Carolina State University*

Melissa McCeney, *Montgomery College*

Marcia McKinley-Baum, *Mount St. Mary's University*

Barbara McMillan, *Alabama Southern University*

Katy Neidhardt, *California Polytechnic State University*

Teri Nicoll-Johnson, *Modesto Junior College*

Patricia Nicosia, *Kettering College of Medical Arts*

Christopher Ostwinkle, *Northeast Iowa Community College*

William Pannell, *El Paso Community College*

Neophytos Papaneophytou, *Borough of Manhattan Community College*

David Payne, *Wallace Community College*

Julie Penley, *El Paso Community College*

John Pierce, *Villanova University*

Deborah Podwika, *Kankakee Community College*

Gregory Pool, *St. Mary's University*

Dennis Russell, *Southeast Technical Institute*

Brian Sexton, *Georgian Court University*

Donald Smith, *Everett Community College*

Jason Spiegelman, *Towson University & Community College of Baltimore County*

David Steitz, *Nazareth College*

Annette Kujawski Taylor, *University of San Diego*

Inger Thompson, *Glendale Community College*

Sarah Ting, *Cerritos College*

Susan Troy, *Northeast Iowa Community College*

Ada Wainwright, *College of DuPage*

Elizabeth Weiss, *Ohio State University*

Linda Weldon, *Community College of Baltimore County—Essex*

Jennifer Zwahr-Castro, *St. Mary's University*

My gratitude extends to more students who shared that most precious commodity—time—in order to help make this text a better learning tool for those who will follow. Students from the following schools gave up an afternoon to participate in one of our focus groups, or offered written feedback by way of their instructor.

Adrian College

Century College

Long Beach City College

Mount San Antonio College

Nassau Community College

Pikes Peak Community College

Shasta College

SUNY College at Fredonia

Southern Nazarene University

University of Akron

University of North Florida

University of Toledo

At Worth Publishers a host of people played key roles in creating this text. The formal planning began as the author-publisher team gathered for a two-day retreat. This happy and creative gathering included John Brink, Thomas Ludwig, Richard Straub, and me from the author team, along with my assistants Kathryn Brownson and Sara Neevel. We were joined by Bedford-Freeman-Worth executives Tom Scotty, Elizabeth Widdicombe, Mark Resmer, and Catherine Woods; editors Christine Brune, Kevin Feyen, Nancy Fleming, Tracey Kuehn, Trish Morgan, and Betty Probert; artistic director Babs Reingold; sales and marketing colleagues John Britch, Kari Ewalt, Mike Howard, Lindsay Johnson, Tom Kling, Matt Ours, and Carlise Stembridge; and by special guests from the academic community Amy Himsel (El Camino College), Jennifer Peluso (Florida Atlantic University), Charlotte VanOyen Witvliet (Hope College), and Jennifer Zwolinski (University of San Diego).

Executive Editor Kevin Feyen has become a valued team leader, thanks to his dedication, creativity, and sensitivity. Senior Publisher Catherine Woods helped construct and execute the plan for this new text and its supplements. Catherine was also a trusted sounding board as we faced a seemingly unending series of discrete decisions along the way. Sharon Prevost coordinated production of the huge supplements package for this edition. Betty Probert efficiently edited and produced the print supplements and, in the process, also helped fine-tune the whole book. Adam Frese provided invaluable support in commissioning and organizing the multitude of reviews, sending information to professors, and handling numerous other daily tasks related to the book's development and production. Lee McKevitt did a splendid job of laying out each page. Bianca Moscatelli and Donna Ranieri worked together to locate the myriad photographic illustrations.

Associate Managing Editor Tracey Kuehn and Project Editor Dana Kasowitz displayed tireless tenacity, commitment, and impressive organization in leading Worth's gifted artistic production team and coordinating editorial input throughout the production process. Production Manager Sarah Segal masterfully held the book to its tight schedule, and Babs Reingold skillfully envisioned and directed creation of the distinctive design and art program. Production Manager Stacey Alexander, along with supplements production editor Jenny Chiu, did their usual excellent work of producing the many supplements.

As you can see, although this book has one author it is a *team* effort. A special salute is due my two book development editors who have invested so much in creating *Psychology in Everyday Life*. My longtime editor Christine Brune saw the need for a very short, accessible, student-friendly introductory psychology text, and she energized and guided the rest of us in bringing her vision to reality. Development editor Nancy Fleming is one of those rare editors who is gifted at "thinking big" about a chapter while also applying her sensitive, graceful, line-by-line touches. Her painstaking, deft editing was a key part of achieving the hoped-for brevity and accessibility.

To achieve our goal of supporting the teaching of psychology, this teaching package not only must be authored, reviewed, edited, and produced, but also made available to teachers of psychology. For their exceptional dedication to doing that, our author team is grateful to Worth Publishers' professional sales and marketing team. We are especially grateful to Executive Marketing Manager Kate Nurre, Associate Director of Market Development Carlise Stembridge, Marketing Manager Lindsay Johnson, National Psychology and Economics Consultant Tom Kling, High School Executive Marketing Manager

Cindi Weiss, and Marketing Assistant Kerri Knipper, both for their tireless attempts to inform our teaching colleagues of our efforts to assist their teaching, and for the joy of working with them.

At Hope College, the supporting team members for this edition included Kathryn Brownson, who researched countless bits of information and proofed hundreds of pages. Kathryn has become a knowledgeable and sensitive adviser on many matters, and Sara Neevel has become our high-tech manuscript developer, par excellence.

I gratefully acknowledge the influence and editing assistance of my writing coach, poet Jack Ridl, whose influence resides in the voice you will be hearing in the pages that follow. He, more than anyone, cultivated my delight in dancing with the language, and taught me to approach writing as a craft that shades into art.

After hearing countless dozens of people say that the Worth Publishers' supplements for my texts have taken their teaching to a new level, I reflect on how fortunate I am to be a part of a team on which everyone produces on-time work marked by the highest professional standards. For their remarkable talents, their long-term dedication, and their friendship, I thank John Brink, Thomas Ludwig, and Richard Straub.

* * *

The day this book went to press was the day I started gathering information and ideas for the next edition. Your input will influence how this book continues to evolve. So, please, do share your thoughts.

Hope College
Holland, Michigan 49422-9000 USA
www.davidmyers.org

content changes

Psychology in Everyday Life, Second Edition, includes 600 new research citations, new pedagogy that reflects the latest in cognitive psychology research on retention, a fresh new design, and many fun new photos and cartoons. In addition, you will find the following, significant content changes in this new second edition.

Chapter 1
Psychology's Roots, Big Ideas, and Critical Thinking Tools

- Contemporary Psychology discussion has been clarified in narrative and tables.

- "Cognitive neuroscience" is now a key term.

- The biopsychosocial perspective has been clarified in narrative and captions.

- New cross-cultural data update the discussion of psychology's worldwide expansion.

- New current events update the introduction.

- Naturalistic Observation section includes new research examples, with two new photos.

- New examples demonstrate the importance of control groups and dependent and independent variables.

- Experimental ethics discussion expanded.

- New scatterplot figure enriches the correlations discussion.

- How to Be a Better Student now includes material on testing as an active learning tool, not just a way to assess learning, with additional emphasis on the SQ3R study method.

Chapter 2 The Biology of Mind and Consciousness

- Captivating new example illustrates the autonomic nervous system in action.

- Expanded discussion and new examples help clarify the concept of neural networks.

- "Pons" has been added to the structures described and illustrated.

- Tools of Discovery discussion of brain-scanning techniques has been updated with new research.

- New figure memorably illustrates the brain's cross-wiring.

- Motor cortex discussion now includes new research (with photos) in developing robotic prosthetic limbs.

- Frontal lobe discussion contains new research on impaired moral judgment, plus recently discovered photo of Phineas Gage after his accident.

- New research updates our understanding of success rates for hemispherectomies in children.

- "Neurogenesis" is now a key term.

- Selective attention discussion now includes new findings on dangers of texting while driving, and a new photo example of inattentional blindness research.

- Discussion of sleep stages updated with new research.

- New research relates sleep deprivation to unwanted weight gain, and also provides data on high school students' sleepiness.

- New data in Sleep Theories discussion outlines the benefits of sleep for creativity.

Chapter 3
Developing Through the Life Span

- New research suggests that pregnant women's drinking primes their children for greater risk later of heavy drinking and alcohol dependence.

- Brain Development includes new research on the effect of frontal lobe development on preschoolers' ability to control their attention and behavior.

- New research updates discussion of benefits of touch on infant development.

- New research extends long-term effects of attachment styles.

- New research describes increased risk of depression if abuse victims carry gene that spurs stress-hormone production.

- New, cross-cultural research results support importance of adult monitoring of young children.

- New research updates parenting styles discussion.

- Teen risk assessment updated with new research.

- New table summarizes Kohlberg's levels of moral thinking.

- Adolescent Social Development now includes data on teen texting and social networking.

- Parent and Peer Relationships has been updated with new research.

- Emerging Adulthood section now includes concept of "sandwich generation."

- New research updates discussion of aging and sexuality.

- Now includes evolutionary psychology explanation of menopause, with new research.

- Sensory Abilities section now includes new research on pitches only teens can hear.

- Includes new neuroscience research on the effects of atrophying frontal lobes later in life, the benefits of exercising, and Alzheimer's.

- New research suggests lessened effects of negative emotions later in life, and updates discussion of Age and Life Satisfaction.

- New research updates discussions of death, dying, grief counseling, and happiness in later life.

- New figure offers a comparative review of the stage theories of Kohlberg, Erikson, and Piaget to help students learn and retain the distinctions.

Chapter 4 Gender and Sexuality

- New gender research sheds light on aggression and power issues, with new photo example.

- Gender and Social Connectedness section enhanced with new global research and ideas, including social networking differences.

- "Gender schema" is now a key term.

- New coverage of APA Task Force report, The Sexualization of Girls, and the media's role.

- New evolutionary psychology research illuminates the discussion of mating preferences.

- Includes new gender-based research on time spent in caregiving versus work for pay.

- New discussion of transgendered individuals, with two new photo examples.

- New discussion of effects of high fetal testosterone on muscles and bones in females.

- Updated global survey data guide the sexual orientation and teen sexuality discussions.

- Includes new APA statements related to sexual orientation.

- New discussions, with figure, of genetic influences on sexual orientation.

Chapter 5 Sensation and Perception

- Chapter has been re-organized and streamlined so that the concepts are now fully integrated rather than presented as sensation followed by perception. For example, earlier discussion of perceptual set (now with the rest of vision) enables better understanding of its relevance to all the senses, and new examples, photos, and figures enrich the discussion.

- Includes new neuroscience research on facial perception.

- New research and photo update discussion of subliminal stimulation.

- Includes new examples of sensory adaptation.

- New gender research suggests noise exposure differences.

- New research examples enrich discussion of sensory interaction.

- New photo helps illustrate structure of the eye.

- New medical research updates discussion of hypnosis for pain relief.

- New table outlines Survival Functions of Basic Tastes, and new research demonstrates importance of taste and of taste expectations.

- Context Effects figure revised to better illustrate how comparisons govern perceptions of color.

- New table and illustration memorably summarize information on the senses.

- Includes new data on belief in extrasensory perception, and new research on lack of evidence for ESP in brain scans.

Chapter 6 Learning

- Chapter has been reorganized and now includes a new section on Biology, Cognition, and Learning.

- "Cognitive learning" is now defined as a key term, early in the chapter.

- New research suggests that learned associations feed our habitual behaviors.

- New evolutionary psychology research, with a new figure, suggests why men so easily learn an association between the color red and romance.

- Role of neutral stimulus in classical conditioning has been clarified in narrative and figures. "Neutral stimulus" is now a key term.

- New section discusses schedules of reinforcement in more detail, including comparison of four schedules of partial reinforcement. New comparison table provides applications to help students understand the differences.

- New research links "sureness and swiftness" to effective criminal punishment. New table illustrates differences between positive and negative punishment.

- New Biology, Cognition, and Learning section discusses biological constraints on classical and operant conditioning; cognitive processes related to classical and operant conditioning; and observational learning from the perspective of cognitive processes.

- Expanded discussion of mirror neurons and imitation in observational learning includes new research and new examples.

- New research updates discussion of cognitive effects on conditioning likes and dislikes.

Chapter 7 Memory

- Reorganized chapter gives students an earlier introduction to memory issues related to the two-track mind (dual processing), with new research citations and examples.

- Biology of memory is further integrated throughout the chapter.

- New research outlines the strength of even ordinary memory ability.

- Discussion of the three-stage information-processing model clarifies working memory and unconscious

processing with illustrative new examples and improved accompanying art.

- New research outlines variability of working memory capacity.

- Serial position and two-track memory figures have been updated and clarified.

- Includes new emphasis on usefulness of testing as an active learning tool, not just a way to assess learning.

- New research applies memory principles to everyday learning, including the benefits of spaced learning, repeated quizzing, and meaningful encoding.

- New research examples and ideas enhance discussion of memory's synaptic changes.

- Stress Hormones and Memory now includes evolutionary psychology explanation and a new photo example from the 2010 China earthquake.

- New research explains function of memory-blunting drug following traumatic events.

- New neuroscience and other research updates discussion of implicit and explicit memories, including the story of famous patient H. M. and the dissection of his brain.

- Discussion of priming and déjà vu updated with new research.

- New research example and photo highlight value of *not* remembering everything.

- New research demonstrates the value of avoiding interference in learning.

- New research story enlivens discussion of Motivated Forgetting.

- Misinformation and Imagination Effects has been condensed, reorganized, and updated, with new research, quotes, stories, and clarified definitions.

- Sleep and the testing effect are now promoted as important variables for memory improvement.

Chapter 8 Thinking, Language, and Intelligence

- New neuroscience research clarifies insight discussion.

- Power of framing illustrated with new research examples.

- Dramatic new examples illustrate the idea that emotion-laden images can make ideas more fearfully memorable.

- New research, with new figure, shows how our brains process word problems.

- Includes new research examples of impressive animal thinking, including chimpanzees' ability to read intent.

- New research examples enhance discussion of risk assessment and emotional reasoning.

- Intuition discussion enriched with new research and new ideas.

- New table summarizes and compares cognitive processes and strategies.

- Discussion of animal thinking and language has been condensed, but core discussion has been enhanced by new research examples.

- New research supports the idea that different abilities interact and feed one another.

- New research example provides window into the world of a savant, with new photo.

- Dramatic new art improves presentation of Gardner's Eight Intelligences.

- New research improves discussions of Sternberg's theories and of creativity.

- New twin research expands discussion of the genetic basis of intelligence.

- New research extends discussion of the high extreme of intelligence.

- New cross-cultural and gender studies, with two new figures, enhance discussion of cultural, ethnic, and gender similarities and differences in intelligence; includes updates on "stereotype threat."

Chapter 9
Motivation and Emotion

- Includes new discussion of how activated motives can hijack our consciousness, with new research.

- Obesity discussion has been reorganized and condensed; now includes new research on the effects of portion sizes and variety of choices.

- Eating Disorders section now includes "binge-eating disorders" concept, along with new research on prevalence and genetic factors.

- New global statistics update the obesity prevalence data.

- Now includes discussion of key environmental factors influencing obesity rates: social influence, sleep loss, and cultural effects on changing food consumption patterns and activity levels.

- The Need to Belong now outlines three basic psychological needs: relatedness, autonomy, and competence, with new research.

- New Social Networking section discusses patterns, social effects, and self-control issues.

- New research updates ostracism discussion.

- New figure illustrates emotional arousal.

- Cognition and Emotion now includes a new discussion, with new research, of the way our two-track mind (automatic emotion and conscious thinking) creates our emotional experience, and new research on the stronger effects of liking a political candidate

emotionally versus agreeing with his/her positions.

- Includes new research on more effective methods of detecting lies, including possible use of brain scans, with new photo example from *Lie to Me* (TV show based on Paul Ekman's research).

- New research supports our remarkable ability to recognize distinct emotions quickly.

- Detecting Emotion in Others now includes new research, with a new "try this" style figure, about anger and its perception as masculine.

- Culture and Emotional Expression enhanced with new research on the culturally universal perceptions of happiness and sadness in music.

- New Japanese research expands the discussion of The Effects of Facial Expressions, with new art.

- Wealth and Well-Being now includes new research on the "diminishing returns" phenomenon (more income does not produce greater happiness) and the idea that more happiness may produce greater incomes/success (rather than the other way around).

- New research supports the benefits of keeping a gratitude journal.

Chapter 10 Stress, Health, and Human Flourishing

- "Stress," "stressor," and "stress reaction" are now distinguished with a memorable new story of Ben's wild wheelchair ride (stuck to the grill of a truck for miles after crossing the road).

- Chapter includes new examples and new research on stress related to job loss and financial worries.

- Stress Reactions now includes a discussion of men's and women's differ-

ing responses to stress, and the effects of oxytocin.

- Stressful Life Events now includes Hurricane Katrina's effect on suicide rates; new photo examples of the 2010 Haiti earthquake and the 2010 collapsed Chilean mine; more research on daily hassles and frustrations (including the effects of perceived discrimination); and variations in stress by gender and age.

- New brain research shows reduced reactions to perceived threats in the presence of a socially supportive spouse.

- Now includes new research on the dangers of unrealistic optimism; the consistency and magnitude of the optimism and positive emotions factors in health; and the reality that job loss, poverty, and diminished control increase stress among adults and children.

- Includes new research linking regular exercise with reduced risk of dementia, and new studies showing possible links between increased depression rates and current sedentary lifestyles.

- New Close-Up Box: Pets are Friends, Too, outlines the health benefits of pets during times of stress.

- New research demonstrates the cluster effects of bad or good health practices in groups.

Chapter 11
Personality

- New table summarizes defense mechanisms.

- Evaluating the Psychoanalytic Perspective has been reorganized and clarified, with new research findings and new examples.

- More new research questions validity of the concept of repression.

- "Big Five" table of personality factors has been revised/improved.

- New research supports the predictive value of rating personality based on photos, social networking profiles, e-mails, and conversational word choice.

- New research expands discussion of self-serving bias.

- Self-Esteem discussion enhanced with new research related to benefits as well as concerns, including increased narcissism.

Chapter 12 Psychological Disorders

- The biopsychosocial discussion of culture-related disorders has been updated, with new research on the global spread of North American disorders and new cross-cultural photo examples.

- Classifying Disorders and Labeling People previews some new categories expected in the upcoming DSM-V.

- Includes new research on age-related development and decline of symptoms in some anxiety disorders.

- Includes new evolutionary psychology research on phobias.

- Discussion of Post-Traumatic Stress Disorder (PTSD) has been enhanced and updated, including new research on genetic factors and new examples and discussion of war-related cases, with reference to Chapter 13's discussion of resilience.

- Substance-Related Disorders discusses new research on the effects of binge-drinking on the birth and death of nerve cells, and new data for tobacco-related deaths and stop-smoking success rates.

- New data update the discussion of early use of alcohol and later development of alcohol dependence.

- Discussion of personality disorders now includes new research on genetic influences and on the interaction of predispositions and childhood abuse.

- New research enhances discussion of rates of depression among college students, as well as gender differences in depression, with new table illustrating seasonal variations in depression for males and females.

- New research expands the discussion of bipolar disorder to include diagnoses among adolescents experiencing prolonged mood swings, and simulated mania in the lab.

- Includes several new photo examples of prominent individuals with psychological disorders.

- Includes new section on suicide, with updated statistics and discussion of risk factors.

- Schizophrenia discussion includes new research on risk factors related to body type and infant nutrition, expanded discussion of brain tissue loss, and new findings from gene research.

Chapter 13 Therapy

- Psychoanalysis discussion has been condensed and clarified.

- "Psychodynamic therapy" receives additional emphasis as a new key term, and is supported by a new example of patient-therapist interaction.

- "Unconditional positive regard" is now a key term.

- More new research highlights the effectiveness of cognitive-behavioral therapy.

- Includes new discussion of "evidence-based practice," which is a key term, with a new figure demonstrating evidence-based clinical decision making.

- Drug Therapies presents new data showing 100 percent increase in use of antidepressants in the past decade.

- Many research updates enhance the discussion of antidepressants, including more support for the power of placebos; brain research indicating why SSRIs may take weeks to work; and support for the idea that fewer patients attempt suicide if treated with antidepressants.

- New neuroscience and other research expands discussion of brain stimulation to provide additional research support for ECT as well as coverage of deep-brain stimulation.

- New Therapeutic Life-Style Change section provides research support for the mental health benefits of engaging in a healthier life style (more sleep, exercise, socializing, and light; better nutrition; less rumination).

- Preventing Psychological Disorders includes new discussion of resilience and post-traumatic growth, as well as new emphasis on community psychology.

Chapter 14 Social Psychology

- New chapter-opening story draws students into the content.

- New current events photo highlights actor and observer perspectives in attribution.

- Attitudes and Actions includes new research and current event examples.

- New research enhances the discussion of role-playing to emphasize the power of the individual in each situation.

- Group Pressure and Conformity now offers new research related to college student populations.

- Additional new research updates the Milgram discussion.

- Deindividuation updated with new Internet examples, including global climate change and terrorism.

- Group Polarization updated with new section, The Internet as Social Amplifier, with new research and current examples.

- New research examples enhance discussion of automatic (implicit) prejudice.

- Discussion of ingroup/outgroup enhanced with new evolutionary psychology research.

- Cognitive Roots of Prejudice enhanced with new research on basic tendency toward social conservatism.

- "Other-race effect" is now a key term, supported by new research and discussion.

- New research enhances the discussion of biochemical influences on aggression.

- The Psychology of Aggression is enhanced with new research examples (father-absent homes, baseball, suicide bombers).

- New research updates the discussion of media models (Internet, TV, music, video games) of sexual aggression, and their detrimental effects.

- Physical Attractiveness updated with new research on humor and on speed dating.

- Now includes Close-Up box, Online Matchmaking.

- Global research updates emphasize the importance of contact in resolving conflicts.

Appendix A Psychology and Work

- New examples and research emphasize the concept of flow.

- New resilience research, examples, and photo enrich Motivating Achievement discussion.

- Leadership discussion improved with new gender studies. Emphasizes the value of having engaged workers and specific goals. Includes new case study, with new photo, of a very engaged recent immigrant.

time management

Or, How to Be a Great Student and Still Have a Life!

—Richard O. Straub University of Michigan, Dearborn

How Are You Using Your Time Now?

Design a Better Schedule
Plan the Term
Plan Your Week
CLOSE-UP: More Tips for Effective Scheduling

Make Every Minute of Your Study Time Count
Take Useful Class Notes
Create a Study Space That Helps You Learn
Set Specific, Realistic Daily Goals
Use SQ3R to Help You Master This Text
Don't Forget About Rewards!

Do You Need to Revise Your New Schedule?

Motivated students: This course at Bunker Hill Community College meets at the increasingly popular time of midnight to 2:00 A.M., allowing shift workers, busy parents, and others to make it to class.

We all face challenges in our schedules. Some of you may be taking midnight courses, others squeezing in an online course in between jobs or after putting children to bed at night. Some of you may be veterans using military benefits to jump-start a new life.

How can you balance all of your life's demands and be successful? Time management. Manage the time you have so that you can find the time you need.

In this section, I will outline a simple, four-step process for improving the way you make use of your time.

1. Keep a time diary to understand how you are using your time. You may be surprised at how much time you're wasting.

2. Design a new schedule for using your time more effectively.

3. Make the most of your study time so that your new schedule will work for you.

4. If necessary, refine your new schedule, based on what you've learned.

How Are You Using Your Time Now?

Although everyone gets 24 hours in the day and seven days in the week, we fill those hours and days with different obligations and interests. If you are like most people, you probably use your time wisely in some ways, and not so wisely in others. Answering the questions in **TABLE 1** on the next page can help you find trouble spots—and hopefully more time for the things that matter most to you.

The next thing you need to know is how you *actually* spend your time. To find out, record your activities in a **time-use diary** for one week. Be realistic. Take notes on how much time you spend attending class, studying, working, commuting, meeting personal and family needs, fixing and eating meals, socializing (don't forget texting and Facebooking), exercising, and anything else that occupies your time, including life's small practical tasks, which can take up plenty of your 24/7.

As you record your activities, take notes on *how you are feeling* at various times of the day. When does your energy slump, and when do you feel most energetic?

Design a Better Schedule

Take a good look at your time-use diary. Where do you think you may be wasting time? Do you spend a lot of time

TABLE 1   Study Habits Survey

Answer the following questions, writing *Yes* or *No* for each line.

1. Do you usually set up a schedule to budget your time for studying, work, recreation, and other activities?
   _____

2. Do you often put off studying until time pressures force you to cram? _____

3. Do other students seem to study less than you do, but get better grades?
   _____

4. Do you usually spend hours at a time studying one subject, rather than dividing that time among several subjects?
   _____

5. Do you often have trouble remembering what you have just read in a textbook?
   _____

6. Before reading a chapter in a textbook, do you skim through it and read the section headings? _____

7. Do you try to predict test questions from your class notes and reading?
   _____

8. Do you usually try to summarize in your own words what you have just finished reading? _____

9. Do you find it difficult to concentrate for very long when you study? _____

10. Do you often feel that you studied the wrong material for a test? _____

Thousands of students have participated in similar surveys. Students who are fully realizing their academic potential usually respond as follows: (1) yes, (2) no, (3) no, (4) no, (5) no, (6) yes, (7) yes, (8) yes, (9) no, (10) no.

Do your responses fit that pattern? If not, you could benefit from improving your time management and study habits. Knowing your areas of weakness will help you set specific goals for improvement and create a plan for reaching them.

commuting, for example? If so, could you use that time more productively? If you take public transportation, commuting is a great time to read and review. If you drive, consider audio review files. (For audio review files for this text, see www.worthpublishers.com/Psych2Go.)

Did you remember to include time for meals, personal care, and other fixed activities?

How much time do you sleep? In the battle to meet all of life's daily commitments and interests, we tend to treat sleep as optional. Do your best to manage your life so that you can get enough sleep to feel rested. You will feel better and be healthier, and you will also do better academically and in relationships with your family and friends. (You will read more about this in Chapter 2.)

Are you dedicating enough time for focused study? Take a last look at your notes to see if any other patterns pop out. Now it's time to create a new and more efficient schedule.

Plan the Term

Before you draw up your new schedule, think ahead. Buy a portable calendar that covers the entire school term, with a writing space for each day. Using the course outlines provided by your instructors, enter the dates of all exams, term-paper deadlines, and other important assignments. Also be sure to enter your own long-range personal plans (work and family commitments, etc.). Carry this calendar with you each day. Keep it up to date, refer to it often, and change it as needed. *Through this process, you will develop a regular schedule that will help you achieve success.*

Plan Your Week

To pass those exams, meet those deadlines, and keep up with your life outside of class, you will need to convert your long-term goals into a daily schedule. Be realistic—you will be living with this routine for the entire school term. Here are some more things to add to that portable calendar.

1. Enter your class times, work hours, and any other fixed obligations. *Be thorough.* Allow plenty of time for such things as commuting, meals, and laundry.

2. Set up a study schedule for each course. Remember what you learned about yourself in the study habits survey (Table 1) and your time-use diary. Close-Up: More Tips for Effective Scheduling offers some detailed guidance drawn from psychology's research.

3. After you have budgeted time for studying, fill in slots for other obligations, exercise, fun, and relaxation.

Make Every Minute of Your Study Time Count

How do you study from a textbook? Many students simply read and reread in a *passive* manner. As a result, they remember the wrong things—the catchy stories but not the main points that show up later in test questions. To make things worse, many students take poor notes during class. Here are some tips that will help you get the most from your class and your text.

Take Useful Class Notes

Even if you record lectures (with your instructor's approval, of course), good notes will boost your understanding and retention. Are yours thorough? Do they form a sensible outline of each lecture? If not, you may need to make some changes.

Keep Each Course's Notes Separate and Organized

If you have all your notes for a course in one location, you will be able to find answers to questions more easily. In addition to electronic note-taking options, two paper options are (1) separate notebooks for each course, or (2) clearly marked sections in a shared ring binder. If pages are removable, you can reorganize as needed, adding new information and weeding out past mistakes. In either case, pages with lots of space—8.5 inches by 11 inches—are a good choice. You'll have room for notes, with a wide margin remaining to hold comments when you review and revise your notes after class.

More Tips for Effective Scheduling

Here are a few other things you will want to keep in mind when you set up your schedule.

Spaced study is more effective than massed study. If you need 3 hours to study one subject, for example, it's best to divide that into shorter periods spaced over several days.

Alternate subjects, but avoid interference. Alternating the subjects you study in any given session will keep you fresh and will, surprisingly, increase your ability to remember what you're learning in each different area. Studying similar topics back-to-back, however, such as two different foreign languages, could lead to *interference* in your learning. (You will hear more about this in Chapter 7.)

Determine the amount of study time you need to do well in each course. The time you need depends upon the difficulty of your courses and the effectiveness of your study methods. Ideally, you would spend at least 1 to 2 hours studying for each hour spent in class. Increase your study time slowly by setting weekly goals that will gradually bring you up to the desired level.

Create a schedule that makes sense. Tailor your schedule to meet the demands of each course. For the course that emphasizes lecture notes, plan a daily review of your notes soon after each class. If you are evaluated for class participation (for example, in a language course), allow time for a review just before the class meets. Schedule study time for your most difficult (or least motivating) courses during hours when you are the most alert and distractions are fewest.

Schedule open study time. Life can be unpredictable. Emergencies and new obligations can throw off your schedule. Or you may simply need some extra time for a project or for review in one of your courses. Try to allow for some flexibility in your schedule each week.

Following these guidelines will help you find a schedule that works for you!

Use an Outline Format

Use roman numerals for major points, letters for supporting arguments, and so on. (See **FIGURE 1** on the next page for a sample.) In some courses, taking notes will be easy, but some instructors may be less organized, and you will have to work harder to form your outline.

Clean Up Your Notes After Class

Try to reorganize your notes soon after class. Expand or clarify your coments and clean up any hard-to-read scribbles while the material is fresh in your mind. Write important questions in the margin next to notes that answer them. (For example: "What are the sleep stages?") This will help you when you review your notes before a test.

Create a Study Space That Helps You Learn

It's easier to study effectively if your work area is well designed.

Organize Your Space

Work at a desk or table, not in your bed or a comfy chair that will tempt you to nap.

Minimize Distractions

Turn the TV off. If you must listen to music to mask outside noise, play soft instrumentals, not vocal selections that will draw your mind to the lyrics.

Ask Others to Honor Your Quiet Time

Tell roommates, family, and friends about your new schedule. Try to find a study place where you are least likely to be disturbed.

Set Specific, Realistic Daily Goals

The simple note "7–8 P.M.: Study psychology" is too broad to be useful. Instead, break your studying into manageable tasks. For example, you will want to subdivide large reading assignments. If you aren't used to studying for long periods, start with relatively short periods of concentrated study, with breaks in between. In this text, for example, you might decide to read one major section before each break. Limit your breaks to 5 or 10 minutes to stretch or move around a bit.

Your attention span is a good indicator of whether you are pacing yourself successfully. At this early stage, it's important to remember that you're in training. If your attention begins to wander, get up immediately and take a short break. It is better to study effectively for 15 minutes and then take a break than to fritter away 45 minutes out of your study hour. As your endurance develops, you can increase the length of study periods.

Use SQ3R to Help You Master This Text

David Myers organized this text by using a system called SQ3R (Survey, Question, Read, Rehearse, Review). Using SQ3R can help you to understand what you read, and to retain that information longer.

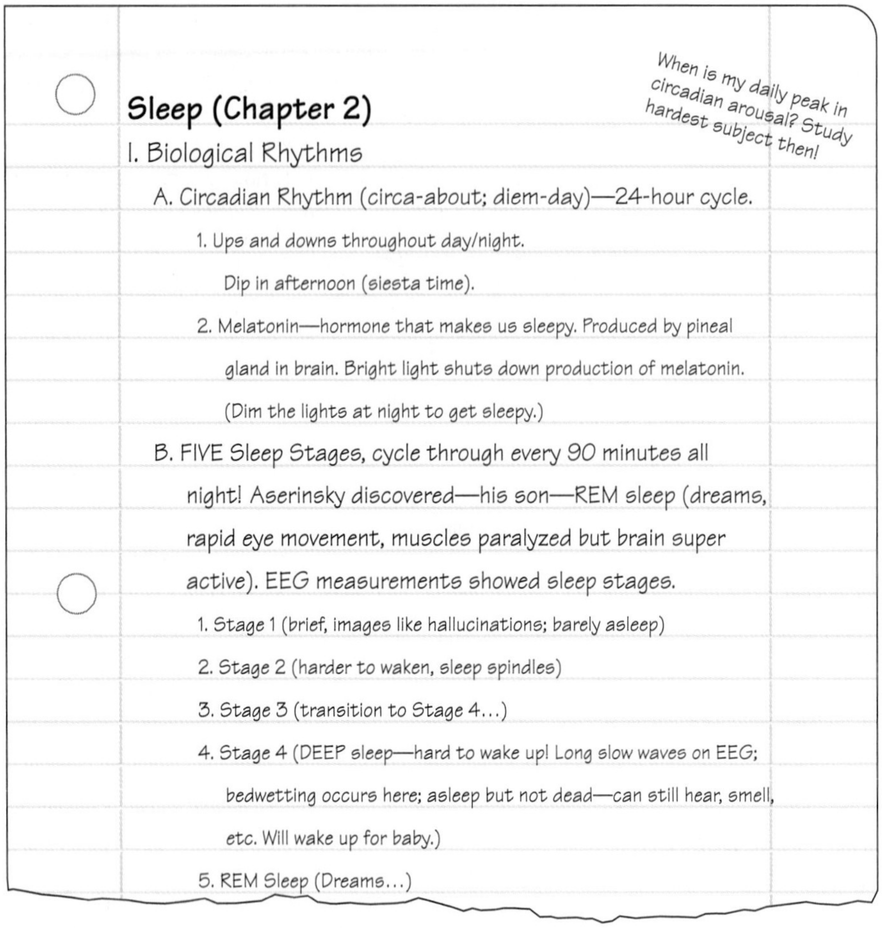

Sleep (Chapter 2)

When is my daily peak in circadian arousal? Study hardest subject then!

I. Biological Rhythms

  A. Circadian Rhythm (circa-about; diem-day)—24-hour cycle.

    1. Ups and downs throughout day/night.

      Dip in afternoon (siesta time).

    2. Melatonin—hormone that makes us sleepy. Produced by pineal gland in brain. Bright light shuts down production of melatonin.

      (Dim the lights at night to get sleepy.)

  B. FIVE Sleep Stages, cycle through every 90 minutes all night! Aserinsky discovered—his son—REM sleep (dreams, rapid eye movement, muscles paralyzed but brain super active). EEG measurements showed sleep stages.

    1. Stage 1 (brief, images like hallucinations; barely asleep)

    2. Stage 2 (harder to waken, sleep spindles)

    3. Stage 3 (transition to Stage 4...)

    4. Stage 4 (DEEP sleep—hard to wake up! Long slow waves on EEG; bedwetting occurs here; asleep but not dead—can still hear, smell, etc. Will wake up for baby.)

    5. REM Sleep (Dreams...)

FIGURE 1 ● **Sample class notes in outline form** Here is a sample from a student's notes taken in outline form from a lecture on sleep.

Applying SQ3R may feel at first as though it's taking more time and effort to "read" a chapter, but with practice, these steps will become automatic.

Survey

Before you read a chapter, *survey* its key parts. Scan the chapter outlines. Note that main sections have numbered learning objective questions to help you focus. Pay attention to headings, which indicate important subtopics, and to words set in bold type. In the last few pages of the chapter, you will see a list of important terms and concepts, followed by a visual Concept Map that gives an overview of the chapter.

Surveying gives you the big picture of a chapter's content and organization. Understanding the chapter's logical sections will help you break your reading into manageable pieces in your study sessions.

Question

As you survey, don't limit yourself to the numbered learning objective questions that appear throughout the chapter. Jotting down additional questions of your own will cause you to look at the material in a new way. (You might, for example, scan this section's headings and ask "What does 'SQ3R' mean?") Information becomes easier to remember when you make it personally meaningful. Trying to answer your questions while reading will keep you in an active learning mode.

Read

As you *read*, keep your questions in mind and actively search for the answers. If you come to material that seems to answer an important question that you haven't jotted down, stop and write down that new question.

Be sure to read everything. Don't skip photo or art captions, graphs, boxes, tables, or quotes. An idea that seems vague when you read about it may become clear when you see it in a graph or table. Keep in mind that instructors sometimes base their test questions on figures and tables.

Rehearse

When you have found the answer to one of your questions, close your eyes and mentally recite the question and its answer. Then *write* the answer next to the question in your own words. Trying to explain something in your own words will help you figure out where there are gaps in your understanding. *Rehearsal* develops the skills you will need when you are taking exams. If you study without ever putting your book and notes aside, you may develop false confidence about what you know. With the material available, you may be able to *recognize* the correct answer to your questions. But will you be able to *recall* it later, when you take an exam without having your mental props in sight?

Test your understanding as often as you can. Testing yourself is part of successful learning, because the act of testing forces your brain to work at remembering, thus establishing the memory more permanently (so you can find it later for the exam!).

Use the self-testing opportunities throughout each chapter, including the Practice Tests at the end of

You will hear more about SQ3R in Chapter 1.

each main section. Also take advantage of the self-testing that is available on the free book companion Web site (www.worthpublishers.com/myers).

Review

After working your way through the chapter, read over your questions and your written answers. Study the visual Concept Map review at the end of the chapter. Take an extra few minutes to create a brief written summary covering all of your questions and answers.

Don't Forget About Rewards!

If you have trouble studying regularly, giving yourself a reward may help. What kind of reward works best? That depends on what you enjoy. You might start by making a list of 5 or 10 things that put a smile on your face. Spending time with a loved one, taking a walk or going for a bike ride, relaxing with a magazine or novel, or watching a favorite show can provide immediate rewards for achieving short-term study goals.

To motivate yourself when you're having trouble sticking to your schedule, allow yourself an immediate reward for completing a specific task. If running makes you smile, change your shoes, grab a friend, and head out the door! You deserve a reward for a job well done.

Do You Need to Revise Your New Schedule?

What if you've lived with your schedule for a few weeks, but you aren't making progress toward your academic and personal goals? What if your studying hasn't paid off in better grades? Don't despair and abandon your program, but do take a little time to figure out what's gone wrong.

Are You Doing Well in Some Courses But Not in Others?

Perhaps you need to shift your priorities a bit. You may need to allow more time for Chemistry, for example, and less time for some other course.

Have You Received a Poor Grade on a Test?

Did your grade fail to reflect the effort you spent preparing for the test? This can happen to even the hardest-working student, often on a first test with a new instructor. This common experience can leave you feeling confused and abused. "What do I have to do to get an A?" "The test was unfair!" "I studied the wrong material!"

Try to figure out what went wrong. Analyze the questions you missed, dividing them into two categories: class-based questions, and text-based questions. How many questions did you miss in each category? If you find far more errors in one category than in the other, you'll have some clues to help you revise your schedule. Depending on the pattern you've found, you can add extra study time to review of class notes, or to studying the text.

Are You Trying to Study Regularly for the First Time and Feeling Overwhelmed?

Perhaps you've set your initial goals too high. Remember, the point of time management is to *identify a regular schedule that will help you achieve success*. Like any skill, time management takes practice. Accept your limitations and revise your schedule to work slowly up to where you know you need to be—perhaps adding 15 minutes of study time per day.

* * *

I hope that these suggestions help make you more successful academically, and that they enhance the quality of your life in general. Having the necessary skills makes any job a lot easier and more pleasant. Let me repeat my warning not to attempt to make too drastic a change in your life-style immediately. Good habits require time and self-discipline to develop. Once established, they can last a lifetime.

REVIEW: TIME MANAGEMENT—OR HOW TO BE A GREAT STUDENT AND STILL HAVE A LIFE!

You will encounter these helpful Concept Maps at the end of each chapter. Use them as a visual aid to organize and review key topics.

1 How Are You Using Your Time Now?

- Identify your areas of weakness.
- Keep a time-use diary.
- Record the time you actually spend on activities.
- Record your energy levels to find your most productive times.

2 Design a Better Schedule

- Decide on your goals for the term and for each week.
- Enter class times, work times, social times (for family and friends), and time needed for other obligations and for practical activities.
- Tailor study times to avoid interference and to meet each course's needs.
- Set time aside for rest and recreation.

3 Make Every Minute of Your Study Time Count

- Take careful class notes (in outline form) that will help you recall and rehearse material covered in lectures.
- Try to eliminate distractions to your study time, and ask friends and family to help you focus on your work.
- Set specific, realistic daily goals to help you focus on each day's tasks.
- Use the SQ3R system (survey, question, read, rehearse, review) to master material covered in your text.
- When you achieve your daily goals, reward yourself with something that you value.

4 Do You Need to Revise Your New Schedule?

- Allocate extra study time for courses that are more difficult, and a little less time for courses that are easy for you.
- Study your test results to help determine a more effective balance in your schedule.
- Make sure your schedule is not too ambitious. Gradually establish a schedule that will be effective for the long term.

1

PSYCHOLOGY'S ROOTS, BIG IDEAS, AND CRITICAL THINKING TOOLS

Hoping to understand themselves and others, millions turn to psychology, as you now do. What do psychologists really know? "What's it like being married to a psychologist?" people have occasionally asked my wife. "Does he use his psychology on you?"

"So, does your Dad, like, analyze you?" my children have been asked many times by friends.

"What do you think of me?" asked one barber, hoping for an instant personality analysis after learning that I am a psychologist.

For these questioners, as for most people whose exposure to psychology comes from popular media, psychologists analyze personality, offer counseling, and dispense ideas about the meaning of dreams, the source of happiness, and the path to love.

Do they? Yes, and much more. Psychology's roots are broad, its ideas are big, and its investigations are scientific.

1

Psychology's Roots

Once upon a time, on a planet in your neighborhood of the universe, there came to be people. These creatures became intensely interested in themselves and in one another. They wondered, "WHO ARE WE? WHY DO WE THINK ◄ AND FEEL AND ACT AS WE DO? AND HOW ARE WE TO UNDERSTAND—AND TO MANAGE—THOSE AROUND US?"[1]

To be human is to be curious about ourselves and the world around us. Before 300 B.C.E., the Greek naturalist and philosopher Aristotle (384–322 B.C.E.) wondered about learning and memory, motivation and emotion, perception and personality. Today we chuckle at some of his guesses, like his suggestion that a meal makes us sleepy by causing gas and heat to collect around the source of our personality, the heart. But credit Aristotle with asking the right questions.

Now, more than 2000 years later, psychology asks similar questions. But with its roots reaching back into philosophy and biology, and its branches spreading out across the world, psychology gathers its answers by scientifically studying how we act, think, and feel.

Psychological Science Is Born

1 **How has psychology's focus changed over time?[2]**

Psychology as we know it was born on a December day in 1879, in a small, third-floor room at a German university. There, Wilhelm Wundt and his assistants created a machine to measure how long it took people to press a telegraph key after hearing a ball hit a platform (Hunt, 1993).[3]

(Most hit the key within about one-tenth of a second.) Wundt's attempt to measure "atoms of the mind"—the fastest and simplest mental processes—was psychology's first experiment. And that modest third-floor room took its place in history as the first psychological laboratory.

Psychology's earliest pioneers— "Magellans of the mind," Morton Hunt called them (1993)—

© Bettmann/Corbis

Wilhelm Wundt: Wundt established the first psychology laboratory at the University of Leipzig, Germany.

came from many disciplines and countries. Wundt was both a philosopher and a physiologist. Charles Darwin, who proposed evolutionary psychology, was an English naturalist. Ivan Pavlov, who taught us much about learning, was a Russian physiologist. Sigmund Freud, a famous personality theorist, was an Austrian physician. Jean Piaget, who explored children's developing minds, was a Swiss biologist. William James, who shared his love of psychology in his 1890 textbook, was an American philosopher.

Few of the early pioneers were women. In the late 1800s, psychology, like most fields, was a man's world. William James helped break that mold when he accepted Mary Calkins as his student. Although Calkins went on to outscore all the male students on the Ph.D. exams, Harvard University denied her a degree. In its place, she was told, she could have a degree from Radcliffe College, Harvard's sister

Margaret Floy Washburn: After Harvard refused to grant Calkins the degree she had earned, Washburn became the first woman to receive a psychology Ph.D. She focused on animal behavior research in *The Animal Mind*.

Center for the History of Psychology Archives of the History of American Psychology, The University of Akron

school for women. Calkins turned down the offer but continued her work, which her colleagues honored by electing her the first female president of the American Psychological Association (APA). Animal behavior researcher Margaret Floy Washburn became the first woman to receive a psychology Ph.D. and the second to become an APA president.

The rest of the story of psychology— the story told by this book—develops at many levels, in the hands of many people, with interests ranging from therapy to the study of nerve cell activity. As you might expect, agreeing on a definition of *psychology* has not been easy.

For the early pioneers, psychology was "the science of mental life." And so it continued until the 1920s, when two larger-than-life American psychologists dismissed this idea. John B. Watson, and later B. F. Skinner, insisted that psychology must be "the scientific study of observable behavior." After all, science is rooted in observation. How can you observe a sensation, a feeling, or a thought? You *can*, however, observe and record people's *behavior* as they respond to different situations. Many agreed, and these **behaviorists**[4] were one of two major forces in psychology well into the 1960s.

© Bettmann/Corbis

Sigmund Freud: The controversial ideas of this famous personality theorist and therapist influenced humanity's self-understanding.

The other major force was *Freudian psychology*. Some students' ideas about psychology focus on Sigmund Freud alone. They wonder: Is psychology all about Freud's teachings on unconscious sexual conflicts and the mind's defenses against its own wishes and impulses? No. Psychology is much more, though Freudian psychology did have an impact. (In chapters to come, we'll look more closely at Freud and others mentioned here.)

---

1. The questions highlighted in orange throughout the text will help you see how psychology applies to everyday life.

2. Throughout this book you will find numbered questions that preview main sections and suggest your learning objective. Keep the question in mind as you read the section to ensure that you are following the main point of the discussion. These learning objective questions are repeated and answered in the Review at the end of each chapter.

3. This book's information sources are cited in parentheses, with name and date. Every citation can be found in the end-of-book References, with complete documentation.

4. Throughout the text, important concepts are **boldfaced.** As you study, you can find these terms defined in a boxed section nearby, and in the Glossary at the end of the book.

As the behaviorists had done in the early 1900s, two other groups rejected the definition of *psychology* that was current in the 1960s. The first, the **humanistic psychologists,** led by Carl Rogers and Abraham Maslow, found both Freudian psychology and behaviorism too limiting.

Mary Evans Picture Library/Alamy

William James and Mary Whiton Calkins: William James was a legendary teacher-writer of psychology. Among his students was Mary Whiton Calkins, who became famous for her memory research and for being the first woman president of the American Psychological Association.

Rather than focusing on childhood memories or learned behaviors, Rogers and Maslow drew attention to ways that a positive environment can enhance our personal growth, and to our needs for love and acceptance.

Wellesley College Archives

The rebellion of another group of psychologists during the 1960s is now known as the *cognitive revolution,* and it led the field back to its early interest in mental processes. But this new view differed in an important way. It intended to study internal thought processes *scientifically,* to find out how our minds perceive, process, and remember information. More recently **cognitive neuroscience** has enriched our understanding of the brain ac-

©Underwood & Underwood/Corbis

John B. Watson and Rosalie Rayner: Working with Rayner, Watson championed psychology as the scientific study of behavior. He and Rayner showed fear could be learned, in experiments on a baby who became famous as "Little Albert."

tivities underlying our mental activities.

This long journey has led to the current definition: **Psychology** is *the science of behavior and mental processes.* Let's unpack this definition. *Behavior* is anything a human or nonhuman animal *does*—any action we can observe and record. Blinking, smiling, talking, and questionnaire marking are all observable behaviors. *Mental processes* are the internal states we infer from behavior—such as thoughts, beliefs, and feelings. For example, I may say that "I feel your pain," but in fact I infer it from the hints you give me—crying out, clutching your side, and gasping.

The key word in psychology's definition is *science.* Psychology, as I will stress again and again, is less a set of findings than a way of asking and answering questions. My aim, then, is not merely to report results but also to show you how psychologists play their game, evaluating opinions and ideas. I hope

Center for the History of Psychology Archives of the History of American Psychology, The University of Akron

you, too, will learn how to play the game—to think smarter when explaining events and making choices in your own life.

Bachrach/Getty Images

B. F. Skinner: This leading behaviorist rejected the idea of studying inner thoughts and feelings. He studied how consequences shape behavior.

Contemporary Psychology

2 **What are psychology's current perspectives and some of its subfields?**

Psychologists' diverse interests make it hard to picture a psychologist at work. You might start by imagining a neuroscientist probing an animal's brain, an intelligence researcher studying how quickly infants become bored with a familiar scene, or a therapist listening closely to a client's depressed thoughts. Psychology's many perspectives, which are described in **TABLE 1.1**, range from the biological to the social-cultural, and its settings range from the laboratory to the clinic. But all share a common goal: to describe and explain behavior and the mind underlying it.

Psychology also relates to many other fields. You'll find psychologists teaching in medical schools, law schools, and

behaviorism the view that psychology (1) should be an objective science that (2) studies behavior without reference to mental processes. Most research psychologists today agree with (1) but not with (2).

humanistic psychology emphasized the growth potential of healthy people and the individual's potential for personal growth.

cognitive neuroscience the interdisciplinary study of the brain activity linked with mental activity (including perception, thinking, memory, and language).

psychology the science of behavior and mental processes.

TABLE 1.1	Psychology's Current Perspectives		
Perspective	**Focus**	**Sample Questions**	**Examples of Subfields Using This Perspective**
Neuroscience	How the body and brain enable emotions, memories, and sensory experiences	How do pain messages travel from the hand to the brain? How is blood chemistry linked with moods and motives?	Biological; cognitive; clinical
Evolutionary	How natural selection explains certain human traits and tendencies	How has our evolutionary past influenced our modern-day mating preferences? Why do humans learn some fears so much more easily than others?	Biological; developmental; social
Behavior genetics	How much our genes and our environment influence our individual differences	To what extent are psychological traits such as intelligence, personality, sexual orientation, and vulnerability to depression products of our genes? Of our environment?	Personality; developmental; legal/forensic
Psychodynamic	How behavior springs from unconscious drives and conflicts	How can someone's personality traits and disorders be explained in terms of their childhood relationships?	Clinical; counseling; personality
Behavioral	How we learn observable responses	How do we learn to fear particular objects or situations? What is the most effective way to alter our behavior, say, to lose weight or stop smoking?	Clinical; counseling; industrial-organizational
Cognitive	How we encode, process, store, and retrieve information	How do we use information in remembering? Reasoning? Solving problems?	Cognitive neuroscience; clinical; counseling; industrial-organizational
Social-cultural	How behavior and thinking vary across situations and cultures	How are we alike as members of one human family? How do we differ as products of our environments?	Developmental; social psychology; clinical; counseling

theological seminaries, and you'll see them working in hospitals, factories, and corporate offices. In this course, you will hear about

- *biological psychologists* exploring the links between brain and mind.
- *developmental psychologists* studying our changing abilities from womb to tomb.
- *cognitive psychologists* experimenting with how we perceive, think, and solve problems.
- *personality psychologists* investigating our persistent traits.
- *industrial-organizational psychologists* studying and advising on behavior in the workplace.
- *counseling psychologists* helping people cope with personal and career challenges by recognizing their strengths and resources.

- *clinical psychologists* assessing and treating mental, emotional, and behavior disorders (as distinct from *psychiatrists,* medical doctors who also prescribe drugs when treating psychological disorders).
- *social psychologists* exploring how we view and affect one another.

Psychology also influences modern culture. Knowledge transforms us. After learning about psychology's findings, people less often judge psychological disorders as moral failures. They less often regard women as men's inferiors. They less often view children as ignorant, willful beasts in need of taming. And as thinking changes, so do actions. "In each case," noted Hunt (1990, p. 206), "knowledge has modified attitudes, and, through them, behavior." Once aware of psychology's well-researched ideas—about how body and mind connect, how we construct our perceptions, how a child's mind grows, how people across the world differ (and are alike)—your own mind may never again be quite the same.

Testing is an important part of learning and remembering. Dive into these Practice Test sections, and every self-testing opportunity!

THE BASICS

1. In 1879, in psychology's first laboratory experiment, _____ and his students measured the time lag between hearing a ball hit a platform and pressing a key.

   a. Charles Darwin
   b. William James
   c. Sigmund Freud
   d. Wilhelm Wundt

2. An important psychology text was published in 1890. Its author was
   a. Wilhelm Wundt.
   b. Mary Whiton Calkins.
   c. Charles Darwin.
   d. William James.

3. The definition of *psychology* has changed several times since the late 1800s. In the early twentieth century, _____ redefined *psychology* as "the scientific study of observable behavior."
   a. John B. Watson
   b. Margaret Floy Washburn
   c. William James
   d. Jean Piaget

4. The perspective in psychology that focuses on how behavior and thought differ from situation to situation and from culture to culture is the
   a. cognitive perspective.
   b. behavioral perspective.
   c. social-cultural perspective.
   d. neuroscience perspective.

5. The perspective in psychology that emphasizes how we learn observable responses is the
   a. cognitive perspective.
   b. behavioral perspective.
   c. social-cultural perspective.
   d. neuroscience perspective.

6. A psychologist who treats emotionally troubled adolescents at a local mental health agency is most likely to be a(n)
   a. biological psychologist.
   b. personality psychologist.
   c. industrial-organizational psychologist.
   d. personality psychologist.

THE BIG PICTURE

1A. What event defined the start of scientific psychology?

IN YOUR EVERYDAY LIFE

▪ How would you have defined *psychology* before taking this class?

Answers: 1. d, 2. d, 3. a, 4. c, 5. b, 6. d. Answers to The Big Picture questions can be found in Appendix B at the end of the book.

---

5. With special thanks to Amy Himsel (El Camino College) for her work on the In Your Everyday Life questions, which help students make the concepts more personally meaningful, and may also function as Discussion Forum prompts.

Four Big Ideas in Psychology

3 What four big ideas run throughout this book?

I have used four of psychology's big ideas to organize material in this book.

1. **Critical thinking** Science supports thinking that examines assumptions, uncovers hidden values, weighs evidence, and tests conclusions. Science-aided thinking is smart thinking.

2. **The biopsychosocial approach** We can view human behavior from three levels—the biological, psychological, and social-cultural. We share a biologically rooted human nature. Yet cultural and psychological influences fine-tune our assumptions, values, and behaviors.

3. **The two-track mind** Today's psychological science explores our *dual-processing* capacity. Our perception, thinking, memory, and attitudes all operate on two levels: conscious (with awareness) and unconscious (without awareness). It has been a surprise to learn how much information processing happens without our awareness.

4. **Exploring human strengths** Psychology today focuses not only on understanding and offering relief from troublesome behaviors and emotions, but also on understanding and building the emotions and traits that help us to thrive.

Let's consider these four big ideas, one by one.

Big Idea 1: Critical Thinking Is Smart Thinking

Whether reading a news report or swapping ideas with others, **critical thinkers** ask questions. How do we know that? Who benefits from this? Is the conclusion based on guesswork and gut feelings, or on evidence? How do we know one event caused the other? How else could we explain things?

In psychology, critical thinking has led to some surprising findings. Believe it or not . . .

- massive losses of brain tissue early in life may have few long-term effects (see Chapter 2).

- within days, newborns can recognize their mother's odor and voice (Chapter 3).

- some people with brain damage can learn new skills, yet at the mind's conscious level be unaware that they have these skills (Chapter 7).

- diverse people—men and women, old and young, rich and middle class, those with disabilities and without—report roughly the same levels of personal happiness (Chapter 9).

- when all else has failed, delivering an electric shock to the brain (electroconvulsive therapy) may snap people out of severe depression (Chapter 13).

This same critical thinking has also debunked some popular beliefs. When we let the evidence speak for itself, we learn that . . .

- sleepwalkers are *not* acting out their dreams (Chapter 2).

- our past is *not* precisely recorded in our brain. Neither brain stimulation nor hypnosis will let us push "play" and relive long-buried memories (Chapter 7).

- most of us do *not* suffer from low self-esteem, and high self-esteem is not all good (Chapter 11).

- opposites do *not* generally attract (Chapter 14).

In later chapters, you'll see many more examples of research in which critical thinking has challenged our beliefs and triggered new ways of thinking.

Big Idea 2: Behavior Is a Biopsychosocial Event

Each of us is part of a larger social system—a family, a group, a society. But each of us is also made up of smaller systems,

---

critical thinking thinking that does not blindly accept arguments and conclusions. Rather, it examines assumptions, uncovers hidden values, weighs evidence, and assesses conclusions.

such as our nervous system and body organs, which are composed of still smaller systems—cells, molecules, and atoms.

If we study this complexity with simple tools, we may end up with partial answers. Consider: Why do grizzly bears hibernate? Is it because hibernation helped their ancestors to survive and reproduce? Because their biology drives them to do so? Because cold climates hinder food gathering during winter? Each of these is a partial truth, but no one is a full answer. For the best possible view, we need to use many *levels of analysis*. The **biopsychosocial approach** considers three influence levels: biological, psychological, and social-cultural (**FIGURE 1.1**). Each viewpoint gives us valuable insights into behavior, and together, they offer us the most complete picture.

Consider gender differences. *Gender* is not the same as *sex*. *Gender* refers to the traits and behaviors we expect in a man or a woman. *Sex* refers to the biological characteristics we inherit, thanks to our genes. To study gender differences, we would want to know as much as possible about biological influences. But we would also want to understand how our **culture**—the ideas and behaviors shared by a group and passed on from one generation to the next—defines *male* and *female*. Even with this much information, our view would be incomplete. We would also need some understanding of *individual* differences arising from personal abilities and learning.

Biological influences:
• genetic predispositions
• genetic mutations
• natural selection of adaptive physiology and behaviors
• genes responding to the environment

Psychological influences:
• learned fears and other learned expectations
• emotional responses
• cognitive processing and perceptual interpretations

Behavior or mental process

Social-cultural influences:
• presence of others
• cultural, societal, and family expectations
• peer and other group influences
• compelling models (such as in the media)

FIGURE 1.1 ● **Biopsychosocial approach: Three paths to understanding** Studying events from many viewpoints gives us a more complete picture than any one perspective could offer.

Studying all these influences, researchers have found some gender differences—in what we dream, in how we express and detect emotion, and in our risk for substance abuse, depression, and eating disorders. Psychologically as well as biologically, women and men differ. But we are also alike. Whether female or male, we learn to walk at about the same age. We experience the same sensations of light and sound. We feel the same pangs of hunger, desire, and fear. We exhibit similar overall intelligence and well-being.

Psychology's biggest and most persistent issue is one part of the biopsychosocial approach: How do we judge the contributions of *nature* (biology) and *nurture* (experience)? Today's psychologists explore this age-old **nature-nurture issue** by asking, for example:

● How are differences in intelligence, personality, and psychological disorders influenced by heredity and by environment?

● Is our *sexual orientation* written in our genes or learned through our experiences?

Diverse Yet Alike

A Smile Is a Smile the World Around

Throughout this book, you will see examples not only of our cultural and gender diversity but also of our shared human nature. People in different cultures vary in when and how often they smile, but a naturally happy smile *means* the same thing anywhere in the world.

David Malan/Getty Images

© DreamPictures/Blend Images/Corbis

Felix Hug/lpi

A nature-made nature-nurture experiment:
Identical twins (right) have the same genes. This makes them ideal participants in studies designed to shed light on hereditary and environmental influences on temperament, intelligence, and other traits. Fraternal twins (above) have different genes but often share the same environment. Twin studies provide a wealth of findings—described in later chapters—showing the importance of both nature and nurture.

©Hola Images/agefotostock   Tony Freeman/Photo Edit

- Should we treat depression as a disorder of the brain or a disorder of thought—or both?

In most cases, *nurture works on what nature endows*. Our species has been graced with a great biological gift: an enormous ability to learn and adapt. Moreover (and you will read this over and over in the pages that follow), every psychological event—every thought, every emotion—is also a biological event.

Big Idea 3: We Operate With a Two-Track Mind (Dual Processing)

From moment to moment we're consciously aware of little of what is happening around and within us. Our conscious mind *feels* like our body's chief executive. But mountains of new research reveal that our brain works on two tracks—the conscious track, and a surprisingly large unconscious, automatic track that is processing information without our awareness. Thinking, memory, perception, language, and attitudes all operate on these two tracks. Today's researchers call it **dual processing.** We know more than we know we know.

A fascinating scientific story illustrates the mind's two tracks. Sometimes

science-aided critical thinking confirms widely held beliefs. But sometimes, as this story illustrates, the truth turns out to be stranger than fiction.

During my time spent at Scotland's University of St. Andrews, I came to know research psychologists Melvyn Goodale and David Milner (2004, 2006). A local woman, whom they call D. F., was overcome by carbon monoxide one day while showering. The resulting brain damage left her unable to recognize objects visually. Yet she was only partly blind, for she acted as if she *could* see. Asked to slip a postcard into a mail slot, she could do so without error. And although she could not report the width of a block in front of her, she could grasp it with just the right finger-thumb distance.

How could this be? HOW COULD A◄ WOMAN WHO IS BLIND GRASP OBJECTS

ACCURATELY? Goodale and Milner knew from animal research that the eye sends information to different brain areas, each of which has a different task. Sure enough, a scan of D. F.'s brain activity revealed normal activity in the area concerned with reaching for and grasping objects, but not in the area concerned with consciously recognizing objects. So, would the reverse damage lead to the opposite symptoms? Indeed, there are a few such patients—who can see and recognize objects but have difficulty pointing toward or grasping them.

We think of our vision as one system: We look, we see, we respond to what we see. Actually, vision is a great example of our dual processing. A *visual perception track* enables us to think about the world—to recognize things and to plan future actions. A *visual action track* guides our moment-to-moment actions.

This big idea—that much of our everyday thinking, feeling, sensing, and acting operates outside our awareness—may be a weird new idea for you. It was for me. I long believed that my own intentions and deliberate choices ruled my life. Of course, in many ways they do. But in the mind's downstairs, as you will see in later chapters, there is much, much more to being human.

---

biopsychosocial approach an integrated approach that incorporates different but complementary views from biological, psychological, and social-cultural perspectives.

culture the enduring behaviors, ideas, attitudes, and traditions shared by a group of people and transmitted from one generation to the next.

nature-nurture issue the longstanding controversy over the relative contributions that genes and experience make to the development of psychological traits and behaviors. Today's psychological science sees traits and behaviors arising from the interaction of nature and nurture.

dual processing the principle that information is often simultaneously processed on separate conscious and unconscious tracks.

Big Idea 4: Psychology Explores Human Strengths as Well as Challenges

Psychology's first hundred years focused on understanding and treating troubles, such as abuse and anxiety, depression and disease, prejudice and poverty. Much of today's psychology continues the exploration of such challenges. To balance this focus on human problems, Martin Seligman and others (2002, 2005) have called for more research on human flourishing. These psychologists use scientific methods to explore "positive emotions, positive character traits, and enabling institutions." They believe that happiness is a by-product of a pleasant, engaged, and meaningful life. Thus, **positive psychology** focuses on building a "good life" that engages our skills, and a "meaningful life" that points beyond ourselves. We can view this movement as having three main supports:

- The first pillar, *positive emotions,* is built of satisfaction with the past, happiness with the present, and optimism about the future.

- The bricks and mortar of the second pillar, *positive character,* are traits such as creativity, courage, compassion, integrity, self-control, leadership, wisdom, and spirituality. Current research examines the roots and fruits of such qualities, sometimes by studying the lives of individuals who offer striking examples.

- The third pillar, *positive groups, communities, and cultures,* supports positive

social forces, including healthy families, friendly neighborhoods, effective schools, socially responsible media, and civil discussions.

Will psychology have a more positive mission in this century? Can it help us all to flourish? Without slighting the need to repair damage and cure disease, an increasing number of scientists worldwide believe it can, and they are helping it happen right now.

Martin E. P. Seligman: "The main purpose of a positive psychology is to measure, understand, and then build the human strengths and the civic virtues."

PRACTICE TEST

THE BASICS

7. A newspaper article describes how a "cure for cancer has been found." A critical thinker probably will

  a. dismiss the article as untrue.

  b. accept the information as a wonderful breakthrough.

  c. question the article, evaluate the evidence, and assess the conclusions.

  d. question the article but accept it as true if the author has an excellent reputation.

8. In the history of psychology, a major topic has been the relative influence of nature and nurture. Nature is to nurture as

  a. personality is to intelligence.

  b. biology is to experience.

  c. intelligence is to biology.

  d. psychological traits are to behaviors.

9. Which one of the following is NOT one of the four big ideas in psychology used to organize material in this book?

  a. Exploring human strengths

  b. The two-track mind

  c. Industrial-organizational psychology

  d. The biopsychosocial approach

THE BIG PICTURE

1B. What are the four big ideas that organize material in this book?

IN YOUR EVERYDAY LIFE

▪ Imagine someone claims she can interpret your dreams or can speak to the dead. How could critical thinking help you check her claims?

▪ Which of the four big ideas is most interesting to you? What was it that attracted your attention to that idea?

Answers: 7. c, 8. b, 9. c. Answers to The Big Picture questions can be found in Appendix B at the end of the book.

Why Do Psychology?

Many people feel guided by their *intuition*—by what they feel in their gut. "Buried deep within each and every one of us, there is an instinctive, heart-felt awareness that provides—if we allow it to—the most reliable guide," offered Britain's Prince Charles (2000).

The Limits of Intuition and Common Sense

4 How do hindsight bias and overconfidence make research findings seem like ordinary common sense?

Prince Charles has much company, judging from the long list of pop psychology books on "intuitive managing," "intuitive trading," and "intuitive healing." Intuition is indeed important. Research shows that, more than we realize, our thinking, memory, and attitudes operate automatically, off screen. Like jumbo jets, we fly mostly on autopilot.

But intuition can lead us astray. Our gut feelings may tell us that lie detectors work and that eyewitness recollections are accurate. But as you will see in chapters to come, hundreds of findings challenge these beliefs.

Hunches are a good starting point, even for smart thinkers. But thinking critically means checking assumptions, weighing evidence, inviting criticism, and testing conclusions. Does the death penalty prevent murders? Whether your gut tells you *Yes* or *No,* you need more evidence. You might ask, *Do states with a death penalty have lower homicide rates? After states pass death-penalty laws, do their homicide rates drop? Do homicide rates rise in states that abandon the death penalty?* If we ignore the answers to such questions (which the evidence suggests are *No, No,* and *No*), our intuition may steer us down the wrong path.

"The first principle is that you must not fool yourself—and you are the easiest person to fool."

Richard Feynman (1997)

With its standards for gathering and sifting evidence, psychological science helps us avoid errors and think smarter. Before moving on to our study of how psychologists use psychology's methods in their research, let's look more closely at two common flaws in intuitive thinking—*hindsight bias* and *overconfidence*.

Did We Know It All Along? Hindsight Bias

Some people think psychology merely proves what we already know and then dresses it in jargon: "So what else is new—you get paid for using fancy methods to tell me what my grandmother knew?" But consider how easy it is to draw the bull's eye *after* the arrow strikes. After the stock market drops, people say it was "due for a correction." After the football game, we credit the coach if a "gutsy play" wins the game and fault the coach for the "stupid play" if it doesn't. After a war or an election, its outcome usually seems obvious. Although history may therefore seem like a series of predictable events, the actual future is seldom foreseen. No one's diary recorded, "Today the Hundred Years War began."

This **hindsight bias** (also called the *I-knew-it-all-along phenomenon*) is easy to demonstrate: Give half the members of a group a true psychological finding, and give the other half an opposite result. Tell the first group, "Psychologists have found that separation weakens romantic attraction. As the saying goes, 'Out of sight, out of mind.'" Ask them to imagine why this might be true. Most people can, and nearly all will then view this true finding as unsurprising—just common sense.

Tell the second group the opposite, "Psychologists have found that separation strengthens romantic attraction. As the saying goes, 'Absence makes the heart grow fonder.'" People given this false statement can also easily explain it, and most will also see it as unsurprising. When two opposite findings both seem like common sense, we have a problem!

Such errors in our recollections and explanations show why we need psychological research. Just asking people how and why they felt or acted as they did can sometimes be misleading. Why? Not because common sense is usually

wrong, but because common sense more easily describes what *has* happened than what *will* happen. As physicist Neils Bohr reportedly said, "Prediction is very difficult, especially about the future."

Of course, many of psychology's findings have been foreseen. We're all behavior watchers, and sometimes we get it right. Many people believe that love breeds happiness, and it does. (We have what Chapter 9 calls a deep "need to belong.") But sometimes Grandmother's intuition, informed by countless casual observations, gets it wrong. Psychological research has overturned many popular ideas—that familiarity breeds contempt, that dreams predict the future, and that emotional reactions coincide with menstrual phase. It has also surprised us with discoveries we had not predicted—that the brain's chemical messengers control our moods and memories, that other animals can pass along their learned habits, that stress affects our capacity to fight disease.

> "We don't like their sound. Groups of guitars are on their way out."
> Decca Records, in turning down a recording contract with the Beatles in 1962

Overconfidence

We humans also tend to be *overconfident*. Consider these three word puzzles (called anagrams), which people like you were asked to unscramble in one study (Goranson, 1978).

WREAT → WATER
ETRYN → ENTRY
GRABE → BARGE

About how many seconds do you think it would have taken you to unscramble each anagram? Once people know the target word, the answer seems obvious—so much so that they become overconfident. They think they would have seen the

Hindsight bias: When drilling the Deepwater Horizon oil well in 2010, oil industry employees took some shortcuts and ignored some warning signs, without intending to put their companies and the environment at serious risk of devastation. *After* the resulting Gulf oil spill, with the benefit of 20/20 hindsight, the foolishness of those judgments became obvious.

positive psychology the scientific study of human functioning, with the goals of discovering and promoting strengths and virtues that help individuals and communities to thrive.

hindsight bias the tendency to believe, after learning an outcome, that we could have predicted it. (Also known as the *I-knew-it-all-along phenomenon.*)

solution in only 10 seconds or so. In reality, the average problem solver spends 3 minutes, as you also might, given a similar puzzle without the solution: OCHSA. (See the footnote below to check your answer.[6])

> Fun anagram solutions from Wordsmith.org:
> Elvis = lives
> Dormitory = dirty room
> Slot machines = cash lost in 'em

ARE WE ANY GOOD AT PREDICTING OUR◄ SOCIAL BEHAVIOR? In one study, students predicted their own behavior at the beginning of the school year (Vallone et al., 1990). Would they drop a course, vote in an upcoming election, call their parents more than twice a month (and so forth)? On average, the students felt 84 percent sure of these self-predictions. But later quizzes about their actual behavior showed their predictions were correct only 71 percent of the time. Even when they were 100 percent sure of themselves, their self-predictions were wrong 15 percent of the time.

The point to remember: Hindsight bias and overconfidence often lead us to overestimate our intuition. But scientific inquiry can help us sift reality from illusion.

The Scientific Attitude

> **5** What are the three key elements of the scientific attitude, and how do they support scientific inquiry?

What makes scientific inquiry so useful for detecting truth? The answer lies in three basic attitudes: *curiosity, skepticism,* and *humility.*

Underlying all science is, first, a hard-headed *curiosity,* a passion to explore and understand without misleading or being misled. Some questions (*Is there life after death?*) are beyond science. To answer them requires a leap of faith. With many other questions (*Can some people read minds?*), the proof is in the pudding. No matter how crazy an idea sounds, the scientist asks, *Does it work?* When put to the test, can its predictions be confirmed?

Magician James Randi uses the scientific approach when testing those claiming to see auras around people's bodies:

Randi: Do you see an aura around my head?

Aura-seer: Yes, indeed.

Randi: Can you still see the aura if I put this magazine in front of my face?

Aura-seer: Of course.

Randi: Then if I were to step behind a wall barely taller than I am, you could determine my location from the aura visible above my head, right?

Randi has told me that no aura-seer has agreed to take this simple test.

When subjected to scientific tests, crazy-sounding ideas sometimes find support. More often, they become part of the mountain of forgotten claims of palm reading, miracle cancer cures, and out-of-body travels. For a lot of bad ideas, science is society's garbage disposal.

Sifting reality from fantasy, sense from nonsense, also requires us to be *skeptical*—not cynical, but also not gullible. "To believe with certainty," says a Polish proverb, "we must begin by doubting." As scientists, psychologists greet statements about behavior and mental processes by asking two questions: *What do you mean?* and *How do you know?*

When ideas compete, skeptical testing can reveal which ones best match the facts. Do parental behaviors determine children's sexual orientation? Can astrologers predict your future based on the position of the planets at your birth? As you will see in later chapters, putting these two claims to the test has led most psychologists to doubt them.

A scientific attitude is more than curiosity and skepticism, however. It also requires *humility*—an awareness that we

can make mistakes, and a willingness to be surprised and follow new roads. In the last analysis, what matters is not my opinion or yours, but the truths nature reveals in response to our questioning. If people or other animals don't behave as our ideas predict, then so much the worse for our ideas. This humble attitude was expressed in one of psychology's early mottos: "The rat is always right."

Historians of science tell us that these attitudes—curiosity, skepticism, and humility—helped make modern science possible.

AP Photo/Alan Diaz

The amazing Randi: Magician and skeptic James Randi has tested and debunked a variety of psychic phenomena.

PRACTICE TEST

THE BASICS

10. *Hindsight bias* refers to our tendency to
a. perceive events as obvious after they happen.
b. assume that two events happened because we wished them to happen.
c. overestimate our ability to predict the future.
d. make judgments that don't follow common sense.

11. As scientists, psychologists view theories with curiosity, skepticism, and humility. This means that they
a. have a negative, cynical approach to other people's research.
b. assume that an article published in a respected journal must be true.
c. believe that every important human question can be tested scientifically.
d. are willing to ask questions and to reject testable claims that cannot be verified by research.

How Do Psychologists Ask and Answer Questions?

Psychologists transform their scientific attitude into practice by using the *scientific method.* They observe events, form theories, and then refine their theories in the light of new observations.

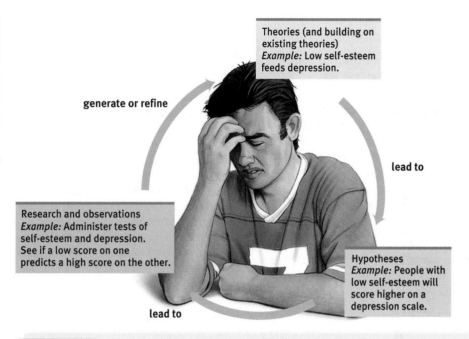

Theories (and building on existing theories)
Example: Low self-esteem feeds depression.

generate or refine

lead to

Research and observations
Example: Administer tests of self-esteem and depression. See if a low score on one predicts a high score on the other.

Hypotheses
Example: People with low self-esteem will score higher on a depression scale.

lead to

FIGURE 1.2 ● **The scientific method** Theory building is a self-correcting process for asking questions and observing nature's answers.

The Scientific Method

6 How do psychological theories guide scientific research?

Chatting with friends and family, we often use *theory* to mean "mere hunch." In science, a **theory** *explains* behaviors or events by offering ideas that *organize* what we have observed. By organizing isolated facts, a theory simplifies. There are too many facts about behavior to remember them all. By linking facts to underlying principles, a theory connects many small dots. The result is a clear picture.

Let's see how this might work with a theory of depression. Imagine that we observe over and over that people with depression describe their past, present, and future in gloomy terms. To organize these observations, we might state, *"Low self-esteem feeds depression."* So far so good: We've created a self-esteem principle that neatly summarizes a long list of facts about people with depression.

But wait—a theory must do more than organize observations. If a theory's principles reflect reality, they will also *predict* events. Thus, a good theory

produces **hypotheses,** predictions that let us test the theory. In this case, the hypothesis might be, *"People with low self-esteem will score higher on a depression test."*

Our next step is to ask people to take two different tests. One will assess self-esteem by asking people to agree or disagree with statements such as, "I have good ideas" and "I am fun to be with." The second test will ask them to agree or disagree with statements that indicate depression.

If our hypothesis is correct, people who report poorer self-images will also score higher on the depression scale **(FIGURE 1.2)**. If not, we will need to reject or revise our theory.

Belief in a theory can bias observations. Believing that depression springs from low self-esteem, we may see what we expect. We may perceive depressed people's neutral comments as self put-downs. As a check on their biases, psychologists use **operational definitions** when they report their studies. These exact descriptions will allow anyone to **replicate** (repeat) the research. Other people can then re-create the study with different participants and

in different situations. If they get similar results, we can be confident that the findings are reliable.

Let's summarize. A good theory:

● effectively *organizes* a range of observations.

● leads to clear *predictions* that anyone can use to check the theory.

● often stimulates research that leads to a revised theory (such as the one in Chapter 13, which better organizes and predicts what we know about depression).

theory an explanation using an integrated set of principles that organizes observations and predicts behaviors or events.

hypothesis a testable prediction, often implied by a theory.

operational definition a statement of the procedures (operations) used to define research variables. For example, *human intelligence* may be operationally defined as what an intelligence test measures.

replication repeating the essence of a research study, usually with different participants in different situations, to see whether the basic finding extends to other participants and circumstances.

We can test our hypotheses and refine our theories in several ways.

- *Descriptive* methods describe behaviors, often by using case studies, surveys, or naturalistic observations.
- *Correlational* methods associate different factors. (You'll see the word *factor* often in descriptions of research. It refers to anything that contributes to a result.)
- *Experimental* methods manipulate factors to discover their effects.

To think critically about popular psychology claims, we need to understand the strengths and weaknesses of these methods.

Description

> **7** How do psychologists use case studies, surveys, and naturalistic observation to observe and describe behavior, and why is random sampling important?

In daily life, all of us observe and describe people, trying to understand why they behave as they do. Professional psychologists do much the same, though more objectively and systematically, using case studies, surveys, and naturalistic observation.

The Case Study

A **case study** examines one individual in great depth, in the hope of revealing things true of us all. Some examples: Medical case studies of people who lost specific abilities after damage to certain brain regions gave us much of our early knowledge about the brain. Jean Piaget, the pioneer researcher on children's thinking, carefully watched and questioned just a few children. Studies of only a few chimpanzees jarred our beliefs about what other animals can understand and communicate.

Intensive case studies are sometimes very revealing. They often suggest directions for further study, and they show us what *can* happen. But individual cases may also mislead us. The individual being studied may be *atypical* (not like those in the larger group).

Viewing such cases as general truths can lead to false conclusions. Indeed, anytime a researcher mentions a finding (*Smokers die younger: 95 percent of men over 85 are nonsmokers*), someone is sure to offer an exception. (*Well, I have an uncle who smoked two packs a day and lived to be 89.*) These contradictory anecdotes—dramatic stories, personal experiences, even psychological case examples—often command attention.

> "Given a thimbleful of [dramatic] facts we rush to make generalizations as large as a tub."
>
> Psychologist Gordon Allport, *The Nature of Prejudice*, 1954

The point to remember: Individual cases can suggest fruitful ideas. What is true of all of us can be seen in any one of us. But just because something is true of one of us (the atypical uncle), that does not mean it will be true of all of us (most long-term smokers suffer ill health and early deaths). We look to methods beyond the case study to uncover general truths.

The Survey

A **survey** looks at many cases in less depth, asking people to report their behavior or opinions. Questions about everything from sexual practices to political opinions get put to the public. Harris and Gallup polls have revealed that 89 percent of Americans say they face high stress, 95 percent believe in God, and 96 percent would like to change something about their appearance. But asking questions is tricky, and your results often depend on the way you word your questions and on who answers them.

> With very large samples, estimates become quite reliable. *E* is estimated to represent 12.7 percent of the letters in written English. *E*, in fact, is 12.3 percent of the 925,141 letters in Melville's *Moby-Dick*, 12.4 percent of the 586,747 letters in Dickens' *A Tale of Two Cities*, and 12.1 percent of the 3,901,021 letters in 12 of Mark Twain's works (*Chance News*, 1997).

Wording Effects Even subtle changes in the order or wording of questions can have major effects. Should violence be allowed to appear in children's television programs? People are much more likely to approve "not allowing" such things than "forbidding" or "censoring" them. In one national survey, only 27 percent of Americans approved of "government censorship" of media sex and violence, though 66 percent approved of "more restrictions on what is shown on television" (Lacayo, 1995). And people are much more approving of "aid to the needy" than of "welfare," and of "revenue enhancers" than of "taxes."

Consider two national surveys taken in 2009. In one, three in four Americans approved of giving people "a choice" of public, government-run health insurance or private health insurance. In the other survey, however, most Americans were *not* in favor of "creating a public health care plan administered by the federal government that would compete directly with private health insurance companies" (Stein, 2009). Because wording is such a delicate matter (*choice* is a word that triggers support), critical thinkers will reflect on how the question's phrasing might affect the opinions people express.

Random Sampling For an accurate picture of a group's experiences and attitudes, there's only one game in town—a *representative sample*—a small group that accurately reflects a larger *population*.

So how do you obtain a representative sample to survey? How could you choose a group that would represent the whole group you want to study and describe—say, the total student population at your school? You would choose a **random sample,** in which every person in the entire group has an equal chance of being picked. You would not want to ask for volunteers, because those extra-nice students who step forward to help out would not necessarily be a random sample of all the students. But you could use a table of random numbers to select a sample after assigning each student a number.

Time and money will affect the size of your sample, but you would try to involve as many people as possible. Why? Because large representative samples are better than small ones. (But a small representative sample of 100 is better than an unrepresentative sample of 500.)

Political pollsters sample voters in national election surveys just this way. Using only 1500 randomly sampled people, drawn from all areas of a country, they can provide a remarkably accurate snapshot of the nation's opinions. Without random sampling, large samples—including call-in phone samples and TV Web site polls—often merely give misleading results.

The point to remember: Before accepting survey findings, think critically. Consider the question wording and the sample. The best basis for generalizing is from a random sample of a population.

Naturalistic Observation

We can also describe behavior by watching and recording it in a natural environment. These **naturalistic observations** may describe parenting practices in different cultures, students' self-seating patterns in American lunchrooms, or chimpanzee family structures in the wild.

In one study, researchers had 52 introductory psychology students don belt-worn tape recorders (Mehl & Pennebaker, 2003). For up to four days, the machines captured 30-second snippets of the stu-

Courtesy of Matthias Mehl

An EAR for naturalistic observation: Researchers have used Electronically Activated Recorders (EAR) to sample naturally occurring slices of daily life (Mehl & Pennebaker, 2003).

dents' waking hours, turning on every 12.5 minutes. By the end of the study, researchers had eavesdropped on more than 10,000 half-minute life slices. What percentage of the time did these researchers find students talking with someone? What percentage captured students at a computer keyboard? The answers: 28 and 9 percent. WHAT PER-◄ CENTAGE OF *YOUR* WAKING HOURS ARE SPENT IN THESE ACTIVITIES?

Like case studies and surveys, naturalistic observation does not *explain* behavior. It *describes* it. Nevertheless, descriptions can be revealing.

Correlation

8 What are positive and negative correlations, and how do they permit prediction without cause-effect explanation?

Describing behavior is a first step toward predicting it. Surveys and naturalistic observations often show us that one trait or behavior is related to another. In such cases, we say the two **correlate.** A statistical measure (the *correlation coefficient*) helps us figure how closely two things vary together, and thus how well either one *predicts* the other. Displaying data in a scatterplot (**FIGURE 1.3**) can help us see correlations.

case study a descriptive technique in which one person is studied in depth in the hope of revealing universal principles.

survey a descriptive technique for obtaining the self-reported attitudes or behaviors of people, usually by questioning a representative, random sample of a population.

random sample a sample that fairly represents a population because each member has an equal chance of inclusion.

naturalistic observation a descriptive technique of observing and recording behavior in naturally occurring situations without trying to change or control the situation.

correlation a measure of the extent to which two events vary together, and thus of how well either one predicts the other. The *correlation coefficient* is the mathematical expression of the relationship, ranging from −1 to +1.

FIGURE 1.3 ● **Scatterplot for height and temperament** This display of data from 20 imagined people (each represented by a data point) reveals an upward slope, indicating a positive correlation.

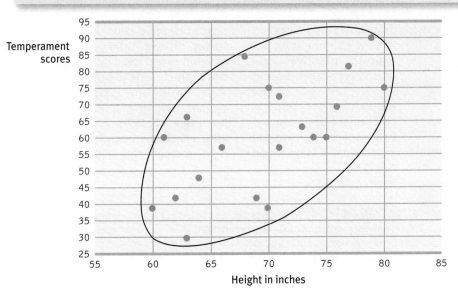

TABLE 1.2	Name the Correlation

For each of the following news reports of correlational research, indicate in the blank whether the reported link is a positive (*P*) correlation or a negative (*N*) correlation.

1. The more TV is on in a young child's home, the less time the child spends reading (Kaiser, 2003). _____

2. The more sexual content teens see on TV, the more likely they are to have sex (Collins et al., 2004). _____

3. The longer children are breast-fed, the greater their later academic achievement (Horwood & Fergusson, 1998). _____

4. The more income rose among a sample of poor families, the fewer psychiatric symptoms their children experienced (Costello et al., 2003). _____

Answers: 1. negative, 2. positive, 3. positive, 4. negative.

Digital Vision/Jupiter Images/Getty

Correlation need not mean causation: Length of marriage correlates with hair loss in men. Does this mean that marriage causes men to lose their hair (or that balding men make better husbands)? In this case, as in many others, a third factor obviously explains the correlation: Golden anniversaries and baldness both accompany aging.

- A *positive correlation* (between 0 and +1.00) indicates a direct relationship, meaning that two things increase together or decrease together. Across people, height correlates positively with weight. The data in Figure 1.3 are positively correlated, because they are generally both rising (moving up and right) together.

- A *negative correlation* (between 0 and –1.00) indicates an *inverse* relationship: As one thing increases, the other decreases. Our earlier example, on the link between self-esteem and depression, might illustrate a negative correlation. If so, people who score low on self-esteem would tend to score high on depression. If the correlation is as low as –1.00, one set of scores goes down precisely as the other goes up, just

as children do on opposite ends of a teeter-totter.

- A coefficient near zero is a weak correlation, indicating little or no relationship.

The point to remember: A correlation coefficient helps us see the world more clearly by revealing the extent to which two things relate. To learn how to spot positive and negative correlations, take the quiz in **TABLE 1.2**.

Correlation and Causation

Correlations help us predict. Self-esteem correlates negatively with (and therefore predicts) depression. But does that mean low self-esteem *causes* depression? If your answer is *yes*, you are not alone. A nearly irresistible error is thinking that such an association proves causation. But no matter how strong the relationship, it does not!

How else might we explain the negative correlation between self-esteem and depression? As **FIGURE 1.4** suggests, we'd get the same correlation between low self-esteem and depression if depression

caused people to be down on themselves. And we'd also get that correlation if something else—a third factor such as heredity or brain chemistry—caused *both* low self-esteem and depression.

This point is so important—so basic to thinking smarter with psychology—that it merits one more example, this one from a survey of over 12,000 adolescents. The more teens feel loved by their parents, the less likely they are to behave in unhealthy ways—having early sex, smoking, abusing alcohol and drugs, behaving violently (Resnick et al., 1997). "Adults have a powerful effect on their children's behavior right through the high school years,"

(1)
Low self-esteem — could cause → **Depression**

or

(2)
Depression — could cause → **Low self-esteem**

or

(3)
Distressing events or biological predisposition — could cause → **Low self-esteem** and **Depression**

FIGURE 1.4 • **Three possible cause-effect relationships** People low in self-esteem are more likely to report depression than are those high in self-esteem. One possible explanation of this negative correlation is that a bad self-image causes depressed feelings. But, as the diagram indicates, other cause-effect relationships are possible.

gushed an Associated Press (AP) story on the study. But no correlation has a built-in cause-effect arrow. Thus, the AP could as well have said, "Well-behaved teens feel their parents' love and approval; out-of-bounds teens more often describe their parents as disapproving jerks."

The point to remember (turn up the volume here): Correlation indicates the *possibility* of a cause-effect relationship, *but it does not prove causation.* Knowing that two events are associated need not tell us anything about which causes the other. Remember this principle and you will be wiser as you read and hear news of scientific studies.

Illusory Correlations

9 How do we form illusory correlations, and why do we perceive order in random sequences?

Correlation coefficients help us see relationships we might otherwise miss. They also help us to avoid "seeing" imaginary relationships. When we *believe* there is a link between two things, we are likely to *notice* and *recall* instances that confirm our belief (Trolier & Hamilton, 1986). These nonexistent relationships are **illusory correlations.**

Have you ever had a thought pop into your mind—say, that you were about to get an unlikely phone call—and then the unlikely event happened? We are espe-cially likely to notice and remember such dramatic or unusual events occurring in sequence. When the call does not follow the thought, we are less likely to note and remember the nonevent.

Illusory correlations help explain many inaccurate beliefs, such as the idea that infertile couples who adopt become more likely to conceive (Gilovich, 1991). And they help explain why for so many years people believed (as many still do) that get-ting chilled and wet causes one to catch a cold, and that weather changes trigger arthritis pain. We are eager to perceive patterns, whether they're there or not.

The point to remember: When we notice random coincidences, we may forget that they are random and instead see them as correlated. Thus, we can easily deceive ourselves by perceiving correlations that do not exist.

Experimentation

10 How do experiments clarify or reveal cause-effect relationships?

Descriptions don't prove causation. Cor-relations don't prove causation. To isolate cause and effect, psychologists have to simplify the world. In our everyday lives, many things affect our actions and influ-ence our thoughts. Psychologists sort out this complexity by using **experiments.** With experiments, researchers can focus on the possible effects of one or more items by (1) *manipulating the factors of in-terest* and (2) *holding constant ("controlling") other factors.* Let's consider a few experi-ments to see how this works.

Random Assignment: Minimizing Differences

Researchers have compared breast-fed infants and infants bottle-fed with for-mula. Several studies show that children's intelligence scores are somewhat higher if they were breast-fed as infants (Kramer et al., 2008). So we can say that mother's milk correlates modestly but positively with later intelligence. But does this mean that the nutrients in mother's milk contribute to brain development? Or that smarter mothers (who more often breast-feed) have smarter children?

How might researchers isolate the ef-fects of mother's milk from the effects of other factors, such as mother's age, educa-tion, and intelligence? The answer? By ex-perimenting. This is just what a British research team did, with parental permis-sion. The researchers **randomly assigned** 424 hospital preterm infants either to for-mula feedings or to breast-milk feedings (Lucas et al., 1992). By doing this, the re-searchers created two groups: an **experi-mental group,** in which babies received the treatment (breast milk), and a **control group** without the treatment. Researchers were then fairly certain that the two groups were otherwise identical. Random assignment, like coin tossing, roughly equalizes the two groups in other charac-teristics (including mother's age, intelli-gence, and so on). This eliminated alternative explanations and supported the conclusion that breast is indeed best for developing intelligence (at least for preterm infants). On intelligence tests taken at age 8, the children who had been nourished with breast milk had signifi-cantly higher scores than their formula-fed counterparts.

Given enough random events, something weird will happen: An event that happens to but 1 in 1 billion people every day occurs about 6 times a day, 2000 times a year. Angelo and Maria Gallina were the beneficiaries of one of those extraordi-nary chance events when they won two California lottery games on the same day.

Jerry Telfer/San Francisco Chronicle

illusory correlation the perception of a rela-tionship where none exists.

experiment a method in which researchers vary one or more factors (independent variables) to ob-serve the effect on some behavior or mental process (the dependent variable).

random assignment assigning participants to experimental and control groups by chance, thus minimizing any differences between the groups.

experimental group the group in an experi-ment that is exposed to the treatment, that is, to one version of the independent variable.

control group the group in an experiment that is not exposed to the treatment and therefore serves as a comparison with the experimental group for evaluating the effect of the treatment.

This experiment inspired a massive follow-up study, with some 17,000 Belarus newborns. Researchers randomly assigned the infants' mothers either to an experimental group in which breast-feeding was promoted or to a control group given a normal pediatric care program (Kramer et al., 2008). At 3 months of age, 43 percent of the infants in the experimental group were being exclusively breast-fed, as were 6 percent in the control group. At 6 years of age, nearly 14,000 of the children were restudied. Those with mothers in the breast-feeding promotion group had IQ scores averaging six points higher than their control group counterparts.

These studies illustrate an important point: If a behavior (such as test performance) changes when we vary an experimental factor (such as infant nutrition), then we know the factor is having an effect. Unlike correlational studies, which uncover *naturally occurring* relationships, an experiment *manipulates* (varies) a factor to determine its effect.

The Double-Blind Procedure: Eliminating Bias

Researchers in the breast-milk experiment were lucky—babies don't have expectations that can affect the experiment's outcome. Adults do.

Consider: Three days into a cold, many of us start taking vitamin C tablets. If we find our cold symptoms lessening, we may credit the pills. But after a few days, a cold is naturally on its way out. Was the remedy truly effective? To find out, we could experiment.

And that is precisely how investigators evaluate new drug treatments and new methods of psychological therapy (Chapter 13). Often, the participants in these studies are *blind* (uninformed) about what treatment, if any, they are receiving. The experimental group receives the treatment. The control group receives a **placebo** (an inactive substance—perhaps a pill with no drug in it).

Many studies use a **double-blind procedure**—neither the participants nor the research assistants collecting the data know which group is receiving the

treatment. In such studies, researchers can check a treatment's actual effects apart from the participants' belief in its healing powers and the staff's enthusiasm for its potential. Just *thinking* you are getting a treatment can boost your spirits, relax your body, and relieve your symptoms. This **placebo effect** is well documented in reducing pain, depression, and anxiety (Kirsch & Sapirstein, 1998). And that is why we can't know how effective a therapy really is unless we control for a possible placebo effect.

Independent and Dependent Variables

Here is an even more potent example: The drug Viagra was approved for use after 21 clinical trials. One trial was an experiment in which researchers randomly assigned 329 men with erectile dysfunction to either an experimental group (Viagra takers) or a control group (placebo takers). It was a double-blind procedure—neither the men nor the person who gave them the pills knew which drug they were receiving. The result: Viagra worked. At peak doses, 69 percent of Viagra-assisted attempts at intercourse were successful, compared with 22 percent

for men receiving the placebo (Goldstein et al., 1998).

This simple experiment manipulated just one factor—the drug Viagra. A manipulated factor is called an **independent variable.** We can vary it independently—without concern for other factors, such as the men's age, weight, and personality, which, thanks to random assignment, should be roughly equal in both groups. Experiments examine the effect of one or more independent variables on some measurable behavior. This affected behavior is called the **dependent variable** because it can vary *depending* on what takes place during the experiment.

Experimenters give both variables precise *operational definitions.* They specify exactly how they are manipulating the independent variable (in this study, the precise drug dosage and timing) and how they are measuring the dependent variable (the questions that assessed the men's responses). These definitions answer the "What do you mean?" question with a level of precision that enables others to repeat the study.

Let's see how this works with the breast-milk experiment (**FIGURE 1.5**). A *variable* is anything that can vary (infant nutrition,

> Note the distinction between random *sampling* (discussed earlier in relation to surveys) and random *assignment* (depicted in Figure 1.5). Through *random sampling*, we may represent a population effectively, because each member of that population has an equal chance of being selected (*sampled*) for participation in our research. *Random assignment* ensures accurate representation among the research groups, because each participant has an equal chance of being placed in (*assigned* to) any of the groups. This helps control outside influences so that we can determine cause and effect.

FIGURE 1.5 ● **Experimentation** To study cause-effect, psychologists may randomly assign some participants to an experimental group, others to a control group. Measuring the dependent variable (intelligence score) will determine the effect of the independent variable (type of milk).

Random assignment
(controlling for other variables, such as parental intelligence and environment)

Group	Independent variable	Dependent variable
Experimental	Breast milk	Intelligence score, age 8
Control	Formula	Intelligence score, age 8

TABLE 1.3	Comparing Research Methods			
Research Method	**Basic Purpose**	**How Conducted**	**What Is Manipulated**	**Weaknesses**
Descriptive	To observe and record behavior	Do case studies, surveys, or naturalistic observations	Nothing	No control of variables; single cases may be misleading.
Correlational	To detect naturally occurring relationships; to assess how well one variable predicts another	Compute statistical association, sometimes among survey responses	Nothing	Does not specify cause-effect.
Experimental	To explore cause-effect	Manipulate one or more factors; use random variable(s) assignment	The independent variable(s)	Sometimes not possible for practical or ethical reasons. Results may not generalize to other contexts.

intelligence). Experiments aim to *manipulate* an *independent* variable (infant nutrition) and *measure* the *dependent* variable (intelligence). An experiment has at least two different groups: an *experimental group* (infants received breast milk) and a *comparison* or *control group* (infants did not receive breast milk). *Random assignment* works to *control all other variables* by equating the groups before any manipulation begins. In this way, an experiment tests the effect of at least one independent variable (what we manipulate) on at least one dependent variable (the outcome we measure).

Let's pause to check your understanding using another simple experiment. To test the effect of perceived ethnicity on the availability of a rental house, researchers sent identically worded e-mails to 1115 Los Angeles-area landlords (Carpusor & Loges, 2006). They varied the senders' name to imply different ethnic groups: "Patrick McDougall," "Said Al-Rahman," and "Tyrell Jackson." Then they tracked the percentage of positive replies. How many e-mails triggered invitations to view the apartment? For McDougall, 89 percent, for Al-Rahman, 66 percent; and for Jackson, 56 percent. In this experiment, what was the independent variable? The dependent variable?[7]

Each of psychology's research methods has strengths and weaknesses (TABLE 1.3). Experiments show cause-effect relationships, but some experiments would not be ethical or practical. (To test the effects of parenting, we're just not going to take newborns and randomly assign them either to their biological parents or to orphanages.)

THE BASICS

12. In psychology, a good theory leads to hypotheses, or predictions that can be tested. When hypotheses are tested, the result is typically
  a. increased skepticism.
  b. rejection of the theory.
  c. confirmation or revision of the theory.
  d. personal bias on the part of the investigator.

13. You wish to take an accurate poll in a certain country by questioning people who truly represent that country's adult population. Therefore, you need to make sure the people you poll are
  a. at least 50 percent males and 50 percent females.
  b. a small but intelligent sample of the population.
  c. a very large sample of the population.
  d. a random sample of the population.

14. A psychologist finds that the more classes in natural childbirth training a woman attends, the less pain medication she requires during childbirth. The relationship between the number of classes attended and the amount of pain medication taken is a(n)
  a. positive correlation.
  b. negative correlation.
  c. cause-effect relationship.
  d. illusory correlation.

15. Knowing that two events are correlated does not tell us which is the cause and

Continued

placebo [pluh-SEE-bo; Latin for "I shall please"] an inactive substance or condition that is sometimes given to control group members in place of the treatment given to the experimental group.

double-blind procedure a procedure in which participants and research staff are ignorant (blind) about who has received the treatment or a placebo.

placebo effect results caused by expectations alone.

independent variable the experimental factor that is manipulated; the variable whose effect is being studied.

dependent variable the outcome factor; the variable that may change in response to manipulations of the independent variable.

---

7. The independent variable, which the researchers manipulated, was the ethnicity-related names. The dependent variable, which they measured, was the positive response rate.

which is the effect. However, it does provide

a. a basis for prediction.
b. an explanation for why things happened the way they did.
c. proof that as one event increases, the other also increases.
d. an indication that some third factor is affecting both events.

16. Some people wrongly perceive that their dreams predict future events. This is an example of a(n)

a. negative correlation.
b. positive correlation.
c. illusory correlation.
d. naturalistic observation.

17. Descriptive and correlational studies describe behavior, detect relationships, and predict behavior. But to *explain* that behavior, psychologists use

a. naturalistic observations.
b. experiments.
c. surveys.
d. case studies.

18. A researcher wants to determine whether noise level affects heart rate. In one group she varies the level of noise in the environment and records participants' heart rate. In this experiment, noise level is the

a. correlation coefficient.
b. illusory correlation.
c. dependent variable.
d. independent variable.

19. To test the effect of a new drug on depression, we randomly assign people to control and experimental groups. Those in the experimental group take a pink pill containing the new drug. Those in the control group take a pink sugar pill. Which statement is true?

a. The drug is the dependent variable.
b. Depression is the independent variable.
c. Control group members take a placebo.
d. Experimental group members take a placebo.

20. A double-blind procedure is often used to prevent a researcher's biases from influencing an experiment's outcome. In this procedure,

a. only the participants will know whether they are in the control group or the experimental group.
b. experimental and control group members will be carefully matched for age, sex, income, and education level.
c. neither the participants nor the researchers will know who is in the experimental and control groups.
d. someone separate from the researcher will ask people to volunteer for either the experimental group or the control group.

THE BIG PICTURE

1D. Let's say we are testing a new blood pressure drug. Why would we learn more about its effectiveness from giving it to half a group of 1000 people than to all 1000 participants?

IN YOUR EVERYDAY LIFE

▪ If you could conduct a study on any psychological question, which would you choose? How would you do it?

Answers: 12. c, 13. d, 14. b, 15. a, 16. c, 17. b, 18. d, 19. c, 20. c. Answers to The Big Picture questions can be found in Appendix B at the end of the book.

Frequently Asked Questions About Psychology

We have reflected on how a scientific approach can restrain biases. We have seen how case studies, surveys, and naturalistic observations help us describe behavior. We have also noted that correlational studies assess the association between two factors, showing how well one predicts the other. We have examined the logic underlying experiments, which use controls and random assignment to isolate the effects of independent variables on dependent variables.

Hopefully, you are now prepared to understand what lies ahead and to think critically about psychological matters. Before we plunge in, let's address some frequently asked questions about psychology.

> **11** How do simplified laboratory conditions help us understand general principles of behavior?

Do you ever wonder whether people's behavior in the laboratory will predict their behavior in real life? For example, does detecting the blink of a faint red light in a dark room have anything useful to say about flying a plane at night? AFTER VIEWING A VIOLENT, SEXUALLY EX- ◄ PLICIT FILM, DOES AN AROUSED MAN'S INCREASED WILLINGNESS TO PUSH BUTTONS THAT HE THINKS WILL ELECTRICALLY SHOCK A WOMAN REALLY SAY ANYTHING ABOUT WHETHER VIOLENT PORNOGRAPHY MAKES A MAN MORE LIKELY TO ABUSE A WOMAN?

Before you answer, consider this. The experimenter *intends* to simplify reality—to create a mini-environment that imitates and controls important features of everyday life. Just as a wind tunnel lets airplane designers re-create airflow forces under controlled conditions, a laboratory experiment lets psychologists re-create psychological forces under controlled conditions.

In aggression studies, deciding whether to push a button that delivers a shock may not be the same as slapping someone in the face, but the *principle* is the same. The experiment's purpose is not to re-create the exact behaviors of everyday life but to test theoretical principles (Mook, 1983). *It is the resulting principles—not the specific findings—that help explain everyday behaviors.* And many investigations show that principles derived in the laboratory *do* typically generalize to the everyday world (Anderson et al., 1999).

The point to remember: Psychologists' concerns lie less with particular behaviors than with the general principles that help explain many behaviors.

12 Why do psychologists study animals, and what ethical guidelines safeguard human and animal research participants?

Many psychologists study animals because they find them fascinating. They want to understand how different species learn, think, and behave. Psychologists also study animals to learn about people. We humans are not *like* animals; we *are* animals, sharing a common biology. Animal experiments have therefore led to treatments for human diseases—insulin for diabetes, vaccines to prevent polio and rabies, transplants to replace defective organs.

> "Rats are very similar to humans except that they are not stupid enough to purchase lottery tickets."
>
> Dave Barry, July 2, 2002

Humans are complex. But the same processes by which we learn are present in rats, monkeys, and even sea slugs. The simplicity of the sea slug's nervous system is precisely what makes it so revealing of the neural mechanisms of learning. Sharing such similarities, should we not respect our animal relatives? "We cannot defend our scientific work with animals on the basis of the similarities between them and ourselves and then defend it morally on the basis of differences," noted Roger Ulrich (1991). The animal protection movement protests the use of animals in psychological, biological, and medical research.

Out of this heated debate, two issues emerge. The basic one is whether it is right to place the well-being of humans above that of animals. In experiments on stress and cancer, is it right that mice get tumors in the hope that people might not? Should some monkeys be exposed to an HIV-like virus in the search for an AIDS vaccine? Is our use and consumption of other animals as natural as the behavior of carnivorous hawks, cats, and whales? The answers to such questions vary by culture. In Gallup surveys in Canada and the United States, about 6 in 10 adults deem medical testing on animals "morally acceptable." In Britain, only 37 percent do (Mason, 2003).

If we give human life first priority, what safeguards should protect the well-being of animals in research? One survey of animal researchers gave an answer. Some 98 percent supported government regulations protecting primates, dogs, and cats, and 74 percent supported regulations providing for the humane care of rats and mice (Plous & Herzog, 2000). Many professional associations and funding agencies already have such guidelines. For example, British Psychological Society guidelines call for housing animals under reasonably natural living conditions, with companions for social animals (Lea, 2000). American Psychological Association guidelines state that researchers must ensure the "comfort, health, and

D. Shapiro, ©Wildlife Conservation Society

Animal research benefiting animals: Thanks partly to research on the benefits of novelty, control, and stimulation, these gorillas are enjoying an improved quality of life in New York's Bronx Zoo. As they would in the wild, they now work for their supper (Stewart, 2002).

humane treatment" of animals and minimize "infection, illness, and pain" (APA, 2002).

Animals have themselves benefited from animal research. One Ohio team of research psychologists measured stress hormone levels in samples of millions of dogs brought each year to animal shelters. They devised handling and stroking methods to reduce stress and ease the dogs' transition to adoptive homes (Tuber et al., 1999). Other studies have helped improve care and management in animals' natural habitats. By revealing our behavioral kinship with animals and the remarkable intelligence of chimpanzees, gorillas, and other animals, experiments have also led to increased empathy and protection for them. At its best, a psychology concerned for humans and sensitive to animals serves the welfare of both.

What about human participants? Does the image of white-coated scientists delivering electric shocks trouble you? If so, you'll be relieved to know that most psychological studies are free of such stress. With people, blinking lights, flashing words, and pleasant social interactions are more common. Moreover, psychology's experiments are mild compared with the stress and humiliation often inflicted by reality TV shows. In one episode of *The Bachelor,* a man dumped his new fiancée—on camera, at the producers' request—for the woman who earlier had finished second (Collins, 2009).

Occasionally, though, researchers do temporarily stress or deceive people, but only when they believe it is essential to a justifiable end, such as understanding and controlling violent behavior or studying mood swings. Some experiments won't work if participants know everything beforehand. (Wanting to be helpful, the participants might try to confirm the researcher's predictions.)

The American Psychological Association's ethics code urges researchers to (1) obtain the participants' informed consent, (2) protect them from harm and discomfort, (3) keep information about individual participants confidential, and (4) fully explain the research afterward. Moreover, most universities now have an ethics committee that screens research proposals and safeguards participants' well-being.

13 How do personal values influence psychologists' research and application? Does psychology aim to manipulate people?

Psychology is definitely not value-free. Values affect what we study, how we study it, and how we interpret results. Consider: Researchers' values influence their choice of topics. Should we study worker productivity or worker morale? Sex discrimination or gender differences?

Conformity or independence? Our values can also color "the facts." As noted earlier, what we want or expect to see can bias our observations and interpretations **(FIGURE 1.6).**

Even the words we use to describe something can reflect our values. Are the sex acts we do not practice *perversions* or *sexual variations?* Labels describe and labels evaluate. One person's *rigidity* is another's *consistency.* One person's *faith* is another's *fanaticism.* Our words—*firm* or *stubborn, careful* or *picky, discreet* or *secretive*—reveal as much about us as they do about those we label.

Applied psychology also contains hidden values. If you defer to "professional" guidance—on raising children,

achieving self-fulfillment, coping with sexual feelings, getting ahead at work— you are accepting value-laden advice. A science of behavior and mental processes can certainly help us reach our goals, but it cannot decide what those goals should be.

Psychology is value-laden. Is it also dangerously powerful, as some worry? Is it an accident that astronomy is the oldest science and psychology the youngest? To some people, exploring the external universe seems far safer than exploring our own inner universe. Might psychology, they ask, be used to manipulate people?

Knowledge, like all power, can be used for good or evil. Nuclear power has been used to light up cities—and to demolish them. Persuasive power has been used to educate people—and to deceive and control them. Although psychology has the power to deceive, its purpose is to enlighten. Every day, psychologists are exploring ways to enhance learning, creativity, and compassion. Psychology speaks to many of our world's great problems—war, climate change, prejudice, family crises, crime—all of which involve attitudes and behaviors. Psychology also speaks to

FIGURE **1.6** ● **What do you see?** Our expectations influence what we perceive. Did you see a duck or a rabbit? Show some friends this image with the rabbit above covered up and see if they are more likely to perceive a duck lying on its back instead. (From Shepard, 1990.)

Mike Kemp/Getty Images

©Roger Shepard

our deepest longings—for nourishment, for love, for happiness. And one of the new developments in this field—positive psychology—has as its goal exploring and promoting human strengths. Many of life's questions are beyond psychology, but even a first psychology course can shine a bright light on some very important ones.

> For study and learning tips for this and any other class you take, see the Close-Up: How to Be a Better Student, on the next page.

PRACTICE TEST

THE BASICS

21. The laboratory environment is designed to
   a. exactly re-create the events of everyday life.
   b. re-create psychological forces under controlled conditions.
   c. create opportunities for naturalistic observation.
   d. minimize the use of animals and humans in psychological research.

22. Professional ethical standards provide guidelines for the treatment of people in research studies. Those guidelines include
   a. protecting participants from harm and discomfort.
   b. obtaining informed consent before participation, and fully explaining the research after.
   c. keeping information about individual participants confidential.
   d. all of these answers.

23. In defending their research with animals, psychologists have noted that animal experimentation
   a. can tell us much about our own physical and mental processes because we share a common biology.
   b. sometimes helps animals as well as humans.
   c. has led to treatments for human diseases.
   d. does all of these things.

THE BIG PICTURE
1E. How are human and animal research subjects protected?

IN YOUR EVERYDAY LIFE
- What other questions or concerns do you have about psychology?

Answers : 21. b, 22. d, 23. d. Answers to The Big Picture questions can be found in Appendix B at the end of the book.

Terms and Concepts to Remember

behaviorism, p. 2

humanistic psychology, p. 3

cognitive neuroscience, p. 3

psychology, p. 3

critical thinking, p. 5

biopsychosocial approach, p. 6

culture, p. 6

nature-nurture issue, p. 6

dual processing, p. 7

positive psychology, p. 8

hindsight bias, p. 9

theory, p. 11

hypothesis, p. 11

operational definition, p. 11

replication, p. 11

case study, p. 12

survey, p. 12

random sample, p. 12

naturalistic observation, p. 13

correlation, p. 13

illusory correlation, p. 15

experiment, p. 15

random assignment, p. 15

experimental group, p. 15

control group, p. 15

placebo [pluh-SEE-bo], p. 16

double-blind procedure, p. 16

placebo effect, p. 16

independent variable, p. 16

dependent variable, p. 16

SQ3R, p. 22

Multiple-choice **self-tests** and more may be found at www.worthpublishers.com/myers

How to Be a Better Student

14 **How can psychology's principles help you to become a better student?**

In this course, you will learn *how to ask and answer important questions*—to think critically as you consider competing ideas and claims. Your mind is not like your stomach, something to be filled passively. Your mind is more like a muscle that grows stronger with exercise. We learn and remember material best when we actively process it—when we put it in our own words, test ourselves, and then review and rehearse it again.

The **SQ3R** study method—**S**urvey, **Q**uestion, **R**ead, **R**ehearse, **R**eview—uses these principles (McDaniel et al., 2009; Robinson, 1970).

- To study a chapter, first *survey,* taking a bird's-eye view as you scan the headings. Notice how the chapter is organized.

- As you prepare to read each section, form a *question* that you should answer. This will keep you in active learning mode. For this section, you might have asked, "How can I master the information in this book and become a better student while I'm at it?"

- Then *read,* actively searching for the answer to your question. At each sitting, read only as much of the chapter as you can absorb without tiring. Usually, a single main section will do—the Frequently Asked Questions About Psychology section you just finished, for example. Relating what you are reading to your own life will help you understand and remember the material. (The "In Your Everyday Life" questions in the Practice Tests at the end of each main section are designed to help you do just that.)

- When you finish reading a section, *rehearse* the section's main ideas, putting them into your own words. Then test yourself. This will not only help you figure out what you know; the testing itself will help you learn and retain the information more effectively.

- Finally, *review:* Read over any notes you have taken. As you do this, keep an eye on the chapter's organization. Then, quickly review the whole chapter.

Survey, question, read, rehearse, review. I have organized this book's chapters with the SQ3R study system in mind. Each chapter begins with a chapter outline that aids your *survey.* Headings and numbered learning objective *questions* suggest issues and concepts you should consider as you *read.* The material is organized into sections of readable length. Practice Tests at the end of main sections will help you *rehearse*—ensuring that you really learn the material before you move on. The list of key terms provides more testing opportunities as you check your mastery of important concepts. Finally, a visual concept map at the end of each chapter

repeats and answers the numbered learning objective questions, and it can help you *review* the material.

You now have five SQ3R pointers to help you become a better student. Here are five more study tips drawn from psychology's research.

1. *Distribute your study time.* One of psychology's oldest findings is that *spaced practice* (perhaps an hour a day, six days a week) promotes better learning than trying to cram everything into one long study blitz. To space your study sessions, you'll need to learn to manage your time carefully. (Richard O. Straub explains time management in a helpful section at the front of this text. He has also written a very useful Study Guide to accompany this text.)

2. *Learn to think critically.* As you read and participate in class, think about people's *assumptions and values.* Do they have a strong perspective or even a bias in their arguments? *Evaluate evidence.* Is it just one person's story? Is it correlational? Is the evidence based on an experiment? *Assess conclusions.* Try to think of other explanations for what you are reading or hearing. Could you come up with another conclusion?

3. *In class, listen actively.* Listen for the main ideas of a lecture. Write them down. Ask questions during and after class. In class, as in your private study, process the information actively and you will understand and remember it better.

4. *Test yourself.* We tend to be overconfident about how much we know. You may understand a chapter as you read it. But you may not be able to hold on to that knowledge unless you devote extra study time to testing your knowledge. Research shows that our retention is greater for material we've been tested on, and the harder we have to think to come up with an answer, the stronger is our learning of that concept!

5. *Be a smart test-taker.* If a test contains both multiple-choice questions and an essay question, turn first to the essay. Read the question carefully, noting exactly what the instructor is asking. On the back of a page, pencil in a list of points you'd like to make and then organize them. Before writing, put aside the essay and work through the multiple-choice questions. (As you do so, your mind may continue to mull over the essay question. Sometimes the other questions will bring important points to mind.) Then reread the essay question, rethink your answer, and start writing. When you finish, proofread your answer to fix spelling and other little mistakes that make you look less competent than you are. When reading multiple-choice questions, don't confuse yourself by trying to imagine how each choice might be the right one. Try instead to answer the question as if it were a fill-in-the-blank. First cover the answers, recall what you know, and complete the sentence in your mind. Then read the answers on the test and find the choice that best matches what you recall.

While connecting psychology to your everyday life, you will learn much more than effective study techniques. Psychology deepens our appreciation for how we perceive, think, feel, and act. By so doing it can enrich our lives and enlarge our vision. Through this book I hope to help guide you toward that end. As educator Charles Eliot said a century ago: "Books are the quietest and most constant of friends, and the most patient of teachers."

SQ3R a study method incorporating five steps: **S**urvey, **Q**uestion, **R**ead, **R**ehearse, **R**eview.

PSYCHOLOGY'S ROOTS, BIG IDEAS, AND CRITICAL THINKING TOOLS

Psychology's Roots

1 **How has psychology's focus changed over time?**

■ First psychological laboratory, 1879, studied the elements of mental experience.

■ Early definition of *psychology:* the "science of mental life."

■ Revised by *behaviorists* in 1920s to "the scientific study of observable behavior."

■ Current definition: "the science of behavior and mental processes."

2 **What are psychology's current perspectives and some of its subfields?**

■ Perspectives: Neuroscience, Evolutionary, Behavior genetics, Psychodynamic, Behavioral, Cognitive, Social-cultural

■ Subfields: Biological, Developmental, Cognitive, Personality, Industrial-organizational, Counseling, Clinical, Social

Four Big Ideas in Psychology

3 **What four big ideas run throughout this book?**

■ *Critical thinking* is smart thinking.

■ Behavior is a *biopsychosocial* event. (Includes studying *nature-nurture* interaction and *cultural* influences.)

■ We operate with a two-track mind *(dual processing).* (Our brains process a surprising amount without our awareness.)

■ Psychology explores human strengths *(positive psychology)* as well as challenges (clinical psychology).

Why Do Psychology?

4 **How do hindsight bias and overconfidence make research findings seem like ordinary common sense?**

■ *Hindsight bias* (the I-knew-it-all-along phenomenon) is believing, after learning the outcome, that we would have foreseen it.

■ Overconfidence is the human tendency to be more confident than correct.

■ Both tendencies lead us to overestimate our intuition and common sense.

5 **What are the three key elements of the scientific attitude, and how do they support scientific inquiry?**

■ Curiosity triggers new ideas.

■ Skepticism encourages attention to the facts.

■ Humility helps us discard predictions that can't be verified by research.

The scientific attitude carries into life as critical thinking.

How Do Psychologists Ask and Answer Questions?

6 **How do psychological theories guide scientific research?**

- *Theories* organize observations and attempt to explain behaviors.
- Theories generate *hypotheses* (predictions that can be tested using descriptive, correlational, or experimental methods).
- Research results may validate the theory, or lead to its rejection or revision.
- The precise language used in *operational definitions* allows *replication* by others. (Similar results increase confidence in original conclusion.)

7 **How do psychologists use case studies, surveys, and naturalistic observation to observe and describe behavior, and why is random sampling important?**

- *Case studies* study one person in depth.
- *Surveys* study many people in less depth, using *random sampling* to fairly represent the population being studied.
- *Naturalistic observation* studies behavior in naturally occurring situations.

8 **What are positive and negative correlations, and how do they permit prediction without cause-effect explanation?**

- In a positive correlation, both items increase or decrease together.
- In a negative correlation, one item increases as the other decreases.
- *Correlations* tell us how well one event predicts another (using a measure called a correlation coefficient), but not whether one event caused the other, or whether some third factor influenced both events.

9 **How do we form illusory correlations, and why do we perceive order in random sequences?**

- An *illusory correlation* is a perceived relationship that does not exist.
- We perceive relationships in random coincidences, because they stand out and are memorable.

10 **How do experiments clarify or reveal cause-effect relationships?**

EXPERIMENTS

- Create a controlled, simplified version of reality.
- Manipulate one factor (the *independent variable*) while controlling others.
- Measure changes in other factors (*dependent variables*).
- Minimize differences between groups (through *random assignment*).
- Compare *experimental group* results with *control group* results.
- May use a *double-blind procedure* to control for the *placebo effect*.

Frequently Asked Questions About Psychology

11 **How do simplified laboratory conditions help us understand general principles of behavior?**

- Studying specific examples in controlled environments can reveal important general principles.

12 **Why do psychologists study animals, and what ethical guidelines safeguard human and animal research participants?**

- Research on animals advances our understanding of other species and sometimes benefits them directly.
- Animal experimentation advances our understanding of ourselves and may help solve human problems.
- Professional ethical standards and other legal guidelines, enforced by ethics committees, protect participants.

13 **How do personal values influence psychologists' research and application? Does psychology aim to manipulate people?**

- Values influence choice of research topics, theories and observations, labels for behavior, and professional advice.
- Psychology's principles could be used for good or evil, but have been used mainly to enlighten and to achieve positive ends.

14 **How can psychology's principles help you to become a better student?**

- The *SQ3R* study method (Survey, Question, Read, Rehearse, Review) can help you learn and remember material.
- Five other principles (spacing practice, thinking critically, listening actively, testing yourself, and being a smart test-taker) can help you use your study time effectively.

2

THE BIOLOGY OF MIND AND CONSCIOUSNESS

Imagine that just moments before your death, someone removed your brain from your body and kept it alive by floating it in a tank of fluid while feeding it enriched blood. Would you still be in there? Further imagine that your still-living brain was transplanted into the body of a person whose own brain had been severely damaged. To whose home should the recovered patient return? If you say the patient should return to your home, you illustrate what most of us believe—that we reside in our head. An acquaintance of mine received a new heart from a woman who had needed a heart-lung transplant. When the two chanced to meet in their hospital ward, she introduced herself: "I think you have my heart." But only her heart; her self, she assumed, still resided inside her skull.

CHAPTER OUTLINE

Biology and Behavior

1 Why are psychologists concerned with human biology?

No principle is more central to today's psychology, or to this book, than this: *Everything psychological—every idea, every mood, every urge—is simultaneously biological.* We may talk separately of biological influences and psychological influences, but they are two sides of the same coin. To think, feel, or act without a body would be like running without legs.

Biological psychologists study the links between our biology and our behavior. These links are a key part of the biopsychosocial approach, which is one of the Four Big Ideas that appear throughout this text. In later chapters, we'll look at some of the ways our thinking and emotions can influence our brain and our health. In this chapter, our exploration of the biology of the mind starts small and builds from the bottom up—from nerve cells to the brain. We'll also see how our brain states form the waking and sleeping mind.

"You're certainly a lot less fun since the operation"

Neural Communication

The human body is complexity built from simplicity. Part of this complexity is our amazing internal communication system, which makes the Internet look like a child's toy telephone. Across the world, researchers are unlocking the mysteries of how our brain uses electrical and chemical processes to take in, organize, interpret, store, and use information. The story begins with the system's basic building block, the neuron, or nerve cell. We'll look first at its structure, and then at how neurons work together.

A Neuron's Structure

2 What are the parts of a neuron?

Neurons differ, but all are variations on the same theme **(FIGURE 2.1)**. Each consists of a cell body and branching fibers. The bushy **dendrite** fibers receive messages and conduct them toward the cell body. From there, the cell's **axon** sends out messages to other **neurons** or to muscles or glands. Dendrites listen. Axons speak.

The messages that neurons carry are nerve impulses called **action potentials.** These electrical signals travel down axons inside your brain at different speeds. Researchers have tracked some trudging along at a sluggish 2 miles per hour, and others racing along at 200 or more miles per hour. WHICH REACTS FASTER, A HUMAN ◀ BRAIN OR A HIGH-SPEED COMPUTER? The computer wins every time. Even our brain's top speed is 3 million times slower than electricity zipping through a wire. Thus, unlike the nearly instant reactions

> "All information processing in the brain involves neurons 'talking to' each other at synapses."
>
> Neuroscientist
> Solomon H. Snyder, 1984

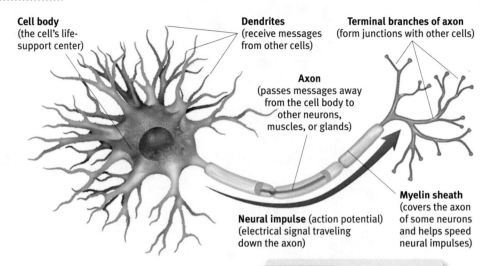

Cell body (the cell's life-support center)

Dendrites (receive messages from other cells)

Terminal branches of axon (form junctions with other cells)

Axon (passes messages away from the cell body to other neurons, muscles, or glands)

Neural impulse (action potential) (electrical signal traveling down the axon)

Myelin sheath (covers the axon of some neurons and helps speed neural impulses)

FIGURE 2.1 • **A typical neuron**

of a high-speed computer, your "quick" reaction to a sudden event, such as a child darting in front of your car, may take a quarter-second or more. Your brain is vastly more complex than a computer, but slower at executing simple responses.

Neurons interweave so tightly that even with a microscope you would have trouble seeing where one ends and another begins. But end they do, at meeting places called **synapses.** At these points, two neurons are separated by a tiny gap less than a millionth of an inch wide. "Like elegant ladies air-kissing so as not to muss their makeup, dendrites and axons don't quite touch," noted poet Diane Ackerman (2004). How then does a neuron send information across the tiny *synaptic gap?* The answer is one of the important scientific discoveries of our age.

How Neurons Communicate

3 How do neurons communicate?

Each neuron is itself a miniature decision-making device, reacting to signals it receives from hundreds, even thousands, of other neurons. Most of these signals are *excitatory,* somewhat like pushing a neuron's gas pedal. Others are *inhibitory,* more like pushing its brake.

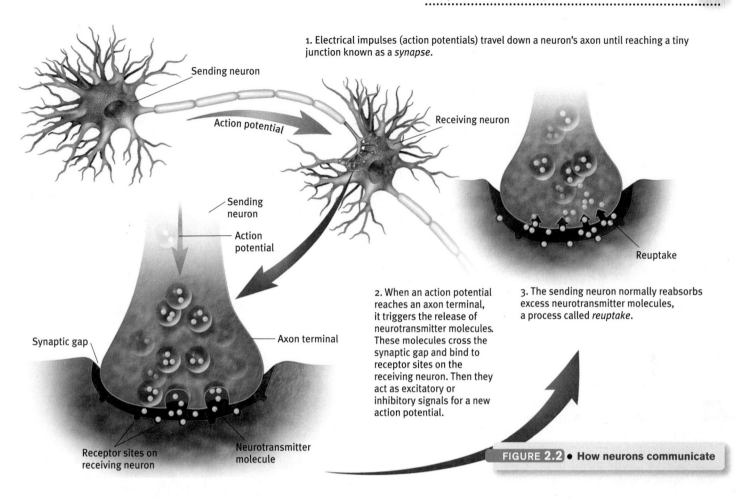

1. Electrical impulses (action potentials) travel down a neuron's axon until reaching a tiny junction known as a *synapse*.

Sending neuron

Action potential

Receiving neuron

Sending neuron

Action potential

Reuptake

Synaptic gap

Axon terminal

2. When an action potential reaches an axon terminal, it triggers the release of neurotransmitter molecules. These molecules cross the synaptic gap and bind to receptor sites on the receiving neuron. Then they act as excitatory or inhibitory signals for a new action potential.

3. The sending neuron normally reabsorbs excess neurotransmitter molecules, a process called *reuptake*.

Receptor sites on receiving neuron

Neurotransmitter molecule

FIGURE 2.2 ● **How neurons communicate**

If excitatory signals minus inhibitory signals exceed a minimum intensity, or **threshold,** the combination triggers an action potential. (Think of it this way: If the excitatory party animals outvote the inhibitory party poopers, the party's on.) The neuron then fires, sending an impulse down its axon, carrying information to another cell.

A neuron's firing doesn't vary in intensity. The neuron's reaction is an **all-or-none response.** Like guns, neurons either fire or they don't. How then do we distinguish a big hug from a gentle touch? A strong stimulus (the hug) can trigger *more* neurons to fire, and to fire more often. But it does not affect the action potential's strength or speed. Squeezing a trigger harder won't make a bullet bigger or faster.

When the action potential reaches the axon's end, your body performs an amazing trick. Your neural system converts an *electrical* impulse into a *chemical* message. At the synapse, the impulse triggers the

release of **neurotransmitter** molecules **(FIGURE 2.2).** Within one 10,000th of a second, these chemical messengers cross the synaptic gap and bind to receptor sites on the receiving neuron. There, they act as excitatory or inhibitory signals, and the process begins again in this new cell. Finally, in a process called *reuptake,* the sending neuron absorbs any excess neurotransmitters left in the gap.

How Neurotransmitters Influence Us

4. How do neurotransmitters affect our mood and behavior?

Dozens of different neurotransmitters travel along their own pathways in the brain, carrying specific but different messages that influence our behavior and emotions. *Serotonin* levels, for example, can make us more or less moody, hungry,

biological psychology a branch of psychology concerned with the links between biology and behavior.

dendrites neuron extensions that receive messages and conduct them toward the cell body.

axon neuron extension that sends messages to other neurons or cells.

neuron a nerve cell; the basic building block of the nervous system.

action potential a nerve impulse.

synapse [SIN-aps] junction between the axon tip of a sending neuron and the dendrite or cell body of a receiving neuron.

threshold level of stimulation required to trigger a neural impulse.

all-or-none response a neuron's reaction of either firing (with a full-strength response) or not firing.

neurotransmitters neuron-produced chemicals that cross synapses to carry messages to other neurons or cells.

TABLE 2.1	Some Neurotransmitters and Their Functions	
Neurotransmitter	**Function**	**Examples of Imbalances**
Serotonin	Affects mood, hunger, sleep, and arousal.	Undersupply linked to depression. Some antidepressant drugs raise serotonin levels.
Dopamine	Influences movement, learning, attention, and emotion.	Oversupply linked to schizophrenia. Undersupply linked to tremors and decreased mobility in Parkinson's disease.
Acetylcholine (ACh)	Enables muscle action, learning, and memory.	With Alzheimer's disease, ACh-producing neurons deteriorate.
Norepinephrine	Helps control alertness and arousal.	Undersupply can depress mood.
GABA (gamma-aminobutyric acid)	A major inhibitory neurotransmitter.	Undersupply linked to seizures, tremors, and insomnia.
Glutamate	A major excitatory neurotransmitter; involved in memory.	Oversupply can overstimulate brain, producing migraines or seizures (which is why some people avoid MSG, monosodium glutamate, in food).

sleepy, or aroused. *Dopamine* levels influence our movement, learning, attention, and emotions. **TABLE 2.1** outlines the effects of these and other neurotransmitters.

In Chapter 1, I promised to show you how psychologists play their game. Here's an example. An exciting neurotransmitter discovery emerged when researchers attached a radioactive tracer to morphine, an **opiate** drug that elevates mood and eases pain (Pert & Snyder, 1973). They noticed that the morphine "unlocked" receptors in brain areas linked with mood and pain sensations. Why would the brain have these "opiate receptors"? Why would it have a chemical lock, unless it also had a natural key to open it? **DOES THE BRAIN HAVE ITS OWN ◄ BUILT-IN PAINKILLERS?**

Further work revealed the answer. The brain does indeed produce its own natural opiates. Pain and vigorous exercise trigger the release of several types of neurotransmitter molecules similar to morphine. These **endorphins** (short for *endogenous* [produced within] *morphine*), as we now call them, help explain good feelings such as the "runner's high," the painkilling effects of acupuncture, and the indifference to pain that sometimes follows severe injuries.

If our natural endorphins lessen pain and boost mood, why not achieve these ends by flooding the brain with artificial opiates such as heroin or morphine? One problem is that this flood of artificial opiates may cause the brain to shut down its own "feel-good" chemistry. If the drugs are then withdrawn, the brain will be deprived of any form of relief. Nature charges a price for suppressing the body's own neurotransmitter production. Ongoing research is, however, leading to new drugs that effectively treat disorders influenced by neurotransmitter imbalances.

As we follow the biology-of-mind story throughout this book, you will hear more about neurotransmitters in our discussions of depression, addictions, and other disorders. But now it's time to consider the body's larger communication network.

PRACTICE TEST

THE BASICS

1. The neuron fiber that carries messages to other neurons is the
   a. dendrite.
   b. axon.
   c. cell body.
   d. synapse.

2. The tiny space between the axon of a sending neuron and the dendrite of a receiving neuron is called the
   a. axon.
   b. dendrite.
   c. synaptic gap.
   d. threshold.

3. A neural impulse is an *all-or-none response*. This means that the signals received by a neuron determine
   a. whether or not an impulse will be generated.
   b. how fast an impulse will be transmitted.
   c. how intense an impulse will be.
   d. whether reuptake will occur.

4. When a neural impulse reaches the end of an axon, it triggers the release of chemical messengers called
   a. dendrites.
   b. synapses.
   c. action potentials.
   d. neurotransmitters.

5. Endorphins are released in the brain in response to
   a. morphine or heroin.
   b. pain or vigorous exercise.
   c. the all-or-none response.
   d. all of these answers.

THE BIG PICTURE
2A. How do neurons communicate with one another?

IN YOUR EVERYDAY LIFE
▪ Can you think of a time when endorphins may have saved you or a friend from feeling intense pain? What happened?

Answers: 1. b, 2. c, 3. a, 4. d, 5. b. Answers to The Big Picture questions can be found in Appendix B at the end of the book.

The Nervous System

5 What are the two major divisions of the nervous system, and what are their basic functions?

To live is to take in information from the world and the body's tissues, to make decisions, and to send back information and orders to the body's tissues. All this happens thanks to our body's **nervous system (FIGURE 2.3)**. The brain and spinal cord form the **central nervous system (CNS),** the body's decision maker. The **peripheral nervous system (PNS)** is responsible for gathering information and for transmitting CNS decisions to other body parts. **Nerves,** electrical cables formed of bundles of axons, link the central nervous system with the body's sensory receptors, muscles, and glands. The optic nerve, for example, bundles a million axons into a single cable carrying the messages each eye sends to the brain (Mason & Kandel, 1991).

The nervous system's information travels through three types of neurons.

- **Sensory neurons** carry messages from the body's tissues and sensory receptors inward to the brain and spinal cord, for processing.
- **Motor neurons** carry instructions from the central nervous system out to the body's tissues.
- **Interneurons** process information between the sensory input and motor output.

Our complexity resides mostly in our interneuron systems. Our nervous system has a few million sensory neurons, a few million motor neurons, and billions and billions of interneurons.

The Peripheral Nervous System

Our peripheral nervous system has two parts—somatic and autonomic. Our **somatic nervous system** controls voluntary movements of our skeletal muscles. As you reach the end of this page, your somatic nervous system will trigger your hand to turn the page. Your **autonomic nervous system** (ANS) controls your glands and the muscles of your internal organs, including those of your heart and digestive system. Like an automatic pilot, this system may be consciously overridden, but usually it operates on its own (autonomously).

HOW DOES THE AUTONOMIC NERVOUS ◄ SYSTEM HELP US COPE WITH CHALLENGES? Through its two subdivisions, the autonomic nervous system arouses and calms us **(FIGURE 2.4** on the next page). If something alarms or challenges you (such as a longed-for job interview), your **sympathetic nervous system** will make you alert and expend energy, preparing you for action. It will increase your heartbeat and your blood pressure, slow your digestion, raise your blood sugar, and cool you with perspiration. When the stress dies down (the interview is over), your **parasympathetic nervous system** will calm you. It will conserve your energy as it decreases your heartbeat, lowers your blood sugar, and so on.

---

opiate chemical, such as opium, morphine, and heroin, that depresses neural activity, temporarily lessening pain and anxiety.

endorphins [en-DOR-fins] "morphine within"—natural, opiatelike neurotransmitters linked to pain control and to pleasure.

nervous system the body's speedy, electrochemical communication network, consisting of all the nerve cells of the central and peripheral nervous systems.

central nervous system (CNS) the brain and spinal cord.

peripheral nervous system (PNS) the sensory and motor neurons connecting the central nervous system (CNS) to the rest of the body.

nerves bundled axons that form neural "cables" connecting the central nervous system with muscles, glands, and sense organs.

sensory neuron neuron that carries incoming information from the sensory receptors to the central nervous system.

motor neuron neuron that carries outgoing information from the central nervous system to the muscles and glands.

interneuron neuron that processes information between sensory inputs and motor outputs.

somatic nervous system peripheral nervous system division controlling the body's skeletal muscles. Also called the *skeletal nervous system.*

autonomic [aw-tuh-NAHM-ik] **nervous system** peripheral nervous system division controlling the glands and the muscles of the internal organs (such as the heart). Its sympathetic subdivision arouses; its parasympathetic subdivision calms.

sympathetic nervous system autonomic nervous system subdivision that arouses the body, mobilizing its energy in stressful situations.

parasympathetic nervous system autonomic nervous system subdivision that calms the body, conserving its energy.

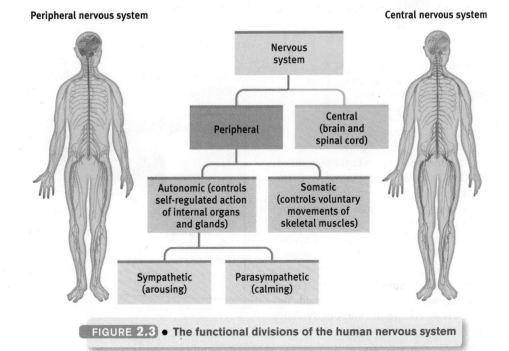

Peripheral nervous system

Central nervous system

- Nervous system
  - Peripheral
    - Autonomic (controls self-regulated action of internal organs and glands)
      - Sympathetic (arousing)
      - Parasympathetic (calming)
    - Somatic (controls voluntary movements of skeletal muscles)
  - Central (brain and spinal cord)

FIGURE 2.3 ● **The functional divisions of the human nervous system**

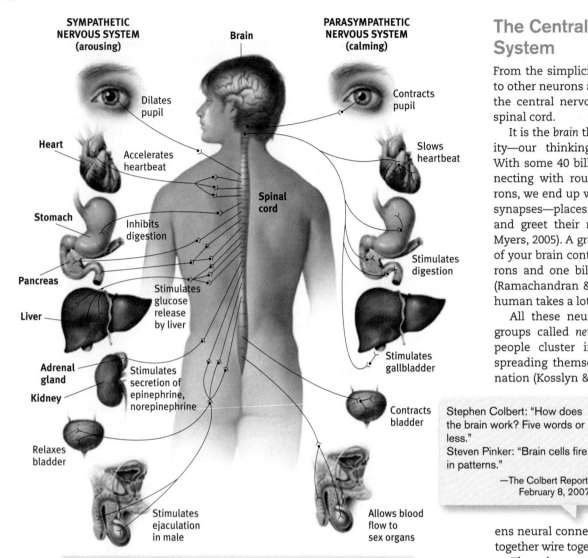

SYMPATHETIC NERVOUS SYSTEM (arousing)

Brain

PARASYMPATHETIC NERVOUS SYSTEM (calming)

Dilates pupil

Contracts pupil

Heart

Accelerates heartbeat

Slows heartbeat

Spinal cord

Stomach

Inhibits digestion

Stimulates digestion

Pancreas

Liver

Stimulates glucose release by liver

Adrenal gland

Stimulates secretion of epinephrine, norepinephrine

Stimulates gallbladder

Kidney

Contracts bladder

Relaxes bladder

Stimulates ejaculation in male

Allows blood flow to sex organs

FIGURE 2.4 ● **The autonomic nervous system arouses and calms** Its sympathetic subdivision arouses and expends energy. Its parasympathetic subdivision calms and conserves energy, allowing routine maintenance activity. For example, sympathetic stimulation speeds up heartbeat, and parasympathetic stimulation slows it.

The Central Nervous System

From the simplicity of neurons "talking" to other neurons arises the complexity of the central nervous system's brain and spinal cord.

It is the *brain* that enables our humanity—our thinking, feeling, and acting. With some 40 billion neurons, each connecting with roughly 10,000 other neurons, we end up with perhaps 400 trillion synapses—places where neurons meet and greet their neighbors (de Courten-Myers, 2005). A grain-of-sand–sized speck of your brain contains some 100,000 neurons and one billion "talking" synapses (Ramachandran & Blakeslee, 1998). Being human takes a lot of nerve.

All these neurons cluster into work groups called *neural networks,* much as people cluster into cities rather than spreading themselves evenly across the nation (Kosslyn & Koenig, 1992). Neurons network with close neighbors by means of short, fast connections. Learning—to speak a foreign language, play guitar, solve a math problem—occurs as feedback strengthens neural connections. Neurons that fire together wire together.

The other part of the central nervous system, the *spinal cord,* is a two-way highway connecting the brain and the peripheral

> Stephen Colbert: "How does the brain work? Five words or less."
> Steven Pinker: "Brain cells fire in patterns."
>
> —The Colbert Report, February 8, 2007

In everyday situations, the sympathetic and parasympathetic divisions work together to steady our internal state. I recently experienced my ANS in action. Before sending me into an MRI machine for a routine shoulder scan, the technician asked if I had issues with claustrophobia (panic feelings when confined). "No, I'm fine," I assured her, with perhaps a hint of macho swagger. Moments later, as I found myself on my back, stuck deep inside a coffin-sized box and unable to move, my sympathetic nervous system had a different idea. As claustrophobia overtook me, my heart began pounding and I felt a desperate urge to escape. Just as I was about to cry out for release, I suddenly felt my calming parasympathetic nervous system kick in. My heart rate slowed, and my body relaxed, though my arousal surged again before the 20-minute confinement ended. "You did well!" the technician said, unaware of my autonomic nervous system's roller coaster ride.

"The body is made up of millions and millions of crumbs."

nervous system. Some nerve fibers carry incoming information from your senses to your brain, while others carry outgoing motor-control information to your body parts. What happens when people suffer damage to the top of their spinal cord? Their brain is literally out of touch with their body. They lose all sensation and voluntary movement in body regions that connect to the spinal cord below its injury. They feel no pain, no pleasure. Men paralyzed below the waist may be capable of an erection (a simple reflex) if their genitals are stimulated (Goldstein, 2000). Females similarly paralyzed may respond with vaginal lubrication. But, depending on where and how completely the spinal cord is severed, people may have no genital responses to erotic images and no genital feeling (Kennedy & Over, 1990; Sipski & Alexander, 1999). To produce physical pain or pleasure, the sensory information must reach the brain.

PRACTICE TEST

THE BASICS

6. The autonomic nervous system controls internal functions, such as your digestion and heart rate. The word *autonomic* means
   a. peripheral.
   b. voluntary.
   c. operating on its own.
   d. arousing.

7. Usually, the sympathetic nervous system arouses us for action, and the parasympathetic nervous system calms us. Together, the two systems make up the
   a. autonomic nervous system.
   b. somatic nervous system.
   c. central nervous system.
   d. spinal cord.

8. The spinal cord is part of the
   a. somatic nervous system.
   b. central nervous system.
   c. autonomic nervous system.
   d. peripheral nervous system.

THE BIG PICTURE

2B. How does information flow through your nervous system as you pick up a fork? Can you summarize this process?

IN YOUR EVERYDAY LIFE
▪ Think back to a time when you felt your autonomic nervous system kick in. What was your body preparing you for?

Answers: 6. c, 7. a, 8. b. Answers to The Big Picture questions can be found in Appendix B at the end of the book.

The Endocrine System

6 What are the endocrine system's functions, and how does the endocrine system interact with the nervous system?

So far, we have focused on the body's electrochemical information system. But your body has a second communication system, the **endocrine system (FIGURE 2.5).** Glands in this system secrete **hormones,** another form of chemical messenger that influences our behaviors and emotions.

Some hormones are chemically identical to neurotransmitters. The endocrine system and nervous system are therefore close relatives. Both produce molecules that act on receptors elsewhere. Like many relatives, they also differ. The speedy nervous system zips messages from eyes to brain to hand in a fraction of a second. Endocrine messages trudge along in the bloodstream, taking several seconds or more to travel from the gland to the target tissue. If the nervous system delivers its messages rather like e-mail, the endocrine system is the body's snail mail.

But slow and steady sometimes wins the race. The effects of endocrine messages tend to outlast those of neural messages. HAVE YOU EVER FELT ANGRY, ◀ FOR NO APPARENT REASON? You may have experienced an "endocrine hangover" from lingering emotion-related hormones.

endocrine [EN-duh-krin] system the body's "slow" chemical communication system; a set of glands that secrete hormones into the bloodstream.

hormones chemical messengers that are manufactured by the endocrine glands, travel through the bloodstream, and affect other tissues.

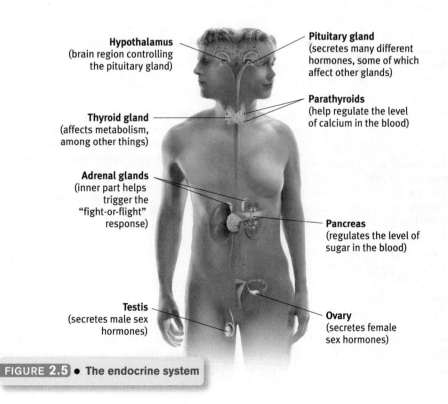

Hypothalamus (brain region controlling the pituitary gland)

Pituitary gland (secretes many different hormones, some of which affect other glands)

Thyroid gland (affects metabolism, among other things)

Parathyroids (help regulate the level of calcium in the blood)

Adrenal glands (inner part helps trigger the "fight-or-flight" response)

Pancreas (regulates the level of sugar in the blood)

Testis (secretes male sex hormones)

Ovary (secretes female sex hormones)

FIGURE 2.5 ● **The endocrine system**

Angry feelings can hang on, beyond our awareness of what set them off. When this happens, we need a little time to "simmer down."

The endocrine system's hormones influence many aspects of our lives: growth, reproduction, metabolism, mood. They work with our nervous system to keep everything in balance as we respond to stress, hard work, and our own thoughts. For example, if a noise at your window sounds like a burglar, your autonomic nervous system may order your **adrenal glands** to release *epinephrine* and *norepinephrine* (also called *adrenaline* and *noradrenaline*). In response, your heart rate, blood pressure, and blood sugar will rise, giving you a surge of energy known as the *fight-or-flight response*. When the "burglar" turns out to be a friend, the hormones—and the feelings of excitement—will linger a while.

The endocrine glands' control center is the **pituitary gland,** a pea-sized structure located in the core of the brain. Pituitary hormones influence growth, and they also send messages to other endocrine glands to release their hormones. For example, the pituitary directs your sex glands to release sex hormones, which in turn influence your brain and behavior.

But the pituitary has its own master—a nearby brain area, the *hypothalamus.* The pituitary doesn't send messages to the sex glands until it receives a signal from the hypothalamus. This feedback system (brain → pituitary → other glands → hormones → brain) reveals the interplay between the nervous and endocrine systems. The nervous system directs endocrine secretions, which then affect the nervous system. In charge of this whole electrochemical orchestra is that master conductor we call the brain.

> "I am a brain, Watson. The rest of me is a mere appendix."
>
> —Sherlock Holmes, in Arthur Conan Doyle's "The Adventure of the Mazarin Stone"

PRACTICE TEST

THE BASICS

9. The endocrine system produces chemical messengers that travel through the bloodstream and influence our behaviors and emotions. These chemical substances are
   a. hormones.
   b. neurotransmitters.
   c. endorphins.
   d. glands.

10. The pituitary gland releases hormones that influence growth and the activity of other glands. The pituitary gland is part of the
    a. endocrine system.
    b. peripheral nervous system.
    c. sympathetic nervous system.
    d. central nervous system.

THE BIG PICTURE
2C. How are the nervous and endocrine systems alike, and how do they differ?

IN YOUR EVERYDAY LIFE
▪ Do you remember feeling the lingering effects of hormones after a really stressful event? How did it feel? How long did it last?

Answers: 9. a, 10. a. Answers to The Big Picture questions can be found in Appendix B at the end of the book.

---

adrenal [ah-DREEN-el] glands pair of endocrine glands that sit just above the kidneys and secrete hormones (epinephrine and norepinephrine) that help arouse the body in times of stress.

pituitary gland most influential endocrine gland. Under the influence of the hypothalamus, the pituitary regulates growth and controls other endocrine glands.

brainstem the oldest part and central core of the brain, beginning where the spinal cord swells as it enters the skull; responsible for automatic survival functions.

medulla [muh-DUL-uh] the base of the brainstem; controls heartbeat and breathing.

The Brain

When you think *about* your brain, you're thinking *with* your brain—sending billions of neurotransmitter molecules across countless millions of synapses. Indeed, say neuroscientists, the *mind is what the brain does.*

Even in a motionless body, the brain—and mind—may, in some cases, be active. One hospitalized 23-year-old woman showed no outward signs of conscious awareness after being in a traffic accident. Nevertheless, when researchers asked her to *imagine* playing tennis or moving around her home, brain scans revealed activity like that of healthy volunteers (Owen et al., 2006). As she imagined playing tennis, for example, an area of her brain controlling arm and leg movements became active.

Close-Up: Tools of Discovery explains how scientists explore the brain-mind connection. For centuries, we had no tools high-powered yet sensitive enough to study the living brain. Now we are living in the golden age of brain science, moving closer and closer to understanding where and how the mind's functions are tied to the brain. To be learning about the brain now is like studying geography while the early explorers were mapping the world. Let's begin our own exploration of the brain.

Older Brain Structures

Brain structures determine our abilities. In sharks and other primitive vertebrates (animals with backbones), a not-too-complex brain mainly handles basic survival functions: breathing, resting, and feeding. In lower mammals, such as rodents, a more complex brain enables emotion and greater memory. In advanced mammals, such as humans, a brain that processes more information enables foresight as well.

This increasing complexity arises from new brain systems built on top of the old, much as new layers cover old ones in the Earth's landscape. Digging down, one discovers the fossil remnants of the past—brainstem components performing for us much as they did for our distant ancestors. Let's start with the brain's basement and work up.

Tools of Discovery—Having Our Head Examined

7 | What are some techniques for studying the brain?

In the past, brain injuries provided clues to brain-mind connections. For example, damage to one side of the brain often caused paralysis on the body's opposite side. Noting this, physicians guessed that the body's right side is wired to the brain's left side, and vice versa. Others linked vision problems with damage to the back of the brain, and speech problems with damage to the left-front brain. Gradually, a map of the brain began to emerge.

Now a new generation of map makers is at work charting formerly unknown territory, stimulating various brain parts and watching the results. Some use microelectrodes to snoop on the messages of individual neurons. Some attach larger electrodes to the scalp to eavesdrop with an **EEG (electroencephalograph)** on the chatter of billions of neurons. Others use scans that peer into the thinking, feeling brain and give us a Supermanlike ability to see what's happening.

The **PET (positron emission tomography) scan** tracks the brain's favorite food, the sugar glucose. Knowing that active neurons are glucose hogs, researchers give the person a form of temporarily radioactive glucose. The PET scan then detects where this "food for thought" goes by locating the radioactivity. Rather like weather radar showing rain activity, PET scan "hot spots" show which brain areas are most active as the person solves math problems, looks at images of faces, or daydreams. (See Figure 2.21 later in this chapter for an example of PET scans.)

MRI (magnetic resonance imaging) scans capture images of brain structures by briefly disrupting activity in brain molecules. Researchers first position the person's head in a strong magnetic field that aligns brain molecules' spinning atoms. With a brief pulse of radio waves, they then disrupt the spinning, which alters the magnetic alignment. As the MRI scanner detects the molecules' location, a detailed picture of soft tissues emerges. These images have revealed, for example, that some people with schizophrenia, a disabling psychological disorder, have enlarged fluid-filled brain areas **(FIGURE 2.6)**.

A special application of MRI, **fMRI (functional MRI),** also reveals the brain's *functions*. Oxygen-laden blood flows to brain areas that are especially active. By comparing MRI scans taken less than a second apart, researchers can watch parts of the brain "light up" as a person thinks or acts in certain ways. As the person looks at a photo, for example, the fMRI shows blood rushing to the back of the brain, which processes visual information (see Figure 2.17). The

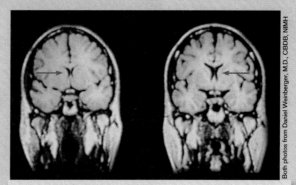

FIGURE 2.6 ● MRI scan of a healthy individual (left) and a person with schizophrenia (right) :: Note the enlarged fluid-filled brain region in the image on the right.

technology enables a very crude sort of mind reading, as some neuroscientists showed after scanning 129 people's brains as they did eight different mental tasks (such as reading, gambling, and rhyming). Later, viewing another person's brain images, they were able, with 80 percent accuracy, to predict which of these mental tasks the person was doing (Poldrack et al., 2009).

What the telescope did for astronomy, these brain-snooping tools are doing for psychology. By revealing how the living, working brain divides its labor, these tools have taught us more about the brain in the past 30 years than we had learned in the prior 30,000 years.

EEG (electroencephalograph) device that uses electrodes placed on the scalp to record waves of electrical activity sweeping across the brain's surface. (The tracing of those brain waves is an *electroencephalogram*.)

PET (positron emission tomography) scan a view of brain activity showing where a radioactive form of glucose goes while the brain performs a given task.

MRI (magnetic resonance imaging) a technique that uses magnetic fields and radio waves to produce computer-generated images of soft tissue. MRI scans show brain anatomy.

fMRI (functional magnetic resonance imaging) a technique for revealing bloodflow and, therefore, brain activity by comparing successive MRI scans. fMRI scans show brain function.

The Brainstem

8 | What are the functions of the brainstem and its related structures?

The brain's oldest and innermost region is the **brainstem (FIGURE 2.7** on the next page**)**. It begins where the spinal cord swells slightly after entering the skull. This slight swelling is the **medulla,** the control center for your heartbeat and breathing. Just above the medulla sits the *pons,* an area that helps coordinate movements. If a cat's brainstem is severed from the rest of the brain above it, the animal will still breathe. It will even run, climb, and groom (Klemm, 1990). But cut off from the brain's higher regions, it won't *purposefully* run or climb to get food.

The brainstem is a crossover point. Here, you'll find a peculiar sort of cross-wiring, with most nerves to and from

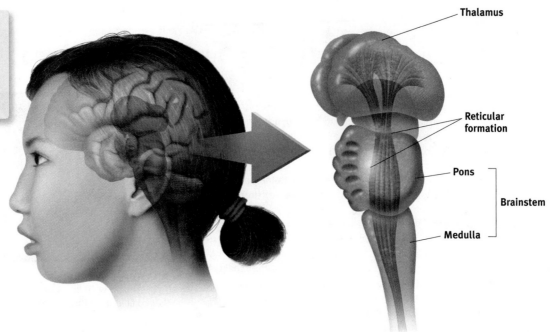

Thalamus

Reticular formation

Pons

Brainstem

Medulla

each side of the brain connecting to the body's opposite side. Thus, the right brain controls the left side of the body, and vice versa **(FIGURE 2.8)**. This cross-wiring is one of the brain's many surprises.

The Thalamus

Sitting at the top of the brainstem is the **thalamus.** This joined pair of egg-shaped structures acts as the brain's sensory switchboard. The thalamus receives information from all your senses except smell, and it forwards the messages to regions of your brain that deal with seeing, hearing, tasting, and touching. You can think of your thalamus as something like an e-mail server. Messages flow through this hub on their way to their final destination. In addition to incoming sensory messages, your thalamus receives replies from some higher

FIGURE **2.8** ● **The body's cross-wiring** Nerves from one side of the brain are mostly linked to the body's opposite side.

Andrew Swift

brain regions. It forwards these replies to your medulla and *cerebellum* for processing.

The Reticular Formation

Inside the brainstem, between your ears, lies your **reticular** ("netlike") **formation.** This finger-shaped network of neurons extends upward from your spinal cord, through your brainstem, and into your thalamus (Figure 2.7). This long structure acts as a filter for some of the sensory messages traveling from your spinal cord to your thalamus, relaying important information to other areas of your brain.

In 1949, researchers discovered that electrically stimulating the reticular formation of a sleeping cat almost instantly produced an awake, alert animal (Moruzzi & Magoun, 1949). When a cat's reticular formation was cut off from higher brain regions, without damaging

the nearby sensory pathways, the effect was equally dramatic. The cat lapsed into a coma and never awakened. The conclusion? The reticular formation enables arousal.

The Cerebellum

At the rear of the brainstem is the **cerebellum,** meaning "little brain," which is what its two wrinkled halves resemble **(FIGURE 2.9).** This baseball-sized structure plays an important role in a lot that happens just outside your awareness. Quickly, answer these questions. How much time has passed since you woke up this morning? Does your chair feel different from the back of your hand? How's your mood? If you answered those questions easily, thank your cerebellum. It helps you judge time, discriminate sounds and textures, and control your emotions (Bower & Parsons, 2003). It also coordinates voluntary movement. If you injured your cerebellum or drugged it with alcohol, you would have trouble walking, keeping your balance, or shaking hands. The cerebellum also helps process and store memories for things we cannot consciously recall, such as why we link the sound of thunder to a flash of lightning. (Stay tuned for more about this in Chapter 7.)

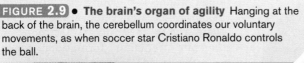

FIGURE 2.9 ● **The brain's organ of agility** Hanging at the back of the brain, the cerebellum coordinates our voluntary movements, as when soccer star Cristiano Ronaldo controls the ball.

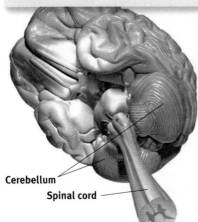

Cerebellum

Spinal cord

Note: These older brain functions all occur without any conscious effort. Once again, we see one of our Big Ideas at work: *Our two-track brain processes most information outside of our awareness.* We are aware of the *results* of our brain's labor, say, our current visual experience, but not of *how* we constructed the visual image. Likewise, whether we are asleep or awake, our brainstem manages its life-sustaining functions, freeing our newer brain regions to dream, think, talk, or savor a memory.

The Limbic System

9 What are the structures and functions of the limbic system? What is the relationship of the hypothalamus to the pituitary gland?

We've traveled through the brain's oldest parts, but we've not yet reached its newest and highest regions, the *cerebral hemispheres* (the two halves of the brain). In between the oldest and newest brain areas lies the **limbic system** (*limbus* means "border"). This system contains the *amygdala,* the *hypothalamus,* and the *hippocampus* **(FIGURE 2.10** on the next page**).** The hippocampus processes conscious memories. Animals or humans who lose their hippocampus to surgery or injury also lose their ability to form new memories of facts and events. Chapter 7 explains how our two-track mind processes our memories. For now, let's look at the limbic system's links to emotions such as fear and anger, and to basic motives such as those for food and sex.

The Amygdala Research has linked the **amygdala**—two lima-bean–sized neural clusters in the limbic system—to aggression and fear. In 1939, researchers surgically removed a rhesus monkey's

PRACTICE TEST

THE BASICS

11. The part of the brainstem that controls heartbeat and breathing is the
   a. cerebellum.   c. reticular formation.
   b. medulla.   d. thalamus.

12. The thalamus receives sensory information and routes it to higher brain regions for processing. The thalamus functions as a(n)
   a. memory bank.   c. breathing regulator.
   b. arousal center.   d. switchboard.

13. The lower brain structure that governs arousal is the
   a. thalamus.   c. reticular formation.
   b. cerebellum.   d. medulla.

14. The part of the brain that coordinates voluntary movement is the
   a. cerebellum.   c. thalamus.
   b. medulla.   d. reticular formation.

THE BIG PICTURE

2D. In what brain region would damage be most likely to disrupt your ability to skip rope? Your ability to hear and taste? In what brain region would damage perhaps leave you in a coma? Without the very breath and heartbeat of life?

IN YOUR EVERYDAY LIFE

■ In what ways has learning about the physical brain influenced your thoughts about human nature?

■ If most information in the brain is processed outside of our awareness, how can we ever really know ourselves?

Answers: 11. b, 12. d, 13. c, 14. a. Answers to The Big Picture questions can be found in Appendix B at the end of the book.

---

thalamus [THAL-uh-muss] area at the top of the brainstem; directs sensory messages to the cortex and transmits replies to the cerebellum and medulla.

reticular formation nerve network running through the brainstem and thalamus; plays an important role in controlling arousal.

cerebellum [sehr-uh-BELL-um] the "little brain" at the rear of the brainstem; functions include processing sensory input and coordinating movement output and balance.

limbic system neural system (including the *hippocampus, amygdala,* and *hypothalamus*) located below the cerebral hemispheres; associated with emotions and drives.

amygdala [uh-MIG-duh-la] two lima-bean–sized neural clusters in the limbic system; linked to emotion.

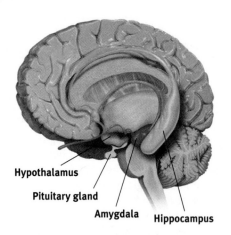

Hypothalamus

Pituitary gland

Amygdala   Hippocampus

FIGURE 2.10 • **The limbic system** This neural system sits between your brain's older parts and its cerebral hemispheres. The limbic system, via the hypothalamus, controls the nearby pituitary gland. Electrical stimulation of a cat's amygdala provokes reactions such as the one shown here, suggesting its role in emotions such as rage.

Jane Burton/Dorling Kindersley/Getty Images

amygdala, turning the normally ill-tempered animal into the most mellow of creatures (Klüver & Bucy, 1939).

What then might happen if we electrically stimulate the amygdala of a normally mellow domestic animal, such as a cat? Do so in one spot and the cat prepares to attack, hissing with its back arched, its pupils wide, its hair on end (Figure 2.10). Move the electrode only slightly within the amygdala, cage the cat with a small mouse, and now it cowers in terror.

These experiments confirm the amygdala's role in emotions such as rage and fear. Still, a critical thinker would be careful here. When we feel or act in aggressive and fearful ways, there is neural activity in all levels of our brain, not just in the amygdala. Stimulating limbic structures other than the amygdala can also trigger aggression or fear. If you charge a car's dead battery, you can activate the engine. Yet the battery is merely one link in an integrated system.

The Hypothalamus Just below (*hypo*) your thalamus is your **hypothalamus,** an important link in the chain of command for bodily maintenance. Some neural clusters in the hypothalamus influence hunger. Others regulate thirst, body temperature, and sexual behavior. Together, they help you maintain a steady internal state.

As the hypothalamus monitors the state of your body, it tunes into your blood chemistry and any incoming orders from other brain parts. For example, picking up signals from your cerebral cortex that you are thinking about sex, your hypothalamus will secrete hormones. These hormones will in turn trigger the nearby "master gland," your *pituitary* (see Figure 2.10), to influence your sex glands to release their hormones. These will intensify the thoughts of sex in your cerebral cortex. (Note the interplay between the nervous and endocrine systems: The brain influences the endocrine system, which in turn influences the brain.)

A remarkable discovery about the hypothalamus illustrates how progress in science often occurs—when curious, smart-thinking investigators keep an open mind. Two young psychologists, James Olds and Peter Milner (1954), were trying to implant electrodes in rats' reticular formations when they made a magnificent mistake. In one rat, they placed the electrode incorrectly. Curiously, the rat kept returning to the location where it had been stimulated by this misplaced electrode, as if seeking more stimulation. On discovering they had actually placed the device in a region of the hypothalamus, Olds and Milner realized they had stumbled upon a brain center that provides pleasurable rewards (Olds, 1975).

In later studies, when rats were allowed to control their own stimulation in these and other areas, they did so at a feverish pace—pressing a pedal up to 7000 times an hour, until they dropped from exhaustion. Moreover, to get this stimulation, they would even cross an electrified floor that a starving rat would not cross to reach food (**FIGURE 2.11**).

FIGURE 2.11 • **Pain for pleasure** This rat has an electrode implanted in a reward center of its hypothalamus. It will cross an electric grid, accepting painful shocks, in order to press a lever that sends impulses to its reward center.

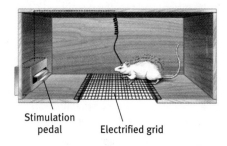

Stimulation pedal

Electrified grid

hypothalamus [hi-po-THAL-uh-muss] a neural structure lying below (*hypo*) the thalamus; directs several maintenance activities (eating, drinking, body temperature), helps govern the endocrine system via the pituitary gland, and is linked to emotion.

Similar reward centers in or near the hypothalamus were later discovered in many other species, including goldfish, dolphins, and monkeys. In fact, animal research has revealed both a general reward system that triggers the release of the neurotransmitter dopamine, and specific centers associated with the pleasures of eating, drinking, and sex. Animals, it seems, come equipped with built-in systems that reward activities essential to survival.

DO HUMANS HAVE LIMBIC CENTERS FOR ◄ PLEASURE? Indeed we do. To calm violent patients, one neurosurgeon implanted electrodes in such areas. Stimulated patients reported mild pleasure. Unlike Olds' rats, however, they were not driven to a frenzy (Deutsch, 1972; Hooper & Teresi, 1986).

* * *

We've finished our tour of the older brain structures. **FIGURE 2.12** will help you place the key brain areas we've discussed, as well as the cerebral cortex, our next topic.

PRACTICE TEST

THE BASICS

15. The limbic system sits between the brain's older parts and the cerebral hemispheres. Two parts of the limbic system are the amygdala and the
   a. pituitary.
   b. hippocampus.
   c. medulla.
   d. cerebellum.

16. A cat's ferocious response to electrical brain stimulation would lead you to suppose that the electrode had been touching the
   a. hippocampus.
   b. pituitary.
   c. hypothalamus.
   d. amygdala.

17. The neural structure that most directly regulates eating, drinking, and body temperature is the
   a. hippocampus.
   b. hypothalamus.
   c. thalamus.
   d. amygdala.

18. The reward centers discovered by Olds and Milner were located in regions of the
   a. pituitary.
   b. amygdala.
   c. hypothalamus.
   d. hippocampus.

THE BIG PICTURE

2E. How is the limbic system involved in fear and anger?

IN YOUR EVERYDAY LIFE

▪ Why do you think humans are not driven to a frenzy, as the rats were, by stimulation of their "reward centers" in the limbic system?

Answers: 15. b, 16. d, 17. b, 18. c. Answers to The Big Picture questions can be found in Appendix B at the end of the book.

The Cerebral Cortex

Older brain networks sustain basic life functions and enable memory, emotions, and basic drives. High above these older

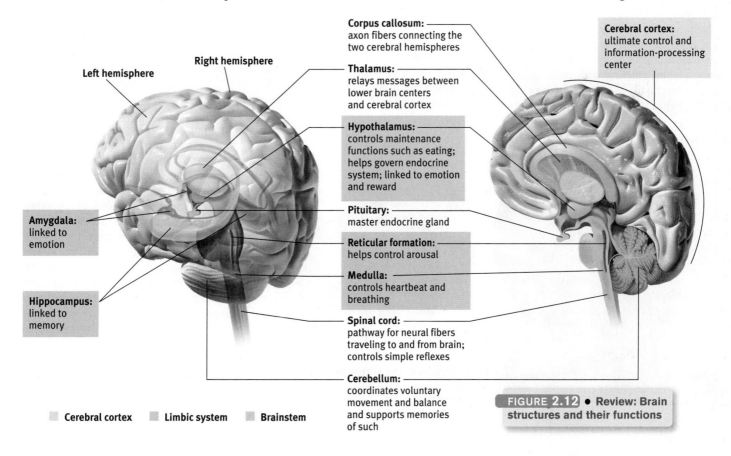

Corpus callosum: axon fibers connecting the two cerebral hemispheres

Thalamus: relays messages between lower brain centers and cerebral cortex

Hypothalamus: controls maintenance functions such as eating; helps govern endocrine system; linked to emotion and reward

Pituitary: master endocrine gland

Reticular formation: helps control arousal

Medulla: controls heartbeat and breathing

Spinal cord: pathway for neural fibers traveling to and from brain; controls simple reflexes

Cerebellum: coordinates voluntary movement and balance and supports memories of such

Cerebral cortex: ultimate control and information-processing center

Right hemisphere

Left hemisphere

Amygdala: linked to emotion

Hippocampus: linked to memory

▪ Cerebral cortex   ▪ Limbic system   ▪ Brainstem

FIGURE 2.12 ● **Review: Brain structures and their functions**

structures is the *cerebrum,* consisting of two large hemispheres that contribute 85 percent of the brain's weight. Covering those hemispheres, like bark on a tree, is the **cerebral cortex,** a thin surface layer of interconnected neurons. Its newer neural networks form specialized work teams that enable your perceiving, thinking, and speaking. The cerebral cortex is your brain's thinking crown, your body's ultimate control and information-processing center.

Structure of the Cortex

10 What are the four lobes of the cerebral cortex, and where are they located?

If you opened a human skull, exposing the brain, you would see a wrinkled organ, shaped somewhat like the meat of an oversized walnut. Without these wrinkles, a flattened cerebral cortex would require triple the area—roughly that of a very large pizza. The brain's ballooning left and right hemispheres are filled mainly with axons connecting the cortex to the brain's other regions.

Each hemisphere's cortex is subdivided into four *lobes,* separated by deep folds **(FIGURE 2.13).** You can roughly trace the four lobes, starting with both hands on your forehead. The **frontal lobes** lie directly behind your forehead. As you move your hands over the top of your head, toward the rear, you're sliding over your **parietal lobes.** Continuing to move down, toward the back of your head, you'll slide over your **occipital lobes.** Now move each hand forward, to the sides of your head, and just above each ear you'll find your **temporal lobes.** Each hemisphere has four lobes. Each lobe carries out many functions. And many functions require the cooperation of several lobes.

Functions of the Cortex

11 What are the functions of the motor cortex, sensory cortex, and association areas?

More than a century ago, surgeons found damaged areas of the cerebral cortex during autopsies of people who had been partially paralyzed or speechless. This rather crude evidence was interesting, but it did not prove that specific parts of the cortex control complex functions like movement or speech. After all, if the entire cortex controlled speech and movement, damage to

Demonstration: Try moving your right hand in a circular motion, as if polishing a car. Now start your right foot doing the same motion synchronized with the hand. Now reverse the foot motion (but not the hand). Tough, huh? But easier if you try moving the *left* foot opposite to the right hand. The left and right limbs are controlled by opposite sides of the brain. So their opposed activities interfere less with one another.

almost any area might show up as a disability. A television with its power cord cut would go dead, but we would be fooling ourselves if we thought we had "localized" the picture in the cord.

Motor Functions Early scientists had better luck showing simpler brain-behavior links. In 1870, for example, German physicians Gustav Fritsch and Eduard Hitzig made an important discovery. By electrically stimulating parts of a dog's cortex, they could make other parts of its body move. The movement happened only when they stimulated an arch-shaped region at the back of the dog's frontal lobe, running roughly ear-to-ear across the top of the brain. Moreover, if they stimulated this region in the left hemisphere, the dog's right leg would move. And if they stimulated part of the right hemisphere, the opposite leg—on the left—reacted. Fritsch and Hitzig had discovered what is now called the **motor cortex.**

Lucky for brain surgeons and their patients, the brain has no sensory receptors. Knowing this, Otfrid Foerster and Wilder Penfield were able to map the motor cortex in hundreds of wide-awake patients, by stimulating different cortical areas and observing the body's responses. They discovered that body areas requiring precise control, such as the fingers and mouth, occupied the greatest amount of cortical space **(FIGURE 2.14).**

As is so often the case in science, new answers triggered new questions. We now know that electrically stimulating the motor cortex can cause body parts to move. What might happen, some researchers are asking, if we implanted a device to detect motor cortex activity? Could such devices cause a robotic limb to move in soldiers who have lost arms or legs during combat? Could they help severely paralyzed people learn to command a cursor to write e-mail or

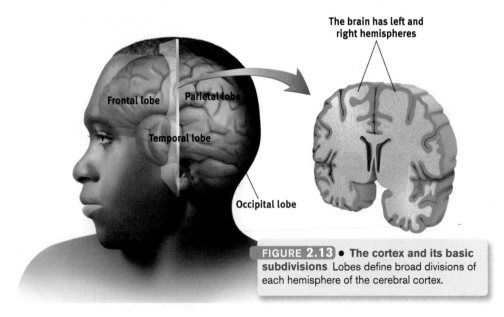

The brain has left and right hemispheres

Frontal lobe Parietal lobe

Temporal lobe

Occipital lobe

FIGURE 2.13 ● **The cortex and its basic subdivisions** Lobes define broad divisions of each hemisphere of the cerebral cortex.

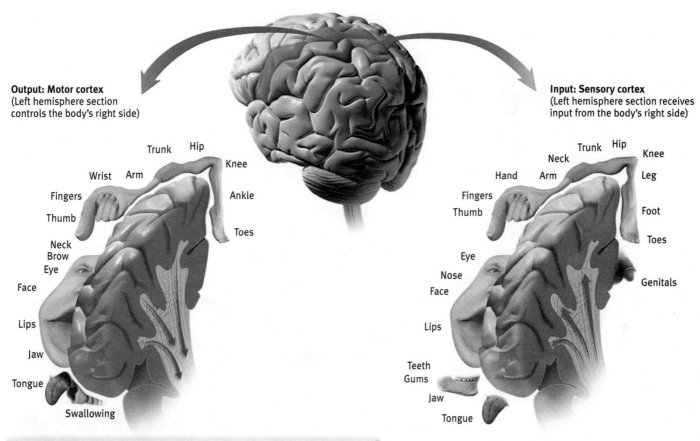

Output: Motor cortex
(Left hemisphere section controls the body's right side)

Trunk Hip
Knee
Wrist Arm
Fingers Ankle
Thumb Toes
Neck
Brow
Eye
Face
Lips
Jaw
Tongue
Swallowing

Input: Sensory cortex
(Left hemisphere section receives input from the body's right side)

Trunk Hip
Neck Knee
Hand Arm Leg
Fingers Foot
Thumb Toes
Eye
Nose Genitals
Face
Lips
Teeth
Gums
Jaw
Tongue

FIGURE 2.14 ● **Left hemisphere tissue devoted to each body part in the motor cortex and the sensory cortex** The amount of cortex devoted to a body part is not proportional to that part's size. Your brain devotes more tissue to sensitive areas and to areas requiring precise control. Thus, your fingers occupy more cortex space than does your upper arm.

work online? All this and more may happen in the near future **(FIGURE 2.15** on the next page).

Sensory Functions The motor cortex sends messages out to the body. What parts of the cortex receive incoming messages from our senses of touch and movement? Penfield supplied the answer. The **sensory cortex,** running parallel to the motor cortex and just behind it at the front of the parietal lobes, carries out this task (Figure 2.14). Stimulate a point on the top of this band of tissue, and a person reports being touched on the shoulder. Stimulate some point on the side, and the person feels something on the face.

The more sensitive a body region, the larger the sensory cortex area devoted to it. WHY DO WE KISS WITH OUR LIPS ◀ RATHER THAN RUB ELBOWS? Our supersensitive lips project to a larger brain area than do our arms (Figure 2.14). Similarly, rats have a large brain area devoted to their whisker sensations, and owls to their hearing sensations.

Your sensory cortex is a very powerful tool for processing information from your skin senses and from movements of your body parts. But it isn't the only area of the cortex that receives input from your senses. If you have normal vision, you are receiving visual information in the *visual*

cerebral [seh-REE-bruhl] **cortex** thin layer of interconnected neurons covering the cerebral hemispheres; the body's ultimate control and information-processing center.

frontal lobes portion of the cerebral cortex lying just behind the forehead; involved in speaking and muscle movements and in making plans and judgments.

parietal [puh-RYE-uh-tuhl] **lobes** portion of the cerebral cortex lying at the top of the head and toward the rear; receives sensory input for touch and body position.

occipital [ahk-SIP-uh-tuhl] **lobes** portion of the cerebral cortex lying at the back of the head; includes areas that receive information from the visual fields.

temporal lobes portion of the cerebral cortex lying roughly above the ears; includes areas that receive information from the ears.

motor cortex cerebral cortex area at the rear of the frontal lobes; controls voluntary movements.

sensory cortex cerebral cortex area at the front of the parietal lobes; registers and processes body touch and movement sensations.

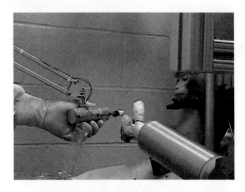

Motorlab, University of Pittsburgh School of Medicine

FIGURE 2.15 ● **Mind over matter** Guided by a tiny, 100-electrode brain implant, monkeys have learned to control a mechanical hand that can grab snacks and put them in their mouth (Velliste et al., 2008). Although not yet permanently effective, such implants are raising hopes that people with paralyzed limbs may someday be able to use their own brain signals to control computers and robotic limbs.

Association Areas So far, we have pointed out small areas of the cortex that receive messages from our senses, and other small areas that send messages to our muscles. Together, these areas occupy about one-fourth of the human brain's thin, wrinkled cover. What, then, goes on in the vast remaining regions of the cortex? In these **association areas** (peach colored in **FIGURE 2.18**), neurons are busy with higher mental functions—many of the tasks that make us human.

Electrically probing an association area won't trigger any observable response. So, unlike the sensory and motor areas, association area functions

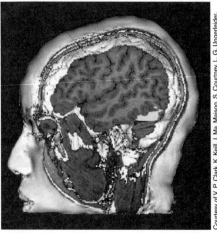

Courtesy of V. P. Clark, K. Keill, J. Ma. Maisog, S. Courtney, L. G. Ungerleider, and J. V. Haxby, National Institute of Mental Health

FIGURE 2.17 ● **Watching the brain in action** As this person looks at a photo, the fMRI (functional MRI) scan shows increased activity (color represents more bloodflow) in the visual cortex in the occipital lobes. When the person stops looking, the region instantly calms down.

cortex in your occipital lobes, at the back of your brain **(FIGURE 2.16)**. A bad enough bash there would make you blind. Stimulated there, you might see flashes of light or dashes of color. (In a sense, we *do* have eyes in the back of our head!) From your occipital lobes, visual information goes to other areas that specialize in tasks such as identifying words, detecting emotions, and recognizing faces **(FIGURE 2.17)**.

Any sound you now hear is processed by your *auditory cortex* in your temporal lobes (see Figure 2.16). Most of this auditory information travels a roundabout route from one ear to the auditory

receiving area above your opposite ear. If stimulated there, you alone might hear a sound. People with schizophrenia sometimes have auditory **hallucinations** (false sensory experiences). MRI scans taken during these hallucinations show active auditory areas in the temporal lobes (Lennox et al., 1999).

Auditory cortex

Visual cortex

FIGURE 2.16 ● **The visual cortex and auditory cortex** The visual cortex of the occipital lobes at the rear of your brain receives input from your eyes. The auditory cortex, in your temporal lobes—above your ears—receives information from your ears.

hallucination false sensory experience, such as hearing something in the absence of an external auditory stimulus.

association areas cerebral cortex area involved primarily in higher mental functions, such as learning, remembering, thinking, and speaking.

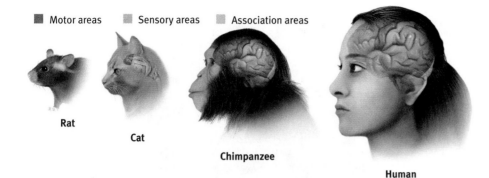

■ Motor areas   ■ Sensory areas   ■ Association areas

Rat

Cat

Chimpanzee

Human

FIGURE 2.18 ● **Areas of the cortex in four mammals** More intelligent animals have increased "uncommitted" or association areas of the cortex. These vast brain areas are responsible for integrating and acting on information received and processed by sensory areas.

can't be neatly mapped. Their silence has led to what Donald McBurney (1996, p. 44) has called "one of the hardiest weeds in the garden of psychology": DO ◄ WE REALLY USE ONLY 10 PERCENT OF OUR BRAIN? Time for some critical thinking: The odds are not 90 percent that a bullet to your brain would land in an area you don't use. Surgically lesioned animals and brain-damaged humans bear witness that association areas are not dormant. Rather, they interpret, integrate, and act on sensory information and link it with stored memories—a very important part of thinking.

Association areas are found in all four lobes. In the frontal lobes, they enable judgments, planning, and processing of new memories. People with damaged frontal lobes may have intact memories, high scores on intelligence tests, and great cake-baking skills. Yet they would not be able to plan ahead to *begin* baking a cake for a loved one's birthday (Huey et al., 2006).

Frontal lobe damage can have even more serious effects. It can alter personality and remove inhibitions. Consider the case of railroad worker Phineas Gage. One afternoon in 1848, Gage, then 25 years old, was using an iron rod to pack gunpowder into a rock. A spark ignited the gunpowder, shooting the rod up through his left cheek and out the top of his skull **(FIGURE 2.19a)**.

To everyone's amazement, he was immediately able to sit up and speak, and after the wound healed he returned to work. But the friendly, soft-spoken Phineas Gage was now irritable, profane, and dishonest. Although his mental abilities and memories were intact, his personality was not. His frontal lobes had been massively damaged, and he was, said his friends, "no longer Gage." Gage eventually lost his job and ended up earning his living as a fairground exhibit.

With his frontal lobes ruptured, Gage's moral compass had disconnected from his behavior. Similar impairments to moral judgment have appeared in more recent studies of people with damaged frontal lobes. Without the frontal lobe brakes on their impulses they, too, became less inhibited. Moreover, their moral judgments seem unrestrained by normal emotions. Would you advocate pushing someone in front of a runaway boxcar to save five others? Most people do not, but those with damage to a brain area behind the eyes often do (Koenigs et al., 2007).

Damage to association areas in other lobes would have different consequences. If a stroke or head injury destroyed part of your parietal lobes, you might lose mathematical and spatial reasoning. If the damaged area was on the underside of the right temporal lobe, which lets you recognize faces, you would still be able to describe facial features and to recognize someone's gender and approximate age. Yet you would be strangely unable to identify the person as, say, your grandmother.

FIGURE 2.19 ● **Phineas Gage reconsidered** (a) Gage's skull was kept as a medical record. Using measurements and modern neuroimaging techniques, researchers have reconstructed the probable path of the rod through Gage's brain (Damasio et al., 1994). (b) This recently discovered photo shows Gage after his accident. The image has been laterally reversed to show the features correctly given that early photos, such as this one, are actually mirror images.

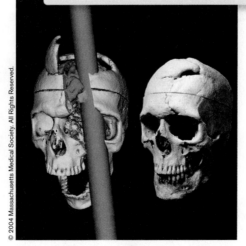

(a)

(b)

Language: Specialization and Integration

12 How does the brain process language?

So far, we have considered the effects of damage to some localized areas of the brain's cortex. But many of our complex abilities are spread across many areas of the brain.

Consider this curious finding: Damage to any one of several cortical areas can impair language. Even more curious, some people with brain damage can speak fluently but cannot read (despite good vision). Others can understand what they read but cannot speak. Still others can write but not read, read but not write, read numbers but not letters, or sing but not speak. This is puzzling, because we tend to think of speaking and reading, or writing and reading, or singing and speaking as merely different examples of one general ability. To sort out this puzzle required a lot of smart thinking by many different scientists, all working toward the same goal: How does the brain process language?

In 1865 French physician Paul Broca discovered that after damage to a specific area of the left frontal lobe (now called **Broca's area**), a person would struggle to form words, yet could often sing familiar songs with ease. A decade later, German investigator Karl Wernicke discovered that after damage to a specific area of the left temporal lobe **(Wernicke's area),** people could speak only meaningless words and were unable to understand others' words. Over the next century, other researchers—like archeologists unearthing dinosaur bones—revealed other fragments of the language-processing answer.

Norman Geschwind assembled all these clues into the explanation you can see in **FIGURE 2.20.** When you read aloud, the words (1) register in your visual cortex, (2) are relayed to another brain area, the *angular gyrus,* which transforms the words into an auditory code that (3) is received and understood in nearby Wernicke's area, and (4) is sent to Broca's area, which (5) controls the motor cortex as it directs

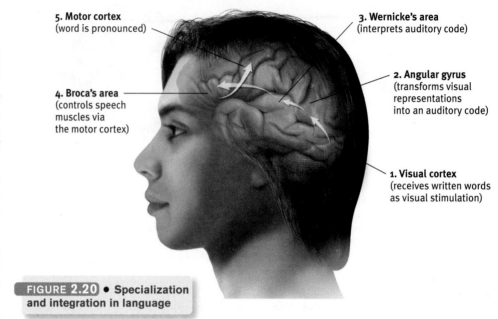

5. Motor cortex
(word is pronounced)

3. Wernicke's area
(interprets auditory code)

2. Angular gyrus
(transforms visual representations into an auditory code)

4. Broca's area
(controls speech muscles via the motor cortex)

1. Visual cortex
(receives written words as visual stimulation)

FIGURE 2.20 • **Specialization and integration in language**

your muscles to pronounce the word. PET scans can track this processing **(FIGURE 2.21).** Any link in the chain can be damaged, and each would impair speech in a different way. With a damaged angular gyrus, you could speak and understand but you wouldn't be able to read. With a damaged Wernicke's area, you wouldn't understand the words. With a damaged Broca's area, you would be unable to speak.

Some funny things have turned up during research on language processing. When you read a word, your brain computes the word's form, sound, and meaning using different neural networks (Posner & Carr, 1992). Thus, fMRI scans show that jokes playing on meaning ("Why don't sharks bite lawyers? . . . Professional courtesy") are processed in a different brain area than jokes playing on words ("What kind of lights did Noah use on the ark? . . . Flood lights") (Goel & Dolan, 2001). Again, we encounter the theme of the two-track mind (dual processing): *What you experience as one continuous stream of perception is actually only*

FIGURE 2.21 • **Brain activity when seeing, hearing, and speaking words**
PET scans such as these detect the activity of different areas of the brain.

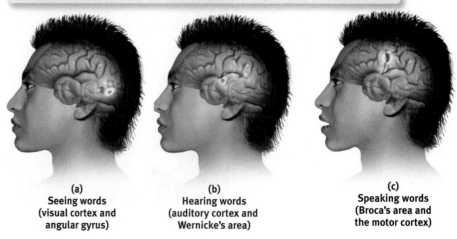

(a)
Seeing words
(visual cortex and angular gyrus)

(b)
Hearing words
(auditory cortex and Wernicke's area)

(c)
Speaking words
(Broca's area and the motor cortex)

the visible tip of a much larger iceberg. Most information processing takes place beneath the surface of conscious awareness.

To sum up, the brain operates by dividing its mental functions—speaking, perceiving, thinking, remembering—into subfunctions. Those subfunctions are localized in particular brain regions, yet the brain acts as a unified whole. Moving your hand; recognizing a face; even perceiving color, motion, and depth—all depend on specific neural networks. Yet complex functions such as listening, learning, and loving involve the coordination of many brain areas. Together, these two principles—*specialization* and *integration*—describe the way our brain functions.

The Brain's Plasticity

13 | **When damaged, can the brain repair or reorganize itself?**

Some of the effects of brain damage described earlier can be traced to two hard facts. (1) Severed neurons, unlike cut skin, usually do not repair themselves. (If your spinal cord were severed, you probably would be permanently paralyzed.) And (2) some brain functions seem forever linked to specific areas. One newborn who suffered damage to the facial recognition areas on both temporal lobes later remained unable to recognize faces (Farah et al., 2000).

But there is good news: The brain's impressive **plasticity** allows it to modify itself after some types of damage. Some brain tissue can *reorganize* in response to damage. Under the surface of our awareness, the brain is constantly changing, building new pathways as it adjusts to little mishaps and new experiences.

Plasticity may also occur after serious damage, especially in young children (Kolb, 1989; see also **FIGURE 2.22**). If a slow-growing left-hemisphere tumor disrupts language, the right hemisphere may compensate (Thiel et al., 2006). If a finger is lost, the sensory cortex that received

its input will begin to pick up signals from the neighboring fingers, which then become more sensitive (Fox, 1984).

As Figure 2.14 shows, the toes region is next to the genitals region of the sensory cortex. So what do you suppose was the sexual intercourse experience of a patient whose lower leg was amputated? "I actually experience my orgasm in my foot. And there it's much bigger than it used to be because it's no longer just confined to my genitals" (Ramachandran & Blakeslee, 1998, p. 36).

Although the brain often attempts self-repair by reorganizing existing tissue, it sometimes attempts to mend itself by producing new neurons. Evidence of this process, known as **neurogenesis,** has been found in adult mice and humans. These baby neurons originate deep in the brain. They may then migrate elsewhere and form connections with neighboring neurons (Gould, 2007).

FIGURE 2.22 • **Brain plasticity** This 6-year-old had surgery to end her life-threatening brain seizures. Although most of an entire hemisphere was removed (see MRI of hemispherectomy at left), her remaining hemisphere compensated by putting other areas to work.

Living Art Enterprises, LLC/Photo Researchers, Inc.
Joe McNally/Joe McNally Photography

Broca's area frontal lobe area, usually in the left hemisphere, that directs the muscle movements involved in speech; controls language expression.

Wernicke's area brain area, usually in the left temporal lobe, involved in language comprehension and expression; controls language reception.

plasticity the brain's ability to change, especially during childhood, by reorganizing after damage or by building new pathways based on experience.

neurogenesis formation of new neurons.

Might new drugs spur the production of new nerve cells? Stay tuned. As you read this sentence, companies are hard at work on such possibilities. In the meantime, we can all benefit from natural promoters of neurogenesis, such as exercise, sleep, and nonstressful but stimulating environments (Iso et al., 2007; Pereira et al., 2007; Stranahan et al., 2006).

PRACTICE ⟨ TEST ⟩

THE BASICS

19. If a neurosurgeon stimulated your right motor cortex, you would most likely
   a. see light.
   b. hear a sound.
   c. feel a touch on the right arm.
   d. move your left leg.

20. Which of the following occupies the greatest amount of space in the sensory cortex?
   a. Knee
   b. Toes
   c. Forehead
   d. Thumb

21. Only about one-fourth of the cerebral cortex is committed to specific sensory or motor functions. The remaining "uncommitted" areas are called
   a. occipital lobes.
   b. temporal lobes.
   c. association areas.
   d. plastic areas.

22. Judging and planning are enabled by the _____ lobes.
   a. occipital
   b. parietal

Continued

c. frontal

d. temporal

23. The area in the brain that, if damaged, might impair your ability to speak words is

a. Wernicke's area.

b. Broca's area.

c. the left occipital lobe.

d. the angular gyrus.

24. The brains of young children are especially plastic. *Plasticity* refers to the

a. formation of new nerve cells deep in the brain.

b. area of sensory cortex devoted to association areas.

c. brain's ability to modify itself after damage.

d. specialization of the brain's right and left hemispheres.

THE BIG PICTURE

2F. Which area of the human brain is most similar to that of primitive animals? Which part of the human brain distinguishes us the most from primitive animals?

IN YOUR EVERYDAY LIFE

- Why do you think our brain evolved into so many interconnected structures with varying functions?

The Big Picture questions can be found in Appendix B at the end of the book.

Answers: 19. d, 20. d, 21. c, 22. c, 23. b, 24. c.

Our Divided Brain

> **14** What is a split brain, and what does it reveal about the functions of our left and right hemispheres?

We have seen that our look-alike left and right hemispheres exhibit an important difference. Language processing seems to reside mostly in the left hemisphere. In fact, research collected over more than a century has shown that an accident, stroke, or tumor in your left hemisphere could leave you unable to read, write, speak, do arithmetic, and understand others. Similar events in the right hemisphere seldom have such dramatic effects.

Does this mean that the right hemisphere is just along for the ride—a silent, "subordinate," or "minor" hemisphere? Many believed this was the case, until 1960, when researchers found that the "minor" right hemisphere was not so limited after all. The unfolding of this discovery is another one of psychology's fascinating stories.

> "You wouldn't want to have a date with the right hemisphere."
> —Michael Gazzaniga, 2002

Splitting the Brain

In 1961, two neurosurgeons speculated that the uncontrollable seizures of some patients with severe epilepsy were caused by abnormal brain activity bouncing back and forth between the two cerebral hemispheres. If so, could they put an end to this neurological tennis game by cutting through the **corpus callosum (FIGURE 2.23)?** This wide band of neural fibers connects the two hemispheres and carries messages between them. The neurosurgeons knew that psychologists Roger Sperry, Ronald Myers, and Michael Gazzaniga had divided the brains of cats and monkeys in this manner, with no serious ill effects.

So the surgeons operated. The result? The seizures all but disappeared. The patients with these **split brains** were surprisingly normal, their personality and intellect hardly affected. Waking from surgery, one even joked that he had a "splitting headache" (Gazzaniga, 1967). By sharing their experiences with us, these patients have greatly expanded our understanding of interactions between the intact brain's two hemispheres.

To appreciate these studies, we need to focus for a minute on the peculiar nature of our visual wiring. As **FIGURE 2.24** illustrates, information from the left half of your field of vision goes to your right hemisphere, and information from the right half of your visual field goes to your left hemisphere, which usually controls speech. Note, however, that each eye receives sensory information from both the right and left visual fields. In an intact brain, data received by either hemisphere are quickly transmitted to the other side across the corpus callosum. In a person with a severed corpus callosum, this information sharing does not take place.

Knowing these facts, Sperry and Gazzaniga could send information to a patient's left hemisphere by having the person stare at a dot and then flashing a stimulus (a word or photo) to the right of the dot. To send a message to the right hemisphere, they would flash the item to the left of the dot.

They could do this with you, too, but in your intact brain the hemisphere receiving the information would instantly pass the news to the other side. Because the split-brain surgery had cut the

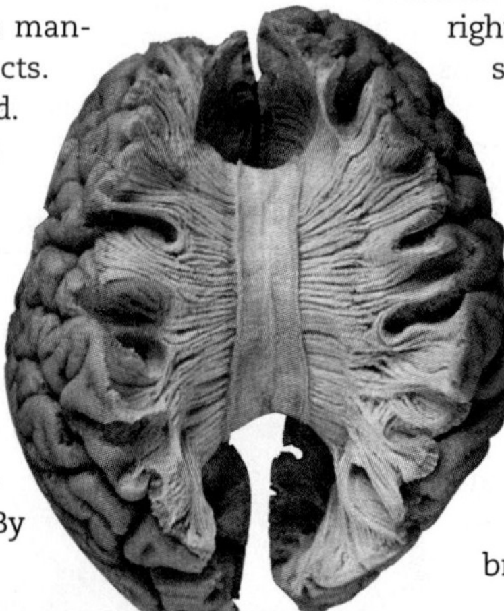

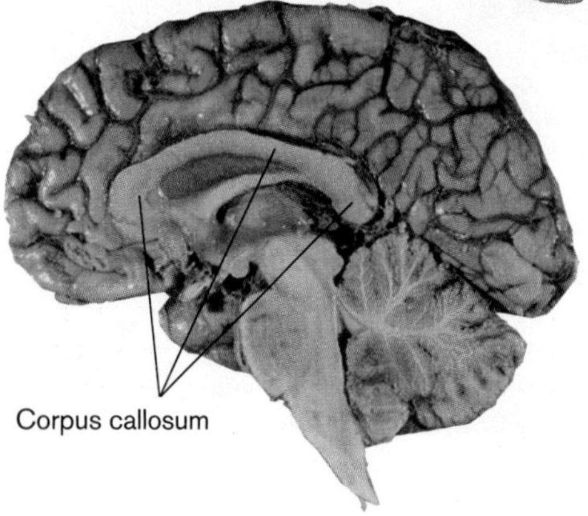

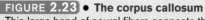

FIGURE 2.23 • **The corpus callosum** This large band of neural fibers connects the two brain hemispheres. To photograph the half brain shown at left, a surgeon separated the hemispheres by cutting through the corpus callosum and lower brain regions. In the view above, brain tissue has been cut back to expose the corpus callosum and bundles of fibers coming out from it.

Corpus callosum

Martin M. Rother (left)
Courtesy of Terence Williams, University of Iowa (above)

communication lines between the hemispheres, the researchers could, with these patients, quiz each hemisphere separately. One way of doing this is to flash the word HEART across the screen in such a way that HE appears to the left of the dot, and ART appears to the right (Figure 2.25b). The patients then report what they see. But there's a catch. Asked to *say* what they see, they report the letters transmitted to the left hemisphere—"ART." Asked to *point* with their left hand to what they see, they point to the letters transmitted to the right hemisphere—"HE" (Figure 2.25c).

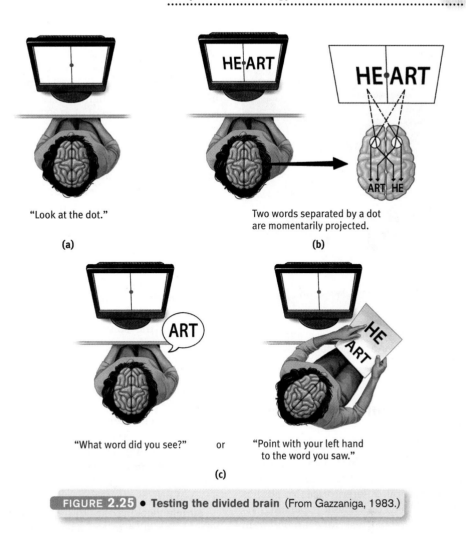

"Look at the dot."

(a)

Two words separated by a dot are momentarily projected.

(b)

"What word did you see?"   or   "Point with your left hand to the word you saw."

(c)

FIGURE 2.25 ● **Testing the divided brain** (From Gazzaniga, 1983.)

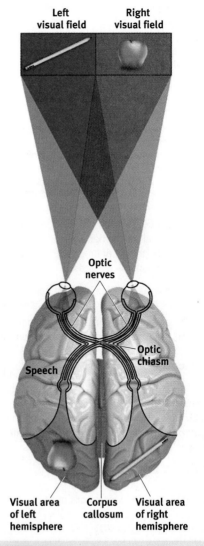

Left visual field   Right visual field

Optic nerves

Optic chiasm

Speech

Visual area of left hemisphere   Corpus callosum   Visual area of right hemisphere

FIGURE 2.24 ● **The information pathway from eye to brain**

After split-brain surgery, a few people have been bothered for a time by the unruly independence of their left hand. It seemed the left hand truly didn't know what the right hand was doing. One hand might unbutton a shirt while the other buttoned it, or put grocery store items back on the shelf after the other hand put them in the cart. It was as if each hemisphere was thinking, "I've half a mind to wear my green (blue) shirt today." Indeed, said Sperry (1964), split-brain surgery leaves people "with two separate minds" **(FIGURE 2.26** on the next page).

Who resolves disagreements when the "two minds" are at odds? If a split-brain patient follows an order sent to the right hemisphere ("Walk"), the left hemisphere won't know why it did so. But rather than say "I don't know," a strange thing happens. The left hemisphere instantly invents—and apparently believes—an explanation ("I'm going into the house to get a Coke"). Thus, Gazzaniga (1989), who has called split-brain patients "the most fascinating people on Earth," concluded that the conscious left hemisphere is an "interpreter" that instantly constructs theories to explain our behavior.

corpus callosum [KOR-pus kah-LOW-sum] large band of neural fibers connecting the two brain hemispheres and carrying messages between them.

split brain condition in which the brain's two hemispheres are isolated by cutting the fibers (mainly those of the corpus callosum) connecting them.

BBC

FIGURE 2.26 ● **Try this!** Joe, a split-brain patient, can simultaneously draw two different shapes.

Right-Left Differences in Intact Brains

So, what about the 99.99+ percent of us with undivided brains? Does each of *our* hemispheres also perform distinct functions? Several different types of studies indicate they do. When a person performs a *perceptual* task, for example, brain waves, bloodflow, and glucose consumption reveal increased activity in the *right* hemisphere. When the person speaks or calculates, activity increases in the left hemisphere.

If you could peek into an operating room at the beginning of some types of brain surgery, you could watch a dramatic demonstration of hemispheric specialization. To locate the patient's language centers, the surgeon injects a sedative into the neck artery feeding blood to the left hemisphere, which usually controls speech. Before the injection, the patient is lying down, arms in the air, chatting with the doctor. Can you predict what will happen when the drug puts the left hemisphere to sleep?

Within seconds, the patient's right arm will fall limp. If the left hemisphere is controlling language, the patient will be speechless until the drug wears off.

To the brain, language is language, whether spoken or signed. Just as hearing people usually use the left hemisphere to process speech, deaf people usually use the left hemisphere to read sign language (Corina et al., 1992; Hickok et al., 2001). Thus, a left-hemisphere stroke disrupts a deaf person's signing, much as it would disrupt a hearing person's speaking (Corina, 1998).

The left hemisphere is adept at making quick, literal interpretations of language. But the right hemisphere excels in high-level language processing (Beeman & Chiarello, 1998; Bowden & Beeman, 1998; Mason & Just, 2004). Given an insight problem—"What word goes with *boot, summer,* and *ground?*"—the right hemisphere more quickly than the left recognizes the solution: *camp.* As one patient explained after a right-hemisphere stroke, "I understand words, but I'm missing the subtleties." The right side of the brain also surpasses the left at copying drawings, recognizing faces, perceiving differences, perceiving emotion, and expressing emotion through the more expressive left side of the face **(FIGURE 2.27).** Right-hemisphere damage can greatly disrupt these abilities.

Simply looking at the two hemispheres, so alike to the naked eye, who would suppose they contribute uniquely to the harmony of the whole? Yet a variety of observations—of people with split brains and those with intact brains—leaves little doubt that we have unified brains with specialized parts.

FIGURE 2.27 ● **Which one is happier?** Look at the center of one face, then the other. Does one appear happier? Most people say the right face does. Some researchers believe we make this choice because our right hemisphere, which is skilled in emotion processing, receives information from the left half of each face (when looking at its center).

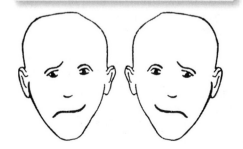

Brain States and Consciousness

> **15** What do we mean by *consciousness*, and how does selective attention direct our perceptions?

In the lively field of neuroscience, researchers are addressing many exciting questions. Among the most interesting are those in the subfield of *cognitive neuroscience*, which studies connections between brain activity and mental processes, including states of consciousness.

Consciousness is our awareness of ourselves and our environment. It arises not from any one brain area but from the coordinated activity of the whole brain (Gaillard et al., 2009). Consciousness lets us reflect on the past, plan for the future, and focus on the present. Psychologists study many aspects of consciousness. In Chapter 12, for example, we'll look closely at consciousness-altering drugs and their effects. In this chapter, we explore the role of attention and the altered states of consciousness we all experience—sleep and dreams.

Selective Attention

Through **selective attention,** our awareness focuses, like a flashlight beam, on a *very* limited aspect of all that we experience. Until reading this sentence, you have been unaware that your shoes are pressing against your feet or that your nose is in your line of vision. Now, suddenly, the spotlight shifts. Your feet feel encased, your nose stubbornly intrudes on the words before you. While focusing on these

words, you've also been blocking other parts of your environment from awareness, though your peripheral vision would let you see them easily. You can change that. As you stare at the X below, notice what surrounds these sentences (the edges of the page, the desktop, the floor).

X

What happens to our attention when we are on the phone? WHY NOT USE A ◄ CELL PHONE WHILE DRIVING? We pay a toll for switching attentional gears, especially when we shift to complex tasks, like noticing and avoiding cars around us. The toll is a slight delay in coping (Rubenstein et al., 2001). In driving-simulation experiments, students talking on cell phones—both hand-held and hands-free—have been slower to detect and respond to traffic signals, billboards, and other cars (Horrey & Wickens, 2006; Strayer & Drews, 2007; Strayer et al., 2003). Twenty-eight percent of vehicle crashes occur when people are talking on cell phones or texting (National Safety Council, 2010). One study tracked long-haul truck drivers for 18 months. The video cameras mounted in their cabs showed they were at 23 times greater risk of a collision while texting (VTTI, 2009). In response to this research, the U.S. government in 2010 banned texting by truckers and bus drivers while driving (Halsey, 2010). But it's not just

truck drivers who are at risk. One in four teen drivers with cell phones admit to texting while driving (Pew, 2009). Multitasking comes at a cost.

We can process only a tiny sliver of the immense ocean of visual stimuli constantly before us. In one famous study, people watched a one-minute videotape in which images of three black-shirted men tossing a basketball were mixed with images of three white-shirted players (Becklen & Cervone, 1983; Neisser, 1979). Researchers told the viewers to press a key each time they saw a black-shirted player pass the ball. Most were so intent on the game that they failed to notice a young woman carrying an umbrella stroll across the screen midway through the tape. During a replay they were amazed to see her! Their attention focused elsewhere, the viewers suffered from **inattentional blindness.**

In a repeat of the experiment, smart-aleck researchers sent a gorilla-suited assistant through the swirl of players (Simons & Chabris, 1999). During its 5- to 9-second cameo appearance, the gorilla paused to thump its chest. Still, half of the pass-counting viewers failed to see it. In another follow-up experiment, only 1 in 4 students absorbed in a cell-phone conversation while crossing a campus square noticed a clown-suited unicyclist in their midst (Hyman et al., 2010). (Most of those not on the phone did notice.) (See **FIGURE 2.28** on the next page.)

Attention directed elsewhere, people also are prone to *change blindness*. After a brief visual interruption, a big Coke bottle may disappear, a railing may rise, clothing color may change, but, more often than not, viewers don't notice (Resnick

States of consciousness: In addition to normal, waking awareness, consciousness comes to us in altered states, including meditating, daydreaming, sleeping, and drug-induced hallucinating.

Kaz Mori/Getty Images

consciousness our awareness of ourselves and our environment.

selective attention focusing conscious awareness on a particular stimulus.

inattentional blindness failure to see visible objects when our attention is directed elsewhere.

FIGURE 2.28 ● **Hard to miss?** Would you notice a clown unicycling past you on campus? In this study, most students on cell phones did *not* notice the clown; students who were off the phone generally did notice.

FIGURE 2.29 ● **Change blindness** While a man (white hair) provides directions to a construction worker, two experimenters rudely pass between them carrying a door. During this interruption, the original worker switches places with another person wearing different colored clothing. Most people, focused on their direction giving, do not notice the switch.

et al., 1997; Simons, 1996; Simons & Ambinder, 2005). **FIGURE 2.29** shows clips from one study in which two-thirds of the people giving directions to a construction worker failed to notice when he was replaced by another worker. Out of sight, out of mind.

> "I love to sleep. Do you? Isn't it great? It really is the best of both worlds. You get to be alive and unconscious."
>
> Comedian Rita Rudner, 1993

PRACTICE TEST

THE BASICS

29. Failure to see visible objects when our attention is occupied elsewhere is called
   a. automatic processing.
   b. awareness unconsciousness.
   c. inattentional blindness.
   d. subconscious processing.

THE BIG PICTURE

2H. Would we function better if we were completely aware of all of our thought processes? Why or why not?

IN YOUR EVERYDAY LIFE

▪ Can you think of a time when you focused your attention on one thing so much that you did not notice something else? What happened?

▪ Do you ever text, watch TV, or talk on the phone while studying? What impact do you think this multitasking has on your learning?

Answer: 29. c. Answers to The Big Picture questions can be found in Appendix B at the end of the book.

Sleep and Dreams

Now playing at an inner theater near you: the premiere showing of a sleeping person's vivid dream. This never-before-seen mental movie features captivating characters wrapped in a plot that is original and unlikely, yet seemingly real.

Waking from a dream, we may wonder how our brain can so creatively, colorfully, and completely construct this inner-space world. Caught for a moment between our dreaming and waking consciousness, we may even be unsure which world is real.

Sleep's mysteries have intrigued scientists for centuries. Now, in laboratories around the world, some of these mysteries are being solved as people sleep, attached to recording devices, while others observe. By recording brain waves and muscle movements, and by waking sleepers, researchers are glimpsing things that a thousand years of common sense never told us.

Biological Rhythms and Sleep

16 What is the circadian rhythm, and what are the stages of our nightly sleep cycle?

Like the ocean, life has its rhythmic tides. Let's look more closely at two of these biological rhythms—our 24-hour biological clock and our 90-minute sleep cycle.

Circadian Rhythm Try pulling an all-nighter, or working an occasional night shift. You will feel groggiest in the middle of the night but may get new energy around the time you would normally wake up. Your body is reacting in part to its own wake-up call. The human body is kept roughly in tune with the 24-hour cycle of day and night by an internal biological clock called the **circadian rhythm** (from the Latin *circa,* "about," and *diem,* "day"). As morning approaches, body temperature rises, then peaks during the day, dips for a time in early afternoon (when many people take naps), and begins to drop again in the evening. Thinking is sharpest and memory most accurate when we are at our daily peak in circadian arousal.

Age and experience can alter our circadian rhythm. At about age 20 (slightly earlier for women), we begin to shift from being evening-energized "owls" to being morning-loving "larks" (Roenneberg et al., 2004). Most college students are owls, with performance improving across the day (May & Hasher, 1998). Most older adults are larks, with performance declining as the day wears on. By mid-evening, when the night has hardly begun for many young adults, retirement homes are typically quiet.

Sleep Stages Sooner or later, sleep overtakes us and consciousness fades as different parts of our brain's cortex stop communicating (Massimini et al., 2005). But rather than emitting a constant dial tone, the sleeping brain has its own biological rhythm.

About every 90 minutes, we cycle through five distinct sleep stages. This basic fact apparently was unknown until 8-year-old Armond Aserinsky went to bed

one night in 1952. His father, Eugene, needed to test an electroencephalograph he had repaired that day (Aserinsky, 1988; Seligman & Yellen, 1987). Placing electrodes near Armond's eyes to record the rolling eye movements then believed to occur during sleep, Aserinsky watched the machine go wild, tracing deep zigzags on the graph paper. Could the machine still be broken? As the night proceeded and the activity recurred, Aserinsky realized that the periods of fast, jerky eye movements were accompanied by energetic brain activity. Awakened during one such episode, Armond reported having a dream. Aserinsky had discovered what we now know as **REM sleep** (rapid *eye movement* sleep).

Similar procedures used with thousands of volunteers showed the cycles were a normal part of sleep (Kleitman, 1960). To appreciate these studies, imagine yourself as a participant. As the hour grows late, you feel sleepy and get ready for bed. A researcher comes in and tapes electrodes to your scalp (to detect your brain waves), on your chin (to detect muscle tension), and just outside the corners of your eyes (to detect eye movements) **(FIGURE 2.30).** Other devices will record your heart rate, respiration rate, and genital arousal.

circadian [ser-KAY-dee-an] **rhythm** internal biological clock; regular bodily rhythms (for example, of temperature and wakefulness) that occur on a 24-hour cycle.

REM (rapid eye movement) sleep recurring sleep stage during which vivid dreams commonly occur. Also known as *paradoxical sleep,* because the muscles are relaxed (except for minor twitches) but other body systems are active.

alpha waves relatively slow brain waves of a relaxed, awake state.

sleep periodic, natural, reversible loss of consciousness—as distinct from unconsciousness resulting from a coma, general anesthesia, or hibernation. (Adapted from Dement, 1999.)

When you are in bed with your eyes closed, the researcher in the next room sees on the EEG the relatively slow **alpha waves** of your awake but relaxed state. As you adapt to all this equipment, you grow tired and, in an unremembered moment, slip into **sleep.** The transition is marked by the slowed breathing and the irregular brain waves of *Stage 1 sleep* **(FIGURE 2.31** on the next page).

During this brief Stage 1 sleep you may experience fantastic images resembling *hallucinations*—sensory experiences that occur without a sensory stimulus.

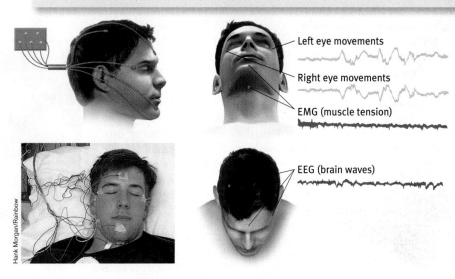

FIGURE 2.30 ● **Measuring sleep activity** As this man sleeps, electrodes attached to an electroencephalograph are picking up weak electrical signals from his brain, eyes, and facial muscles. (From Dement, 1978.)

Left eye movements

Right eye movements

EMG (muscle tension)

EEG (brain waves)

Hank Morgan/Rainbow

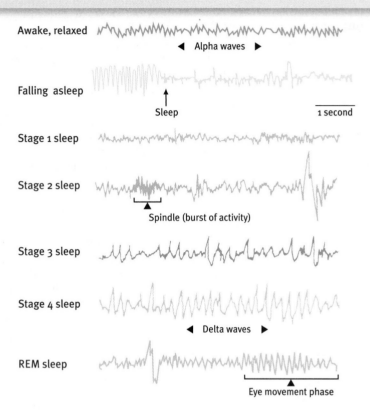

Awake, relaxed

◄ Alpha waves ►

Falling asleep

↑ Sleep   1 second

Stage 1 sleep

Stage 2 sleep

▲ Spindle (burst of activity)

Stage 3 sleep

Stage 4 sleep

◄ Delta waves ►

REM sleep

Eye movement phase

responds to sound stimuli during sleep (Kutas, 1990). And one of this book's themes emerges again: *We process most information outside our conscious awareness (dual processing).*

REM Sleep About an hour after you first dive into sleep, a strange thing happens. You reverse course. From Stage 4, to Stage 3, and through Stage 2 (where you spend about half your night), you enter the most puzzling sleep phase—REM sleep **(FIGURE 2.32).** And the show begins. For about 10 minutes, your brain waves become rapid and saw-toothed. Your heart rate rises and your breathing becomes rapid and irregular. (If you are a snorer, your snoring usually stops.) Every half-minute or so, your eyes dart around in a brief burst of activity behind closed lids. These eye movements announce the beginning of a dream—often emotional, usually storylike, and richly hallucinatory.

Except during very scary dreams, your genitals become aroused during REM sleep. You have an erection or increased vaginal lubrication and clitoral engorgement, regardless of whether the dream's content is sexual (Karacan et al., 1966).

You may have a sensation of falling (at which moment your body may suddenly jerk) or of floating weightlessly. These sensations may later be woven into your memories. People who claim to have been abducted by aliens—often shortly after getting into bed—commonly recall being floated off or pinned down on their beds (Clancy, 2005).

You then relax more deeply and begin about 20 minutes of *Stage 2 sleep,* with its periodic *sleep spindles*—bursts of rapid, rhythmic brain-wave activity (see Figure 2.31). Although you could still be awakened without too much difficulty, you are now clearly asleep.

For the next few minutes, you go through the transitional *Stage 3* to the *deep sleep of Stage 4.* (Some classifications now omit the transitional stage and call deep sleep Stage 3.) In deep sleep, your brain

emits large, slow *delta* waves. These two slow-wave stages last about 30 minutes, during which you are hard to awaken. (It is at the end of the deep sleep of Stage 4 that children may wet the bed.)

Even when you are deeply asleep, your perceptual window is not completely shut. You move around on your bed, but you manage not to fall out. The roar of a passing motorcycle may leave your deep sleep undisturbed, but a baby's cry can quickly interrupt it, as can the sound of your name. EEG recordings confirm that the brain's auditory cortex

Some sleep deeply, some not: The fluctuating sleep cycle enables safe sleep for these soldiers on the battlefield. One benefit of communal sleeping is that someone will probably be awake or easily roused in the event of a threat.

FIGURE 2.32 ● **The stages in a typical night's sleep** Most people pass through the five-stage sleep cycle (graph a) several times each night. As the night goes on, the periods of Stage 4 sleep and then Stage 3 grow shorter, and periods of REM sleep increase. Graph b plots these trends, based on data from 30 young adults. (From Cartwright, 1978; Webb, 1992.)

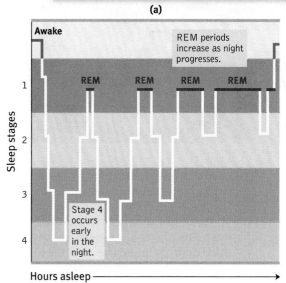

(Many men troubled by *erectile dysfunction* [impotence] still have sleep-related erections, suggesting the problem is not between their legs.)

Your brain's motor cortex is active during REM sleep, but your brainstem blocks its messages. This leaves your muscles relaxed, so much so that, except for an occasional finger, toe, or facial twitch, you are essentially paralyzed. Moreover, you cannot easily be awakened. Thus, REM sleep is sometimes called *paradoxical* sleep; the body is internally aroused and externally calm—except for those darting eyes.

The sleep cycle repeats itself about every 90 minutes. As the night wears on, deep Stage 4 sleep grows shorter and disappears. REM sleep periods get longer (see Figure 2.32b). By morning, we have spent 20 to 25 percent of an average night's sleep— some 100 minutes—in REM sleep. **DOES EVERYONE DREAM?** ◀ Thirty-seven percent of people report rarely or never having dreams "that you can remember the next morning" (Moore,

Horses, which spend 92 percent of each day standing and can sleep standing, must lie down for muscle-paralyzing REM sleep (Morrison, 2003).

2004). Yet even they, more than 80 percent of the time, will recall a dream if awakened during REM sleep. Each year we spend about 600 hours experiencing some 1500 dreams, or more than 100,000 dreams over a typical lifetime—dreams mostly swallowed by the night but not acted out, thanks to REM's protective paralysis.

Why Do We Sleep?

 How do our sleep patterns differ? What four theories describe our need to sleep?

The idea that "everyone needs 8 hours of sleep" is untrue. Newborns sleep nearly two-thirds of their day, most adults no more than one-third. Still, there is more to our sleep differences than age. Allowed to sleep unhindered, most adults will regularly sleep at least 9 hours a night (Coren, 1996). Some, however, thrive with fewer than 6 hours a night. Genetics seems to play a role. When researchers checked sleep patterns among

fraternal and identical twins, only the identical twins were strikingly similar (Webb & Campbell, 1983).

But we should not overstress biology. Remember another of this book's themes: *Individual and social-cultural forces also affect behavior.* Sleep patterns are culturally influenced. In industrialized nations, people now sleep less than they did a century ago. Thanks to modern light bulbs, shift work, and social diversions, those who would have gone to bed at 9:00 P.M. are now up until 11:00 P.M. or later. In sleep as in waking behavior, environment and biology interact.

Bright light at night can disrupt our biological clock, tricking the brain into thinking it's morning. The process begins in the retinas in our eyes, which contain light-sensitive proteins. Normally, morning light sounds an internal alarm by activating these proteins, which then signal neural clusters in the brain (Foster, 2004).

The brain interprets these signals as orders to decrease production of the sleep-inducing hormone *melatonin*.

So our sleep patterns differ from person to person and from culture to culture. But why do we need to sleep?

Theories About Sleep's Functions Psychologists believe sleep may have evolved for four reasons.

2004 Gallup poll: "Usually, how many hours of sleep do you get at night?"
5 or less   14%
6   26%
7   28%
8   25%
2004 average = 6.8 hours
1942 average = 7.6 hours

1. *Sleep protects.* When darkness shut down the day's hunting, food gathering, and travel, our distant ancestors were better off asleep in a cave, out of harm's way. Those who didn't try to navigate around rocks and cliffs at night were more likely to leave descendants. This fits a broader principle: A species' sleep patterns tend to suit its place in nature. Animals with the most need to graze and the least ability to hide tend to sleep less. Elephants and horses sleep 3 to 4 hours a day, gorillas 12 hours, and cats 14 hours. For bats and Eastern chipmunks, both of which sleep 20 hours, to live is hardly more than to eat and to sleep (Moorcroft, 2003).

Sleep and development: During our first months, we spend less and less time asleep—from newborns' 16 hours a day down to 12 by age 2 (Snyder & Scott, 1972).

2. *Sleep helps us recover.* Sleep helps restore and repair brain tissue. Bats and many other small animals burn a lot of calories, producing a lot of *free radicals,* molecules that are toxic to neurons. Sleeping a lot gives resting neurons time to repair themselves (Siegel, 2003). Think of it this way: When consciousness leaves the highway, the brain's road crews repair potholes while traffic is light.

3. *Sleep helps us remember and think creatively.* During sleep, we restore and rebuild our memories of the day's experiences. People trained to perform tasks recall them better after a night's sleep than after several hours awake (Walker & Stickgold, 2006). Sleep also feeds creative thinking. After working on a task, then sleeping on it, people solve problems more insightfully than do those who stay awake (Wagner et al., 2004). They also are better at spotting connections among novel pieces of information (Ellenbogen et al., 2007). To think smart and see connections, it often pays to sleep on it.

4. *Sleep may play a role in the growth process.* During deep sleep, the pituitary gland releases a growth hormone. As we age, we release less of this hormone and spend less time in deep sleep (Pekkanen, 1982).

Given all the benefits of sleep, it's no wonder that sleep loss hits us so hard.

Sleep Deprivation and Sleep Disorders

18 How does sleep loss affect us, and what are the major sleep disorders?

If our body yearns for sleep but does not get it, we begin to feel terrible. Trying to stay awake, we will eventually lose. In the tiredness battle, sleep always wins.

The Effects of Sleep Loss Today more than ever, our sleep patterns leave us not only sleepy but also drained of energy and feelings of well-being. After a succession of 5-hour nights, we run up a sleep debt that cannot be repaid with one long 10-hour sleep. "The brain keeps an accurate

count of sleep debt for at least two weeks," reported sleep researcher William Dement (1999, p. 64).

Teenagers average less than 7 hours of sleep—nearly 2 hours less each night than their counterparts enjoyed a century ago (Holden, 1993; Maas, 1999). And they regret it: Four in five American teens and three in five 18- to 29-year-olds wish they could get more sleep on weekdays (Mason, 2003, 2005). Small wonder so many fall asleep in class. When the going gets boring, the students start snoring. Even when awake, they often function below their peak.

Sleep deprivation can suppress immune cells that fight off viral infections and cancer (Beardsley, 1996; Irwin et al., 1994). Chronic sleep debt alters metabolism and hormonal functioning in ways that mimic aging. These effects can contribute to high blood pressure and memory impairment (Spiegel et al., 1999; Taheri, 2004). Sleep deprivation also makes us irritable, slows performance, and impairs creativity, concentration, and communication (Harrison & Horne, 2000).

Sleepless: After teaching a world-record-breaking, 72-hour English class in Shanghai, this teacher is clearly suffering. Sleep-deprived people experience a depressed immune system, impaired concentration, and greater vulnerability to accidents.

CAN LACK OF SLEEP MAKE YOU FAT? ◄
Yes, sleep deprivation can make you fatter. It increases *ghrelin,* a hunger-arousing hormone, and decreases its hunger-suppressing partner, *leptin.* It also increases *cortisol,* a stress hormone that stimulates fat production. Sure enough, children and adults who sleep less than normal are fatter than those who sleep more (Chen et al., 2008; Knutson et al., 2007; Schoenborn & Adams, 2008). Experimental sleep deprivation of adults increases appetite and eating (Nixon et al., 2008; Patel et al., 2006; Spiegel et al., 2004; Van Cauter et al., 2007). This may help explain the common weight gain among sleep-deprived college and university students.

Less sleep can also mean more accidents. Twice each year, most of us participate in a sleep-manipulation experiment—the "spring forward" to "daylight savings" time and "fall backward" to "standard" time. A search of millions of records showed that in both Canada and the United States, accidents increased immediately after the time change that shortened sleep (Coren, 1996).

Major Sleep Disorders To manage your life with enough sleep to awaken naturally and well rested is to be more alert, productive, happy, healthy, and safe. But for many people, that goal is hard to achieve. The major sleep disorders include *insomnia; narcolepsy; sleep apnea;* and *sleepwalking, sleeptalking,* and *night terrors.*

No matter what their normal need for sleep, some 1 in 10 adults, and 1 in 4 older adults, complain of **insomnia.** These people have ongoing problems in falling or staying asleep, not just an occasional loss of sleep when anxious or excited.

The most popular quick fixes for true insomnia—sleeping pills and alcohol—can make things worse because they reduce REM sleep. Such aids also lead to *tolerance*—a state in which increasing doses are needed to produce an effect. An ideal sleep aid would mimic the natural chemicals that are abundant during

> "Sleep faster, we need the pillows."
> Yiddish proverb

> "Sleep is like love or happiness. If you pursue it too ardently it will elude you."
> Wilse Webb, 1992 (p. 170)

TABLE 2.2	Looking for a Better Night's Sleep?
Exercise regularly, but not in the late evening. (Late afternoon is best.)
Avoid caffeine, especially in the afternoon or later, and avoid food and drink near bedtime. The exception would be a glass of milk, which provides raw materials for the manufacture of serotonin, a neurotransmitter that promotes sleep.
Relax before bedtime, using dimmer light.
Sleep on a regular schedule (rise at the same time even after a restless night) and avoid naps.
Reassure yourself that a temporary loss of sleep causes no great harm.
If all else fails, settle for less sleep, either going to bed later or getting up earlier.

sleep, without side effects. Until scientists can supply this magic pill, experts have offered some tips for getting better quality sleep **(TABLE 2.2).**

Falling asleep is not the problem for people with **narcolepsy** (from *narco,* "numbness," and *lepsy,* "seizure"), who have sudden attacks of overwhelming sleepiness, usually lasting less than 5 minutes. Narcolepsy attacks can occur at the worst times, perhaps just after taking a terrific swing at a softball or when laughing loudly, shouting angrily, or having sex (Dement, 1978, 1999). In severe cases, the person collapses directly into a brief period of REM sleep, with loss of muscle control. People with narcolepsy—1 in 2000 of us, estimates the Stanford University Center for Narcolepsy (2002)—must therefore live with extra caution. As a traffic menace, "snoozing is second only to boozing," said the American Sleep Disorders Association, and those with narcolepsy are especially at risk (Aldrich, 1989).

Sleep apnea also puts millions of people—1 in 20 of us—at increased risk of traffic accidents (Teran-Santos et al., 1999). *Apnea* means "with no breath," and people with this condition stop breathing during sleep. Then, after an airless minute or so, their blood oxygen drops enough to jolt them awake, and they snort in air for a few seconds. This process repeats hundreds of times each night, depriving them of slow-wave sleep. Apnea sufferers don't

recall these episodes the next day. So, despite feeling fatigued and depressed, many are unaware of their disorder (Peppard et al., 2006).

Sleep apnea is linked with obesity, particularly among men. Other warning signs are loud snoring, daytime sleepiness and irritability, lack of energy, and (possibly) high blood pressure (Dement, 1999). If one doesn't mind looking a little goofy in the dark (imagine a snorkeler at a slumber party), the treatment—a mask-like device with an air pump that keeps the sleeper's airway open—can effectively relieve apnea symptoms.

Sleepwalking and *sleeptalking* are usually childhood disorders, and, like narcolepsy, they run in families. If a fraternal twin sleepwalks, the odds are about 1 in 3 that the other twin will also sleepwalk. But if twins are identical, sharing the same genes, the odds increase to 1 in 2. The same is true for sleeptalking (Hublin et al., 1997, 1998). Sleepwalking is usually harmless. After returning to bed on their own or with the help of a family member, few sleepwalkers recall their trip the next morning.

insomnia recurring problems in falling or staying asleep.

narcolepsy sleep disorder in which a person has uncontrollable sleep attacks, sometimes lapsing directly into REM sleep.

sleep apnea a sleep disorder in which a sleeping person repeatedly stops breathing until blood oxygen is so low it awakens the person just long enough to draw a breath.

Stress robs sleep: Urban police officers, especially those under stress, report poorer sleep quality and less sleep than average (Neylan et al., 2002). The sleep of these Iraq war soldiers may also be disturbed.

Sleepwalking happens during Stage 4 sleep. So do *night terrors,* which are not nightmares. During an attack, a child may sit up or walk around, talk nonsense, and appear terrified. The child's heart and breathing rates may double. Luckily, children remember little or nothing of the fearful event the next day (Hartmann, 1981). Children have the deepest and longest Stage 4 sleep, so it's no surprise that they most often have night terrors and sleepwalking. As deep Stage 4 sleep decreases with age, these disorders become more and more rare.

Did Brahms need his own lullabies?: Cranky, overweight, and nap-prone, Johannes Brahms exhibited common symptoms of sleep apnea (Margolis, 2000).

PRACTICE TEST

THE BASICS

30. Our body temperature tends to rise and fall in tune with a biological clock, which is called

a. the circadian rhythm.
b. narcolepsy.
c. REM sleep.
d. an alpha wave.

31. During Stage 1 sleep, a person is most likely to experience

a. sleep spindles.
b. hallucinations.
c. night terrors or nightmares.
d. rapid eye movements.

32. The deepest stage of sleep, when the brain emits large, slow waves, is _____ sleep.

a. Stage 2
b. Stage 4
c. REM
d. paradoxical

33. In a normal night's sleep, we cycle through five stages. As the night progresses, the REM stage

a. gradually disappears.
b. becomes briefer and briefer.
c. remains about the same.
d. becomes longer and longer.

34. Which of the following is NOT one of the theories that tries to explain why we need sleep?

a. Sleep has survival value.
b. Sleep helps us restore and repair brain tissue.
c. Sleep rests the eyes.

d. Sleep plays a role in the growth process.

35. Narcolepsy is a sleep disorder in which a person _____; sleep apnea is a sleep disorder in which a person _____.

a. has persistent problems falling asleep; experiences rising blood-oxygen levels
b. experiences rising blood-oxygen levels; has persistent problems falling asleep
c. repeatedly stops breathing; suffers attacks of overwhelming sleepiness
d. suffers attacks of overwhelming sleepiness; repeatedly stops breathing

THE BIG PICTURE

21. Most teens in the United States start school early—by 7:30 or 8:00 A.M. Critics say that early to rise is not making kids wise, it's making them sleepy. Do you think later start times would help remedy the tired-teen problem?

IN YOUR EVERYDAY LIFE

▪ What have you learned about sleep that you could apply to yourself?

to The Big Picture questions can be found in Appendix B at the end of the book.

Answers: 30. a, 31. b, 32. b, 33. d, 34. c, 35. d. Answers

Dreams

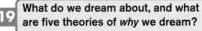 **What do we dream about, and what are five theories of *why* we dream?**

Our two-track mind is clearly at work during sleep. Consider all the events happening outside our conscious awareness. We may stop breathing (sleep apnea), stroll around (sleepwalking), talk to imaginary people (sleeptalking), or *dream.*

Each of us spends about six years of our life in dreams—adventures that remain locked behind our moving eyelids and usually vanish with the new day. The discovery of the link between REM sleep and dreaming gave us a key to that lock. Now, instead of relying on a dreamer's hazy recall hours or days after waking, researchers can catch dreams as they happen. They can awaken people during or within three minutes after a REM sleep period and hear a vivid account.

What We Dream REM **dreams**—the sleeping mind's hallucinations—are vivid, emotional, and bizarre. Unlike daydreams, the dreams of REM sleep are so vivid we may confuse them with reality. Awakening from a nightmare, a 4-year-old may scream in fear of the bear in the house.

Few dreams are sweet. For both women and men, 8 in 10 dreams are bad dreams (Domhoff, 1999). Common themes are failing in an attempt to do something; being attacked, pursued, or rejected; or experiencing misfortune (Hall et al., 1982). Dreams with sexual imagery occur less often than you might think. In one study, only 1 in 10 dreams among young men and 1 in 30 among young women had sexual overtones (Domhoff, 1996). More commonly, the story line of our dreams—what Sigmund Freud called their **manifest content**—features people and places from the day's experiences (De Koninck, 2000).

Our two-track mind is also monitoring our environment while we sleep. Sensory stimuli—a particular odor or a phone's ringing—may be instantly and ingeniously woven into a dream story. In a classic experiment, researchers lightly sprayed cold water on dreamers' faces (Dement & Wolpert, 1958). Compared with sleepers who did not get the cold-water treatment, these people were more likely to dream about a waterfall, a leaky roof, or even about being sprayed by someone.

> A popular sleep myth: If you dream you are falling and hit the ground (or if you dream of dying), you die. Unfortunately, those who could confirm these ideas are not around to do so. Some people, however, have had such dreams and are alive to report them.

Why We Dream Dream theorists have proposed several explanations of why we dream, including the following.

Freud's wish-fulfillment theory. In 1900, offering what he thought was "the most valuable of all the discoveries it has been my good fortune to make," Freud proposed that dreams act as a safety valve, discharging feelings that cannot be expressed in public. He viewed a dream's remembered story line (its manifest content) as a censored, symbolic version of its **latent content,** the unconscious drives and wishes that would be threatening if expressed directly. Most dreams have no openly sexual imagery. Freud nevertheless believed that most adult dreams could be "traced back by analysis to erotic wishes." Thus, a gun appearing in a dream could be a penis in disguise.

Freud's critics say it is time to wake up from Freud's dream theory, which is a scientific nightmare. Scientific studies offer "no reason to believe any of Freud's specific claims about dreams and their purposes," noted dream researcher William Domhoff (2000). Maybe a dream about a gun is really a dream about a gun. Legend has it that even Freud, who loved to smoke cigars, agreed that "sometimes, a cigar is just a cigar." Other critics have noted that dreams may be interpreted in many different ways.

Information-processing: The sleep-memory link. The information-processing perspective proposes that dreams may help sift, sort, and fix the day's events in our memory. Some sleep studies support this view. When tested the next day after learning a task, those deprived of both slow-wave and REM sleep did not do as well as those who slept undisturbed (Stickgold et al., 2000, 2001). To sleep, perchance to remember. Students, take note. Sleep researcher Robert Stickgold (2000) believes many of you suffer from a kind of sleep bulimia, binge sleeping on the weekend. From his information-processing perspective he warns, "If you don't get good sleep and enough sleep after you learn new stuff, you won't integrate it effectively into your memories." In one study, high-achieving secondary students with top grades averaged 25 minutes more sleep a night and went to bed 40 minutes earlier than their lower-achieving classmates (Wolfson & Carskadon, 1998).

Brain scans confirm the link between REM sleep and memory. Brain regions that are active as rats learn to navigate a maze (or as people learn to perform a visual-discrimination task) are active again later during REM sleep (Louie & Wilson, 2001; Maquet, 2001). So precise are these activity patterns that scientists can tell where in the maze the rat would be if awake.

Physiological function: Developing and preserving neural pathways. Perhaps dreams—or the brain activity linked to

Maxine

© 2001 Mariam Henley
www.maxine.net — © 2001 Mariam Henley — mkhenley@prodigy.net

---

dream sequence of images, emotions, and thoughts passing through a sleeping person's mind.

manifest content according to Freud, the remembered story line of a dream.

latent content according to Freud, the underlying meaning of a dream.

Diverse Yet Alike

People in hunter-gatherer tribes, such as these people in the Republic of Cameroon, often dream of animals; urban Japanese rarely do (Mestel, 1997). Yet we all dream repeatedly while asleep.

REM sleep—give the sleeping brain a work-out that helps it develop. We know that stimulating experiences preserve and expand the brain's neural pathways. Infants, whose neural networks are fast developing, spend much of their abundant sleep time in REM sleep.

The activation-synthesis theory: Making sense of neural static. This theory proposes that dreams are born when random neural activity spreads upward from the brainstem (Antrobus, 1991; Hobson, 2003, 2004). Our ever-alert brain attempts to make sense of the activity, pasting the random bits of information into a meaningful image, much as children construct storybooks from snippets of magazine photos.

The cognitive-development perspective. Some dream researchers see dreams as a reflection of brain maturation and cognitive development (Domhoff, 2003; Foulkes, 1999). For example, before age 9, children's dreams seem more like a slide show and less like an active story in which the child is an actor. Dreams at all ages tend to feature the kind of thinking and talking we demonstrate when awake. They seem to draw on our current knowledge and concepts we understand.

There is one thing dream theorists agree on: We need REM sleep. Deprived of it in sleep labs or in real life, people return more and more quickly to the REM stage when finally allowed to sleep undisturbed. They literally sleep like babies—with increased REM sleep, a phenomenon called **REM rebound.** Withdrawing REM-suppressing sleeping pills also increases REM sleep, often with nightmares.

* * *

We have glimpsed the truth of this chapter's overriding principle: *Everything psychological is simultaneously biological.* You and I are privileged to live in a time when the pace of discoveries about the interplay of our biology and our behavior and mental processes is truly breathtaking. Yet what is unknown still dwarfs what is known. We can describe the brain. We can learn the functions of its parts. We can study how the parts communicate. We can observe sleeping and waking brains. But how do we get mind out of meat? How does the electrochemical whir in a hunk of tissue the size of a head of lettuce give rise to a feeling of joy, a creative idea, or a crazy dream?

The mind seeking to understand the brain—that is indeed among the ultimate scientific challenges. And so it will always be. To paraphrase scientist John Barrow, a brain simple enough to be understood is too simple to produce a mind able to understand it.

PRACTICE TEST

THE BASICS

36. According to Sigmund Freud, dreams are the key to understanding our inner conflicts. In interpreting dreams, Freud was most interested in their

a. information-processing function.
b. physiological function.
c. manifest content, or story line.
d. latent content, or symbolic meaning.

37. Some theories of dreaming propose that dreams serve a physiological purpose. One such theory suggests that dreams

a. are the brain's attempt to make sense of random neural activity.
b. provide a rest period for overworked brains.
c. serve as a safety valve for unfulfilled desires.
d. prevent the brain from being disturbed by periodic stimulation.

38. The tendency for REM sleep to increase following REM sleep deprivation is called

a. neural static.
b. activation synthesis.
c. REM rebound.
d. brain maturation.

THE BIG PICTURE

2J. Do you normally remember your dreams? How do sleep researchers find out what people are dreaming about?

IN YOUR EVERYDAY LIFE

■ Which explanation for why we dream makes the most sense to you? How well does it explain your own dreams?

REM rebound the tendency for REM sleep to increase following REM sleep deprivation.

Answers: 36. d, 37. a, 38. c. Answers to The Big Picture questions can be found in Appendix B at the end of the book.

Terms and Concepts to Remember

biological psychology, p. 28

dendrites, p. 28

axon, p. 28

neuron, p. 28

action potential, p. 28

synapse [SIN-aps], p. 28

threshold, p. 29

all-or-none response, p. 29

neurotransmitters, p. 29

opiate, p. 30

endorphins [en-DOR-fins], p. 30

nervous system, p. 31

central nervous system (CNS), p. 31

peripheral nervous system (PNS), p. 31

nerves, p. 31

sensory neuron, p. 31

motor neuron, p. 31

interneuron, p. 31

somatic nervous system, p. 31

autonomic [aw-tuh-NAHM-ik]
nervous system, p. 31

sympathetic nervous system, p. 31

parasympathetic nervous system, p. 31

endocrine [EN-duh-krin] system, p. 33

hormones, p. 33

adrenal [ah-DREEN-el] glands, p. 34

pituitary gland, p. 34

EEG (electroencephalograph), p. 35

PET (positron emission tomography)
scan, p. 35

MRI (magnetic resonance imaging), p. 35

fMRI (functional MRI), p. 35

brainstem, p. 35

medulla [muh-DUL-uh], p. 35

thalamus [THAL-uh-muss], p. 36

reticular formation, p. 36

cerebellum [sehr-uh-BELL-um], p. 36

limbic system, p. 37

amygdala [uh-MIG-duh-la], p. 37

hypothalamus [hi-po-THAL-uh-muss],
p. 38

cerebral [seh-REE-bruhl] cortex, p. 40

frontal lobes, p. 40

parietal [puh-RYE-uh-tuhl] lobes, p. 40

occipital [ahk-SIP-uh-tuhl] lobes, p. 40

temporal lobes, p. 40

motor cortex, p. 40

sensory cortex, p. 41

hallucination, p. 42

association areas, p. 42

Broca's area, p. 44

Wernicke's area, p. 44

plasticity, p. 45

neurogenesis, p. 45

corpus callosum
[KOR-pus kah-LOW-sum], p. 46

split brain, p. 46

consciousness, p. 49

selective attention, p. 49

inattentional blindness, p. 49

circadian [ser-KAY-dee-an] rhythm,
p. 51

REM (rapid eye movement) sleep,
p. 51

alpha waves, p. 51

sleep, p. 51

insomnia, p. 55

narcolepsy, p. 55

sleep apnea, p. 55

dream, p. 57

manifest content, p. 57

latent content, p. 57

REM rebound, p. 58

Multiple-choice **self-tests** and more may be found at www.worthpublishers.com/myers

THE BIOLOGY OF MIND AND CONSCIOUSNESS

Biology and Behavior

Why are psychologists concerned with human biology?

1

- Everything psychological is simultaneously biological.
- The links between biology and behavior are a key part of the biopsychosocial approach.
- *Biological psychologists* study these links.

Neural Communication

What are the parts of a neuron?

2

- *Neurons* are basic units of the *nervous system*.
- Neurons contain a cell body, *dendrites,* and an *axon.*

How do neurons communicate?

3

NEURONS

- transmit information in a chemistry-to-electricity process.
- send signals *(action potentials)* down their axons.
- receive incoming excitatory or inhibitory signals through their dendrites and cell body.
- fire in an *all-or-none response* when combined incoming signals are strong enough to pass a *threshold.* Response triggers release of chemical messengers *(neurotransmitters)* across the tiny gap *(synapse)* separating a sending neuron from a receiving cell.

How do neurotransmitters affect our mood and behavior?

4

SPECIFIC NEUROTRANSMITTERS, SUCH AS SEROTONIN AND DOPAMINE,

- travel designated pathways in the brain.
- affect particular behaviors and emotions, such as hunger, movement, and arousal.

Endorphins are natural *opiates* released in response to pain and intense exercise.

The Nervous System

What are the two major divisions of the nervous system, and what are their basic functions?

5

- The *nervous system's* two major divisions are the *central nervous system (CNS)* and the *peripheral nervous system (PNS).* CNS *interneurons* communicate with PNS *motor neurons* and *sensory neurons.*
- In the CNS, the brain enables thinking, feeling, and acting. The spinal cord connects the PNS to the brain.
- In the PNS, the *somatic nervous system* controls voluntary movements of the skeletal system. The *autonomic nervous system (ANS)* controls the involuntary muscles and the glands.
- The subdivisions of the PNS are the *sympathetic nervous system* (which arouses) and the *parasympathetic nervous system* (which calms).

The Endocrine System

What are the endocrine system's functions, and how does the endocrine system interact with the nervous system?

6

- The *endocrine system* is the body's slower information system. Its glands secrete *hormones,* which influence brain and behavior.
- In times of stress or danger, the ANS activates the *adrenal glands'* fight-or-flight response.
- The *pituitary* (the endocrine system's master gland) triggers other glands, including sex glands, to release hormones, which then affect the brain and behavior.

The Brain

What are some techniques for studying the brain?

7

TO STUDY THE BRAIN, RESEARCHERS

- consider the effects of brain damage.
- use *MRI* scans to reveal brain structures.
- use *EEG* recordings and *PET* and *fMRI* (functional MRI) scans to reveal brain activity.

...are the functions of the brainstem and its ... lated structures?

8

- The *brainstem* controls automatic survival functions.
- The *medulla* controls heartbeat and breathing.
- The *reticular formation* controls arousal and attention.
- The *thalamus* is the brain's sensory switchboard.
- The *cerebellum* processes sensory input and coordinates muscle movement.

Brain States and Consci[ousness]

15 **What do we mean by *consciousness*, and how [does] attention direct our perceptions?**

- *Consciousness:* our awareness of ourselves and ou[r ...]
- *Selective attention* (for example, *inattentional blind[ness]*): We can focus attention on only a small part of the world around us.

16 **What is the circadian rhythm, and what are the stages of our nightly sleep cycle?**

- The *circadian rhythm:* internal biological clock; regulates daily cycles of alertness and sleepiness.
- Nightly sleep cycles every 90 minutes through recurring stages.
- Stage 1: brief, near-waking; *hallucinations* (sensations such as falling or floating) may occur.
- Stage 2: includes characteristic bursts of rhythmic brain waves
- Stage 3 is transitional sleep, and Stage 4 is deep sleep. These stages involve large, slow delta waves and shorten as night goes on.
- *REM (rapid eye movement) sleep:* internal arousal; outward paralysis. Includes most dreaming. Lengthens as night goes on.

17 **How do our sleep patterns differ? What four theories describe our need to sleep?**

- Life-span, genetic, and social-cultural factors affect *sleep* patterns.
- We sleep for: protection, maintenance, memory processing, and physical development.

18 **How does sleep loss affect us, and what are the major sleep disorders?**

RISKS OF SLEEP DEPRIVATION:

- Fatigue, irritability
- Depressed immune system
- Impaired concentration, creativity, communication, and performance
- Obesity, memory impairment

MAJOR SLEEP DISORDERS:

- *Insomnia* (recurring wakefulness)
- *Narcolepsy* (sudden, uncontrollable sleepiness or REM sleep)
- *Sleep apnea* (the stopping of breathing while asleep)
- Sleepwalking, sleeptalking, and night terrors

19 **What do we dream about, and what are five theories of *why* we dream?**

- Most dreams are bad dreams—of personal failures, dangers, or misfortunes.

DREAM THEORIES INCLUDE:

- Freud's wish-fulfillment theory.
- information-processing: the sleep-memory link.
- physiological function: developing and preserving neural pathways.
- the activation-synthesis theory: making sense of neural static.
- the cognitive-development perspective.

10

11

12

13

14

3
DEVELOPING THROUGH THE LIFE SPAN

Developmental psychology is the study of how we change (physically, cognitively, and socially) as we journey from conception to death. In some ways we become older versions of our former selves. An outgoing, playful 3-year-old, for example, may morph into a happy, wise-cracking 18-year-old, and finally into a jolly, playful grandparent. An abused and neglected child may later have difficulty forming close, trusting relationships.

Development also can bring surprises. My formerly shy little preschooler is now a young adult, living confidently in South Africa. There, Little-Miss-Hide-Behind-My-Legs has been a youth development worker who loves engaging adolescents from low-income townships.

The power of utterly unexpected life developments can be seen in the true story of Alexander (Bandura, 2008). Alexander was born in 1755, on a tiny Caribbean island. His parents were not married, and his father deserted the family. His mother was imprisoned and died. His guardian committed suicide. When his aunt, uncle, and grandfather also died, Alexander's few belongings were sold, leaving him penniless.

Alexander's luck turned when a local minister raised funds to send him to King's College (now Columbia University). From there, he went on to become one of the Founding Fathers of the United States and a leading author of the U.S. Constitution. As first Secretary of the Treasury, he helped create the country's banking and currency systems.

If you have ever had a ten-dollar bill, you have seen Alexander— Alexander Hamilton. His life—first as a penniless immigrant, and later as a respected statesman—shows how great achievements may arise from humble beginnings. In other ways, the apple did not fall far from the tree. His own stormy life, which ended after he was shot in a duel with Aaron Burr, was plagued by some of the instability and infidelity that also plagued his parents' lives.

① **What are the three major issues studied by developmental psychologists?**

We humans travel many of the same paths because we are alike in so many ways. We share most of our genes. As infants, we arrive able to sense and learn about our world. We begin walking around age 1 and talking by age 2. As children, we play together in preparation for life's work. As adults, we all smile and cry, love and loathe. As mortals, we all die.

We also differ. For better or worse, our experiences become part of who we are. In this chapter, we explore human development across the life span, from womb to tomb. **Developmental psychologists'** observations and experiments have shed light on three major issues.

1. *Nature and nurture:* How does our genetic inheritance (*our nature*) interact with our experiences (*the nurture we receive*) to influence our development?

2. *Continuity and stages:* What parts of development are gradual and continuous, like riding an escalator? What parts change abruptly in separate stages, like climbing rungs on a ladder?

3. *Stability and change:* Which of our traits persist through life? How do we change as we age?

You will read about these issues throughout this chapter. We also will focus on nature and nurture at the end of our infancy and childhood development discussion; continuity and stages at the end of our adolescent development discussion; and stability and change at the end of our adult development discussion.

Prenatal Development and the Newborn

Conception

② **How does conception occur, and what are chromosomes, DNA, genes, and the genome?**

Nothing is more natural than a species reproducing itself, yet nothing is more wondrous. With humans, the process starts when a woman's ovary releases a mature egg—a cell roughly the size of the period at the end of this sentence. The 200 million or more sperm deposited during intercourse begin their race upstream. Like space voyagers approaching a huge planet, the sperm approach a cell 85,000 times their own size. Only a small number will reach the egg. Those that do will release digestive enzymes that eat away its protective coating **(FIGURE 3.1a)**. As soon as one sperm penetrates that coating (Figure 3.1b), the egg's surface will block out the others. Before half a day passes, the egg nucleus and the sperm nucleus will fuse. The two have become one. Consider it your most fortunate of moments. Among 200 million sperm, the one needed to make you, in combination with that one particular egg, won the race.

Contained within the new single cell is a master code that will interact with your experience, creating you—a being in many ways like all other humans, but in other ways like no other human. Every cell in every part of your body will contain a copy of this genetic code.

Each of the trillions of cells you will eventually have will carry this code in its **chromosomes.** These threadlike structures contain the **DNA** we hear so much about. **Genes** are pieces of DNA, and they can be active (*expressed*) or inactive. Events in your environment can "turn them on," much as a cup of hot water "turns on" a teabag and lets it "express" itself as a refreshing cup of tea.

When turned on, your genes will guide your development. **FIGURE 3.2** summarizes these elements that make up your **heredity.**

Genetically speaking, every other human is close to being your identical twin. It is our shared genetic profile—our human **genome**—that makes us humans, rather than chimpanzees or tulips. "Your DNA and mine are 99.9 percent the same," noted former Human Genome

Diverse Yet Alike

The Nurture of Nature
Parents everywhere wonder: Will my baby grow up to be peaceful or aggressive? Homely or attractive? Successful or struggling at every step? What comes built in, and what is nurtured—and how? Research reveals that nature and nurture together shape our development—every step of the way.

FIGURE 3.1 ● **Life is sexually transmitted** (a) Sperm cells surround an ovum. (b) As one sperm penetrates the egg's jellylike outer coating, a series of events begins that will cause sperm and egg to fuse into a single cell. If all goes well, that cell will subdivide again and again to emerge 9 months later as a 100-trillion-cell human being.

(a)

(b)

"Thanks for almost everything, Dad."

Project director Francis Collins (2007). "At the DNA level, we are clearly all part of one big worldwide family."

The slight person-to-person variations found at particular gene sites in the DNA give clues to our uniqueness—why one person has a disease that another does not, why one person is short and another tall, why one is happy and another depressed. Most human traits are influenced by many genes. How tall you are, for example, reflects the height of your face, the length of your leg bones, and so forth. Complex human traits such as intelligence, happiness, and aggressiveness are similarly influenced by a whole orchestra of genes (Holden, 2008).

Our human differences are also shaped by our **environment**—by every external influence, from maternal nutrition while in the womb, to social support while nearing the tomb. Your height, for example, may be influenced by your diet and even by accidental injuries during growth.

Heredity and environment **interact.** HOW DO ◄ NATURE AND NURTURE INTERACT IN OUR DEVELOPMENT? Let's imagine two babies with two different sets of genes. Ashley

> "We share half our genes with the banana."
>
> Evolutionary biologist Robert May, president of Britain's Royal Society, 2001

FIGURE 3.2 ● **The genes: Their location and composition** Contained in the nucleus of each cell in your body are chromosomes. Each chromosome contains a coiled chain of the molecule DNA. Genes are DNA segments that, when expressed (turned on), direct the production of proteins and influence our individual biological development.

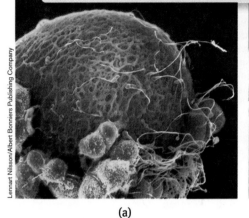

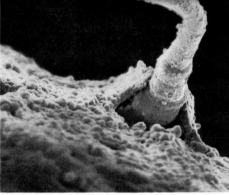

Chromosome

Gene

DNA

Cell

Nucleus

developmental psychology branch of psychology that studies physical, cognitive, and social change throughout the life span.

chromosomes threadlike structures made of DNA molecules that contain the genes.

DNA (deoxyribonucleic acid) a molecule containing the genetic information that makes up the chromosomes.

genes the biochemical units of heredity that make up the chromosomes; a segment of DNA.

heredity the genetic transfer of characteristics from parents to offspring.

genome the complete instructions for making an organism, consisting of all the genetic material in that organism's chromosomes.

environment every external influence, from prenatal nutrition to social support in later life.

interaction the interplay that occurs when the effect of one factor (such as environment) depends on another factor (such as heredity).

is a beautiful child and is also sociable and easygoing. Kalie is plain, shy, and colicky. Ashley's pretty, smiling face elicits affectionate and stimulating care, which in turn helps her develop into an even warmer and more outgoing person. Kalie's fussiness often leaves her caretakers tired and stressed. As the two children grow older, Ashley, naturally outgoing, more often seeks activities and friends that increase her social confidence. Shy Kalie has few friends and becomes even more withdrawn.

What has caused these differences? *Environments trigger gene activity. And our genetically influenced traits evoke significant responses in others.* Ashley and Kalie were very different when they began life. Their appearances and characteristics caused other people to react differently to them. These responses, in turn, strengthened Ashley's and Kalie's inborn tendencies. From conception onward, heredity and experience will dance together.

Prenatal Development

3 How does life develop before birth, and how do teratogens put prenatal development at risk?

Fertilized eggs are called **zygotes.** Fewer than half of them survive beyond the first two weeks (Grobstein, 1979; Hall, 2004). But for you and me, good fortune prevailed. One cell became 2, then 4—each just like the first—until this cell division had produced some 100 identical cells within the first week. Then the cells began to specialize. How identical cells do this—as

Jun Sato/Getty Images

Rob Rich/Getty Images

if one decides "I'll become a brain, you become intestines!"—is a puzzle that scientists are just beginning to solve.

About 10 days after conception, the zygote attaches to the wall of the mother's uterus. So begins about 37 weeks of the closest human relationship. The tiny clump of cells forms two parts. The inner cells become the **embryo** (**FIGURE 3.3**). The outer cells become the *placenta,* the life-link between embryo and mother.

Over the next 6 weeks, the embryo's organs begin to form and function. The heart begins to beat.

For about 1 in 270 sets of parents, though, there is a bonus. Two heartbeats will reveal that the zygote, during its early days of development, has split into two (**FIGURE 3.4**). If all goes well, two genetically identical babies will start life together some eight months later.

Identical twins are nature's own human clones.

Prenatal development	
zygote:	conception to 2 weeks
embryo:	2 weeks through 8 weeks
fetus:	9 weeks to birth

They share not only the same genes but also the same conception and uterus, and usually the same birth date and cultural history. **Fraternal twins** develop from separate fertilized eggs. They share the same prenatal environment but not the same genes. Genetically, they are no more similar than nontwin brothers and sisters. (Turn the page to read more on how psychologists use twin studies to judge the influences of heredity and environment in Close-Up: Twin and Adoption Studies.)

By 9 weeks after conception, an embryo looks unmistakably human. It is now a **fetus** (Latin for "offspring" or "young one"). By the sixth month, organs such as the stomach have developed enough to give the fetus a chance of survival if born prematurely.

Remember: *Heredity and environment interact.* This is true even in the prenatal period. In addition to transferring nutrients and oxygen from mother to fetus, the placenta screens out many harmful substances. But some slip by. Among them are **teratogens** (pronounced tuh-RAT-uh-jens), agents such as viruses and drugs that can damage an embryo or fetus. This is one reason pregnant women are advised not to drink alcoholic beverages. A pregnant woman never drinks alone. As alcohol enters her bloodstream—and her fetus'—it depresses activity in both their central nervous systems.

If she is a persistent heavy drinker, the fetus will be at risk for birth defects and mental retardation. For 1 in about 800 infants, the effects are visible as **fetal alcohol syndrome (FAS),** marked by a small, misproportioned head and lifelong brain abnormalities (May & Gossage, 2001). Even light drinking can harm the fetal brain (Braun, 1996; Ikonomidou et al., 2000). A pregnant woman's alcohol use may also prime her offspring to like alcohol. Teens whose mothers drank while pregnant are at risk for heavy drinking and alcohol dependence. In experiments, when pregnant rats drink alcohol, their young offspring later display a liking for alcohol's odor (Youngentob et al., 2007).

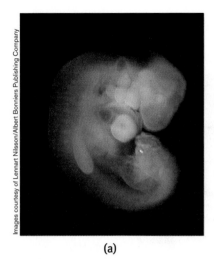

(a)

(b)

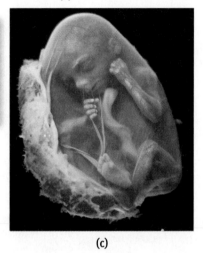

(c)

FIGURE 3.3 ● **Prenatal development**
(a) The embryo grows and develops rapidly. At 40 days, the spine is visible and the arms and legs are beginning to grow. (b) By the end of the second month, when the fetal period begins, facial features, hands, and feet have formed. (c) As the fetus enters the fourth month, its 3 ounces could fit in the palm of your hand.

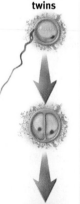

Identical twins   Fraternal twins

Same sex only   Same or opposite sex

FIGURE 3.4 ● **Same fertilized egg, same genes; different eggs, different genes**
Identical twins develop from a single fertilized egg, fraternal twins from two different eggs.

Even as newborns, we search out sights and sounds linked with other humans. We turn our heads in the direction of human voices. We gaze longer at a drawing of a facelike image (turn the page for **FIGURE 3.5**). We prefer to look at objects 8 to 12 inches away. Wonder of wonders, that just happens to be the approximate distance between a nursing infant's eyes and its mother's eyes (Maurer & Maurer, 1988).

We seem especially attuned to that human who is our mother. **CAN NEW-◄ BORNS DISTINGUISH THEIR OWN MOTHER'S SMELL AND THE SOUND OF HER VOICE IN A SEA OF OTHERS?** Indeed they can. Within days after birth, our brain has picked up and stored the smell of our mother's body. Week-old nursing babies, placed between a gauze pad from their mother's bra and one from another nursing mother, usually turn toward the pad that carries their mother's smell (MacFarlane, 1978). And what do you suppose happens if you give 3-week-olds a pacifier that sometimes turns on recordings of their mother's voice and sometimes the voice of a stranger? The infants will suck more

The Competent Newborn

4 What are some of the newborn's abilities and traits?

As newborns, we arrive with automatic **reflex** responses ideally suited for our survival. New parents are often in awe of the finely tuned set of reflexes by which their baby gets food. When something touches their cheek, babies turn toward that touch, open their mouth, and actively *root* for a nipple. Finding one, they quickly close on it and begin *sucking*. Sucking has its own set of reflexes—*tonguing, swallowing,* and *breathing*. Failing to find satisfaction, the hungry baby may *cry*—a behavior parents find highly unpleasant, and very rewarding to relieve.

zygote the fertilized egg; it enters a 2-week period of rapid cell division and develops into an embryo.

embryo the developing human organism from about 2 weeks after fertilization through the second month.

identical twins twins who develop from a single fertilized egg that splits in two, creating two genetically identical siblings.

fraternal twins twins who develop from separate fertilized eggs. They are genetically no closer than non-twin brothers and sisters, but they share a prenatal environment.

fetus the developing human organism from 9 weeks after conception to birth.

teratogen an agent, such as a chemical or virus, that can reach the embryo or fetus during prenatal development and cause harm.

fetal alcohol syndrome (FAS) physical and cognitive abnormalities in children caused by a pregnant woman's heavy drinking. In severe cases, symptoms include noticeable facial misproportions.

reflex an unlearned, automatic response to a sensory stimulus.

Twin and Adoption Studies

5 How do twin and adoption studies help us understand the effects of nature and nurture?

In procreation, a woman and a man shuffle their gene decks and deal a life-forming hand to their child-to-be, who is then subjected to countless influences beyond their control. How might researchers tease apart the influences of nature and nurture? To do so, they would need to

- vary the home environment while controlling heredity.
- vary heredity while controlling the home environment.

Happily for our purposes, nature has done this work for us.

Identical Versus Fraternal Twins

Identical twins have identical genes. Do these shared genes mean that identical twins also *behave* more similarly than fraternal twins (Bouchard, 2004)? Studies of some 800,000 twin pairs worldwide provide a consistent answer. Identical twins are more similar than fraternals in their abilities, personal traits, and interests (Johnson et al., 2009; Loehlin & Nichols, 1976).

Next question: Could shared experiences rather than shared genes explain these similarities? Again, studies of twin pairs give some answers.

Separated Twins

On a chilly February morning in 1979, some time after divorcing his first wife, Linda, Jim Lewis awoke next to his second wife, Betty. Determined that this marriage would work, Jim left love notes to Betty around the house. As he lay there he thought about his son, James Alan, and his faithful dog, Toy.

Jim loved his basement woodworking shop where he had built furniture, including a white bench circling a tree. Jim also liked to drive his Chevy, watch stock-car racing, and drink Miller Lite beer. Except for an occasional migraine, Jim was healthy. His blood pressure was a little high, perhaps related to his chain-smoking. He had gained weight but had shed some of the extra pounds. After a vasectomy, he was done having children.

What was extraordinary about Jim Lewis, however, was that at that moment (I am not making this up) there was another man named Jim for whom all these things were also true.[1] This other Jim—Jim Springer—just happened, 38 years earlier, to have been Jim Lewis' womb-mate. Thirty-seven days after their birth, these genetically identical twins were separated and adopted by two blue-collar families. They grew up with no contact until the day Jim Lewis received a call from his genetic clone (who, having been told he had a twin, set out to find him).

One month later, the brothers became the first of 126 separated twin pairs tested by psychologist Thomas Bouchard and his colleagues (Holden, 2009). Given tests measuring their personality, intelligence, heart rate, and brain waves, the Jim twins were virtually as alike as the same person tested twice. Their voice patterns were so

Identical twins: Jim Lewis and Jim Springer are people two.

©2006 Bob Sacha

similar that, hearing a playback of an earlier interview, Jim Springer guessed "That's me." Wrong—it was his brother.

This and other research on separated identical twins supports the idea that genes matter.

Twin similarities do not impress Bouchard's critics, however. If any two strangers were to spend hours comparing their behaviors and life histories, wouldn't they also discover many coincidental similarities? Moreover, critics note, identical twins share an appearance and the responses it evokes, so they have probably had similar experiences. Bouchard replies that the life choices made by separated fraternal twins are not as dramatically similar as those made by separated identical twins.

Biological Versus Adoptive Relatives

The separated twin studies control heredity while varying environment. Nature's second type of real-life experiment—adoption—controls environment while varying heredity. Adoption creates two groups: genetic relatives (biological parents and siblings) and environmental relatives (adoptive parents and siblings). For any given trait we study, we can therefore ask three questions:

- How much do adopted children resemble their biological parents, who contributed their genes?
- How much do they resemble their adoptive parents, who contribute a home environment?
- While sharing a home environment, do adopted siblings also come to share traits?

By providing children with loving, nurturing homes, adoption matters. Yet researchers asking these questions about *personality* agree on one stunning finding, based on studies of hundreds of adoptive families. *Non-twin siblings who grow up together, whether biologically related or not, do not much resemble one another in personality* (McGue & Bouchard, 1998; Plomin et al., 1998; Rowe, 1990). In traits such as outgoingness and agreeableness, adoptees are more similar to their biological parents than to their caregiving adoptive parents. This heredity effect shows up in macaque monkeys' personalities as well (Maestripieri, 2003).

In the pages to come, twin and adoption study results will shed light on how nature and nurture influence intelligence, disordered behavior, and many other traits.

---

1. Actually, this description of the two Jims errs in one respect: Jim Lewis named his son James Alan. Jim Springer named his James Allan.

Prepared to feed and eat: Animals, including humans, are predisposed to respond to their offspring's cries for nourishment.

vigorously when they hear their now-familiar mother's voice (Mills & Melhuish, 1974).

Very young infants are competent, indeed. They see what they need to see. They smell and hear well. They are already using their sensory equipment to learn. Guided by biology and experience, those sensory and perceptual abilities will develop continuously over the next months.

Yet newborns also differ. As most parents will tell you after having their second child, babies differ even before gulping their first breath. This difference

FIGURE 3.5 ● Newborns' preference for faces When shown these two forms with the same three elements, newborns spent nearly twice as long looking at the facelike image on the left (Johnson & Morton, 1991). Newborns—average age just 53 minutes in one study—seem to have an inborn preference for looking toward faces (Mondloch et al., 1999).

is **temperament,** or emotional excitability—whether reactive, intense, and fidgety, or easygoing, quiet, and placid. Anxious, inhibited infants have high and variable heart rates. Physically, they become very aroused when facing new or strange situations (Kagan & Snidman, 2004). From the first weeks of life, *difficult* babies are more irritable, intense, and unpredictable. *Easy* babies are cheerful and relaxed, with predictable feeding and sleeping schedules (Chess & Thomas, 1987).

Temperament, which is rooted in our biology, is one aspect of personality. Identical twins, who have identical genes, have more similar personalities, including temperament, than do fraternal twins. Such evidence supports the idea that our biologically rooted temperament helps form our enduring personality (McCrae et al., 2000, 2007; Rothbart, 2007).

PRACTICE TEST

THE BASICS

1. Developmental psychologists tend to focus on three major issues. Which of the following is NOT one of those issues?
   a. Nature and nurture
   b. Reflexes and unlearned behaviors
   c. Stability and change
   d. Continuity and stages

2. The first two weeks of prenatal development, the period of the _____ is a time of rapid cell division. The period of the _____ lasts from 9 weeks after conception until birth.
   a. zygote; embryo
   b. zygote; fetus
   c. embryo; fetus
   d. fetus; embryo

3. Teratogens are agents that pass through the placenta's screen and may harm an embryo or fetus. Which of the following is a known teratogen?
   a. Oxygen   c. Alcohol
   b. Sugar   d. Onions

4. From the very first weeks of life, some infants are intense and anxious, while others are easygoing and relaxed. These differences are usually explained as differences in
   a. automatic reflex responses.
   b. diet.
   c. temperament.
   d. parental responsiveness.

5. In seeking to understand genetic influences on personality, adoption studies
   a. compare adopted children with non-adopted children.
   b. evaluate whether adopted children's traits more closely resemble those of their adoptive parents or those of their biological parents.
   c. assess the effect of prior neglect on adopted children.
   d. assess the effect of children's age at adoption.

THE BIG PICTURE

3A. Your friend, who is a regular drinker, hopes to become pregnant soon and has stopped drinking. Why is this a good idea?

IN YOUR EVERYDAY LIFE

■ What impresses you the most about infants' abilities, and why?

■ What do you think about the idea that, genetically speaking, we are all nearly identical twins?

Answers: 1. b, 2. b, 3. c, 4. c, 5. b. Answers to The Big Picture questions can be found in Appendix B at the end of the book.

temperament a person's characteristic emotional reactivity and intensity.

Infancy and Childhood

During infancy, a baby grows from newborn to toddler, and during childhood from toddler to teenager. We all traveled this path, with its physical, cognitive, and social milestones.

As a flower unfolds in accord with its genetic instructions, so did we, in the orderly biological growth process called **maturation.** Maturation dictates much of our shared path. We stand before we walk. We use nouns before adjectives. Some experiences, such as severe deprivation or abuse, can throw us off our path and slow development. Others, such as having caretakers who talk and read to us, can speed us on our way. Maturation (nature) sets the basic course of development; experience (nurture) adjusts it. Once again, we see genes and scenes interacting.

Physical Development

6 How do the brain and motor skills develop during infancy and childhood?

Brain Development

In your mother's womb, your developing brain formed nerve cells at the explosive rate of nearly one-quarter million per *minute.* This brain-cell production line was so efficient that you arrived in the world with most of the brain cells you would ever have—or need. However, the wiring among these cells—your nervous system— was immature. After birth, these neural networks had a wild growth spurt, branching and linking in patterns that would eventually enable you to walk, talk, and remember.

> "It is a rare privilege to watch the birth, growth, and first feeble struggles of a living human mind."
>
> Annie Sullivan, in Helen Keller's *The Story of My Life,* 1903

From ages 3 to 6, the most rapid brain growth was in your frontal lobes, the seat of rational planning. During those years, your ability to control your attention and behavior developed rapidly (Garon et al., 2008; Thompson-Schill et al., 2009). Your

"This is the path to adulthood. You're here."

frontal lobes have continued developing into adolescence and beyond. Last to develop are the association areas—those linked with thinking, memory, and language. As they do, mental abilities surge (Chugani & Phelps, 1986; Thatcher et al., 1987).

The neural pathways supporting language and agility continue their rapid growth into puberty. Then, a use-it-or-lose-it *pruning process* shuts down unused links and strengthens others (Paus et al., 1999; Thompson et al., 2000).

Your genes laid down the basic design of your brain, rather like the lines of a coloring book, but experience fills in the details. In experiments showing how early experiences leave their "marks" in the brain, researchers separated young rats into two groups (Rosenzweig, 1984; Renner & Rosenzweig, 1987). Rats in one group lived alone, with little to interest or distract them. The other rats shared a cage, complete with objects and activities that might exist in a natural "rat world" **(FIGURE 3.6)**. In this enriched environment, rats developed a heavier and thicker brain cortex.

The environment's effect was so great that if you viewed brief video clips, you could tell from the rats' activity and curiosity whether they had lived in solitary confinement or in the enriched setting (Renner & Renner, 1993). After 60 days in the enriched environment, some rats'

brain weight increased 7 to 10 percent. The number of synapses, forming the networks between the cells (see Figure 3.6), mushroomed by about 20 percent (Kolb & Whishaw, 1998).

Touching or massaging infant rats and premature human babies has similar benefits (Field et al., 2006, 2007). In hospital intensive care units, caretakers now massage premature infants to help them develop faster neurologically, gain weight more rapidly, and go home sooner.

Nature and nurture together sculpt our synapses. Brain maturation provides us with an abundance of neural connections. Experience—sights and smells, touches and tugs—activate and strengthen some neural pathways while others weaken from disuse. Similar to paths through a forest, less-traveled neural pathways gradually disappear and popular ones are broadened.

During early childhood—while excess connections are still on call—youngsters can most easily master such skills as the grammar and accent of another language. But we seem to have a **critical period** for some skills. Lacking any exposure to spoken, written, or signed language before adolescence, a person will never master any language (see Chapter 8). Likewise, lacking visual experience during the early years, a person whose vision is restored by cataract removal will never achieve normal perceptions (see Chapter 5). Without stimulation, the brain cells normally assigned to vision will die during the pruning process or be diverted to other uses. For normal brain development, early stimulation is critical. The maturing brain's rule: Use it or lose it.

The brain's development does not, however, end with childhood. Throughout life, whether we are learning to type or skateboard, we perform with increasing skill as experience sculpts our neural tissue.

Motor Development

As their muscles and nervous system mature, infants begin to control their movements. With occasional exceptions, the sequence of physical (motor) development is universal. Babies sit unsup-

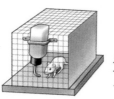

Impoverished environment

Impoverished rat brain cell

Enriched environment

Enriched rat brain cell

FIGURE 3.6 ● **Experience affects brain development** In this experiment, some rats lived alone in an environment without playthings. Others lived together in an environment enriched with playthings changed daily. In 14 of 16 repetitions of the experiment, rats in the enriched setting developed more cerebral cortex (relative to the rest of the brain's tissue) than was found in those raised in the impoverished environment (Renner & Rosenzweig, 1987; Rosenzweig, 1984).

ported before they crawl, and they walk before they run (**FIGURE 3.7**).

Heredity plays a major role in motor development. Identical twins typically begin sitting up and walking on nearly the same day (Wilson, 1979). The rapid development of the cerebellum (at the back of the brain; see Chapter 2) helps create our eagerness to walk at about age 1. Experience before that time has a limited effect. This is also true for other physical skills, including bowel and bladder control. If a child's muscles and brain have not yet matured, don't expect pleading or punishment to produce successful toilet training.

Cognitive Development

7 How did Piaget view the developmental stages of a child's mind, and how does current thinking about cognitive development differ?

"Who knows the thoughts of a child?" wondered poet Nora Perry. Developmental psychologists aim to know. To see how they study thinking and learning in very young children, consider a surprise dis-

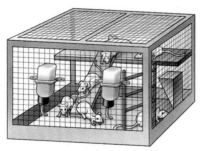

Evan Kafka/Getty Images

FIGURE 3.7 ● **Physical development:** Sit, crawl, walk, run—the sequence of events is the same the world over. In the United States, 25 percent of all babies walk by age 11 months, 50 percent within a week after their first birthday, and 90 percent by age 15 months (Frankenburg et al., 1992). Depending on the culture, babies may reach these milestones sooner or later, but the *sequence* doesn't vary.

covery. In 1965, Carolyn Rovee-Collier was finishing her doctoral work in psychology. She was also a new mom, whose colicky 2-month-old, Benjamin, could be calmed by moving a crib mobile. Weary of hitting the mobile, she strung a cloth ribbon connecting the mobile to Benjamin's foot. Soon, he was kicking his foot to move the mobile.

Thinking about her unintended home experiment, Rovee-Collier realized that, contrary to popular opinion in the 1960s, babies are capable of learning. To know for sure that little Benjamin wasn't just a whiz kid, Rovee-Collier had to repeat the

experiment with other infants (Rovee-Collier, 1989, 1999). Sure enough, they, too, soon kicked more when hitched to a mobile, both on the day of the experiment and the day after. They had learned the link between moving legs and moving mobile. If, however, she hitched them to a different mobile the next day, the infants showed no learning. Their actions indicated that they remembered the original mobile and recognized the difference. Moreover, when tethered to a familiar mobile a month later, they remembered the association and again began kicking.

Jean Piaget (pronounced Pee-ah-ZHAY) spent a half-century doing as Rovee-Collier did—studying how a child's mind develops. Thanks partly to Piaget's pioneering work, we now understand that a child's mind is not a miniature model of an adult's. Children reason *differently*, in "wildly illogical ways about problems whose solutions are self-evident to adults" (Brainerd, 1996).

Bill Anderson/Photo Researchers, Inc.

Jean Piaget (1896–1980): "If we examine the intellectual development of the individual or of the whole of humanity, we shall find that the human spirit goes through a certain number of stages, each different from the other" (1930).

maturation biological growth processes leading to orderly changes in behavior, independent of experience.

critical period a period early in life when exposure to certain stimuli or experiences is needed for proper development.

Piaget's interest began in 1920, when he was developing questions for children's intelligence tests in Paris. Looking over the test results, Piaget noticed something interesting. At certain ages, children made strikingly similar mistakes. Where others saw childish mistakes, Piaget saw intelligence at work.

Decades of observation convinced Piaget that a child's mind develops through a series of stages. This upward march begins with the newborn's simple reflexes, and it ends with the adult's abstract reasoning power. Moving through these stages, Piaget believed, is like climbing a ladder. A child can't easily move to a higher rung without first having a firm footing on the one below. Tools for thinking and reasoning differ in each stage. Thus, you can tell an 8-year-old that "getting an idea is like having a light turn on in your head," and the child will understand. A 2-year-old won't get the analogy. WOULD A 2-YEAR-OLD UNDERSTAND THAT A ◄ MINIATURE SLIDE IS TOO SMALL FOR SLIDING, OR THAT A MINIATURE CAR IS MUCH TOO SMALL TO GET INTO? (See **FIGURE 3.8**.) No. But an adult mind likewise can reason in ways that an 8-year-old won't understand.

Piaget believed that the force driving us up this intellectual ladder is our struggle to make sense of our experiences. His core idea is that "children are active thinkers, constantly trying to construct more advanced understandings of the world"

TABLE 3.1	Piaget's Stages of Cognitive Development	
Typical Age Range	**Stage and Description**	**New Developments**
Birth to nearly 2 years	*Sensorimotor* Experiencing the world through senses and actions (looking, hearing, touching, mouthing, and grasping)	• Object permanence • Stranger anxiety
About 2 to 6 or 7 years	*Preoperational* Representing things with words and images; using intuitive rather than logical reasoning	• Pretend play • Egocentrism
About 7 to 11 years	*Concrete operational* Thinking logically about concrete events; grasping concrete analogies and performing arithmetical operations	• Conservation • Mathematical transformations
About 12 through adulthood	*Formal operational* Reasoning abstractly	• Abstract logic • Potential for mature moral reasoning

(Siegler & Ellis, 1996). Part of this active thinking is building **schemas**, which are concepts or mental molds into which we pour our experiences. By adulthood we have built countless schemas, ranging from what a dog is to what love is.

Let's turn now to the stages Piaget proposed for the development of **cognition**—all the mental activities associated with thinking, knowing, remembering, and communicating. Somewhere on your journey from egghood to childhood you became conscious. When was that, and how did your mind unfold thereafter?

Pretend play

Piaget's Theory and Current Thinking

Piaget believed that children construct their understanding of the world as they interact with it. Their minds go through spurts of change, he believed, as they move from one level to the next. **TABLE 3.1** summarizes the four stages in Piaget's theory.

Sensorimotor Stage The **sensorimotor stage** begins at birth and lasts to nearly age 2. In this stage, babies take in the world through their senses and actions— through looking, hearing, touching, mouthing, and grasping.

Very young babies seem to live in the present. In one test, Piaget showed an infant an appealing toy and then flopped his hat over it. Before the age of 6 months, the infant acted as if the toy no

FIGURE 3.8 • **Scale errors** Children age 18 to 30 months may fail to take the size of an object into account when trying to perform impossible actions with it. At left, a 21-month-old attempts to slide down a miniature slide. At right, a 24-month-old opens the door to a miniature car and tries to step inside (DeLoache et al., 2004).

Doug Goodman

FIGURE 3.9 ● **Object permanence** Infants younger than 6 months seldom understand that things continue to exist when they are out of sight. But for this older infant, out of sight is definitely not out of mind.

longer existed: Out of sight was out of mind. Such very young infants lack **object permanence**—the awareness that objects continue to exist when out of sight **(FIGURE 3.9)**. By about 8 months, infants begin to show that they do remember things they can no longer see. If you hide a toy, an 8-month-old will momentarily look for it. Within another month or two, the infant will look for it even after several seconds have passed.

So does object permanence in fact blossom at 8 months, much as tulips blossom in spring? Today's researchers think not. They believe object permanence unfolds gradually, and they view development as more continuous than Piaget did.

They also think that young children are more competent than Piaget and his followers believed. For example, babies seem to have an inborn grasp of simple physics. Like adults staring in disbelief at a magic trick (the *"Whoa!"* look), infants look longer at an unexpected and unfamiliar scene of a car seeming to pass through a solid object. They also stare longer at a ball stopping in midair, or at an object that seems to magically disappear (Baillargeon, 1995, 2008; Wellman & Gelman, 1992).

Preoperational Stage Piaget believed that until about age 6 or 7, children are in a **preoperational stage**—too young to perform *mental operations* (such as imagining an action and mentally reversing it).

Conservation Consider a 5-year-old, who objects that there is too much milk in a tall, narrow glass. "Too much" may become an acceptable amount if you pour that milk into a short, wide glass. Focusing only on the height dimension, the child cannot perform the operation of mentally pouring the milk back into the tall glass. Before about age 6, said Piaget, young children lack the concept of **conservation**—the idea that quantity remains the same even if it changes shape **(FIGURE 3.10** on the next page).

Pretend Play A child who can perform mental operations can think in symbols and therefore begins to enjoy *pretend play*. Contemporary researchers have found symbolic thinking at an earlier age than Piaget supposed. One researcher showed children a model of a room and hid a model toy in it (a miniature stuffed dog behind a miniature couch) (DeLoache & Brown, 1987). The 2½-year-olds easily remembered where to find the miniature toy in the model, but that knowledge didn't transfer to the real world. They could not use the model to locate an actual stuffed dog behind a couch in a real room. Three-year-olds—only 6 months older—usually went right to the actual stuffed animal in the real room, showing they *could* think of the model as a symbol for the room. Piaget did not view the change from one stage to another as an abrupt shift. Even so, he probably would have been surprised to see symbolic thinking at such a young age.

Egocentrism Piaget also believed that preschool children are **egocentric:** They have difficulty imagining things from another's point of view. Asked to "show Mommy your picture," 2-year-old Gabriella holds the picture up facing her own eyes. Told to hide, 3-year-old Gray puts his hands over his eyes, assuming that if he can't see you, you can't see him.

Contemporary research supports preschoolers' egocentrism. This is helpful information when a TV-watching

schema a concept or framework that organizes and interprets information.

cognition all the mental activities associated with thinking, knowing, remembering, and communicating.

sensorimotor stage in Piaget's theory, the stage (from birth to about 2 years of age) during which infants know the world mostly in terms of their sensory impressions and motor activities.

object permanence the awareness that things continue to exist even when not perceived.

preoperational stage in Piaget's theory, the stage (from about 2 to 6 or 7 years of age) in which a child learns to use language but cannot yet perform the mental operations of concrete logic.

conservation the principle (which Piaget believed to be a part of concrete operational reasoning) that properties such as mass, volume, and number remain the same despite changes in shapes.

egocentrism in Piaget's theory, the preoperational child's difficulty taking another's point of view.

Bianca Moscatelli/Worth Publishers

FIGURE 3.10 • **Piaget's test of conservation** This preoperational child does not yet understand the principle of conservation of volume. When the milk is poured into a tall, narrow glass, it suddenly seems like "more" than when it was in the shorter, wider glass. In another year or so, she will understand that the volume stays the same even though it looks different.

preschooler blocks your view of the screen. The child probably assumes that you see what she sees. At this age, children simply are not yet able to take another's viewpoint. Even we adults may overestimate the extent to which others share our views. **HAVE YOU EVER MISTAK-◀ ENLY ASSUMED THAT SOMETHING WOULD BE CLEAR TO A FRIEND BECAUSE IT WAS CLEAR TO YOU?** Or sent an e-mail mistakenly thinking that the receiver would "hear" your "just kidding" intent (Epley et al., 2004; Kruger et al., 2005)? As children, we were even more likely to commit this thinking error.

Theory of Mind When Little Red Riding Hood realizes her "grandmother" is really a wolf, she swiftly revises her ideas about the creature's intentions and races away. Preschoolers develop this ability to read others' mental states when they begin forming a **theory of mind.**

When children can imagine another person's viewpoint, all sorts of new skills emerge. They can tease, because they now understand what makes a playmate angry. They may be able to convince a sibling to share. Knowing what might make a parent buy a toy, they may try to persuade.

Between about 3½ and 4½, children worldwide use their new theory-of-mind skills to realize that others may hold *false* beliefs (Callaghan et al., 2005; Sabbagh et al., 2006). Researchers illustrated this by asking preschoolers to tell them what

was inside a Band Aids box (Jenkins & Astington, 1996). Expecting Band Aids, the children were surprised to see that the box actually contained pencils. Then came the theory-of-mind question. Asked what a child who had never seen the box would think was inside, 3-year-olds typically answered "pencils." By age 4 to 5, children knew better. They anticipated their friends' false belief that the box would hold Band Aids.

Children with **autism** have an impaired theory of mind (Klein & Kihlstrom, 1998; Yirmiya et al., 1998). They have difficulty reading other people's thoughts and feelings. Most children learn that another child's pouting mouth signals sadness, and that twinkling eyes mean happiness or mischief. A child with autism fails to

understand these signals (Frith & Frith, 2001). The underlying cause seems to be poor communication among brain regions that normally work together to let us take another's viewpoint. This effect appears to result from an unknown number of autism-related genes interacting with the environment (Blakeslee, 2005; Wickelgren, 2005).

Concrete Operational Stage By about 6 or 7 years of age, said Piaget, children enter the **concrete operational stage.** Given concrete materials, they begin to grasp conservation. Understanding that change in form does not mean change in quantity, they can mentally pour milk back and forth between glasses of different shapes. They also enjoy jokes that allow them to use this new understanding:

AP Photo/Steven Senne

Autism: This therapist is using music to help a young man with autism to improve his language skills. Autism is marked by limited communication ability and difficulty understanding others' states of mind.

Mr. Jones went into a restaurant and ordered a whole pizza for his dinner. When the waiter asked if he wanted it cut into 6 or 8 pieces, Mr. Jones said, "Oh, you'd better make it 6, I could never eat 8 pieces!" (McGhee, 1976)

Piaget believed that during the concrete operational stage, children fully gain the mental ability to understand simple math and conservation. When my daughter, Laura, was 6, I was astonished at her inability to reverse simple arithmetic. Asked, "What is 8 plus 4?" she required 5 seconds to compute "12," and another 5 seconds to then compute 12 minus 4. By age 8, she could answer a reversed question instantly.

As Piaget was forming his theory of stages of cognitive development, Russian psychologist Lev Vygotsky was also studying how children think and learn. He noted that by age 7, children are more and more able to think in words and to use words to work out solutions to problems. They do this, he said, by no longer thinking aloud. Instead they internalize their culture's language and rely on inner speech (Ferbyhough, 2008). Parents who say *"No, no!"* when pulling a child's hand away from a cake are giving the child a self-control tool. When the child later needs to resist temptation, he may likewise think *"No!"*

Lev Vygotsky (1896–1934): Vygotsky, pictured here with his daughter, was a Russian developmental psychologist. He studied how children's minds feed on the language of social interaction.

James V. Wertsch/Washington University

Talking to themselves, whether out loud or inside their heads, helps children to control their behavior and emotions and to master new skills. And when parents give children words, they provide, said Vygotsky, a *scaffold* upon which children can step to higher levels of thinking. (For more on children's development of language, see Chapter 8.)

Formal Operational Stage By age 12, said Piaget, our reasoning expands to include abstract thinking. We are no longer limited to purely concrete reasoning, based on actual experience. As children approach adolescence, many become capable of abstract *if . . . then* thinking: *If* this happens, *then* that will happen. Piaget called this new systematic reasoning ability **formal operational** thinking. (Stay tuned for more about adolescents' thinking abilities later in this chapter.)

Reflecting on Piaget's Theory What remains of Piaget's ideas about the child's mind? Plenty—enough to merit his being singled out by *Time* magazine as one of the last century's 20 most influential scientists and thinkers, and to be rated in a survey of British psychologists as the greatest twentieth-century psychologist (*Psychologist,* 2003). Piaget identified significant cognitive milestones and stimulated worldwide interest in how the mind develops. His emphasis was less on the ages at which children typically reach specific milestones than on their sequence. Studies around the globe, from Algeria to North America, have confirmed that human cognition unfolds basically in the sequence Piaget described (Lourenco & Machado, 1996; Segall et al., 1990).

Although today's researchers see development as more continuous than did Piaget, his insights can help teachers and parents understand young children. We will all be happier if we remember that young children cannot think with adult logic and cannot take another's viewpoint. What seems simple and obvious to us—getting off a teeter-totter will cause a friend on the other end to crash—may never occur to a 3-year-old. We should also remember that children are not

empty containers waiting to be filled with knowledge. By building on what children already know, we can engage them in concrete demonstrations and stimulate them to think for themselves. Finally, psychologists remind us, we should realize that children's cognitive immaturity is adaptive (Bjorklund & Green, 1992). It is nature's strategy for keeping children close to protective adults and providing time for learning and socialization.

Social Development

From birth, babies all over the world are social creatures, developing an intense bond with their caregivers. Infants come to prefer familiar faces and voices, then to coo and gurgle when given their mother's or father's attention. HAVE YOU ◄ EVER WONDERED WHY TINY INFANTS CAN HAPPILY BE HANDED OFF TO ADMIRING VISITORS, BUT WHEN THE BABY REACHES A CERTAIN AGE ONLY MOM WILL DO? Soon after object permanence emerges and children become mobile, a curious thing happens. At about 8 months, they develop **stranger anxiety.** They may react to strangers by crying and reaching for familiar caregivers. "No! Don't leave me!" their distress seems to say. At about this age, children have schemas for familiar

---

theory of mind people's ideas about their own and others' mental states—about their feelings, perceptions, and thoughts, and the behaviors these might predict.

autism a disorder that appears in childhood and is marked by deficient communication, social interaction, and understanding of others' state of mind.

concrete operational stage in Piaget's theory, the stage of cognitive development (from about 6 or 7 to 11 years of age) during which children gain the mental operations that enable them to think logically about concrete events.

formal operational stage in Piaget's theory, the stage of cognitive development (normally beginning about age 12) during which people begin to think logically about abstract concepts.

stranger anxiety the fear of strangers that infants commonly display, beginning by about 8 months of age.

Diverse Yet Alike

Stranger Anxiety

A newly emerging ability to evaluate people as unfamiliar and possibly threatening helps protect babies 8 months and older. Babies display this same adaptive response, whether in the United States or Togo, West Africa.

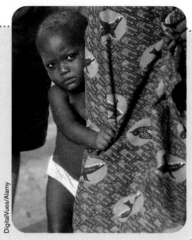

faces—mental images of how caretakers should look. When the new face does not fit into one of these remembered images, they become distressed (Kagan, 1984). Once again, we see an important principle: *The brain, mind, and social-emotional behavior develop together.*

Origins of Attachment

8 | How do the bonds of attachment form between caregivers and infants?

By 12 months, infants typically cling tightly to a parent when they are frightened or expect separation. Reunited after being apart, they shower the parent with smiles and hugs. No social behavior is more striking than this intense and mutual infant-parent bond. This **attachment** bond is a powerful survival impulse that keeps infants close to their caregivers.

Infants become attached to people—typically their parents—who are comfortable and familiar. For many years, psychologists reasoned that infants grew attached to those who satisfied their need for nourishment. It made sense. But an accidental finding overturned this idea.

During the 1950s, University of Wisconsin psychologists Harry Harlow and Margaret Harlow bred monkeys for their learning studies. They separated the infant monkeys from their mothers shortly after birth. To isolate them from diseases and ensure they were treated equally, the

researchers placed each infant in a sanitary individual cage with a cheesecloth baby blanket (Harlow et al., 1971). Then came a surprise: When the monkeys' blankets were taken to be laundered, they became distressed.

Imagine yourself as one of the Harlows, trying to figure out why the monkey infants were so intensely attached to their blankets. Remember, at the time, psychologists believed that infants became attached to those who nourish them. Might comfort be the key? How could you test that idea? To pit the drawing power of a food source against the contact comfort of the blanket, the Harlows created two artificial mothers. One was a bare wire cylinder with a wooden head and an attached feeding bottle. The other was a cylinder wrapped with terry cloth.

For the monkeys, it was no contest. They overwhelmingly preferred the comfy cloth mother **(FIGURE 3.11)**. Like other infants clinging to their live mothers, the monkey babies would cling to their cloth mothers when anxious. When exploring their environment, they used her as a *secure base,* acting as though they were attached to her by an invisible elastic band that stretched only so far before pulling them back. Researchers soon learned that other qualities—rocking, warmth, and feeding—made the cloth mother even more appealing.

Human infants, too, become attached to parents who are soft and warm and who rock, pat, and feed. Much parent-infant emotional communication occurs via touch (Hertenstein et al., 2006), which can be either soothing (snuggles) or arousing (tickles). The human parent also provides a safe haven for a distressed child and a secure base from which to explore.

FIGURE 3.11 ● **The Harlows' mothers**
The Harlows' infant monkeys much preferred contact with a comfortable cloth mother, even while feeding from a wire nourishing mother.

Attachment Differences

9 Why do secure and insecure attachments matter, and how does an infant develop basic trust?

What accounts for children's attachment differences? Trying to answer this question, Mary Ainsworth (1979) designed the *strange situation* experiment. She observed mother-infant pairs at home during their first six months. Later she observed the 1-year-old infants in a strange situation (usually a laboratory playroom) without their mothers. Such research shows that about 60 percent of infants display *secure attachment*. In their mother's presence, they play comfortably, happily exploring their new environment. When she leaves, they become upset. When she returns, they seek contact with her.

Other infants show *insecure attachment*, marked either by *anxiety* or *avoidance* of trusting relationships. They are less likely to explore their surroundings. They may even cling to their mother. When she leaves, some cry loudly and remain upset. Others seem not to notice or care about her departure and return (Ainsworth, 1973, 1989; Kagan, 1995; van IJzendoorn & Kroonenberg, 1988).

Ainsworth (1979) found that sensitive, responsive mothers—those who noticed what their babies were doing and responded appropriately—had infants who were securely attached. Insensitive, unresponsive mothers—mothers who attended to their babies when they felt like doing so but ignored them at other times—often had infants who were insecurely attached. The Harlows' monkey studies, with unresponsive artificial mothers, produced even more striking effects. When put in strange situations without their artificial mothers, the deprived infants were terrified **(FIGURE 3.12)**.

BUT IS ATTACHMENT STYLE ENTIRELY◀ THE RESULT OF PARENTING? OR IS ATTACHMENT STYLE ALSO AFFECTED BY OUR GENETICALLY INFLUENCED TEMPERAMENT? As we saw earlier in this chapter, some babies are, from the time of their birth, noticeably *difficult*—irritable, intense, and

Harlow Primate Laboratory, University of Wisconsin

FIGURE 3.12 • **Social deprivation and fear** In the Harlows' experiments, monkeys raised with artificial mothers were terror-stricken when placed in strange situations without those mothers. (Today's climate of greater respect for animal welfare prevents such primate studies.)

unpredictable. Others are *easy*—cheerful, relaxed, and feeding and sleeping on predictable schedules (Chess & Thomas, 1987). By neglecting such inborn differences, critics say, parenting studies are like "comparing foxhounds reared in

Father care: Fathers are not just mobile sperm banks. Across nearly 100 studies worldwide, father love is linked, at about the same level as is mother love, with their offspring's health and well-being (Rohner & Veneziano, 2001). Among the Aka people of Central Africa, fathers form an especially close bond with their infants and may be found holding or within reach of their babies 47 percent of the time (Hewlett, 1991).

© Barry Hewlett

kennels with poodles reared in apartments" (Harris, 1998). To separate nature and nurture, we would need to vary parenting while controlling temperament. (Pause and think: If you were a researcher, how might you do this?)

One researcher's solution was to randomly assign 100 temperamentally difficult infants to two groups. Half of the 6- to 9-month-olds were in the experimental group, in which mothers received personal training in sensitive responding. The other half were in a control group, in which mothers did not receive this training (van den Boom, 1990, 1995). At 12 months of age, 68 percent of the infants in the first group were rated securely attached, as were only 28 percent of the control group infants. Other studies support the idea that such programs can increase parental sensitivity and, to some extent, infant attachment security (Bakermans-Kranenburg et al., 2003; Van Zeijl et al., 2006).

Whether children live with one parent or two, are cared for at home or in a daycare center, live in North America or the Kalahari Desert, their anxiety over separation from parents peaks at around 13 months, then gradually declines **(FIGURE 3.13** on the next page**)**. As the power of early attachment relaxes, we begin to move out into a wider range of situations, communicate with strangers more freely, and stay attached emotionally to loved ones despite distance.

Attachment Styles and Later Relationships As we mature, our secure base and safe haven shift—from parents to peers and partners (Cassidy & Shaver, 1999). But at all ages we are social creatures. We gain strength when someone offers, by words and actions, a safe haven: "I will be here. I am interested in you. Come what may, I will actively support you" (Crowell & Waters, 1994).

attachment an emotional tie with another person; shown in young children by their seeking closeness to the caregiver, and showing distress on separation.

FIGURE 3.13 • **Infants' distress over separation from parents** In an experiment, two groups of infants were left by their mothers in an unfamiliar room. In both groups, the percentage who cried when the mother left peaked at about 13 months (from Kagan, 1976). Whether the infant had experienced day care made little difference.

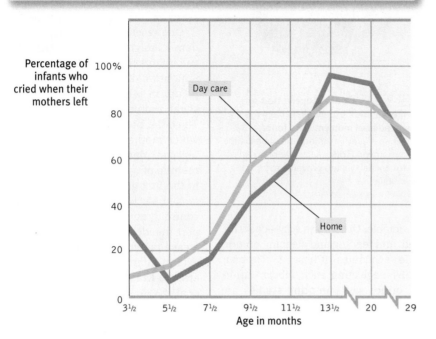

DO OUR EARLY ATTACHMENTS FORM THE ◄ FOUNDATION FOR ADULT RELATIONSHIPS, INCLUDING OUR COMFORT WITH INTIMACY? Many researchers now believe they do (Birnbaum et al., 2006; Fraley, 2002).

Developmental theorist Erik Erikson (1902–1994), working with his wife, Joan Erikson, believed that securely attached children approach life with a sense of **basic trust**—a sense that the world is predictable and reliable. This lifelong attitude of trust rather than fear, they said, flows from children's interactions with sensitive, loving caregivers. Our adult styles of romantic love likewise exhibit either secure, trusting attachment; insecure, anxious attachment; or the avoidance of attachment (Feeney & Noller, 1990; Shaver & Mikulincer, 2007). These adult attachment styles in turn affect relationships with one's own children, as avoidant people find parenting more stressful (Rholes et al., 2006).

Deprivation of Attachment If secure attachment nurtures social competence, what happens when circumstances prevent a child from forming attachments? In all of

psychology, there is no sadder research literature. Some of these babies were reared in institutions without a regular caregiver's stimulation and attention. Others were locked away at home under conditions of abuse or extreme neglect. Most were withdrawn, frightened, even speechless. Those abandoned in Romanian orphanages during the 1980s looked "frighteningly like Harlow's monkeys" (Carlson, 1995). The longer they were institutionalized, the more they bore lasting emotional scars (Chisholm, 1998; Nelson et al., 2009).

The Harlows' monkeys bore similar scars if reared in total isolation, without even an artificial mother. As adults, when placed with other monkeys their age, they either cowered in fright or lashed out in aggression. When they reached sexual maturity, most were incapable of mating. Females who did have babies were often neglectful, abusive, even murderous toward them.

In humans, too, the unloved sometimes become the unloving. Some 30 percent of those who have been abused

do later abuse their own children. This is four times the U.S. national rate of child abuse (Dumont et al., 2007; Widom, 1989a,b). Abuse victims are at greater risk for depression if they carry a gene variation that spurs stress hormone production (Bradley et al., 2008). As we will see again and again, behavior and emotion arise from a particular environment interacting with particular genes.

Extreme childhood trauma can leave footprints on the brain. Normally placid golden hamsters that are repeatedly threatened and attacked while young grow up to be cowards when caged with same-sized hamsters, or bullies when caged with weaker ones (Ferris, 1996). Young children who are terrorized through physical abuse or wartime atrocities (being beaten, witnessing torture, and living in constant fear) often suffer other lasting wounds. Many have reported nightmares, depression, and an adolescence troubled by substance abuse, binge eating, or aggression (Kendall-Tackett et al., 1993, 2004; Polusny & Follette, 1995; Trickett & McBride-Chang, 1995). So too with childhood sexual abuse. Especially if severe and prolonged, it places children at increased risk for health problems, psychological disorders, substance abuse, and criminality (Freyd et al., 2005; Tyler, 2002).

Still, many children successfully survive abuse. It's true that most abusive parents—and many condemned murderers—were indeed abused. It is also true that most children growing up in harsh conditions don't become violent criminals or abusive parents. They show great *resilience*—they bounce back and somehow go on to lead a better life.

Parenting Styles

10 What are three primary parenting styles, and what outcomes are associated with them?

Child-rearing practices vary. Some parents are strict, some are lax. Some show little affection, some liberally hug and kiss. DO PARENTING-STYLE DIFFERENCES ◄ AFFECT CHILDREN?

Diverse Yet Alike

Cultures Vary

Parents everywhere care about their children, but raise and protect them differently depending on the surrounding culture. Parents raising children in New York City keep them close. In Scotland's Orkney Islands' town of Stromness, social trust has enabled parents to park their toddlers outside shops.

Reuters/Phil Noble

Copyright Steve Reehl

The most heavily researched aspect of parenting has been how, and to what extent, parents seek to control their children. Investigators have identified three parenting styles:

1. *Authoritarian* parents impose rules and expect obedience: "Don't interrupt." "Keep your room clean." "Don't stay out late or you'll be grounded." "Why? Because I said so."

2. *Permissive* parents submit to their children's desires, make few demands, and use little punishment.

3. *Authoritative* parents are both demanding and responsive. They exert control not only by setting rules and enforcing them but also by explaining the reasons. And, especially with older children, they encourage open discussion and allow exceptions when making the rules.

Too hard, too soft, and just right, these styles have been called. Studies reveal that children with the highest self-esteem, self-reliance, and social competence usually have warm, concerned, *authoritative* parents (Baumrind, 1996; Buri et al., 1988; Coopersmith, 1967). Those with authoritarian parents tend to have less social skill and self-esteem, and those with permissive parents tend to be more aggressive and immature.

A word of caution: *Correlation is not causation.* The association between certain parenting styles (being firm but open) and certain childhood outcomes (social competence) is correlational. Perhaps you can imagine other possible explanations for this parenting-competence link.

It's also important to remember that parenting doesn't happen in a vacuum. One of the forces that influences parenting styles is culture.

Culture and Child-Rearing *Culture,* as we noted in Chapter 1, is the set of behaviors, attitudes, values, and traditions shared by a group of people and transmitted from one generation to the next (Brislin, 1988). In Chapter 4, we'll explore the effects of culture on gender. In later chapters we'll consider the influence of culture on psychological disorders and social interactions. For now, let's look at the way that child-rearing practices reflect cultural values.

Cultural values vary from place to place and, even in the same place, from one time to another. Do you prefer children who are independent, or children who comply with what others think? The Westernized culture of the United States today favors independence. "You are responsible for yourself," Western families and schools tell their children. "Follow your conscience. Be true to yourself. Discover your

gifts. Think through your personal needs." But a half-century and more ago, Western cultural values placed greater priority on obedience, respect, and sensitivity to others (Alwin, 1990; Remley, 1988). "Be true to your traditions," parents then taught their children. "Be loyal to your heritage and country. Show respect toward your parents and other superiors." Cultures can change.

Many Asians and Africans live in cultures that value emotional closeness. Rather than being given their own bedrooms and entrusted to day care, infants and toddlers may sleep with their mothers and spend their days close to a family member (Morelli et al., 1992; Whiting & Edwards, 1988). These cultures encourage a strong sense of *family self*—a feeling that what shames the child shames the family, and what brings honor to the family, brings honor to the self.

Children across place and time have thrived under various child-rearing systems. Upper-class British parents traditionally handed off routine caregiving to nannies, then sent their children off to

basic trust according to Erik Erikson, a sense that the world is predictable and trustworthy; said to be formed during infancy by appropriate experiences with responsive caregivers.

boarding school at about age 10. These children generally grew up to be pillars of British society. Sending children away would be shocking to an African Gusii family. Their babies nurse freely but spend most of the day on their mother's back, with lots of body contact but little face-to-face and language interaction. When the mother becomes pregnant, the toddler is weaned and handed over to another family member. Westerners may wonder about the negative effects of the lack of verbal interaction, but then the African Gusii would in turn wonder about Western mothers pushing their babies around in strollers and leaving them in playpens and car seats (Small, 1997). Such diversity in child-rearing cautions us against presuming that our way is the only way to rear children successfully.

Thinking About Nature and Nurture

The unique gene combination created when our mother's egg engulfed our father's sperm helped form us, as individuals. Genes predispose both our shared humanity and our individual differences.

But it also is true that our experiences form us. In the womb, in our families, and in our peer social relationships, we learn ways of thinking and acting. Even differences initiated by our nature may be amplified by our nurture. We are not formed by either nature or nurture, but by the interaction between them. Biological, psychological, and social-cultural forces interact (**FIGURE 3.14**).

Mindful of how others differ from us, however, we often fail to notice the similarities stemming from our shared biology. Regardless of our culture, we humans share the same life cycle. We speak to our infants in similar ways and respond similarly to their coos and cries (Bornstein et al., 1992a,b). All over the world, the children of warm and supportive parents feel better about themselves and are less hostile than are the children of punishing and rejecting parents (Rohner, 1986; Scott et al., 1991). Although Hispanic, Asian, Black, and White Americans differ in

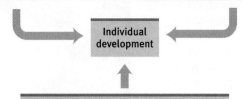

FIGURE 3.14 • **The biopsychosocial approach to development**

Biological influences:
• Shared human genome
• Individual genetic variations
• Prenatal environment

Psychological influences:
• Gene-environment interaction
• Neurological effect of early experiences
• Responses evoked by our own traits
• Beliefs, feelings, and expectations

Individual development

Social-cultural influences:
• Parental influences
• Peer influences
• Cultural emphasis on group or individual
• Chance events
• Other social influences

school achievement and delinquency, the differences are "no more than skin deep." To the extent that family structure, peer influences, and parental education predict behavior in one of these ethnic groups, they do so for the others as well. Compared with the person-to-person differences within groups, the differences between groups are small.

PRACTICE TEST

THE BASICS

6. The orderly biological growth process called maturation explains why
   a. children need training to learn bowel and bladder control.
   b. most children begin walking by about 12 to 15 months.
   c. enriching experiences may affect brain tissue.
   d. boys walk before they crawl.

7. Researchers raised some rats in an enriched environment and others in a deprived environment with no objects or activities to stimulate them. At the end of the experiment,
   a. the brains of the rats living in the enriched environment developed a heavier, denser cortex.
   b. the brains of the deprived rats developed a heavier, denser cortex.
   c. the brains of the two groups of rats showed no differences.
   d. the rats living in the deprived environment experienced a critical period.

8. As an infant's muscles and nervous system mature, more complicated skills emerge. Which of the following is true of motor-skill development?
   a. It is determined ONLY by genetic factors.
   b. The sequence is universal.
   c. The timing is universal.
   d. Environment determines maturation of muscles and nerves.

9. During Piaget's preoperational stage (from about age 2 to 6 or 7), the young child's thinking is
   a. abstract.
   b. negative.
   c. conservative.
   d. egocentric.

10. The principle of conservation explains why a pint of milk remains a pint, whether we pour it into a tall, thin pitcher or a short, wide one. Children gain the mental ability to understand conservation during the
    a. sensorimotor stage.
    b. preoperational stage.
    c. concrete operational stage.
    d. formal operational stage.

11. Piaget's theory of cognitive development has enriched our understanding of how children think. However, many researchers believe that
    a. development is more continuous than Piaget realized.
    b. children do not progress as rapidly as Piaget predicted.
    c. few children ever reach the concrete operational stage.
    d. there is no way of testing much of Piaget's theoretical work.

12. After about 8 months of age, infants show distress when faced with a new baby-sitter. Their response is an example of
    a. conservation.
    b. stranger anxiety.
    c. abstract thinking.
    d. maturation.

13. In a series of experiments, the Harlows found that monkeys raised with artificial mothers tended, when afraid, to cling to
    a. the wire mother who held the feeding bottle.
    b. the cloth mother who offered comfortable contact.
    c. only their real, live mother.
    d. other infant monkeys.

14. Parents who use the _____ parenting style tend to have children with high self-esteem, self-reliance, and social competence.
    a. authoritative
    b. authoritarian
    c. permissive
    d. independent

THE BIG PICTURE

3B. Use Piaget's first three stages of cognitive development to explain why young children are not just miniature adults in the way they think.

3C. How is our development affected by both nature and nurture?

IN YOUR EVERYDAY LIFE

▪ What kinds of mistakes do you think parents of the past made? What mistakes do you think contemporary parents might be making?

▪ What are the skills you practiced the most as a child? Which have you continued to use? How do you think this affected your brain development?

▪ Imagine your friend says, "Personality (or intelligence) is in the genes." How would you respond?

Answers: 6. b, 7. a, 8. b, 9. d, 10. c, 11. a, 12. b, 13. b, 14. a. Answers to The Big Picture questions can be found in Appendix B at the end of the book.

Adolescence

During **adolescence** we morph from child to adult. Adolescence starts with a physical event—bodily changes that mark the beginning of sexual maturity. It ends with a social event—independent adult status, which means that in cultures where teens are self-supporting, adolescence hardly exists.

Physical Development

11 | **What defines adolescence, and what major physical changes occur during adolescence?**

Adolescence begins with **puberty,** the time when we are maturing sexually. Puberty follows a surge of hormones, which may intensify moods. This outpouring of hormones triggers two years of rapid physical development, usually beginning at about age 11 in girls and at about age 13 in boys.

A girl's puberty starts with breast development, often beginning by age 10 (Brody, 1999). The first menstrual period, called **menarche** (meh-NAR-key), usually occurs within a year of age 12. Girls who have been prepared for menarche usually experience it as a positive event. As adults, most women remember having had mixed feelings—pride, excitement, embarrassment, and a tinge of fear—in response to this important life transition (Greif & Ulman, 1982; Woods et al., 1983).

Most men similarly recall their first ejaculation (*spermarche*). This landmark event usually occurs as a nighttime event at about age 14 (Fuller & Downs, 1990).

adolescence the transition period from childhood to adulthood, extending from puberty to independence.

puberty the period of sexual maturation, during which a person becomes capable of reproducing.

menarche [meh-NAR-key] the first menstrual period.

Height differences: Throughout childhood, boys and girls are similar in height. At puberty, girls surge ahead briefly, but then boys overtake them at about age 14. (Data from Tanner, 1978.)

David Young-Wolff/Photo Edit

Just as in the earlier life stages, we all go through the same *sequence* of changes in puberty. All girls, for example, develop breast buds and visible pubic hair before they have their first period. The timing of such changes is less predictable. Some girls start their growth spurt at 9, others as late as age 16. Maturing earlier or later than your peers has little effect on adult physical features, such as your final height.

Adolescents' brains are a work in progress. Frontal lobe maturation lags behind the emotional limbic system's development. When puberty's hormonal surge combines with limbic system development and unfinished frontal lobes, it's no wonder teens feel stressed. Impulsiveness, risky behaviors, and emotional storms—slamming doors and turning up the music—happen. Not yet fully equipped for making long-term plans and curbing impulses, young teens sometimes give in to the lure of smoking, which adult smokers could tell them they will later regret. Teens typically know the risks, but often weigh the benefits of risky behaviors more heavily (Reyna & Farley, 2006; Steinberg, 2007). As teens become young adults, their developing frontal lobes can better communicate with other brain regions. That brings improved judgment, impulse control, and the ability to plan for the long term.

> "If a gun is put in the control of the prefrontal cortex of a hurt and vengeful 15-year-old, and it is pointed at a human target, it will very likely go off."
>
> National Institutes of Health brain scientist Daniel R. Weinberger, "A Brain Too Young for Good Judgment," 2001

"Young man, go to your room and stay there until your cerebral cortex matures."

So, when Junior drives recklessly and academically self-destructs, should his parents reassure themselves that "he can't help it; his frontal cortex isn't yet fully grown"? They can at least take hope: The brain with which Junior begins his teens differs from the brain with which he will end his teens. In fact, his frontal lobes will continue maturing until about age 25 (Beckman, 2004). In 2004, the American Psychological Association joined seven other medical and mental health associations in filing briefs with the U.S. Supreme Court. These petitions argued against the death penalty for 16- and 17-year-olds. They presented evidence for the teen brain's immaturity "in areas that bear upon adolescent decision-making." Teens are "less guilty by reason of adolescence," suggested psychologist Laurence Steinberg and law professor Elizabeth Scott (2003; Steinberg et al., 2009). In 2005, by a 5-to-4 margin, the Court agreed, declaring juvenile death penalties unconstitutional.

Cognitive Development

12 How did Piaget and Kohlberg describe cognitive and moral development during adolescence?

During the early teen years, reasoning is often self-focused. Adolescents may think their private experiences are unique, something parents just couldn't understand: "But, Mom, you don't really know how it feels to be in love" (Elkind, 1978). Capable of thinking about their own thinking and about other people's thinking, they also begin imagining what other people are thinking about them. (They might worry less if they understood their peers' similar self-absorption.) Gradually, though, most begin to reason more abstractly.

Developing Reasoning Power

When adolescents achieve the intellectual summit Jean Piaget called *formal operations,* they apply their new abstract-thinking tools to the world around them. They may debate human nature, good and evil, truth and justice. Having left behind the concrete images of early childhood, they may search for a deeper meaning of life (Elkind, 1970; Worthington, 1989). They can now reason logically. And they can spot hypocrisy and detect inconsistencies in others' reasoning (Peterson et al., 1986). (Can you remember having a heated debate with your parents? Did you perhaps even vow silently never to lose sight of your own ideals?)

Developing Morality

A crucial task of childhood and adolescence is developing the psychological muscles for controlling impulses. Much of our morality is rooted in unconscious, gut-level reactions, such as disgust or liking. Our conscious mind then tries to make sense of these feelings (Haidt, 2006). Yet to be a moral person is to *think* morally (sorting right from wrong) and to *act* accordingly.

Moral Thinking Piaget (1932) believed that children's moral judgments build on their cognitive development. Agreeing with Piaget, Lawrence Kohlberg (1981, 1984) sought to describe the development of *moral reasoning,* the thinking that occurs as we consider right and wrong. Kohlberg posed moral dilemmas—for example, should a man steal medicine to save his wife's life? He then asked children, adolescents, and adults whether the action was right or wrong. He believed their answers would give evidence of stages of moral thinking. His findings led him to propose three basic levels of moral thinking, preconventional, conventional, and postconventional (**TABLE 3.2**). Kohlberg claimed these levels form a moral ladder. As with all stage theories, the sequence never changes. We begin on the bottom rung and rise to varying heights.

What does cross-cultural research tell us about Kohlberg's theory? In various cultures, children do move from Kohlberg's preconventional level into his conventional level (Edwards, 1981, 1982; Snarey, 1985, 1987). The postconventional level appears more culturally limited. This stage appears mostly among people who

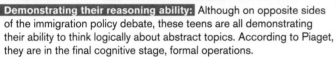

Demonstrating their reasoning ability: Although on opposite sides of the immigration policy debate, these teens are all demonstrating their ability to think logically about abstract topics. According to Piaget, they are in the final cognitive stage, formal operations.

prize *individualism*—giving priority to one's own goals rather than to group goals (Eckensberger, 1994; Miller & Bersoff, 1995). These people are found mostly in the European and North American educated middle class. Kohlberg's theory, say its critics, is biased against *collectivist* (group-centered) societies, such as China and India.

Moral Action Today's character-education programs focus both on moral reasoning and on *doing* the right thing. They teach children *empathy* for others' feelings. They also teach the self-discipline needed to restrain one's own impulses— to delay small pleasures now to earn bigger rewards later. Those who have learned to *delay gratification* have become more socially responsible, academically successful, and productive (Funder & Block, 1989; Mischel et al., 1988, 1989). In service-learning programs, teens tutor, clean up their neighborhoods, and assist the elderly. Everyone seems to benefit. The teens' sense of competence and their desire to serve increase, while their school absenteeism and drop-out rates decrease (Andersen, 1998; Piliavin, 2003). Moral action feeds moral attitudes.

Moral reasoning: Survivors of the 2010 Haiti earthquake were faced with a moral dilemma: Should they take household necessities? Their reasoning likely reflected different levels of moral thinking, even if they behaved similarly.

TABLE 3.2	Kohlberg's Levels of Moral Thinking	
Level (approximate age)	**Focus**	**Example**
Preconventional morality (before age 9)	Self-interest; obey rules to avoid punishment or gain concrete rewards.	"If you save your wife, you'll be a hero."
Conventional morality (early adolescence)	Uphold laws and rules to gain social approval or maintain social order.	"If you steal the drug, everyone will think you're a criminal."
Postconventional morality (adolescence and beyond)	Actions reflect belief in basic rights and self-defined ethical principles.	"People have a right to live."

Social Development

13 According to Erikson, what stages—and accompanying tasks and challenges— mark our psychosocial development?

Erik Erikson (1963) believed that we must resolve a specific crisis at each stage of life. Thus, each stage has its own *psychosocial* task. Young children wrestle with issues of *trust*, then *autonomy* (independence), then *initiative*. School-age children strive for *industry*—feeling able and productive. The adolescent's task is

Identity vs. role confusion

Paul Burns/Getty Images

Stage (approximate age)	Issues	Description of Task
Infancy (to 1 year)	If needs are dependably met, infants develop a sense of basic trust.	Trust vs. mistrust
Toddlers (1 to 3 years)	Toddlers learn to exercise their will and do things for themselves, or they doubt their abilities.	Autonomy vs. shame and doubt
Preschool (4 to 6 years)	Preschoolers learn to initiate tasks and carry out plans, or they feel guilty about efforts to be independent.	Initiative vs. guilt
Elementary school (7 to about 12 years)	Children learn the pleasure of applying themselves to tasks, or they feel inferior.	Industry vs. inferiority
Adolescence (12 to about 18 years)	Teenagers work at refining a sense of self by testing roles and then blending them into a single identity, or they become confused about who they are.	Identity vs. role confusion
Young adulthood (20s to early 40s)	Young adults struggle to form close relationships and to gain the capacity for intimate love, or they feel socially isolated.	Intimacy vs. isolation
Middle adulthood (40s to 60s)	In middle age, people discover a sense of contributing to the world, usually through family and work, or they may feel a lack of purpose.	Generativity vs. stagnation
Late adulthood (late 60s and up)	When reflecting on his or her life, the older adult may feel a sense of satisfaction or failure.	Integrity vs. despair

TABLE 3.3 Erikson's Stages of Psychosocial Development

Blend Images/Punchstock

Industry vs. inferiority

to blend past, present, and future possibilities into a clearer sense of self. Adolescents wonder, "Who am I as an individual? What do I want to do with my life? What values should I live by? What do I believe in?" Such questions, said Erikson, are part of the adolescent's *search for identity* **(TABLE 3.3)**.

Forming an Identity

To refine their sense of identity, adolescents in Western cultures usually try out different "selves" in different situations. They may act out one self at home, another with friends, and still another at school or online. But sometimes these separate worlds overlap. DO YOU REMEM-◄ BER HAVING YOUR FRIEND WORLD AND FAMILY WORLD BUMP INTO EACH OTHER, AND WONDERING, "WHICH SELF SHOULD I BE? WHICH IS THE REAL ME?" In time, however, most of us make peace with our

various selves, blending them into a stable and comfortable sense of who we are—an **identity.**

For both adolescents and adults, our group identities are often formed by how we differ from those around us. When living in Britain, I become conscious of my Americanness. When spending time with my daughter in Africa, I become conscious of my minority (White) race. When surrounded by women, I am mindful of my gender identity. For international students, for those of a minority ethnic group, for people with a disability, for those on a team, a **social identity** often forms around their distinctiveness.

But not always. Erikson noticed that some adolescents bypass this period. Some forge their identity early, simply by taking on their parents' values and expectations. Others may adopt the identity of a partic-

ular peer group—jocks, preps, geeks, goths.

Cultural values may influence teens' search for an identity. Traditional, less individualistic cultures tend to inform adolescents about who they are, rather than encouraging them to decide on their own. In individualistic Western cultures, young people may continue to try out possible roles well into their late teen years, when many people begin attending college or working full time. During

"How was my day? How was my day? Must you micromanage my life?"

Diverse Yet Alike

Who Shall I Be Today?

By varying the way they look, adolescents try out different "selves." Although we eventually form a consistent and stable sense of identity, the self we present may change with the situation.

the early to mid-teen years, self-esteem falls and, for girls, depression scores often increase. Then, during the late teens and twenties, self-image bounces back (Robins et al., 2002; Twenge & Campbell, 2001; Twenge & Nolen-Hoeksema, 2002).

Erikson believed that the adolescent identity stage is followed in young adulthood by a developing capacity for **intimacy,** the ability to form emotionally close relationships. With a clear and comfortable sense of who you are, said Erikson, you are ready for close relationships. Such relationships are, for most of us, a source of great pleasure.

Parent and Peer Relationships

14 To what extent are adolescent lives shaped by parental and peer influences?

As adolescents in Western cultures seek to form their own identities, they begin to pull away from their parents (Shanahan et al., 2007). The preschooler who can't be close enough to her mother, who loves to touch and cling to her, becomes the 14-year-old who wouldn't be caught dead holding hands with Mom. The transition occurs gradually, but this period is typically a time of diminishing parental influence and growing peer influence. As ancient Greek philosopher Aristotle long ago recognized, we humans are "the social animal." At all ages, but especially during childhood and the teen years, we seek to fit in with our groups and are influenced by them (Harris, 1998, 2000).

- Children who hear English spoken with one accent at home and another in the neighborhood and at school will invariably adopt the accent of the peers, not the parents. Accents reflect culture, "and children get their culture from their peers," noted Judith Harris (2007).

- Teens who start smoking typically have friends who model smoking, suggest its pleasures, and offer cigarettes (Rose et al., 1999, 2003). Part of this peer similarity may result from a *selection effect,* as kids seek out peers with similar attitudes and interests. Those who smoke (or don't) may select as friends those who also smoke (or don't).

- When researchers used a beeper to sample the daily experiences of American teens, they found them unhappiest when alone and happiest when with friends (Csikszentmihalyi & Hunter, 2003).

By adolescence, arguments with parents occur more often, usually over ordinary things—household chores, bedtime, homework (Tesser et al., 1989). For a minority of families, these arguments lead to real splits and great stress (Steinberg & Morris, 2001). But most disagreements are at the level of harmless bickering. And most adolescents—6000 of them in 10 countries, from Australia to Bangladesh to Turkey—say they like their parents (Offer et al., 1988). "We usually get along but . . . ," adolescents often report (Galambos, 1992; Steinberg, 1987).

Positive parent-teen relations and positive peer relations often go hand-in-hand. High school girls who have the most affectionate relationships with their mothers tend also to enjoy the most intimate friendships with girlfriends (Gold & Yanof, 1985). And teens who feel close to their parents tend to be healthy and happy and to do well in school (Resnick et al., 1997). But pause now to think critically. Look what happens if you state this association another way: Teens in trouble are more likely to have tense relationships with parents and other adults. Remember: *Correlations don't prove cause and effect.*

"Men resemble the times more than they resemble their fathers."

Ancient Arab proverb

---

identity our sense of self; according to Erikson, the adolescent's task is to solidify a sense of self by testing and integrating various roles.

social identity the "we" aspect of our self-concept; the part of our answer to "Who am I?" that comes from our group memberships.

intimacy in Erikson's theory, the ability to form close, loving relationships; a primary developmental task in early adulthood.

How Much Credit (or Blame) Do Parents Deserve?

15 **Does parenting matter?**

Parents usually feel enormous satisfaction in their children's successes, and feel guilt or shame over their failures. They beam over the child who wins an award. They wonder where they went wrong with the child repeatedly called into the principal's office for sassing the teacher. Freudian psychiatry and psychology have been among the sources of such ideas, by blaming problems from asthma to schizophrenia on "bad mothering." Society reinforces such parent-blaming. Believing that parents shape their offspring as a potter molds clay, people readily praise parents for their children's virtues and blame them for their children's vices.

But do parents really damage these future adults by being (take your pick from the toxic-parent lists) overbearing—or uninvolved? Pushy—or ineffectual? Overprotective—or distant? Are children really so easily wounded? If so, should we then blame our parents for our failings, and ourselves for our children's failings? Or does all the talk of wounding fragile children through parental mistakes trivialize the brutality of real abuse?

"So I blame you for everything—whose fault is that?"

Parents do matter. The power of parenting is clearest at the extremes: the abused who become abusive, the neglected who become neglectful, the loved but firmly handled children who become self-confident and socially competent. The power of the family environment also appears in the remarkable academic and vocational successes of children of people who fled from Vietnam and Cambodia—successes attributed to close-knit, supportive, even demanding families (Caplan et al., 1992).

But how much does parenting matter? As twin and adoption studies show, shared environmental influences—including the home influences siblings share—typically account for less than 10 percent of children's personality differences. In the words of Robert Plomin and Denise Daniels (1987), "Two children in the same family [are on average] as different from one another as are pairs of children selected randomly from the population." To developmental psychologist Sandra Scarr (1993), this meant that "parents should be given less credit for kids who turn out great and blamed less for kids who don't." Knowing that children are not easily sculpted by parental nurture, perhaps parents can relax a bit more and love their children for who they are.

Does this then mean that adoptive parenting is a fruitless venture? No. The genetic leash may limit the family environment's influence on personality, but parents do influence their children's attitudes, values, manners, faith, and politics (Brodzinsky & Schechter, 1990). A pair of adopted children or identical twins *will*, if reared together, have more similar religious beliefs, especially during adolescence (Kelley & De Graaf, 1997; Koenig et al., 2005; Rohan & Zanna, 1996).

Child neglect, abuse, and parental divorce are rare in adoptive homes, in part because adoptive parents are carefully screened. Despite a somewhat greater risk of psychological disorder, most adopted children thrive, especially when adopted as infants (Benson et al., 1994; Wierzbicki, 1993). Seven in eight report feeling strongly attached to one or both adoptive parents. As children of self-giving parents, they themselves grow up to be more self-giving than average (Sharma et al., 1998). Many score higher than their biological parents on intelligence tests, and most grow into happier and more stable adults. Regardless of personality differences between parents and their adoptees, children benefit from adoption. Parenting matters!

As we saw earlier, heredity does much of the heavy lifting in forming personality differences, and parent-peer influences do much of the rest. (For more on parent-peer influences, see Thinking Critically About: How Much Credit [or Blame] Do Parents Deserve?) Teens are herd animals. They talk, dress, and act more like their peers than their parents. In 2008, according to a Nielsen study, the average American 13- to 17-year-old sent or received more than 1700 text messages a month (Steinhauer & Holson, 2008). Many adolescents become absorbed by social networking, sometimes with a compulsive use that produces "Facebook fatigue." For better (support groups) and for worse (online predators and extremist groups), online communication prompts intimate self-disclosure (Subrahmanyam & Greenfield, 2008; Valkenburg & Peter, 2009).

For those who feel excluded, the pain is acute. "The social atmosphere in most high schools is poisonously clique-driven and exclusionary," observed social psychologist Elliot Aronson (2001). Most excluded teens "suffer in silence. . . . A small number act out in violent ways against their classmates." Those who withdraw are vulnerable to loneliness, low self-esteem, and depression (Steinberg & Morris, 2001). Peer approval matters.

Teens see their parents as having more influence in other areas—for example, in shaping their religious faith and in thinking about college and career choices

Nine times out of ten, it's all about peer pressure.

(*Emerging Trends,* 1997). A Gallup Youth Survey revealed that most share their parents' political views (Lyons, 2005).

Howard Gardner (1998) has concluded that parents and peers are complementary:

> Parents are more important when it comes to education, discipline, responsibility, orderliness, charitableness, and ways of interacting with authority figures. Peers are more important for learning cooperation, for finding the road to popularity, for inventing styles of interaction among people of the same age. Youngsters may find their peers more interesting, but they will look to their parents when contemplating their own futures. Moreover, parents [often] choose the neighborhoods and schools that supply the peers.

The investment in raising a child buys many years not only of joy and love but of worry and irritation. Yet for most people who become parents, a child is one's biological and social

legacy—one's personal investment in the human future. To paraphrase psychiatrist Carl Jung, we reach backward into our parents and forward into our children, and through their children into a future we will never see, but about which we must therefore care.

Emerging Adulthood

16 | **What are the characteristics of emerging adulthood?**

In the Western world, adolescence now roughly equals the teen years. At earlier times, and in other parts of the world today, this has not always been the case (Baumeister & Tice, 1986). Shortly after sexual maturity, such young people would assume adult responsibilities and status. The event might be celebrated with an elaborate initiation—a public *rite of passage.* The new adult would then work, marry, and have children.

In the Western world, when schooling became compulsory, independence was put on hold until after graduation. Educational goals rose, and so did the age of independence. Now, from Europe to Australia, adolescents are taking more time to finish college, leave the nest, and establish careers. In the United States, the average age at first marriage has increased more than 4 years since 1960 (to 28 for men, 26 for women).

Delayed independence has overlapped with an earlier onset of puberty. Earlier puberty seems to be related both to girls' increased body fat (which can support pregnancy and nursing) and to weakened parent-child bonds, including absent fathers (Ellis, 2004).

Together, later independence and earlier sexual maturity have stretched the once-brief interlude between child and adult (**FIGURE 3.15** on the next page). In prosperous communities, the time from 18 to the mid-twenties is an increasingly not-yet-settled phase of life, which some now call **emerging adulthood** (Arnett, 2006, 2007). No longer adolescents, these emerging adults,

> "I love u guys."
> Colorado school hostage Emily Keyes' final text message to her parents before being murdered, 2006.

having not yet assumed adult responsibilities and independence, feel "in between." After high school, those who enter the job market or go to college may be managing their own time and priorities more than ever before. Yet they may be doing so from their parents' home—unable to afford their own place and perhaps still emotionally dependent as well. Adulthood emerges, gradually. Thus some middle-aged adults describe themselves as a *sandwich generation,* caught between providing support to their aging parents on the one side and their emerging adult children or grandchildren on the other (Riley & Bowen, 2005).

Thinking About Continuity and Stages

Let's stop now and consider the second developmental issue introduced at the beginning of this chapter—*continuity and stages.* Do adults differ from infants as a giant redwood differs from its seedling—differences mostly created by constant, gradual growth? Or do we change in some ways like the caterpillar that becomes a butterfly—in distinct stages?

Generally speaking, researchers who emphasize experience and learning view development as a slow, ongoing process. Those who emphasize the influence of our biology tend to see development as a process of maturation, as we pass through a series of stages or steps, guided by instructions programmed into our genes. Progress through the various stages may be quick or slow, but we all pass through the stages in the same order. We crawl before we stand. We walk before we run.

---

emerging adulthood a period from about age 18 to the mid-twenties, when many in Western cultures are no longer adolescents but have not yet achieved full independence as adults.

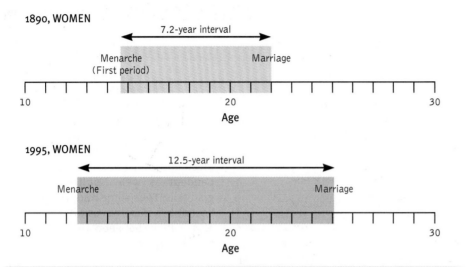

1890, WOMEN

7.2-year interval

Menarche
(First period)   Marriage

10   20   30
                          Age

1995, WOMEN

12.5-year interval

Menarche   Marriage

10   20   30
                          Age

FIGURE 3.15 ● **Transition to adulthood is being stretched from both ends** In the 1890s, the average time between a woman's first menstrual period and marriage, which typically marked a transition to adulthood, was about 7 years. Today, in industrialized countries it is about 12 years (Guttmacher, 1994, 2000). Although many adults are unmarried, later marriage combines with prolonged education and earlier menarche to help stretch out the transition to adulthood.

Are there clear-cut stages of psychological development, as there are physical stages such as walking before running? We have considered the stage theories of Jean Piaget on cognitive development, Lawrence Kohlberg on moral development, and Erik Erikson on psychosocial development (summarized in **FIGURE 3.16**). And we have seen their stage theories criticized. Young children have some abilities Piaget attributed to later stages. Kohlberg's work reflected a world-view found primarily in individualistic cultures, and he emphasized thinking over acting. And as you will see in the next section, adult life does not progress through a fixed, predictable series of steps. Chance events can influence us in ways we would never have predicted.

Although research casts doubt on the idea that life proceeds through neatly defined, age-linked stages, the concept of *stage* remains useful. The human brain does experience growth spurts during childhood and puberty that correspond roughly to Piaget's stages (Thatcher et al., 1987). And stage theories help us focus our attention on the forces and interests that affect us at different points in the life span. This close attention can help us understand how people of one age think and act differently when they arrive at a later age.

THE BASICS

15. Adolescence is marked by the onset of
    a. autonomy.
    b. puberty.
    c. frontal lobe maturation.
    d. parent-child conflict.

16. Puberty is the time of maturing sexually. Girls begin puberty at about the age of _____, boys at about the age of _____.

    a. 12; 14   c. 11; 13
    b. 14; 12   d. 13; 11

17. According to Piaget, the ability to think abstractly indicates
    a. concrete operational thought.
    b. egocentrism.
    c. formal operational thought.
    d. conservation.

18. According to Kohlberg, preconventional morality focuses on _____; conventional morality is more concerned with _____.

    a. upholding laws and social rules; self-interest

FIGURE 3.16 ● **Comparing the stage theories**

Lawrence Kohlberg

| Preconventional morality | Conventional morality | (Postconventional morality?) |

Erik Erikson

| Basic trust | Autonomy | Initiative | Industry | Identity | Intimacy | Genera-tivity | Integrity |

Jean Piaget

| Sensorimotor | Preoperational | Concrete operational | Formal operational |

Birth 1 2 3 4 5 6 7 8 9 10 11 12 13 14   Death

b. self-interest; basic ethical principles

c. upholding laws and social rules; basic ethical principles

d. self-interest; upholding laws and social rules

19. Erikson contended that each stage of life has its own special psychosocial task or challenge. The primary task during adolescence is to

a. attain formal operations.

b. search for an identity.

c. develop a sense of intimacy with another person.

d. live independent of parents.

20. Studies comparing personalities of parents and their adopted children show that children's personality differences are mainly due to

a. adoptive parenting practices.

b. heredity.

c. interactions with adopted siblings.

d. interactions with schoolmates.

21. Some Western developmental psychologists refer to the time period when a person has not yet reached the full independence of adulthood as

a. emerging adulthood.

b. adolescence.

c. formal operations.

d. young adulthood.

THE BIG PICTURE

3D. In Western cultures, how has the transition from childhood to adulthood changed in the last century?

3E. How is our development affected by both continuity and stages?

IN YOUR EVERYDAY LIFE

■ What are the most positive or most negative things you remember about your own adolescence? Who do you credit or blame more—your parents or your peers?

■ Think about a difficult decision you had to make as a teenager. What did you do? Would you do things differently now?

■ What do you think makes a person an adult? Do you feel like an adult? Why or why not?

Answers to The Big Picture questions can be found in Appendix B at the end of the book.

Answers: 15. b, 16. c, 17. c, 18. d, 19. b, 20. b, 21. a.

Adulthood

At one time, psychologists viewed the center-of-life years between adolescence and old age as one long plateau. No longer. Those who follow the unfolding of people's adult lives now believe our development continues across the life span.

Earlier in this chapter, we considered many qualities and events we all share in life's early years. Making such statements about the adult years is much more difficult. If we know that James is a 1-year-old and Jamal is a 10-year-old, we can say a great deal about each child. Not so with adults who differ by a decade. The 20-year-old may be a parent who supports a child or a child who gets an allowance. The new mother may be 25 or 45. The boss may be 30 or 60.

Nevertheless, our life courses are in some ways similar. Physically, cognitively, and especially socially, we are at age 60 different from our 25-year-old selves. In the discussion that follows, we recognize

> "I am still learning."
> Michelangelo, 1560, at age 85

these differences and use three terms: *early adulthood* (roughly twenties and thirties), *middle adulthood* (to age 65), and *late adulthood* (the years after 65). Remember, though, that within each of these stages, people vary widely in physical, psychological, and social development.

Physical Development

17 How do our bodies and sensory abilities change from early to late adulthood?

Young Adulthood

Our physical abilities—our muscular strength, reaction time, sensory keenness, and cardiac output—all crest by our mid-twenties. Like the declining daylight at the end of summer, the pace of our physical decline is a slow creep. Athletes are often the first to notice. World-class sprinters and swimmers peak by their early twenties. Women, who mature earlier than men, also peak earlier. But few of us notice. Unless our daily lives require us to be in top physical condition, we hardly perceive the early signs of decline.

TOO MUCH COFFEE MAN BY SHANNON WHEELER

LIFE:

PLAY, SCHOOL, PLAY, SCHOOL, PLAY, SCHOOL, PLAY, SCHOOL, FIRST LOVE, BRIEF HAPPINESS, BREAK UP, REGRET, SCHOOL, SCHOOL, SCHOOL, SCHOOL, SCHOOL, SCHOOL, SCHOOL, SCHOOL, SCHOOL, SCHOOL, SCHOOL, SCHOOL, SCHOOL, SCHOOL, SCHOOL, PLAY, WORK, PLAY, WORK, PLAY, WORK, PLAY, WORK, IDEALISM, EFFORT, REJECTION, FAILURE, WORK, EFFORT, FAILURE, COMPROMISE, WORK, WORK, WORK, WORK, WORK, WORK, PLAY, COMMITMENT, WORK, WORK, WORK, WORK, WORK, WORK, PLAY, WORK, WORK, WORK, WORK, WORK, WORK, WORK, WORK, PLAY, WORK, WORK, WORK, WORK, WORK, WORK, WORK, WORK, PLAY, WORK, WORK, WORK, WORK, WORK, WORK, WORK, WORK, PLAY, WORK, WORK, WORK, WORK, WORK, WORK, WORK, WORK, PLAY, WORK, WORK, WORK, WORK, WORK, WORK, WORK, WORK, PLAY, WORK, WORK, WORK, WORK, WORK, WORK, WORK, WORK, PLAY, WORK, WORK, WORK, WORK, WORK, WORK, WORK, WORK, PLAY, WORK, WORK, WORK, WORK, WORK, WORK, WORK, WORK, PLAY, WORK, WORK, WORK, WORK, WORK, WORK, WORK, WORK, PLAY, WORK, WORK, WORK, WORK, WORK, WORK, WORK, WORK, PLAY, WORK, WORK, WORK, WORK, WORK, WORK, WORK, WORK, PLAY, WORK, WORK, WORK, WORK, WORK, WORK, WORK, WORK, PLAY, WORK, WORK, WORK, WORK, WORK, WORK, WORK, WORK, PLAY, RETIRE, PLAY, DIE.

©Shannon Wheeler

Stages of the life cycle

Adult abilities vary widely: Ninety-three-year-olds: Don't try this. In 2008, George Blair maintained his place in the record books as the world's oldest barefoot water skier.

Rick Doyle/Corbis

Middle Adulthood

During early and middle adulthood, physical vigor has less to do with age than with a person's health and exercise habits. Many of today's sedentary 25-year-olds find themselves huffing and puffing up two flights of stairs. When they make it to the top and glance out the window, they may see their physically fit 50-year-old neighbor jog by on a daily 4-mile run.

Physical decline is gradual, but as most athletes know, the pace of that decline gradually picks up (**FIGURE 3.17**). As a 67-year-old whose daily exercise is usually playing basketball, I now play only a half-court game. The good news is that even diminished vigor is enough for normal activities.

Aging also brings a gradual decline in fertility. For a 35- to 39-year-old woman, the chances of getting pregnant after a single act of intercourse are only half those of a woman 19 to 26 (Dunson et al., 2002). A woman's foremost biological sign of aging is the onset of **menopause,** the end of the menstrual cycle, usually within a few years of age 50. Does she see this as a sign that she is losing her femininity and growing old? Or does she view it as liberation from menstrual periods and fears of pregnancy? The answer depends on her expectations and attitudes.

"Happy fortieth. I'll take the muscle tone in your upper arms, the girlish timbre of your voice, your amazing tolerance for caffeine, and your ability to digest french fries. The rest of you can stay."

There is no male menopause—no end of fertility or sharp drop in sex hormones. Men do experience a more gradual decline in sperm count, testosterone level, and speed of erection and ejaculation.

> "For some reason, possibly to save ink, the restaurants had started printing their menus in letters the height of bacteria."
>
> Dave Barry, *Dave Barry Turns Fifty,* 1998

Late Adulthood

Is old age "more to be feared than death" (Juvenal, *Satires*)? Or is life "most delightful when it is on the downward slope" (Seneca, *Epistulae ad Lucilium*)? What is it like to grow old?

Although physical decline begins in early adulthood, we are not usually acutely aware of it until later life. Vision changes. We have trouble seeing fine details, and our eyes take longer to adapt to changes in light levels. As the eye's pupil shrinks and its lens grows cloudy, less light reaches the *retina*—the light-sensitive inner portion of the eye. In fact, a 65-year-old retina receives only about one-third as much light as its 20-year-old counterpart (Kline & Schieber, 1985). Thus, to see as well as a 20-year-old when reading or driving, a 65-year-old needs three times as much light—a reason for buying cars with untinted windshields. This also explains why older people sometimes ask younger people, "Don't you need better light for reading?"

Muscle strength, reaction time, and stamina also diminish noticeably. The fine-tuned senses of smell, hearing, and distance perception that we took for granted in our twenties and thirties are now distant memories (**FIGURE 3.18**). In later life, the stairs get steeper, the print gets smaller, and people seem to mumble more.

Clever manufacturers have found a new market in this age-related difference in hearing. Some stores have reduced teen loitering by installing a device that emits a shrill, high-pitched

FIGURE 3.17 • **Gradually accelerating decline** An analysis of aging and batting averages of all twentieth-century major league baseball players revealed a gradual but accelerating decline in players' later years (Schall & Smith, 2000). The career performance record of the great Willie Mays followed this curve.

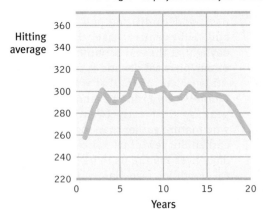

Baseball averages—18 players with 20-year careers

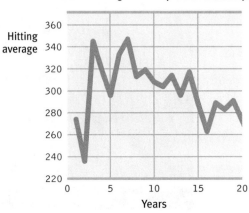

Baseball averages over 20 years for Willie Mays

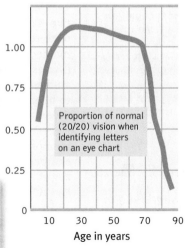

Proportion of normal (20/20) vision when identifying letters on an eye chart

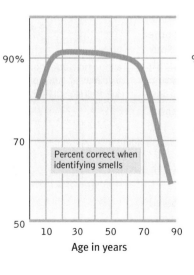

Percent correct when identifying smells

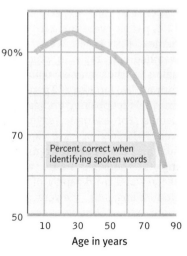

Percent correct when identifying spoken words

FIGURE 3.18 ● **The aging senses** Sight, smell, and hearing all are less acute among those over age 70. (From Doty et al., 1984.)

sound that almost no one over 30 can hear (Barr, 2008; Lyall, 2005). Other teens have learned they can use that pitch to their advantage by downloading cell-phone ring tones that their middle-aged instructors cannot hear (Vitello, 2006).

In late adulthood, there is both bad and good news about health. The bad news: The body's disease-fighting immune system weakens, putting older adults at higher risk for life-threatening ailments, such as cancer and pneumonia. The good news: Thanks partly to a lifetime's collection of antibodies, those over 65 suffer fewer short-term ailments, such as common flu and cold viruses. They are, for example, half as likely as 20-year-olds and one-fifth as likely as preschoolers to suffer upper respiratory flu each year (National Center for Health Statistics, 1990). No wonder older workers have lower absenteeism rates (Rhodes, 1983).

> "The things that stop you having sex with age are exactly the same as those that stop you riding a bicycle (bad health, thinking it looks silly, no bicycle)."
> Alex Comfort, *The Joy of Sex,* 2002

For both men and women, sexual activity also remains satisfying after middle age. In one survey of people over 60, 39 percent said they were satisfied with the amount of sex they were having, and another 39 percent said they wished for sex more frequently (Leary, 1998). When does sexual desire diminish? In another sexuality survey, age 75 was the point when most women and nearly half the

men reported little sexual desire (DeLamater & Sill, 2005).

Aging levies another tax as well. The small, gradual net loss of brain cells begins in young adulthood. By age 80, the brain has lost about 5 percent of its former weight. This loss is a bit slower in women, who worldwide live an average 4 years longer than men (CIA, 2008). But in both women and men, some of the brain regions that shrink during aging are the areas important to memory (Schacter, 1996). The frontal lobes, which help restrain impulsivity, also shrink, which helps explain older people's occasional blunt comments and questions ("Have you put on weight?") (Von Hippel, 2007).

> If you are within five years of 20, what experiences from your last year will you likely never forget? (When you are 70, this is the time of your life you may best remember.)

Cognitive Development
Aging and Memory

18 **In what ways do memory and intelligence change as we age?**

As we age, we remember some things well. Looking back in later life, people asked to recall the one or two most important events over the last half-century tend to

name events from their teens or twenties (Conway et al., 2005; Rubin et al., 1998). Whatever one experienced around this time of life—World War II, the civil rights movement, the Vietnam war, or the Iraq war—becomes pivotal (Pillemer, 1998; Schuman & Scott, 1989). Our teens and twenties are also the time when we experience many memorable "firsts"—first date, first job, first day at college, first meeting your parents-in-law. This period is indeed a peak time for some types of learning and remembering.

Up through the teen years, we process information with greater and greater speed (Fry & Hale, 1996; Kail, 1991). This neural processing slows in late adulthood. Compared with teens and young adults, older people take a bit more time to react, to solve perceptual puzzles, even to remember names (Bashore et al., 1997; Verhaeghen & Salthouse, 1997). The lag is greatest on complex tasks (Cerella, 1985; Poon, 1987). At video games, most 70-year-olds are no match for a 20-year-old.

menopause the end of menstruation. In everyday use, it can also mean the biological transition a woman experiences from before to after the end of menstruation.

Consider one experiment in which 1205 people were invited to learn some names (Crook & West, 1990). They watched videotapes in which 14 individuals said their names, using a common format: "Hi, I'm Larry." Then the same individuals reappeared and gave additional details. For example, saying "I'm from Philadelphia" gave viewers visual and voice cues for remembering the person's name. After a second and third replay of the introductions, all viewers remembered more names, but younger adults were consistently better than older adults.

Perhaps it is not surprising, then, that nearly two-thirds of people over age 40 say their memory is worse than it was 10 years ago (KRC, 2001). In fact, how well older people remember depends on the task. When asked to *recognize* words they had earlier tried to memorize, people showed only a minimal decline in memory. When asked to *recall* that information without clues, the decline was greater (**FIGURE 3.19**).

Aging and Intelligence

WHAT HAPPENS TO OUR BROADER INTEL-◄ LECTUAL POWERS AS WE AGE? The answer again depends on the task and the type of ability it represents (Cattell, 1963; Horn, 1982).

- **Crystallized intelligence**—one's accumulated knowledge, as reflected in vocabulary and analogies tests—*increases* into middle age.

- **Fluid intelligence**—one's ability to reason speedily and abstractly, as when solving unfamiliar logic problems—*decreases* slowly up to age 75 or so, then more rapidly, especially after age 85.

We can see this pattern in the intelligence scores of a national sample of adults. After adjustments for education, word power scores (reflecting crystallized intelligence) increase until later life (Salthouse, 2004). Nonverbal, puzzle-solving intelligence declines (Park et al., 2002). With age we lose and we win. We lose recall memory and processing speed, but we gain vocabulary and

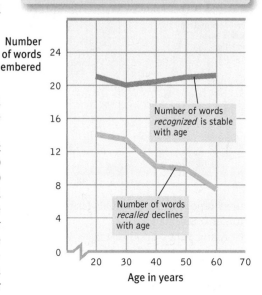

FIGURE 3.19 ● **Recall and recognition in adulthood** In this experiment, the ability to *recall* new information declined during early and middle adulthood, but the ability to *recognize* new information did not. (From Schonfield & Robertson, 1966.)

knowledge. Our decisions also become less distorted by negative emotions such as anxiety, depression, or anger (Blanchard-Fields, 2007; Carstensen & Mikels, 2005).

These age-related cognitive differences help explain some curious findings about creativity. Mathematicians and scientists produce much of their most creative work during their late twenties or early thirties. In literature, history, and philosophy, people tend to produce their best work in their forties, fifties, and beyond, after accumulating more knowledge (Simonton, 1988, 1990). Poets, for example, who depend on fluid intelligence, reach their peak output earlier than prose authors, who need a deeper knowledge reservoir. This finding holds in every major literary tradition, for both living and dead languages.

Life-span trends in our cognitive abilities reflect a theme we have seen before in this chapter. Our biology and our experiences interact. Despite normal age-related cognitive changes, mental and physical exercise can make a difference.

> "In youth we learn, in age we understand."
>
> Marie Von Ebner-Eschenbach, *Aphorisms*, 1883

Practice helps sustain specific cognitive skills. In mock air traffic control tests, experienced older controllers remained adept on well-practiced tasks (Nunes & Kramer, 2009). Across 20 other studies, active older adults again tended to be mentally quick older adults. When sedentary older adults were randomly assigned to aerobic exercise programs, their memory improved and their judgment sharpened (Colcombe et al., 2004; Hertzog et al., 2008; Nazimek, 2009). "Use it or lose it" is indeed sound advice.

Fit body, fit mind. Physical exercise feeds the brain and stimulates brain cell development and connections, thanks partly to increased oxygen and nutrient flow (Coleman & Flood, 1986; Kempermann et al., 1998). Exercise also promotes the birth of new nerve cells in the hippocampus, a brain area important for memory (Pereira et al., 2007).

Studies in several countries support the idea that age is less a predictor of abilities such as memory and intelligence than is proximity to death. Thus, tell me whether someone is 5 months or 5 years from death and, regardless of age, you've given me a clue to that person's mental ability. Researchers call this near-death drop *terminal decline* (Backman & MacDonald, 2006; Wilson et al., 2007).

Social Development

19 What are adulthood's two primary commitments, and how do the social clock and chance events influence us?

Adulthood's Commitments

Two basic aspects of our lives dominate adulthood. Erik Erikson called them *intimacy* (forming close relationships) and *generativity* (being productive and supporting future generations). Sigmund Freud (1935) put it most simply: The healthy adult, he said, is one who can *love* and *work*.

Love We typically flirt, fall in love, and commit—one person at a time. "Pair-bonding is a trademark of the human animal," observed anthropologist Helen Fisher (1993). From an evolutionary perspective, this pairing makes sense. Parents who cooperated to nurture their children to maturity were more likely to have their gene-carrying children survive and reproduce.

Bonds of love are most satisfying and enduring when two adults share similar interests and values and offer mutual emotional and material support. One of the ties that binds couples is *self-disclosure*—revealing intimate aspects of oneself to others (see Chapter 14).

The chances that a marriage will last also increase when couples marry after age 20 and are well educated. Shouldn't this mean that fewer marriages would end in divorce today? Compared with their counterparts of 50 years ago, people in Western countries *are* better educated and marrying later. But no—ironically, we are nearly twice as likely to divorce today. Both Canada and the United States now have about one divorce for every two marriages. In Europe, divorce is only slightly less common. The divorce rate partly reflects women's increased ability to support themselves, but it also reflects other changes. Both men and women now expect more than an enduring bond when they marry. Most hope for a mate who is a wage earner, caregiver, intimate friend, and warm and responsive lover.

MIGHT TEST-DRIVING A RELATIONSHIP◄ WITH A LIVE-IN "TRIAL MARRIAGE" MINIMIZE DIVORCE RISK? In a 2001 Gallup survey of American twenty-somethings, 62 percent thought it would (Whitehead & Popenoe, 2001). In reality, in Europe, Canada, and the United States, those living together before marriage have had *higher* rates of divorce and marital troubles than those who have not lived together (Dush et al., 2003; Popenoe & Whitehead, 2002). The risk appears greatest for those who live together before becoming engaged (Kline et al., 2004; Rhoades et al., 2009). These couples tend to

Love: Intimacy, attachment, commitment—love by whatever name—is central to healthy and happy adulthood.

Blend Images/Alamy

be initially less committed to the ideal of enduring marriage, and they become even less marriage-supporting while living together.

Nonetheless, the institution of marriage endures. Worldwide, reports the United Nations, 9 in 10 heterosexual adults marry. And marriage is a predictor of happiness, health, sexual satisfaction, and income. Neighborhoods with high marriage rates typically have low rates of crime, delinquency, and emotional disorders among children. Since 1972, surveys of 49,000 Americans have revealed that 40 percent of married adults report being "very happy," compared wth 23 percent of unmarried adults (Myers & Scanzoni, 2005). Part of this happiness seems to come from having a partner who is a close, supportive companion—someone who sees you as special. Lesbian couples, too, report greater well-being than those who are alone (Peplau & Fingerhut, 2007; Wayment & Peplau, 1995).

Often, love bears children. For most people, this most enduring of life changes is a happy event. "I feel an overwhelming love for my children unlike anything I feel for anyone else," said 93 percent of American mothers in a national survey (Erickson & Aird, 2005). Many fathers feel the same. A few weeks after the birth of my first child I was suddenly struck by a realization: "So *this* is how my parents felt about me!"

Children eventually leave home. This departure is a significant and sometimes difficult event. For most people in middle adulthood, though, an empty nest is a happy place (Adelmann et al., 1989; Glenn, 1975). Compared with middle-aged women with children still at home, those living in an empty nest report greater happiness and greater enjoyment of their marriage. Many parents experience a "postlaunch honeymoon," especially if they maintain close relationships with their children (White & Edwards, 1990). As Daniel Gilbert (2006) concludes, "The only known symptom of 'empty nest syndrome' is increased smiling."

Work Having work that fits your interests provides a sense of competence and accomplishment. For many adults, the answer to "Who are you?" depends a great deal on the answer to "What do you do?"

crystallized intelligence accumulated knowledge and verbal skills; tends to increase with age.

fluid intelligence ability to reason speedily and abstractly; tends to decrease during late adulthood.

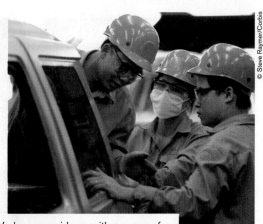

Thinkstock Images/Jupiterimages

© Steve Raymer/Corbis

Job satisfaction and life satisfaction: Work can provide us with a sense of identity and competence and opportunities for accomplishment. Perhaps this is why challenging and interesting occupations enhance people's happiness.

Choosing a career path is difficult, especially in today's changing work environment. (See Appendix A: Psychology at Work for more on building work satisfaction.)

For women, the once-rigid sequence—of student to worker to wife to at-home mom to worker again—has loosened. Contemporary women who choose to occupy these roles do so in any order or all at once. Nevertheless, for both men and women, there exists a **social clock**—a culture's definition of "the right time" to leave home, get a job, marry, have children, and retire. It's the expectation people have in mind when saying "I married early" or "I started college late." Today the clock still ticks, but people feel freer about being out of sync with it.

Chance Events

Simple chance, not maturation, often sends us down one road rather than another (Bandura, 1982). Romantic attraction, for example, is often influenced by chance encounters. Psychologist Albert Bandura (2005) recalled the ironic true story of a book editor who came to one of Bandura's lectures on the "Psychology of Chance Encounters and Life Paths"—and ended up marrying the woman who happened to sit next to him.

Consider one study of identical twins and their spouses. Twins, especially identical twins, make similar choices of friends, clothes, vacations, jobs, and so on. So, if your identical twin became engaged to someone, wouldn't you (being in so many ways the same as your twin) expect to also feel attracted to this person? Surprisingly, only half the identical twins recalled really liking their co-twin's selection, and only .5 percent said, "I could have fallen for my twin's partner." This finding fits one explanation of romantic love: Given repeated exposure to someone after childhood, you may become attached to almost any available person who has a roughly similar background and level of attractiveness and who returns your affections (Lykken & Tellegen, 1993).

> "Love—why, I'll tell you what love is: It's you at 75 and her at 71, each of you listening for the other's step in the next room, each afraid that a sudden silence, a sudden cry, could mean a lifetime's talk is over."
>
> Brian Moore, *The Luck of Ginger Coffey*, 1960

Death and Dying

20 How do people vary in their responses to a loved one's death?

Perhaps the saddest event most of us will have to cope with is the death of a close relative or friend. Usually, the most difficult separation is from one's spouse or partner—a loss suffered by five times more women than men. When, as usually happens, death comes at an expected late-life time—the "right time" on the social clock—the grieving usually passes (**FIGURE 3.20**).

When the death of a loved one comes suddenly and before its expected time, grief is especially severe. The sudden illness that claims a 45-year-old life partner, or the accidental death of a child, may trigger a year or more of memory-filled mourning. Eventually, this may give way to a mild depression, sometimes lasting several years (Lehman et al., 1987). For some, the loss is unbearable. One study tracked more than 17,000 people who had suffered the death of a child under 18. In the five years following that death, 3 percent of them were hospitalized in a psychiatric unit. This rate is 67 percent higher than the rate found in a control group of parents who had not lost a child (Li et al., 2005).

WHY DO GRIEF REACTIONS VARY SO WIDELY? Some cultures encourage public weeping and wailing. Others expect mourners to hide their emotions. In all cultures, some individuals grieve more intensely and openly. Some popular beliefs, however, are not confirmed by scientific studies.

- Those who immediately express the strongest grief do not purge their grief faster (Bonanno & Kaltman, 1999; Wortman & Silver, 1989).

- Therapy and self-help groups offer support for grieving survivors, but there is similar healing power in the passing of time and the support of friends—and also in giving support and help to others (Brown et al., 2008).

Diverse Yet Alike

Grief reactions vary across cultures. Himba mourners in Namibia may gather quietly near their sacred fire. New Zealanders may continue a Scottish tradition of bagpiped funeral music.

FIGURE 3.20 • **Life satisfaction before, during the year of, and after a spouse's death** In periodic lifetime surveys of more than 30,000 Germans, researchers identified 513 married people who had not remarried after the death of a spouse. They found that life satisfaction began to dip during the year before the spouse's death, dropped significantly during the year of the death itself, and then eventually rebounded to nearly the earlier level (Lucas et al., 2003).

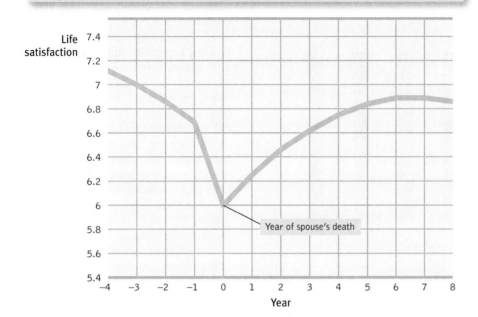

After a spouse's death, those who talk often with others or who receive grief counseling adjust about as well as those who grieve more privately (Bonanno, 2009; Genevro, 2003; Stroebe et al., 2001, 2002, 2005).

• Terminally ill and grief-stricken people do not go through identical stages, such as denial before anger (Nolen-Hoeksema & Larson, 1999). Given similar losses, some people grieve hard and long, others grieve less (Ott et al., 2007).

Well-Being Across the Life Span

21 **What factors affect our well-being in later life?**

To live is to grow older. This moment marks the oldest you have ever been and the youngest you will henceforth be. That means we all can look back with satisfaction or regret, and forward with hope or dread. When asked what they would have done differently if they could relive their lives, people most often answer, "Taken my education more seriously and worked harder at it" (Kinnier & Metha, 1989; Roese & Summerville, 2005). Other regrets—"I should have told my father I loved him," "I regret that I never went to Europe"—also focus less on mistakes made than on the things one *failed* to do (Gilovich & Medvec, 1995).

From early adulthood to midlife, people's sense of identity, confidence, and self-esteem typically grows stronger (Miner-Rubino et al., 2004; Robins & Trzesniewski, 2005). In later life, challenges arise. Income often shrinks as work is taken away. The body declines, recall fades, and energy wanes. Family members and friends die or move away. The great enemy, death, looms ever closer. Small wonder that most believe that happiness declines in later life (Lacey et al., 2006; Lachman et al., 2008). Data collected from nearly 170,000 people in 16 nations show otherwise (Inglehart, 1990).

> How will you look back on your life 10 years from now? Are you making choices that someday you will recollect with satisfaction?

People over 65 report as much happiness and satisfaction with life as younger people do (**FIGURE 3.21** on the next page).

> "At 20 we worry about what others think of us. At 40 we don't care what others think of us. At 60 we discover they haven't been thinking about us at all."
>
> Anonymous

If anything, positive feelings grow after midlife and negative feelings give way (Charles et al., 2001; Mroczek, 2001). Older adults increasingly express positive emotions (Pennebaker & Stone, 2003). Compared with younger adults, they pay less attention to negative information and are slower to perceive negative faces (Carstensen & Mikels, 2005). Brain areas that process emotions show less activity in response to negative events, but they continue to respond at the same levels to positive events (Mather et al., 2004; Williams et al., 2006).

Throughout the life span, the bad feelings tied to negative events fade faster than the good feelings linked with positive events (Walker et al., 2003). This contributes to most older people's sense that life, on balance, has been mostly good. The positivity of later life is comforting. As the years go by, feelings mellow (Costa et al., 1987; Diener et al., 1986). Highs become less high, lows less low.

For all of us, life eventually ends. Although death may be unwelcome, facing death with dignity and openness helps people complete the life cycle with a sense of life's meaningfulness and unity. Many treasure the feeling that their existence has been good and that life and death are parts of an ongoing cycle. Erik Erikson called this feeling a sense of *integrity*—an ability to look back with satisfaction, knowing one's life has been meaningful and worthwhile.

social clock the culturally preferred timing of social events such as marriage, parenthood, and retirement.

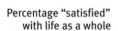

FIGURE 3.21 ● **Age and life satisfaction** With the tasks of early adulthood behind them, many older adults have more time to pursue personal interests. No wonder their satisfaction with life remains high, and may even rise if they are healthy and active. As this graph based on multinational surveys shows, age differences in life satisfaction are trivial. (Data from Inglehart, 1990.)

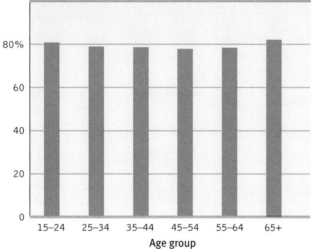

Percentage "satisfied" with life as a whole

Age group

Thinking About Stability and Change

It's time to address our third developmental issue. As we follow lives through time, do we find more evidence for stability or change? If reunited with a long-lost grade-school friend, do we instantly realize that "it's the same old Andy"? Or do people we befriend during one period of life seem like total strangers at a later period? (At least one man would choose the second option. He failed to recognize a former classmate at his 40-year college reunion. That angry classmate eventually pointed out that she was his long-ago first wife!)

Developmental psychologists' research reveals that we experience both stability and change. Some of our characteristics, such as temperament, are very stable. As we noted earlier in this chapter, temperament seems to be something we're born with. When a research team studied 1000 people from age 3 to 26, they were struck by the consistency of temperament and emotionality across time (Caspi et al., 2003). The widest smilers in childhood photos are, years later, the ones most likely to enjoy enduring marriages (Hertenstein et al., 2009). "As at 7, so at 70," says a Jewish proverb.

We cannot, however, predict all of our eventual traits based on our first three years of life (Kagan et al., 1978, 1998). Some traits, such as social attitudes, are much less stable than temperament (Moss & Susman, 1980). Older children and adolescents can learn new ways of coping. It is true that delinquent children have high rates of work problems, substance abuse, and crime, but many confused and troubled children have blossomed into mature, successful adults (Moffitt et al., 2002; Roberts et al., 2001;

As adults grow older, there is continuity of self.

Thomas & Chess, 1986). Happily for them, life is a process of becoming.

In some ways, we *all* change with age. Most shy, fearful toddlers begin opening up by age 4. In the years after adolescence, most people become calmer and more self-disciplined, agreeable, and self-confident (McCrae & Costa, 1994; Roberts et al., 2003, 2006). Conscientiousness increases especially during the twenties, and agreeableness during the thirties (Srivastava et al., 2003). As people grow older, personality gradually stabilizes (Terracciano et al., 2006). Many a 20-year-old goof-off has matured into a 40-year-old business or cultural leader. (If you are the former, you aren't done yet.) *Such changes can occur without changing a person's position relative to others of the same age.* The hard-driving young adult may mellow by later life, yet still be a relatively hard-driving senior citizen.

Life requires *both* stability and change. Stability gives us our identity. It lets us depend on others and be concerned about the healthy development of the children in our lives. Our trust in our ability to change gives us hope for a brighter future and lets us adapt and grow with experience.

PRACTICE TEST

THE BASICS

22. Our physical abilities tend to peak by our
   a. late teens.
   b. mid-twenties.
   c. mid-thirties.
   d. late forties.

23. By age 65, a person would be most likely to experience a decline in the ability to
   a. recall and name all the items on a grocery list.
   b. remember important events from their teens or twenties.
   c. decide whether a statement is true or false.
   d. do well on a vocabulary test.

24. Freud defined the healthy adult as one who is able to love and work. Erikson agreed, observing that the adult struggles to attain intimacy and

a. affiliation.

b. identity.

c. industry.

d. generativity.

25. Most older adults report

    a. more depression than younger people.

    b. less confidence than younger people.

    c. satisfaction levels comparable to those of younger people.

    d. more negative thinking than younger people experience.

26. Which statement is true about stability and change throughout the life span?

    a. Once we reach adolescence, our attitudes are set for life and do not change.

b. Our temperament takes a while to develop as we learn through experience.

c. Our temperament tends to be very stable throughout our lives.

d. A shy child usually becomes an outgoing adult.

THE BIG PICTURE

3F. What are some of the most significant challenges and rewards of growing older?

3G. How is our development affected by both stability and change?

IN YOUR EVERYDAY LIFE

▪ Imagining the future, how do you think you might change? How might you stay the same?

Answers: 22. b, 23. a, 24. d, 25. c, 26. c. Answers to The Big Picture questions can be found in Appendix B at the end of the book.

Terms and Concepts to Remember

developmental psychology, p. 64	reflex, p. 67	stranger anxiety, p. 75
chromosomes, p. 64	temperament, p. 69	attachment, p. 76
DNA (deoxyribonucleic acid), p. 64	maturation, p. 70	basic trust, p. 78
genes, p. 64	critical period, p. 70	adolescence, p. 81
heredity, p. 64	schema, p. 72	puberty, p. 81
genome, p. 64	cognition, p. 72	menarche [meh-NAR-key], p. 81
environment, p. 65	sensorimotor stage, p. 72	identity, p. 84
interaction, p. 65	object permanence, p. 73	social identity, p. 84
zygote, p. 66	preoperational stage, p. 73	intimacy, p. 85
embryo, p. 66	conservation, p. 73	emerging adulthood, p. 87
identical twins, p. 66	egocentrism, p. 73	menopause, p. 90
fraternal twins, p. 66	theory of mind, p. 74	crystallized intelligence, p. 92
fetus, p. 66	autism, p. 74	fluid intelligence, p. 92
teratogen, p. 66	concrete operational stage, p. 74	social clock, p. 94
fetal alcohol syndrome (FAS), p. 66	formal operational stage, p. 75	

Multiple-choice **self-tests** and more may be found at www.worthpublishers.com/myers

DEVELOPING THROUGH THE LIFE SPAN

Developmental psychologists study physical, cognitive, and social changes throughout the life span.

1 What are the three major issues studied by developmental psychologists?
- Nature and nurture
- Continuity and stages
- Stability and change

Prenatal Development and the Newborn

2 How does conception occur, and what are chromosomes, DNA, genes, and the genome?
- At conception, one sperm cell fuses with one egg cell.
- *Genes* (*DNA* segments that form the *chromosomes*) are the basic units of *heredity.* When expressed in particular *environments,* genes guide development.
- A *genome* is the shared genetic profile that distinguishes each species.
- Heredity and environment *interact* to influence development.

3 How does life develop before birth, and how do teratogens put prenatal development at risk?
- From conception to 2 weeks, the *zygote* is in a period of rapid cell development.
- By 6 weeks, the *embryo's* body organs begin to form and function.
- By 9 weeks, the *fetus* is recognizably human.
- *Identical twins* develop from a single fertilized egg that splits into two; *fraternal twins* develop from separate fertilized eggs.
- *Teratogens* are potentially harmful agents that can pass through the placental screen and interfere with normal development.

4 What are some of the newborn's abilities and traits?
- Newborns' sensory systems and *reflexes* aid their survival and social interactions with adults.
- Inborn *temperament*—emotional excitability—heavily influences our developing personality.

5 How do twin and adoption studies help us understand the effects of nature and nurture?
- Studies of separated identical twins allow researchers to maintain the same genes while testing the effects of different home environments. Studies of adoptive families let researchers maintain the same home environment while studying the effects of genetic differences.
- *Nature and nurture:* Our heredity (nature) and our environment (nurture) interact. The biopsychosocial approach studies this interaction.

6

7

8 How do the bonds of attachment form between caregivers and infants?
- Infants develop *stranger anxiety* soon after object permanence.
- Infants form *attachments* with caregivers who are comfortable, familiar, and responsive.

9 Why do secure and insecure attachments matter, and how does an infant develop basic trust?
- Attachment styles differ (secure or insecure) due to the child's individual temperament and the responsiveness of the child's caregivers.
- Securely attached children develop *basic trust* and tend to have healthier adult relationships.
- Neglect or abuse can disrupt the attachment process and put children at risk for physical, psychological, and social problems.

10 **What are three primary parenting styles, and what outcomes are associated with them?**

■ Parenting styles—permissive, authoritative, and authoritarian—often reflect cultural influences.

■ Children with the highest self-esteem, self-reliance, and social competence tend to have authoritative parents.

Adolescence

11 **What defines adolescence, and what major physical changes occur during adolescence?**

■ *Adolescence* begins with *puberty,* a time of sexual maturation.

■ The brain's frontal lobes mature during adolescence and the early twenties, enabling improved judgment, impulse control, and long-term planning.

12 **How did Piaget and Kohlberg describe cognitive and moral development during adolescence?**

■ In Piaget's view, formal operations (abstract reasoning) develop in adolescence. Research indicates that these abilities begin to emerge earlier than Piaget believed.

■ Kohlberg proposed a stage theory of moral thinking: preconventional morality (self-interest), conventional morality (gaining others' approval or doing one's duty), and postconventional morality (only in some people; agreed-upon rights or universal ethical principles).

■ Kohlberg's critics note that true morality is both moral actions and moral thinking. And the postconventional level represents morality only from the perspective of an individualist, middle class.

13 **According to Erikson, what stages—and accompanying tasks and challenges—mark our psychosocial development?**

■ Erikson proposed eight stages of psychosocial development across the life span.

■ Erikson believed we need to achieve the following challenges: trust, autonomy, initiative, industry, *identity* (in adolescence), *intimacy* (in young adulthood), generativity, and integrity.

14 **To what extent are adolescent lives shaped by parental and peer influences?**

■ During adolescence, parental influence diminishes and peer influence increases.

■ Nature and nurture—genes and experiences—interact to guide our development.

15 **Does parenting matter?**

■ Parents influence our manners, and political and religious beliefs.

■ Language and other behaviors are shaped by peer groups, as children adjust to fit in.

16 **What are the characteristics of emerging adulthood?**

■ *Emerging adulthood* is the period from age 18 to the mid-twenties, when many young people in Western cultures are not yet fully independent.

■ *Continuity and stages:* Development is more continuous than stage theorists believed. Still, it is important to consider the effects of growth spurts and the changing forces and interests that affect us at different points in our lives.

Adulthood

17 **How do our bodies and sensory abilities change from early to late adulthood?**

■ Muscular strength, reaction time, sensory abilities, and cardiac output begin to decline in the late twenties.

■ Around age 50, *menopause* ends women's period of fertility. Men do not undergo a similar sharp drop in hormone levels or fertility.

18 **In what ways do memory and intelligence change as we age?**

■ Recall begins to decline, especially for meaningless information. Recognition memory remains strong.

■ *Fluid intelligence* (speedy, abstract reasoning) declines in later life. *Crystallized intelligence* (accumulated knowledge) does not.

19 **What are adulthood's two primary commitments, and how do the social clock and chance events influence us?**

■ Adulthood's two major commitments are love (Erikson's intimacy—forming close relationships) and work (productive activity, or what Erikson called generativity).

■ The *social clock* is a culture's expected timing for social events, such as marriage and retirement.

■ Chance encounters affect many of our important decisions, such as our choice of romantic partners.

20 **How do people vary in their responses to a loved one's death?**

■ Normal grief reactions vary widely.

■ Death of a loved one is much harder to accept when it comes before its expected time.

21 **What factors affect our well-being in later life?**

■ Most older people retain a sense of well-being, partly due to the tendency to focus more on positive emotions and memories.

■ Many experience what Erikson called a sense of integrity—a feeling that one's life has been meaningful.

■ *Stability and change:* Development is lifelong. People's traits continue to change in later life. There is also an underlying consistency to most people's temperament and personality traits.

4

GENDER AND SEXUALITY

n 1972, as the young chair of our psychology department, I was proud to make the announcement: We had concluded our search for a new colleague. We had found just who we were looking for—a bright, warm, enthusiastic woman about to receive her Ph.D. in developmental psychology. The vote was unanimous. Alas, our elderly chancellor rejected our recommendation. "As a mother of a preschooler," he said, "she should be home with her child, *not* working full time." No amount of pleading or arguing (for example, that it might be possible to parent a child while employed) could change his mind. So, with a heavy heart, I drove to her city to explain, face to face, my embarrassment in being able to offer her only a temporary position.

In this case, all's well that ends well. She accepted a temporary position and quickly became a beloved, tenured colleague who went on to found our college's women's studies program. But today, she and I marvel at the swift transformation in our culture's thinking about gender. In a thin slice of history, our ideas about the "proper" behavior for women and men have undergone an extreme makeover. Both women and men are now recognized as "fully capable of effectively carrying out organizational roles at all levels" (Wood & Eagly, 2002). Women's employment in formerly male occupations and men's employment in formerly female occupations have increased. And as this was happening, our views of what is "masculine" and what is "feminine" have also changed, as have our ideas about what we seek in a mate (Twenge, 1997).

In this chapter, we'll look at some of the ways nature and nurture interact to form us as males and females. We'll see what researchers tell us about how much males and females are alike, and how and why they differ. Along the way, we'll take a close look at human sexuality. As part of that close look, we'll see how evolutionary psychologists explain our sexuality.

Let's start by considering what gender is and how it develops.

Gender Development

Humans everywhere share an irresistible urge to organize the world into simple categories. Among the ways we classify people—as tall or short, slim or fat, smart or dull—one stands out. Before or at your birth, everyone wanted to know, "Boy or girl?" From that time on, your biological sex helped define your **gender,** the characteristics our society defines as *male* or *female*.

HOW MUCH DOES BIOLOGY CONTRIBUTE◄ TO OUR GENDER CHARACTERISTICS, AND WHAT PORTION OF OUR DIFFERENCES IS SOCIALLY CONSTRUCTED? Before we try to answer those questions, let's consider some gender similarities and differences.

How Are We Alike? How Do We Differ?

1 What are some gender similarities and differences in aggression, social power, and social connectedness?

In most ways, we are alike. Men and women are not from different planets—Mars and Venus—but from the same planet Earth. Tell me whether you are male or female and you give me no clue to your intelligence. You tell me little about the mechanisms by which you see, hear, learn, and remember. Your "opposite" sex is, in reality, your very similar sex. At conception, you received 23 chromosomes from your mother and 23 from your father. Of those 46 chromosomes, 45 are *unisex*—the same for males and females. (More about that other chromosome later in this chapter.)

But males and females do differ, and differences command attention. Some are obvious. Compared with the average man, the average woman enters puberty two years sooner, and her life span is five years longer. She carries 70 percent more fat, has 40 percent less muscle, and is 5 inches shorter. She expresses emotions more freely, can smell fainter odors, and is offered help more often. She can become sexually re-aroused immediately

after orgasm. She is also doubly vulnerable to depression and anxiety, and her risk of developing an eating disorder is 10 times greater than the average man's. Yet, he is some 4 times more likely to commit suicide or become dependent on alcohol. He is also more likely to be diagnosed with autism, color-blindness, and ADHD as a child, and with antisocial personality disorder as an adult. Choose your gender and pick your vulnerability.

Psychologists have been especially interested in three areas of male-female differences: aggression, social power, and social connectedness.

Gender and Aggression

In surveys, men admit to more **aggression** than women do. This aggression gender gap pertains to harmful *physical* aggression rather than verbal, *relational* aggression (such as excluding someone). The gap appears in everyday life in various cultures and at various ages (Archer, 2009).

In dating relationships, violent acts, such as slaps and thrown objects, are often mutual (Straus, 2008). But men's

Gender difference in aggression: Around the world, fighting, violent crime, and blowing things up are mostly men's activities. This is why many were surprised to hear that *female* suicide bombers were responsible for the 2010 Moscow subway bombing that killed dozens.

Vladmir Fedorenko/AFP/Getty Images

tendency to behave more aggressively can be seen in experiments where they deliver what they believe are more painful electric shocks (Bettencourt & Kernahan, 1997). Violent crime rates illustrate the gender difference even more strikingly. The male-to-female arrest ratio for murder, for example, is 9 to 1 in both the United States and Canada (FBI, 2008; Statistics Canada, 2008). Throughout the world, fighting, warring, and hunting are primarily men's activities (Wood & Eagly, 2002, 2007). Men also express more support for war (Newport, 2007).

Gender and Social Power

Close your eyes and imagine two adults standing side by side. The one on the left is dominant, forceful, and independent. The one on the right is submissive, nurturing, and socially connected.

Did you see the person on the left as a man, and the one on the right as a woman? If so, you are not alone.

Around the world, from Nigeria to New Zealand, people perceive such power differences between men and women (Williams & Best, 1990). Indeed, in most societies men *do* place more importance on power and achievement and *are* socially dominant (Schwartz & Rubel, 2005). When political leaders are elected, they usually are men, who held 82 percent of the seats in the world's governing parliaments in 2009 (IPU, 2010). When groups form, whether as juries or companies, leadership tends to go to males (Colarelli et al., 2006). And when paychecks arrive, those in traditionally male occupations receive more.

As leaders, men tend to be more *directive,* even authoritarian, issuing orders for others to follow. Women tend to be more *democratic,* more welcoming of subordinates' participation in decision making (Eagly, 2007, 2009; van Engen & Willemsen, 2004). When people interact, men are more likely to utter opinions, women to express support (Aries, 1987; Wood, 1987). Men tend to act as powerful people often do. They smile less often than women do, and they are more likely to talk assertively, interrupt, initiate touches, and stare (Hall, 1987; Leaper & Ayres, 2007).

Gender and power: At the 2007 European Union leaders summit, there was a sea of suits, but one (Germany's Angela Merkel) was not like the others.

Such behaviors help sustain men's greater social power.

Gender differences in power grow smaller as we age. With maturity, middle-aged women become more assertive, and men become more empathic—more able to walk in others' shoes (Maccoby, 1998).

Gender and Social Connectedness

The gender gap extends also to relationships. Many psychologists view adolescence as a time when we struggle to create a separate *identity*—a unique, independent self. To Carol Gilligan and her colleagues (1982, 1990), this "normal" struggle describes males more than females. Gilligan believes females differ from males in two important ways. Females are less concerned with viewing themselves as separate individuals. And they are more concerned with relationships, with *making connections*. That tendency was clear in one analysis of more than half a million people's responses to various interest inventories. The results showed that "men prefer working with things and women prefer working with people" (Su et al., 2009).

These male-female social differences surface early. In children's play, boys typically form large groups. Their games tend to be active and competitive, with little intimate discussion (Rose & Rudolph, 2006). Girls usually play in smaller groups, often with one friend. Their play is less competitive, and they tend to act out social relationships. Both in play and in other settings, females are more open to feedback and more likely to react to it (Maccoby, 1990; Roberts, 1991).

These differences continue with age. In their teen years, girls spend more time with friends and on social networking Internet sites, and less time alone (Pryor et al., 2007; Wong & Csikszentmihalyi, 1991). As adults, men enjoy doing activities *side-by-side*, and they tend to talk with others to communicate solutions. Women take more pleasure in talking *face-to-face* (Wright, 1989), and they tend to talk with others to explore relationships (Tannen, 1990). As friends, women also talk more often and more openly (Berndt, 1992; Dindia & Allen, 1992). This may help explain a gender difference in phone communication. In France, women make 63 percent of telephone calls. When talking to a woman, female callers stay connected longer (7.2 minutes) than men do when talking to another man (4.6 minutes) (Smoreda & Licoppe, 2000).

Perhaps we should not be surprised, then, that relationship-oriented women provide most of the care to the very young and the very old. In one survey of American adults, women were five times more likely than men to claim primary responsibility "for taking care of your children" (*Time,* 2009). In their interests and vocations, women worldwide emphasize caring and relate more to people (Eagly, 2009; Schwartz & Rubel-Lifschitz, 2009). They also have purchased 85 percent of greeting cards (*Time,* 1997). Although many people (69 percent) say they have a close relationship with their father, more (90 percent) feel close to their mother (Hugick, 1989). When wanting someone who will understand them and share their worries and hurts, both men and women usually turn to women. Both also report their friendships with women to be more intimate, enjoyable, and nurturing (Rubin, 1985; Sapadin, 1988).

What explains our male-female differences? Are we shaped by our biology? By our experiences? A biopsychosocial view suggests both are at work. Gender diversity, like so many other aspects of our development, is a byproduct of the interplay of our biology, our personal history, and our current situation (Eagly, 2009).

The Nature of Gender: Our Biology

2 How is biological sex determined, and how do sex hormones influence development and gender differences?

In areas where we face similar challenges—regulating heat with sweat, preferring foods that nourish, growing

---

gender in psychology, the biologically and socially influenced characteristics by which members of a culture define *male* and *female*.

aggression physical or verbal behavior intended to hurt someone.

calluses where the skin meets friction—men and women are similar. Even when describing the ideal mate, both put traits such as "kind," "honest," and "intelligent" at the top of their lists. But in mating-related areas, *evolutionary psychologists* contend, guys act like guys whether they are elephants or elephant seals, rural peasants or corporate presidents. Our biology may influence our gender differences in two ways: genetically, through our differing *sex chromosomes,* and physiologically, from our differing concentrations of *sex hormones.*

As we noted earlier, males and females are variations on a single form—of 46 chromosomes, 45 are unisex. So great is this similarity that until seven weeks after conception, you were anatomically the same as someone of the other sex. Then that forty-sixth chromosome kicked in. Male or female, your sex was determined by your father's contribution to your twenty-third pair of chromosomes, the two sex chromosomes. You received an **X chromosome** from your mother. From your father, you received the one chromosome that is not unisex—either an X chromosome, making you a girl, or a **Y chromosome,** making you a boy.

The Y chromosome includes a single gene that, about the seventh week after conception, throws a master switch triggering the testes to develop and to produce the principal male hormone, **testosterone.** This hormone starts the development of external male sex organs. Females also have testosterone, but less of it.

Another key period for the development of male-female differences falls during the fourth and fifth prenatal months. During this period, sex hormones bathe the fetal brain and influence its wiring. Different patterns for males and females develop under the influence of the male's greater testosterone and the female's ovarian hormones (Hines, 2004; Udry, 2000). High fetal testosterone sometimes produces females with more masculine muscular and skeletal features. For those who later engage in athletic competitions, this may give them an edge over other females (Kolata, 2010).

In adulthood, male and female brains differ in some areas. Parts of the frontal lobes (an area involved in verbal fluency), for example, are thicker in women. Part of the parietal cortex, a key area for space perception, is thicker in men.

Despite normal male hormones and testes, some male infants are born without a penis or with a very small one. In such cases, biology's power to influence gender development is clear. Until recently, pediatricians and other medical experts often recommended surgery to create a female identity for these children. One study reviewed 14 cases of boys who had undergone early sex-reassignment surgery and had been raised as girls. Six later declared themselves to be males, 5 were living as females, and 3 had unclear gender identity (Reiner & Gearhart, 2004).

The dramatic difference between *gender* (the characteristics that people associate with male and female) and *sex* (the biology of male and female) was equally and tragically clear in another case, in which a little boy had lost his penis during a botched circumcision. His parents followed a psychiatrist's advice to raise him as a girl rather than as a damaged boy. Alas, "Brenda" Reimer was not like other girls. "She" didn't like dolls. She tore her dresses with rough-and-tumble play. At puberty she wanted no part of kissing boys. Finally, Brenda's parents explained what had happened, whereupon this young person immediately rejected the assigned female identity. He cut his

Reuters/Michael Dalder

hair and took a male name, David. He eventually married a woman and became a stepfather. And, sadly, he later committed suicide (Colapinto, 2000).

Gender scrutiny: Dramatic improvements in South African track star Caster Semenya's race times prompted the International Association of Athletics Federations to undertake gender testing in 2009. Media leaks threw her into the international spotlight for 11 months. Before being officially cleared to continue competing as a woman, Semenya declared, "God made me the way I am and I accept myself. I am who I am" (*YOU,* 10 September 2009).

Sex-reassignment surgery is no longer recommended for genetic males in cases like these. Indeed, "sex matters," concluded the National Academy of Sciences (2001).

The transgendered mayor: When Stu Rassmussen was elected Silverton, Oregon's mayor he was a guy in pants. When reelected he was openly transgendered and wore a dress and makeup to his installation.

Courtesy of Nick Downes

Kimberly A. C. Wilson/The Oregonian

In combination with the environment, sex-related genes and physiology "result in behavioral and cognitive differences between males and females."

Some individuals are *transgendered*, meaning that their gender identity feels mismatched with their biological sex (Bering, 2010). A person may feel like a man in a woman's body, or a woman in a man's body. Some may express their feelings by dressing as a person of the other biological sex typically would. *Gender identity* (one's sense of being male or female) is distinct from *sexual orientation* (the direction of one's sexual attraction). Most cross-dressers are biological males, the majority of whom are attracted to females (APA, 2010).

The Nurture of Gender: Our Culture

3 What is the importance of gender roles in development?

If nurture cannot undo biology in cases like David Reimer's, does this mean that biology is destiny? *No.* For most of us, nurture finishes the job that biology begins.

Gender Roles

Sex indeed matters. But from a biopsychosocial perspective, culture and the immediate situation matter, too. *Culture* is everything shared by a group and transmitted across generations. We can see culture's shaping power in the social expectations that guide men's and women's behavior.

In psychology, as in the theater, a **role** refers to a cluster of actions, the behaviors we expect of those who occupy a particular social position. **Gender roles** are the behaviors a culture expects of its men and women. Traditionally, American men were expected to initiate dates, drive the car, and pick up the check. Women were expected to decorate the home, buy and care for the children's clothes, and select the wedding gifts. About 90 percent of the time in two-parent families, Mom has stayed home with a sick child, arranged for the baby-sitter, and called the doctor (Maccoby, 1995). Even today, compared

The gendered tsunami: In Sri Lanka, Indonesia, and India, the gendered division of labor helps explain the excess of female deaths from the 2004 tsunami. In some villages, 80 percent of those killed were women, who were mostly at home when the storm hit. The men were more likely to be out at sea fishing or doing out-of-the-home chores (Oxfam, 2005).

with employed women, employed men in the United States spend about an hour and a half more on the job and about one hour less on household activities and caregiving each day (Amato et al., 2007; Bureau of Labor Statistics, 2004; Fisher et al., 2006).

Gender roles can smooth social relations, avoiding irritating discussions about whose job it is to get the car fixed, and who should make the kids breakfast. But these quick and easy assumptions come at a cost. If we don't fit people's expectations of roles, we may feel anxious.

Gender roles vary from culture to culture. People who live in nomadic societies and travel from place to place gathering food have only a minimal division of labor by sex. Boys and girls receive much the same upbringing. In agricultural societies, where women work in the fields close to home and men roam more freely herding livestock, children are typically guided into more distinct gender roles (Segall et al., 1990; Van Leeuwen, 1978).

Among industrialized countries, gender roles and attitudes vary widely (UNICEF, 2006). Would you say life is more

satisfying when both spouses work for pay and share child care? If so, you would agree with most people in 41 of 44 countries, according to a Pew Global Attitudes survey (2003). Even so, the culture-to-culture differences were huge, ranging from Egypt, where people disagreed 2 to 1, to Vietnam, where people agreed 11 to 1.

Gender ideas can change from one generation to the next. When families emigrate from Asia to Canada and the United States, for example, the parents carry with them the old culture's ideas about what it means to be a man or a woman. Their children often grow up with peers with very different attitudes about gender roles. Daughters, especially, may feel torn between the "old ways" and "new ways" (Dion & Dion, 2001).

Even within the same culture, attitudes about gender roles change over time. In 1960, of every 30 U.S. students entering law school, 1 was a woman. By 2005, half were (Cynkar, 2007; Glater, 2001). Ideas about men's and women's roles have changed.

How Do We Learn to Be Male or Female?

However our culture defines the behaviors expected of males and females, most boys will, in time, display these "masculine" traits and interests. Most girls will

---

X chromosome the sex chromosome found in both men and women. Females have two X chromosomes; males have one X chromosome and one Y chromosome.

Y chromosome the sex chromosome found only in males. When paired with an X chromosome from the mother, it produces a male child.

testosterone the most important male sex hormone. Stimulates the growth of the male sex organs in the fetus and the development of the male sex characteristics during puberty. Females have testosterone, but less of it.

role a set of expectations about a social position, defining how those in the position ought to behave.

gender role a set of expected behaviors for males or for females.

display "feminine" ones. How does this happen? **HOW DO WE ACQUIRE OUR GEN-◄ DER IDENTITY, OUR SENSE OF BEING MALE OR FEMALE?**

Social learning theory assumes that children learn **gender identity** by observing and imitating others' gender-linked behaviors and by being rewarded or punished for acting in certain ways themselves. ("Nicole, you're such a good mommy to your dolls," or "Big boys don't cry, Alex.") Some critics object, saying that differences in the way parents rear boys and girls aren't enough to explain **gender typing**—the way some children seem more attuned than others to traditional male or female roles (Lytton & Romney, 1991). In fact, even in families that discourage traditional gender typing, children organize themselves into "boy worlds" and "girl worlds," each guided by rules for what boys and girls do. So, modeling and rewarding by parents can't be the whole story.

Cognition (thinking) also matters. In your own childhood, as you struggled to understand the world, you—like other children—formed *schemas,* or concepts that helped you make sense of your world. One of these was your **gender schema,** your framework for organizing boy-girl characteristics (Bem, 1987, 1993). This gender schema then became a lens through which you viewed your experiences **(FIGURE 4.1).**

Gender schemas begin to form early in life, and social learning helps to form them. Before age 1, you began to discriminate male and female voices and faces (Martin et al., 2002). After age 2, language forced you to begin organizing your world on the basis of gender. English, for example, uses the pronouns *he* and *she;* other languages classify objects as masculine ("*le train*") or feminine ("*la table*").

Young children are "gender detectives" (Martin & Ruble, 2004). Once they grasp that two sorts of people exist—and that they are of one sort—they search for clues about gender, and they find them in language, dress, toys, and songs. Girls, they may decide, are the ones with long hair. Having divided the human world in half, 3-year-olds will then like their own

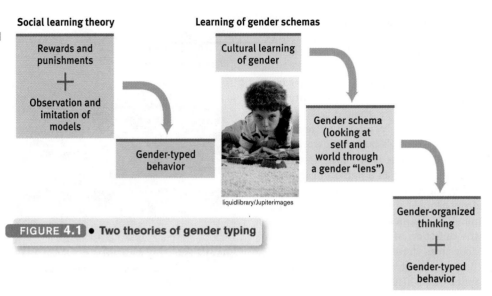

Social learning theory

Rewards and punishments

+

Observation and imitation of models

→ Gender-typed behavior

Learning of gender schemas

Cultural learning of gender

liquidlibrary/Jupiterimages

→ Gender schema (looking at self and world through a gender "lens")

→ Gender-organized thinking

+

Gender-typed behavior

FIGURE 4.1 • **Two theories of gender typing**

kind better and seek them out for play. And having compared themselves with their concept of gender, they will adjust their behavior accordingly. ("I am male—thus, masculine, strong, aggressive," or "I am female—therefore, feminine, sweet, and helpful.") These rigid boy-girl comparisons peak at about age 5 or 6. If the new neighbor is a boy, a 6-year-old girl may assume he just cannot share her interests. For young children, gender looms large.

PRACTICE TEST

THE BASICS

1. Females and males are very similar to each other. But one way they differ is that
   a. women are more physically aggressive than men.
   b. men are more democratic than women in their leadership roles.
   c. girls tend to play in small groups, while boys tend to play in large groups.
   d. women are more likely to commit suicide.

2. The fertilized egg will develop into a boy if it receives
   a. an X chromosome from its mother.
   b. an X chromosome from its father.
   c. a Y chromosome from its mother.
   d. a Y chromosome from its father.

3. Gender roles vary across cultures and over time. *Gender role* refers to our
   a. sense of being male or female.
   b. expectations about the way males and females should behave.
   c. biological sex.
   d. unisex characteristics.

4. When children have developed a *gender identity,* they
   a. exhibit traditional masculine or feminine behaviors.
   b. have a masculine or feminine appearance.
   c. have a sense of being male or female.
   d. have an unclear biological sex.

THE BIG PICTURE

4A. What are gender roles, and what do their variations tell us about our human capacity for learning and adaptation?

IN YOUR EVERYDAY LIFE

▪ How gender-typed are you? What has influenced your feelings of masculinity or femininity?

Answers: 1. c, 2. d, 3. b, 4. c. Answers to The Big Picture questions can be found in Appendix B at the end of the book.

Human Sexuality

One aspect of our gender is our sexuality. As we have seen, gender roles vary from place to place and from time to time within the same place. It's not surprising, then, that sexual expression also varies dramatically with time and culture. Among American women born before 1900, a mere 3 percent reported having had premarital sex by age 18 (Smith, 1998). A century later, about half of U.S. ninth- to twelfth-graders reported having had sexual intercourse (CDC, 2010). Teen intercourse rates have been higher in Western Europe but much lower in Arab and Asian countries and among North Americans of Asian descent (McLaughlin et al., 1997; Wellings et al., 2006).

In European and U.S. history, the pendulum of sexual values has swung back and forth. The early 1800s' eroticism gave way to the conservative Victorian era of the late 1800s. The free-thinking flapper era of the 1920s was replaced by the stricter family-values period of the 1950s, which gave way to the end-of-century pleasure-seeking "me generation" (Twenge, 2006). The pendulum may have begun a new swing toward commitment in the twenty-first century. Teen birth rates have declined since 1991, and virgins (52 percent in 2007) now outnumber nonvirgins among U.S. 15- to 19-year-olds (CDC, 2008).

Attitudes toward homosexuality also vary with time and culture. In U.S. Gallup surveys, support for gay marriage increased from 27 percent in 1996 to 40 percent in 2009. Should homosexuality "be accepted in society"? Only 1 in 10 people in some predominantly Muslim countries said it should, as did more than 3 in 4 people in several West European countries (Speulda & McIntosh, 2004).

Later in this chapter, we'll return to these topics. But let's look first at some more basic aspects of our sexuality.

The Physiology of Sex

The first extensive descriptions of sexual behavior in the United States appeared in mid-twentieth-century surveys (Kinsey et al., 1948, 1953). In the 1960s, the studies of gynecologist-obstetrician William Masters and his collaborator Virginia Johnson (1966) made headlines. Before reviewing their findings, we need to know more about the hormones affecting sexual behavior.

Hormones and Sexual Behavior

4 How do hormones influence our sexuality, and what stages mark the human sexual response cycle?

Among the forces driving sexual behavior are the *sex hormones*. The main male sex hormone, as we saw earlier, is *testosterone*. The main female sex hormones are the **estrogens,** such as estradiol. Sex hormones influence us at many points in the life span.

- During the prenatal period, they direct our development as males or females.

- During puberty, a surge in sex hormones ushers us into adolescence.

- After puberty and well into the late adult years, sex hormones help activate sexual behavior.

In most mammals, fertility and sex overlap. Females become sexually receptive ("in heat") when their estrogen levels peak at ovulation. In experiments, researchers can cause female animals to become receptive by injecting them with estrogens. Researchers cannot so easily manipulate the sexual behavior of male animals (Feder, 1984). Nevertheless, male rats that have had their testes (which manufacture testosterone) surgically removed will gradually lose much of their interest in receptive females. They gradually regain it if injected with testosterone.

Hormones do influence human sexual behavior, but in a looser way. Among women with mates, sexual desire rises slightly at ovulation (Pillsworth et al., 2004). "How do we know this?" a critical thinker might ask. We know because of studies like the one that invited women with partners to keep a sexual activity diary. On the days around ovulation, intercourse was 24 percent more frequent (Wilcox et al., 2004). Other studies find that women fantasize more about sex with desirable partners and wear more sexually attractive clothing around ovulation (Haselton et al., 2006; Pillsworth & Haselton, 2006; Sheldon et al., 2006).

Another study found that men's testosterone levels increased when they were exposed to the scent of an ovulating woman's T-shirt (Miller & Maner, 2010). In a study of 5300 lap dances by 18 strip-club lap dancers, hourly tips almost doubled on the days near ovulation, compared with days during menstruation (Miller et al., 2007).

Women more than other mammalian females are responsive to testosterone level (van Anders & Dunn, 2009). You may recall that women have testosterone, though at lower levels than are found in men. If a woman's natural testosterone level drops, as happens with removal of the ovaries or adrenal glands, her sexual interest may wane. But testosterone-replacement therapy can often restore sexual desire, arousal, and activity (Buster et al., 2005; Davis et al., 2003; Kroll et al., 2004).

In men, normal fluctuations in testosterone levels (from man to man and from hour to hour) have little effect on sexual drive (Byrne, 1982). Indeed, male hormones sometimes vary *in response* to sexual stimulation. In one study, heterosexual male volunteers talked separately with a male student and with a female student. In both cases, their testosterone levels rose with the social arousal, but especially after talking with the female (Dabbs et al., 1987, 2000). Thus, sexual arousal can be a *cause* as well as a result of increased testosterone levels.

Large hormonal surges or declines do affect men and women's desire. These shifts tend to occur at two predictable points in the life span, and sometimes at an unpredictable third point.

social learning theory the theory that we learn social behavior by observing and imitating and by being rewarded or punished.

gender identity one's sense of being male or female.

gender typing taking on a traditional masculine or feminine role.

gender schema a culturally learned concept of what it means to be male and female.

estrogens sex hormones secreted in greater amounts by females than by males. In nonhuman female mammals, estrogen levels peak during ovulation, promoting sexual receptivity.

1. *During puberty, a surge in sex hormones triggers the development of sex characteristics.* Interest in dating and sexual stimulation usually increases at this time. If the hormonal surge is prevented—as it was during the 1600s and 1700s for boys who were castrated to preserve their soprano voices for Italian opera—sex characteristics and sexual desire do not develop normally (Peschel & Peschel, 1987).

2. *In later life, estrogen levels fall, and women experience menopause* (Chapter 3). As sex hormone levels decline, the frequency of sexual fantasies and intercourse declines as well (Leitenberg & Henning, 1995).

3. *For some, surgery or drugs may cause hormonal shifts.* When adult men are castrated, sex drive typically falls as testosterone levels decline (Hucker & Bain, 1990). If male sex offenders take a drug that reduces testosterone level to that of a boy's before puberty, they also lose much of their sexual urge (Money et al., 1983).

The Sexual Response Cycle

In their studies of sexual behavior, Masters and Johnson recorded the physiological responses of 382 female and 312 male volunteers who masturbated or had intercourse. With the help of this somewhat atypical sample (people able and willing to display arousal and orgasm while being observed in a laboratory), the researchers identified a four-stage **sexual response cycle,** similar in men and women. Here are the stages:

1. *Excitement:* The genital areas become engorged with blood, which causes a woman's clitoris and a man's penis to swell. A woman's vagina expands and secretes lubricant.

2. *Plateau:* Excitement peaks as breathing, pulse, and blood pressure rates continue to increase. A man's penis becomes fully engorged. A woman's vaginal secretion continues to increase and her clitoris retracts. Orgasm feels imminent.

"I love the idea of there being two sexes, don't you?"

3. *Orgasm:* Muscle contractions appear all over the body and are accompanied by further increases in breathing, pulse, and blood pressure rates. (Later studies showed that a woman's arousal and orgasm aid conception. They help propel semen from the penis, position the uterus to receive sperm, and draw the sperm farther inward [Furlow & Thornhill, 1996].) In the excitement of the moment, men and women are hardly aware of all this as their rhythmic genital contractions create a pleasurable feeling of sexual release. The feeling apparently is much the same for both sexes. One panel of experts could not reliably distinguish between descriptions of orgasm written by men and those written by women (Vance & Wagner, 1976). In another study, PET scans showed that the same brain regions were active in men and women during orgasms (Holstege et al., 2003a,b).

4. *Resolution:* The body gradually returns to its unaroused state as genital blood vessels release their accumulated blood. This happens relatively quickly if orgasm has occurred, relatively slowly otherwise. (It's like the nasal tickle that goes away rapidly if you have sneezed, slowly otherwise.) Men then enter a **refractory period,** a resting period that lasts from a few minutes to a day or more, during which they are incapable of another orgasm. A woman's much shorter refractory period may enable her to have another orgasm if restimulated during or soon after resolution.

Sexually Transmitted Infections

5 What are STIs, and how can they be prevented?

Rates of *sexually transmitted infections* (STIs, also called STDs for *sexually transmitted diseases*) are rising. Two-thirds of new infections occur in people under 25 (ASHA, 2003). Teenage girls, because of their less mature biological development and lower levels of protective antibodies, seem especially vulnerable (Guttmacher, 1994; Morell, 1995). About 40 percent of sexually experienced 14- to 19-year-old U.S. females have an STI (CDC, 2008).

To comprehend the mathematics of sexually transmitted infection, imagine this scenario. Over the course of a year, Pat has sex with 9 people. Over the same period, each of Pat's partners has sex with 9 other people, who in turn have sex with 9 others. How many "phantom" sex partners (past partners of partners) will Pat have? The actual number—511—is more than five times the estimate given by the average student (Brannon & Brock, 1994).

Condoms offer no protection against certain skin-to-skin STIs and only partial protection against the human papillomaviruses (HPV). Most HPVs can, however, be prevented by vaccination (Medical Institute, 1994; NIH, 2001). Condoms do reduce other risks. The risk of getting HIV (*human immunodeficiency virus*—the virus that causes **AIDS**) from an infected partner is 10 times higher for those who do not use condoms (Pinkerton & Abramson, 1997). Although AIDS is also transmitted by other means, such as needle sharing during drug use, its sexual transmission is most common.

Women's AIDS rates are increasing fastest, partly because the virus is passed from male to female much more often than from female to male. A man's semen can carry more of the virus than can a woman's vaginal and cervical secretions. The HIV-infected semen can also linger for days in a woman's vagina and cervix, increasing the time of exposure (Allen & Setlow, 1991; WHO, 2004).

Most U.S. AIDS cases have been people in midlife and younger—ages 25 to 44

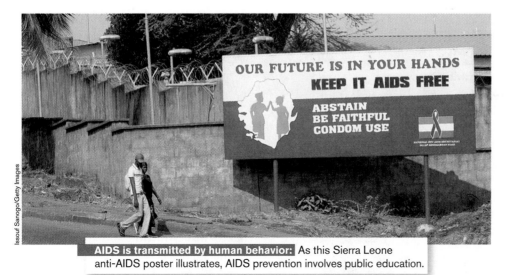

AIDS is transmitted by human behavior: As this Sierra Leone anti-AIDS poster illustrates, AIDS prevention involves public education.

form our perceptions and direct our actions. So what sexual scripts do today's media write on our minds? An average hour of prime-time television on the three major U.S. networks contains approximately 15 sexual acts, words, and innuendos. The partners are usually unmarried, with no prior romantic relationship, and few communicate any concern for birth control or sexually transmitted infections (Brown et al., 2002; Kunkel, 2001; Sapolsky & Tabarlet, 1991). The more sexual content adolescents view (even when controlling for other predictors of early sexual activity), the more likely they are to perceive their peers as sexually active, to develop sexually permissive attitudes, and to have early intercourse (Escobar-Chaves et al., 2005; Martino et al., 2005; Ward & Friedman, 2006). (See Close-Up: The Sexualization of Girls on the next page.)

One response to these facts of life has been a greater emphasis on teen abstinence within some comprehensive sex education programs. A National Longitudinal Study of Adolescent Health among 12,000 teens found several predictors of sexual restraint.

- *High intelligence* Teens with high (rather than average) intelligence test scores are more likely to delay sex. They evidently appreciate the risk of pregnancy and other negative outcomes. They also tend to be more focused on future achievement than on here-and-now pleasures (Halpern et al., 2000).

(U.S. Centers for Disease Control and Prevention, 2007). Given AIDS' long incubation period, this means that many of these young people were infected as teens. In 2009, the death of 1.8 million AIDS victims worldwide left behind countless grief-stricken partners and millions of orphaned children (UNAIDS, 2010). Sub-Saharan Africa is home to two-thirds of those infected with HIV, and medical treatment and care for the dying are sapping the region's social resources.

> "Condoms should be used on every conceivable occasion."
> Anonymous

Teen Pregnancy

6 What factors influence teenagers' sexual behaviors and use of contraceptives?

WHY DO U.S. TEENS, WHEN COMPARED◄ WITH EUROPEAN TEENS, HAVE A LOWER RATE OF INTERCOURSE BUT HIGHER RATES OF PREGNANCY AND ABORTION? One reason is that they have lower rates of contraceptive use (Call et al., 2002; Sullivan/Anderson, 2009). Some related findings:

> "All of us who make motion pictures are teachers, teachers with very loud voices."
> Film producer George Lucas, Academy Award ceremonies, 1992

Ignorance Most teens overestimate their peers' sexual activity. The idea that "everybody is doing it" may influence their own behavior (Child Trends, 2001).

Guilt related to sexual activity One survey found that 72 percent of sexually active 12- to 17-year-old American girls said they regretted having had sex (Reuters, 2000). Such feelings may reduce further sexual activity. But if passion overwhelms intentions, it can also reduce attempts at birth control (Gerrard & Luus, 1995).

Minimal communication about birth control Many teens are uncomfortable talking about contraception with parents, partners, and peers. Those who talk freely with friends or parents, and are in an exclusive relationship with a partner with whom they communicate openly, are more likely to use contraceptives (Aspy et al., 2007; Milan & Kilmann, 1987).

Alcohol use Sexually active teens are typically alcohol-using teens (Zimmer-Gembeck & Helfand, 2008). Alcohol depresses the brain centers that control judgment, inhibition, and self-awareness. As a result, a few pre-sex drinks may translate into not using condoms (Kotchick et al., 2001). Alcohol's tendency to break down normal restraints is a fact well known to sexually coercive males.

TV and movies model unsafe sex Media help write the "social scripts" that help

sexual response cycle the four stages of sexual responding described by Masters and Johnson—excitement, plateau, orgasm, and resolution.

refractory period a resting period after orgasm, during which a man cannot achieve another orgasm.

AIDS (acquired immune deficiency syndrome) a life-threatening, sexually transmitted infection caused by the *human immunodeficiency virus* (HIV). AIDS depletes the immune system, leaving the person vulnerable to infections.

The Sexualization of Girls

Have you noticed? Just about all media—TV, the Internet, music videos and lyrics, movies, magazines, sports media, and advertising—share a tendency. They portray women and even girls as sexual objects, while emphasizing unrealistic beauty standards. HOW DO MEDIA MODELS AFFECT YOUNG GIRLS WHO ARE STUDYING AND TRYING TO LIVE UP TO THESE MODELS OF FEMININITY? The frequent result, reports the 2007 American Psychological Association (APA) Task Force on the Sexualization of Girls, is harm to their self-image and unhealthy sexual development.

Sexualization occurs when girls

- are led to value themselves in terms of their sexual appeal.
- compare themselves to narrowly defined beauty standards.
- see themselves as sexual beings for others' use.

In experiments, the task force reported, being made self-conscious about one's body, such as by wearing a swimsuit, disrupts thinking when doing math computations or logical reasoning. Sexualization also contributes to eating disorders and depression, and to unrealistic expectations regarding sexuality.

Mindful of today's sexualizing media, the APA has some suggestions for countering these messages. Parents, teachers, and others can teach girls "to value themselves for who they are rather than how they look." They can teach boys "to value girls as friends, sisters, and girlfriends, rather than as sexual objects." And they can help girls and boys develop "media literacy skills" that enable them to recognize and resist the message that women are sexual objects and that a thin, sexy look is all that matters.

© T. Arroyo/JPegFoto/PictureGroup via AP Images

- *Religious engagement* Actively religious teens and young adults have lower pregnancy rates because they more often reserve sex for marital commitment (Lucero et al., 2008).

- *Father's presence* In studies that followed hundreds of New Zealand and U.S. girls from age 5 to 18, a father's absence was linked to sexual activity before age 16 and teen pregnancy (Ellis et al., 2003). These associations held even after adjusting for other adverse influences, such as poverty.

- *Participation in service-learning programs* Several experiments have found that pregnancy rates among teens who volunteered as tutors or participated in community projects were lower

than those of teens randomly assigned to control conditions (Kirby, 2002; O'Donnell et al., 2002). Does service learning promote a sense of personal competence, control, and responsibility? Does it encourage more future-oriented thinking? Or does it simply reduce opportunities for unprotected sex? Researchers are searching for these answers.

We have seen that exposure to mass media portrayals of sexual behavior correlates with the sexualization of girls and with teen pregnancy. Sexually explicit material may also influence our attitudes about our partners and relationships.

The Psychology of Sex

7 How do external and imagined stimuli contribute to sexual arousal?

We might compare human sex hormones, especially testosterone, to the fuel in a car. Without fuel, a car will not run. Our hormonal fuel is equally essential. But our sexual motivation is fueled by more than hormones. It also requires the psychological stimuli—external and imagined—that turn on the engine, keep it running, and shift it into high gear.

External Stimuli

Many studies confirm that men become aroused when they see, hear, or read erotic material. It should not be surprising, then, to hear that most sexually explicit materials are sold to men. What may be surprising, though, is that most women—at least the less inhibited women who volunteer to participate in such studies—report or exhibit nearly as much arousal to the same stimuli (Heiman, 1975; Stockton & Murnen, 1992).

With repeated exposure, the emotional response to any erotic stimulus often grows weaker. During the 1920s, when Western women's hemlines first rose to the knee, an exposed leg was a mildly erotic stimulus. So were (by today's standards) modest two-piece swimsuits and movie scenes of a mere kiss. Today, few Westerners would be aroused by such images.

"Fill'er up with testosterone."

Repeatedly viewing images of women being sexually coerced—and seeming to enjoy it—appears to follow a similar path. In studies, viewers have become more accepting of the false idea that women enjoy rape. They also tended to be more willing to hurt women (Malamuth & Check, 1981; Zillmann, 1989).

Simply looking at images of sexually attractive women and men can also affect people's attitudes toward their own partners and relationships. After male collegians viewed sexually attractive women on TV or in magazines, they often found an average woman, or their own girlfriend or wife, less attractive (Kenrick & Gutierres, 1980; Kenrick et al., 1989; Weaver et al., 1984). Viewing X-rated sex films has similarly tended to diminish people's satisfaction with their own sexual partners (Zillmann, 1989). Some sex researchers suspect that reading or watching erotica may create expectations that few men and women can fulfill.

Imagined Stimuli

The brain, it has been said, is our most important sex organ. The stimuli inside our heads—our imagination—can influence sexual arousal and desire. People who, because of a spinal cord injury, have no genital sensation, can still feel sexual desire (Willmuth, 1987).

Wide-awake people become sexually aroused not only by memories of prior sexual activities but also by fantasies. In one survey of masturbation-related fantasies, 19 percent of women and 10 percent of men reported imagining being "taken" by someone overwhelmed with desire for them (Hunt, 1974). Fantasy is not reality, however. There's a big difference between fantasizing that Johnny Depp just won't take No for an answer and having a hostile stranger actually force himself on you (Brownmiller, 1975).

About 95 percent of both men and women say they have had sexual fantasies. Men (whether gay or straight) fantasize about sex more often, more physically, and less romantically. They also prefer less personal and faster-paced sexual content in books and videos (Leitenberg & Henning, 1995).

* * *

We have considered some of the research on the biological and psychological aspects of human sexuality. It's important to remember, though, that scientific research on human sexuality does not aim to define the personal meaning of sex in our own lives. (See Thinking Critically About: Sex and Human Values.) We could know every available fact about sex—that the initial spasms of male and female orgasm come at 0.8-second intervals, that the female nipples expand 10 millimeters at the peak of sexual arousal, that systolic blood pressure rises some 60 points, and respiration rate to 40 breaths per minute—but fail to understand the human significance of sexual intimacy.

Surely one significance of sexual intimacy is its expression of our profoundly social nature. Sex is a socially significant act. Men and women can achieve orgasm alone, yet most people find greater satisfaction while embracing their loved one. Our sexuality fuels a yearning for closeness. At its human best, sex is life-uniting and love-renewing.

Image Source/Getty Images

Sex and Human Values

Recognizing that values are both personal and cultural, most sex researchers and educators try to keep their writings on sexual behavior value free. But the very words we use to describe behaviors can reflect our personal values. Whether we label certain sexual behaviors as "perversions" or as part of an "alternative sexual life-style" depends on our attitude toward the behaviors. Labels describe, but they also evaluate.

Yet sex education separated from the context of human values may give some students the idea that sexual intercourse is simply a recreational activity. Diana Baumrind (1982), a University of California child-rearing expert, has observed that an implication that adults are neutral about adolescent sexual activity is unfortunate, because "promiscuous recreational sex poses certain psychological, social, health, and moral problems that must be faced realistically."

Perhaps we can agree that the knowledge provided by sex research is preferable to ignorance, and yet also agree that researchers' values should be stated openly, enabling us to debate them and to reflect on our own values.

In the remaining pages of this chapter, we'll consider two special topics: *sexual orientation* (the direction of our sexual interests), and evolutionary psychology's explanation of our sexual motivation.

PRACTICE TEST

THE BASICS

5. A striking effect of hormonal changes on human sexual behavior is the
   a. end of sexual desire in men over 60.
   b. sharp rise in sexual interest at puberty.
   c. decrease in women's sexual desire at the time of ovulation.
   d. increase in testosterone levels in castrated males.

6. In describing the sexual response cycle, Masters and Johnson noted that
   a. a plateau phase follows orgasm.
   b. men experience a refractory period during which they cannot experience orgasm.
   c. the feeling that accompanies orgasm is stronger in men than in women.
   d. testosterone is released equally in women and men.

7. The use of condoms during sex
   a. protects against all STIs.
   b. reduces the risk of getting HIV.
   c. protects against skin-to-skin STIs.
   d. increases the risk of getting a human papillomavirus.

8. Factors contributing to unplanned teen pregnancies include ignorance, guilt, lack of communication about options, mass media modeling of promiscuity, and
   a. low levels of testosterone during adolescence.
   b. higher intelligence level.
   c. the decreased rates of sexually transmitted diseases.
   d. alcohol use.

9. An example of an external stimulus that might influence sexual behavior is
   a. blood level of testosterone.
   b. the onset of puberty.
   c. a sexually explicit film.
   d. an erotic fantasy or dream.

THE BIG PICTURE
4B. What factors affect sexual expression?

IN YOUR EVERYDAY LIFE
▪ What do you think would be an effective strategy for reducing teen pregnancy?

Answers: 5. b, 6. b, 7. b, 8. d, 9. c. Answers to The Big Picture questions can be found in Appendix B at the end of the book.

Sexual Orientation

8 What does current research tell us about why some people are attracted to members of their own sex and others are attracted to members of the other sex?

We express the *direction* of our sexual interest in our **sexual orientation**—our enduring sexual attraction toward members of our own sex (*homosexual orientation*) or the other sex (*heterosexual orientation*). As far as we know, all cultures in all times have been predominantly heterosexual (Bullough, 1990). Some cultures have condemned homosexuality. (In Kenya and Nigeria, 98 percent have thought homosexuality is "never justified" [Pew, 2006].) Other have accepted it. But in both cases, heterosexuality prevails and homosexuality endures.

Estimates based on data from the 2000 U.S. Census suggest that 2.5 percent of the population is gay or lesbian (Tarmann, 2002). About 3 or 4 percent of men and 1 or 2 percent of women are exclusively homosexual. A much smaller number (fewer than 1 percent) report being actively bisexual, and many of them say they had an isolated homosexual experience (Mosher et al., 2005). Most people surveyed say they have had an occasional homosexual fantasy.

The overwhelming majority of the U.S. population—some 97+ percent—is heterosexual, or *straight*.

WHAT DOES IT FEEL LIKE TO BE THE "ODD◀ MAN (OR WOMAN) OUT" IN A STRAIGHT CULTURE? If you are heterosexual, one way to

> In one British survey of 18,876 people, 1 percent reported being *asexual*, having "never felt sexually attracted to anyone at all" (Bogaert, 2006).

> Studies indicate that men who describe themselves as bisexual tend to respond like homosexual men; they typically have genital arousal mostly to same-sex erotic stimuli (Rieger et al., 2005).

understand is to imagine how you would feel if you were socially isolated for openly admitting or displaying your feelings toward someone of the other sex. How would you react if you overheard people making crude jokes about heterosexual people? And how would you answer if your family members were pleading with you to change your heterosexual life-style and to enter into a homosexual marriage?

Facing such reactions, homosexual people often struggle with their sexual orientation. They may at first try to ignore or deny their desires, hoping they will go away. But they don't. Some may try to change, through psychotherapy, willpower, or prayer. But the feelings typically persist, as do those of heterosexual people—who are similarly incapable of becoming homosexual (Haldeman, 1994, 2002; Myers & Scanzoni, 2005).

Most of today's psychologists therefore view sexual orientation as neither willfully chosen nor willfully changed. "Efforts to change sexual orientation are unlikely to be successful and involve some risk of harm," declared a 2009 American Psychological Association report. In 1973, the American Psychiatric Association dropped homosexuality from its list of "mental illnesses." In 1993, the World Health Organization did the same, as did Japan's and China's psychiatric associations in 1995 and 2001. Some have noted that rates of depression and attempted suicide are higher among gays and lesbians. Many psychologists believe, however, that these symptoms may result from experiences with bullying, harassment, and discrimination (Sandfort et al., 2001; Warner et al., 2004). "Homosexuality, in and of itself, is not associated with mental disorders or emotional or social problems," declared the American Psychological Association (2007).

Thus, sexual orientation in some ways is like handedness: Most people are one way, some the other. A very few are ambidextrous. Regardless, the way one is endures.

Personal values affect sexual orientation less than they affect other forms of sexual behavior: Compared with people who rarely attend religious services, for example, those who attend regularly are one-third as likely to have lived together before marriage, and they report having had many fewer sex partners. But (if male) they are just as likely to be homosexual (Smith, 1998).

Let me qualify that. Compared with men's sexual orientation, women's tends to be less strongly felt and may be more variable (Chivers, 2005; Diamond, 2007; Peplau & Garnets, 2000). Men's lesser *erotic plasticity* (sexual variability) is apparent across time, across cultures, across situations, and across differing levels of education, religious engagement, and peer influence (Baumeister, 2000). Adult women's sexual drive and interests are more flexible and changing than are adult men's. Women, more than men, for example, prefer to alternate periods of high sexual activity with periods of almost none. They are also somewhat more likely than men to report bisexual attractions.

Environment and Sexual Orientation

So our sexual orientation is something we do not choose and (especially for males) seemingly cannot change. WHERE, THEN, ◄ DO THESE ENDURING PREFERENCES— HETEROSEXUAL OR HOMOSEXUAL—COME FROM? Let's look first at possible environmental influences on sexual orientation. To see if you can predict the findings that have emerged from hundreds of studies, try answering (Yes or No) to the following questions:

1. Is homosexuality linked with problems in a child's relationships with parents, such as with a domineering mother and an ineffectual father, or a possessive mother and a hostile father?

2. Does homosexuality involve a fear or hatred of people of the other gender, leading individuals to direct their sexual desires toward members of their own sex?

3. Is sexual orientation linked with levels of sex hormones currently in the blood?

4. As children, were many homosexuals molested, seduced, or otherwise sexually victimized by an adult homosexual?

The answer to all these questions appears to be *No* (Storms, 1983). In a search for possible environmental influences on sexual orientation, Kinsey Institute investigators interviewed nearly 1000 homosexuals and 500 heterosexuals. They assessed nearly every imaginable psychological cause of homosexuality—parental relationships, childhood sexual experiences, peer relationships, dating experiences (Bell et al., 1981; Hammersmith, 1982). Their findings: Homosexuals were no more likely than heterosexuals to have been sexually abused, smothered by maternal love, or neglected by their father. Consider this: If "distant fathers" were more likely to produce homosexual sons, then shouldn't boys growing up in father-absent homes more often be gay? (They are not.) And shouldn't the rising number of such homes have led to a noticeable increase in the gay population? (It has not.)

A bottom line has emerged from a half-century's theory and research. If there are environmental factors that influence sexual orientation, we do not yet know what they are.

Biology and Sexual Orientation

The lack of evidence for environmental causes of homosexuality has led researchers to explore possible biological influences. Researchers have looked at homosexuality in other species, gay-straight brain differences, and the influence of genetics and prenatal hormones.

Same-Sex Attraction in Other Species

In Boston's Public Gardens, caretakers have solved the mystery of why a much-loved swan couple's eggs never hatch. Both swans are female. In New York City's Central Park Zoo, penguins Silo and Roy spent several years as devoted same-sex partners. At least occasional same-sex relations have been observed in several hundred species (Bagemihl, 1999). Grizzlies, gorillas, monkeys, flamingos, and owls are all on the long list. Among rams, for example, some 7 to 10 percent (to sheep-breeding ranchers, the "duds") display same-sex attraction by shunning ewes and seeking to mount other males (Perkins & Fitzgerald, 1997). Some degree of homosexuality seems to be a natural part of the animal world.

sexual orientation an enduring sexual attraction toward members of either our own sex (homosexual orientation) or the other sex (heterosexual orientation).

Juliet and Juliet: Boston's beloved swan couple, "Romeo and Juliet," were discovered actually to be, as are many other animal partners, a same-sex pair.

Gay-Straight Brain Differences

Researcher Simon LeVay (1991) studied sections of the hypothalamus taken from deceased heterosexual and homosexual people. (The hypothalamus is a brain structure linked to emotion.) As a gay man, LeVay wanted to do "something connected with my gay identity." To avoid biasing the results, he did a *blind study,* without knowing which donors were gay or straight. After nine months of peering through his microscope at a cell cluster that seemed to come in different sizes, he consulted the donor records. The cell cluster was reliably larger in heterosexual men than in women and homosexual men. "I was almost in a state of shock," LeVay said (1994). "I took a walk by myself on the cliffs over the ocean. I sat for half an hour just thinking what this might mean."

It should not surprise us that brains differ with sexual orientation. Remember, *everything psychological is simultaneously biological.* But when did the brain difference begin? At conception? During childhood or adolescence? Did experience produce the difference? Or was it genes or prenatal hormones (or genes via prenatal hormones)?

LeVay does not view this cell cluster as an "on-off button" for sexual orientation. Rather, he believes it is an important part of a brain pathway active during sexual behavior. He agrees that sexual behavior patterns could influence the brain's anatomy. (Neural pathways in our brain do grow stronger with use.) In fish, birds, rats, and humans, brain structures vary with experience—including sexual experience (Breedlove, 1997). But LeVay believes it more likely that brain anatomy influences sexual orientation. His hunch seems confirmed by the discovery of a similar difference found between the 7 to 10 percent of male sheep that display same-sex attraction and the 90+ percent attracted to females (Larkin et al., 2002; Roselli et al., 2002, 2004). Moreover, such differences seem to develop soon after birth, perhaps even before birth (Rahman & Wilson, 2003).

> "Gay men simply don't have the brain cells to be attracted to women."
>
> Simon LeVay, *The Sexual Brain,* 1993

Since LeVay's discovery, other researchers have reported additional gay-straight brain differences. One is an area of the hypothalamus that governs sexual arousal (Savic et al., 2005). When straight women are given a whiff of a scent derived from men's sweat (which contains traces of male hormones), this area becomes active. Gay men's brains respond similarly to the men's scent. Straight men's brains do not. They show the arousal response only to a female hormone sample. In a similar study, lesbians' responses differed from those of straight women (Kranz & Ishai, 2006; Martins et al., 2005).

A third brain difference appears in the fibers connecting the right and left hemispheres. A section of the anterior commissure (similar to the corpus callosum) is one-third larger in homosexual men than in heterosexual men (Allen & Gorski, 1992). Such studies support the idea that, in some areas, homosexual men's brains are similar to women's brains in ways not found in heterosexual men (Gladue, 1994).

Genetic Influences

Three lines of evidence suggest a genetic influence on sexual orientation.

- "Homosexuality does appear to run in families," note Brian Mustanski and Michael Bailey (2003). Homosexual men have more homosexual relatives on their mother's side than on their father's. And the relatives on the mother's side also produce more offspring than do the maternal relatives of heterosexual men (Camperio-Ciani et al., 2004, 2009; Zietsch et al., 2008).

- Twin studies support the idea that genes influence sexual orientation. Identical twins (who have identical genes) are somewhat more likely than fraternal twins (whose genes are not identical) to share a homosexual orientation. However, sexual orientations differ in many identical twin pairs (especially female twins). This means that other factors besides genes play a role.

- Laboratory experiments on fruit flies have altered a single gene and changed the flies' sexual orientation and behavior (Dickson, 2005). During courtship, females acted like males (pursuing other females) and males acted like females (Demir & Dickson, 2005).

Brain anatomy and genetics are two of the biological influences on sexual orientation. The third appears to be prenatal exposure to hormones or other biochemical substances in the womb.

Prenatal Influences

Twins share not only genes, but also a prenatal environment. Two sets of findings indicate that the prenatal environment matters.

First, in humans, a critical period of brain development seems to fall between the middle of the second and fifth months after conception (Ellis & Ames, 1987; Gladue, 1990; Meyer-Bahlburg, 1995). Exposure to the hormone levels typically experienced by female fetuses during this period may predispose a person (female or male) to be attracted to males in later life. When pregnant sheep are injected with testosterone during a similar critical period, their female offspring later show homosexual behavior (Money, 1987).

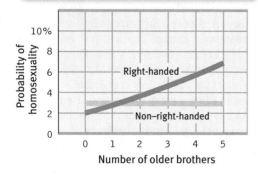

FIGURE 4.2 ● **The fraternal birth order effect** Researcher Ray Blanchard (2008) offers these approximate curves depicting a man's likelihood of homosexuality as a function of his number of older brothers. This correlation has been found in several studies, but only among right-handed men (as about 9 in 10 men are).

Second, the mother's immune system may play a role in the development of sexual orientation. Men who have older brothers are somewhat more likely to be gay—about one-third more likely for each additional older brother (Blanchard, 1997, 2008; Bogaert, 2003). If the odds of homosexuality are roughly 2 percent among first sons, they would rise to nearly 3 percent among second sons, 4 percent for third sons, and so on for each additional older brother (see **FIGURE 4.2**). The reason for this curious effect—called the *older-brother* or *fraternal birth-order effect*—is unclear. But the explanation does seem biological. The effect does not occur among adopted brothers (Bogaert, 2006). Researchers suspect the mother's immune system may have a defensive response to substances produced by male fetuses. After each pregnancy with a male fetus, the maternal antibodies may become stronger and may prevent the fetal brain from developing in a typical male pattern.

Gay-Straight Trait Differences

On several traits, homosexual individuals of both sexes fall midway between heterosexual females and males. Consider, for example, the spatial abilities of gay and straight people (Cohen, 2002; Gladue, 1994; McCormick & Witelson, 1991; Sanders & Wright, 1997). On mental rotation tasks such as the one illustrated in **FIGURE 4.3,** the scores of homosexual males and females fall between those of heterosexual males and heterosexual females. **TABLE 4.1** lists some biological and behavioral traits that show similar gay-straight differences. (See also LeVay, 2010.)

* * *

The consistency of the genetic, prenatal, and brain findings supports a biological explanation of sexual orientation (Rahman & Wilson, 2003). This helps explain why sexual orientation is so difficult to change, and why a BBC Internet survey of more than 200,000 people found the same gay-straight differences worldwide (Lippa 2007a,b, 2008). Our sexual orientation is, it now appears, a natural and enduring disposition.

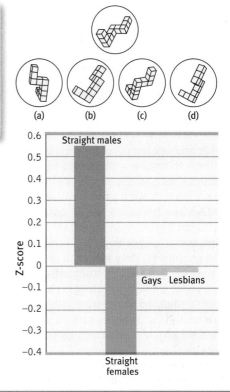

FIGURE 4.3 • **Spatial abilities and sexual orientation** Which two of the four figures can be rotated to match the target figure at the top? Straight males tend to solve this problem more easily than straight females, with gays and lesbians scoring somewhere in between. (From Rahman et al., 2003, with 60 people tested in each group.)

Answer: Figures a and d.

(a)   (b)   (c)   (d)

TABLE 4.1 **Biological Factors in Sexual Orientation**

Gay-straight trait differences

Studies—some in need of replication—indicate that homosexuals and heterosexuals differ in the following biological and behavioral traits.

- spatial abilities
- fingerprint ridge counts
- auditory system development
- handedness
- occupational preferences
- relative finger lengths

- gender nonconformity
- age of onset of puberty in males
- male body size
- sleep length
- physical aggression
- walking style

On average (the evidence is strongest for males), results for gays and lesbians fall between those of straight men and straight women. Three biological influences—brain, genetic, and prenatal—may contribute to these differences.

Brain differences

- One hypothalamic cell cluster is smaller in women and gay men than in straight men.
- Anterior commissure is larger in gay men than in straight men.
- Gay men's hypothalamus reacts as do straight women's to the smell of sex-related hormones.

Genetic influences

- Shared sexual orientation is higher among identical twins than among fraternal twins.
- Sexual attraction in fruit flies can be genetically manipulated.
- Male homosexuality often appears to be transmitted from the mother's side of the family.

Prenatal influences

- Altered prenatal hormone exposure may lead to homosexuality in humans and other animals.
- Right-handed men with several older biological brothers are more likely to be gay, possibly due to a maternal immune-system reaction.

An Evolutionary Explanation of Human Sexuality

9 How do evolutionary psychologists use natural selection to explain human sexuality?

Hunger and sex are different sorts of motivations. Hunger responds to a need. If we do not eat, we die. Sex is not in this sense a need. If we do not have sex, we may feel like dying, but we do not. Why, then, is our sexuality so important to us? **Evolutionary psychologists** have proposed an answer. They ask us to remember that life is sexually transmitted. As the pleasure we take in eating is nature's inventive method of getting our body nourishment, so the pleasure of sex is our genes' way of preserving and spreading themselves. When two people are attracted, they hardly stop to think of themselves as guided by their genes. But sexual motivation is nature's clever way of making people procreate, thus enabling our species' survival.

At the dawn of human history, our ancestors faced certain questions: Who is my ally, who my foe? What food should I eat? With whom should I mate? Some early humans answered those questions more successfully than others. (Those who deemed leopards "nice to pet" were probably not in the group that contributed their genes to later generations.)

As carriers of our prehistoric ancestors' genes, we are biologically prepared to act as they did. In generations past, men who were attracted to young, healthy women would have produced more offspring than those who were as attracted to older or less healthy women. And today, across a wide range of cultures studied (**FIGURE 4.4**), men still have eyes for women whose age and features imply fertility (Buss, 1994). That, say evolutionary psychologists, is because of **natural selection**—nature selects traits and appetites that contribute to survival and reproduction. Thus, what these men are really attracted to, suggest Douglas Kenrick and his colleagues (2009), are

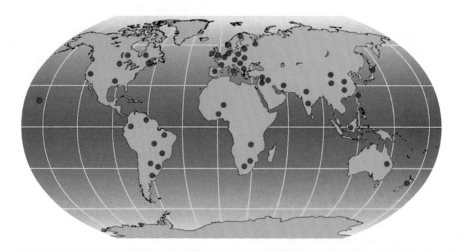

FIGURE 4.4 ● **Worldwide mating preferences** In a wide range of cultures studied (indicated by the red dots), men more than women preferred physical features suggesting youth and health—and reproductive potential. Women more than men preferred mates with resources and social status. Researchers credit (or blame) natural selection (Buss, 1994).

"female features that were associated with fertility in the ancestral past."

In areas where men and women have faced similar adaptive challenges, they have reacted in similar ways. Whether male or female, we eat the same foods, avoid the same predators, and perceive, learn, and remember in much the same ways. Evolutionary psychology is a one-stop shop that explains our species' universal tendencies to give and receive parental care, to recognize emotions, and to fear some things and desire others (Schloss, 2009). Only in areas where men and women faced differing adaptive challenges—most obviously in behaviors related to reproduction—do we differ.

> "It's not that gay men are oversexed; they are simply men whose male desires bounce off other male desires rather than off female desires."
>
> Steven Pinker, *How the Mind Works*, 1997

Gender Differences in Sexuality

And differ we do. Consider women's and men's sex drive. WHO DESIRES MORE FREQUENT SEX? THINKS MORE ABOUT SEX? MASTURBATES MORE OFTEN? SACRIFICES MORE TO GAIN SEX? INITIATES MORE SEX? VIEWS MORE PORNOGRAPHY? The answers, worldwide: *Men, men, men, men, men,* and *men* (Baumeister et al., 2001;

Lippa, 2009; Petersen & Hyde, 2009). To see if you can predict such gender differences, take the quiz in **TABLE 4.2.**

Evolutionary psychologists summarize findings like those in Table 4.2 by saying that men have a more *recreational* approach to sex, while women have a more *relational* approach (Schmitt, 2005). This difference also appears in surveys that compare homosexual men and women. Gay men (like straight men) report more interest in uncommitted sex, more responsiveness to visual sexual stimuli, and more concern with their partner's physical attractiveness (Bailey et al., 1994; Doyle, 2005). Gay male couples report having sex

"Not tonight, hon, I have a concussion."

TABLE 4.2 Predict the Responses

Researchers asked samples of U.S. men and women whether they agreed or disagreed with the following statements. For each item below, give your best guess about the percentage of men and women who agreed with the statement.

Statement	Percentage of men who agreed	Percentage of women who agreed
1. If two people really like each other, it's all right for them to have sex even if they've known each other for a very short time.	_____	_____
2. I can imagine myself being comfortable and enjoying "casual" sex with different partners.	_____	_____
3. Affection was the reason I first had intercourse.	_____	_____
4. I think about sex every day, or several times a day.	_____	_____

Answers: (1) men, 58 percent; women, 34 percent; (2) men, 48 percent; women, 12 percent; (3) men, 25 percent; women, 48 percent; (4) men, 54 percent; women, 19 percent.

Sources: (1) Pryor et al., 2005; (2) Bailey & others, 2000; (3 and 4) Adapted from Laumann et al., 1994.

more often than do lesbian couples (Peplau & Fingerhut, 2007). And in the first year of Vermont's same-sex civil unions, and among the first 12,000 Massachusetts same-sex marriages, a striking fact emerged. Although men are roughly two-thirds of the gay population, they were only about one-third of those electing legal partnership (Rothblum, 2007; Crary, 2009).

Natural Selection and Mating Preferences

Evolutionary psychologists use natural selection to explain why men and women differ more in the bedroom than in the boardroom. Our natural yearnings are our genes' way of reproducing themselves. "Humans are living fossils—collections of mechanisms produced by prior selection pressures," said evolutionary psychologist David Buss (1995).

The explanation goes like this. Most women incubate and nurse one infant at a time. Men, however, can spread their genes by mating with many females. In our ancestral history, men most often sent their genes into the future by pairing widely,

women by pairing wisely. Thus, women often feel attracted to men who seem mature, dominant, bold, and affluent—traits that reflect a capacity to support and protect (Buss, 1996, 2000; Geary, 1998; Singh, 1995). Women also prefer stick-around dads over walk-away cads. Long-term mates contribute protection and support, which give their offspring greater survival prospects (Gangestad & Simpson, 2000). Women's more relational approach to sex has adaptive benefits. A woman's best chances for sending her genes into

Valerie Hache/AFP/Getty Images

The mating game: Evolutionary psychologists are not surprised that older men, and not just Harrison Ford, 68 (pictured here with his wife, Calista Flockhart, 46), often prefer younger women whose features suggest fertility.

the future lie in finding a long-term mate who will protect her offspring.

For a man, there is a genetic tradeoff between seeking to distribute his genes widely and being willing to co-parent to ensure his offspring's survival. Even so, say evolutionary psychologists, the same principle is at work: Nature selects behaviors that increase the likelihood of sending one's genes into the future. As mobile gene machines, we are designed to prefer whatever worked for our ancestors in their environments. They were predisposed to act in ways that would leave grandchildren. Had they not been, we wouldn't be here. And as carriers of their genetic legacy, we are similarly predisposed.

Critiquing the Evolutionary Perspective

10 What do critics say of evolutionary explanations of human behavior, and how do evolutionary psychologists respond?

Most critics of evolutionary psychology's explanation of human sexuality accept Charles Darwin's theory of evolution, which has been an organizing principle for biology for a long time. As Jared Diamond (2001) notes, "Virtually no contemporary scientists believe that Darwin was basically wrong." Evolutionary psychologists have adapted Darwin's theory and applied evolutionary principles to psychology. Darwin would have been pleased. In concluding *On the Origin of Species,* he predicted "open fields for far more important researches. Psychology will be based on a new foundation" (1859, p. 346).

But critics say there is a weakness in the reasoning used by evolutionary psychologists. Evolutionary psychology often

evolutionary psychology the study of how our behavior and mind have changed in adaptive ways over time due to natural selection.

natural selection the adaptive process; among the range of inherited trait variations, those that lead to increased reproduction and survival will most likely be passed on to succeeding generations.

starts with an effect (such as the gender sexuality difference) and works backward to propose an explanation. To see the problem, let's imagine a different observation and reason backward. If men were uniformly loyal to their mates, might we not reason that the children of these committed, supportive fathers would more often survive to pass on their fathers' genes? Might not this bond with one woman also increase the otherwise slim odds of conceiving a child, while preventing her from mating with competing men? Might not a ritualized bond—a marriage—also spare women from male advances and chronic harassment? Such suggestions are, in fact, evolutionary explanations for why humans tend to pair off monogamously. One can hardly lose at hindsight explanation, which is, said Stephen Jay Gould (1997), mere "speculation [and] guesswork."

Some also worry about the social consequences of evolutionary psychology's approach. Does it suggest that genes *are* destiny? Does it mean that any effort to remake society is useless (Rose, 1999)? Does it mean that men don't need to take responsibility for their sexual behavior? Could it be used to justify "high-status men marrying a series of young, fertile women" (Looy, 2001)?

Other critics remind us that cultural expectations can bend the genders. If men are socialized to value lifelong commitment, they may sexually bond with one partner. If women are socialized to accept casual sex, they may willingly have sex with many partners.

Cultural expectations can also shape our mate preferences. Show Alice Eagly and Wendy Wood (1999; Wood & Eagly, 2002) a culture with gender inequality—where men are providers and women are homemakers—and they will show you a culture where men strongly desire youth and domestic skill in their potential mates, and where women seek status and earning potential in their mates. Show Eagly and Wood a culture with gender equality, and they will show you a culture with smaller gender differences in mate preferences.

Evolutionary psychologists agree that much of who we are is not hard-wired.

What's considered attractive varies somewhat with time and place. And they reassure us that the sexes, having faced similar adaptive problems, are far more alike than different. They stress that the tight genetic leash that predisposes a dog's retrieving, a cat's pouncing, or an ant's building is looser on humans. The genes selected during our ancestral history give us a great capacity to learn and to adapt and survive, whether living in igloos or tree houses.

But they ask us to remember the power of evolutionary principles to explain by offering testable predictions. We can, for example, scientifically test hypotheses such as: Do we tend to favor others to the extent that they share our genes or can later return our favors? (The answer is *Yes*.) And they remind us that our great capacity to learn gives us hope. Genes and experience together wire the brain.

PRACTICE TEST

THE BASICS

10. Current research suggests several possible influences on male sexual orientation. Which of the following is NOT one of those influences?

   a. Certain cell clusters in the hypothalamus

   b. A domineering mother and ineffectual father

   c. A section of fibers connecting the right and left hemispheres of the brain

   d. Exposure to hormone levels typically experienced by female fetuses

11. Evolutionary psychologists are most likely to focus on

   a. how we differ from one another.

   b. the social consequences of sexual behaviors.

   c. natural selection of the fittest adaptations.

   d. cultural expectations about the "right" ways for men and women to behave.

THE BIG PICTURE

4C. Which factors have researchers thus far found to be *unrelated* to the development of our sexual orientation?

IN YOUR EVERYDAY LIFE

• Especially among younger people, there is increasing acceptance of homosexuals. Yet strong disapproval of same-sex relationships persists in the population at large. Why do you think this is the case?

• How has reading about the causes of sexual orientation influenced your views on homosexuality?

• What do you think about the evolutionary perspective on sexual behavior? To what extent do you think genetics affects our sexual behavior?

Answers: 10. b, 11. c. Answers to The Big Picture questions can be found in Appendix B at the end of the book.

Thinking About Gender, Sexuality, and Nature-Nurture Interaction

Our ancestral history helped form us as a species. Where there is variation, natural selection, and heredity, there will be evolution. Our genes form us. This is a great truth about human nature.

But our culture and experiences also form us. If their genes and hormones predispose males to be more physically aggressive than females, culture may magnify this gender difference by encouraging males to be macho and females to be the kinder, gentler sex. If men are encouraged toward roles that demand physical power, and women toward more nurturing roles, each may act accordingly. By exhibiting the actions expected of those who fill such roles, they will shape their own behaviors. Presidents in time become more presidential, servants more servile. Gender roles similarly shape us.

Today, in our culture, gender roles are converging. Brute strength has become increasingly irrelevant to power and status (think Bill Gates and Oprah Winfrey). From 1960 into the next century, women soared from 6 percent to 50 percent of U.S. medical students (AMA, 2010). In the mid-1960s, U.S. married women devoted *seven times* as many hours to housework as did their husbands; by 2003 this gap had shrunk to two times as much (Bianchi et al., 2000, 2006). Such swift change signals that biology does not fix gender roles.

For Those Troubled by the Scientific Understanding of Human Origins

I know from my mail that some readers feel troubled by the naturalism and evolutionism of contemporary science. They worry that a science of behavior (and evolutionary science in particular) will destroy our sense of the beauty, mystery, and spiritual significance of the human creature. For those concerned, I offer some reassuring thoughts.

When Isaac Newton explained the rainbow in terms of light of differing wavelengths, British poet John Keats feared that Newton had destroyed the rainbow's mysterious beauty. Yet, nothing about the science of optics need diminish our appreciation for the drama of a rainbow arching across a rain-darkened sky.

When Galileo assembled evidence that the Earth revolved around the Sun, not vice versa, he did not offer absolute proof for his theory. Rather he offered an explanation that pulled together a variety of observations, such as the changing shadows cast by the Moon's mountains. His explanation eventually won the day because it described and explained things in a way that made sense, that hung together. Darwin's theory of evolution likewise offers an organizing principle that makes sense of many observations.

Some people of faith may find the scientific idea of human origins troubling. Many others find that it fits with their own spirituality. Pope John Paul II in 1996 welcomed a science-religion dialogue, finding it noteworthy that evolutionary theory "has been progressively accepted by researchers, following a series of discoveries in various fields of knowledge."

Meanwhile, many people of science are awestruck at the emerging understanding of the universe and the human creature. It boggles the mind—the entire universe popping out of a point some 14 billion years ago, and instantly inflating to cosmological size. Had the energy of this Big Bang been the tiniest bit less, the universe would have collapsed back on itself. Had it been the tiniest bit more, the result would have been a soup too thin to support life. Had gravity been a teeny bit stronger or weaker, or had the weight of a carbon proton been a wee bit different, our universe just wouldn't have worked.

What caused this almost-too-good-to-be-true, finely tuned universe? Why is there something rather than nothing? How did it come to be, in the words of Harvard-Smithsonian astrophysicist Owen Gingerich (1999), "so extraordinarily right, that it seemed the universe had been expressly designed to produce intelligent, sentient beings"? Is there a benevolent superintelligence behind it all? On such matters, a humble, awed, scientific silence is appropriate, suggested philosopher Ludwig Wittgenstein: "Whereof one cannot speak, thereof one must be silent."

Rather than fearing science, we can welcome its enlarging our understanding and awakening our sense of awe. In a short 4 billion years, life on Earth has come from nothing to structures as complex as a 6-billion-unit strand of DNA and the incomprehensible intricacy of the human brain. Nature seems cunningly and ingeniously devised to produce extraordinary, self-replicating, information-processing systems—us (Davies, 1992, 1999, 2004). Although we appear to have been created from dust, over eons of time, the end result is a priceless creature, one rich with potential beyond our imagining.

IF NATURE AND NURTURE JOINTLY FORM◄ US, ARE WE "NOTHING BUT" THE PRODUCT OF NATURE AND NURTURE? ARE WE RIGIDLY DETERMINED?

We *are* the product of nature and nurture, but we are also an open system. Genes are all-pervasive but not all-powerful; people may defy their genetic bent to reproduce, by electing celibacy. Culture, too, is all-pervasive but not all-powerful; people may defy peer pressures and do the opposite of the expected. To excuse our failings by blaming our nature is handing over responsibility for our fate to bad genes or bad influences.

In reality, we are both the creatures and the creators of our worlds. So many things about us—including our gender identity and mating behaviors—are the product of our genes and environments. Nevertheless, the stream of causation that shapes the future runs through our present choices. Our decisions today design our environments tomorrow. Mind matters. The human environment is not like the weather—something that just happens. We are its architects. Our hopes, goals, and expectations influence our future. And that is what enables cultures to vary and to change so quickly.

Terms and Concepts to Remember

gender, p. 102	gender role, p. 105	sexual response cycle, p. 108
aggression, p. 102	social learning theory, p. 106	refractory period, p. 108
X chromosome, p. 104	gender identity, p. 106	AIDS, p. 108
Y chromosome, p. 104	gender typing, p. 106	sexual orientation, p. 112
testosterone, p. 104	gender schema, p. 106	evolutionary psychology, p. 116
role, p. 105	estrogens, p. 107	natural selection, p. 116

Multiple-choice **self-tests** and more may be found at www.worthpublishers.com/myers

GENDER AND SEXUALITY

Gender Development

1 **What are some gender similarities and differences in aggression, social power, and social connectedness?**

■ *Gender* is a social definition of what it means to be male or female in a particular culture.

■ Males and females are similar in their overall genetic makeup and in their functioning.

■ Male-female differences include size, age of onset of puberty, and life expectancy.

■ Psychological differences include the greater tendencies for men to express physical *aggression* and to hold social power, and for women to form social connections.

2 **How is biological sex determined, and how do sex hormones influence development and gender differences?**

■ The twenty-third chromosome determines sex, with the mother contributing an *X chromosome* and the father contributing either an X chromosome (for a girl baby) or a *Y chromosome* (for a boy baby).

■ A Y chromosome triggers additional *testosterone* release and the formation of male sex organs.

3 **What is the importance of gender roles in development?**

■ *Gender roles* vary depending on cultural expectations, which change over time and place.

■ *Social learning theory:* Children learn male and female behaviors through imitation and reinforcement.

■ *Gender schemas:* Children pick up their concepts of male and female from the surrounding culture.

Human Sexuality

4 **How do hormones influence our sexuality, and what stages mark the human sexual response cycle?**

■ The main sex hormones are testosterone (greater in males) and the *estrogens* (greater in females).

■ These hormones direct sexual development in the prenatal period; trigger development of sexual characteristics in adolescence; and help activate sexual behavior from puberty to late adulthood.

■ Masters and Johnson described four stages in the human *sexual response cycle:* excitement, plateau, orgasm, and resolution. Males then enter a *refractory period* in which renewed arousal and orgasm are impossible.

5 **What are STIs, and how can they be prevented?**

■ Using condoms helps protect against most sexually transmitted infections (especially *AIDS*), but not those that are transmitted skin-to-skin.

■ HPV may be prevented by vaccination.

6 **What factors influence teenagers' sexual behaviors and use of contraceptives?**

■ Ignorance

■ Guilt about sexual behavior

■ Poor communication about options

■ Alcohol use

■ Media modeling of casual unsafe sex

7 **How do external and imagined stimuli contribute to sexual arousal?**

■ Erotic material and other external stimuli can trigger sexual arousal in both men and women.

■ Viewing sexually coercive material can lead to increased acceptance of violence toward women.

■ Viewing sexually explicit materials can cause men to devalue their own partners.

■ Imagined stimuli (fantasies) help trigger sexual arousal.

Sexual Orientation

8 **What does current research tell us about why some people are attracted to members of their own sex and others are attracted to members of the other sex?**

■ About 3 or 4 percent of men and 1 or 2 percent of women are homosexual, and *sexual orientation* seems to be enduring.

■ There is no evidence that environmental factors influence sexual orientation.

■ Evidence for biological influences on homosexuality comes from same-sex attraction in other species; gay-straight differences in brain characteristics and other traits; higher rates of homosexuality in certain families; and higher rates among individuals exposed to abnormal levels of hormones during critical periods of prenatal development.

Thinking About Gender, Sexuality, and Nature-Nurture Interaction

■ Nature and nurture interact in the development of our gender-related traits and our mating behaviors.

An Evolutionary Explanation of Human Sexuality

9 **How do evolutionary psychologists use natural selection to explain human sexuality?**

■ *Evolutionary psychologists* attempt to understand how *natural selection* has shaped behaviors found in all people.

■ They reason that men's more recreational attitude toward sex results from their ability to spread their genes widely by mating with many females, and women's more relational approach to sex results from their need to incubate and nurse one infant at a time.

10 **What do critics say of evolutionary explanations of human behavior, and how do evolutionary psychologists respond?**

■ Critics point out the problem in starting with an effect (male/female differences in sexuality) and working back to an explanation and suggest that cultural and social factors are being underestimated.

■ Evolutionary psychologists agree we are not entirely hardwired but suggest there is value in the testable predictions that evolutionary principles can offer.

5

SENSATION AND PERCEPTION

My friend, Heather Sellers, an acclaimed writer and teacher, cannot recognize faces. Her vision is perfect, but her perception is not. In her book, *You Don't Look Like Anyone I Know* (2010), she tells of awkward moments resulting from her lifelong *prosopagnosia*—face blindness.

In college . . . I returned from the bathroom and plunked myself down in the wrong booth, facing the wrong man. I remained unaware he was not my date even as my date (a stranger to me) accosted Wrong Booth Guy, and then stormed out. . . . I do not recognize myself in photos or videos. I can't recognize my stepsons in the soccer pick-up line; I failed to determine which husband was mine at a party, in the mall, at the market.

People sometimes see Sellers as snobby. "Why did you walk past me?" a neighbor might later ask. Hoping to avoid offending others, Sellers sometimes fakes recognition. She smiles at people she passes, in case she knows them, and may pretend to know the person with whom she is talking. But there is an upside to these perception failures. When encountering someone who previously irritated her, she typically won't feel ill will. She doesn't recognize the person.

1 What is the difference between sensation and perception?

Sellers' curious mix of "perfect vision" and face blindness illustrates the distinction between *sensation* and *perception*. When she looks at a friend, her **sensation** is normal. Her senses detect the same information yours would, and they transmit that information to her brain. And her **perception**—the processes by which her brain organizes and interprets the sensory input—is *almost* normal. Thus, she may recognize people from their hair, walk, voice, or peculiar build—just not from their face. Her experience is much like yours or mine if we were struggling to recognize a specific penguin in a group of waddling penguins.

Most of us have an area on the underside of our brain's right hemisphere that helps us recognize a familiar human face as soon as we detect it—in only one-seventh of a second (Jacques & Rossion, 2006). This ability is an example of a broader principle. Nature's sensory gifts enable each animal to obtain essential information. Some examples:

- Frogs, which feed on flying insects, have cells in their eyes that fire only in response to small, dark, moving objects. A frog could starve to death knee-deep in motionless flies. But let one zoom by and the frog's "bug detector" cells snap awake.

- Male silkworm moths' odor receptors can detect one-billionth of an ounce of sex attractant per second released by a female one mile away. That is why there continue to be silkworms.

- Human ears are most sensitive to sound frequencies that include human voices, especially a baby's cry.

We begin our exploration of such sensory gifts by considering some basic principles of how we sense and perceive.

Basic Principles of Sensation and Perception

Twenty-four hours a day, all kinds of stimuli from the outside world bombard your body. Meanwhile, in a silent, cushioned, inner world, your brain floats in utter darkness. By itself, it sees nothing. It hears nothing. It feels nothing. SO, HOW ◀ DOES THE WORLD OUT THERE GET IN? How do a campfire's flicker, crackle, and smoky scent activate neural connections in our brain? And how, from this living neurochemistry, do we construct our conscious experience of the fire's motion and temperature, its aroma and beauty? To find the answers to these questions, let's look at some processes that cut across all of our sensory systems.

From Energy to Neural Impulse

2 What three steps are basic to all our sensory systems?

Every second of every day, your sensory systems perform an amazing feat: They convert one sort of energy into another. Vision processes light energy. Hearing processes sound waves. All your senses

- *receive* sensory stimulation, often using specialized receptor cells.

- *transform* that stimulation into neural impulses.

- *deliver* the neural information to your brain.

The process of converting one form of energy into another form that your brain can use is called **transduction.** Later in this chapter, we'll focus on individual sensory systems. How do we see? Hear? Feel pain? Taste? Smell? Keep our balance? In each case, we'll consider these three steps—receiving, transforming, and delivering the information to the brain. We'll also look at some of the ways our experiences and expectations guide our mind as it interprets what our senses gather.

First, though, let's explore some strengths and weaknesses in our ability to detect and interpret stimuli in the vast sea of energy around us.

Thresholds

3 How do absolute thresholds and difference thresholds differ, and what is Weber's law?

At this moment, you and I are being struck by X-rays and radio waves, ultraviolet and infrared light, and sound waves of very high and very low frequencies. To all of these we are blind and deaf. Other animals with differing needs detect a world that lies beyond our experience (Hughes, 1999). Birds stay on course using a magnetic compass. Bats and dolphins locate prey using sonar, bouncing sounds off objects. Bees navigate on cloudy days by detecting aspects of sunlight we cannot see. The shades on our senses are open just a crack, giving us only a tiny glimpse of the energy around us. But for our needs, this is enough.

Absolute Thresholds

To some kinds of stimuli we are amazingly sensitive. From a mountain peak on an utterly dark, clear night, most of us could see a candle flame atop another mountain 30 miles away. We could feel the wing of a bee falling on our cheek. We could even smell a single drop of perfume in a three-room apartment (Galanter, 1962).

Our awareness of these faint stimuli illustrates our **absolute thresholds**—the minimum stimulation needed to detect a particular light, sound, pressure, taste, or odor 50 percent of the time. To test your absolute threshold for sounds, for example, a hearing specialist would send tones, at varying levels, into each of your ears. The tester would then record whether or not you could hear each tone. The test results would show the point where half the time you could detect the sound and half the time you could not. That 50-50 point would define your absolute threshold for that sound.

Stimuli you cannot detect 50 percent of the time are **subliminal**—below your absolute threshold (**FIGURE 5.1**). Under certain conditions, you can be affected by stimuli so weak that you don't notice them. An unnoticed image or word can briefly **prime** your response to a later question. Let's see how this might work in a laboratory experiment. You've been asked to view slides of people and to give them either positive or negative ratings. But the trickster researchers also flash another image an instant before showing you each slide. Some of the flashed images will be emotionally positive (kittens, a romantic couple) and some will be negative (a werewolf, a dead body). You will consciously perceive these images only as flashes of light. Will they affect your ratings?

In this real experiment, people somehow looked nicer if their photo immediately followed unperceived kittens rather than an unperceived werewolf (Krosnick et al., 1992). This *priming effect* happened even though the viewer's brain did not have enough time to consciously perceive the flashed images. As other experiments confirm, we may evaluate a stimulus even when we are not aware of it (Ferguson & Zayas, 2009). Once again, we see the two-track mind at work: *Much of our information processing occurs automatically, out of sight, off the radar screen of our conscious mind.*

> The LORD is my shepherd;
>   I shall not want.
> He maketh me to lie down
>   in green pastures:
>   he leadeth me
>   beside the still waters.
> He restoreth my soul:
>   he leadeth me
>   in the paths of righteousness
>   for his name's sake.
> Yea, though I walk through the valley
>   of the shadow of death,
>   I will fear no evil:
>   for thou art with me;
>   thy rod and thy staff
>   they comfort me.
> Thou preparest a table before me
>   in the presence of mine enemies:
>   thou anointest my head with oil,
>   my cup runneth over.
> Surely goodness and mercy
>   shall follow me
>   all the days of my life:
> and I will dwell
>   in the house of the LORD
>   for ever.

CAN WE BE CONTROLLED BY SUBLIMINAL◀ MESSAGES? For more on that question, see Thinking Critically About: Can Subliminal Messages Control Our Behavior? on the next page.

Difference Thresholds

To function effectively, we need absolute thresholds low enough to allow us to detect important sights, sounds, textures, tastes, and smells. We also need to detect small differences among stimuli. A musician must detect tiny differences when tuning an instrument. Parents must detect the sound of their own child's voice amid other children's voices. Even after living two years in Scotland, sheep *baa's* all sound alike to my ears. But not to

The difference threshold: In this world literature classic poem, the Twenty-third Psalm, each line of the typeface changes imperceptibly. How many lines did you read before detecting a just noticeable difference?

those of ewes, which I have observed streaking, after shearing, directly to the *baa* of their lamb amid the chorus of other distressed lambs.

Psychologists call the minimum difference a person (or a sheep) can detect between any two stimuli half the time the **difference threshold** (or the *just noticeable difference [jnd]*.) That detectable difference increases with the size of the stimulus. Thus, if you add 1 ounce to a 10-ounce weight, you will detect the difference. If you add 1 ounce to a 100-ounce weight, you will not.

More than a century ago, Ernst Weber noted something so simple but so true that we refer to it as **Weber's law** and

sensation the process by which our sensory receptors and nervous system take in stimulus energies from our environment.

perception the process by which our brain organizes and interprets sensory information, transforming it into meaningful objects and events.

transduction changing one form of energy into another. In sensation, the transforming of stimulus energies, such as sights, sounds, and smells, into neural impulses our brain can interpret.

absolute threshold the minimum stimulation needed to detect a particular stimulus 50 percent of the time.

subliminal below our absolute threshold for conscious awareness.

priming activating, often unconsciously, associations in our mind, thus setting us up to perceive or remember objects or events in certain ways.

difference threshold the minimum difference between two stimuli required for detection 50 percent of the time. We experience the difference threshold as a *just noticeable difference* (or *jnd*).

Weber's law the principle that, to be perceived as different, two stimuli must differ by a constant minimum proportion (rather than a constant amount).

FIGURE 5.1 ● **Absolute threshold** Can I detect this sound? An *absolute threshold* is the intensity at which a person can detect a stimulus half the time. Hearing tests locate these thresholds for various frequency levels.

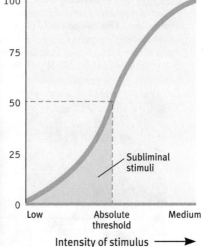

Percentage of correct detections

Intensity of stimulus ⟶

Subliminal stimuli

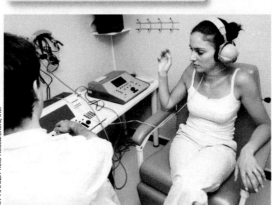

©PHANIE/Photo Researchers, Inc.

Can Subliminal Messages Control Our Behavior?

4 **Can we be persuaded by subliminal stimuli?**

Hoping to penetrate our unconscious, marketers offer audio and video programs to help us lose weight, stop smoking, or improve our memories. Soothing ocean sounds may mask messages we cannot consciously hear, such as "I am thin," "Cigarettes taste bad," or "I do well on tests. I have total recall of information." These subliminal messages, below our absolute threshold of awareness, supposedly change our lives. Such claims make two assumptions: (1) We can unconsciously sense subliminal stimuli. (2) Without our awareness, these stimuli have extraordinary persuasive powers. Can we? Do they?

As we have seen, subliminal *sensation* is a fact. Remember that an "absolute" threshold is merely the point at which we can detect a stimulus *half the time*. At or slightly below this threshold, we will still detect the stimulus some of the time.

But does this mean that claims of subliminal *persuasion* are also facts? Can subliminal recordings really help us make lasting behavioral changes, such as eating less or quitting smoking? Research results from 16 experiments on the influence of subliminal self-help recordings reached the same conclusion. The effect of subliminal stimuli is subtle and fleeting, with no powerful, enduring influence on behavior. Not one of the recordings helped more than a placebo (Greenwald et al., 1991, 1992). And placebos, you may remember, work only because we *believe* they will work.

still apply it. This law states that for an average person to perceive a difference, two stimuli must differ by a constant minimum *proportion*—not a constant *amount*. The exact proportion varies, depending on the stimulus. Two lights, for example, must differ in intensity by 8 percent. Two objects must differ in weight by 2 percent. And two tones must differ in frequency by only 0.3 percent (Teghtsoonian, 1971).

Sensory Adaptation

5 **What function does sensory adaptation serve?**

Entering your neighbors' living room, you smell a musty odor. You wonder how they can stand it, but within minutes you no longer notice it. **Sensory adaptation** has come to your rescue. When we are constantly exposed to a stimulus that does not change, we become less aware of it because our nerve cells fire less frequently. (To experience sensory adaptation, move your watch up your wrist an inch. You will feel it—but only for a few moments.)

Why, then, if we stare at an object without flinching, does it *not* vanish from sight? Because, unnoticed by us, our eyes are always moving. This continual flitting from one spot to another ensures that stimulation on the eyes' receptors is always changing.

> "My suspicion is that the universe is not only queerer than we suppose, but queerer than we can suppose."
>
> J.B.S. Haldane, *Possible Worlds*, 1927

What if we actually could stop our eyes from moving? Would sights seem to vanish, as odors do? To find out, psychologists have devised clever instruments that maintain a constant image on the eye's inner surface. Imagine that we have fitted a volunteer, Mary, with one of these instruments—a miniature projector mounted on a contact lens **(FIGURE 5.2a).** When Mary's eye moves, the image from the projector moves as well. So everywhere that Mary looks, the scene is sure to go.

If we project images through this instrument, what will Mary see? At first, she will see the complete image. But within a few seconds, as her sensory system begins to tire, things get weird. Bit by bit, the image vanishes, only to reappear and then disappear—often in fragments (Figure 5.2b).

Although sensory adaptation reduces our sensitivity, it offers an important benefit: freedom to focus on *informative* changes in our environment without being distracted by background chatter. Stinky or heavily perfumed people don't notice their odor because, like you and me, they adapt to what's constant and only detect change. Our sensory receptors are alert to novelty; bore them with repetition and they free our attention for more important things. We will see this

FIGURE 5.2 ● Sensory adaptation: Now you see it, now you don't! (a) To test the visual system's reaction to constant, unchanging stimulation, researchers mounted a projector on a contact lens. This device made the projected image move as the eye moved. At first, the person saw the whole image, but soon it began to break into fragments that faded and reappeared, like those in frame (b). (From "Stabilized images on the retina" by R. M. Pritchard. Copyright © 1961, Scientific American, Inc. All Rights Reserved.)

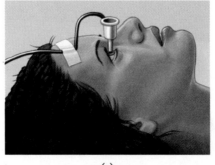

(a)

(b)

principle again and again: *We perceive the world not exactly as it is, but as it is useful for us to perceive it.*

Our sensitivity to changing stimulation helps explain television's attention-getting power. Cuts, edits, zooms, pans, and sudden noises demand attention. Even TV researchers marvel at its attention-grabbing power. One noted that even during interesting conversations, "I cannot for the life of me stop from periodically glancing over to the screen" (Tannenbaum, 2002).

Sensory adaptation and sensory thresholds are important ingredients in our perceptions of the world around us. But much of what we perceive comes not just from what's "out there" but also from what's behind our eyes and between our ears.

Perceptual Set

6 How do our expectations, assumptions, and contexts affect our perceptions?

As everyone knows, to see is to believe. As we also know, but less fully appreciate, to believe is to see. Through experience, we come to *expect* certain results. Those expectations may give us a **perceptual set,** a set of mental tendencies and assumptions that greatly influence what we perceive.

> When shown the phrase:
> Mary had a
> a little lamb
> many people perceive what they expect, and miss the repeated word. Did you?

Perceptual set can influence what we hear, taste, feel, and see. In 1972, a British

IT'S AMAZING HOW PEOPLE SLOW DOWN WHEN YOU POINT A HAIR DRYER AT THEM.

FIGURE 5.3 • **Believing is seeing** What do you perceive in these photos? Is this Nessie, the Loch Ness monster, or a log?

newspaper published photos of a "monster" in Scotland's Loch Ness—"the most amazing pictures ever taken," stated the paper. If this information creates in you the same expectations it did in most of the paper's readers, you, too, will see the monster in the photo in **FIGURE 5.3.** But when a skeptical researcher approached the photos with different expectations, he saw a curved tree trunk—as had others the day the photo was shot (Campbell, 1986). With this different perceptual set, you may now notice that the object is floating motionless, with no ripples in the water around it—hardly what we would expect of a lively monster.

Perceptual set can also affect what we hear. Consider the kindly airline pilot who, on a takeoff run, looked over at his unhappy co-pilot and said, "Cheer up." Expecting to hear the usual "Gear up," the co-pilot promptly raised the wheels—before they left the ground (Reason & Mycielska, 1982).

Perceptual set similarly affects taste. One experiment invited some bar patrons to sample free beer (Lee et al., 2006). When researchers added a few drops of vinegar to a brand-name beer, the tasters preferred it—unless they had been told they were drinking vinegar-laced beer. Then they expected, and usually experienced, a worse taste. In another experiment, preschool children, by a 6 to 1 margin,

thought french fries tasted better when served in a McDonald's bag rather than a plain bag (Robinson et al., 2007).

Context Effects

The effects of perceptual set show how experience helps us construct perception. But the immediate context also plays a role. Some examples:

- What is above the woman's head in **FIGURE 5.4** on the next page? When East Africans were asked this question, most said that the woman was balancing a metal box or can on her head, and the family was sitting under a tree. Most Westerners, for whom corners and boxlike architecture are more common, said the woman was sitting under a window, indoors with her family. Cultural context helps form our perceptions.

- Does the pursuing monster in **FIGURE 5.5** on the next page look aggressive? Does the pursued one seem frightened? If so, you experienced a context effect, because the images are identical.

---

sensory adaptation reduced sensitivity in response to constant stimulation.

perceptual set a mental predisposition to perceive one thing and not another.

FIGURE 5.4 ● **Culture and context effects** What is above the woman's head? East African and Western viewers respond differently to this question, and their answers reflect their experiences in their own cultures. (Adapted from Gregory & Gombrich, 1973.)

● How tall is the shorter player in **FIGURE 5.6**? He seemed quite short when matched in a semi-pro game against the world's tallest basketball player, 7'9" Sun Ming Ming from China. In a different context, he would appear taller than normal.

Even hearing sad rather than happy music can tilt our minds toward hearing a sad meaning in spoken words—*mourn-*

FIGURE 5.5 ● **Fooling our size-distance perceptions** Which monster is bigger? Measure them to see.

From Shepard (1990).

FIGURE 5.6 ● **Big and "little"** The "little guy" shown here is actually a 6'9" former Hope College basketball center who towers over most of us.

ing rather than *morning, die* rather than *dye, pain* rather than *pane* (Halberstadt et al., 1995).

Even our emotions can become contexts that shove our social perceptions in one direction or another. Spouses who feel loved and appreciated perceive less

threat in stressful marital events—"He's just having a bad day" (Murray et al., 2003). Professional referees, if told a soccer team has a history of aggressive behavior, will assign more penalty cards when watching recorded play (Jones et al., 2002). Lee Ross invites us to recall our own perceptions in different contexts: "Ever notice that when you're driving you hate pedestrians, the way they saunter through the crosswalk, almost daring you to hit them, but when you're walking you hate drivers?" (Jaffe, 2004).

* * *

The processes we've discussed so far are features shared by all our sensory systems. Let's turn now to the ways those systems are unique. We'll start with vision, the sense that people prize the most.

PRACTICE TEST

THE BASICS

1. The process by which we organize and interpret sensory information is called
   a. sensation.
   b. sensory adaptation.
   c. transduction.
   d. perception.

2. Subliminal stimuli are
   a. too weak to be processed by the brain in any way.
   b. consciously perceived more than 50 percent of the time.
   c. always strong enough to affect our behavior.
   d. below our absolute threshold for conscious awareness.

3. Another term for difference threshold is
   a. just noticeable difference.
   b. sensory adaptation.
   c. absolute threshold.
   d. subliminal stimulation.

4. Weber's law states that for a difference to be perceived, two stimuli must differ by
   a. a fixed or constant energy amount.
   b. a constant minimum proportion.
   c. a constantly changing amount.
   d. more than 7 percent.

5. Sensory adaptation helps us focus on
   a. visual stimuli.
   b. auditory stimuli.
   c. constant features of the environment.
   d. important changes in the environment.

6. Our perceptual set influences what we perceive. This mental tendency reflects our
   a. experiences, assumptions, and expectations.
   b. perceptual adaptation.
   c. priming ability.
   d. difference thresholds.

THE BIG PICTURE

5A. What is the rough distinction between sensation and perception?

IN YOUR EVERYDAY LIFE

▪ What types of sensory adaptation have you experienced in the last 24 hours?

▪ Can you recall a time when your expectations influenced how you perceived a person (or group of people)? What happened?

Answers: 1. d, 2. d, 3. a, 4. b, 5. c, 6. a. Answers to The Big Picture questions can be found in Appendix B at the end of the book.

FIGURE 5.7 ● **The wavelengths we see** What we see as light is only a tiny slice of a wide spectrum of electromagnetic energy. The wavelengths visible to the human eye (shown enlarged) extend from the shorter waves of blue-violet light to the longer waves of red light.

White light

Prism

400   500   600   700

Part of spectrum visible to humans

Gamma rays	X-rays	Ultra-violet rays		Infrared rays	Radar	Broadcast bands
10^{-5}	10^{-3}	10^{-1}	10^{1}	10^{3} 10^{5}	10^{7} 10^{9}	10^{11} 10^{13}

Wavelength in nanometers (billionths of a meter)

Vision

Your eyes receive light energy and transform it into neural messages that your brain then processes into what you consciously see. How does such a taken-for-granted yet remarkable thing happen?

Light Energy: From the Environment Into the Brain

7 **What are the characteristics of the energy we see as light?**

When you see a red-breasted robin, what strikes your eyes are not bits of the colors gray or red but pulses of energy that your visual system perceives as these colors. What we see as visible light is but a thin slice of the wide spectrum of electromagnetic energy

shown in **FIGURE 5.7**. On one end of this spectrum are the short gamma waves, no longer than the diameter of an atom. On the other end of the spectrum are the mile-long waves of radio transmission. In between is the narrow band we can see as visible light. Other portions are visible to other animals. Bees, for instance, cannot see what we perceive as red but can see ultraviolet light.

Adaptive eyes: Bees can detect ultraviolet light (left), which allows them to detect a "landing field" of pollen. When it comes to flowers, we see the ones in the middle. We don't normally need to see well at night. Night vision goggles (right), however, allow soldiers to see infrared rays (heat) in order to maneuver in the dark.

Edward Kinsman/Photo Researchers, Inc.   Edward Kinsman/Photo Researchers, Inc.   Chris Hondros/Getty Images

The light we see travels in waves, and the shape of those waves influences what we see. Light's **wavelength**—the distance from one wave peak to the next (**FIGURE 5.8a**)—determines its **hue** (the color we experience, such as a robin's red breast). A light wave's *amplitude,* or height, determines its **intensity**—the amount of energy it contains. Intensity influences brightness (Figure 5.8b).

Understanding the characteristics of the physical energy we see as light is one part of understanding vision. But to appreciate how we transform that energy into color and meaning, we need to know more about vision's window, the eye.

The Eye

8 How does the eye transform light energy into neural messages?

What color are your eyes? Asked this question, most people describe the color of their *irises.* This doughnut-shaped ring of muscle adjusts the size of your *pupil,* which controls the amount of light entering your eye. After passing through your *cornea* (the eyeball's protective covering) and pupil, light hits the *lens* in your eye. The lens then focuses the light into an image on your eyeball's inner surface, the **retina.**

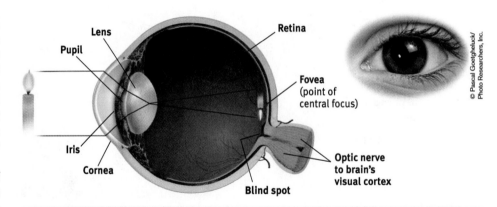

FIGURE 5.9 ● **The eye** Light rays reflected from a candle pass through the cornea, pupil, and lens. The curve and thickness of the lens change to bring nearby or distant objects into focus on the retina. Rays from the top of the candle strike the bottom of the retina and those from the left side of the candle strike the right side of the retina. The candle's image appears on the retina upside-down and reversed.

For centuries, scientists knew that when an image of an object passes through a small opening, it casts an inverted mirror image on a dark wall behind. If the retina receives this sort of upside-down image, as in **FIGURE 5.9**, how can we see the world right side up? Eventually, the answer became clear: The retina doesn't "see" a whole image. Rather, its millions of receptor cells behave like the prankster engineering students who make news by taking a car

apart and rebuilding it in a friend's third-floor bedroom. The retina's cells convert the stream of light energy into neural impulses and forward those to the brain, where they are reassembled into what we perceive as an upright object.

The Retina

Let's follow a single light-energy particle into your eye. First, it makes its way through the retina's outer layer of cells to its buried receptor cells, the **rods** and **cones** (**FIGURE 5.10**). There, the light energy triggers chemical changes that nudge nearby *bipolar cells,* causing them to send out neural signals. These signals in turn activate neighboring *ganglion cells,* whose axons twine together like strands of a rope to form the **optic nerve.** That nerve will carry the information to your brain, where your *thalamus* stands ready to distribute the information. The optic nerve can send nearly 1 million messages at once through its nearly 1 million ganglion fibers. We pay a small price for this high-speed eye-to-brain highway. Where the optic nerve leaves the eye, there are no receptor cells—creating a **blind spot** (**FIGURE 5.11**). Close one eye and you won't see a black hole on your TV screen, however. Without seeking your approval, your brain fills in the hole.

Rods and cones differ in where they're found and in what they do (**FIGURE 5.12**).

FIGURE 5.8 ● **The physical properties of waves** (a) Waves vary in *wavelength,* the distance between successive peaks. *Frequency,* the number of complete wavelengths that can pass a point in a given time, depends on the length of the wave. The shorter the wavelength, the higher the frequency. (b) Waves also vary in *amplitude,* the height from peak to trough. Wave amplitude determines the *intensity* of colors and sounds.

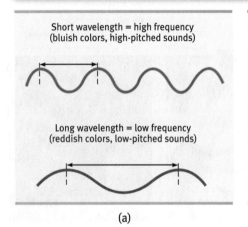

(a)

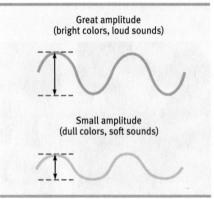

(b)

FIGURE **5.10** • **The retina's reaction to light**

2. Chemical reaction in turn activates bipolar cells.

1. Light entering eye triggers photochemical reaction in rods and cones at back of retina.

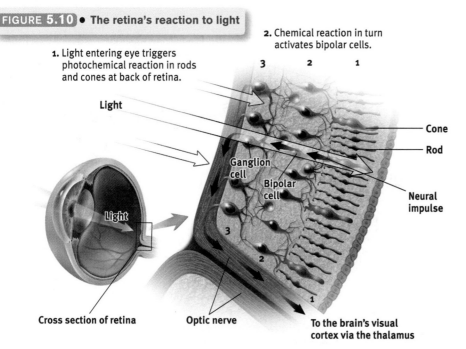

Light

Cone

Rod

Ganglion cell

Bipolar cell

Neural impulse

Light

Cross section of retina

Optic nerve

To the brain's visual cortex via the thalamus

3. Bipolar cells then activate the ganglion cells, the axons of which converge to form the optic nerve. This nerve transmits information to the visual cortex (via the thalamus) in the brain.

Omikron/Photo Researchers, Inc.

FIGURE **5.12** • **Rod-shaped rods and cone-shaped cones** As the scanning electron microscope shows, rods and cones are well named. The rods are more sensitive to light than are the color-sensitive cones, which is why the world looks colorless at night. Some night-loving animals, such as toads, mice, rats, and bats, have retinas made up almost entirely of rods, allowing them to function well in dim light. These creatures probably have very poor color vision.

Cones cluster around the retina's area of central focus. Many have their own hotline to the brain—each one transmits to a single bipolar cell that helps relay the cone's individual message to the visual cortex. These direct connections preserve the cones' precise information, making them better able to detect fine detail.

Rods have no such hotline; they share bipolar cells with other rods, sending combined messages. Stop for a minute and experience this rod-cone difference in sensitivity to details. Pick a word in this sentence and stare directly at it, focusing its image on the cones in the center of your eye. Notice that words a few inches off to the side appear blurred?

wavelength the distance from the peak of one light or sound wave to the peak of the next.

hue the dimension of color that is determined by the wavelength of light; what we know as the color names *blue, green,* and so forth.

intensity the amount of energy in a light wave or sound wave, which we perceive as brightness or loudness, as determined by the wave's amplitude.

retina the light-sensitive inner surface of the eye; contains the receptor rods and cones plus layers of neurons that begin the processing of visual information.

rods retinal receptors that detect black, white, and gray; necessary for peripheral and twilight vision, when cones don't respond.

cones retinal receptor cells that are concentrated near the center of the retina; in daylight or well-lit conditions, cones detect fine detail and give rise to color sensations.

optic nerve the nerve that carries neural impulses from the eye to the brain.

blind spot the point at which the optic nerve leaves the eye; this part of the retina is "blind" because it has no receptor cells.

FIGURE **5.11** • **The blind spot** There are no receptor cells where the optic nerve leaves the eye (Figure 5.10). This creates a blind spot in our vision. To demonstrate, close your left eye, look at the spot, and move the page to a distance from your face (about a foot) at which the car disappears. The blind spot does not normally impair your vision, because your eyes are moving and because one eye catches what the other misses.

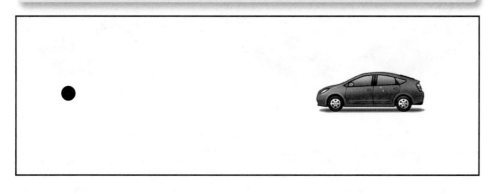

TABLE 5.1	Receptors in the Human Eye	
	Cones	**Rods**
Number	6 million	120 million
Location in retina	Center	Periphery
Sensitivity in dim light	Low	High
Color sensitive?	Yes	No
Detail sensitive?	Yes	No

Their image strikes the outer regions of your retina, where most rods are found. Thus, when driving or biking, you can detect a car in your peripheral vision well before perceiving its color.

Cones enable you to perceive color. In dim light they don't function well, and you don't see colors. Rods, which enable black-and-white vision, remain sensitive in dim light. Several rods will funnel their faint energy output onto a single bipolar cell. Thus, cones and rods each provide a special sensitivity—cones to detail and color, and rods to faint light (**TABLE 5.1**).

Visual Information Processing

9 | What roles do feature detection and parallel processing play in the brain's visual information processing?

After processing by the retina's receptor cells, information travels up the optic nerve to the brain. Any given retinal area relays its information to a corresponding location in the visual cortex in the back of your brain (**FIGURE 5.13**).

Feature Detection

David Hubel and Torsten Wiesel (1979) received a Nobel Prize for their work on **feature detectors.** These specialized nerve cells in the brain's visual cortex receive information from individual ganglion cells in the retina. Feature detector cells get their name from their ability to respond to a scene's specific features—to particular edges, lines, and angles. These cells pass this information to other cortical areas,

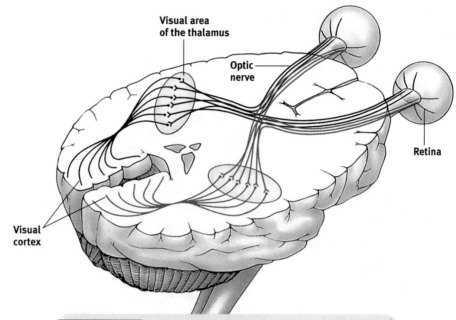

FIGURE 5.13 ● **Pathway from the eyes to the visual cortex** The retina's ganglion axons form the optic nerve, which runs to the thalamus to connect with neurons that run to the visual cortex.

where teams of cells respond to more complex patterns, such as recognizing faces. The resulting brain activity is so specific that, with the help of brain scans, "we can tell if a person is looking at a shoe, a chair, or a face," noted one researcher (Haxby, 2001).

Parallel Processing

One of the most amazing aspects of visual information processing is the brain's ability to divide a scene into its parts.

Using **parallel processing,** the brain assigns different teams of nerve cells to process simultaneously a scene's color, movement, form, and depth (**FIGURE 5.14**). We then construct our perceptions by integrating the work of these different visual teams (Livingstone & Hubel, 1988).

Destroy or disable the neural workstation for a visual subtask, and something peculiar results, as happened to "Mrs. M." (Hoffman, 1998). Since a stroke damaged areas near the rear of both sides of her

FIGURE 5.14 ● **Parallel processing** Studies of patients with brain damage suggest that the brain delegates the work of processing a robin's color, motion, form, and depth to different areas. After taking a scene apart, the brain integrates these parts into a whole perceived image.

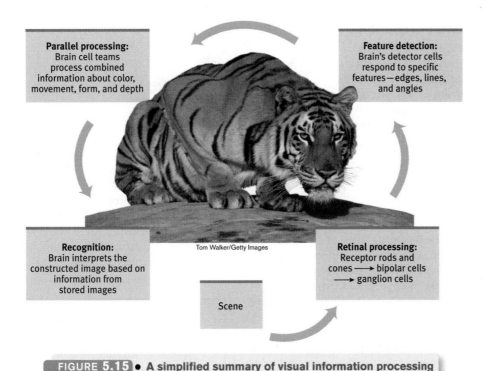

Parallel processing: Brain cell teams process combined information about color, movement, form, and depth

Feature detection: Brain's detector cells respond to specific features—edges, lines, and angles

Recognition: Brain interprets the constructed image based on information from stored images

Tom Walker/Getty Images

Retinal processing: Receptor rods and cones ⟶ bipolar cells ⟶ ganglion cells

Scene

FIGURE 5.15 ● **A simplified summary of visual information processing**

brain, she has been unable to perceive movement. People in a room seem "suddenly here or there but I have not seen them moving." Pouring tea into a cup is a challenge because the fluid appears frozen—she cannot perceive it rising in the cup.

> "I am fearfully and wonderfully made."
> King David, Psalm 139:14

sends formless nerve impulses to several areas of your brain, which integrates the information and discovers meaning. And that is how we transfer information across time and space from my mind to yours. That all of this happens instantly, effortlessly, and continuously is indeed awesome.

* * *

Think about the wonders of visual processing. As you look at that tiger in the zoo, information enters your eyes, where it is taken apart and turned into millions of neural impulses that are sent to your brain. As your brain buzzes with activity, various areas focus on different aspects of the bird's image. Finally, in some as yet mysterious way, these separate teams pool their work to produce a meaningful image. You compare this with previously stored images and recognize it—a crouching tiger **(FIGURE 5.15)**.

Think, too, about what is happening as you read this page. The printed letters reflect light rays into your retina, which

PRACTICE TEST

THE BASICS

7. The characteristic of light that determines the color we experience, such as blue or green, is
    a. intensity.
    b. wavelength.
    c. amplitude.
    d. rods.

8. The blind spot in your retina is located where
    a. there are rods but no cones.
    b. there are cones but no rods.
    c. the optic nerve leaves the eye.
    d. the bipolar cells meet the ganglion cells.

9. Rods and cones are the eye's receptor cells. Cones are especially sensitive to _____ light and are responsible for our _____ vision.
    a. bright; black-and-white
    b. dim; color
    c. bright; color
    d. dim; black-and-white

10. The cells in the visual cortex that respond to certain lines, edges, and angles are called
    a. rods and cones.
    b. feature detectors.
    c. bug detectors.
    d. ganglion cells.

11. The brain is capable of processing many aspects of an object or problem at the same time. We call this ability
    a. parallel processing.
    b. movement processing.
    c. feature detecting.
    d. bipolar processing.

THE BIG PICTURE

5B. What is the rapid sequence of events that occurs when you see and recognize someone you know?

IN YOUR EVERYDAY LIFE

■ People often compare the human eye to a camera. Do you think this is an accurate comparison? Why or why not?

Answers: 7. b, 8. c, 9. c, 10. b, 11. a. Answers to The Big Picture questions can be found in Appendix B at the end of the book.

Visual Organization

🔟 **What was the main message of Gestalt psychology, and how do figure-ground and grouping principles help us perceive forms?**

It's one thing to understand how we see shapes and colors. BUT HOW DO WE OR- ◀ GANIZE AND INTERPRET THOSE SIGHTS (OR SOUNDS OR TASTES OR SMELLS) SO THAT THEY BECOME MEANINGFUL PERCEPTIONS—A ROSE IN BLOOM, A FAMILIAR FACE, A SUNSET?

feature detector nerve cell in the brain that responds to specific features of a stimulus, such as edges, lines, and angles.

parallel processing the processing of many aspects of a problem or scene at the same time; the brain's natural mode of information processing for many functions, including vision.

Early in the twentieth century, a group of German psychologists noticed that people have a tendency to organize pieces of information into a **gestalt,** a German word meaning a "form" or a "whole." For example, look at **FIGURE 5.16.** Note that the individual elements of this figure, called a *Necker cube,* are really nothing but eight blue circles, with three white lines meeting near the center. When we view these elements all together, however, we see a cube that sometimes reverses direction.

Over the years, the Gestalt psychologists demonstrated some principles we use to organize our sensations into perceptions. Underlying all of them is a basic truth: *Our brain does more than register information about the world.* Perception is not just opening a shutter and letting a picture print itself on the brain. We filter incoming information and we construct perceptions. Mind matters.

Form Perception

Imagine designing a video-computer system that, like your eye-brain system, can recognize faces at a glance. What abilities would it need?

Figure and Ground To start with, the video-computer system would need to separate faces from their backgrounds. Likewise, in our eye-brain system, our first perceptual task is to perceive any object (the *figure*) as distinct from its surroundings (the *ground*). Among the voices you hear at a party, the one you attend to becomes the figure; all others are part of the ground. As you read, the words are the figure; the white paper is the ground. Sometimes, the same stimulus can trigger more than one perception. In **FIGURE 5.17,** for example, the **figure-ground** relationship continually reverses as we see the arrows, then the men running. But always we perceive a figure standing out from a ground.

Grouping While telling figure from ground, we (and our video-computer system) also organize the figure into a *meaningful* form. Some basic features of a scene—such as color, movement, and light-dark contrast—we process instantly and automatically (Treisman, 1987). Our mind brings order and form to stimuli by following certain rules for **grouping.** These rules, identified by the Gestalt psychologists, illustrate how the perceived whole differs from the sum of its parts (Quinn et al., 2002; Rock & Palmer, 1990). Three examples:

Proximity We group nearby figures together. We see not six separate lines, but three sets of two lines.

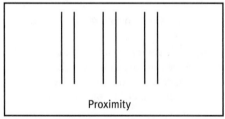

Proximity

Time Saving Suggestion, ©2003 Roger Shepard

FIGURE **5.17** ● **Reversible figure and ground.**

Continuity We perceive smooth, continuous patterns rather than discontinuous ones. This pattern could be a series of alternating semicircles, but we perceive it as two continuous lines—one wavy, one straight.

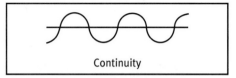

Continuity

Closure We fill in gaps to create a complete, whole object. Thus, we assume that the circles on the left are complete but partially blocked by the (illusory) triangle. Add nothing more than little lines to close off the circles, and your brain stops constructing a triangle.

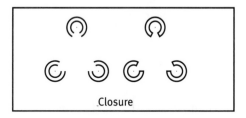

Closure

Depth Perception

11 How do we use monocular and binocular cues to see the world in three dimensions?

From the two-dimensional images falling on our retinas, our amazing brain creates three-dimensional perceptions. **Depth perception** lets us estimate an object's distance from us. At a glance, we can, for example, estimate the distance of an oncoming car. This ability is partly present at birth. Eleanor Gibson and Richard Walk (1960) discovered this using a model of a cliff with a drop-off area (which was covered by sturdy glass). These experiments were a product of Gibson's scientific curiosity, which kicked in while she was picnicking on the rim of the Grand Canyon. She wondered: WOULD A TODDLER PEERING OVER THE RIM PERCEIVE THE DANGEROUS DROP-OFF AND DRAW BACK?

Back in their laboratory, Gibson and Walk placed 6- to 14-month-old infants on the edge of a safe canyon—a **visual cliff (FIGURE 5.18).** Their mothers then coaxed them to crawl out onto the glass. Most infants refused to do so, indicating that they could perceive depth.

Had they *learned* to perceive depth? Learning seemed to be part of the answer, because crawling, no matter when it begins, seems to increase an infant's fear of heights. Yet, the researchers observed, mobile newborn animals come prepared to perceive depth. Even those with no visual experience—including young kittens, a day-old goat, and newly hatched chicks—will not venture across the visual cliff. Thus, it seems that biological maturation prepares us to be wary of heights, and experience amplifies that fear.

How do we do it? *How* do we perceive depth—transforming two differing two-dimensional retinal images into a single three-dimensional perception? Our brain constructs these perceptions using information supplied by one or both eyes.

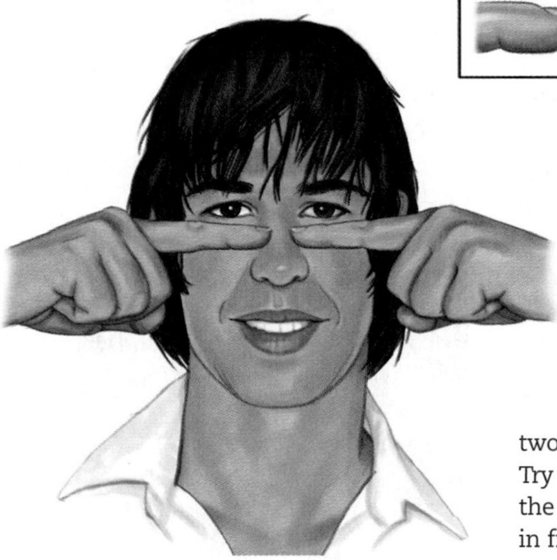

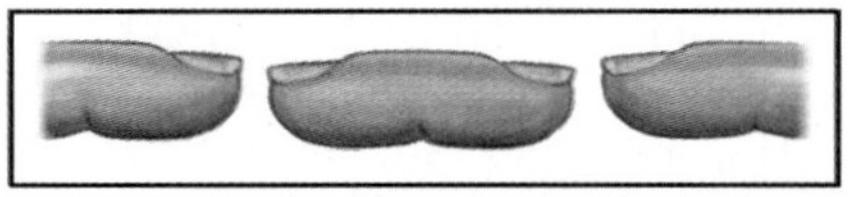

Binocular Cues People who see with two eyes perceive depth thanks partly to **binocular cues.** Here's an example. With both eyes open, hold two pens or pencils in front of you and touch their tips together. Now do so with one eye closed. With one eye, the task becomes more difficult.

We use binocular cues to judge the distance of nearby objects. One such cue is **retinal disparity.** Because your eyes are about 2½ inches apart, your retinas receive slightly different images of the world. By comparing these two images, your brain can judge how close an object is to you. The greater the difference between the

FIGURE 5.19 • **The floating finger sausage** Hold your two index fingers about 5 inches in front of your eyes, with their tips half an inch apart. Now look beyond them and note the weird result. Move your fingers out farther and the retinal disparity—and the finger sausage—will shrink.

two retinal images, the closer the object. Try it. Hold your two index fingers, with the tips about half an inch apart, directly in front of your nose, and your retinas will receive quite different views. If you close one eye and then the other you can see the difference. (You may also create a finger sausage, as in **FIGURE 5.19.**) At a greater distance—say, when you hold your fingers at arm's length—the disparity, or difference, is smaller.

We could easily build this feature into our seeing computer. Movie makers can exaggerate retinal disparity by filming a scene with two cameras placed a few inches apart. Viewers then wear glasses that allow the left eye to see only the

gestalt an organized whole. Gestalt psychologists emphasized our tendency to integrate pieces of information into meaningful wholes.

figure-ground the organization of the visual field into objects (the *figures*) that stand out from their surroundings (the *ground*).

grouping the perceptual tendency to organize stimuli into meaningful groups.

depth perception the ability to see objects in three dimensions, although the images that strike the retina are two dimensional; allows us to judge distance.

visual cliff a laboratory device for testing depth perception in infants and young animals.

binocular cue a depth cue, such as retinal disparity, that depends on the use of two eyes.

retinal disparity a binocular cue for perceiving depth. By comparing images from the two eyes, the brain computes distance—the greater the disparity (difference) between the two images, the closer the object.

FIGURE 5.18 • **Visual cliff** Eleanor Gibson and Richard Walk devised this structure to find out whether crawling infants and newborn animals can perceive depth. Even when coaxed, most infants refuse to climb onto the sturdy glass covering the miniature cliff.

Innervisions

image from the left camera, and the right eye to see only the image from the right camera. The resulting 3-D effect, as *Avatar* movie fans will recall, mimics or exaggerates normal retinal disparity.

Monocular Cues How do we judge whether a person is 10 or 100 yards away? Retinal disparity won't help us here, because there won't be much difference between the images cast on our right and left retinas. At such distances, we depend on **monocular cues** (depth cues available to each eye separately). See **FIGURE 5.20** for some examples.

FIGURE 5.20 • Monocular depth cues

Relative height
We perceive objects higher in our field of vision as farther away. Because we assume the lower part of a figure-ground illustration is closer, we perceive it as figure (Vecera et al., 2002). Turn the illustration upside-down and the black will become ground, like a night sky.

Relative size
If we assume two objects are similar in size, *most* people perceive the one that casts the smaller retinal image as farther away.

Interposition
Interpose means "to come between." If one object partially blocks our view of another, we perceive it as closer. The depth cues provided by interposition make this an impossible scene.

Relative motion
As we move, objects that are actually stable may appear to move. If while riding on a bus you fix your gaze on some point—say, a house—the objects beyond the fixation point will appear to move with you. Objects in front of the point will appear to move backward. The farther an object is from the fixation point, the faster it will seem to move.

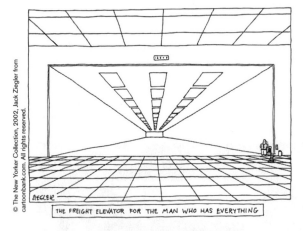

Linear perspective
Parallel lines appear to meet in the distance. The sharper the angle of convergence, the greater the perceived distance.

Direction of passenger's motion ⟶

Light and shadow
Shading produces a sense of depth consistent with our assumption that light comes from above. If you turn this illustration, the hollow will become a hill.

Perceptual Constancy

12 How do perceptual constancies help us construct meaningful perceptions?

So far, we have noted that our video-computer system must perceive objects as we do—as having a distinct form and location (as well as motion). Its next task is to recognize objects without being deceived by changes in their color, shape, and size—an ability we call **perceptual constancy.**

Color Constancy Color does not reside in an object. Our experience of color depends on an object's context. If you viewed an isolated tomato through a paper tube, its color would seem to change as the light—and thus the wavelengths reflected from its surface—changed. But if you viewed that tomato without the tube, as one item in a bowl of fresh vegetables, its color would remain roughly constant as the lighting shifts. This perception of consistent color is known as **color constancy.**

> "From there to here, from here to there, funny things are everywhere."
> Dr. Seuss, *One Fish, Two Fish, Red Fish, Blue Fish*, 1960

Though we take color constancy for granted, this ability is truly remarkable. A blue poker chip under indoor lighting will, in sunlight, reflect wavelengths that match those reflected by a sunlit gold chip (Jameson, 1985). Yet bring a goldfinch indoors and it won't look like a bluebird. The color is not in the bird's feathers. You and I see color thanks to our brain's ability to decode the meaning of the light reflected by an object *relative to the objects surrounding it.* **FIGURE 5.21** dramatically illustrates the ability of a blue object to appear very different in three different contexts. Yet we have no trouble seeing these disks as blue. Paint manufacturers have learned this lesson. Knowing that your perception of a paint color will be determined by other colors in your home, many now offer trial samples you can test in that context. The take-home lesson: *Comparisons govern our perceptions.*

Shape and Size Constancies Thanks to *shape constancy,* we usually perceive the form of familiar objects, such as the door in **FIGURE 5.22,** as constant even while our retinas receive changing images of them.

Thanks to *size constancy,* we perceive objects as having a constant size, even while our distance from them varies. We assume a car is large enough to carry people, even when we see its tiny image from two blocks away. This assumption also shows the close connection between perceived *distance* and perceived *size.*

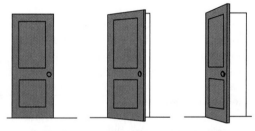

FIGURE 5.22 ● **Shape constancy** A door casts an increasingly trapezoidal image on our retinas as it opens. Yet we still perceive it as rectangular.

Perceiving an object's distance gives us cues to its size. Likewise, knowing its general size—that the object is a car—provides us with cues to its distance.

Even in size-distance judgments, however, we consider an object's context. The monsters in Figure 5.5 (page 128) cast identical images on our retinas. Using linear perspective as a cue (see Figure 5.20), our brain assumes that the pursuing monster is farther away. We therefore perceive it as larger. It isn't.

The interplay between perceived size and perceived distance helps explain several well-known illusions. FOR EXAMPLE, THE MOON LOOKS UP TO 50 PERCENT LARGER NEAR THE HORIZON THAN WHEN HIGH IN THE SKY. CAN YOU IMAGINE WHY? One reason is that cues to objects' distances make the horizon Moon—like the distant monster in Figure 5.5—appear farther away. If it's farther away, our brain assumes, it must be larger than the Moon high in the night sky (Kaufman & Kaufman, 2000). Take away the distance cues—by looking at the horizon Moon (or each monster) through a paper tube—and the object will immediately shrink.

monocular cue a depth cue, such as interposition or linear perspective, available to either eye alone.

perceptual constancy perceiving objects as unchanging (having consistent color, brightness, shape, and size) even as illumination and retinal images change.

color constancy perceiving familiar objects as having consistent color, even if changing illumination alters the wavelengths reflected by the object.

FIGURE 5.21 ● **Color depends on context** Believe it or not, these three blue disks are identical in color (a). Remove the surrounding context and see what results (b).

R. Beau Lotto at University College, London

(a)   (b)

Mistaken judgments like these reveal the workings of our normally effective perceptual processes. The perceived relationship between distance and size is usually valid. But under special circumstances it can lead us astray—as when helping to create the Moon illusion.

Form perception, depth perception, and perceptual constancy illuminate how we organize our visual experiences. Perceptual organization applies to our nonvisual senses, too. It explains why we perceive a clock's steady tick not as a *tick-tick-tick-tick* but as grouped sounds, say, *TICK-tick, TICK-tick*. Perception, though, is more than organizing stimuli. Perception also requires what would be a challenge to our video-computer system: interpretation—finding meaning in what we perceive.

Visual Interpretation

The debate over whether our perceptual abilities spring from our nature or our nurture has a long history. To what extent do we learn to perceive? German philosopher Immanuel Kant (1724–1804) maintained that knowledge comes from our *inborn* ways of organizing sensory experiences. Psychology's findings support this idea. We do come equipped to process sensory information. But British philosopher John Locke (1632–1704) argued that through our experiences we also *learn* to perceive the world. Psychology also supports this idea. We do learn to link an object's distance with its size. **SO, JUST HOW** ◄ **IMPORTANT IS EXPERIENCE? HOW MUCH DOES IT SHAPE OUR PERCEPTUAL INTERPRETATIONS?**

Experience and Visual Perception

13 What does research on restored vision, sensory deprivation, and perceptual adaptation reveal about the effects of experience on perception?

Restored Vision and Sensory Deprivation Writing to John Locke, a friend wondered: If "a man born blind, and now adult, [was] taught by his touch to distinguish between a cube and a sphere" could he, if made to see, visually distinguish the two? Locke's

Learning to see: At age 3, Mike May lost his vision in an explosion. Decades later, after a new cornea restored vision to his right eye, he got his first look at his wife and children. Alas, although signals were now reaching his visual cortex, it lacked the experience to interpret them. May could not recognize expressions, or faces, apart from features such as hair. Yet he can see an object in motion and has learned to navigate his world and to marvel at such things as dust floating in sunlight (Abrams, 2002).

answer was *No*, because the man would never have learned to see the difference.

This clever question has since been put to the test with a few dozen adults who, though blind from birth, have gained sight (Gregory, 1978; von Senden, 1932). Most were born with cataracts—clouded lenses that allowed them to see only light and shadows, rather as someone might see a foggy image through a Ping-Pong ball sliced in half. After surgery that removed the cataracts, the patients could tell the difference between figure and ground, and they could sense colors. This suggests that we are born with these aspects of perception. But much as Locke supposed, they often could not visually recognize objects that were familiar by touch.

In experiments with infant kittens and monkeys, researchers have outfitted the young animals with goggles through which they could see only diffuse, unpatterned light (Wiesel, 1982). After infancy, when the goggles were removed, these animals' reactions were much like those

of humans born with cataracts. Their eyes were healthy. Their retinas still sent signals to their visual cortex. But the brain's cortical cells had not developed normal connections. Thus, the animals remained functionally blind to shape. Experience guides and sustains the brain's development as it forms pathways that affect our perceptions.

In both humans and animals, similar sensory restrictions later in life do no permanent damage. When researchers cover an adult animal's eye for several months, its vision will be unaffected after the eye patch is removed. When surgeons remove cataracts that develop during late adulthood, most people are thrilled at the return to normal vision. The effect of sensory restriction on infant cats, monkeys, and humans suggests there is a *critical period* (Chapter 3) for normal sensory and perceptual development. Nurture sculpts what nature has endowed.

Perceptual Adaptation Given a new pair of glasses, we may feel a little strange, even dizzy. Within a day or two, we adjust. Our **perceptual adaptation** to changed visual input makes the world seem normal again. But imagine a far more dramatic new pair of glasses—one that shifts the apparent location of objects 40 degrees to the left. When you first put them on and

Perceptual adaptation: "Oops, missed," thinks researcher Hubert Dolezal as he views the world through inverting goggles. Yet, believe it or not, kittens, monkeys, and humans can adapt to an upside-down world.

toss a ball to a friend, it sails off to the left. Walking forward to shake hands with the person, you veer to the left.

Could you adapt to this distorted world? Chicks cannot. When fitted with such lenses, they continue to peck where food grains *seem* to be (Hess, 1956; Rossi, 1968). But we humans adapt to distorting lenses quickly. Within a few minutes, your throws would again be accurate, your stride on target. Remove the lenses and you would experience an aftereffect. At first your throws would err in the *opposite* direction, sailing off to the right. But again, within minutes you would adjust.

Indeed, given an even more radical pair of glasses—one that literally turns the world upside down—you could still adapt. Psychologist George Stratton (1896) experienced this when he invented, and for eight days wore, a device that flipped left to right *and* up to down, making him the first person to experience a right-side-up retinal image while standing upright. The ground was up, the sky was down.

At first, when Stratton wanted to walk, he found himself searching for his feet, which were now "up." Eating was nearly impossible. He became nauseated and depressed. But Stratton persisted, and by the eighth day he could comfortably reach for an object in the right direction and walk without bumping into things. When Stratton finally removed the headgear, he readapted quickly.

In later experiments, people wearing the optical gear have even been able to ride a motorcycle, ski the Alps, and fly an airplane (Dolezal, 1982; Kohler, 1962). The world around them still seemed above their heads or on the wrong side. But by actively moving about in these topsy-turvy worlds, they adapted to the context and learned to coordinate their movements.

PRACTICE TEST

THE BASICS

12. Gestalt psychologists identified principles by which we organize our perceptions. Our minds bring order and form to stimuli by following certain rules for

   a. color constancy.
   b. depth perception.
   c. shape constancy.
   d. grouping.

13. In listening to a concert, you attend to the solo instrument and perceive the orchestra as accompaniment. This illustrates the organizing principle of

   a. figure-ground.
   b. shape constancy.
   c. grouping.
   d. depth perception.

14. The visual cliff experiments suggest that

   a. infants have not yet developed depth perception.
   b. crawling human infants and very young animals perceive depth.
   c. we have no way of knowing whether infants can perceive depth.
   d. unlike other species, humans are able to perceive depth in infancy.

15. Depth perception is our ability to

   a. group similar items in a gestalt.
   b. perceive objects as having a constant shape or form.
   c. judge distances.
   d. fill in the gaps in a figure.

16. Two examples of monocular cues are interposition and

   a. closure.
   b. retinal disparity.
   c. linear perspective.
   d. continuity.

17. Perceiving a tomato as consistently red, despite lighting shifts, is an example of

   a. shape constancy.
   b. color constancy.
   c. a binocular cue.
   d. continuity.

18. In some cases, surgeons have restored vision to patients who have been blind from birth. The newly sighted individuals were able to sense colors but had difficulty

   a. recognizing objects by touch.
   b. recognizing objects by sight.
   c. distinguishing figure from ground.
   d. distinguishing between bright and dim light.

19. In experiments, people have worn glasses that turned their visual fields upside down. After a period of adjustment, they learned to function quite well. This ability is called

   a. context effect.
   b. perceptual set.
   c. sensory interaction.
   d. perceptual adaptation.

THE BIG PICTURE

5C. What do we mean when we say that, in perception, the whole is greater than the sum of its parts?

IN YOUR EVERYDAY LIFE

▪ What would your life be like without perceptual constancy?

Answers: 12. d, 13. a, 14. b, 15. c, 16. c, 17. b, 18. b, 19. d. Answers to The Big Picture questions can be found in Appendix B at the end of the book.

The Nonvisual Senses

For humans, vision is the major sense. More of our brain cortex is devoted to vision than to any other sense. Yet without our senses of hearing, touch, taste, smell, and body position and movement, our experience of the world would be vastly diminished.

Hearing

Like our other senses, our hearing, or **audition,** helps us adapt and survive. We hear a wide range of sounds, but the ones we hear best are those in a range similar to that of the human voice. We also are remarkably sensitive to faint sounds, such as a child's whimper. (If our ears were much more sensitive, we would hear a constant hiss from the movement of air molecules.) Our ancestors' survival may have depended on this keen hearing when hunting or being hunted.

We are also acutely sensitive to sound differences. Among thousands of possible

---

perceptual adaptation in vision, the ability to adjust to an artificially displaced or even inverted visual field.

audition the sense or act of hearing.

voices, we easily detect a friend's on the phone, from the moment she says "Hi." A fraction of a second after such events stimulate the ear's receptors, millions of neurons have worked together to extract the essential features, compare them with past experience, and identify the sound (Freeman, 1991). For hearing as for seeing, we wonder: How do we do it?

The Stimulus Input: Sound Waves

14 What are the characteristics of the air pressure waves that we hear as meaningful sounds?

Hit a piano key and you will unleash the energy of sound waves. Jostling molecules of air, each bumping into the next, create waves of compressed and expanded air, like the ripples on a pond circling out from a tossed stone. Our ears detect these brief air pressure changes.

Like light waves, sound waves vary in shape. The *amplitude* of sound waves determines their *loudness*. Their length, or **frequency,** determines the **pitch** we experience. Long waves have low frequency—and low pitch. Short waves have high frequency—and high pitch. Sound waves produced by a violin are much

shorter and faster than those produced by a cello or a bass guitar.

We measure sounds in *decibels,* with zero decibels representing the absolute threshold for hearing. Normal conversation registers at about 60 decibels. A whisper falls at about 20 decibels, and a passing subway train at about 100 decibels. Prolonged exposure to any sounds above 85 decibels can produce hearing loss.

Decoding Sound Waves

15 How does the ear transform sound energy into neural messages?

The intricate process that transforms vibrating air into nerve impulses, which our brain decodes as sounds, begins when sound waves enter the outer ear. In the first step of a mechanical chain reaction, the outer ear channels the waves into the auditory canal, where they bump against the *eardrum,* a tight membrane, causing it to vibrate **(FIGURE 5.23a).** In the middle ear, a piston made of three tiny bones picks up the vibrations and transmits them to the **cochlea,** a snail-shaped tube in the inner ear. The incoming vibrations then cause the cochlea's membrane (the *oval window*) to vibrate, creating ripples in the fluid inside the cochlea (Figure 5.23b). The ripples bend the *hair cells* lining the cochlea's surface, like wind bending a wheat field. The hair cell movements in turn trigger impulses in nerve cells. Axons from those nerve cells combine to form the *auditory nerve,* which carries the neural messages to the *auditory cortex* in the brain's temporal lobe. From vibrating air to moving piston to fluid waves to electrical impulses to the brain: We hear!

My vote for the most magical part of the hearing process is the hair cells— "quivering bundles that let us hear" thanks to their "extreme sensitivity and extreme speed" (Goldberg, 2007). A cochlea has 16,000 of them, which sounds like a lot until we

compare that with an eye's 130 million or so receptors. But consider their responsiveness. Deflect the tiny bundles of *cilia* on the tip of a hair cell by the width of an atom—the equivalent of displacing the top of the Eiffel Tower by half an inch—and the alert hair cell triggers a neural response (Corey et al., 2004).

At the highest perceived frequency, hair cells can turn neural current on and off a thousand times per second! As you might expect of something so sensitive, they are, however, delicate. Blast them with hunting rifle shots or blaring iPods, as teen boys more than girls do, and the hair cells' cilia will begin to wither or fuse. No wonder men's hearing tends to be less acute than women's (Zogby, 2006).

Most hearing loss results from damage to hair cells. They have been likened to shag carpet fibers. Walk around on them and they will spring back with a quick vacuuming. But leave a heavy piece of furniture on them for a long time and they may never rebound. As a general rule, any noise we cannot talk over may be harmful, especially if we are exposed to it often or for a long time (Roesser, 1998). And if our ears ring after exposure to loud machinery or music, we have been bad to our unhappy hair cells. As pain alerts us to possible bodily harm, ringing of the ears alerts us to possible hearing damage. It is hearing's version of bleeding. People who spend many hours behind a power mower, above a jackhammer, or in a loud nightclub should wear earplugs. "Condoms or, safer yet, abstinence," say sex educators. "Earplugs or walk away," say hearing educators.

AP Photo/Mark J. Terrill

The sounds of music: A violin's short, fast waves create a high pitch. A cello's longer, slower waves create a lower pitch. Differences in the waves' height, or amplitude, also create differing degrees of loudness.

Joern Rynio/Getty Images

That Baylen may hear: When Super Bowl–winning quarterback Drew Brees celebrated New Orleans' 2010 victory amid pandemonium, he used ear muffs to protect the vulnerable hair cells of his son, Baylen.

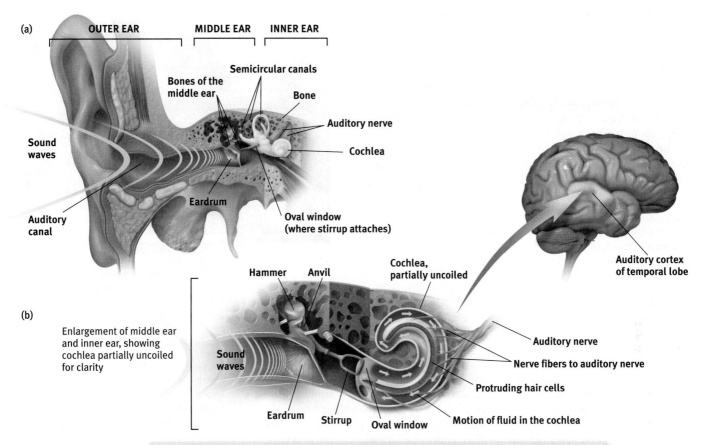

(a) OUTER EAR MIDDLE EAR INNER EAR

Semicircular canals

Bones of the middle ear

Bone

Auditory nerve

Cochlea

Sound waves

Eardrum

Auditory canal

Oval window (where stirrup attaches)

Auditory cortex of temporal lobe

(b) Enlargement of middle ear and inner ear, showing cochlea partially uncoiled for clarity

Hammer   Anvil

Cochlea, partially uncoiled

Sound waves

Eardrum   Stirrup   Oval window

Auditory nerve

Nerve fibers to auditory nerve

Protruding hair cells

Motion of fluid in the cochlea

FIGURE 5.23 ● **Hear here: How we transform sound waves into nerve impulses that our brain interprets** (a) The outer ear funnels sound waves to the eardrum. The bones of the middle ear (hammer, anvil, and stirrup) amplify and relay the eardrum's vibrations through the oval window into the fluid-filled cochlea. (b) As shown in this detail of the middle and inner ear, the resulting pressure changes in the cochlear fluid cause the hair cells to bend. Hair cell movements trigger impulses at the base of the nerve cells, whose fibers join together to form the auditory nerve. That nerve sends neural messages to the thalamus and on to the auditory cortex.

How Do We Locate Sounds?

WHY DON'T WE HAVE ONE BIG EAR— ◄ PERHAPS ABOVE OUR ONE NOSE? "The better to hear you," as the wolf said to Red Riding Hood. The placement of our two ears allows us to hear two slightly different messages. We benefit in two ways. If a car to the right honks, your right ear receives a more *intense* sound, and it receives sound slightly *sooner* than your left ear (FIGURE 5.24). Because sound travels 750 miles per hour and our ears are only 6 inches apart, the intensity difference and the time lag are very small. Lucky for us, our supersensitive sound system can detect such tiny differences (Brown & Deffenbacher, 1979; Middlebrooks & Green, 1991).

So, how well do we do at locating a sound that comes from directly ahead, behind, overhead, or beneath us? Not very well. Why? Because such sounds strike both ears at the same time.

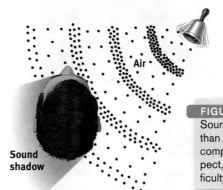

Air

Sound shadow

frequency the number of complete wavelengths that pass a point in a given time (for example, per second).

pitch a tone's experienced highness or lowness; depends on frequency.

cochlea [KOHK-lee-uh] a coiled, bony, fluid-filled tube in the inner ear; sound waves traveling through the cochlear fluid trigger nerve impulses.

FIGURE 5.24 ● **Why two ears are better than one** Sound waves strike one ear sooner and more intensely than the other. From this information, our nimble brain can compute the sound's location. As you might therefore expect, people who lose all hearing in one ear often have difficulty locating sounds.

You can try this yourself by sitting with closed eyes while a friend snaps fingers around your head. You will easily point to the sound when it comes from either side, but you will likely make some mistakes when it comes from directly ahead, behind, above, or below. That is why, when trying to pinpoint a sound, you cock your head, so that your two ears will receive slightly different messages.

Touch

16 What are the four basic touch sensations, and which of them has identifiable receptors?

If you had to lose one sense, which would you give up? If you could have only one, which would you keep?

Although not the first sense to come to mind, touch might be a good choice for keeping. Right from the start, touch is essential to our development. Infant monkeys allowed to see, hear, and smell—but not touch—their mothers become desperately unhappy. Those separated by a screen with holes that allow touching are much less miserable. As we noted in Chapter 3, premature babies gain weight faster and go home sooner if they are stimulated by hand massage. As lovers, we yearn to touch—to kiss, to stroke, to snuggle.

Humorist Dave Barry may be right to jest that your skin "keeps people from seeing the inside of your body, which is repulsive, and it prevents your organs from falling onto the ground." But skin does

much more. Our "sense of touch" is actually a mix of distinct skin senses for *pressure, warmth, cold,* and *pain*. Other skin sensations are variations of the basic four. For example, stroking side-by-side pressure spots creates a tickle. Repeated gentle stroking of a pain spot creates an itching sensation. Touching side-by-side cold and pressure spots triggers a sense of wetness (which you can experience by touching dry, cold metal.)

Surprisingly, there is no simple relationship between what we feel at a given spot and the type of specialized nerve ending found there. Only pressure has identifiable receptors.

Touch sensations involve more than the feelings on our skin, however. A self-produced tickle activates a smaller area of the brain's cortex than the same tickle would from something or someone else (Blakemore et al., 1998). (The brain is wise enough to be most sensitive to unexpected stimulation.)

Pain

17 What influences our feelings of pain, and how can we treat pain?

SHOULD WE BE THANKFUL FOR OCCA- ◀ SIONAL PAIN? Yes. Pain is your body's way of telling you something has gone wrong.

A pain-free, problematic life: Ashlyn Blocker (right), shown here with her mother and sister, has a rare genetic disorder. She feels neither pain nor extreme hot and cold. She must frequently be checked for accidentally self-inflicted injuries that she herself cannot feel. "Some people would say that [feeling no pain] is a good thing," says her mother. "But no, it's not. Pain's there for a reason. It lets your body know something's wrong and it needs to be fixed. I'd give anything for her to feel pain" (quoted by Bynum, 2004).

When drawing your attention to a burn, a break, or a sprain, pain tells you to change your behavior immediately. Stay off that turned ankle! The rare people born without the ability to feel pain may experience severe injury or even die before early adulthood. Without the discomfort that makes us shift positions, their joints can fail from excess strain.

Diverse Yet Alike

As William James wrote in his *Principles of Psychology* (1890), "Touch is both the alpha and omega of affection."

Without the warnings of pain, infections can run wild, and injuries can accumulate (Neese, 1991).

Many more people live with chronic pain, which is rather like an alarm that won't shut off. The suffering of those who cannot escape the pain of backaches, arthritis, headaches, and cancer-related problems prompts two questions: WHAT◀ IS PAIN? AND HOW MIGHT WE CONTROL IT?

Understanding Pain Pain experiences vary widely from person to person. The pain we feel is in part a property of our senses, of the region where we feel it. But our pain system differs from some of our other senses. We don't have a simple neural cord running from a sensing device on our skin to a specific area in our brain. No one type of stimulus triggers pain (as light triggers vision). And we have no special receptors (like the retina's rods and cones) for pain. In fact, at low intensities, the stimuli that produce pain also cause other sensations, including warmth or coolness, smoothness or roughness.

Pain is a physical event, but it is also a product of our attention, our expectations, and our culture. The brain-pain connection is clear in the clever *rubber hand illusion,* in which a participant's own hand is out of sight beneath a visible fake hand (**FIGURE 5.25**). Even just "stroking" the fake hand with a laser light produces, for most people, an illusory sensation of

warmth or touch in their unseen real hand (Durgin et al., 2007). Touch is not only a bottom-up property of your senses but also a top-down product of your brain and your expectations.

With pain, as with sights and sounds, the brain sometimes gets its signals crossed. Consider people's experiences of *phantom limb sensations.* After having a limb amputated, some 7 in 10 people feel pain or movement in limbs that no longer exist (Melzack, 1992, 1993). Some try to step off a bed onto a phantom leg or to lift a cup with a phantom hand. Even those born without a limb sometimes feel sensations in the missing part. The brain, notes Ronald Melzack, comes prepared to anticipate "that it will be getting information from a body that has limbs" (1998).

Phantoms may haunt our other senses, too. People with hearing loss often experience the sound of silence: *tinnitus,* a phantom sound of ringing in the ears. Those who lose vision to glaucoma, cataracts, diabetes, or macular degeneration may experience phantom sights—nonthreatening hallucinations (Ramachandran & Blakeslee, 1998). And damage to nerves in the systems for tasting and smelling can give rise to phantom tastes or smells, such as ice water that seems sickeningly sweet, or fresh air that reeks of rotten food (Goode, 1999). The point to remember: *We see, hear, taste, smell, and feel pain with our brain.*

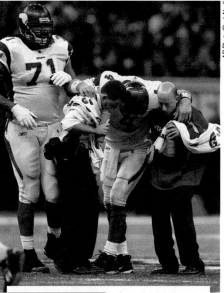

Playing with pain: In a 2010 Super Bowl playoff game, Vikings quarterback Brett Favre seriously injured his ankle and hamstring. He was taken out of the game briefly but came back and played through the pain, which reclaimed his attention after the game's end.

Controlling Pain If pain is where body meets mind—if pain is both a physical and a psychological event—then it should be treatable both physically and psychologically.

We have some built-in pain controls. Our brain releases a natural painkiller—*endorphins*—in response to severe pain or even vigorous exercise. Soothed by the release of endorphins, our experience of pain may be greatly diminished. People who carry a gene that boosts the normal supply of endorphins are less bothered by pain, and their brains are less responsive to it (Zubieta et al., 2003). Others, who carry a gene that disrupts the neural pain circuit, may be unable to experience pain (Cox et al., 2006). These discoveries point the way toward future pain medications that mimic the genetic effects.

When endorphins combine with distraction, amazing things can happen. Sports injuries may go unnoticed until the after-game shower (thus demonstrating that the pain in sprain is mainly in

> "Pain is increased by attending to it."
>
> Charles Darwin, *Expression of Emotions in Man and Animals,* 1872

FIGURE 5.25 ● **The rubber hand illusion** When Dublin researcher Deirdre Desmond simultaneously touches a volunteer's real and fake hands, the volunteer feels as though the seen fake hand is her own.

the brain). During a 1989 basketball game, Ohio State University player Jay Burson broke his neck—and kept playing.

Health care professionals understand the value of distractions and may divert attention with a pleasant image (*"Think of a warm, comfortable environment"*) or a request to perform some task (*"Count backward by 3s"*) (Fernandez & Turk, 1989; McCaul & Malott, 1984). A well-trained nurse may distract needle-shy patients by chatting with them and asking them to look away when the needle is inserted. For burn victims receiving excruciating wound care, an even more effective distraction comes from immersion in a computer-generated 3-D world **(FIGURE 5.26)**. Functional MRI (fMRI) scans reveal that playing in the virtual reality reduces the brain's pain-related activity (Hoffman, 2004).

The brain-pain connection is also clear in our *memories* of pain. The pain we experience may not be the pain we remember. In experiments, and after medical procedures, people tend to overlook how long a pain lasted. Their memory snapshots may instead record its *peak moment* and also how much pain they felt at the *end*. Researchers discovered this when they asked people to put one hand

in painfully cold water for 60 seconds, and then the other hand in the same painfully cold water for 60 seconds, followed by a slightly less painful 30 seconds more (Kahneman et al., 1993). Which of these experiences would you expect to recall as most painful?

Curiously, when asked which trial they would prefer to repeat, most preferred the longer trial, with more net pain—but less pain at the end. A physician used this principle with patients undergoing colon exams—lengthening the discomfort by a minute, but lessening its intensity at the end (Kahneman, 1999). Patients experiencing this taper-down treatment later recalled the exam as less painful than those whose pain ended abruptly. (As a painful root canal is coming to an end, if the oral surgeon asks if you'd like to go home, or to have a few more minutes of milder discomfort, there's a case to be made for prolonging your hurt.)

Because pain is in the brain, hypnosis may also bring relief.

Hypnosis and Pain Relief Imagine you are about to be hypnotized. The hypnotist invites you to sit back, fix your gaze on a spot high on the wall, and relax. In a quiet, low voice the hypnotist suggests,

"Your eyes are growing tired. . . . Your eyelids are becoming heavy . . . now heavier and heavier. . . . They are beginning to close. . . . You are becoming more deeply relaxed. . . . Your breathing is now deep and regular. . . . Your muscles are becoming more and more relaxed. Your whole body is beginning to feel like lead."

After a few minutes of this *hypnotic induction*, you may experience **hypnosis.** Hypnotists have no magical mind-control power; they merely focus people on certain images or behaviors. To some extent, we are all open to suggestion. But highly hypnotizable people—such as the 2 percent who can carry out a suggestion not to smell or react to an open bottle of ammonia—are especially suggestible and imaginative (Barnier & McConkey, 2004; Silva & Kirsch, 1992).

HAS HYPNOSIS PROVED USEFUL IN RE-◀ LIEVING PAIN? Yes it has. When unhypnotized people put their arms in an ice bath, they feel intense pain within 25 seconds (Druckman & Bjork, 1994; Patterson, 2004). When hypnotized people do the same after being given suggestions to feel no pain, they indeed report feeling little pain. As some dentists know, light hypnosis can reduce fear, and thus hypersensitivity to pain.

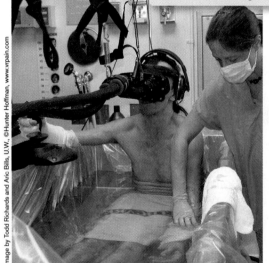

FIGURE 5.26 • **Virtual-reality pain control** For burn victims undergoing painful skin repair, escaping into virtual reality (like the icy playground shown here) can be a powerful distraction. With attention focused elsewhere, pain and the brain's response to painful stimulation decrease, as shown in the fMRI scans on the right. The calmer brain on the lower right belongs to a person playing in a virtual reality environment.

No distraction

Distraction

Hypnosis inhibits pain-related brain activity. In surgical experiments, hypnotized patients have required less medication, recovered sooner, and left the hospital earlier than unhypnotized control patients (Askay & Patterson, 2007; Patterson & Jensen, 2003). Nearly 10 percent of us can become so deeply hypnotized that even major surgery can be performed without anesthesia. The surgical use of hypnosis has flourished in Europe, where one Belgian medical team has performed more than 5000 surgeries with a combination of hypnosis, local anesthesia, and a mild sedative (Song, 2006).

Psychologists have proposed two explanations for how hypnosis works. One theory proposes that hypnosis produces a *dissociation*—a split—between normal sensations and conscious awareness. Dissociation theory seeks to explain why, when no one is watching, hypnotized people may carry out *posthypnotic suggestions* (which are made during hypnosis but carried out after the person is no longer hypnotized). It also offers an explanation for why people hypnotized for pain relief may show brain activity in areas that receive sensory information, but not in areas that normally process pain-related information.

Those who reject the hypnosis-as-dissociation view believe that hypnosis is instead a form of normal *social influence* (Lynn et al., 1990; Spanos & Coe, 1992). In

this view, hypnosis is a by-product of normal social and mental processes. Like actors caught up in their roles, people begin to feel and behave in ways appropriate for "good hypnotic subjects." They may allow the hypnotist to direct their attention and fantasies away from pain.

Taste

18 How are our senses of taste and smell similar, and what is sensory interaction?

Our sense of taste involves several basic sensations, which until recently were thought to be *sweet, sour, salty,* and *bitter* (McBurney & Gent, 1979). In recent decades, many researchers have searched for specialized fibers that might act as nerve pathways for the four taste sensations. During this search, they discovered a receptor for a fifth basic taste sensation—the savory, meaty taste of *umami*. You may have experienced umami as the flavor enhancer monosodium glutamate, often used in Chinese or Thai food.

Tastes exist for more than our pleasure. Nice tastes attracted our ancestors to protein- or energy-rich foods that enabled their survival (see **TABLE 5.2** on the next page). Unpleasant tastes warned them away from new foods that might contain toxins and lead to food poisoning, which can be especially deadly for children. HOW DO THE TASTE PREFERENCES ◄ OF TODAY'S 2- TO 6-YEAR-OLDS REFLECT OUR INHERITED BIOLOGICAL WISDOM? At this age, children are typically fussy eaters and often turn away from new

meat dishes or bitter-tasting vegetables, such as spinach and brussels sprouts (Cooke et al., 2003). But another tool in our early ancestors' survival kit was learning. Across the globe, frustrated parents are happy to see that, given repeated small tastes of disliked new foods, children typically learn to accept these foods (Wardle et al., 2003).

Taste is a chemical sense. You've surely noticed the little bumps on the top and sides of your tongue. Inside each bump are 200 or more taste buds. Each bud contains a pore. Projecting into each of these pores are antennalike hairs from 50 to 100 taste receptor cells. These hairs carry information about molecules of food chemicals back to your taste receptor cells. Some receptors respond mostly to sweet-tasting molecules, others to salty-, sour-, umami-, or bitter-tasting ones. All send their messages to your brain.

It doesn't take much to trigger those responses. If a stream of water is pumped across your tongue, the addition of a concentrated salty or sweet taste for but one-tenth of a second will get your attention (Kelling & Halpern, 1983). When a friend asks for "just a taste" of your soft drink, you can squeeze off the straw after an eyeblink.

Taste receptors reproduce themselves every week or two, so if you burn your tongue with hot food it hardly matters. However, as you grow older, it may matter more, because the number of taste buds in your mouth will decrease, as will your taste sensitivity (Cowart, 1981). (No wonder adults enjoy strong-tasting foods that children resist.) Smoking and alcohol can speed up the loss of taste buds.

Essential as taste buds are, there's more to taste than meets the tongue.

Lauren Burke/Getty Images

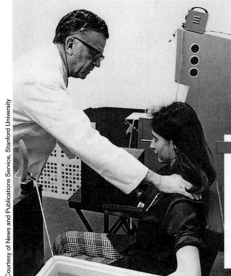

Courtesy of News and Publications Service, Stanford University

Dissociation or social influence?: This hypnotized woman being tested by famous researcher Ernest Hilgard showed no pain when her arm was placed in an ice bath. But asked to press a key if some part of her felt the pain, she did so. To Hilgard (1986, 1992), this was evidence of dissociation, or divided consciousness. The social influence perspective, however, maintains that people responding this way are caught up in playing the role of "good subject."

hypnosis a social interaction in which one person (the hypnotist) suggests to another (the subject) that certain perceptions, feelings, thoughts, or behaviors will spontaneously occur.

TABLE 5.2	The Survival Functions of Basic Tastes
Taste	**Indicates**
Sweet	Energy source
Salty	Sodium essential to physiological processes
Sour	Potentially toxic acid
Bitter	Potential poisons
Umami	Proteins to grow and repair tissue

(Adapted from Cowart, 2005.)

Expectations can influence taste. When told a sausage roll was "vegetarian," people in one experiment found it decidedly inferior to its identical partner labeled "meat" (Allen et al., 2008). In another experiment, being told that a wine cost $90 rather than its real $10 price made it taste better and triggered more activity in a brain area that responds to pleasant experiences (Plassman et al., 2008).

Smell also affects taste. Hold your nose, close your eyes, and have someone feed you various foods. You may not be able to tell a slice of apple from a slice of raw potato. To savor a taste, we normally breathe its aroma through our nose—which is why eating is not much fun when you have a bad cold. Smell can also *change* our perception of taste. Add a strawberry odor and a drink will seem sweeter. This is **sensory interaction** at work—the principle that one sense may influence another. Smell + texture + taste = flavor.

Sensory interaction also influences what we hear (**FIGURE 5.27**). If I (as a person with hearing loss) watch a video with subtitles, I have no trouble hearing the words I am seeing. If I then mistakenly think I don't need these captions and turn them off, I suddenly realize I really do need them. But what do you suppose happens if we *see* a speaker saying one syllable (*ga*) while we *hear* another (*ba*)? Surprise: We may

Anouk de Maar/Getty Images

perceive a third syllable (*da*) that blends both inputs. This peculiar interaction is known as the *McGurk effect,* after its discoverers, psychologist Harry McGurk and his assistant John MacDonald (1976).

Our senses—tasting, smelling, hearing, seeing, touching—are not totally separate information channels. In interpreting the world, our brain blends their inputs. It even blends our sensory and social judgments. After holding a warm drink rather than cold one, people are more likely to rate someone more warmly and behave more generously (Williams & Bargh, 2008). Physical warmth promotes social warmth. And after being given the cold shoulder by others in an experiment, people judge the room as colder than do those treated warmly (Zhong & Leonardelli, 2008). Social exclusion literally feels cold.

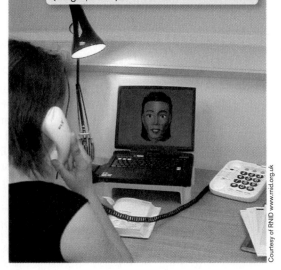

FIGURE 5.27 • Sensory interaction
When a hard-of-hearing listener *sees* an animated face forming words being spoken, the words become easier to understand (Knight, 2004).

Courtesy of RNID www.rnid.org.uk

Smell

Inhale, exhale. Inhale, exhale. Breaths come in pairs—except at two moments: birth and death. Between those two moments, you will daily inhale and exhale nearly 20,000 breaths of life-sustaining air, bathing your nostrils in a stream of scent-laden molecules. **IS IT◄ TRUE THAT WE INHALE SOMETHING OF WHATEVER OR WHOEVER IT IS WE SMELL?** *Yes.* Our experience of smell (*olfaction*) is strikingly intimate.

Smell, like taste, is a chemical sense. We smell something when molecules of a substance carried in the air reach a tiny cluster of 5 million or more receptor cells at the top of each nasal cavity. These olfactory receptor cells, waving like sea anemones on a reef, respond selectively—to the aroma of a cake baking, to a wisp of smoke, to a friend's fragrance. Instantly (bypassing the brain's sensory switchboard, the thalamus), they alert the brain.

Aided by smell, a mother fur seal returning to a beach crowded with pups will find her own. Human mothers and nursing infants also quickly learn to recognize each other's scents (McCarthy, 1986). Our sense of smell is, however, less impressive than our senses of seeing and hearing. Looking out across a garden, we see its forms and colors in wonderful detail and hear a variety of birds singing. Yet we smell few of the garden's scents without sticking our nose into the blossoms.

Odor molecules come in many shapes and sizes—so many, in fact, that it takes hundreds of different receptors, designed by a large family of genes, to recognize these molecules (Miller, 2004). We do not have one distinct receptor for each detectable odor. Instead, different combinations of receptors send messages to the brain's olfactory cortex. As the English alphabet's 26 letters can combine to form many words, so olfactory receptors can produce different patterns to identify the 10,000 odors we can detect (Malnic et al., 1999). These different combinations activate different neural patterns (Zou & Buck, 2006). And that is what allows us to smell

The nose knows: Humans have 10 to 20 million olfactory receptors. A bloodhound has some 200 million (Herz, 2001).

Bodies in space: These high school competitive cheer team members can thank their inner ears for the information that enables their brains to monitor their bodies' position so expertly.

the difference between fresh-brewed and hours-old coffee.

Odors can evoke memories **(FIGURE 5.28)**. Though it's difficult to recall odors by name, we have a remarkable capacity to recognize long-forgotten odors and their associated personal tales (Engen, 1987; Schab, 1991). Pleasant odors can call up pleasant memories (Ehrlichman & Halpern, 1988). The smell of the sea, the

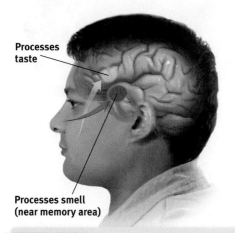

Processes taste

Processes smell (near memory area)

FIGURE 5.28 • **Taste, smell, and memory** Information from the taste buds (yellow arrow) travels to an area between the frontal and temporal lobes of the brain. It registers in an area not far from where the brain receives information from our sense of smell, which interacts with taste. The brain's circuitry for smell (red arrow) also connects with areas involved in memory storage, which helps explain why a smell can trigger a memory.

scent of a perfume, or an aroma of a favorite relative's kitchen can bring to mind a happy time. It's a link one British travel agent chain understood well. To evoke memories of lounging on sunny, warm beaches, the company once piped the aroma of coconut sunscreen into its shops (Fracassini, 2000).

Body Position and Movement

19 What sensory systems monitor our body's position and movement?

With only the five familiar senses we have so far considered, you could not put food in your mouth, stand up, or reach out and touch someone. Just the "simple" act of moving your arms to grasp someone's hand requires a sixth sense that will inform you about the current position of your arms and hands and their changing positions as you move them. Just taking one step forward requires feedback from, and instructions to, some 200 muscles. The brain power engaged in all this dwarfs even that involved in reasoning. Let's take a closer look.

You came equipped with millions of position and motion sensors. They are all over your body—in your muscles, tendons, and joints—and they are continually feeding information to your brain. Twist your

wrist one degree, and these sensors provide an immediate update. This sense of your body parts' position and movement is **kinesthesis.**

You can momentarily imagine being blind or deaf. Close your eyes, plug your ears, and experience the dark stillness. BUT WHAT WOULD IT BE LIKE TO LIVE WITH- ◄ OUT BEING ABLE TO SENSE THE POSITIONS OF YOUR LIMBS WHEN YOU WAKE DURING THE NIGHT? Ian Waterman of Hampshire, England, knows. In 1972, at age 19, Waterman contracted a rare viral infection that destroyed the nerves that enabled his sense of light touch and of body position and movement. People with this condition report feeling disconnected from their body, as though it is dead, not real, not theirs (Sacks, 1985). With prolonged practice, Waterman has learned to walk and eat—by visually focusing on his limbs and directing them accordingly. But if the lights go out, he crumples to the floor (Azar, 1998).

sensory interaction the principle that one sense may influence another, as when the smell of food influences its taste.

kinesthesis [kin-ehs-THEE-sehs] the system for sensing the position and movement of individual body parts.

For all of us, vision interacts with kinesthesis. Stand with your right heel in front of your left toes. Easy. Now close your eyes and you will probably wobble.

Working hand-in-hand with kinesthesis is our **vestibular sense.** This companion sense monitors your head's (and thus your body's) position and movement. Controlling this sense of equilibrium are two structures in your inner ear. The first, your *semicircular canals,* look like a three-dimensional pretzel (Figure 5.23a). The second, connecting those canals with the cochlea, is the *vestibular sacs,* which contain fluid that moves when your head rotates or tilts. When this movement stimulates hairlike receptors, sending messages to the cerebellum at the back of your brain, you sense your body position and maintain your balance.

If you twirl around and then come to an abrupt halt, it takes a few seconds for the fluid in your semicircular canals and for your kinesthetic receptors to return to their neutral state. The aftereffect fools your dizzy brain with the sensation that you're still spinning. This illustrates a principle underlying perceptual illusions: *Mechanisms that normally give us an accurate experience of the world can, under special conditions, fool us.* Understanding how we get fooled provides clues to how our perceptual system works.

TABLE 5.3 summarizes the sensory systems we have discussed so far.

Sensation, as we have seen, is one of the two streams that feed the river of perception; the other is cognition. If perception is the product of these two sources, what can we say about extrasensory perception, which claims that perception can occur apart from sensory input? For more on that question, see Thinking Critically About: ESP—Perception Without Sensation?

Within our ordinary sensation and perception lies much that is truly extraordinary. A century of research has revealed many of the secrets of sensation and perception, yet for future generations of researchers there remain profound and genuine mysteries to solve.

TABLE 5.3	Summarizing the Senses	
Sensory System	**Source**	**Receptors**
Vision	Light waves striking the eye	Rods and cones in the retina
Hearing	Sound waves striking the outer ear	Cochlear hair cells in the inner ear
Touch	Pressure, warmth, cold on the skin	Skin receptors detect pressure, warmth, cold, and pain
Taste	Chemical molecules in the mouth	Basic tongue receptors for sweet, sour, salty, bitter, and umami
Smell	Chemical molecules breathed in through the nose	Millions of receptors at top of nasal cavity
Body position—kinesthesis	Any change in position of a body part, interacting with vision	Kinesthetic sensors all over the body
Body movement—vestibular sense	Movement of fluids in the inner ear caused by head/body movement	Hairlike receptors in the inner ear's semicircular canals and vestibular sacs

Sensory information travels to these areas of the brain's cerebral cortex:

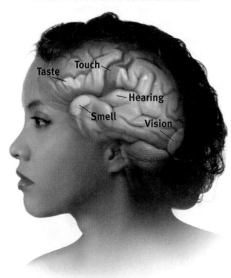

vestibular sense the sense of body movement and position, including the sense of balance.

THINKING CRITICALLY ABOUT

ESP—Perception Without Sensation?

20 | **How do ESP claims hold up when put to the test by scientists?**

Without sensory input, are we capable of **extrasensory perception (ESP)?** Nearly half of Americans believe we are (AP, 2007; Moore, 2005).

▶ ARE THERE INDEED PEOPLE—*ANY* PEOPLE—WHO CAN READ MINDS, SEE THROUGH WALLS, OR FORETELL THE FUTURE? Before we evaluate claims of ESP, let's review them. The most testable and, for this chapter, most relevant ESP claims focus on:

Telepathy: mind-to-mind communication.

Clairvoyance: perceiving remote events, such as a house on fire in another state.

Precognition: perceiving future events, such as an unexpected death in the next month.

Closely linked with these are claims of *psychokinesis,* or "mind over matter," such as levitating a table or influencing the roll of a die. (The claim is illustrated by the wry request, "Will all those who believe in psychokinesis please raise my hand?")

Facts or Fantasies?

Most research psychologists and scientists—including 96 percent of the scientists in one U.S. National Academy of Sciences survey—are skeptical of ESP claims (McConnell, 1991). No greedy—or charitable—psychic has been able to predict the outcome of a lottery jackpot, or to make billions on the stock market, much less always to win at "rocks, paper, and scissors." The new-century psychics failed to anticipate the big-news events such as the horror of 9/11. (Where were the psychics on 9/10 when we needed them?) In 26 years, unusual predictions have almost never come true, and psychics have virtually never anticipated any of the year's headline events (Emery, 2004).

Moreover, the hundreds of visions offered by psychics working with the police have been no more accurate than guesses made by others (Nickell, 1994, 2005; Reiser, 1982). But their sheer volume does increase the odds of an occasional correct guess, which psychics can then report to the media. Police departments are wise to all this. When researchers asked the police departments of America's 50 largest cities whether they ever had used psychics, 65 percent said *No* (Sweat & Durm, 1993). Of those that had, not one had found them helpful.

Are the spontaneous "visions" of everyday people any more accurate? Do our dreams foretell the future, or do they only seem to do so when we recall or reconstruct them in light of what has already happened? Two Harvard psychologists tested the prophetic power of dreams after aviator Charles Lindbergh's baby son was kidnapped and murdered in 1932, but before the body was discovered

> "A person who talks a lot is sometimes right."
>
> Spanish proverb

(Murray & Wheeler, 1937). When invited to report their dreams about the child, 1300 visionaries replied. How many accurately saw the child dead? Five percent. And how many also correctly anticipated the body's location—buried among trees? Only 4 of the 1300. Although this number was surely no better than chance, to those 4 dreamers the accuracy of their *apparent* prior knowledge must have seemed uncanny.

Given the billions of events in the world each day, and given enough days, some stunning coincidences are sure to occur. By one careful estimate, chance alone would predict that more than a thousand times a day someone on Earth will think of another person and then within the next five minutes will learn of that person's death (Charpak & Broch, 2004). Thus, when pondering the explanation of an astonishing event, we should "give chance a chance" (Lilienfeld, 2009). With enough time and people, the improbable becomes inevitable.

That became the experience of comics writer John Byrne (2003). Six months after his Spider-Man story about a New York blackout appeared, New York suffered its massive 1977 blackout. A later Spider-Man story line involved a major earthquake in Japan, "and again," Byrne recalled, "the real thing happened in the month the issue hit the stands." When working on a Superman comic book, Byrne "had the Man of Steel fly to the rescue when disaster beset the NASA space shuttle. The 1986 *Challenger* tragedy happened almost immediately thereafter" (with time for the issue to be redrawn). "Most recent, and chilling, came when I was writing and drawing Wonder Woman and did a story in which the title character was killed as a prelude to her becoming a goddess." The issue cover "was done as a newspaper front page, with the headline 'Princess Diana Dies.' (Diana is Wonder Woman's real name.) That issue went on sale on a Thursday. The following Saturday . . . I don't have to tell you, do I?"

Testing ESP

When faced with claims of mind reading or out-of-body travel or communication with the dead, how can we separate bizarre ideas from those that sound bizarre but are true? At the heart of science is a simple answer: *Test them to see if they work.* If they do, so much the better for the ideas. If they don't, so much the better for our skepticism.

How might we test ESP claims in a controlled experiment? An experiment differs from a staged demonstration. In the laboratory,

extrasensory perception (ESP) the controversial claim that perception can occur apart from sensory input, such as through *telepathy, clairvoyance,* and *precognition.*

(Continued)

the experimenter controls what the "psychic" sees and hears. On stage, the "psychic" controls what the audience sees and hears.

The search for a valid and reliable test of ESP has resulted in thousands of experiments. Some 380 of them have assessed people's efforts to influence computer-generated random sequences of ones and zeros. In some small experiments, the tally of the desired number has exceeded chance by 1 or 2 percent, an effect that disappears when larger experiments are added to the mix (Bösch et al., 2006a,b; Radin et al., 2006; Wilson & Shadish, 2006).

> "A psychic is an actor playing the role of a psychic."
>
> Psychologist magician
> Daryl Bem, 1984

Another set of experiments invited "senders" to telepathically transmit one of four visual images to "receivers" deprived of sensation in a nearby chamber (Bem & Honorton, 1994). The result? A 32 percent accurate response rate, surpassing the chance rate of 25 percent. But follow-up studies have (depending on who was summarizing the results) either failed to replicate the phenomenon or produced mixed results (Bem et al., 2001; Milton & Wiseman, 2002; Storm, 2000, 2003).

If ESP nevertheless exists, might it subtly register in the brain? To find out, researchers had a sender try to transmit one of two pictures telepathically to a receiver (most were the other half of a couple, friend, or twin pair) lying in an fMRI machine. The receivers' correct guesses were at a level of chance (50.0 percent), and their brains responded no differently when viewing the ESP-sent pictures. "These findings," concluded the researchers, "are the strongest evidence yet obtained against the existence of paranormal mental phenomena" (Moulton & Kosslyn, 2008).

One skeptic, magician James Randi, had a longstanding offer (which expired in 2010) of $1 million to be given "to anyone who proves a genuine psychic power under proper observing conditions" (Randi, 1999). French, Australian, and Indian groups have similar offers of up to 200,000 euros (CFI, 2003). And $50 million was made available for information leading to Osama bin Laden's capture. Large as these sums are, the scientific seal of approval would be worth far more. To silence those who say there is no ESP, one need only produce a single person who can demonstrate a single, reproducible ESP event. (To silence those who say pigs can't talk would take only one talking pig.) So far, no such person has emerged.

Courtesy of Claire Cole

Testing psychic powers in the British population: Psychologist Richard Wiseman created a "mind machine" to see if people could influence or predict a coin toss. Using a touch-sensitive screen, visitors to British festivals were given four attempts to call heads or tails, playing against a computer that kept score. By the time the experiment ended, nearly 28,000 people had predicted 110,972 tosses—with 49.8 percent correct.

PRACTICE TEST

THE BASICS

20. The amplitude of a light wave determines our perception of brightness. The amplitude of a sound wave determines our perception of
  a. loudness. c. audition.
  b. pitch. d. frequency.

21. The frequency of sound waves determines their pitch. The _____ the waves, the lower their frequency, and the _____ their pitch.
  a. shorter; higher
  b. longer; lower
  c. lower; longer
  d. higher; shorter

22. The snail-shaped tube in the inner ear, where sound waves are converted into neural activity, is called the
  a. piston.
  b. cilia.
  c. cochlea.
  d. auditory nerve.

23. Of the four skin senses that make up our sense of touch, only _____ has its own identifiable receptor cells.
  a. pressure c. cold
  b. warmth d. pain

24. Which of the following options has NOT been proven to reduce pain?
  a. Distraction
  b. Hypnosis
  c. Phantom limb sensations
  d. Endorphins

25. The taste of the food we eat is greatly enhanced by its smell or aroma. This influence of one sense on another is an example of
  a. sensory adaptation.
  b. chemical sensation.
  c. kinesthesis.
  d. sensory interaction.

26. The receptors for the vestibular sense are located in the
  a. skin. c. inner ear.
  b. brain. d. skeletal muscles.

27. There is some evidence to suggest that the following ESP phenomenon may have a scientific base of support.
  a. Telepathy
  b. Clairvoyance
  c. Precognition
  d. None of these answers

THE BIG PICTURE

5D. What are the basic steps in transforming sound waves into perceived sound?

5E. How does our system for sensing smell differ from our sensory systems for vision, touch, and taste?

IN YOUR EVERYDAY LIFE

■ How would you respond if, after you were injured, a friend said, "The pain is just in your head"?

Answers: 20. a, 21. b, 22. c, 23. a, 24. c, 25. d, 26. c, 27. d. Answers to The Big Picture questions can be found in Appendix B at the end of the book.

Terms and Concepts to Remember

sensation, p. 124

perception, p. 124

transduction, p. 124

absolute threshold, p. 124

subliminal, p. 124

priming, p. 125

difference threshold, p. 125

Weber's law, p. 125

sensory adaptation, p. 126

perceptual set, p. 127

wavelength, p. 130

hue, p. 130

intensity, p. 130

retina, p. 130

rods, p. 130

cones, p. 130

optic nerve, p. 130

blind spot, p. 130

feature detectors, p. 132

parallel processing, p. 132

gestalt, p. 134

figure-ground, p. 134

grouping, p. 134

depth perception, p. 134

visual cliff, p. 135

binocular cues, p. 135

retinal disparity, p. 135

monocular cues, p. 136

perceptual constancy, p. 137

color constancy, p. 137

perceptual adaptation, p. 138

audition, p. 139

frequency, p. 140

pitch, p. 140

cochlea [KOHK-lee-uh], p. 140

hypnosis, p. 144

sensory interaction, p. 146

kinesthesis [kin-ehs-THEE-sehs], p. 147

vestibular sense, p. 148

extrasensory perception (ESP), p. 149

Multiple-choice **self-tests** and more may be found at www.worthpublishers.com/myers

Basic Principles of Sensation and Perception

1 | What is the difference between sensation and perception?

- *Sensation:* Sensory receptors receive information and transmit it to the brain.
- *Perception:* Our brain organizes and interprets that information.

2 | What three steps are basic to all our sensory systems?

- Receiving sensory input.
- Transforming that input into neural impulses *(transduction).*
- Delivering neural information to our brain.

3 | How do absolute thresholds and difference thresholds differ, and what is Weber's law?

- *Absolute threshold:* minimum stimulation needed for detection 50 percent of the time.
- *Difference threshold:* minimum change needed to detect a difference between two stimuli 50 percent of the time.
- *Weber's law:* Our difference threshold increases in proportion to the stimulus.

4 | Can we be persuaded by subliminal stimuli?

- We do sense some stimuli *subliminally*—less than 50 percent of the time—but those sensations don't have lasting behavioral effects.

5 | What function does sensory adaptation serve?

- We grow less sensitive to constant sensory input.
- *Sensory adaptation* makes us aware of changes in our environment.

6 | How do our expectations, assumptions, and contexts affect our perceptions?

- Perception is influenced by our *perceptual set*—our mental tendencies and assumptions.
- Physical, emotional, and cultural context can create expectations about what we will perceive, thus affecting those perceptions.

Vision

7 | What are the characteristics of the energy we see as light?

- The visible light we experience is a thin slice of the broad spectrum of electromagnetic energy.
- The *hue* (blue, green, etc.) and brightness we perceive depend on the light's *wavelength* and *intensity.*

8 | How does the eye transform light energy into neural messages?

- Light entering the eye is focused on our *retina*—the inner surface of the eye.
- The retina's light-sensitive *rods* and color-sensitive *cones* convert the light energy into neural impulses.
- Those impulses travel along the *optic nerve* to the brain.

9 | What roles do feature detection and parallel processing play in the brain's visual information processing?

- In the visual cortex, *feature detectors* respond to specific features of the visual information (lines, edges, etc.).
- Through *parallel processing,* the brain processes different aspects of visual information (color, movement, depth, and form) separately but at the same time.

10 | What was the main message of Gestalt psychology, and how do figure-ground and grouping principles help us perceive forms?

- *Gestalt* psychologists showed that the brain organizes bits of sensory information into meaningful forms.
- To recognize an object, we must first perceive it as distinct (see it as a *figure*) from its surroundings (the *ground*).
- We bring order and form to sensory input by organizing it into meaningful *groups*, following such rules as proximity, continuity, and closure.

11 | How do we use monocular and binocular cues to see the world in three dimensions?

- Humans and many other species perceive depth at, or very soon after, birth.
- We transform two-dimensional retinal images into three-dimensional *depth perceptions* by use of *binocular cues* (such as *retinal disparity*) and *monocular cues* (such as relative height, relative size, interposition, relative motion, linear perspective, and light and shadow).

12 How do perceptual constancies help us construct meaningful perceptions?

- *Perceptual constancy:* ability to recognize an object regardless of its changing angle, distance, or illumination.
- *Color constancy:* ability to perceive consistent color under changing light.
- Shape and size constancies: help explain visual illusions, such as the Moon illusion.

13 What does research on restored vision, sensory deprivation, and perceptual adaptation reveal about the effects of experience on perception?

- Some perceptual abilities (such as color and figure-ground perception) are inborn.
- A critical period exists for other abilities (such as perceiving shapes visually). Without early experience, these abilities (and brain areas associated with them) do not develop normally.
- Given eyeglasses that shift the world slightly to the left or right, turn it upside down, or reverse it, people can, through *perceptual adaptation,* learn to move about with ease.

The Nonvisual Senses

14 What are the characteristics of the air pressure waves that we hear as meaningful sounds?

- Sound waves vary in amplitude (perceived as loudness) and in *frequency* (perceived as *pitch*—a tone's highness or lowness).
- Sound energy is measured in decibels.

15 How does the ear transform sound energy into neural messages?

- Sound waves travel through the auditory canal, causing tiny vibrations in the eardrum.
- The bones of the middle ear transmit the vibrations to the *cochlea,* causing waves of movement in hair cells.
- This movement triggers nerve cells to send signals along the auditory nerve to the brain's auditory cortex.
- Small differences in the loudness and timing of the sounds received by each ear allow us to locate sounds.

16 What are the four basic touch sensations, and which of them has identifiable receptors?

- Our sense of touch involves pressure, warmth, cold, and pain. Only pressure has identifiable receptors.

17 What influences our feelings of pain, and how can we treat pain?

- Pain is a combination of biological, psychological, and social-cultural influences. Treatments may manage pain from any or all of these perspectives.
- *Hypnosis,* which increases our response to suggestions, can help relieve pain.

18 How are our senses of taste and smell similar, and what is sensory interaction?

- Both taste and smell are chemical senses.
- Taste involves five basic sensations—sweet, sour, salty, bitter, and umami.
- Taste receptors in the taste buds carry messages to an area between the frontal and temporal lobes of the brain.
- Receptors for smell, located at the top of each nasal cavity, send messages to the brain. These cells work together, combining their messages into patterns that vary, depending on the different odors they detect.
- *Sensory interaction* is the influence of one sense on another.

19 What sensory systems monitor our body's position and movement?

- *Kinesthetic sense:* monitors the position and movement of individual body parts. Sensors all over the body send messages to the brain.
- *Vestibular sense:* monitors the position and movement of our head (and therefore our whole body). Its receptors in the inner ear send messages to the cerebellum.

ESP—Perception Without Sensation?

20 How do ESP claims hold up when put to the test by scientists?

- Researchers have not been able to replicate (reproduce) *extrasensory perception* (ESP) effects under controlled conditions.

LEARNING

In the early 1940s, University of Minnesota graduate students Marian Breland and Keller Breland witnessed the power of a new learning technology. Their mentor, B. F. Skinner, would become famous for *shaping* rat and pigeon behaviors, by delivering well-timed rewards as the animals inched closer and closer to a desired behavior. Impressed with Skinner's results, the Brelands began shaping the behavior of cats, chickens, parakeets, turkeys, pigs, ducks, and hamsters (Bailey & Gillaspy, 2005). The rest is history. The company they formed spent the next half-century training more than 15,000 animals from 140 species for movies, traveling shows, amusement parks, corporations, and the government. And along the way, the Brelands themselves mentored others, including Sea World's first director of training.

While writing a book about such animal trainers, Amy Sutherland wondered if shaping had uses closer to home (2006a,b). If baboons could be trained to skateboard and elephants to paint, might "the same techniques . . . work on that stubborn but lovable species, the American husband"? Step by step, she "began thanking Scott if he threw one dirty shirt into the hamper. If he threw in two, I'd kiss him [and] as he basked in my appreciation, the piles became smaller." After two years of "thinking of my husband as an exotic animal species," she reports, "my marriage is far smoother, my husband much easier to love."

Like husbands and other animals, much of what we do we learn from experience. Indeed, nature's most important gift may be our *adaptability*—our capacity to learn new behaviors that help us cope with our changing world. We can learn how to build grass huts or snow shelters, submarines or space stations, and thereby adapt to almost any environment.

Learning breeds hope. What is learnable we may be able to teach—a fact that encourages animal trainers, and also parents, educators, and coaches. What has been learned we may be able to change by new learning—an assumption underlying stress management and counseling programs. No matter how unhappy or unloving we are, we can learn and change.

No topic is closer to the heart of psychology than *learning,* a relatively permanent behavior change due to experience. (Learning acquires information, and memory—our next chapter topic—retains it.) In earlier chapters we considered the learning of sleep patterns, of gender roles, of visual perceptions. In later chapters we will see how learning shapes our thoughts, our emotions, our personalities, and our attitudes. This chapter examines some core processes of three types of learning: *classical conditioning, operant conditioning,* and *cognitive learning.*

How Do We Learn?

1 **What are some basic forms of learning?**

Our minds naturally connect events that occur in sequence. One way we **learn** is by association. Suppose you see and smell freshly baked bread, eat some, and find it satisfying. The next time you see and smell fresh bread, you expect that eating it will again be satisfying. So, too, with sounds. If you associate a sound with a frightening consequence, hearing the sound alone may trigger your fear. As one 4-year-old said after watching a TV character get mugged, "If I had heard that music, I wouldn't have gone around the corner!" (Wells, 1981).

WHY ARE HABITS SO HARD TO BREAK? ◀ Learned associations also feed our habitual behaviors (Wood & Neal, 2007). Habits form when we repeat behaviors in a given context—sleeping in the same comfy position in bed, walking familiar routes on campus, eating buttery popcorn in a movie theater. As the behavior becomes associated with the context, our next experience of that context will automatically trigger the behavior. Such associations can make it hard to kick a smoking habit. When back in the smoking context, the urge to light up can be powerful (Siegel, 2005).

Other animals also learn by association. To protect itself, the sea slug *Aplysia* withdraws its gill when squirted with water. If the squirts continue, as happens naturally in choppy water, the withdrawal response weakens. But if the sea slug repeatedly receives an electric shock just after being squirted, its response to the squirt instead grows stronger. The animal has learned that the squirt signals an upcoming shock.

Complex animals can learn to link outcomes with their own responses. An aquarium seal will repeat behaviors, such as slapping and barking, that prompt people to toss it a herring.

By linking two events that occur close together, both animals are exhibiting **associative learning.** The sea slug associates the squirt with an upcoming shock; the seal associates slapping and barking with a herring treat. Each animal has learned something important to its survival: predicting the immediate future.

This process of learning associations is *conditioning,* and it takes two main forms:

- In *classical conditioning,* we learn to associate two stimuli and thus to anticipate events. (A **stimulus** is any event or situation that evokes a response.) We learn that a flash of lightning will be followed by a crack of thunder, so

when lightning flashes nearby, we start to brace ourselves (**FIGURE 6.1**).

- In *operant conditioning,* we learn to associate a response (our behavior) and its consequence. Thus, we (and other animals) learn to repeat acts followed by good results (**FIGURE 6.2**) and avoid acts followed by bad results.

Conditioning is not the only form of learning. Through **cognitive learning** we acquire mental information that guides our behavior. *Observational learning,* one form of cognitive learning, lets us learn from others' experiences. Chimpanzees, for example, sometimes learn behaviors merely by watching others perform them. If one animal sees another solve a puzzle and gain a food reward, the observer may perform the trick more quickly. So, too, in humans: We look and we learn.

By learning, we humans are able to adapt to our environments. We learn to expect and prepare for significant events such as food or pain (*classical conditioning*). We learn to repeat acts that bring good results and to avoid acts that bring bad results (*operant conditioning*). We learn new behaviors by observing events and by watching others, and through language we learn things we have neither experienced nor observed (*cognitive learning*).

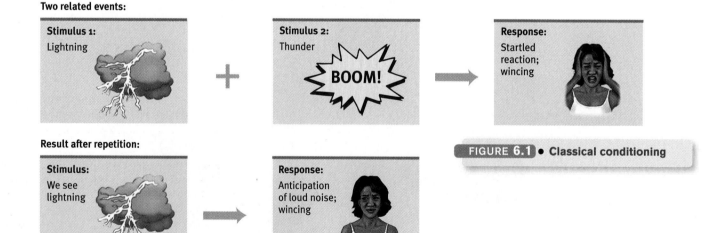

Two related events:

Stimulus 1: Lightning

+

Stimulus 2: Thunder — BOOM!

Response: Startled reaction; wincing

Result after repetition:

Stimulus: We see lightning

Response: Anticipation of loud noise; wincing

FIGURE 6.1 • **Classical conditioning**

FIGURE 6.2 ● Operant conditioning

(a) Response: balancing a ball   **(b)** Consequence: receiving food   **(c)** Behavior strengthened

Classical Conditioning

For many people, the name Ivan Pavlov (1849–1936) rings a bell. His early twentieth-century experiments—now psychology's most famous research—are classics. The process he explored we justly call **classical conditioning.**

Pavlov's Experiments

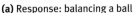

2 How does classical conditioning demonstrate associative learning?

For his studies of digestion, Pavlov (who held a medical degree) earned Russia's first Nobel Prize in 1904. But his novel experiments on learning, which consumed the last three decades of his life, earned this feisty scientist his place in history.

Sovfoto

Ivan Pavlov: "Experimental investigation . . . should lay a solid foundation for a future true science of psychology" (1927).

PEANUTS

© 1989 United Feature Syndicate, Inc.

PEANUTS reprinted by permission of United Feature Syndicate, Inc.

Pavlov's new direction came when his creative mind seized on an incidental observation. Without fail, putting food in a dog's mouth caused the animal to salivate. Moreover, the dog began salivating not only to the taste of the food but also to the mere sight of the food or the food dish or the person delivering the food, or even the sound of that person's approaching footsteps. At first, Pavlov considered these "psychic secretions" an annoyance. Then he realized they pointed to a simple but important form of learning.

Pavlov and his assistants tried to imagine what the dog was thinking and feeling as it drooled in anticipation of the food. This only led them into fruitless debates. So to make their studies more objective, they experimented. To rule out other possible influences,

they isolated the dog in a small room, placed it in a harness, and attached a device to measure its saliva. From the next room, they presented food—first by sliding in a food bowl, later by blowing meat

learning a relatively permanent behavior change due to experience.

associative learning learning that certain events occur together. The events may be two stimuli (as in classical conditioning) or a response and its consequences (as in operant conditioning).

stimulus any event or situation that evokes a response.

cognitive learning the acquisition of mental information, whether by observing events, by watching others, or through language.

classical conditioning a type of learning in which we learn to link two or more stimuli and anticipate events.

powder into the dog's mouth at a precise moment. They then paired various **neutral stimuli (NS)**—events the dog could see or hear but didn't associate with food—with food in the dog's mouth. If a sight or sound regularly signaled the arrival of food, would the dog learn the link? If so, would it begin salivating in anticipation of the food?

The answers proved to be *Yes* and *Yes*. Just before placing food in the dog's mouth to produce salivation, Pavlov sounded a tone. After several pairings of tone and food, the dog got the message. Anticipating the meat powder, it began salivating to the tone alone. In later experiments, a buzzer, a light, a touch on the leg, even the sight of a circle set off the drooling.

A dog doesn't *learn* to salivate in response to food in its mouth. Food in the mouth automatically, *unconditionally*, triggers this response. Thus, Pavlov called the drooling an **unconditioned response (UR)**. And he called the food an **unconditioned stimulus (US)**.

Salivating in response to a tone, however, is learned. Because it is *conditional* upon the dog's linking the tone with the food (**FIGURE 6.3**), we call this response the **conditioned response (CR)**. The stimulus that used to be neutral (in this case, a previously meaningless tone that now triggers drooling) is the **conditioned stimulus (CS)**. Remembering the difference between these two kinds of stimuli and responses is easy: Conditioned = learned; *unconditioned* = *unlearned*.

A second example, drawn from more recent experiments, may help. An experimenter sounds a tone just before delivering an air puff to your eye. After several repetitions, you blink to the tone alone. What is the NS? The US? The UR? The CS? The CR?[1]

---

1. NS = tone before procedure; US = air puff; UR = blink to air puff; CS = tone after procedure; CR = blink to tone

> Remember:
> **NS** = **N**eutral **S**timulus
> **US** = **U**nconditioned **S**timulus
> **UR** = **U**nconditioned **R**esponse
> **CS** = **C**onditioned **S**timulus
> **CR** = **C**onditioned **R**esponse

If Pavlov's demonstration of associative learning was so simple, what did he do for the next three decades? What discoveries did his research factory publish in his 532 papers on salivary conditioning (Windholz, 1997)? He and his associates identified five major conditioning processes: *acquisition, extinction, spontaneous recovery, generalization,* and *discrimination*.

Acquisition

3 What parts do acquisition, extinction, spontaneous recovery, generalization, and discrimination play in classical conditioning?

Acquisition is the first stage in classical conditioning. This is the point when Pavlov's dogs learned the link between the NS (the tone, the light, the touch) and the US (the food). To understand this stage, Pavlov and his associates had to

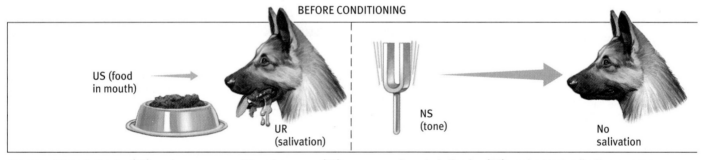

BEFORE CONDITIONING

An unconditioned stimulus (US) produces an unconditioned response (UR).

A neutral stimulus (NS) produces no salivation response.

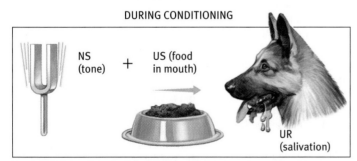

DURING CONDITIONING

The unconditioned stimulus is repeatedly presented just after the neutral stimulus. The unconditioned stimulus continues to produce an unconditioned response.

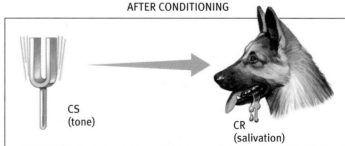

AFTER CONDITIONING

The previously neutral stimulus alone now produces a conditioned response (CR), thereby becoming a conditioned stimulus (CS).

FIGURE 6.3 ● **Pavlov's classic experiment** Pavlov presented a neutral stimulus (a tone) just before an unconditioned stimulus (food in mouth). The neutral stimulus then became a conditioned stimulus, producing a conditioned response.

confront the question of timing. How much time should pass between presenting the neutral stimulus and the food? In most cases, not much—half a second usually works well.

What do you suppose would happen if the food (US) appeared before the tone (NS) rather than after? Would conditioning occur? Not likely. With only a few exceptions, conditioning doesn't happen when the NS follows the US. *Remember, classical conditioning is biologically adaptive because it helps humans and other animals prepare for good or bad events.* To Pavlov's dogs, the originally neutral tone became a CS after signaling an important biological event—the arrival of food (US). To deer in the forest, the snapping of a twig (CS) may signal a predator's approach (US). If the good or bad event has already occurred, the tone or the sound won't help the animal prepare.

More recent research on male Japanese quail shows how a CS can signal another important biological event (Domjan, 1992, 1994, 2005).

Joern Rynio/Getty Images

Tracy Morgan/Getty Images

> Check yourself: If the aroma of cake baking sets your mouth to watering, what is the US? The CS? The CR?
>
> Answers: The cake and its taste are the US. The associated aroma is the CS. Salivation to the aroma is the CR.

Just before presenting a sexually approachable female quail, the researchers turned on a red light. Over time, as the red light continued to announce the female's arrival, the light caused the male quail to become excited. They developed a preference for their cage's red-light district. When a female appeared, they mated with her more quickly and released more semen and sperm (Matthews et al., 2007). All in all, the quail's capacity for classical conditioning gives it a reproductive edge.

CAN OBJECTS, SIGHTS, AND SMELLS ASSOCIATED WITH SEXUAL PLEASURE BECOME CONDITIONED STIMULI FOR SEXUAL AROUSAL IN HUMANS, TOO? Indeed they can (Byrne, 1982). Onion breath does not usually produce sexual arousal. But when repeatedly paired with a passionate kiss, it can become a CS and do just that (**FIGURE 6.4**). The larger lesson: *Conditioning helps an animal survive and reproduce—by responding to cues that help it gain food, avoid dangers, locate mates, and produce offspring* (Hollis, 1997).

Extinction and Spontaneous Recovery

What would happen, Pavlov wondered, if after conditioning, the CS occurred repeatedly without the US? If the tone sounded again and again, but no food appeared, would the tone still trigger drooling? The answer was mixed. The dogs salivated less and less, a reaction known as **extinction,** a drop-off in responses when a CS (tone) no longer signals an upcoming US (food). But a different picture emerged when Pavlov allowed several hours to pass before sounding the tone. After the delay, the dogs would again begin drooling to the tone (**FIGURE 6.5** on the next page). This **spontaneous recovery**—the reappearance of a (weakened) CR after a pause—suggested to Pavlov that extinction was suppressing the CR rather than eliminating it.

---

neutral stimulus (NS) in classical conditioning, a stimulus that elicits no response before conditioning.

unconditioned response (UR) in classical conditioning, an unlearned, naturally occurring response (such as salivation) to an unconditioned stimulus (US) (such as food in the mouth).

unconditioned stimulus (US) in classical conditioning, a stimulus that unconditionally—naturally and automatically—triggers a response (UR).

conditioned response (CR) in classical conditioning, a learned response to a previously neutral (but now conditioned) stimulus (CS).

conditioned stimulus (CS) in classical conditioning, an originally irrelevant stimulus that, after association with an unconditioned stimulus (US), comes to trigger a conditioned response (CR).

acquisition in classical conditioning, the initial stage, when we link a neutral stimulus and an unconditioned stimulus so that the neutral stimulus begins triggering the conditioned response. (In operant conditioning, the strengthening of a reinforced response.)

extinction in classical conditioning, the weakening of a conditioned response when an unconditioned stimulus does not follow a conditioned stimulus. (In operant conditioning, the weakening of a response when it is no longer reinforced.)

spontaneous recovery the reappearance, after a pause, of an extinguished conditioned response.

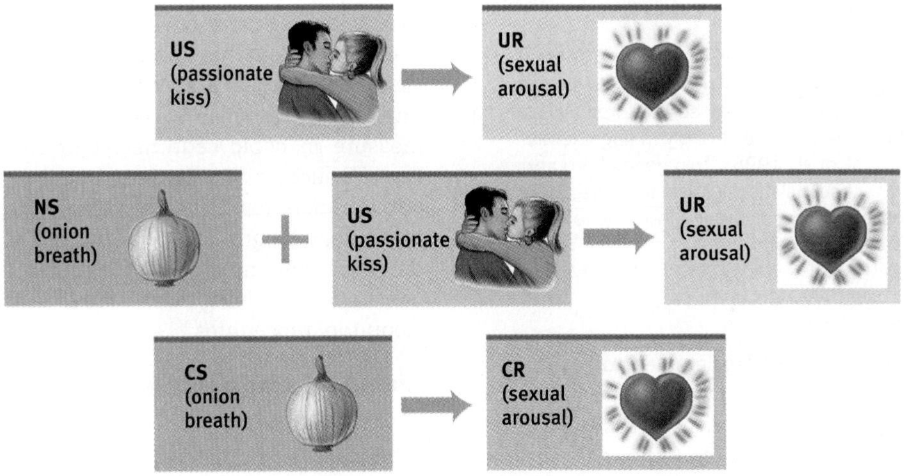

US (passionate kiss) → UR (sexual arousal)

NS (onion breath) + US (passionate kiss) → UR (sexual arousal)

CS (onion breath) → CR (sexual arousal)

FIGURE 6.4 • **An unexpected CS** Psychologist Michael Tirrell (1990) recalled: "My first girlfriend loved onions, so I came to associate onion breath with kissing. Before long, onion breath sent tingles up and down my spine. Oh what a feeling!"

FIGURE 6.5 • **Acquisition, extinction, and spontaneous recovery** The rising curve (simplified here) shows that the CR rapidly grows stronger as the NS and US are repeatedly paired (acquisition). The CS weakens when it is presented alone (extinction). After a pause, the CR reappears (spontaneous recovery).

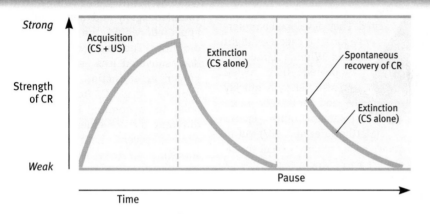

Generalization

Pavlov and his students noticed that a dog conditioned to the sound of one tone also responded somewhat to the sound of a new and different tone. Likewise, a dog conditioned to salivate when rubbed would also drool a bit when scratched or when touched on a different body part (Windholz, 1989). This tendency to respond to stimuli similar to the CS is called **generalization.**

Generalization can be adaptive, as when toddlers taught to fear moving cars also become afraid of moving trucks and motorcycles. And generalized fears can linger. One Argentine writer who had been tortured still flinches when he sees black shoes—his first glimpse of his torturers as they approached his cell. This generalized fear response was found in laboratory studies comparing abused

Stimulus generalization

"I don't care if she's a tape dispenser. I love her."

with nonabused children (Pollak et al., 1998). When an angry face appears on a computer screen, abused children's brain-wave responses are dramatically stronger and longer lasting (**FIGURE 6.6**).

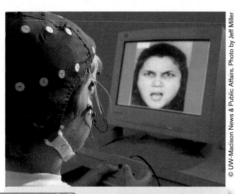

FIGURE 6.6 • **Why child abuse puts children at risk** Abused children's sensitized brains react more strongly to angry faces (Pollak et al., 1998). This generalized anxiety response may help explain their greater risk of psychological disorder. Child abuse leaves tracks in the brain.

Discrimination

Pavlov's dogs also learned to respond to the sound of a particular tone and *not* to other tones. This learned ability to *distinguish* between a conditioned stimulus (which predicts the US) and other irrelevant stimuli is called **discrimination**. Being able to recognize differences is adaptive. Slightly different stimuli can be

followed by vastly different results. Confronted by a guard dog, your heart may race; confronted by a guide dog, it probably will not.

Pavlov's Legacy

4 Why is Pavlov's work important, and how is it being applied?

What remains today of Pavlov's ideas? A great deal. Most psychologists now agree that classical conditioning is a basic form of learning. Judged by today's knowledge of the interplay of our biology, psychology, and social-cultural environment, Pavlov's ideas were incomplete. But if we see further than Pavlov did, it is because we stand on his shoulders.

Why does Pavlov's work remain so important? If he had merely taught us that old dogs can learn new tricks, his experiments would long ago have been forgotten. Why should we care that dogs can be conditioned to drool at the sound of a tone? The importance lies first in this finding: *Many other responses to many other stimuli can be classically conditioned in many other creatures*—in fact, in every species tested, from earthworms to fish to dogs to monkeys to people (Schwartz, 1984). Thus, classical conditioning is one way that virtually all animals learn to adapt to their environment.

Second, *Pavlov showed us how a process such as learning can be studied objectively.* He was proud that his methods were not based on guesswork about a dog's mind. The salivary response is a behavior we can measure in cubic centimeters of saliva. Pavlov's success therefore suggested a scientific model for how the young field of psychology might proceed—by isolating the basic building blocks of complex behaviors and studying them with objective laboratory procedures.

Classical Conditioning in Everyday Life

Other chapters in this text—on motivation and emotion, stress and health, psychological disorders, and therapy—show how Pavlov's principles can influence human health and well-being. Two examples:

- Drugs used to treat cancer can trigger nausea and vomiting more than an hour following treatment. Patients may then develop classically conditioned nausea (and sometimes anxiety) to the sights, sounds, and smells associated with the clinic (Hall, 1997). Merely entering the clinic's waiting room or seeing the nurses can provoke these feelings (Burish & Carey, 1986).

- Former crack cocaine users often feel a craving when they are again with people or in places they associate with previous highs. Thus, drug counselors advise addicts to steer clear of people and settings that may trigger these cravings.

For years, people wondered what became of "Little Albert." Not until 2009 did some psychologist-sleuths identify him. It seems he was Douglas Merritte, the son of a campus hospital wet nurse who received $1 for her tot's participation. Sadly, this famous child died of a disease at age 6 (Beck et al., 2009, 2010).

DOES PAVLOV'S WORK HELP US UNDERSTAND OUR OWN EMOTIONS? John B. Watson thought so. He believed that human emotions and behavior, though biologically influenced, are mainly a bundle of conditioned responses (1913). Working with an 11-month-old, Watson and Rosalie Rayner (1920; Harris, 1979) showed how specific fears might be conditioned. Like most infants, "Little Albert" feared loud noises but not white rats. Watson and Rayner presented a white rat and, as Little Albert reached to touch it, struck a hammer against a steel bar just behind his head. After seven repeats of seeing the rat and hearing the frightening noise, Albert burst into tears at the mere sight of the rat. Five days later, he had generalized this startled-fear reaction to the sight of a rabbit, a dog, and a sealskin coat, but not to dissimilar objects, such as toys.

The treatment of Little Albert would be unacceptable by today's ethical standards. Also, some psychologists, noting that the infant's fear wasn't learned quickly, had difficulty repeating Watson and Rayner's findings with other children. Nevertheless, Little Albert's learned fears led many psychologists to wonder whether each of us might be a walking storehouse of conditioned emotions. If so, might extinction procedures or even new conditioning help us change our unwanted responses to emotion-arousing stimuli?

Comedian-writer Mark Malkoff extinguished his fear of flying by doing just that. With support from AirTran, he faced his fear, living on an airplane for 30 days and taking 135 flights, which had him in the air 14 hours a day. After a week and a half, Malkoff's fear had faded, and he began playing games with fellow passengers (NPR, 2009). In Chapter 13 we will see more examples of how psychologists use conditioning techniques to treat emotional disorders and promote personal growth.

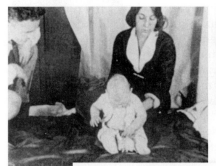

Little Albert's classically conditioned fear: In Watson and Rayner's experiments, "Little Albert" learned to fear a white rat after repeatedly experiencing a loud noise as the rat was presented. In this experiment, what was the US? The UR? The NS? The CS? The CR?

Answers: The US was the loud noise; the UR was the startled-fear response; the NS was the rat before it was paired with the noise; the CS was the rat after pairing; the CR was fear.

PRACTICE TEST

THE BASICS

1. *Learning* is defined as "a relatively permanent behavior change due to
   a. instinct."
   b. mental processes."
   c. experience."
   d. formal education."

2. Two forms of associative learning are classical conditioning, in which we associate _____, and operant conditioning, in which we associate _____.
   a. two responses; a response and a consequence
   b. two stimuli; two responses
   c. two stimuli; a response and a consequence
   d. two responses; two stimuli

3. In Pavlov's experiments, dogs learned to drool in response to a tone. The tone is therefore a(n)
   a. conditioned stimulus.
   b. unconditioned stimulus.
   c. conditioned response.
   d. unconditioned response.

4. Dogs can learn to respond (by salivating) to one kind of stimulus (a circle, for example) and not to another (a square). This process is an example of
   a. generalization.
   b. discrimination.
   c. acquisition.
   d. spontaneous recovery.

Continued

generalization in classical conditioning, the tendency, after conditioning, to respond similarly to stimuli that resemble the conditioned stimulus.

discrimination in classical conditioning, the learned ability to distinguish between a conditioned stimulus and other irrelevant stimuli.

5. After Watson and Rayner classically conditioned a small child to fear a white rat, the child later showed some fear in response to a rabbit, a dog, and a sealskin coat. The child's fear of objects that resembled the rat illustrates

a. extinction.
b. generalization.
c. spontaneous recovery.
d. discrimination between two stimuli.

THE BIG PICTURE

6A. As we develop, we learn cues that lead us to expect and prepare for good and bad events. We learn to repeat behaviors that bring rewards. And we learn through language, and by observing events and people. What do psychologists call these three types of learning?

6B. In slasher movies, sexually arousing images of women are sometimes paired with violence against women. Based on classical conditioning principles, what might be an effect of this pairing?

IN YOUR EVERYDAY LIFE

▪ How have your emotions or behaviors been classically conditioned?

Answers: 1. c, 2. c, 3. a, 4. b, 5. b. Answers to The Big Picture questions can be found in Appendix B at the end of the book.

Operant Conditioning

It's one thing to classically condition a dog to drool at the sound of a tone, or a child to fear moving cars. To teach an elephant to walk on its hind legs or a child to say *please*, we must turn to another type of learning—*operant conditioning*.

Classical conditioning and operant conditioning are both forms of associative learning, yet their difference is straightforward:

● In classical conditioning, an animal (dog, child, sea slug) forms associations between two events it does not control. This type of learning involves *respondent behavior*—actions that are automatic responses to a stimulus (such as salivating in response to meat powder and later in response to a tone).

● In **operant conditioning,** animals associate their own actions with consequences. Actions followed by a rewarding event increase; those followed by a punishing event decrease. Behavior that operates on the environment to *produce* rewarding or punishing events is called *operant behavior*.

We can therefore distinguish classical from operant conditioning by asking two questions. *Is the animal learning associations between events it does not control* (classical conditioning)? *Or is it learning associations between its behavior and resulting events* (operant conditioning)?

Skinner's Experiments

5 How is operant behavior reinforced and shaped?

In college, B. F. Skinner (1904–1990) was an English major and aspiring writer. Seeking a new direction, he entered graduate school in psychology. This decision led to pioneering studies in control, in which he taught pigeons such unpigeonlike behaviors as walking in a figure eight, playing Ping-Pong, and keeping a missile on course by pecking at a target on a screen.

For his studies, Skinner designed an **operant chamber,** popularly known as a *Skinner box* (**FIGURE 6.7**). The box has a bar or button that an animal presses or pecks to release a food or water reward. An attached recording device tracks these responses. This design creates a stage on

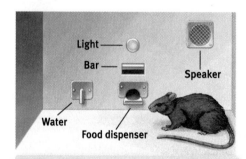

FIGURE 6.7 ● **A Skinner box** Inside the box, the rat presses a bar or button for a food reward. Outside, a measuring device (not shown here) records the animal's accumulated responses.

Light
Bar
Speaker
Water
Food dispenser

Reuters/Corbis

Reinforcers vary with circumstances: What is reinforcing (a heat lamp) to one animal (a cold meerkat) may not be to another (an overheated child). What is reinforcing in one situation (a cold snap at the Taronga Zoo in Sydney) may not be in another (a sweltering summer day).

which rats and other animals act out Skinner's concept of **reinforcement:** any event that strengthens (increases the frequency of) a preceding response. What is reinforcing depends on the animal and the conditions. For people, it may be praise, attention, or a paycheck. For hungry and thirsty rats, food and water work well. Skinner's operant conditioning experiments have done far more than teach us how to pull habits out of a rat. They have explored the precise conditions that foster efficient and enduring learning.

Vitaly Titov & Maria Sidelnikova/Shutterstock

Shaping Behavior

Imagine that you wanted to condition a hungry rat to press a bar. Like Skinner, you could tease out this action with **shaping,** gradually guiding the rat's actions toward the desired behavior. First, you would watch how the animal naturally

Shaping rats to save lives: This Gambian giant pouched rat has been shaped to sniff out and approach the smell of land mines. After successfully locating a mine during training in Mozambique, the rat receives a bite of banana.

behaves, so that you could build on its existing behaviors. You might give the rat a bit of food each time it approaches the bar. Once the rat is approaching regularly, you would give the treat only when it moves close to the bar, then closer still. Finally, you would require it to touch the bar to get food. With this method of *successive approximations,* you reward responses that are ever-closer to the final desired behavior. By giving rewards only for desired behaviors and ignoring all other responses, researchers and animal trainers gradually shape complex behaviors.

Shaping can also help us understand what nonverbal organisms perceive. Can a dog see red and green? Can a baby hear the difference between lower- and higher-pitched tones? If we can shape them to respond to one stimulus and not to another, then we know they can perceive the difference. Such experiments have even shown some animals can form concepts. When experimenters reinforced pigeons for pecking after seeing a human face, but not after seeing other images, the pigeons learned to recognize human faces (Herrnstein & Loveland, 1964). After being trained to discriminate among classes of events or objects—flowers, people, cars, chairs—pigeons can usually identify the category in which a new pictured object belongs (Bhatt et al., 1988; Wasserman, 1993).

In everyday life, we continually reward and shape others' behavior, said Skinner, though we may not mean to do so. Billy's whining, for example, annoys his parents, but look how they respond:

Billy: Could you tie my shoes?

Father: (Continues reading paper.)

Billy: Dad, I need my shoes tied.

Father: Uh, yeah, just a minute.

Billy: DAAAAD! TIE MY SHOES!

Father: How many times have I told you not to whine? Now, which shoe shall we do first?

Billy's whining is reinforced, because he gets something desirable—his dad's attention. Dad's response is reinforced because it ends something unpleasant—Billy's whining.

Or consider a teacher who pastes gold stars on a wall chart after the names of children scoring 100 percent on spelling tests. As everyone can then see, some children always score 100 percent. The others, who take the same test and may have worked harder than the academic all-stars, get no stars. USING OPERANT◄ CONDITIONING PRINCIPLES, WHAT ADVICE COULD YOU OFFER THE TEACHER TO HELP ALL STUDENTS DO THEIR BEST WORK?[2]

Types of Reinforcers

6 **What are the basic types of reinforcers?**

Up to now, we've mainly been discussing **positive reinforcement,** which strengthens a response by *presenting* a typically pleasurable stimulus after a response. But, as we saw in the whining Billy story, there are *two* basic kinds of reinforcement (**TABLE 6.1** on the next page). **Negative reinforcement** strengthens a response by *reducing or removing* something undesirable or unpleasant. Billy's whining was *positively* reinforced, because Billy got something

---

2. You might advise the teacher to apply operant conditioning principles. To shape students, reinforce them all for gradual improvements.

---

operant conditioning a type of learning in which behavior is strengthened if followed by a reinforcer or diminished if followed by a punisher.

operant chamber a box (also known as a *Skinner box*) with an attached recording device to track the rate at which an animal presses the box's bar to obtain a reinforcer. Used in operant conditioning research.

reinforcement in operant conditioning, any event that *strengthens* the behavior it follows.

shaping an operant conditioning procedure in which reinforcers guide actions closer and closer toward a desired behavior.

positive reinforcement increases behaviors by presenting positive stimuli, such as food. A positive reinforcer is anything that, when *presented* after a response, strengthens the response.

negative reinforcement increases behaviors by stopping or reducing negative stimuli, such as shock. A negative reinforcer is anything that, when *removed* after a response, strengthens the response. (Note: Negative reinforcement is *not* punishment.)

HI AND LOIS

TABLE 6.1 Ways to Increase Behavior

Operant Conditioning Term	Description	Examples
Positive reinforcement	Give something that's desired.	Praise a dog that comes when you call it.
		Pay a person who paints your house.
Negative reinforcement	End something that's undesired.	End pain by taking painkillers.
		End loud beeping noise by fastening seat belt.

desirable—his father's attention. His dad's response to the whining (doing what Billy wanted) was *negatively* reinforced, because it got rid of Billy's annoying whining. Similarly, taking aspirin may relieve your headache and pushing the snooze button will silence your annoying alarm. These welcome results provide negative reinforcement and increase the odds that you will repeat these behaviors. For drug addicts, the negative reinforcement of escaping withdrawal pangs can be a compelling reason to resume using (Baker et al., 2004). Note that *negative reinforcement is not punishment.* (Some friendly advice: Repeat the last five words in your mind.) Rather, negative reinforcement *removes* a punishing event. Whether it works by getting rid of something we don't enjoy, or by giving us something we do enjoy, *reinforcement is any consequence that strengthens behavior.*

Primary and Conditioned Reinforcers Getting food when hungry or having a painful headache go away is innately satisfying. These **primary reinforcers** are unlearned. **Conditioned reinforcers,** also called *secondary reinforcers,* get their power through learned associations with primary reinforcers. If a rat in a Skinner box learns that a light reliably signals a food delivery, the rat will work to turn on the light. The light has become a secondary reinforcer linked with food. Our lives are filled with conditioned reinforcers— money, good grades, a pleasant tone of voice—each of which has been linked with a more basic reward. Conditioned reinforcers greatly enhance our ability to influence one another.

Immediate and Delayed Reinforcers Unlike rats, which are shaped by immediate reinforcers, humans respond to delayed reinforcers: the paycheck at the end of the week, the good grade at the end of the semester, the trophy at the end of the season. Indeed, learning to control one's impulses in order to achieve more valued rewards is a big step toward maturity (Logue, 1998a,b). Sometimes, however, small but immediate pleasures (the enjoyment of watching late-night TV, for example) blind us to big but delayed consequences (tomorrow's sluggishness). For many teens, the immediate gratification of risky, unprotected sex in passionate moments prevails over the delayed gratification of safe sex or saved sex (Loewenstein & Furstenberg, 1991). And for too many of us, the immediate rewards of today's gas-guzzling vehicles, air travel, and air conditioning prevail over the bigger future consequences of climate change, rising seas, and extreme weather.

"Oh, not bad. The light comes on, I press the bar, they write me a check. How about you?"

Reinforcement Schedules

7 How do continuous and partial reinforcement schedules affect behavior?

In most of our examples, the desired response has been reinforced every time it occurs. But **reinforcement schedules** vary, and they influence our learning. With **continuous reinforcement,** learning occurs rapidly, which makes this the best choice for mastering a new behavior. But there's a catch: Extinction also occurs rapidly. When reinforcement stops— when we stop delivering food after the rat presses the bar—the behavior soon stops. If a normally dependable candy machine fails to deliver a chocolate bar twice in a row, we stop putting money into it (although a week later we may exhibit spontaneous recovery by trying again).

Real life rarely provides continuous reinforcement. Salespeople don't make a sale with every pitch. But they persist because their efforts are occasionally rewarded. And that's the good news about **partial (intermittent) reinforcement** schedules, in which responses are sometimes reinforced, sometimes not. Learning is slower to appear, but *resistance to extinction* is greater than with continuous reinforcement. Imagine a pigeon that has learned to peck a key to obtain food. If you gradually phase out the food delivery until it occurs only rarely, in no predictable pattern, the pigeon may peck 150,000 times without a reward (Skinner, 1953). Slot machines reward gamblers in much the same way—occasionally and unpredictably. And like pigeons, slot players keep trying, again and again. With intermittent reinforcement, hope springs eternal.

Lesson for parents: Partial reinforcement also works with children. WHAT◄ HAPPENS WHEN WE *OCCASIONALLY* GIVE IN TO CHILDREN'S TANTRUMS FOR THE SAKE OF PEACE AND QUIET? We have intermittently reinforced the tantrums. This is the very best procedure for making a behavior persist.

Skinner (1961) and his collaborators compared four schedules of partial reinforcement. Some are rigidly fixed, some unpredictably variable.

Fixed-ratio schedules reinforce behavior after a set number of responses. Frequent-flyer programs may offer a free flight to faithful customers who have traveled 25,000 miles. Coffee shops may reward us with a free drink after every 10 purchased. In the laboratory, rats may be reinforced on a fixed ratio of, say, one food pellet for every 30 responses. Once conditioned, the rats will pause only briefly to munch on the pellet before returning to a high rate of responding.

Variable-ratio schedules provide reinforcers after an unpredictable number of responses. This is what slot-machine players and fly-casting anglers experience—unpredictable reinforcement—and what makes gambling and fly fishing so hard to extinguish even when both are getting nothing for something. Because reinforcers increase as the number of responses increases, variable-ratio schedules produce high rates of responding.

Fixed-interval schedules reinforce the first response after a fixed time period. Animals on this type of schedule tend to respond more frequently as the time for reinforcement draws near. People waiting for an important letter check more often as delivery time approaches. A hungry cook peeks into the oven frequently to see if cookies are brown. Pigeons peck keys more rapidly as the time for reward draws near. This produces a choppy stop-start pattern rather than a steady rate of response.

Variable-interval schedules reinforce the first response after unpredictable time intervals. At varying times, the "You've got mail" message finally rewards persistence in rechecking for e-mail. And at unpredictable times, a food pellet rewarded Skinner's pigeons for persistence in pecking a key. Variable-interval schedules tend to produce slow, steady responding. This makes sense, because there is no knowing when the waiting will be over (**TABLE 6.2**). In general, response rates are higher when reinforcement is linked to the number of re-

TABLE 6.2	Schedules of Reinforcement	
	Fixed	**Variable**
Ratio	*Every so many:* reinforcement after every *nth* behavior, such as buy 10 coffees, then get 1 free, or get paid per shirt sewn	*After an unpredictable number:* reinforcement after a random number of behaviors, as when playing slot machines or fly-casting
Interval	*Every so often:* reinforcement for behavior after a fixed time, such as Tuesday discount prices	*Unpredictably often:* reinforcement for behavior after a random amount of time, as in checking for e-mail

sponses (a ratio schedule) rather than to time (an interval schedule). But responding is more consistent when reinforcement is unpredictable (a variable schedule) than when it is predictable (a fixed schedule).

Animal behaviors differ, yet Skinner (1956) contended that the reinforcement principles of operant conditioning are universal. It matters little, he said, what response, what reinforcer, or what species you use. The effect of a given reinforcement schedule is pretty much the same: "Pigeon, rat, monkey, which is which? It doesn't matter. . . . Behavior shows astonishingly similar properties."

Punishment

8 | How does punishment affect behavior, and what is the difference between punishment and negative reinforcement?

Reinforcement increases a behavior; **punishment** does the opposite. A *punisher* is any consequence that *decreases* the frequency of the behavior it follows. (See **TABLE 6.3** on the next page for some types of punishment.) Swift and sure punishers can powerfully restrain behaviors. The rat

that is shocked after touching a forbidden object and the child who is burned by touching a hot stove will learn not to repeat those behaviors.

Sureness and swiftness also mark effective criminal punishment (Darley & Alter, in press). Studies show that the threat of severe sentences does not deter criminal behavior, which is often impulsive.

primary reinforcer an event that is innately reinforcing, often by satisfying a biological need.

conditioned reinforcer (also known as *secondary reinforcer*) an event that gains its reinforcing power through its link with a primary reinforcer.

reinforcement schedule a pattern that defines how often a desired response will be reinforced.

continuous reinforcement reinforcing a desired response every time it occurs.

partial (intermittent) reinforcement reinforcing a response only part of the time; results in slower acquisition but much greater resistance to extinction than does continuous reinforcement.

fixed-ratio schedule in operant conditioning, a reinforcement schedule that reinforces a response only after a specified number of responses.

variable-ratio schedule in operant conditioning, a reinforcement schedule that reinforces a response after an unpredictable number of responses.

fixed-interval schedule in operant conditioning, a reinforcement schedule that reinforces a response only after a specified time has elapsed.

variable-interval schedule in operant conditioning, a reinforcement schedule that reinforces a response at unpredictable time intervals.

punishment an event that decreases the behavior it follows.

TABLE 6.3	Types of Punishment	
Type of Punisher	Description	Possible Examples
Positive punishment	Administer an aversive stimulus	Spanking; receiving a parking ticket
Negative punishment	Withdraw a desirable stimulus	Time-out from privileges (such as time with friends); revoked driver's license

Thus, when Arizona introduced an exceptionally harsh sentence for first-time drunk drivers, it did not affect the drunk-driving rate. But when Kansas City stepped up police patrols in a high crime area so that the sureness and swiftness of punishment increased, crime dropped dramatically.

How should we interpret punishment studies in relation to parenting practices? **SHOULD WE PHYSICALLY PUNISH CHILDREN ◄ TO CHANGE THEIR BEHAVIOR? Many** psychologists and supporters of nonviolent parenting say *No,* pointing out four major drawbacks of physical punishment (Gershoff, 2002; Marshall, 2002).

1. *Punished behavior is suppressed, not forgotten. This temporary state may (negatively) reinforce parents' punishing behavior.* The child swears, the parent swats, the parent hears no more swearing and feels the punishment successfully stopped the behavior. No wonder spanking is a hit with so many U.S. parents of 3- and 4-year-olds—more than 9 in 10 of whom acknowledge spanking their children (Kazdin & Benjet, 2003).

2. *Punishment teaches discrimination.* Was the punishment effective in putting an end to the swearing? Or did the child simply learn that it's not okay to swear around the house, but it is okay to swear elsewhere?

3. *Punishment can teach fear.* The child may associate the fear not only with the undesirable behavior but also with the person who delivered the punishment or the place it occurred. Thus, children may learn to fear a punishing teacher and try to avoid school. For such reasons, most European countries and most U.S. states now ban hitting children in schools (stophitting.com, 2009). Eleven countries, including those in Scandinavia, further outlaw hitting by parents, giving children the same legal protection given to spouses (EPOCH, 2000).

4. *Physical punishment may increase aggressiveness by modeling aggression as a way to cope with problems.* Studies find that spanked children are at increased risk for aggression (and depression and low self-esteem). We know, for example, that many aggressive delinquents and abusive parents come from abusive families (Straus et al., 1997).

Children see, children do? Children who often experience physical punishment tend to display more aggression.

Some researchers note a problem. Well, yes, they say, physically punished children may be more aggressive for the same reason that people who have undergone psychotherapy are more likely to suffer depression—because they had pre-existing problems that triggered the treatments (Larzelere, 2000, 2004). Which is the chicken and which is the egg? The correlations don't hand us an answer.

If one adjusts for preexisting antisocial behavior, then an occasional single swat or two to misbehaving 2- to 6-year-olds looks more effective (Baumrind et al., 2002; Larzelere & Kuhn, 2005). That is especially so if two other conditions are met:

1. The swat is used only as a backup when milder disciplinary tactics, such as a time-out (removing them from reinforcing surroundings), fail.

2. The swat is combined with a generous dose of reasoning and reinforcing.

Remember: *Punishment tells you what not to do; reinforcement tells you what to do.* This dual approach can be effective. Children with self-destructive behaviors may be mildly punished (say, with a squirt of water in the face) when they bite themselves, or bang their heads, but also rewarded (with positive attention and food) when they behave well. In high school classrooms, teachers can give feedback on papers by saying "No, but try this . . ." and "Yes, that's it!" Such responses reduce unwanted behavior while reinforcing more desirable alternatives.

Parents of delinquent youths may not know how to reinforce desirable behavior without screaming or hitting (Patterson et al., 1982). Training programs can help them translate dire threats ("You clean up your room this minute or no dinner!") into positive incentives ("You're welcome at the dinner table after you get your room cleaned up"). Stop and think about it. Aren't many threats of punishment just as forceful, and perhaps more effective, when rephrased positively? Thus, "If you don't get your homework done, there'll be no car!" would better be phrased as . . .

David Strickler/The Image Works

What punishment often teaches, said Skinner, is how to avoid it. Most psychologists now favor an emphasis on reinforcement: *Notice people doing something right and affirm them for it.*

Skinner's Legacy

9 Why were Skinner's ideas controversial, and how are educators, managers, and parents applying operant principles?

B. F. Skinner stirred a hornet's nest with his outspoken beliefs. He repeatedly insisted that external influences (not internal thoughts and feelings) shape behavior. And he urged people to use operant principles to influence others' behavior at school, work, and home. Knowing that behavior is shaped by its results, he said we should use rewards to evoke more desirable behavior.

Skinner's critics objected, saying that he dehumanized people by neglecting their personal freedom and trying to control their actions. Skinner's reply: External consequences already haphazardly control people's behavior. So why not steer those consequences toward human betterment? Wouldn't reinforcers be more humane than the punishments used in homes, schools, and prisons? And if it is humbling to think that our history has shaped us, doesn't this very idea also give us hope that we can shape our future?

Applications of Operant Conditioning

In later chapters we will see how psychologists apply operant conditioning principles to help people moderate high blood pressure or gain social skills. Reinforcement technologies are also at work in schools, workplaces, and homes (Flora, 2004).

At School A generation ago, Skinner and others worked toward a day when machines and textbooks would shape learning in small steps, by immediately reinforcing correct responses. Such machines and texts, they said, would revolutionize education and free teachers to focus on each student's special needs.

Falk/Photo Researchers, Inc.

B. F. Skinner: "I am sometimes asked, 'Do you think of yourself as you think of the organisms you study?' The answer is yes. So far as I know, my behavior at any given moment has been nothing more than the product of my genetic endowment, my personal history, and the current setting" (1983).

Stand in Skinner's shoes for a moment and imagine two math teachers, each with a class of students ranging from whiz kids to slow learners. Teacher A gives the whole class the same lesson, knowing that the bright kids will breeze through the math concepts and slower ones will be frustrated and fail. With so many different children, how could one teacher guide them individually?

Teacher B, faced with a similar class, paces the material according to each student's rate of learning and provides prompt feedback, with positive reinforcement, to both the slow and the fast learners. Thinking as Skinner did, how might you achieve the individualized instruction of Teacher B?

Computers were Skinner's final hope. "Good instruction demands two things," he said. "Students must be told immediately whether what they do is right or wrong and, when right, they must be directed to the step to be taken next." Thus, the computer could be Teacher B—pacing math drills to the student's rate of learning, quizzing the student to find gaps in understanding, giving immediate feedback, and keeping flawless records.

To the end of his life, Skinner (1986, 1988, 1989) believed his ideal was achievable. Although the predicted education revolution has not occurred, today's interactive student software, Web-based learning, and online testing bring us closer than ever before to achieving this ideal.

At Work Skinner's ideas also show up in the workplace. Knowing that reinforcers influence productivity, many organizations have invited employees to share the risks and rewards of company ownership. Others focus on reinforcing a job well done. Rewards are most likely to increase productivity if the desired performance has been well defined and is achievable.

Lauren Burke/Getty Images

Computer-assisted learning: Computers have helped realize Skinner's goal of individually paced instruction with immediate feedback.

HOW MIGHT MANAGERS SUCCESSFULLY◄ MOTIVATE THEIR EMPLOYEES? *Reward specific, achievable behaviors, not vaguely defined "merit."*

Operant conditioning also reminds us that reinforcement should be *immediate*. IBM legend Thomas Watson understood. When he observed an achievement, he wrote the employee a check on the spot (Peters & Waterman, 1982). But rewards need not be material, or lavish. An effective manager may simply walk the floor and sincerely affirm people for good work, or write notes of appreciation for a completed project. As Skinner said, "How much richer would the whole world be if the reinforcers in daily life were more effectively contingent on productive work?"

At Home As we have seen, parents can learn from operant conditioning practices. Parent-training researchers remind us that by saying "Get ready for bed" but caving in to protests or defiance, parents reinforce such whining and arguing. Exasperated, they may then yell or gesture menacingly. When the child, now frightened, obeys, that in turn reinforces the parents' angry behavior. Over time, a destructive parent-child relationship develops.

To disrupt this cycle, parents should remember the basic rule of shaping: *Notice people doing something right and affirm them for it.* Give children attention and other reinforcers when they are behaving *well* (Wierson & Forehand, 1994). Target a specific behavior, reward it, and watch it increase. When children misbehave or are defiant, do not yell at or hit them. Simply explain the misbehavior and give them a time-out.

Operant conditioning principles can also help us change our own behaviors. For some tips, see Close-Up: Using Operant Conditioning to Build Your Own Strengths.

Contrasting Classical and Operant Conditioning

10 What are the major similarities and differences between classical and operant conditioning?

Both classical and operant conditioning are forms of *associative learning* (**TABLE 6.4**). In both, we *acquire* behaviors that may

Using Operant Conditioning to Build Your Own Strengths

WANT TO STOP SMOKING? EAT LESS? STUDY OR EXERCISE MORE? To reinforce your own desired behaviors and extinguish the undesired ones, psychologists suggest taking four steps.

1. *State your goal in measurable terms, and announce it.* You might, for example, aim to boost your study time by an hour a day and share that goal with some close friends.

2. *Monitor how often you engage in your desired behavior.* You might log your current study time, noting under what conditions you do and don't study. (When I began writing textbooks, I logged how I spent my time each day and was amazed to discover how much time I was wasting.)

"I wrote another five hundred words. Can I have another cookie?"

3. *Reinforce the desired behavior.* To increase your study time, give yourself a reward (a snack or some activity you enjoy) only after you finish your extra hour of study. Agree with your friends that you will join them for weekend activities only if you have met your realistic weekly studying goal.

4. *Reduce the rewards gradually.* As your new behaviors become habits, give yourself a mental pat on the back instead of a cookie.

later become *extinct* and then *spontaneously reappear*. We often *generalize* our responses but learn to *discriminate* among different stimuli.

But these two forms of learning also differ: Through classical conditioning, we associate different events that we don't control, and we respond automatically **(respondent behaviors)**. Through operant conditioning, we link our own behaviors that act on our environment to produce rewarding or punishing events **(operant behaviors)** with their consequences.

As we shall next see, our *biology* and our *thought processes* influence both classical and operant conditioning.

respondent behavior behavior that occurs as an automatic response to some stimulus.

operant behavior behavior that operates on the environment, producing consequences.

PRACTICE TEST

THE BASICS

6. Salivating in response to a tone paired with food is a(n) _____; pressing a bar to obtain food is a(n) _____.
   a. primary reinforcer; conditioned reinforcer
   b. conditioned reinforcer; primary reinforcer
   c. operant behavior; respondent behavior
   d. respondent behavior; operant behavior

7. One way to change behavior is to reward natural behaviors in small steps, as they get closer and closer to the desired behavior. This process is called
   a. shaping.
   b. punishment.
   c. acquisition.
   d. classical conditioning.

TABLE 6.4	Comparison of Classical and Operant Conditioning	
	Classical Conditioning	Operant Conditioning
Basic idea	Learning associations between events we don't control.	Learning associations between our own behavior and its consequences.
Response	Involuntary, automatic.	Voluntary, operates on environment.
Acquisition	Associating events; CS announces US.	Associating response with a consequence (reinforcer or punisher).
Extinction	CR decreases when CS is repeatedly presented alone.	Responding decreases when reinforcement stops.
Spontaneous recovery	The reappearance, after a rest period, of an extinguished CR.	The reappearance, after a rest period, of an extinguished response.
Generalization	Responding to stimuli similar to the CS.	Responses to similar stimuli are also reinforced.
Discrimination	Learning to distinguish between a CS and other stimuli that do not signal a US.	Learning that some responses, but not others, will be reinforced.

8. Your dog is barking so loudly that it's making your ears ring. You clap your hands, the dog stops barking, your ears stop ringing, and you think to yourself, "I'll have to do that when he barks again!" The end of the dog's barking was for you a
   a. positive reinforcer.
   b. negative reinforcer.
   c. delayed reinforcer.
   d. punishment.

9. Continuous reinforcement is reinforcing the desired response every time it occurs. _____ reinforcement is reinforcing a desired response only some of the times it occurs.
   a. Negative
   b. Partial
   c. Delayed
   d. Aversive

10. A restaurant is running a special deal. After you buy four meals at full price, your fifth meal will be free. This is an example of a _____ schedule of reinforcement.
   a. fixed-ratio
   b. variable-ratio
   c. fixed-interval
   d. variable-interval

11. An old saying states that "a burnt child dreads the fire." In operant conditioning, the burning would be an example of a

a. conditioned reinforcer.
b. negative reinforcer.
c. punisher.
d. positive reinforcer.

THE BIG PICTURE
6C. *Positive reinforcement, negative reinforcement, positive punishment,* and *negative punishment* are tricky concepts for many students. Can you fit the right term in the four boxes in the table below? I will do the first one (positive reinforcement) for you.

Types of Stimulus	Give It	Take It Away
Desired (for example, a compliment):	Positive reinforcement	
Undesired/ aversive (for example, an insult):		

IN YOUR EVERYDAY LIFE
■ Can you recall a time when a teacher, coach, family member, or employer helped you learn something by shaping your behavior in little steps until you achieved your goal?

■ Think of a bad habit of yours or of someone you know. How could you use operant conditioning to break it?

Big Picture questions can be found in Appendix B at the end of the book.
Answers: 6. d, 7. a, 8. b, 9. b, 10. a, 11. c. Answers to The

Biology, Cognition, and Learning

From drooling dogs, running rats, and pecking pigeons, we have learned much about the basic processes of learning. But conditioning principles don't tell us the whole story. Once again we see one of this book's big ideas at work. Our learning is the product of the interaction of biological, psychological, and social-cultural influences.

Biological Constraints on Conditioning

11 **What limits does biology place on conditioning?**

Charles Darwin proposed that natural selection favors traits that aid survival. In the middle of the twentieth century, researchers enriched the study of conditioning by showing that there are *biological constraints* on learning. Each species comes prepared to learn those things crucial to its survival.

Limits on Classical Conditioning

The idea that environments are the whole story—that almost any stimulus (whether a taste, sight, or sound) can

John Garcia: As the laboring son of California farmworkers, Garcia attended school only in the off-season during his early childhood years. After entering junior college in his late twenties, and earning his Ph.D. in his late forties, he received the American Psychological Association's Distinguished Scientific Contribution Award "for his highly original, pioneering research in conditioning and learning." He was also elected to the National Academy of Sciences.

Courtesy of John Garcia

serve equally well as a conditioned stimulus—ended in the 1960s, with a discovery by John Garcia and Robert Koelling (1966). They noticed that rats would avoid a taste—but not sights or sounds—associated with becoming sick, even hours later. This makes adaptive sense. For rats, the easiest way to identify tainted food is to taste it; if sickened after sampling a new food, they avoid it thereafter. This response, which psychologists call *taste aversion*, makes it tough to wipe out an invasion of "bait-shy" rats by poisoning.

Humans, too, seem biologically prepared to learn some things rather than others. If you become violently ill four hours after eating a tainted hamburger, you will probably develop an aversion to the taste of hamburger but usually not to the sight of the associated restaurant, its plates, the people you were with, or the music you heard there.

Taste aversion: As an alternative to killing wolves and coyotes that preyed on sheep, some ranchers have sickened the animals with lamb laced with a drug.

blickwinkel/Alamy

Though Garcia and Koelling's taste-aversion research began with the discomfort of some laboratory animals, it later enhanced the welfare of many others. In one taste-aversion study, coyotes and wolves were tempted into eating sheep carcasses laced with a sickening poison. Ever after, they avoided sheep meat (Gustavson et al., 1974, 1976). Two wolves penned with a live sheep seemed actually to fear it. The study not only saved the sheep from their predators, but also saved the sheep-shunning coyotes and wolves from angry ranchers and farmers who had wanted to destroy them. In later experiments, conditioned taste aversion has successfully prevented baboons from raiding African gardens, raccoons from attacking chickens, and ravens and crows from feeding on crane eggs. In all cases, research helped preserve both the prey and their predators, who occupy an important ecological niche (Garcia & Gustavson, 1997).

Such research supports Darwin's principle that natural selection favors traits that aid survival. Our ancestors who readily learned taste aversions were unlikely to eat the same toxic food again and were more likely to survive and leave descendants. Nausea, like anxiety, pain, and other bad feelings, serves a good purpose. Like a low-oil warning on a car dashboard, each alerts the body to a threat (Neese, 1991).

This tendency to learn behaviors favored by natural selection may help explain why we humans seem naturally disposed to learn associations between the color red and women's sexuality. Female primates display red when nearing ovulation. In human females, enhanced bloodflow produces the red blush of flirtation and sexual excitation. DOES THE ◄ FREQUENT PAIRING OF RED AND SEX— WITH VALENTINE'S HEARTS, RED-LIGHT DISTRICTS, AND RED LIPSTICK—NATURALLY ENHANCE MEN'S ATTRACTION TO WOMEN? Experiments (**FIGURE 6.8**) suggest that, without men's awareness, it does (Elliot & Niesta, 2008).

Courtesy of Kathryn Brownson, Hope College

FIGURE 6.8 ● Romantic red In a series of experiments that controlled for other factors (such as the brightness of the image), men (but not women) found women more attractive and sexually desirable when framed in red (Elliot & Niesta, 2008).

Limits on Operant Conditioning

As with classical conditioning, nature sets limits on each species' capacity for operant conditioning. Mark Twain (1835–1910) said it well: "Never try to teach a pig to sing. It wastes your time and annoys the pig."

We most easily learn and retain behaviors that reflect our biological predispositions. Thus, using food as a reinforcer, you could easily condition a hamster to dig or to rear up, because these are among the animal's natural food-searching behaviors. But you won't be so successful if you use food to try to shape face washing and other hamster behaviors that normally have no link to food or hunger (Shettleworth, 1973). Similarly, you could easily teach pigeons to flap their wings to avoid being shocked, and to peck to obtain food. That's because fleeing with their wings and eating with their beaks are natural pigeon behaviors. However, pigeons have a hard time learning to peck to avoid a shock, or to flap their wings to obtain food (Foree & LoLordo, 1973). The principle: *Our biology predisposes us to learn associations that are naturally adaptive.*

Cognitive Processes and Classical Conditioning

12 How do cognitive processes influence conditioning and learning?

John B. Watson, of the "Little Albert" research discussed earlier in this chapter, was one of many psychologists who built on Pavlov's work. The two researchers shared many beliefs. They rejected "mentalistic" concepts (such as consciousness) that referred to inner thoughts, feelings, and motives (Watson, 1913). They also maintained that the basic laws of learning are the same for all animals—whether dogs or humans. Thus, the science of psychology should study how organisms respond to stimuli in their environments, said Watson. "Its theoretical goal is the prediction and control of behavior." This view, that psychology should be an objective science based on observable behavior, was called **behaviorism,** and it influenced North American psychology during the first half of the twentieth century.

Later research has shown that Pavlov's and Watson's views of learning underestimated two important sets of influences. The first, as we have seen, is the way that biological predispositions limit our learning. The second is the effect of our *cognitive processes*—our thoughts, perceptions, and expectations—on learning. For example, people being treated for alcohol dependence may be given alcohol spiked with a nauseating drug. However, their *awareness* that the drug, not the alcohol, causes

John B. Watson: Watson (1924) admitted to "going beyond my facts" when offering his famous boast: "Give me a dozen healthy infants, well-formed, and my own specified world to bring them up in and I'll guarantee to take any one at random and train him to become any type of specialist I might select—doctor, lawyer, artist, merchant-chief, and, yes, even beggar-man and thief, regardless of his talents, penchants, tendencies, abilities, vocations, and race of his ancestors."

Brown Brothers

the nausea tends to weaken the association between drinking alcohol and feeling sick. In classical conditioning, it is (especially with humans) not simply the CS–US pairing, but also the thought that counts.

Cognitive Processes and Operant Conditioning

B. F. Skinner granted the biological underpinnings of behavior and the existence of private thought processes. Nevertheless, many psychologists criticized him for discounting the importance of these influences.

A mere eight days before dying of leukemia in 1990, Skinner stood before the American Psychological Association convention. In this final address, he again rejected the growing belief that cognitive processes (thoughts, perceptions, expectations) have a necessary place in the science of psychology and even in our understanding of conditioning. For Skinner, thoughts

Natural athletes: Animals can most easily learn and retain behaviors that draw on their biological predispositions, such as small dogs' inborn ability to stand on their hind legs.

Karen Moskowitz/Getty Images

and emotions were behaviors that follow the same laws as other behaviors.

Nevertheless, the evidence of cognitive processes cannot be ignored. For example, rats exploring a maze, given no obvious rewards, seem to develop a **cognitive map,** a mental representation of the maze. When an experimenter then places food in the maze's goal box, these rats run the maze as quickly and efficiently as other rats that were previously reinforced with food for this result. Like people sightseeing in a new town, the exploring rats seemingly experienced **latent learning** during earlier tours. That learning became apparent only when there was some reason to demonstrate it.

The cognitive perspective has also shown us the limits of rewards. Promising people a reward for a task they already enjoy can backfire. Excessive rewards can destroy **intrinsic motivation**—the desire to do something well, for its own sake. In experiments, children have been promised a payoff for playing with an interesting puzzle or toy. Later, they played with the toy *less* than other children do (Deci et al., 1999; Tang & Hall, 1995). Likewise, rewarding children with toys or candy for reading shortens the time they spend reading (Marinak & Gambrell, 2008). It is as if they think, "If I have to be bribed into doing this, it must not be worth doing for its own sake."

behaviorism the view that psychology (1) should be an objective science that (2) studies behavior without reference to mental processes. Most research psychologists today agree with (1) but not with (2).

cognitive map a mental image of the layout of one's environment.

latent learning learning that is not apparent until there is an incentive to demonstrate it.

intrinsic motivation a desire to perform a behavior for its own sake.

Diverse Yet Alike

We learn from our experience—whether in a Chinese shopping mall or the Amazon jungle—and form cognitive maps of our environments.

Greg Elms/Lonely Planet/Getty Images

Victor Englebert/Photo Researchers, Inc

To sense the difference between intrinsic motivation and **extrinsic motivation** (behaving to gain external rewards or avoid threatened punishment), think about your experience in this course. Are you feeling pressured to finish this reading before a deadline? Worried about your grade? Eager for the credits that will count toward graduation? If *Yes,* then you are extrinsically motivated (as, to some extent, almost all students must be). Are you also finding the material interesting? Does learning it make you feel more competent? If there were no grade at stake, might you be curious enough to want to learn the material for its own sake? If *Yes,* intrinsic motivation also fuels your efforts.

Nevertheless, rewards used to signal a job well done—not to bribe or to control someone—can be effective (Boggiano et al., 1985). "Most improved player" awards, for example, can boost feelings of competence and increase enjoyment of a sport. Rightly administered, rewards can raise performance and spark creativity (Eisenberger & Rhoades, 2001; Henderlong & Lepper, 2002).

TABLE 6.5 compares the biological and cognitive influences on classical and operant conditioning.

Learning by Observation

13 **What is observational learning, and how does it differ from associative learning?**

Cognition is certainly a factor in **observational learning,** in which higher animals, especially humans, learn, without direct experience, by watching and imitating others. A child who sees his sister burn her fingers on a hot stove learns not to touch it. We learn all kinds of specific behaviors by observing and imitating others, a process called **modeling.**

Picture this scene from an experiment by Albert Bandura, the pioneering researcher of observational learning (Bandura et al., 1961). A preschool child works on a drawing. An adult in another part of the room is building with Tinkertoys. As the child watches, the adult gets up and for nearly 10 minutes pounds, kicks, and throws around the room a large, inflated Bobo doll, yelling, "Sock him in the nose. . . . Hit him down. . . . Kick him."

Albert Bandura:
"The Bobo doll follows me wherever I go. The photographs are published in every introductory psychology text and virtually every undergraduate takes introductory psychology. I recently checked into a Washington hotel. The clerk at the desk asked, 'Aren't you the psychologist who did the Bobo doll experiment?' I answered, 'I am afraid that will be my legacy.' He replied, 'That deserves an upgrade. I will put you in a suite in the quiet part of the hotel'" (2005).

Courtesy of Albert Bandura, Stanford University

TABLE 6.5	Biological and Cognitive Influences on Conditioning	
	Classical Conditioning	**Operant Conditioning**
Cognitive processes	Expecting the CS to signal the arrival of the US.	Expecting a response will be reinforced or punished; latent learning can occur without reinforcement; excessive rewards may destroy intrinsic motivation.
Biological predispositions	Biological tendencies to associate some stimuli more easily than others.	Biological tendency to learn behaviors similar to the species' natural behaviors.

The child is then taken to another room filled with appealing toys. Soon the experimenter returns and tells the child she has decided to save these good toys "for the other children." She takes the now-frustrated child to a third room containing a few toys, including a Bobo doll. Left alone, what does the child do?

Compared with other children in the study, those who viewed the model's actions were much more likely to lash out at the doll. Apparently, observing the aggressive outburst lowered their inhibitions. But *something more* was also at work, for the children imitated the very acts they had observed and used the very words they had heard (**FIGURE 6.9**).

In one of those quirky events that appear in the growth of science, researchers made an amazing discovery. That "something more" is part of the biology of our mind.

Mirrors in the Brain

On a 1991 hot summer day in Parma, Italy, a lab monkey awaited its researchers' return from lunch. The researchers had implanted wires next to its motor cortex, in a frontal lobe brain region that enabled the monkey to plan and enact movements. The monitoring device would alert the researchers to activity in that region of the monkey's brain. When the monkey moved a peanut into its mouth, for example, the device would buzz. That day, as one of the researchers entered the lab, ice cream cone in hand, the monkey stared at him. As the student raised the cone to lick it, the monkey's monitor buzzed—as if the motionless monkey had itself made some movement (Blakeslee, 2006; Iacoboni, 2009).

The same buzzing had been heard earlier, when the monkey watched humans or other monkeys move peanuts to their mouths. The flabbergasted researchers, led by Giacomo Rizzolatti (2002, 2006), had stumbled onto a previously unknown type of neuron. These **mirror neurons** provide a neural basis for everyday imitation and observational learning. When a monkey grasps, holds, or tears something, these neurons fire. And they likewise fire when the monkey observes another doing so. When one monkey sees, its neurons mirror what another monkey does.

It's not just monkey business. Imitation occurs in various animal species, but it is most striking in humans. Our catch-phrases, hem lengths, ceremonies, foods, traditions, vices, and fads—all spread by one person copying another. Imitation shapes even very young humans' behavior. Shortly after birth, a baby may imitate an adult who sticks out his tongue. By 8 to 16 months, infants imitate various novel gestures (Jones, 2007). By age 12 months, they begin looking where an adult is looking (Brooks & Melzoff, 2005). By 14 months, children imitate acts modeled on TV (Melzoff & Moore, 1997). And by 2½ years, when many of their mental abilities are near those of adult chimpanzees, young humans surpass chimps at social tasks such as imitating another's solution to a problem (Herrmann et al., 2007). Children see, children do.

extrinsic motivation a desire to perform a behavior to gain a reward or avoid a punishment.

observational learning learning by observing others.

modeling the process of observing and imitating a specific behavior.

mirror neuron neuron that fires when we perform certain actions and when we observe others performing those actions; neural basis for imitation and observational learning.

FIGURE 6.9 ● **The famous Bobo doll experiment**
Notice how the children's actions directly imitate the adult's.

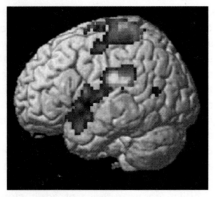
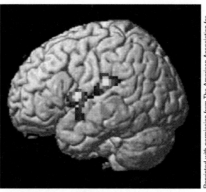

Pain

Empathy

Reprinted with permission from The American Association for the Advancement of Science, Subiaul et al., Science 305: 407–410 (2004) © 2004 AAAS.

FIGURE 6.10 ● **Experienced and imagined pain in the brain** Brain activity related to actual pain (left) is mirrored in the brain of an observing loved one (right). Empathy in the brain shows up in areas that process emotions, but not in the areas that register physical pain.

Our mirror neurons make emotions contagious. We grasp others' states of mind—often feeling what they feel—by mental *simulation* (by mentally imagining their experience). We find it harder to frown when viewing a smile than when viewing a frown (Dimberg et al., 2000, 2002). We find ourselves yawning after observing another's yawn, laughing when others laugh. (People with autism display less of this imitative yawning and reduced mirror-neuron activity—they have "broken mirrors" [Ramachandran & Oberman, 2006; Senju et al., 2007; Williams et al., 2006].) When watching a film of a scorpion crawling up someone's leg, we tighten up. Observing a passionate kiss, we may notice our own lips puckering. Seeing a loved one's pain, our face mirrors their emotion. And so does our brain (**FIGURE 6.10**). In this fMRI scan, the pain imagined by an empathic romantic partner has triggered some of the same brain activity experienced by the loved one actually having the pain (Singer et al., 2004). The bottom line: *Our brain's mirror neurons underlie our intensely social nature.*

Applications of Observational Learning

So the big news from Bandura's studies and the mirror-neuron research is that we look, we mentally imitate, and we learn. Models—in our family or neighborhood, or on TV—may have effects—good or bad.

Prosocial Effects The good news is that **prosocial behavior** (positive, helpful) models can have prosocial effects. To encourage children to read, read to them and surround them with books and people who read. To increase the odds that your children will practice your religion, worship and attend religious activities with them. People who model nonviolent, helpful behavior can prompt similar behavior in others. India's Mahatma Gandhi and America's Martin Luther King Jr. both drew on the power of modeling, making nonviolent action a powerful force for social change in both countries. Parents are also powerful models. European Christians who risked their lives to rescue Jews from the Nazis usually had a close relationship with at least one parent who modeled a strong moral or humanitarian concern. This was also true for U.S. civil rights activists in the 1960s (London, 1970; Oliner & Oliner, 1988).

Antisocial Effects The bad news is that observational learning may have *antisocial effects*. This helps us understand how abusive parents might have aggressive children, and why many men who beat their wives had wife-battering fathers (Stith et al., 2000). Critics note that being aggressive could be passed along by parents' genes. But in monkeys, we know it can also be environmental. In study after study, young monkeys reared apart from their mothers and subjected to high levels of aggression grew up to be aggressive themselves (Chamove, 1980). The lessons we learn as children are not easily unlearned as adults, and they are sometimes visited on future generations.

TV programs teach powerful lessons to young observers. While watching, children may "learn" that bullying is an ef-

Model of giving: Children, such as this boy volunteering with his dad for a neighborhood revitalization project, learn positive behaviors and attitudes from the prosocial models in their lives.

Jeff Greenberg/Photo Edit

fective way to control others, that free and easy sex brings pleasure without later misery or disease, or that men should be tough and women gentle. And they have ample time to learn such lessons. During their first 18 years, most children in developed countries spend more time watching TV than they spend in school. In the United States, where 9 in 10 teens watch TV daily, someone who lives to 75 will have spent 9 years staring at the tube (Gallup, 2002; Kubey & Csikszentmihalyi, 2002).

TV viewers are learning about life from a rather peculiar storyteller, one with a taste for violence. Before finishing elementary school, they will have observed some 8000 TV murders and 100,000 other violent acts (Huston et al., 1992). During one closely studied year, nearly 6 in 10 U.S. network and cable programs featured violence, 74 percent of those acts went unpunished, and the victims usually showed no pain. Nearly half the events were portrayed as "justified," and nearly half the attackers were attractive (Donnerstein, 1998). To see how these factors contribute to the violence-viewing effect, see Thinking

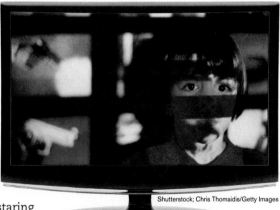
Shutterstock; Chris Thomaidis/Getty Images

Critically About: Does Viewing Media Violence Trigger Violent Behavior? on the next page. But before moving on, try the self-test in **TABLE 6.6**, So, How Did I Learn That?

TV's greatest effect may stem from what it displaces. Children and adults who spend four hours a day watching TV spend four fewer hours in active pursuits—talking, studying, playing, reading, or socializing with friends. What would you have done with your extra time if you had never watched TV, and how might you therefore be different?

TABLE 6.6 So, How Did I Learn That?

Time for a self-check! Can you match the learning examples in Items 1–5 to the following concepts?:

    a. *Classical conditioning*   d. *Observational learning*
    b. *Operant conditioning*   e. *Biological predispositions*
    c. *Latent learning*

1. Knowing the way from your bed to the bathroom in the dark.

2. Your little brothers getting in a fight after watching a violent action movie.

3. Salivating when you smell brownies in the oven.

4. Disliking the taste of chili after being violently sick a few hours after eating chili.

5. Your dog racing to greet you on your arrival home.

5. b. Through *operant conditioning* your dog may have come to associate your arrival with attention, petting, and a treat.
4. e. You are *biologically predisposed* to develop a conditioned taste aversion to foods associated with illness.
3. a. Through *classical conditioning* you have associated the smell with the anticipated tasty result.
2. b. *Observational learning* may have contributed to their imitating the behaviors modeled by the actors.
1. c. You've probably learned your way by *latent learning*.

PRACTICE TEST

THE BASICS

12. Taste-aversion research showed that when rats get sick after sampling a new food, they learn to avoid certain tastes but not the sights or sounds connected to the place they became sick. This finding supports the idea that
    a. animals learn to react to similar stimuli in similar ways.
    b. conditioning has survival value by helping animals adapt to their environment.
    c. psychologists should only study observable behavior.
    d. organisms can be conditioned to any stimulus.

13. We now know that cognitive processes (thoughts, perceptions, and expectations) play an important role in learning. Evidence for the effect of these processes comes from studies in which rats
    a. spontaneously recover previously learned behavior.
    b. develop cognitive maps.
    c. exhibit respondent behavior.
    d. generalize responses.

14. Rats were carried through a maze without any opportunity to walk around or explore, and they were given no reward when they left the maze. In later trials in which food was given at the end of the maze, these rats immediately did as well as others that had received rewards for running the maze. The rats that had learned without reinforcement demonstrate
    a. modeling.
    b. biological predisposition.
    c. shaping.
    d. latent learning.

15. Children learn many social behaviors by imitating parents and other models. This type of learning is called
    a. observational learning.
    b. reinforced learning.

Continued

prosocial behavior positive, constructive, helpful behavior. The opposite of antisocial behavior.

THINKING CRITICALLY ABOUT

Does Viewing Media Violence Trigger Violent Behavior?

Was the judge who in 1993 tried two British 10-year-olds for their murder of a 2-year-old right to suspect that the pair had been influenced by "violent video films"? Were the American media right to think that the teen assassins who killed 13 of their Columbine High School classmates had been influenced by repeated exposure to *Natural Born Killers* and splatter games such as *Doom*? To understand whether violence viewing leads to violent behavior, researchers have done both correlational and experimental studies (Anderson & Gentile, 2008).

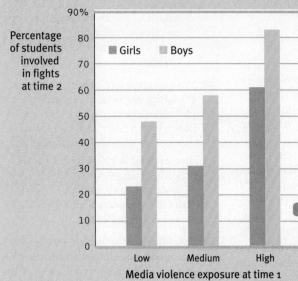

Percentage of students involved in fights at time 2

■ Girls ■ Boys

Low Medium High
Media violence exposure at time 1

Correlational studies do support this link.

● In the United States and Canada, homicide rates doubled between 1957 and 1974, just when TV was introduced and spreading. Moreover, census regions with later dates for TV service also had homicide rates that jumped later.

● Elementary-school children with heavy exposure to media violence (via TV, videos, and video games) also tend to get into more fights (**FIGURE 6.11**). As teens, they also are at greater risk for violent behavior (Boxer et al., 2009).

But as we know from Chapter 1, correlation does not prove causation. So these studies do not prove that viewing violence causes aggression (Freedman, 1988; McGuire, 1986). Maybe aggressive children prefer violent programs. Maybe abused or neglected children are both more aggressive and more often left in front of the TV.

Critical thinking leads to smart thinking. To pin down causation, psychologists use experiments. In this case, researchers randomly assigned some viewers to observe violence and others to watch entertaining nonviolence. Does viewing cruelty prepare people, when irritated, to react more cruelly? To some extent, it does. This is especially so when an attractive person commits seemingly justified,

FIGURE 6.11 ● **Heavy exposure to media violence predicts future aggressive behavior** Researchers studied more than 400 third- to fifth-graders. After controlling for existing differences in hostility and aggression, the researchers reported increased aggression in those heavily exposed to violent TV, videos, and video games (Gentile et al., 2004).

---

c. operant conditioning.
d. classical conditioning.

16. _____ famous Bobo doll experiments demonstrated that children learn by observing others' behaviors.

a. Skinner's
b. Watson's
c. Bandura's
d. Pavlov's

17. Correlational studies show a link between viewing violence on TV and behaving aggressively, but they don't *prove* that violence *causes* aggression.

However, most experts agree that repeated viewing of TV violence

a. makes all viewers significantly more aggressive.
b. has little effect on viewers.
c. dulls the viewers' sensitivity to violence.
d. makes viewers angry and frustrated.

THE BIG PICTURE

6D. In what ways do biological and cognitive factors affect what we learn by way of conditioning?

6E. Jason's parents and older friends all smoke, but they advise him not to. Juan's

parents and friends don't smoke, but they say nothing to discourage him from doing so. Will Jason or Juan be more likely to start smoking?

IN YOUR EVERYDAY LIFE

▪ Is your behavior in this class influenced more by intrinsic motivation or extrinsic motivation?

▪ Who has been a significant role model for you? What did you learn from observing this person? Are you a role model for someone else?

The Big Picture questions can be found in Appendix B at the end of the book.

Answers: 12. b, 13. b, 14. d, 15. a, 16. c, 17. c. Answers to

Violence viewing leads to violent play: Research has shown that viewing media violence does lead to increased expression of aggression in the viewers, as with these boys imitating pro wrestlers.

realistic violence that goes unpunished and causes no visible pain or harm (Donnerstein, 1998).

This *violence-viewing effect* seems to stem from at least two factors. One is *imitation* (Geen & Thomas, 1986). As children watch, their mirror neurons simulate the behavior, and after this rehearsal they become more likely to act it out. Thus, in one experiment, violent play increased sevenfold immediately after children viewed *Power Rangers* episodes (Boyatzis et al., 1995). As happened in the Bobo doll experiment, children often precisely imitated the model's violent acts—in this case, flying karate kicks.

Prolonged exposure to violence also *desensitizes* viewers. They become more indifferent to it when later viewing a brawl, whether on TV or in real life (Rule & Ferguson, 1986). Adult males who spent three evenings watching sexually violent movies became progressively less bothered by the rapes and slashings. Compared with those in a control group, the film watchers later expressed less sympathy for domestic violence victims, and they rated the victims' injuries as less severe (Mullin & Linz, 1995).

Drawing on such findings, the American Academy of Pediatrics (2009) has advised pediatricians that "media violence can contribute to aggressive behavior, desensitization to violence, nightmares, and fear of being harmed." Indeed, an evil psychologist could hardly imagine a better way to make people indifferent to brutality than to expose them to a graded series of scenes, from fights to killings to the mutilations in slasher movies (Donnerstein et al., 1987). Watching cruelty fosters indifference.

"Don't you understand? This is life, this is what is happening. We can't switch to another channel."

Terms and Concepts to Remember

learning, p. 156
associative learning, p. 156
stimulus, p. 156
cognitive learning, p. 156
classical conditioning, p. 157
neutral stimulus, p. 158
unconditioned response (UR), p. 158
unconditioned stimulus (US), p. 158
conditioned response (CR), p. 158
conditioned stimulus (CS), p. 158
acquisition, p. 158
extinction, p. 159
spontaneous recovery, p. 159
generalization, p. 160

discrimination, p. 160
operant conditioning, p. 162
operant chamber, p. 162
reinforcement, p. 162
shaping, p. 162
positive reinforcement, p. 163
negative reinforcement, p. 163
primary reinforcer, p. 164
conditioned reinforcer, p. 164
reinforcement schedule, p. 164
continuous reinforcement, p. 164
partial (intermittent) reinforcement, p. 164
fixed-ratio schedule, p. 165
variable-ratio schedule, p. 165

fixed-interval schedule, p. 165
variable-interval schedule, p. 165
punishment, p. 165
respondent behavior, p. 168
operant behavior, p. 168
behaviorism, p. 171
cognitive map, p. 171
latent learning, p. 171
intrinsic motivation, p. 171
extrinsic motivation, p. 172
observational learning, p. 172
modeling, p. 172
mirror neuron, p. 173
prosocial behavior, p. 174

How Do We Learn?

1 **What are some basic forms of learning?**

- *Learning:* Relatively permanent behavior change due to experience.
- *Associative learning:* We learn that certain events occur together.
- *Cognitive learning:* Acquiring mental information, such as by observation or language, that guides our behavior.

Classical Conditioning
(LEARNING TO ASSOCIATE TWO STIMULI)

2 **How does classical conditioning demonstrate associative learning?**

- *UR (unconditioned response)* occurs naturally (such as salivation), in response to some *stimulus.*
- *US (unconditioned stimulus)* naturally and automatically (without learning) triggers the unlearned response (as food in the mouth triggers salivation).
- *CS (conditioned stimulus)* is originally an *NS (neutral stimulus,* such as a tone) that, through learning, becomes associated with some unlearned response (salivating).
- *CR (conditioned response)* is the learned response (salivating) to the originally neutral but now conditioned stimulus.

3 **What parts do acquisition, extinction, spontaneous recovery, generalization, and discrimination play in classical conditioning?**

- First stage: association of NS with US *(acquisition).*
- *Extinction* occurs if the CS appears repeatedly by itself (without the US).
- Responses may reappear after pause *(spontaneous recovery).*
- Responses may be triggered by stimuli similar to CS *(generalization)* but not by dissimilar stimuli *(discrimination).*

4 **Why is Pavlov's work important, and how is it being applied?**

- *Classical conditioning* is one way all animals adapt to their environment.
- Pavlov also taught us how to study a process objectively.
- Classical conditioning is applied to further human health and well-being, such as in the control of emotions.

Operant Conditioning
(LEARNING TO ASSOCIATE A RESPONSE AND ITS CONSEQUENCES)

5 **How is operant behavior reinforced and shaped?**

- B. F. Skinner and others *shaped* the behavior of rats and pigeons placed in *operant chambers* by rewarding the closer and closer approximations of a desired behavior.
- *Reinforcement:* Any event that strengthens a preceding response.

6 **What are the basic types of reinforcers?**

- *Positive reinforcers:* presented after a desired response.
- *Negative reinforcers:* cause an aversive stimulus to be withdrawn.
- *Primary reinforcers:* unlearned.
- *Conditioned reinforcers:* learned through association with primary reinforcers.
- Reinforcers may be immediate or delayed.

7 **How do continuous and partial reinforcement schedules affect behavior?**

- *Continuous reinforcement:* Faster acquisition; less resistance to extinction.
- *Partial reinforcement:* Slower acquisition; greater resistance to extinction. Includes the following four schedules.
- *Fixed-ratio schedules:* Offer rewards after a set number of responses.
- *Variable-ratio schedules:* Offer rewards after an unpredictable number of responses.
- *Fixed-interval schedules:* Offer rewards after set time periods.
- *Variable-interval schedules:* Offer rewards after unpredictable time periods.

8 **How does punishment affect behavior, and what is the difference between punishment and negative reinforcement?**

PUNISHMENT:

- Administering undesirable consequence (spanking) or withdrawing something desirable (favorite toy).
- Aims to decrease frequency of a behavior (child's disobedience).
- Negative reinforcement aims to *increase* frequency of a behavior (such as putting on your seat belt) by taking away something undesirable (the annoying beeping).

UNDESIRABLE SIDE EFFECTS OF PUNISHMENT:

- Suppressing rather than changing behavior.
- Teaching aggression and creating fear.
- Encouraging discrimination (undesirable behavior appears when the punisher is not present).
- Fostering depression and feelings of hopelessness.

9 Why were Skinner's ideas controversial, and how are educators, managers, and parents applying operant principles?

- Critics say that Skinner tried to dehumanize and control people. Skinner replied that external forces shape us anyway, so why not direct those forces.
- Teachers can shape students' behaviors.
- Interactive media can provide immediate feedback.
- Managers can boost productivity and morale by rewarding well-defined and achievable behaviors.
- Parents can reward desirable behaviors.
- We can use these principles to reinforce our own desired behaviors and extinguish undesirable ones.

10 What are the major similarities and differences between classical and operant conditioning?

- Both types of conditioning are forms of associative learning and involve acquisition, extinction, spontaneous recovery, generalization, and discrimination.
- Classical conditioning: We associate events we do not control and respond automatically.
- Operant conditioning: We link our behaviors with their consequences.

Biology, Cognition, and Learning

11 What limits does biology place on conditioning?

- Organisms come prepared to learn tendencies, such as taste aversions, that aid their survival.
- Despite operant training, animals may revert to biologically predisposed patterns.

12 How do cognitive processes influence conditioning and learning?

- More than Pavlov and Skinner supposed, expectations influence conditioning.
- *Cognitive mapping* and *latent learning* illustrate learning that occurs without immediate consequences.
- Excess rewards can undermine *intrinsic motivation* for an activity.

13 What is observational learning, and how does it differ from associative learning?

- *Observational learning,* as shown in Bandura's Bobo doll experiment, involves learning by watching, rather than learning associations between different events.
- *Mirror neurons* demonstrate a neural basis for observational learning, which influences both antisocial and *prosocial behavior.*

7

MEMORY

Imagine life without being able to form new conscious memories. For 55 years after having brain surgery to stop severe seizures, this was life for Henry Molaison, or H. M., as psychologists knew him until his 2008 death. H. M. was intelligent and did daily crossword puzzles. Yet, reported neuroscientist Suzanne Corkin (2005), "I've known H. M. since 1962, and he still doesn't know who I am." For about 20 seconds during a conversation he could keep something in mind. When distracted, he would lose what was just said or what had just occurred.

My own father suffered a similar problem after a small stroke at age 92. His upbeat personality was intact. He enjoyed poring over family photo albums and telling stories about his pre-stroke life. But he could not tell me what day of the week it was, or what he'd had for dinner. Told repeatedly of his brother-in-law's death, he was surprised and saddened each time he heard the news.

At the other extreme are people who would be gold medal winners in a memory Olympics. Russian journalist Shereshevskii, or S, had merely to listen while other reporters scribbled notes (Luria, 1968). You and I could parrot back a string of 7 or so numbers. S could repeat up to 70, if they were read about 3 seconds apart in an otherwise silent room. Moreover, he could recall these numbers (and words, too) backwards as easily as forward. His accuracy was perfect, even when recalling a list 15 years later. "Yes, yes," he might recall. "This was a series you gave me once when we were in your apartment. . . . You were sitting at the table and I in the rocking chair. . . . You were wearing a gray suit. . . ."

Amazing? Yes, but consider your own impressive memory. You remember countless voices, sounds, and songs; tastes, smells, and textures; faces, places, and happenings. Imagine viewing 2500 slides of faces and places for 10 seconds each. Later, you see 280 of these slides, paired with others you've never seen before. Actual participants in this experiment recognized 90 percent of the slides they had viewed in the first round (Haber, 1970).

Memory is learning we retain over time. How does our brain pluck information out of the world around us and tuck that information away for later use? How can we remember things we have not thought about for years, yet forget the name of someone we just met? Why will you be likely later in this chapter to misrecall this sentence: *"The angry rioter threw the rock at the window"*? In this chapter, we'll consider these fascinating questions and more—including how we can improve our own memories.

CHAPTER OUTLINE

Studying Memory

1 What three processes are involved in building a memory, and how do the concepts of unconscious processing and working memory update the three-stage information-processing model?

How does our brain construct **memories**? Building a memory is somewhat like the way I processed information in creating this book. First, I viewed countless items of information, including some 100,000 journal article titles. Most of it I ignored, but I *selected* some things for *temporary storage* in my briefcase, to process later. Most of those items I eventually threw out. The rest—about 3000 articles and news items—I organized and filed for long-term storage. Later, I *retrieved* that information and drew from it as I spun this story of today's psychology. We build memories in a similar way. To remember any event, we must

- *get information into our brain,* a process called **encoding.**
- *retain* that information, a process called **storage.**
- later *get the information back out,* a process called **retrieval.**

Architects make miniature models of houses to help clients imagine living in their future homes. Similarly, psychologists create models of memory to help us think about how our brain forms and retrieves memories. Let's consider one of those models.

An Information-Processing Model

Richard Atkinson and Richard Shiffrin (1968) designed a memory model based on a computer's information-processing system. They proposed that we form memories in three stages.

1. We first record to-be-remembered information as a fleeting **sensory memory.**

2. From there, we process information into **short-term memory,** where we encode it through *rehearsal.*

3. Finally, information moves into **long-term memory** for later retrieval.

Other psychologists have updated this model to include two important newer concepts:

- Some information takes a shortcut on its way to long-term storage. These memories are formed through *unconscious processing,* without our awareness. As we have seen so many times in this text, our mind operates on two tracks. It processes some information out in the open, with our full attention. But another show is quietly going on behind the scenes.

- Short-term memory, the model's second stage, is not just a temporary shelf for holding incoming information. It's an active desktop where your brain processes important new information and links it with material stored in long-term memory. To focus on the active processing that takes place in this middle stage, psychologists use the term **working memory.** Right now, you are using your working memory to link the information you're reading with information you have previously stored.

In **FIGURE 7.1,** this updated information-processing model is summarized. Later in this chapter, we'll examine its three stages in more detail. First, though, let's consider how some information slips into memory through the mind's back door.

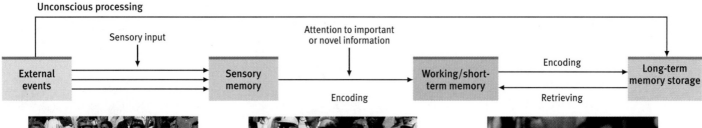

Unconscious processing

Sensory input

Attention to important or novel information

External events → Sensory memory → Encoding → Working/short-term memory → Encoding → Long-term memory storage

Retrieving

Sensory memory registers incoming information, allowing your brain to capture for a moment a sea of faces.

We pay attention to and encode important or novel stimuli—in this case, an angry face in the crowd.

If we stare at the face long enough (rehearsal), or if we're sufficiently disturbed by it (it's deemed "important"), we will encode it for long-term storage, and we may, an hour later, be able to call up an image of the face.

FIGURE 7.1 • **A modified three-stage information-processing model of memory**

Two Memory Tracks

2 How do automatic and effortful processing help us encode sights, sounds, and other sensations?

Two-Track Processing: Automatic Versus Effortful

As you walked to class today, your mind processed your journey without your awareness. But your mind would have switched into another gear if a friend had called to make a last-minute change in a meeting place. WHY DO WE REMEMBER ◄ SOME THINGS EASILY AND OTHERS ONLY IF WE STUDY HARD? With the help of our two-track minds, we **automatically process** vast amounts of everyday information. And we remember new and important information through **effortful processing** (FIGURE 7.2).

What Do We Process Automatically? With little or no conscious effort, you automatically process information about

- *space.* While studying, you often encode the place on a page where certain material appears. Later, when you try to recall the difference between automatic and effortful processing, you may picture the text on this page.

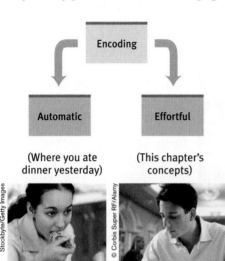

Encoding

Automatic
(Where you ate dinner yesterday)

Effortful
(This chapter's concepts)

Stockbyte/Getty Images

© Corbis Super RF/Alamy

FIGURE 7.2 ● Automatic versus effortful processing

- *time.* While going about your day, your mind is working behind the scenes, jotting down the sequence of the day's events. Later, when you realize you've left your coat somewhere, you can call up that sequence and retrace your steps.

- *frequency.* Your behind-the-scenes mind also takes notes about how many times things have happened, thus enabling you to realize, "This is the third time I've run into her today!"

Automatic processing happens so effortlessly that it is difficult to shut off. When you see words in your native language, perhaps on the side of a delivery truck, you can't help but read them and register their meaning. *Learning* to read wasn't automatic. You may recall working hard to pick out letters and connect them to certain sounds. But with experience and practice, your reading became automatic. Imagine now learning to read reversed sentences like this:

.citamotua emoceb nac gnissecorp luftroffE

At first, this requires effort, but after enough practice, you would also perform this task much more automatically. We develop many skills in this way. We learn to drive, to text, to speak a new language with great effort, but then these tasks become automatic.

What Requires Effortful Processing? Effortful processing requires close attention and effort. The work you put into remembering people's names (or this chapter's information) will produce durable and accessible memories. You can boost your memory of new information through **rehearsal** (conscious repetition). A pioneering researcher, Hermann Ebbinghaus (1850–1909), showed this long ago by studying his own learning and forgetting of new verbal material.

Put yourself in Ebbinghaus' shoes. How could you produce new items to learn? Ebbinghaus' answer was to form a list of all possible nonsense syllables by sandwiching a vowel between two consonants. Then, for a particular experiment, he would randomly select a sample of the syllables, practice them, and test himself. To get a feel for his experiments, rapidly read aloud the following list, repeating it eight times (from Baddeley, 1982). Then, without looking, try to recall the items:

JIH, BAZ, FUB, YOX, SUJ, XIR, DAX, LEQ, VUM, PID, KEL, WAV, TUV, ZOF, GEK, HIW.

The day after learning such a list, Ebbinghaus recalled only a few of the syllables. But were they entirely forgotten? No. The more often he practiced the list aloud on day 1, the fewer times he would have to practice it to learn it on day 2 (FIGURE 7.3 on the next page). Here, then, was a simple beginning principle: The amount we remember depends on the time we spend learning. Even after you think you know material, additional rehearsal (*overlearning*) increases learning.

memory the persistence of learning over time through the encoding, storage, and retrieval of information.

encoding the process of getting information into the memory system.

storage retaining of encoded information over time.

retrieval the process of getting information out of memory storage.

sensory memory the immediate, very brief recording of sensory information in the memory system.

short-term memory activated memory that holds a few items briefly (such as the seven digits of a phone number while dialing) before the information is stored or forgotten.

long-term memory the relatively permanent and limitless storehouse of the memory system. Includes knowledge, skills, and experiences.

working memory a view of short-term memory that stresses conscious, active processing of information, whether newly encoded or retrieved from long-term memory.

automatic processing unconscious encoding of everyday information, such as space, time, frequency, and well-learned word meanings.

effortful processing encoding that requires attention and conscious effort.

rehearsal the conscious repetition of information, either to maintain it in consciousness or to encode it for storage.

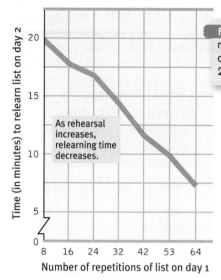

As rehearsal increases, relearning time decreases.

Time (in minutes) to relearn list on day 2

Number of repetitions of list on day 1

FIGURE **7.3** ● **Ebbinghaus' retention curve** The more times he practiced a list of nonsense syllables on day 1, the less time he would need to relearn it on day 2. (From Baddeley, 1982.)

For novel verbal information, practice—effortful processing—does indeed make perfect.

We retain information (such as our new classmates' names) even better if we spread rehearsal over time. This **spacing effect** (Cepeda et al., 2006; Kornell & Bjork, 2008) is the reason teachers have urged you to study regularly throughout the term rather than only cramming the night before an exam. Repeated quizzing of previously studied material, called the *testing effect*, also helps. Testing does more than assess learning; it improves it (Roediger & Karpicke, 2006). In life, as in your studies, spreading out learning helps you retain information far into the future. And the longer you need to remember something, the more spread out your study times should be (Cepeda et al., 2008).

Even with rehearsal, however, we won't remember all items in a list equally well. As we struggle to recall the list, we will probably remember the last and first items better than those in the middle **(FIGURE 7.4)**. This is the **serial position effect** (Reed, 2000). Perhaps we remember the last items better because they are still in working memory, and we briefly have access to them. After a delay—after we shift our attention away from those last items—our recall is best for the first items.

Time spent rehearsing is an important part of effortful processing. But memory is not a single, unified, conscious system. Memories formed without conscious effort follow a different set of rules.

Two-Track Storage: Facts Versus Skills

3 **What are implicit and explicit memories, and what brain structures enable each?**

A memory-to-be enters by way of the senses, then makes its way into the brain's depths. Precisely where it goes depends on the type of information. This is dramatically illustrated by those who, as in the cases of Henry Molaison and my father (mentioned in this chapter's introduction), suffer brain damage that leaves them unable to form new memories.

Neurologist Oliver Sacks (1985, pp. 26–27) described one such patient, Jimmie, who was stuck in the year of his injury, 1945. Jimmie had formed no new memories after that year. Asked in 1975 to name the U.S. President, he replied, "FDR's dead. Truman's at the helm." When Jimmie gave his age as 19, Sacks set a mirror before him: "Look in the mirror and tell me what you see. Is that a 19-year-old looking out from the mirror?"

Jimmie turned pale, gripped the chair, cursed, then became frantic: "What's going on? What's happened to me? Is this a nightmare? Am I crazy? Is this a joke?" When his attention was directed to some children playing baseball, his panic ended, the dreadful mirror forgotten.

Sacks showed Jimmie a photo from *National Geographic*. "What is this?" he asked.

"It's the Moon," Jimmie replied.

"No, it's not," Sacks answered. "It's a picture of the Earth taken from the Moon."

"Doc, you're kidding? Someone would've had to get a camera up there!"

"Naturally."

"Hell! You're joking—how the hell would you do that?" Jimmie's wonder was that of a bright young man from the 1940s amazed by his travel back to the future.

Careful testing of people with injuries like Jimmie's reveals something even stranger. Although they are unable to recall new facts or anything they have done recently, they can learn new skills and can be classically conditioned.

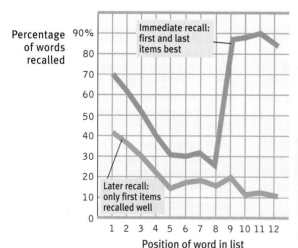

Percentage of words recalled

Immediate recall: first and last items best

Later recall: only first items recalled well

Position of word in list

China Photos/Getty Images

FIGURE **7.4** ● **The serial position effect** Which names will Hu Jintao (President of the People's Republic of China) remember best when he finishes making his way through this long line of dignitaries from Taiwan?

Answer: Immediately, Hu Jintao would probably remember best the first and last people he greeted. Later, he would probably remember best the first people in line.

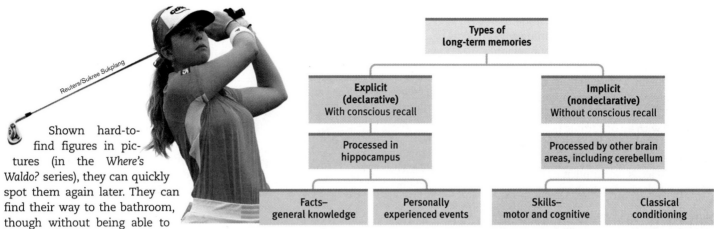

Shown hard-to-find figures in pictures (in the *Where's Waldo?* series), they can quickly spot them again later. They can find their way to the bathroom, though without being able to tell you where it is. They can master mirror-image writing, jigsaw puzzles, and even complicated job skills (Schacter, 1992, 1996; Xu & Corkin, 2001). However, *they do all these things with no awareness of having learned them.*

We can see the two-track memory system at work in people with Jimmie's type of brain injury **(FIGURE 7.5).** Whatever has destroyed their conscious recall has left their capacity for unconscious processing intact. They can learn *how* to do something—to play golf, for example. And they can form an **implicit** (unconscious) **memory** of their new skill. But they may not *be aware* that they can play golf. They won't form **explicit** (conscious) **memories** of learning the sport or playing on a particular golf course. If they continue to practice, their game will improve steadily. Yet they will have no conscious

	Types of long-term memories	
Explicit (declarative) With conscious recall		**Implicit (nondeclarative)** Without conscious recall
Processed in hippocampus		**Processed by other brain areas, including cerebellum**
Facts—general knowledge / **Personally experienced events**		**Skills—motor and cognitive** / **Classical conditioning**

FIGURE 7.5 ● Two-track memory We process and store our memories for facts and skills separately. Thus, people with brain injuries may lose conscious (explicit) memory (the awareness of being able to play golf), yet retain memory for material they cannot consciously recall (implicit memory; the ability to play golf).

memories of the facts associated with their new skills. Even Alzheimer's patients, whose explicit memories for people and events are lost, have shown an ability to form new implicit memories (Lustig & Buckner, 2004).

Our explicit and implicit memory systems involve separate brain regions. We know this from scans of the brain in action, and from autopsies of people who had suffered from different types of memory loss. New explicit memories of names, images, and events are laid down via the *hippocampus,* a limbic system neural center that is our brain's equivalent of a "save" button. When brain scans capture the brain forming an explicit memory, they reveal hippocampus activity. The hippocampus seems to act as a loading dock where the brain registers and temporarily stores the elements of a remembered episode. But then, like older files shifted to a basement storeroom, memories migrate for storage elsewhere. This process is called *memory consolidation.*

CAN A GOOD NIGHT'S SLEEP IMPROVE◄ EXAM GRADES? It can, because sleep supports memory consolidation, both in humans and in rats. Removing a rat's hippocampus 3 hours after it learns the location of some tasty new food prevents long-term memory formation. Removing the hippocampus 48 hours later does not (Tse et al., 2007). During sleep,

the hippocampus and brain cortex display rhythmic patterns of activity, as if they were talking to each other (Ji & Wilson, 2007; Mehta, 2007). Researchers suspect that the brain is replaying the day's experiences as it transfers them to the cortex for long-term storage.

You could lose your hippocampus and still lay down implicit memories for skills (such as golfing) and conditioned associations. Memory loss following brain damage left one patient unable to recognize her physician as, each day, he shook her hand and introduced himself. One day, after reaching for his hand, she yanked hers back, for the physician had pricked her with a tack in his palm. When he next introduced himself, she refused to shake his hand but couldn't explain why. Having been classically conditioned, she just wouldn't do it (LeDoux, 1996).

off the mark.com   by Mark Parisi

THE BAD NEWS IS WE LEFT A CLAMP IN YOUR TEMPORAL LOBE... THE GOOD NEWS IS THAT YOU WON'T REMEMBER WHAT I JUST SAID...

offthemark.com ©2007 MARK PARISI DIST. BY UFS INC.

spacing effect the tendency for distributed study or practice to yield better long-term retention than is achieved through massed study or practice.

serial position effect the tendency to recall best the last and first items in a list.

implicit memory retaining learned skills or conditioning, often without conscious awareness of this learning.

explicit memory memories of facts and personal events that you can consciously retrieve.

We form and store the implicit memories created by classical conditioning with the help of our *cerebellum,* the brain region extending out from the rear of the brainstem. Humans with a damaged cerebellum cannot develop certain conditioned reflexes. They can't, for example, associate a tone with an oncoming puff of air, so they don't blink in anticipation of the puff (Daum & Schugens, 1996; Green & Woodruff-Pak, 2000). Implicit memory formation needs the cerebellum.

PRACTICE TEST

THE BASICS

1. The psychological terms for taking in information, retaining it, and later getting it back out are
   a. retrieval, encoding, and storage.
   b. encoding, storage, and retrieval.
   c. storage, encoding, and retrieval.
   d. retrieval, storage, and encoding.

2. In what order does our brain process an external event into a memory that can last a lifetime?
   a. Long-term memory, sensory memory, working/short-term memory
   b. Working/short-term memory, sensory memory, long-term memory
   c. Working/short-term memory, long-term memory, sensory memory
   d. Sensory memory, working/short-term memory, long-term memory

3. Rehearsal—the conscious repetition of information you want to remember—is part of
   a. automatic processing.
   b. effortful processing.
   c. implicit memory formation.
   d. retrieval.

4. When we are tested immediately after viewing a list of words, we tend to recall the first and last items more readily than those in the middle. This tendency is called the _____ effect.
   a. serial position
   b. spacing
   c. rehearsal
   d. effortful processing

5. Hippocampus damage will typically not affect the ability to learn new skills, such as riding a bike, which is an example of
   a. explicit memory.
   b. implicit memory.
   c. operant conditioning.
   d. classical conditioning.

6. The cerebellum plays an important role in forming and storing implicit memories created by
   a. classical conditioning.
   b. effortful processing.
   c. explicit memory.
   d. rehearsal.

THE BIG PICTURE

7A. What two important new concepts now update the classic three-stage information-processing model?

IN YOUR EVERYDAY LIFE

■ What has your memory system encoded, stored, and retrieved today?

Answers: 1. b, 2. d, 3. b, 4. a, 5. b, 6. a. Answers to The Big Picture questions can be found in Appendix B at the end of the book.

Building Memories

We have considered the types of memories the human brain processes and stores. And we have seen that different brain areas process explicit (conscious) memories of things we know and have experienced and implicit (unconscious) memories of skills and conditioned responses. Now let's see how information gets in, gets retained, and gets retrieved.

> Here is another sentence I will ask you about later: *The fish attacked the swimmer.*

Encoding: Getting Information In

4 **What are the most common and effective ways of encoding information?**

Processing our experiences is like sorting through e-mail. Some items we instantly trash. Others we open, read, and retain, encoding their meaning or image and mentally organizing the information.

Encoding Meaning

While processing verbal information, our active mind makes connections between new information and what we already know or imagine. These connections guide us as we interpret and encode sounds. For example, whether we hear *eye-screem* as "ice cream" or "I scream" depends on both the context (snack shop or horror film) and our experience. This all happens in our working memory, that temporary work site where we organize information and solve problems.

Can you repeat the sentence about the rioter (from this chapter's opening page)? Was the sentence "The angry rioter threw the rock *through* the window" or "The angry rioter threw the rock *at* the window"? If the first looks more correct, you—like the participants in the original study—may have recalled the meaning you encoded, not the words that were written (Brewer, 1977). In making such mistakes, our minds are like theater directors who, given a raw script, imagine a finished stage production (Bower & Morrow, 1990). Asked later what we heard or read, we recall not the text itself but *the meaning we encoded* while listening or reading. Thus, studying for an exam, you may remember your lecture notes with your encoded meaning rather than the lecture itself.

Given too raw a script, we may have trouble finding any meaning, as students did when asked to remember the following recorded passage (Bransford & Johnson, 1972).

The procedure is actually quite simple. First you arrange things into different groups. Of course, one pile may be sufficient depending on how much there is to do.... After the procedure is completed one arranges the materials into different groups again. Then they can be put into their appropriate places. Eventually they will be used once more and the whole cycle will then have to be repeated. However, that is part of life.

Hearing the paragraph you just read, without a meaningful context, students remembered little of it. But when they were told the paragraph described doing laundry (something meaningful to them), they remembered much more of it—as you probably could now if you read it again.

Such research illustrates another important principle: You will more easily remember what you read and hear if you translate it into personally meaningful information. From his experiments on himself, memory researcher Hermann Ebbinghaus estimated that learning meaningful material required one-tenth the effort needed to learn nonsense material. As memory researcher Wayne Wickelgren (1977, p. 346) noted, "The time you spend thinking about material you are reading and relating it to previously stored material is about the most useful thing you can do in learning any new subject matter."

Encoding Images

If you could recall the rock-throwing rioter sentence, it was probably not only because of the meaning you encoded but also because that sentence lent itself to visual **imagery.** We more easily remember things we can process visually as well as meaningfully (Marschark et al., 1987; Paivio, 1986). Our earliest memories—probably of something that happened at age 3 or 4—involved visual imagery. As adults, we may struggle to remember formulas, definitions, and dates, yet we can easily remember mental pictures—where we were yesterday, who was with us, where we sat, and what we wore. High-imagery words—those that lend themselves to *visual encoding*—are more easily remembered than low-imagery words. (When I quiz you later, which three of these words—*bicycle, void, cigarette, known, fire, process*—will you most likely recall?)

Storage: Retaining Information

5 What are the duration and capacity of sensory, short-term, and long-term memory?

At the heart of memory is storage. If you later recall something you experienced, you must, somehow, have stored and retrieved it. How much can we store in our memory, and how does our brain change as we store our memories?

Storage Capacities

Sensory memory is truly fleeting—like lightning flashes in the brain. In one classic experiment, George Sperling showed people three rows of three letters each for only 1/20th of a second (**FIGURE 7.6**). After the nine letters disappeared from the screen, people could recall only about half of them.

Was it because they had too little time to see them? No—Sperling demonstrated that people actually *can* see and recall all the letters, but only for a moment. Rather than ask them to recall all nine letters at once, he sounded a high, medium, or low tone immediately *after* flashing the nine letters. This cue directed people to report only the letters of one row—the top, middle, or bottom, depending on the tone. Now they rarely missed a letter, showing that all nine letters were briefly available for recall.

Our *short-term memories* have a very limited life. Unless our working memory rehearses or meaningfully encodes information, it quickly disappears. During your finger's trip from phone book to phone, your memory of a telephone number may evaporate. To find out how quickly memories fade, researchers asked people to remember three-consonant groups, such as *CHJ* (Peterson & Peterson, 1959). To prevent rehearsal, the participants were distracted by counting backwards from 100

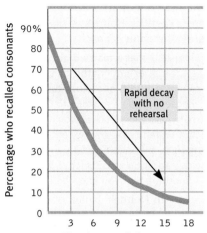

FIGURE 7.7 ● **Short-term memory decay** Unless rehearsed, verbal information may be quickly forgotten. (From Peterson & Peterson, 1959.)

by threes. Without active processing, memories of the consonants disappeared. After 3 seconds, people recalled the letters only about half the time; after 12 seconds, they seldom recalled them at all (**FIGURE 7.7**).

We also have limited *short-term memory capacity.* Typically, we can store about seven bits of information (give or take two) in short-term memory. George Miller (1956) enshrined this recall capacity as the *Magical Number Seven, plus or minus two.* (The Magical Number Seven is the newest member of the list of magical sevens—the seven wonders of the world, the seven seas, the seven deadly sins, the seven primary colors, the seven musical scale notes, the seven days of the week—seven magical sevens.) Not surprisingly, when some phone companies began requiring callers to dial a three-digit area code in addition to a seven-digit number, people had trouble retaining the just-looked-up number.

FIGURE 7.6 ● **Momentary photographic memory** When George Sperling (1960) flashed a group of letters similar to this for 1/20th of a second, people could recall only about half of the letters. But when signaled to recall a particular row *immediately* after the letters had disappeared, they could do so with near-perfect accuracy.

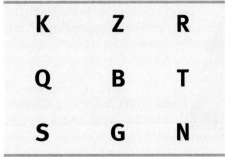

---

imagery mental pictures; a powerful aid to effortful processing, especially when combined with encoding meaning.

In Arthur Conan Doyle's A *Study in Scarlet,* Sherlock Holmes offers a popular theory of memory capacity.

> I consider that a man's brain originally is like a little empty attic, and you have to stock it with such furniture as you choose.... It is a mistake to think that that little room has elastic walls and can distend to any extent. Depend upon it, there comes a time when for every addition of knowledge you forget something that you knew before.

Contrary to Holmes' belief, our *long-term memory capacity* has no real limit and sometimes endures for a lifetime. The point is vividly shown by those who have performed amazing memory feats.

How the Brain Stores Memories

6 What biological changes enable memory storage?

I marveled at my aging mother-in-law, a retired pianist and organist. At age 88 her blind eyes could no longer read music. But let her sit at a keyboard and she would flawlessly play any of hundreds of songs, including some she had not thought of for 20 years. Where did her brain store those thousands of note patterns?

Some twentieth-century memory researchers believed that vivid flashbacks triggered by brain stimulation during surgery offered an answer. Our whole past, not just well-practiced music, seemed to be "in there," just waiting to be relived. Further research disproved this idea. The vivid flashbacks were creations of a stressed brain, not real memories (Loftus & Loftus, 1980). Other research has shown that we do not store information as li-

Clark's Nutcracker: Among animals, one contender for the gold medal for memory would be a mere birdbrain—the Clark's Nutcracker. During winter and early spring, this bird can locate up to 6000 caches of pine seeds it had buried earlier. (Shettleworth, 1993.)

© Tim Zurowski/All Canada Photos/Corbis

braries store their books, in neat, precise locations. Instead, the brain assigns aspects of a memory to various work groups of neurons (Tsien, 2007). Thus, the ongoing quest to understand how our brain learns and remembers has sparked the study of neurons and their meeting places.

Synaptic Changes Memories begin as impulses whizzing through neural circuits, somehow leaving permanent tracks in our brain. Where do these changes occur? The available clues point to the *synapses*—the sites where nerve cells communicate with one another by means of chemical messengers. We know that experience modifies the brain's neural networks. Increased activity in a particular pathway strengthens connections between neurons (see Chapter 3).

Eric Kandel and James Schwartz (1982) were able to catch a memory leaving tracks in neurons of the California sea slug. This simple animal's nerve cells are unusually large and accessible, and researchers have been able to observe how they change during learning. Using electric shocks, they have classically conditioned sea slugs to withdraw their gills when squirted with water, much as we might jump when lightning strikes nearby. By observing the slugs' neural connections before and after this conditioning, Kandel and Schwartz pinpointed changes. As a slug learns, its neurons release more of the neurotransmitter *serotonin* at certain synapses. These synapses then become more sensitive and transmit signals more efficiently.

As synapses become more efficient, so do neural circuits. Sending neurons now release their neurotransmitters more easily. Receiving neurons may grow additional receptor sites. This process, called **long-term potentiation (LTP),** helps us understand how our brain learns and re-

On the previous page, in the discussion of encoding imagery, I gave you six words and told you I would quiz you about them later. How many of those words can you now recall? Of these, how many are high-imagery words? How many are low-imagery?

Memory slug: The much-studied California sea slug, *Aplysia,* has increased our understanding of the neural basis of learning.

Marty Snyderman/Visuals Unlimited, Inc.

members (Lynch, 2002; Whitlock et al., 2006). Blocking LTP interferes with learning (Lynch & Staubli, 1991). Mutant mice that lack an enzyme needed for LTP can't learn their way out of a maze (Silva et al., 1992). And rats given a drug that enhances LTP can learn to run a maze with half the usual number of mistakes (Service, 1994).

After LTP has occurred, an electric current passing through the brain won't disrupt old memories. Before LTP, very recent memories can be wiped out. This often happens when depressed people are given electroconvulsive therapy (Chapter 13). CAN SPORTS INJURIES WIPE OUT RECENT◄ MEMORIES? Indeed they can. Football players and boxers knocked unconscious typically have no memory of events just before the knock-out (Yarnell & Lynch, 1970). Their working memory had no time to process the information into long-term memory before the shutdown.

Emotion-Laden Memories Arousal can sear certain events into the brain (Birnbaum et al., 2004; Strange & Dolan, 2004). Excitement or stress (perhaps a time you performed in front of a crowd) triggers our glands to produce stress hormones. These hormones make more glucose energy available to fuel brain activity, signaling the brain that something important has happened. At the

Retrieval: Getting Information Out

7 How do psychologists assess memory with recall, recognition, and relearning?

Remembering an event requires more than getting information into our brain and storing it there. To most people, memory is **recall,** the ability to draw information out of storage and into conscious awareness. To a psychologist, memory is more than that. **Recognizing** or more quickly **relearning** information also shows that something has been learned and retained.

Long after you cannot recall most of your high school classmates, you could probably recognize their yearbook pictures from a photo lineup and pick them out from a list of names. One research team found that people who had graduated 25 years earlier could not recall many of their old classmates, but they could recognize 90 percent of their pictures and names (Bahrick et al., 1975).

Our recognition memory is quick and vast. "Is your friend wearing a new or old outfit?" *Old.* "Is this five-second movie clip from a film you've ever seen?" *Yes.* "Have you ever before seen this person—this minor variation on the same old human features (two eyes, one nose, and so on)?"

Severe stress sears in memories: Significantly stressful events, such as the disastrous 2010 earthquake that left these ethnic Tibetans homeless in China's remote and mountainous Yushu county, may become a permanent part of survivors' memories.

same time, emotion-processing clusters in the brain boost activity in memory-forming areas (Buchanan, 2007). The result is "stronger, more reliable memories" (McGaugh, 1994, 2003). After horrific experiences—a wartime ambush, a house fire, a rape—vivid memories of the event may intrude again and again. The persistence of such memories is adaptive. These memories help alert us to potential dangers.

Weaker emotion means weaker memories. Given a drug that blocks stress hormone effects, people later have trouble remembering the details of an upsetting story (Cahill, 1994). Research is under way on a drug that could blunt intrusive memories if taken soon after a traumatic experience. One experiment gave such drugs to victims of car accidents, rapes, and other traumas. For 10 days following their horrific event, they received either the drug (propranolol) or a placebo. When tested three months later, half the placebo group, but none of the drug-treated group, showed signs of stress disorder (Pitman et al., 2002, 2005). (If you suffered a trauma, would you want such a drug?)

Which is more important—your experiences or your memories of them?

WHY ARE SOME MEMORIES SO MUCH◀ MORE CRISP AND CLEAR THAN OTHERS? Emotion-triggered hormonal changes help explain why we form enduring, very clear memories of exciting or shocking events. Some psychologists call them **flashbulb memories**—it's as if the brain commands, "Capture this!" Ask any adult American where he or she first heard the news on 9/11—that fateful day that the *New York Times* called "one of those moments in which history splits and we define the world as 'before and after.'" Five years later, 95 percent of surveyed Americans said they remembered where they were (Pew, 2006). Moreover, people's 9/11 memories remained consistent over the next two to three years (Conway et al., 2009; Kvavilashvili et al., 2009).

Our memories of dramatic experiences remain bright and clear in part because we rehearse them, thinking about them and describing them to others. But sometimes, even our flashbulb memories err (Talarico & Rubin, 2003). As we will see later in this chapter, rehearsal can feed the construction of false memories.

long-term potentiation (LTP) an increase in a synapse's firing potential. Believed to be a neural basis for learning and memory.

flashbulb memory a clear memory of an emotionally significant moment or event.

recall memory demonstrated by retrieving information learned earlier, as on a fill-in-the-blank test.

recognition memory demonstrated by identifying items previously learned, as on a multiple-choice test.

relearning memory demonstrated by time saved when learning material a second time.

Remembering things past: Even if Oprah Winfrey and Brad Pitt had not become famous, their high school classmates would most likely still recognize their yearbook photos.

Both photos: Spanky's Yearbook Archive

No. Before our mouth can form an answer to any of millions of such questions, our mind knows, and knows that it knows.

Speed of relearning also reveals memory. If you once learned something and then forgot it, you probably will relearn it more quickly. When you re-study material for a final exam or resurrect a language you used in early childhood, mastering the material is easier the second time around. Tests of recognition and of time spent relearning confirm the point: *We remember more than we can recall.*

Retrieval Cues

8 How can retrieval cues help us access stored memories, and how do contexts and moods influence retrieval?

Imagine a spider suspended in the middle of her web, held up by the many strands extending outward from her in all directions to different points. To trace a pathway to the spider, you would need to begin at one of these anchor points and follow the attached strand down into the web.

Retrieving a memory is similar. Memories are held in storage by a web of associations, each piece of information connected to many others. Here's a simplified example of how a memory web is constructed. Suppose you encode into your memory the name of the person sitting next to you in class. With that name, you will also encode other bits of information, such as

> **Review:**
> * Multiple-choice questions test our
>   a. recall.
>   b. recognition.
>   c. relearning.
> * Fill-in-the-blank questions test our _____.
>
> Answers: Multiple-choice questions test recognition. Fill-in-the-blank questions test recall.

your surroundings, mood, seating position, and so on. These bits serve as **retrieval cues,** anchor points for pathways you can follow to access your classmate's name when you need to recall it later. The more retrieval cues you've encoded, the better your chances of finding a path to the memory suspended in this web of information.

The best retrieval cues come from associations formed at the time we encode a memory. **WHY DOES** ◄ **THE SMELL OF POPCORN TRIGGER MEMORIES OF WATCHING MOVIES?** Because tastes, smells, and sights can open pathways to our memories. To recall something, we may mentally place ourselves

in the original context. Doing so gives us visual cues that can lead us to the searched-for memory. After losing his sight, British theologian John Hull (1990, p. 174) described his difficulty recalling such details: "I knew I had been somewhere, and had done particular things with certain people, but where? I could not put the conversations . . . into a context. There was no background, no features against which to identify the place. Normally, the memories of people you have spoken to during the day are stored in frames which include the background."

Here's a question to test your memory. Do you recall the second sentence I asked you to remember in the introduction to Building Memories? If not, does the word *shark* open a pathway? Experiments show that *shark* (likely the image you visualized and stored) is a better retrieval cue than the sentence's actual word, *fish* (Anderson et al., 1976). *(The fish attacked the swimmer.)*

Context Effects Returning to the context where you experienced something can *prime* (activate) your memory of it. Researchers discovered this when they had scuba divers listen to a list of words in two different settings, either 10 feet underwater or sitting on the beach (Godden & Baddeley, 1975). The divers recalled more words when they were retested in the same place **(FIGURE 7.8)**.

You may have experienced similar context effects. Imagine this: While taking notes from this book, you realize you need to sharpen your pencil. You get up and walk to another room, and then cannot recall why you came. After returning to your desk, it hits you: "I wanted to sharpen this pencil!" What happens to create this frustrating experience? In one context (desk, reading psychology), you realize your pencil needs sharpening. In another room, in a different context, you have few cues to lead you back to that thought. When you are once again at your desk, you are back in the context in which you encoded the thought ("This pencil is dull").

Sometimes, being in a context similar to one we've been in before may trigger

WELL, FOR CRYING-OUT LOUD! AL TOWBRIDGE! WHAT IS IT, NINE YEARS, SEVEN MONTHS, AND TWELVE DAYS SINCE I LAST RAN INTO YOU? TEN-THIRTY-TWO A.M., A SATURDAY, FELCHER'S HARDWARE STORE. YOU WERE BUYING SEALER FOR YOUR BLACKTOP DRIVEWAY. TELL ME, AL, HOW DID THAT SEALER WORK? DID IT HOLD UP?

MR. TOTAL RECALL

© The New Yorker Collection, 1987, W. Miller from cartoonbank.com. All Rights Reserved.

FIGURE 7.8 • **The effect of context on memory** Words heard underwater were best recalled underwater; words heard on land were best recalled on land. (Adapted from Godden & Baddeley, 1975.)

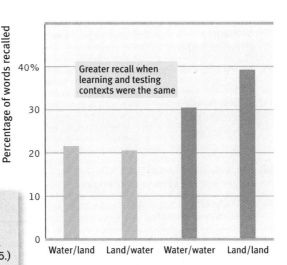

Greater recall when learning and testing contexts were the same

Percentage of words recalled

Water/land Land/water Water/water Land/land

Different contexts for hearing and recall | Same contexts for hearing and recall

feelings of **déjà vu** (French for "already seen"). WHAT CAUSES DÉJÀ VU? Two-thirds ◄ of us have had this fleeting, eerie sense that "I've been in this exact situation before." Well-educated, imaginative young adults are most likely to experience déjà vu, especially when tired or stressed (Brown, 2003, 2004; McAneny, 1996). Some wonder, "How could I recognize a situation I'm now in for the first time?" Others may suspect extraordinary causes: "Could I have experienced this in a previous life?" or "Did I dream of this place?"

Posing the question differently—"Why do I feel as though I recognize this situation?"—we can see how our memory system might produce déjà vu (Alcock, 1981). Our current situation may be loaded with retrieval cues that take us down paths leading to earlier, similar experiences. Thus, if you are in a restaurant where you often meet a friend for lunch, and you see a stranger who walks and talks like that friend, the similarity may trigger an eerie feeling of recognition. Having awakened a shadow of that earlier experience, you may think, "I've seen that person in this situation before."

Déjà vu seems to be a feeling of familiarity without remembering the source (Cleary, 2008). Sometimes a situation seems familiar because it resembles

> "Do you ever get that strange feeling of vujà dé? Not déjà vu; vujà dé. It's the distinct sense that, somehow, something just happened that has never happened before. Nothing seems familiar. And then suddenly the feeling is gone. Vujà dé."
>
> George Carlin (1937–2008), *Funny Times*, December 2001

several other similar experiences (Lampinen, 2002). Imagine you briefly encountered my dad, my brothers, my sister, and my children. Then, a few weeks later, you meet me. You might think, "I've been with this guy before." Although no one in my family looks or acts just like me (lucky them), their looks and gestures are somewhat like mine. I might form a "global match" to what you had experienced.

Moods and Memories Words, images, and contexts are not our only retrieval cues. An event in the past may have aroused a specific *emotion*, such as fear, anger, or joy. Later, when we again feel that emotion, we may recall the event associated with it (Fiedler et al., 2001).

We have all experienced mood effects. If you have a terrible evening—your date canceled, you lost your iPod, and now you've absent-mindedly washed your colored clothes with bleach—your sour mood may bring to mind memories of other unhappy times. If a friend or family member walks in at this point, your mind may fill with bad memories of that person. Being angry or depressed sours memories. This tendency to recall events that fit our mood is

called **mood-congruent memory.** If put in a great mood—whether under hypnosis or just by the day's events (a World Cup soccer victory for the German participants in one study)—people recall the world through rose-colored glasses (DeSteno et al., 2000; Forgas et al., 1984; Schwarz et al., 1987). They judge themselves competent and effective, other people as kind and giving, and happy events as more common than unhappy ones.

Knowing this mood-memory connection, we should not be surprised that in some studies *currently* depressed people recall their parents as rejecting and punishing. *Formerly* depressed people describe their parents in more positive ways—much as do those who have never been depressed (Lewinsohn & Rosenbaum, 1987; Lewis, 1992). Similarly, adolescents' ratings of parental warmth in one week give little clue to how they will rate their parents six weeks later (Bornstein et al., 1991). When teens are down, their parents seem inhuman. As moods brighten, those devil parents sprout wings and become angels.

"I can't remember what we're arguing about, either. Let's keep yelling, and maybe it will come back to us."

retrieval cue any stimulus (event, feeling, place, and so on) linked to a specific memory.

déjà vu that eerie sense that "I've experienced this before." Cues from the current situation may unconsciously trigger retrieval of an earlier experience.

mood-congruent memory the tendency to recall experiences that are consistent with your current good or bad mood.

Our mood's effect on retrieval helps explain why our moods persist. When happy, we recall happy events and therefore see the world as a happy place, which helps prolong our good mood. When depressed, we recall sad events, which darkens our interpretations of current events. For those predisposed to depression, this process can help maintain a vicious, dark cycle.

Mood-congruent memory is part of a larger concept called *state-dependent memory*. What we learn in one state may be more easily recalled when we are again in that state. What people learn when drunk, for example, they don't recall well in any state (alcohol disrupts storage). But they recall it slightly better when again drunk. Someone who hides money when drunk may forget the location until drunk again.

PRACTICE TEST

THE BASICS

7. The process of forming mental images as we encode information in memory is called
   a. picturing.
   b. visual encoding.
   c. rehearsing.
   d. imagining.

8. Our short-term memory capacity is about
   a. 20 items.
   b. 18 items.
   c. 7 items.
   d. 3 items.

9. A neural basis for learning and memory is LTP, which refers to
   a. emotion-triggered hormonal changes.
   b. the effect of mood on memory.
   c. an increase in a synapse's firing potential.
   d. the link between familiarity and déjà vu.

10. To access a memory, we think of things associated with that memory, such as odors, images, or emotions, which are all examples of
    a. relearning.
    b. storage.

c. imagery.
d. retrieval cues.

11. The feeling that "I've been here before" is known as
    a. déjà vu.
    b. retrieval.
    c. relearning.
    d. an explicit memory.

12. The tendency to recall experiences consistent with our current emotions is called
    a. emotional memory.
    b. déjà vu.
    c. automatic processing.
    d. mood-congruent memory.

THE BIG PICTURE

7B. What would be the most effective strategy to learn and retain a list of names of key historical figures for a week? For a year?

7C. Your friend tells you that her father experienced brain damage in an accident. She wonders if psychology can explain why he can still play checkers very well but has a hard time holding a sensible conversation. What can you tell her?

IN YOUR EVERYDAY LIFE

▪ How do you make psychology terms more personally meaningful so you remember them better? Could you do this more often?

▪ Can you recall a time when stress helped you remember something? Has stress ever made it more difficult to remember something?

▪ In what ways do you notice your moods coloring your memories, perceptions, or expectations?

Answers: 7. b, 8. c, 9. c, 10. d, 11. a, 12. d. Answers to The Big Picture questions can be found in Appendix B at the end of the book.

Forgetting

9 What are some possible reasons for when and why we forget?

If a memory-enhancing pill becomes available, it had better not be too effective. To discard the clutter of useless information—outfits worn last month, e-mail addresses now out of date, restaurant orders already cooked and served—is surely a blessing. Remember meeting the Russ-

"Oh, is that today?"

ian memory whiz S earlier in this chapter? His junk heap of memories dominated his consciousness. He had difficulty thinking abstractly—generalizing, organizing, evaluating. So does a woman named A. J. (Jill Price in real life). She reports that her extraordinary memory interferes with her life, with one memory cuing another (Parker et al., 2006): "It's like a running movie that never stops."

More often, however, our quirky memories fail us when we least expect it.

The woman who can't forget: "A. J." in real life is Jill Price. With writer Bart Davis, Price told her story in a 2008 published memoir. She remembers every day of her life since age 14 with detailed clarity, including both the joys and the unforgotten hurts.

My own memory can easily call up such episodes as that wonderful first kiss with the woman I love, or trivial facts like the air mileage from London to Detroit. Then it abandons me when I'm trying to recall that new colleague's name or where I left my hat, after failing to encode, store, or retrieve the information. Memory researcher Daniel Schacter (1999) has listed seven ways our memories fail us—the seven sins of memory, he called them.

Three sins of forgetting and retrieval:

1. *Absent-mindedness*—inattention to details leads to encoding failure (our mind is elsewhere as we lay down our phone).

2. *Transience*—memory loss (we forget former classmates as unused information fades).

3. *Blocking*—inability to access stored information (seeing an actor in an old movie, we feel the name on the tip of our tongue but cannot get it out).

Three sins of distortion:

4. *Misattribution*—confusing the source of information (forgetting who said what or remembering a dream as an actual event).

5. *Suggestibility*—the lingering effects of misinformation (a leading question—"Did Mr. Jones touch your private parts?"—later becomes a young child's false memory).

6. *Bias*—belief-colored recollections (current bad feelings toward a friend may change a memory of initial good feelings).

One sin of intrusion:

7. *Persistence*—unwanted memories (being haunted by images of a sexual assault).

Let's first consider encoding failures, then storage decay and retrieval failures.

Encoding Failure

Much of what we sense we never notice, and what we fail to encode, we will never remember **(FIGURE 7.9)**. Age can affect encoding efficiency. The brain areas that

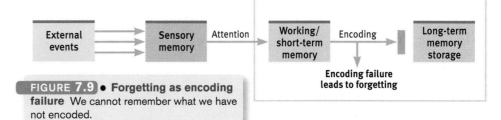

FIGURE 7.9 • **Forgetting as encoding failure** We cannot remember what we have not encoded.

jump into action when young adults encode new information are less responsive in older adults. This slower encoding helps explain age-related memory decline (Grady et al., 1995).

But no matter how young we are, we pay conscious attention to only a limited portion of the vast number of sights and sounds bombarding us. Consider something you have looked at countless times: What letters accompany the number 5 on your phone? For people who don't text, the question is surprisingly tough. This detail is not personally meaningful, and few of them have made the effort to encode it. We encode some information—where we had dinner yesterday—automatically. Other types of information, such as the concepts in this chapter, require effort and attention. Without this effortful processing, many memories never form.

Shutterstock

Storage Decay

Even after encoding something well, we sometimes later forget it. Hermann Ebbinghaus (1885), who was a master of nonsense-syllable learning, also studied how long memories last. After learning lists of nonsense syllables, he measured how much he remembered at various times, from 20 minutes to 30 days later. The result was his famous *forgetting curve:* The course of forgetting is rapid at first, then levels off with time (Wixted & Ebbesen, 1991). People studying Spanish as a foreign language showed this forgetting curve for Spanish vocabulary (Bahrick, 1984). Compared with others who had just completed a high school or college Spanish course, people 3 years out of school had forgotten much of what they had learned. However, what they remembered then, they still remembered 25 and more years later. Their forgetting had leveled off **(FIGURE 7.10)**.

FIGURE 7.10 • **The forgetting curve for Spanish learned in school** Compared with others just completing a Spanish language-learning course, people 3 years out of the course remembered much less. Compared with the 3-year group, however, those who studied Spanish even longer ago did not forget much more. (Adapted from Bahrick, 1984.)

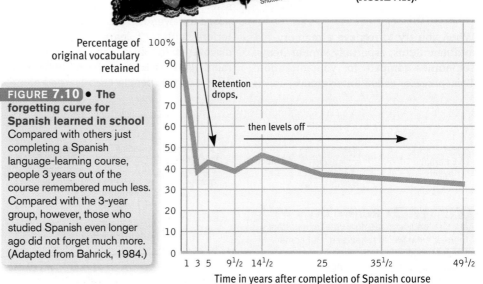

Percentage of original vocabulary retained

Retention drops, then levels off

Time in years after completion of Spanish course

One explanation for these forgetting curves is a gradual fading of the **memory trace,** physical changes in the brain as a memory forms. Researchers are getting closer to solving the mystery of the physical storage and decay of memories. But memories fade for many reasons, including other learning that disrupts our retrieval.

Retrieval Failure

10 How does interference cause forgetting? Do people seem to repress emotionally painful experiences?

We can compare forgotten events to books you can't find in your local library. Some aren't available because they were never acquired (not encoded). Others have been discarded (stored memories decay).

But there is a third possibility. The book may be there but irretrievable because we don't have enough information to look it up. Sometimes information feels like it's just beyond our reach. WHAT ◀ CAUSES THOSE FRUSTRATING "TIP OF THE TONGUE" MEMORY PROBLEMS? These are retrieval problems **(FIGURE 7.11).** (Deaf people fluent in sign language experience a parallel "tip of the fingers" phenomenon [Thompson et al., 2005]). Given retrieval cues *("It begins with an M")*, you may easily retrieve the memory. Often, forgetting is not memories discarded but memories not retrieved.

Interference

When you try to retrieve a memory, old and new items, especially similar items, sometimes compete for your attention. This process, called **interference,** is an

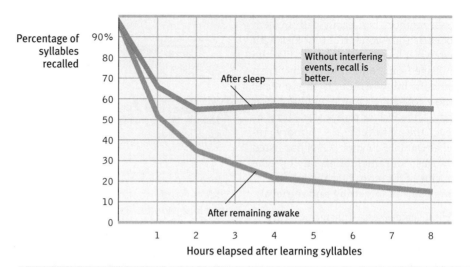

Percentage of syllables recalled

Without interfering events, recall is better.

After sleep

After remaining awake

Hours elapsed after learning syllables

FIGURE 7.12 • **Interference** People forgot more when they stayed awake and experienced other new material. (From Jenkins & Dallenbach, 1924.)

important cause of forgetting. If you're at a party and someone gives you a phone number, you may be able to recall it the next day. But if two more people give you their numbers, each of those numbers will interfere with your memory of the others. Likewise, if you get a new ATM card password, your memory of your old ATM password may interfere with your remembering the new sequence. A typical student faces eight demands for passwords (Brown et al., 2004). As you collect more and more information, your mental attic never fills, but it gets cluttered.

New learning in the hour before we fall asleep is protected because we are exposed to fewer distractions that could interfere with our learning. Researchers discovered this in a now-classic experiment (Jenkins & Dallenbach, 1924). Day after day, two people each learned some

nonsense syllables. When they tried to recall them after a night's sleep, they could retrieve more than half the items **(FIGURE 7.12).** But when they learned the material and then stayed awake and involved with other activities, they forgot more, and sooner. Later experiments have confirmed that the hour before a night's sleep is a good time to commit information to memory (Benson & Feinberg, 1977; Fowler et al., 1973; Nesca & Koulack, 1994). But not the *seconds* just before sleep. Information presented then doesn't have a chance to get encoded, so we seldom remember it later (Wyatt & Bootzin, 1994). Nor do we remember recorded information played during sleep, although our ears register it (Wood et al., 1992). Without opportunity for rehearsal, most cognitive learning doesn't occur.

But we should not overstate the point. Sometimes old information can help us learn new information. Knowing Latin may actually help us to learn French. It is when old and new information compete with each other, as in learning Spanish soon after learning French, that interference occurs.

Motivated Forgetting

To remember our past is often to revise it. Years ago, the huge cookie jar in our kitchen was jammed with freshly baked

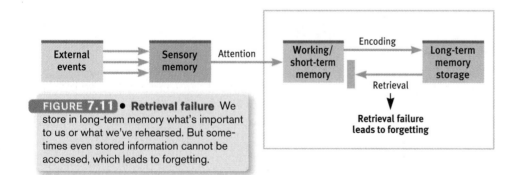

FIGURE 7.11 • **Retrieval failure** We store in long-term memory what's important to us or what we've rehearsed. But sometimes even stored information cannot be accessed, which leads to forgetting.

External events → Sensory memory → Attention → Working/ short-term memory → Encoding → Long-term memory storage → Retrieval → Retrieval failure leads to forgetting

chocolate chip cookies. Still more were cooling across racks on the counter. Twenty-four hours later, not a crumb was left. Who had taken them? During that time, my wife, three children, and I were the only people in the house. So while memories were still fresh, I conducted a little memory test. Andy admitted wolfing down as many as 20. Peter thought he had eaten 15. Laura guessed she had stuffed her then-6-year-old body with 15 cookies. My wife, Carol, recalled eating 6, and I remembered consuming 15 and taking 18 more to the office. We sheepishly accepted responsibility for 89 cookies. Still, we had not come close; there had been 160.

© Johansky, Peter/Index Stock/Cor

Why were we so far off in our estimates of the number of cookies we had eaten? As **FIGURE 7.13** reminds us, we automatically encode sensory information in amazing detail. So was it an *encoding* problem? (Did we just not notice what we had eaten?) Was it a *storage* problem? (Might our memories of cookies, like Ebbinghaus' memory of nonsense syllables, have melted away almost as fast as the cookies themselves?) Or was the information still intact but *not retrievable* because it would be embarrassing to remember?[1]

Sigmund Freud might have argued that our memory systems self-censored this information. He proposed that we **repress** painful or unacceptable memories to protect our self-concept and to minimize anxiety. But the repressed memory lingers, he believed, and can be retrieved by some later cue or during therapy. Repression was central to Freud's theory (see Chapter 11) and was a popular idea in mid-twentieth-century psychology. In one study, 9 in 10 university students agreed that "memories for painful experiences are sometimes pushed into unconsciousness" (Brown et al., 1996). Therapists often assume it. Today, increasing numbers of memory researchers think repression rarely, if ever, occurs. More typically, we have trouble forgetting traumatic experiences. People's efforts to forget often succeed when the material is neutral, but not when it is emotional (Payne & Corrigan, 2007). Thus, we may have intrusive memories of the very traumatic experiences we would most like to forget.

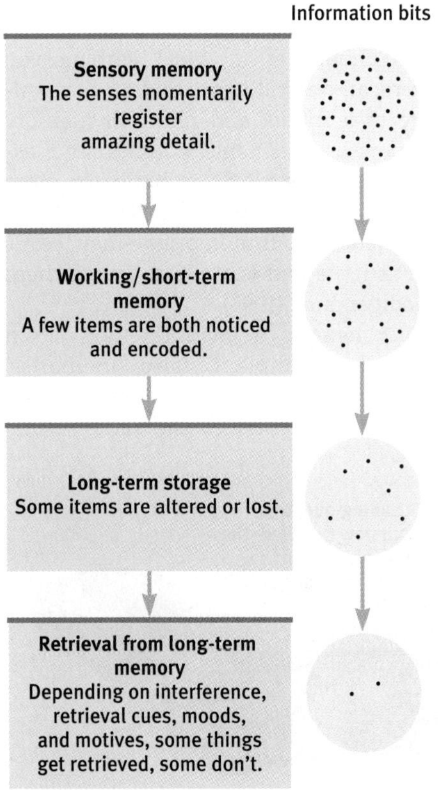

---

1. One of my cookie-scarfing sons, on reading this in his father's textbook years later, confessed he had fibbed "a little."

Information bits

Sensory memory
The senses momentarily register amazing detail.

Working/short-term memory
A few items are both noticed and encoded.

Long-term storage
Some items are altered or lost.

Retrieval from long-term memory
Depending on interference, retrieval cues, moods, and motives, some things get retrieved, some don't.

FIGURE 7.13 ● When do we forget?
Forgetting can occur at any memory stage. As we process information, we filter, alter, or lose much of it.

PRACTICE TEST

THE BASICS

13. Which of the following is NOT one of Schacter's seven sins of memory?

a. Misattribution
b. Persistence
c. Mood congruence
d. Absent-mindedness

14. The Ebbinghaus forgetting curve showed that after an initial decline, memory for new information tends to
a. increase slightly.
b. decrease noticeably.
c. decrease greatly.
d. level out.

15. The hour before sleep is a good time to memorize information because
a. our minds are clearer at night.
b. we'll dream about what we learned.
c. fewer distractions interfere with our learning.
d. we're too tired in the morning to memorize effectively.

16. Sigmund Freud believed that we block painful or unacceptable memories from consciousness, through a mechanism called
a. repression.
b. interference.
c. effortful processing.
d. blocking of recall.

THE BIG PICTURE
7D. What are three ways we forget, and how does each of these happen?

IN YOUR EVERYDAY LIFE
▪ Most people wish for a better memory. Is that true of you? Do you ever wish you were better at forgetting certain memories?

Picture questions can be found in Appendix B at the end of the book.

Answers: 13. c, 14. d, 15. c, 16. a. Answers to The Big

memory trace enduring physical changes in the brain as a memory forms.

interference the blocking of recall as old or new learning disrupts the recall of other memories.

repression in psychoanalytic theory, the basic defense mechanism that banishes from consciousness the thoughts, feelings, and memories that arouse anxiety.

Memory Construction

11 How do misinformation, imagination, and source amnesia influence our memories?

Picture yourself having this experience:

> You go to a fancy restaurant for dinner. You are seated at a table with a white tablecloth. You study the menu. You tell the server you want broiled salmon, a baked potato with sour cream, and a salad with blue cheese dressing. You also order some white wine from the wine list. A few minutes later the server returns with your salad. Later the rest of the meal arrives. You enjoy it all, except the salmon is a bit overdone.

Were I immediately to quiz you on this paragraph (adapted from Hyde, 1983), you could surely retrieve plenty of details. For example, without looking back, answer the following questions:

1. What kind of salad dressing did you order?
2. Was the tablecloth red-checked?
3. What did you order to drink?
4. Did the server give you a menu?

You were probably able to recall exactly what you ordered, and maybe even the color of the tablecloth. We do have a large capacity for storing and reproducing the little details of our daily experience. But did the server give you a menu? Not in the paragraph given. Nevertheless, many answer *Yes*. We often *construct* our memories as we encode them. We may also *alter* our memories as we withdraw them from our memory bank. Like scientists who infer a dinosaur's appearance from its remains, we infer our past from stored tidbits of information plus what we later imagined, expected, saw, and heard.

We don't just retrieve memories, we reweave them (Gilbert, 2006). Every time we "replay" a memory, we replace the original with a slightly modified version (Hardt et al., 2010). (Memory researchers call this process *reconsolidation*.) So, in a

sense, said Joseph LeDoux (2009), "Your memory is only as good as your last memory. The fewer times you use it, the more pristine it is." This means that, to some degree, "all memory is false" (Bernstein & Loftus, 2009).

So how do we interpret this in everyday life? CAN WE TRUST EYEWITNESS TES-◄ TIMONY IN COURT CASES? Let's examine some of the ways we rewrite our past.

Misinformation and Imagination Effects

In more than 200 experiments, involving more than 20,000 people, Elizabeth Loftus has shown how eyewitnesses reconstruct their memories when questioned after a crime or an accident. In one, two groups of people watched a film of a traffic accident and then answered questions about what they had seen (Loftus & Palmer, 1974). Those asked, "How fast were the cars going when they *smashed* into each other?" gave higher speed estimates than those asked, "How fast were the cars going when they *hit* each other?" A week later, when asked whether they recalled seeing any broken glass, people who had heard *smashed* were more than twice as likely to report seeing glass fragments **(FIGURE 7.14)**. In fact, the film showed no broken glass.

In many follow-up experiments, others have witnessed an event. Then they have received or not received misleading information about it. And then they have

taken a memory test. The repeated result is a **misinformation effect.** Exposed to misleading information, we tend to misremember.

Because the misinformation effect happens outside our awareness, it's nearly impossible to sift the suggested ideas out of the larger pool of real memories (Schooler et al., 1986). Perhaps you can recall describing a childhood experience to a friend, and filling in memory gaps with reasonable guesses and assumptions. We all do it, but after more retellings, those guessed details—now absorbed into our memories—may feel as real as if we had actually observed them (Roediger et al., 1993).

Just hearing a vivid retelling of an event may implant false memories. Should we be surprised that digitally altered photos produced the same result?

Leading question: "About how fast were the cars going when they *smashed* into each other?"

Depiction of actual accident

Memory construction

FIGURE 7.14 • **Memory construction** When people who had seen the film of a car accident were later asked a leading question, they recalled a more serious accident than they had witnessed. (From Loftus, 1979.)

DOONESBURY

By Garry Trudeau DOONESBURY © 1994 G. B. Trudeau. Reprinted with permission of UNIVERSAL PRESS SYNDICATE.

In one experiment, researchers altered photos from a family album to show some family members taking a hot-air balloon ride. After viewing these childhood photos three times over two weeks, half the participants "remembered" the faked experience, often in rich detail (Wade et al., 2002). The human mind comes with built-in Photoshopping software.

Another experiment falsely suggested to some Dutch university students that, as children, they had become ill after eating egg salad (Geraerts et al., 2008). After absorbing that suggestion, a significant minority were less likely to eat egg-salad sandwiches, both immediately and four months later.

Such experiments can help us understand why some people have been wrongly convicted of crimes. Of 200 people who were later proven innocent by DNA testing, 79 percent had been misjudged based on faulty eyewitness identification

© D. Hurst/Alamy

> "Memory is insubstantial. Things keep replacing it. Your batch of snapshots will both fix and ruin your memory. . . . You can't remember anything from your trip except the wretched collection of snapshots."
>
> Annie Dillard, "To Fashion a Text," 1988

(Garrett, 2008). This research also explains why "hypnotically refreshed" memories of crimes often contain errors. If the hypnotist asks leading questions ("*Did you hear loud noises?*"), witnesses may weave that false information into their memory of the event.

Even repeatedly *imagining* fake actions and events can create false memories. American and British university students were asked to imagine certain childhood events, such as breaking a window with their hand or having a skin sample removed from a finger. One in four of them later recalled the imagined event as something that had really happened (Garry et al., 1996; Mazzoni & Memon, 2003).

Misinformation and imagination effects occur partly because visualizing something and actually perceiving it activate similar brain areas (Gonsalves et al., 2004). Imagined events also later seem more familiar, and familiar things seem more real. The

more vividly we can imagine things, the more likely they are to become memories (Loftus, 2001; Porter et al., 2000).

Source Amnesia

Among the frailest parts of a memory is its source. Have you ever recognized someone but had no idea where you had met the person? Or dreamed about an event and later wondered whether it really happened? Or misrecalled how you learned about something (Henkel et al., 2000)? If so, you experienced **source amnesia**—you retained the memory of the event but not of the context in which you acquired it. Source amnesia, along with the misinformation effect, is at the heart of many false memories. Authors and songwriters sometimes suffer from it. They think an idea came from their own creative imagination, when in fact they are unintentionally plagiarizing something they earlier read or heard.

---

misinformation effect a memory that has been corrupted by misleading information.

source amnesia faulty memory for how, when, or where information was learned or imagined.

Psychologist Donald Thompson became part of his own research on memory distortion when police brought him in for questioning about a rape. Although he was a near-perfect match to the victim's memory of the rapist, Thompson had an airtight alibi. Just before the rape occurred, he was being interviewed on live TV and could not possibly have made it to the crime scene. Then it came to light that the victim had been watching the interview—ironically about face recognition—and had experienced source amnesia. She had confused her memories of Thompson with those of the rapist (Schacter, 1996).

Children's Eyewitness Recall

12 How reliable are young children's eyewitness reports, and why are reports of repressed and recovered memories so hotly debated?

Constructed memories *feel* like real memories. If memories can be sincere, yet sincerely wrong, how can jurors decide cases in which children's memories of sexual abuse are the only evidence?

Stephen Ceci (1993) thinks "it would be truly awful to ever lose sight of the enormity of child abuse." Yet Ceci and Maggie Bruck's (1993, 1995) studies have made them aware of how easily children's memories can be molded. For example, they asked 3-year-olds to show on anatomically correct dolls where a pediatrician had touched them. Of the children who had not received genital examinations, 55 percent pointed to either genital or anal areas.

In other experiments, the researchers studied the effect of suggestive interviewing techniques (Bruck & Ceci, 1999, 2004). In one study, children chose a card from a deck of possible happenings, and an adult then read the card to them. For example, "Think real hard, and tell me if this ever happened to you. Can you remember going to the hospital with a mousetrap on your finger?" In weekly interviews, the same adult repeatedly asked children to think about several real and fictitious

events. After 10 weeks of this, a new adult asked the same questions. The stunning result: 58 percent of preschoolers produced false (often vivid) stories about one or more events they had never experienced (Ceci et al., 1994). Here's one of those stories.

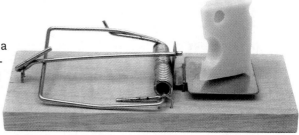
© Darren Matthews/Alamy

> My brother Colin was trying to get Blowtorch [an action figure] from me, and I wouldn't let him take it from me, so he pushed me into the wood pile where the mousetrap was. And then my finger got caught in it. And then we went to the hospital, and my mommy, daddy, and Colin drove me there, to the hospital in our van, because it was far away. And the doctor put a bandage on this finger.

Given such detailed stories, professional psychologists who specialize in interviewing children could not reliably separate the real memories from the false ones. Nor could the children themselves. The above child, reminded that his parents had told him several times that the mousetrap event never happened—that he had imagined it—protested. "But it really did happen. I remember it!"

Does this mean that children can never be accurate eyewitnesses? No—not if a neutral person asks nonleading questions soon after the event, using words the children can understand. Interviewed this way, children often accurately recall what happened and who did it (Goodman & Quas, 2008; Pipe et al., 2004).

Repressed or Constructed Memories of Abuse?

There are two tragedies related to adult recollections of childhood abuse. One happens when people don't believe abuse survivors who finally share their secret. The other happens when truly innocent people are falsely accused. What, then, shall we say about clinicians who have guided people in "recovering" memories of childhood abuse? Were these well-intentioned therapists triggering false memories that would damage innocent adults? Or were they uncovering the truth?

The research on source amnesia and the misinformation effect raises concerns

about therapist-guided recovered memories. Some therapists have reasoned with patients that "people who've been abused often have your symptoms, so you probably were abused. Let's see if, aided by hypnosis or drugs, or helped to dig back and visualize your trauma, you can recover it." Patients exposed to such techniques may then form an image of a threatening person. With rehearsal, the image grows more vivid, as it did for the little boy who came to believe he had caught his finger in a mousetrap. The patient ends up stunned, angry, and ready to confront or sue the remembered abuser. The equally stunned parent, relative, or clergy member vigorously denies the accusation.

Don Shrubshell

Elizabeth Loftus: "The research findings for which I am being honored now generated a level of hostility and opposition I could never have foreseen. People wrote threatening letters, warning me that my reputation and even my safety were in jeopardy if I continued along these lines. At some universities, armed guards were provided to accompany me during speeches." (Elizabeth Loftus, on receiving the Association for Psychological Science's William James Fellow Award, 2001.)

Critics are not questioning the professionalism of most therapists. Nor are they questioning the accusers' sincerity; even if false, their memories are heartfelt. Critics' charges are specifically directed against clinicians who use "memory work" techniques, such as "guided imagery," hypnosis, and dream analysis to recover memories. "Thousands of families were cruelly ripped apart," with "previously loving adult daughters" suddenly accusing fathers (Gardner, 2006). Irate clinicians have countered that those who argue that recovered memories of abuse never happen are adding to abused people's trauma and playing into the hands of child molesters.

> "When memories are 'recovered' after long periods of amnesia, particularly when extraordinary means were used to secure the recovery of memory, there is a high probability that the memories are false."
>
> Royal College of Psychiatrists Working Group on Reported Recovered Memories of Child Sexual Abuse (Brandon et al., 1998)

In an effort to find a sensible common ground that might resolve psychology's "memory war," professional organizations (the American Medical, American Psychological, and American Psychiatric Associations, among others) have set up study panels and issued public statements. Those committed to protecting abused children and those committed to protecting wrongly accused adults agree on the following.

- **Sexual abuse happens.** And it happens more often than we once supposed. There is no characteristic "survivor syndrome"—no group of symptoms that lets us spot victims of sexual abuse (Kendall-Tackett et al., 1993). However, sexual abuse can leave its victims at risk for problems ranging from sexual dysfunction to depression (Freyd et al., 2007).

- **Injustice happens.** Some innocent people have been falsely convicted. And some guilty people have avoided punishment by casting doubt on their truth-telling accusers.

- **Forgetting happens.** Many of those actually abused were either very young when it happened or may not have understood the meaning of their experience—circumstances under which forgetting is common. Forgetting isolated past events, both negative and positive, is an ordinary part of everyday life.

- **Recovered memories are commonplace.** Cued by a remark or an experience, we all recover memories of long-forgotten events, both pleasant and unpleasant. What many psychologists question is twofold. Does the unconscious mind *forcibly repress* painful experiences? And can these experiences be retrieved by certain therapist-aided techniques (McNally & Geraerts, 2009)? (Memories that surface naturally are more likely to be verified [Geraerts et al., 2007]).

- **Memories of things happening before age 3 are unreliable.** WHY CAN'T WE REMEMBER LEARNING TO TALK AND WALK? ◄ We cannot reliably recall happenings of any sort from our first three years. This *infantile amnesia* happens because our brain pathways are not yet developed enough to form the kinds of memories we will form later in life. Psychologists therefore doubt "recovered" memories of abuse during infancy (Gore-Felton et al., 2000; Knapp & VandeCreek, 2000). The older the child was when suffering sexual abuse, and the more severe the abuse, the more likely it is to be remembered (Goodman et al., 2003).

- **Memories "recovered" under hypnosis or under the influence of drugs are especially unreliable.** Under hypnosis, people will incorporate all kinds of suggestions into their memories, even memories of past lives.

- **Memories, whether real or false, can be emotionally upsetting.** Both the accuser and the accused may suffer when what was born of mere suggestion becomes, like an actual trauma, a stinging memory that drives bodily stress (McNally, 2003, 2007). Some people knocked unconscious in unremembered accidents know this all too well. They have developed stress disorders after being haunted by memories they constructed from photos, news reports, and friends' accounts (Bryant, 2001).

So, does repression of threatening memories ever occur? Or is this concept—the cornerstone of Freud's theory and of so much popular psychology—misleading? In Chapter 11, we will return to this hotly debated issue. For now, this much appears certain: The most common response to a traumatic experience (witnessing a loved one's murder, being terrorized by a hijacker or a rapist, losing everything and everyone in a natural disaster) is not banishing the experience into the unconscious. Rather, such experiences are typically etched on the mind as vivid, persistent, haunting memories (Porter & Peace, 2007). As Robert Kraft (2002) said of the experience of those trapped in the Nazi death camps, "Horror sears memory, leaving . . . the consuming memories of atrocity."

TODAY'S SPECIAL GUEST

BRUNDAGE MORNALD, OF BATTLE CREEK, MONTANA

UNDER HYPNOSIS, MR. MORNALD RECOVERED LONG-BURIED MEMORIES OF A PERFECTLY NORMAL, HAPPY CHILDHOOD.

18. You recognize a face in a crowd, but you can't recall how you know this person. This is an example of
    a. the misinformation effect.
    b. interference.
    c. source amnesia.
    d. repression.

19. Children may be accurate eyewitnesses if
    a. interviewers give the children hints about what really happened.
    b. a neutral person asks nonleading questions soon after the event, in words the children can understand.
    c. the children have a chance to talk with involved adults before the interview.
    d. interviewers use precise technical and medical terms.

20. Psychologists involved in the study of memories of abuse tend to DISAGREE about which of the following statements?
    a. Memories of events that happened before age 3 are not reliable.
    b. We tend to repress extremely upsetting memories.
    c. Memories can be emotionally upsetting.
    d. Sexual abuse happens.

THE BIG PICTURE

7E. What—given the commonality of source amnesia—might life be like if we remembered all our waking experiences and all our dreams?

IN YOUR EVERYDAY LIFE

▪ If you were on a jury in a trial involving recovered memories of abuse, do you think you could be impartial? Would it matter whether the defendant was a parent accused of sexual abuse, or a therapist being sued for creating a false memory?

▪ Think of a memory you frequently recall. How might you have changed it without conscious awareness?

Answers: 17. b, 18. c, 19. b, 20. b. Answers to The Big Picture questions can be found in Appendix B at the end of the book.

Improving Memory

13 How can you improve your memory so that you do better in this and other courses?

Biology's findings benefit medicine. Botany's findings benefit agriculture. CAN ◄ PSYCHOLOGY'S RESEARCH ON MEMORY BENEFIT YOUR PERFORMANCE IN CLASS AND ON TESTS? You bet! Sprinkled throughout this chapter and summarized here for easy reference are concrete suggestions that could help you remember information when you need it.

Study repeatedly. Overlearn. To learn a name, say it to yourself after being introduced. Wait a few seconds and say it again. Wait a bit longer and say it a third time. To learn a concept, give yourself many separate study sessions. Take advantage of life's little intervals— riding on the bus, walking across campus, waiting for class to start.

Space out study. Cramming just before a test produces overconfidence. Spreading out your studying over many days and weeks produces better results.

Thinking and memory: Actively thinking as we read, by rehearsing and relating ideas, and by making the material meaningful, yields the best retention.

Spend more time rehearsing or actively thinking about the material. New memories are weak; exercise them and they will strengthen. To memorize specific facts or figures, Thomas Landauer (2001) has advised us to "rehearse the name or number you are trying to memorize, wait a few seconds, rehearse again, wait a little longer, rehearse again, then wait longer still and rehearse yet again. The waits should be as long as possible without losing the information."

Make the material meaningful. You can build a network of retrieval cues by taking text and class notes in your own words. You can increase retrieval cues by forming as many associations as possible. Apply the concepts to your own life. Form images. Understand and organize information. Relate the material to what you already know or have experienced. As William James (1890) suggested, "Knit each new thing on to some acquisition already there." Restate concepts in your own words. Mindlessly repeating someone else's words won't provide such cues. On an exam, you may find yourself stuck when a question uses phrasing different from the words you memorized.

Activate retrieval cues. Mentally re-create the situation and the mood in which your original learning occurred. Return to the same location. Jog your memory by allowing one thought to cue the next.

Minimize interference. Study before sleeping. Do not schedule back-to-back study times for topics that are likely to interfere with each other, such as Spanish and French.

Sleep more. During sleep, the brain organizes and consolidates information for long-term memory. Sleep deprivation disrupts this process.

Test your own knowledge, both to rehearse it and to find out what you don't yet know. Test your learning using the Practice Tests at the end of text sections and in this book's study guide or on its Web site (www.worthpublish-ers.com/myers). But don't let your ability to recognize information fool you. Outline sections on a blank page. Try defining the terms and concepts listed at each chapter's end before turning back to their definitions.

PRACTICE TEST

THE BASICS

21. Which of the following is NOT a good suggestion for improving your memory?
    a. Cram just before a test rather than spacing out your studying.
    b. Make the material you are reading as personally meaningful as possible.
    c. Overlearn by studying repeatedly.
    d. Study in a way that reduces the interference of other topics and distractions.

THE BIG PICTURE

7F. What are the recommended memory strategies you just read about? (One advised rehearsing to-be-remembered material. What were the others?)

IN YOUR EVERYDAY LIFE

▪ Which of the study and memory strategies suggested in this section do you plan to try?

Answers: 21. a. Answers to The Big Picture questions can be found in Appendix B at the end of the book.

Terms and Concepts to Remember

memory, p. 182	rehearsal, p. 183	relearning, p. 189
encoding, p. 182	spacing effect, p. 184	retrieval cue, p. 190
storage, p. 182	serial position effect, p. 184	déjà vu, p. 191
retrieval, p. 182	implicit memory, p. 185	mood-congruent memory, p. 191
sensory memory, p. 182	explicit memory, p. 185	memory trace, p. 194
short-term memory, p. 182	imagery, p. 187	interference, p. 194
long-term memory, p. 182	long-term potentiation (LTP), p. 188	repression, p. 195
working memory, p. 182	flashbulb memory, p. 189	misinformation effect, p. 196
automatic processing, p. 183	recall, p. 189	source amnesia, p. 197
effortful processing, p. 183	recognition, p. 189	

Multiple-choice **self-tests** and more may be found at www.worthpublishers.com/myers

Studying Memory

1 **What three processes are involved in building a memory, and how do the concepts of unconscious processing and working memory update the three-stage information-processing model?**

- *Memory* is the persistence of learning over time through the *encoding, storage,* and *retrieval* of information.

- Atkinson and Shiffrin's classic three-stage model of memory: (1) We register fleeting *sensory memories;* (2) some are processed into *short-term memories;* (3) even fewer are encoded for *long-term memory* and later retrieval.

- Today's researchers note that we register much information unconsciously, bypassing the first two stages (sensory and short-term).

- The term *working memory* is better than short-term memory for describing the more active role in this second stage, where we work to connect new input with older stored memories.

2 **How do automatic and effortful processing help us encode sights, sounds, and other sensations?**

- We unconsciously and *automatically* process some types of information, such as space, time, and frequency.

- *Effortful processing,* including *rehearsal* that is *spaced* out over time, requires conscious attention and deliberate effort.

- When learning a list, our later recall is often best for items learned first, which we may have rehearsed more (the *serial position effect*).

3 **What are implicit and explicit memories, and what brain structures enable each?**

- *Explicit* (conscious) *memories* of general knowledge, facts, and experiences are processed by the hippocampus.

- *Implicit* (unconscious) *memories* of skills and conditioned responses are processed by other parts of the brain, including the cerebellum.

Building Memories

4 **What are the most common and effective ways of encoding information?**

- Effortful encoding of meaning and *imagery* improves long-term retention.

5 **What are the duration and capacity of sensory, short-term, and long-term memory?**

- We lose sensory memories almost immediately, unless those memories are further processed.

- In our short-term memory, we can focus on and process only about seven items of information. Without rehearsal, information disappears from short-term memory within seconds.

- We have an unlimited capacity for storing information permanently in long-term memory.

6 **What biological changes enable memory storage?**

- *Long-term potentiation (LTP)* involves an increase in a synapse's firing potential; this is a neural basis of learning and memory.

- Intense emotions trigger hormonal changes that arouse brain areas and can produce strong memories. Especially vivid events can form *flashbulb memories.*

7 **How do psychologists assess memory with recall, recognition, and relearning?**

- *Recall:* retrieving information we learned earlier (fill-in-the-blank test).

- *Recognition:* identifying items previously learned (multiple-choice test).

- *Relearning:* more quickly mastering material that has been previously learned.

8 **How can retrieval cues help us access stored memories, and how do contexts and moods influence retrieval?**

- *Retrieval cues,* such as context and *mood,* are information bits linked with the original encoded memory.

Forgetting

9 **What are some possible reasons for when and why we forget?**

- Encoding failure (information never enters the memory system) from absent-mindedness, transience, or blocking.
- Storage decay (encoded information is later forgotten) through mis-attribution, suggestibility, or bias; measured by a gradual fading of the *memory trace* in the brain.
- Retrieval failure (inability to access stored information), often caused by interference.

10 **How does interference cause forgetting? Do people seem to repress emotionally painful experiences?**

- Retrieval failure may be caused by *interference* from older and newer memories.
- Freud believed, but modern research does not support, the idea that we *repress* painful memories.

Memory Construction

11 **How do misinformation, imagination, and source amnesia influence our memories?**

- We construct our memories, using both stored and new information as well as our imaginations.
- *Misinformation* (exposure to misleading information) and imagination effects corrupt our stored memories of what actually happened. *Source amnesia* leads to faulty memories of how, when, or where we learned something.

12 **How reliable are young children's eyewitness reports, and why are reports of repressed and recovered memories so hotly debated?**

- Children's eyewitness reports are subject to the same memory influences that distort adult reports.
- Incest and abuse happen more than was once supposed. But unless the victim was a child too young to remember, such traumas are usually remembered vividly, not repressed.

Improving Memory

13 **How can you improve your memory so that you do better in this and other courses?**

- Study repeatedly.
- Schedule spaced (not crammed) study times.
- Actively rehearse information to be learned.
- Make well-organized, vivid, and personally meaningful associations.
- Return to contexts and moods that are rich with association.
- Minimize interference.
- Plan for a complete night's sleep.
- Self-test to rehearse information and find gaps in your memory.

8

THINKING, LANGUAGE, AND INTELLIGENCE

We have studied the human brain—three pounds of wet tissue the size of a small cabbage, yet containing circuitry more complex than the planet's telephone networks. From this complex circuitry emerge two images—the rational and competent human, and the irrational and error-prone human.

We saw the thoughtful and competent human take form in the amazing abilities of newborns. We relished the power of the human sensory system, translating light and shapes into clear and colorful perceived images. We assessed our memory's almost unlimited capacity and the ease with which our two-track mind processes information, with and without awareness. Little wonder that our species has had the collective genius to invent the camera, the car, and the computer; to unlock the atom and crack the genetic code; to travel out to space and into the oceans' depths.

Yet we have also seen that our species is kin to the other animals, influenced by the same principles that produce learning in rats and pigeons. We have noted that we not-so-wise humans are easily fooled by perceptual illusions, fake psychic claims, and false memories.

In this chapter, we find more examples of these two images—the rational and the irrational human. We will consider how our active brain uses and misuses the information it receives, perceives, stores, and retrieves. We will look at our flair for language. And we will reflect on how deserving we are of the meaning of our species' name, *Homo sapiens*—wise human.

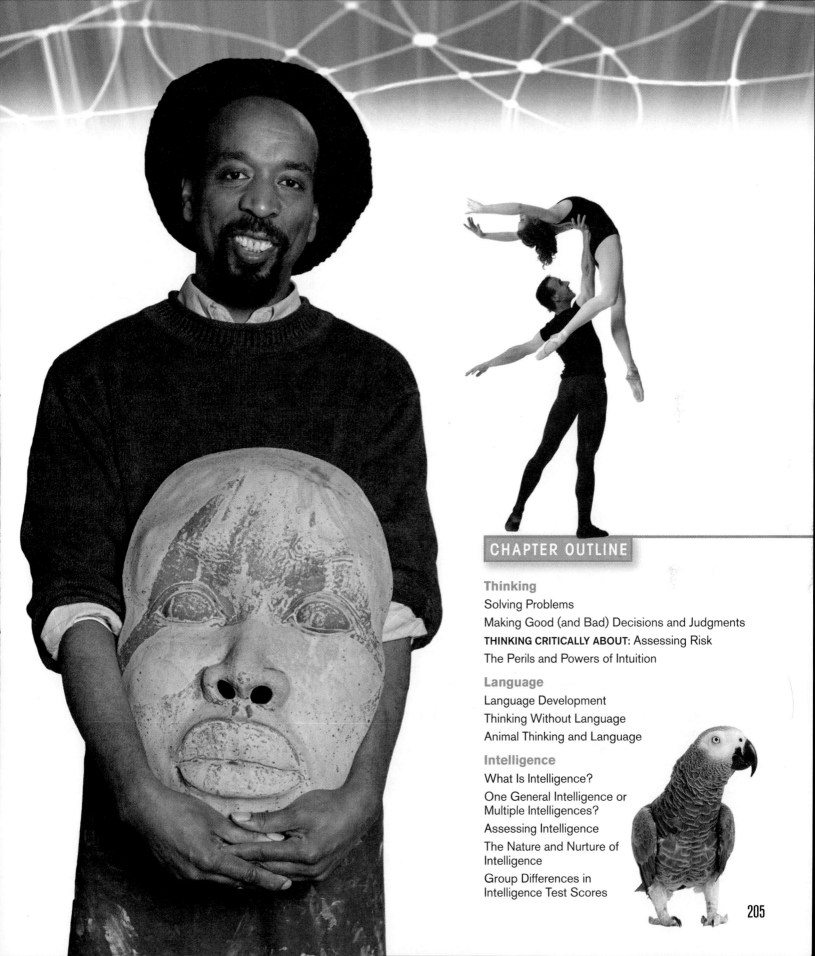

Thinking

Psychologists who study **cognition** focus on the mental activities associated with thinking, knowing, remembering, and communicating information. Among these activities are the ways we solve problems, make decisions, form judgments, and assess risk.

Solving Problems

1 What are some cognitive strategies we use to solve problems?

One tribute to our rationality is our impressive skill in solving problems and coping with new situations. What's the best route around this traffic jam? How should we handle a friend's criticism? How can we get in the house without our keys?

Some problems we solve through *trial and error*. Thomas Edison tried thousands of light bulb filaments before stumbling upon one that worked. For other problems, we use **algorithms,** step-by-step procedures that guarantee a solution. But following the steps in an algorithm takes time and effort—sometimes a lot of time and effort. To find a word using the 10 letters in *SPLOYOCHYG*, for example, you could construct a list, with each letter in each of the 10 positions. But your list of 907,200 different combinations would be very long! In such cases, we often resort to **heuristics,** simpler thinking strategies. Thus, you might reduce the number of options in the *SPLOYOCHYG* example by grouping letters that often appear together (*CH* and *GY*) and avoiding rare combinations (such as *YY*). By using heuristics and then applying trial and error, you may hit on the answer. Have you guessed it?[1]

Sometimes we puzzle over a problem, and suddenly the pieces fall together in a flash of **insight.** (Such sudden *Aha!* moments are the result of a series of

Halfdark/Jupiterimages

brain states that can be measured in the laboratory [Kounios & Beeman, 2009].) Ten-year-old Johnny Appleton's insight solved a problem that had stumped many adults: how to rescue a young robin that had fallen into a narrow, 30-inch-deep hole in a cement-block wall. Johnny's solution: slowly pour in sand, giving the bird enough time to keep its feet on top of the constantly rising mound (Ruchlis, 1990).

Teams of researchers have identified brain activity associated with sudden flashes of insight (Jung-Beeman et al., 2004; Sandkühler & Bhattacharya, 2008). They gave people a problem: Think of a word that will form a compound word or phrase with each of three words in a set (such as *pine, crab,* and *sauce*), and press a button to sound a bell when you know the answer. (If you need a hint: The word is a fruit.[2]) To see what brain activity enables insight, the researchers mapped the problem solver's brain activity, using fMRIs (functional MRIs) or EEGs. In the first experiment, about half the solutions were by a sudden Aha! insight. Before the Aha! moment, their frontal lobes (which are involved in focusing attention) were active. There was also a burst of activity in their right temporal lobe, just above the ear (**FIGURE 8.1**).

Insight gives us a sense of satisfaction, a feeling of happiness. The joy of a joke is similarly a sudden "I get it!" reaction to a surprise ending or a double meaning. See for yourself, with these two jokes rated funniest (among 2 million ratings of 40,000 submitted jokes) in an Internet humor study (Wiseman, 2002). First, the runner-up.

> Sherlock Holmes and Dr. Watson are going camping. They pitch their tent under the stars and go to sleep. Sometime in the middle of the night Holmes awakens Watson.
>
> *Holmes:* "Watson, look up at the stars, and tell me what you deduce."

FIGURE 8.1 ● **The Aha! moment** A burst of right temporal lobe activity accompanies insight solutions to word problems (Jung-Beeman et al., 2004).

From Mark Jung-Beekman, Northwestern University, and John Kounios, Drexel University

> *Watson:* "I see millions of stars and even if a few of those have planets, it's quite likely there are some planets like Earth, and if there are a few planets like Earth out there, there might also be life. What does it tell you, Holmes?"
>
> *Holmes:* "Watson, you idiot, somebody has stolen our tent!"

And drum roll, please, for the winner.

> A couple of New Jersey hunters are out in the woods when one of them falls to the ground. He doesn't seem to be breathing, his eyes are rolled back in his head. The other guy whips out his cell phone and calls the emergency services. He gasps to the operator: "My friend is dead! What can I do?" The operator, in a calm, soothing voice, says: "Just take it easy. I can help. First, let's make sure he's dead." There is a silence, then a shot is heard. The guy's voice comes back on the line: "OK, now what?"

Making Good (and Bad) Decisions and Judgments

2 What obstacles hinder smart thinking?

Each day holds hundreds of judgments and decisions. Is it worth the bother to take an umbrella? Can I trust this person?

---

1. Answer to SPLOYOCHYG problem: PSYCHOLOGY

2. The word is *apple*: pineapple, crabapple, applesauce.

Should I shoot the basketball or pass to the player who's hot? As we judge the odds and make our decisions, we seldom take the time and effort to reason systematically. We just follow our *intuition,* our fast, automatic, unreasoned feelings and thoughts. After interviewing leaders in government, business, and education, one social psychologist concluded that these leaders "often do not use a reflective problem-solving approach. How do they usually arrive at their decisions? If you ask, they are likely to tell you . . . they do it mostly by *the seat of their pants*" (Janis, 1986).

Quick-Thinking Heuristics

When we need to act quickly, those mental shortcuts we call *heuristics* often do help us overcome analysis paralysis. Without awareness, we make automatic intuitive judgments. But cognitive psychologists Amos Tversky and Daniel Kahneman (1974) showed how these shortcuts can lead even the smartest people into quick but dumb judgments. Consider the **availability heuristic,** which operates when we base our judgments on how quickly and easily an event comes to mind. The faster we can remember an instance of some event (a broken promise, for example), the more we expect it to happen again (MacLeod & Campbell, 1992). Mentally

"*The problem is I can't tell the difference between a deeply wise, intuitive nudge from the Universe and one of my own bone-headed ideas!*"

"In creating these problems, we didn't set out to fool people. All our problems fooled us, too." (Amos Tversky, 1985)

"Intuitive thinking [is] fine most of the time. . . . But sometimes that habit of mind gets us in trouble." (Nobel laureate Daniel Kahneman, 2005)

available events *are* more likely to repeat—but not always. To see this, try answering this question: Does the letter *k* appear more often as the first or third letter in English words?

Did you guess that *k* occurs more frequently as the first letter? Most people do, because words beginning with *k* come to mind more easily than words having *k* as their third letter. Actually, *k* appears more often as the third letter. So far in this chapter, words such as *know, kingdom,* and *kin* are outnumbered 20 to 4 by words such as *make, likely, asked,* and *acknowledged.*

The availability heuristic can lead us astray in our judgments of other people, too. Anything that makes information "pop" into mind—its vividness, recency, or distinctiveness—can make it more available to our memory. If someone from a particular ethnic group commits a terrorist act, as happened on September 11, 2001, our readily available memory of the dramatic event may shape our impression of the whole group. At such times, we may ignore statistical reality: Numbers can be numbing. We remember vivid images, and those images often distort our judgment of risks and probable outcomes (see Thinking Critically About: Assessing Risk on the next page).

Sometimes heuristics can lead to **fixation**—an inability to see a problem

from a fresh perspective. Once we get hung up on an incorrect view of a problem, it's hard to approach it from a different angle. If you can't solve the matchstick problem in **FIGURE 8.2**, you may be experiencing fixation. (Turn the page to see the solution in **FIGURE 8.4**.)

FIGURE 8.2 ● **The matchstick problem** How would you arrange six matches to form four equilateral triangles?

From "Problem Solving" by M. Scheerer. Copyright © 1963 by Scientific American, Inc. All Rights Reserved.

cognition the mental activities associated with thinking, knowing, remembering, and communicating.

algorithm a methodical, logical rule or procedure that guarantees you will solve a particular problem. Contrasts with the usually speedier—but also more error-prone—use of *heuristics*.

heuristics simple thinking strategies that often allow us to make judgments and solve problems efficiently; usually speedier but also more error-prone than *algorithms*.

insight a sudden realization of the solution to a problem; it contrasts with strategy-based solutions.

availability heuristic estimating the likelihood of an event based on its availability in memory; if instances come readily to mind (perhaps because of their vividness), we assume such events are common.

fixation the inability to see a problem from a new perspective; an obstacle to problem solving.

THINKING CRITICALLY ABOUT

Assessing Risk

Lars Christensen/Shutterstock

3 **How can we improve our risk assessment?**

Why do we fear the wrong things? Can you guess how many Americans (questioned in a 2006 Gallup survey) said they were "not afraid at all" to fly? Only 40 percent chose this answer. Yet mile for mile, those same Americans were 170 times more likely to die in an automobile or pickup truck crash than on a scheduled flight in the years 2005 to 2007 (National Safety Council, 2010). Why do we judge terrorism to be a greater risk than accidents?

In a late 2001 essay, I calculated that if—because of 9/11—we flew 20 percent less and instead drove half those unflown miles, about 800 more people would die in the next year (Myers, 2001). German psychologist Gerd Gigerenzer (2004, 2006) later checked this estimate against actual accident data. (*Why didn't I think of that?*) U.S. traffic deaths did indeed increase significantly in the last three months of 2001 (**FIGURE 8.3**). By the end of 2002, Gigerenzer estimated, 1600 Americans had "lost their lives on the road by trying to avoid the risk of flying." Long after 9/11, the dead terrorists were still killing Americans by sending them back to their cars.

From 2002 to 2005, air travel gradually recovered. Some 2.5 billion passengers flew on U.S. commercial flights. Of those on a major airline, none died (McMurray, 2006; Miller, 2005). Meanwhile, traffic accidents claimed 172,000 American lives. For most people, flying's greatest danger is the drive to the airport.

How can our intuition about risk be so wrong? Psychologists have identified four forces that can feed fear and cause us to ignore higher risks.

© Transtock/Corbis

1. *We fear what our ancestral history has prepared us to fear.* Human emotions were road-tested in the Stone Age. Our old brain prepares us to fear yesterday's risks: snakes, lizards, and spiders (which combined now kill a tiny fraction of the number killed by modern-day threats, such as cars and cigarettes). Yesterday's risks also prepare us to fear confinement and heights, and therefore flying.

2. *We fear what we cannot control.* Driving we control; flying we do not.

3. *We fear what is immediate.* The dangers of flying are mostly squeezed into the moments of takeoff and landing. The dangers of driving are spread across many moments to come, each trivially dangerous.

4. Thanks to the availability heuristic, *we fear what is most readily available in memory.* We remember vivid images, like that of United Flight 175 slicing into the World Trade Center. Vivid images form powerful, available memories that serve as a measuring tape as we intuitively judge risks. Thousands of car trips lull us into a comfortable safe feeling. Similarly, we remember (and fear) widespread disasters—hurricanes, earthquakes—that kill people dramatically, in bunches. But we fear too little the less dramatic threats that claim lives quietly, one by one, and in the distant future. Bill Gates has noted that each year a half-million children worldwide die from rotavirus. This is the equivalent of four 747s full of children crashing *every day,* and we hear nothing of it (Glass, 2004). Dramatic outcomes capture our attention; probabilities don't.

As one risk analyst explained, "If it's in the news, don't worry about it. The very definition of *news* is 'something that hardly ever happens'" (Schneier, 2007). But the news, and our own memorable experiences, can make us fear the least likely events. Although many people fear dying in a terrorist attack on an airplane, the last decade produced one terrorist attempt for every 10.4 million flights—less than one-twentieth the chance of your being struck by lightning (Silver, 2009).

The point to remember: Critical thinkers—smart thinkers—will check their fears against the facts and resist those who try to lead us to fear the wrong things.

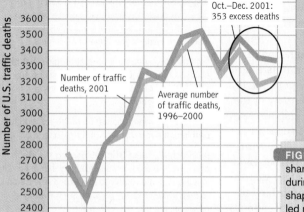

FIGURE 8.3 ● **Scaring us onto deadly highways** Images of 9/11 etched a sharper image in our minds than did the millions of fatality-free flights on U.S. airlines during 2002 and after. Dramatic events are readily available to memory, and they shape our perceptions of risk. In the three months after 9/11, those faulty perceptions led more people to travel, and some to die, by car. (Adapted from Gigerenzer, 2004.)

Confirmation Bias

HAVE YOU EVER HAD AN ARGUMENT WITH ◄ SOMEONE AND SEARCHED FOR EVIDENCE TO SUPPORT YOUR VIEWS? We all seek evidence for our ideas more eagerly than we seek evidence *against* them (Klayman & Ha, 1987; Skov & Sherman, 1986). This tendency is **confirmation bias,** as Peter Wason (1960) demonstrated in a now-classic study. He gave students a set of three numbers (2-4-6) and told them the sequence was based on a rule. Their task was to guess the rule. (It was simple: Each number must be larger than the one before it.) Before giving their answers, students formed their own three-number sets, and Wason told them whether their sets worked with his rule. Once they felt *certain* they had the rule, they were to announce it. The result? They were seldom right but never in doubt. Most students formed a wrong idea ("Maybe it's counting by twos") and then searched only for evidence confirming the wrong rule (by testing 6-8-10, 100-102-104, and so forth).

In real-life disagreements, said Wason (1981), "ordinary people evade facts, become inconsistent, or systematically defend themselves against the threat of new information." The process can have grave results. The U.S. war against Iraq was launched on the belief that the late Saddam Hussein was hiding weapons of mass destruction (WMDs). That belief turned out to be false. When a U.S. Senate committee (with members from both political parties) investigated, they found flaws in the judgment process, including confirmation bias (U.S. Senate Select Committee on Intelligence, 2004). Administration analysts "had a tendency to accept information which supported [their beliefs] . . . more readily than information which contradicted" them. Sources denying such weapons were viewed to be "either lying or not knowledgeable about Iraq's problems, while those sources who reported ongoing WMD activities were seen as having provided valuable information."

Overconfidence: Was There Ever Any Doubt?

Using heuristics and seeking confirmation often leads to **overconfidence.** We overestimate the accuracy of our beliefs and decisions. Often, however, we're more confident than correct. When answering such questions as, "Is absinthe a liqueur or a precious stone?" only 60 percent of people in one study answered correctly. (It's a licorice-flavored liqueur.) Yet those answering felt, on average, 75 percent confident. Even those who felt 100 percent certain of their answer were wrong about 15 percent of the time (Fischhoff et al., 1977).

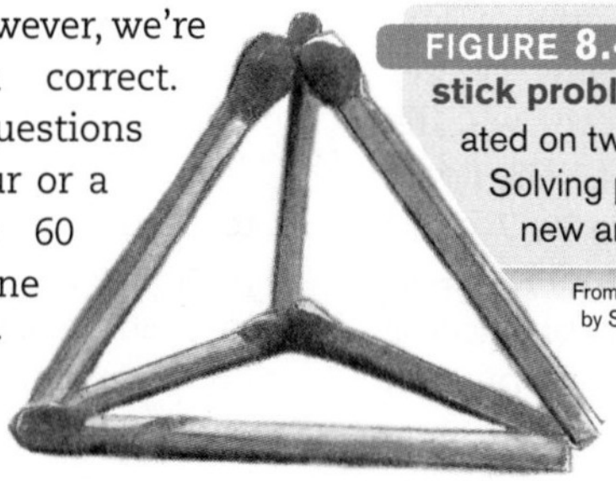

History is full of leaders who were more confident than correct. It was an overconfident Lyndon Johnson who waged war with North Vietnam and an overconfident George W. Bush who marched into Iraq to save us from supposed weapons of mass destruction. And classrooms are full of overconfident students who expect to finish assignments and write papers ahead of schedule (Buehler et al., 1994). In fact, the projects generally take about twice the number of days predicted.

We tend to overestimate our future free time (Zauberman & Lynch, 2005). Thinking we will have more free time next month than we do today, we happily accept invitations, only to discover we're just as busy when the day rolls around. When taking out loans or credit debt, we may also overestimate our future money. Despite our painfully wrong estimates, we remain overly confident of our next prediction.

Overconfidence can have adaptive value. Believing that their decisions are right and they have time to spare, self-confident people live more happily. They make tough decisions more easily, and they seem more believable than others (Baumeister, 1989; Taylor, 1989).

Moreover, we can learn from our mistakes. When given prompt and clear feedback—as weather forecasters receive after each day's predictions—we learn to be more realistic about the accuracy of our judgments (Fischhoff, 1982). The wisdom to know when we know a thing and when we do not is born of experience.

Framing: Let Me Put It This Way . . .

Framing is the way we present an issue, and its effects can be striking. Imagine two surgeons explaining the risk of surgery in two different but equally logical ways. One tells patients that 10 percent of people will die during this surgery. The other tells patients that 90 percent will

FIGURE 8.4 ● **Solution to the matchstick problem** Were you, by chance, fixated on two-dimensional solutions? Solving problems often requires taking a new angle on the situation.

From "Problem Solving" by M. Scheerer. Copyright © 1963 by Scientific American, Inc. All Rights Reserved.

Bianca Moscatelli/Worth Publishers

Predict your own behavior: When will you finish reading this chapter?

confirmation bias a tendency to search for information that supports our preconceptions and to ignore or distort evidence that contradicts them.

overconfidence the tendency to be more confident than correct—to overestimate the accuracy of our beliefs and judgments.

framing the way an issue is posed; framing can significantly affect decisions and judgments.

survive. In surveys, both patients and physicians said the risk seems greater when they hear that 10 percent will die (Marteau, 1989; McNeil et al., 1988; Rothman & Salovey, 1997). Similarly, 9 in 10 college students rated a condom as effective if told it has a "95 percent success rate" in stopping the HIV virus. Only 4 in 10 judged it effective when told it has a "5 percent failure rate" (Linville et al., 1992).

Framing can be a powerful tool of persuasion for people who want you to share their viewpoint. For example, politicians may frame their position on public assistance as "aid to the needy" if for it and "welfare" if not. People told that a chemical exposure will kill 10 of every 10 million people (imagine 10 dead people!) feel more frightened than if told the fatality risk is a mere 0.000001 (Kraus et al., 1992).

Retailers understand the power of framing. They may mark up their "regular prices" to appear to offer huge savings on "sale prices." A $100 coat marked down from $150 by Store X can seem like a better deal than the same coat priced regularly at $100 by Store Y (Urbany et al., 1988). Try it yourself. WHICH SOUNDS◄ MORE TEMPTING, A HAMBURGER THAT IS "75 PERCENT LEAN" OR "25 PERCENT FAT"? Would you feel better about receiving a discount for paying cash or being charged a fee for using your credit card? The price difference is the same. The effect is not (Levin & Gaeth, 1988; Sanford et al., 2002).

Framing has also been used to nudge people toward decisions that benefit them or society (Thaler & Sunstein, 2008).

- *Why choosing to be an organ donor depends on where you live.* In many European countries as well as in the United States, people can decide whether they want to be organ donors when renewing their driver's license. In some countries, the default option is *yes*, but people can "opt out." Nearly 100 percent of the people in the opt-out countries agree to be donors. In the United States, Britain, and Germany, the default option has been *no*, but people can "opt in." In those countries, only about 25 percent agree to be donors (Johnson & Goldstein, 2003).

- *How to help employees decide to save for their retirement.* A 2006 U.S. pension law recognized the framing effect. Before that law, employees who wanted to contribute to a 401(k) retirement plan typically had to choose a lower take-home pay, which few people will do. Companies can now automatically enroll people in the plan but allow them to opt out (which would raise the employee's take-home pay). In both plans, the decision to contribute is the employee's. But under the new opt-out arrangement, enrollments soared from 49 to 86 percent (Madrian & Shea, 2001).

The point to remember: Those who understand the power of framing can use it to influence our decisions.

Our Beliefs Live On—Despite the Evidence

That our judgments can flip-flop dramatically is startling. Equally startling is our unwillingness to give up our beliefs even when the evidence proves us wrong. **Belief perseverance** often fuels social conflict, as it did in one study of people with opposing views of the death penalty (Lord et al., 1979). Both sides were asked to read the same material—two reports on new research. One report showed that the death penalty lowers the crime rate. The other report showed that the death penalty has no effect on the crime rate. Were people's views changed by reading these studies? Not a bit. Each side was very impressed by the study supporting its own beliefs, and each was quick to criticize the other study. Thus, showing the two groups the *same* mixed evidence actually *increased* their disagreement about the value of capital punishment.

So how can we avoid belief perseverance? A simple remedy is to *consider the opposite*. In a repeat of the death penalty study, researchers asked some participants to be "as *objective* and *unbiased* as possible" (Lord et al., 1984). This plea did nothing to reduce people's biases in judging the evidence. They also asked another group to consider "whether you would have made the same high or low evaluations had exactly the same study

produced results on the *other* side of the issue." In this group, people's views did change. After imagining the *opposite* findings, they judged the evidence in a much less biased way.

The more we come to appreciate why our beliefs might be true, the more tightly we cling to them. Once we have explained to ourselves why we believe a child is "gifted" or "learning disabled," or why candidate X or Y will be more likely to help working folks, we tend to ignore evidence that challenges our belief. Prejudice persists. Once beliefs form and get justified, it takes more compelling evidence to change them than it did to create them.

The Perils and Powers of Intuition

4 When is intuition useful?

We have seen how our unreasoned thinking can plague our efforts to solve problems, to assess risks, and to make wise decisions and form valid judgments. Moreover, these perils of intuition persist. They appear even when people are offered extra pay for thinking smart, even when they are asked to justify their answers, and even when they are expert physicians or clinicians (Shafir & LeBoeuf, 2002). Should we then conclude that we fail to live up to our species' name, *Homo sapiens* (wise human)?

Let's not abandon hope for our species so easily. Throughout this book, you have also seen intuition's powers. Here is a summary of some of the high points (see also **TABLE 8.1**).

- *Intuition is huge.* More than we realize, thinking occurs off-screen, with the results occasionally displayed on-screen.

- *Intuition is adaptive.* Our instant, intuitive reactions enable us to react quickly. Our fast and frugal heuristics, for example, enable us to intuitively assume that fuzzy-looking objects are far away—which they usually are, except on foggy mornings. Our learned associations surface as gut feelings—

TABLE 8.1	Comparing Cognitive Processes and Strategies		
Process or Strategy	**Description**	**Powers**	**Perils**
Algorithm	Methodical rule or procedure	Guarantees solution	Requires time and effort
Intuition	Fast, automatic, unthinking feelings and thoughts; includes insight, heuristics, and other forms of unconscious processing	Is based on our experience; huge and adaptive	Can lead us to overfeel and underthink
Insight	Sudden Aha! reaction	Provides instant realization of solution	May not happen
Heuristics	Simple thinking shortcuts, such as the *availability heuristic,* which estimates likelihood based on how easily events come to mind	Lets us act quickly and efficiently	Puts us at risk for errors
Fixation	Inability to view problems from a new angle	Focuses thinking	Hinders creative problem solving
Confirmation bias	Tendency to search for support for our own views and ignore contradictory evidence	Lets us quickly recognize supporting evidence	Hinders recognition of contradictory evidence
Overconfidence	Overestimating the accuracy of our beliefs and judgments	Allows us to be happy and to make decisions easily	Puts us at risk for errors
Framing	Wording a question or statement so that it evokes a desired response	Can influence others' decisions	Can produce a misleading result
Belief perseverance	Ignoring evidence that proves our beliefs are wrong	Supports our enduring beliefs	Closes our minds to new ideas

the intuitions of our two-track mind. If a stranger looks like someone who previously harmed or threatened us, we may—without consciously recalling the earlier experience—react warily.

- *Intuition is recognition born of experience.* We see this in chess masters playing "blitz chess," where every move is made after barely more than a glance. They can look at a board and intuitively know the right move (Burns, 2004). We see it in experienced nurses, firefighters, art critics, car mechanics, and hockey players. And in you, too, for anything in which you have developed a deep and special strength. In each case, what feels like instant intuition is a speedy use of expert skill and knowledge. As Nobel laureate psychologist-economist Herbert Simon (2001) observed, intuition is analysis "frozen into habit."

- *Intuition can sometimes be perilous, guiding us in the wrong direction.* This is especially so when we overfeel and underthink, as we do when judging risks. Today's psychological science enhances our appreciation for intuition. But it also reminds us to check

Intuition is recognition born of experience.

belief perseverance clinging to beliefs and ignoring evidence that proves they are wrong.

our intuitions against reality. Our two-track mind makes sweet harmony as smart, critical thinking listens to the creative whispers of our vast unseen mind. Together, they help us judge evidence, test conclusions, and plan for the future. At its best, intuition feeds our expertise, our creativity, our love, and our spirituality.

PRACTICE TEST

THE BASICS

1. The most systematic procedure for solving a problem is
   a. a heuristic.
   b. an algorithm.
   c. insight.
   d. intuition.

2. A major obstacle to problem solving is fixation, which is
   a. a tendency to base our judgments on vivid memories.
   b. the art of framing the same question in two different ways.
   c. an inability to view a problem from a new perspective.
   d. the tendency to overestimate the accuracy of our own beliefs and judgments.

3. Flying home for the holidays, Jill's brother was on a plane that had to make an emergency landing when an engine caught fire. Jill now thinks she'll be safer if she drives to her family's Thanksgiving gathering. Her decision was influenced by
   a. belief perseverance.
   b. the availability heuristic.
   c. insight.
   d. confirmation bias.

4. Politicians know that the way an issue is presented can affect our decisions and judgments. They understand the power of
   a. belief perseverance.
   b. fixation.
   c. confirmation bias.
   d. framing.

THE BIG PICTURE

8A. The availability heuristic is a quick-and-easy but sometimes misleading guide to judging reality. What is the availability heuristic?

IN YOUR EVERYDAY LIFE

- What are the things you fear? Are some of those fears out of proportion to statistical risk? Are there other areas of your life where you need to take more precautions?

- Can you recall a time when contradictory information challenged one of your views? Was it hard for you to consider the opposite view? Did you change your mind?

Answers: 1. b, 2. c, 3. b, 4. d. Answers to The Big Picture questions can be found in Appendix B at the end of the book.

Language

Imagine an alien species that could pass thoughts from one head to another merely by setting air molecules in motion between them. Perhaps these weird creatures, with their wireless mind-to-mind communication, could star in a future Spielberg movie? Actually, we are those creatures! When we speak, we send air pressure waves banging against other people's eardrums as we transfer thoughts from our brain into theirs. As Steven Pinker (1998) noted, we sometimes sit for hours "listening to other people make noise as they exhale, because those hisses and squeaks contain *information*." And thanks to all those funny sounds created from the air pressure waves we send out, we get people's attention and we get them to do things (Guerin, 2003). Depending on how you vibrate the air after opening your mouth, you may get slapped or kissed.

Language—our spoken, written, or signed words and the ways we combine them as we think and communicate—is the most obvious indication of our thinking power. When our capacity for language evolved, our species took a giant step forward (Diamond, 1989). With language, we humans can transmit civilization's knowledge from one generation to the next. Many animals know only what they see. Thanks to language, we know much that we've never seen.

Language also connects us. If you were able to retain one cognitive ability,

what would it be? Without sight or hearing, you could still have friends, family, and a job. But without language, could you have these things? "Language is so fundamental to our experience, so deeply a part of being human, that it's hard to imagine life without it" (Boroditsky, 2009).

Language Development

Make a quick guess: How many words did you learn during the years between your first birthday and your high school graduation? Ready? Although you use only 150 words for about half of what you say, you probably learned about 60,000 words in your native language during those years (Bloom, 2000; McMurray, 2007). That averages nearly 3500 words each year, or nearly 10 each day! How you did it—how the 3500 words could so far outnumber the roughly 200 words your schoolteachers consciously taught you each year—is one of the great human wonders.

Could you even now state all your language's rules of *syntax* (the correct way to string words together to form sentences)? Most of us cannot. Yet, before you were able to add 2 + 2, you were creating your own original sentences and applying these rules. As a preschooler, your ability to understand and speak your language was so great it would put to shame high schoolers struggling to learn a foreign language.

We humans have an astonishing knack for language. Without blinking, we sample tens of thousands of words in our memory, effortlessly combine them with near-perfect syntax, and spew them out three words a second (Vigliocco & Hartsuiker, 2002). Seldom do we form sentences in our minds before speaking them. Rather, they organize themselves on the fly as we speak. We also fine-tune our language to our social and cultural setting, following rules for speaking (*How far apart should we stand?*) and listening (*Is it OK to interrupt?*). Given how many ways there are to mess up, it's amazing that we effortlessly master this social dance. So, when and how does it happen?

When Do We Learn Language?

5 What stages do young children move through as they begin to develop language?

TABLE 8.2	Summary of Language Development
Month (approximate)	**Stage**
4	Babbles many speech sounds ("ah-goo").
10	Babbling resembles household language ("ma-ma").
12	One-word stage ("Kitty!").
24	Two-word speech ("Get ball.").
24+	Language develops rapidly into complete sentences.

Children's language development moves from simplicity to complexity. Infants start without language (*in fantis* means "not speaking"). Yet by 4 months of age, babies can recognize differences in speech sounds (Stager & Werker, 1997). They can also read lips. They prefer to look at a face that matches a sound, so we know they can recognize that *ah* comes from wide open lips and *ee* from a mouth with corners pulled back (Kuhl & Meltzoff, 1982). This marks the beginning of the development of babies' *receptive language,* their ability to understand what is said to and about them. Babies' *productive language,* their ability to produce words, matures after their receptive language.

Around 4 months of age, babies enter a **babbling stage** in which they seem to sample all the sounds they can make, such as *ah-goo.* Babbling is not an imitation of adult speech. We know this because babbling includes sounds from various languages, including those not spoken in the household. From this early babbling, a listener could not identify an infant as being, say, French, Korean, or Ethiopian.

By the time infants are about 10 months old, their babbling has changed so that a trained ear can identify the language of the household (de Boysson-Bardies et al., 1989). **DO DEAF INFANTS BABBLE IN SIGN LANGUAGE?** They do, and those who observe their parents' fluent signing begin to babble more with their hands (Petitto & Marentette, 1991).

Without exposure to other languages, babies lose their ability to hear and produce sounds and tones found outside their native language (Pallier et al., 2001). Thus, by adulthood those who speak only English cannot discriminate certain sounds in Japanese

Scott Hancock/Getty Images

speech. Nor can Japanese adults with no training in English hear the difference between the English *r* and *l.* For a Japanese-speaking adult, *la-la-ra-ra* may sound like the same syllable repeated. This can make life challenging if the Japanese speaker is told that a train station is "just after the next light." The next what? After the street veering right, or farther down, after the traffic light?

Around their first birthday, most children enter the **one-word stage.** They already know that sounds carry meanings. They now begin to use sounds—usually only one barely recognizable syllable, such as *ma* or *da*—to communicate meaning. But family members quickly learn to understand, and gradually the infant's language sounds more like the family's language. Across the world, baby's first words are often nouns that label objects or people (Tardif et al., 2008). At this one-word stage, a single word ("Doggy!") may equal a sentence ("Look at the dog out there!").

At about 18 months, children's word learning explodes, jumping from about a word each week to a word each day. By their second birthday, most have entered the **two-word stage (TABLE 8.2).** They start uttering two-word sentences in **telegraphic speech.** Like today's text messages or yesterday's telegrams that charged by

"Got idea. Talk better. Combine words. Make sentences."

© 1994 by Sidney Harris.

the word (TERMS ACCEPTED. SEND MONEY.), a 2-year-old's speech contains mostly nouns and verbs (*Want juice*). Also like telegrams, it follows rules of syntax: The words are in a sensible order.

language our spoken, written, or signed words and the ways we combine them to communicate meaning.

babbling stage beginning at about 4 months, the stage of speech development in which the infant spontaneously utters various sounds at first unrelated to the household language.

one-word stage the stage in speech development, from about age 1 to 2, during which a child speaks mostly in single words.

two-word stage beginning about age 2, the stage in speech development during which a child speaks mostly two-word statements.

telegraphic speech early speech stage in which a child speaks like a telegram—"go car"—using mostly nouns and verbs.

English-speaking children typically place adjectives before nouns—*white house* rather than *house white*. Spanish reverses this order, as in *casa blanca*.

Moving out of the two-word stage, children quickly begin speaking in longer phrases (Fromkin & Rodman, 1983). What might happen if they got a late start on learning a particular language, perhaps after surgery to enable hearing, or after being adopted by a family in another country? For these children, language development follows the same sequence, but the pace is often faster (Ertmer et al., 2007; Snedeker et al., 2007). (But stay tuned. As you will see next, there is a limit on how long language learning can be delayed.)

By early elementary school, children understand complex sentences. They can enjoy a joke with a double meaning: "You never starve in the desert because of all the sand-which-is there."

How Do We Learn Grammar?

6 How do children acquire grammar, and when is the best time to master a language?

Linguist Noam Chomsky has argued that all languages share a *universal grammar*. Thus, all human languages have the same grammatical building blocks, such as nouns, verbs, and adjectives. Moreover, said Chomsky, we humans are born with a built-in readiness—a predisposition—to learn grammar rules. This predisposition helps explain why preschoolers pick up language so readily and use grammar so well. It happens so naturally—as naturally as birds learn to fly—that training hardly helps. Once again, we see biology and experience working together.

We are not, however, born with a built-in *specific* language. Babies born in Mexico learn to speak Spanish, not Chinese. We learn readily the specific grammar of the language we experience, whether it is spoken or signed (Bavelier et al., 2003). No matter what that language is, we start speaking mostly in nouns (*kitty, da-da*) rather than verbs and adjectives (Bornstein et al., 2004).

Creating a language: Young deaf children in Nicaragua were brought together as if on a desert island (actually a school). They drew upon sign gestures from their own home to create their own Nicaraguan Sign Language, complete with words and intricate grammar. Our biological predisposition for language does not create language in a vacuum. But activated by a social context, nature and nurture work creatively together (Osborne, 1999; Sandler et al., 2005; Senghas & Coppola, 2001).

Susan Meiselas/Magnum Photos

In *The Fragile Species* (1992), Lewis Thomas observed, "Childhood is the time for language, no doubt about it. Young children, the younger the better, are good at it; it is child's play. It is a onetime gift to the species." Childhood seems to represent a *critical period* for mastering certain aspects of language (Hernandez & Li, 2007). Deaf children who gain hearing with *cochlear implants* by age 2 develop better oral speech than do those who receive implants after age 4 (Greers, 2004). For deaf or hearing children, later-than-usual exposure to language—at age 2 or 3—unleashes their brain's idle language capacity, producing a rush of language. But there is no similar rush of learning if children are not exposed to either a spoken or a signed language until age 7. Such deprived children lose their ability to master *any* language.

After the language window closes, even learning a second language becomes more difficult. Have you learned a second language as an adult? If so, you almost certainly speak it with the accent of your first. And you probably also remember that learning the grammar of the second language required a lot of effort.

The older we are when moving to a new country, the harder it will be to learn the new language (Hakuta et al., 2003). This was clear in one study of Korean and Chinese immigrants (Johnson & Newport, 1991). They were asked to read 276 English sentences, such as "Yesterday the hunter shoots a deer," and to score each sentence as either grammatically correct or incorrect. All these test-takers had lived in the United States for approximately 10 years. Some had arrived as very young children, others as adults. As **FIGURE 8.5** reveals, those who had learned their second language early learned it best.

The impact of early experiences is also evident in language learning in children who are deaf from birth. The 90+ percent

FIGURE 8.5 • **New language learning gets harder with age** Young children have a readiness to learn language. Ten years after coming to the United States, Asian immigrants took a grammar test. Those who arrived before age 8 understood American English grammar as well as native speakers did. Those who arrived later did not. (From Johnson & Newport, 1991.)

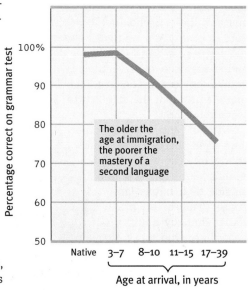

The older the age at immigration, the poorer the mastery of a second language

Percentage correct on grammar test

Native   3–7   8–10   11–15   17–39

Age at arrival, in years

who are born to hearing parents who do not use sign language typically experience written but not signed language during their early years. Like immigrants who learn a new language after childhood, those who learn to sign as teens or adults can master the basic words and learn to order them. But compared with natively deaf children exposed to sign language from birth, they never become as fluent in producing and comprehending subtle grammatical differences (Newport, 1990).

Natively deaf children who learn sign language after age 9 learn it better if they were previously exposed to a language, such as written and lip-formed English. And natively deaf children who learn to sign in infancy have an easier time learning English (Mayberry et al., 2002). The striking conclusion: When a young brain does not learn *any* language, its language-learning capacity never fully develops. Brain scans show the difference. The late-learners show less activity in brain regions that become active when native signers read sign language (Newman et al., 2002). Without nourishment, a flower's growth will be stunted. So, too, will children typically become linguistically stunted if isolated from language during the critical period for its acquisition.

Thinking Without Language

7 How can thinking in images be useful?

To turn on the cold water in your bathroom, in which direction do you turn the handle? To answer this question, you probably thought not in words but in images—perhaps a mental picture of your hand turning the faucet.

Indeed, we often think in images. Pianist Liu Chi Kung showed the value of this process. One year after placing second in a worldwide piano competition, Liu was imprisoned during China's cultural revolution. Soon after his release, after seven years without touching a piano, he was back on tour. The critics judged his playing to be better than ever, and his fans wondered how he had continued to develop without practice. "I did

practice," said Liu, "every day. I rehearsed every piece I had ever played, note by note, in my mind" (Garfield, 1986).

Mental practice is now an accepted part of training for many athletes, including Olympic athletes (Suinn, 1997). One experiment observed the University of Tennessee women's basketball team (Savoy & Beitel, 1996). Over 35 games, researchers tracked the team's skill at shooting free throws following standard physical practice or mental practice. After physical practice, the team scored about 52 percent of their shots. After mental practice, that score rose to 65 percent. During mental practice, players had repeatedly imagined making foul shots under various conditions, including being "trash-talked" by their opposition. In a dramatic conclusion, Tennessee won that season's national championship game in overtime, thanks in part to their foul shooting.

So how does mental practice work its magic? Once you have learned a skill, even *watching* that event will flip a switch in the brain, triggering activity in the same areas that are active when you are actually using that skill. As ballet dancers watch ballet videos, functional MRI scans (fMRIs) show the brain dancing along (Calvo-Merino et al., 2004).

Just imagining an event can likewise trigger brain activity. **FIGURE 8.6** shows an fMRI of a person imagining the experience of pain. Those thoughts activated neural networks that normally become active during *actual* pain (Grèzes & Decety, 2001). **CAN WE USE MENTAL RE-◄ HEARSAL TO HELP REACH OUR ACADEMIC GOALS?** Definitely! One study demonstrated this with two groups of introductory psychology students facing a midterm exam one week later (Taylor et al., 1998). (A third control group did not engage in any mental simulation.) The first group spent five minutes each day imagining themselves scanning the posted grade list, seeing their A, beaming with joy, and feeling proud. This daily *outcome simulation* had little effect, adding only 2 points to their average exam score. A second group spent five minutes each day imagining themselves effectively

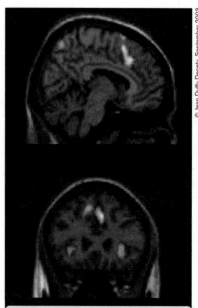

FIGURE 8.6 • **The power of imagination** These fMRIs show a person imagining the experience of pain (top) in comparison to a person experiencing real pain (bottom). The thoughts alone activated some of the same brain areas that become active during the actual experience of pain.

studying—reading the chapters, going over notes, eliminating distractions, declining an offer to go out. This daily *process simulation* paid off—the group began studying sooner in real life, spent more time at it, and beat the other students' average by 8 points.

The point to remember: Mental practice is more effective if you spend your fantasy time planning how to get somewhere, rather than just fantasizing on the imagined destination.

* * *

Experiments on thinking without language bring us back to a question raised earlier in this chapter: How deserving are we of our name *Homo sapiens*? Let's pause to issue an interim report card. On decision making and judgment, our smart but error-prone species might rate a B–. On problem solving, where humans are inventive yet subject to confirmation bias and fixation, we would probably receive better marks, perhaps a B+. On cognitive efficiency, our fallible but quick heuristics earn us an A. And when it comes to language and the processing that occurs outside of consciousness, the awestruck experts would surely award the human species an A+. Inside our dual-track brain, many streams of activity flow at once, function automatically, and only occasionally surface as conscious words.

PRACTICE TEST

THE BASICS

5. The one-word stage of speech development is usually reached at about
   a. 4 months.   c. 1 year.
   b. 6 months.   d. 2 years.

6. According to Chomsky, we _____ to learn the grammar rules of language.
   a. must receive instruction
   b. are born with a built-in readiness
   c. need rewards for babbling and other early verbal behaviors
   d. must imitate and drill

THE BIG PICTURE

8B. If children are not yet speaking, is there any reason to think they would benefit from parents and other caregivers reading to them?

8C. What is "mental practice," and how can it help you prepare for an upcoming event?

IN YOUR EVERYDAY LIFE

▪ Do you think that young children should be required to learn a second language? Why or why not?

▪ How could you use mental practice to improve your performance in some area of your life?

Answers: 5. c, 6. b. Answers to The Big Picture questions can be found in Appendix B at the end of the book.

Animal Thinking and Language

8 Do animals display cognitive skills? What are the arguments for and against their ability to exhibit language?

If in our use of language we humans are, as an ancient psalm says, "little lower than God," where do other animals fit in the scheme of things? Are they "little lower than human"? Let's see what the research on animal thinking and language can tell us.

Do Animals Share Our Thinking Skills?

Animals are smarter than many humans realize. Let's consider some of psychology's findings in this area.

Forming Concepts Even pigeons—mere birdbrains—can sort objects (pictures of cars, cats, chairs, flowers) into categories, or *concepts*. Shown a picture of a never-before-seen chair, the pigeon will reliably peck a key that represents "chairs" (Wasserman, 1995). The great apes—a group that includes chimpanzees and gorillas—also form concepts, such as "cat" and "dog." After monkeys learn these concepts, certain frontal lobe neurons in their brains fire in response to new "cat-like" images, others to new "doglike" images (Freedman et al., 2001).

Numerical Ability Until his death in 2007, Alex, an African Grey parrot, displayed jaw-dropping numerical skills (Pepperberg, 2006). He named and categorized objects. Most surprisingly, he could comprehend numbers up to 6. He could speak the number of objects. He could add two small clusters of objects and announce the sum. He could indicate which of two numbers was greater. And he gave correct answers when shown various groups of objects. Asked, for example, "What color four?" (meaning "What's the color of the objects of which there are four?"), he spoke the answer.

Life on white/Alamy

Displaying Insight In an experiment with Sultan, a chimpanzee, psychologist Wolfgang Köhler (1925) showed that we are not the only creatures to display insight (discussed earlier in this chapter). He placed a piece of fruit and a long stick outside Sultan's cage, beyond his reach. Inside the cage, he placed a short stick, which Sultan grabbed, using it to try to reach the fruit. After several failed attempts, he dropped the stick and seemed to survey the situation. Then suddenly, as if thinking "Aha!" Sultan jumped up and seized the short stick again. This time, he used it to pull in the longer stick—which he then used to reach the fruit.

Tool Use Forest-dwelling chimpanzees are one of many species using tools (Boesch-Achermann & Boesch, 1993). They select different tools for different purposes—a heavy stick for making holes, a light, flexible stick for fishing for termites (Sanz et al., 2004). They break off the reed or stick, strip off any leaves, and carry it to a termite mound. Then they twist it just so and carefully remove it. Termites for lunch! (This is very reinforcing for a chimpanzee.) One anthropologist, trying to mimic the animal's deft fishing moves, failed miserably.

Researchers have found at least 39 local customs related to chimpanzee tool use, grooming, and courtship (Whiten & Boesch, 2001). One group may slurp termites directly from a stick, another group may pluck them off individually. One group may break nuts with a stone hammer, another with a wooden hammer.

Cultural Transmission Group differences in chimpanzees' tool use, along with differing styles of communication and hunting, are not genetic. Rather, they are the chimpanzee version of cultural diversity. Like humans, chimpanzees invent behaviors and transmit cultural patterns to their peers and offspring **(FIGURE 8.7a)**. So do orangutans (van Schaik et al., 2003). And so do some Australian dolphins (Figure 8.7b), which have learned to break off and wear sponges to protect their snouts when probing the sea floor for fish (Krützen et al., 2005).

Several experiments have brought chimpanzee cultural transmission into the laboratory (Horner et al., 2006). If Chimpanzee A obtains food either by sliding or by lifting a door, Chimpanzee B will then typically do the same to get food. And so will Chimpanzee C after observing Chimpanzee B. Across a chain of six animals, chimpanzees see, and chimpanzees do.

Other Cognitive Skills A baboon knows everyone's voice within its 80-member troop (Jolly, 2007). Sheep can recognize and remember individual faces (Morell, 2008). Chimpanzees and two species of monkeys can even read your intent. They

(a)

(b)

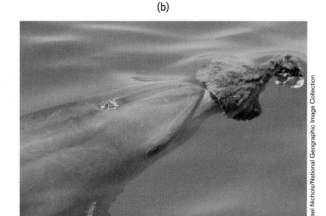

FIGURE 8.7 ● **Cultural transmission** (a) On the western bank of one Ivory Coast river in Africa, a youngster watches as its mother uses a stone hammer to open a nut. On the river's other side, a few miles away, chimpanzees do not follow this custom. (b) This bottlenose dolphin lives in Shark Bay, Western Australia. It is a member of a small group that uses marine sponges as a protective nose guard when probing the sea floor for fish.

would show more interest in a food container that you have intentionally grasped rather than one you flopped your hand on, as if by accident (Wood et al., 2007). Great apes, dolphins, and elephants have also demonstrated self-awareness (by recognizing themselves in a mirror). And as social creatures, chimpanzees have shown altruism, cooperation, and group aggression. But do they, like humans, exhibit language?

Do Animals Have Language?

Without doubt, animals show impressive comprehension and communication. Consider vervet monkeys. They sound different alarm cries for different predators: a barking call for a leopard, a cough for an eagle, and a chuttering for a snake. Hearing the leopard alarm, other vervets climb the nearest tree. Hearing the eagle alarm, they rush into the bushes. Hearing the snake chutter, they stand up and scan the ground (Byrne, 1991). But is this language, in the sense that humans use language? This question has launched thousands of studies, most of them with chimpanzees.

In the late 1960s, psychologists Allen Gardner and Beatrix Gardner (1969)

Johan Swanepoel/Alamy

aroused enormous scientific and public interest when they taught sign language to the chimpanzee Washoe (c. 1965–2007). After four years, Washoe could use 132 signs; by age 32, Washoe was using 181 signs (Sanz et al., 1998). One *New York Times* reporter, having learned sign language from his deaf parents, visited Washoe and exclaimed, "Suddenly I realized I was conversing with a member of another species in my native tongue."

During the 1970s, as more and more reports came in, it seemed apes might indeed be "little lower than human." Some were stringing signs together to form sentences, as Washoe did, signing, "You me go out, please." Some word combinations seemed very creative—saying *water bird* for "swan" or *elephant baby* for a long-nosed Pinocchio doll, or *apple which-is orange* for "orange" (Patterson, 1978; Rumbaugh, 1977).

By the late 1970s, some psychologists were growing skeptical. Were the chimps language champs or were the researchers chumps? Here is a summary of some points that have been raised by the skeptics.

- Ape vocabularies and sentences are simple, rather like those of a 2-year-old child. And unlike speaking or signing children, who easily soak up dozens of new words a week (and 60,000 by adulthood), apes gain their limited vocabularies only with great difficulty (Wynne, 2004, 2008). Saying that apes can learn language because they can sign words is like saying humans can fly because they can jump.

Comprehending canine: Border collie Rico has a 200 (human) word vocabulary. If asked to retrieve a toy with a name he has never heard, Rico will pick out a new toy from a group of familiar items (Kaminski et al., 2004). Hearing that name for the second time four weeks later, Rico more often than not retrieves the same toy.

- Chimpanzees can make signs or push buttons in sequence to get a reward. But pigeons, too, can peck a sequence of keys to get grain (Straub et al., 1979). The apes' signing might be nothing more than aping their trainers' signs and learning that certain arm movements produce rewards (Terrace, 1979).

- Studies of perceptual set show that when information is unclear, we tend to see what we want or expect to see. Interpreting chimpanzee signs as language may be little more than the trainers' wishful thinking (Terrace, 1979). When Washoe signed *water bird*, she may have been separately naming *water* and *bird*.

- "Give orange me give eat orange me eat orange . . ." is a far cry from the exquisite syntax of a 3-year-old (Anderson, 2004; Pinker, 1995). To the child, "You tickle" and "Tickle you" communicate different ideas. A chimpanzee, lacking human syntax, might use the same sequence of signs for both phrases.

Controversy can stimulate progress. In this case, it triggered more evidence of chimpanzees' abilities to think and communicate. One surprising finding was that Washoe trained her adopted son Loulis to use the signs she had learned. It

But is this language? Chimpanzees' ability to express themselves in American Sign Language raises questions about the very nature of language. Here, the trainer is asking, "What is this?" The sign in response is "Baby." Does the response constitute language?

started like this. After her second infant died, Washoe became withdrawn when told, "Baby dead, baby gone, baby finished." Two weeks later, researcher caretaker Roger Fouts (1992, 1997) signed better news: "I have baby for you." Washoe reacted with instant excitement. Hair on end, she swaggered and panted while signing over and again, "Baby, my baby." It took several hours for Washoe and the foster infant, Loulis, to warm to each other. But then she broke the ice by signing, "Come baby" and cuddling Loulis. In the months that followed, Loulis picked up 68 signs. He did this simply by observing Washoe and three other language-trained chimps signing together, without human assistance.

Even more stunning was a report that Kanzi, a bonobo, could understand *syntax* in English spoken to him (Savage-Rumbaugh et al., 1993, 2009). Kanzi happened onto language while observing his adoptive mother during her language training. To those who don't understand syntax, "Can you show me the light?" and "Can you bring me the [flash]light?" and "Can you turn the light on?" would all seem the same. Kanzi, who appears to have the grammatical abilities of a human 2-year-old, knows the difference. He also knows many spoken words, such as *snake, bite,* and *dog*. Given stuffed animals and asked—for the first time—to "make the dog bite the snake," he put the snake to the dog's mouth.

For chimpanzees as for humans, say some researchers, early life is a critical time for learning language. Without early exposure to speech or word symbols, adult chimpanzees will not gain language competence (Rumbaugh & Savage-Rumbaugh, 1994).

So, how should we interpret these studies? Are humans the only language-using species? If by *language* we mean verbal or signed expression of complex grammar, most psychologists would now agree that humans alone possess language. If we mean, more simply, an ability to

"Although humans make sounds with their mouths and occasionally look at each other, there is no solid evidence that they actually communicate with each other."

communicate through a meaningful sequence of symbols, then apes are indeed capable of language.

* * *

Studies of animal thinking and language have moved psychologists toward a greater appreciation of other species' remarkable abilities (Friend, 2004; Rumbaugh & Washburn, 2003). In the past, many psychologists doubted that animals could plan, form concepts, count, use tools, show compassion, or use language (Thorpe, 1974). Today, thanks to animal researchers, we know better. Other animals exhibit insight, show family loyalty, communicate with one another, care for one another, and transmit cultural patterns across generations. Some even understand the syntax of human speech. Accepting and working out what this means in terms of the moral rights of other animals is an unfinished task for our own thinking species.

PRACTICE TEST

THE BASICS

7. Of the examples discussed in this section, the problem-solving behavior that most closely resembled insight was
   a. Loulis the chimpanzee's ability to learn signs by observing Washoe.
   b. Sultan the chimpanzee's use of a short stick to pull in a long stick.
   c. Kanzi the bonobo's ability to understand subtle grammatical differences in English sentences.
   d. Washoe the chimpanzee's use of sign language to request her baby.

8. There is much controversy over whether apes can be taught to use language in the way that humans do. However, most researchers agree that apes can

   a. communicate through symbols.
   b. imitate most human speech sounds.
   c. master language in adulthood.
   d. do better than a human 3-year-old in language skills.

THE BIG PICTURE

8D. If your dog barks at a stranger at the front door, does this qualify as language? What if the dog yips in a telltale way to let you know she needs to go out?

IN YOUR EVERYDAY LIFE

▪ Can you think of a time when you felt an animal was communicating with you? How might you put such intuition to a test?

Answers: 7, b, 8, a. Answers to The Big Picture questions can be found in Appendix B at the end of the book.

Intelligence

So far, we have considered how humans as a group think and communicate. But we humans also differ from one another in these abilities. One of psychology's heated questions is whether each of us has some general mental capacity that can be measured and assigned a number. School boards, courts, and scientists debate the usefulness of tests of intelligence and aptitude. Is it fair to use such tests to rank individuals and decide who can enter a particular training program, college, or job? How shall we interpret group differences? Do they reflect nature (heredity) or nurture (environment)? What about our other not-so-easily-measured abilities? Let's consider some findings from a century of research.

What Is Intelligence?

9 What is intelligence? Is it a single general ability or several distinct abilities?

In many research studies, *intelligence* has been defined as whatever intelligence tests measure, which has tended to be school smarts. But intelligence is not a quality like height or weight, which has the same meaning in all generations, all around the globe. People assign the term *intelligence* to the qualities that enable success in their own time and in their own culture (Sternberg & Kaufman, 1998). In the Amazon rain forest, intelligence may be understanding the medicinal qualities of local plants. In a North American high school, it may be mastering difficult concepts in tough courses. In both locations, **intelligence** is the ability to learn from experience, solve problems, and use knowledge to adapt to new situations.

You probably know some people with talents in science or history, and others gifted in athletics, art, music, or dance. You may also know a terrific artist who is stumped by the simplest math problem, or a brilliant math student with little talent for writing term papers. Are all these people intelligent? Could you rate their intelligence on a single scale? Or would you need several different scales? Simply put: Is intelligence a single overall ability or several specific abilities?

One General Intelligence or Multiple Intelligences?

Charles Spearman (1863–1945) believed we have one **general intelligence** (often shortened to *g*) that is at the heart of all of our intelligent behavior, from navigating the sea to excelling in school. He granted that people often have special, outstanding abilities. But he noted that those who score high in one area, such as verbal intelligence, typically score higher than average in other areas, such as spatial or reasoning ability. Spearman's belief stemmed in part from his work with *factor analysis*, a statistical tool that searches for clusters of related items.

Other psychologists have questioned the extent of the *g* factor, or common skill set. Howard Gardner (1983, 2006), for example, views intelligence as multiple abilities that come in several packages. He asks us to consider studies of people with brain damage, who may lose one ability while others remain intact. He sees other evidence of multiple intelligences in people with **savant syndrome.** Despite their island of brilliance, people with savant syndrome often score low on intelligence tests and may have limited or no language ability (Treffert & Wallace, 2002). Some can render incredible works of art or musical performances. Others can compute numbers as quickly and accurately as an electronic calculator, or identify almost instantly the day of the week that matches any given date in history (Miller, 1999).

Four out of five people with savant syndrome are males. Many also have *autism*, a developmental disorder (see Chapter 3). The late memory whiz Kim Peek (who did not have autism) was the inspiration for the movie *Rain Man*. In 8 to 10 seconds, he could read and remember a page. During his lifetime, he learned 9000 books, including Shakespeare's plays and the Bible, by heart. He learned maps from the front of phone books, and he could provide MapQuest-like travel directions within any major U.S. city. Yet he could not button his clothes. And he had little capacity for abstract concepts. Asked by his father at a restaurant to "lower your voice," he slid lower in his chair to lower his voice box. Asked for Lincoln's Gettysburg Address, he responded, "227 North West Front Street. But he only stayed there one night—he gave the speech the next day" (Treffert & Christensen, 2005).

Gardner has identified a total of eight *relatively independent intelligences*, including the verbal and mathematical

---

intelligence mental quality consisting of the ability to learn from experience, solve problems, and use knowledge to adapt to new situations.

general intelligence (*g*) a general intelligence factor that, according to Spearman and others, underlies specific mental abilities and is therefore measured by every task on an intelligence test.

savant syndrome a condition in which a person otherwise limited in mental ability has an exceptional specific skill, such as in computation or drawing.

Islands of genius: Savant syndrome: After a 30-minute helicopter ride and a visit to the top of a skyscraper, British artist Stephen Wiltshire, who has savant syndrome, began seven days of drawing that reproduced the Tokyo skyline.

© The Stephen Wiltshire Gallery

aptitudes assessed by standard tests **(FIGURE 8.8)**. Thus, the computer programmer, the poet, the street-smart adolescent who becomes a crafty executive, and the basketball team's playmaking point guard exhibit different kinds of intelligence (Gardner, 1998). To Gardner, a general intelligence score is like the overall rating of a city—which tells you something but doesn't give you much specific information about its schools, streets, or nightlife.

Wouldn't it be wonderful if the world were so just that a weakness in one area would always be balanced by genius in some other area? Alas, say Gardner's critics, the world is not just (Ferguson, 2009; Scarr, 1989). Recent research, using factor analysis, has confirmed that there is a general intelligence factor (Johnson et al., 2008). *g* matters. Some of Gardner's intelligences, such as logical-mathematical and spatial, correlate with each other—and with *g*. Some others, such as musical abil-

> "You have to be careful, if you're good at something, to make sure you don't think you're good at other things that you aren't necessarily so good at. . . . Because I've been very successful at [software development] people come in and expect that I have wisdom about topics that I don't."
>
> Bill Gates, 1998

ity, don't represent what most psychologists would consider intelligence. And general intelligence scores also predict performance on various complex tasks and in various jobs (Gottfredson, 2002a,b, 2003a,b). In one overview of 127 studies, an academic intelligence score that predicted graduate school success also predicted later job success (Kuncel et al., 2004).

But we do well to remember that the recipe for success is not simple. As in so many realms of life, success has two ingredients: *can do* (ability) and *will do* (motivation) (Lubinski, 2009). High intelligence may get you into a profession (via the schools and training programs that open doors). *Grit*—your motivation and drive—will make you

successful once you're there. Highly successful people tend to be conscientious, well connected, and doggedly energetic. These qualities often translate into dedicated hard work. Researchers discovered

Spatial intelligence genius: In 1998, World Checkers Champion Ron "Suki" King of Barbados set a new record by simultaneously playing 385 players in 3 hours and 44 minutes. Thus, while his opponents often had hours to plot their game moves, King could only devote about 35 seconds to each game. Yet he still managed to win all 385 games!

Courtesy of Cameras on Wheels

FIGURE 8.8 • **Gardner's eight intelligences**

that expert performers—in chess, dancing, sports, computer programming, music, and medicine—all had spent a decade in intense, daily practice (Ericsson, 2002, 2007; Ericsson et al., 2007). More than 300 studies of college and university students confirm the point. Study habits and study skills are important for academic success (Credé & Kuncel, 2008).

> "[Einstein] showed that genius equals brains plus tenacity squared."
>
> Walter Isaacson, "Einstein's Final Quest," 2009

Are Creativity and Emotional Sensitivity Forms of Intelligence?

10 How do psychologists define creativity and emotional intelligence?

Creativity There was no question about the intelligence of seventeenth-century genius Pierre de Fermat. He dared scholars of his day to solve various mathematical problems. Three centuries later, one of those problems continued to baffle the greatest mathematical minds, even after a $2 million prize had been offered for cracking the puzzle.

Princeton math professor Andrew Wiles had searched for the answer. After more than 30 years, he was on the brink of a solution. Then, one morning, out of the blue, an "incredible revelation" struck him. "It was so . . . beautiful . . . so simple and so elegant. I couldn't understand how I'd missed it and I just stared at it in disbelief for 20 minutes. Then during the day I walked around the department, and I'd keep coming back to my desk looking to see if it was still there. It was still there. I couldn't contain myself, I was so excited. It

bitt24/Shutterstock

was the most important moment of my working life" (Singh, 1997, p. 25).

Wiles' incredible revelation illustrates **creativity**—the ability to produce ideas that are both novel and valuable. Creativity requires a certain level of aptitude (a score of about 120 on a standard intelligence test helps), but it is not the same thing as aptitude. The intelligence test scores of exceptionally creative architects, mathematicians, scientists, and engineers are often no higher than those of their less creative peers (MacKinnon & Hall, 1972; Simonton, 2000).

What is creativity? Robert Sternberg (1988, 2003) believes it has five necessary parts.

> **creativity** the ability to produce new and valuable ideas.

1. *Expertise*—a well-developed base of knowledge—furnishes the ideas, images, and phrases we use as mental building blocks. The more blocks we have, the more chances we have to combine them in novel ways. Wiles' well-developed base of mathematical knowledge gave him access to many different combinations of ideas and methods.

2. *Imaginative thinking skills* let us see things in novel ways, recognize patterns, and make connections. Having mastered a problem's basic elements, we can redefine or explore the problem in a new way. Wiles' imaginative solution combined two partial solutions.

3. A *venturesome personality* seeks new experiences, tolerates gray areas, takes risks, and continues despite obstacles. Wiles said he worked in near-isolation from the mathematics community, partly to stay focused and avoid distraction.

4. *Intrinsic motivation* arises from our internal feelings rather than outside rewards or external pressures (extrinsic motivation) (Amabile & Hennessey, 1992). Creative people seem driven by the pleasure and challenge of the work itself, not by meeting deadlines, impressing people, or making money. As Wiles said, "I was so obsessed by this problem that for eight years I was thinking about it all the time—when I woke up in the morning to when I went to sleep at night" (Singh & Riber, 1997).

5. A *creative environment* sparks, supports, and refines creative ideas. Colleagues are an important part of creative environments. In one study of 2026 leading scientists and inventors, the best known of them had been mentored, challenged, and supported by their relationships with colleagues (Simonton, 1992). Many creative environments foster contemplation. Jonas Salk solved a problem that led to the polio vaccine while in a monastery. Later, when he designed the Salk Institute, he provided contemplative spaces where scientists could work without interruption (Sternberg, 2006).

Emotional Intelligence Is being in tune with yourself and others also a form of intelligence? Howard Gardner (1999) has suggested that it is. We can respect emotional sensitivity, creativity, and motivation as important but different. But if we stretch *intelligence* to include everything we prize, that word will lose its meaning, he warned. Other psychologists disagree. They define *social intelligence* as the know-how involved in understanding social situations and managing yourself successfully (Cantor & Kihlstrom, 1987). Psychologist Edward Thorndike first proposed the concept in 1920, noting that "the best mechanic in a factory may fail as a foreman for lack of social intelligence" (Goleman, 2006, p. 83). Like Thorndike, later psychologists have marveled that high-aptitude people are "not, by a wide margin, more effective . . . in achieving better marriages, in successfully raising their children, and in achieving better mental and physical well-being" (Epstein & Meier, 1989).

Researchers have focused on a critical part of social intelligence, **emotional intelligence,** with its four abilities (Mayer et al., 2002; Salovey & Grewal, 2005).

- *Perceiving* emotions (recognizing them in faces, music, and stories)
- *Understanding* emotions (predicting them and how they may change and blend)

Imaginative thinking: Cartoonists often display creativity as they see things in new ways or make unusual connections. Cartoonist Gary Larson described his creative process in *The Complete Far Side* (2003), "If you would allow me any talent, it's simply this: I can, for whatever reason, reach down into my own brain, feel around in all the mush, find and extract something from my persona, and then graft it onto an idea."

"For the love of God, is there a doctor in the house?"

Everyone held up their crackers as David threw the cheese log into the ceiling fan.

- *Managing* emotions (knowing how to express them in varied situations)
- *Using* emotions to enable adaptive or creative thinking

Emotionally intelligent people are self-aware. Those who score high on emotional intelligence tests enjoy higher-quality interactions with friends (Lopes et al., 2004). They avoid being hijacked by overwhelming depression, anxiety, or anger. They can read others' emotions and know what to say to soothe a grieving friend, encourage a workmate, and manage a conflict.

These emotional intelligence high scorers also perform modestly better on the job (Van Rooy & Viswesvaran, 2004). On and off the job, they can delay gratification in pursuit of long-range rewards, rather than being overtaken by immediate impulses. Simply said, they are emotionally smart. Thus they often succeed in career, marriage, and parenting situations where academically smarter (but emotionally less intelligent) people fail (Ciarrochi et al., 2006).

* * *

To summarize, we might compare mental abilities to physical abilities. Athleticism is not one thing but many. The ability to run fast is distinct from the strength needed for power lifting, which is distinct from the eye-hand coordination required to throw a ball on target. A champion weightlifter rarely has the potential to be a skilled ice skater. Yet there remains some tendency for good things to come packaged together. Running

"You're wise, but you lack tree smarts."

speed and throwing accuracy, for example, often correlate, thanks to general athletic ability. Similarly, intelligence involves several distinct abilities, which correlate enough to define a small general intelligence factor. Let's turn next to how psychologists have designed tests to assess these mental abilities.

Assessing Intelligence

How do we assess intelligence? As noted earlier, *intelligence* can be considered to be whatever **intelligence tests** measure. So, what are these tests, and what makes them trustworthy? Answering those questions begins with a look at why psychologists created tests of mental abilities and how they have used those tests.

What Do Intelligence Tests Test?

11 When and why were intelligence tests created, and how do today's tests differ from early intelligence tests?

Barely a century ago, psychologists began designing tests to assess people's abilities. Some measured **aptitude** (ability to learn). Others assessed **achievement** (what people have already learned).

Alfred Binet: Predicting School Achievement
Modern intelligence testing traces its birth to early twentieth-century France, where a new law required all children to attend school. French officials knew that some children, including many newcomers to Paris, would need special classes. But how could the schools make fair judgments about children's learning potential? Teachers might assess children who had little prior education as slow learners. Or they might sort children into classes on the basis of their social backgrounds. To minimize bias, France's minister of public education in 1904 gave Alfred Binet and others, including Théodore Simon, the task of studying this problem.

Binet and Simon began by assuming that all children follow the same course of intellectual development but that some develop more rapidly. A "dull" child's test

Alfred Binet (1857–1911):
Adaptations of Binet's pioneering intelligence test were sometimes used to discriminate against immigrant and minority groups. But his intent was to match children with appropriate schooling.

National Library of Medicine

results should therefore be the same as a typical younger child's, and a "bright" child's results the same as a typical older child's. Binet and Simon now had a clear goal. They would measure each child's **mental age,** the level of performance typically associated with a certain chronological age. The average 8-year-old, for example, has a mental age of 8. An 8-year-old with a below-average mental age (perhaps performing at the level of a typical 6-year-old) would struggle with schoolwork considered normal for 8-year-olds.

Binet and Simon tested a variety of reasoning and problem-solving questions on Binet's two daughters, and then on "bright" and "backward" Parisian schoolchildren. The items they developed eventually predicted how well French children would handle their schoolwork.

---

emotional intelligence the ability to perceive, understand, manage, and use emotions.

intelligence test a method for assessing an individual's mental aptitudes and comparing them with those of others, using numerical scores.

aptitude test a test designed to predict a person's future performance; *aptitude* is the capacity to learn.

achievement test a test designed to assess what a person has learned.

mental age a measure of intelligence test performance devised by Binet; the chronological age that most typically corresponds to a given level of performance. Thus, a child who does as well as the average 8-year-old is said to have a mental age of 8.

Lewis Terman: Measuring Innate IQ Soon after Binet's death in 1911, others adapted his tests for wider use. One of them was Lewis Terman (1877–1956), a Stanford University professor. Terman found that the Paris-developed questions and age norms worked poorly with California schoolchildren. He adapted some items, added others, and established new standards for various ages. He also extended the upper end of the test's range from teenagers to "superior adults." He gave his revision the name it retains today—the **Stanford-Binet.**

William Stern's contribution to intelligence testing was the famous term **intelligence quotient,** or **IQ.** The IQ was simply a person's mental age divided by chronological age and multiplied by 100 to get rid of the decimal point.

Thus, an average child, whose mental age (8) and chronological age (8) are the same, has an IQ of 100. But an 8-year-old who answers questions at the level of a typical 10-year-old has an IQ of 125:

$$IQ = \frac{\text{mental age of } 10}{\text{chronological age of } 8} \times 100 = 125$$

The original IQ formula worked fairly well for children but not for adults. (Should a 40-year-old who does as well on the test as an average 20-year-old be assigned an IQ of only 50?) Most current intelligence tests, including the Stanford-Binet, no longer compute an IQ (though the term IQ still lingers in everyday vocabulary as short for "intelligence test score"). Instead, they represent the test-taker's performance *relative to the average performance of others the same age.* This average performance is arbitrarily assigned a score of 100, and about two-thirds of all test-takers fall between 85 and 115.

David Wechsler: Separate Scores for Separate Skills Psychologist David Wechsler created what is now the most widely used intelligence test, the **Wechsler Adult Intelligence Scale (WAIS).** There is a version for school-age children (the *Wechsler Intelligence Scale for Children* [WISC]), and another for preschool children. The WAIS consists of 11 subtests broken into verbal and performance areas **(FIGURE 8.9).** It yields both an overall

intelligence score and separate scores for verbal comprehension, perceptual organization, working memory, and processing speed. Striking differences among these scores can provide clues to strengths or weaknesses. For example, a low verbal comprehension score combined with high scores on other subtests could indicate a reading or language disability. Other comparisons can help a therapist establish a rehabilitation plan for a stroke patient. In such ways, tests help realize Binet's aim: to identify opportunities for improvement and strengths that teachers and others can build upon.

Three Tests of a "Good" Test

 12 **By what criteria can we judge intelligence tests?**

To be widely accepted, a psychological test must be *standardized, reliable,* and *valid.* The Stanford-Binet and Wechsler tests meet these requirements.

Was the Test Standardized? The number of correct answers you score on an intelligence test would tell you almost nothing. To know how well you performed, you would need some basis for comparison. That's why test-makers give new tests to a representative sample of people. The scores from this pretested group become the basis for future comparisons. If you later take the test following the same procedures, your score will be meaningful when compared with others. This process is called **standardization.**

If we make a graph of test-takers' scores, they typically form a bell-shaped pattern called the **normal curve.** No matter what attributes we measure—heights, weights, or mental aptitudes—people's scores tend to form this shape. The highest point is the midpoint, or the average score. On an intelligence test, we give this average score a value of 100 **(FIGURE 8.10).** Moving out from the average, toward either extreme, we find fewer and fewer

VERBAL (samples from the six subtests)

Similarities
    In what way are wool and cotton alike?

Arithmetic Reasoning
    If eggs cost 60 cents a dozen, what does 1 egg cost?

Comprehension
    Why do people buy fire insurance?

PERFORMANCE (samples from the five subtests)

Picture Arrangement
    The pictures below tell a story. Put them in the right order to tell the story.

Block Design
    Using the four blocks, make one just like this.

FIGURE 8.9 ● **Sample items from the Wechsler Adult Intelligence Scale (WAIS) subtests** (Adapted from Thorndike & Hagen, 1977.)

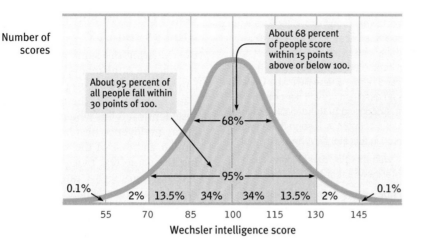

FIGURE 8.10 ● **The normal curve** Scores on aptitude tests tend to form a normal, or bell-shaped, curve around an average score. For the Wechsler scale, for example, the average score is 100.

people. For the Stanford-Binet and the Wechsler tests, a person's score indicates whether that person's performance fell above or below the average. A performance higher than all but 2 percent of all scores earns an intelligence score of 130. A performance lower than 98 percent of all scores earns an intelligence score of 70.

Is the Test Reliable? Knowing where you stand in comparison to the standardizing group still won't tell you much unless the test has **reliability.** A reliable test gives consistent scores, no matter who takes the test or when they take it. To check a test's reliability, researchers test many people many times. They may retest people using the same test, or they may split the test in half and see whether odd-question scores and even-question scores agree. If the two sets of scores generally agree, the test is reliable. The tests we have considered so far—the Stanford-Binet, the WAIS, and the WISC—all score very high for reliability. When retested, people's scores generally match their first score closely.

Is the Test Valid? High reliability does not ensure a test's **validity**—the extent to which the test actually measures or predicts what it promises. Imagine cutting six inches off the end of a tape measure and then using it to measure people's heights. Your results would be very reliable. No matter how many times you measured, people's heights would be the same. But your results would not be valid—you wouldn't be giving the information you promised—real heights.

We expect intelligence tests to have *predictive validity.* They should predict future performance. To some extent, intelligence tests do have predictive ability. But as critics are fond of noting, past grades—which reflect both aptitude and motivation—are better predictors of future achievements. DO INTELLIGENCE◀ TESTS PREDICT WHETHER YOU WILL HAVE A SUCCESSFUL AND HAPPY LIFE? "The IQ test was invented to predict academic performance, nothing else. If we wanted something that would predict life success, we'd have to invent another test completely," noted the social psychologist Robert Zajonc (1984b).

PRACTICE TEST

THE BASICS

9. The existence of savant syndrome seems to support
   a. Stern's concept of IQ.
   b. Spearman's notion of general intelligence, or *g* factor.
   c. Gardner's theory of multiple intelligences.
   d. Binet's concept of mental age.

10. Which of the following is NOT a characteristic of a creative person?
    a. Expertise
    b. Extrinsic motivation
    c. A venturesome personality
    d. Imaginative thinking skills

11. Emotionally intelligent people are characterized by
    a. the tendency to seek immediate gratification.
    b. the ability to understand their own emotions but not those of others.
    c. high academic intelligence.
    d. self-awareness.

12. The intelligence quotient, or IQ, of a 6-year-old with a mental age of 9 would be
    a. 67.
    b. 133.
    c. 86.
    d. 150.

Continued

Stanford-Binet the widely used American revision (by Terman at Stanford University) of Binet's original intelligence test.

intelligence quotient (IQ) defined originally as the ratio of mental age *(ma)* to chronological age *(ca)* multiplied by 100 (thus, $IQ = ma \div ca \times 100$). On contemporary intelligence tests, the average performance for a given age is assigned a score of 100.

Wechsler Adult Intelligence Scale (WAIS) the WAIS is the most widely used intelligence test; contains verbal and performance (nonverbal) subtests.

standardization defining scores by comparing them with the performance of a pretested standardization group.

normal curve the bell-shaped curve that describes the distribution of many physical and psychological attributes. Most scores fall near the average, and fewer and fewer scores lie near the extremes.

reliability the extent to which a test yields consistent results, as assessed by the consistency of scores on two halves of the test, on alternate forms of the test, or on retesting.

validity the extent to which a test measures or predicts what it is supposed to.

13. The Wechsler Adult Intelligence Scale (WAIS) is best able to tell us
    a. what part of an individual's intelligence is determined by genetic inheritance.
    b. whether the test-taker will succeed in a job.
    c. how the test-taker compares with other adults in vocabulary and arithmetic reasoning.
    d. whether the test-taker has specific skills for music and the performing arts.

14. The Stanford-Binet, the Wechsler Adult Intelligence Scale, and the Wechsler Intelligence Scale for Children are known to have very high reliability. This means that
    a. a pretest has been given to a representative sample.
    b. the test yields consistent results, for example, on retesting.
    c. the test measures what it is supposed to measure.
    d. the results of the test will predict future behavior, such as college grades or success in business.

THE BIG PICTURE

8E. Joseph, a Harvard Law School student, has a straight-*A* average, writes for the *Harvard Law Review*, and will clerk for a Supreme Court justice next year. His grandmother, Judith, is very proud of him, saying he is way more intelligent than she ever was. But Joseph is also very proud of Judith: As a young woman, she was imprisoned by the Nazis. When the war ended, she walked out of Germany, contacted an agency helping refugees, and began a new life in the United States as an assistant chef in her cousin's restaurant. According to the definition of *intelligence* in this chapter, is Joseph the only intelligent person in this story? Why or why not?

8F. What was the purpose of Binet's pioneering intelligence test?

IN YOUR EVERYDAY LIFE

- The concept of multiple intelligences suggests that different people have different gifts. What are yours?

Answers: 9. c, 10. b, 11. d, 12. d, 13. c, 14. b. Answers to The Big Picture questions can be found in Appendix B at the end of the book.

The Nature and Nurture of Intelligence

13 Is intelligence influenced more by heredity or by environment?

Intelligence runs in families. But why? Are our intellectual abilities mostly inherited? Or are they molded by our environment? Few issues in psychology arouse so much passion. Let's look at some of the evidence.

What Do Twin and Adoption Studies Tell Us?

Does sharing the same genes also mean sharing the same mental abilities? As you can see from **FIGURE 8.11**, which summarizes many studies, the answer is clearly *Yes*. Identical twins who grow up together have intelligence test scores nearly as similar as those of the same person taking the same test twice (Haworth et al., 2009; Lykken, 1999). (Fraternal twins, who typically share only half their genes, have much less similar scores.) Even when identical twins are adopted by two different families, their scores are very similar. Genes matter.

But shared environment matters, too. Fraternal twins, who are genetically no more alike than any other siblings—but who are treated more alike because they are the same age—tend to score more alike than other siblings. And studies show that adoption of mistreated or neglected children enhances their intelligence scores (van IJzendoorn & Juffer, 2005, 2006). So, should we expect biologically unrelated children adopted into the same family to share similar aptitudes?

Seeking to untangle genes and environment, researchers have compared the intelligence test scores of adopted children with those of their family members.

FIGURE 8.11 ● **Intelligence: Nature and nurture** The most genetically similar people have the most similar intelligence scores. Remember: 1.0 indicates a perfect correlation; zero indicates no correlation at all. (Data from McGue et al., 1993.)

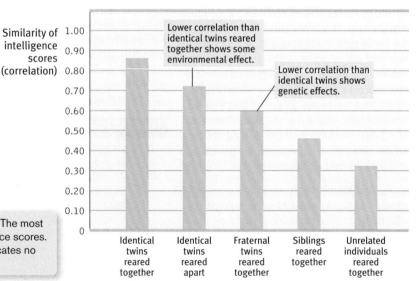

Similarity of intelligence scores (correlation)

Lower correlation than identical twins reared together shows some environmental effect.

Lower correlation than identical twins shows genetic effects.

Identical twins reared together | Identical twins reared apart | Fraternal twins reared together | Siblings reared together | Unrelated individuals reared together

"I told my parents that if grades were so important they should have paid for a smarter egg donor."

These include their *biological parents* (the providers of their genes), their *adoptive parents* (the providers of their home environment), and their *adoptive siblings* (who share that home environment). During childhood, adoptive siblings' test scores correlate modestly. What do you think happens as the years go by and adopted children settle in with their adoptive families? Would you expect the effect of family environment to grow stronger and the genetic effect to shrink?

If you said *Yes,* I have a surprise for you. Mental similarities between adopted children and their adoptive families *lessen* with age, dropping to roughly zero by adulthood (McGue et al., 1993). Similarities with *biological* parents become more apparent as adopted children gain life experience (Bouchard, 1995, 1996b). Adopted children's verbal ability scores, for example, become more like those of their biological parents over time **(FIGURE 8.12)**. Further evidence of the power of genetic influences comes from studies of identical twins. Their mental similarities increase from childhood to adulthood and remain stable into their eighties (Deary et al., 2009; Plomin et al., 1997).

What Is Heritability?

Heritability of intelligence is the portion of the variation among people's test scores that we can assign to genetic factors. This genetically influenced portion is often estimated to be about 50 percent. Does this mean *your* genes are responsible for 50 percent of *your* intelligence and *your* environment is responsible for the rest? *No.* It means we credit heredity with 50 percent of the *variation in intelligence among people being studied.* This point is so often misunderstood that I repeat: Heritability never applies to an *individual,* only to *why people in a group differ from one another.*

Heredity's influence on the range of test scores varies from study to study. Where environments vary widely, as they do among children of less-educated parents, environmental differences are better

> A check on your understanding of heritability: If environments become more equal, the heritability of intelligence would
> a. increase.
> b. decrease.
> c. be unchanged.
>
> Answer: Heritability—variation explained by genetic influences—will *increase* as environmental variation *decreases.*

FIGURE 8.12 • **Adopted children resemble birth parents** As the years went by in their adoptive families, children's verbal ability scores became modestly more like their *biological* parents' scores. (Adapted from Plomin & DeFries, 1998.)

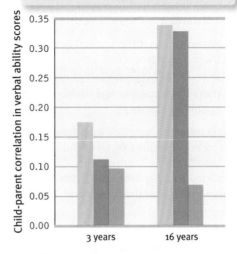

- Children and their birth parents
- Adopted children and their birth parents
- Adopted children and their adoptive parents

predictors of intelligence scores (Rowe et al., 1999). To see why, consider humorist Mark Twain's fantasy of raising boys in barrels until age 12, feeding them through a hole. Let's take his joke a step further and say we'll give all those boys an intelligence test at age 12. Since their environments were all equal, any differences in their test scores could only be due to their heredity. In this "study," heritability would be nearly 100 percent. But what if a mad scientist cloned 100 boys and raised them in drastically different environments (some in barrels and others in mansions)? In this case, their heredity would be equal, so any test-score differences could only be due to their environment. The environmental effect would be 100 percent, and heritability would be zero.

In the real world, your genes and your environment work together. Suppose that (thanks to your genes) you are just slightly taller and quicker than others (Flynn, 2003, 2007). If you try out for a basketball team, you will likely be picked. Once on the team, you will probably play more often than others (getting more practice and experience) and you will receive more coaching. The same would be true for your separated identical twin— who might, *not just for genetic reasons,* also become a basketball star. *Our genes shape the experiences that shape us.* If you have a natural aptitude for academics, you will more likely stay in school, read books, and ask questions—all of which will increase your brain power. In these gene-environment interactions, small genetic advantages can trigger social experiences that multiply our original skills.

heritability the portion of variation among individuals that we can attribute to genes. The heritability of a trait may vary, depending on the population and the environment.

How Does Environment Influence Intelligence?

We have seen that biology and experience intertwine. Nowhere is this more apparent than in the most hopeless human environments. Severe deprivation can leave footprints on the brain, as J. McVicker Hunt (1982) observed in one Iranian orphanage. The typical child Hunt observed there could not sit up unassisted at age 2 or walk at age 4. The little care the infants received was not in response to their crying, cooing, or other behaviors, so the children developed little sense of personal control over their environment. They were instead becoming passive "glum lumps." Extreme deprivation was crushing native intelligence.

Hunt was aware of both the dramatic effects of early experiences and the impact of early intervention. He began a training program for caregivers, teaching them to play language-fostering games with 11 infants. They learned to imitate the babies' babbling. They engaged them in vocal follow-the-leader. And, finally, they taught the infants sounds from the Persian language. The results were dramatic. By 22 months of age, the infants could name more than 50 objects and body parts. They so charmed visitors that most were adopted—an impressive new success rate for the orphanage.

Elena Schweitzer/ Shutterstock

So malnutrition, sensory deprivation, and social isolation can retard normal brain development. Does this mean that an "enriched" environment can "give

Josef Polleross / The Image Works

Devastating neglect: Some Romanian orphans, such as this child in the Lagunul Pentro Copii orphanage in 1990, had minimal interaction with caregivers. They suffered delayed development.

your child a superior intellect," as some popular books claim? CAN WE TURN HEALTHY NORMAL BABIES INTO GENIUSES? Most experts are doubtful (Bruer, 1999). All babies should have normal exposure to sights, sounds, and speech. Beyond that, Sandra Scarr's (1984) verdict is still widely shared: "Parents who are very concerned about providing special educational lessons for their babies are wasting their time." There is no environmental recipe for fast-forwarding a normal infant into a genius.

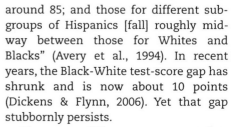
Dorling Kindersley/Getty Images

Group Differences in Intelligence Test Scores

If there were no group differences in aptitude scores, psychologists could politely debate hereditary and environmental influences in their ivory towers. But there are group differences. What are they? And what do they mean?

Ethnic Differences

> **14** How do psychologists explain ethnic group differences in intelligence test scores?

Fueling the group differences debate are two disturbing but agreed-upon facts:

- Racial groups differ in their average intelligence test score.

- High-scoring people (and groups) are more likely to have high levels of education and income.

A statement by 52 intelligence researchers described some of these differences. "The bell curve for Whites is centered roughly around IQ 100; the bell curve for American Blacks roughly around 85; and those for different subgroups of Hispanics [fall] roughly midway between those for Whites and Blacks" (Avery et al., 1994). In recent years, the Black-White test-score gap has shrunk and is now about 10 points (Dickens & Flynn, 2006). Yet that gap stubbornly persists.

There are differences among other groups as well (Steele, 1990; Zeidner, 1990). In New Zealand, people of European descent outscore people of native Maori descent. In Israel, Jews outscore Arabs. In Japan, most Japanese outscore the Burakumin, a stigmatized minority group.

One more agreed-upon fact is that *group* differences provide little basis for judging individuals. Women outlive men by six years, but knowing that this book's editor is a woman doesn't tell me how long she will live. Even Charles Murray and Richard Herrnstein (1994), whose writings drew attention to Black-White intelligence-score differences, reminded us that "millions of Blacks have higher IQs than the average White."

So what shall we make of these group differences in intelligence scores? As we have seen, heredity contributes to *individual* differences in intelligence. Does that mean it also contributes to *group* differences? Some psychologists believe it does, perhaps because of the world's differing climates and survival challenges (Herrnstein & Murray, 1994; Lynn, 2008; Rushton & Jensen, 2010).

But we have also seen that group differences in a heritable trait may be entirely environmental, as in our earlier boys-in-barrels versus boys-in-mansions example. Consider one of nature's experiments: Allow some children to grow up hearing their culture's dominant language, while others, born deaf, do not. Then give both groups an intelligence test rooted in the dominant language. In group comparisons on such tests, people who can hear (those who have expertise in the dominant language) get higher scores than those who were born deaf (Braden, 1994). Within each group, the differences between individuals are mainly a reflection of genetic differences. Between the two groups, the difference is mainly environmental **(FIGURE 8.13)**.

Might ethnic group differences be similarly environmental? Consider:

Genetics research reveals that under the skin, the races are remarkably alike (Cavalli-Sforza et al., 1994; Lewontin, 1982). The average genetic difference between two Icelandic villagers or between two Kenyans greatly exceeds the group difference between Icelanders and Kenyans. Moreover, looks can deceive. Genetic studies show that light-skinned Europeans and dark-skinned Africans are more closely related than are dark-skinned Africans and dark-skinned Aboriginal Australians.

In prosperous country X everyone eats all they want. In country Y the rich are well fed, but the semistarved poor are often thin. In which country will the heritability of body weight be greater?

Answer: Heritability—differences due to genes—will be greater in country X, where environmental differences in nutrition are minimal.

Race is not a neatly defined category. Some scholars argue that there is a reality to race, noting that there are genetic markers for race and that medical risks (such as skin cancer or high blood pressure) vary by race (Rowe, 2005). Other social scientists think race is no longer a meaningful term. They view race as primarily a social category that has no well-defined biological boundaries (Helms et al., 2005; Smedley & Smedley, 2005; Sternberg et al., 2005). People from many different ancestries may label themselves—or be labeled by others—as members of the same race. Moreover, with increasingly mixed ancestries, fewer and fewer people fit neatly into any one category.

Within the same population, there are generation-to-generation differences in intelligence test scores. Test scores of today's better-fed, better-educated, and more test-prepared population exceed the scores of the 1930s population (Flynn, 2007). The two generations differ by the same margin that the intelligence test score of the average White today exceeds that of the average Black. No one attributes the generational group difference to genetics.

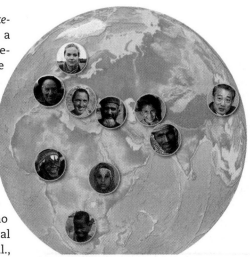

Nature's own morphing: Nature draws no sharp boundaries between races, which blend gradually one into the next around the Earth. But the human urge to classify causes people to socially define themselves in racial categories, which become catchall labels for physical features, social identity, and nationality.

© Paul Almasy/Corbis; © Rob Howard/ Corbis; © Barbara Bannister; Gallo Images/ Corbis; © David Turnley/Corbis; © Dave Bartruff/Corbis; © Haruyoshi Yamaguchi/Corbis; © Richard T. Nowitz/Corbis; © Owen Franken/Corbis; © Paul Almasy/Corbis; © John-Francis Bourke/zefa/Corbis

White and Black infants tend to score equally well on an infant intelligence measure (preference for looking at novel stimuli—a crude predictor of future intelligence scores [Fagan, 1992]).

Schools and culture matter. A country's rich-poor wealth gap correlates with its

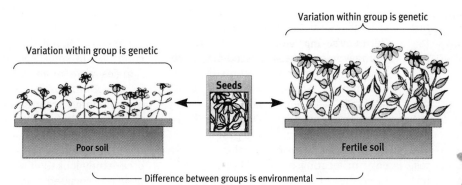

FIGURE 8.13 ● Group differences and environmental impact Even if the variation between members within a group reflects genetic differences, the average difference between groups may be wholly due to the environment. Imagine that seeds from the same mixture are sown in different soils. Although height differences *within* each window box will be genetic, the height difference *between* the two groups will be environmental. (From Lewontin, 1976.)

foodfolio/Alamy

social class IQ gap (Nisbett, 2009). More-over, educational policies—such as kindergarten attendance, school discipline, and instructional time per year—predict national differences in intelligence and knowledge tests (Rindermann & Ceci, 2009). An example: Asian students outperform North American students on math achievement and aptitude tests. This difference may reflect culture more than inborn abilities (Fagan & Holland, 2007). Compared with Americans, Asian students attend school 30 percent more days per year, and they spend much more time studying math in school and at home (Geary et al., 1996; Larson & Verma, 1999; Stevenson, 1992).

In different eras, different ethnic groups have experienced golden ages—periods of remarkable achievement. Twenty-five-hundred years ago, it was the Greeks and the Egyptians, then the Romans. In the eighth and ninth centuries, genius seemed to reside in the Arab world. Five hundred years ago, the Aztec Indians and the peoples of Northern Europe took the lead. Today, we marvel at Asians' technological genius. In today's United States, Jews are 2 percent of the population, but their creative roles are much higher. They form 21 percent of Ivy League student bodies, 37 percent of Academy Award-winning directors, and 51 percent of Pulitzer Prize winners for nonfiction (Brooks, 2010). Cultures rise and fall over centuries; genes do not. That fact makes it difficult to believe in the natural genetic superiority of any ethnic group.

> "Do not obtain your slaves from Britain, because they are so stupid and so utterly incapable of being taught."
> Cicero, 106–43 B.C.E.

Gender Differences

15 Are there gender differences in cognitive abilities?

In science, as in everyday life, differences, not similarities, excite interest. Compared with the many ways men and women are physically alike, our physical sex differences are relatively minor. DO◄ MEN AND WOMEN THINK ALIKE? *Yes* and *No.* In the ways we think and feel and act, gender similarities vastly outnumber

World Math Olympics champs: After outscoring thousands of their U.S. peers, these young people became the U.S. Math Team in 2002 and placed third in the worldwide competition.

Robert Strawn/National Academy of Sciences/Einstein Statue, sculptor, Robert Berks

gender differences. In a 1932 testing of all Scottish 11-year-olds, for example, girls' average intelligence score was 100.6 and boys' was 100.5 (Deary et al., 2003, 2009). So far as *g* is concerned, boys and girls, men and women, are the same species. Yet most people find differences, such as those that follow, more newsworthy.

Verbal memory Females excel at verbal fluency and remembering words (Halpern et al., 2007). They are better spellers. By the end of high school, only 30 percent of males spell better than the average female (Lubinski & Benbow, 1992). And, year after year, among nearly 200,000 students taking Germany's Test for Medical Studies, young women have surpassed men in remembering facts from short medical case descriptions (Stumpf & Jackson, 1994). (My wife, who remembers many of my experiences for me, tells me that if she died I'd be a man without a past.)

Nonverbal memory Females have an edge in locating objects (Halpern, 2000). In studies of more than 100,000 adolescents, females also modestly surpassed males in memory for picture associations (Hedges & Nowell, 1995). Females are also more sensitive to touch, taste, and odor, which may provide them with more tags to find memories.

Emotion-detecting ability Females are better emotion detectors. This fact emerged from studies in which hundreds of men and women viewed brief film clips of portions of a person's emotionally expressive face or body, sometimes with a garbled voice added (McClure, 2000; Rosenthal et al., 1979). For example, they watched a 2-second scene revealing only the face of an upset woman. Then they guessed whether the woman was criticizing someone for being late or was talking about her divorce. Who guessed right more often? Women did.

Math aptitudes Another gender gap emerged in an analysis of teen math achievement among 493,495 students in 69 countries (Else-Quest et al., 2010; Hyde & Mertz, 2009). But the gap varied across countries. In some countries, males and females were more equally represented in school enrollment, research jobs, and parliamentary representation. And in those countries, genders were more equal in math achievement, and there were more "profoundly gifted females." Another study looked at the extent to which people associated "male" with "science." The findings, based on more than half a million people in 34 countries, were striking. The stronger a culture's male-science stereotype, the greater its gender difference in science and math achievement (Nosek et al., 2009). With gender as with ethnicity, culture matters. In Western countries, almost all participants in past International Mathematics Olympiads have been males. In non-Western countries, such as China, more females have reached the top levels (Halpern, 1991).

Spatial abilities The most reliable male edge appears in spatial ability tests like the one shown in **FIGURE 8.14**. The solution requires speedily rotating three-dimensional objects in one's mind (Collins & Kimura, 1997; Halpern, 2000). Today, such skills help when fitting suitcases into a car trunk, playing chess, or doing certain types of geometry problems. From an evolutionary perspective, those same skills would have helped our ancestral fathers track prey and make their way home (Geary, 1995, 1996; Halpern et al., 2007). The survival of our ancestral mothers may have benefited more from a keen memory for the location of edible plants—a legacy that lives today in women's superior memory for objects and their location.

But experience also matters. One experiment found that playing action video games boosts spatial abilities (Feng et al., 2007). And you probably won't be surprised to know that among entering American collegians, 23 percent of men and 4 percent of women report playing video/computer games six or more hours a week (Pryor et al., 2010).

Greater male variability Finally, intelligence research consistently reports another peculiar gender gap. Males' mental ability scores tend to vary more

Nature or nurture? At this 2005 Google Inc.-sponsored computer coding competition, programmers competed for cash prizes and possible jobs. What do you think accounted for the fact that only one of the 100 finalists was female?

than females' do (Halpern et al., 2007; Johnson et al., 2009; Machin & Pekkarinen, 2008). Thus, boys outnumber girls at both the low extremes and the high extremes (Kleinfeld, 1998; Strand et al., 2006). Boys are, therefore, more often found in special education classes. They talk later. They stutter more.

Are Test Questions Biased?

16 Are intelligence tests biased and discriminatory?

Knowing there are group differences in intelligence test scores leads us to wonder whether those differences are built into the tests. ARE INTELLIGENCE TESTS BIASED FOR OR AGAINST SOME PEOPLE? The answer depends on how we define *bias*.

One way a test can be biased is if scores are influenced by a person's cultural experience. This in fact happened to Eastern European immigrants in the early 1900s. Lacking the experience to answer questions about their new culture, many were classified as feebleminded.

The *scientific* meaning of *bias* hinges on the test's validity. For an intelligence test, this means it should predict future behavior for all groups of test-takers, not just for some. For example, if the SAT accurately predicted the college achievement of women but not that of men, then the test would be biased. Almost all psychologists agree that the major U.S. aptitude tests are *not* biased in this scientific meaning of the term (Hunt & Carlson, 2007; Neisser et al., 1996; Wigdor & Garner, 1982). Their predictive validity is roughly the same for women and men, for Blacks and Whites, and for rich and poor. If an intelligence test score of 95 predicts slightly below-average grades, that rough prediction usually applies equally to both genders and all ethnic and economic groups.

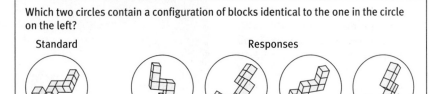

Which two circles contain a configuration of blocks identical to the one in the circle on the left?

Standard　　　　　　　　　Responses

FIGURE 8.14 • **The mental rotation test** This is a test of spatial abilities. Which two responses show a rotated view of the standard? (From Vandenberg & Kuse, 1978.)

Answers: first and fourth alternatives.

Test-Takers' Expectations Our expectations and attitudes can influence our perceptions and behaviors. They also influence our performance on tests. Sometimes we are driven by **stereotype threat**—the fear that our performance will support others' stereotypes of our group (Nguyen & Ryan, 2008; Walton & Spencer, 2009). In one study, for example, Black students performed at a lower level on verbal aptitude tests under conditions designed to make them feel such threat (Steele et al., 2002). In other studies, equally capable men and women have had different results on a difficult math test. The women did not perform as well as the men—except when they had been led to expect that women usually do as well as men on the test (Spencer et al., 1999). Without this helpful hint, the women seem to have been concerned that they could not do well. This feeling then influenced them to live *down* to their own expectations. Stereotype threat helps explain why women have scored higher on math tests when no male test-takers were in the group. And it helps explain why Blacks have scored higher when tested by Blacks than when tested by Whites (Danso & Esses, 2001; Inzlicht & Ben-Zeev, 2000).

Could remedial "minority support" programs function as a stereotype threat, eroding test and school performance? Some researchers think they could, by "telling" students that they probably couldn't succeed otherwise (Steele, 1995, 1997). Over time, such students may detach their self-esteem from academics and look for recognition elsewhere. Indeed, from eighth to twelfth grade, African-American boys have tended to underachieve. During these years, the disconnect between their grades and their self-esteem becomes pronounced (Osborne, 1997). One experiment randomly assigned some African-American seventh-graders to write for 15 minutes about their most important values (Cohen et al., 2006). That simple exercise in self-affirmation had the apparent effect of boosting their grades. Their semester grade point average rose by 0.26 in a first experiment and 0.34 in a repeat of that experiment. College programs that challenge minority students to believe in their potential, or to focus on the idea that intelligence is not fixed, have had similarly good results. Students' grades were markedly higher, and their dropout rates were lower (Wilson, 2006).

* * *

All these findings show that intelligence test scores reflect many things—the test-takers' innate abilities, their attitudes and expectations, and their cultural experience. In this sense, the tests are biased. But they are not biased in the scientific sense of making valid predictions for all groups.

Do intelligence tests discriminate against some people? Again, the answer can be *Yes* or *No*. In one sense, *Yes*, their purpose is to discriminate—to show differences among individuals, according to their abilities. But in another sense, intelligence tests are designed to reduce discrimination. Recall that intelligence testing began with Alfred Binet. The French government hired him so that France would not have to rely on teachers' personal judgments about how well children would do in school programs. Aptitude tests are meant to give people a fair chance at school and job placement. They are meant to replace others' judgments about who you know, how you dress, or whether you are the "right kind of person." Civil service aptitude tests, for example, were devised to select people for U.S. government jobs more fairly and objectively, by reducing the political, racial, and ethnic discrimination that preceded their use. Without access to aptitude test scores, those who award jobs and admissions would rely more on other considerations, such as their personal values.

Perhaps, then, our goals for tests of mental abilities should be threefold. First, we should realize the benefits Binet foresaw—to enable schools to recognize who

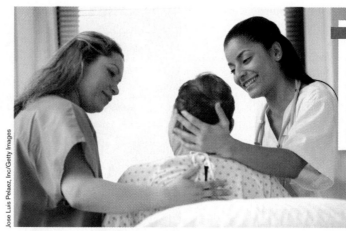

Untestable compassion: Intelligence test scores are only one part of the picture of a whole person. They don't measure the abilities, talent, and commitment of, for example, people who devote their lives to helping others.

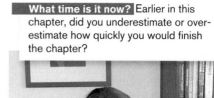

What time is it now? Earlier in this chapter, did you underestimate or overestimate how quickly you would finish the chapter?

stereotype threat a self-confirming concern that we will be evaluated based on a negative stereotype.

might profit most from early intervention. Second, we must remain alert to misinterpreting intelligence test scores as measures of a person's worth and fixed potential. And finally, we must remember that the competence sampled by general intelligence tests is important; it helps people succeed in some life paths. But it reflects only one aspect of personal competence. Our emotional intelligence matters, too, as do other forms of creativity, talent, and character. The carpenter's spatial ability differs from the programmer's logical ability, which differs from the poet's verbal ability. There are many ways of being successful. Our differences are best seen as variations of human adaptability.

PRACTICE TEST

THE BASICS

15. The strongest support for heredity's influence on intelligence is the finding that

a. identical twins, but not other siblings, have nearly identical intelligence test scores.

b. the correlation between intelligence test scores of fraternal twins is higher than that for other siblings.

c. separated fraternal twins living in different environments tend to have similar intelligence test scores.

d. rich children have higher intelligence test scores than impoverished children.

16. To say that the heritability of intelligence is about 50 percent means that 50 percent of

a. an individual's intelligence is due to genetic factors.

b. the similarities between men and women are attributable to genes.

c. the variation in intelligence within a group of people is attributable to genetic factors.

d. intelligence is due to the mother's genes and the rest is due to the father's genes.

17. The experience that has the clearest, most profound effect on intellectual development is

a. being enrolled in school by age 4.

b. growing up in an economically disadvantaged home or neighborhood.

c. being raised in a very neglectful home or institution.

d. being exposed to very stimulating toys and lessons in infancy.

18. Stereotype threat can lead to poor performance on tests by

a. building racial, ethnic, or gender bias into the questions.

b. framing questions so that some people won't understand them.

c. punishing creative answers.

d. undermining test-takers' belief that they can do well on the test.

THE BIG PICTURE

8G. As society succeeds in creating equality of opportunity, it will also increase the heritability of ability. The heritability of intelligence scores will be greater in a society marked by equal opportunity than in a society of peasants and aristocrats. Why?

IN YOUR EVERYDAY LIFE

▪ How have environmental influences shaped your ability to reach your academic potential?

Answers: 15. a, 16. c, 17. c, 18. d. Answers to The Big Picture questions can be found in Appendix B at the end of the book.

Terms and Concepts to Remember

cognition, p. 206	one-word stage, p. 213	Stanford-Binet, p. 224
algorithm, p. 206	two-word stage, p. 213	intelligence quotient (IQ), p. 224
heuristics, p. 206	telegraphic speech, p. 213	Wechsler Adult Intelligence Scale (WAIS), p. 224
insight, p. 206	intelligence, p. 219	
availability heuristic, p. 207	general intelligence (*g*), p. 219	standardization, p. 224
fixation, p. 207	savant syndrome, p. 219	normal curve, p. 224
confirmation bias, p. 209	creativity, p. 221	reliability, p. 225
overconfidence, p. 209	emotional intelligence, p. 222	validity, p. 225
framing, p. 209	intelligence test, p. 223	heritability, p. 227
belief perseverance, p. 210	aptitude test, p. 223	stereotype threat, p. 232
language, p. 212	achievement test, p. 223	
babbling stage, p. 213	mental age, p. 223	

Multiple-choice **self-tests** and more may be found at www.worthpublishers.com/myers

Thinking

COGNITION: ALL THE MENTAL ACTIVITIES ASSOCIATED WITH THINKING, KNOWING, REMEMBERING, AND COMMUNICATING.

1 What are some cognitive strategies we use to solve problems?

- *Algorithms:* Time-consuming but thorough strategies (such as a step-by-step description for evacuating a building during a fire) that guarantee a solution to a problem.
- *Heuristics:* Strategies that are simpler and quicker (such as running for an exit if you smell smoke), but can lead to incorrect solutions.
- *Insight:* An Aha! reaction, a sudden flash of inspiration that is not based on any strategy.

2 What obstacles hinder smart thinking?

- *The availability heuristic:* Judging the likelihood of events based on how readily they come to mind (not on how likely they are to actually occur).
- *Fixation:* Inability to take fresh perspectives on a problem.
- *Confirmation bias:* Searching for evidence that confirms rather than challenges our ideas.
- *Overconfidence:* Believing we know more than we do.
- *Framing:* The wording of questions, which affects how we respond to them.
- *Belief perseverance:* Our tendency to cling to our ideas, ignoring evidence that disproves them.

3 How can we improve our risk assessment?

- Realize that we are predisposed to fear what our ancestors feared, what we feel we cannot control, what is immediate, and what is most available to our memory.
- Test our fears against the facts.

4 When is intuition useful?

- Intuition involves fast, automatic, unreasoned feelings and thoughts.
- When we gain expertise in a field, we grow adept at making quick, shrewd judgments.

Language

LANGUAGE: WORDS AND THE WAYS WE COMBINE THEM TO COMMUNICATE MEANING.

5 What stages do young children move through as they begin to develop language?

- By about 4 months of age, infants *babble,* making a wide range of sounds found in languages all over the world.
- By about 10 months, babbling contains only the sounds of the household language.
- By about 12 months, babies speak in *one-word* sentences.
- *Two-word (telegraphic)* phrases happen around 24 months, followed by full sentences soon after.

6 How do children acquire grammar, and when is the best time to master a language?

- We are predisposed to learn language, but the particular language we learn is the result of our experience.
- Childhood is a critical period for learning language.

7 How can thinking in images be useful?

- Thinking in images can provide useful mental practice if we focus on the steps needed to reach our goal rather than fantasizing about having achieved the goal.

8 Do animals display cognitive skills? What are the arguments for and against their ability to exhibit language?

- Other animals form concepts, display insight, use and create tools, have numerical ability, and transmit cultural innovations.
- Animals do communicate among themselves. Some animals (especially chimpanzees) can learn a limited vocabulary of human signs and symbols. Others (bonobos) can recognize human syntax (word order). But only humans possess language—verbal or signed expressions of complex grammar.

Intelligence

INTELLIGENCE: THE ABILITY TO LEARN FROM EXPERIENCE, SOLVE PROBLEMS, AND ADAPT TO NEW SITUATIONS.

9 What is intelligence? Is it a single general ability or several distinct abilities?

- A *general intelligence (g)* factor seems to run through many aptitudes.
- *Savant syndrome* and abilities lost after brain injuries suggest that we have multiple types of mental aptitudes.
- Gardner proposed eight intelligences (linguistic, logical-mathematical, musical, spatial, bodily-kinesthetic, intrapersonal, interpersonal, and naturalist).

10 How do psychologists define creativity and emotional intelligence?

- *Creativity* is the ability to produce novel and valuable ideas.
- Creativity correlates with developed expertise, imaginative thinking skills, a venturesome personality, intrinsic motivation, and a creative environment.
- Beyond a score of about 120, intelligence test scores don't predict creativity.
- *Emotional intelligence* is the ability to perceive, understand, manage, and use emotions.

11 When and why were intelligence tests created, and how do today's tests differ from early intelligence tests?

- *Aptitude tests* measure the ability to learn; *achievement tests* measure what we have already learned.
- *Intelligence tests* assess a person's mental aptitudes and compare them with those of others.
- In the early 1900s, Alfred Binet and Théodore Simon developed tests to measure children's *mental age* and predict their progress in the Paris school system.
- Lewis Terman's *Stanford-Binet* test was an adaptation of Binet's work for use in the United States. William Stern devised a formula (the *intelligence quotient*) to state test scores as a single number.
- David Wechsler designed the most widely used individual intelligence tests, the *Wechsler Adult Intelligence Scale (WAIS)* and the Wechsler Intelligence Scale for Children (WISC).

12 By what criteria can we judge intelligence tests?

- All good tests must be *standardized* by comparisons with a pretested group. Test-takers' scores usually form a bell-shaped *normal curve*.
- Tests must also be *reliable* (yielding dependably consistent scores) and *valid* (measuring or predicting what they are supposed to).

13 Is intelligence influenced more by heredity or by environment?

- *Heritability* is the amount of variation among individuals that can be attributed to genes.
- Twin and adoption studies reveal an important genetic contribution to intelligence.
- Studies of children raised in impoverished, enriched, or culturally different environments show that life experiences also affect intelligence test performance.
- Heredity and environment interact: Our genes shape the environments that influence us.

14 How do psychologists explain ethnic group differences in intelligence test scores?

- Environmental differences predict ethnic group differences in test scores.

15 Are there gender differences in cognitive abilities?

- Girls score higher on verbal and nonverbal memory; on sensitivity to touch, taste, and odor; and on reading others' emotions.
- Boys score higher on spatial relations tests, and higher on math tests in some cultures, and they outnumber girls at the high and low extremes of school achievement.

16 Are intelligence tests biased and discriminatory?

- Intelligence tests need to be sensitive to performance differences caused by cultural experience.
- Expectations influence our performance on tests, as when we feel a *stereotype threat* (fearing others' negative judgment of our group).
- Experts consider the major intelligence tests to be unbiased, in the sense that they predict as well for one group as for another.

9

MOTIVATION
AND
EMOTION

Having bagged nearly all of Colorado's tallest peaks, many of them solo and in winter, experienced climber Aron Ralston went canyon hiking alone one Saturday spring morning in 2003. The outing seemed so risk-free he did not bother to tell anyone where he was going. In Utah's narrow Bluejohn Canyon, just 150 yards above his final drop, he was climbing over an 800-pound rock when disaster struck. The rock shifted and pinned his right wrist and arm. He was, as the title of his book says, caught *Between a Rock and a Hard Place*.

Realizing that no one would be rescuing him, Ralston tried with all his might to dislodge the rock. Then, with his dull pocket knife, he tried chipping away at the rock. When that failed, he rigged up ropes to lift the rock. Alas, nothing worked. Hour after hour, then cold night after cold night, he was stuck.

By Tuesday, he had run out of food and water. On Wednesday, as thirst and hunger gnawed, he began saving and sipping his own urine. Using his video recorder, he said his good-byes to family and friends, for whom he now felt intense love. "So again love to everyone. Bring love and peace and happiness and beautiful lives into the world in my honor. Thank you. Love you."

On Thursday, surprised to find himself still alive, Ralston had a seemingly divine insight into his reproductive future. In his vision, he saw a preschool boy being scooped up by a one-armed man. With this inspiration, he summoned his remaining strength and his enormous will to live. Over the next hour, he willfully broke his bones and then proceeded to use that dull knife to cut off his arm. After slowing his bloodflow with a tourniquet, he chopped the last piece of skin and, after 127 hours, broke free. Then, holding his bleeding half-arm close, he climbed down the 65-foot cliff and hiked 5 miles before finding someone. He describes the moment when he broke free. "[I was] just reeling with this euphoria . . . having been dead and standing in my grave, leaving my last will and testament, etching 'Rest in peace' on the wall, all of that, gone and then replaced with having my life again. It was undoubtedly the sweetest moment that I will ever experience" (Ralston, 2004).

Aron Ralston's thirst and hunger, his sense of belonging to others, and his brute will to live and become a father highlight the force of *motivation:* a need or desire that *energizes* behavior and *directs* it toward a goal. His intense emotional experiences of love and joy demonstrate the close ties between our feelings, or *emotions,* and our motivated behaviors. In this chapter, we explore both of these human forces—our motivations and our emotions.

CHAPTER OUTLINE

Motivational Concepts

1 What is motivation, and what are three key perspectives that help us understand motivated behaviors?

Our **motivations** arise from the interplay between nature (the bodily "push") and nurture (the "pulls" from our thought processes and culture). Let's consider three perspectives psychologists have used in their attempt to understand motivated behaviors. *Drive-reduction theory* focuses on how our inner pushes and external pulls interact. *Arousal theory* focuses on our search for the "right" level of stimulation. And Abraham Maslow's *hierarchy of needs* describes how some of our needs take priority over others.

Drive-Reduction Theory

Drive-reduction theory assumes that our unmet **physiological needs** (such as hunger or thirst) create an aroused state. This physical arousal translates into a psychological **drive**—a motivated state that *pushes* us to reduce the need by, say, eating or drinking.

We also are *pulled* by **incentives**—environmental stimuli that attract or repel us, depending on our individual learning histories. Thus, the aroma of good food will motivate a hungry person. Whether that aroma comes from fresh-baked bread or toasted ants will depend on your culture and experience.

"What do you think . . . should we get started on that motivation research or not?"

When there is both a need and an incentive, we feel strongly driven. If I skip lunch and then smell baking bread, I will feel a strong hunger drive. In the presence of that drive, the baking bread becomes a powerful incentive. *For each motive, we can therefore ask, "How are we pushed by our inborn bodily needs and pulled by incentives in the environment?"*

Arousal Theory

When we are motivated to satisfy our basic needs, we are *aroused* (physically energized or tense). Behaviors that meet these needs, such as eating when we're hungry, reduce our arousal. (Imagine sitting lazily around the table after Thanksgiving dinner.) But other motivated behaviors actually *increase* arousal **(FIGURE 9.1)**. Well-fed animals with no clear, need-based drive will leave a safe shelter to explore. From taking such risks, animals gain information and resources (Renner, 1992).

Curiosity drives monkeys to monkey around trying to figure out how to unlock a latch that opens nothing, or how to open a window that allows them to see outside their room (Butler, 1954). It drives 9-month-old infants who check out every corner of the house. It drives the scientists whose work this text discusses. And it drives adventurers such as Aron Ralston. Asked why he wanted to climb Mount Everest, George Mallory answered, "Because it is there." Those who, like Mallory and Ralston, enjoy high arousal are most likely to enjoy intense music, novel foods, and risky behaviors (Zuckerman, 1979).

When we humans find that all our biological needs have been met, we may feel bored and seek stimulation to increase our arousal. But not *too* much stimulation, for that brings stress, and we then look for a way to decrease arousal. This search for just the right level of arousal thus energizes and directs our behavior.

A Hierarchy of Needs

Some needs are more important than others. At this moment, with your needs for air and water satisfied, other motives are directing your behavior. But if you were deprived of water, your thirst would take over your thoughts. Just ask Aron Ralston. And if your air supply was cut off, your thirst would disappear.

Abraham Maslow (1970) viewed these and other motives as a pyramid—a **hierarchy of needs (FIGURE 9.2)**. At the pyramid's base are our physiological

Diverse Yet Alike

FIGURE 9.1 ● These Israeli college students exploring at an archeological site (left) and this Berber shepherd boy in Morocco meeting a digital camera for the first time (right) are all driven by their curiosity, and they are maintaining a desired level of arousal.

Self-transcendence needs
Need to find meaning and identity beyond the self

Self-actualization needs
Need to live up to our fullest and unique potential

Esteem needs
Need for self-esteem, achievement, competence, and independence; need for recognition and respect from others

Belongingness and love needs
Need to love and be loved, to belong and be accepted; need to avoid loneliness and separation

Safety needs
Need to feel that the world is organized and predictable; need to feel safe, secure, and stable

Physiological needs
Need to satisfy hunger and thirst

FIGURE 9.2 • Maslow's hierarchy of needs Once our lower-level needs are met, we are prompted to satisfy our higher-level needs (Koltko-Rivera, 2006; Maslow, 1970). For survivors of recent Pakistani flooding, such as these people at a food distribution station, satisfying very basic needs for water, food, and safety become top priority. Higher-level needs such as respect, self-actualization, and finding meaning often take a back seat during such times.

needs, such as those for food and water. Only after these needs are met, said Maslow (1971), do we try to meet our need for safety, and then to satisfy the uniquely human needs to give and receive love and to enjoy self-esteem. At the peak of the pyramid are the highest human needs. At the *self-actualization* level, people seek to realize their own potential. At the very top is *self-transcendence*, which Maslow proposed near the end of his life. At this level, some people strive for meaning, purpose, and identity that is *transpersonal*—beyond *(trans)* the self (Koltko-Rivera, 2006).

There are exceptions to Maslow's hierarchy. For example, people have starved themselves to make a political statement. Nevertheless, the simple idea that some needs are more basic than others gives us a framework for thinking about motivation. Surveys in 39 nations support this basic idea (Oishi et al., 1999). In poorer nations, money—and the food and shelter it buys—more strongly commands attention and predicts feelings of well-being. In wealthy nations, where most are able to meet their basic needs, home-life satisfaction is a better predictor of well-being.

Let's take a closer look now at two specific motives, beginning at the basic level with *hunger* and working up to the higher-level *need to belong*. As you read about these motives, watch for ways that incentives (the psychological "pull") interact with bodily needs (the biological "push").

PRACTICE TEST

THE BASICS

1. An example of a physiological need is _____ . An example of a psychological drive is _____ .
   a. hunger; a "push" to find food
   b. a "push" to find food; hunger
   c. curiosity; a "push" to reduce arousal
   d. a "push" to reduce arousal; curiosity

2. Motivated behaviors satisfy a variety of needs. When feeling bored, we may look for ways to
   a. reduce physiological needs.
   b. search out respect from others.
   c. increase arousal.
   d. ensure stability.

3. Jan walks into a friend's kitchen, smells bread baking, and begins to feel very hungry. The smell of baking bread is a(n)

   a. psychological drive.
   b. physiological need.
   c. incentive.
   d. aroused state.

4. According to Abraham Maslow, our most basic needs are physiological needs, including the need for food, water, and oxygen; just above these are
   a. safety needs.
   b. self-esteem needs.
   c. belongingness needs.
   d. psychological needs.

THE BIG PICTURE

9A. While on a long road trip, you suddenly feel very hungry. You see a diner that looks pretty deserted and creepy, but you are *really* hungry, so you stop anyway. What motivational perspective would most easily explain this behavior, and why?

IN YOUR EVERYDAY LIFE

▪ How often do you satisfy what Maslow called "self-actualization" needs? What about "self-transcendence" needs?

▪ Does boredom ever motivate you to do things just to figure out something new? When was the last time that happened, and what did you find?

Answers: 1. a, 2. c, 3. c, 4. a. Answers to The Big Picture questions can be found in Appendix B at the end of the book.

motivation a need or desire that energizes and directs behavior.

drive-reduction theory the idea that a physiological need creates an aroused state (a drive) that motivates us to satisfy the need.

physiological need a basic bodily requirement.

drive an aroused, motivated state often created when the body is deprived of some substance it needs.

incentive a positive or negative environmental stimulus that motivates behavior.

hierarchy of needs Maslow's pyramid of human needs; at the base are physiological needs. These basic needs must be satisfied before higher-level safety needs, and then psychological needs, become active.

Hunger

The power of physiological needs was vividly demonstrated in World War II prison camps. David Mandel (1983), a Nazi concentration camp survivor, recalled how a starving "father and son would fight over a piece of bread. Like dogs." One father, whose 20-year-old son stole his bread from under his pillow while he slept, went into a deep depression, asking over and over how his son could do such a thing. The next day the father died. "Hunger does something to you that's hard to describe," Mandel explained.

To learn more about the results of semistarvation, Ancel Keys (the creator of Army K rations) and his research team did a now-classic study (Keys et al., 1950). They first fed 36 male volunteers just enough to maintain their initial weight. Then, for six months, they cut this food level in half. The effects soon became visible. Without thinking about it, the men began conserving energy. They appeared sluggish and dull. After dropping rapidly, their body weights eventually stabilized at about 25 percent below their starting weights. As Maslow would have guessed, the men became food-obsessed. They talked food. They daydreamed food. They collected recipes, read cookbooks, and feasted their eyes on tasty but forbidden food. Preoccupied with their unmet basic need, they lost interest in sex and social activities. As one man reported, "If we see a show, the most interesting part of it is contained in scenes where people are eating. I couldn't laugh at the funniest picture in the world, and love scenes are completely dull."

The semistarved men's preoccupations illustrate how motives can hijack our consciousness. As journalist Dorothy Dix (1861–1951) observed, "Nobody wants to kiss when they are hungry." When we're hungry, thirsty, fatigued, or sexually aroused, little else seems to matter. When we're not, food, water, sleep, or sex just doesn't seem like that big a thing in life, now or ever. (You may recall from Chapter 7 a parallel effect of our current good or bad mood on our memories.) Shop for food on an empty stomach and you are more likely to see those jelly-filled doughnuts as just what you've always loved and will be wanting tomorrow. Motives matter mightily.

"Never hunt when you're hungry."

The Physiology of Hunger

2 **What physiological factors cause us to feel hungry?**

Deprived of a normal food supply, Keys' volunteers were clearly hungry. WHAT◄ TRIGGERS OUR FEELINGS OF HUNGER? Are the pangs of an empty stomach the source of hunger? So it seemed to A. L. Washburn. Working with Walter Cannon (Cannon & Washburn, 1912), Washburn agreed to swallow a balloon that was attached to a recording device **(FIGURE 9.3)**. When inflated to fill his stomach, the balloon tracked his stomach contractions. Washburn supplied information about his *feelings* of hunger by pressing a key each time he felt a hunger pang. The discovery: Washburn was indeed having stomach contractions whenever he felt hungry.

Can hunger exist without stomach pangs? To answer that question, researchers removed some rats' stomachs and created a direct path to their small intestines (Tsang, 1938). Did the rats continue to eat? Indeed they did. Some hunger persists similarly in humans whose stomachs have been removed as a treatment for ulcers or cancer. So the pangs of an empty stomach cannot be the *only* source of hunger. What else might trigger hunger?

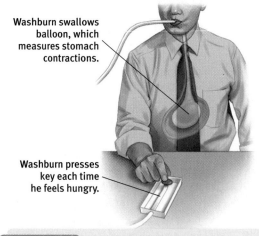

Washburn swallows balloon, which measures stomach contractions.

Washburn presses key each time he feels hungry.

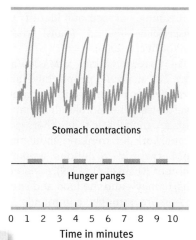

Stomach contractions

Hunger pangs

0 1 2 3 4 5 6 7 8 9 10
Time in minutes

FIGURE 9.3 ● **Monitoring stomach contractions**

Body Chemistry and the Brain

Somehow, somewhere, your body is keeping tabs on the energy it takes in and the energy it uses. If this weren't true, you would be unable to maintain a stable body weight. A major source of energy in your body is the blood sugar **glucose.** If your blood glucose level drops, your stomach, intestines, and liver will send messages to your brain. Your brain, which is automatically monitoring your blood chemistry and your body's internal state, will then trigger hunger.

How does the brain integrate these messages and sound the alarm? The work is done by several neural areas, some housed deep in the brain within the hypothalamus **(FIGURE 9.4)**. This neural traffic intersection includes areas that influence eating. For example, one neural arc (called the *arcuate nucleus*) has a center that secretes appetite-stimulating hormones, and another center that secretes appetite-suppressing hormones. Explorations of this and other neural areas reveal that when an appetite-enhancing center is stimulated electrically, well-fed animals begin to eat. If the area is destroyed, even starving animals have no interest in food. The opposite occurs when electrically stimulating an appetite-suppressing area: An animal will stop eating. Destroy this area and animals will become extremely fat (Duggan & Booth, 1986; Hoebel & Teitelbaum, 1966) **(FIGURE 9.5)**.

Blood vessels connect the hypothalamus to the rest of the body, so it can

Richard Howard

FIGURE 9.5 ● **Hunger signals in the hypothalamus** Destroying an appetite-suppressing area of the hypothalamus caused this rat's weight to triple.

respond to our current blood chemistry and other incoming information. One of its tasks is monitoring levels of appetite hormones, such as *ghrelin,* a hunger-arousing hormone secreted by an empty stomach. During bypass surgery for severe obesity, surgeons seal off part of the stomach. The remaining stomach then produces much less ghrelin, and the person's appetite lessens (Lemonick, 2002). Other appetite hormones include insulin, leptin, orexin, and PYY **(FIGURE 9.6)**.

The interaction of appetite hormones and brain activity suggests that the body has some sort of "weight thermostat." When semi-starved rats fall below their normal weight, this system signals the body to restore the lost weight. The rats' hunger increases and their energy

output decreases. If body weight rises—as happens when rats are force-fed—hunger decreases and energy output increases. In this way, rats (and humans) tend to hover around a stable weight, or **set point**, influenced in part by heredity (Keesey & Corbett, 1983).

glucose the form of sugar that circulates in the blood and provides the major source of energy for body tissues. When its level is low, we feel hunger.

set point the point at which your "weight thermostat" is supposedly set. When your body falls below this weight, increased hunger and a lowered metabolic rate may combine to restore lost weight.

— Orexin

Ghrelin

Insulin

Leptin

PYY

FIGURE 9.4 ● **The hypothalamus** The hypothalamus (colored red) performs various body maintenance functions. One of these functions is control of hunger.

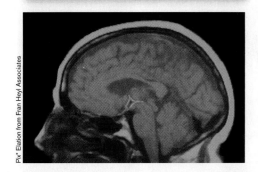

Pix* Elation from Fran Hey Associates

FIGURE 9.6 ● **The appetite hormones**

Ghrelin: Hormone secreted by empty stomach; sends "I'm hungry" signals to the brain.
Insulin: Hormone secreted by pancreas; controls blood glucose.
Leptin: Protein hormone secreted by fat cells; when abundant, causes brain to increase metabolism and decrease hunger.
Orexin: Hunger-triggering hormone secreted by hypothalamus.
PYY: Digestive tract hormone; sends "I'm *not* hungry" signals to the brain.

We humans vary in our **basal metabolic rate,** a measure of how much energy we use to maintain basic body functions when our body is at rest. But we share a common response to decreased food intake: Our basal metabolic rate drops, as it did for the participants in Keys' experiment. After 24 weeks of semistarvation, they stabilized at three-quarters of their normal weight, although they were taking in only *half* their previous calories. How did their bodies achieve this dieter's nightmare? They reduced the amount of energy they were using—partly by being less active, but partly by dropping their basal metabolic rate by 29 percent.

Some researchers have suggested that the idea of a biologically *fixed* set point is too rigid to explain some things. One thing it doesn't address is that slow, steady changes in body weight can alter a person's set point (Assanand et al., 1998). Another is that when we have unlimited access to various tasty foods, we tend to overeat and gain weight (Raynor & Epstein, 2001). And set points don't explain why psychological factors influence hunger. For all these reasons, some prefer the looser term *settling point* to indicate the level at which a person's weight settles in response to caloric intake and energy use. As we will see next, these factors are influenced by environment as well as biology.

The Psychology of Hunger

3 What psychological and cultural factors affect our eating behavior and feelings of hunger? How do eating disorders illustrate the power of psychological influences?

We have seen that our eagerness to eat is pushed by our body chemistry and brain activity. Yet there is more to hunger than meets the stomach. This was strikingly apparent when trickster researchers tested two patients who had no memory for events occurring more than a minute ago (Rozin et al., 1998). If offered a second lunch 20 minutes after eating a normal lunch, both patients readily ate it . . . and usually a third meal offered 20 minutes after they finished the second. This suggests that one

"Never get a tattoo when you're drunk and hungry."

part of our decision to eat is our memory of the time of our last meal. As time passes, we think about eating again, and that thought triggers feelings of hunger.

Environmental stimuli also matter. We eat more when given supersized servings, bigger food packages, larger serving containers, and more variety (Herman & Polivy, 2008; Wansink, 2007). Offered ice cream, people take and eat more when given a big bowl and big scoop. Consider this: Over the next 40 years you will eat about 20 tons of food. If during those years you give in to the environmental stimuli bombarding you, and you increase your daily intake by just .01 ounce more than required for your energy needs, you will gain 24 pounds (Martin et al., 1991).

Andrew Paterson/Alamy

Peter Zijlstra/Shutterstock

Psychological influences on eating behavior affect all of us at some point. But their effect is most striking when an abnormal desire to be thin overrides normal reactions to hunger (see Close-Up: Eating Disorders).

Taste Preference: Biology or Culture?

Both body chemistry and environment play a role in our feelings of hunger and in what we hunger for—our taste preferences. **WHEN FEELING TENSE OR DEPRESSED, DO YOU CRAVE STARCHY, CARBOHYDRATE-LADEN FOODS?** Carbohydrates such as pasta, chips, and sweets help boost levels of the neurotransmitter serotonin, which has calming effects. When stressed, even rats find it extra rewarding to scarf Oreos (Artiga et al., 2007; Boggiano et al., 2005).

Our preferences for sweet and salty tastes are genetic and universal. Other taste preferences are learned. People given highly salted foods, for example, develop a liking for excess salt (Beauchamp, 1987). People who become violently ill after eating a particular food often develop a dislike of it. (The frequency of children's illnesses provides many chances for them to learn to avoid certain foods.)

Culture affects taste preferences, too. Bedouins enjoy eating the eye of a camel, which most North Americans would find

Diverse Yet Alike

People everywhere learn to enjoy the fatty, bitter, or spicy foods common in their culture. For Yupik Alaska Natives but not for most other North Americans, *akutaq* (sometimes called "Eskimo ice cream" and traditionally made with reindeer fat, seal oil, and wild berries) is a tasty treat (left). For Peruvians, roasted guinea pig is similarly delicious (right).

Eating Disorders

Our bodies are naturally disposed to maintain a normal weight, storing energy reserves in case food becomes unavailable. But psychological influences can overwhelm biological wisdom. Nowhere is this more painfully clear than in eating disorders.

- In **anorexia nervosa,** people—usually female adolescents—starve themselves. Anorexia often begins as an attempt to lose weight, but the dieting doesn't end. Even when far below normal weight (typically, by 15 percent or more), the self-starved person feels fat, fears weight gain, and focuses obsessively on losing weight, sometimes exercising excessively. If hunger conquers these feelings, food binges may occur followed by purges and depression. At some point in their lifetime, 0.6 percent of Americans meet the criteria for anorexia nervosa (Hudson et al., 2007). Many people with the disorder come from competitive, high-achieving families. They tend to have low self-esteem, to set impossible standards, and to fret about falling short of expectations (Polivy & Herman, 2002; Sherry & Hall, 2009).

- In **bulimia nervosa,** food binges alternate with vomiting, laxative use, fasting, and excessive exercise. Unlike anorexia, bulimia is marked by weight shifts within or above normal ranges, making this disorder easier to hide. Binge-purge eaters are preoccupied with food (especially sweet and high-fat foods) and obsessed with their weight and appearance. They experience bouts of depression and anxiety, most severe during and following binges (Hinz & Williamson, 1987; Johnson et al., 2002). About 1 percent of Americans, mostly women in their late teens or early twenties, have had bulimia.

- In **binge-eating disorder,** significant binge eating is followed by remorse. But people with the disorder do not purge, fast, or exercise excessively after their food binges. At some point during their lifetime, 2.8 percent of Americans have had binge-eating disorder (Hudson et al., 2007).

So, how can we explain eating disorders? Heredity may bend some people in their direction. Identical twins share these disorders somewhat more often than fraternal twins do (Culbert et al., 2009; Klump et al., 2009).

Reuters/Philippe Wojazer

"Skeletons on parade": A newspaper article used this headline in criticizing superthin models. Do such models make self-starvation fashionable?

But environment plays a bigger role. Body ideals vary across culture and time. In India, women students rate their ideal body size as close to their actual shape. In impoverished areas of the world, including much of Africa—where plump means prosperous and thinness can signal poverty or illness—bigger is better (Knickmeyer, 2001; Swami et al., 2010).

Bigger does not seem better in Western cultures, where the rise in eating disorders over the last 50 years has coincided with a dramatic increase in women having a poor body image (Feingold & Mazzella, 1998). Part of the pressure on women surely stems from the doctored images of unnaturally thin models and celebrities (Tovee et al., 1997). Viewing such images, women—especially those who can't resist comparing their bodies with others'—often feel ashamed, depressed, and dissatisfied with their own bodies (Myers & Crowther, 2009; Posavac et al., 1998; Stice & Shaw, 1994).

In one study, researchers tested media influences by giving some adolescent girls (but not others) a 15-month subscription to a teen fashion magazine (Stice et al., 2001). Vulnerable girls (those who felt dissatisfied, idealized thinness, and lacked social support) receiving the magazine showed increased body dissatisfaction and eating disorder tendencies. Thus, the eating disorders of today's Western world seem to be reflecting a weight-obsessed culture.

anorexia nervosa an eating disorder in which a person (usually an adolescent female) maintains a starvation diet despite being significantly (15 percent or more) underweight.

bulimia nervosa an eating disorder in which a person alternates binge eating (usually of high-calorie foods) with purging (by vomiting or laxative use), fasting, or excessive exercise.

binge-eating disorder significant binge eating, followed by distress, disgust, or guilt, but without the purging, fasting, or excessive exercise that marks bulimia nervosa.

---

repulsive. North Americans and Europeans also shun horse, dog, and rat meat, all of which are prized elsewhere.

Rats tend to avoid unfamiliar foods (Sclafani, 1995). So do we, especially those that are animal-based. This surely was adaptive for our ancestors by protecting them from potentially toxic substances.

We also may learn to prefer some tastes because they are adaptive. In hot climates (where food spoils more quickly), recipes often include spices that inhibit

basal metabolic rate the body's resting rate of energy output.

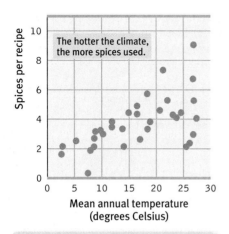

Spices per recipe / Mean annual temperature (degrees Celsius) — "The hotter the climate, the more spices used."

FIGURE 9.7 ● **Hot cultures like hot spices** (Sherman & Flaxman, 2001).

the growth of bacteria **(FIGURE 9.7)**. India averages nearly 10 spices per meat recipe, Finland 2 spices. Pregnancy's food dislikes—and the nausea associated with them—are another example of adaptive taste preferences. These dislikes peak about the tenth week, when the developing embryo is most vulnerable to toxins.

Obesity and Weight Control

4 What factors predispose some people to become and remain obese?

WHY ARE SO MANY OF US OVERWEIGHT, ◄ WHILE OTHERS WHO EAT THE SAME AMOUNT DON'T ADD A POUND? Why do so few overweight people win the battle of the bulge?

The answers lie partly in our history. Fat is an ideal form of stored energy. It is a fuel reserve that can carry us through famine periods, which were common in our prehistoric ancestors' world. (Think of that spare tire around the middle as an energy storehouse—biology's counterpart to a hiker's waist-borne snack pack.) In Europe in earlier centuries, obesity signaled wealth and social status, as it does in other parts of the world today (Furnham & Baguma, 1994).

Our hungry distant ancestors were well served by a simple rule: *When you find energy-rich fat or sugar, eat it!* That rule is no longer adaptive in a world where food and sweets are abundantly available.

Pretty much everywhere this book is being read, people have a growing problem. Worldwide, more than 1 billion people are overweight (WHO, 2007), and 300 million of them are clinically *obese* (defined as a body mass index of 30 or more) **(FIGURE 9.8)**. In the United States alone, 34 percent of all adults are obese—more than double the rate of 40 years ago. Among children and teens, obesity rates have quadrupled (Flegal et al., 2010; NCHS, 2007).

Fitness matters more than carrying a little extra weight (Dolan et al., 2007; Gibbs, 2005). But significant obesity can shorten your life and reduce your quality of life. It increases the risk of diabetes, high blood pressure, heart disease, gallstones, joint pain, arthritis, and certain types of cancer (Olshansky et al., 2005). The risks are greater for apple-shaped people who carry their weight in pot bellies than for pear-shaped people with ample hips and thighs (Greenwood, 1989; Price et al., 2006).

The Social Effects of Obesity

Obesity can also be socially toxic, by affecting both how others treat you and how you feel about yourself. Obese people know the unfair stereotype: slow, lazy, and sloppy (Crandall, 1994, 1995; Ryckman et al., 1989). Widen people's images on a video monitor, making them look fatter, and observers suddenly rate them as less sincere, less friendly, meaner, and more obnoxious (Gardner & Tockerman, 1994).

In personal ads, men often state their preference for slimness, and women

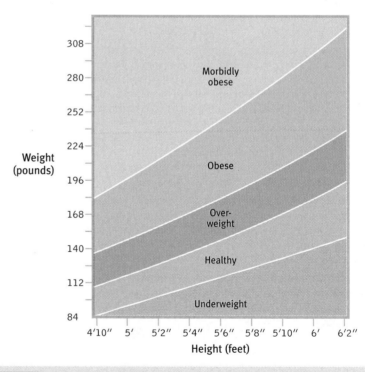

FIGURE **9.8** ● **Obesity measured as body mass index (BMI)** U.S. government guidelines encourage a body mass index (BMI) under 25. The World Health Organization and many countries define *obesity* as a BMI of 30 or more. The zones in this graph are based on BMI measurements for these heights and weights. BMI is calculated by using the following formula:

$$\frac{\text{Weight in kg (pounds} \times 0.45)}{\text{Squared height in meters (inches} \div 39.4)^2} = \text{BMI}$$

often advertise it (Miller et al., 2000; Smith et al., 1990). In the workplace, the social effects are equally clear. In one study of 370 obese 16- to 24-year-old women, two-thirds of them were still obese seven years later. They were less likely to be married, and they were also making less money—$7000 a year less—than an equally intelligent comparison group of some 5000 women who were not obese (Gortmaker et al., 1993).

In another study, viewers rated applicants in videotaped mock job interviews. The "applicants" were in fact professional actors, who appeared as either normal-weight or overweight, thanks to makeup and body padding that made them look 30 pounds heavier (Pingitore et al., 1994). When appearing to be overweight, the same person—using the same sentences, voice, and gestures—was rated less worthy of hiring. The weight bias was especially strong against women.

Weight discrimination has been found at every stage of the employment cycle—hiring, placement, promotion, compensation, discipline, and discharge (Roehling et al., 1999, 2007). Anti-fat prejudice even extends to job seekers who are *seen* with an obese person (Hebl & Mannix, 2003).

The Losing Battle

So, why don't obese people just drop that excess baggage? Because their bodies fight back. Let's consider some evidence.

A Sluggish Metabolism People get fat by taking in more calories than they use. The energy equivalent of a pound of fat is 3500 calories. Many dieters therefore believe they will lose a pound for every 3500 calories they cut from their diet. Surprise: This conclusion is false. Our bodies are designed to survive periods of famine. One way of adapting to starvation is to burn off fewer calories. When an overweight person's body drops below its previous set point (or settling point), the person's hunger increases and metabolism decreases. In one classic experiment, obese patients' daily food intake was reduced from 3500 to 450 calories for a month (Bray, 1969). Despite this drastic cut, participants lost only 6 percent of

their weight. Their bodies reacted as though they were being starved, and their metabolic rates dropped about 15 percent (**FIGURE 9.9**). That's why reducing food intake by 3500 calories may not equal a 1-pound weight loss. That's also why a rigorous diet can produce early rapid losses followed by a plateau. And that's why we can regain weight by eating amounts of food that only maintained our weight before we dieted. After a diet ends, our body is still in famine mode, trying to conserve energy. So how does this work if two people weigh and look the same, but one has dieted to

reach that weight? The formerly overweight one will likely need to eat fewer calories to maintain that weight. (Who said life is fair?)

An Explosion of Fat Cells Compared with other tissue, fat takes fewer calories to maintain. Body fat depends on the size and number of our fat cells. A typical adult has 30 to 40 billion of these mini fuel tanks, half of which lie near the skin's surface. The total number of fat cells depends on our heredity and personal history. Each fat cell can vary from nearly empty, like a dead balloon, to stuffed full. In an obese person, fat cells

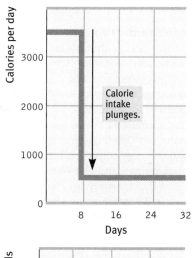

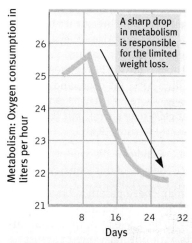

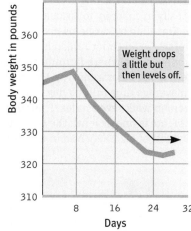

FIGURE 9.9 • **Dealing with dieting** These graphs show the effects of a severe diet on obese patients' body weight and metabolism (Bray, 1969). The students above are at a yearlong therapeutic boarding school for overweight teens that is designed to help increase metabolism with required exercise, to boost self-esteem in a supportive atmosphere, and to provide nutritional and academic counseling along with strict dietary requirements.

FIGURE 9.10 ● **Fat cells** Our bodies store energy in fat cells, which grow larger and more numerous if we become obese. If we then lose weight, the fat cells shrink in size, but their number doesn't decrease. (Adapted from Jules Hirsch, 2003.)

Never obese   Obese   Reduced obese

may swell to two or three times their normal size. Then—surprise—they divide, or they trigger nearby immature fat cells to divide (Hirsch, 2003). This can result in up to 75 billion total fat cells, and the new total never decreases (**FIGURE 9.10**). A dieter's fat cells may shrink, but they won't disappear (Sjöstrum, 1980).

A Genetic Handicap It's true. Our genes influence the size of our jeans. Consider:

- Given an obese parent, a boy is three times, and a girl six times, more likely to be obese than their counterparts with normal-weight parents (Carrière, 2003).

- Adopted children share meals with their adoptive siblings and parents. Yet their body weights most closely resemble those of their biological family (Grilo & Pogue-Geile, 1991).

- Identical twins have closely similar weights, even when reared apart (Plomin et al., 1997; Stunkard et al.,

1990). Fraternal twins' weights are much less similar. Such studies suggest that genes explain two-thirds of the person-to-person differences in body mass (Maes et al., 1997).

Environmental Influences

The strongest evidence that environment influences weight comes from our fattening world. Although the developed nations lead the trend, people *across the globe* are getting heavier. Since 1989, the percentage of overweight people in Mexico has expanded from 1 in 10 to today's nearly 7 in 10 (Popkin, 2007). So, why the change?

Too little activity Americans live in a culture that is a lot like an animal feedlot. Farmers fatten animals by giving them lots of food and little exercise. That formula works for humans, too. One long-term study of 50,000 nurses controlled for exercise, smoking, age, and diet. The researchers found that for every two-hour increase in daily TV watching, the nurses' obesity rates increased by 23 percent and their diabetes rates by 7 percent (Hu et al., 2003). TV watching is linked with obesity in children, too (**FIGURE 9.11**).

Siede Preis/Jupiterimages

Traveling by car helps us hoard fat. Ontario's Old Order Amish live in communities where farming and gardening are labor intensive. Men walk an average nine miles a day, and women walk seven miles. Their obesity rate is one-seventh the U.S. rate (Bassett et al., 2004). And in the United

States, a similar trend is found among people who live in areas that require a lot of walking (such as urban centers). The more sedentary folks who live in car-dependent suburbs weigh more (Ewing et al., 2003).

Too much unhealthy food Compared with people in the early 1900s, Americans are eating a higher-fat, higher-sugar diet. The ready availability of all-you-can-eat food buffets, make-your-own waffles, and free-refill soft drinks offers a fast path to weight gain—and to diabetes at younger ages (Popkin, 2007). Since 1960, the average adult's waist size has increased by nearly five inches (Ford et al., 2003; NCHS, 1970). The seats that hold our growing population are also wider. Washington State Ferries abandoned a 50-year-old standard of 18 inches per person. "Eighteen-inch butts are a thing of the past," explained a spokesperson (Shepherd, 1999). New York City agrees. It has mostly replaced its 17.5-inch bucket-style subway seats with bucketless seats for Big Apple bottoms (Hampson, 2000). Airline seat widths, having remained unchanged, feel more crowded. The "bottom" line: Today's people need more room.

Sleep loss Studies in France, Japan, Spain, the United States, and Switzerland show that children and adults who skimp on sleep are more vulnerable to obesity (Keith et al., 2006; Taheri, 2004a,b). With sleep deprivation, the levels of leptin (which reports body fat to the brain) fall and levels of ghrelin (the stomach hormone that stimulates appetite) rise. Taken together, sleep loss, Big Macs, large fries, sugar-laden drinks, and inactivity form a weapon of mass inflation.

Too much food, and too little: It is ironic that in a world where 800 million still live with hunger, obesity rates continue to rise in Western countries, endangering the lives of the severely overweight (Pinstrup-Andersen & Cheng, 2007; Popkin, 2007).

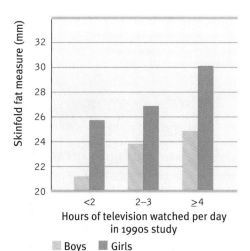

FIGURE 9.11 • **American idle: Couch potatoes beware—TV watching correlates with obesity** (Robinson, 1999).

Social influence A final environmental force is social influence. One 32-year study of 12,067 people found that people are most likely to become obese when a friend becomes obese (Christakis & Fowler, 2007). If that friend is a close mutual friend, the odds almost triple. Moreover, the correlation among friends' weights is not simply a matter of seeking out similar people as friends. Friends matter.

> "We put fast food on every corner, we put junk food in our schools, we got rid of [physical education classes], we put candy and soda at the checkout stand of every retail outlet you can think of. The results are in. It worked."
>
> Harold Goldstein, Executive Director of the California Center for Public Health Advocacy, 2009, when imagining a vast U.S. national experiment to encourage weight gain

* * *

These findings also reinforce a familiar lesson from Chapter 8's study of intelligence. There can be high levels of *heritability* (genetic influence on individual differences) without heredity being the only explanation of group differences. Genes mostly determine why you are heavier or leaner than your friends. Environment mostly determines why you and your friends are heavier than your parents and grandparents were at your age.

Setting Realistic Goals

Our eating behavior once again demonstrates one of this book's big ideas: Biological, psychological, and social-cultural factors interact. We have seen many biological and psychological forces working against those who want to shed excess pounds. Indeed, short of drastic surgery to tie off part of the stomach and small intestine, most who have succeeded on weight-loss programs have eventually regained most of the weight (Mann et al., 2007).

SO WHAT ADVICE CAN◄ PSYCHOLOGY OFFER TO THE NEARLY TWO-THIRDS OF AMERICAN WOMEN AND HALF OF MEN WHO SAY THEY WANT TO LOSE WEIGHT? About half of those women and men say they are "seriously trying" (Moore, 2006). What are their chances?

Permanent weight loss is not easy. For some helpful hints, see Close-Up: Waist Management on the next page.

THE BASICS

5. Hunger occurs in response to
   a. high blood glucose and low levels of ghrelin.
   b. low blood glucose and high levels of ghrelin.
   c. a low basal metabolic rate.
   d. a high basal metabolic rate.

6. Which of the following is a genetically disposed response to food?
   a. Disgust at the idea of eating cats and dogs
   b. An interest in novel foods
   c. A preference for sweet and salty foods
   d. Disliking carbohydrates

7. Which of the following is true of the eating disorder bulimia nervosa?
   a. People with bulimia continue to want to lose weight even when they are underweight.
   b. Bulimia is marked by weight fluctuations within or above normal ranges.
   c. Bulimia patients have food binges but do not purge.
   d. If one twin is diagnosed with bulimia, the chances of the other twin's sharing the disorder are greater if they are fraternal rather than identical twins.

8. Obese people find it very difficult to lose weight permanently for several reasons, including the fact that
   a. with dieting, fat cells shrink and then disappear.
   b. the settling point of obese people is lower than average.
   c. with dieting, basal metabolic rate increases.
   d. there is a genetic influence on body weight.

THE BIG PICTURE

9B. Sanjay recently adopted the typical college diet high in fat and sugar. He knows he may gain weight, but he figures it's no big deal because he can lose the extra pounds in the future. How would you evaluate Sanjay's plan?

IN YOUR EVERYDAY LIFE

▪ Do you usually eat only when your body sends hunger signals? How much does the sight or smell of delicious food tempt you even when you're full?

▪ Have you or a loved one ever tried unsuccessfully to lose weight? What happened? What weight-loss strategies might have been more successful?

Answers: 5. b, 6. c, 7. b, 8. d. Answers to The Big Picture questions can be found in Appendix B at the end of the book.

Waist Management

People struggling with extreme obesity should seek medical help. For others seeking to lose less weight, researchers offer these tips.

Begin only if you feel motivated and self-disciplined. For most people, the first step in permanent weight loss is setting moderate goals and having realistic expectations. Long-term success will require modifying your life-style, eating habits, and exercise routines.

Minimize exposure to tempting food cues. Keep tempting foods out of the house. Food shop only on a full stomach, and avoid the sweets and chips aisles. Limit meals to a few simple foods. Given more variety, we eat more.

Exercise regularly and get enough sleep. In a U.S. Centers for Disease Control study of 107,000 adults, only 1 in 5 of those trying to lose weight was following government guidelines for calories and exercise (Serdula et al., 1999). Brisk walking, running, or swimming empties fat cells, builds muscle, and makes you feel better. Exercise is especially effective when supported by 7 to 8 hours of sleep a night. The combination speeds up metabolism and helps lower your settling point (Bennett, 1995; Kolata, 1987; Thompson et al., 1982).

Eat healthy foods. Eat whole grains, fruits, and vegetables. Use healthy fats (such as those found in olive oil and fish), which help regulate appetite and artery-clogging cholesterol (Taubes, 2001, 2002). Better crispy greens than Krispy Kremes.

Don't starve all day and scarf at night. This pattern, common among overweight people, slows metabolism. By late morning, most of us are more alert and less fatigued if we have eaten a balanced breakfast (Spring et al., 1992).

Be aware of social influences. Ever notice that you eat more when out with friends? They can distract you from monitoring your eating (Ward & Mann, 2000).

Joe R. Liuzzo

Long-term success: Tammy and Jeffrey Munson are in the National Weight Control Registry, which tracks people who have lost at least 30 pounds and kept the weight off for at least a year. She lost 147 pounds, and he lost 100 pounds. "We broke the bed when we were first married," said Jeffrey. They had, at the time the second photo was taken, been slim for 8 years, thanks to healthier eating and exercise. "You eat a lot of good stuff and a little bad stuff, and you'll be fine," noted Tammy (*New York Times,* May 25, 1999).

Beware of the binge. Drinking alcohol or feeling anxious or depressed can unleash your urge to eat (Herman & Polivy, 1980). Once you break your diet, you may think "What the heck," and then binge (Polivy & Herman, 1985, 1987). But a lapse doesn't have to become a full collapse. You can stray from a healthy diet without abandoning it.

The Need to Belong

> **5** What are some results of our need to belong? How does social networking influence us?

The social stigma attached to obesity may bother us as much or more than the health concerns. Why? We are what Greek philosopher Aristotle called the *social animal.* Cut off from friends or family—alone in prison or at a new school or in a foreign land—most people feel keenly their lost connections with important others. This deep *need to belong* seems a basic human motivation (Baumeister & Leary, 1995). Josh Silverman (2008), president of Internet communication company Skype, understands the need to belong: "There's no question in my mind about what stands at the heart of the communication revolution—the human desire to connect." And connect we do.

The Benefits of Belonging

Social bonds boosted our ancestors' chances of survival. These bonds helped keep children close to their caregivers, protecting them from many threats. As adults, those who formed attachments were more likely to reproduce and co-nurture their offspring to maturity. To be "wretched" literally means, in its Middle English origin (*wrecche*), to be without kin nearby.

The need to connect: Six days a week, women from the Philippines work as "domestic helpers" in 154,000 Hong Kong households. On Sundays, they throng to the central business district to picnic, dance, sing, talk, and laugh. "Humanity could stage no greater display of happiness," reported one observer (*Economist,* 2001).

Survival also was supported by cooperation. In solo combat, our ancestors were not the toughest predators. But as hunters, they learned that six hands were better than two. As food gatherers, they gained protection from their enemies by traveling in groups. Those who felt a need to belong survived and reproduced most successfully, and their genes now rule.

People in every society on Earth belong to groups (and, as Chapter 14 explains, prefer and favor "us" over "them"). With the need to belong satisfied by close, supportive relationships, we feel included, accepted, and loved, and our self-esteem rides high. Indeed, *self-esteem* is a measure of how valued and accepted we feel (Leary & others, 1998). When our need for relatedness is satisfied in balance with two other basic psychological needs—*autonomy* (a sense of personal control) and *competence*—the result is a deep sense of well-being (Deci & Ryan, 2002; Patrick et al., 2007; Sheldon & Niemiec, 2006). To feel free, capable, and connected is to enjoy a good life.

Is it surprising, then, that so much of our social behavior aims to increase our feelings of belonging? To win friendship and avoid rejection, we generally conform to group standards. We monitor our behavior, hoping to make a good impression. We spend billions on clothes, cosmetics, and diet and fitness aids—all motivated by our search for love and acceptance.

By drawing a sharp circle around "us," the need to belong feeds both deep attachments and menacing threats. Out of our need to define a "we" come loving families, faithful friendships, and team spirit, but also teen gangs, ethnic rivalries, and fanatic nationalism.

For good or for bad, we work hard to form and maintain our relationships. Familiarity breeds liking, not contempt. Thrown together in groups at school, at work, in a tornado shelter, we behave like magnets, moving closer, forming bonds. Parting, we feel distress. We promise to call, to write, to come back for reunions.

Even when bad relationships break, people suffer. In one 16-nation survey, and in repeated U.S. surveys, separated and divorced people have been half as likely as married people to say they were "very happy" (Inglehart, 1990; NORC, 2007). After such separations, loneliness and anger—and sometimes even a strange desire to be near the former partner—linger. For those in abusive relationships, the fear of being alone sometimes seems worse than the certainty of emotional or physical pain. Children who move through a series of foster homes also know the fear of being alone. After repeated breaks in budding attachments, children may have difficulty forming deep attachments. The evidence is clearest at the extremes—children who grow up in institutions without a sense of belonging to anyone, or who are locked away at home and severely neglected. They become pathetic creatures, withdrawn, frightened, speechless.

When something threatens or dissolves our social ties, anxiety, loneliness, jealousy, or guilt may overwhelm us. Life may feel empty, pointless. For those moving alone to new places, the stress and loneliness can be depressing. Such findings have influenced U.S. policies. After years of placing individual refugee and immigrant families in isolated communities, U.S. agencies today encourage *cluster migration* (Pipher, 2002). The second refugee Sudanese family settling in a town generally has an easier adjustment than the first.

The Pain of Being Shut Out

Sometimes our need to belong is denied. CAN YOU RECALL A TIME WHEN YOU FELT◄ EXCLUDED OR IGNORED OR SHUNNED? Perhaps you received the silent treatment. Perhaps others avoided you, looked away, mocked you, or shut you out in some other way.

This is *ostracism*—social exclusion (Williams, 2007, 2009). Worldwide, humans use many forms of ostracism—exile, imprisonment, solitary confinement—to punish, and therefore control, social behavior. For children, even a brief time-out in isolation can be punishing. Being shunned threatens our need to belong

A violent response to social exclusion: Although most socially excluded teens do not commit violence, ostracism "weaves through case after case of school violence," reports Kipling Williams (2007). This teen, described by a classmate as someone his peers taunted as "freak, dork, nerd, stuff like that," went on a shooting spree at his suburban California high school, killing 2 and wounding 13 (Bowles & Kasindorf, 2001).

(Williams & Zadro, 2001). Lea, a lifelong victim of the silent treatment by her mother and grandmother, described the effect. "It's the meanest thing you can do to someone, especially if you know they can't fight back. I never should have been born." Like Lea, people often respond to ostracism with depressed moods, initial efforts to restore their acceptance, and then withdrawal. After two years of silent treatment by his employer, Richard reported, "I came home every night and cried. I lost 25 pounds, had no self-esteem, and felt that I wasn't worthy."

Rejected and powerless, people may seek new friends. Or they may turn nasty, as did college students made to feel rejected in one series of experiments (Baumeister et al., 2002; Twenge et al., 2001, 2002, 2007). Some students were told that a personality test they had taken showed that they were "the type likely to end up alone later in life." Others heard that people they had met didn't want them in a group that was forming. Still others heard good news. These lucky people would have "rewarding relationships throughout life," or "everyone chose you as someone they'd like to work with." How did students react after being told they weren't wanted or would end up alone? They were much more likely to engage in self-defeating behaviors and to underperform on aptitude tests. They also were more likely to act in mean or aggressive ways (blasting people with noise, for example) when they later interacted with those who had excluded them. "If intelligent, well-adjusted, successful . . . students can turn aggressive in response to a small laboratory experience of social exclusion," noted the research team, "it is disturbing to imagine the aggressive tendencies that might arise from . . . chronic exclusion from desired groups in actual social life." (At the end of the experiments, the study was fully explained and the participants left feeling reassured.)

The bottom line: Social isolation and rejection foster depressed moods or emotional numbness, and they can trigger aggression (Baumeister et al., 2009; Gerber & Wheeler, 2009). They also put us at risk for mental decline and ill health (Cacioppo & Hawkley, 2009). But if feelings of acceptance and connection build, so do self-esteem, positive feelings, and desires to help rather than hurt others (Buckley & Leary, 2001).

Social Networking

As social creatures, we live for connection. One researcher (Vaillant, 2009) was asked what he had learned from studying 238 Harvard University men from the 1930s to the end of their lives. He replied, "The only thing that really matters in life are your relationships to other people." A South African Zulu saying captures the idea: *Umuntu ngumuntu ngabantu*—"a person is a person through other persons."

Mobile Networks and Social Media

Look around and see humans connecting: talking, texting, posting, chatting, social gaming, e-mailing. The changes in how we connect have been fast and vast.

- Cell phones have been history's most rapidly adopted technology. By the end of 2009, 4.6 billion of us worldwide were using them (ITU, 2010). Asia and Europe lead the way, but American youth are catching up: 85 percent of 15- to 18-year-olds are cell-phone users (Kaiser, 2010).

- In all age groups, texting and e-mailing are displacing phone talking, which now accounts for less than half of U.S. mobile network traffic (Wortham, 2010).

- HOW MANY TEEN CELL- ◄ PHONE USERS WERE TEXTING IN 2009? Ninety percent of U.S. teens, up from 50 percent in 2006. Half (mostly females) were sending 50 or more texts daily; one-third were sending 200 (Lenhart, 2010). For many, it's as though friends, for better or worse, are always present.

- How many of us are using social networking sites, such as Facebook? In 2009, among online teens and under-30 adults, 75 percent were using these sites, as were 40 percent of those over 30 (Lenhart et al., 2010). The numbers are growing. If a "critical mass" of your friends are on a social network, its lure becomes hard to resist. If you don't check in, you may feel you're missing out. Such is our need to belong.

The Social Effects of Social Networking

By connecting like-minded people, the Internet serves as a social amplifier. It also functions as an online dating matchmaker (more on those topics in Chapter 14). As electronic communication becomes part of the "new normal," researchers are exploring how these changes affect our relationships.

Are Social Networking Sites Making Us More, or Less, Socially Isolated? Do lonely people use social networks to fill their social void? Do online relationships divert time from existing "real-world" relationships?

In the Internet's early years, when online communication in chat rooms and during social games was mostly between strangers, the answers appeared to be *Yes* and *Yes* (Kraut et al., 1998; Mesch, 2001; Nie, 2001). Adolescents and adults who spent more time on the Internet spent less time with friends, and their offline relationships suffered as a result. Even today, social networkers are less likely to know their real-world neighbors. A recent national survey also found they are "64 percent less likely than non-Internet users to rely on neighbors for help in caring for themselves or a family member" (Pew, 2009).

ICP-UK/Alamy

But some things are changing. The Internet is diversifying our social networks. (I am now connected to other hearing-technology advocates around the world.) And despite the decrease in neighborliness, social networking is mostly strengthening our connections with people we already know, enhancing our existing real-world friendships (DiSalvo, 2010; Valkenburg & Peter, 2009). If your Facebook or MySpace page helps you connect with friends, stay in touch with extended family, or find support in facing challenges, then you are not alone.

Does Electronic Communication Stimulate Healthy Self-Disclosure? As we will see in Chapter 10, confiding in others can be a healthy way of coping with day-to-day challenges. When communicating electronically rather than face-to-face, we often are less focused on others' reactions, less self-conscious, and thus less inhibited. We become more willing to share joys, worries, and vulnerabilities. Sometimes this is taken to an extreme, as when "sexting" teens send nude photos of themselves, or hate groups post messages promoting bigotry or crimes. More often, however, the increased self-disclosure serves to deepen friendships (Valkenburg & Peter, 2010).

Thomas Northcut/
Jupiterimages

Do Social Networking Profiles and Posts Reflect People's Actual Personalities? We've all heard stories of Internet predators hiding behind false personalities, values, and motives. Generally, however, social networks reveal people's real personalities. In one study, participants completed a personality test twice. In one test, they described their "actual personality"; in the other, they described their "ideal self." Volunteers then used the participants' Facebook profiles to create an independent set of personality ratings. The ratings based on Facebook profiles were much closer to the participants' actual personalities than to their ideal personalities (Back et al., 2010). In another study, people who seemed most likable

on their Facebook page also seemed most likable in face-to-face meetings (Weisbuch et al., 2009). So, your Facebook profile may indeed be the real you!

Does Social Networking Promote Narcissism? A secure and positive self-esteem can benefit our health and well-being, but self-esteem gone awry becomes *narcissism*. Narcissistic people are self-important, self-focused, and self-promoting. Some personality tests assess narcissism with items such as "I like to be the center of attention." Those who score high on these items are more active on social networking sites. They collect more superficial "friends." They offer more staged, glamorous photos. And, not surprisingly, they *seem* more narcissistic to strangers viewing their pages (Buffardi & Campbell, 2008).

Social networking sites are not just a gathering place for narcissists. They are also a feeding trough. In one study, (Twenge et al., 2010), college students were randomly assigned either to edit and explain their MySpace page for 15 minutes, or to use that time to study and explain a Google Maps routing. After completing their tasks, all were tested. Who then scored higher on a narcissism measure? Those who had spent the time focused on themselves.

Maintaining Balance and Focus

So social networks connect us. But they can also, as you've surely noticed, become a gigantic time- and attention-sucking

diversion. In both Taiwan and the United States, excessive Internet socializing and gaming have been associated with lower grades (Chen & Fu, 2008; Kaiser Foundation, 2010). In one U.S. survey, 47 percent of the heaviest users of the Internet and other media were receiving mostly C grades or lower, as were 23 percent of the lightest users (Kaiser Foundation, 2010). Except for seven hours or so (think sleep), the heaviest users may be almost constantly connected.

In today's world, each of us is challenged to find a healthy balance between our real-world time with people and our online sharing. Experts offer some practical suggestions for balancing online connecting with real-world responsibilities.

- *Monitor your time.* Keep a log of how you use your time. Then ask yourself, "Does my time use reflect my priorities? Am I spending more time online than I intended? Is my time online interfering with school or work performance? Have family or friends commented on this?"

- *Monitor your feelings.* Ask yourself, "Am I emotionally distracted by online gaming, gambling, or pornography? When I get up from my computer, how do I feel?"

- *"Hide" your more distracting online friends.* And in your own postings, practice the golden rule. Before you post, ask yourself, "Is this something I'd care about reading if someone else posted it?"

• *Periodically turn off your cell phone or leave it in another room.* Selective attention—the flashlight of your mind—can be in only one place at a time. "One of the most stubborn, persistent [aspects] of the mind," notes cognitive psychologist Daniel Willingham (2010), "is that when you do two things at once, you don't do either one as well as when you do them one at a time." When you want to study or work productively, squelch the temptation to check for texts, posts, and e-mails. And disable sound alerts and pop-ups. These distractions can interrupt your work and hijack your attention just when you've managed to get focused.

• *Try a Facebook fast (give it up for a day or a week) or a time-controlled Facebook diet (check in only after homework is done, or only during a lunch break).* Take notes on what you're losing and gaining on your new "diet."

PRACTICE TEST

THE BASICS

9. Decades of evidence indicate that we normally have a strong need to belong. Which of the following is NOT part of this evidence?

a. Students made to feel rejected and unwanted developed aggressive tendencies.

b. Social exclusion—such as exile or solitary confinement—is considered a severe form of punishment.

c. Gang members are not subject to the need to belong.

d. Children who are extremely neglected become withdrawn, frightened, and speechless.

10. Social networking tends to

a. strengthen your relationships with people you already know.

b. increase self-disclosure.

c. reveal your true personality.

d. do all of these things.

THE BIG PICTURE

9C. How might the evolutionary perspective, drive-reduction theory, and arousal theory explain our need to belong?

IN YOUR EVERYDAY LIFE

▪ Do you think that texting, e-mailing, or posting on Facebook increases your sense of belonging or leaves you feeling more isolated?

Answers: 9. c, 10. d. Answers to The Big Picture questions can be found in Appendix B at the end of the book.

Theories of Emotion

6 | What are the three parts of an emotion, and what theories help us to understand our emotions?

Motivated behavior is often connected to powerful emotions. I will never forget the day I went to a huge store to drop off film and brought along Peter, my toddler first-born child. As I set Peter down on his feet and prepared to complete the paperwork, a passerby warned, "You'd better be careful or you'll lose that boy!" Not more than a few breaths later, after dropping the film in the slot, I turned and found no Peter beside me.

With mild anxiety, I peered around one end of the counter. No Peter in sight. With slightly more anxiety, I peered around the other end. No Peter there, either. Now, with my heart pounding, I circled the neighboring counters. Still no Peter anywhere. As anxiety turned to panic, I began racing up and down the store aisles. He was nowhere to be found. Hearing my alarm, the store manager used the public-address system to ask customers to assist in looking for a missing child. Soon after, I passed the customer who had warned me. "I told you that you were going to lose him!" he scorned. With visions of kidnapping (strangers routinely adored that beautiful child), I braced for the possibility that my neglect had caused me to lose what I loved above all else, and—dread of all dreads—that I might have to return home and face my wife without our only child.

Courtesy of David G. Myers

RubberBall/Alamy

But then, as I passed the customer service counter yet again, there he was, having been found and returned by some obliging customer! In an instant, the arousal of dread spilled into ecstasy. Clutching my son, with tears suddenly flowing, I found myself unable to speak my thanks and stumbled out of the store awash in grateful joy.

Where do such emotions come from? Why do we have them? What are they made of? Emotions don't exist just to give us interesting experiences. They are our body's adaptive response, increasing our chances of survival. When we face challenges, emotions focus our attention and energize our action. Our heart races. Our pace quickens. All our senses go on high alert. Receiving unexpected good news, we may find our eyes tearing up. We raise our hands in triumph. We feel joy and a newfound confidence.

As my panicked search for Peter illustrates, **emotions** are a mix of

• *bodily arousal* (heart pounding).

• *expressive behaviors* (quickened pace).

• *conscious experience* including thoughts ("Is this a kidnapping?") and feelings (panic, fear, and later joy).

The puzzle for psychologists has been figuring out how these three pieces fit together. To do that, we need answers to two major questions:

1. A chicken-and-egg debate: Does your bodily arousal come *before* or *after* your emotional feelings? (Did I first notice my racing heart and faster step, and then feel terror about losing Peter? Or did my sense of fear come first, stirring my heart and legs to respond?)

2. How do *thinking* (cognition) and *feeling* interact? Does cognition always come before emotion? (Did I think about a kidnapping threat before I reacted emotionally?)

Theories of emotion differ in their answers to these questions.

James-Lange Theory: Arousal Comes Before Emotion Common sense tells most of us that we cry because we are sad, lash out because we are angry, tremble because we are afraid. First comes conscious awareness, then the feeling. But to pioneering psychologist William James, this commonsense view of emotion had things backwards. Rather, "We feel sorry because we cry, angry because we strike, afraid because we tremble" (1890, p. 1066). James' idea was also proposed by Danish physiologist Carl Lange, and thus is called the **James-Lange theory.** Perhaps you can recall a time when your car skidded on slick pavement. As it veered crazily, you countersteered and regained control. Just after the skid ended, you noticed your racing heart and then, shaking with fright, you felt the whoosh of emotion. Your feeling of fear followed your body's response.

Cannon-Bard Theory: Arousal and Emotion Happen at the Same Time Physiologist Walter Cannon (1871–1945) disagreed with James and Lange. Does a racing heart

Joy expressed is joy felt: According to the James-Lange theory, we don't just smile because we share our teammates' joy. We also share the joy because we are smiling with them.

signal fear, anger, or love? The body's responses—heart rate, perspiration, and body temperature—are too similar to cause the different emotions, and they change too slowly to trigger sudden emotions, said Cannon. He, and later another physiologist, Philip Bard, concluded that our bodily arousal and emotional experience occur together. So, according to the **Cannon-Bard theory,** your heart begins pounding as you experience fear. The emotion-triggering stimulus travels to your sympathetic nervous system, causing your body's arousal, at the same time that it travels to your brain's cortex, causing your awareness of emotion. Your pounding heart does not cause your feeling of fear, nor does your feeling of fear cause your pounding heart. Bodily responses and experienced emotions are separate.

Comparing Cannon-Bard and James-Lange Let's check your understanding of the James-Lange and Cannon-Bard theories. If your brain could not sense your heart pounding or your stomach churning, how would this affect your experienced emotions?

According to Cannon and Bard, you would experience emotions normally. They believed emotions occur separately from (and at the same time as) the body's arousal. According to James and Lange, your experienced emotions would be much less intense. They believed that to experience emotion, you must first perceive your body's arousal.

The James-Lange theory finds support in studies of people with severed spinal cords, including a survey of 25 soldiers who suffered such injuries in World War II (Hohmann, 1966). Those with *lower-spine injuries,* who had lost sensation only in their legs, reported little change in the intensity of their emotions before and after their spinal injuries. Those with *high spinal cord injury,* who could feel nothing below the neck, did report changes. Some reactions were much less intense than before the injuries. Anger, one man confessed, "just doesn't have the heat to it that it used to. It's a mental kind of anger." Other emotions, those expressed mostly in body areas above the neck, were felt *more* intensely. These men

reported increases in weeping, lumps in the throat, and getting choked up when saying good-bye, worshipping, or watching a touching movie. Such evidence has led some researchers to view feelings as "mostly shadows" of our bodily responses and behaviors (Damasio, 2003).

But most researchers now agree that our experienced emotions involve cognition (Averill, 1993; Barrett, 2006). Whether we fear the man behind us on the dark street depends entirely on whether we interpret his actions as threatening or friendly.

So, with James and Lange we can say that our body's reactions are an important ingredient of emotion. And with Cannon and Bard we can say that our experience of emotion is more than *reading* our body's responses. We *interpret* those responses.

Schachter-Singer Two-Factor Theory: Arousal + Label = Emotion Stanley Schachter and Jerome Singer (1962) proposed a third theory: Our physical reactions and our thoughts (perceptions, memories, and interpretations) together create emotion. In their **two-factor theory,** emotions therefore have two ingredients: physical arousal and cognitive appraisal. Like James and Lange, Schachter and Singer believed that our experience of emotion grows from our awareness of our body's arousal. Yet like Cannon and Bard, Schachter and Singer also believed that our physical reactions to emotions are similar (**FIGURE 9.12** on the next page). Thus, in their view, an emotional experience requires a conscious interpretation of the arousal. We'll revisit the James-Lange,

emotion a response of the whole organism, involving (1) bodily arousal, (2) expressive behaviors, and (3) conscious experience.

James-Lange theory the theory that our experience of emotion is our awareness of our physiological responses to emotion-arousing stimuli.

Cannon-Bard theory the theory that an emotion-arousing stimulus simultaneously triggers (1) physiological responses and (2) the subjective experience of emotion.

two-factor theory Schachter and Singer's theory that to experience emotion we must (1) be physically aroused and (2) cognitively label the arousal.

FIGURE 9.12 • Theories of emotion

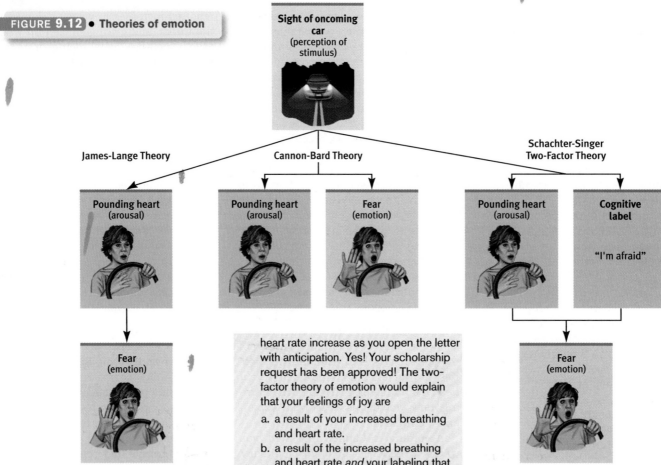

Sight of oncoming car
(perception of stimulus)

James-Lange Theory

Pounding heart
(arousal)

Fear
(emotion)

Cannon-Bard Theory

Pounding heart
(arousal)

Fear
(emotion)

Schachter-Singer Two-Factor Theory

Pounding heart
(arousal)

Cognitive label

"I'm afraid"

Fear
(emotion)

Cannon-Bard, and Schachter-Singer two-factor theories as we consider other research on emotions in this chapter.

PRACTICE TEST

THE BASICS

11. The James-Lange theory states that our experience of an emotion is a result of our physiological response to a stimulus; we are afraid because our heart pounds. The Cannon-Bard theory proposes that the physiological response (like heart pounding) and the subjective experience of, say, fear
    a. are unrelated.
    b. occur simultaneously.
    c. occur in the opposite order (with feelings of fear first).
    d. are cognitive functions.

12. When you pick up your mail, you see a long-awaited letter from your school's financial aid office. Your breathing and heart rate increase as you open the letter with anticipation. Yes! Your scholarship request has been approved! The two-factor theory of emotion would explain that your feelings of joy are
    a. a result of your increased breathing and heart rate.
    b. a result of the increased breathing and heart rate *and* your labeling that arousal as joy.
    c. causing the increased breathing and heart rate.
    d. unrelated to your increased breathing and heart rate.

THE BIG PICTURE

9D. Christine is holding her 8-month-old baby when a fierce dog appears out of nowhere and, with teeth bared, leaps for the baby's face. Christine immediately ducks for cover to protect the baby, screams at the dog, then notices that her heart is banging in her chest and she's broken out in a cold sweat. How would the James-Lange, Cannon-Bard, and two-factor theories explain Christine's emotional reaction?

IN YOUR EVERYDAY LIFE

▪ Can you remember a time when you began to feel upset or uneasy and only later labeled those feelings? What was that like?

Answers: 11. b, 12. b. Answers to The Big Picture questions can be found in Appendix B at the end of the book.

Embodied Emotion

Whether you are falling in love or grieving a loved one's death, you need little convincing that emotions involve the body. Feeling without a body is like breathing without lungs. Some physical responses are easy to notice, others happen without your awareness. Indeed, many take place at the level of your brain's neurons.

Emotions and the Autonomic Nervous System

7 **What bodily changes accompany emotions?**

As we saw in Chapter 2, in a crisis your *autonomic nervous system (ANS)* mobilizes your body for action **(FIGURE 9.13)**.

Autonomic Nervous System Controls Physiological Arousal

Sympathetic division (arousing)		Parasympathetic division (calming)
Pupils dilate	EYES	Pupils contract
Decreases	SALIVATION	Increases
Perspires	SKIN	Dries
Increases	RESPIRATION	Decreases
Accelerates	HEART	Slows
Inhibits	DIGESTION	Activates
Secrete stress hormones	ADRENAL GLANDS	Decrease secretion of stress hormones
Reduced	IMMUNE SYSTEM FUNCTIONING	Enhanced

FIGURE 9.13 ● **Emotional arousal** In a crisis, the ANS' sympathetic division arouses us. When the crisis passes, the parasympathetic division calms us.

Alarmed by the sound of a motorcycle slowing down behind you on a dark street, your muscles tense, your stomach develops butterflies, your mouth becomes dry. To provide energy, your liver pours extra sugar into your bloodstream. To help burn the sugar, your breathing increases to supply needed oxygen. Your digestion slows, allowing blood to move away from your internal organs and toward your muscles. With blood sugar driven into the large muscles, running becomes easier. Your pupils open wider, letting in more light. To cool your stirred-up body, you perspire. If wounded, your blood would clot more quickly.

After your next crisis, think of this: Without any conscious effort, your body's response to danger is wonderfully coordinated and adaptive—preparing you to fight or flee. When the crisis passes, the ANS gradually calms the body, as stress hormones slowly leave your bloodstream.

> "No one ever told me that grief felt so much like fear. I am not afraid, but the sensation is like being afraid. The same fluttering in the stomach, the same restlessness, the yawning. I keep on swallowing."
> C. S. Lewis, *A Grief Observed*, 1961

The Physiology of Emotions

8 How do our body states relate to specific emotions? How effective are polygraphs in using body states to detect lies?

Imagine another scene. You are conducting an experiment, measuring the body's responses to different emotions. In each of four rooms, you have someone watching a movie. In the first, the person is viewing a horror show. In the second, the viewer watches an anger-provoking film. In the third, someone is watching a sexually arousing film. In the fourth, the person is viewing an utterly boring movie. From the control center, you are tracking each person's physical responses, measuring perspiration, breathing, and heart rate. Do you think you could tell who is frightened? Who is angry? Who is sexually aroused? Who is bored?

With training, you could probably pick out the bored viewer. But the bodily differences among fear, anger, and sexual arousal would be much more difficult to spot by measuring perspiration, breathing, and heart rates (Barrett, 2006). Different emotions do not have sharply different biological signatures.

Despite similar bodily responses, sexual arousal, fear, and anger *feel* different. If sexually stimulated, you will experience a genital response. If afraid, you may feel a clutching, sinking sensation in your chest and a knot in your stomach. If angry, you may feel "hot under the collar" and be aware of a pressing inner tension. Fear and anger also *look* different. People may appear "paralyzed with fear" or "ready to explode."

So, does research pinpoint any distinct body- or brain-pattern indicators of each emotion? *Yes.* With the help of some sophisticated laboratory tools, you could find some clues. For example, the finger temperatures and hormone secretions that accompany fear and rage do sometimes differ (Ax, 1953; Levenson, 1992). Fear and joy, although they prompt similar increased heart rate, stimulate different facial muscles. During fear, your brow muscles tense. During joy, muscles in your cheeks and under your eyes pull into a smile (Witvliet & Vrana, 1995).

Emotional arousal: Intense, happy excitement and panicky fear are accompanied by similar states of bodily arousal. That allows us to flip rapidly between the two emotions.

AP Photo/HO

Brain scans show that emotions differ in the brain circuits they use (Panksepp, 2007). When you experience negative emotions such as disgust, your right frontal cortex is more active than your left frontal cortex. The right frontal lobe is also more active in depression-prone people and in those with generally negative personalities (Harmon-Jones et al., 2002). One man, having lost part of his right frontal lobe in brain surgery, became (his not-unhappy wife reported) less irritable and more affectionate (Goleman, 1995). My father, after a right-hemisphere stroke at age 92, lived the last two years of his life with happy gratitude and nary a complaint or negative emotion.

When you experience positive moods—when you are enthusiastic, energized, and happy—your left frontal lobe will be more active. Increased left frontal lobe activity is found in people with positive personalities—jolly infants and alert, energetic, and persistently goal-directed adults (Davidson, 2000, 2003; Urry et al., 2004). Indeed, the more a person's baseline frontal lobe activity tilts left, the more upbeat the person typically is. (When you're happy and you know it, your brain will surely show it.)

To sum up, we can't easily see differences in emotions from tracking heart rate, breathing, and perspiration. But facial expressions and brain activity do vary with the emotion. DO WE, LIKE ◀ PINOCCHIO, GIVE OFF TELLTALE SIGNS

WHEN WE LIE? For more on that question, see Thinking Critically About: Do Lie Detectors Lie?)

Cognition and Emotion

9 What is the role of cognition in emotion? What two tracks does the brain use in processing emotions?

How does what we *think* affect how we *feel*? Can we experience emotion apart from thinking? Or do we become what we think?

Cognition Can Define Emotion

Sometimes our arousal spills over from one event to the next, influencing our response. Imagine arriving home after a fast run and finding a message that you got a longed-for job. With arousal lingering from the run, will you feel more excited than you would be if you heard this news after awakening from a nap?

To see whether this *spillover effect* exists, researchers injected college men with the hormone epinephrine, which triggers feelings of arousal (Schachter & Singer, 1962). Picture yourself as a participant: After receiving the injection, you go to a waiting room. You find yourself with another person (actually an accomplice of the experimenters) who is acting either joyful or irritated. As you observe

this person, you begin to feel your heart race, your body flush, and your breathing become more rapid. If you had been told to expect these effects from the injection, what would you feel? The actual volunteers felt little emotion—because they attributed their arousal to the drug. But if you had been told the injection would produce no effects, what would you feel? Perhaps you would react as another group of participants did. They "caught" the apparent emotion of the other person in the waiting room. They became happy when the accomplice was acting joyful, and testy when the accomplice was acting irritated.

We can experience a stirred-up state as one emotion or another very different one, depending on how we interpret and label it. As happiness researcher Daniel Gilbert (2006) quipped, "Feelings that one interprets as fear in the presence of a sheer drop may be interpreted as lust in the presence of a sheer blouse." Dozens of experiments have demonstrated this spillover effect. Insult people who have just been aroused by pedaling an exercise bike or watching rock videos, and they interpret and label their arousal as a response to the insult. Their anger will exceed that of people similarly provoked but not previously aroused. Likewise, sexually aroused people have angrier reactions in anger-provoking situations. So what do you think might happen if a person who has just experienced an angry or fearful event becomes sexually involved? The lingering arousal may intensify sexual passion (Palace, 1995). Just as the Schachter-Singer two-factor theory predicts, arousal + label = emotion. Arousal—from emotions as diverse as anger, fear, and sexual excitement—can indeed spill from one emotion to another (Reisenzein, 1983; Sinclair et al., 1994; Zillmann, 1986). *The point to remember:* Arousal fuels emotion; cognition channels it.

©Kim Steele/Blend Images/Corbis

Do Lie Detectors Lie?

Do we in any way give ourselves away when we lie? The creators and users of the *lie detector,* or **polygraph,** believe we do. Polygraphs are sensitive machines that measure breathing, heart rate, and perspiration. Changes indicate an emotional response. Imagine yourself attached to one of these machines, trying to relax. An examiner will ask you questions and monitor your responses. He asks you, "In the last 20 years, have you ever taken something that didn't belong to you?" This item is a *control question,* aimed at making everyone a little nervous. If you lie and say "*No!*" (as many people do), your nervousness will register as arousal, which the polygraph will detect. This response will give the examiner a baseline, a useful comparison for your responses to *critical questions* ("Did you ever steal anything from your previous employer?"). If your responses to critical questions are weaker than to control questions, the examiner will infer you are telling the truth. The idea is that only a thief becomes nervous when denying a theft.

Critics of this idea point out two problems. First, our bodily arousal is much the same from one emotion to another. Our bodies react to anxiety, irritation, and guilt in very similar ways. Second, many innocent people *do* get nervous when accused of a crime or bad act. Many rape victims, for example, "fail" these tests because they have strong emotional reactions while telling the truth about the

Lie to Me: In this TV series, the character of Dr. Cal Lightman (left), based on Paul Ekman and his research, reads faces and body language to detect lies uncannily well. In real life, Ekman has trained law enforcement officers to detect deceit in facial expressions with some success (Ekman, 2003).

rapist (Lykken, 1991). About one-third of the time, polygraph test results are wrong **(FIGURE 9.14).**

A 2002 U.S. National Academy of Sciences report noted that "no spy has ever been caught [by] using the polygraph." It is not for lack of trying. The CIA is one of several U.S. agencies that together have spent millions of dollars testing tens of thousands of employees. Did the test catch Aldrich Ames, a Russian spy within the CIA who enjoyed an unexplained lavish life-style? Ames "took scores of polygraph tests and passed them all," notes physicist Robert Park (1999). "Nobody thought to investigate the source of his sudden wealth—after all, he was passing the lie detector tests."

A more effective approach to lie detection uses a *guilty knowledge test,* which also assesses a suspect's bodily responses. But in this test, the questions focus on specific crime-scene details known only to the police and the guilty person (Ben-Shakhar & Elaad, 2003). If a camera and computer had been stolen, for example, only a guilty person should react strongly to the brand names of the stolen items. Given enough such specific probes, an innocent person will seldom be wrongly accused.

Several twenty-first-century research teams are exploring new ways to nab liars. Some are comparing the words or microfacial expressions of truth tellers and liars. Others are going straight to the seat of deceit—the brain (Langleben & Dattilio, 2008). Stay tuned. Pinocchio's giveaway lying signal may turn out to be not the length of his nose, but rather the telltale activity in his brain.

FIGURE 9.14 ● **How often do lie detectors lie?** In one study, polygraph experts interpreted the test results of 100 people who had been suspects in theft crimes (Kleinmuntz & Szucko, 1984). Half the suspects were guilty and had confessed. The other half had been proven innocent. If the polygraph experts had been the judges, more than one-third of the innocent would have been declared guilty, and one-fourth of the guilty would have been declared innocent.

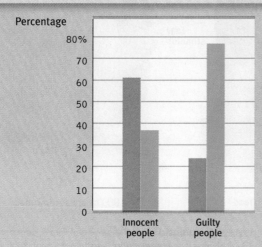

Percentage

- ■ Judged innocent by polygraph
- ■ Judged guilty by polygraph

polygraph a machine, commonly used in attempts to detect lies, that measures some bodily responses (such as changes in perspiration, heart rate, and breathing) accompanying emotion.

Diverse Yet Alike

Whether it's arousal from a soccer match in Belgium (left) or from a political demonstration in Israel (right), these feelings can similarly spill over into anger, which can lead to rioting and violence.

Emotion and the Two-Track Brain

Is the heart always subject to the mind? Must we always interpret our arousal before we can experience an emotion? No, said Robert Zajonc (pronounced ZI-yence; 1980, 1984a). He contended that we actually have many emotional reactions apart from, or even before, our interpretation of a situation. CAN YOU RECALL LIKING SOME- ◄ THING OR SOMEONE IMMEDIATELY, WITHOUT KNOWING WHY? These reactions often reflect the unconscious processing that takes place in our two-track mind.

Our emotional responses are the final step in a process that can follow two different pathways in our brain. Research on neurological processes shows that some of our emotions (especially more complex feelings, like hatred and love) travel a "high road." A stimulus following the high road would travel (by way of the thalamus) to the brain's cortex (FIGURE 9.15a). There, it would be analyzed and labeled before the order is sent out, via the amygdala (an emotion-control center), to respond.

But sometimes our emotions (especially simple likes, dislikes, and fears) take what Joseph LeDoux (2002) calls the "low road," a neural shortcut that bypasses the cortex (Figure 9.15b). Following the low-road pathway, a fear-provoking stimulus would travel (again by way of the thalamus) directly to the amygdala. This shortcut, bypassing the conscious cortex, enables our greased-lightning emotional

response ("Life in danger!") before our brain interprets the exact source of danger. So speedy is the amygdala response that we may not be aware of what's happened (Dimberg et al., 2000). In one fascinating experiment, researchers used fMRI (functional MRI) scans to observe the amygdala's response to subliminally presented fearful eyes (FIGURE 9.16) (Whalen et

al., 2004). Although they were flashed too quickly for people to consciously perceive them, the fearful eyes did trigger increased amygdala activity. A control condition that presented the whites of happy eyes did not trigger this activity.

The amygdala's structure makes it easier for our feelings to hijack our thinking than for our thinking to rule our feelings

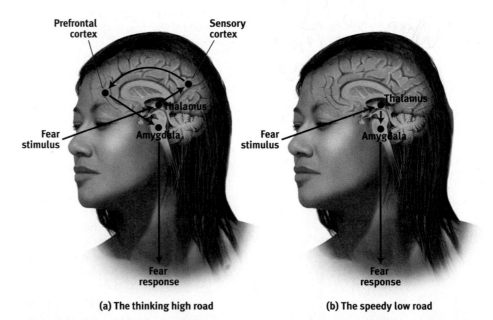

(a) The thinking high road

(b) The speedy low road

FIGURE **9.15** ● **The brain's pathways for emotions** In the two-track brain, sensory input may be routed (a) to the cortex (via the thalamus) for analysis and then transmission to the amygdala; or (b) directly to the amygdala (via the thalamus) for an instant emotional reaction.

(LeDoux & Armony, 1999). It sends more neural projections up to the cortex than it receives back. Thus, in the forest, we can jump when we hear rustling in the bushes nearby, and leave it to our cortex (via the high road) to decide later whether the sound was made by a snake or by the wind. Such an experience supports Zajonc's belief that *some* of our emotional reactions involve no deliberate thinking.

Emotion researcher Richard Lazarus (1991, 1998) agreed that our brains process vast amounts of information outside of our conscious awareness, and that some emotional responses do not require *conscious* thinking. Much of our emotional life operates via the automatic, effortless, speedy low road. But, he asked, how would we *know* what we are reacting to if we did not in some way appraise the situation? The appraisal may be effortless and we may not be conscious of it, but it is still a mental function. To know whether a stimulus is good or bad, the brain must have some idea of what it is (Storbeck et al., 2006). Thus, said Lazarus,

TABLE 9.1	Perspectives on Emotion	
Theory	**Explanation of Emotions**	**Example**
James-Lange	Our awareness of our specific bodily response to emotion-arousing stimuli	We observe our heart racing after a threat and then feel afraid.
Cannon-Bard	Bodily response + simultaneous subjective experience	Our heart races as we experience fear.
Schachter-Singer	Two factors: General arousal + a cognitive label	Arousal could be labeled as fear or excitement, depending on context.
Zajonc; LeDoux	Instant, before cognitive appraisal	We automatically react to a sound in the night before appraising it.
Lazarus	Appraisal ("Is it good or bad?") defines emotion	The sound is "just the wind."

emotions arise when we *appraise* an event as harmless or dangerous, whether we truly *know* it is or not. We appraise the sound of the rustling bushes as the presence of a threat. Later, we learn that it was "just the wind."

Let's sum up (see also **TABLE 9.1**). As Zajonc and LeDoux have demonstrated, some emotional responses—especially simple likes, dislikes, and fears—involve no conscious thinking. We may fear a big spider, even if we "know" it is harmless. Such responses are difficult to alter by changing our thinking. We may automatically like one person more than another. This instant appeal can even influence our political decisions if we vote (as many people do) for the candidate we like over the candidate expressing positions closer to our own (Westen, 2007).

But other emotions—including moods such as depression, and complex feelings such as hatred and love—are, as Lazarus, Schachter, and Singer predicted, greatly affected by our interpretations, memories, and expectations. For these emotions, we have more conscious control. As you will see in Chapter 12, learning to *think* more positively about ourselves and the world around us can help us *feel* better.

A dramatic testimony to the interplay of emotion and cognition comes from a study of seemingly emotionless patients with a history of brain damage (Damasio, 1994, 2003). Its focus was a simple card-game task. Over a number of trials, people could make or lose money. People without brain damage tended to make money. As they repeated the task, the unconscious track of their brain triggered emotions that helped them figure things out before their conscious reasoning kicked in. The emotionless patients with damaged brains did not have these feelings to inform their thinking and they typically *lost* money. Once again we see that the two-track mind includes a smart unconscious. Automatic emotion and conscious thinking together weave the fabric of our minds (Forgas, 2008).

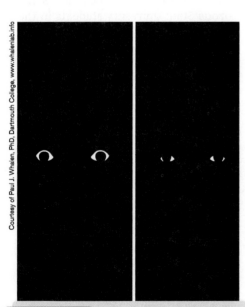

Courtesy of Paul J. Whalen, PhD, Dartmouth College, www.whalenlab.info

FIGURE 9.16 ● The brain's sensitivity to threats Researchers flashed fearful eyes (left) too briefly for viewers to consciously perceive them. But fMRI scans revealed that viewers got the message. Their alert amygdala became more active—a response not triggered when happy eyes (right) were presented (Whalen et al., 2004).

PRACTICE TEST

THE BASICS

13. Research on arousal indicates that if we are physically aroused by swimming, then heckled by an onlooker, we may interpret our arousal as anger and

a. become less physically aroused.
b. feel angrier than usual.
c. feel less angry than usual.
d. act joyful.

Continued

14. Zajonc and LeDoux maintain that some of our emotional reactions occur before we have had the chance to label or interpret them. Lazarus disagreed. These psychologists differ about whether emotional responses occur in the absence of

   a. physical arousal.
   b. learning.
   c. cognition.
   d. autonomic nervous system responses.

THE BIG PICTURE

9E. How do the two divisions of the autonomic nervous system help us respond to and recover from a crisis, and why is this relevant to the study of emotions?

IN YOUR EVERYDAY LIFE

▪ Can you think of a recent time when you noticed your body's reactions to a stressful experience? How did you interpret the situation? What emotion did you feel?

Answers: 13. b, 14. c. Answers to The Big Picture questions can be found in Appendix B at the end of the book.

Expressed Emotion

There is a simple method of detecting people's emotions: Read their body language, listen to their voice tones, and study their faces. People's expressive behavior reveals their emotion. Does this nonverbal language vary with culture, or is it the same everywhere? And do our expressions influence what we feel?

Detecting Emotion in Others

10 How do we use facial expressions to communicate? Do women and men differ in these abilities?

All of us communicate without words. Westerners "read" a firm handshake as evidence of an outgoing, expressive personality (Chaplin et al., 2000). A glance or a stare can communicate intimacy, submission, or dominance (Kleinke, 1986). When two people are passionately in love, they typically spend time—quite a bit of time—gazing into each other's eyes

(Rubin, 1970). Would such gazes stir these feelings between strangers? To find out, researchers asked male-female pairs of strangers to gaze intently for two minutes either at each other's hands or into each other's eyes. After separating, the eye-gazers reported feeling a tingle of attraction and affection (Kellerman et al., 1989).

Most of us read nonverbal cues fairly well. Shown 10 seconds of video from the end of a speed-dating interaction, people can often detect whether one person is attracted to the other (Place et al., 2009). We are especially good at detecting nonverbal threats. A single angry face will "pop out" of a crowd faster than a single happy one (Fox et al., 2000; Hansen & Hansen, 1988; Öhman et al., 2001). Even when hearing another language, most people can easily detect anger (Scherer et al., 2001).

Some of us are especially skilled at decoding emotional cues. In one study, hundreds of people were asked to name the emotion in brief film clips they watched. The clips showed portions of a person's emotionally expressive face or body, sometimes accompanied by a garbled voice (Rosenthal et al., 1979). For example, one 2-second scene revealed only the face of an upset woman. After watching the scene, viewers would state whether the woman was criticizing someone for being late or was talking about her divorce. Given such "thin

Obvious emotions: Graphic novel authors use facial expressions and other design elements to express emotion, reducing the need to explain how the characters are feeling.

slices," women have generally surpassed men at reading people's emotional cues (Hall, 1984, 1987). Women have also surpassed men in other assessments of emotional cues, such as deciding whether a male-female couple is a genuine romantic couple or a posed phony couple (Barnes & Sternberg, 1989).

Women's skill at decoding emotions may help explain why women respond with greater emotion in both positive and negative situations (Grossman & Wood, 1993; Sprecher & Sedikides, 1993; Stoppard & Gruchy, 1993). In studies of 23,000 people, from 26 cultures around the world, women more than men have reported themselves open to feelings (Costa et al., 2001). These findings support the extremely strong perception that emotionality is "more true of women." In one survey, nearly 100 percent of 18- to 29-year-old Americans perceived emotionality as a woman's characteristic (Newport, 2001).

One exception: Anger strikes most people as a more masculine emotion. Try it yourself. Imagine an angry face. What gender is the person? If you're like 3 in 4 Arizona State University students in the original study, you imagined an angry male (Becker et al., 2007). The researchers also found that when a gender-neutral face was made to look angry, most people perceived it as male. If the face was smiling, they were more likely to perceive it as female (**FIGURE 9.17**).

ARE THERE GENDER DIFFERENCES IN ◀ EMPATHY? If you have *empathy,* you identify with others and imagine what it must be like to walk in their shoes. You rejoice with those who rejoice and weep with those who weep. In surveys, women are far more likely than men to describe themselves as empathic. Actually, measures of body responses, such as one's heart rate while seeing another's distress, reveal a much smaller gender gap (Eisenberg & Lennon, 1983).

Nevertheless, females are more likely to *express* empathy—to cry and to report distress when observing someone in distress. As **FIGURE 9.18** shows, this gender difference was clear in videotapes of men and women watching film clips that were sad (children with a dying parent), happy (slapstick comedy), or frightening (a man

© APA/Vaughn Becker

FIGURE 9.17 ● **Male or female?** Researchers manipulated a gender-neutral face. People were more likely to see it as a male when it wore an angry expression, and as a female when it wore a smile (Becker et al., 2007).

nearly falling off the ledge of a tall building) (Kring & Gordon, 1998; Vigil, 2009). Women also tend to experience emotional events, such as viewing pictures of mutilation, more deeply, with more brain activation in areas sensitive to emotion. And they remember the scenes better three weeks later (Canli et al., 2002).

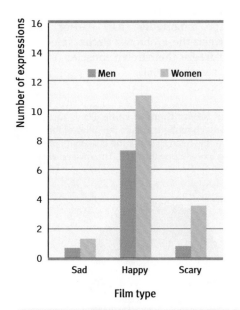

FIGURE 9.18 ● **Gender and expressiveness** Male and female film viewers did not differ dramatically in self-reported emotions or physiological responses. But the women's faces *showed* much more emotion. (From Kring & Gordon, 1998.)

Culture and Emotional Expression

11 Are nonverbal expressions of emotion universally understood, and do they influence our feelings?

The meaning of *gestures* varies with culture. Former U.S. President Richard Nixon learned this while traveling in Brazil. He made the North American "A-OK" sign, but in Brazil that was a crude insult. The importance of cultural definitions of gestures was again demonstrated in 1968, when North Korea publicized photos of supposedly happy officers from a captured U.S. Navy spy ship. In the photo, three men had raised their middle fingers, telling their captors it was a "Hawaiian good luck sign" (Fleming & Scott, 1991).

DO FACIAL EXPRESSIONS HAVE DIFFERENT MEANINGS IN DIFFERENT CULTURES? To find out, researchers showed photographs of different facial expressions to people in different parts of the world and asked them to guess the emotion (Ekman et al., 1975, 1987, 1994; Izard, 1977, 1994). You can try this matching task yourself by pairing the six emotions with the six faces of **FIGURE 9.19** on the next page.

Regardless of your cultural background, you probably did pretty well. A

smile's a smile the world around. Ditto for anger, and to a lesser extent the other basic expressions (Elfenbein & Ambady, 1999). (There is no culture where people frown when they are happy.) We do slightly better when judging emotional displays from our own culture (Elfenbein & Ambady, 2002, 2003a,b). Nevertheless, different cultures tend to categorize emotions—as anger, fear, and so on—in similar ways.

Musical expressions also cross cultures. Happy and sad music feels happy and sad around the world. Whether you live in an African village or a European city, fast-paced music seems happy, and slow-paced music seems sadder (Fritz et al., 2009).

Do these shared categories reflect shared cultural experiences, such as movies and TV programs that are seen around the world? Apparently not. Paul Ekman and his team asked isolated people in New Guinea to respond to such statements as, "Pretend your child has died." When North American collegians viewed the videotaped responses, the students read the New Guineans' facial reactions easily.

So we can say that facial muscles speak a fairly universal language. This discovery would not have surprised Charles Darwin, who wrote *The Expression of the Emotions in Man and Animals* in 1872. Darwin believed that in prehistoric times, before our ancestors communicated in words, they communicated threats, greetings, and submission with facial expressions. Such expressions helped them survive and became part of our shared heritage. A sneer, for example, retains elements of an animal's baring its teeth in a snarl. Emotional expressions may enhance our survival in other ways, too. Surprise raises our eyebrows and widens our eyes, helping us take in more information. Disgust wrinkles our nose, closing out foul odors.

Smiles are social as well as emotional events. Bowlers seldom smile when they score a strike; they smile when they turn to face their companions (Jones et al., 1991; Kraut & Johnston, 1979). Olympic

> "For news of the heart, ask the face."
> Guinean proverb

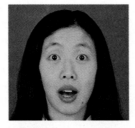
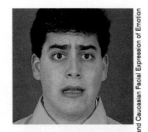
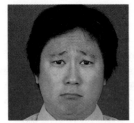

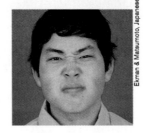

Ekman & Matsumoto, Japanese and Caucasian Facial Expression of Emotion

FIGURE 9.19 ● **Culture-specific or culturally universal expressions?** As people of differing cultures, do our faces speak differing languages? Which face expresses disgust? Anger? Fear? Happiness? Sadness? Surprise? (From Matsumoto & Ekman, 1989.)

Answers, from left to right, top to bottom: happiness, surprise, fear, sadness, anger, disgust.

gold-medal winners typically don't smile when they are awaiting their ceremony. But they wear broad grins when interacting with officials and facing the crowd and cameras (Fernández-Dols & Ruiz-Belda, 1995). Thus, a glimpse at competitors' spontaneous expressions following an Olympic judo competition gives a very good clue to who won, no matter what their country. Even natively blind athletes, who have never observed smiles, display the same social smiles in such situations (Matsumoto & Willingham, 2006, 2009).

The Effects of Facial Expressions

As famed psychologist William James struggled with feelings of depression and grief, he came to believe that we can control our emotions by going "through the outward movements" of any emotion we want to experience. "To feel cheerful," he advised, "sit up cheerfully, look around cheerfully, and act as if cheerfulness were already there."

Was James right? CAN OUR OUTWARD◄ EXPRESSIONS AND MOVEMENTS TRIGGER OUR INNER FEELINGS AND EMOTIONS? You can test his idea: Fake a big grin. Now scowl. Can you feel the "smile therapy" difference? Participants in dozens of experiments have felt a difference. For

example, researchers (Laird et al., 1974, 1984, 1989) tricked students into making a frowning expression by asking them to "contract these muscles" and "pull your brows together." (The students thought they were helping the researchers attach facial electrodes.) The result? The students reported feeling a little angry. Students similarly tricked into smiling felt happier, found cartoons funnier, and recalled happier memories than did the frowners. So, too, with other basic emotions. For example, people reported feeling fear when made to construct a fearful expression: "Raise your eyebrows. And open your eyes wide. Move your whole head back, so that your chin is tucked in a little bit, and let your mouth relax and hang open a little" (Duclos et al., 1989). This **facial feedback effect** has been repeated many times, in many places, for many basic emotions (**FIGURE 9.20**). Just activating one of the smiling muscles by holding a pen in the teeth (rather than with the lips, which activates a frowning muscle) is enough to make cartoons seem more amusing (Strack et al., 1988).

So, your face is more than a billboard that displays your feelings; it also feeds your feelings. No wonder depressed patients reportedly feel better after between-the-eyebrows Botox injections that freeze their frown muscles (Finzi & Wasserman, 2006).

FIGURE 9.20 ● **How to make people smile without telling them to smile** Do as Kazuo Mori and Hideko Mori (2009) did with students in Japan: Attach rubberbands to the sides of the face with adhesive bandages, and then run them either over the head or under the chin. With cheeks raised as though in a smile, most students reported feeling more happy than sad. The reverse was true for those with their cheeks pulled down.

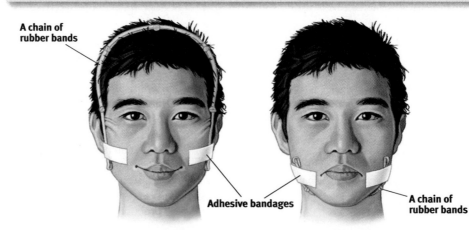

A chain of rubber bands

Adhesive bandages

A chain of rubber bands

Other studies have noted a similar *behavior feedback effect* (Snodgrass & others, 1986). Try it. Walk for a few minutes with short, shuffling steps, keeping your eyes downcast. Now walk around taking long strides, with your arms swinging and your eyes looking straight ahead. Can you feel your mood shift? Going through the motions awakens the emotions.

You can use your understanding of feedback effects to become more empathic—to feel what others feel. See what happens if you let your own face mimic another person's expression. Acting as another acts helps us feel what another feels (Vaughn & Lanzetta, 1981). Indeed, natural mimicry of others' emotions helps explain why emotions are contagious (Dimberg et al., 2000; Neumann & Strack, 2000).

PRACTICE TEST

THE BASICS

15. People in different cultures are most likely to differ in their interpretations of

   a. adults' facial expressions.
   b. children's facial expressions.
   c. frowns.
   d. gestures.

16. When people are tricked into assuming fearful expressions, they often report feeling a little fearful. This result is known as the _____ effect.

   a. facial feedback
   b. culture-specific
   c. natural mimicry
   d. emotional contagion

THE BIG PICTURE

9F. Who tends to express more emotion—men or women? How do we know the answer to that question?

IN YOUR EVERYDAY LIFE

▪ Imagine one situation in which you would like to change the way you feel. How could you do so by altering your facial expressions or the way you carry yourself?

Answers: 15. d, 16. a. Answers to The Big Picture questions can be found in Appendix B at the end of the book.

Experienced Emotion

12 | **What are the basic emotions, and what are the causes and consequences of anger?**

How many distinct emotions are there? Carroll Izard (1977) isolated 10 basic emotions (joy, interest-excitement, surprise, sadness, anger, disgust, contempt, fear, shame, and guilt). Most are present in infancy. Let's take a closer look at anger and happiness. What functions do they serve? What influences our experience of each?

Anger

What makes us angry? People asked to recall or keep careful records of their experiences with anger reported becoming at least mildly angry several times a week, sometimes several times a day (Averill, 1983). The anger was often a response to friends' or loved ones' perceived misdeeds. In most cases, the acts seemed willful, unjustified, and avoidable.

What do we do with our anger? In a Gallup survey of teens, more boys than girls reported walking away from the situation or working it off with exercise. Girls more often reported talking with a friend, listening to music, or writing (Ray, 2005).

Like a boomerang, our anger comes back to strike us when it fuels physically or verbally aggressive acts we later regret.

"I thought it would be nice if we had a forum where we could get together and have screaming tantrums."

Anger also primes prejudice. After 9/11, Americans who responded with more anger than fear also displayed more intolerance for immigrants and Muslims (DeSteno et al., 2004; Skitka et al., 2004).

Anger can harm us in another way. Chronic anger is linked to heart disease (more on this in Chapter 10). Does this mean that we should, as some popular books and articles advise, release our angry feelings by lashing out at those who offend us? **SHOULD CHILDREN BE◄ TOLD TO "VENT" ANGRY FEELINGS?** Are "recovery" therapists right to encourage us to rage at our dead parents, imaginatively curse the boss, or confront our childhood abuser?

The vent-your-anger advice assumes that we can achieve emotional release, or **catharsis,** through aggressive action or fantasy. Experimenters report that *sometimes* when people lash out at a provoker, they may indeed calm down. But this tends to be true only *if* they direct their strike at the provoker, *if* their behavior seems justified, and *if* their target is not threatening (Geen & Quanty, 1977; Hokanson & Edelman, 1966). In short, expressing anger can be *temporarily* calming if it does not leave us feeling guilty or anxious.

More often, expressing anger breeds more anger. For one thing, it may trigger another round of angry interactions, turning a minor conflict into a major confrontation. For another, expressing anger can magnify anger. (Recall the behavior feedback research: *Acting* angry can make us *feel* angrier.) The backfire potential of catharsis appeared in one study of 100 frustrated engineers and technicians just laid off by an aerospace company (Ebbesen et al., 1975). Researchers asked some workers questions

facial feedback effect the tendency of facial muscle states to trigger corresponding feelings such as fear, anger, or happiness.

catharsis emotional release. The catharsis hypothesis maintains that "releasing" aggressive energy (through action or fantasy) relieves aggressive urges.

that released angry feelings, such as, "What instances can you think of where the company has not been fair with you?" After expressing their anger, the workers later filled out a questionnaire that assessed their attitudes toward the company. Had the opportunity to "drain off" their feelings reduced their anger? Quite the contrary. These people expressed more anger than those who had discussed neutral topics.

> "Anger will never disappear so long as thoughts of resentment are cherished in the mind."
>
> The Buddha, 500 B.C.E.

Other studies support this finding. In one, people who had been provoked were asked to wallop a punching bag while thinking about the person who had angered them. Later, when given a chance for revenge, these people became even more aggressive. "Venting to reduce anger is like using gasoline to put out a fire," concluded the researcher, Brad Bushman (2002).

Striking back sometimes reduces tension temporarily and gives a squirt of pleasure (Ramirez et al., 2005). But in the long run, any such pleasure reinforces the outbursts, reduces inhibitions, and may be habit forming. If stressed teachers find they can drain off some of their tension by exploding at a student, then the next time they feel irritated and tense they may be more likely to do it again. Think about it: The next time you are angry you are likely to repeat whatever relieved your anger in the past.

Anger is not always wrong. Used wisely, it can communicate strength and competence (Tiedens, 2001). It can benefit a relationship when it expresses a complaint in ways that help solve the conflict rather than give it a fresh start. This means not only keeping silent about trivial irritations but also communicating important ones clearly and firmly. A nonaccusing statement of feeling—perhaps letting your housemates know that "I get irritated when I have to wash everyone's dirty dishes"—can help end the conflicts that cause anger.

What if someone else's behavior really hurts you, and you cannot resolve the conflict? The age-old response of forgiveness may be your best answer. Without letting the offender off the hook or inviting further harm, forgiveness releases anger and calms the body. To explore the bodily effects of forgiveness, researchers invited college students to recall an incident where someone had hurt them (Witvliet et al., 2001). As the students mentally rehearsed forgiveness, their negative feelings—and their perspiration, blood pressure, heart rate, and facial tension—all were lower than when they rehearsed their grudges.

A cool culture: Domestic violence is rare in Micronesia. This photo of community life on Pulap Island suggests one possible reason: Family life takes place in the open on this island. Relatives and neighbors who witness angry outbursts can step in before the emotion escalates into child, spouse, or elder abuse.

Wolfgang Kaehler

Happiness

13 **What are the causes and consequences of happiness?**

Our state of happiness or unhappiness colors our thoughts and our actions. Happy people perceive the world as a safer place. They make decisions and cooperate more easily. They live healthier and more energized and satisfied lives (Briñol et al., 2007; Lyubomirsky et al., 2005). When your mood is gloomy, life as a whole seems depressing and meaningless. Let your mood brighten, and your thinking broadens and becomes more playful and creative (Amabile et al., 2005; Fredrickson, 2006). Your relationships, your self-image, and your hopes for the future seem more promising.

This helps explain why college students' happiness helps predict their life course. In one study, women who smiled happily in 1950s college yearbook photos were more likely to be married, and happily so, in middle age (Harker & Keltner, 2001). In another study, which surveyed thousands of U.S. college students in 1976 and restudied them at age 37, happy students had gone on to earn significantly more money than their less happy peers (Diener et al., 2002).

Moreover—and this is one of psychology's most consistent findings—when we feel happy we more often help others. In study after study, a mood-boosting experience (finding money, succeeding on a challenging task, recalling a happy event) has made people more likely to give money, pick up someone's dropped papers, volunteer time, and do other good deeds. Psychologists call it the **feel-good, do-good phenomenon** (Salovey, 1990). Happiness doesn't just feel good, it does good.

Doing good also promotes good feeling. Some happiness coaches and instructors harness this force by asking their clients to perform a daily "random act of kindness" and to record how it made them feel.

William James was writing about the importance of happiness ("the secret motive for all [we] do") as early as 1902. With the rise of positive psychology in the twenty-first century, the study of happiness has become a significant area of research. It is a key part of one of our big ideas in this text—psychology explores human strengths as well as challenges. Part of happiness research is the study of **subjective well-being**—our feelings of happiness (sometimes defined as a high ratio of positive to negative feelings) or sense of satisfaction with life. This information, combined with *objective* measures of well-being, such as a person's physical and economic condition, is helping us understand our quality of life judgments.

The Short Life of Emotional Ups and Downs

WHEN YOU ARE DOWN, DOES YOUR MOOD ◄ USUALLY REBOUND WITHIN A DAY OR TWO? How about when you're feeling up? Is that mood also hard to sustain? Over the long run, our emotional ups and downs

Take heart! Tomorrow will be a new day: Car trouble can happen at the worst possible times. But this man's bad mood will almost certainly clear by tomorrow, when he may even experience a better-than-normal good mood.

Human resilience: Seven weeks after her 1994 wedding, Anna Putt of South Midlands, England, shown here with her husband, Des, suffered a brainstem stroke that left her "locked-in." For months afterward, she recalls, "I was paralyzed from the neck down and was unable to communicate. These were VERY frightening times. But with encouragement from family, friends, faith, and medical staff, I tried to keep positive." In the ensuing three years, she became able to "talk" (by nodding at letters), to steer an electric wheelchair with her head, and to use a computer (by nodding while wearing spectacles that guide a cursor). Despite her paralysis, she reports that "I enjoy going out in the fresh air. My motto is 'Don't look back, move forward.' God would not want me to stop trying and I have no intention of doing so. Life is what you make of it!"

tend to balance out. This is true even over the course of the day. Positive emotion rises over the early to middle part of most days and then drops off (Kahneman et al., 2004; Watson, 2000). So, too, with day-to-day moods. A stressful event—an argument, a sick child, a car problem—triggers a bad mood. No surprise there. But by the next day, the gloom nearly always lifts (Affleck et al., 1994; Bolger et al., 1989; Stone & Neale, 1984). If anything, people tend to rebound from bad days to a *better*-than-usual good mood the following day.

Even when negative events drag us down for longer periods, our bad mood usually ends. Romantic breakups feel devastating, but eventually the wound heals. Faculty members denied tenure expect their lives to be deflated. Actually,

5 to 10 years later, their happiness level is about the same as for those who were given tenure (Gilbert et al., 1998).

Grief over the loss of a loved one or anxiety after a severe trauma can linger. But usually, even tragedy is not permanently depressing. People who become blind or paralyzed usually recover near-normal levels of day-to-day happiness. So do those who must go on kidney dialysis or have permanent colostomies (Gerhart et al., 1994; Riis et al., 2005; Smith et al., 2009). A major disability does often leave people somewhat less happy than the average person, yet considerably happier than able-bodied people with depression (Kübler et al., 2005; Lucas, 2007a,b; Schwartz & Estrin, 2004). "If you are a paraplegic," explains Daniel Kahneman (2005), "you will gradually start thinking of other things, and the more time you spend thinking of other things the less miserable you are going to be." Contrary to what many people believe, most patients "locked in" a motionless body do not say they want to die (Bruno et al., 2008; Smith & Delargy, 2005). The surprising reality: *We overestimate the duration of our emotions and underestimate our resilience, our ability to bounce back.*

Wealth and Well-Being

WOULD YOU BE HAPPIER IF YOU MADE ◄ MORE MONEY? In a 2006 Gallup poll, 73 percent of Americans thought they would be. How important is "Being very well off financially"? *Very important,* say many entering U.S. collegians (**FIGURE 9.21** on the next page).

feel-good, do-good phenomenon our tendency to be helpful when already in a good mood.

subjective well-being self-perceived happiness or satisfaction with life. Used along with measures of objective well-being (for example, physical and economic indicators) to evaluate our quality of life.

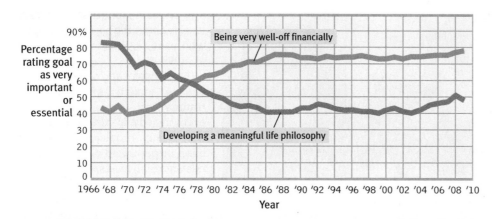

FIGURE 9.21 ● **The changing materialism of entering college students** Yearly surveys of more than 200,000 entering U.S. college students have, since 1970, revealed an increasing desire for wealth. (From *The American Freshman* surveys, UCLA, 1966 to 2009.)

greater wealth—enabling twice as many cars per person, not to mention iPods, laptops, and smart phones—also buy more happiness? As **FIGURE 9.22** shows, the average American, though certainly richer, is not a bit happier. In 1957, some 35 percent said they were "very happy," as did slightly fewer—32 percent—in 2008. Ditto China, where living standards have risen but happiness has not (Brockmann et al., 2009). These findings lob a bombshell at modern materialism: *Economic growth in affluent countries has provided no apparent boost to morale or social well-being.*

Why Can't Money Buy Happiness?

Why is it that, beyond poverty, more and more money does not buy more and more happiness? More generally, why do

To a point, wealth does correlate with well-being. Consider:

- In most countries, and especially in poor countries, individuals with lots of money are typically happier than those who struggle to afford life's basic needs (Diener & Biswas-Diener, 2009; Howell & Howell, 2008).

- People in rich countries are also more satisfied and somewhat happier than those in poor countries (Diener et al., 2009; Inglehart, 2009; Lucas & Schimmack, 2009).

So, it seems that money enough to buy your way out of hunger and hopelessness also buys some happiness. But once one has enough money for comfort and security, piling up more and more matters less and less.

And consider this: During the last four decades, the average U.S. citizen's buying power almost tripled. Did this

"But on the positive side, money can't buy happiness—so who cares?"

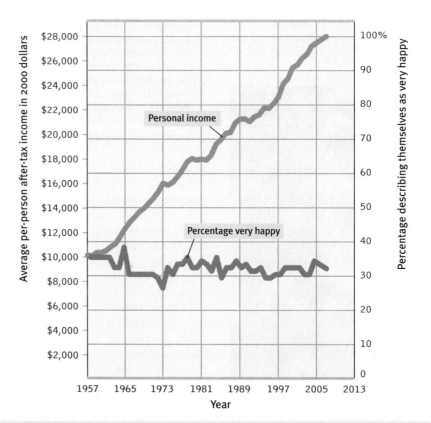

FIGURE 9.22 ● **Does money buy happiness?** Money surely helps us to avoid certain types of pain. Yet, though buying power has almost tripled since the 1950s, the average American's reported happiness has remained almost unchanged. (Happiness data from National Opinion Research Center surveys; income data from *Historical Statistics of the United States* and *Economic Indicators.*)

our emotions seem to be attached to elastic bands that pull us back from highs or lows? Psychology has proposed two answers. Each of them suggests that happiness is relative.

My Happiness Is Relative to My Own Experience The **adaptation-level phenomenon** describes our tendency to judge events in comparison to our past experiences. We draw on those experiences to establish *neutral* levels, points at which sounds seem neither loud nor soft, temperatures neither hot nor cold, events neither pleasant nor unpleasant. We then notice and react to variations up or down from these levels.

So, could we ever create a permanent social paradise? Probably not (Campbell, 1975; Di Tella & MacCulloch, 2008). People who have experienced a recent windfall—from a lottery, an inheritance, or a surging economy—typically feel joy and satisfaction (Diener & Oishi, 2000; Gardner & Oswald, 2007). So would you if you woke up tomorrow with all your wishes granted—perhaps a world with no bills, no ills, perfect grades, someone who loves you unreservedly. But after a time, you would gradually adapt, and you would adjust your neutral level to include these new experiences. Before long, you would again sometimes feel joy and satisfaction (when events exceed your expectations), sometimes feel let down (when they fall below), and sometimes feel neutral. *The point to remember:* Feelings of satisfaction and dissatisfaction, success and failure are judgments we make about ourselves, based on our prior experience.

"Money won't make you happy, Waldron. So instead of a raise, I'm giving a Prozac."

"Researchers say I'm not happier for being richer, but do you know how much researchers make?"

My Happiness Is Relative to Your Success We are always comparing ourselves with others. And whether we feel good or bad depends on our perception of just how successful those others are (Lyubomirsky, 2001). We are slow-witted or clumsy only when others are smarter or more agile. This sense that we are worse off than others with whom we compare ourselves is the concept of **relative deprivation.**

Some examples: During World War II, U.S. Air Corps soldiers experienced a relatively rapid promotion rate. Nevertheless, individual soldiers were frustrated about their own comparatively slow promotion rates (Merton & Kitt, 1950). Seeing so many others being promoted apparently inflated the soldiers' expectations. And when expectations soar above achievements, the result is disappointment. Relative deprivation showed up again when Alex Rodriguez

"I have also learned why people work so hard to succeed: It is because they envy the things their neighbors have. But it is useless. It is like chasing the wind. . . . It is better to have only a little, with peace of mind, than be busy all the time with both hands, trying to catch the wind."

Ecclesiastes 4:4

achieved a 10-year, $275 million baseball contract. His deal surely made him temporarily happy, but it likely also lowered other star players' satisfaction with their smaller multimillion-dollar contracts. And here's a larger example. The economic surge that has made some urban Chinese newly wealthy appears to have fueled among other Chinese a sense of relative deprivation (Burkholder, 2005a,b).

Just as comparing ourselves with those who are better off creates envy, so counting our blessings as we compare ourselves with those worse off boosts our contentment. In one study, University of Wisconsin–Milwaukee women considered others' deprivation and suffering (Dermer et al., 1979). They viewed vivid depictions of how grim life was in Milwaukee in 1900. They imagined and then wrote about various personal tragedies, such as being burned and disfigured. Later, the women expressed greater satisfaction with their own lives. Similarly, when mildly depressed people read about someone who is even more depressed, they feel somewhat better (Gibbons, 1986). "I cried because I had no shoes," states a Persian saying, "until I met a man who had no feet."

adaptation-level phenomenon our tendency to form judgments (of sounds, of lights, of income) relative to a neutral level defined by our past experiences.

relative deprivation the perception that we are worse off relative to those with whom we compare ourselves.

HI & LOIS

Predictors of Happiness

Happy people share many characteristics (TABLE 9.2). But what makes one person so filled with joy, day after day, and others so gloomy? Here, as in so many other areas, the answer is found in the interplay between nature and nurture.

Genes matter. Studies of 254 identical and fraternal twins indicate that heredity accounts for about 50 percent of the difference among people's happiness ratings (Lykken & Tellegen, 1996). Identical twins raised apart are often similarly happy.

But our personal history and our culture matter, too. On the personal level, as we saw earlier, our emotions tend to balance around a level defined by our experiences. On the cultural level, groups vary in the traits they value. Self-esteem matters more to Westerners, who value individualism. Social acceptance matters more to those in other cultures that stress family and community (Diener et al., 2003).

Depending on our genes, our outlook, and our recent experiences, our happiness seems to fluctuate around our "happiness set point," which disposes some people to be ever upbeat and others more negative. Even so, our satisfaction with life is not fixed (Fujita & Diener, 2005; Mroczek & Spiro, 2005). As researchers studying human strengths will tell you, happiness rises and falls, and it can be influenced by factors that are under our

"I could cry when I think of the years I wasted accumulating money, only to learn that my cheerful disposition is genetic."

control (Sin & Lyubomirsky, 2009). For more on this idea, see Close-Up: Want to Be Happier?

Anger, happiness, and other emotions have this in common: They are biopsychosocial phenomena. Our genetic predispositions, brain activity, outlooks, experiences, relationships, and cultures jointly form us.

PRACTICE TEST

THE BASICS

17. When you move into a new apartment, you find the street noise irritatingly loud, but after a while, it no longer bothers you. This illustrates the

a. relative deprivation principle.
b. adaptation-level principle.
c. feel-good, do-good phenomenon.
d. catharsis principle.

18. Those who support catharsis believe that we can get rid of anger by venting—by expressing our feelings in actions or words directed at the person who offended us. Such expressions of anger can

a. be temporarily calming if they do not produce feelings of guilt or anxiety.
b. strengthen the original feelings of anger and cause disagreements to escalate.
c. teach people that anger is a rewarding response that can be repeated on other occasions.
d. have all of these results.

19. There will always be someone more successful, more accomplished, or richer with whom to compare yourself. In psychology, this observation is embodied in the

a. relative deprivation principle.
b. adaptation-level principle.
c. need to belong.
d. feel-good, do-good phenomenon.

20. One of the most consistent findings of psychological research is that happy people are also

a. more likely to express anger.
b. generally luckier than others.
c. concentrated in the wealthier nations.
d. more likely to help others.

THE BIG PICTURE

9G. What things do (and do not) predict self-reported happiness?

IN YOUR EVERYDAY LIFE

■ Have you ever noticed your sadness or anger decreasing as you realized others had it worse than you? What was that like?

■ Can you name two specific changes you could make this week to enhance your happiness?

Picture questions can be found in Appendix B at the end of the book.

Answers: 17. b, 18. d, 19. a, 20. d. Answers to The Big

TABLE 9.2	Happiness Is . . .
Researchers Have Found That Happy People Tend to	**However, Happiness Seems Not Much Related to Other Factors, Such as**
Have high self-esteem (in individualistic countries).	Age.
Be optimistic, outgoing, and agreeable.	Gender (women are more often depressed, but also more often joyful).
Have close friendships or a satisfying marriage.	Education level.
Have work and leisure that engage their skills.	Parenthood (having children or not).
Have a meaningful religious faith.	Physical attractiveness.
Sleep well and exercise.	

Source: Summarized from DeNeve & Cooper (1998), Diener et al. (2003), Headey et al. (2010), Lucas et al. (2004), Myers (1993, 2000), Myers & Diener (1995, 1996), and Steel et al. (2008).

Want to Be Happier?

Your happiness, like your cholesterol level, is genetically influenced. Yet as cholesterol is also influenced by diet and exercise, so happiness is to some extent under your personal control. Here are some research-based suggestions for building your personal strengths to increase your satisfaction with life.

Realize that enduring happiness doesn't come from financial success. We adapt to change by adjusting our expectations. Neither wealth, nor any other circumstance we long for, will guarantee happiness.

Take control of your time. Happy people feel in control of their lives. To master your use of time, set goals and break them into daily aims. This may be frustrating at first because we all tend to overestimate how much we will accomplish in any given day. The good news is that we generally *underestimate* how much we can accomplish in a year, given just a little progress every day.

Act happy. As you saw earlier in this chapter, people who have been manipulated into a smiling expression felt better. So put on a happy face. Talk as if you feel positive self-esteem, are optimistic, and are outgoing. We can often act our way into a happier state of mind.

Seek work and leisure that engage your skills. Happy people often are in a zone called *flow*—absorbed in tasks that challenge but don't overwhelm them. The most expensive forms of leisure (sitting on a yacht) often provide less flow experience than simpler forms, such as gardening, socializing, or craft work. Frequent small positive experiences make for more lasting happiness than big but rare positive events.

Join the "movement" movement. Aerobic exercise can relieve mild depression and anxiety as it promotes health and energy. Sound minds reside in sound bodies. Off your duffs, couch potatoes!

Photodisc/Jupiterimages

Give your body the sleep it wants. Happy people live active lives yet save time for renewing sleep. Many people—high school and college students, especially—suffer from sleep debt. The result is fatigue, diminished alertness, and gloomy moods.

Give priority to close relationships. Intimate friendships with those who care deeply about you can help you weather difficult times. Resolve to nurture your closest relationships by not taking your loved ones for granted. This means displaying to them the sort of kindness you display to others, affirming them, playing together, and sharing together.

Focus beyond self. Reach out to those in need. Happiness increases helpfulness (those who feel good do good). But doing good also makes us feel good.

Count your blessings and record your gratitude. Keeping a gratitude journal heightens well-being (Emmons, 2007; Seligman et al., 2005). Try pausing each day to savor good moments, and to record positive events and why they occurred. Express your gratitude to others.

Nurture your spiritual self. For many people, faith provides a support community, a reason to focus beyond self, and a sense of purpose and hope. That helps explain why people active in faith communities report greater-than-average happiness and often cope well with crisis.

Digested from David G. Myers, The Pursuit of Happiness *(Harper).*

Terms and Concepts to Remember

motivation, p. 238
drive-reduction theory, p. 238
physiological needs, p. 238
drive, p. 238
incentive, p. 238
hierarchy of needs, p. 238
glucose, p. 241
set point, p. 241

basal metabolic rate, p. 242
anorexia nervosa, p. 243
bulimia nervosa, p. 243
binge-eating disorder, p. 243
emotion, p. 252
James-Lange theory, p. 253
Cannon-Bard theory, p. 253
two-factor theory, p. 253

polygraph, p. 257
facial feedback effect, p. 262
catharsis, p. 263
feel-good, do-good phenomenon, p. 264
subjective well-being, p. 265
adaptation-level phenomenon, p. 267
relative deprivation, p. 267

Multiple-choice **self-tests** and more may be found at www.worthpublishers.com/myers

MOTIVATION AND EMOTION

Motivational Concepts

1 **What is motivation, and what are three key perspectives that help us understand motivated behaviors?**

- *Motivation:* The energizing and directing of our behavior.
- *Drive-reduction theory*: We feel motivated when pushed by a *physiological need* to reduce a *drive* (such as thirst), or when pulled by an *incentive* in our environment (ice-cold drink).
- Arousal theory: We also feel motivated to behave in ways that maintain arousal (for example, curiosity-driven behaviors).
- Maslow's *hierarchy of needs:* Our levels of motivation form a pyramid shape. Lower-level needs (hunger, thirst, safety) must be met before we attend to higher-level needs (love, respect, self-actualization, finding meaning).

Hunger

2 **What physiological factors cause us to feel hungry?**

- Empty-stomach pangs and low levels of blood *glucose* motivate hunger.
- The brain's hypothalamus is involved in hunger control.
- Appetite hormones heighten or reduce hunger.
- To maintain a stable weight *(set point)*, the body adjusts its *basal metabolic rate* of energy use, in part according to how much food we eat.

3 **What psychological and cultural factors affect our eating behavior and feelings of hunger? How do eating disorders illustrate the power of psychological influences?**

- Our memory of when we last ate affects our expectation of when we should eat again.
- We universally prefer certain tastes (such as sweet and salty).
- We learn other taste preferences from family and culture.
- Some taste aversions (such as to foods that have made us ill) have survival value.
- Cultural pressures, low self-esteem, negative emotions, and perhaps a genetic factor seem to interact with stressful life experiences to produce *anorexia nervosa, bulimia nervosa,* and *binge-eating disorder*.

4 **What factors predispose some people to become and remain obese?**

- Fat cells store a concentrated fuel reserve for our bodies—perfect for feast/famine times, but no longer adaptive.
- Heredity and environment interact in influencing body weight. Genes determine the number of fat cells we are born with, but our personal history affects whether those fat cells will grow and multiply.
- Weight-loss challenges: The size but not the number of fat cells is reduced by a diet; fat cells require less energy than muscle cells to maintain; and metabolism decreases (and hunger increases) when body weight drops.
- Ways to increase odds of dieting success: Reduce exposure to food cues and negative social influences, boost metabolism through exercise, get enough sleep, develop healthy eating patterns (type of food and time of day), and embrace the lifelong nature of these changes yet be prepared to recover from a lapse.

The Need to Belong

5 **What are some results of our need to belong? How does social networking influence us?**

- Social bonds are adaptive and help us to be healthier and happier.
- When shunned by others, people suffer from stress and depression and may engage in self-defeating or antisocial behavior.
- Social networking is one way of forming and fostering relationships, in part through self-disclosure. Maintaining a balance between real-world and electronic connections can help us avoid the social media pitfalls of poor real-world performance, social isolation, and narcissism.

Theories of Emotion

6 **What are the three parts of an emotion, and what theories help us to understand our emotions?**

- *Emotion:* whole-body response involving bodily arousal, expressive behaviors, and conscious experience.
- *James-Lange theory:* Emotional feelings follow our body's response to the emotion-arousing stimuli. (We observe our heart pounding and feel fear.)
- *Cannon-Bard theory:* Our body responds to emotion at the same time that we experience that emotion. (Neither causes the other.)
- *Two-factor theory:* Emotions involve physical arousal (pounding heart), which is given a cognitive label ("I'm afraid").

7

8 **How do our body states relate to specific emotions? How effective are polygraphs in using body states to detect lies?**

- The large-scale body changes that accompany sexual arousal, fear, and anger are very similar (increased perspiration, breathing, and heart rate), though they feel different.
- The small-scale body changes are different. For example, fear stimulates different facial muscles than joy does.
- Emotions use different circuits in the brain. For example, greater activity in the left frontal lobe signals positive rather than negative moods.
- *Polygraphs* (lie detectors) attempt to measure physical evidence of emotions, but they are not accurate enough to justify widespread use.

9 **What is the role of cognition in emotion? What two tracks does the brain use in processing emotions?**

- The emotion we experience may be influenced by our interpretation of our feelings.
- Emotions may be processed on one of two tracks in the brain—the analyzing "high-road" slow path (thalamus, cortex, and then amygdala), or the instant response "low-road" path (thalamus straight to the amygdala).
- Zajonc and LeDoux argued that simple emotions (such as likes, dislikes, and fears) may occur instantly, without conscious appraisal.
- Lazarus and Schachter and Singer argued that conscious appraisal and labeling are key parts of more complex emotions (such as moods, hatred, and love).

Expressed Emotion

10 **How do we use facial expressions to communicate? Do women and men differ in these abilities?**

- We are good at detecting emotions from facial expressions, especially if the message is a threat.
- Women surpass men at reading emotional cues, at expressing most emotions (but not anger), and at deep processing of emotions in the brain.

11 **Are nonverbal expressions of emotion universally understood, and do they influence our feelings?**

- Facial expressions, such as those of happiness and fear, are roughly similar all over the world.
- The meaning of gestures varies by culture.
- Expressions communicate emotion to others but also amplify the feelings we experience (*facial feedback effect*).

Experienced Emotion

12 **What are the basic emotions, and what are the causes and consequences of anger?**

- The basic emotions: joy, interest–excitement, surprise, sadness, anger, disgust, contempt, fear, shame, and guilt.
- Anger is caused by frustrating or insulting events that we interpret as willful, unjustified, and avoidable.
- Venting our anger *(catharsis)* may be temporarily calming, but expressing anger can actually make us angrier.

13 **What are the causes and consequences of happiness?**

- Good moods boost our perception of the world, ability to think creatively, health, energy levels, and willingness to help others (the *feel-good, do-good phenomenon*).
- Even significantly good or bad events don't usually change our *subjective well-being* for long.
- Our happiness level depends on our comparisons with our own experiences, including recent ones (the *adaptation-level phenomenon*), and on our comparisons with others (*relative deprivation*).
- Tips for increasing happiness levels: Focus beyond finances, take charge of your schedule, act happy, seek meaningful work and leisure, exercise, sleep enough, foster friendships, focus beyond the self, and nurture gratitude and spirituality.

STRESS, HEALTH, AND HUMAN FLOURISHING

Consider: How much stress did you experience yesterday? When Gallup pollsters put that question to a national sample of Americans in 2008 and 2009, almost half (48 percent) said they experienced stress during "a lot of the day yesterday" (Newport & Pelham, 2009). And you?

For many students, the transition to college (or back to college) adds to daily stress. Debt piles up. Deadlines loom. New relationships present new challenges. Family demands continue. A big exam or a class presentation makes you tense. Then, stuck in traffic and late to class or work, your mood turns sour. It's enough to give you a headache or to disrupt your sleep. No wonder 85 percent of college students surveyed in 2009 reported sometimes or frequently experiencing stress during the past three months (AP, 2009).

Stress often strikes without warning. Imagine being 21-year-old Ben Carpenter on the world's wildest and fastest wheelchair ride. As he crossed an intersection on a sunny summer afternoon in 2007, the light changed. A large truck, whose driver didn't see him, started moving into the intersection. As they bumped, Ben's wheelchair turned to face forward, and its handles got stuck in the truck's grille. Off they went, the driver unable to hear Ben's cries for help. As they sped down the highway about an hour from my home, passing motorists caught the bizarre sight of a truck pushing a wheelchair at 50 miles per hour and started calling 911. (The first caller: "You are not going to believe this. There is a semi truck pushing a guy in a wheelchair on Red Arrow highway!") Lucky for Ben, one passerby was an undercover police officer. Pulling a quick U-turn, he followed the truck to its destination a couple of miles from where the wild ride had started, and informed the disbelieving driver that he had a passenger hooked in his grille. "It was very scary," said Ben, who has muscular dystrophy.

In this chapter we explore stress—what it is and how it affects us. We also take a close look at some ways we can reduce the stress in our lives, so that we can flourish in both body and mind.

Stress: Some Basic Concepts

1 How does our appraisal of an event affect our stress response, and what are the three main types of stressors?

Stress is a slippery concept. We sometimes use the word informally to describe threats or challenges ("Ben was under a lot of stress"), and at other times to describe our responses ("Ben experienced acute stress"). To a psychologist, the dangerous truck ride was a *stressor*. Ben's physical and emotional responses were a *stress reaction*. And the process by which he related to the threat was *stress*. Thus, **stress** is the process of appraising and responding to a threatening or challenging event.

Stress arises less from the event itself than from how we appraise it (Lazarus, 1998). If you have prepared for an important math test, you may welcome it as a challenge. You will be aroused and focused, and you will probably do well **(FIGURE 10.1)**. Championship athletes, successful entertainers,

James Hoenstine/Shutterstock

Extreme stress: Ben Carpenter experienced the wildest of rides after his wheelchair got stuck in a truck's grille.

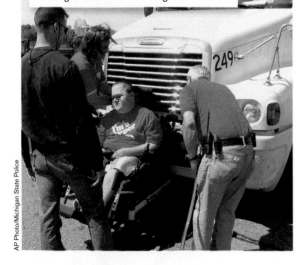

AP Photo/Michigan State Police

and great teachers and leaders all thrive and excel when aroused by a challenge (Blascovich et al., 2004). Bouncing back from a serious illness or a lost job, we may feel a stronger sense of self-esteem and a deeper sense of purpose. Tough challenges, especially early in life, can foster personal growth and emotional resilience (Landauer & Whiting, 1979).

Stressors that we appraise as threats, not challenges, can instead lead to strong *negative* reactions. Suppose a personal crisis prevented you from preparing for your math test. You will appraise this event as a threat that could destroy your hope for a good grade, and your response will be distress.

Extreme or prolonged stress can harm us. Children who suffer severe or repeated abuse are later at risk of chronic disease (Repetti et al., 2002). Troops who had stress reactions after heavy combat in the Vietnam war later suffered high rates of circulatory, digestive, respiratory, and infectious diseases (Boscarino, 1997). Job loss, especially later in one's working life, increases the risk of heart problems and death (Gallo et al., 2006; Sullivan & von Wachter, 2009).

So, there is an interplay between our heads and our health. Before we explore that interplay, let's take a closer look at stressors and stress reactions.

Stressors—Things That Push Our Buttons

Stressors fall into three main types: catastrophes, significant life changes, and daily hassles. All can be toxic.

Catastrophes are unpredictable large-scale events, such as wars, earthquakes, and famines. Nearly everyone appraises catastrophes as threatening. We often give aid and comfort to one another after such events, but the damage to emotional and physical health can be significant. In surveys taken in the three weeks after the 9/11 terrorist attacks, for example, two-thirds of Americans said they were having some trouble concentrating and sleeping (Wahlberg, 2001). In the four months after Hurricane Katrina, New Orleans reportedly experienced a tripled suicide rate (Saulny, 2006).

Misery often has company during catastrophes, but significant life changes may leave us experiencing stress alone. Even happy life events, such as getting married, can be stressful. Not only getting married, but other changes—leaving

SW Productions/Jupiterimages

Stressful event
(tough math test)

Appraisal

Challenge
("I've got to apply
all I know.")

Threat
("Yikes! This is
beyond me!")

Response

Aroused, focused

Stressed to
distraction

FIGURE 10.1 • **Stress appraisal** The events of our lives flow through a psychological filter. How we appraise an event influences how much stress we experience and how effectively we respond.

Toxic stress: On the day of its 1994 earthquake, Los Angeles experienced a fivefold increase in sudden-death heart attacks. Most occurred in the first two hours after the quake and near its center and were unrelated to physical exertion (Muller & Verrier, 1996). The 2010 Haiti earthquake surely also triggered stress-related ills.

home, becoming divorced, having a loved one die—often happen during young adulthood. The stress of those years was clear in a recent survey. People in the survey were asked this question: "Are you trying to take on too many things at once?" Women and younger adults reported the highest stress levels (APA, 2009). About half of people in their twenties reported experiencing stress during "a lot of the day yesterday" (Newport & Pelham, 2009). Only one-fifth of those over 65 gave that response.

> "It's not the large things that send a man to the madhouse . . . no, it's the continuing series of small tragedies . . . not the death of his love but the shoelace that snaps with no time left."
>
> American author
> Charles Bukowski (1920–1994)

How does stress related to life changes affect our health? Long-term studies indicate that people recently widowed, fired, or divorced are more disease-prone (Dohrenwend et al., 1982; Strully, 2009). In one study of 96,000 widowed people, their risk of death doubled in the week following their partner's death (Kaprio et al., 1987). Experiencing a cluster of crises (perhaps losing a job while falling behind in schoolwork *and* losing a relationship) puts one even more at risk.

Events don't have to remake our lives to cause stress. Stress comes from *daily hassles*—rush-hour traffic, irritating housemates, long lines at the store, too many things to do, e-mail spam, and loud cell-phone talkers (Lazarus, 1990; Pascoe & Richman, 2009; Ruffin, 1993). Some people can simply shrug off such hassles. For others, however, these little stressors add up and take a toll on health and well-being.

Many Americans experience more significant daily hassles: low wages; stretching to make ends meet; poor health; no health insurance; solo parenting; day-care, school, and neighborhood problems; perceived discrimination; and unreachable goals. Any of these stressors can lead to high blood pressure and other health problems.

Stress Reactions—From Alarm to Exhaustion

2 How does the body respond to stress?

The stress response is part of a unified mind-body system. Walter Cannon (1929) first realized this in the 1920s. He found that extreme cold, lack of oxygen, and emotion-arousing events all trigger an outpouring of stress hormones from the adrenal glands. When your brain sounds an alarm, your *sympathetic nervous system* responds. It increases your heart rate and respiration, diverts blood from your digestive organs to your skeletal muscles, dulls your feeling of pain, and releases sugar and fat from your body's stores. All this prepares your body for the wonderfully adaptive **fight-or-flight response** (see Figure 9.13 in Chapter 9).

Hans Selye (1936, 1976) extended Cannon's findings. His studies of animals' reactions to various stressors, such as electric shock and surgery, helped make stress a major concept in both psychology and medicine. Selye discovered that the body's adaptive response to stress was so general that it was like a single burglar alarm that sounds, no matter what intrudes. He named this response the **general adaptation syndrome (GAS),** and he saw it as a three-stage process **(FIGURE 10.2** on the next page). Let's say you suffer a physical or emotional trauma. In Phase 1, you have an *alarm reaction,* as your sympathetic nervous system is suddenly activated. Your heart rate zooms. Blood flows to your skeletal muscles. You feel the faintness of shock.

With your resources mobilized, you are ready to fight back. During Phase 2, *resistance,* your temperature, blood pressure, and respiration remain high. Your adrenal glands pump stress hormones into your bloodstream. You are fully engaged, summoning all your resources to meet the challenge.

As time passes, with no relief from stress, your body's reserves begin to run out. You have reached Phase 3, *exhaustion.*

stress the process by which we perceive and respond to certain events, called *stressors,* that we appraise as threatening or challenging.

fight-or-flight response an emergency response, including activity of the sympathetic nervous system, that mobilizes energy and activity for attacking or escaping a threat.

general adaptation syndrome (GAS) Selye's concept of the body's adaptive response to stress in three stages—alarm, resistance, exhaustion.

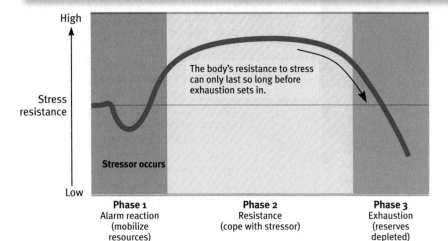

FIGURE 10.2 ● **Selye's general adaptation syndrome** When a gold and copper mine in Chile collapsed in 2010, family and friends rushed to the scene, fearing the worst. Many of those holding vigil outside the mine were nearly exhausted with the stress of waiting and worrying when, after 18 days, they received news that all 33 of the miners inside were alive and well!

The body's resistance to stress can only last so long before exhaustion sets in.

High

Stress resistance

Low

Stressor occurs

Phase 1
Alarm reaction
(mobilize
resources)

Phase 2
Resistance
(cope with stressor)

Phase 3
Exhaustion
(reserves
depleted)

With exhaustion, you become more vulnerable to illness or even, in extreme cases, collapse and death. Although your body copes well with temporary stress, prolonged stress can damage it. So, too, with rats. The most fearful and easily stressed rats die sooner (after about 600 days) than their more confident siblings, which average 700-day life spans (Cavigelli & McClintock, 2003).

Fortunately, there are other options for dealing with stress. One is a common response to a loved one's death: Withdraw. Pull back. Conserve energy. Faced with an extreme disaster, such as a ship sinking, some people become paralyzed by fear. Another stress response, found especially among women, is to seek and give support (Taylor et al., 2000, 2006). This **tend-and-befriend** response is demonstrated in the outpouring of help after natural disasters.

Facing stress, men more often than women tend to socially withdraw, turn to alcohol, or become aggressive. Women more often respond to stress by nurturing and banding together. This may in part be due to *oxytocin*, a stress-moderating hormone associated with pair-bonding in animals and released by cuddling, massage, and breast feeding in humans (Taylor, 2006).

It often pays to spend our resources in fighting or fleeing an external threat. But we do so at a cost. When our stress is momentary, the cost is small. When stress persists, we may pay a much higher price, with lowered resistance to infections and other threats to mental and physical health.

PRACTICE TEST

THE BASICS

1. _____ are events that we appraise as challenging or threatening.
   a. Adrenals
   b. Stress reactions
   c. Stressors
   d. Fight-or-flight responses

2. The number of short-term illnesses and stress-related psychological disorders was higher than usual in the months following an earthquake. Such findings suggest that
   a. daily hassles can ruin our health.
   b. experiencing a very stressful event makes us more vulnerable to physical and mental disorders.
   c. the amount of stress we feel is not related to the number of bad events we experience.
   d. small, bad events don't stress us, but large ones can be toxic.

3. In Selye's general adaptation syndrome (GAS), the first stage, an alarm reaction, is followed by
   a. a fight-or-flight response.
   b. resistance then exhaustion.
   c. challenge then recovery.
   d. stressful life events.

THE BIG PICTURE

10A. How does our stress response work?

IN YOUR EVERYDAY LIFE

▪ In what ways have you experienced the stress adaptation phases of alarm, resistance, and exhaustion in your life as a student?

Answers: 1. c, 2. b, 3. b. Answers to The Big Picture questions can be found in Appendix B at the end of the book.

Stress Effects and Health

3 **How does stress influence our immune system?**

Throughout this text, we have seen that everything psychological is also biological. To experience this, think for a moment about biting into a section of a perfectly ripe orange. Imagine the sweet, tangy juice flooding across your tongue. Did you begin to salivate a bit? Our psychological states have real effects on our body. Stress contributes to high blood pressure and headaches. Stress also leaves us less able to fight off disease. A relatively new field—**psychoneuroimmunology**—has emerged to study these mind-body interactions (Kiecolt-Glaser, 2009). That mouthful of a word makes sense when said slowly. Your emotions *(psycho)* affect your brain *(neuro),* which controls the stress hormones that influence your disease-fighting *immune* system. And this new field is the study of *(ology)* those interactions.

You can think of your immune system as a complex security system. When it functions properly, it keeps you healthy by capturing and destroying bacteria, viruses, and other invaders. Four types of cells are active in these search-and-destroy missions **(FIGURE 10.3).** Two are types of white blood cells, called **lymphocytes.** *B lymphocytes* release antibodies that fight bacterial infections. *T lymphocytes* attack cancer cells, viruses, and foreign substances—even "good" ones, such as transplanted organs. The third agent is the *macrophage* ("big eater"), which identifies, pursues, and ingests harmful invaders and worn-out cells. And, finally, the *natural killer cells* (NK cells) pursue diseased cells (such as those infected by viruses or cancer). Your age, nutrition, genetics, body temperature, and stress all influence your immune system's activity.

When your immune system doesn't function properly, it can err in two directions. Responding too strongly, it may attack the body's own tissues, causing some forms of arthritis or an allergic reaction. Underreacting, it may allow a dormant herpes virus to erupt or cancer cells to multiply. Women have stronger immune systems, making them less likely than men to get infections. But this very strength also makes women more susceptible to self-attacking diseases, such as lupus and multiple sclerosis (Morell, 1995; Pido-Lopez et al., 2001).

Your immune system becomes less active when your body is flooded with stress hormones. Immune suppression appears when animals are stressed by physical

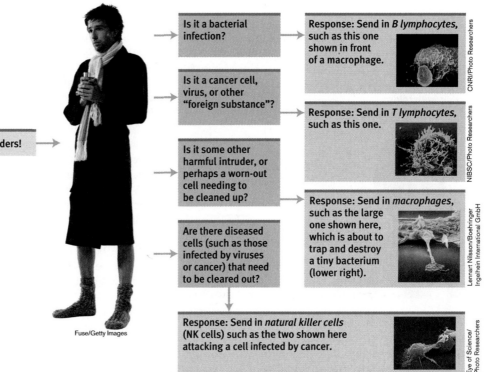

Intruders!

Is it a bacterial infection?

Is it a cancer cell, virus, or other "foreign substance"?

Is it some other harmful intruder, or perhaps a worn-out cell needing to be cleaned up?

Are there diseased cells (such as those infected by viruses or cancer) that need to be cleared out?

Response: Send in *B lymphocytes,* such as this one shown in front of a macrophage.

Response: Send in *T lymphocytes,* such as this one.

Response: Send in *macrophages,* such as the large one shown here, which is about to trap and destroy a tiny bacterium (lower right).

Response: Send in *natural killer cells* (NK cells) such as the two shown here attacking a cell infected by cancer.

Fuse/Getty Images

CNRI/Photo Researchers

NIBSC/Photo Researchers

Lennart Nilsson/Boehringer Ingelhein International GmbH

Eye of Science/Photo Researchers

FIGURE 10.3 • **A simplified view of immune responses**

restraints, unavoidable electric shocks, noise, crowding, cold water, social defeat, or separation from their mothers (Maier et al., 1994). In one such study, monkeys were housed with new roommates—three or four new monkeys—each month for six months (Cohen et al., 1992). If you know the stress of adjusting to a new roommate, you can imagine how trying it would be to repeat this experience monthly. By the end of the experiment, the socially stressed monkeys' immune systems were weaker than those of other monkeys left in stable groups. Human immune systems react similarly. Two examples:

- *Surgical wounds heal more slowly in stressed people.* In one experiment, two groups of dental students received punch wounds (small holes punched in the skin). Punch-wound healing was 40 percent slower in the group wounded three days before a major exam than in the group wounded during summer vacation (Kiecolt-Glaser et al., 1998). Marriage conflict also slows punch-wound healing (Kiecolt-Glaser et al., 2005).

- *Stressed people are more vulnerable to colds.* Researchers dropped a cold virus in the noses of stressed and relatively unstressed people **(FIGURE 10.4** on the next page**).** Among those living stress-filled lives, 47 percent developed colds. Among those living relatively free of stress, only 27 percent did (Cohen et al., 1999, 2003, 2006a,b).

tend and befriend under stress, people (especially women) often provide support to others *(tend)* and bond with and seek support from others *(befriend).*

psychoneuroimmunology the study of how psychological, neural, and endocrine processes combine to affect our immune system and health.

lymphocytes the two types of white blood cells that are part of the body's immune system: *B lymphocytes* release antibodies that fight bacterial infections; *T lymphocytes* attack cancer cells, viruses, and foreign substances.

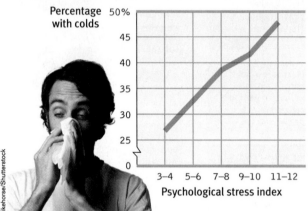

FIGURE 10.4 • **Stress and colds** People with the highest life-stress scores were also most vulnerable when exposed to an experimentally delivered cold virus (Cohen et al., 1999).

Percentage with colds

Psychological stress index

The stress effect on immunity makes sense. It takes energy to track down invaders, produce swelling, and maintain fevers (Maier et al., 1994). Stress hormones drain this energy away from the disease-fighting white blood cells. **WHEN WE ARE ILL, WHY IS IT WE WANT ONLY TO REST AND SLEEP?** Your body makes those demands in part to cut back on the energy your muscles usually use. Stress does the opposite. It creates a competing energy need. During an aroused fight-or-flight reaction, your stress responses draw energy away from your disease-fighting immune system and send it to your muscles and brain (see Figure 9.13 in Chapter 9). This leaves you more vulnerable to illness. *The bottom line:* Stress does not make us sick, but it does reduce our immune system's ability to function, which leaves us less able to resist infection.

Let's look now at some ways that stress might affect AIDS, cancer, and heart disease.

Stress and AIDS

We know that stress suppresses immune functioning. What does this mean for people suffering from AIDS (acquired immune deficiency syndrome)? People with AIDS already have a damaged immune system. The name of the virus that triggers AIDS tells us that. "HIV" stands for *human immunodeficiency virus.* Stress can't give people AIDS. But could stress and negative emotions speed the transition from HIV infection to AIDS in someone already infected? Might stress predict a faster decline in those with AIDS? The answer to both questions seems to be *Yes* (Bower et al., 1998; Kiecolt-Glaser & Glaser, 1995; Leserman et al., 1999). HIV-infected men who experience stressful events, such as the loss of a partner, show somewhat greater immune suppression and travel a faster course in this disease.

COULD REDUCING STRESS HELP◀ CONTROL AIDS? The answer again appears to be *Yes.* Educational programs, grief support groups, talk therapy, and exercise programs that reduce distress have all had good results for HIV-positive people (Baum & Posluszny, 1999; Schneiderman, 1999). But the benefits of stress-reduction programs are small, compared with available drug treatments.

Although AIDS is now more treatable than ever before, preventing HIV infection is a far better option. This is the focus of many educational programs, such as the ABC (abstinence, being faithful, condom use) program that has been used with seeming success in the African country of Uganda (Altman, 2004; USAID, 2004).

Stress and Cancer

Stress does not create cancer cells. But in a healthy, functioning immune system, lymphocytes, macrophages, and NK cells search out and destroy cancer cells and cancer-damaged cells. If stress weakens the immune system, might this weaken a person's ability to fight off cancer? To find out, researchers have implanted tumor cells in rodents, or given them *carcinogens* (cancer-producing substances). They then exposed some of the rodents to uncontrollable stress, such as inescapable shocks, which weakened their immune systems. These rodents were indeed more prone to developing cancer (Sklar & Anisman, 1981). Their tumors developed sooner and grew larger than in nonstressed rodents.

Does this stress-cancer link also hold with humans? The results are mixed. Some studies find that people are at increased risk for cancer within a year after experiencing depression, helplessness, or grief. In one large study, the risk of colon cancer was 5.5 times greater among people with a history of workplace stress than among those who reported no such problems. This difference was not due to group differences in age, smoking, drinking, or physical characteristics (Courtney et al., 1993). Other studies, however, have found no link between stress and human cancer (Edelman & Kidman, 1997; Fox, 1998; Petticrew et al., 1999, 2002). Concentration camp survivors and former prisoners of war, for example, do not have elevated cancer rates. So this research story is still being written.

There is a danger in hyping reports on attitudes and cancer. Can you imagine how a woman dying of breast cancer might react to a report on the effects of stress on the speed of decline in cancer patients? She could wrongly blame herself for her illness. ("If only I had been more expressive, relaxed, and hopeful.") Healthy people around her could fall back on a "wellness macho" attitude and take credit for their "healthy character," laying a guilt trip on the cancer patient. ("She has cancer? That's what you get for holding your feelings in and being so nice.") Dying thus becomes the ultimate failure.

It's important enough to repeat: *Stress does not create cancer cells.* At worst, it may

> "I didn't give myself cancer."
> Mayor Barbara Boggs Sigmund
> (1939–1990),
> Princeton, New Jersey

affect their growth by weakening the body's natural defenses against multiplying cancer cells (Antoni & Lutgendorf, 2007). Although a relaxed, hopeful state may enhance these defenses, we should be aware of the thin line that divides science from wishful thinking. The powerful biological processes at work in advanced cancer or AIDS are not likely to be completely derailed by avoiding stress or maintaining a relaxed but determined spirit (Anderson, 2002; Kessler et al., 1991).

Stress and Heart Disease

4 How does stress make people more vulnerable to coronary heart disease, especially people with Type A personalities?

Stress is much more closely linked to **coronary heart disease,** North America's leading cause of death. In this disease, the blood vessels that nourish the heart muscle gradually close. High blood pressure and a family history of the disease increase the risk of coronary heart disease. So do smoking, obesity, a high-fat diet, physical inactivity, and a high cholesterol level. Stress and personality also play a big role, as Meyer Friedman, Ray Rosenman, and their colleagues discovered in 1956 (Friedman & Ulmer, 1984).

To test the effects of stress on heart disease, these researchers measured the blood cholesterol level and clotting speed of 40 U.S. male tax accountants at different times of year. From January through March, the test results were completely normal. Then, as the accountants began scrambling to finish their clients' tax returns before the April 15 filing deadline, their cholesterol and clotting measures rose to dangerous levels. In May and June, with the deadline past, the measures returned to normal. Stress predicted heart attack risk for the accountants, with rates going up during their most stressful times. The researchers' hunch had paid off, launching a classic nine-year study of more than 3000 healthy men, aged 35 to 59.

At the start of the study, the researchers interviewed each man for 15 minutes, noting his work and eating habits, manner of talking, and other behavioral patterns. Some men reacted very strongly. These men, whom they labeled **Type A,** were competitive, hard-driving, impatient, time-conscious, supermotivated, verbally aggressive, and easily angered. The roughly equal number who were more easygoing they called **Type B.** Which group do you suppose turned out to be the most coronary-prone?

Nine years later, 257 men in the study had suffered heart attacks, and 69 percent of them were Type A. Moreover, not one of the "pure" Type Bs—the most mellow and laid-back of their group—had suffered a heart attack.

As often happens in science, this exciting discovery provoked enormous public interest. But after that initial honeymoon period, researchers wanted to know more. Was the finding reliable? If so, what exactly is so toxic about the Type A profile: Time-consciousness? Competitiveness? Anger? Further research revealed the answer. Type A's toxic core is negative emotions—especially anger (Smith, 2006; Williams, 1993). Type A individuals are more often "combat ready." When these people are harassed or challenged by a stressor, they react aggressively. As their often-active sympathetic nervous system redistributes bloodflow to the muscles, it pulls blood away from internal organs. One of these internal organs, the liver, which normally removes cholesterol and fat from the blood, can't do its job. Excess cholesterol and fat continue to circulate in the blood and are deposited around the heart. Further stress—

TYPE **A** PERSONALITY

Because it's there!

TYPE **B** PERSONALITY

Because it's there!

Bannerman © 7/94

sometimes conflicts brought on by their own abrasiveness—may trigger altered heart rhythms. In people with weakened hearts, this altered pattern can cause sudden death (Kamarck & Jennings, 1991). We see again that our hearts and minds interact in important ways.

Hundreds of other studies of young and middle-aged men and women have confirmed the finding that people who react with anger over little things are the most coronary-prone (Chida & Hamer, 2008; Chida & Steptoe, 2009). One study followed 13,000 middle-aged people for five years. Among those with normal blood pressure, people who had scored high on anger were three times more likely to have had heart attacks, even after researchers controlled for smoking and weight (Williams et al., 2000). Another study followed 1055 male medical students over an average of 36 years. Those who had reported being hot-tempered were five times more likely to have had a heart attack by age 55 (Chang et al., 2002). As others have noted, rage "seems

"The fire you kindle for your enemy often burns you more than him."—Chinese proverb

PhotoSpin, Inc./Alamy

coronary heart disease the clogging of the vessels that nourish the heart muscle; the leading cause of death in North America and many other countries.

Type A Friedman and Rosenman's term for competitive, hard-driving, impatient, verbally aggressive, and anger-prone people.

Type B Friedman and Rosenman's term for easygoing, relaxed people.

to lash back and strike us in the heart muscle" (Spielberger & London, 1982).

Depression, too, can be lethal, as the evidence from 57 studies indicates (Wulsin et al., 1999). People with high scores for depression are four times more likely than their low-scoring counterparts to develop further heart problems (Frasure-Smith & Lesperance, 2005). In a British study that followed 61,349 people over three to six years, depression predicted risk of death as well as did smoking (Mykletun et al., 2009). Although explanations of the depression–heart disease association range from unhealthy life-style habits to a biological clogging of the arteries, this much seems clear: Depression is disheartening.

* * *

We can view the stress effect on our disease resistance as a price we pay for the benefits of stress (**FIGURE 10.5**). Stress invigorates our lives. It arouses and motivates us. An unstressed life would not be challenging or productive.

PRACTICE TEST

THE BASICS

4. Stress hormones suppress immune system cells that ordinarily attack bacteria, viruses, cancer cells, and other foreign substances. Which of the following is NOT one of those cell types?

   a. Lymphocytes
   b. Macrophages
   c. NK cells
   d. Neurons

5. People are at increased risk for cancer a year or so after experiencing depression, helplessness, or grief. In describing this link between negative emotions and cancer, researchers are quick to point out that

   a. accumulated stress causes cancer.
   b. anger is the negative emotion most closely linked to cancer.
   c. stress does not create cancer cells, but it weakens the body's natural defenses against them.
   d. feeling optimistic about the chances of survival ensures that a cancer patient will get well.

6. Heart attacks occur more often in Type A people, who are hard-driving, verbally aggressive, and anger-prone. The "toxic ingredient" most closely linked to coronary heart disease is

   a. living a fast-paced life-style.
   b. working in a competitive job.
   c. meeting deadlines and challenges.
   d. often feeling angry and negative.

THE BIG PICTURE

10B. A Chinese proverb warns, "The fire you kindle for your enemy often burns you more than him." How is this true of Type A individuals?

IN YOUR EVERYDAY LIFE

▪ Do you think you are Type A, Type B, or somewhere in between? In what ways has this been helpful to you, and in what ways has this been a challenge?

Answers: 4, d, 5, c, 6, d. Answers to The Big Picture questions can be found in Appendix B at the end of the book.

Human Flourishing

Stressors are unavoidable. That's the reality we live with. One way we can develop our strengths and protect our health is to learn better ways to cope with our stress. In one study, the single personality trait shared by 169 people over the age of 100 was their ability to manage stress well (Perls et al., 1999).

Coping With Stress

> 5 **What are two basic ways that people cope with stress?**

To prevent illness and promote our well-being, we need to find new ways to feel, think, and act when we are dealing with stressors. We address some stressors directly, with **problem-focused coping.** For example, if our impatience leads to a family fight, we may go directly to that family member to work things out. We tend to use problem-focused strategies when we feel a sense of control over a situation and think we can change the circumstances, or at least change ourselves to deal with the circumstances more capably. We turn to **emotion-focused coping** when we can-

---

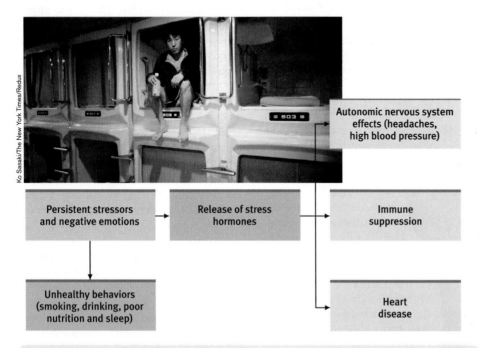

Autonomic nervous system effects (headaches, high blood pressure)

Persistent stressors and negative emotions → Release of stress hormones → Immune suppression

Unhealthy behaviors (smoking, drinking, poor nutrition and sleep)

Heart disease

Ko Sasaki/The New York Times/Redux

FIGURE 10.5 ● **Stress can have a variety of health-related consequences** This is especially so when stress is experienced by angry, depressed, or anxious people. Job and income loss caused by the recent economic recession has created stress for many people, such as this jobless Japanese man living in a Tokyo "capsule hotel."

not—or *believe* we cannot—change a situation. If, despite our best efforts, we cannot get along with that family member, we may search for relief from stress by confiding in friends and reaching out for support and comfort.

Emotion-focused strategies can move us toward better long-term health, as when we attempt to gain emotional distance from a damaging relationship or keep busy with hobbies to avoid thinking about an old addiction. Emotion-focused strategies can be nonadaptive, however, as when students worried about not keeping up with the reading in class go out to party to get it off their minds. Sometimes a problem-focused strategy (catching up with the reading) will reduce stress more effectively and promote long-term health and satisfaction.

Our success in coping depends on several factors. Let's look at four of them: personal control, an optimistic outlook, social support, and finding meaning in life's ups and downs.

Personal Control

6 How do our sense of control and our outlook on life influence stress and health?

Personal control is our sense of seeing ourselves in control of our environment. Psychologists study the effect of personal control (or any personality factor) in two ways:

1. They *correlate* people's feelings of control with their behaviors and achievements.

2. They *experiment*, by raising or lowering people's sense of control and noting the effects.

Control, Morale, and Health WHY DO WE◄ FEEL HELPLESS, HOPELESS, AND DE-PRESSED AFTER EXPERIENCING A SERIES OF BAD EVENTS BEYOND OUR CONTROL? Psychologists call this state **learned helplessness.** Researcher Martin Seligman (1975, 1991) and others studied the conditions that can create feelings of passive resignation in animals and people **(FIGURE 10.6).** For example, dogs were strapped in a harness and given repeated shocks, with

| Uncontrollable bad events | → | Perceived lack of control | → | Generalized helpless behavior |

FIGURE 10.6 ● **Learned helplessness** When animals and people experience no control over repeated bad events, they often learn helplessness.

no opportunity to avoid them. When later placed in another situation where they *could* escape the punishment by simply leaping a hurdle, the dogs cowered as if without hope. Other dogs that were able to escape the first shocks did not react this way. They learned they were in control, and they easily escaped the shocks in the new situation.

Animal studies show—and human studies confirm—that feelings of losing control trigger physical symptoms. Stress hormone levels rise. Blood pressure increases. And immune responses drop (Rodin, 1986; Sapolsky, 2005). Captive animals experience more stress and are more vulnerable to disease than are wild animals (Roberts, 1988). Feelings of loss of control happen when rats cannot avoid shocks. They happen when people in high-density neighborhoods, prisons, and even college dorms are crowded together (Fleming et al., 1987; Ostfeld et al., 1987).

Knowing all this, psychologists have proposed measures that increase control and improve health and morale (Humphrey et al., 2007; Ruback et al., 1986; Wener et al., 1987). These include allowing prisoners to move chairs and control room lights and the TV, having workers participate in decision making, and offering nursing home patients choices about their environment.

In one Gallup poll, workers were asked whether they were allowed to personalize their workspace. Those who answered *Yes* were 55 percent more likely also to report high engagement with their work (Krueger & Killham, 2006). And in another famous study, when nursing home patients were encouraged to exert more control, 93 percent of them became more alert, active, and happy (Rodin, 1986). "Per-

ceived control is basic to human functioning," observed researcher Ellen Langer (1983, p. 291). "For the young and old alike," environments should enhance people's sense of control over their world. No wonder iPods and DVRs, which enhance our control of the content and timing of our entertainment, are so popular.

Happy to have control: After working on the building—alongside Habitat for Humanity volunteers—for several months, this family is finally experiencing the joy of having their own new home.

problem-focused coping attempting to reduce stress directly—by changing the stressor or the way we interact with that stressor.

emotion-focused coping attempting to reduce stress by avoiding or ignoring a stressor and attending to emotional needs related to our stress reaction.

personal control our sense of controlling our environment rather than feeling helpless.

learned helplessness the hopelessness and passive resignation an animal or human learns when unable to avoid repeated aversive events.

The verdict of these studies is reassuring on a larger scale. Under conditions of personal freedom and empowerment, people thrive. Indeed, the citizens of stable democracies report higher levels of happiness (Inglehart et al., 2008). Shortly before the democratic revolution in the former East Germany, researchers compared the telltale body language of working-class men in East and West Berlin bars (Oettingen & Seligman, 1990). Compared with their counterparts on the other side of the Wall, the empowered West Berliners much more often laughed, sat upright rather than slumped, and had upturned rather than downturned mouths.

So, some freedom and control is better than none. DOES EVER-INCREASING CHOICE ◄ BREED EVER-HAPPIER LIVES? Perhaps not. Barry Schwartz (2000, 2004) has suggested that the "excess of freedom" in today's Western cultures actually makes for decreased life satisfaction, increased depression, and, sometimes, behavior paralysis. We consumers can be staggered by too many choices. After choosing among 30 brands of jam or chocolate, people have expressed less satisfaction, compared with those who chose from only 6 options (Iyengar & Lepper, 2000). This *tyranny of choice* brings information overload and a greater likelihood that we will feel regret over some of the things we left behind.

Who's at the Controls? Do you believe that your life is out of control? That the world is run by a few powerful people? That getting a good job depends mainly on being in the right place at the right time? Or do you more strongly believe that you control your own fate? That each of us can influence our government's decisions? That being a success is a matter of hard work?

Hundreds of studies have compared people who differ in their perceptions of control. On the one side are those who have what psychologist Julian Rotter called an **external locus of control**—the view that chance or outside forces control their fate. On the other are those who perceive an **internal locus of control,** who believe they control their own destiny.

IN REAL LIFE, DOES IT MATTER WHETHER ◄
YOU FEEL YOU CONTROL YOUR OWN FATE?

Rubes®   By Leigh Rubin

> YOU SEEM TO HAVE TROUBLE ACCEPTING RESPONSIBILITY.

> IT'S MY PARENTS' FAULT.

7-6

Creators Syndicate, Inc.
© 1993 Leigh Rubin!

Apparently it does. In study after study, "internals" achieve more in school and work, act more independently, enjoy better health, and feel less depressed than do "externals" (Lefcourt, 1982; Ng et al., 2006). One study followed 7551 British people for two decades. Those who had expressed a more internal locus of control at age 10 exhibited less obesity, hypertension, and distress at age 30 (Gale et al., 2008).

If *feeling* an internal locus of control lowers stress, does *actively* controlling or self-managing our behavior likewise reduce stress? *Self-control*—the ability to control impulses and delay gratification—predicts good adjustment, better grades, and social success (Tangney et al., 2004). Do you plan your day's activities and then live out your day as you had planned? In one study, students who fit this profile were at low risk for depression (Nezlek, 2001).

Self-control is not a constant state, like having brown eyes. Rather, self-control, like a muscle, temporarily weakens after being used, regains energy with rest, and grows stronger with exercise (Baumeister & Exline, 2000). Hungry people who had exercised self-control and resisted the temptation to eat chocolate chip cookies gave up sooner when later asked to perform a tedious task. This decrease in mental energy has also appeared in other experiments. Imagine yourself as a participant in an experiment that demands your full attention and energy. When you see the word green printed in red ink, you must quickly state the color of the printed word ("red," not "green"). After expending self-control on this task, people who participated in this experiment were temporarily less restrained in their aggressive responses when provoked and in their sexual thoughts and behaviors (DeWall et al., 2007; Gaillot & Baumeister, 2007).

Decreased mental energy after exercising self-control is a short-term effect. The long-term effect of exercising self-control is *increased* self-control, much as work-out programs strengthen muscles. Strengthened self-control appears both in people's performance on laboratory tasks and in their improved self-management of eating, drinking, smoking, and household chores (Oaten & Cheng, 2006a,b). *Develop self-discipline in one area of your life and your strengthened self-control may spill over into other areas as well, making for a less stressed life.*

Is the Glass Half Full or Half Empty?

Another part of coping with stress is your outlook—what you expect from the world. **Optimists** agree with statements such as, "In uncertain times, I usually expect the best" (Scheier & Carver, 1992). People with an optimistic outlook expect to have more control and to cope better with stressful events. **Pessimists** expect

"We just haven't been flapping them hard enough."

things to go badly. If they perform poorly, they see it as evidence of their lack of ability or of a situation that is beyond their control (Noel et al., 1987; Peterson & Barrett, 1987). They often make statements like, "I can't do this!" or "There is nothing I can do about it."

▶ WHO REALLY COPES BETTER WITH STRESS—OPTIMISTS OR PESSIMISTS? Optimists tend to enjoy better health than pessimists. During a semester's last month, students previously identified as optimistic reported less fatigue and fewer coughs, aches, and pains. And during the stressful first few weeks of law school, those who were optimistic ("It's unlikely that I will fail") enjoyed better moods and stronger immune systems (Segerstrom et al., 1998). Optimists also respond to stress with smaller increases in blood pressure, and they recover more quickly from heart bypass surgery.

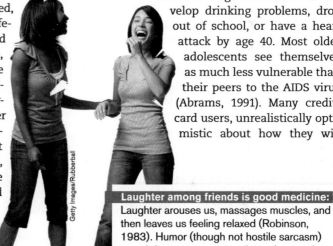
PhotosIndia.com LLC/Alamy

Does optimists' better health translate into a longer life? Possibly. One study asked 795 Americans aged 64 to 79 years if they were "hopeful about the future." Five years later, 29 percent of those answering *No* had died—more than double the 11 percent of deaths among those who said *Yes* (Stern et al., 2001). The optimism–long-life correlation also appeared in a famous study of 180 Catholic nuns. At about 22 years of age, each of these women had written a brief autobiography. In the decades that followed, they lived similar lifestyles. Those who had expressed happiness, love, and other positive feelings in their autobiographies lived an average seven years longer than did the more negative nuns (Danner et al., 2001). By age 80, only 24 percent of the most positive-spirited had died, compared with 54 percent of those expressing few positive emotions.

Positive thinking pays dividends, but so does a dash of realism (Schneider, 2001). Can you remember a time when you were *realistically* anxious about failing in some future event? Perhaps you were short of money and worried about being able to pay a bill on time. Perhaps you had fallen behind on your reading and feared you would do badly on an exam. CAN ANX- ◀ IETY CAUSE US TO TRY EXTRA HARD TO AVOID FAILURE? Realistic anxiety over possible *future* failures often has this effect (Goodhart, 1986; Norem, 2001; Showers, 1992). Students concerned about failing an upcoming exam may

> "God grant us the serenity to accept the things we cannot change, courage to change the things we can, and wisdom to know the difference."
>
> Alcoholics Anonymous Serenity Prayer (attributed to Reinhold Niebuhr)

study more, and therefore outperform equally able but more confident peers. This may help explain the impressive academic achievements of some Asian-American students. Compared with European-Americans, these students express somewhat greater pessimism (Chang, 2001). Success requires enough optimism to provide hope and enough pessimism to keep us on our toes.

Excessive optimism can also blind us to real risks (Weinstein, 1980, 1982, 1996). Most college students display an *unrealistic optimism*. They view themselves as less likely than their average classmate to develop drinking problems, drop out of school, or have a heart attack by age 40. Most older adolescents see themselves as much less vulnerable than their peers to the AIDS virus (Abrams, 1991). Many credit-card users, unrealistically optimistic about how they will

Getty Images/Rubberball

Laughter among friends is good medicine: Laughter arouses us, massages muscles, and then leaves us feeling relaxed (Robinson, 1983). Humor (though not hostile sarcasm) may defuse stress, ease pain, and strengthen immune activity (Ayan, 2009; Berk et al., 2001; Kimata, 2001). People who laugh a lot also tend to have lower rates of heart disease (Clark et al., 2001).

external locus of control the perception that chance or outside forces beyond our personal control determine our fate.

internal locus of control the perception that we control our own fate.

optimism the anticipation of positive outcomes. Optimists are people who expect the best and expect their efforts to lead to good things.

pessimism the anticipation of negative outcomes. Pessimists are people who expect the worst and doubt that their goals will be achieved.

Robert Biswas-Diener/The Strengths Project

Optimism against all odds: *The Strengths Project* profiled "Gita" in India, who remains upbeat and is flourishing despite having lost her daughter to suicide. She is shown here with her beloved granddaughter, whose blood disorder requires frequent, expensive treatments that have left them impoverished. Yet she still finds joy in life's small pleasures. "We are a community," she says proudly. "We respect one another and help each other during hard times."

use their charge cards, elect cards with low fees and high interest (Yang et al., 2006). Blinded by optimism, people young and old deny the effects of smoking, engage in unprotected sex, and suffer high interest payments. As famed basketball player Magic Johnson said (1993) after contracting the HIV virus, "I didn't think it could happen to me."

Social Support

7 | How do social support and meaning in life influence health?

Social support—feeling liked and encouraged by intimate friends and family—is another coping strategy that promotes both happiness and health. That striking fact emerged in seven massive investigations. For several years, each study followed thousands of people—some with, and others without, close social ties. The studies reached similar conclusions. People are less likely to die early if supported by close relationships (Uchino, 2009). Some find this support system with friends, family, fellow workers, members of a faith community, or other support groups.

Others find their support in a happy marriage. People in low-conflict marriages live longer, healthier lives than the unmarried (Kaplan & Kronick, 2006; Wilson & Oswald, 2002). This correlation holds regardless of age, sex, race, and income (National Center for Health Statistics, 2004). One seven-decades–long study found that at age 50, healthy aging is better predicted by a good marriage than by a low cholesterol level (Vaillant, 2002). Even pets can help us cope with stress. (See Close-Up: Pets Are Friends, Too).

HOW CAN SOCIAL SUPPORT HELP US ◀ FIGHT ILLNESS? It does so in at least two ways. First, it calms our cardiovascular system, lowering blood pressure and stress hormones (Uchino et al., 1996, 1999). To see if social support might calm people's response to threats, one research team subjected happily married women, while lying in an fMRI machine, to the threat of electric shock to an ankle (Coan et al., 2006). During the experiment, some women held their husband's hand.

Pets Are Friends, Too

Have you ever wished for a friend who would love you just as you are? One who would never judge you? Who would be there for you, no matter your mood? For many tens of millions of people that friend exists, and it is a loyal dog or a friendly cat.

Many people describe their pet as a beloved family member who helps them feel calm, happy, and valued. Can pets also help people handle stress? If so, might pets have healing power? Karen Allen reports that the answers are *Yes* and *Yes*. For example, women's blood pressure rises as they struggle with challenging math problems in the presence of a best friend or even a spouse, but much less so in the presence of their dog (Allen, 2003). Studies show that pets increase the odds of survival after a heart attack. They relieve depression among AIDS patients. And they lower the level of fatty acids in the blood that increase the risk of heart disease.

So, would pets be good medicine for people who do not have pets? To find out, Allen experimented. The participants were a group of stockbrokers. They all lived alone, described their work as stressful, and had high blood pressure. She randomly selected half to adopt an animal shelter cat or dog. Did these new companions help their owners handle stress better? Indeed they did. When later facing stress, all participants experienced higher blood pressure. But among the new pet owners, the increase was only half as high as the increases in the no-pet group. The effect was greatest for pet owners with few social contacts or friends. Allen's conclusion: For lowering blood pressure, pets are no substitute for effective drugs and exercise. But for those who enjoy animals, and especially for those who live alone, they are a healthy pleasure.

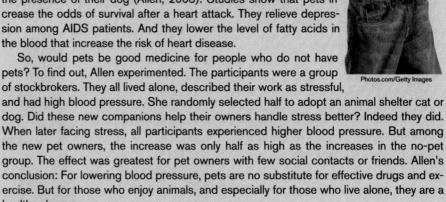
Photos.com/Getty Images

Others held the hand of an unknown person or no hand at all. While awaiting the occasional shocks, the women's brains reacted differently. Those who held their husband's hand had less activity in threat-responsive areas. This soothing benefit was greatest for women reporting the highest-quality marriages.

Second, social support fosters stronger *immune functioning*. Cancer patients' spouses who received ample social support showed this effect (Baron et al., 1990). So did volunteers in studies of resistance to cold viruses (Cohen et al., 1997, 2004). In those studies, two groups of healthy volunteers inhaled nose drops loaded with a cold virus and were quarantined and observed for five days. (The volunteers received $800 each to endure this experience.) The researchers then took a cold, hard look at the results, after controlling for age, race, sex, smoking, and other health habits. People with close social ties in their everyday lives were least likely to catch a cold. If they did catch one, they produced less mucus. The effect of social ties is nothing to sneeze at.

If we are aiming to exercise more, drink less, quit smoking, or stay slender, our social ties can tug us toward or away from our goal. Studies of networks of thousands of people followed over years of time suggest that clusters of friends may "infect" one another with either bad health practices or good ones (Christakis & Fowler, 2009). Obesity, for example, spreads within networks in ways that seem not merely to reflect people's seeking out similar others.

Finding Meaning

For many people, an important part of coping with stress is making sense of bad events and finding some redeeming purpose in their suffering (Taylor, 1983). Those with a strong sense of meaning have a purpose for which to live, strong values, and a sense of personal competence and self-worth. Close relationships offer an opportunity for "open heart therapy," a chance to *confide* painful feelings (Frattaroli, 2006). Confiding is good for both soul and body. Talking or writing about our experiences helps us make sense of our stress and find meaning in it (Esterling et al., 1999). This effect is clear in studies of Holocaust survivors, victims of childhood sexual abuse, and other trauma survivors (Pennebaker et al., 1984, 1989, 1990). In one study, researchers contacted the surviving spouses of people who had committed suicide or died in car accidents. Those who bore their grief alone had more health problems than those who could express it openly. In other studies, people who managed to find meaning in a family member's death and to draw something positive out of it were less distressed a year and more later (Nolen-Hoeksema & Davis, 2002).

So we see that a strong sense of meaning can have health consequences (Baumeister & Vohs, 2002). One study looked at this effect in 40 HIV-positive men who had recently lost a partner to AIDS. Those who said they had found meaning in the loss showed stronger immune system functioning, and they were also less likely to die during a follow-up period (Bower et al., 1998). Likewise, psychiatrist Viktor Frankl (1962), who had been imprisoned in a Nazi concentration camp, observed that his fellow inmates who retained a sense of meaning more often survived.

Managing Stress Effects

Having a sense of control, nurturing an optimistic outlook, building our social support, and finding meaning in hard times can help us experience less stress and thus improve our health. What do we do when we cannot avoid stress? At such times, we need to *manage* our stress. Aerobic exercise, relaxation, meditation, and spirituality may help us gather inner strength and lessen stress effects.

Aerobic Exercise

8 How effective is aerobic exercise as a way to manage stress and improve well-being?

Aerobic exercise is sustained activity—such as jogging, swimming, or biking—that increases heart and lung fitness. It's hard to find bad things to say about exercise. By one estimate, moderate exercise adds not only to your quantity of life—two additional years, on average—but also to your quality of life, with more energy and better mood (Seligman, 1994).

Exercise helps fight heart disease. It strengthens your heart, increases blood-flow, keeps blood vessels open, and lowers both blood pressure and the blood pressure reaction to stress (Ford, 2002; Manson, 2002). Compared with inactive adults, people who exercise suffer half as many heart attacks (Powell et al., 1987; Visich & Fletcher, 2009). Exercise makes the muscles hungry for the fats that, if not used by the muscles, contribute to clogged arteries (Barinaga, 1997).

CAN AEROBIC EXERCISE REDUCE ◀ STRESS, DEPRESSION, AND ANXIETY? Many studies suggest it can. For example, half of Americans report exercising 30 or more minutes three times a week or more (Mendes, 2009). In studies, these active people also manage stressful events better, are more self-confident and energetic, and feel less depressed and fatigued than their inactive peers (McMurray, 2004; Puetz et al., 2006). But we could state this observation another way: Stressed and depressed people exercise less. It's that old correlation problem again—cause and effect are not clear.

To sort out cause and effect, researchers experiment. They randomly assign stressed, depressed, or anxious people either to an aerobic exercise group or to a control group. One such experiment randomly assigned mildly depressed female college students to

The mood boost: When energy or spirits are sagging, few things reboot the day better than exercising (as I can vouch from my daily noontime basketball).

three groups. One-third participated in a program of aerobic exercise. Another third took part in a program of relaxation exercises, and the remaining third (the control group) formed a no-treatment group (McCann & Holmes, 1984). As **FIGURE 10.7** on the next page shows, 10 weeks later the women in the aerobic exercise program reported the greatest decrease in depression. Many of them had, quite literally, run away from their troubles.

More than 150 other studies have confirmed that exercise reduces depression and anxiety. Some findings indicate that aerobic exercise counteracts depression in two ways. First, it increases arousal. Second, it does naturally what some prescription drugs do chemically: It increases the brain's serotonin activity. Aerobic exercise has therefore taken a place, along with antidepressant drugs and psychotherapy, on the list of effective

aerobic exercise sustained activity that increases heart and lung fitness; may also reduce depression and anxiety.

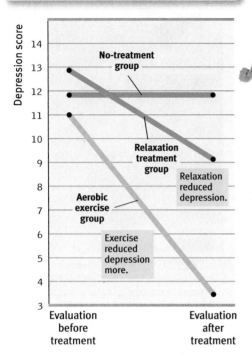

FIGURE 10.7 • **Aerobic exercise reduced depression** (From McCann & Holmes, 1984.)

No-treatment group

Relaxation treatment group

Aerobic exercise group

Relaxation reduced depression.

Exercise reduced depression more.

Depression score

Evaluation before treatment

Evaluation after treatment

treatments for depression and anxiety (Arent et al., 2000; Berger & Motl, 2000; Dunn et al., 2005). In later life, exercise also predicts better mental functioning and less risk of dementia (Kramer & Erickson, 2007).

Relaxation and Meditation

9 In what ways might relaxation and spiritual engagement influence stress and health?

Aerobic exercise reduces depression and anxiety. But did you notice in Figure 10.7 that women in the relaxation treatment group also experienced reduced depression? More than 60 studies have found that relaxation procedures can also provide relief from headaches, high blood pressure, anxiety, and insomnia (Nestoriuc et al., 2008; Stetter & Kupper, 2002). Such findings would not surprise Meyer Friedman and his colleagues. These researchers used relaxation in a program designed to help Type A heart attack survivors reduce their risk of future attacks. They randomly assigned

hundreds of these middle-aged men to one of two groups. The first group received standard advice from cardiologists about medications, diet, and exercise habits. The second group received similar advice, but they also were taught ways of modifying their life-style. They learned to slow down and relax by walking, talking, and eating more slowly. They learned to smile at others and laugh at themselves. They learned to admit their mistakes, to take time to enjoy life, and to renew their religious faith. The training paid off (**FIGURE 10.8**). During the next three years, the group that learned to modify their life-style had half as many repeat heart attacks as did the first group. This, wrote Friedman, was a truly spectacular reduction. After suffering a heart attack at age 55, Friedman started taking his own behavioral medicine—and lived to age 90 (Wargo, 2007).

Lev Olkha/Shutterstock

Cardiologist Herbert Benson (1996) became intrigued with reports that experienced meditators could lower their blood pressure, heart rate, and oxygen consumption and raise their fingertip temperature. His research led him to what he now calls the *relaxation response.* HOW CAN ◄ WE CONSCIOUSLY RELAX OUR BODY? Try this. Sit quietly in a comfortable position. Close your eyes. Relax your muscles, starting with your feet, then your calves, and upward through your thighs, shoulders, neck, and head. Breathe slowly and as you exhale each breath, repeat a focus word, phrase, or prayer—something drawn from your own belief system. When other thoughts intrude, don't worry, just return to your repetition and continue for 10 to 20 minutes. When finished, sit quietly for another minute or

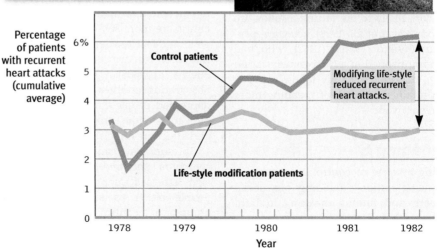

David Madison/Jupiterimages

FIGURE 10.8 • **Recurrent heart attacks and life-style modification** The San Francisco Recurrent Coronary Prevention Project offered counseling from a cardiologist to survivors of heart attacks. Those who were also guided in modifying their Type A life-style suffered fewer repeat heart attacks. (From Friedman & Ulmer, 1984.)

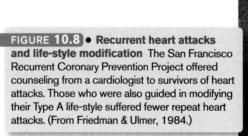

Percentage of patients with recurrent heart attacks (cumulative average)

Control patients

Modifying life-style reduced recurrent heart attacks.

Life-style modification patients

1978   1979   1980   1981   1982

Year

two, then open your eyes and sit for a few more moments.

Tibetan Buddhists deep in meditation and Franciscan nuns deep in centering prayer report a diminished sense of self, space, and time. Brain scans reveal the footprints these mystical experiences leave in the brain. A part of the brain that tracks our location in space is less active than usual, and an area involved in focused attention is more active (Cahn & Polich, 2006; Newberg & D'Aquili, 2001). Another difference appears in the brain's left frontal lobe. In Buddhist monks who are experienced in meditation, this brain area shows a high level of activity that is usually associated with positive emotions.

Was this high rate of activity a result of meditation, or simply a correlation that had nothing to do with cause and effect? To find out, researchers experimented, comparing "before" and "after" brain scans of volunteers who were *not* experienced meditators. First, they took baseline scans of the volunteers' normal levels of brain activity. Then they randomly assigned people either to a control group or to an eight-week course in "mindfulness meditation" (Davidson et al., 2003). Finally, they compared the meditation participants' "after" scans with their pre-course baselines and with the scans from the control group. The meditation group showed noticeably more left hemisphere brain activity after the training, and they also had improved immune functioning.

Spirituality and Health

A wealth of studies has revealed another curious correlation, called the *faith factor*. Religiously active people tend to live longer than those who are not religiously active. For example, one 16-year study tracked 3900 Israelis living in one of two groups of communities. The first group contained 11 religiously orthodox collective settlements. The second contained 11 matched, nonreligious collective settlements (Kark et al., 1996). Researchers found that "belonging to a religious collective was associated with a strong protective effect" not explained by age or economic differences. In every age group, religious community members were about half as likely to have died as were their nonreligious counterparts.

How should we interpret such findings? Skeptical researchers remind us, of course, that correlations can leave many factors uncontrolled (Sloan et al., 1999, 2000, 2002, 2005). Here's one obvious possibility: Women are more religiously active than men, and women outlive men. Does religious involvement reflect this gender-longevity link? *No.* Although stronger among women, the spirituality-longevity correlation is also found among men (McCullough et al., 2000, 2005). In study after study— some lasting 28 years, and some studying more than 20,000 people—the faith factor holds (Chida et al., 2009; Hummer et al., 1999; Schnall et al., 2008). And it holds after researchers control for age, sex, race, ethnicity, education, and region. In one study, this effect translated into a life expectancy at age 20 of 83 years for attenders at religious services (more than weekly) and 75 years for nonattenders **(FIGURE 10.9** on the next page).

WILL NONATTENDERS WHO START ATTENDING SERVICES AND CHANGE NOTHING ELSE LIVE 8 YEARS LONGER? Again, the answer is *No.* But these findings do indicate that religious involvement is a *predictor* of health and longevity, just as nonsmoking and exercise are. Can you imagine what might account for this correlation?

First, religiously active people have healthier life-styles; for example, they smoke and drink less (Koenig & Vaillant, 2009; Park, 2007; Strawbridge et al., 2001). Health-oriented, vegetarian Seventh Day Adventists have a longer-than-usual life expectancy (Berkel & de Waard, 1983). Compared with other Israelis, those who are religiously orthodox eat less fat. But such life-style differences

---

Diverse Yet Alike

The Faith Factor

Across diverse cultures, people experience and express their spirituality in faith communities.

Bob Daemmrich/Photo Edit

AAMIR QURESHI/AFP/Getty Images

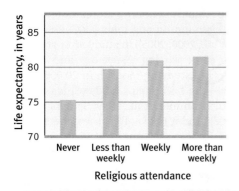

FIGURE 10.9 ● **Religious attendance and life expectancy** (Data from Hummer et al., 1999.)

are not great enough to explain the dramatically reduced death rates in the religious settlements, say the Israeli researchers. In the American studies, too, about 75 percent of the longevity difference remained when researchers controlled for unhealthy behaviors, such as inactivity and smoking (Musick et al., 1999).

Could social support explain the faith factor (Ai et al., 2007; George et al., 2002)? In Judaic, Christian, and Islamic religions, faith is a communal experience. To belong to one of these faith communities is to have access to a support network. Religiously active people are there for one another when misfortune strikes. Moreover, religion encourages marriage, another predictor of health and longevity. In

the Israeli religious settlements, for example, divorce has been almost nonexistent. But even after controlling for social support, gender, unhealthy behaviors, and preexisting health problems, much of the original correlation remains (George et al., 2000; Powell et al., 2003).

Researchers therefore speculate about a third set of influences that help protect religiously active people from stress and enhance their well-being. Those benefits may flow from a stable worldview, a sense of hope for the long-term future, feelings of ultimate acceptance, and the relaxed meditation of prayer or Sabbath observance **(FIGURE 10.10)**.

The religion-health correlation has yet to be fully explained. But these findings, noted Harold Pincus (1997), former deputy medical director of the American Psychiatric Association, "have made clear that anyone involved in providing health care services . . . cannot ignore . . . the important connections between spirituality, religion, and health."

＊＊＊

Let's summarize: Sustained emotional reactions to stressful events can be damaging. However, research on stress and coping indicates that some qualities and influences can help us flourish by making us emotionally and physically stronger. These include a sense of control, an optimistic outlook, healthy habits, social support, relaxation, a sense of meaning, and spirituality **(FIGURE 10.11)**.

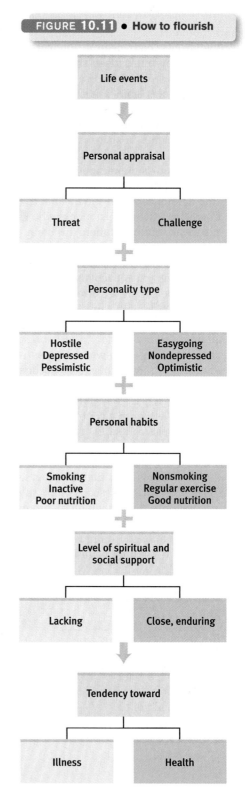

FIGURE 10.11 ● **How to flourish**

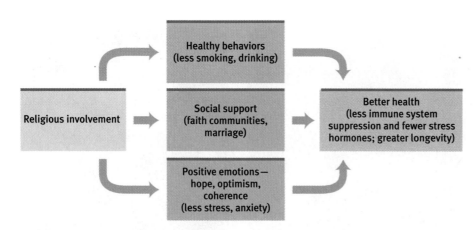

FIGURE 10.10 ● **Possible explanations for the correlation between religious involvement and health/longevity**

PRACTICE TEST

THE BASICS

7. To cope with stress, we tend to use _____ strategies when we feel in control of our world, and to use _____ strategies when we believe we cannot change a situation.

    a. emotion-focused; problem-focused
    b. problem-focused; emotion-focused
    c. internal locus; external locus
    d. external locus; internal locus

8. People who have a strong social support system tend to live longer than those who do not, supporting the idea that

    a. social ties can be a source of stress.
    b. gender influences longevity.
    c. Type A behavior is responsible for many premature deaths.
    d. social support has a beneficial effect on health.

9. A dog will respond with learned helplessness if it has received repeated shocks and has had

    a. the opportunity to escape.
    b. no control over the shocks.
    c. ample social support.
    d. a Type B personality.

10. The *faith factor* is a research finding that

    a. optimists tend to be healthier than pessimists.
    b. our expectations influence our feelings of stress.
    c. religiously active people tend to live longer than those who are not religiously active.
    d. our mind and our body interact to influence our health and well-being.

THE BIG PICTURE

10C. How do problem-focused coping and emotion-focused coping differ? What are some examples of each?

10D. What are some of the tactics we can use to manage stress successfully?

IN YOUR EVERYDAY LIFE

▪ Can you remember a time when you felt better after discussing a problem with a loved one, or even after playing with your pet? How did it help you to cope?

▪ What strategies have you used to cope with stress in your own life? How well are they working? What other strategies could you try?

▪ How much control do you feel you have over your life? What changes could you make to increase your sense of control?

Answers: 7. b, 8. d, 9. b, 10. c. Answers to The Big Picture questions can be found in Appendix B at the end of the book.

Terms and Concepts to Remember

stress, p. 274

fight-or-flight response, p. 275

general adaptation syndrome (GAS), p. 275

tend and befriend, p. 276

psychoneuroimmunology, p. 277

lymphocytes, p. 277

coronary heart disease, p. 279

Type A, p. 279

Type B, p. 279

problem-focused coping, p. 280

emotion-focused coping, p. 280

personal control, p. 281

learned helplessness, p. 281

external locus of control, p. 282

internal locus of control, p. 282

optimism, p. 282

pessimism, p. 282

aerobic exercise, p. 285

Multiple-choice **self-tests** and more may be found at www.worthpublishers.com/myers

STRESS, HEALTH, AND HUMAN FLOURISHING

Stress: Some Basic Concepts

1 **How does our appraisal of an event affect our stress response, and what are the three main types of stressors?**

- *Stress* is the process by which we appraise and respond to stressors—events that challenge or threaten us.

- If we appraise an event as challenging, we will be aroused and focused in preparation for success.

- If we appraise an event as a threat, we will experience a stress reaction, and our health may suffer.

- The three main types of stressors are catastrophes, significant life changes, and daily hassles.

2 **How does the body respond to stress?**

- Cannon viewed our body's response to stress as *fight-or-flight*.

- Selye saw our response as a three-stage (alarm-resistance-exhaustion) *general adaptation syndrome (GAS)*.

- People may also react to stress by withdrawing (more common in men) or by showing a *tend-and-befriend* response (more common in women), such as when helping others after natural disasters.

Stress Effects and Health

3 **How does stress influence our immune system?**

- Stress takes energy away from the immune system, inhibiting the activities of its B and T *lymphocytes*, macrophages, and natural killer cells. This leaves us more vulnerable to illness and disease.

- *Psychoneuroimmunology* is the study of these mind-body interactions.

- Although stress does not cause diseases such as AIDS and cancer, it may affect their progression.

4 **How does stress make people more vulnerable to coronary heart disease, especially people with Type A personalities?**

- Stress is directly connected to *coronary heart disease,* North America's number one cause of death.

- Heart disease has been linked with the competitive, hard-driving, impatient, and (especially) anger-prone *Type A* personality. *Type B* personalities are more relaxed and easygoing and less likely to experience heart disease.

- The fight-or-flight stress reaction may divert blood from the liver to the muscles, leaving excess cholesterol circulating in the bloodstream. Stress can also trigger altered heart rhythms.

Human Flourishing

5 **What are two basic ways that people cope with stress?**

- We use direct, *problem-focused coping* strategies when we feel a sense of control over a situation, and these are usually most effective.

- When lacking that sense of control, we may need to use *emotion-focused coping* strategies to protect our long-term well-being. These strategies can be harmful if misused.

6 **How do our sense of control and our outlook on life influence stress and health?**

- Feelings of loss of *personal control* can trigger physical symptoms, such as increased stress hormones and rising blood pressure.

- Those with an *internal locus of control* achieve more in school and work, act more independently, enjoy better health, and feel less depressed than do those with an *external locus of control*.

- Those who develop and maintain self-control achieve more academic and social success and are healthier.

- *Optimists* (those expecting positive outcomes) tend to be in better health than *pessimists*. Yet realistic anxiety over possible future failures can help motivate us to do better.

7 **How do social support and meaning in life influence health?**

- We can significantly reduce our stress and increase our health by building and maintaining relationships with family and friends, and by finding meaning even in difficult times.

8 **How effective is aerobic exercise as a way to manage stress and improve well-being?**

- *Aerobic exercise* improves physical functioning, which leads to greater well-being.

- Exercise also reduces stress, depression, and anxiety by increasing arousal and by increasing serotonin activity.

9 **In what ways might relaxation and spiritual engagement influence stress and health?**

- Relaxation and meditation can help us manage stress by altering brain activity and by improving immune function.

- Counseling Type A heart attack survivors to slow down and relax has helped lower rates of recurring attacks.

- Religious involvement predicts better health and longevity. This may be explained by the healthier life-styles of religiously active people, the social support that comes along with practicing a faith in community, and the sense of meaning that people find in their faith.

11

PERSONALITY

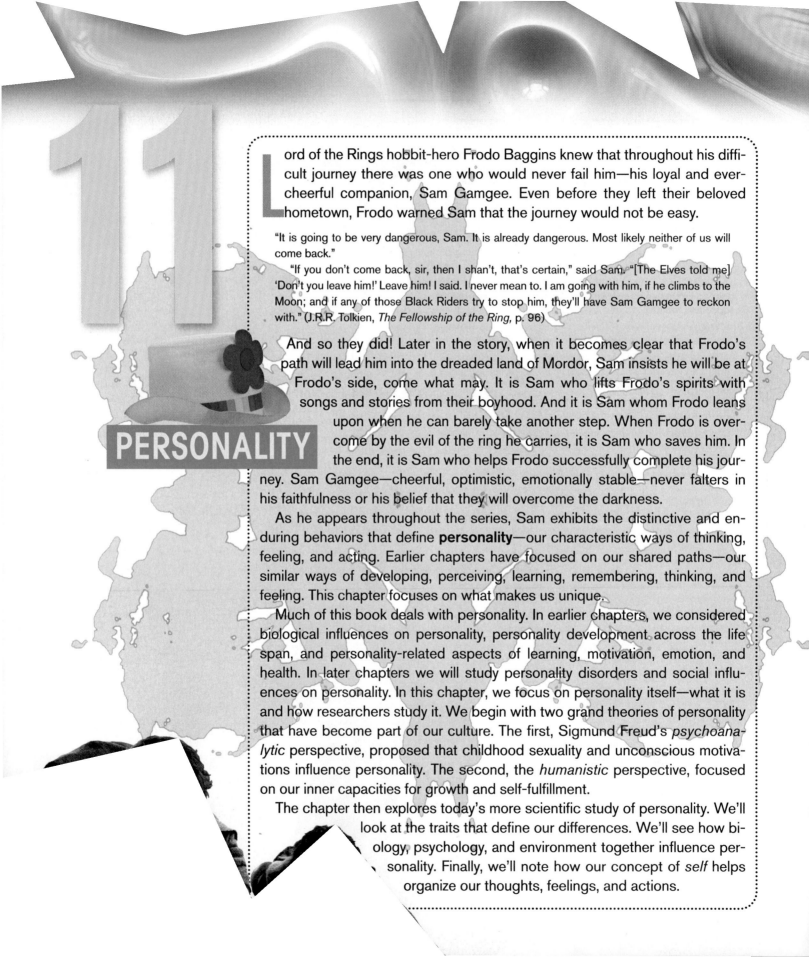

Lord of the Rings hobbit-hero Frodo Baggins knew that throughout his difficult journey there was one who would never fail him—his loyal and ever-cheerful companion, Sam Gamgee. Even before they left their beloved hometown, Frodo warned Sam that the journey would not be easy.

"It is going to be very dangerous, Sam. It is already dangerous. Most likely neither of us will come back."

"If you don't come back, sir, then I shan't, that's certain," said Sam. "[The Elves told me] 'Don't you leave him!' Leave him! I said. I never mean to. I am going with him, if he climbs to the Moon; and if any of those Black Riders try to stop him, they'll have Sam Gamgee to reckon with." (J.R.R. Tolkien, *The Fellowship of the Ring,* p. 96)

And so they did! Later in the story, when it becomes clear that Frodo's path will lead him into the dreaded land of Mordor, Sam insists he will be at Frodo's side, come what may. It is Sam who lifts Frodo's spirits with songs and stories from their boyhood. And it is Sam whom Frodo leans upon when he can barely take another step. When Frodo is overcome by the evil of the ring he carries, it is Sam who saves him. In the end, it is Sam who helps Frodo successfully complete his journey. Sam Gamgee—cheerful, optimistic, emotionally stable—never falters in his faithfulness or his belief that they will overcome the darkness.

As he appears throughout the series, Sam exhibits the distinctive and enduring behaviors that define **personality**—our characteristic ways of thinking, feeling, and acting. Earlier chapters have focused on our shared paths—our similar ways of developing, perceiving, learning, remembering, thinking, and feeling. This chapter focuses on what makes us unique.

Much of this book deals with personality. In earlier chapters, we considered biological influences on personality, personality development across the life span, and personality-related aspects of learning, motivation, emotion, and health. In later chapters we will study personality disorders and social influences on personality. In this chapter, we focus on personality itself—what it is and how researchers study it. We begin with two grand theories of personality that have become part of our culture. The first, Sigmund Freud's *psychoanalytic* perspective, proposed that childhood sexuality and unconscious motivations influence personality. The second, the *humanistic* perspective, focused on our inner capacities for growth and self-fulfillment.

The chapter then explores today's more scientific study of personality. We'll look at the traits that define our differences. We'll see how biology, psychology, and environment together influence personality. Finally, we'll note how our concept of *self* helps organize our thoughts, feelings, and actions.

The Psychoanalytic Perspective

1 **How did Sigmund Freud's treatment of psychological disorders lead to his view of the unconscious mind?**

In the popular mind, Sigmund Freud is to psychology's history what Elvis Presley is to rock music's history. Ask 100 people on the street to name a deceased psychologist, suggested Keith Stanovich (1996, p. 1), and "Freud would be the winner hands down." His influence lingers in books, movies, and psychological therapies. Who was Freud, what did he teach, and why do we still study his work?

After graduating from the University of Vienna medical school, Freud specialized in nervous disorders. Before long, he began hearing complaints that made no medical sense. One patient had lost all feeling in one hand. Yet there is no nerve pathway that, if damaged, would numb the entire hand and nothing else. Freud wondered: What could cause such disorders? His search for the answer led in a direction that would challenge our self-understanding.

Exploring the Unconscious

Could these strange disorders have mental rather than physical causes? Freud decided they could. Many meetings with patients led to Freud's "discovery" of the

Sigmund Freud (1856–1939): "I was the only worker in a new field."

unconscious. In Freud's view, this deep well keeps unacceptable thoughts, wishes, feelings, and memories hidden away, beyond our awareness. But despite our attempts, bits and pieces of these ideas seep out. Thus, patients might have an odd loss of feeling in their hand because they have an unconscious fear of touching their genitals. Or their unexplained blindness might be caused by unconsciously not wanting to see something that makes them anxious.

Basic to Freud's theory was his belief that the mind is mostly hidden. Below the surface is this large unconscious region in which unacceptable passions and thoughts lurk. Freud believed we *repress* these unconscious feelings and ideas, forcibly blocking them from awareness, because admitting them would be too unsettling. Nevertheless, he said, these repressed feelings and ideas powerfully influence us.

For Freud, nothing was ever accidental. He saw the unconscious seeping not only into people's troubling symptoms but also, in disguised forms, into their work, their beliefs, and their daily habits. He also glimpsed the unconscious in slips of the tongue and pen, as when a financially stressed patient, not

> "I know how hard it is for you to put food on your family."
>
> George W. Bush, 2000

wanting any large pills, said, "Please do not give me any bills, because I cannot swallow them." Jokes, too, were expressions of repressed sexual and aggressive tendencies traveling in disguise. Dreams, he said, were the "royal road to the unconscious." He thought the dream we remember is really a censored version of our unconscious wishes.

Hoping to unlock the door to the unconscious, Freud first tried hypnosis, but with poor results. He then turned to **free association,** telling patients to relax and say whatever comes to mind, no matter how unimportant or silly. Freud believed that free association would trace a path from the troubled present into a patient's distant past. The chain of thought would lead back into the patient's unconscious, the hiding place of painful past memo-

"Good morning, beheaded—uh, I mean beloved."

ries, often from childhood. His goal was to find these forbidden thoughts and release them.

Personality Structure

2 **How did Freud view personality structure?**

Freud called his treatment and the underlying theory of personality **psychoanalysis.** In his view, human personality arises from a conflict between impulse and restraint. He believed that we are born with aggressive, pleasure-seeking biological impulses. As we are socialized, we internalize social restraints against these basic urges. Personality is the result of our efforts to resolve this basic conflict—to express these impulses in ways that bring satisfaction without guilt or punishment.

To understand the mind's conflicts, Freud proposed three interacting systems: the *id, ego,* and *superego.* Psychologists have found it useful to view the mind's structure as an iceberg (**FIGURE 11.1**).

The **id** stores unconscious energy. It tries to satisfy our basic drives to survive, reproduce, and be aggressive. The id operates on the *pleasure principle:* It seeks immediate gratification. To see the id's power, think of newborn infants crying out the moment they feel a need, wanting satisfaction now. Or think of people who abuse drugs, partying now rather than sacrificing today's pleasure for future success and happiness (Keough et al., 1999).

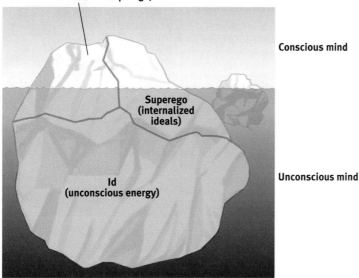

Ego
(mostly conscious; makes peace
between the id and the superego)

Conscious mind

Superego
(internalized
ideals)

Unconscious mind

Id
(unconscious energy)

FIGURE 11.1 ● **Freud's idea of the mind's structure** Icebergs hide most of their bulk beneath the surface of the water. Psychologists often use this image to show Freud's idea that the mind is mostly hidden beneath the surface of our awareness. Unlike the parts of a frozen iceberg, however, the id, ego, and superego interact.

of **psychosexual stages,** from oral to genital (**TABLE 11.1** on the next page). In each stage, the id's pleasure-seeking energies focus on an *erogenous zone,* a distinct pleasure-sensitive area of the body.

Freud believed that during the third stage, the *phallic stage,* boys seek genital stimulation, and they develop unconscious sexual desires for their mother. They feel jealousy and hatred for their father, who is a rival for their mother's attention. These feelings lead to guilt and a lurking fear that their father will punish them, perhaps by castration.

The mind's second part, the **ego,** operates on the *reality principle.* The ego is the conscious mind. It tries to satisfy the id's impulses in realistic ways that will bring long-term pleasure rather than pain or destruction.

"Fifty is plenty." "Hundred and fifty."
The ego struggles to reconcile the demands of superego and id, said Freud.

As the ego develops, the young child learns to cope with the real world. Beginning around age 4 or 5, Freud theorized, a child's ego begins to recognize the demands of the **superego,** the voice of our moral compass or *conscience.* The superego forces the ego to consider not only the real but the ideal. It focuses on how one *ought* to behave in a perfect world. It judges actions and produces positive feelings of pride or negative feelings of guilt.

The superego's demands often oppose the id's. It is the ego's job to reconcile the two. As the personality "executive," the ego juggles the impulsive demands of the id, the restraining demands of the superego, and the real-life demands of the external world.

Personality Development

3 What were Freud's stages of development, and how did he view "fixation" at a given stage?

Freud was convinced that personality forms during life's first few years. He said that children pass through a series

personality an individual's characteristic pattern of thinking, feeling, and acting.

unconscious according to Freud, a reservoir of mostly unacceptable thoughts, wishes, feelings, and memories. According to contemporary psychologists, information processing of which we are unaware.

free association in psychoanalysis, a method of exploring the unconscious in which the person relaxes and says whatever comes to mind, no matter how trivial or embarrassing.

psychoanalysis Freud's theory of personality that attributes thoughts and actions to unconscious motives and conflicts; the techniques used in treating psychological disorders by seeking to expose and interpret unconscious tensions.

id a reservoir of unconscious psychic energy that, according to Freud, strives to satisfy basic sexual and aggressive drives. The id operates on the *pleasure principle,* demanding immediate gratification.

ego the largely conscious, "executive" part of personality that, according to Freud, balances the demands of the id, superego, and reality. The ego operates on the *reality principle,* satisfying the id's desires in ways that will realistically bring pleasure rather than pain.

superego the part of personality that, according to Freud, represents internalized ideals and provides standards for judgment (the conscience).

psychosexual stages the childhood stages of development (oral, anal, phallic, latency, genital) during which, according to Freud, the id's pleasure-seeking energies focus on distinct erogenous zones.

TABLE 11.1	Freud's Psychosexual Stages
Stage	**Focus**
Oral (0–18 months)	Pleasure centers on the mouth—sucking, biting, chewing
Anal (18–36 months)	Pleasure focuses on bowel and bladder elimination; coping with demands for control
Phallic (3–6 years)	Pleasure zone is the genitals; coping with incestuous sexual feelings
Latency (6 to puberty)	Dormant sexual feelings
Genital (puberty on)	Maturation of sexual interests

"Oh, for goodness' sake! Smoke!"

Freud called this collection of feelings the **Oedipus complex,** after the Greek legend of Oedipus, who unknowingly killed his father and married his mother.

Children learn to cope with these feelings by repressing them, said Freud. They identify with the "rival" parent and try to become like him or her. It's as though something inside the child decides, "If you can't beat 'em [the same sex parent], join 'em." Through this **identification** process, children's superegos gain strength as they take on many of their parent's values. Freud believed that identification with the same-sex parent provides what psychologists now call our *gender identity*—our sense of being male or female.

Identification: I want to be like Dad.

Science Cartoons Plus

"I heard that as soon as we become aware of our sexual impulses, whatever they are, we'll have to hide them."

Other conflicts could arise at other childhood stages. But whatever the stage, a conflict that isn't resolved may cause trouble in adulthood. The result, Freud believed, would be **fixation,** locking the person's pleasure-seeking energies at the unresolved stage. A child who is either orally overindulged or orally deprived (perhaps by abrupt, early weaning) might become stalled at the oral stage, for example. As an adult, this orally fixated person might continue to seek oral gratification by smoking and excessive eating. In such ways, Freud suggested, the twig of personality is bent at an early age.

Defense Mechanisms

4 | How do Freud's defense mechanisms protect us from anxiety?

Anxiety, said Freud, is the price we pay for civilization. As members of social groups, we must control our sexual and aggressive impulses, not act them out. But sometimes the ego fears losing control of this inner war between the id and superego. The presumed result is a dark cloud of generalized anxiety. We feel unsettled but are unsure why.

Freud proposed that the ego distorts reality in an effort to protect itself from anxiety. **Defense mechanisms** achieve this goal by disguising threatening impulses and preventing them from reaching consciousness. Note that *all defense mechanisms function indirectly and unconsciously.* Just as the body unconsciously defends itself against disease, so also does the ego unconsciously defend itself against anxiety. For example, **repression** banishes anxiety-arousing wishes and feelings from consciousness. According to Freud, *repression underlies all the other defense mechanisms.* However, because repression is often incomplete, repressed urges may appear as symbols in dreams or as slips of the tongue in casual conversation. **TABLE 11.2** describes six other well-known defense mechanisms.

TABLE 11.2	Six Defense Mechanisms

Freud believed that *repression,* the basic mechanism that banishes anxiety-arousing impulses, enables other defense mechanisms.

Defense mechanism	Unconscious process employed to avoid anxiety-arousing thoughts or feelings	Example
Regression	Retreating to a more infantile psychosexual stage, where some psychic energy remains fixated.	A little boy reverts to the oral comfort of thumb sucking in the car on the way to his first day of school.
Reaction formation	Switching unacceptable impulses into their opposites.	Repressing angry feelings, a person displays exaggerated friendliness.
Projection	Disguising one's own threatening impulses by attributing them to others.	An El Salvadoran saying captures the idea: "The thief thinks everyone else is a thief."
Rationalization	Offering self-justifying explanations in place of the real, more threatening unconscious reasons for one's actions.	A habitual drinker says she drinks with her friends "just to be sociable."
Displacement	Shifting sexual or aggressive impulses toward a more acceptable or less threatening object or person.	A little girl kicks the family dog after her mother sends her to her room.
Denial	Refusing to believe or even perceive painful realities.	A partner denies evidence of his loved one's affair.

Regression: Faced with a mild stressor, children and young orangutans will regress, retreating to the comfort of earlier behaviors.

Neo-Freudians and Psychodynamic Theory

5 How did the neo-Freudians view Freud's original theory, and what is the more contemporary psychodynamic theory?

Freud's writings caused a lot of debate, but he soon attracted followers. Several young, ambitious physicians formed an inner circle around the strong-minded Freud. These *neo-Freudians,* such as Alfred Adler, Karen Horney [HORN-eye], and Carl Jung [Yoong] (all pictured on the next page), accepted Freud's basic ideas:

• Personality is made up of id, ego, and superego.

• The unconscious is key.

• Personality is shaped in childhood.

• We use defense mechanisms to ward off anxiety.

But the neo-Freudians differed from Freud in two important ways. First, they placed more emphasis on the role of the *conscious* mind. And second, they doubted that sex and aggression were all-consuming motivations. Instead, they tended to emphasize loftier motives and social interactions.

Freud died in 1939. Since then, some of his ideas have been incorporated into **psychodynamic theory.** Theorists and clinicians who study personality from a psychodynamic perspective assume, with Freud, that much of our mental life is unconscious. They believe we often struggle with inner conflicts among our wishes, fears, and values, and respond defensively. And they agree that childhood shapes our personality and ways of becoming attached to others. But in other ways, they differ from Freud. "Most contemporary dynamic theorists and therapists are not wedded to the idea that sex is the basis of personality," noted psychologist Drew Westen (1996). They "do not talk about ids and egos, and do not go around classifying their patients as oral, anal, or phallic characters."

Oedipus [ED-uh-puss] **complex** according to Freud, a boy's sexual desires toward his mother and feelings of jealousy and hatred for the rival father.

identification the process by which, according to Freud, children incorporate their parents' values into their developing superegos.

fixation according to Freud, a lingering focus of pleasure-seeking energies at an earlier psychosexual stage, in which conflicts were unresolved.

defense mechanisms in psychoanalytic theory, the ego's protective methods of reducing anxiety by unconsciously distorting reality.

repression in psychoanalytic theory, the basic defense mechanism that banishes anxiety-arousing thoughts, feelings, and memories from consciousness.

psychodynamic theory a Freud-influenced perspective that sees behavior, thinking, and emotions as reflecting unconscious motives.

Alfred Adler (1870–1937): Adler believed that childhood feelings of insecurity can drive behavior, triggering strivings for power and superiority. Adler coined the term *inferiority complex.*

Karen Horney (1885–1952): Horney proposed that children's feelings of dependency give rise to feelings of helplessness and anxiety. These feelings trigger adult desires for love and security. Horney believed Freud's views of personality showed a masculine bias.

Carl Jung (1875–1961): Jung shared Freud's view of the power of the unconscious. He also proposed a human *collective unconscious,* derived from our species' experiences in the distant past. Today's psychology rejects the idea that experiences can be inherited.

Assessing Unconscious Processes

6 | What are projective tests, how are they used, and how are they criticized?

Personality tests reflect the basic ideas of particular personality theories. So, what might be the tool of choice for someone working in the Freudian tradition?

To find a way into the unconscious mind, you would need a sort of "psychological X-ray." The test would have to see through the top layer of social politeness, revealing hidden conflicts and impulses. **Projective tests** aim to provide this view by asking test-takers to describe an unclear image or tell a story about it. The image itself has no real meaning. Anything test-takers read into it can be considered a projection of their unconscious feelings and conflicts. (Recall that in Freudian theory, *projection* is a defense mechanism that disguises threatening impulses by "seeing" them in other people.)

The most widely used projective test, the **Rorschach inkblot test,** was introduced in 1921. Swiss psychiatrist Hermann Rorschach [ROAR-shock] based it

> "We don't see things as they are; we see things as we are."
> The Talmud

on a game he and his friends played as children. They would drip ink on paper, fold it, and then say what they saw in the resulting blot (Sdorow, 2005). The assumption is that what you see in a series of 10 inkblots reflects your inner feelings and conflicts. Do you see an attacking animal in the blot in **FIGURE 11.2?** Perhaps you feel like attacking someone.

Is this a reasonable assumption? Let's see how well the Rorschach test measures up to the two primary criteria of a good test (see Chapter 8):

- *Reliability* (consistency of results): Raters trained in different Rorschach scoring systems show little agreement (Sechrest et al., 1998).

- *Validity* (predicting what it's supposed to): The Rorschach test is not very successful at predicting behavior or at discriminating between groups (for example, identifying who is suicidal and who is not). Inkblot results diagnose many normal adults as disordered (Wood et al., 2003, 2006).

Thus, the test has neither much reliability nor great validity. A research-based, computer-aided coding and interpreta-

tion tool aims to improve agreement among raters and enhance the test's validity (Erdberg, 1990; Exner, 2003). But Freud himself might have been uncomfortable with a tool that tried to diagnose patients based on tests. He probably would have been more interested in the therapist-patient interactions that take place during the test.

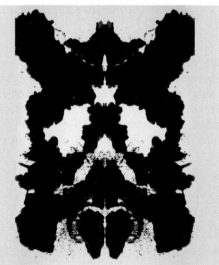

FIGURE 11.2 ● **The Rorschach test** In this projective test, people tell what they see in a series of symmetrical inkblots.

"*The forward thrust of the antlers shows a determined personality, yet the small sun indicates a lack of self-confidence. . . .*"

Evaluating the Psychoanalytic Perspective

7 How does contemporary psychology assess Freud's ideas?

"Many aspects of Freudian theory are indeed out of date, and they should be: Freud died in 1939, and he has been slow to undertake further revisions," observed Drew Westen (1998). In Freud's time, there were no neurotransmitter or DNA studies. More than seven decades of research—all the scientific breakthroughs in human development, thinking, and emotion announced during your parents' and your grandparents' time—were yet to come. Criticizing Freud's theory by comparing it with current concepts is therefore, some say, like comparing Henry Ford's Model T with today's hybrid cars. (How tempting it always is to judge people in the past from our perspective in the present.)

Does Developmental Research Support Freud's Views of Childhood? Developmental psychologists now see our development as lifelong, not fixed in childhood. They doubt that infants' neural networks are mature enough to process emotional trauma in the ways Freud assumed. Some think Freud overestimated parental influence and underestimated peer influence

(and abuse). They also doubt that conscience and gender identity form as the child resolves the Oedipus complex at age 5 or 6. We gain our gender identity earlier and become masculine or feminine even without a same-sex parent present. And they note that Freud's ideas about childhood sexuality have a shaky basis, in part because Freud didn't believe his female patients' stories of childhood sexual abuse. He apparently thought such stories reflected childhood sexual wishes and conflicts (Esterson, 2001; Powell & Boer, 1994). Today, we understand how Freud's questioning might have created false memories of abuse, but we also know that childhood sexual abuse does happen.

Does Memory Research Support Freud's Idea of Repression? Freud's entire psychoanalytic theory rests on his assumption that the human mind often *represses* offending wishes. Repression supposedly banishes emotions into the unconscious until they resurface, like long-lost books in a dusty attic. Today's memory researchers find that we do sometimes spare our egos by neglecting threatening information (Green et al., 2008). Yet they also find that repression, if it ever occurs, is a rare mental response to terrible trauma. "Repression folklore is . . . partly refuted, partly untested, and partly untestable," said Elizabeth Loftus (1995). Even those who have witnessed a parent's murder or survived Nazi death camps retain their unrepressed memories of the horror (Helmreich, 1992, 1994; Malmquist, 1986; Pennebaker, 1990). "Dozens of formal studies have yielded not a single convincing case of repression in the entire literature on trauma," concludes personality researcher John Kihlstrom (1990).

Some researchers believe that extreme, prolonged stress, such as the stress some severely abused children experience, might disrupt memory by damaging the hippocampus (Schacter, 1996). But the far more common reality is that high stress and associated stress hormones *enhance* memory. Indeed, rape, torture, and other traumatic events haunt survivors, who experience unwanted

flashbacks. They are seared onto the soul. "You see the babies," said Holocaust survivor Sally H. (1979). "You see the screaming mothers. You see hanging people. You sit and you see that face there. It's something you don't forget."

Does Cognitive Research Support Freud's View of the Unconscious? New ideas about why we dream do not support Freud's belief that dreams disguise unfulfilled wishes lurking in our unconscious. And slips of the tongue can be explained as competition between similar word choices in our memory network. Someone who says "I don't want to do that—it's a lot of brothel" may simply be blending *bother* and *trouble* (Foss & Hakes, 1978).

Freud was right about at least one thing. We indeed have limited access to all that goes on in our minds (Erdelyi, 1985, 1988, 2006; Kihlstrom, 1990). Our two-track mind has a vast out-of-sight realm. But the unconscious mind studied by cognitive researchers today is not a place for storing our censored anxiety-producing thoughts and seething passions. Rather, it is a part of our two-track mind, where cooler information processing occurs without our awareness, such as

- the right hemisphere activity that enables the split-brain patient's left hand to carry out an instruction the patient cannot verbalize (Chapter 2).
- the parallel processing of different aspects of vision and thinking, and the schemas that automatically control our perceptions and interpretations (Chapter 5).

projective test a personality test, such as the Rorschach test, that provides an unclear image designed to trigger projection of the test-taker's unconscious thoughts or feelings.

Rorschach inkblot test the most widely used projective test, a set of 10 inkblots, designed by Hermann Rorschach; seeks to identify people's inner feelings by analyzing their interpretations of the blots.

- the implicit memories that operate without our conscious recall, and even among those with amnesia (Chapter 7).

- the emotions that activate instantly, before conscious analysis (Chapter 9).

- the self-concept and stereotypes that automatically and unconsciously influence how we process information about ourselves and others (Chapter 14).

More than we realize, we fly on autopilot, guided by off-screen, out-of-sight, unconscious information processing. The unconscious mind is huge.

Although researchers find little support for Freud's idea that defense mechanisms disguise sexual and aggressive impulses, they do find evidence for mechanisms that defend self-esteem. For example, people do tend to see their traits and attitudes in others (Baumeister et al., 1998). Freud called this *projection*. Today's researchers call it the *false consensus effect*—the tendency to overestimate the extent to which others share our beliefs and behaviors. People who cheat on their taxes or break speed limits tend to think many others do the same. Defense mechanisms don't work exactly as Freud supposed. They seem motivated less by the seething impulses he imagined than by our need to protect our self-image.

Can Freud's Theory Be Tested Scientifically? As smart thinkers, we must ask the same question about Freud's theory that we ask about other theories. You may recall from Chapter 1 that a good theory organizes observations and predicts behaviors or events. How does Freudian theory stand up to the test?

Freud's theory rests on few objective observations, and it has produced few hypotheses to verify or reject. (For Freud, his own interpretations of patients' free associations, dreams, and slips were evidence enough.) Moreover, say the critics, Freud's theory offers after-the-fact explanations of behaviors and traits, but it fails to predict them. If you feel angry at your mother's death, you illustrate his theory because "your unresolved childhood dependency needs are threatened." If you do not feel angry, you again illustrate his theory because "you are repressing your anger." That, said Calvin Hall and Gardner Lindzey (1978, p. 68), "is like betting on a horse after the race has been run."

Freud's supporters object. To criticize Freudian theory for not making testable predictions is, they say, like criticizing baseball for not being an aerobic exercise, something it was never intended to be. Freud never claimed that psychoanalysis was predictive science. He merely claimed that, looking back, psychoanalysts could find meaning in our state of mind (Rieff, 1979).

Freud's supporters also note that some of his ideas *are* enduring. It was Freud who drew our attention to the unconscious and the irrational, when such ideas were not popular. Freud also drew our attention to the importance of human sexuality. He made us aware of the tension between our biological impulses and our social well-being. He challenged our self-righteousness, pointed out our self-protective defenses, and reminded us of our potential for evil.

No wonder, then, that in popular culture, Freud's legacy lives on. Can you see his influence in the idea that childhood experiences mold personality? That dreams have meaning? That many behaviors have

disguised motives? His early twentieth-century concepts have crept into our twenty-first-century language. Without realizing their source, we may speak of *ego, repression, projection, sibling rivalry, Freudian slips,* and *fixation.* Freud's ideas may not stand up as current psychological science, but as Martin Seligman noted (1994), "Hollywood, the talk shows, many therapists, and the general public still love them."

PRACTICE TEST

THE BASICS

1. Freud believed that we block unacceptable thoughts, wishes, feelings, and memories from our consciousness. He called this process of blocking
   a. free association.
   b. repression.
   c. anxiety.
   d. identification.

2. Freud called the *conscience,* or the part of the personality that internalizes ideals,
   a. the ego.
   b. the superego.
   c. the reality principle.
   d. repression.

3. According to the psychoanalytic view, conflicts unresolved at any of the psychosexual stages may lead to
   a. dormant sexual feelings.
   b. fixation in that stage.
   c. conscious blocking of impulses.
   d. a distorted identity.

4. All defense mechanisms distort or disguise reality, and all are
   a. conscious.
   b. unconscious.
   c. fixations.
   d. rationalizations.

5. In general, neo-Freudians such as Adler and Horney accepted many of Freud's views but placed more emphasis on
   a. motives beyond sex and aggression.
   b. social interactions.
   c. the role of the conscious mind.
   d. all of these factors.

6. Contemporary psychologists do NOT agree with the Freudian idea that
   a. we have limited access to all that goes on in our minds.

b. we use some defenses to protect our self-image.

c. life involves tension between biological impulses and social restraint.

d. we often repress the memory of traumatic events.

THE BIG PICTURE

11A. What, according to Freud, were some of the important defense mechanisms, and what do they defend against?

11B. How does today's psychological science assess Freud's theory?

IN YOUR EVERYDAY LIFE

■ How would you describe *your* personality? What are your typical patterns of thinking, feeling, and acting?

■ What did you think or know about Freud before you read this chapter? Have your thoughts changed now that you have learned more about him?

Answers: 1. b, 2. b, 3. b, 4. b, 5. d, 6. d. Answers to The Big Picture questions can be found in Appendix B at the end of the book.

The Humanistic Perspective

8 What were Abraham Maslow's and Carl Rogers' humanistic psychology perspectives?

In the 1960s, some psychologists decided that psychology needed some fresh ideas and a new direction. They thought Freud's views were too negative. They were equally uncomfortable with the strict behaviorism of John Watson and B. F. Skinner (see Chapter 6), judging it to be too mechanical. This movement helped produce *humanistic psychologists* such as Abraham Maslow (1908–1970) and Carl Rogers (1902–1987). In contrast to Freud's emphasis on disorders born out of dark

Abraham Maslow: "Any theory of motivation that is worthy of attention must deal with the highest capacities of the healthy and strong person as well as with the defensive maneuvers of crippled spirits" (*Motivation and Personality*, 1970).

conflicts, the humanistic psychologists focused on the ways "healthy" people strive for self-determination and self-realization. In contrast to behaviorism's objective laboratory experiments, they asked people to report their own experiences and feelings.

Abraham Maslow's Self-Actualizing Person

Abraham Maslow proposed that human motivations form a pyramid-shaped **hierarchy of needs** (see Chapter 9). At the base are bodily needs. If those are met, we become concerned with the next-higher level of needs, personal safety. If we feel secure, we then seek to love, to be loved, and to love ourselves. With our love needs satisfied, we seek self-esteem (feelings of self-worth). Having achieved self-esteem, we seek the top-level needs for **self-actualization** and **self-transcendence.** These motives, at the pyramid's peak, involve reaching our full potential.

Maslow (1970) formed his ideas by studying healthy, creative people rather than troubled clinical cases. His description of self-actualization grew out of his study of people, such as Abraham Lincoln, who had lived rich and productive lives. They were self-aware and self-accepting. They were open and spontaneous. They were loving and caring. They didn't worry too much about other people's opinions. Yet they were not self-centered. Curious about the world, they focused their energies on a particular task, often regarding that task as their life mission. Most enjoyed a few deep relationships rather than many shallow ones. Many had been moved by spiritual or personal peak *experiences* that were beyond normal consciousness.

These, said Maslow, are mature adult qualities. These healthy people had outgrown their mixed feelings toward their parents. They had found their calling. They had "acquired enough courage to be unpopular, to be unashamed about being openly virtuous." HOW MANY OF US ARE ◄ LIKELY TO BECOME SELF-ACTUALIZING ADULTS? Maslow's work with college students led him to believe that the best candidates were likable, caring young people who are "privately affectionate to those of their elders who deserve it," and "secretly uneasy about the cruelty, meanness, and mob spirit so often found in young people."

Carl Rogers' Person-Centered Perspective

Carl Rogers agreed that people have self-actualizing tendencies. Rogers believed that people are basically good. Like acorns, we are primed to reach our potential if we are given a growth-promoting environment. People nurture our growth, and we nurture theirs, in three ways (Rogers, 1980).

● If we are *genuine* to another person, we are open with our own feelings. We drop our false fronts and are transparent and self-disclosing.

● If we are *accepting,* we offer the other person what Rogers called **unconditional positive regard.** This is an

---

hierarchy of needs Maslow's pyramid of human needs; at the base are physiological needs that must be satisfied before higher-level safety needs, and then psychological needs, become active.

self-actualization according to Maslow, the psychological need that arises after basic physical and psychological needs are met and self-esteem is achieved; the motivation to fulfill our potential.

self-transcendence according to Maslow, the striving for identity, meaning, and purpose beyond the self.

unconditional positive regard according to Rogers, an attitude of total acceptance toward another person.

© Bettmann/Corbis

attitude of total acceptance. We value the person even knowing the person's failings. We all find it a huge relief to drop our pretenses, confess our worst feelings, and discover that we are still accepted. In a good marriage, a close family, or an intimate friendship, we are free to be ourselves without fearing what others will think.

- If we are *empathic,* we share another's feelings and reflect that person's meanings back to them. "Rarely do we listen with real understanding, true empathy," said Rogers. "Yet listening, of this very special kind, is one of the most potent forces for change that I know."

Genuineness, acceptance, and empathy are the water, sun, and nutrients that enable people to grow like vigorous oak trees, according to Rogers. For "as persons are accepted and prized, they tend to develop a more caring attitude toward themselves" (Rogers, 1980, p. 116). As persons are empathically heard, "it becomes possible for them to listen more accurately to the flow of inner experiencing."

Rogers called for genuineness, acceptance, and empathy in the relationship between therapist and client. But he also believed that these three qualities nurture growth between any two human beings—between leader and group, teacher and student, manager and staff member, parent and child, friend and friend.

"Just remember, son, it doesn't matter whether you win or lose—unless you want Daddy's love."

A father *not* offering unconditional positive regard.

The picture of empathy: Being open and sharing confidences is easier when the listener shows real understanding. Within such relationships people can relax and fully express their true selves.

Writer Calvin Trillin (2006) recalls an example of parental genuineness and acceptance at a camp for children with severe disorders, where his wife, Alice, worked. L., a "magical child," had genetic diseases that meant she had to be tube-fed and could walk only with difficulty. Alice recalled,

... One day, when we were playing duck-duck-goose, I was sitting behind her and she asked me to hold her mail for her while she took her turn to be chased around the circle. It took her a while to make the circuit, and I had time to see that on top of the pile [of mail] was a note from her mom. Then I did something truly awful. . . . I simply had to know what this child's parents could have done to make her so spectacular, to make her the most optimistic, most enthusiastic, most hopeful human being I had ever encountered. I snuck a quick look at the note, and my eyes fell on this sentence: "If God had given us all of the children in the world to choose from, L., we would only have chosen you." Before L. got back to her place in the circle, I showed the note to Bud, who was sitting next to me. "Quick. Read this," I whispered. "It's the secret of life." . . .

Maslow and Rogers would have smiled knowingly. For them, a central feature of personality is one's **self-concept**—all the thoughts and feelings we have in response to the question, "Who am I?" If our self-concept is positive, we tend to act and perceive the world positively. If it is negative—if in our own eyes we fall far short of our *ideal self*—we feel dissatisfied and unhappy. A worthwhile goal for all of us—therapists, parents, teachers, and friends—is therefore to help others know, accept, and be true to themselves, said Rogers.

Evaluating the Humanistic Perspective

9 | What have critics said about humanistic psychology?

Humanistic psychology's message has been heard, and its impact has been far-reaching. Maslow's and Rogers' ideas have influenced counseling, education, child-rearing, and management.

These theorists have also influenced—sometimes in ways they did not intend—much of today's popular psychology. IS A ◄ POSITIVE SELF-CONCEPT THE KEY TO HAPPINESS AND SUCCESS? Do acceptance and empathy nurture positive feelings about ourselves? Are people basically good and capable of improving? Many would answer *Yes, Yes,* and *Yes.* Nine in ten people responding to a 1992 *Newsweek* Gallup poll rated self-esteem as very important for "motivating a person to work hard and succeed."

Many psychologists have criticized the humanistic perspective. First, said the critics, its concepts are vague and based on the theorists' personal opinions, rather than on scientific methods. Consider Maslow's description of self-actualizing people as open, spontaneous, loving, self-accepting, and productive. Is this a scientific description? Or is it merely a description of Maslow's own values and ideals, as viewed in his own personal heroes (Smith, 1978)? Imagine another theorist with a different set of heroes, such as Napoleon and former Vice President Dick Cheney. This theorist might have described self-actualizing people as "desiring power," "aggressive," and "self-assured."

Other critics objected to the attitudes encouraged by humanistic psychology. Rogers, for example, said, "The only question which matters is, 'Am I living in a way which is deeply satisfying to me, and which truly expresses me?'" (quoted by Wallach & Wallach, 1985). Could such attitudes—trusting and acting on our feelings, being true to ourselves, fulfilling ourselves—lead to self-indulgence, selfishness, and a lack of moral restraints (Campbell & Specht, 1985; Wallach & Wallach, 1983)?

Humanistic psychologists have countered that a secure, nondefensive self-acceptance is actually the first step toward loving others. Indeed, people who feel liked and accepted—for who they are, not just for their achievements—show less-defensive attitudes (Schimel et al., 2001).

A final criticism has been that humanistic psychology fails to appreciate our human capacity for evil. Faced with global climate change, overpopulation, terrorism, and the spread of nuclear weapons, we may be paralyzed by either of two ways of thinking. One is a naive optimism that denies the threat ("People are basically good; everything will work out"). The other is a dark despair ("It's hopeless; why try?"). Action requires enough realism to fuel concern and enough optimism to provide hope. Humanistic psychology,

said the critics, encourages the needed hope but not the equally necessary realism about evil.

"We do pretty well when you stop to think that people are basically good."

PRACTICE TEST

THE BASICS

7. Maslow based his description of self-actualizing people on
   a. Freudian theory.
   b. case histories of people with disorders.
   c. controlled laboratory experiments.
   d. his study of healthy, creative people.

8. Rogers believed that we can help people reach their full potential by providing an environment of total acceptance, which he called
   a. self-esteem.
   b. unconditional positive regard.
   c. self-actualization.
   d. the "ideal self."

9. In the humanistic perspective, a central feature of personality is the
   a. human capacity for evil.
   b. reality principle.
   c. unconscious.
   d. self-concept.

THE BIG PICTURE

11C. What does it mean to be "empathic"? To be "self-actualized"?

IN YOUR EVERYDAY LIFE

▪ Has someone in your life accepted you unconditionally? Has this person helped you know yourself better or improve your self-image?

Answers: 7. d, 8. b, 9. d. Answers to The Big Picture questions can be found in Appendix B at the end of the book.

The Trait Perspective

10 How do psychologists use traits to describe personality?

Both the Freudian and the humanistic perspectives viewed personality as the product of forces acting upon us. Both perspectives attempted to *explain* how personality develops. **Trait** researchers are less concerned with *explaining* individual traits than with *describing* them. To them,

personality is a *stable and enduring pattern of behavior,* such as Sam Gamgee's consistent loyalty and optimism.

Searching for Basic Personality Traits

Imagine that you've been hired by an Internet dating service. Your job is to construct a questionnaire that will help people describe themselves to those seeking dates and mates. What personality traits might give an accurate sense of the person filling out the questionnaire? You might begin by thinking of how we describe an apple. We place it along several trait dimensions. It's relatively large or small; it's red or green; it's sweet or sour. By likewise placing people on trait dimensions, we can begin to describe them.

An even better way to identify a person's personality is to identify **factors**—clusters of behavior tendencies that occur together. People who describe themselves as outgoing, for example, may also say that they like excitement and practical jokes and dislike quiet reading. This cluster of behaviors reflects a basic factor, or trait—in this case, *extraversion.*

So how many traits will be just the right number for your Internet-dating questionnaire? If psychologists Hans Eysenck and Sybil Eysenck [EYE-zink] had been hired to do your job, they would have said two. They believed that we can reduce many normal human variations to the two shown in **FIGURE 11.3** on the next page: *extraversion-introversion* and *emotional stability-instability.* People in 35 countries around the world, from China to Uganda to Russia, have taken the *Eysenck Personality Questionnaire.* In their answers, the extraversion and emotionality factors emerged as basic personality dimensions (Eysenck, 1990, 1992).

---

self-concept all our thoughts and feelings about ourselves, in answer to the question, "Who am I?"

trait a characteristic pattern of behavior or a tendency to feel and act in a certain way, as assessed by self-reports on a personality test.

factor a cluster of behavior tendencies that occur together.

UNSTABLE

Moody   Touchy
Anxious   Restless
Rigid   Aggressive
Sober   Excitable
Pessimistic   Changeable
Reserved   Impulsive
Unsociable   Optimistic
Quiet   Active

INTRODUCED ———— **EXTRAVERTED**

Passive   Sociable
Careful   Outgoing
Thoughtful   Talkative
Peaceful   Responsive
Controlled   Easygoing
Reliable   Lively
Even-tempered   Carefree
Calm   Leadership

STABLE

FIGURE 11.3 ● **Two personality factors** Map makers can tell us a lot by using two axes (north-south and east-west). Two primary personality factors (extraversion-introversion and stability-instability) are similarly useful as axes for describing personality variation. Varying combinations define other, more specific traits. (From Eysenck & Eysenck, 1963.) Those who are naturally introverted, such as primatologist Jane Goodall, may be particularly gifted in field studies. Successful politicians, including French President Nicolas Sarkozy, are often natural extraverts.

The Eysencks believed that extraversion and emotionality are genetically influenced. Recent research supports this belief. Brain-activity scans suggest that extraverts seek stimulation because their normal brain arousal is relatively low. Also, a frontal lobe area involved in restraining behavior is less active in extraverts than in introverts (Johnson et al., 1999).

As you may recall from the twin and adoption studies discussed in Chapter 3, our genes have much to say about the temperament and behavioral style that help define our personality. Developmental psychologist Jerome Kagan, for example, has attributed differences in children's shyness to differences in their autonomic nervous systems. An infant with a reactive autonomic nervous system responds quickly and dramatically to stress. A less fearful and more curious child often has a less reactive autonomic nervous system.

The Big Five Factors

11 Which traits seem to provide the most useful information about personality variation?

It helps to know that a potential date is an introvert or an extravert, or even that the person is emotionally stable or unstable. But as the designer of the dating questionnaire, you'd probably prefer more information about the test-taker's personality.

Diverse Yet Alike

Whether we are at Doshisha University in Kyoto, Japan, or at the University of California, Los Angeles, our personality traits can be described using the Big Five factors.

The *Minnesota Multiphasic Personality Inventory (MMPI)* might help. *Personality inventories,* including the famous MMPI, are long sets of questions covering a wide range of feelings and behaviors. Although the MMPI was originally developed to identify emotional disorders, it also assesses people's personality traits. But for a dating questionnaire, this might be too much information. (COULD ASTROL-

▶OGY OFFER CLUES TO PEOPLE'S TRAITS? See Thinking Critically About: How to Be a "Successful" Astrologer on the next page.) Let's see what else personality researchers have to offer.

Today's trait researchers often use an expansion of the Eysencks' introverted/extraverted and stable/unstable factors. It's called the *Big Five* because it measures five factors—*conscientiousness, agreeableness, neuroticism, openness,* and *extraversion* (TABLE 11.3) (Costa & McCrae, 2006; John & Srivastava, 1999). Where people fall on these five dimensions says much of what there is to say about their personality.

The recent wave of Big Five research has explored various questions:

- *How stable are these traits?* In adulthood, the Big Five traits are quite stable. Some tendencies (emotional instability, extraversion, and openness) fade a bit during early and middle adulthood. Others (conscientiousness and agreeableness) increase (McCrae et al., 1999; Vaidya et al., 2002). Conscientiousness typically rises most during our twenties, as we mature and learn to manage our jobs and relationships. Agreeableness increases the most during people's thirties and continues to increase through their sixties (Srivastava et al., 2003).

- *Do we inherit these traits?* Roughly 50 percent of our individual differences on the Big Five can be credited to our genes (Loehlin et al., 1998).

- *How well do these traits apply to various cultures?* The Big Five dimensions describe personality in various cultures reasonably well (Schmitt et al., 2007; Yamagata et al., 2006). "Features of personality traits are common to all human groups," concluded Robert McCrae and 79 co-researchers (2005) from their 50-culture study.

If you work the Big Five traits into your dating questionnaire, your mission should be accomplished—assuming people act the same way at all times and in all situations. Next, we ask, do they?

PRACTICE TEST

THE BASICS

10. Trait theory often describes personality in terms of clusters of characteristic behaviors or traits that tend to occur together. These clusters are called
    a. maps.   c. factors.
    b. axes.   d. dimensions.

11. A personality inventory is a(n)
    a. set of questions covering a wide range of feelings and behaviors.
    b. brain scan tracking variations in arousal.
    c. single trait scale used to measure emotionality.
    d. handwriting analysis that offers clues to personal traits.

12. Most trait researchers today believe that the Big Five factors offer the best descriptions of personality. Which of the following is NOT one of the Big Five?
    a. Conscientiousness
    b. Sadness
    c. Extraversion
    d. Agreeableness

THE BIG PICTURE

11D. What are some advantages of assessing personality by using the Big Five factors?

IN YOUR EVERYDAY LIFE

- Where would you place yourself on the Big Five personality dimensions—conscientiousness, agreeableness, neuroticism, openness, and extraversion? Would your family and friends agree with you?

Answers: 10. c, 11. a, 12. b. Answers to The Big Picture questions can be found in Appendix B at the end of the book.

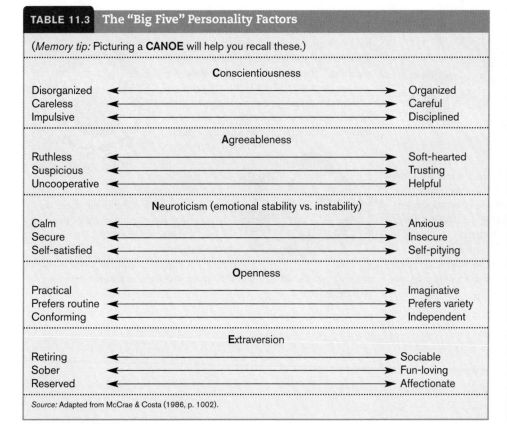

TABLE 11.3	The "Big Five" Personality Factors

(Memory tip: Picturing a **CANOE** will help you recall these.)

Conscientiousness

Disorganized	←————————————→	Organized
Careless	←————————————→	Careful
Impulsive	←————————————→	Disciplined

Agreeableness

Ruthless	←————————————→	Soft-hearted
Suspicious	←————————————→	Trusting
Uncooperative	←————————————→	Helpful

Neuroticism (emotional stability vs. instability)

Calm	←————————————→	Anxious
Secure	←————————————→	Insecure
Self-satisfied	←————————————→	Self-pitying

Openness

Practical	←————————————→	Imaginative
Prefers routine	←————————————→	Prefers variety
Conforming	←————————————→	Independent

Extraversion

Retiring	←————————————→	Sociable
Sober	←————————————→	Fun-loving
Reserved	←————————————→	Affectionate

Source: Adapted from McCrae & Costa (1986, p. 1002).

How to Be a "Successful" Astrologer

Can we figure out people's traits from the alignment of the stars and planets at the time of their birth? From their handwriting?

Astronomers scoff at astrology: The stars and planets have shifted in the thousands of years since astrologers first made their predictions (Kelly, 1997, 1998). Humorists mock it: "No offense," writes Dave Barry, "but if you take the horoscope seriously your frontal lobes are the size of Raisinets." Psychologists instead ask questions: Can astrologers beat chance when given someone's birth date and asked to identify the person from a short list of personality descriptions? Can people pick out their own horoscope from such a list?

The consistent answers have been: *No* and *No* (British Psychological Society, 1993; Carlson, 1985; Kelly, 1997). Can handwriting experts do better than chance at telling people's jobs after examining several pages of their handwriting? Again, the answer is *No* (Beyerstein & Beyerstein, 1992; Dean et al., 1992). Still, experts—and introductory psychology students—often *perceive* correlations between personality and handwriting even where there are none (King & Koehler, 2000).

How do astrologers persuade thousands of newspapers and millions of people worldwide to buy their advice? Ray Hyman (1981), a palm reader turned research psychologist, revealed some tricks of the trade.

The first technique is the "stock spiel." Each of us is in some ways like no one else and in other ways just like everyone. That some things are true of us all allows the "seer" to offer statements that seem impressively accurate. "I sense that you worry about things more than you let on, even to your best friends."

A second technique is to "read" our clothing, physical features, gestures, and reactions. An expensive wedding ring and black dress might, for example, suggest a wealthy woman who was recently widowed.

You, too, could read such clues, says Hyman. If people seek you out for a reading, start with some safe sympathy: "I sense you're having some problems lately. You seem unsure what to do. I get the feeling another person is involved." Then give them what they want to hear, and tell them it is their duty to cooperate by relating your message to their specific experiences. Later they will recall that you predicted those specific details.

Phrase statements as questions, and when you detect a positive response assert the statement strongly. Finally, be a good listener, and later, in different words, reveal to people what they earlier revealed to you.

Better yet, beware of those who, by exploiting people with these techniques, are fortune takers rather than fortune tellers.

The Social-Cognitive Perspective

12 How does the social-cognitive perspective view personality?

In some ways, our personality seems to stay reliably the same. Cheerful, friendly children tend to become cheerful, friendly adults. But it's also true that a fun-loving jokester can suddenly be serious and respectful at a job interview. DO◀ THE PERSONALITY TRAITS WE EXPRESS CHANGE FROM ONE SITUATION TO ANOTHER? The short answer is *Yes*.

The **social-cognitive perspective** on personality is especially interested in the many ways our individual traits and thoughts interact with our social world as we move from one situation to another. Let's take a closer look at this idea.

We bring a lot of baggage to any social situation we enter. We bring our past learning, often picked up through conditioning or by observing others. We also bring our ways of thinking about specific situations. But situations themselves place different demands on us. Most of us know the general social rules for acceptable behavior at a grandparent's funeral, for example. We also know that a different set of rules outlines what's acceptable at a friend's New Year's Eve party. In the end, our behavior in any situation is in part the result of our own characteristics and in part the result of the situation. For psychologists who study personality from a social-cognitive perspective, this interaction is a fascinating area of research. Roughly speaking, the short-term, outside influences on behavior are the focus of social psychology (see Chapter 14), and the lasting, inner influences are the focus of personality psychology. In actuality, behavior always depends on the interaction of persons with situations.

The Person

Are some people dependably conscientious and others unreliable, some cheerful and others grumpy, some friendly and

"Mr. Coughlin over there was the founder of one of the first motorcycle gangs."

outgoing and others shy? To be useful indicators of personality, traits would have to persist over time. Friendly people, for example, would have to act friendly at different times and places. In such cases, we could say that personality is stable.

Some researchers who have followed lives through time (especially those who have studied infancy) are impressed with personality change. Others are struck by personality stability during adulthood. Data from 152 long-term studies reflect both of these trends. The studies compared early trait scores with scores for the same traits seven years later. These comparisons were done for several different age groups, and for each group, the scores were positively correlated. But the correlations were strongest for comparisons done in adulthood. For young children, the correlation between early and later scores was +0.3. For collegians, the correlation was +0.54. For 70-year-olds, the correlation was +0.73. (Remember that 0 indicates no relationship, and +1.0 would mean that one score perfectly predicts the other.)

As people grow older, their personality stabilizes. Interests may change—the devoted collector of tropical fish may become the devoted gardener. Careers may change—the determined salesperson may become a determined social worker. Relationships may change—the hostile spouse may start over with a new partner.

The consistency of specific *behaviors* from one situation to the next is another matter. People are not always predictable.

What relationship would you expect to find between a student's being conscientious on one occasion (say, showing up for class on time) and being conscientious on another occasion (say, turning in assignments on time)? If you've noticed how outgoing you are in some situations and how reserved you are in others, perhaps you said, "very little." That's what researchers have found—only a small correlation (Mischel, 1968, 1984, 2004). This inconsistency makes personality test scores weak predictors of behaviors. A person's score on an extraversion test predicts that person's behavior *across many different situations*. It does not neatly predict how sociable that individual will be *on any given occasion*.

If we remember such results, we will be more careful about labeling other people (Mischel, 1968, 1984, 2004). We will be slower to respond when asked whether someone is likely to violate parole, commit suicide, or be an effective employee. Years in advance, science can tell us the phase of the Moon for any given date. A day in advance, meteorologists can often predict the weather. But we are much further from being able to predict how *you* will feel and act tomorrow.

Does this mean that psychological science has nothing meaningful to say about personality traits? *No!* People's *average* outgoingness, happiness, or carelessness over *many* situations is predictable (Epstein, 1983a,b). Extraverts really do talk more. We know this because researchers collected snippets of people's daily experience via wearable recording devices (Mehl et al., 2006).

Even when we try to restrain them, our traits may assert themselves. During my noontime pickup basketball games with friends, I keep vowing to cut back on my jabbering and joking. But without fail, the irrepressible chatterbox reoccupies my body moments later.

social-cognitive perspective views behavior as influenced by the interaction between persons (and their thinking) and their social context.

Our personality traits influence our health, our thinking, and our job performance (Hogan, 1998; Roberts et al., 2007). Our traits even lurk in some unexpected places.

- *Music preferences:* Your playlist says a lot about who you are. Classical, jazz, blues, and folk music lovers tend to be open to experience and verbally intelligent. Country, pop, and religious music lovers tend to be cheerful, outgoing, and conscientious (Rentfrow & Gosling, 2003).

- *Dorm rooms and offices:* Our personal spaces—our scattered papers or neat surfaces—display our personality. After just a few minutes' inspection of someone's living and working spaces, you could give a fairly accurate summary of their conscientiousness, openness to new experience, and even emotional stability (Gosling, 2008).

- *Personal Web sites:* Personal Web sites and social networking profiles offer important clues to whether you are extraverted, conscientious, and open to experiences. Personal Web sites are a canvas for self-expression (Gosling et al., 2007; Marcus et al., 2006). Even mere photos, with their associated clothes, expressions, and postures, can give clues to personality (Naumann et al., 2009).

Alex Segre/Alamy

- *E-mail:* If you have ever felt you could detect someone's personality from the writing voice in their e-mail, you are right!! What a cool, exciting finding!!! (If you catch my drift.) People's ratings of others' personalities, based solely on their e-mails, correlate with actual personality test scores on measures such as extraversion and neuroticism (Gill et al., 2006; Oberlander & Gill, 2006). Extraverts, for example, use more adjectives.

To sum up, averaging our behavior across many occasions reveals distinct personality traits. Personality traits exist, and they leave tracks in our lives. We differ. And our differences matter.

The Situation

Situations also differ. And as powerful as our personality traits are, they don't give us control over every situation. At any moment, the immediate situation powerfully influences our behavior, *especially when the situation makes clear demands.* We can better predict drivers' behavior at traffic lights from knowing the color of the lights than from knowing the drivers' personalities.

Sometimes, in unfamiliar, formal situations—perhaps as a guest in the home of a person from another culture—our

Our spaces express our personalities: Even at "zero acquaintance," people can catch a glimpse of others' personality from looking at their Web site, dorm room, or office. So, what's your read on University of Texas researcher Samuel Gosling?

John Langford Photography

traits remain hidden as we carefully attend to social cues. In familiar, informal situations—just hanging out with friends—we feel more relaxed, and our traits emerge (Buss, 1989). In these informal situations, our expressive styles—our animation, manner of speaking, and gestures—are impressively consistent. Viewing "thin slices" of someone's behavior—even just three 2-second clips of a teacher—can tell us a lot about the person's basic traits (Ambady & Rosenthal, 1992, 1993).

The Interaction

So our personal traits interact with our environment to influence our behavior. Albert Bandura (1986, 2006, 2008) called this process **reciprocal determinism.** "Behavior, internal personal factors, and environmental influences," he said, "all operate as interlocking determinants of each other" **(FIGURE 11.4)**. We can see this in children's TV-viewing habits. Their history of watching TV (past behavior) influences their viewing preferences (internal factor), which influence how TV (environmental factor) affects their current behavior. Where a behaviorist might assume that environment *determines* behavior, a social-cognitive theorist explores the *interaction* among the three sets of influences.

1. *Different people choose different environments.* Choices are part of life. What school do you attend? What do you read? What shows do you watch? What music do you download? With whom do you enjoy spending time? All these choices are part of an environment you are choosing, based partly on your personality (Ickes et al., 1997). You choose your environment, and then it shapes you.

2. *Our personalities shape how we interpret and react to events.* For example, anxious people pay more attention to potentially threatening events (Eysenck et al., 1987). If you perceive the world as threatening, you will watch for threats and be prepared to defend yourself.

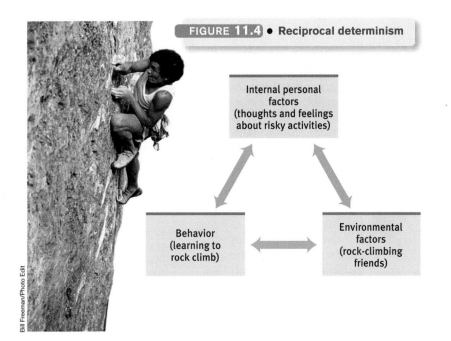

FIGURE **11.4** • Reciprocal determinism

Internal personal factors
(thoughts and feelings about risky activities)

Behavior
(learning to rock climb)

Environmental factors
(rock-climbing friends)

Bill Freeman/Photo Edit

Exploring the Self

13 How do we use our possible selves to develop an integrated personality, and how does self-esteem help in the process?

We can think of our *self-image* as our internal view of our personality. Underlying this idea is the notion that the **self** is the center of personality—the organizer of our thoughts, feelings, and actions.

Consider the concept of *possible selves* (Cross & Markus, 1991; Markus & Nurius, 1986). Your possible selves include your visions of the self you dream of becoming—the rich self, the successful self, the loved

Getty Images/Image Source

Trying out a possible self: As an apprentice, this young man has a chance to see how it feels to be a woodworker, while learning valuable life skills in the process.

---

3. *Our personalities help create situations to which we react.* How we view and treat people influences how they then treat us. If you expect a family member to be angry, you may give that person a cold shoulder, touching off the very anger you expect. Do you have an easygoing, upbeat personality? If so, you will probably enjoy close, supportive friendships (Donnellan et al., 2005; Kendler, 1997).

In such ways, we are both the products and the architects of our environments. Boiling water turns an egg hard and a potato soft. A threatening environment turns one person into a hero, another into a scoundrel. *The point to remember:* At every moment, we are influenced by past behavior, our social context, and our personality.

PRACTICE TEST

THE BASICS

13. The social-cognitive perspective focuses on how people's traits and thoughts interact with their
   a. genes.
   b. behaviors.
   c. emotions.
   d. social context.

14. Personality tests are best at predicting our
   a. behavior on a specific occasion.
   b. average behavior across many situations.
   c. feelings, not our thoughts.
   d. thoughts, not our feelings.

15. Reciprocal determinism is the idea that personal factors, environment, and _____ interact and influence one another.
   a. behavior
   b. thoughts and feelings
   c. culture
   d. expectations

THE BIG PICTURE

11E. How do our personality traits typically interact with the situations in which we find ourselves?

IN YOUR EVERYDAY LIFE

■ Look around your personal spaces, such as your bedroom, car, or even your Facebook profile. How do you think these spaces reflect your personality?

■ How have your experiences shaped your personality? How has your personality helped shape your environment?

Answers: 13. d, 14. b, 15. a. Answers to The Big Picture questions can be found in Appendix B at the end of the book.

---

reciprocal determinism the interacting influences of behavior, internal personal factors, and environment.

self your image and understanding of who you are; in modern psychology, the idea that this is the center of personality, organizing your thoughts, feelings, and actions.

and admired self. Your possible selves also include the self you fear becoming—the unemployed self, the lonely self, the academically failed self. Possible selves motivate us by laying out specific goals and calling forth the energy to work toward them. University of Michigan students in a combined undergraduate and medical school program earned higher grades if they had a clear vision of themselves as successful doctors.

Carried too far, our self-focus can lead us to fret that others are noticing and evaluating us. Researchers demonstrated this **spotlight effect** by having some students wear Barry Manilow T-shirts and enter a room filled with other students (Gilovich, 1996). Feeling self-conscious, the T-shirt wearers guessed that nearly half of the other students would notice the shirt as they walked in. How many did notice? Fewer than one in four. We stand out less than we imagine, even with dorky clothes or bad hair, and even after a blunder like setting off a library alarm (Gilovich & Savitsky, 1999; Savitsky et al., 2001).

Knowing about the spotlight effect can be empowering. When public speakers understand that their natural nervousness is not obvious to the audience, their speaking performance improves (Savitsky & Gilovich, 2003).

Self-Esteem: The Good News and the Bad

If we like our self-image, we'll probably have high **self-esteem.** This feeling of high self-worth will translate into fewer sleepless nights and less pressure to conform. We'll be more persistent at difficult tasks. We'll be less shy, anxious, and lonely, and, in the future, we'll be just plain happier (Greenberg, 2008; Orth et al., 2008, 2009; Swann et al., 2007).

CAN WE BOOST PEOPLE'S SELF-ESTEEM◀ BY REPEATEDLY REMINDING THEM OF THEIR GOOD POINTS? AND WOULD THIS IMPROVE THEIR LIVES? Much research challenges

the idea that high self-esteem is really "the armor that protects kids" from life's problems (Baumeister, 2006; Dawes, 1994; Leary, 1999; Seligman, 1994, 2002). Problems and failures lower self-esteem. So, maybe self-esteem simply reflects reality. Maybe it's a side effect of meeting challenges and getting through difficulties. Maybe kids with high self-esteem do better in school because doing better in school boosts self-esteem. Maybe self-esteem is a gauge that reports the state of our relationships with others. If so, isn't pushing the gauge artificially higher much like forcing a car's low-fuel gauge to display "full"? If feeling good *follows* doing well, the best boost will come from children's own hard-won achievements, not from repeatedly telling them how wonderful they are. As one researcher observed, "When kids increase in self-control, their grades go up later. But when kids increase their self-esteem, there is no effect on their grades" (Duckworth et al., 2009).

There is, however, an important *effect* of low self-esteem. People who feel negative about themselves also tend to be negative toward others (Amabile, 1983; Baumgardner et al., 1989; Pelham, 1993). Researchers have temporarily deflated people's self-image—for example, by telling them they did poorly on a test or by insulting them. These participants were

then more likely to insult others or to express racial prejudice (Ybarra, 1999).

But inflated self-esteem also causes problems. When studying insult-triggered aggression, researchers found that "conceited, self-important individuals turn nasty toward those who puncture their bubbles of self-love" (Baumeister, 2001; Bushman et al., 2009). Some find it helpful to separate self-esteem into two categories—*defensive* and *secure* (Lambird & Mann, 2006; Ryan & Deci, 2004).

- *Defensive self-esteem is fragile.* Its goal is to sustain itself, which makes failures and criticism feel threatening. Defensive self-esteem feeds anger and disorder (Crocker & Park, 2004). Like low self-esteem, it correlates with aggressive and antisocial behavior (Donnellan et al., 2005).

- *Secure self-esteem is less fragile.* It relies less on other people's evaluations. If we feel accepted for who we are, and not for our looks, wealth, or fame, we are free of pressures to succeed. We can focus beyond ourselves, losing ourselves in relationships and purposes larger than self. Secure self-esteem thus leads to greater quality of life. Such findings are in line with Maslow's and Rogers' ideas about the benefits of a healthy self-image.

If deflating people's self-image can lower self-esteem, will groups that have faced discrimination—members of minority groups, for example—have low self-esteem? The evidence says *No*. Comparisons of more than a half-million people reveal slightly *higher* self-esteem scores for Black than for White children, adolescents, and young adults (Gray-Little & Hafdahl, 2000; Twenge & Crocker, 2002).

Members of stigmatized groups (people of color, those with disabilities, and, in some cases, women) appear to maintain their self-esteem in three ways (Crocker & Major, 1989):

- They value the things at which they excel.

- They attribute problems to prejudice.

- They do as everyone does—they compare themselves to people in their own group.

Self-Serving Bias

14 What evidence points to a self-serving bias?

Carl Rogers (1958) once objected to the idea that humanity's problems arise from too much self-love, or pride. He noted that most people he had known "despise themselves, regard themselves as worthless and unlovable."

One of psychology's most surprising but firmly established recent conclusions indicates the opposite. Most of us actually have a good reputation with ourselves. We display a **self-serving bias**—a readiness to perceive ourselves favorably (Mezulis et al., 2004; Myers, 2010). Consider:

People accept more responsibility for good deeds than for bad, and for successes than for failures. Athletes often privately credit their victories to their own talent. Their losses are the result of bad breaks, lousy officials, or the other team's amazing performance. In a half-dozen studies, most students who received poor grades on an exam criticized the exam, not themselves. On insurance forms, drivers have explained accidents in such words as: "An invisible car came out of nowhere, struck my car, and vanished." "As I reached an intersection, a hedge sprang up, obscuring my vision, and I did not see the other car." "A pedestrian hit me and went under my car." The question "What have I done to deserve this?" is

> "If you are like most people, then like most people, you don't know you're like most people. Science has given us a lot of facts about the average person, and one of the most reliable of these facts is the average person doesn't see herself as average."
>
> Daniel Gilbert, *Stumbling on Happiness,* 2006

one we usually ask of our troubles, not our successes.

Most people see themselves as better than average. This is true for nearly any common, socially desirable behavior. In national surveys, most business executives say they are more ethical than the average executive. Most business managers and college professors (90 percent or more of each) rate their performance as superior to that of their average peer. This tendency is less striking in Asia, where people value modesty (Heine & Hamamura, 2007). Yet self-serving biases have been observed worldwide: among Dutch, Australian, and Chinese students; Japanese drivers; Indian Hindus; and French people of most walks of life. In every one of 53 countries surveyed, people expressed self-esteem above the midpoint of the most widely used scale (Schmitt & Allik, 2005).

Most people (this is a fun finding) even see themselves as more immune than others to self-serving bias (Pronin, 2007). We also are quicker to believe flattering descriptions of ourselves than unflattering ones, and we are im-

AND GOD CREATED SELF-WORTH

© Shannon Wheeler

pressed with psychological tests that make us look good.

Self-serving bias often underlies conflicts. Some blame their spouse for marriage problems. All of us tend to see our own group (whether it's our school, our ethnic group, or our country) as superior. "Aryan pride" fueled Nazi horrors. No wonder religion and literature so often warn against the perils of self-love and pride.

So, if the self-serving bias is so common, **WHY DO SO MANY PEOPLE PUT THEM-SELVES DOWN?** For four reasons: First, some negative thoughts—"How could I have been so stupid!"—*protect us from repeating mistakes.* Second, self put-downs are sometimes meant to *prompt positive feedback.* Saying "No one likes me" may at least get you "But not everyone has met you!" Third, these put-downs help *prepare us for possible failure.* The coach who talks about the superior strength of the upcoming opponent makes a loss understandable, a victory noteworthy. Finally, we may be putting down *our old selves,* not our current selves (Wilson & Ross, 2001). Chumps yesterday, but champs today: "At 18, I was a jerk; today I'm more sensitive."

Despite our self-serving bias, all of us some of the time, and some of us much of the time, do feel inferior. As we saw in Chapter 9, this often happens when we compare ourselves with those who are a step or two higher on the ladder of status, looks, income, or ability. The deeper and more frequently we have such feelings, the more unhappy, even depressed, we are. Positive self-esteem predicts happiness and persistence after failure (Baumeister et al., 2003). So maybe it helps that, for most people, thinking has a naturally positive bias.

spotlight effect overestimating others' noticing and evaluating our appearance, performance, and blunders (as if we presume a spotlight shines on us).

self-esteem our feelings of high or low self-worth.

self-serving bias our readiness to perceive ourselves favorably.

Culture and the Self

15 How does the view of self differ in individualist and collectivist cultures?

The meaning of *self* varies from culture to culture. Imagine that someone were to rip away your social connections, leaving you alone in a foreign land. How much of your identity would remain intact? Your answer may depend on your culture, and whether it gives greater priority to the *independent self* or to the *interdependent self*.

If you are an **individualist,** alone in a foreign land, you would retain a lot of your identity. The very core of your being, the sense of "me," the awareness of your personal convictions and values would be intact. Individualists give higher priority to personal goals. They define their identity mostly in terms of personal traits. They strive for personal control and individual achievement.

The United States, with its relatively big "I" and small "we," is mostly an individualist culture. Some 85 percent of Americans say it is possible "to pretty much be who you want to be" (Sampson, 2000). Being more self-contained, individualists also move in and out of social groups more easily. They feel relatively free to switch places of worship, leave one job for another, or even leave their extended families and migrate to a new place. Marriage is often for as long as they both shall love.

If set adrift in a foreign land as a **collectivist,** you might experience a much greater loss of identity. Cut off from family, groups, and loyal friends, you would lose the connections that have defined who you are. *Group identifications* provide a sense of belonging and a set of values in collectivist cultures. In Korea, for example, people place less value on expressing a consistent, unique self-concept, and more on tradition and shared practices (Choi & Choi, 2002).

Collectivists are like athletes who take more pleasure in their team's victory than in their own performance. They find satisfaction in advancing their groups' interests, even at the expense of personal needs. Preserving group spirit and avoiding social embarrassment are important goals. Collectivists therefore avoid direct confrontation, blunt honesty, and uncomfortable topics. They often defer to others' wishes and display polite humility (Markus & Kitayama, 1991). In new groups, they may be shy and more easily embarrassed than are individualists (Singelis et al., 1995, 1999). Compared with Westerners, people in Japanese and Chinese cultures, for example, show greater shyness toward strangers and greater concern for social harmony and loyalty (Bond, 1988; Cheek & Melchior, 1990; Triandis, 1994). Elders and superiors receive respect, and duty to one's family may trump personal career preference.

Interdependence: This young man is helping a fellow student who became trapped in the rubble that was their school after a devastating earthquake shook China in 2008. By identifying strongly with family and other groups, Chinese people tend to have a collectivist sense of "we" and an accompanying support network of care, which may have helped them struggle through the aftermath of this disaster.

People in competitive, individualist cultures have more personal freedom (**TABLE 11.4**). They take more pride in personal achievements, are less geographically bound to their families, and enjoy more privacy. But these benefits come at

TABLE 11.4	Value Contrasts Between Individualism and Collectivism	
Concept	**Individualism**	**Collectivism**
Self	Independent (identity from individual traits).	Interdependent (identity from belonging to groups).
Life task	Discover and express your own uniqueness.	Maintain connections, fit in, perform your role.
What matters	Me—personal achievement and fulfillment; rights and liberties; self-esteem.	Us—group goals and solidarity; social responsibilities and relationships; family duty.
Coping method	Change reality.	Adjust to reality.
Morality	Defined by the individual (self-based).	Defined by social networks (duty-based).
Relationships	Many, often temporary or casual; confrontation is acceptable.	Few, close, and enduring; harmony is valued.
Attributing behavior	Behavior reflects the individual's personality and attitudes.	Behavior reflects social norms and roles.

Sources: Adapted from Thomas Schoeneman (1994) and Harry Triandis (1994).

Individualist proverb: "The squeaky wheel gets the grease."
Collectivist proverb: "The quacking duck gets shot."

the cost of more loneliness, divorce, homicide, and stress-related disease (Popenoe, 1993; Triandis et al., 1988). People in individualist cultures also demand more romance and personal fulfillment in marriage, which puts relationships under more pressure (Dion & Dion, 1993). In one survey, "keeping romance alive" was rated as important to a good marriage by 78 percent of U.S. women but only 29 percent of Japanese women (*American Enterprise*, 1992).

* * *

From Freud's psychoanalysis and Maslow's and Rogers' humanistic perspective, to the trait and social-cognitive theories, to today's study of the self, our understanding of personality has come a long way! This is a good base from which to explore Chapter 12's questions: How and why do some people suffer from disordered thinking and emotions?

THE BASICS

16. The *spotlight effect* is our tendency to
    a. perceive ourselves favorably and perceive others unfavorably.
    b. try out many possible selves.
    c. become excessively critical when made to feel insecure.
    d. overestimate others' attention to and evaluation of our appearance, performance, and blunders.

17. People tend to accept responsibility for their successes and to blame circumstances or bad luck for their failures. This is an example of
    a. defensive self-esteem.
    b. secure self-esteem.
    c. self-serving bias.
    d. possible selves.

18. Researchers have found a correlation between low self-esteem and life problems. This finding proves
    a. that life problems cause low self-esteem.
    b. that low self-esteem leads to life problems.
    c. that some third factor causes both low self-esteem and life problems.
    d. nothing—correlations allow predictions, but they don't prove cause and effect.

THE BIG PICTURE

11F. What is the difference between defensive self-esteem and secure self-esteem, and which one provides a higher quality of life?

11G. How do individualist and collectivist cultures differ?

IN YOUR EVERYDAY LIFE

▪ What possible selves do you dream of—or fear—becoming? To what extent do these imagined selves motivate you now?

▪ Do you consider yourself to be more of a collectivist or an individualist? How do you think this has influenced your behavior, emotions, or thoughts?

Answers: 16. d, 17. c, 18. d. Answers to The Big Picture questions can be found in Appendix B at the end of the book.

individualism giving priority to our own goals over group goals and defining our identity in terms of personal traits rather than group membership.

collectivism giving priority to goals of our group (often our extended family or work group) and defining our identity accordingly.

Terms and Concepts to Remember

personality, p. 292
unconscious, p. 294
free association, p. 294
psychoanalysis, p. 294
id, p. 294
ego, p. 295
superego, p. 295
psychosexual stages, p. 295
Oedipus [ED-uh-puss] complex, p. 296
identification, p. 296
fixation, p. 296

defense mechanisms, p. 296
repression, p. 296
psychodynamic theory, p. 297
projective test, p. 298
Rorschach inkblot test, p. 298
hierarchy of needs, p. 301
self-actualization, p. 301
self-transcendence, p. 301
unconditional positive regard, p. 301
self-concept, p. 302
trait, p. 303

factor, p. 303
social-cognitive perspective, p. 307
reciprocal determinism, p. 308
self, p. 309
spotlight effect, p. 310
self-esteem, p. 310
self-serving bias, p. 311
individualism, p. 312
collectivism, p. 312

PERSONALITY

Personality—an individual's characteristic pattern of thinking, feeling, and acting.

The Psychoanalytic Perspective

1 **How did Sigmund Freud's treatment of psychological disorders lead to his view of the unconscious mind?**

- In treating patients whose disorders had no clear physical explanation, Freud concluded that these problems reflected unacceptable and *unconscious* thoughts and feelings.
- To explore the unconscious, Freud analyzed dreams and urged his patients to use the technique of *free association*.
- Personality includes *id* (pleasure-seeking impulses), *ego* (reality-oriented executive), and *superego* (internalized set of ideals).
- Children develop through *psychosexual stages*—oral, anal, phallic, latency, and genital stages. Freud believed that our personalities are influenced by how we have resolved conflicts at each stage, and whether we have remained *fixated* at any stage.

2 **How did Freud view personality structure?**

- In *psychoanalysis* (Freud's theory of personality), personality is a result of conflict among the mind's three systems: the *id* (pleasure-seeking impulses), *ego* (reality-oriented executive), and *superego* (internalized set of ideals, or conscience).

3 **What were Freud's stages of development, and how did he view "fixation" at a given stage?**

- Freud believed children pass through five *psychosexual stages* (oral, anal, phallic, latency, and genital); unresolved conflicts at any stage can leave a person's pleasure-seeking impulses *fixated* (stalled) at that stage.

4 **How do Freud's defense mechanisms protect us from anxiety?**

- Tensions between the demands of id and superego cause anxiety.
- The ego copes by using *defense mechanisms,* such as *repression,* which is the basic mechanism underlying and enabling all the others.

5 **How did the neo-Freudians view Freud's original theory, and what is the more contemporary psychodynamic theory?**

- The neo-Freudians accepted many of Freud's ideas but stressed social motives more than sex or aggression.
- *Psychodynamic theory* is a more modern perspective that rejects Freud's emphasis on sexual motivation but retains his focus on unconscious motives and the influence of childhood experiences on adult personality and attachment patterns.

6 **What are projective tests, how are they used, and how are they criticized?**

- *Projective tests* attempt to assess personality by showing people vague stimuli with many possible interpretations; answers reveal unconscious motives.
- One such test, the *Rorschach inkblot test,* has low reliability and validity.

7 **How does contemporary psychology assess Freud's ideas?**

- Freud rightly drew our attention to the vast unconscious, to the struggle to cope with anxiety and sexuality, and to the conflict between biological impulses and social restraints.
- Researchers question whether repression ever occurs, but there is support for some of Freud's defense mechanisms.
- Freud's view of the unconscious as a collection of repressed and unacceptable thoughts, wishes, feelings, and memories has not survived scientific scrutiny.
- Freud offered after-the-fact explanations, which are hard to test scientifically.
- Research does not support many of Freud's specific ideas, such as development being fixed in childhood. (We now know it is lifelong.)

The Humanistic Perspective
SOUGHT TO TURN PSYCHOLOGY'S ATTENTION TOWARD HUMAN GROWTH POTENTIAL.

8 **What were Abraham Maslow's and Carl Rogers' humanistic psychology perspectives?**

- Maslow: Human motivations form a *hierarchy of needs;* if basic needs are fulfilled, people will strive toward *self-actualization* and *self-transcendence.*
- Rogers: People are basically good; showing *unconditional positive regard* and being genuine, accepting, and empathic can help others develop a more realistic and positive *self-concept.*

9 **What have critics said about humanistic psychology?**

- Humanistic psychology helped renew interest in the concept of self.
- Humanistic psychology's concepts were vague, subjective, and self-centered, and its assumptions naively optimistic.

The Trait Perspective

10 **How do psychologists use traits to describe personality?**

- *Trait* theorists see personality as a stable and enduring pattern of behavior. They describe our differences rather than trying to explain them.
- They identify *factors*—clusters of behavior tendencies that occur together.

11 **Which traits seem to provide the most useful information about personality variation?**

- The Big Five personality factors—conscientiousness, agreeableness, neuroticism, openness, and extraversion (CANOE)—currently offer the clearest picture of personality.
- These factors are stable and appear to be found in all cultures.

The Social-Cognitive Perspective

12 **How does the social-cognitive perspective view personality?**

- The *social-cognitive perspective* views personality as the product of the interaction between our individual traits and the social world around us.
- Social cognitive researchers apply principles of learning, cognition, and social behavior to personality.
- *Reciprocal determinism:* Behavior, internal personal factors, and environmental factors interact and influence one another.
- A person's average traits are predictable over many different situations, but not in any one particular situation.

Exploring the Self

13 **How do we use our possible selves to develop an integrated personality, and how does self-esteem help in the process?**

- The *self* is the center of personality, organizing our thoughts, feelings, and actions.
- Considering possible selves helps motivate us toward positive development, but focusing too intensely on ourselves can lead to the *spotlight effect*.
- High *self-esteem* (our feeling of self-worth) is beneficial, but unrealistically high self-esteem is dangerous (linked to aggressive behavior) and fragile.

14 **What evidence points to a self-serving bias?**

- *Self-serving bias* is evident in our tendency to perceive ourselves favorably, as when viewing ourselves as better than average, or when accepting credit for our successes but not blame for our failures.

15 **How does the view of self differ in individualist and collectivist cultures?**

- *Individualism:* Self-reliant; defines the self in terms of personal goals and attributes.
- *Collectivism:* Socially connected; gives priority to group goals, social identity, and commitments.

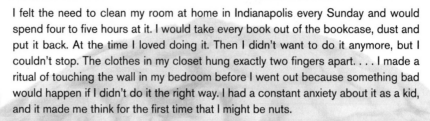

12

PSYCHOLOGICAL DISORDERS

I felt the need to clean my room at home in Indianapolis every Sunday and would spend four to five hours at it. I would take every book out of the bookcase, dust and put it back. At the time I loved doing it. Then I didn't want to do it anymore, but I couldn't stop. The clothes in my closet hung exactly two fingers apart. . . . I made a ritual of touching the wall in my bedroom before I went out because something bad would happen if I didn't do it the right way. I had a constant anxiety about it as a kid, and it made me think for the first time that I might be nuts.

Marc, diagnosed with obsessive-compulsive disorder (from Summers, 1996)

Whenever I get depressed it's because I've lost a sense of self. I can't find reasons to like myself. I think I'm ugly. I think no one likes me. . . . I become grumpy and short-tempered. Nobody wants to be around me. I'm left alone. Being alone confirms that I am ugly and not worth being with. I think I'm responsible for everything that goes wrong.

Greta, diagnosed with depression (from Thorne, 1993, p. 21)

Voices, like the roar of a crowd, came. I felt like Jesus; I was being crucified. It was dark. I just continued to huddle under the blanket, feeling weak, laid bare and defenseless in a cruel world I could no longer understand.

Stuart, diagnosed with schizophrenia (from Emmons et al., 1997)

Now and then, all of us feel, think, or act the way disturbed people do much of the time. We, too, get anxious, depressed, withdrawn, or suspicious, just less intensely and more briefly. So it's no wonder that we sometimes see ourselves in the psychological disorders we study. "To study the abnormal is the best way of understanding the normal," proposed William James (1842–1910).

Either personally or through friends or family, many of us will know the confusion and pain of unexplained physical symptoms, irrational fears, or a feeling that life is not worth living. Worldwide, some 450 million people suffer from mental or behavioral disorders (WHO, 2008a,b). The National Institute of Mental Health (2008a) estimates that 26 percent of adult Americans "suffer from a diagnosable mental disorder in a given year" (TABLE 12.1). Rates and symptoms vary by culture, but no known society is free of two terrible disorders: depression and schizophrenia (Baumeister & Härter, 2007; Draguns, 1990a,b, 1997). This chapter examines these and other disorders, and the next chapter considers their *treatment*. But first, let's address some basic questions.

What Is a Psychological Disorder?

Most of us would agree that a family member who is depressed and refuses to get out of bed for three months has a psychological disorder. But what should we say about a grieving mother who can't resume her usual social activities three months after her child has died? Where do we draw the line between clinical depression and understandable grief? Between bizarre irrationality and zany creativity? Between abnormality and normality?

Defining Psychological Disorders

1 What is a psychological disorder, and how do psychologists distinguish between normal and disordered behavior?

To a psychologist, a **psychological disorder** is an ongoing pattern of thoughts, feelings, or actions that are *deviant, distressful,* and *dysfunctional* (Comer, 2004).

"They're trying to figure out whether it's a chemical thing or I'm just a crybaby."

Deviant Behavior Being *deviant* means being different from most other people who share your culture. Even within a culture, what people consider deviant varies with the situation. Mass killing may be viewed as heroic (on the battlefield) or horrific (on a playground). In our Western culture, hearing voices is deviant. But in cultures that practice ancestor worship, people who claim to talk with the dead may be seen as gifted (Friedrich, 1987).

What people consider deviant also varies with time. In 1952, the American Psychiatric Association listed homosexuality as a psychological disorder. In 1973, it dropped homosexuality as a disorder because fewer and fewer mental health workers viewed homosexuality as a psychological problem. Also in the 1950s, many viewed high-energy children as normal children running wild. Today, many of those children would be diagnosed with *attention-deficit hyperactivity disorder (ADHD)*. Times change, and views of what's deviant change with them.

Distressful Behavior But there is more to a disorder than being deviant. Olympic gold medalists differ from most of us in their physical abilities, and society honors them. For deviant behavior to be considered disordered, it usually causes *distress* to the person or to others. Marc, Greta, and Stuart were all clearly distressed by their behaviors. If the distress becomes extreme, the disordered behavior may also be judged dangerous. If Greta's depression deepens, for example, she may develop suicidal thoughts and be considered a danger to herself.

Dysfunctional Behavior *Dysfunctional* behaviors interfere with normal day-to-day life. An intense fear of spiders may be deviant, but if it doesn't interfere with your life, it isn't a disorder. Marc's obsessive cleaning and other rituals interfered with his work and leisure. Even typical behaviors can become dysfunctional. Many students have occasional sad moods. If these feelings persist and become disabling, they may signal a disorder. We sometimes refer to dysfunctional behaviors as *maladaptive*.

Understanding Psychological Disorders

2 How is our understanding of psychological disorders affected by whether we use a medical model or a biopsychosocial approach?

The way we view a problem influences how we try to solve it. In earlier times, people often thought that strange behaviors were evidence that strange forces were at work. Had you lived during the Middle Ages, you might have said "The devil made him do it." To drive out demons, "mad" people were sometimes

TABLE 12.1	Percentage of Americans Reporting Certain Psychological Disorders in the Past Year	
Disorder		**Percentage**
Generalized anxiety		3.1
Social phobia		6.8
Phobia of specific object or situation		8.7
Mood disorder		9.5
Obsessive-compulsive disorder (OCD)		1.0
Schizophrenia		1.1
Post-traumatic stress disorder (PTSD)		3.5
Attention-deficit hyperactivity disorder (ADHD)		4.1
Any mental disorder		26.2

Source: National Institute of Mental Health, 2008.

Diverse Yet Alike

Young men of the West African Wodaabe tribe put on elaborate makeup and costumes to attract women. Young American men may buy flashy cars with loud stereos to do the same. Each culture would view the other's behavior as abnormal.

Carol Beckwith

Jupiterimages

caged or given "therapies" such as beatings, genital mutilations, removal of teeth or lengths of intestine, or transfusions of animal blood (Farina, 1982).

Reformers such as Philippe Pinel (1745–1826) in France opposed such brutal treatments. Madness is not demon possession, he insisted, but a sickness of the mind caused by severe stress and inhumane conditions. Curing the sickness requires "moral treatment," including boosting patients' morale by unchaining them and talking with them. He and others worked to replace brutality with gentleness, isolation with activity, and filth with clean air and sunshine.

George Wesley Bellows, *Dance in a Madhouse*, 1907. © 1997 The Art Institute of Chicago

"Moral treatment": Under Philippe Pinel's influence, hospitals sometimes sponsored patient dances, often called "lunatic balls," depicted in this painting by George Bellows (*Dance in a Madhouse*).

The Medical Model

By the 1800s, a medical breakthrough prompted further reform. Researchers discovered that syphilis, a sexually transmitted infection, invades the brain and distorts the mind. This discovery triggered an excited search for physical causes of other mental disorders, and for treatments that would cure them. Hospitals replaced madhouses, and the **medical model** of mental disorders was born. This model is reflected in words we still use today. We speak of the mental *health* movement. A mental *illness* needs to be *diagnosed* on the basis of its *symptoms*. It needs to be *cured* through *therapy*, which may include *treatment* in a psychiatric *hospital*. Recent discoveries that abnormal brain structures and biochemistry contribute to some disorders have energized the medical perspective.

The Biopsychosocial Approach

To call psychological disorders "sicknesses" tilts research heavily toward the influence of biology and away from the influence of our personal histories and social and cultural surroundings. But as we have seen throughout this text, our behaviors, our thoughts, and our feelings are formed by the interaction of our biology, our psychology, and our social-cultural environment. As individuals, we differ in the amount of stress we experience and in the ways we cope with stress.

Cultures also differ in the sources of stress they produce and in the ways of coping they provide.

The environment's influence on disorders can be seen in culture-related symptoms (Beardsley, 1994; Castillo, 1997). Anxiety, for example, may be exhibited in different ways in different cultures. In Latin American cultures, people may suffer from *susto,* a condition marked by severe anxiety, restlessness, and a fear of black magic. In Japanese culture, people may experience *taijin-kyofusho*—social anxiety about their appearance, combined with a readiness to blush and a fear of eye contact. The eating disorders *anorexia nervosa* and *bulimia nervosa* occur mostly in North American and other Western cultures. Increasingly, however, such North American disorders are, along with McDonalds and MTV, spreading the globe (Watters, 2010).

Other disorders, such as depression and schizophrenia, also occur worldwide.

psychological disorder deviant (atypical), distressful, and dysfunctional patterns of thoughts, feelings, or behaviors.

medical model the concept that diseases, in this case psychological disorders, have physical causes that can be diagnosed, treated, and, in most cases, cured, often through treatment in a hospital.

From Asia to Africa and across the Americas, people with schizophrenia often act irrationally and speak in disorganized ways. Disorders, it seems, reflect genes and physiology, as well as psychological dynamics and cultural circumstances. The biopsychosocial approach reminds us that mind and body are inseparable. We are mind embodied.

Classifying Disorders—and Labeling People

3 How and why do clinicians classify psychological disorders, and why do some psychologists criticize the use of diagnostic labels?

In biology, classification creates order and helps us communicate. To say that an animal is a "mammal" tells us a great deal—that it is warm-blooded, has hair or fur, and produces milk to feed its young. In psychiatry and psychology, classification serves the same ends. To classify a disorder as "schizophrenia" also tells us a great deal. It says that the person speaks in a disorganized way, has bizarre beliefs, shows either little emotion or inappropriate emotion, or is socially withdrawn. "Schizophrenia" is a quick way of describing a complex set of behaviors.

But diagnostic classification does more than give us a thumbnail sketch of a person's disordered behavior. In psychiatry and psychology, classification also attempts to predict the disorder's future course and to suggest treatment. It prompts research into causes. Indeed, to study a disorder we must first name and describe it.

Our current best scheme for describing disorders and estimating how often they occur is the American Psychiatric Association's *Diagnostic and Statistical Manual of Mental Disorders,* now in its "text-revised" fourth edition (**DSM-IV-TR**). Many examples in this chapter were drawn from case illustrations accompanying the DSM-IV-TR.

A new edition, DSM-V, is slated to appear in 2013. In 2010, the American Psychiatric Association released the first draft of that revision (Carey, 2010; DSM5.org; Miller & Holden, 2010). Some diagnostic labels

© 1992 by Sidney Harris.

"I'm always like this, and my family was wondering if you could prescribe a mild depressant."

are changing. "Mental retardation," for example, becomes "intellectual disability." Some new categories, such as "hypersexual disorder," "hoarding disorder," and "binge-eating disorder" have been added.

The DSM-IV-TR categories and diagnostic guidelines have been fairly reliable **(TABLE 12.2)**. If one psychiatrist or psychologist diagnoses someone as having, say, "agoraphobia," the chances are good that another mental health worker will independently give the same diagnosis. To reach a diagnosis, clinicians answer a series of objective questions about observable behaviors, such as, "Is the person afraid to leave home?"

In one study, 16 psychologists used DSM guidelines in interviews with 75 patients with disorders. The psychologists' task was to diagnose each patient as having (1) depression, (2) generalized anxiety, or (3) some other disorder (Riskind et al., 1987). Another psychologist then viewed a videotape of each interview and offered a second, independent opinion. For 83 percent of the patients, the two opinions agreed.

TABLE 12.2 **How Are Psychological Disorders Diagnosed?**

Based on assessments, interviews, and observations, many clinicians diagnose by answering the following questions from the five levels, or *axes,* of the DSM-IV-TR. (Chapters in parentheses locate the topics discussed elsewhere in this text.)

Axis I Is a *Clinical Syndrome* present?
Using specifically defined criteria, clinicians may select none, one, or more syndromes from the following list:

- Disorders usually first diagnosed in infancy, childhood, and adolescence
- Delirium, dementia, amnesia, and other cognitive disorders (Chapter 7)
- Mental disorders due to a general medical condition
- Substance-related disorders
- Schizophrenia and other psychotic disorders
- Mood disorders
- Anxiety disorders
- Somatoform disorders
- Factitious disorders (intentionally faked)
- Dissociative disorders
- Eating disorders (Chapter 9)
- Sexual disorders and gender identity disorder
- Sleep disorders (Chapter 2)
- Impulse-control disorders not classified elsewhere
- Adjustment disorders
- Other conditions that may be a focus of clinical attention

Axis II Is a *Personality Disorder* or *Mental Retardation* present?
Clinicians may or may not also select one of these two conditions.

Axis III Is a *General Medical Condition,* such as diabetes, hypertension, or arthritis, also present?

Axis IV Are *Psychosocial* or *Environmental Problems,* such as school or housing issues, also present?

Axis V What is the *Global Assessment* of this person's functioning?
Clinicians assign a code from 0–100.

Shutterstock

Nevertheless, the DSM has its critics. Some have been concerned that it casts too wide a net and brings "almost any kind of behavior within the compass of psychiatry" (Eysenck et al., 1983). Others note that as the number of disorder categories has swelled (from 60 in the 1950s DSM to 400 today), so has the number of adults who meet the criteria for at least one of them. According to the U.S. National Institute of Mental Health (2008), 26 percent of all adults meet those criteria in any year, and 46 percent have met them at some time in their lives (Kessler et al., 2005).

Other critics register a more basic complaint—that these labels are just society's value judgments. CAN THE LABEL◀ WE ASSIGN TO A PERSON CAUSE US TO VIEW THAT PERSON DIFFERENTLY? Indeed it can (Farina, 1982). Labels can change reality by putting us on the alert for evidence that confirms our view. When teachers are told certain students are "gifted," they may act in ways that bring out the creative behavior they expect (Snyder, 1984). If we hear that a new coworker is a difficult person, we may treat him suspiciously. He may in turn respond to us as a difficult person would. Labels can be self-fulfilling.

The biasing power of labels was clear in a now-classic study. David Rosenhan (1973) and seven others went to hospital admissions offices, complaining of "hearing voices" saying *empty, hollow,* and *thud.* Apart from this complaint and giving false names and occupations, they answered questions truthfully. All eight of these normal people were misdiagnosed with disorders.

Should we be surprised? Surely not. As one psychiatrist noted, if someone swallowed blood, went to an emergency room, and spat it up, would we blame a doctor for diagnosing a bleeding ulcer? But what followed the diagnosis was startling. Until being released an average of 19 days later, these eight "patients" showed no other symptoms. Yet after analyzing their (quite normal) life histories, clinicians were able to "discover" the causes of their disorders, such as having mixed emotions about a parent. Even the patients' routine note-taking behavior was misinterpreted as a symptom.

In another study, people watched videotaped interviews. If told the people being interviewed were job applicants, the viewers perceived them as normal (Langer et al., 1974, 1980). Others were told they were watching psychiatric or cancer patients. These viewers perceived the same people as "different from most people." Labels matter. Therapists who thought they were watching an interview of a psychiatric patient described him as "frightened of his own aggressive impulses," a "passive, dependent type," and so forth. As Rosenhan discovered, a label can have "a life and an influence of its own."

The power of labels is just as real outside the laboratory. Getting a job or finding a place to rent can be a challenge for people recently released from a mental hospital. The shame seems to be lifting as people better understand that many psychological disorders are diseases of

Accurate portrayal: Popular movies, such as *Silence of the Lambs* and *Psycho,* have often portrayed those with psychological disorders as aggressive and dangerous. The TV show *Law & Order: Criminal Intent* has portrayed more typical suffering and personal disruption.

© USA Network/Courtesy Everett Collection

Shutterstock

the brain, not failures of character (Solomon, 1996). Public figures have helped foster this understanding by speaking openly about their own struggles with disorders such as depression. The more contact we have with people with disorders, the more accepting our attitudes are (Kolodziej & Johnson, 1996).

Despite their risks, we can't forget the *benefits* of diagnostic labels. Mental health professionals have good reasons for using labels. These shortcuts help them communicate about their cases, pinpoint underlying causes, and share information about effective treatments.

DSM-IV-TR the American Psychiatric Association's *Diagnostic and Statistical Manual of Mental Disorders,* a widely used system for classifying psychological disorders.

PRACTICE TEST

THE BASICS

1. Although some psychological disorders appear in only one culture, others are universal. For example, in every known culture some people have
   a. bulimia nervosa.
   b. anorexia nervosa.
   c. schizophrenia.
   d. susto.

2. If a lawyer washes his hands 100 times a day for no apparent reason and has no time left to meet with his clients, the hand washing will probably be labeled disordered because it is, among other things,
   a. distressing and dysfunctional.
   b. not explained by the medical model.
   c. harmful to others.
   d. untreatable.

3. A therapist focusing mostly on disorders as sicknesses and suggesting patients should be treated in hospitals is using a
   a. social-cultural perspective.
   b. biopsychosocial approach.
   c. medical model.
   d. diagnostic model.

Continued

4. A psychologist working with a distressed person is trying to get more information on the person's medical history, personal background, and social environment. This psychologist is using a _____ approach.

   a. medical
   b. deviant-dysfunctional
   c. biopsychosocial
   d. diagnostic labels

5. Most psychologists and psychiatrists currently use _____ to classify psychological disorders.

   a. the DSM-IV-TR
   b. in-depth histories of patients
   c. input from patients' family and friends
   d. the theories of Pinel, Rosenhan, and others

THE BIG PICTURE

12A. What is the biopsychosocial perspective, and why is it important in our understanding of psychological disorders?

12B. What is the value, and what are the dangers, of labeling individuals with disorders?

IN YOUR EVERYDAY LIFE

▪ As his fans already know, comedian and TV personality Howie Mandel suffers from obsessive-compulsive disorder and a severe germ phobia. How do you think being labeled has helped or hurt Mandel?

Answers: 1. c, 2. a, 3. c, 4. c, 5. a. Answers to The Big Picture questions can be found in Appendix B at the end of the book.

Anxiety Disorders

> 4 | What are the main anxiety disorders, and how do they differ from the ordinary worries and fears we all experience?

Anxiety is part of life. Have you ever felt anxious when speaking in front of a class, peering down from a high ledge, or waiting to play in a big game? We all feel anxious at times. We may occasionally feel enough anxiety to avoid making eye contact or talking with someone—"shyness," we call it. Fortunately for most of us, our uneasiness is not intense and persistent.

Coping with disorder: "The only way I knew how to deal with it was to write a song about it," musician Billie Joe Armstrong of Green Day explained. He was referring to his song "Basket Case," which relates a personal struggle with anxiety disorders.

Some of us, however, are more prone to notice and remember threats (Mitte, 2008). This tendency may place us at risk for one of the **anxiety disorders,** marked by distressing, persistent anxiety or by maladaptive behaviors that reduce anxiety. For example, a man with a fear of social settings may avoid going out. This behavior is maladaptive because it reduces his anxiety but does not help him cope with his world.

In this section we focus on five anxiety disorders:

- *Generalized anxiety disorder,* in which a person is constantly tense and uneasy for no apparent reason.

- *Panic disorder,* in which a person experiences sudden episodes of intense dread.

- *Phobias,* in which a person feels irrationally and intensely afraid of a specific object or situation.

- *Obsessive-compulsive disorder,* in which a person is troubled by repetitive thoughts or actions.

- *Post-traumatic stress disorder,* in which a person has lingering memories, nightmares, and possibly other symptoms for weeks after a severely threatening, uncontrollable event.

Generalized Anxiety Disorder

Tom is a 27-year-old electrician. For the past two years, he has been bothered by dizziness, sweating palms, irregular heartbeat, and ringing in his ears. He feels edgy and sometimes finds himself shaking. Tom has been fairly successful at hiding his symptoms from his family and co-workers, but sometimes he has to leave work. He allows himself few other social contacts. Neither his family doctor nor a neurologist has been able to find any physical problem.

Tom's unfocused, out-of-control, negative feelings suggest **generalized anxiety disorder.** The symptoms of this disorder are commonplace; their persistence is not. People with this condition worry continually, and they are often jittery, on edge, and sleep deprived. Concentration is difficult, as attention switches from worry to worry. Their tension may leak out through furrowed brows, twitching eyelids, trembling, sweating, or fidgeting.

One of the worst features of this disorder is that the person cannot identify the tension's cause, and therefore cannot deal with or avoid it. To use Sigmund Freud's term, the anxiety is *free-floating.* Generalized anxiety disorder and depression often go hand in hand, but even without depression this disorder tends to be disabling (Hunt et al., 2004; Moffit et al., 2007b). Moreover, it may lead to physical problems, such as high blood pressure.

Two-thirds of those with generalized anxiety disorder are women. Anxiety strikes women more often than men. This "gender bias" appeared in a Gallup poll taken eight months after 9/11. More U.S. women (34 percent) than men (19 percent) said they were still less willing than before 9/11 to go into skyscrapers or fly on planes. And in early 2003, more women (57 percent) than men (36 percent) said they were "somewhat worried" about becoming a terrorist victim (Jones, 2003).

Many people with generalized anxiety disorder were treated badly and inhibited as children (Moffitt et al., 2007a). As time passes, however, emotions tend to mellow. By age 50, generalized anxiety disorder becomes rare (Rubio & López-Ibor, 2007).

Panic Disorder

Panic disorder is an anxiety tornado. It strikes suddenly, does its damage, and disappears. Anxiety suddenly escalates into a terrifying panic attack—a minutes-long feeling of intense fear that something horrible is about to happen. Irregular heartbeat, chest pains, shortness of breath, choking, trembling, or dizziness may accompany the panic. One woman recalled suddenly feeling "hot and as though I couldn't breathe. My heart was racing and I started to sweat and tremble and I was sure I was going to faint. Then my fingers started to feel numb and tingly and things seemed unreal. It was so bad I wondered if I was dying and asked my husband to take me to the emergency room. By the time we got there (about 10 minutes) the worst of the attack was over and I just felt washed out" (Greist et al., 1986).

Panic attack symptoms are often misread as a heart attack or some other serious physical ailment. Smokers have at least a doubled risk of a panic attack (Zvolensky & Bernstein, 2005). Because nicotine is a stimulant, lighting up doesn't lighten up.

Phobias

We all live with some fears. People with **phobias** are consumed by a persistent, irrational fear and avoidance of some object or situation. Marilyn, an otherwise healthy and happy 28-year-old, so fears thunderstorms that she feels anxious as soon as a weather forecaster mentions possible storms later in the week. If her husband is away and a storm is forecast, she may stay with a close relative. During a storm, she hides from windows and buries her head to avoid seeing the lightning. *Specific phobias* such as Marilyn's typically focus on particular animals, insects, heights, blood, or closed spaces **(FIGURE 12.1)**.

Not all phobias are so specific. *Social phobia* is shyness taken to an extreme. Those with a social phobia have an intense fear of being judged by others. They avoid threatening social situations, such as speaking in a group, eating out, or

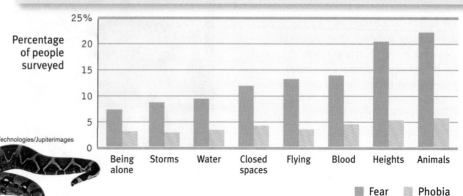

FIGURE 12.1 • **Some common and uncommon specific fears** Researchers surveyed people to identify the most common events or objects they feared. A strong fear becomes a phobia if it provokes a compelling but irrational desire to avoid the dreaded object or situation. (From Curtis et al., 1998.)

going to parties. Finding themselves in such a situation, they will sweat, tremble, or have diarrhea.

After several panic attacks, people may come to fear the fear itself. This may trigger *agoraphobia,* fear or avoidance of situations in which panic may strike, escape might be difficult, and help unavailable. People with agoraphobia may avoid being outside the home, in a crowd, on a bus, or on an elevator.

Obsessive-Compulsive Disorder (OCD)

As with generalized anxiety and phobias, we can see aspects of our own behavior in **obsessive-compulsive disorder (OCD).**

SNAPSHOTS

Obsessing about obsessive-compulsive disorder.

Obsessive thoughts (recall Marc's focus on cleaning his room) are unwanted and so repetitive it may seem they will never go away. *Compulsive behaviors* are responses to those thoughts (cleaning and cleaning and cleaning).

All of us are at times obsessed with senseless or offensive thoughts that will not go away. Have you ever caught yourself behaving compulsively, perhaps rigidly checking, ordering, and cleaning before guests arrive, or lining up books and pencils "just so" before you begin studying? On a small scale, obsessive thoughts and compulsive behaviors are

anxiety disorders psychological disorders characterized by distressing, persistent anxiety or maladaptive behaviors that reduce anxiety.

generalized anxiety disorder an anxiety disorder in which a person is continually tense, fearful, and in a state of autonomic nervous system arousal.

panic disorder an anxiety disorder marked by unpredictable minutes-long episodes of intense dread in which a person experiences terror and accompanying chest pain, choking, or other frightening sensations.

phobia an anxiety disorder marked by a persistent, irrational fear and avoidance of a specific object or situation.

obsessive-compulsive disorder (OCD) an anxiety disorder characterized by unwanted repetitive thoughts (obsessions) and/or actions (compulsions).

part of everyday life. They cross the fine line between normality and disorder when they *interfere* with everyday life and cause us distress. Checking to see if you locked the door is normal; checking 10 times is not. Washing your hands is normal; washing so often that your skin becomes raw is not. Normal rehearsals and fussy behaviors become a disorder when the obsessive thoughts are so haunting, the compulsive rituals so senselessly time-consuming, that effective functioning becomes impossible.

Post-Traumatic Stress Disorder (PTSD)

As an Army infantry scout during the Iraq war, Jesse "saw the murder of children and women. It was just horrible for anyone to experience." After calling in a helicopter strike on one house where he had seen ammunition crates carried in, he heard the screams of children from within. "I didn't know there were kids there," he recalled. Back home in Texas, he suffered "real bad flashbacks" (Welch, 2005).

Jesse is not alone. In one study of 103,788 veterans returning from Iraq and Afghanistan, 25 percent were diagnosed with a psychological disorder (Seal et al., 2007). The most frequent diagnosis was **post-traumatic stress disorder (PTSD).** Typical symptoms include recurring haunting memories and nightmares, a numb feeling of social withdrawal, jumpy anxiety, and trouble sleeping (Hoge et al., 2004, 2006, 2007; Kessler, 2000). Many battle-scarred veterans have been diagnosed with PTSD. Survivors of accidents, disasters, and violent and sexual assaults (including an estimated two-thirds of prostitutes) have also experienced these symptoms (Brewin et al., 1999; Farley et al., 1998; Taylor et al., 1998).

The greater one's emotional distress during a trauma, the higher the risk for post-traumatic symptoms (Ozer et al., 2003). One in 3 Vietnam veterans who had experienced heavy combat were diagnosed with PTSD (Dohrenwend et al., 2006; U.S. Centers for Disease Control

Bringing the war home: During his three deployments to Iraq, this Marine Staff Sergeant suffered traumatic brain injury. After his return home, he was diagnosed with post-traumatic stress disorder. He regularly travels two hours each way with his wife to Bethesda Naval Hospital for psychiatric and medical appointments.

Whitney Shefte/The Washington Post via Getty Images

Vietnam Experience Study, 1988). One in 10 veterans who had never seen combat received that diagnosis. Similar rates were found among New Yorkers who witnessed the 9/11 attacks. PTSD diagnoses among survivors who had been inside the World Trade Center during the attack were double the rates found among those who were outside (Bonanno et al., 2006). The more frequent and severe the trauma, the worse the long-term outcomes tend to be (Golding, 1999). In the thirty years after the Vietnam war, veterans who came home with a PTSD diagnosis had twice the normal likelihood of dying (Crawford et al., 2009).

About half of us will experience at least one traumatic event in our lifetime. WHY DO SOME PEOPLE DEVELOP PTSD◄ AFTER A TRAUMATIC EVENT, BUT OTHERS DON'T? Some people may have more sensitive emotion-processing limbic systems that flood their bodies with stress hormones (Kosslyn, 2005; Ozer & Weiss, 2004). The odds of getting this disorder after a traumatic event are higher for women (about 1 in 10) than for men (1 in 20) (Olff et al., 2007; Ozer & Weiss, 2004).

But most people, male and female, display an impressive *survivor resiliency*, or ability to recover after severe stress (Bonanno, 2004, 2005, 2006). For more on human resilience, and on the "post-traumatic growth" that some experience, see Chapter 13.

Some psychologists believe that PTSD has been overdiagnosed, due partly to a broader definition of *trauma* (Dobbs, 2009; McNally, 2003). Too often, say these critics, PTSD gets stretched to include normal bad memories and dreams after a bad experience. In such cases, procedures commonly used to treat PTSD may make people feel worse (Wakefield & Spitzer, 2002). For example, survivors may be "debriefed" right after a trauma and asked to revisit the experience and vent their emotions. This tactic has been generally ineffective and sometimes harmful (Devilly et al., 2006; McNally et al., 2003; Rose et al., 2003).

Understanding Anxiety Disorders

5 | How do learning and biology contribute to the feelings and thoughts that mark anxiety disorders?

Anxiety is both a feeling and a thought—a doubt-laden appraisal of one's safety or social skill. How do these anxious feelings and thoughts arise? Sigmund Freud's psychoanalytic theory (Chapter 11) proposed that, beginning in childhood, people repress certain impulses, ideas, and feelings. He thought this submerged mental energy sometimes leaks out, appearing as odd symptoms, such as anxious hand washing. Few of today's psychologists interpret anxiety disorders this way. Most believe that two modern perspectives—learning and biological—are more helpful.

The Learning Perspective

Fear Conditioning When bad events happen unpredictably and uncontrollably, anxiety often develops (Field, 2006; Mineka & Zinbarg, 2006). In experiments, researchers have shown how classical conditioning can produce fear and anxiety. You may recall from Chapter 6 that infants have learned to fear furry objects that were paired with loud noises. And by giving rats unpredictable electric shocks, researchers have created anxious animals (Schwartz, 1984). The rats—like assault victims who report feeling anxious when returning to the scene of the crime—then become uneasy in their lab environment. That environment has become a cue for fear.

Such research helps explain how panic-prone people come to associate anxiety with certain cues and why anxious people are so attentive to possible threats. In one survey, 58 percent of those with social phobia said their disorder began after a traumatic event (Ost & Hugdahl, 1981).

How might conditioning magnify a single painful and frightening event into a full-blown phobia? The answer lies in two specific learning processes: stimulus generalization and reinforcement.

Stimulus generalization occurs when a person experiences a fearful event and later develops a fear of similar events. My car was once struck by another whose driver missed a stop sign. For months afterward, I felt a twinge of unease when any car approached from a side street. My fear eventually disappeared, but for others, fear may linger and grow. Marilyn's phobia may have similarly generalized after a terrifying or painful experience during a thunderstorm.

Once phobias and compulsions arise, *reinforcement* helps maintain them. Anything that helps us avoid or escape from a feared situation reduces our anxiety. This feeling of relief can reinforce phobic behaviors. Fearing a panic attack, a person may decide not to leave the house. Reinforced by feeling calmer, the person is likely to repeat that maladaptive behavior in the future (Antony et al., 1992). So, too, with compulsive behaviors. If washing your hands relieves your feelings of anxiety, you may wash your hands again when anxiety returns.

Observational Learning We may also learn fear by observing others' fears. DO◄ WE LEARN TO FEAR WHAT OUR MOTHER OR FATHER FEARS? Without meaning to, parents often transmit fears to their children. The watchful offspring of wild monkeys pick up their parents' fear of snakes (Mineka, 1985). In humans, too, just observing someone receiving a mild electric shock after a conditioned stimulus produces fear learning. What the observer learns by watching is very similar to what the shocked person learns from direct experience (Olsson & Phelps, 2004).

The Biological Perspective

There is, however, more to anxiety than conditioning and observational learning. The biological perspective can help us gain insight into some important questions. WHY WILL SOME OF US DEVELOP◄ LASTING PHOBIAS AFTER SUFFERING TRAUMAS? WHY ARE SOME OF US MORE VULNERABLE TO LEARNED FEARS? WHY DO WE ALL LEARN SOME FEARS MORE EASILY THAN OTHERS?

Genes Genes matter. Among monkeys, fearfulness runs in families. A monkey reacts more strongly to stress if its close biological relatives have sensitive, high-strung temperaments (Suomi, 1986). So, too, with people. Some of us are predisposed to anxiety. If one identical twin has an anxiety disorder, the other is also likely to

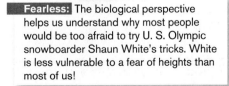

have it (Hettema et al., 2001; Kendler et al., 1992, 1999, 2002a,b). Even when raised separately, identical twins may develop similar phobias (Carey, 1990; Eckert et al., 1981). One pair of separated identical twins independently became so afraid of water that, even at age 35, they would wade into the ocean backwards and only up to their knees.

The Brain Pair a genetic predisposition with a traumatic event, and the result may be an anxiety disorder. Our experiences alter our brain, paving new pathways. Fear-learning experiences leave tracks in the brain. These fear pathways create easy inroads for more fear experiences (Armony et al., 1998).

Generalized anxiety, panic attacks, PTSD, and even obsessions and compulsions are biologically measurable. Brain scans of people with OCD, for example, reveal higher-than-normal activity in brain areas involved in impulse control and habitual behaviors. Specific brain areas become very active during behaviors such as compulsive hand washing, checking, ordering, or hoarding (Mataix-Cols et al., 2004, 2005). When the disordered brain detects that something is amiss, it seems to generate a mental hiccup of repeating thoughts or actions (Gehring et al., 2000).

Natural Selection No matter how fearful or fearless we are, we humans seem biologically prepared to fear the threats our ancestors faced—spiders and snakes, closed spaces and heights, storms and darkness. (In the distant past, those who did not fear these threats were less likely to survive and leave descendants.) Thus, even in Britain, which has only one poisonous snake species, people often fear snakes. And we have these fears at very young ages. Preschool children detect

Fearless: The biological perspective helps us understand why most people would be too afraid to try U. S. Olympic snowboarder Shaun White's tricks. White is less vulnerable to a fear of heights than most of us!

post-traumatic stress disorder (PTSD) an anxiety disorder characterized by haunting memories, nightmares, social withdrawal, jumpy anxiety, and/or insomnia lingering for four weeks or more after a traumatic experience.

snakes in a scene faster than they spot flowers, caterpillars, or frogs (LoBue & DeLoache, 2008). Our Stone Age fears are easy to condition and hard to extinguish (Davey, 1995; Öhman, 1986).

Our modern fears may also have an evolutionary explanation. For example, a modern fear of flying may have grown from a fear of confinement and heights, which can be traced to our biological past.

Moreover, consider what people tend *not* to learn to fear. World War II air raids produced remarkably few lasting phobias. As the air strikes continued, the British, Japanese, and German populations did not become more and more panicked. Rather, they grew more indifferent to planes outside their immediate neighborhood (Mineka & Zinbarg, 1996). Evolution has not prepared us to fear bombs dropping from the sky.

Our phobias focus on dangers our ancestors faced. Our compulsive acts typically exaggerate behaviors that helped them survive. Grooming had survival value; it detected insects and infections. Gone wild, it becomes compulsive hair pulling. Cleaning up helped people stay healthy. Out of control, it becomes ritual hand washing. Checking territorial boundaries helped ward off enemies. In OCD, it becomes checking and rechecking an already locked door (Rapoport, 1989).

The biological perspective explains a great deal, but it cannot explain all aspects of anxiety disorders. It cannot, for example, explain the sharp increase in the anxiety levels of U.S. children and college students over the last half-century. That increase appears related to modern-day concerns—unrealistic expectations, a greater focus on the self than on the community, and a loss of social support (Twenge, 2000). Nevertheless, it is clear that biology underlies anxiety.

Martin Harvey/Jupiterimages

Dissociative and Personality Disorders

Dissociative Disorders

6 What are dissociative disorders, and why are they controversial?

Among the most bewildering disorders are the rare **dissociative disorders.** The person's conscious awareness is said to become separated—*to dissociate*—from painful memories, thoughts, and feelings. In this state, people may suddenly lose their memory or change their identity, often in response to an overwhelmingly stressful situation.

Dissociation itself is not so rare. Now and then, any one of us may have a fleeting sense of being unreal, of being separated from our body, of watching ourselves as if in a movie. A massive dissociation of self from ordinary consciousness occurs in **dissociative identity disorder (DID).** At different times, two or more distinct identities seem to control the person's behavior, each with its own voice and mannerisms. Thus, the person may be prim and proper one moment, loud and flirtatious the next. Typically, the original personality denies any awareness of the other(s).

Skeptics have raised some serious questions about DID. First, they find it suspicious that this disorder has such a short history. Between 1930 and 1960, the number of DID diagnoses in North America was 2 per decade. By the 1980s, when the DSM contained the first formal code for this disorder, the number of reported cases had exploded to more than 20,000 (McHugh, 1995a). The average number of displayed personalities also mushroomed—from 3 to 12 per patient (Goff & Simms, 1993).

Second, note the skeptics, DID is much less common outside North America, although in other cultures some people are said to be "possessed" by an alien spirit (Aldridge-Morris, 1989; Kluft, 1991). In Britain, DID—which some consider "a wacky American fad" (Cohen, 1995)—is

Multiple personalities: Chris Sizemore's story, told in the book and movie, *The Three Faces of Eve,* gave early visibility to what is now called *dissociative identity disorder.*

rare. In India and Japan, it is essentially nonexistent. Such findings, say skeptics, point to a cultural explanation. They propose that this disorder is created by therapists in a particular social context (Merskey, 1992). Rather than being provoked by trauma, dissociative symptoms tend to be exhibited by suggestible, fantasy-prone people (Giesbrecht et al., 2008, 2010).

Third, instead of being a real disorder, some ask, could DID be an extension of the way we vary the "selves" we present, as when we display a goofy, loud self while hanging out with friends, and a subdued, respectful self around grandparents? If so, say the critics, clinicians who discover multiple personalities may merely have triggered role-playing by fantasy-prone people. After all, patients

"Would it be possible to speak with the personality that pays the bills?"

do not enter therapy saying, "Allow me to introduce myselves." Rather, note these skeptics, some therapists go fishing for multiple personalities: "Have you ever felt like another part of you does things you can't control? Does this part of you have a name? Can I talk to the angry part of you?" Once patients permit a therapist to talk, by name, "to the part of you that says those angry things," they begin acting out the fantasy. Like actors who lose themselves in their roles, vulnerable patients may "become" the parts they are acting out. The result may be the experience of another self.

Other researchers and clinicians believe DID is a real disorder. They find support for this view in the distinct brain and body states associated with differing personalities (Putnam, 1991). DID patients have exhibited activity in brain areas linked with traumatic memories (Elzinga et al., 2007).

If DID is a real disorder, how can we best understand it? Both the psychoanalytic and the learning perspectives interpret DID symptoms as ways of dealing with anxiety. Psychoanalysts see them as defenses against the anxiety caused by unacceptable impulses. In this view, an immoral second personality could allow the discharge of forbidden impulses. Learning theorists see dissociative disorders as behaviors reinforced by anxiety reduction.

Other psychologists include dissociative disorders under the umbrella of post-traumatic disorders. In this view, DID would be a natural, protective response to traumatic experiences during childhood (Putnam, 1995; Spiegel, 2008). Many DID patients recall suffering physical, sexual, or emotional abuse as children (Gleaves, 1996; Lilienfeld et al., 1999). In one study of 12 murderers diagnosed with DID, 11 had suffered severe abuse, even torture, in childhood (Lewis et al., 1997). One had been set afire by his parents. Another had been used in child pornography and was scarred from being made to sit on a stove burner. Some critics wonder, however, whether vivid imagination or therapist suggestion contributes to such recollections (Kihlstrom, 2005).

So the debate continues. On one side are those who believe multiple personalities are the desperate efforts of people trying to detach from a horrific existence. On the other are the skeptics who think DID is a condition constructed out of the therapist-patient interaction and acted out by fantasy-prone, emotionally vulnerable people.

Personality Disorders

7 What characteristics are typical of personality disorders in general, and what biological and psychological factors are associated with antisocial personality disorder?

There is little debate about the reality of **personality disorders.** These disruptive, inflexible, and enduring behavior patterns interfere with a person's social functioning. Some people with these disorders withdraw and avoid social contact. Others interact but do so without responding emotionally.

The most troubling and heavily researched personality disorder is **antisocial personality disorder.** (You may have heard the older terms *sociopath* or *psychopath.*) A person with this disorder is typically a male who shows no conscience in his actions, even toward friends and family. When an antisocial personality combines a keen intelligence with no conscience, the result may be a charming and clever con artist—or worse.

---

dissociative disorders disorders in which conscious awareness becomes separated (dissociated) from previous memories, thoughts, and feelings.

dissociative identity disorder (DID) a rare dissociative disorder in which a person exhibits two or more distinct and alternating personalities. Formerly called *multiple personality disorder.*

personality disorders psychological disorders characterized by inflexible and enduring behavior patterns that impair social functioning.

antisocial personality disorder a personality disorder in which the person (usually a man) exhibits a lack of conscience for wrongdoing, even toward friends and family members. May be aggressive and ruthless or a clever con artist.

Antisocial personality? Dennis Rader, known as the "BTK killer" in Kansas, was convicted in 2005 of killing 10 people over a 30-year span. Rader exhibited the extreme lack of conscience that marks antisocial personality disorder.

Lack of conscience usually becomes plain before age 15, as the person begins to lie, steal, fight, or display unrestrained sexual behavior (Cale & Lilienfeld, 2002). Not all such children become antisocial adults. Those who do (about half of them) will generally be unable to keep a job, irresponsible as a spouse and parent, and violent or otherwise criminal (Farrington, 1991). DO ALL CRIMINALS HAVE ANTISOCIAL◄ PERSONALITY DISORDER? Definitely not. Most criminals show concern for their friends and family members.

Antisocial personalities behave impulsively, and then feel and fear little (Fowles & Dindo, 2009). The results can be horrifying, as they were in the case of Henry Lee Lucas. He killed his first victim when he was 13. He felt little regret then or later. He confessed that, during his 32 years of crime, he had brutally beaten, suffocated, stabbed, shot, or mutilated some 360 women, men, and children. For the last 6 years of his reign of terror, Lucas teamed with Elwood Toole, who reportedly slaughtered about 50 people he "didn't think was worth living anyhow" (Darrach & Norris, 1984).

Antisocial personality disorder is woven of both biological and psychological strands. No single gene codes for a complex behavior such as crime. There does, however, seem to be a genetic tendency toward a fearless and uninhibited life. Twin and adoption studies reveal that biological relatives of people with antisocial and unemotional tendencies are at increased risk for antisocial behavior (Livesley & Jang, 2008).

The genetic vulnerability of those with antisocial personality disorder appears as low arousal. Awaiting events that most people would find unnerving, such as electric shocks or loud noises, they show little bodily arousal (Hare, 1975; van Goozen et al., 2007). Long-term studies have shown that their levels of stress hormones were lower than average when they were youngsters, before committing any crime (FIGURE 12.2). Even at age 3, children who were slow to develop conditioned fears were later more likely to commit a crime (Gao et al., 2010).

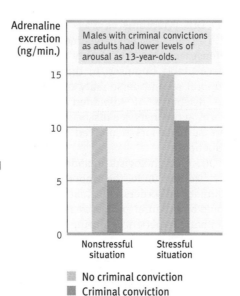

Adrenaline excretion (ng/min.)

Males with criminal convictions as adults had lower levels of arousal as 13-year-olds.

No criminal conviction
Criminal conviction

FIGURE 12.2 ● **Cold-blooded arousability and risk of crime** Levels of the stress hormone adrenaline were measured in two groups of 13-year-old Swedish boys. In both stressful and nonstressful situations, those who would later be convicted of a crime (as 18- to 26-year-olds) had showed relatively low arousal as 13-year-olds. (From Magnusson, 1990.)

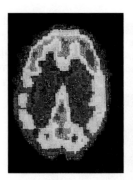
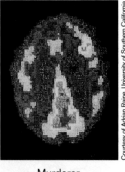

Normal | Murderer

FIGURE 12.3 ● **Murderous minds** PET scans illustrate reduced activation (less red and yellow) in a murderer's frontal lobes. This brain area helps brake impulsive, aggressive behavior. (From Raine, 1999.)

Genetic influences, often in combination with childhood abuse, help wire the brain (Dodge, 2009). One researcher compared PET scans of 41 murderers' brains with those from people of similar age and sex (Raine, 1999, 2005). He found reduced activity in the murderers' frontal lobes, an area of the brain that helps control impulses (FIGURE 12.3). This reduction was apparent in those who murdered impulsively. In a follow-up study, researchers found that violent repeat offenders had 11 percent less frontal lobe tissue than normal (Raine et al., 2000). This helps explain another finding. People with antisocial personality disorder fall far below normal in aspects of thinking such as planning, organization, and inhibition, which are all frontal lobe activities (Morgan & Lilienfeld, 2000).

PRACTICE TEST

11. Psychologists debate whether dissociative identity disorder is a real disorder because

   a. people in other cultures are possessed by alien spirits.

   b. it was reported frequently in the 1920s but rarely today.

   c. it is almost never reported outside North America.

   d. its symptoms are nearly identical to those of obsessive-compulsive disorder.

12. A personality disorder, such as antisocial personality, is characterized by
   a. the presence of multiple personalities.
   b. disorganized thinking.
   c. enduring and maladaptive personality traits.
   d. an elevated level of autonomic nervous system arousal.

THE BIG PICTURE

12D. The psychoanalytic and learning perspectives agree that dissociative identity disorder symptoms are ways of dealing with anxiety. How do their explanations differ?

12E. How do biological and psychological factors contribute to antisocial personality disorder?

IN YOUR EVERYDAY LIFE

▪ Dissociative identity disorder is rare, but feeling like a "different person" at times is common. Can you recall ever feeling like a "different person" because of the situation you were in? What was that like?

Answers to The Big Picture questions can be found in Appendix B at the end of the book.

Answers: 11. c, 12. c.

Substance-Related Disorders

8 | What is a substance-related disorder, and what are tolerance, addiction, and dependence?

As we will see in the next chapter, psychiatrists sometimes prescribe drugs to treat the disorders we've been discussing. But there is another category of disorder in which maladaptive drug use is a major symptom.

Most of us manage to use some nonprescription drugs—caffeine, alcohol, and painkillers, for example—in moderation and without disrupting our lives. But some of us develop self-harming **substance-related disorders.** Such people may have trouble completing school work, maintaining healthy relationships, or holding a job. They may be unable to care for their children. They may drive dangerously or lose control of machinery while "under the influence." Conflicts over getting, using, or

---

TABLE 12.3	**Drug Use or Abuse?**

The following DSM guidelines are used to determine when a person crosses the line from drug use to substance abuse.

Maladaptive use of a substance is shown by one of the following:
- Failure to meet obligations.
- Repeated use in situations where it is physically dangerous.
- Continued use despite problems caused by the substance.
- Repeated substance-related legal problems.

---

not using the substance may be frequent enough to interfere with their daily life. The substances they are using are **psychoactive drugs,** chemicals that change perceptions and mood.

A drug's overall effect depends not only on its *biological* effects but also on the *psychology* of the user's expectations, which vary with *cultures* (Ward, 1994). If one culture assumes that a particular drug produces good feelings or aggression or sexual arousal, and another does not, each culture may find its expectations fulfilled. In the pages that follow, we'll take a closer look at these interacting forces in the use and potential abuse of particular psychoactive drugs. (See **TABLE 12.3** for the DSM guidelines for substance abuse.) But first, let's see how our bodies react to the ongoing use of psychoactive drugs, which helps explain why these substances can lead to deviant, distressful, and dysfunctional behaviors.

Anton Prado Photo/Shutterstock

Tolerance, Addiction, and Dependence

WHY MIGHT A PERSON WHO RARELY◄ DRINKS ALCOHOL GET BUZZED ON ONE CAN OF BEER, WHILE A LONG-TERM DRINKER SHOWS FEW EFFECTS UNTIL THE SECOND SIX-PACK? The answer is **tolerance.** With continued use of alcohol and some other drugs, the user's brain chemistry adapts to offset the drug's effect. To experience the same result, the user needs to take larger and larger doses of the substance. These ever-increasing doses can become a serious threat to health. In some cases,

they lead to **addiction:** The person craves and uses the substance despite its unpleasant consequences.

Regular users often try to fight their addiction. But abruptly stopping the drug can lead to undesirable side effects known as **withdrawal.** Heavy coffee drinkers who skip their usual caffeine fix know the feeling when a headache or grogginess strikes. With more serious drugs like heroin, the physical pain and intense cravings of withdrawal are evidence of **physical dependence.**

People can also develop **psychological dependence,** particularly for stress-relieving drugs, such as alcohol. Although not always physically addictive, such

---

substance-related disorders a maladaptive pattern of substance use leading to clinically significant impairment or distress.

psychoactive drug a chemical substance that alters perceptions and mood.

tolerance the diminishing effect with regular use of the same dose of a drug, requiring the user to take larger and larger doses before experiencing the drug's effect.

addiction compulsive drug craving and use.

withdrawal the discomfort and distress that follow discontinuing the use of an addictive drug.

physical dependence a physiological need for a drug, marked by unpleasant withdrawal symptoms when the drug is discontinued.

psychological dependence a psychological need to use a drug, such as to relieve negative emotions.

TABLE 12.4	What Is Substance Dependence?

According to the DSM, the presence of three or more of the following indicates *dependence* on a substance.

- Tolerance (a lessening effect requires larger doses)
- Withdrawal (discomfort and distress when discontinued)
- Taking the substance longer or in greater amounts than intended
- Little desire or effort to regulate use
- Much time devoted to obtaining the substance
- Normal activities abandoned or reduced
- Continued use despite knowledge that using the substance worsens problems

drugs may nevertheless become an important part of the person's life, often as a way of relieving negative emotions. For someone who is either physically or psychologically dependent, obtaining and using the drug can become the day's main focus **(TABLE 12.4)**.

Types of Psychoactive Drugs

The three major categories of psychoactive drugs—*depressants, stimulants,* and *hallucinogens*—all do their work at the brain's synapses. They stimulate, inhibit, or mimic the activity of the brain's own chemical messengers, the neurotransmitters. As noted earlier, our culturally influenced expectations also play a role in the way these drugs affect us (Ward, 1994).

Depressants

9 How do depressants, such as alcohol, influence neural activity and behavior?

Depressants are drugs such as alcohol, barbiturates, and opiates that calm (depress) neural activity and slow body functions. Let's take a closer look at alcohol.

Alcohol True or false? In large amounts, alcohol is a depressant; in small amounts, it is a stimulant. *False.* Low doses of alcohol may, indeed, enliven a drinker, but they do so by acting as a *disinhibitor*—they slow brain activity that controls judgment and inhibitions. (This activity is part of what happens when

you think about doing something, decide it's a *really* bad idea, and then don't do it.) Alcohol is an equal-opportunity drug. It increases helpful tendencies, as when tipsy restaurant patrons leave big tips (M. Lynn, 1988). And it increases harmful tendencies—as when sexually aggressive college men lower their dates' inhibitions by getting them to drink (Abbey, 1991; Mosher & Anderson, 1986). One University of Illinois campus survey showed that before sexual assaults, 80 percent of the male attackers and 70 percent of the female victims had been drinking (Camper, 1990). Another survey of 89,874 American collegians found alcohol or drugs involved in 79 percent of unwanted sexual intercourse experiences (Presley et al., 1997). Each year, drinking contributes to 1400 U.S. college student deaths, 70,000 sexual assaults, and 500,000 injuries (Hingson et al., 2002).

"That is not one of the seven habits of highly effective people."

In one survey of 18,000 students at 140 colleges and universities, almost 9 in 10 students reported abuse by intoxicated peers. That abuse included sleep and study interruption, insults, sexual advances, and property damage (Wechsler et al., 1994). In a follow-up survey, 44 percent of students admitted binge drinking within the previous two weeks (Wechsler et al., 2002). *The point to remember:* The urges you would feel if sober are the ones you will more likely act upon after drinking.

Slowed neural processing. Low doses of alcohol relax the drinker by slowing sympathetic nervous system activity. With larger doses, reactions slow, speech slurs, and skilled performance declines. Paired with lack of sleep, alcohol is a potent sedative. Add these physical effects to lowered inhibitions, and the result can be deadly. Worldwide, several hundred thousand lives are lost each year in alcohol-related accidents and violent crime. When sober, most drinkers believe that driving under the influence of alcohol is wrong, and they insist they would not do so. That belief disappears as blood-alcohol level rises and moral judgments become fuzzy. Most will drive home from a bar, even if given a breathalyzer test and told they are intoxicated (Denton & Krebs, 1990; MacDonald et al., 1995).

Memory disruption. Some people drink to forget their troubles. And forget they do—alcohol disrupts the processing of recent experiences into long-term memories. Thus, heavy drinkers may not recall people they met the night before or what they said or did while drunk. These blackouts result in part because alcohol suppresses REM sleep, the part of the sleep cycle that helps fix the day's experiences into permanent memories. Heavy drinking can also have long-term effects on the brain. In rats, at a development period corresponding to human adolescence, binge drinking contributes to the death of nerve cells and reduces the birth rates of new nerve cells. It also impairs the growth of synaptic connections (Crews et al., 2006, 2007).

In those with **alcohol dependence,** prolonged and excessive drinking can shrink the brain. Women **(FIGURE 12.4)** are

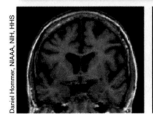

FIGURE 12.4 • **Alcohol dependence shrinks the brain** MRI scans show brain shrinkage in women with alcohol dependence (left) compared with women in a control group (right).

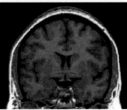

Scan of woman with alcohol dependence

Scan of woman without alcohol dependence

especially vulnerable because they have less of a stomach enzyme that digests alcohol (Wuethrich, 2001). Girls and young women can become addicted to alcohol more quickly than boys and young men do. They also suffer lung, brain, and liver damage at lower consumption levels (CASA, 2003).

A strong correlation between early drinking and later dependence appeared in a national survey of 43,000 adults. Of those who began drinking alcohol before age 14, about half (47 percent) later became alcohol dependent (Hingson et al., 2006). Of those who began drinking at age 21 or after, only 9 percent showed this dependency. These correlations remained after researchers controlled for smoking, family alcohol history, and antisocial behaviors.

Few college and university students believe they have an alcohol problem. In fact, many meet the criteria for alcohol dependence (**TABLE 12.5**). College and university students drink more alcohol than their nonstudent peers. They spend more on alcohol than on books and other beverages combined. Fraternity and sorority members drink three times as much as other students (Atwell, 1986; Malloy, 1994; Slutske, 2005). As students mature with age, they drink less (Marlatt, 1991).

Effects of expectations. As with other psychoactive drugs, users' expectations influence their behavior. When people *believe* that alcohol affects social behavior in certain ways, and

believe, rightly or wrongly, that they have been drinking alcohol, they will behave accordingly (Leigh, 1989). In one experiment, researchers gave college male volunteers (for a study on "alcohol and sexual stimulation"), either an alcoholic or a nonalcoholic drink (Abrams & Wilson, 1983). (Both had strong tastes that masked any alcohol.) In each group, half the participants thought they were drinking alcohol and half thought they were not. After watching an erotic movie clip, the men who *thought* they had consumed alcohol were more likely to report having strong sexual fantasies and feeling guilt-free. Being able to explain their sexual responses as reactions to alcohol released their inhibitions—whether or not they had actually consumed any alcohol. If, as commonly believed, liquor is the quicker pick-her-upper, the effect lies partly in that powerful sex organ, the mind.

Barbiturates Like alcohol, the **barbiturate** drugs, or *tranquilizers,* depress nervous system activity. Barbiturates such as Nembutal, Seconal, and Amytal are sometimes prescribed to induce sleep or reduce anxiety. In larger doses, they can impair memory and judgment. If combined with alcohol, the total depressive effect on body functions can lead to death. This sometimes happens when people take a sleeping pill after an evening of heavy drinking.

Drinking disaster demo: Firefighters re-enacted the trauma of an alcohol-related car accident, providing a memorable demonstration for these high school students. Alcohol consumption leads to feelings of invincibility, which become especially dangerous behind the wheel of a car.

Opiates The **opiates**—opium and its offshoots, morphine and heroin—also depress nervous system activity. Pupils constrict, breathing slows, and *lethargy* (a feeling of extreme relaxation) sets in, as blissful pleasure replaces pain and anxiety. For this short-term pleasure, opiate users may pay a long-term price: a gnawing craving for another fix, a need for progressively larger doses (as tolerance develops), and the extreme discomfort of withdrawal. When repeatedly flooded with an artificial opiate, the brain eventually stops producing *endorphins,* its own feel-good opiates. If the artificial opiate is then withdrawn, the brain lacks the normal level of these natural painkillers.

TABLE 12.5	Warning Signs of Alcohol Dependence
• Drinking binges
• Regretting things done or said when drunk
• Feeling low or guilty after drinking
• Failing to honor a resolve to drink less
• Drinking to reduce depression or anxiety
• Avoiding family or friends when drinking

depressants drugs (such as alcohol, barbiturates, and opiates) that reduce (depress) neural activity and slow body functions.

alcohol dependence (popularly known as alcoholism). Alcohol use marked by tolerance, withdrawal if suspended, and a drive to continue use.

barbiturates drugs that depress the activity of the central nervous system, reducing anxiety but impairing memory and judgment.

opiates opium and its derivatives, such as morphine and heroin; they depress neural activity, temporarily lessening pain and anxiety.

Those who cannot or choose not to endure this state may pay an ultimate price—death by overdose. Methadone, a synthetic opiate drug prescribed as a substitute for heroin or for relief of chronic pain, can also produce tolerance and dependence.

Stimulants

10 How do the major stimulants affect neural activity and behavior?

A **stimulant** excites neural activity and speeds up body functions. Pupils dilate. Heart and breathing rates increase. Blood-sugar levels rise, causing a drop in appetite. Energy and self-confidence also rise.

Stimulants include caffeine, nicotine, the **amphetamines,** cocaine, methamphetamine, and Ecstasy (NIDA, 2002, 2005). People use stimulants to feel alert, lose weight, or boost mood or athletic performance. Unfortunately, stimulants can be addictive. You may know this if you are one of the many people who use caffeine daily in your coffee, tea, soda, chocolate, or energy drinks. If cut off from your usual dose, you may crash into fatigue, headaches, irritability, and depression (Silverman et al., 1992).

Nicotine One of the most addictive stimulants is **nicotine,** found in cigarettes and other tobacco products. ARE TOBACCO◀ PRODUCTS AS ADDICTIVE AS HEROIN AND COCAINE? *Yes.* If you are a smoker who has tried to kick your habit, you probably aren't surprised. Addicted customers are loyal customers. And about 1 billion of them will be rewarded for their loyalty with a tobacco-related death (WHO, 2008c).

"There is an overwhelming medical and scientific consensus that cigarette smoking causes lung cancer, heart disease, emphysema, and other serious diseases in smokers. Smokers are far more likely to develop serious diseases, like lung cancer, than nonsmokers."

Philip Morris Companies Inc., 1999

As with other addictions, smokers become *dependent,* and they develop *tolerance.* A burning cigarette is a portable nicotine dispenser. Within 7 seconds

James Devaney/WireImage

Nic-a-teen: Virtually nobody starts smoking past the vulnerable teen years. Eager to hook customers whose addiction will give them business for years to come, cigarette companies target teens. Portrayals of smoking by popular actors, such as Robert Pattinson in *Remember Me,* entice teens to imitate.

(twice as fast as intravenous heroin), a rush of nicotine signals the central nervous system to release a flood of neurotransmitters **(FIGURE 12.5).** Epinephrine

and norepinephrine diminish appetite and boost alertness and mental efficiency. Dopamine and opioids calm anxiety and reduce sensitivity to pain (Nowak, 1994; Scott et al., 2004).

These mood-altering effects are very reinforcing, and they are especially potent when balanced against the punishment of nicotine-withdrawal symptoms, which include craving, insomnia, anxiety, and irritability. The combined package keeps people smoking, even among the 8 in 10 smokers who wish they could stop (Jones, 2007). Each year, fewer than 1 in 7 smokers who want to quit will be able to resist. Even those who know they are committing slow-motion suicide may be unable to stop (Saad, 2002).

Nevertheless, repeated attempts seem to pay off. Half of all Americans who have ever smoked have quit, and more than 90 percent did so on their own. The acute craving and withdrawal symptoms do go away gradually over six months (Ward et

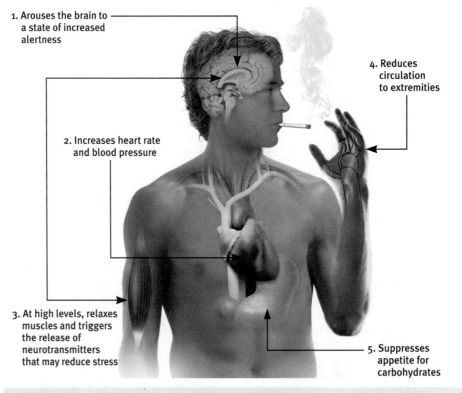

1. Arouses the brain to a state of increased alertness

2. Increases heart rate and blood pressure

3. At high levels, relaxes muscles and triggers the release of neurotransmitters that may reduce stress

4. Reduces circulation to extremities

5. Suppresses appetite for carbohydrates

FIGURE 12.5 ● **Where there's smoke . . . : The physiological effects of nicotine** Nicotine reaches the brain within 7 seconds, twice as fast as intravenous heroin. Within minutes, the amount in the blood soars.

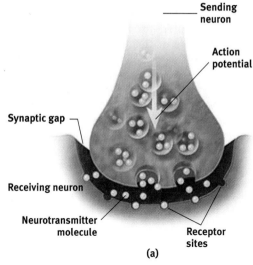

Sending neuron

Action potential

Synaptic gap

Receiving neuron

Neurotransmitter molecule

Receptor sites

(a)

Neurotransmitters carry a message from a sending neuron across a synapse to receptor sites on a receiving neuron.

Reuptake

(b)

The sending neuron normally reabsorbs excess neurotransmitter molecules, a process called *reuptake*.

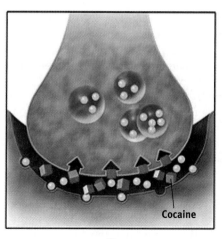

Cocaine

(c)

By binding to the sites that normally reabsorb neurotransmitter molecules, cocaine blocks reuptake of dopamine, norepinephrine, and serotonin (Ray & Ksir, 1990). The extra neurotransmitter molecules therefore remain in the synapse, intensifying their normal mood-altering effects and producing a euphoric rush. When the cocaine level drops, the absence of these neurotransmitters produces a crash.

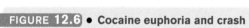

FIGURE 12.6 • **Cocaine euphoria and crash**

al., 1997). After a year's abstinence, only 10 percent return to smoking (Hughes et al., 2008).

Cocaine Cocaine users travel a fast track from flying high to crashing to earth. The recipe for Coca-Cola originally included an extract of the coca plant, creating a tonic laced with a small amount of cocaine for tired elderly people. Between 1896 and 1905, Coke was indeed "the real thing." But no longer. Cocaine is now snorted, injected, or smoked. It enters the bloodstream quickly, producing a rush of *euphoria*—feelings of great happiness and well-being. Those feelings continue until the brain's supply of the neurotransmitters dopamine, serotonin, and norepinephrine drops off (**FIGURE 12.6**). Then, within a mere 15 to 30 minutes, a crash of agitated depression follows. Many regular cocaine users chasing this high become addicted. In the lab, cocaine-addicted monkeys have pressed levers more than 12,000 times to gain one cocaine injection (Siegel, 1990).

In a national survey, 3 percent of U.S. high school seniors reported having tried cocaine during the past year (Johnston et al., 2010). Nearly half of them had smoked *crack*. This faster-working, potent

crystal form of cocaine produces a briefer but more intense high, followed by a more intense crash. The craving for more wanes after several hours, only to return several days later (Gawin, 1991).

Cocaine's psychological effects depend in part on the dosage and form consumed. But as with all psychoactive drugs, the situation and the user's expectations and personality play a role. Given a placebo, cocaine users who *thought* they were taking cocaine often had a cocaine-like experience (Van Dyke & Byck, 1982).

Methamphetamine The highly addictive **methamphetamine** triggers the release of the neurotransmitter dopamine, which stimulates brain cells that enhance energy and mood. The drug's powerful effects include eight or so hours of heightened energy and mood. Its aftereffects may include irritability, insomnia, high blood pressure, seizures, periods of disorientation, and occasional violent behavior. Over time, methamphetamine use appears to permanently reduce the brain's normal output of dopamine.

Ecstasy **Ecstasy** is the street name for **MDMA** (methylenedioxymethamphetamine). This powerful drug is both a

stimulant and a mild hallucinogen. (*Hallucinogens*, as we will see in the next section, distort perceptions and lead to false sensory images.) Ecstasy is an amphetamine derivative that triggers the brain's release of dopamine. But its major effect is releasing stored serotonin and blocking

stimulants drugs (such as caffeine, nicotine, and the more powerful amphetamines, cocaine, and Ecstasy) that excite neural activity and speed up body functions.

amphetamines drugs that stimulate neural activity, causing speeded-up body functions and associated energy and mood changes.

nicotine a stimulating and highly addictive psychoactive drug in tobacco.

methamphetamine a powerfully addictive drug that stimulates the central nervous system with speeded-up body functions and associated energy and mood changes; over time, appears to reduce baseline dopamine levels.

Ecstasy (MDMA) a synthetic stimulant and mild hallucinogen. Produces euphoria and social intimacy, but with short-term health risks and longer-term harm to serotonin-producing neurons and to mood and cognition.

its reuptake, thus prolonging serotonin's feel-good flood (Braun, 2001). Users feel the effect about a half-hour after taking an Ecstasy pill. For three or four hours, they experience euphoria. They feel intimately connected to the people around them. ("I love everyone.")

During the late 1990s, Ecstasy's popularity soared as a "club drug" taken at night clubs and all-night raves (Landry, 2002). There are, however, reasons not to be ecstatic about Ecstasy. One is its ability to cause dehydration. With prolonged dancing, Ecstasy's side effects can lead to severe overheating, increased blood pressure, and death. Long-term, repeated use can also damage serotonin-producing neurons. Serotonin does more than just make us feel good. It helps regulate our body rhythms (including sleep), our disease-fighting immune system, and our memory and other cognitive functions (Laws & Kokkalis, 2007; Pacifici et al., 2001; Schilt et al., 2007). Ecstasy interferes with all of these functions. The decreased serotonin output can be permanent and can lead to a permanently depressed mood (Croft et al., 2001; McCann et al., 2001; Roiser et al., 2005). Ecstasy delights for the night but darkens our tomorrows.

Hallucinogens

11 | What are the physiological and psychological effects of LSD and marijuana?

Among the least addictive drugs are the **hallucinogens.** These substances distort perceptions and call up sensory images (such as sounds or sights) without any input from the senses. This helps explain why these drugs are also called *psychedelics,* meaning "mind-manifesting." Some are synthetic. The best known synthetic hallucinogens are MDMA (Ecstasy), discussed earlier, and LSD. Others, such as the mild hallucinogen marijuana, are natural substances.

LSD In 1943, Albert Hofmann reported perceiving "an uninterrupted stream of fantastic pictures, extraordinary shapes with an intense, kaleidoscopic play of colors" (Siegel, 1984). Hofmann, a

chemist, created and accidentally ingested **LSD** (lysergic acid diethylamide). LSD, like Ecstasy, interferes with the serotonin neurotransmitter system. LSD and other powerful hallucinogens are chemically similar to one type of serotonin and can therefore block its actions (Jacobs, 1987). An LSD "trip" can take users to unexpected places. Emotions may vary from euphoria to detachment to panic, depending in part on the person's current mood and expectations.

The odds of getting hooked after trying various drugs:
Marijuana: 9 percent
Alcohol: 15 percent
Cocaine: 17 percent
Heroin: 23 percent
Tobacco: 32 percent
Source: National Academy of Science, Institute of Medicine (Brody, 2003).

Even so, the perceptual distortions and hallucinations have some things in common. Whether provoked to hallucinate by drugs, loss of oxygen, or extreme sensory deprivation, the brain hallucinates in basically the same way (Siegel, 1982). The experience typically begins with simple geometric forms, such as a criss-cross, a cobweb, or a spiral. The next phase consists of more meaningful images. Some may be seen in front of a tunnel, others may be replays of past emotional experiences. As the hallucination peaks, users frequently feel separated from their bodies. Dreamlike scenes feel so real that people may become panic-stricken or harm themselves.

These sensations are strikingly similar to the **near-death experience.** This altered state of consciousness is reported by about one-third of those who survive a brush with death, as when revived from cardiac arrest (Moody, 1976; Ring, 1980; Schnaper, 1980). Many experience visions of tunnels **(FIGURE 12.7)**, bright lights or beings of light, a replay of old memories, and out-of-body sensations (Siegel, 1980). Oxygen deprivation and other insults to the brain can produce hallucinations. Following temporal lobe seizures, for example, patients have reported similarly profound mystical experiences. So have solitary sailors and polar explorers while enduring monotony, isolation, and cold (Suedfeld & Mocellin, 1987). Under stress, the brain can manufacture seeming near-death experiences.

Marijuana For 5000 years, hemp has been cultivated for its fiber. The leaves and flowers of this plant, which are sold as *marijuana,* contain **THC** (delta-9-tetrahydrocannabinol). Marijuana is a difficult drug to classify. Whether smoked (getting to the brain in a mere 7 seconds) or eaten (producing slower, less intense effects), THC produces a mix of effects. Marijuana is a mild hallucinogen, increasing sensitivity to colors, sounds, tastes, and smells. But like alcohol, marijuana also relaxes, disinhibits, and may produce a euphoric high. Both drugs impair the motor coordination, perceptual skills, and reaction time necessary for safely operating an automobile or other machine. "THC causes animals to misjudge events," reported Ronald Siegel (1990, p. 163). "Pigeons wait too long to respond to buzzers or lights that tell them food is available for brief periods; and rats turn the wrong way in mazes."

FIGURE 12.7 ● **Near-death vision or hallucination?** Psychologist Ronald Siegel (1977) reported that people under the influence of hallucinogenic drugs often see "a bright light in the center of the field of vision. . . . The location of this point of light create[s] a tunnel-like perspective." This is very similar to others' reported near-death experiences.

TABLE 12.6	A Guide to Selected Psychoactive Drugs		
Drug	**Type**	**Pleasurable Effects**	**Negative Aftereffects**
Alcohol	Depressant	Initial high followed by relaxation and disinhibition	Impaired reactions, depression, memory loss, organ damage
Heroin	Depressant	Rush of euphoria, relief from pain	Depressed physiology, agonizing withdrawal
Caffeine	Stimulant	Increased alertness and wakefulness	In high doses, anxiety, restlessness, and insomnia; uncomfortable withdrawal
Nicotine	Stimulant	Arousal and relaxation, sense of well-being	Heart disease, cancer
Cocaine	Stimulant	Rush of euphoria, confidence, energy	Cardiovascular stress, suspiciousness, depressive crash
Methamphetamine	Stimulant	Euphoria, alertness, energy	Irritability, insomnia, high blood pressure, seizures
Ecstasy (MDMA)	Stimulant; mild hallucinogen	Euphoria, disinhibition	Dehydration, overheating, depressed mood, impaired cognitive and immune functioning
LSD	Hallucinogen	Visual "trip"	Risk of panic
Marijuana	Mild hallucinogen	Enhanced sensation, relief of pain, distortion of time, relaxation	Impaired learning and memory, increased risk of psychological disorders, lung damage from smoke

Marijuana and alcohol differ in other ways. The body eliminates alcohol within hours. THC and its by-products linger in the body for a month or more, which means that regular users may achieve a high with smaller amounts of the drug than would be needed by an occasional user. This is contrary to the usual path of tolerance, in which repeat users need to take larger doses to feel the same effect.

A user's experience can vary with the situation. If the user feels anxious or depressed, marijuana may intensify these feelings. The more often the person uses it, the greater the risk of anxiety, depression, or, possibly, schizophrenia. These correlations held even after researchers controlled for other drug use and personal traits (Hall, 2006; Murray et al., 2007; Patton et al., 2002). Marijuana also disrupts memory formation and interferes with immediate recall of information learned only a few minutes before. Such effects on thinking outlast the period of smoking (Pope & Yurgelun-Todd, 1996; Smith, 1995).

Some states have passed laws allowing marijuana to be used for medical purposes to relieve the pain, nausea, and severe weight loss associated with diseases such as cancer and AIDS (Watson et al., 2000). In such cases, the Institute of Medicine recommends medical inhalers to deliver the THC. Marijuana smoke, like cigarette smoke, is toxic and can cause cancer and other conditions. How does marijuana alter thinking, movements, and moods and relieve pain? Scientists shed light on this question when they made an exciting discovery. Dense groups of THC-sensitive receptors exist in our brain's frontal lobes, limbic system, and motor cortex (Iversen, 2000). Why would our brain be equipped with THC-sensitive receptors? The answer had to be that something very much like THC regularly passes through the brain and binds with these receptors. These THC-like molecules may naturally control pain. If so, this would help explain why marijuana is effective for pain relief.

* * *

TABLE 12.6 summarizes the psychoactive drugs discussed in this section. They share some features. All trigger negative aftereffects that counter the drug's immediate positive effects. These negative aftereffects grow stronger with repetition. As the opposing, negative aftereffects grow stronger, larger and larger doses are typically needed to produce the desired positive effect. (This process is *tolerance*.) These increasingly larger doses produce even worse aftereffects in the drug's absence. (This process is *withdrawal*.) The worsening aftereffects in turn create a need to switch off the withdrawal symptoms by taking yet more of the drug. (This process is *addiction*.)

hallucinogens psychedelic ("mind-manifesting") drugs, such as LSD, that distort perceptions and evoke sensory images in the absence of sensory input.

LSD a powerful hallucinogenic drug; also known as *acid (lysergic acid diethylamide)*.

near-death experience an altered state of consciousness reported after a close brush with death (such as through cardiac arrest); often similar to drug-induced hallucinations.

THC the major active ingredient in marijuana; triggers a variety of effects, including mild hallucinations.

Understanding Substance Abuse

What biological, psychological, and social-cultural factors help explain why some people abuse mind-altering drugs?

Substance abuse by North American youth increased during the 1970s. Then, with increased drug education and a shift toward more realism in media portrayals of the effects of drugs, substance abuse declined sharply. After the early 1990s, the cultural antidrug voice softened, and drugs for a time have again been glamorized in some music and films **(FIGURE 12.8)**.

For many adolescents, occasional drug use represents thrill seeking. WHY DO◄ SOME ADOLESCENTS BUT NOT OTHERS BECOME REGULAR DRUG ABUSERS? In search of answers, researchers have tried to sort out biological, psychological, and social-cultural influences.

Biological Influences

Are some of us biologically vulnerable to particular drugs? Some evidence indicates we are (Crabbe, 2002).

- Adopted individuals are more likely to develop alcohol dependence if one or both biological parents have a history of it.

- Having an identical twin with alcohol dependence puts one at increased risk for alcohol problems (Kendler et al., 2002). This increased risk is not found among fraternal twins.

- Boys who at age 6 are excitable, impulsive, and fearless (genetically influenced traits) are more likely as teens to smoke, drink, and abuse other drugs (Masse & Tremblay, 1997).

- Some genes are more common among people and animals predisposed to alcohol dependence. These genes may, for example, produce deficiencies in the brain's natural dopamine reward system.

- Researchers have bred rats and mice that prefer alcoholic drinks to water. One such strain has low levels of a brain chemical called NPY. What do you think was the result when researchers bred mice to produce *higher-than-normal* amounts of NPY? Those mice were very sensitive to alcohol's sedating effect, and they drank little (Thiele et al., 1998).

Psychological and Social-Cultural Influences

Throughout this text, you have seen a recurring theme. Biological, psychological, and social-cultural influences interact to produce behavior. So, too, with substance abuse. Feeling that one's life is meaningless and directionless is a psychological influence that puts youth and young adults at risk (Newcomb & Harlow, 1986). This feeling is common among school dropouts who try to make their way in life without job skills, without privilege, and with little hope. The ups and downs of marijuana usage among young people seem predicted by another psychological factor—their perception of the risk involved in using marijuana. When perceived risk rises, usage falls (Johnston et al., 2007).

Sometimes, the psychological influence is obvious. Many heavy users of alcohol, marijuana, and cocaine have experienced significant stress or failure and are depressed. Monkeys develop a taste for alcohol when stressed by permanent separation from their mothers at birth (Small, 2002). Girls with a history of depression, eating disorders, or sexual or physical abuse are at risk for substance addiction. So are youth undergoing school or neighborhood transitions (CASA, 2003; Logan et al., 2002). By temporarily dulling the pain of self-awareness, alcohol and other drugs may offer a way to avoid coping with depression, anger, anxiety, or insomnia. As Chapter 6 explains, behavior is often controlled more by its immediate consequences than by its later ones.

Especially for teenagers, substance abuse can also have social roots. The media offer easy access to models who drink and smoke. For example, in the real world, alcohol accounts for one-sixth or less of beverage use. In TV land, people drink alcohol more often than other drinks—coffee, tea, soft drinks, or water—combined (Gerbner, 1990). Teens are also exposed to smoking in movies. Those with high exposure are three times as likely as other teens to try smoking and to become smokers. And that correlation is not a result of personality, parenting

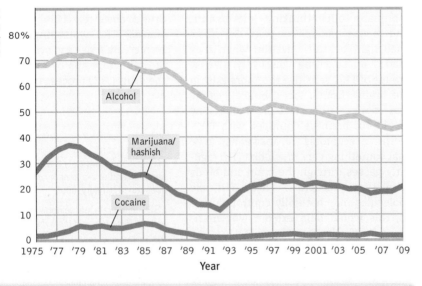

FIGURE 12.8 ● **Trends in drug use** The percentage of U.S. high school seniors who said they had used alcohol, marijuana, or cocaine during the past 30 days peaked in the late 1970s. (From Johnston et al., 2010.)

SNAPSHOTS

Once upon a time, peer pressure caused Bob to start smoking.

RESTAURANT

Twenty years later, it forces him to quit.

(c) Love A|41

© Jason Love

style, or family economics, which researchers controlled for (Heatherton & Sargent, 2009). Rates of substance abuse also vary across cultural and ethnic groups. Among the Amish, Mennonites, Mormons, and Orthodox Jews, alcohol and other substance addiction rates are extremely low (Trimble, 1994). Among African-American teens, rates of drinking, smoking, and cocaine use are sharply lower than among other U.S. teens (Johnston et al., 2007).

For substance abuse as for real estate, location makes a difference. Those whose genetic predispositions nudge them toward substance abuse will find more opportunities and less supervision in cities (Legrand et al., 2005). Relatively drug-free small towns and rural areas tend to exert an influence in the opposite direction.

Regardless of location, peers influence attitudes about drugs. Peers throw the parties and provide (or don't provide) the drugs. If an adolescent's friends abuse drugs, the odds are that he or she will, too. If the friends do not, the opportunity may not even arise.

Peer influence is more than what friends do and say. Adolescents' expectations—what they *believe* their friends are doing and favoring—influence their behavior. One study surveyed sixth-graders

in 22 U.S. states. How many believed their friends had smoked marijuana? About 14 percent. How many of those friends said they had smoked it? Only 4 percent (Wren, 1999). College students are not immune to such misperceptions. Drinking dominates social occasions partly because students overestimate their fellow students' enthusiasm for alcohol (Moreira et al., 2009; Prentice & Miller, 1993; Self, 1994). As always with correlations, the traffic between friends' drug use and our own may be two-way. Our friends influence us, but we also select as friends those who share our likes and dislikes.

Teens rarely abuse drugs if they understand the physical and psychological costs, do well in school, feel good about themselves, and are in a peer group that disapproves of early drinking and abusing drugs (Bachman et al., 2007; Hingson, 2006). These findings suggest three tactics for preventing and treating substance abuse and addiction among young people.

- Educate people about the long-term costs of a drug's temporary pleasures.
- Boost people's self-esteem and purpose in life.
- Modify peer associations or "inoculate" youth against peer pressures by training them in refusal skills.

In Chapter 13, we'll consider treatments for substance abuse in more detail.

PRACTICE TEST

THE BASICS

13. Continued use of a psychoactive drug produces tolerance. This usually means that the user will
    a. feel physical pain and intense craving.
    b. be irreversibly addicted to the substance.
    c. need to take larger doses to get the desired effect.
    d. be able to take smaller doses to get the desired effect.

14. The depressants include alcohol, barbiturates,
    a. and opiates.
    b. cocaine, and morphine.
    c. caffeine, nicotine, and marijuana.
    d. and amphetamines.

15. Because alcohol _____, it may make a person more helpful or more aggressive.
    a. causes alcoholic blackouts
    b. destroys REM sleep
    c. produces hallucinations
    d. lowers inhibitions

16. Nicotine and cocaine stimulate neural activity, speed up body functions, and
    a. induce sensory hallucinations.
    b. interfere with memory.
    c. induce a temporary sense of well-being.
    d. lead to heroin use.

17. Long-term use of Ecstasy can
    a. depress sympathetic nervous system activity.
    b. deplete the brain's supply of epinephrine.
    c. deplete the brain's supply of dopamine.
    d. damage serotonin-producing neurons.

18. Near-death experiences are strikingly similar to the hallucinations evoked by
    a. heroin.
    b. cocaine.
    c. LSD.
    d. alcohol.

19. Use of marijuana
    a. impairs motor coordination, perception, reaction time, and memory.
    b. inhibits people's emotions.
    c. leads to dehydration and overheating.
    d. stimulates brain cell development.

20. Social explanations for drug use often focus on the effect of peer influence. An important *psychological* contributor to drug use is
    a. inflated self-esteem.
    b. the feeling that life is meaningless and directionless.
    c. genetic predispositions.
    d. overprotective parents.

Continued

Mood Disorders

13 What are the main mood disorders, and why do people attempt suicide?

Just as most of us have indirectly or directly had some experience with substance-related disorders, many of us have also had close encounters with **mood disorders.** These disorders, which are characterized by emotional extremes, appear in two principal forms. *Major depressive disorder* is a prolonged state of hopeless depression. *Bipolar disorder* is an alternation between depression and overexcited hyperactivity.

Anxiety is a response to the threat of future loss. Depressed mood is often a response to past and current loss. To feel bad in reaction to very sad events (such as the death of a loved one) is to be in touch with reality. In such times, depression is like a car's oil light—a signal that warns us to stop and take appropriate measures.

In the past year, have you at some time "felt so depressed that it was difficult to function"? If so, you were not alone. In one national survey, 31 percent of American collegians

answered Yes to that question (ACHA, 2009). The college years are an exciting time, but they can also be very stressful. Perhaps you wanted to go to college right out of high school but couldn't afford it, and now you are struggling to find time for school amid family and work responsibilities. Perhaps social stresses, such as a relationship gone sour or a feeling of being excluded, have made you feel isolated or plunged you into despair. Dwelling on these thoughts may leave you feeling deeply discouraged about your life or your future. You may lack the energy to get things done or even to force yourself out of bed. You may be unable to concentrate, eat, or sleep normally. Occasionally you may even wonder if you would be better off dead.

These feelings are more likely to strike during the dark months of winter than the bright days of summer. For some people, winter darkness means more blue moods. When asked "Have you cried today?" Americans answered *Yes* doubly often in the winter (**TABLE 12.7**). For others, recurring depression during winter's dark months constitutes a *seasonal affective disorder*.

From an evolutionary perspective, depression makes sense. As social psychologist Daniel Gilbert (2006) warned, "If someone offered you a pill that would make you permanently happy, you would be well advised to run fast and run far. Emotion is a compass that tells us what to do, and a compass that is perpetually stuck on NORTH is worthless."

Depression helps us face and solve problems. Biologically speaking, life's purpose is survival and reproduction, not happiness. Coughing, vomiting, and various forms of pain protect our body from dangerous toxins. Depression similarly protects us from dangerous thoughts and feel-

TABLE 12.7	Percentage Answering *Yes* When Asked "Have You Cried Today?"	
	Men	**Women**
In August	4%	7%
In December	8%	21%

Source: *Time*/CNN survey, 1994

ings. It slows us down, focuses our mind, defuses aggression, and cuts back on risk taking (Allen & Badcock, 2003; Andrews & Thomson, 2009). Grinding temporarily to a halt, as we do when feeling threatened or finding that our goals are beyond our reach, gives us time to think hard and consider our options (Wrosch & Miller, 2009). After reassessing our life, we may redirect our energy in more promising ways. There is sense to suffering. But sometimes depression becomes seriously maladaptive. **HOW DO WE RECOGNIZE THE◄ FINE LINE BETWEEN A NORMAL BLUE MOOD AND ABNORMAL DEPRESSION?**

Major Depressive Disorder

Joy, contentment, sadness, and despair are different points on a continuum, points at which any of us may be found at any given moment. The difference between a blue mood after bad news and **major depressive disorder** is like the difference between gasping for breath after a hard run and having chronic asthma. Major depressive disorder occurs when signs of depression last two or more weeks and are not caused by drugs or a medical condition. These signs include lethargy (extreme lack of energy), feelings of worthlessness, or loss of interest in family, friends, and activities. To sense what major depression feels like, suggest some clinicians, imagine combining the anguish of grief with the exhaustion you feel after pulling an all-nighter.

Although phobias are more common, depression is the number one reason people seek mental health services. Worldwide, it is the leading cause of disability. In any given year, 5.8 percent of men and 9.5 percent of women will have

Brad Wenner/Getty Images

a depressive episode (World Health Organization, 2001). With or without therapy, most of these people will temporarily or permanently return to their previous nondepressed state.

Bipolar Disorder

In **bipolar disorder,** people bounce from one emotional extreme to the other. When a depressive episode ends, an intensely happy, hyperactive, wildly optimistic state called **mania** follows. But before long, the elated mood either returns to normal or plunges again into depression.

If depression is living in slow motion, mania is fast forward. During this phase, people are typically overtalkative, overactive, and elated. They feel little need for sleep. They show fewer sexual inhibitions. They are easily irritated if crossed. Feeling extreme optimism and self-esteem, they find advice annoying. Yet they need protection from their poor judgment, which may lead to reckless spending or unsafe sex.

In milder forms, mania's energy and free-flowing thinking can fuel creativity. George Frideric Handel (1685–1759), who many believe suffered a mild form of bipolar disorder,

> "All the people in history, literature, art, whom I most admire: Mozart, Shakespeare, Homer, El Greco, St. John, Chekhov, Gregory of Nyssa, Dostoevsky, Emily Brontë: not one of them would qualify for a mental-health certificate."
>
> Madeleine L'Engle, *A Circle of Quiet,* 1972

composed his nearly four-hour-long *Messiah* during three weeks of intense, creative energy (Keynes, 1980). Bipolar disorder strikes more often among people who rely on emotional expression and vivid imagery, such as poets and artists, and less often among those who rely on precision and logic, such as architects, designers, and journalists (Jamison, 1993, 1995; Kaufman & Baer, 2002; Ludwig, 1995).

Bipolar disorder is as maladaptive as major depressive disorder, but it is much less common. It afflicts as many men as women. The diagnosis is on the rise among adolescents, whose mood swings, sometimes prolonged, range from rage to bubbly. The trend was clear in U.S. National Center for Health Statistics annual physician surveys. Between 1994 and 2003, bipolar diagnoses in under-20 people showed an astonishing 40-fold increase—from an estimated 20,000 to 800,000 (Carey, 2007; Flora & Bobby, 2008; Moreno et al., 2007). The new popularity of the diagnosis has been a boon to companies whose drugs are prescribed to lessen the mood swings. This surge in diagnoses has prompted debate over whether normal mood swings are sometimes being labeled abnormal and medicated.

George C. Beresford/Hulton Getty Pictures Library

The Granger Collection

George Napolitano/FilmMagic

Creativity and bipolar disorders:
There are many creative artists, composers, writers, and musical performers with bipolar disorder, including (left to right) Madonna, Virginia Woolf, Samuel Clemens (Mark Twain), and Tim Burton.

Jemal Countess/Getty Images

Suicide

Each year nearly 1 million despairing people worldwide will elect a permanent solution to what might have been a temporary problem (WHO, 2008c). During the recent economic recession, the National Suicide Prevention Lifeline has experienced a dramatic increase in calls for help. In one year, calls increased by more than 20 percent (from 42,406 in April 2008, to 51,465 in April 2009).

The risk of suicide is at least five times greater for those who have been depressed than for the general population (Bostwick & Pankratz, 2000). People seldom, however, commit suicide while in the depths of depression, when energy and initiative are lacking. It is when they begin to rebound and become capable of following through that the risk increases.

Suicide is not necessarily an act of hostility or revenge. Elderly people sometimes choose death as an alternative to current or future suffering. People of all ages may view suicide as a way of switching off unendurable pain and relieving a perceived burden on family members. "People desire death when two fundamental needs are frustrated to the point of extinction," notes Thomas Joiner (2006, p. 47): "The need to belong with or connect to others, and the need to feel effective with or to influence others." Looking back, families and friends may recall signs that they believe should have forewarned them—

mood disorders psychological disorders characterized by emotional extremes. See *major depressive disorder, mania,* and *bipolar disorder.*

major depressive disorder a mood disorder in which a person experiences, in the absence of drugs or a medical condition, two or more weeks of significantly depressed moods, feelings of worthlessness, and diminished interest or pleasure in most activities.

bipolar disorder a mood disorder in which the person alternates between the hopelessness and lethargy of depression and the overexcited state of mania. (Formerly called *manic-depressive disorder.*)

mania a mood disorder marked by a hyperactive, wildly optimistic state.

verbal hints, giving possessions away, or withdrawal and preoccupation with death. But few who talk or think of suicide (a number that includes one-third of all adolescents and college students) actually attempt it. Only about 1 in 25 who make the attempt will complete the act (AAS, 2009). Nevertheless, about 30,000 will kill themselves. Most will have discussed it beforehand.

The point to remember: If a friend talks suicide to you, it's important to listen and to direct the person to professional help. Anyone who threatens suicide is at least sending a signal of feeling desperate or beyond hope.

Understanding Mood Disorders

14 How do the biological and social-cognitive perspectives help explain mood disorders?

From thousands of studies of the causes, treatment, and prevention of mood disorders, researchers have pulled out some common threads. Any theory of depression must explain at least the following (Lewinsohn & others, 1985, 1998, 2003).

Behaviors and thoughts change with depression. People trapped in a depressed mood are inactive and feel unmotivated. They are sensitive to negative happenings. They recall negative information. And they expect negative outcomes (my team will lose, my grades will fall, my love will fail). When the mood lifts, these behaviors and thoughts disappear. Nearly half the time, people with depression also have symptoms of another disorder, such as anxiety or substance abuse.

Depression is widespread. Depression is one of two disorders found worldwide. (The other is schizophrenia.) This suggests that depression's causes, too, must be common.

Women's risk of major depression is nearly twice as high as men's. When Gallup, during 2009, asked more than a quarter-million Americans if they had

ever been diagnosed with depression, 13 percent of men and 22 percent of women said *Yes* (Pelham, 2009). This gender gap has been found worldwide (**FIGURE 12.9**). The trend begins in adolescence; preadolescent girls are not more depression-prone than boys are (Hyde et al., 2008).

The depression gender gap fits a bigger pattern. Women are generally more vulnerable to disorders involving internal states, such as depression, anxiety, and inhibited sexual desire. Men's disorders tend to be more external—alcohol abuse, antisocial conduct, lack of impulse control. When women get sad, they often get sadder than men do. When men get mad, they often get madder than women do.

Most major depressive episodes end on their own. Most people suffering major depression eventually return to normal. The plague of depression comes and, a few weeks or months later, it goes. About half the time, it recurs within two years (Burcusa & Iacono, 2007). Recovery is more likely to endure when

- the first episode strikes later in life.
- there were few previous episodes.
- the person experiences minimal stress.
- there is ample social support (Belsher & Costello, 1988; Fergusson & Woodward, 2002; Kendler et al., 2001).

Stressful events often precede depression. A family member's death, a job loss, a marital crisis, or a physical assault increase one's risk of depression. One long-term study tracked rates of depression in 2000 people (Kendler, 1998). Among those who had experienced no stressful life event in the preceding month, the risk of depression was less than 1 percent. Among those who had experienced three such events in that month, the risk was 24 percent.

With each new generation, depression is striking earlier (now often in the late teens) and affecting more people. This has been true in Canada, the United States, England, Germany, Italy, France, Lebanon, New Zealand, Taiwan, and Puerto Rico (Collishaw et al., 2007; Cross-National Collaborative Group, 1992). In North America, today's young adults are three times more likely than their grandparents to report having recently—or ever—suffered depression. This is true even though their grandparents have been at risk for many more years.

The increased risk among young adults appears partly real, but it may also reflect cultural differences between generations. Today's young people are more willing to talk openly about their depression. Psychological processes may also be at work. We tend to forget many negative experiences over time, so older generations may

The emotional lives of men and women?

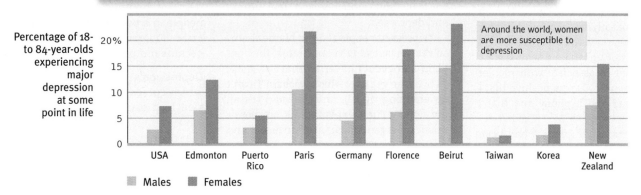

FIGURE 12.9 ● **Gender and major depression** Interviews with 38,000 adults in 10 countries confirmed what many smaller studies had found. Women's risk of major depression is nearly double that of men's. Lifetime risk of depression also varies by culture—from 1.5 percent in Taiwan to 19 percent in Beirut. (Data from Weissman et al., 1996.)

Percentage of 18- to 84-year-olds experiencing major depression at some point in life

Around the world, women are more susceptible to depression

USA   Edmonton   Puerto Rico   Paris   Germany   Florence   Beirut   Taiwan   Korea   New Zealand

Males   Females

overlook depressed feelings they had in earlier years. Both of these tendencies are examples of reasons why the biopsychosocial perspective is so useful in studying psychological disorders.

Biological Influences

Depression is a whole-body disorder. It involves genetic predispositions and biochemical imbalances as well as negative thoughts and a gloomy mood.

Genes and Depression We have long known that mood disorders run in families. The risk of major depression and bipolar disorder increases if you have a parent or sibling with the disorder (Sullivan et al., 2000). If one identical twin is diagnosed with major depressive disorder, the chances are about 1 in 2 that at some time the other twin will be, too. If one identical twin has bipolar disorder, the chances are 7 in 10 that the other twin will at some point be diagnosed similarly. Among fraternal twins, the corresponding odds are just under 2 in 10 (Tsuang & Faraone, 1990). The greater similarity among identical twins holds even among twins reared apart (DiLalla et al., 1996). Moreover, adopted people with mood disorders often have close biological relatives who have mood disorders, become dependent on alcohol, or commit suicide (Wender et al., 1986). "Emotions are postcards from our genes," observed Henry Plotkin (1994).

The Depressed Brain Scanning devices open a window on the brain's activity during depressed and manic states. During depression, brain activity slows. During mania, it increases (**FIGURE 12.10**). The left frontal lobe, which is active during positive emotions, is less active during depressed times (Davidson et al., 2002).

At least two neurotransmitter systems are at work during these periods of activity and inactivity. *Norepinephrine* increases arousal and boosts mood. It is scarce during depression and overabundant during mania. *Serotonin* is also scarce or inactive during depression (Carver et al., 2008; Plomin & McGuffin, 2003).

In Chapter 13, we will see how drugs that relieve depression tend to make more norepinephrine or serotonin available to the depressed brain. Repetitive physical exercise, such as jogging, which increases serotonin, can have a similar effect (Ilardi, 2009; Jacobs, 1994).

Psychological and Social Influences

Biological influences contribute to depression, but in the nature-nurture dance, thinking and acting also play a part. The *social-cognitive perspective* explores how people's assumptions and expectations influence what they perceive.

Depressed people see life through dark glasses. They have intensely negative views of themselves, their situation, and their future. Expecting the worst,

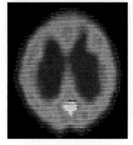
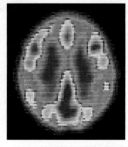
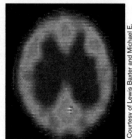

FIGURE 12.10 ● **The ups and downs of bipolar disorder** PET scans show that brain energy consumption rises and falls with the patient's emotional switches. Red areas are where the brain is using energy most rapidly.

Depressed state (May 17)   **Manic state** (May 18)   **Depressed state** (May 27)

Courtesy of Lewis Baxter and Michael E. Phelps, UCLA School of Medicine they magnify bad experiences and minimize good ones. Listen to Norman, a college professor, recalling his depression (Endler, 1982, pp. 45–49).

> I [despaired] of ever being human again. I honestly felt subhuman, lower than the lowest vermin. Furthermore, I . . . could not understand why anyone would want to associate with me, let alone love me. . . . I was positive that I was a fraud and a phony and that I didn't deserve my Ph.D. . . . I didn't deserve the research grants I had been awarded; I couldn't understand how I had written books and journal articles. . . . I must have conned a lot of people.

Negative Thoughts and Negative Moods Interact Self-defeating beliefs may arise from learned helplessness. As we saw in Chapter 10, both dogs and humans act depressed, passive, and withdrawn after experiencing uncontrollable painful events. Learned helplessness is more common in women, who may respond more strongly to stress (Hankin & Abramson, 2001; Mazure et al., 2002; Nolen-Hoeksema, 2001, 2003). Do you agree or disagree with the statement, "I feel frequently overwhelmed by all I have to do?" In a survey of women and men entering American colleges, 38 percent of the women agreed. Only 17 percent of the men agreed (Pryor et al., 2006). (Did your answer fit that pattern?)

Why are women nearly twice as vulnerable to depression (Kessler, 2001)? This higher risk may relate to women's tendency to *overthink,* to brood or ruminate (Nolan-Hoeksema, 2003). Women often vividly recall both wonderful and horrid experiences. Men recall their experiences more vaguely (Seidlitz & Diener, 1998). This gender difference in emotional memory may feed women's greater tendency to linger mentally on the meaning of negative events. It may also help explain why fewer men than women report being frequently overwhelmed on entering college.

But why do life's unavoidable failures lead some people—women and men—and not others to become depressed? The answer lies partly in their *explanatory style*—who or what they blame for their failures. Think how you might feel if you failed a test. If you can blame someone else ("What an unfair test!"), you are more likely to feel angry. If you blame yourself, you probably will feel stupid and depressed.

Depressed people tend to blame themselves. As **FIGURE 12.11** illustrates, they explain bad events in terms that are *stable* ("I'll never get over this"), *global* ("I can't do anything right"), and *internal* ("It's all my fault"). Their explanations are pessimistic, overgeneralized, self-focused, and self-blaming. The result may be a depressing sense of hopelessness (Abramson et al., 1989; Panzarella et al., 2006). As Martin Seligman has noted, "A recipe for severe depression is preexisting pessimism encountering failure" (1991, p. 78).

Critics point out a chicken-and-egg problem nesting in the social-cognitive explanation of depression. Which comes first? The pessimistic explanatory style, or the depressed mood? Certainly, the negative explanations *coincide* with a depressed mood, and they are *indicators* of depression (Barnett & Gotlib, 1988). But do they *cause* depression, any more than a speedometer's reading 70 mph *causes* a car's speed? Before or after being depressed, people's thoughts are less negative. Perhaps a depressed mood *triggers* negative thoughts. If you temporarily put people in a bad or sad mood, their memories, judgments, and expectations do become more pessimistic.

Depression's Vicious Cycle No matter which comes first, rejection and depression feed each other. Depression, as we have seen, is often brought on by events that disrupt our sense of who we are and why we are worthy. The stressful experience may be losing a job, getting divorced or rejected, and suffering physical trauma. Such disruptions in turn lead to brooding, which is rich soil for growing negative feelings. And that negativity—being withdrawn, self-focused, and complaining—can cause others to reject us (Furr & Funder, 1998; Gotlib & Hammen, 1992). Indeed, people with depression are at high risk for divorce, job loss, and other stressful life events. Weary of the person's fatigue, hopeless attitude, and lethargy, a spouse may threaten to leave,

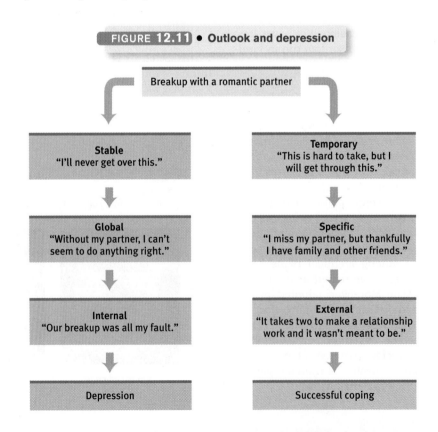

FIGURE **12.11** • **Outlook and depression**

Breakup with a romantic partner

Stable
"I'll never get over this."

Temporary
"This is hard to take, but I will get through this."

Global
"Without my partner, I can't seem to do anything right."

Specific
"I miss my partner, but thankfully I have family and other friends."

Internal
"Our breakup was all my fault."

External
"It takes two to make a relationship work and it wasn't meant to be."

Depression

Successful coping

or a boss may begin to question the person's competence. New losses and stress then plunge the already depressed person into even deeper misery. Misery may love another's company, but company does not love another's misery.

We can now assemble pieces of the depression puzzle **(FIGURE 12.12)**: (1) Stressful events interpreted through (2) a brooding, negative explanatory style create (3) a hopeless, depressed state that (4) hampers the way the person thinks and acts. These thoughts and actions in turn fuel (1) negative experiences such as rejection. Depression is a snake that bites its own tail.

It is a cycle we can all recognize. When we feel down, we think negatively and remember bad experiences. On the brighter side, if we recognize the cycle, we can break out of it. Each of the four points offers an exit. We could reverse our self-blame and negative outlook. We could turn our attention outward. We could engage in more pleasant activities and more competent behavior.

Britain's Prime Minister Winston Churchill called depression a "black dog" that periodically hounded him. President Abraham Lincoln was so withdrawn and brooding as a young man that his friends

feared he might take his own life (Kline, 1974). As their lives remind us, people can and do struggle through depression. Most regain their capacity to love, to work, to hope, and even to succeed at the highest levels.

PRACTICE TEST

THE BASICS

21. The most common reason for seeking mental health services is
    a. substance abuse.
    b. depression.
    c. bipolar disorder.
    d. obsessive-compulsive disorder.

22. Bipolar disorder affects
    a. more women than men.
    b. more men than women.
    c. women and men equally.
    d. primarily scientists and doctors.

23. Rates of depression
    a. are higher among women than among men.
    b. vary by culture.
    c. are rising with each new generation.
    d. are characterized by all of these factors.

24. Psychologists who emphasize the importance of negative perceptions, beliefs, and thoughts in depression are working within the _____ perspective.
    a. psychoanalytic
    b. biological
    c. behavioral
    d. social-cognitive

THE BIG PICTURE

12G. What does it mean to say that "depression is a whole-body disorder"?

IN YOUR EVERYDAY LIFE

▪ Can you think of a time when being in a sad mood has actually helped you in some ways? Did you reevaluate your situation or make new plans for the future?

▪ How has student life affected your moods? What advice would you have for new students?

FIGURE 12.12 • **The vicious cycle of depressed thinking** Cognitive therapists attempt to break this cycle, as we will see in Chapter 13, by changing the way depressed people process events. Psychiatrists prescribe medication to try to alter the biological roots of persistently depressed moods.

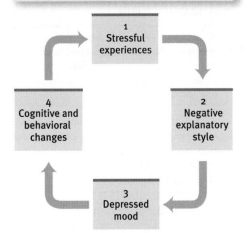

Schizophrenia

During their most severe periods, people with **schizophrenia** live in a private inner world, preoccupied with the strange ideas and images that haunt them. The word itself means "split" (*schizo*) "mind" (*phrenia*). But in this disorder, the mind is not split into multiple personalities. Rather, the mind has suffered a split from reality that shows itself in disorganized thinking, disturbed perceptions, and inappropriate emotions and actions.

As you can imagine, these traits profoundly disrupt social relationships and make it difficult to hold a job. Given a supportive environment, some eventually recover to enjoy a normal life or to experience only occasional bouts of schizophrenia. Others remain socially withdrawn and isolated for much of their life.

Symptoms of Schizophrenia

> **15** What symptoms characterize schizophrenia, and what are chronic and acute schizophrenia?

The term *schizophrenia* covers a cluster of disorders that share some features and differ in others. One difference is between those who have *positive symptoms* and those who have *negative symptoms*. Symptoms are "positive" in the sense that inappropriate behaviors are *present*. People may have hallucinations or talk in disorganized and deluded ways. They may laugh or cry or lash out in rage at inappropriate times.

Symptoms are "negative" in the sense that actions or feelings are *absent* when you might expect them to be present. People may have toneless voices, expressionless faces, or mute and rigid bodies. Because schizophrenia is a cluster of disorders, these varied symptoms may have more than one cause.

---

schizophrenia a group of severe disorders characterized by disorganized and delusional thinking, disturbed perceptions, and inappropriate emotions and actions.

Craig Geiser

2006

Art by someone diagnosed with schizophrenia:
Commenting on the kind of art work shown here
(from Craig Geiser's 2010 art exhibit in
Michigan), poet and art critic John Ashbery
wrote: "The lure of the work is strong, but so is the
terror of the unanswerable riddles it proposes."

Disorganized Thinking

Imagine trying to communicate with Maxine, a young woman whose thoughts spill out in no logical order. Her biographer, Susan Sheehan (1982, p. 25), observed her saying aloud to no one in particular, "This morning, when I was at Hillside [Hospital], I was making a movie. I was surrounded by movie stars. . . . I'm Mary Poppins. Is this room painted blue to get me upset? My grandmother died four weeks after my eighteenth birthday."

As this strange speech illustrates, the thinking of a person with schizophrenia is fragmented and often distorted by false beliefs called **delusions.** Maxine believed she was Mary Poppins. People with paranoid tendencies often believe they are being threatened or pursued.

Disorganized thinking may appear as *word salad,* jumbled ideas that make no sense even within sentences. One young man begged for "a little more allegro in the treatment," and suggested that "liberationary movement with a view to the widening of the horizon" will "ergo extort some wit in lectures."

Disturbed Perceptions

Delusions are false *beliefs. Hallucinations* are false *perceptions.* People with schizophrenia sometimes see, feel, taste, or smell things that are not there. Most often, however, the hallucinations are sounds, often voices making insulting remarks or giving orders. The voices may tell the person that she is bad or that she must burn herself with a cigarette lighter. When the unreal seems real, the resulting perceptions are at best bizarre, at worst terrifying. Imagine your own reaction if a dream broke into your waking consciousness. Stuart Emmons described his experience: "When someone asks me to explain schizophrenia I tell them, you know how sometimes in your dreams you are in them yourself and some of them feel like real nightmares? My schizophrenia was like I was walking through a dream. But everything around me was real. At times, today's world seems so boring and I wonder if I would like to step back into the schizophrenic dream, but then I remember all the scary and horrifying experiences" (Emmons et al., 1997).

Inappropriate Emotions and Actions

The emotions of schizophrenia are often utterly inappropriate, split off from reality. Maxine laughed after recalling her grandmother's death. On other occasions, she cried when others laughed, or became angry for no apparent reason. Others with schizophrenia lapse into an emotionless *flat affect,* a zombielike state of no apparent feeling.

Inappropriate motor behavior takes many forms. Some patients perform senseless, compulsive acts, such as continually rocking or rubbing an arm. Others may remain motionless for hours (a condition called *catatonia*) and then become agitated.

Onset and Development of Schizophrenia

Nearly 1 in 100 people will develop schizophrenia this year, joining the estimated 24 million worldwide who suffer this dreaded

disorder (WHO, 2008b). It typically strikes as young people are maturing into adulthood. It knows no national boundaries, and it affects both men and women. Men tend to be struck earlier, more severely, and slightly more often (Picchioni & Murray, 2007). In studies of Swedish and Danish men, the risk was highest for those who were thin and young, and for those who had not been breast-fed (Sørensen et al., 2005, 2006; Zammit et al., 2007).

For some, schizophrenia appears suddenly, seemingly as a reaction to stress. For others, as was the case with Maxine, schizophrenia develops gradually, emerging from a long history of social inadequacy. This may help explain why people predisposed to schizophrenia often are found in the lower socioeconomic levels, or even homeless.

One rule holds true around the world (World Health Organization, 1979): When schizophrenia is a slow-developing process (called *chronic,* or *process, schizophrenia*), recovery is doubtful. Social withdrawal, a negative symptom, is common among those with chronic schizophrenia. Men more often exhibit negative symptoms and chronic schizophrenia (Räsänen et al., 2000).

Recovery is much more likely when a well-adjusted person develops schizophrenia rapidly (called *acute,* or *reactive, schizophrenia*) following some sort of stress. People with reactive schizophrenia more often have the positive symptoms that respond to drug therapy (Fenton & McGlashan, 1991, 1994; Fowles, 1992).

Understanding Schizophrenia

16 | What do we know about the brain chemistry, functions, and structures associated with schizophrenia, and what have we learned about prenatal risk factors?

Schizophrenia is the most dreaded psychological disorder. It is also one of the most heavily researched. Most of the new research studies link it with abnormal brain tissue and activity, and with genetic predispositions. Schizophrenia is a disease of the brain exhibited in symptoms of the mind.

Brain Abnormalities

Could chemical imbalances in the brain explain schizophrenia? Scientists have long known that strange behavior can have strange chemical causes. Have you ever heard the phrase "mad as a hatter"? The saying dates back to the behavior of British hatmakers whose brains were slowly poisoned as they used their tongue and lips to moisten the brims of mercury-laden felt hats (Smith, 1983). Could schizophrenia symptoms have a similar biochemical key? Scientists are tracking the mechanisms by which chemicals produce hallucinations and other symptoms.

Dopamine Overactivity One possible answer emerged when researchers examined schizophrenia patients' brains after death. They found an excess number of *dopamine* receptors (Seeman et al., 1993; Wong et al., 1986). What could this mean? Perhaps a high level of dopamine could intensify brain signals, creating positive symptoms such as hallucinations and paranoia. Sure enough, other evidence confirmed this idea. Drugs that block dopamine receptors often lessen the positive symptoms of schizophrenia. Drugs that increase dopamine levels, such as amphetamines and cocaine, sometimes intensify them (Seeman, 2007; Swerdlow & Koob, 1987).

Abnormal Brain Activity and Anatomy Brain scans show that abnormal brain activity and brain structures accompany schizophrenia. Some patients have abnormally low activity in the brain's frontal lobes, which are critical for reasoning, planning, and problem solving (Morey et al., 2005; Pettegrew et al., 1993; Resnick, 1992).

One study took PET scans of brain activity while people were hallucinating (Silbersweig et al., 1995). When patients heard a voice or saw something, their brain became vigorously active in several core regions. One was the thalamus, the structure that filters incoming sensory signals and transmits them to the brain's cortex. Another PET scan study of people

Ralph Hutchings/Visuals Unlimited, Inc.

with paranoia found increased activity in the amygdala, a fear-processing center (Epstein et al., 1998).

In schizophrenia, areas of the brain become enlarged and fill with fluid; cerebral tissue also shrinks (Goldman et al., 2009; Wright et al., 2000). "People with schizophrenia are losing brain tissue at a more rapid rate than healthy people," notes researcher Nancy Andreasen (2008). The greater the shrinkage, the more severe the thought disorder (Collinson et al., 2003; Nelson et al., 1998; Shenton, 1992). Some studies have even found brain abnormalities in people who would *later* develop this disorder (Boos et al., 2007; Job et al., 2006).

The bottom line of various studies is clear. Schizophrenia involves not one isolated brain abnormality but problems with several brain regions and their interconnections (Andreasen, 1997, 2001).

Prenatal Environment and Risk

What causes the brain abnormalities that are found in people with schizophrenia? Some researchers blame low birth weight

Chris Usher

Studying schizophrenia: Psychiatrist E. Fuller Torrey is collecting the brains of hundreds of those who died as young adults and suffered disorders such as schizophrenia and bipolar disorder. Torrey is making tissue samples available to researchers worldwide.

or lack of oxygen during delivery (Buka et al., 1999; Zornberg et al., 2000). Famine may also increase risks. People conceived during the peak of World War II's Dutch famine developed schizophrenia at twice the normal rate. Those conceived during the famine of 1959 to 1961 in eastern China also displayed this doubled rate (St. Clair et al., 2005; Susser et al., 1996).

Let's consider another possible culprit. Might a midpregnancy viral infection impair fetal brain development (Patterson, 2007)? Can you imagine some ways to test this fetal-virus idea? Scientists have asked these questions.

- *Are people at increased risk of schizophrenia if, during the middle of their fetal development, their country experienced a flu epidemic?* The repeated answer is Yes (Mednick et al., 1994; Murray et al., 1992; Wright et al., 1995).

- *Are people who are born in densely populated areas, where viral diseases spread more readily, at greater risk for schizophrenia?* The answer, confirmed in a study of 1.75 million Danes, is Yes (Jablensky, 1999; Mortensen, 1999).

- *Are people born during the winter and spring months—after the fall-winter flu season—also at increased risk?* The answer is again Yes, and the risk increases from 5 to 8 percent (Torrey et al., 1997, 2002).

- *In the Southern Hemisphere, where the seasons are the reverse of the Northern Hemisphere, are the months of above-average schizophrenia births similarly reversed?* Again, the answer is Yes. In Australia, people born between August and October are at greater risk. But there is an exception. For people born in the Northern Hemisphere, who later moved to Australia, the risk is greater if they were born between January and March (McGrath et al., 1995, 1999).

delusions false beliefs, often of persecution or grandeur, that may accompany schizophrenia and other disorders.

- *Are mothers who report being sick with influenza during pregnancy more likely to bear children who develop schizophrenia?* In one study of nearly 8000 women, the answer was Yes. The schizophrenia risk increased from the customary 1 percent to about 2 percent. But that increase applied only to mothers who were infected during their second trimester (Brown et al., 2000).

- *Does blood drawn from pregnant women whose offspring develop schizophrenia suggest a viral infection?* In a huge California study, which collected blood samples from some 20,000 pregnant women during the 1950s and 1960s, the answer was again Yes. Some children born of those pregnancies were later diagnosed with schizophrenia. Antibodies in the blood samples indicated whether the women had been exposed to influenza. When the exposure took place during the first half of the pregnancy, the child's risk of developing schizophrenia tripled. Exposure to flu during the second half of the pregnancy produced no such increase (Brown et al., 2004).

Taken together, these lines of evidence suggest a key to the schizophrenia puzzle: Prenatal viral infections can contribute to the development of schizophrenia. This finding strengthens the U.S. government recommendation that "women who expect to be more than three months pregnant during the flu season" should have a flu shot (CDC, 2006).

Genetics and Risk

17 | Does research indicate a genetic contribution to schizophrenia?

Prenatal viruses increase the odds that a child will develop schizophrenia. But many women get the flu during their second trimester of pregnancy, and only 2 percent of their children develop schizophrenia. WHY DOES PRENATAL EXPOSURE TO THE FLU ◄ VIRUS PUT SOME CHILDREN AT RISK BUT NOT OTHERS? Could the answer be that some people are more vulnerable because they have inherited a predisposition to this disorder? The evidence indicates the answer is Yes. For most people, the odds of being

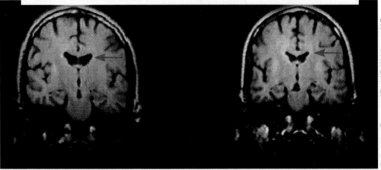

Schizophrenia in identical twins: When twins differ, only the one afflicted with schizophrenia typically has enlarged, fluid-filled cranial cavities (left) (Suddath et al., 1990). The difference between the twins implies some nongenetic factor, such as a virus, is also at work.

Both photos: Courtesy of Daniel R. Weinberger, M.D., NIH–NIMH/NSC

Schizophrenia   No schizophrenia

diagnosed with schizophrenia are nearly 1 in 100. For those who have a sibling or parent with schizophrenia, the odds increase to 1 in 10. And if the affected sibling is an identical twin, the odds are close to 5 in 10 **(FIGURE 12.13)**. Those odds are unchanged even if the twins are reared apart (Plomin et al., 1997). (Only a dozen or so of these cases are on record.)

But wait! Identical twins also share a prenatal environment. So it is possible that shared germs as well as shared genes produce identical twin similarities. And there is some evidence to support this idea.

About two-thirds of identical twins also share a placenta and the blood it supplies. The other sets of identical twins have two separate placentas. Sharing a

placenta raises the odds of later sharing a schizophrenia diagnosis. If identical twins had separate placentas, the chances are 1 in 10. If they shared a placenta, the co-twin's chances of having the disorder are 6 in 10 (Davis et al., 1995a,b; Phelps et al., 1997). A likely explanation: Identical twins who share a placenta are more likely to share the same prenatal viruses.

How, then, could we untangle the genetic influences from the environmental influences on this disorder? Adoption studies offer some clues. Children adopted by someone who develops schizophrenia seldom "catch" the disorder. Rather, adopted children have a higher risk of developing schizophrenia if one of their *biological* parents has this disorder.

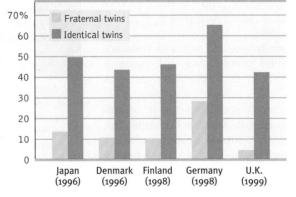

FIGURE 12.13 ● **Risk of developing schizophrenia** The lifetime risk of developing schizophrenia varies for family members of a person with this disorder. The closer the genetic relationship, the higher the risk. Across countries, barely more than 1 in 10 fraternal twins, but some 5 in 10 identical twins, share a schizophrenia diagnosis. (Adapted from Gottesman, 2001.)

Schizophrenia risk for twins of those diagnosed with schizophrenia

70%

- Fraternal twins
- Identical twins

60
50
40
30
20
10
0

Japan (1996)   Denmark (1996)   Finland (1998)   Germany (1998)   U.K. (1999)

Adoption studies confirm that the genetic link is real (Gottesman, 1991).

The search is on for specific genes that might lead to schizophrenia-related brain abnormalities. Some of these genes influence the activity of dopamine and other neurotransmitters in the brain. Part of the search has focused on comparing DNA samples from several thousand people, some who have been diagnosed with schizophrenia, some who do not have this disorder. The somewhat discouraging news is that the number of culprit genes is turning out to be huge. Researchers have turned up thousands of gene differences, each exerting small effects (International Schizophrenia Consortium, 2009). Moreover, environmental factors—such as prenatal viral infections, nutritional deprivation, and oxygen deprivation at birth—may somehow help to "turn on" the genes that put some of us at higher risk for this disease. As we have seen in so many different contexts, our genes sculpt our brain, and our brain interacts with our environment to direct our behavior. Neither hand claps alone.

* * *

Most of us can relate more easily to the ups and downs of mood disorders than to the strange thoughts, perceptions, and behaviors of schizophrenia. Sometimes our thoughts do jump around, but we do not talk nonsensically. Occasionally, we feel unjustly suspicious of someone, but we do not believe the world is plotting against us. Often, our perceptions err, but rarely do we see or hear things that are not there. We have felt regret after laughing at someone's misfortune, but we rarely giggle in response to bad news. At times we just want to be alone, but we do not live in social isolation. However, millions of people around the world do talk strangely, suffer delusions, hear nonexistent voices, see things that are not there, laugh or cry at inappropriate times, or withdraw into private imaginary worlds. The quest to solve the cruel puzzle of schizophrenia therefore continues, more vigorously than ever.

PRACTICE TEST

THE BASICS

25. People with schizophrenia may hear voices when no one is speaking. This is an example of a(n)
    a. flat emotion.
    b. inappropriate emotion.
    c. word salad.
    d. hallucination.

26. A person who has schizophrenia and has positive symptoms is most likely to experience
    a. catatonia.
    b. delusions.
    c. withdrawal.
    d. flat emotion.

27. Chances for recovery from schizophrenia are best when
    a. onset is sudden, in response to stress.
    b. deterioration occurs gradually.
    c. no environmental causes can be identified.
    d. there is a detectable brain abnormality.

THE BIG PICTURE

12H. What factors contribute to the onset and development of schizophrenia?

IN YOUR EVERYDAY LIFE

▪ Now that you know more about schizophrenia, do you think the media accurately portray the behavior of people with this disorder? Why or why not?

Answers: 25. d, 26. b, 27. a. Answers to The Big Picture questions can be found in Appendix B at the end of the book.

Terms and Concepts to Remember

psychological disorder, p. 318

medical model, p. 319

DSM-IV-TR, p. 320

anxiety disorders, p. 322

generalized anxiety disorder, p. 322

panic disorder, p. 323

phobia, p. 323

obsessive-compulsive disorder (OCD), p. 323

post-traumatic stress disorder (PTSD), p. 324

dissociative disorders, p. 326

dissociative identity disorder (DID), p. 326

personality disorders, p. 327

antisocial personality disorder, p. 327

substance-related disorders, p. 329

psychoactive drug, p. 329

tolerance, p. 329

addiction, p. 329

withdrawal, p. 329

physical dependence, p. 329

psychological dependence, p. 329

depressants, p. 330

alcohol dependence, p. 330

barbiturates, p. 331

opiates, p. 331

stimulants, p. 332

amphetamines, p. 332

nicotine, p. 332

methamphetamine, p. 333

Ecstasy (MDMA), p. 333

hallucinogens, p. 334

LSD, p. 334

near-death experience, p. 334

THC, p. 334

mood disorders, p. 338

major depressive disorder, p. 338

bipolar disorder, p. 339

mania, p. 339

schizophrenia, p. 343

delusions, p. 344

Multiple-choice self-tests and more may be found at www.worthpublishers.com/myers

What Is a Psychological Disorder?

1 **What is a psychological disorder, and how do psychologists distinguish between normal and disordered behavior?**

■ What is considered "abnormal" varies with context, culture, and time in history.

■ Psychologists define *psychological disorder* as an ongoing pattern of thoughts, feelings, or behaviors that are deviant (different from your cultural norm), distressful, and dysfunctional (interfering with everyday life).

2 **How is our understanding of psychological disorders affected by whether we use a medical model or a biopsychosocial approach?**

■ The *medical model:* Psychological disorders are considered mental illnesses, diagnosed based on symptoms, and cured through therapy, sometimes in a hospital.

■ The biopsychosocial approach: Disordered behavior comes from the interaction of biological characteristics (genes and physiology), psychological dynamics, and social-cultural circumstances.

3 **How and why do clinicians classify psychological disorders, and why do some psychologists criticize the use of diagnostic labels?**

■ The Diagnostic and Statistical Manual of Mental Disorders *(DSM-IV-TR)* lists and describes psychological disorders.

■ Diagnostic labels provide a common language and shared concepts for communications and research.

■ Labels can create preconceptions that cause us to view a person differently, and then look for evidence to confirm that view.

Anxiety Disorders

4 **What are the main anxiety disorders, and how do they differ from the ordinary worries and fears we all experience?**

■ It's common to feel uneasy; when those feelings are intense and persistent they may be classified as disordered.

■ *Anxiety disorders*: distressing, persistent anxiety or maladaptive behaviors that reduce anxiety.

■ *Generalized anxiety disorder*: continuing state of tension and apprehension for no apparent reason.

■ *Panic disorder:* anxiety escalating into episodes of intense dread.

■ *Phobia:* irrational fear and avoidance of a specific object or situation.

■ *Obsessive-compulsive disorder:* Persistent and repetitive thoughts (obsessions) and actions (compulsions).

■ *Post-traumatic stress disorder:* four or more weeks of haunting memories, nightmares, social withdrawal, jumpy anxiety, and sleep problems following a traumatic event.

5 **How do learning and biology contribute to the feelings and thoughts that mark anxiety disorders?**

■ Freud's now-dated view: Anxiety disorders discharge repressed impulses.

■ The learning perspective: Anxiety disorders come from fear conditioning (including stimulus generalization and reinforcement of fearful behaviors) and observational learning.

■ The biological perspective: Anxiety disorders result from inherited temperament differences; learned fears that have altered brain pathways; and outdated, inherited responses that had survival value for our distant ancestors.

Dissociative and Personality Disorders

6 **What are dissociative disorders, and why are they controversial?**

■ *Dissociative disorders:* Conscious awareness becomes separated from previous memories, thoughts, and feelings.

■ Skeptics say: *Dissociative identity disorder* (*DID;* multiple personality disorder) increased dramatically in the late twentieth century. DID is rarely found outside North America. Critics say DID may reflect role-playing by people who are vulnerable to therapists' suggestions.

7 **What characteristics are typical of personality disorders in general, and what biological and psychological factors are associated with antisocial personality disorder?**

■ *Personality disorders:* enduring, maladaptive patterns of behavior that impair social functioning.

■ *Antisocial personality disorder:* aggressive, fearless behavior and lack of conscience; attributed to genetic influences, sometimes in combination with childhood abuse.

Substance-Related Disorders

8 **What is a substance-related disorder, and what are tolerance, addiction, and dependence?**

- *Substance-related disorder:* Maladaptive pattern of substance use that leads to significant self-harm or distress.
- *Tolerance:* requiring larger doses of a drug to achieve the same effect; produced by continued use of the drug.
- *Addiction:* compulsive drug craving and use.
- In *physical dependence,* the need for the drug is physiological, and ending the drug use may produce *withdrawal* symptoms.
- In *psychological dependence,* the person relies on the drug to relieve stress or negative emotions, but may not be physically addicted.

9 **How do depressants, such as alcohol, influence neural activity and behavior?**

- *Depressants* (alcohol, *barbiturates, opiates*) dampen neural activity and slow body functions.
- Alcohol disinhibits, increasing the likelihood that we will act on our impulses, whether helpful or harmful.
- Alcohol slows neural processing, disrupts memory, and shrinks the brain in those with *alcohol dependence* (marked by tolerance, withdrawal if use is suspended, and a drive to continue using).

10 **How do the major stimulants affect neural activity and behavior?**

- *Stimulants* (caffeine, *nicotine, amphetamines, methamphetamine,* cocaine, *Ecstasy*) excite neural activity, speed up body functions, and lead to heightened energy and mood. All are highly addictive.
- Methamphetamine may permanently reduce dopamine levels.
- Ecstasy (MDMA), which is also a mild hallucinogen, may damage serotonin-producing neurons and impair physical and cognitive functions.

11 **What are the physiological and psychological effects of LSD and marijuana?**

- *Hallucinogens* (*LSD,* marijuana) distort perceptions and evoke hallucinations (sensory images in the absence of sensory input), some of which resemble the altered consciousness of *near-death experiences.*
- *THC,* the major ingredient in marijuana, contributes to pain relief.

12 **What biological, psychological, and social-cultural factors help explain why some people abuse mind-altering drugs?**

- Some people are biologically more vulnerable to drugs.
- Psychological factors (stress, depression, hopelessness) and social-cultural influences (peer pressure, cultural values) also affect drug use.

Mood Disorders

13 **What are the main mood disorders, and why do people attempt suicide?**

- *Mood disorders:* characterized by emotional extremes.
- *Major depressive disorder:* two or more weeks of seriously depressed moods and feelings of worthlessness, with little interest in most activities. Not caused by drugs or a medical condition.
- *Bipolar disorder:* mood swings between depression and *mania* (hyperactive and wildly optimistic, impulsive feelings and behavior).
- People with depression and those with chronic pain are more likely than others to attempt suicide. People who talk about suicide should be taken seriously.

14 **How do the biological and social-cognitive perspectives help explain mood disorders?**

- Biological influences: Genetic predispositions and abnormalities in brain structures and functions.
- Psychological and social influences: Cycles of self-defeating beliefs, learned helplessness, a negative outlook, and stressful experiences.

Schizophrenia

15 **What symptoms characterize schizophrenia, and what are chronic and acute schizophrenia?**

- *Schizophrenia* (a group of disorders; typically strikes during late adolescence) includes symptoms of disorganized and *delusional* thinking (with false beliefs), disturbed perceptions, and inappropriate emotions and actions.
- Positive symptoms: the presence of inappropriate behaviors; negative symptoms: the absence of appropriate behaviors.
- Chronic, or process, schizophrenia is slow-developing and difficult to treat. Acute, or reactive, schizophrenia comes on rapidly following stress and is more likely to respond to treatment.

16 **What do we know about the brain chemistry, functions, and structures associated with schizophrenia, and what have we learned about prenatal risk factors?**

- People with schizophrenia have more receptors for dopamine, which may intensify the positive symptoms of schizophrenia.
- Brain scans reveal abnormal activity in the frontal lobes, thalamus, and amygdala.
- Brain abnormalities associated with schizophrenia include enlarged, fluid-filled cerebral cavities and loss of cerebral cortex.
- Low birth weight, famine, or a mid-pregnancy virus may impair fetal brain development.

17 **Does research indicate a genetic contribution to schizophrenia?**

- When one identical twin has schizophrenia, the other is more likely but not certain to get it as well.
- A genetic predisposition seems to interact with environmental factors to produce schizophrenia.

THERAPY

Kay Redfield Jamison, an award-winning clinical psychologist and world expert on the emotional extremes of bipolar disorder, knows her subject firsthand. "For as long as I can remember," she recalled in *An Unquiet Mind*, "I was frighteningly, although wonderfully, beholden to moods. Intensely emotional as a child, mercurial as a young girl, first severely depressed as an adolescent, and then unrelentingly caught up in the cycles of manic-depressive illness by the time I began my professional life, I became, both by necessity and intellectual inclination, a student of moods" (1995, pp. 4–5). Her life was blessed with times of intense sensitivity and passionate energy. But like her father's, it was also at times plagued by reckless spending, racing conversation, and sleeplessness, alternating with swings into "the blackest caves of the mind."

Then, "in the midst of utter confusion," she made a sane and profoundly helpful decision. Risking embarrassment, she made an appointment with a therapist, a psychiatrist she would visit weekly for years to come.

> He kept me alive a thousand times over. He saw me through madness, despair, wonderful and terrible love affairs, disillusionments and triumphs, recurrences of illness, an almost fatal suicide attempt, the death of a man I greatly loved, and the enormous pleasures and aggravations of my professional life. . . . He was very tough, as well as very kind, and even though he understood more than anyone how much I felt I was losing—in energy, vivacity, and originality—by taking medication, he never was seduced into losing sight of the overall perspective of how costly, damaging, and life threatening my illness was. . . . Although I went to him to be treated for an illness, he taught me . . . the total beholdenness of brain to mind and mind to brain (pp. 87–89).

"Psychotherapy heals," Jamison reports. "It makes some sense of the confusion, reins in the terrifying thoughts and feelings, returns some control and hope and possibility from it all."

In this chapter, we consider some of the options available to therapists and the people who seek their help.

Treating Psychological Disorders

1 How do psychotherapy, biomedical therapy, and an eclectic approach to therapy differ?

The long history of efforts to treat psychological disorders has included a bewildering mix of harsh and gentle methods. Well-meaning individuals have cut holes in people's heads and restrained, bled, or "beat the devil" out of them. They have administered drugs and electric shocks. But they also have given warm baths and massages and placed people in sunny, serene environments. And they have talked with their patients about childhood experiences, current feelings, and maladaptive thoughts and behaviors.

Reformers Philippe Pinel, Dorothea Dix, and others pushed for gentler, more humane treatments and for constructing mental hospitals. Since the 1950s, the introduction of effective drug therapies and community-based treatment programs have emptied most of those hospitals.

Today's therapies can be classified into two main categories. The therapist's training and expertise as well as the disorder itself influence the choice of treatment. In **psychotherapy,** a trained therapist uses psychological techniques to assist someone seeking to overcome difficulties or achieve personal growth. **Biomedical therapy** offers medication or other biological treatments.

Some therapists combine techniques. Jamison received psychotherapy in her meetings with her psychiatrist, and she took medications to control her

The history of treatment: Visitors to eighteenth-century mental hospitals paid to gawk at patients, as though they were viewing zoo animals. William Hogarth's (1697–1764) painting (left) captured one of these visits to London's St. Mary of Bethlehem hospital (commonly called Bedlam). Benjamin Rush (1746–1813), a founder of the movement for more humane treatment of the mentally ill, designed the chair on the right "for the benefit of maniacal patients." He believed the restraints would help them regain their sanity.

The Granger Collection

wild mood swings. Indeed, half of all psychotherapists describe themselves as taking an **eclectic approach,** using a blend of therapies. Many patients receive psychotherapy combined with medication.

Hemera Technologies/Jupiterimages

Let's look first at the psychotherapy options for those who are treated with these "talk therapies."

Bettmann/CORBIS

Dorothea Dix (1802–1887): "I . . . call your attention to the state of the Insane Persons confined within this Commonwealth, in cages."

The Psychological Therapies

Among the dozens of types of psychotherapy, we will look at only the most influential. Each is built on one or more of psychology's major theories: psychoanalytic, humanistic, behavioral, and cognitive. Most of these techniques can be used one-on-one or in groups.

Psychoanalysis

2 What are the aims, methods, and criticisms of psychoanalysis?

Sigmund Freud's **psychoanalysis** was the first of the psychological therapies. Few clinicians today practice therapy as Freud did, but his work deserves discussion as part of the foundation for treating psychological disorders.

Goals

Psychoanalytic theory presumes that healthier, less anxious living becomes possible when people release the energy they had previously devoted to id-ego-superego conflicts (see Chapter 11). Freud's therapy aimed to bring patients' repressed or disowned feelings into conscious awareness. By helping them reclaim their unconscious thoughts and feelings and giving them *insight* into the origins of their disorders, he aimed to help them take responsibility for their own growth.

Techniques

Psychoanalysis is historical reconstruction. Psychoanalytic theory emphasizes the formative power of childhood experiences, their ability to mold the adult.

"I'm more interested in hearing about the eggs you're hiding from yourself."

Thus, it aims to excavate the past in hope of loosening its bonds on the present. After discarding hypnosis as an unreliable excavator, Freud turned to *free association.*

Imagine yourself as a patient using free association. First, you relax, perhaps by lying on a couch. As the psychoanalyst sits out of your line of vision, you say aloud whatever comes to your mind. At one moment, you're relating a childhood memory. At another, you're describing a dream or recent experience. It sounds easy, but soon you notice how often you edit your thoughts as you speak. You pause for a second before uttering an embarrassing thought. You omit what seems trivial, irrelevant, or shameful. Sometimes your mind goes blank or you clutch, unable to remember important details. You may joke or change the subject to something less threatening.

To the analyst, these mental blocks indicate **resistance.** They hint that anxiety lurks and you are defending against sensitive material. The analyst will note your resistances and then provide insight into their meaning. If offered at the right

moment, this **interpretation**—of, say, your not wanting to talk about your mother—may illuminate the underlying wishes, feelings, and conflicts you are avoiding. The analyst may also offer an explanation of how this resistance fits with other pieces of your psychological puzzle, including those based on analysis of your dream content.

Over many such sessions, your relationship patterns surface in your interaction with your therapist. You may find yourself experiencing strong positive or negative feelings for your analyst. The analyst may suggest you are **transferring** feelings, such as dependency or mingled love and anger, that you experienced in earlier relationships with family members or other important people. By exposing such feelings, you may gain insight into your current relationships.

Relatively few U.S. therapists now offer traditional psychoanalysis. Its underlying theory is not supported by scientific research (Chapter 11). Analysts' interpretations cannot be proven or disproven. And psychoanalysis takes time and money, often years of several expensive sessions each week. Some of these problems have been addressed in a contemporary psychodynamic perspective that has evolved from psychoanalysis.

Psychodynamic Therapy

3 How is psychodynamic therapy derived from psychoanalysis? How does it differ?

Psychodynamic therapists don't talk much about id, ego, and superego. Instead they try to help people understand their current symptoms by focusing on themes across important relationships, including childhood experiences and the therapist relationship. Rather than lying on a couch, out of the therapist's line of vision, patients meet with their therapist face to face. But these meetings take place once or twice a week (rather than several times weekly) for only a few weeks or months (rather than several years).

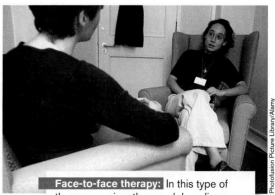

Face-to-face therapy: In this type of therapy session, the couch has disappeared. But the influence of psychoanalytic theory may not have, especially if the therapist seeks information from the patient's childhood and helps the patient reclaim unconscious feelings.

In these meetings, patients explore and gain perspective on defended-against thoughts and feelings. Therapist David Shapiro (1999, p. 8) illustrates with the case of a young man who had told women that

psychotherapy treatment involving psychological techniques; consists of interactions between a trained therapist and someone seeking to overcome psychological difficulties or achieve personal growth.

biomedical therapy prescribed medications or procedures that act directly on the person's physiology.

eclectic approach an approach to psychotherapy that, depending on the client's problems, uses techniques from various forms of therapy.

psychoanalysis Sigmund Freud's therapeutic technique. Freud believed that the patient's free associations, resistances, dreams, and transferences—and the therapist's interpretations of them—released previously repressed feelings, allowing the patient to gain self-insight.

resistance in psychoanalysis, the blocking from consciousness of anxiety-laden material.

interpretation in psychoanalysis, the analyst's noting supposed dream meanings, resistances, and other significant behaviors and events in order to promote insight.

transference in psychoanalysis, the patient's transfer to the analyst of emotions linked with other relationships (such as love or hatred for a parent).

psychodynamic therapy a Freud-influenced perspective that sees behavior, thinking, and emotions in terms of unconscious motives.

"You say, 'Off with her head' but what I'm hearing is, 'I feel neglected.'"

he loved them, when knowing well that he didn't. They expected it, so he said it. But then with his wife, who wishes he would say that he loves her, he finds he "cannot" do that—"I don't know why, but I can't."

Therapist: Do you mean, then, that if you could, you would like to?

Patient: Well, I don't know. . . . Maybe I can't say it because I'm not sure it's true. Maybe I don't love her.

Further interactions reveal that he can't express love because it would feel "mushy" and "soft" and therefore unmanly. He is "in conflict with himself, and he is cut off from the nature of that conflict." Shapiro noted that with such patients, who are estranged from themselves, psychodynamic therapists "are in a position to introduce them to themselves. We can restore their awareness of their own wishes and feelings, and their awareness, as well, of their reactions against those wishes and feelings."

Humanistic Therapies

4 **What are the basic themes of humanistic therapy, and what are the goals of Rogers' client-centered approach?**

The humanistic perspective (Chapter 11) has emphasized people's potential for self-fulfillment. Not surprisingly, humanistic therapies attempt to reduce the conflicts that interfere with natural development and growth. This is a goal that humanistic therapies share with psychoanalytic therapies. But humanistic therapists differ from psychoanalytic therapists in many other ways:

- *Humanistic therapists aim to boost people's self-fulfillment by helping them grow in self-awareness and self-acceptance.*
- *Promoting this growth, not curing illness, is the focus of therapy.* Thus, those in therapy are called "clients" or just "persons" rather than "patients" (a change many other therapists have adopted).
- *The path to growth is taking immediate responsibility for one's feelings and actions, rather than uncovering possible hidden causes.*

- *Conscious thoughts are more important than the unconscious.*
- *The present and future are more important than the past.* The goal is to explore feelings as they occur, rather than achieving insights into the childhood origins of the feelings.

All of these themes are present in the widely used humanistic technique that Carl Rogers (1902–1987) developed and called **client-centered therapy.** This therapy, now often called *person-centered therapy,* focuses on the person's conscious self-perceptions. It is *nondirective*—the therapist listens, without judging or interpreting, and refrains from directing the client toward certain insights.

Rogers (1961, 1980) believed that most people already possess the resources for growth. He encouraged therapists to foster that growth by exhibiting *genuineness, acceptance,* and *empathy.* By being *genuine,* therapists will express their true feelings. By being *accepting,* therapists may help clients feel freer and more open to change. By showing *empathy,* by sensing and reflecting their clients' feelings, therapists can help clients experience a deeper self-understanding and self-acceptance (Hill & Nakayama, 2000). As Rogers (1980, p. 10) explained,

Hearing has consequences. When I truly hear a person and the meanings that are important to him at that moment, hearing not simply his words, but him, and when I let him know that I have heard his own private personal meanings, many things happen. There is first of all a grateful look. He feels released. He wants to tell me more about his world. He surges forth in a new sense of freedom. He becomes more open to the process of change.

I have often noticed that the more deeply I hear the meanings of the person, the more there is that happens. Almost always, when a person realizes he has been deeply heard, his eyes moisten. I think in some real sense he is weeping for joy. It is as though he were saying, "Thank God, somebody heard me. Someone knows what it's like to be me."

To Rogers, "hearing" was **active listening.** The therapist echoes, restates, and clarifies what the client expresses (verbally or nonverbally). The therapist also acknowledges those expressed feelings. Active listening is now an accepted part of counseling practices in many schools, colleges, and clinics. Counselors listen attentively. They interrupt only to restate and confirm feelings, to accept what was said, or to check their understanding of something. In the following brief excerpt, note how Rogers tried to provide a psychological mirror that would help the client see himself more clearly.

Active listening: Carl Rogers (right) empathized with a client during this group therapy session.

Michael Rougier/*Life* Magazine © Time Warner, Inc.

Rogers: Feeling that now, hm? That you're just no good to yourself, no good to anybody. Never will be any good to anybody. Just that you're completely worthless, huh?—Those really are lousy feelings. Just feel that you're no good at all, hm?

Client: Yeah. (*Muttering in low, discouraged voice*) That's what this guy I went to town with just the other day told me.

Rogers: This guy that you went to town with really told you that you were no good? Is that what you're saying? Did I get that right?

Client: M-hm.

Rogers: I guess the meaning of that if I get it right is that here's somebody that meant something to you and what does he think of you? Why, he's told you that he thinks you're no good at all. And that just really knocks the props out from under you. (*Client weeps quietly.*) It just brings the tears. (*Silence of 20 seconds*)

Client: (*Rather defiantly*) I don't care though.

Rogers: You tell yourself you don't care at all, but somehow I guess some part of you cares because some part of you weeps over it. (Meador & Rogers, 1984, p. 167)

Can a therapist be a perfect mirror, critics have asked, without selecting and interpreting what is reflected? Rogers agreed that no one can be totally nondirective. Nevertheless, he said, the therapist's most important contribution is to accept and understand the client. Given a nonjudgmental, grace-filled environment that provides **unconditional positive regard,** people may accept even their worst traits and ► feel valued and whole. HOW CAN WE DEVELOP OUR OWN COMMUNICATION STRENGTHS BY LISTENING MORE ACTIVELY IN OUR FRIENDSHIPS? These three hints may help:

1. *Summarize.* Check your understanding by repeating your friend's statements in your own words.

2. *Invite clarification.* "What might be an example of that?" may encourage your friend to say more.

3. *Reflect feelings.* "It sounds frustrating" might mirror what you're sensing from your friend's body language and intensity.

Behavior Therapies

5 | How do behavior therapy's assumptions and techniques differ from those of psychoanalytic and humanistic therapies? What are exposure therapies and aversive conditioning?

The therapies we have considered so far assume that self-awareness and psychological well-being go hand in hand. Psychodynamic therapists expect people's problems to lessen as they gain insight into their unresolved and unconscious tensions. Humanistic therapists expect people's problems to lessen as they get in touch with their feelings. **Behavior therapists,** however, doubt the healing power of self-awareness. (You can become aware of why you are highly anxious during exams and still be anxious.) Rather than searching beneath the surface for inner causes, they assume that problem behaviors *are* the problems. They view learning principles as useful tools for eliminating unwanted behaviors. They see phobias or sexual disorders, for example, as learned behaviors. If so, why not replace them with new useful behaviors learned through classical or operant conditioning?

Classical Conditioning Techniques

One cluster of behavior therapies derives from principles developed in Ivan Pavlov's conditioning experiments (Chapter 6). As Pavlov and others showed, we learn various behaviors and emotions through classical conditioning. If we're attacked by a dog, we may thereafter have a conditioned fear response when other dogs approach. (Our fear generalizes, and all dogs become conditioned stimuli.)

Could maladaptive symptoms also be examples of conditioned responses? If so, might reconditioning be a solution? Learning theorist O. H. Mowrer thought so. He developed a successful conditioning therapy for chronic bed-wetters, using a liquid-sensitive pad connected to an alarm. If the sleeping child wets the pad (which is on the bed), moisture triggers the alarm, waking the child. With sufficient repetition, this association of urinary relaxation with waking stops the bed-wetting. The treatment has been effective in three out of four cases, and the success provided a boost to the child's self-image (Christophersen & Edwards, 1992; Houts et al., 1994).

Let's broaden the discussion now. What triggers your worst fear responses? CAN WE UNLEARN FEAR RESPONSES ◄ THROUGH NEW CONDITIONING? Many people have. One example: The fear of riding

What's the nature of the trouble, and when did it begin?

Let's drive it around and see what happens.

FREUDIAN

BEHAVIOR THERAPIST

J. Harris

Science Cartoons Plus

client-centered therapy a humanistic therapy, developed by Carl Rogers, in which the therapist uses techniques such as active listening within a genuine, accepting, empathic environment to promote clients' growth. (Also called *person-centered therapy.*)

active listening empathic listening in which the listener echoes, restates, and clarifies. A feature of Rogers' client-centered therapy.

unconditional positive regard a caring, accepting, nonjudgmental attitude, which Carl Rogers believed would help clients develop self-awareness and self-acceptance.

behavior therapy therapy that applies learning principles to the elimination of unwanted behaviors.

in an elevator is often a learned fear response to the stimulus of being in a confined space. **Counterconditioning** pairs the trigger stimulus (the enclosed space of the elevator) with a new response (relaxation) that cannot coexist with fear. Behavior therapists have successfully counterconditioned many people with a fear of confined spaces.

Exposure therapies and *aversive conditioning* illustrate counterconditioning. The goal of both is replacing unwanted responses with new responses.

Exposure Therapies Picture this scene. Behavioral psychologist Mary Cover Jones is working with 3-year-old Peter, who is petrified of rabbits and other furry objects. To rid Peter of his fear of rabbits, Jones plans to associate the fear-evoking rabbit with the pleasurable, relaxed response associated with eating. As Peter begins his midafternoon snack, she introduces a caged rabbit on the other side of the huge room. Peter, eagerly munching away on his crackers and drinking his milk, hardly notices. On succeeding days, she gradually moves the rabbit closer and closer. Within two months, Peter is holding the rabbit in his lap, even stroking it while he eats. Moreover, his fear of other furry objects has also gone away, having been *countered,* or replaced, by a relaxed state that cannot coexist with fear (Fisher, 1984; Jones, 1924).

Unfortunately for many who might have been helped by Jones' procedures, her story of Peter and the rabbit did not enter psychology's lore when it was reported in 1924. It was more than 30 years before psychiatrist Joseph Wolpe (1958; Wolpe & Plaud, 1997) refined Jones' counterconditioning technique into the **exposure therapies** used today. These therapies, in a variety of ways, try to change people's reactions by repeatedly exposing them to stimuli that trigger unwanted reactions. We all experience this process in ▶ everyday life. WHY WOULD SOMEONE WHO HAS MOVED TO A NEW APART-

Kim Reinick/Shutterstock

Creativ Studio Heinemann/ Jupiterimages

Shutterstock

MENT BE ANNOYED BY LOUD TRAFFIC SOUNDS NEARBY BUT ONLY FOR A WHILE? With repeated exposure, the person adapts to the noise. So, too, with people who have fear reactions to specific events. Exposed repeatedly to the situation that once terrified them, they can learn to react less anxiously (Wolitzky-Taylor et al., 2008). Therapist-guided exposure also helps people conquer compulsive behaviors (Rosa-Alcázar et al., 2008).

One form of exposure therapy widely used to treat phobias is **systematic desensitization.** You cannot be anxious and relaxed at the same time. Therefore, if you can repeatedly relax when facing anxiety-provoking stimuli, you can gradually eliminate your anxiety. The trick is to proceed gradually. If you feared public speaking, a behavior therapist might first ask you to make a list of anxiety-triggering speaking situations. Your list would range from situations that cause you to feel mildly anxious (perhaps speaking up in a small group of friends) to those that provoke feelings of panic (having to address a large audience).

In the next step, the therapist would train you in *progressive relaxation.* You would learn to relax one muscle group after another, until you achieved a comfortable, complete relaxation. Then the therapist might ask you to imagine, with your eyes closed, a mildly anxiety-arousing situation: You are having coffee with a group of friends and are trying to decide whether to speak up. If you feel any anxiety while imagining this scene, you will signal by raising your finger. Seeing the signal, the therapist will instruct you to switch off the mental image and go back to deep relaxation. This imagined scene is repeatedly paired with relaxation until you feel no trace of anxiety.

The therapist will then move to the next item on your list, again using relaxation techniques to desensitize you to each imagined situa-

tion. After several sessions, you will move to actual situations and practice what you had only imagined before. You will begin with relatively easy tasks and gradually move to more anxiety-filled ones. Conquering your anxiety in an actual situation, not just in your imagination, will raise your self-confidence (Foa & Kozak, 1986; Williams, 1987). Eventually, you may even become a confident public speaker.

A newer option is **virtual reality exposure therapy.** You would don a head-mounted display unit that projects a three-dimensional virtual world in front of your eyes. The lifelike scenes (which shift as your head turns) will be tailored to your particular fear. Experimentally treated fears include flying, heights, particular animals, and public speaking (Parsons & Rizzo, 2008; Westerhoff, 2007). If you fear flying, you could peer out a virtual window

Bob Mahoney/The Image Works

Virtual reality exposure therapy: Within the confines of a room, virtual reality technology exposes people to vivid simulations of feared stimuli, such as a plane's takeoff.

of a simulated plane. You would feel the engine's vibrations and hear it roar as the plane taxis down the runway and takes off. In studies comparing control groups with people participating in virtual reality exposure therapy, the therapy has provided greater relief from real-life fear (Hoffman, 2004; Krijn et al., 2004).

Aversive Conditioning Exposure therapies substitute a relaxed, positive response for a negative response to a *harmless* stimulus. **Aversive conditioning** substitutes a negative response for a positive response to a *harmful* stimulus. Exposure therapies help you learn what you *should* do. Aversive conditioning helps you to learn what you *should not* do.

The procedure is simple: It associates the unwanted behavior with unpleasant feelings. To treat nail biting, one can paint the fingernails with a yucky-tasting nail polish (Baskind, 1997). To treat alcohol dependence, the therapist offers the client appealing drinks laced with a drug that produces severe nausea. By linking alcohol with violent nausea (recall the taste-aversion experiments with rats and coyotes in Chapter 6), the therapist seeks to transform the person's reaction to alcohol from positive to negative (**FIGURE 13.1**).

Does aversive conditioning work? In the short run it may. In one classic study,

685 patients with alcohol dependence completed an aversion therapy program at a hospital (Wiens & Menustik, 1983). Over the next year, they returned for several booster treatments in which alcohol was paired with sickness. At the end of that year, 63 percent were still successfully abstaining. But after three years, only 33 percent had remained abstinent.

The problem, as we saw in Chapter 6, is that our thoughts can interfere with conditioning processes. People know that outside the therapist's office they can drink without fear of nausea. Their ability to isolate the aversive conditioning situation from all other situations can limit the treatment's effectiveness. Thus, therapists often use aversive conditioning in combination with other treatments.

Operant Conditioning

6 | What is the basic idea of operant conditioning therapies?

A basic concept in operant conditioning (Chapter 6) is that our behaviors are influenced by their consequences. Knowing this, behavior therapists can practice *behavior modification*. They reinforce behaviors they consider desirable. And they fail to reinforce—or sometimes punish—behaviors they consider undesirable.

Using operant conditioning to solve specific behavior problems has raised hopes for some seemingly hopeless cases. Children with an intellectual disability have been taught to care for themselves. Socially withdrawn children with autism have learned to interact. People with schizophrenia have been helped to behave more rationally in their hospital ward. In each case, therapists used positive reinforcers to *shape* behavior. In a step-by-step manner, they rewarded behaviors that came closer and closer to the desired behaviors.

In extreme cases, treatment must be intensive. One study worked with 19 withdrawn, uncommunicative 3-year-olds with autism. For two years, 40 hours each week, the children's parents attempted to shape their behavior (Lovaas, 1987). They positively reinforced desired behaviors and ignored or punished aggressive and self-abusive behaviors. The combination worked wonders for some children. By first grade, 9 of the 19 were functioning successfully in school and exhibiting normal intelligence. Among comparable children not undergoing this treatment, only one child showed similar improvement.

counterconditioning a behavior therapy procedure that uses classical conditioning to evoke new responses to stimuli that are triggering unwanted behaviors; includes *exposure therapies* and *aversive conditioning*.

exposure therapies behavioral techniques, such as *systematic desensitization* and *virtual reality exposure therapy*, that treat anxieties by exposing people (in imagination or actual situations) to the things they fear and avoid.

systematic desensitization a type of exposure therapy that associates a pleasant relaxed state with gradually increasing, anxiety-triggering stimuli. Commonly used to treat phobias.

virtual reality exposure therapy an anxiety treatment that progressively exposes people to electronic simulations of their greatest fears, such as airplane flying, spiders, or public speaking.

aversive conditioning a type of counterconditioning that associates an unpleasant state (such as nausea) with an unwanted behavior (such as drinking alcohol).

FIGURE 13.1 ● **Aversion therapy for alcohol dependence** After repeatedly imbibing an alcoholic drink mixed with a drug that produces severe nausea, some people with a history of alcohol abuse develop at least a temporary conditioned aversion to alcohol.

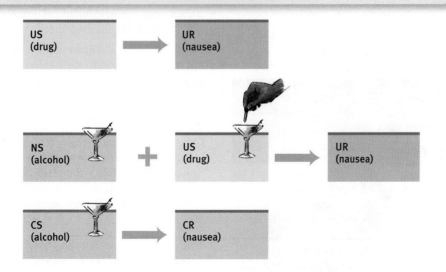

The rewards used to modify behavior vary, because people differ in what they consider rewarding. For some, the reinforcing power of attention or praise is enough. Others require concrete rewards, such as food. In institutional settings, therapists may create a **token economy.** When people display appropriate behavior, such as getting out of bed, washing, dressing, eating, talking meaningfully, cleaning their rooms, or playing cooperatively, they receive a token or plastic coin. Later, they can exchange a number of these tokens for rewards, such as candy, TV time, day trips, or better living quarters. Token economies have been used successfully in various settings (homes, classrooms, hospitals, institutions for the delinquent) and among members of various populations (including disturbed children and people with schizophrenia and other mental disabilities).

Cognitive Therapies

7 **What are the goals and techniques of the cognitive therapies?**

People with specific fears and problem behaviors respond to behavior therapy. But how would you modify the wide assortment of behaviors that accompany major depression? Or those associated with generalized anxiety, where unfocused anxiety doesn't lend itself to a neat list of anxiety-triggering situations? The same *cognitive revolution* that profoundly changed other areas of psychology during the last half-century influenced therapy as well.

The **cognitive therapies** assume that our thinking colors our feelings **(FIGURE 13.2).** Between the event and our response lies the mind. Self-blaming and overgeneralized explanations of bad events are

Simon C Ford/Alamy

Cognitive therapy for eating disorders aided by journaling: Cognitive therapists guide people toward new ways of explaining their good and bad experiences. By recording each day's positive events and how she has enabled them, this young woman may become more mindful of her self-control and more optimistic in her outlook.

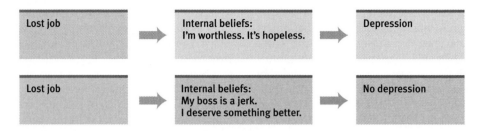

FIGURE 13.2 ● **A cognitive perspective on psychological disorders** The person's emotional reactions are produced not directly by the event but by the person's thoughts in response to the event.

often an important part of the vicious cycle of depression (see Chapter 12). The depressed person interprets a suggestion as criticism, disagreement as dislike, praise as flattery, friendliness as pity. Dwelling on such thoughts sustains the bad mood. Cognitive therapists aim to help people change their minds with new ways of thinking.

Beck's Therapy for Depression

Cognitive therapist Aaron Beck's original training was in Freudian techniques, including dream analysis. Depressed people, he found, often reported dreams with negative themes of loss, rejection, and abandonment. These thoughts extended into their waking thoughts, even into therapy, as clients recalled and rehearsed their failings and worst impulses (Kelly, 2000). Beck and his colleagues (1979) wondered: How could they reverse their clients' negativity about themselves, their situations, and their futures?

Beck's answer was the approach we call cognitive therapy. Gentle questioning seeks to reveal irrational thinking and then to persuade people to remove the dark glasses through which they view life (Beck et al., 1979, pp. 145–146):

Client: I agree with the descriptions of me but I guess I don't agree that the way I think makes me depressed.

Beck: How do you understand it?

Client: I get depressed when things go wrong. Like when I fail a test.

Beck: How can failing a test make you depressed?

Client: Well, if I fail I'll never get into law school.

Beck: So failing the test means a lot to you. But if failing a test could drive people into clinical depression, wouldn't you expect everyone who failed the test to have a depression? . . . Did everyone who failed get depressed enough to require treatment?

Client: No, but it depends on how important the test was to the person.

Beck: Right, and who decides the importance?

Client: I do.

Beck: And so, what we have to examine is your way of viewing the test (or the way that you think about the test) and how it affects your chances of getting into law school. Do you agree?

Client: Right.

Beck: Do you agree that the way you interpret the results of the test will affect you? You might feel depressed, you might have trouble sleeping, not feel like eating, and you might even wonder if you should drop out of the course.

Client: I have been thinking that I wasn't going to make it. Yes, I agree.

Beck: Now what did failing mean?

Client: (*tearful*) That I couldn't get into law school.

Beck: And what does that mean to you?

Client: That I'm just not smart enough.

Beck: Anything else?

Client: That I can never be happy.

Beck: And how do these thoughts make you feel?

Client: Very unhappy.

Beck: So it is the meaning of failing a test that makes you very unhappy. In fact, believing that you can never be happy is a powerful factor in producing unhappiness. So, you get yourself into a trap—by definition, failure to get into law school equals "I can never be happy."

American writer Mark Twain (1835–1910) would probably have applauded the cognitive therapy movement. More than a century ago, he commented, "Life does not consist mainly, or even largely, of facts and happenings. It consists mainly of the storm of thoughts that are forever blowing through one's mind." We often think in words. Therefore, getting people to change what they say to themselves is an effective way to change their thinking. WHY DO SOME WELL-PREPARED STUDENTS◄ BECOME ANXIOUS BEFORE TAKING AN EXAM? Many students make matters worse with self-defeating thoughts like these: "This exam's probably going to be impossible. All these other students

seem so relaxed and confident. I wish I were better prepared. Anyhow, I'm so nervous I'll forget everything." To change such negative self-talk, therapists teach people to alter their thinking in stressful situations (Meichenbaum, 1977, 1985). Sometimes it may be enough simply to say more positive things to yourself. "Relax. The exam may be hard, but it will be hard for everyone else, too. I studied harder than most people. Besides, I don't need a perfect score to get a good grade." Experiments show that training people to "talk back" to negative thoughts can be effective. With such training, depression-prone children and adolescents have shown a modestly reduced rate of future depression (Brunwasser et al., 2009; Stice et al., 2009). When it comes to our emotions, it's the thought that counts.

Cognitive-Behavioral Therapy

"The trouble with most therapy," said therapist Albert Ellis (1913–2007), "is that it helps you to feel better. But you don't get better. You have to back it up with action, action, action." **Cognitive-behavioral therapy** takes a double-barreled approach to depression and other disorders. This integrated approach aims not only to alter the way people *think* but also to alter the way they *act*. Like other cognitive therapies, it seeks to make people aware of their irrational negative thinking and to replace it with new ways of thinking. Like other behavior therapies, it trains people to practice the more positive approach in everyday settings.

In one study, people with obsessive-compulsive behaviors learned to relabel their compulsive thoughts (Schwartz et al., 1996). Feeling the urge to wash their hands again, they would tell themselves, "I'm having a compulsive urge." They would explain to themselves that the

hand-washing urge was a result of their brain's abnormal activity, which they had previously viewed in PET scans. Then, instead of giving in, they would spend 15 minutes in an enjoyable, alternative behavior, such as practicing an instrument, taking a walk, or gardening. This helped "unstick" the brain by shifting attention and engaging other brain areas. For two or three months, the weekly therapy sessions continued, with relabeling and refocusing practice at home. By the study's end, most participants' symptoms had diminished, and their PET scans revealed normalized brain activity. Other studies confirm cognitive-behavioral therapy's effectiveness for those suffering anxiety or depression (Covin et al., 2008).

Group and Family Therapies

8 What are the benefits of group therapy, including family therapy?

Except for traditional psychoanalysis, most therapies may also occur in small groups. Group therapy does not provide the same degree of therapist involvement with each client. However, it saves therapists' time and clients' money, and it often is no less effective than individual therapy (Fuhriman & Burlingame, 1994). Therapists frequently suggest group therapy for families having conflicts or for individuals whose behavior distresses others. Up to 90 minutes a week, the therapist guides the interactions of 6 to 10 people as they confront issues and react to one another.

token economy an operant conditioning procedure in which people earn a token for exhibiting a desired behavior and can later exchange the tokens for privileges or treats.

cognitive therapy therapy that teaches people new, more adaptive ways of thinking; based on the assumption that thoughts intervene between events and our emotional reactions.

cognitive-behavioral therapy a popular integrative therapy that combines cognitive therapy (changing self-defeating thinking) with behavior therapy (changing behavior).

PEANUTS

Drawing by Charles Schulz; © 1956 Reprinted by permission of United Feature Syndicate, Inc.

Family therapy: The therapist helps family members understand how their ways of relating to one another create problems. The treatment's emphasis is not on changing the individuals, but on changing their relationships and interactions.

The social context of group sessions offers some unique benefits. It can be a relief to find that others, despite their calm appearance, share your problems and your troubling feelings. It can also be helpful to receive feedback as you try out new ways of behaving. Hearing that you look poised, even though you feel anxious and self-conscious, can be very reassuring.

One special type of group interaction, **family therapy,** assumes that no person is an island. We live and grow in relation to others, especially our families, yet we also work to find an identity outside of our family. These two opposing tendencies can create stress for the individual and the family. This helps explain why therapists tend to view families as systems, in which each person's actions trigger reactions from others. To change these negative interactions, the therapist often attempts to guide family members toward positive relationships and improved communication.

PRACTICE TEST

THE BASICS

1. A psychotherapist who encourages people to relate their dreams, and who searches for the unconscious roots of their problems is drawing from

   a. psychoanalysis.
   b. humanistic therapies.
   c. client-centered therapy.
   d. nondirective therapy.

2. According to psychoanalytic theory, developing strong feelings for the analyst is an important part of the psychoanalytic process and is called

   a. transference.
   b. resistance.
   c. interpretation.
   d. empathy.

3. Compared with psychoanalysts, humanistic therapists are more likely to emphasize

   a. hidden or repressed feelings.
   b. childhood experiences.
   c. psychological disorders.
   d. self-fulfillment and growth.

4. Especially important to Rogers' client-centered therapy is the technique of active listening, in which the therapist

   a. engages in free association.
   b. exposes the patient's resistances.
   c. restates and clarifies the client's statements.
   d. directly challenges the client's self-perceptions.

5. Behavior therapists apply learning principles to the treatment of problems such as phobias and alcohol dependence. In such treatment, the goal is to

   a. identify and treat the underlying causes of the problem.
   b. foster transference and active listening.
   c. eliminate the unwanted behavior.
   d. improve communication and social sensitivity.

6. To produce new responses to old stimuli, behavior therapists often use counterconditioning techniques, such as exposure therapy and

   a. resistance.
   b. aversive conditioning.
   c. transference.
   d. active listening.

7. Systematic desensitization is commonly used in the treatment of

   a. phobias.   c. nail biting.
   b. depression.   d. bed-wetting.

8. Token economies are an application of

   a. classical conditioning.
   b. counterconditioning.
   c. cognitive therapy.
   d. operant conditioning.

9. Cognitive-behavioral therapists help people to

   a. restate and clarify statements about repressed feelings.
   b. search for childhood experiences that might explain self-defeating thoughts and actions.
   c. transfer negative feelings to the therapist so they can be resolved.
   d. change their self-defeating ways of thinking and act out those changes in their daily behavior.

10. In family therapy, the therapist assumes that

   a. only one family member needs to change.
   b. each person's actions trigger reactions from other family members.
   c. in dysfunctional families the parents should focus on improving the way they interact with each other.
   d. all of these conditions exist.

THE BIG PICTURE

13A. What is the major distinction between the underlying assumptions in psychodynamic therapies and in behavior therapies?

13B. How do the humanistic and cognitive therapies differ?

Answers: 1. a, 2. a, 3. d, 4. c, 5. c, 6. b, 7. a, 8. d, 9. d, 10. b. Answers to The Big Picture questions can be found in Appendix B at the end of the book.

Evaluating Psychotherapies

Many Americans have great confidence in psychotherapy's effectiveness. "Seek counseling" or "Ask your mate to find a therapist," advice columnists often advise. Before 1950, psychiatrists were the primary providers of mental health care. Today, psychotherapy is also offered by many clinical and counseling psychologists; clinical social workers; pastoral, marital, abuse, and school counselors; and psychiatric nurses.

Is the faith that millions of people worldwide place in these therapists justified? The question, though simply put, is not simply answered.

Is Psychotherapy Effective?

9 Why do clients and clinicians tend to overestimate the effectiveness of therapy?

If you and I were to undergo psychotherapy, how would we assess its effectiveness? By how we feel about our progress? By how our therapist feels about it? By how our friends and family feel about it? By how our behavior has changed?

Clients' Perceptions

If clients' testimonials were the only measuring stick, we could strongly assert that psychotherapy is effective. Consider 2900 *Consumer Reports* readers who reported on their experiences with mental health professionals (1995; Kotkin et al., 1996; Seligman, 1995). How many were at least "fairly well satisfied"? Almost 90 percent (as was Kay Redfield Jamison, as we saw at this chapter's beginning). Among those who recalled feeling *fair* or *very poor* when beginning therapy, 9 in 10 now were feeling *very good, good,* or at least *so-so.* We have their word for it—and who should know better?

But client testimonials don't persuade everyone. Critics point out some reasons for skepticism.

- *Clients may need to justify their investment of effort and money.*

- *Clients generally speak kindly of their therapists.* Even if their problems remain, clients "work hard to find something positive to say. The therapist had been very understanding, the client had gained a new perspective, he learned to communicate better, his mind was eased, anything at all so as not to have to say treatment was a failure" (Zilbergeld, 1983, p. 117).

- *People often enter therapy in crisis.* When, with the normal ebb and flow of events, the crisis passes, people may assume their improvement was a result of the therapy.

Clinicians' Perceptions

If clinicians' perceptions were proof of therapy's effectiveness, we would have even more reason to celebrate. Case studies of successful treatment abound. Furthermore, therapists are like the rest of us. They treasure compliments from people they've tried to help—in this case, clients saying goodbye or later expressing their gratitude. The problem is that clients justify entering psychotherapy by emphasizing their

family therapy therapy that treats the family as a system. Views an individual's unwanted behaviors as influenced by or directed at other family members.

unhappiness. They justify leaving by emphasizing their well-being. And they stay in touch only if they are satisfied. This means that therapists are most aware of the failures of *other* therapists—those whose clients, having experienced only temporary relief, are now seeking a new therapist for their recurring problems. Thus, the same person, suffering from the same old anxiety, depression, or marital difficulty, may be a "success" story in several therapists' files.

Outcome Research

How, then, can we objectively assess psychotherapy's effectiveness? What *outcomes* can we expect—what types of people and problems are best helped, and by what type of psychotherapy?

In search of answers, psychologists have turned to controlled research studies. This is a well-traveled path. In the 1800s, skeptical medical doctors asked similar questions and transformed their field into a science. They began to realize that many patients got better on their own and that most of the fashionable treatments (bleeding, purging) were doing no good. Sorting fact from superstition required following patients, and keeping records of

Feng Li/Getty Images

Trauma: These women are mourning the tragic loss of lives and homes in the 2010 earthquake in China. Those who suffer through such trauma may benefit from counseling, though many people recover on their own, or with the help of supportive relationships with family and friends. "Life itself still remains a very effective therapist," noted psychodynamic therapist Karen Horney (*Our Inner Conflicts,* 1945).

what happened with and without a particular treatment. Typhoid fever patients, for example, often improved after being bled, convincing most doctors that the treatment worked. Then came the shock. A control group was given mere bed rest, and after five weeks of fever, 70 percent improved. The study showed that bleeding was worthless (Thomas, 1992).

In the twentieth century, psychology, with its many different therapy options, faced a similar challenge. British psychologist Hans Eysenck (1952) launched a spirited debate when he summarized 24 studies of psychotherapy outcomes. He found that two-thirds of those receiving psychotherapy for disorders not involving hallucinations or delusions improved markedly. To this day, no one disputes that optimistic estimate.

Why, then, are we still debating psychotherapy's effectiveness? Because Eysenck also reported similar improvement among *untreated* persons, such as those who were on waiting lists for treatment. With or without psychotherapy, he said, roughly two-thirds improved noticeably. Time was a great healer.

An avalanche of criticism greeted Eysenck's conclusions. Some pointed out errors in his analysis. Others noted that he based his ideas on only 24 studies.

Now, more than a half-century later, there are hundreds. The best of these are *randomized clinical trials*. Researchers randomly assign people on a waiting list to therapy or to no therapy. Later, they evaluate everyone and compare the outcomes.

When researchers used statistical methods to combine the results of 475 investigations (Smith et al., 1980), psychotherapists welcomed the result (**FIGURE** 13.3). The average therapy client ends up better off than 80 percent of the untreated individuals on waiting lists.

Newer research summaries confirm that psychotherapy, including psychodynamic therapy, works (Kopta et al., 1999; Leichsenring & Rabung, 2008; Shadish et al., 2000). Consider one ambitious study done by the National Institute of Mental Health. Experienced therapists at three research sites were trained in one of three depression treatment methods: cognitive therapy, interpersonal therapy, and a standard drug therapy. Then, 239 participants suffering from depression were randomly assigned to one of these therapists or to a control group. People in the control group received a placebo (a sugar pill) and supportive attention, encouragement, and advice. Participants in all three treatment groups improved more than did those in the control group. At the end

of the full 16-week program, the depression lifted for slightly more than half the people in each of the three treatment groups. Only 29 percent of those in the control group showed similar improvement (Elkin et al., 1989). The results echo the earlier outcome studies: *Those not undergoing therapy often improve, but those undergoing therapy are more likely to improve.*

It's good to know that psychotherapy, in general at least, is somewhat effective. But distressed people—and those paying for their therapy—really want an answer to a different question. How effective are particular treatments for specific problems? So what can we tell these people?

Which Psychotherapies Work Best?

10 | What psychotherapies are most effective—and for what problems?

The early statistical summaries and surveys did not find that any one type of psychotherapy is generally better than others (Smith et al., 1977, 1980). Newer studies have similarly found little connection between clients' outcomes and their clinicians' experience, training, supervision, and licensing (Bickman, 1999; Luborsky et al., 2002; Wampold, 2007). The *Consumer Reports* client survey shared this result. Were they treated by a psychiatrist, psychologist, or social worker? Were they seen in a group or individual context? Did the therapist have extensive or relatively limited training and experience? It didn't matter. Clients seemed equally satisfied (Seligman, 1995).

So was the dodo bird in *Alice in Wonderland* right: "Everyone has won and all must have prizes"? Not quite. Some forms of psychotherapy get prizes for *particular* problems. Behavioral conditioning therapies, for example, have had especially good results with specific behavior problems, such as bed-wetting, phobias, compulsions, marital problems, and sexual disorders (Bowers & Clum, 1988; Hunsley & Di Giulio, 2002; Shadish & Baldwin, 2005). And newer studies confirm cognitive therapy's effectiveness in coping with anxiety, post-traumatic stress disorder,

FIGURE 13.3 • **Treatment versus no treatment** In 475 studies, the outcome for the average therapy client was better than that for 80 percent of the untreated people. (Adapted from Smith et al., 1980.)

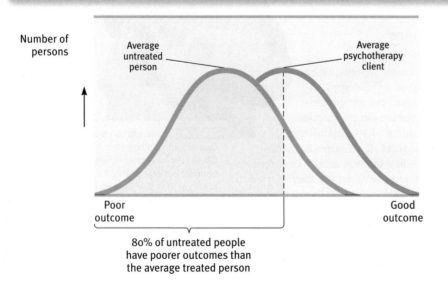

Number of persons

Average untreated person

Average psychotherapy client

Poor outcome

Good outcome

80% of untreated people have poorer outcomes than the average treated person

and depression (Baker et al., 2008; Stewart & Chambliss, 2009).

But no prizes—and little or no scientific support—go to certain other psychotherapies (Arkowitz & Lilienfeld, 2006). We would all therefore be wise to avoid the following unsupported approaches.

- *Energy therapies* propose to manipulate people's invisible energy fields.
- *Recovered-memory therapies* aim to unearth "repressed memories" of early childhood abuse (Chapter 7).
- *Rebirthing therapies* engage people in reenacting the supposed trauma of their birth.
- *Facilitated communication* has an assistant touch the typing hand of a child with autism.
- *Crisis debriefing* forces people to rehearse and "process" their recent traumatic experiences.

But this list of discredited therapies raises another question. Who should decide which psychotherapies get prizes and which do not? This question lies at the heart of a controversy—some call it psychology's civil war. **WHAT ROLE** ◄ **SHOULD SCIENCE PLAY IN CLINICAL PRACTICE, AND HOW MUCH SHOULD SCIENCE GUIDE HEALTH-CARE PROVIDERS AND INSURERS IN SETTING PAYMENT POLICIES FOR PSYCHOTHERAPY?** On one side are research psychologists who use scientific methods to extend the list of well-defined and validated therapies for various disorders. They worry that many clinicians "give more weight to their personal experience than to science" (Baker

© 1994 by Sidney Harris—"Stress Test," Rutgers University Press.

"I utilize the best from Freud, the best from Jung, and the best from my Uncle Marty, a very smart fellow."

Clinical decision making

Patient's values, characteristics, preferences, circumstances

Clinical expertise

Best available research evidence

FIGURE 13.4 ● **Evidence-based clinical decision making** Ideal clinical decision making is a three-legged stool, upheld by research evidence, clinical expertise, and knowledge of the patient.

et al., 2008). On the other side are the nonscientist therapists who view their practices as more art than science, something that cannot be described in a manual or tested in an experiment. People are too complex and psychotherapy is too intuitive for a cookie-cutter approach, many therapists say.

Between them stand the science-oriented clinicians calling for *evidence-based* decision making (**FIGURE 13.4**). Therapists then make informed decisions based on research evidence, clinical expertise, and knowledge of the patient. If we make mental health professionals accountable for effectiveness, everyone gains, say these clinicians. The public will be protected from false therapies. And therapists will be protected from accusations of sounding like snake-oil vendors—"Trust me, I know it works, I've seen it work."

How Do Psychotherapies Help People?

11 What three benefits are provided by all forms of effective psychotherapy? How do differences in culture and values influence the relationship between a therapist and a client?

How can it be that therapists' training and experience do not seem to influence clients' outcomes? The answer seems to

be that all psychotherapies offer three basic benefits (Frank, 1982; Goldfried & Padawer, 1982; Strupp, 1986; Wampold, 2001, 2007). These benefits are *hope for demoralized people; a new perspective on oneself and the world;* and *an empathic, trusting, caring relationship.*

Hope for Demoralized People

People seeking therapy typically feel anxious, depressed, self-disapproving, and not capable of turning things around. What any psychotherapy offers is the expectation that things can and will get better. This belief, apart from any therapy technique, may improve morale, create feelings of inner strength, and reduce symptoms (Prioleau et al., 1983). Each therapy, in its own way, may therefore harness the person's own healing powers. And that helps us understand why all sorts of treatments—including some folk-healing rites with no scientific support for their effectiveness—may produce cures (Frank, 1982).

A New Perspective

Every psychotherapy also offers people an explanation of their symptoms. Therapy is a new experience that can help people change their behaviors and their views of themselves. Armed with a believable fresh perspective, they may approach life with new energy.

An Empathic, Trusting, Caring Relationship

No matter what technique they use, effective psychotherapists are empathic. They seek to understand people's experience. They communicate care and concern. And they earn trust through respectful listening, reassurance, and advice. These qualities were clear in taped therapy sessions from 36 recognized master therapists (Goldfried et al., 1998). Some were cognitive-behavioral therapists. Others were psychodynamic therapists. Regardless, they were strikingly similar during the most significant parts of their sessions. At key moments, the empathic therapists of both types would help clients evaluate themselves, link one aspect of their life with another, and

A caring relationship: Effective counselors, such as this chaplain working aboard a ship, form a bond of trust with their patients.

gain insight into their interactions with others. The emotional bond between therapist and client—the *therapeutic alliance*—is a key aspect of effective psychotherapy (Klein et al., 2003; Wampold, 2001). One U.S. National Institute of Mental Health depression-treatment study confirmed that the most effective therapists were those who were perceived as most empathic and caring and who established the closest therapeutic bonds with their clients (Blatt et al., 1996).

That all psychotherapies offer hope through a fresh perspective offered by a caring person is what also enables paraprofessionals (briefly trained caregivers) to assist so many troubled people so effectively (Christensen & Jacobson, 1994). These three common elements are also part of what the growing numbers of self-help and support groups offer their members. And they are part of what traditional healers have offered (Jackson, 1992). Healers everywhere—special people to whom others disclose their suffering, whether psychiatrists, witch doctors, or shamans—have listened in order to understand and to empathize, reassure, advise, console, interpret, or explain (Torrey, 1986). Such qualities may also explain why people who feel supported by close relationships—who enjoy the fellowship and friendship of caring people—are less likely to need or seek therapy (Frank, 1982; O'Connor & Brown, 1984).

* * *

To recap, people who seek help usually improve. So do many of those who do not undergo psychotherapy, and that is a tribute to our human resourcefulness and our capacity to care for one another. Nevertheless, though the therapist's orientation and experience appear not to matter much, people who receive some psychotherapy usually improve more than those who do not. People with clear-cut, specific problems tend to improve the most.

Culture and Values in Psychotherapy

All psychotherapies offer hope. Nearly all psychotherapists attempt to enhance their clients' sensitivity, openness, personal responsibility, and sense of purpose (Jensen & Bergin, 1988). But in matters of cultural and moral diversity, therapists differ from one another and may differ from their clients (Delaney et al., 2007; Kelly, 1990).

These differences can create a mismatch when a therapist from one culture interacts with a client from another. In North America, Europe, and Australia, for example, many therapists reflect the majority culture's *individualism,* which often gives priority to personal desires and identity. Clients with a *collectivist* perspective, as with many from Asian cultures, may assume people will be more mindful of others' expectations. These clients may have trouble relating to therapies that require them to think only of their own well-being. Such differences help explain the reluctance of some minority populations to use mental health services (Sue, 2006). In one experiment, Asian-American clients matched with counselors who shared their cultural values (rather than mismatched with those who did not) perceived more counselor empathy and felt more alliance with the counselor (Kim et al., 2005).

Another area of potential value conflict is religion. Highly religious people may prefer and benefit from religiously similar therapists (Smith et al., 2007; Wade et al., 2007; Worthington et al., 1996). They may have trouble establishing an emotional bond with a therapist who does not share their values

Albert Ellis, who advocated an aggressive "rational-emotive" therapy, and Allen Bergin, co-editor of the *Handbook of Psychotherapy and Behavior Change,* illustrated how sharply psychotherapists can differ, and how those differences can affect their view of a healthy person. Ellis (1980) assumed that "no one and nothing is supreme," that "self-gratification" should be encouraged, and that "unequivocal love, commitment, service, and . . . fidelity to any interpersonal commitment, especially marriage, leads to harmful consequences." Bergin (1980) assumed the opposite—that "because God is supreme, humility and the acceptance of divine authority are virtues," that "self-control and committed love and self-sacrifice are to be encouraged," and that "infidelity to any interpersonal commitment, especially marriage, leads to harmful consequences."

Bergin's and Ellis' values differed radically. However, they agreed that *psychotherapists' personal beliefs and values influence their practice.* Clients tend to adopt their therapists' values (Worthington et al., 1996). For that reason, some psychologists believe therapists should express those values more openly. (For therapy options see Close-Up: A Consumer's Guide to Psychotherapists.)

A Consumer's Guide to Psychotherapists

Life for everyone is marked by a mix of serenity and stress, blessing and bereavement, good moods and bad. So when should we seek a mental health professional's help? The American Psychological Association offers these common trouble signals:

- Feeling worthless and withdrawing from others
- Deep and lasting depression
- Self-destructive behavior, such as alcohol and drug abuse
- Disruptive fears
- Sudden mood shifts
- Wanting to harm yourself
- Compulsive rituals, such as hand washing
- Sexual difficulties
- Hearing voices or seeing things that others don't experience

In looking for a therapist, you may want to have a preliminary consultation with two or three. You can describe your problem and learn each therapist's treatment approach. You can ask questions about the therapist's values, credentials (**TABLE 13.1**), and fees. And you can assess your own feelings about each of them. The emotional bond between therapist and client is perhaps the most important factor in effective therapy.

TABLE 13.1 Therapists and Their Training

Type	Description
Clinical psychologists	Most are psychologists with a Ph.D. or Psy.D., supplemented by a supervised internship. About half work in agencies and institutions, half in private practice.
Psychiatrists	Psychiatrists are medical doctors who specialize in the treatment of psychological disorders and who, as M.D.s, can prescribe medications.
Clinical or psychiatric social workers	A social work graduate program plus postgraduate supervision prepares professionals to offer psychotherapy, mostly to people with everyday personal and family problems. About half have earned the National Association of Social Workers' designation of clinical social worker.
Counselors	Marriage and family counselors specialize in family relations problems. Pastoral counselors are a source of help for countless people.

PRACTICE TEST

THE BASICS

11. The most *enthusiastic* view of psychotherapy's effectiveness comes from
a. outcome research.
b. controlled studies.
c. reports of clinicians and clients.
d. a government study of treatment for depression.

12. Studies show that _____ therapy is most effective overall.
a. cognitive-behavioral
b. humanistic
c. psychodynamic
d. no one type of

13. Which of the following is NOT one of the three benefits offered by all forms of effective therapy?

a. Hope for demoralized people
b. One-on-one meetings with a professional therapist
c. A fresh perspective
d. A caring relationship

THE BIG PICTURE
13C. What is evidence-based clinical decision making, and who benefits from it?

IN YOUR EVERYDAY LIFE
- How might you use the general helping principles discussed in this chapter during a conversation with a friend who is having family problems?

Answers: 11. c, 12. d, 13. b. Answers to The Big Picture questions can be found in Appendix B at the end of the book.

The Biomedical Therapies

Psychotherapy is one way to treat psychological disorders. The other, often used with the most serious disorders, is *biomedical therapy*. This form of treatment changes the brain's functioning by altering its chemistry with drugs, or affecting its circuitry with electrical stimulation, magnetic impulses, or psychosurgery. Psychologists can provide psychological therapies. But with a few exceptions, only psychiatrists (as medical doctors) offer biomedical therapies.

Drug Therapies

12 What are the different drug therapies, and what are some of the side effects of those treatments?

By far the most widely used biomedical treatments today are the drug therapies.

Since the 1950s, drug researchers have written a new chapter in the treatment of people with severe disorders. Thanks to drug therapies and support from community mental health programs, the resident population of U.S. state and county mental hospitals has dropped to a small fraction of what it was a half-century ago (**FIGURE 13.5**). In the decade between 1996 and 2005 alone, the number of Americans prescribed antidepressant drugs doubled, from 13 to 27 million (Olfson & Marcus, 2009).

Almost any new treatment, including drug therapy, is greeted by an initial wave of enthusiasm as many people apparently improve. But that enthusiasm often diminishes on closer examination. To judge the effectiveness of a new treatment, we also need to know the rates of

- normal recovery among untreated people.
- recovery due to the *placebo effect,* which arises from the positive expectations of patients and mental health workers alike.

To control for these influences when testing a new drug, researchers give half the patients the drug, and the other half a similar-appearing placebo. Because neither the staff nor the patients know who gets which, this is called a *double-blind technique.*

The good news: In double-blind studies, several types of drugs have proven useful in treating psychological disorders.

Antipsychotic Drugs

Accidents sometimes launch revolutions. In this instance, an accidental discovery launched a treatment revolution for people with *psychoses.* The discovery was that some drugs used for other medical purposes calmed the hallucinations or delusions that are part of the split from reality for these patients. **Antipsychotic drugs,** such as chlorpromazine (sold as Thorazine), reduce patients' overreactions to irrelevant stimuli. Thus, they provide the most help to schizophrenia patients experiencing positive symptoms, such as auditory hallucinations and paranoia (Lehman et al., 1998; Lenzenweger et al., 1989). People with negative symptoms, such as apathy and withdrawal, often do not respond well to antipsychotic drugs. Newer-generation drugs (with names such as risperidone, olanzapine, and clozapine) sometimes enable "awakenings" in these individuals. They may also help those who have positive symptoms but have not responded to other drugs.

Antipsychotic drugs mimic certain neurotransmitters. Some block the activity of dopamine by occupying its receptor

"If this doesn't help you don't worry, it's a placebo."

sites. This finding reinforces the idea that an overactive dopamine system contributes to schizophrenia. Further support for this idea comes from a side effect of L-dopa, a drug sometimes given to people with Parkinson's disease (a disease in which a person produces too little dopamine). L-dopa raises dopamine levels, but it has an occasional side effect. Can you guess the side effect of a drug that raises dopamine levels? If you guessed hallucinations, you're right.

Antipsychotics also have powerful side effects. Some produce sluggishness, tremors, and twitches similar to those of Parkinson's disease (Kaplan & Saddock, 1989). Long-term use of antipsychotics can also produce *tardive dyskinesia,* with involuntary movements of the facial muscles (such as grimacing), tongue, and limbs. Although not more effective in controlling schizophrenia symptoms, many of the newer-generation antipsychotics have fewer of these effects. These drugs do not

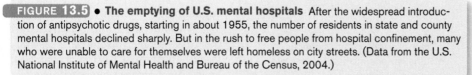

FIGURE 13.5 ● **The emptying of U.S. mental hospitals** After the widespread introduction of antipsychotic drugs, starting in about 1955, the number of residents in state and county mental hospitals declined sharply. But in the rush to free people from hospital confinement, many who were unable to care for themselves were left homeless on city streets. (Data from the U.S. National Institute of Mental Health and Bureau of the Census, 2004.)

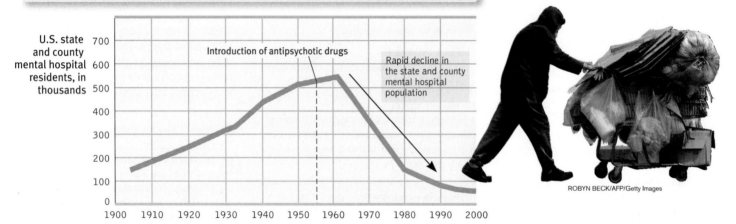

ROBYN BECK/AFP/Getty Images

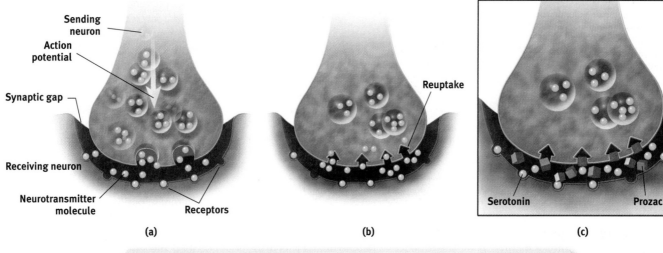

Message is sent across synaptic gap.

Message is received; excess neurotransmitter molecules are reabsorbed by sending neuron.

Prozac partially blocks normal reuptake of the neurotransmitter serotonin; excess serotonin in synapse enhances its mood-lifting effect.

Sending neuron

Action potential

Synaptic gap

Receiving neuron

Neurotransmitter molecule

Receptors

Reuptake

Serotonin

Prozac

(a)   (b)   (c)

FIGURE 13.6 ● **Biology of antidepressants** Shown here is the action of Prozac, which partially blocks the reuptake of serotonin.

seem to increase death risk, but they may increase the risk of obesity and diabetes (Delport-Bedoya et al., 2008; Lieberman et al., 2005, 2006; Tiihonen et al., 2009).

Despite their drawbacks, antipsychotics, combined with life-skills programs and family support, have given new hope to many people with schizophrenia. Hundreds of thousands of patients have left the wards of mental hospitals and returned to work and to near-normal lives (Leucht et al., 2003).

Antianxiety Drugs

Like alcohol, **antianxiety drugs,** such as Xanax or Ativan, depress central nervous system activity (and so should not be used in combination with alcohol). These drugs are often used in combination with psychological therapy. They calm anxiety as the person learns to cope with frightening situations and fear-triggering stimuli.

One criticism made of antianxiety drugs is that they may reduce symptoms without resolving underlying problems, especially if these substances are used as an ongoing treatment. "Popping a Xanax" at the first sign of tension can produce psychological dependence; this immediate relief reinforces a person's tendency to take drugs when anxious. Heavy use can

also lead to physical dependence. Regular users who stop taking antianxiety drugs may experience increased anxiety, insomnia, and other withdrawal symptoms.

Antidepressant Drugs

The **antidepressant drugs** were named for their ability to lift people up from a state of depression. Until recently, this was their main use. These drugs are now also used to treat anxiety disorders, such as obsessive-compulsive disorder. They work by increasing the availability of norepinephrine or serotonin. These neurotransmitters elevate arousal and mood and are scarce during depression. Fluoxetine, which tens of millions of users worldwide have known as Prozac, partially blocks the normal reuptake of excess serotonin from synapses (**FIGURE 13.6**). One possible side effect of this drug is diminished sexual desire.

Prozac, and its cousins Zoloft and Paxil, are called *selective-serotonin-reuptake-inhibitors (SSRIs)* because they slow (inhibit) the synaptic vacuuming up (reuptake) of serotonin. SSRIs begin to influence neurotransmission within hours. Their full psychological effect may take four weeks, possibly because these drugs

© John Greim/Agefotostock

PROZAC 20 mg

promote the birth of new brain cells (Becker & Wojtowicz, 2007; Jacobs, 2004).

Antidepressant drugs are not the only way to give our mood a lift. Aerobic exercise helps calm people who feel anxious and energize those who feel depressed. Cognitive therapy, which helps people reverse their habits of thinking negatively, can boost the drug-aided relief from depression and reduce post-treatment relapses (Hollon et al., 2002; Keller et al., 2000; Vittengl et al., 2007). The best approach seems to be attacking depression from both above and below (Goldapple et al., 2004; TADS, 2004). Antidepressant drugs work from the bottom up to affect the emotion-forming limbic system. Cognitive-behavioral therapy works from the top down to change thought processes.

antipsychotic drugs drugs used to treat schizophrenia and other forms of severe thought disorders.

antianxiety drugs drugs used to control anxiety and agitation.

antidepressant drugs drugs used to treat depression and some anxiety disorders. Different types work by altering the availability of various neurotransmitters.

Drug or placebo effect? For many people, depression lifts while taking an antidepressant drug. But people given a placebo may experience the same effect. Double-blind clinical trials suggest that, especially for those with severe depression, antidepressant drugs do have at least a modest clinical effect.

"Our psychopharmacologist is a genius."

Everyone agrees that people with depression often improve after a month on antidepressant drugs. But after allowing for natural recovery (the return to normal called *spontaneous recovery*) and the placebo effect, how big is the drug effect? Not big, report some researchers (Kirsch et al., 1998, 2002). In double-blind clinical trials, placebos produced improvement comparable to about 75 percent of the active drug's effect. Analysis of data from 45 studies showed similar results. When people with depression were given antidepressants, about 4 in 10 improved. When given placebos, about 3 in 10 improved (Khan et al., 2000). Among those with mild rather than severe depression, the therapeutic effect is close to that of a placebo (Fournier et al., 2010; Kirsch et al., 2008; Olfson & Marcus, 2009). "Given these results, there seems little reason to prescribe antidepressant medication to any but the most severely depressed patients, unless alternative treatments have failed," Kirsch concluded (BBC, 2008).

IS DRUG THERAPY AS EFFECTIVE AS THE◄ TV ADS SUGGEST? In many cases, the drugs don't change lives as dramatically as the ads suggest. But many of the drugs are also less frightening than warnings posted on the Internet would have us believe. Some people taking Prozac, for example, have committed suicide, but their numbers seem fewer than we would expect from the millions of depressed people who take the medication. Prozac users who commit suicide are like cell-phone users who get brain cancer. Given the millions of people taking this drug, or the millions using cell phones, alarming anecdotes tell us nothing.

The question critical thinkers want answered is this: Do people in these groups have a *higher rate* of suicide or brain cancer? In each case, the answer appears to be No (Grunebaum et al., 2004; Paulos, 1995; Søndergård et al., 2006a,b). Three recent studies of between 70,000 and 439,000 patients reached the same conclusion. In the long run, patients attempt fewer suicides if treated with antidepressant drugs (Gibbons et al., 2007; Simon & Savarino, 2007; Søndergård et al., 2006).

Mood-Stabilizing Medications

In addition to antipsychotic, antianxiety, and antidepressant drugs, psychiatrists have *mood-stabilizing drugs* in their arsenal. One of them, depakote, was originally used to treat epilepsy. It was also found effective in controlling the manic episodes associated with bipolar disorder.

"First of all I think you should know that last quarter's sales figures are interfering with my mood-stabilizing drugs."

Another, the simple salt *lithium*, effectively levels the emotional highs and lows of this disorder. Australian physician John Cade discovered this in the 1940s when he administered lithium to a patient with severe mania. Cade's reasoning was misguided. He thought lithium had calmed excitable guinea pigs, when actually it had made them sick. But less than a week after taking the lithium, Cade's patient became perfectly well (Snyder, 1986).

Although we do not understand why, lithium works. About 7 in 10 people with bipolar disorder benefit from a long-term daily dose of this cheap salt (Solomon et al., 1995). Their risk of suicide is but one-sixth that of patients with bipolar disorder not taking lithium (Tondo et al., 1997). Kay Redfield Jamison (1995, pp. 88–89) described the effect. "Lithium prevents my seductive but disastrous highs, diminishes my depressions, clears out the wool and webbing from my disordered thinking, slows me down, gentles me out, keeps me from ruining my career and relationships, keeps me out of a hospital, alive, and makes psychotherapy possible."

Brain Stimulation

13 How are brain stimulation and psychosurgery used in treating specific disorders?

Electroconvulsive Therapy

A more controversial form of biomedical treatment, **electroconvulsive therapy (ECT),** manipulates the brain by shocking it. When ECT was first introduced in 1938, the wide-awake patient was strapped to a table and jolted with roughly 100 volts of electricity to the brain. The procedure, which produced racking convulsions and brief unconsciousness, gained a barbaric image. Although that image lingers, ECT has changed. Today, the patient receives a general anesthetic and a muscle relaxant to prevent convulsions. A psychiatrist then delivers to the patient's brain 30- to 60-seconds of electric current, in briefer pulses, sometimes only to the brain's right side. Within 30 minutes, the patient wakens and remembers nothing of the treatment or of the preceding hours (**FIGURE 13.7**).

FIGURE **13.7** ● **Electroconvulsive therapy** Although controversial, ECT is often an effective treatment for depression that does not respond to drug therapy. "Electroconvulsive" is no longer accurate because patients are now given a drug that prevents convulsions.

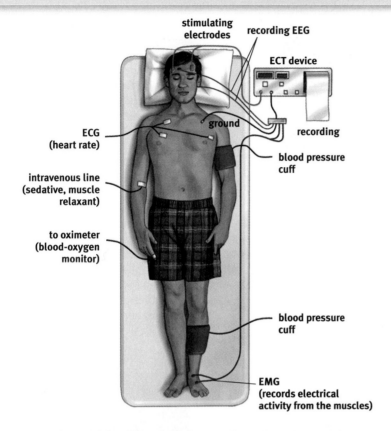

stimulating electrodes

recording EEG

ECT device

ground

recording

ECG (heart rate)

blood pressure cuff

intravenous line (sedative, muscle relaxant)

to oximeter (blood-oxygen monitor)

blood pressure cuff

EMG (records electrical activity from the muscles)

electroconvulsive therapy (ECT) a biomedical therapy for severely depressed patients in which a brief electric current is sent through the brain of an anesthetized patient.

Alternative Neurostimulation Therapies

Hopes are now rising for gentler alternatives that jump-start the depressed brain. *Vagus nerve stimulation* stimulates a nerve in the neck, via an electrical device implanted in the chest. The device periodically sends signals to the brain's mood-related limbic system (Fitzgerald & Daskalakis, 2008; Marangell et al., 2007).

Another new experimental procedure, *deep-brain stimulation,* is administered by a pacemaker that controls implanted electrodes (Lozano et al., 2008; Mayberg et al., 2005). The stimulation inhibits activity in a brain area that feeds negative emotions and thinking. With deep stimulation, some patients whose depression did not respond to drugs or ECT have found their depression lifting. Others became more responsive to drugs or psychotherapy. But investigators caution that more research is needed (Hamani et al., 2009; Rabins et al., 2009).

ECT promotor: In her book, *Shock: The Healing Power of Electroconvulsive Therapy* (2006), Kitty Dukakis writes, "I used to . . . be unable to shake the dread even when I was feeling good, because I knew the bad feelings would return. ECT has wiped away that foreboding. It has given me a sense of control, of hope."

Would you agree to ECT for a loved one? The decision would be difficult, but this treatment works. Shocking as it may seem, study after study confirms that ECT can effectively treat severe depression in patients who have not responded to drug therapy (Fink, 2009; UK ECT Review Group, 2003). After three such sessions each week for two to four weeks, 80 percent or more of those receiving ECT improve markedly. They show some memory loss for the treatment period but no apparent brain damage (Bergsholm et al., 1989; Coffey, 1993). Modern ECT causes less memory disruption than earlier versions did (HMHL, 2007). A *Journal of the American Medical Association* editorial concluded that "the results of ECT in treating severe depression are among the most positive treatment effects in all of medicine" (Glass, 2001). ECT reduces suicidal thoughts and is credited with saving many from suicide (Kellner et al., 2005).

How does ECT relieve severe depression? One patient compared ECT to the smallpox vaccine, which was saving lives before we knew how it worked. Perhaps the brief electric current calms neural centers where overactivity produces depression. ECT, like antidepressant drugs and exercise, also appears to boost the production of new brain cells (Bolwig & Madsen, 2007).

No matter how impressive the results, the idea of administering an electric shock to a person's brain still strikes many as barbaric, especially given our ignorance about why ECT works. Moreover, about 4 in 10 ECT-treated patients relapse into depression within six months (Kellner et al., 2006). Nevertheless, in the minds of many psychiatrists and patients, ECT is a lesser evil than severe depression's misery, anguish, and risk of suicide. As research psychologist Norman Endler (1982) reported after ECT alleviated his deep depression, "A miracle had happened in two weeks."

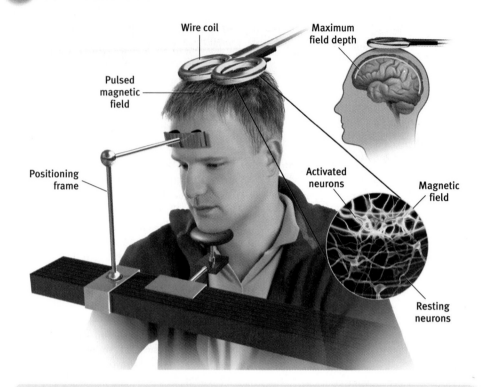

Wire coil

Pulsed magnetic field

Positioning frame

Maximum field depth

Activated neurons

Magnetic field

Resting neurons

FIGURE 13.8 ● **Magnets for the mind** In rTMS, a painless magnetic field is sent through the skull to the surface of the brain. Pulses can stimulate or dampen activity in various areas. (From George, 2003.)

Depressed moods also seem to improve when repeated pulses of magnetic energy are applied to a person's brain. In a painless procedure called **repetitive transcranial magnetic stimulation (rTMS),** a coiled wire held close to the skull sends a magnetic field through the skull to the brain **(FIGURE 13.8).** Unlike deep-brain stimulation, the magnetic energy penetrates only to the brain's surface. And unlike ECT, the rTMS procedure produces no seizures, memory loss, or other side effects. Wide-awake patients receive this treatment daily for two to four weeks.

Initial studies have found "modest" positive benefits of rTMS (Daskalakis et al., 2008; López-Ibor et al., 2008). How it works is not yet clear. One possible explanation is that the stimulation energizes the brain's left frontal lobe, which is relatively inactive during depression (Helmuth, 2001). Repeated stimulation may cause nerve cells to form new functioning circuits through the process of long-term potentiation. (See Chapter 7 for more details on LTP.)

Psychosurgery

Because its effects are irreversible, **psychosurgery**—surgery that removes or destroys brain tissue—is the most drastic and the least-used biomedical intervention for changing thoughts and behaviors. In the 1930s, Portuguese physician Egas Moniz developed what would become the best-known psychosurgical operation: the **lobotomy.** To calm uncontrollably emotional and violent patients, Moniz cut the nerves connecting the frontal lobes with the emotion-controlling centers of the inner brain. His crude but easy and inexpensive procedure took only about 10 minutes. After shocking the patient into a coma, he (and later other neurosurgeons) would hammer an instrument shaped like an icepick through each eye socket driving it into the brain. He then wiggled the instrument to sever connections running up to the frontal lobes. Tens of thousands of severely disturbed people were given lobotomies between 1936 and 1954, and Moniz was honored with a Nobel Prize (Valenstein, 1986).

Although the intention was simply to disconnect emotion from thought, the effect was often more drastic. A lobotomy usually decreased the person's misery or tension. But it also produced a permanently listless, immature, uncreative personality. During the 1950s, after some 35,000 people had been lobotomized in the United States alone, calming drugs became available and psychosurgery was largely abandoned. Today, lobotomies are history, and other psychosurgery is used only in extreme cases. For example, if a patient suffers uncontrollable seizures, surgeons can destroy the specific nerve clusters that cause or transmit the convulsions. MRI-guided precision surgery is also occasionally done to cut the circuits involved in severe obsessive-compulsive disorder (Sachdev & Sachdev, 1997). Because these procedures are irreversible, neurosurgeons perform them only as a last resort.

New York Times Co./Getty Images

Failed lobotomy: This 1940 photo shows Rosemary Kennedy (center) at age 22 with brother (and future U.S. president) John and sister Jean. A year later her father, on medical advice, approved a lobotomy that was promised to control her reportedly violent mood swings. The procedure left her confined to a hospital with an infantile mentality until her death in 2005 at age 86.

Therapeutic Life-Style Change

14 How, by adopting a healthier life-style, might people find some relief from depression?

The effectiveness of the biomedical therapies reminds us of a fundamental lesson. *We find it convenient to talk of separate psychological and biological influences, but everything psychological is also biological.* Every thought and feeling depends on the functioning brain. Every creative idea, every moment of joy or anger, every period of depression emerges from the electrochemical activity of the living brain. The influence is two-way. When psychotherapy relieves obsessive-compulsive behavior, PET scans reveal a calmer brain (Schwartz et al., 1996).

For years, we have trusted our bodies to physicians and our minds to psychiatrists and psychologists. That neat separation no longer seems valid. Stress affects body chemistry and health. And chemical imbalances, whatever their cause, can produce psychological disorders.

That lesson is being applied by Stephen Ilardi and his colleagues (2009) in training seminars promoting *therapeutic life-style change.* Human brains and bodies were designed for physical activity and social engagement, they note. Our ancestors hunted, gathered, and built in groups, with little evidence of disabling depression. Indeed, those whose way of life entails strenuous physical activity, strong community ties, sunlight exposure, and plenty of sleep (think of Amish farming communities) rarely experience major depression. "Simply put: humans were never designed for the sedentary, disengaged, socially isolated, poorly nourished, sleep-deprived pace of twenty-first-century American life."

Other studies confirm that exercise reduces depression and anxiety and is therefore a useful adjunct to antidepressant drugs and psychotherapy (Dunn et al., 2005; Stathopoulou et al., 2006). Not only is exercise about as effective as drugs, some research suggests it better prevents symptom recurrence (Babyak et al., 2000; Salmon, 2001).

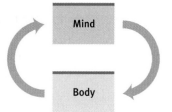

Rubberball/Nicole Hill/Jupiterimages

The Ilardi team was also impressed by research showing that regular aerobic exercise rivals the healing power of antidepressant drugs, and that a complete night's sleep boosts mood and energy. So they invited small groups of people with depression to undergo a 12-week training program with the following goals:

- *Aerobic exercise,* 30 minutes a day, at least three times weekly (increases fitness and vitality, stimulates endorphins)
- *Adequate sleep,* with a goal of 7 to 8 hours a night (increases energy and alertness, boosts immunity)
- *Light exposure,* at least 30 minutes each morning with a light box (amplifies arousal, influences hormones)
- *Social connection,* with less alone time and at least two meaningful social engagements weekly (helps satisfy the human need to belong)
- *Anti-rumination,* by identifying and redirecting negative thoughts (enhances positive thinking)
- *Nutritional supplements,* including a daily fish oil supplement with omega-3 fatty acids (aids in healthy brain functioning)

In one study of 74 people, 77 percent of those who completed the program experienced relief from depressive symptoms, compared with a 19 percent rate in those assigned to a treatment-as-usual control condition. Future research will seek to replicate this striking result of life-style change. Researchers will also try to identify which parts of the treatment (some are found in other therapies) produce the therapeutic effect. But there seems little reason to doubt the truth of the Latin adage, *Mens sana in corpore sano:* "A healthy mind in a healthy body" (**FIGURE 13.9**).

* * *

TABLE 13.2 on the next page summarizes some aspects of the therapies discussed in this chapter.

FIGURE 13.9 • **Mind-body interaction** The biomedical therapies assume that mind and body are a unit: Affect one and you will affect the other.

Mind

Body

Preventing Psychological Disorders

15 What may help prevent psychological disorders?

We have seen that life-style change can help *reverse* some of the symptoms of psychological disorders. Might such change also *prevent* some disorders by building individuals' **resilience**—an ability to cope with stress and recover from adversity? Faced with unforeseen trauma, most adults exhibit resilience. This was true of New Yorkers in the aftermath of 9/11, especially those who enjoyed supportive close relationships and who had not recently experienced other stressful events (Bonanno et al., 2007). More than 9 in 10 New Yorkers, although stunned and grief-stricken by 9/11, did

repetitive transcranial magnetic stimulation (rTMS) the application of repeated pulses of magnetic energy to the brain; used to stimulate or suppress brain activity.

psychosurgery surgery that removes or destroys brain tissue in an effort to change behavior.

lobotomy a psychosurgical procedure once used to calm uncontrollably emotional or violent patients. The procedure cut the nerves connecting the frontal lobes to the emotion-controlling centers of the inner brain.

resilience the personal strength that helps most people cope with stress and recover from adversity and even trauma.

TABLE 13.2	Comparing Therapies		
Therapy	**Presumed Problem**	**Therapy Aim**	**Therapy Technique**
Psychodynamic	Unconscious conflicts and urges	Promote insight into repressed material.	Psychoanalysis; therapist's interpretations of patient's memories and feelings.
Client-centered	Blocking of self-acceptance	Enable growth via unconditional positive regard, genuineness, and empathy.	Active reflective listening.
Behavior	Dysfunctional behaviors	Relearn adaptive behaviors; extinguish problem ones.	Classical conditioning via exposure or aversion therapy; operant conditioning, as in token economies.
Cognitive	Self-harmful thoughts	Promote positive thinking.	Training people to dispute negative thoughts and attributions.
Biomedical	Brain or neurotransmitter malfunctions	Restore healthy biological state.	Drugs; brain stimulation; exercise.

not have a dysfunctional stress reaction. By the following January, the stress symptoms of those who did were mostly gone (Person et al., 2006). Even in groups of combat-stressed veterans and political rebels who have survived dozens of episodes of torture, most do not later exhibit PTSD (Mineka & Zinbarg, 1996).

Psychologist Peter Suedfeld (1998, 2000) documented this resilience among Holocaust survivors, most of whom went on to live productive lives. "It is not always true that 'What doesn't kill you makes you stronger,' but it is often true," Suedfeld reported. "What doesn't kill you may reveal to you just how strong you really are." He speaks from experience. As a boy, Suedfeld survived the Holocaust, though his mother did not. Fellow survivor Ervin Staub has described "altruism born of suffering" (Staub & Vollhardt, 2008). Although nothing justifies terror and victimization, those who have suffered, he reports, often develop a greater-than-usual sensitivity to suffering. They have a greater empathy for others who suffer, an increased sense of responsibility, and an enlarged capacity for caring. Staub is a living example of his own work. He was spared from being sent to the Auschwitz death camps, thanks to a heroic intervention. Since that time, his lifelong mission has been to understand why some people perpetrate evil, some stand by, and some help.

Other evidence that struggling with challenging crises can lead to *post-traumatic growth* comes from cancer survivors (Tedeschi & Calhoun, 2004). Many have reported a greater appreciation for life, more meaningful relationships, increased personal strength, changed priorities, and a richer spiritual life. Out of even our worst experiences some good can come. Suffering can lead to new sensitivity and strength. **WHAT MIGHT WE DO TO FOSTER◄ SUCH GROWTH AND HUMAN FLOURISHING?**

We have seen that psychotherapies and biomedical therapies tend to locate the cause of psychological disorders within the person with the disorder. These therapies try to treat people by giving them insight into their problems, by changing their thinking, or by helping them gain control with drugs. Yet according to the preventive view, it is not just the person who needs treatment, but also the person's social context. Many psychological disorders are understandable responses to a disturbing and stressful society. Better to prevent a problem by reforming a sick situation and by developing people's coping competencies than to wait for a problem to arise and then treat it.

> "It is better to prevent than to cure."
> Peruvian folk wisdom

A story about the rescue of a drowning person from a rushing river illustrates the importance of prevention. Having successfully given first aid to the first victim, the rescuer spots another struggling person and pulls her out, too. After a half-dozen repetitions, the rescuer suddenly turns and starts running away while the river sweeps yet another person into view. "Aren't you going to rescue that fellow?" asks a bystander. "Heck no," the rescuer replies. "I'm going upstream to find out what's pushing all these people in."

Preventive mental health is upstream work. It seeks to prevent psychological casualties by identifying and wiping out the conditions that cause them. Poverty, meaningless work, constant criticism, unemployment, racism, and sexism can undermine people's sense of competence, personal control, and self-esteem (Albee, 1986). Such stresses increase their risk of depression, alcohol dependence, and suicide.

To prevent psychological casualties, said George Albee, caring people should therefore support programs that control or eliminate these stressful situations. We eliminated smallpox not by treating the afflicted but by vaccinating the healthy. We conquered yellow fever by controlling mosquitoes. Preventing psychological problems means empowering those who have learned an attitude of helplessness and changing environments that breed loneliness. Better to drain the swamps than just swat the mosquitos.

Prevention therefore means renewing disintegrating families and bolstering parents' and teachers' skills at nurturing children's achievements and resulting self-concept. Indeed, "Everything aimed at improving the human condition, at making life more fulfilling and meaningful, may be considered part of primary prevention of mental or emotional disturbance" (Kessler & Albee, 1975, p. 557).

Among the upstream prevention workers are *community psychologists.* Mindful of how people interact with their environments, they focus on creating environments that support psychological health. Through their research and social action, community psychologists aim to empower people and to enhance their competence, health, and well-being.

* * *

> "Mental disorders arise from physical ones, and likewise physical disorders arise from mental ones."
>
> The *Mahabharata,* c. 200 C.E.

Toxic environments and pessimism are not, however, the whole story of psychological disorders. Anxiety disorders, major depression, bipolar disorder, substance abuse, and schizophrenia are in part biological events. Again, we see one of this book's big ideas. *A human being is an integrated biopsychosocial system.* We now know that stress affects body chemistry and health. And chemical imbalances, whatever their cause, can produce schizophrenia and depression. Every creative idea, every moment of joy or anger, every period of depression emerges from the electrochemical activity of the living brain.

PRACTICE TEST

THE BASICS

14. The expectation that a treatment will be effective can by itself cause some improvement. Psychologists call this the _____ effect.
a. placebo
b. biomedical
c. spontaneous recovery
d. psychotic

15. Despite their benefits in treating symptoms of schizophrenia, some antipsychotic drugs have unpleasant side effects, including
a. hyperactivity.
b. convulsions and momentary memory loss.
c. sluggishness, tremors, and twitches.
d. paranoia.

16. The _____ drugs can cause death if they are taken in combination with alcohol because both alcohol and these drugs depress central nervous system activity.
a. antipsychotic   c. antidepressant
b. antianxiety   d. SSRI

17. One substance that often brings relief to patients suffering the highs and lows of bipolar disorder is
a. rTMS.   c. lithium.
b. Xanax.   d. clozapine.

18. Electroconvulsive therapy (ECT) can be an effective treatment for

a. severe obsessive-compulsive disorder.
b. severe depression.
c. schizophrenia.
d. generalized anxiety disorder.

19. _____ seeks to identify and alleviate conditions that put people at risk for psychological disorders.
a. Biomedical therapy
b. Behavior therapy
c. rTMS
d. Preventive mental health

THE BIG PICTURE

13D. How do researchers evaluate the effectiveness of particular drug therapies?

13E. How does the placebo effect bias patients' attitudes about the effectiveness of biomedical therapies?

13F. What is the difference between preventive mental health and psychotherapy or biomedical therapy?

IN YOUR EVERYDAY LIFE

▪ What were your impressions of biomedical therapies before reading this chapter? Are any of your views different now? Why or why not?

▪ Which life-style changes could you make to improve your resilience and enhance your mental health?

Answers: 14. a, 15. c, 16. b, 17. c, 18. b, 19. d. Answers the The Big Picture questions can be found in Appendix B at the end of the book.

Terms and Concepts to Remember

psychotherapy, p. 352	unconditional positive regard, p. 355	family therapy, p. 360
biomedical therapy, p. 352	behavior therapy, p. 355	antipsychotic drugs, p. 366
eclectic approach, p. 352	counterconditioning, p. 356	antianxiety drugs, p. 367
psychoanalysis, p. 352	exposure therapies, p. 356	antidepressant drugs, p. 367
resistance, p. 353	systematic desensitization, p. 356	electroconvulsive therapy (ECT), p. 368
interpretation, p. 353	virtual reality exposure therapy, p. 356	repetitive transcranial magnetic stimulation (rTMS), p. 370
transference, p. 353	aversive conditioning, p. 357	
psychodynamic therapy, p. 353	token economy, p. 358	psychosurgery, p. 370
client-centered therapy, p. 354	cognitive therapy, p. 358	lobotomy, p. 370
active listening, p. 354	cognitive-behavioral therapy, p. 359	resilience, p. 371

Multiple-choice **self-tests** and more may be found at www.worthpublishers.com/myers

Treating Psychological Disorders

1 How do psychotherapy, biomedical therapy, and an eclectic approach to therapy differ?

- *Psychotherapy* involves an interaction between a trained therapist and a person seeking to overcome difficulties or achieve personal growth.
- *Biomedical therapy* involves treatment with drugs, medical procedures, or other biological therapies.
- Therapists who take an *eclectic approach* combine different techniques tailored to the client's problems.

The Psychological Therapies

2 What are the aims, methods, and criticisms of psychoanalysis?

- Freud's *psychoanalysis* aimed to help people (1) gain insight into the unconscious origins of their disorders, and (2) work through the accompanying feelings.
- Methods included free association, dream analysis, *interpretation* of *resistance,* and *transference* to the therapist of feelings experienced in other important relationships.

3 How is psychodynamic therapy derived from psychoanalysis? How does it differ?

- Like psychoanalysis, *psychodynamic therapy* focuses on childhood experiences, therapist interactions, unconscious feelings, and unresolved conflicts. Yet it is briefer and focuses primarily on current symptom relief.

4 What are the basic themes of humanistic therapy, and what are the goals of Rogers' client-centered approach?

- Therapy promotes clients' self-awareness and self-acceptance.
- Personal growth requires taking responsibility for your feelings and actions.
- Therapy's focus is promoting growth rather than curing illness.
- Conscious thoughts are more important than the unconscious.
- *Client-centered therapy:* Therapists foster clients' growth through *active listening* and by being genuine, accepting, and empathic, with an attitude of *unconditional positive regard.*

5 How do behavior therapy's assumptions and techniques differ from those of psychoanalytic and humanistic therapies? What are exposure therapies and aversive conditioning?

- *Behavior therapists* use conditioning principles to modify problem behaviors, rather than seeking insight into the source of those behaviors as psychoanalysis and humanistic therapy would do.
- *Counterconditioning* applies classical conditioning techniques (such as *exposure therapy* and *aversive conditioning*) to teach clients new responses to stimuli that trigger unwanted behaviors.
- Exposure therapies help reduce anxiety by exposing people over and over to the feared item or experience.
- Through aversive conditioning, people learn a negative response to a harmful stimulus.

6 What is the basic idea of operant conditioning therapies?

- Behavior can be modified by changing the consequences.
- Therapists may use a *token economy,* in which desired behavior earns privileges.

7 What are the goals and techniques of the cognitive therapies?

- *Cognitive therapies,* such as Beck's therapy for depression, aim to train people to think in healthier ways.
- *Cognitive-behavioral therapy* helps clients to develop new, healthier ways of acting as well as thinking.

8 What are the benefits of group therapy, including family therapy?

- Group therapy can help more people for less money.
- Clients may benefit from knowing others have similar problems and from getting feedback and reassurance.
- *Family therapy* treats a family as a system and attempts to guide family members toward positive relationships and better communication.

Evaluating Psychotherapies

9 Why do clients and clinicians tend to overestimate the effectiveness of therapy?

- Clients justify their investment, tend to speak kindly of their therapists, and sometimes are healed by time alone.
- Therapists tend to track only their "success" stories.
- Outcome research has found that people who remain untreated often improve, but those who receive psychotherapy are more likely to improve.

10 What psychotherapies are most effective—and for what problems?

- No one psychotherapy is superior to all others.
- Behavior therapies work best with specific behavior problems, such as phobias.
- Cognitive therapy is effective in reducing depression and suicide risk.
- Effective clinical decision making relies upon a clear understanding of the patient, therapist expertise, and available research evidence.

11 What three benefits are provided by all forms of effective psychotherapy? How do differences in culture and values influence the relationship between a therapist and a client?

- All effective psychotherapies offer (1) new hope; (2) a fresh perspective; and (3) an empathic, trusting, caring relationship.
- Cultural and value differences can create stress about therapy's goals and prevent the formation of a strong emotional bond between the client and therapist. People can avoid these conflicts by asking potential therapists about their treatment approach and values.

The Biomedical Therapies

12 What are the different drug therapies, and what are some of the side effects of those treatments?

- Drug therapy is the most widely used biomedical therapy.
- *Antipsychotic drugs,* used in treating schizophrenia and other disorders, alter the availability of some neurotransmitters. Side effects can include tardive dyskinesia or increased risk of obesity and diabetes.
- *Antianxiety drugs,* which depress central nervous system activity, are used to treat anxiety disorders, often in combination with psychotherapy. These drugs can be physically and psychologically addictive.
- *Antidepressant drugs,* which increase the availability of serotonin or norepinephrine, are used for depression and anxiety disorders. Side effects may include decreased sexual desire, and their effectiveness is relatively low.
- Mood-stabilizing drugs, such as lithium, are often prescribed for those with bipolar disorder.

13 How are brain stimulation and psychosurgery used in treating specific disorders?

- In *electroconvulsive therapy (ECT),* a brief electric current is sent through the brain.
- ECT is an effective treatment for severely depressed people who have not responded to other therapy.
- Newer alternative treatments for depression include vagus nerve stimulation, deep-brain stimulation, and *repetitive transcranial magnetic stimulation (rTMS).*
- The irreversible *psychosurgical* procedures are used only as a last resort. *Lobotomies* are no longer performed.

14 How, by adopting a healthier life-style, might people find some relief from depression?

- Our bodies and minds affect each other. Research suggests that aerobic exercise, adequate sleep and sunlight, social connections, anti-rumination strategies, and good nutrition may relieve symptoms of depression.

Preventing Psychological Disorders

15 What may help prevent psychological disorders?

- Changing stressful social contexts and teaching people to cope better with stress may help them become more *resilient,* enabling recovery from adversity.
- Community psychologists work to prevent psychological disorders by turning destructive environments into more nurturing places that foster competence, health, and well-being.

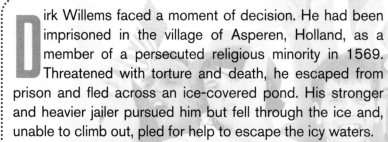

14

SOCIAL PSYCHOLOGY

Dirk Willems faced a moment of decision. He had been imprisoned in the village of Asperen, Holland, as a member of a persecuted religious minority in 1569. Threatened with torture and death, he escaped from prison and fled across an ice-covered pond. His stronger and heavier jailer pursued him but fell through the ice and, unable to climb out, pled for help to escape the icy waters.

With his freedom in front of him, Willems acted with ultimate selflessness. He turned back and rescued his pursuer, who, under orders, took him back to captivity. A few weeks later Willems was condemned to be "executed with fire, until death ensues." For his martyrdom, present-day Asperen has named a street in honor of its folk hero (Toews, 2004).

What drives people to feel contempt for someone of a religious minority, such as Dirk Willems, and then to act so spitefully? And what motivates the selflessness of his response, and of so many who have died trying to save others? Indeed, what motivates any of us when we volunteer kindness and generosity—or ill will and neglect—toward others?

As such examples demonstrate, we are social animals. We may assume the best or the worst in others. We may approach them with closed fists or open arms. But as the novelist Herman Melville remarked, "We cannot live for ourselves alone. Our lives are connected by a thousand invisible threads." *Social psychologists* explore these connections by scientifically studying how we *think about, influence,* and *relate to* one another.

An etching of Dirk Willems by Dutch artist Jan Luyken (from *The Martyrs Mirror,* **1685**)

Personality psychologists (Chapter 11) study the personal traits and dynamics that explain why *different people* may act differently *in a given situation,* such as the one Willems faced. (Would you have helped the jailer out of the icy water?) **Social psychologists** study the social influences that explain why *the same person* will act differently in *different situations.* Might the jailer have acted differently—opting not to march Willems back to jail—under differing circumstances?

Social Thinking

When the unexpected occurs, we want to understand, to explain why people act as they do. Our search for answers—whether in a crisis or in everyday life—often leaves us with two choices. We can attribute the behavior to the person's stable, enduring traits. Or we can attribute it to the situation (Heider, 1958).

The Fundamental Attribution Error

1 What are three main focuses of social psychology? How does the fundamental attribution error describe how we tend to explain others' behavior compared with our own?

In class, we notice that Juliette seldom talks. Over coffee, Jack talks nonstop. That must be the sort of people they are, we decide. Juliette must be shy and Jack outgoing. Are they? Perhaps. People do have enduring personality traits. But all too often, our attributions (our explanations) are wrong. We fall prey to the **fundamental attribution error:** We overestimate the influence of personality and underestimate the influence of situations. In class, Jack may be as quiet as Juliette. Catch Juliette at a party and you may hardly recognize your quiet classmate.

Researchers demonstrated this tendency in an experiment with college students (Napolitan & Goethals, 1979). They had students talk, one at a time, with a young woman who acted either cold and critical or warm and friendly. Before the talks, the researchers told half the students that the woman's behavior would be normal and natural. They told the other half the truth—that they had instructed her to *act* friendly (or unfriendly).

Did hearing the truth affect students' impressions of the woman? Not at all! If the woman acted friendly, both groups decided she really was a warm person. If she acted unfriendly, both decided she really was a cold person. In other words, they attributed her behavior to her personal traits, *even when they were told that her behavior was part of the experimental situation.*

The fundamental attribution error appears more often in some cultures than in others. Individualistic Westerners more often attribute behavior to people's personal traits. People in East Asian cultures are more sensitive to the power of situations (Masuda & Kitayama, 2004). This difference appeared in experiments in which people were asked to view scenes, such as a big fish swimming. Americans focused more on the individual fish and Japanese people on the whole scene (Chua et al., 2005; Nisbett, 2003).

To see how easily we make the fundamental attribution error, answer this question: Is your psychology instructor shy or outgoing? If you're tempted to answer "outgoing," remember that you know your instructor from one situation—the classroom, which demands outgoing behavior. Your instructor (who observes his or her own behavior not only in the classroom, but also with family, friends, and colleagues) might say, "Me, outgoing? It all depends on the situation. In class or with good friends, yes, I'm outgoing. But at professional meetings I'm really rather shy." Outside the classroom, professors seem less professorial, students less studious.

So, when we explain *our own* behavior, we are sensitive to how behavior changes with the situation (Idson & Mischel, 2001). We also are sensitive to the power of the situation when we explain the behavior of people we have seen in many different contexts. When are we most likely to commit the fundamental attribution error? The odds are highest when a stranger acts badly. Having never seen this person in other situations, we assume he must be a bad person. But outside the stadium, that bare-bellied, red-faced man screaming at the referee may be a great neighbor and a good father.

If we could take the observer's point of view, would we become more aware of our own personal style? To test this idea, researchers have reversed the perspectives of actor and observer. They filmed some interactions and then had participants view a replay of the situation—filmed from the other person's perspective. It worked. The viewers reversed their explanations of the behaviors (Lassiter & Irvine, 1986; Storms, 1973). Seeing the world from the actor's perspective, the observers better appreciated the situation.

As we act, our eyes look outward; we see others' faces, not our own. Reflecting on our past selves of 5 or 10 years ago also switches our perspective. Our present self adopts the observer's perspective and attributes our past behavior mostly to our traits (Pronin & Ross, 2006). In another 5 or 10 years, your today's self may seem like another person.

The way we explain others' actions, attributing them to the person or the situation, can have important real-life effects (Fincham & Bradbury, 1993; Fletcher et al., 1990). A person must decide whether to attribute another's friendliness to romantic or sexual interest. A jury must decide whether a shooting was malicious or in self-defense. A voter must judge whether a candidate's promises will be kept or forgotten. A partner must decide whether a loved one's tart-tongued remark reflects a bad day or a mean disposition.

Finally, consider the political effects of attribution. How can we explain poverty or unemployment? In Britain, India, Australia, and the United States (Furnham, 1982; Pandey et al., 1982; Wagstaff, 1982; Zucker & Weiner, 1993), political conservatives have tended to place the blame on the personal traits of the poor and unemployed. "People generally get what

"Otis, shout at that man to pull himself together."

they deserve. Those who don't work are often freeloaders. Anybody who takes the initiative can still get ahead." Political liberals (and social scientists) are more likely to blame past and present situations. "If you or I had to live with the same poor education, lack of opportunity, and discrimination, would we be any better off?"

The point to remember: Our attributions—to someone's disposition or to the situation—have real consequences.

Attitudes and Actions

> **2** What is an attitude, and how do attitudes and actions affect each other?

Attitudes are feelings, often based on our beliefs, that can influence how we respond to particular objects, people, and events. If we *believe* someone is mean, we may *feel* dislike for the person and *act* unfriendly. That helps explain a noteworthy finding. If people in a country intensely dislike the leaders of another country, their country is more likely to produce terrorist acts against that country (Krueger & Malecková, 2009). Hatred spawns violence.

Attitudes Affect Actions

Attitudes affect our behavior, but other factors, including the situation, also influence behavior. Attitudes are especially likely to affect behavior when

external influences are minimal, the attitude is stable, specific to the behavior, and easily recalled (Glasman & Albarracín, 2006). One experiment used vivid, easily recalled information to persuade people that sustained tanning put them at risk for future skin cancer. One month later, 72 percent of the participants, and only 16 percent of those in a waitlist control group, had lighter skin (McClendon & Prentice-Dunn, 2001).

Actions Affect Attitudes

People also come to believe in what they have stood up for. Many streams of evidence confirm that *attitudes follow behavior* (**FIGURE 14.1**).

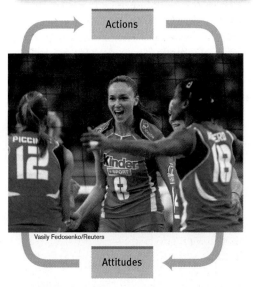

FIGURE 14.1 ● **Attitudes follow behavior** Cooperative actions, such as those performed by people on sports teams, feed mutual liking. Such attitudes, in turn, promote positive behavior.

Actions

Attitudes

Vasily Fedosenko/Reuters

social psychology the scientific study of how we think about, influence, and relate to one another.

fundamental attribution error the tendency, when analyzing another's behavior, to overestimate the influence of personal traits and underestimate the effects of the situation.

attitude feelings, often based on our beliefs, that predispose us to respond in a particular way to objects, people, and events.

Actor and observer perspectives make for differing attributions: During the heated U.S. presidential primaries in 2008, then-candidate Barack Obama was criticized for seeming—in this camera shot that faces him—to turn a cold shoulder to his opponent, Hillary Clinton. Obama later explained that he had greeted her earlier, and here was turning to speak to (as a picture taken from behind him might have shown) the unseen person to his left. In laboratory experiments, when a camera shows the actor's perspective, observers better appreciate the situation's influence.

Doug Mills/New York Times/Redux

The Foot-in-the-Door Phenomenon How would you react if someone induced you to act against your beliefs? In many cases, people change their attitudes. During the Korean war, many U.S. prisoners of war were held in camps run by Chinese communists. Without using brutality, the captors gained prisoners' cooperation in various activities. Some merely ran errands or accepted favors. Others made radio appeals and false confessions. Still others informed on other prisoners and revealed military information. When the war ended, 21 prisoners chose to stay with the communists. More returned home "brainwashed"—convinced that communism was good for Asia.

How did the Chinese captors achieve these amazing results? A key ingredient was their effective use of the **foot-in-the-door phenomenon.** They knew that people who agree to a small request will find it easier to agree later to a larger one. The Chinese began with harmless requests, such as copying a trivial statement, but gradually made bigger demands (Schein, 1956). The next statement to be copied might contain a list of the flaws of capitalism. Then, to gain privileges, the prisoners took part in group discussions, wrote self-criticisms, or made public confessions. After taking this series of small steps, the Americans often changed their beliefs to be more in line with their public acts. The point is simple. To get people to agree to something big, start small and build (Cialdini, 1993). A trivial act makes the next act easier. Give in to a temptation and you will find the next temptation harder to resist.

In dozens of experiments, researchers have coaxed people into acting against their attitudes or violating their moral standards, with the same result. Doing becomes believing. After giving in to a request to harm an innocent victim—by making nasty comments or delivering electric shocks—people begin to look down on their victim. After speaking or writing in support of a position they have doubts about, they begin to believe their own words.

Fortunately, the attitudes-follow-behavior principle works as well for good deeds as for bad. After U.S. schools were desegregated and the 1964 Civil Rights Act was passed, White Americans expressed lower levels of racial prejudice. And as Americans in different regions came to act more alike—thanks to more uniform national standards against discrimination—they began to think more alike. Experiments confirm the observation: Moral action strengthens moral convictions.

Role-Playing Affects Attitudes How many new **roles** have you adopted recently? Becoming a college student is a new role. Perhaps you've started a new relationship or even become engaged or married. If so, you may have realized that people expected you to behave a little differently. At first, your behaviors may have felt phony, because you were *acting* a role. Soldiers may at first feel they are playing war games. Newlyweds may feel they are "playing house." Before long, however, what began as play-acting in the theater of life becomes *you*. (This belief is reflected in the Alcoholics Anonymous saying, "Fake it until you make it.")

Role-playing morphed into real life in one famous study in which male college students volunteered to spend time in a mock prison (Zimbardo, 1972). Psychologist Philip Zimbardo randomly assigned some volunteers to be guards. He gave them uniforms, clubs, and whistles and instructed them to enforce certain rules. Others became prisoners, locked in barren cells and forced to wear humiliating outfits. For a day or two, the volunteers self-consciously played their roles. Then it became clear that the "play" had become real—too real. Most guards developed bad attitudes. Some set up cruel and degrading routines. One by one, the prisoners broke down, rebelled, or became passively resigned. After only six days, Zimbardo called off the study.

Diverse Yet Alike

The Power of the Situation

In his 1972 Stanford Prison simulation, Philip Zimbardo created a toxic situation (left). Those assigned to the guard role soon degraded the prisoners. In real life in 2004, some U.S. military guards abused Iraqi prisoners at the U.S.-run Abu Ghraib prison (right). To Zimbardo (2004, 2007), it was a bad barrel rather than a few bad apples that led to the atrocities: "When ordinary people are put in a novel, evil place, such as most prisons, Situations Win, People Lose."

Philip G. Zimbardo, Inc.

Associated Press

Role-playing can train people to become torturers in the real world, too (Staub, 1989). In the early 1970s, the Greek military government eased men into their roles. First, a trainee stood guard outside an interrogation cell. After this "foot-in-the-door" step, he stood guard inside. Only then was he ready to become actively involved in the questioning and torture. What we do, we gradually become.

Yet people differ. In Zimbardo's prison simulation, and in other atrocity-producing situations, some people gave in to the situation and others did not (Carnahan & McFarland, 2007; Haslam & Reicher, 2007; Mastroianni & Reed, 2006; Zimbardo, 2007). Person and situation interact.

Cognitive Dissonance: Relief From Tension

We have seen that actions can affect attitudes, sometimes turning prisoners into collaborators, doubters into believers, and guards into abusers. But why? One explanation is that when we become aware of a mismatch between our attitudes and actions, we experience mental discomfort, or *cognitive dissonance*. To relieve such tension, according to Leon Festinger's **cognitive dissonance theory,** we often bring our attitudes into line with our actions. Dozens of experiments have explored this cognitive dissonance

phenomenon. Many of them have made people feel responsible for behavior that clashed with their attitudes. As a participant in one of these experiments, you might agree for a mere $2 to help a researcher by writing an essay that supports something you don't believe in (perhaps a tuition increase). Feeling responsible for the statements (which are inconsistent with your attitudes), you would probably feel dissonance, especially if you thought an administrator would be reading your essay. How could you reduce the uncomfortable tension? One way would be to start believing your phony words. At such times, it's as if we tell ourselves, "If I chose to do it (or say it), I must believe in it." Thus, we may change our attitudes to help justify the act.

Some believe that the pressure to reduce dissonance helps explain the evolution of American attitudes toward the U.S. invasion of Iraq. When the war began, the stated reason for the invasion was the presumed threat of Saddam Hussein's weapons of mass destruction (WMD). Would the war be justified if Iraq did not have WMD? Only 38 percent of Americans said it would be (Gallup, 2003). Nearly 80 percent believed such weapons would be found (Duffy, 2003; Newport et al., 2003). When no WMD were found,

many Americans felt dissonance. These feelings deepened as information about the war's human and financial costs poured in. Scenes of chaos in Iraq, and inflamed anti-American and pro-terrorist sentiments in some parts of the world, increased the tension.

To reduce dissonance, some Americans revised their memories of the main reason for going to war. The invasion now became a movement to liberate an oppressed people and promote democracy in the Middle East. Before long, 58 percent of Americans—a majority—said they supported the war even if no WMD were found (Gallup, 2003). Support for the war continued above 50 percent until late 2004, then fell when hopes for a flourishing peace faded.

The attitudes-follow-behavior principle has a heartening implication. We cannot directly control all our feelings, but we can influence them by altering our behavior. (Recall from Chapter 9 the emotional effects of facial expressions and of body postures.) If we are down in the dumps, we can do as cognitive therapists advise and talk in more positive, self-accepting ways with fewer self–put-downs. If we are unloving, we can become more loving by behaving as if we were so—by doing thoughtful things, expressing affection, giving support.

The point to remember: Cruel acts shape the self. But so do acts of good will. Act as though you like someone, and you soon may. Changing our behavior can change how we think about others and how we feel about ourselves.

MANKOFF

"Look, I have my misgivings, too, but what choice do we have except stay the course?"

---

foot-in-the-door phenomenon the tendency for people who have first agreed to a small request to comply later with a larger request.

role a set of expectations about a social position, defining how those in the position ought to behave.

cognitive dissonance theory the theory that we act to reduce the discomfort (dissonance) we feel when two of our thoughts (cognitions) clash. For example, when we become aware that our attitudes and our actions don't match, we may change our attitudes so that we feel more comfortable.

THE BASICS

1. You see a community theater's presentation of *Alice in Wonderland,* in which your new neighbor plays the wicked Queen of Hearts. If you make the fundamental attribution error, you will assume that

   a. she must be a mean person to be able to play that role so well.

   b. she may be a nice person outside her role.

   c. she could just as easily have played the part of sweet Alice.

   d. she was highly influenced by the costume, set, and fellow actors' expectations.

2. During the Korean war, the Chinese "brainwashed" captured American soldiers to think that communism was a good thing for Asia. A key ingredient in this process was their use of

   a. the fundamental attribution error.

   b. the foot-in-the-door phenomenon.

   c. the behavior-follows-attitudes principle.

   d. role-playing.

3. Cognitive dissonance theory attempts to explain why

   a. people who act against their attitudes tend to change their attitudes.

   b. people who act against their attitudes tend to change their behavior.

   c. agreeing to a small request increases the likelihood that we will agree to a larger request.

   d. people talk one way and act another.

THE BIG PICTURE

14A. Driving to school one snowy day, Marco narrowly misses a car that slides through a red light. "Slow down! What a terrible driver," he thinks to himself. Moments later, Marco himself slips through an intersection and yelps, "Wow! These roads are awful. The city plows need to get out here." What social psychology principle has Marco just demonstrated? Explain.

IN YOUR EVERYDAY LIFE

▪ Do you have an attitude or tendency you would like to change? How could you use the attitudes-follow-behavior idea to change it?

Answers: 1. a, 2. b, 3. a. Answers to The Big Picture questions can be found in Appendix B at the end of the book.

Social Influence

Social psychology's great lesson is the enormous power of social influence. We conform to the desires of those around us. We follow orders. We behave as others in our group behave. On campus, jeans are the dress code; on New York's Wall Street, dress suits are the norm. Let's examine the pull of these social strings. How strong are they? How do they operate? When do we break them?

Conformity and Obedience

3 **What do experiments on conformity and obedience reveal about the power of social influence?**

Fish swim in schools. Birds fly in flocks. And humans, too, tend to go with their group, to think what it thinks and do what it does. Behavior is contagious. If one of us laughs, coughs, yawns, or stares at the sky, others in our group will soon do the same. Like the chameleon lizards that take on the color of their surroundings, we humans take on the emotional tones of those around us (Totterdell et al., 1998). We are natural mimics, unconsciously imitating others' expressions, postures, and voice tones.

Researchers demonstrated this *chameleon effect* in a clever experiment (Chartrand & Bargh, 1999). They had students work in a room beside another person, who was actually the experimenter's assistant. Sometimes the assistants rubbed their own face. Sometimes they shook their foot. Sure enough, the students tended to rub their face when with the face-rubbing person and shake their foot when with the foot-shaking person.

Automatic mimicry helps us to *empathize,* to feel what others feel. This helps explain why we feel happier around happy people than around depressed ones. The more we mimic, the greater our empathy, and the more people tend to like us.

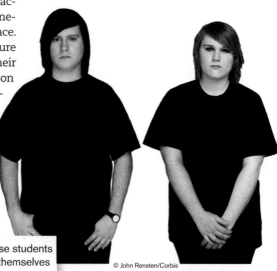

Conforming to nonconformity: Are these students asserting their individuality, or identifying themselves with others of the same microculture?

© John Rensten/Corbis

Group Pressure and Conformity

To study **conformity**—adjusting our behavior or thinking toward some group standard—Solomon Asch (1955) devised a simple test. As a participant in what you believe is a study of visual perception, you arrive in time to take a seat at a table with five other people. The experimenter asks the group to state, one by one, which of three comparison lines is identical to a standard line. You see clearly that the answer is Line 2, and you await your turn to say so. Your boredom begins to show when the next set of lines proves equally easy.

Now comes the third trial, and the correct answer seems just as clear-cut **(FIGURE 14.2).** But the first person gives what strikes you as a wrong answer: "Line 3." When the second person and then the third and fourth give the same wrong answer, you sit up straight and squint. When the fifth person agrees with the first four, you feel your heart begin to pound. The experimenter then looks to you for your answer. Torn between the agreement voiced by the five other respondents and the evidence of your own eyes, you feel tense and suddenly unsure of yourself. You hesitate before answering, wondering whether you should suffer the pain of being the oddball. What answer do you give?

FIGURE 14.2 • **Asch's conformity experiments** Which of the three comparison lines on the right is equal to the standard line? The photo on the left (from one of the experiments) was taken after five people, who were actually working for Asch, had answered, "Line 3." The student in the center shows the severe discomfort that comes from disagreeing with the responses of other group members.

William Vendivert/Scientific American

Standard line   Comparison lines
1   2   3

In Asch's experiments, college students experienced this conflict. Answering questions alone, the students were wrong less than 1 percent of the time. But the odds were quite different when several others—confederates working for the experimenter—answered incorrectly. Although most people told the truth even when others did not, Asch was disturbed by his result. More than one-third of the time, these "intelligent and well-meaning" college students were then "willing to call white black" by going along with the group.

Experiments reveal that we are more likely to conform when we

- are made to feel incompetent or insecure.
- are in a group with at least three people.
- are in a group in which everyone else agrees. (If just one other person disagrees, the odds that we also will disagree greatly increase.)
- admire the group's status and attractiveness.
- have not already committed ourselves to any response.
- know that others in the group will observe our behavior.
- are from a culture that strongly encourages respect for social standards.

Why do we so often think what others think and do what they do? Why in college residence halls do students' attitudes become more similar to those living near them (Cullum & Harton, 2007)? **WHY DO WE CLAP WHEN OTHERS CLAP, EAT AS OTHERS EAT, BELIEVE WHAT OTHERS BELIEVE, EVEN SEE WHAT OTHERS SEE?** Sometimes it's to avoid rejection or to gain social approval. So *we respond to social norms*. But groups also *provide information* that open-minded people will benefit from. "Those who never retract their opinions love themselves more than they love truth," observed Joseph Joubert, an eighteenth-century French essayist.

Is conformity good or bad? The answer depends on our values. When people conform to influences that support what we approve, we applaud them for being "open-minded" and "sensitive" enough to be "responsive." When they conform to influences that support what we disapprove, we scorn their "blind, thoughtless willingness" to give in to others' wishes.

"Have you ever noticed how one example—good or bad—can prompt others to follow? How one illegally parked car can give permission for others to do likewise? How one racial joke can fuel another?"

Marian Wright Edelman, *The Measure of Our Success*, 1992

David Katzenstein/Photolibrary

Tattoos: Yesterday's nonconformity, today's conformity? As tattoos become perceived as fashion conformity, their popularity may wane.

Our values, as we saw in Chapter 11, are influenced by our culture. Western Europeans and people in most English-speaking countries tend to prize individualism. People in many Asian, African, and Latin American countries place a higher value on honoring group standards. It's perhaps not surprising, then, that in social influence experiments across 17 countries, conformity rates are lower in individualist cultures (Bond & Smith, 1996). In the United States, for example, university students tend to see themselves as less conforming than others (Pronin et al., 2007). We are, in our own eyes, individuals amid a flock of sheep.

Obedience

Social psychologist Stanley Milgram (1963, 1974), a student of Solomon Asch, knew that people often give in to social pressure. But how would they respond to outright commands? To find out, he undertook experiments that have become social psychology's most famous and most hotly debated.

conformity adjusting our behavior or thinking to coincide with a group standard.

Stanley Milgram (1933–1984): This social psychologist's obedience experiments "belong to the self-understanding of literate people in our age" (Sabini, 1986).

Imagine yourself as one of the nearly 1000 people who took part in Milgram's 20 experiments. You have responded to an ad for participants in a Yale University psychology study of the effect of punishment on learning. Professor Milgram's assistant asks you and another person to draw slips from a hat to see who will be the "teacher" and who will be the "learner." You draw the "teacher" slip and are asked to sit down in front of a machine, which has a series of labeled switches. The "learner" is led to a nearby room and strapped into a chair. From the chair, wires run through the wall to "your" machine. You are given your task: Teach and then test the learner on a list of word pairs. If the learner gives a wrong answer, you are to flip a switch to deliver a brief electric shock. For the first wrong answer, you will flip the switch labeled "15 Volts—Slight Shock." With each succeeding error, you will move to the next higher voltage. The researcher demonstrates by flipping the first switch. Lights flash, relay switches click on, and an electric buzzing fills the air.

The experiment begins, and you deliver the shocks after the first and second wrong answers. If you continue, you hear the learner grunt when you flick the third, fourth, and fifth switches. After you flip the eighth switch ("120 Volts—Moderate Shock"), the learner cries out that the shocks are painful. After the tenth switch ("150 Volts—Strong Shock"), he begins shouting. "Get me out of here! I won't be in the experiment anymore! I refuse to go on!" You draw back, but the experimenter prods you. "Please continue—the experiment requires that you continue." You resist, but the experimenter insists, "It is absolutely essential that you continue," or "You have no other choice, you *must* go on."

If you obey, you hear the learner shriek in agony as you continue to raise the shock level after each new error. After the 330-volt level, the learner refuses to answer and falls silent. Still, the experimenter pushes you toward the final, 450-volt switch. Ask the question, he says, and if no correct answer is given, administer the next shock level.

Would you follow an experimenter's commands to shock someone? At what level would you refuse to obey? Milgram asked that question in a survey before he started his experiments. Most people were sure they would stop playing such a sadistic-seeming role soon after the learner first indicated pain, certainly before he shrieked in agony. Forty psychiatrists agreed with that prediction when Milgram asked them. Were the predictions accurate? Not even close. When Milgram actually conducted the experiment with men aged 20 to 50, he was astonished. More than 60 percent complied fully—right up to the last switch. Even when Milgram ran a new study, with 40 new teachers, and the learner complained of a "slight heart condition," the results were the same. A full 65 percent of the new teachers obeyed every one of the experimenter's commands right up to 450 volts **(FIGURE 14.3)**.

How can we explain these findings? We know that cultures change over time. Are people today less likely to obey an order to hurt someone? To find out, researchers have replicated Milgram's basic experiment (Burger, 2009). Seventy percent of the participants obeyed up to the 150-volt point, a slight reduction from Milgram's result. And in a French reality TV show replication, 80 percent of people, egged on by a cheering audience, obeyed and tortured a screaming victim (de Moraes, 2010).

Could Milgram's findings reflect some aspect of gender behavior found only in males? No. In 10 later studies, women obeyed at rates similar to men (Blass, 1999).

Did the teachers figure out the hoax—that no real shock was being delivered and the learner was in fact an assistant who was pretending to feel pain? Did they realize the experiment was really testing their willingness to obey commands to inflict punishment? No, the teachers typically displayed genuine distress. They perspired, trembled, laughed nervously, and bit their lips.

In later experiments, Milgram discovered some things that did influence people's behavior. When he varied some details of the situation, the percentage of participants who fully obeyed ranged from 0 to 93 percent. Obedience was highest when

- the person giving the orders was close at hand and was perceived to be a legitimate authority figure.

- the authority figure was supported by a respected, well-known institution (Yale University).

- the victim was depersonalized or at a distance, even in another room. (Similarly, many soldiers in combat either do not fire their rifles at an enemy they can see or do not aim them properly. Such refusals to kill are rare among soldiers who operate long-distance artillery or aircraft weapons [Padgett, 1989].)

"Drive off the cliff, James, I want to commit suicide."

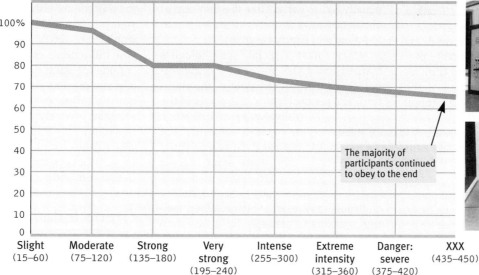

Percentage of participants who obeyed experimenter (y-axis: 0 to 100%)

The majority of participants continued to obey to the end

Shock levels in volts (x-axis):
Slight (15–60), Moderate (75–120), Strong (135–180), Very strong (195–240), Intense (255–300), Extreme intensity (315–360), Danger: severe (375–420), XXX (435–450)

© 1965 By Stanley Milgram, from the film *Obedience*, dist. by Penn State, Media Sales

- there were no role models for defiance. (Teachers did not see any other participant disobey the experimenter.)

The power of legitimate, close-at-hand authorities is dramatically apparent in stories of those who followed orders to carry out the Holocaust atrocities. Obedience alone does not explain the Holocaust. Anti-Semitic ideology produced eager killers as well (Mastroianni, 2002). But obedience was a factor. In the summer of 1942, nearly 500 middle-aged German reserve police officers were dispatched to German-occupied Jozefow, Poland. On July 13, the group's visibly upset commander informed his recruits, mostly family men, of their orders. They were to round up the village's Jews, who were said to be aiding the enemy. Able-bodied men would be sent to work camps, and all the rest were to be shot on the spot.

The commander gave the recruits a chance to refuse to participate in the executions. Only about a dozen immediately refused. Within 17 hours, the remaining 485 officers killed 1500 helpless women, children, and elderly, shooting them in the back of the head as they lay face down. Hearing the pleas of the victims, and seeing the gruesome results, some 20 percent of the officers did eventually

disobey. They did so either by missing their victims or by wandering away and hiding until the slaughter was over (Browning, 1992). In real life, as in Milgram's experiments, those who resisted did so early, and they were the minority.

Standing up for democracy: Some individuals—roughly one in three in Milgram's experiments—resist social coercion. This unarmed man single-handedly challenged an advancing line of tanks in Tiananmen Square in 1989. This was one day after the Chinese government had suppressed a student uprising there.

Another story was being played out in the French village of Le Chambon. There, French Jews were being sheltered by villagers who openly defied orders to cooperate with the "New Order." The villagers' ancestors had themselves been persecuted. Their pastors had been teaching them to "resist whenever our adversaries will demand of us obedience contrary to the orders of the Gospel" (Rochat, 1993). Ordered by police to give a list of sheltered Jews, the head pastor modeled defiance. "I don't know of Jews, I only know of human beings." These resistors had no idea how long and terrible the war would be, or how much punishment and poverty they would suffer. But early on, they made a commitment to resist. After that, they drew support from their beliefs, their role models, their interactions with one another, and their own early actions. They remained defiant to the war's end.

Lessons From the Conformity and Obedience Studies

4 | **What do the social influence studies teach us about ourselves? How much power do we have as individuals?**

How do the laboratory experiments on social influence relate to everyday social behavior? Psychology's experiments aim not to re-create the exact behaviors of everyday life but to explore what influences them. Solomon Asch and Stanley Milgram devised experiments that forced a choice: Do I adhere to my own standards or do I respond to others? That's a dilemma we all face frequently.

In Milgram's experiments and its modern replications (Burger, 2009), participants were also torn. Should they respond to the pleas of the victim or the orders of the experimenter? Their moral sense warned them not to harm another. But that same sense also prompted them to obey the experimenter and to be a good research participant. With kindness and obedience on a collision course, obedience usually won.

> "I was only following orders."
> Adolf Eichmann, Director of Nazi deportation of Jews to concentration camps

These experiments demonstrated that strong social influences can make people conform to falsehoods or give in to cruelty. Milgram saw this as the most basic lesson of his work. "Ordinary people, simply doing their jobs, and without any particular hostility on their part, can become agents in a terrible destructive process" (1974, p. 6). Using the foot-in-the-door effect, Milgram began with a little tickle of electricity and escalated step by step. In the minds of those throwing the switches, the small action became justified, making the next act tolerable.

In any society, great evils sometimes grow out of people's acceptance of lesser evils. The Nazi leaders suspected that most German civil servants would resist shooting or gassing Jews directly. But they found them surprisingly willing to handle the paperwork of the Holocaust (Silver & Geller, 1978). Milgram found a similar reaction in his experiments. When he asked 40 men to administer the learning test while someone else did the shocking, 93 percent complied. Cruelty does not require devilish villains. All it takes is ordinary people corrupted by an evil situation. Ordinary students may follow orders to haze initiates into their group. Ordinary employees may follow orders to

produce and market harmful products. Ordinary soldiers may follow orders to torture prisoners (Lankford, 2009).

In Jozefow and Le Chambon, as in Milgram's experiments, those who resisted usually did so early. After the first acts of obedience or resistance, attitudes began to follow and justify behavior.

What have social psychologists learned about the power of the individual? *Social control* (the power of the situation) and *personal control* (the power of the individual) interact. Much as water dissolves salt but not sand, so rotten situations turn some people into bad apples while others resist (Johnson, 2007).

People may resist coercion. When feeling pressured, perhaps in a situation where "groupthink" threatens decision making, we may react by doing the opposite of what is expected (Brehm & Brehm, 1981). Rosa Parks' refusal to sit at the back of the bus ignited the U.S. civil rights movement.

The power of one or two individuals to sway majorities is *minority influence* (Moscovici, 1985). In studies of groups in

Gandhi: As the life of Mahatma Gandhi powerfully testified, a consistent and persistent minority voice can sometimes sway the majority. The nonviolent appeals and fasts of the Hindu nationalist and spiritual leader were instrumental in winning India's independence from Britain in 1947.

which one or two individuals consistently express a controversial attitude or an unusual perceptual judgment, one finding repeatedly stands out. When you are the minority, you are far more likely to sway the majority if you hold firmly to your position and don't waffle. This tactic won't make you popular, but it may make you influential, especially if your self-confidence stimulates others to consider *why* you react as you do. Even when a minority's influence is not yet visible, people may privately develop sympathy for the minority position and rethink their views (Wood et al., 1994). The powers of social influence are enormous, but so are the powers of the committed individual.

Group Influence

5 How does the presence of others influence our actions, via social facilitation, social loafing, or deindividuation?

Imagine yourself standing in a room, holding a fishing pole. Your task is to wind the reel as fast as you can. On some occasions you wind in the presence of another participant who is also winding as fast as possible. Will the other's presence affect your own performance?

In one of social psychology's first experiments, Norman Triplett (1898) found that adolescents *would* wind a fishing reel faster in the presence of someone doing the same thing. He and later social psychologists studied how the presence of others affects our behavior. Group influences operate in such simple groups—one person in the presence of another—and in more complex groups.

Social Facilitation

Triplett's finding—that our responses on an individual task are stronger in the presence of others—is called **social facilitation.** Later studies revealed that the presence of others sometimes helps and sometimes hurts performance (Guerin, 1986; Zajonc, 1965). Why? Because when others observe us, we

Social facilitation: Skilled athletes often find they are "on" before an audience. What they do well, they do even better when people are watching.

become aroused, and this arousal amplifies our other reactions. It strengthens our most *likely* response—the correct one on an easy task, an incorrect one on a difficult task. Thus, when others observe us, we perform well-learned tasks *more* quickly and accurately. But on new and difficult tasks, we perform *less* quickly and accurately.

This effect helps answer an interesting question. IS THERE REALLY SUCH A THING AS THE HOME-TEAM ADVANTAGE? Yes—studies of more than 80,000 college and professional athletic events in Canada, the United States, and England show that the home team advantage is real **(TABLE 14.1)**. An enthusiastic audience seems to energize the home sports team. In about 6 in 10 games (somewhat fewer for baseball and football, somewhat more for basketball and soccer), home teams win.

The point to remember: What you do well, you are likely to do even better in front of an audience, especially a friendly audience. What you normally find difficult may seem all but impossible when you are being watched.

Social facilitation also helps explain a funny effect of crowding. Comedians and actors know that a "good house" is a full

one. What they may not know is that crowding triggers arousal, which, as you have seen, strengthens other reactions. Comedy routines that are mildly amusing to people in an uncrowded room seem funnier in a densely packed room (Aiello et al., 1983; Freedman & Perlick, 1979). And when you seat participants close to one another, they like a friendly person even more, an unfriendly person even less (Schiffenbauer & Schiavo, 1976; Storms & Thomas, 1977). HOW CAN WE IN- CREASE THE CHANCES OF LIVELY INTERAC- TION AT SOCIAL GATHERINGS? Try choosing a room or setting up seating that will just barely hold everyone.

Social Loafing

Does the presence of others have the same effect when people perform a task as a group? IN A TEAM TUG-OF-WAR, DO PEOPLE EXERT MORE THAN, LESS THAN, OR THE SAME AMOUNT OF EFFORT AS IN A ONE-ON-ONE TUG-OF-WAR? If you said, "less than," you're right. In one experiment, students who believed three others were also pulling behind them exerted only 82 percent as much effort as when they knew they were pulling alone (Ingham et al., 1974). And consider what happened when blindfolded people seated in a group clapped or shouted as loud as they could while hearing (through headphones) other

Working hard, or hardly working? In group projects, such as car washes, social loafing often occurs, as individuals free-ride on the efforts of others.

TABLE 14.1	Home Advantage in Major Team Sports	
Sport	Games Studied	Home Team Winning Percentage
Baseball	23,034	53.5%
Football	2,592	57.3
Ice hockey	4,322	61.1
Basketball	13,596	64.4
Soccer	37,202	69.0

Source: From Courneya & Carron (1992).

people clapping or shouting (Latané, 1981). In one round of noise making, the participants believed the researchers could identify their individual sounds. In another round, they believed their clapping and shouting was blended with other people's. When they thought they were part of a group effort, the participants produced about one-third less noise than when clapping "alone."

This diminished effort is called **social loafing** (Jackson & Williams, 1988; Latané, 1981). Experiments in the United States, India, Thailand, Japan, China, and Taiwan have recorded social loafing on various tasks. It was especially common among men in individualistic cultures (Karau & Williams, 1993). What causes social loafing? Three things:

social facilitation stronger responses on simple or well-learned tasks in the presence of others.

social loafing the tendency for people in a group to exert less effort when pooling their efforts toward attaining a common goal than when individually accountable.

- People acting as part of a group feel less accountable, so they worry less about what others think of them.

- Group members may not believe their individual contributions make a difference (Harkins & Szymanski, 1989; Kerr & Bruun, 1983).

- Loafing itself—when group members share equally in the benefits regardless of how much they contribute, some may slack off. (If you've worked on group assignments, you're probably already aware of this cause of social loafing!) People who are not highly motivated, who don't identify strongly with the group, may *free-ride* on others' efforts.

Deindividuation

We've seen that the presence of others can arouse people or it can make them feel less responsible. But sometimes the presence of others does both. The uninhibited behavior that results can range from a food fight to vandalism or rioting. This process of losing self-awareness and self-restraint, called **deindividuation,** often occurs when group participation makes people feel aroused and anonymous. In one experiment, some female students dressed in depersonalizing Ku Klux Klan-style hoods. Others in a control group did not wear the hoods. Those whose identities were hidden delivered twice as much electric shock to a victim (Zimbardo, 1970). (As in all such experiments, the "victim" did not actually receive the shocks.)

Deindividuation thrives, for better or for worse, in many different settings. The anonymity of Internet discussion boards and blog comment sections can unleash mocking or cruel words. Tribal warriors who depersonalize themselves with face paints or masks are more likely than those with exposed faces to kill, torture, or mutilate captured enemies (Watson, 1973). Whether in a mob, at a rock concert, at a ballgame, or at worship, when we shed self-awareness and self-restraint, we become more responsive to the group experience—bad or good.

Group Polarization

6 How can group interaction enable group polarization and groupthink?

Over time, differences between groups of college students tend to grow. If the first-year students at College X tend to be more artistic, and those at College Y tend to be business-savvy, those differences will probably be even greater by the time they graduate.

In each case, the beliefs and attitudes students bring to a group grow stronger as they discuss their views with others who share them. This process, called **group polarization,** can have positive results, as when low-prejudice students become even more accepting while discussing racial issues. But sometimes the results are far from positive. As **FIGURE 14.4** shows, when high-prejudice students discuss racial issues, they become *more* prejudiced (Myers & Bishop, 1970).

Researchers captured group polarization in a 2005 "Deliberation Day" experiment

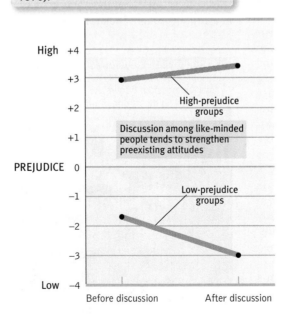

FIGURE 14.4 • **Group polarization** If a group is like-minded, discussion strengthens its prevailing opinions. Talking about racial issues increased prejudice in a high-prejudice group of high school students and decreased it in a low-prejudice group (Myers & Bishop, 1970).

(Schkade et al., 2006). They chose a random sample of people from the voter rolls of liberal Boulder, Colorado. They then divided the sample into five-person groups to discuss global climate change, affirmative action, and same-sex civil unions. In Colorado Springs, the researchers followed the same procedure with its more conservative voters. After the discussions, those in Boulder had moved further left, and those in Colorado Springs further right.

The polarizing effect of interaction among like-minded people applies also to suicide terrorists. The terrorist mentality does not erupt suddenly on a whim (McCauley, 2002; McCauley & Segal, 1987; Merari, 2002). It usually begins slowly, among people who get together because of a grievance. As group members interact in isolation (sometimes with other "brothers" and "sisters" in camps), their views grow more and more extreme. Increasingly, they divide the world into "us" against "them" (Moghaddam, 2005; Qirko, 2004).

The Internet provides an easily accessible medium for group polarization. For more on that topic, see Thinking Critically About: The Internet as Social Amplifier.

Groupthink

So group interaction can influence our personal decisions. **DOES GROUP INTERAC-◀ TION EVER DISTORT IMPORTANT NATIONAL DECISIONS?** It does, and one famous decision led to what is now known as the "Bay of Pigs fiasco." In 1961, President John F. Kennedy and his advisers decided to invade Cuba with 1400 CIA-trained Cuban exiles. The invaders were easily captured and soon linked to the U.S. government. When the invaders were so easily captured, Kennedy wondered in hindsight, "How could I have been so stupid?"

Reading a historian's account of the ill-fated blunder, social psychologist Irving Janis (1982) thought the decision-making procedures leading to the invasion might give some clues.

THINKING CRITICALLY ABOUT

The Internet as Social Amplifier

I cut my eye teeth in social psychology with experiments on *group polarization*—the tendency for face-to-face discussion to amplify group members' preexisting opinions. Never then did I imagine the potential dangers, or the creative possibilities, of polarization in *virtual* groups.

Electronic communication and social networking have created virtual town halls where people can isolate themselves from those whose opinions differ. As the Internet connects the like-minded and pools their ideas, global climate-change skeptics, UFO abductees, and conspiracy theorists find support for their shared ideas and suspicions. White supremacists may become more racist. Obama-despisers may grow more hostile. And militia members may become more terror prone. In the echo chambers of virtual worlds, as in the real world, separation + conversation = polarization.

But the Internet-as-social-amplifier can also work for good. Social networking sites, such as Facebook, connect friends and family members sharing common interests or coping with challenges. Peacemakers, cancer survivors, and bereaved parents can find strength and solace from kindred spirits. By amplifying shared concerns and ideas, Internet-enhanced communication can also foster social ventures. (I know this personally from social networking with others with hearing loss to transform American assistive listening technology.)

The point to remember: By linking and magnifying the inclinations of like-minded people, the Internet can be very, very bad, but also very, very good.

Hemera Technologies/Jupiterimages

deindividuation the loss of self-awareness and self-restraint occurring in group situations that foster arousal and anonymity.

group polarization strengthening of a group's preexisting attitudes through discussions within the group.

groupthink the mode of thinking that occurs when the desire for harmony in a decision-making group overrides a realistic appraisal of alternatives.

Here's what he discovered. The morale of the popular and recently elected president and his advisers was soaring. Their confidence was almost unlimited. To preserve the good feeling, group members with differing views kept quiet, especially after President Kennedy voiced his enthusiasm for the scheme. Since no one spoke strongly against the idea, everyone assumed the support was unanimous. **Groupthink** was at work. The desire for harmony had replaced realistic judgment.

Groupthink later contributed to the escalation of the Vietnam war, the Chernobyl nuclear reactor accident in Russia, and the U.S. space shuttle *Challenger* explosion (Esser & Lindoerfer, 1989; Reason, 1987).

Most recently, groupthink surfaced in U.S. discussions of the Iraq war. The bipartisan U.S. Senate Intelligence Committee (2004) reported that "personnel involved in the Iraq WMD [weapons of mass destruction] issue demonstrated several aspects of groupthink: examining few alternatives, selective gathering of information, pressure to conform within the group or withhold criticism, and collective rationalization." This mode of thinking led analysts to "interpret ambiguous evidence as conclusively indicative of a WMD program as well as ignore or minimize evidence that Iraq did not have [WMD] programs."

In the Iraq war discussions, as in others, groupthink was fed by overconfidence, conformity, self-justification, and group polarization. HOW CAN WE PREVENT ◀ GROUPTHINK? Knowing that two heads are often better than one, leaders can welcome open debate, invite experts' critiques of developing plans, and assign people to identify possible problems. *The point to remember:* None of us is as smart as all of us, especially when we welcome open debate.

PRACTICE TEST

THE BASICS

4. We are *most likely* to conform to a group if
   a. the group members have many different opinions.
   b. we are feeling competent and secure.
   c. the group consists of at least three people.
   d. other group members cannot observe our behavior.

5. In Milgram's experiments, the "teachers" were most likely to obey the commands to deliver high-voltage shocks to "learners" when
   a. the learner was at a distance from the teacher.
   b. the learner was close at hand.
   c. other teachers refused to go along with the experimenter.
   d. the person giving the order was another teacher.

6. Social facilitation—improved performance in the presence of others—occurs with
   a. any physical task.
   b. any mental task.
   c. a well-learned task.
   d. new learning.

7. When people are part of a group working toward a common goal, their individual efforts decrease. This process is called
   a. minority influence.
   b. social facilitation.
   c. social loafing.
   d. group polarization.

Continued

8. Deindividuation—losing self-awareness and self-control in a group situation that fosters arousal and anonymity—is best illustrated by
   a. performing better in front of an audience.
   b. rioting at a mass rally.
   c. avoiding responsibility in a group clean-up effort.
   d. denying your own opinions in the face of a unanimous group opinion.

9. In like-minded groups, discussion strengthens the prevailing opinion. This effect is called
   a. groupthink.
   b. minority influence.
   c. group polarization.
   d. social facilitation.

10. When a group's desire for harmony overrides its realistic analysis of other options, _____ has occurred.
    a. group polarization
    b. groupthink
    c. social facilitation
    d. deindividuation

THE BIG PICTURE

14B. What are some examples of social situations in which people are more likely to be obedient?

14C. You are organizing a group meeting of fiercely competitive political candidates. To add to the fun, friends have suggested handing out masks of the candidates' faces for supporters to wear. Based on what you read about deindividuation, what do you think might happen if people wear those masks?

IN YOUR EVERYDAY LIFE

• What example of social influence have you experienced this week? How did you respond to the power of the situation?

• What could you do to discourage social loafing in a group project assigned for a class?

Social Relations

We have sampled how we *think about* and *influence* one another. Now we come to social psychology's third focus—how we *relate* to one another. What causes us to harm or to help or to fall in love? How can we transform the closed fists of aggression into the open arms of compassion? We will ponder the bad and the good: from prejudice and aggression to attraction, altruism, and peacemaking.

Prejudice

7 What are the three parts of prejudice, and how has prejudice changed over time?

Prejudice means "prejudgment." It is an unjustifiable and usually negative attitude toward a group—often a different cultural, ethnic, or gender group. Prejudice is a three-part mixture of

> "Unhappily the world has yet to learn how to live with diversity."
> Pope John Paul II, Address to the United Nations, 1995

• *beliefs* (called **stereotypes**).

• *emotions* (for example, hostility, envy, or fear).

• predispositions to *action* (to discriminate).

To *believe* that obese people are gluttonous, to *feel* dislike for an obese person, and to be hesitant to hire or date an obese person is to be prejudiced. Prejudice is a negative *attitude*. **Discrimination** is a negative *behavior*.

Our ideas influence what we notice and how we interpret events. In one 1970s study, most White participants who saw a White man shoving a Black man said they were "horsing around." When they saw a Black man shoving a White man, they interpreted the same act as "violent" (Duncan, 1976). Our preconceived ideas color our perceptions.

How Prejudiced Are People?

To learn about levels of prejudice, we can assess what people say and what they do. Americans say that gender and racial attitudes have changed dramatically in the last half-century. Nearly everyone agrees that women and men should receive the same pay for doing the same job and that children of all races should attend the same schools.

The one-third of Americans who in 1937 told Gallup they would vote for a qualified woman whom their party nominated for president soared to 89 percent in 2007 (Gallup Brain, 2008; Jones & Moore, 2003). Support for all forms of racial contact, including interracial marriage **(FIGURE 14.5)** and voting for "a Black candidate" for president, has also dramatically increased. Among 18- to 29-year-old Americans, 9 in 10 now say they would be fine with a family member

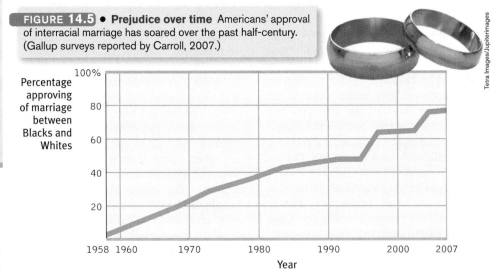

FIGURE 14.5 • **Prejudice over time** Americans' approval of interracial marriage has soared over the past half-century. (Gallup surveys reported by Carroll, 2007.)

Percentage approving of marriage between Blacks and Whites

Year

Tetra Images/Jupiterimages

Automatic Prejudice

Again and again throughout this book, we have seen that the human mind processes thoughts, memories, and attitudes on two different tracks. Sometimes that processing is *explicit*—on the radar screen of our awareness. More often, it is *implicit*—below the radar, out of sight. Modern studies indicate that prejudice is often implicit, an automatic attitude that is more of an unthinking knee-jerk response than a decision. Consider these findings on U.S. racial prejudice.

Implicit Racial Associations Even people who deny harboring racial prejudice may carry negative associations (Greenwald et al., 1998). For example, 9 in 10 White respondents took longer to identify pleasant words (such as *peace* and *paradise*) as "good" when presented with Black-sounding names (such as *Latisha* and *Darnell*) rather than White-sounding names (such as *Katie* and *Ian*). Such tests are useful for studying automatic prejudice. But critics caution against using them to assess or label individuals as prejudiced (Blanton et al., 2006, 2007, 2009).

Race-Influenced Perceptions Our expectations influence our perceptions. Consider the shooting of an unarmed man in the doorway of his Bronx apartment building several years ago. The officers thought he had pulled a gun from his pocket. In fact, he had pulled out his wallet. Curious about this shooting, two research teams reenacted the situation (Correll et al., 2002, 2007; Greenwald et al., 2003). They asked people to press buttons quickly to "shoot" or not shoot men who suddenly appeared on screen. Some of the on-screen men held a gun. Others held a harmless object, such as a flashlight or bottle. People (both Blacks and Whites, in one study) more often shot Black men holding the harmless object.

Reflexive Bodily Responses Even people who *consciously* express little prejudice may give off telltale signals as their body responds selectively to another person's race. Neuroscientists can detect these signals when people look at images of White and Black faces. The viewers' implicit prejudice shows up in different responses in their facial muscles and in their amygdala, an emotion-processing center (Cunningham et al., 2004; Eberhardt, 2005; Vanman et al., 2004).

Are you sometimes aware that you have feelings you would rather not have about other people? If so, remember this: It is what we do with our feelings that matters. We can monitor our feelings and actions and replace old habits with new ones based on new friendships.

Social Roots of Prejudice

8 What factors contribute to the social roots of prejudice, and how does scapegoating illustrate the emotional roots of prejudice?

Why does prejudice arise? Social inequalities and social divisions are partly responsible.

Social Inequalities Some people have money, power, and prestige. Others do not. In this situation, the "haves" usually develop attitudes that justify things as they are. The **just-world phenomenon** assumes that good is rewarded and evil is punished. From this it is but a short leap to assume that those who succeed must be good and those who suffer must be bad. Such reasoning enables the rich to see both their own wealth and the poor's misfortune as justly deserved.

---

marrying someone of a different race (Pew, 2010).

Yet as *open* prejudice wanes, *subtle* prejudice lingers. Despite increased verbal support for interracial marriage, many people admit that in socially intimate settings (dating, dancing, marrying) they would feel uncomfortable with someone of another race. Recent experiments illustrate that prejudice can be not only subtle but also automatic and unconscious (see Close-Up: Automatic Prejudice).

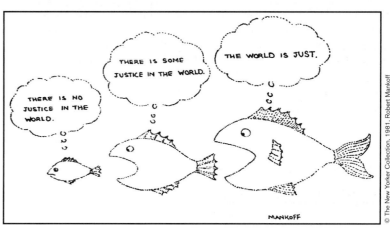

THERE IS SOME JUSTICE IN THE WORLD.

THE WORLD IS JUST.

THERE IS NO JUSTICE IN THE WORLD.

MANKOFF

ARE WOMEN NATURALLY UNASSERTIVE◀ BUT SENSITIVE? This common perception is a stereotype. These traits just happen to "justify" holding women responsible for the caretaking tasks they have traditionally performed (Hoffman & Hurst, 1990). In an extreme case, slave "owners" developed attitudes that they then used to "justify" slavery. Their stereotypes of the people they enslaved included traits of being innately lazy, ignorant, and irresponsible. Stereotypes rationalize inequalities.

Victims of discrimination may react with either self-blame or anger (Allport, 1954). Either reaction can feed prejudice through the classic *blame-the-victim* dynamic. Do the circumstances of poverty breed a higher crime rate? If so, that higher crime rate can be used to justify discrimination against those who live in poverty.

Us and Them: Ingroup and Outgroup We have inherited our Stone Age ancestors' need to belong, to live and love in groups. We cheer for our groups, kill for them, die for them. Indeed, we define who we are partly in terms of our groups. Through our *social identities* we associate ourselves with certain groups and contrast ourselves with others (Hogg, 1996; Turner, 1987). When Marc identifies himself as a man, an American, a political Independent, a Hudson Community College student, a Catholic, and a part-time letter carrier, he knows who he is, and so do we.

Evolution prepared us, when encountering strangers, to make instant judgments: friend or foe? Those from our group, those who look like us, and also those who *sound* like us— with accents like our own—we instantly tend to like, from childhood onward (Kinzler et al., 2009). Mentally drawing a circle defines "us," the **ingroup.** But the social definition of who you are also states who you are not. People outside that circle are "them," the **outgroup.** An **ingroup bias**—a favoring of our own group—soon

> "All good people agree,
> And all good people say
> All nice people, like Us,
> are We
> And everyone else is They."
>
> Rudyard Kipling, "We and They,"
> 1926

The ingroup: Scotland's famed "Tartan Army" soccer fans, shown here during a match against archrival England, share a social identity that defines "us" (the Scottish ingroup) and "them" (the English outgroup).

follows. Even forming us-them groups by tossing a coin creates this bias. In experiments, people have favored their own new group when dividing any rewards (Tajfel, 1982; Wilder, 1981).

Emotional Roots of Prejudice

Prejudice springs not only from the divisions of society but also from the passions of the heart. When threatened, people cling more tightly to their prejudices. Facing the terror of death heightens patriotism and produces anger and aggression toward "them"—those who threaten our world (Pyszczynski et al., 2002). **Scapegoat theory** proposes that when things go wrong, finding someone to blame can provide an outlet for anger. Following 9/11, negative stereotypes blossomed. Some outraged people lashed out at innocent Arab-Americans. Others called for eliminating Saddam Hussein, the Iraqi leader whom Americans had been grudgingly tolerating. "Fear and anger create aggression, and aggression against citizens of different ethnicity or race creates racism and, in turn, new forms of terrorism," noted Philip Zimbardo (2001). A decade after 9/11, anti-Muslim animosities still flared, with mosque burnings and efforts to block an Islamic community center near Ground Zero.

Evidence for the scapegoat theory of prejudice comes from two sources.

• Prejudice levels tend to be high among economically frustrated people.

• In experiments, a temporary frustration increases prejudice. Students made to feel temporarily insecure have often restored their self-esteem by speaking badly of a rival school or another person (Cialdini & Richardson, 1980; Crocker et al., 1987). Those made to feel loved and supported have become more open to and accepting of others who differ (Mikulincer & Shaver, 2001).

Cognitive Roots of Prejudice

9 What cognitive processes help create and maintain prejudice?

Prejudice springs from the culture's divisions, the heart's passions, and also from the mind's natural workings.

Forming Categories One way we simplify our world is to sort things into categories. A chemist sorts molecules into categories of "organic" and "inorganic." Therapists discuss symptoms of psychological disorders and treatments by referring to diagnostic categories. But when we categorize people into social or ethnic groups, we often overestimate their similarities.

"They"—the members of that other group—seem to look alike. In personality and attitudes, too, they seem more alike than they really are, while "we" differ from one another (Bothwell et al., 1989). To those in one ethnic group, members of another often seem more alike than they really are in attitudes, personality, and appearance. This greater recognition for own-race faces—called the **other-race effect,** or *own-race bias*—emerges during infancy, between 3 and 9 months of age (Kelly et al., 2007).

Remembering Vivid Cases Cognitive psychologists tell us that we often judge the likelihood of events by recalling vivid cases that readily come to mind. In a classic experiment, researchers showed two groups of student volunteers lists containing information about 50 men (Rothbart et al., 1978). The first group's list included 10 men arrested for *nonviolent* crimes, such as forgery. The second group's list included 10 men arrested for *violent* crimes, such as assault. Later, both groups were asked how many men on their list had committed *any* sort of crime. The second group overestimated the number. Vivid (violent) cases are readily available to our memory and feed our stereotypes (**FIGURE 14.6**).

Believing the World Is Just Another thought process that helps build stereotypes is the just-world phenomenon described earlier in this chapter. If the world is just, "people must get what they deserve." As one German civilian is said to have remarked when visiting the Bergen-Belsen concentration camp shortly after World War II, "What terrible criminals these prisoners must have been to receive such treatment."

People have a basic tendency to justify their culture's social systems (Jost et al., 2009; Kay et al., 2009). We're inclined to see the way things are as the way they ought to be. This natural conservatism makes it difficult to legislate major social changes, such as civil rights laws or Social Security or health care reform. But once such policies are in place, our natural system justification tends to preserve them.

Aggression

10 What biological factors predispose us to be aggressive?

The most destructive force in our social relations is aggression. In psychology, **aggression** is any verbal or physical behavior intended to hurt or destroy, be it passing along a vicious rumor or engaging in a physical assault.

Aggressive behavior emerges when biology interacts with experience. For a gun to fire, the trigger must be pulled. With some people, as with hair-trigger guns, it doesn't take much to trip an explosion. Let's look first at some biological factors that influence our thresholds for aggressive behavior. Then we'll turn to the psychological factors that pull the trigger.

The Biology of Aggression

Is aggression an unlearned instinct? The wide variation from culture to culture, era to era, and person to person argues against that idea. But biology does *influence* aggression at three levels—genetic, neural, and biochemical.

In the last 25 years, guns have caused some 800,000 suicidal, homicidal, and accidental deaths in the United States. Compared with people of the same sex, race, age, and neighborhood, those who keep a gun in the home (ironically, often for protection) are nearly three times more likely to be murdered in the home—nearly always by a family member or close acquaintance. For every self-defense use of a gun in the home, there have been 4 unintentional shootings, 7 criminal assaults or homicides, and 11 attempted or completed suicides (Kellermann et al., 1993, 1997, 1998).

ingroup "us"—people with whom we share a common identity.

outgroup "them"—those perceived as different or apart from our group.

ingroup bias the tendency to favor our own group.

scapegoat theory the theory that prejudice offers an outlet for anger by providing someone to blame.

other-race effect the tendency to recall faces of one's own race more accurately than faces of other races.

aggression any physical or verbal behavior intended to hurt or destroy.

Genetic Influences Genes influence aggression. We know this because animals have been bred for aggressiveness. The effect of genes also appears in human twin studies. If one identical twin admits to "having a violent temper," the other twin will often independently admit the same (Miles & Carey, 1997; Rowe et al., 1999). Fraternal twins are much less likely to respond similarly.

Neural Influences There is no one spot in the brain that controls aggression. Aggression is a complex behavior, and it occurs in particular contexts. But animal and human brains do have neural systems that, when stimulated, either inhibit or produce aggressive behavior (Moyer, 1983). Here are some examples.

- Researchers implanted a radio-controlled electrode in the brain of the domineering leader of a caged monkey colony. The electrode was in a brain area that, when stimulated, inhibits aggression. When researchers placed the control button for the electrode in the colony's cage, one small monkey learned to push it every time the boss became threatening.

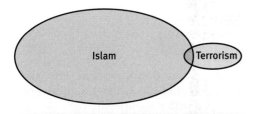

FIGURE 14.6 • Vivid cases feed stereotypes The 9/11 Muslim terrorists created, in many minds, an exaggerated stereotype of Muslims as terror-prone. Actually, reported a National Research Council panel on terrorism, most terrorists are not Muslim. "The vast majority of Islamic people have no connection with and do not sympathize with terrorism" (Smelser & Mitchell, 2002).

"It's a guy thing."

- Neurosurgeons implanted an electrode in the brain of a mild-mannered woman to diagnose a disorder. The electrode was in her amygdala, within her limbic system. Because the brain has no sensory receptors, she did not feel the stimulation. But at the flick of a switch she snarled, "Take my blood pressure. Take it now," then stood up and began to strike the doctor.

- Studies of violent criminals have revealed diminished activity in the frontal lobes, which help control impulses. If the frontal lobes are damaged, inactive, disconnected, or not yet fully mature, aggression may be more likely (Amen et al., 1996; Davidson et al., 2000; Raine, 1999, 2005).

Biochemical Influences Our genes engineer our individual nervous systems, which operate electrochemically. The hormone testosterone, for example, circulates in the bloodstream and influences the neural systems that control aggression. A raging bull will become a gentle Ferdinand when castration reduces its testosterone level. The same is true of mice. When injected with testosterone, the gentle, castrated mice again become aggressive.

Humans are less sensitive to hormonal changes. But as men age, their testosterone levels—and their aggressiveness—drop off. Hormonally charged 17-year-olds mature into hormonally quieter and gentler 70-year-olds. Also, violent criminals tend to be muscular young males with higher-than-average testosterone levels, lower-than-average intelligence scores, and low levels of the neurotransmitter serotonin (Dabbs et al., 2001a; Pendick, 1994). Drugs that sharply reduce their testosterone also subdue their aggressive tendencies.

Another substance that sometimes circulates in the bloodstream—alcohol—*unleashes* aggressive responses to frustration. In police data and prison surveys, as in experiments, aggression-prone people are more likely to drink, and more likely to become violent when they are intoxicated (White et al., 1993). Among inmates convicted of violent offenses, 4 in 10 had been drinking at the time of the crime (Karberg & James, 2005). Alcohol's effects are both biological and psychological (Bushman, 1993; Ito et al., 1996; Taylor & Chermack, 1993). (Just *thinking* you've imbibed alcohol has some effect; but so, too, does drinking alcohol unknowingly in a drink.)

The Psychology of Aggression

11 What psychological factors trigger aggression? How does viewing multimedia violence affect aggressive behavior?

A lean, mean fighting machine—the testosterone-laden female hyena: Unusual prenatal development pumps testosterone into female hyena fetuses. The result is revved-up young females that seem born to fight.

This reaction is called the **frustration-aggression principle.** Frustration creates anger, which can spark aggression. One analysis of 27,667 hit-by-pitch incidents between 1960 and 2004 revealed this link in major league baseball (Timmerman, 2007). Pitchers were most likely to hit batters when

- they had been frustrated by the previous batter hitting a home run.
- the current batter hit a home run the last time at bat.
- a teammate had been hit by a pitch in the previous half inning.

The frustration-aggression link also appeared after 9/11, when Americans responded with a readiness to fight. Terrorism similarly may spring from a desire for revenge, following the death or injury of a friend or family member. Contrary to the popular idea that poverty breeds terrorists, suicide bombers and those who support them actually tend to be neither uneducated nor desperately poor (Krueger, 2007). The 9/11 suicide bombers, for example, were mostly educated men from wealthy Saudi Arabia (McDermott,

> "We could avoid two-thirds of all crime simply by putting all able-bodied young men in cryogenic sleep from the age of 12 through 28."
>
> David T. Lykken, *The Antisocial Personalities,* 1995

Biological factors create the hair trigger for aggression. But what psychological factors pull that trigger?

Being Frustrated or Rejected Suffering sometimes builds character. Too often, however, when we are miserable we make others miserable (Berkowitz, 1983, 1989).

2005). Frustration (and aggression) arise less from deprivation than from the gap between reality and expectations, which may rise with education and attainments.

Another aversive event, rejection, can also trigger aggression (Catanese & Tice, 2005; Gaertner & Iuzzini, 2005). In a series of studies (Twenge & others, 2001, 2002, 2003), researchers told participants that some people they had met didn't want them in their group, or that a personality test indicated they "were likely to end up alone later in life." Later, participants led to feel socially excluded were more likely to put down those who had insulted them, or even deliver a blast of noise to them. Rejection-induced aggression has also been a theme in various North American and European school shootings, committed by youths who had been shunned, mocked, and/or bullied by peers.

Learning That Aggression Is Rewarding Experience can teach us that aggression pays. Animals that have successfully fought to get food or mates become increasingly ferocious. Children whose aggression successfully intimidates other children may become more aggressive. Terrorism, which aims to terrorize, is rewarded by massive publicity and frightened and inconvenienced people. "Kill one, frighten 10,000," asserts an ancient Chinese proverb. Once established, aggressive behavior patterns are difficult to change.

Observing Models of Aggression As Chapter 6 points out, we observe and we learn. We often imitate what a model, even an aggressive model, says and does. To foster a kinder, gentler world, we had best model and reward sensitivity and cooperation from an early age.

Parent-training programs often advise parents to avoid modeling violence by screaming and hitting. Instead, parents should reinforce desirable behaviors and frame statements positively. ("When you finish loading the dishwasher, you can go play," rather than "If you don't load the dishwasher, there'll be no playing.") Parents of

"Why do we kill people who kill people to show that killing people is wrong?"
National Coalition to Abolish the Death Penalty, 1992

Aggression-replacement program: Part of the rehabilitation of these juvenile offenders at the Missouri Division of Youth Services' Rosa Parks Center involves learning anger management and peaceful ways to resolve disputes. Here they "circle up" to resolve a problem peacefully.

delinquent youngsters typically discipline with beatings and give in to (and thus reward) their children's tears and temper tantrums (Patterson et al., 1982, 1992).

One *aggression-replacement program* worked with juvenile offenders and gang members and their parents. It taught both generations new ways to control anger, and more thoughtful approaches to moral reasoning (Goldstein et al., 1998). The result? The youths' repeat-rates dropped.

Different cultures model, reinforce, and evoke different tendencies toward violence. For example, crime rates are higher (and average happiness is lower) in countries marked by a wide gulf between rich and poor (Triandis, 1994). In the United States, cultures and families that experience minimal father care also have high violence rates (Myers, 2000; Triandis, 1994). Even after controlling for parental education, race, income, and teen motherhood, American male youths from father-absent homes have double their peers' incarceration rate (Harper & McLanahan, 2004).

Parents are not the only aggression models. In the United States and elsewhere, TV, films, and video games offer supersized portions of violence. (See Thinking Critically About: Do Video Games Teach, or Release, Violence? on the next page.)

Repeatedly viewing on-screen violence tends to make us less sensitive to cruelty. It also primes us to respond aggressively when provoked. And it teaches us **social scripts**—culturally provided mental files for how to act. When we find ourselves in new situations, uncertain how to behave, we rely on social scripts. After so many games and action films, youngsters may acquire a script that plays in their head when they face real-life conflicts. Challenged, they may "act like a man" by intimidating or eliminating the threat.

Likewise, after exposure to the sexual commentary and behavior in the short-term relationships featured in many prime-time TV shows, youths may acquire *sexual scripts* they later enact in real-life relationships (Kunkel et al., 2001; Sapolsky & Tabarlet, 1991). Music lyrics also write social scripts. In one set of experiments, German university men who listened to woman-hating song lyrics administered the most hot chili sauce to a woman and recalled more negative feelings and beliefs about women. Man-hating song lyrics had a similar effect on the aggressive behavior of women listeners (Fischer & Greitemeyer, 2006).

Sexual scripts depicted in X-rated films are often toxic. People heavily exposed to televised crime perceive the world as more dangerous. People heavily exposed to pornography see the world as more sexual. Repeatedly watching X-rated films, even nonviolent films, has many effects (Kingston et al., 2009). One's own partner seems less attractive (Chapter 4). Extramarital sex seems less troubling (Zillmann, 1989). Women's friendliness seems more sexual. Sexual aggression seems less serious (Harris, 1994).

frustration-aggression principle the principle that frustration—the blocking of an attempt to achieve some goal—creates anger, which can generate aggression.

social script culturally modeled guide for how to act in various situations.

Do Video Games Teach, or Release, Violence?

Most abused children don't become abusive adults. Most social drinkers don't become alcohol dependent. And most youths who spend hundreds of hours with mass-murder simulators don't become teen assassins. Nevertheless, violent video games became an issue for public debate after teenagers in more than a dozen places seemed to mimic the carnage in the shooter games they had so often played (Anderson, 2004a).

In 2002, two Grand Rapids, Michigan, teens and a man in his early twenties spent part of a night drinking beer and playing Grand Theft Auto III. Using simulated cars, they ran down pedestrians, then beat them with fists, leaving a bloody body behind (Kolker, 2002). These same teens and man then went out for a real drive. Spotting a 38-year-old man on a bicycle, they ran him down with their car, got out, stomped and punched him, and returned home to play the game some more. (The victim, a father of three, died six days later.)

Such violent mimicry causes some to wonder. WHAT WILL BE THE EFFECT OF ACTIVELY ROLE-PLAYING AGGRESSION? WILL YOUNG PEOPLE BECOME LESS SENSITIVE TO VIOLENCE AND MORE OPEN TO VIOLENT ACTS? Nearly 400 studies of 130,000 people offer an answer. Video games can prime aggressive thoughts, decrease empathy, and increase aggression (Anderson et al., 2010). University men who spent the most hours playing violent video games also tended to be the most physically aggressive (Anderson & Dill, 2000). (For example, they more often acknowledged having hit or attacked someone else.) And people randomly assigned to play a game involving bloody murders with groaning victims (rather than to play nonviolent Myst) became more hostile. On a follow-up task, they also were more likely to blast intense noise at a fellow student.

Studies of young adolescents reveal that those who play a lot of violent video games see the world as more hostile (Gentile, 2009). Compared with nongaming kids, they get into more arguments and fights and get worse grades.

Ah, but is this merely because naturally hostile kids are drawn to such games? Apparently not. Comparisons of gamers and nongamers who scored low in hostility revealed a difference in the number of fights they reported. Almost 4 in 10 violent-game players

Desensitizing people to violence?

© Sylent-Press/ullstein bild/The Image Works

had been in fights. Only 4 in 100 of the nongaming kids reported fights (Anderson, 2004a). Due to the more repetitive and active participation of game play, and to its rewarding violence, violent video games seem to have even greater effects than exposure to violent television and movies.

Other researchers are unimpressed by such findings (Ferguson & Kilburn, 2010). They note that from 1996 to 2006, youth violence was declining while video game sales were increasing. Moreover, some point out that avid game players develop speedy reaction times and enhanced visual skills (Dye et al., 2009).

Maybe so, reply the video game effect researchers, but the effects of violent gaming are comparable to the toxic effects of asbestos or second-hand smoke exposure (Bushman et al., 2010). This much seems clear. We don't feel better if we "blow off steam" by venting our emotions (Chapter 9). Instead, playing violent video games increases aggressive thoughts, emotions, and behaviors. As the Greek philosopher Aristotle observed, "We are what we repeatedly do."

In one experiment (Zillmann & Bryant, 1984), some undergraduates viewed six brief, sexually explicit films each week for six weeks. A control group viewed films with no sexual content during the same six-week period. Three weeks later, both groups read a newspaper report about a man convicted but not yet sentenced for raping a hitchhiker. They were then asked to suggest an appropriate prison term. Did viewing the sexually explicit films affect that group's suggestions? *Yes.* Sentences recommended by those viewers were only half as long as the sentences recommended by the control group.

Research on the effects of violent versus nonviolent erotic films indicates that it's not the sexual content of films that most directly affects men's aggression against women. It's the behavior modeled in the acts of sexual *violence*, whether in R-rated slasher films or X-rated films. A statement by 21 social scientists noted, "Pornography that portrays sexual aggression as pleasurable for the victim increases the acceptance of the use of coercion in sexual relations" (Surgeon General, 1986). Contrary to much popular opinion, viewing such scenes does not provide an outlet for bottled-up impulses. Rather, "in laboratory studies measuring short-term effects, exposure to violent pornography increases punitive behavior toward women."

* * *

To sum up, research reveals biological, psychological, and social-cultural influences on aggressive behavior. Complex behaviors, including violence, have many causes, making any single explanation an oversimplification. Asking what causes violence is therefore like asking what causes cancer. Those who study the effects of asbestos exposure on cancer rates may remind us that asbestos is indeed a cancer cause, but it is only one among many. Like so much else, aggression is a biopsychosocial phenomenon.

Attraction

12 | How do proximity, attractiveness, and similarity influence whom we befriend or fall in love with?

Pause a moment and think about your relationships with two people—a close friend, and someone who stirs in you feelings of romantic love. These special sorts of attachments help us cope with all other relationships. What is the psychological chemistry that binds us together? Social psychology suggests some answers.

The Psychology of Attraction

We endlessly wonder how we can win others' affection and what makes our own affections flourish or fade. DOES FAMILIARITY BREED CONTEMPT, OR AFFECTION? DO BIRDS OF A FEATHER FLOCK TOGETHER, OR DO OPPOSITES ATTRACT? IS BEAUTY ONLY SKIN DEEP, OR DOES ATTRACTIVENESS MATTER GREATLY? Let's address these questions by considering three ingredients of our liking for one another: proximity, physical attractiveness, and similarity.

Photodisc/Jupiterimages

Familiarity breeds acceptance: When this rare white penguin was born in the Sydney, Australia, zoo, his tuxedoed peers shunned him. Zookeepers thought they would need to dye him black to gain acceptance. But after three weeks of contact, the other penguins came to accept him.

AP Photo/The Mat-Su Valley Frontiersman, Robert DeBerry; Anchorage Daily News Out

Proximity Before friendships become close, they must begin. *Proximity*—geographic nearness—is friendship's most powerful predictor. Being near another person gives us opportunities for aggression, but much more often it breeds liking. Study after study reveals that people are most inclined to like, and even to marry, those who are nearby. We are drawn to those who live in the same neighborhood, sit nearby in class, work in the same office, share the same parking lot, eat in the same dining hall. Look around. Mating starts with meeting. (For a twenty-first-century technology that connects people not in physical proxim-

ity, see Close-Up: Online Matchmaking on the next page.)

Psychologists call this the **mere exposure effect.** Repeated exposure to novel stimuli increases our liking for them. This applies to nonsense syllables, musical selections, geometric figures, Chinese characters, human faces, and the letters of our own name (Moreland & Zajonc, 1982; Nuttin, 1987; Zajonc, 2001). People are even somewhat more likely to marry someone whose first or last name resembles their own (Jones et al., 2004).

So, within certain limits, familiarity breeds fondness (Bornstein, 1989, 1999). Researchers demonstrated this by having four equally attractive women

The mere exposure effect: The mere exposure effect applies even to ourselves. Because the human face is not perfectly symmetrical, the face we see in the mirror is not the same as the one our friends see. Most of us prefer the familiar mirror image, while our friends like the reverse (Mita et al., 1977). The Sarah Palin known to us all is at left. The person she sees in the mirror each morning is shown at right, and that's the photo she would probably prefer.

mere exposure effect the phenomenon that repeated exposure to novel stimuli increases liking of them.

Online Matchmaking

If you have not found a romantic partner in your immediate proximity, why not cast a wider net? In the United States, 16 million people have tried online dating and matchmaking services, as have an estimated 14 million more in China, 10 million in India, and tens of millions in other countries (Cullen & Masters, 2008).

"I can't wait to see what you're like online."

Although published research on the effectiveness of Internet matchmaking services is sparse, this much seems well established: Some people dishonestly represent their age, attractiveness, occupation, or other details, and thus are not who they seem to be. Nevertheless, Katelyn McKenna and John Bargh and their colleagues have offered a surprising finding: Compared with relationships formed in person, Internet-formed friendships and romantic relationships are more likely to last beyond two years (Bargh et al., 2002, 2004; McKenna et al., 2002; McKenna & Bargh, 1998, 2000). In one of their studies, people disclosed more, with less posturing, to those whom they met online. When conversing online with someone for 20 minutes, they felt more liking for that person than they did for someone they had met and talked with face to face. This was true even when (unknown to them) it was the same person! Small wonder that Internet friendships often feel as real and important to people as in-person relationships.

---

silently attend a 200-student class for zero, 5, 10, or 15 class sessions (Moreland & Beach, 1992). At the end of the course, students were shown slides of each woman and asked to rate her attractiveness. The most attractive? The ones they'd seen most often. These ratings would come as no surprise to the young Taiwanese man who wrote more than 700 letters to his girlfriend, urging her to marry him. She did marry—the mail carrier (Steinberg, 1993).

No face is more familiar than your own. And that helps explain a curious finding about voter preferences. Researchers showed people images of the 2004 presidential candidates, John Kerry and George W. Bush. What the researchers did not tell these voters was that the images had been altered. They were actually blends of the voter's own features and a candidate's features **(FIGURE 14.7)**. Which candidate did these voters prefer? The one whose face incorporated some of

their own features (Bailenson et al., 2008). In me I trust.

The mere exposure effect had survival value for our ancestors. What was familiar was generally safe and approachable. What was unfamiliar was more often dangerous and threatening. Evolution

may have hard-wired into us the tendencies to bond with those who are familiar and to be wary of those who are unfamiliar (Zajonc, 1998). If so, gut-level prejudice against those who are culturally different could be a primitive, automatic emotional response (Devine, 1995). It's

> **FIGURE 14.7** • **I like the candidate who looks a bit like dear old me** Voters viewed images of presidential candidates. Researchers had secretly incorporated some of the voters' features into the blended photos (Bailenson et al., 2008). Without conscious awareness of their own features, the participants became more likely to favor the candidate who shared those features.

Voter

George W. Bush

60:40 Blend

"I'm going to have to recuse myself."

"...So I told my plastic surgeon, 'Do whatever it takes — just make me look YOUNG again.'"

what we do with our knee-jerk prejudice that matters, suggest researchers. Do we let those feelings control our behavior? Or do we monitor our feelings and act in ways that reflect our conscious valuing of human equality?

Physical Attractiveness So proximity offers contact. WHAT MOST AFFECTS OUR ◀ FIRST IMPRESSIONS? THE PERSON'S SINCERITY? INTELLIGENCE? PERSONALITY? Research indicates that the answer is physical appearance. This finding is unnerving for most of us who were taught that "beauty is only skin deep" and that "appearances can be deceiving."

In one early study, researchers randomly matched new students for a Welcome Week dance (Walster et al., 1966). Before the dance, the researchers gave each student a battery of personality and aptitude tests, and they rated each student's level of physical attractiveness. On the night of the blind date, the couples danced and talked for more than two hours and then took a brief intermission to rate their dates. What determined whether they liked each other? Only one thing seemed to matter: Appearance. Both the men and the women liked good-looking dates best. Women are more likely than men to

say that another's looks don't affect them (Lippa, 2007). But studies show that a man's looks do affect women's behavior (Feingold, 1990; Sprecher, 1989; Woll, 1986). Speed-dating experiments confirm that attractiveness influences first impressions for both sexes, especially when meeting lots of people in fleeting encounters (Belot & Francesconi, 2006; Finkel & Eastwick, 2008).

Physical attractiveness also predicts how often people date and how popular they feel. It affects initial impressions of people's personalities. We don't assume that attractive people are more honest or compassionate, but we do perceive them as healthier, happier, more sensitive, more successful, and more socially skilled (Eagly et al., 1991; Feingold, 1992; Hatfield & Sprecher, 1986). Attractive, well-dressed people make a more favorable impression on potential employers, and they tend to be more successful in their jobs (Cash & Janda, 1984; Langlois et al., 2000; Solomon, 1987). There is a premium for beauty in the workplace, and a penalty for plainness or obesity (Engemann & Owyang, 2005).

Judging from their gazing times, even babies seem to prefer attractive over unattractive faces (Langlois et al., 1987). So do some *blind* people. University of Birmingham professor John Hull (1990, p. 23) discovered this after going blind himself. A colleague's remarks about a woman's beauty can strangely affect his feelings. He finds this "deplorable . . . but I still feel it. . . . What can it matter to me what sighted men think of women . . . yet I do care what sighted men think, and I do not seem able to throw off this prejudice."

For those of us who find the importance of looks unfair and unenlightened, two attractiveness findings may be reassuring. First, people's attractiveness is

Percentage of Men and Women Who "Constantly Think About Their Looks"		
	Men	Women
Canada	18%	20%
United States	17	27
Mexico	40	45
Venezuela	47	65

From Roper Starch survey, reported by McCool (1999).

surprisingly unrelated to their self-esteem and happiness (Diener et al., 1995; Major et al., 1984). Except after comparing ourselves with superattractive people, few of us (thanks, perhaps, to the mere exposure effect) view ourselves as unattractive (Thornton & Moore, 1993). Second, strikingly attractive people are sometimes suspicious that praise for their work may simply be a reaction to their looks. Less attractive people are more likely to accept praise as sincere (Berscheid, 1981).

Moreover, beauty is in the eye of the culture. Hoping to look attractive, people across the globe have pierced their nose, lengthened their neck, bound their feet, and dyed or painted their skin and hair. Cultural ideals also change over time. In the United States, the soft, voluptuous Marilyn Monroe ideal of the 1950s has been replaced by today's lean yet busty ideal.

If we're not born attractive, we may try to buy beauty. Americans now spend more on beauty supplies than on education and social services combined. Still not satisfied, millions undergo plastic surgery, Botox skin smoothing, teeth

Photodisc/Getty Images

Extreme makeover: In 2009, Americans spent $10.5 billion on nearly 10 million cosmetic procedures (ASAPS, 2010), such as this woman experienced thanks to the TV show *Extreme Makeover*. If money were no concern, might you ever do the same?

whitening or capping, and laser hair removal (Wall, 2002).

Do any aspects of attractiveness cross place and time? *Yes.* As we noted in Chapter 4, men in many cultures, from Australia to Zambia, find women more attractive if they have a youthful appearance. Women are attracted to healthy looking men, but especially to those who seem mature, dominant, and affluent (Cunningham et al., 2005; Langlois et al., 2000).

Our feelings also influence our attractiveness judgments. Imagine two people: One is polite and humorous, the other is rude and abusive. Which one is more attractive? Most people perceive the polite and humorous person as more attractive (Lewandowski et al., 2007). Our feelings influence our perceptions. In a Rodgers and Hammerstein musical, Prince Charming asks Cinderella, "Do I love you because you're beautiful, or are you beautiful because I love you?" Chances are it's both. As we see our loved ones again and again, their physical imperfections grow less noticeable and their attractiveness grows more apparent (Beaman & Klentz, 1983; Gross & Crofton, 1977). Shakespeare said it in *A Midsummer Night's Dream:* "Love looks not with the eyes, but with the mind." Come to love someone and watch beauty grow.

Similarity So you've met someone, and your appearance has made a decent first impression. What now influences whether you will become friends? As you get to know each other, will the chemistry be better if you are opposites or if you are alike? In real life, birds that flock together usually are of a feather. Compared with randomly paired people, friends and couples are far more likely to share attitudes, beliefs, and interests (and, for that matter, age, religion, race, education, intelligence, smoking behavior, and economic status). Journalist Walter Lippmann was right to suppose that love lasts "when the lovers love many things together, and not merely each other."

Proximity, attractiveness, and similarity are not the only forces that influence attraction. We also like those who like us. This is especially so when our self-image is low. When we believe someone likes us, we feel good and respond warmly. Our warm response in turn leads them to like us even more (Curtis & Miller, 1986). To be liked is powerfully rewarding.

Indeed, all the findings we have considered so far can be explained by a simple *reward theory of attraction*. We will like those whose behavior is rewarding to us, and we will continue relationships that offer more rewards than costs. When people live or work in close proximity

Diverse Yet Alike

In the Eye of the Beholder

Conceptions of attractiveness vary by culture and over time. Yet some adult physical features, such as a youthful form and face, seem attractive everywhere.

with us, it costs less time and effort to develop the friendship and enjoy its benefits. When people are attractive, they are aesthetically pleasing, and associating with them can be socially rewarding. When people share our views, they reward us by confirming our own.

Romantic Love

13 How does physical arousal affect passionate love? What predicts enduring companionate love?

Sometimes people move from initial impressions, to friendship, to the more intense, complex, and mysterious state of romantic love. If love endures, temporary passionate love will mellow into a lingering companionate love (Hatfield, 1988).

Passionate Love A key ingredient of **passionate love** is arousal. The two-factor theory of emotion (Chapter 9) can help us understand this intense positive absorption in another (Hatfield, 1988). That theory makes two assumptions:

- Emotions have two ingredients—arousal and appraisal.
- Arousal from any source can enhance an emotion, depending on how we interpret and label the arousal.

In tests of this theory, college men have been aroused by fright, by running in place, by viewing erotic materials, or by listening to humorous or repulsive monologues. They were then introduced to an attractive woman and asked to rate her (or their girlfriend). Unlike unaroused men, these men interpreted their stirred-up state as a response to the woman or girlfriend, and they felt more attracted to her (Carducci et al., 1978; Dermer & Pyszczynski, 1978; White & Kight, 1984).

A sample experiment: Researchers studied people crossing two bridges above British Columbia's rocky Capilano River (Dutton & Aron, 1974, 1989). One, a swaying footbridge, was 230 feet above

Mike Flippo/Shutterstock

the rocks. The other was low and solid. The researchers had an attractive young woman stop men coming off each bridge and ask their help in filling out a short questionnaire. She then offered her phone number in case they wanted to hear more about her project. Which men accepted the number and later called the woman? Far more of those who had just crossed the high bridge—which left their hearts pounding. To be revved up and to associate some of that arousal with a desirable person is to feel the pull of passion. Adrenaline makes the heart grow fonder.

> "When two people are under the influence of the most violent, most insane, most delusive, and most transient of passions, they are required to swear that they will remain in that excited, abnormal, and exhausting condition continuously until death do them part."
>
> George Bernard Shaw, "Getting Married," 1908

Companionate Love Passionate romantic love seldom endures. The intense absorption in the other, the thrill of the romance, the giddy "floating on a cloud" feeling typically fades. ARE THE FRENCH CORRECT IN SAYING ◀ THAT "LOVE MAKES THE TIME PASS AND TIME MAKES LOVE PASS"? Not really. The evidence indicates that, as love matures, it becomes a steadier **companionate love**—a deep, affectionate attachment (Hatfield, 1988).

There may be adaptive wisdom to this change from passion to affection (Reis & Aron, 2008). Passionate love often produces children, whose survival is aided by the parents' waning obsession with one another. Failure to appreciate passionate love's limited half-life can doom a relationship (Berscheid & others, 1984). Indeed, recognizing the short duration of passionate love, some societies judge such feelings to be a poor reason for marrying. Better, these cultures say, to choose (or have someone choose for you) a partner who shares your background and interests. Non-Western cultures, where people rate love less important for marriage, do have lower divorce rates (Levine et al., 1995). Do you think you could be happy in a marriage someone else arranged for you, by matching you with someone who shared your interests and traits? Many people in many cultures around the world live seemingly happy lives in such marriages.

One key to a gratifying and enduring relationship is **equity.**

Love is an ancient thing: In 2007, skeletons of a 5000- to 6000-year-old "Romeo and Juliet" young couple were unearthed, locked in an embrace, near Rome.

AP Photo/Archaeological Society SAP, ho

passionate love an aroused state of intense positive absorption in another, usually present at the beginning of a love relationship.

companionate love the deep affectionate attachment we feel for those with whom our lives are intertwined.

equity a condition in which people receive from a relationship in proportion to what they give to it.

Courtship and Matrimony (From the collection of Werner Nekes)

YNOMIRTAM

COURTSHIP

Sometimes passionate love becomes enduring companionate love, sometimes not (turn the picture upside-down): What, in addition to similar attitudes and interests, predicts long-term loving attachment?

Answer: equity and self-disclosure

When equity exists—when both partners receive in proportion to what they give—the chances for sustained and satisfying companionate love are good (Gray-Little & Burks, 1983; Van Yperen & Buunk, 1990). In one national survey, "sharing household chores" ranked third, after "faithfulness" and a "happy sexual relationship," on a list of nine things Americans associated with successful marriages. "I like hugs. I like kisses. But what I really love is help with the dishes," summarized the Pew Research Center (2007).

Equity's importance extends beyond marriage. Mutually sharing self and possessions, making decisions together, giving and getting emotional support, promoting and caring about one another's welfare—all of these acts are at the core of every type of loving relationship (Sternberg & Grajek, 1984). It's true for lovers, for parent and child, and for intimate friends.

Another vital ingredient of loving relationships is **self-disclosure,** revealing intimate details about ourselves—our likes and dislikes, our dreams and worries, our proud and shameful moments.

As one person reveals a little, the other returns the gift. The first then reveals more, and on and on, as friends or lovers move to deeper and deeper intimacy (Baumeister & Bratslavsky, 1999).

One study marched pairs of students through 45 minutes of increasingly self-disclosing conversation—from "When did you last sing to yourself" to "When did you last cry in front of another person? By yourself?" Others spent the time with small-talk questions, such as "What was your high school like?" (Aron et al., 1997). By the experiment's end, those experiencing the escalating intimacy felt remarkably close to their conversation partner, much closer than did the small-talkers.

In the mathematics of love, self-disclosing intimacy + mutually supportive equality = enduring companionate love.

Michael Newman/Photo Edit

Keep it deep: In a naturalistic observation study, Mathias Mehl and his colleagues (2010) equipped 79 undergraduates with a device that recorded 30-second snippets five times an hour over four days. Those who spent relatively more of their day having deep or substantive discussions rather than small talk were also happier.

Altruism

14 What is altruism? When are we most—and least—likely to intervene as bystanders?

Altruism is an unselfish concern for the welfare of others, such as Dirk Willems exemplified in rescuing his jailer. Another heroic example of altruism occurred in an underground New York City subway station. Construction worker Wesley Autrey and his 6- and 4-year-old daughters were waiting for their train when they saw a nearby man collapse in a convulsion. The man then got up, stumbled to the platform's edge, and fell onto the tracks. With train headlights approaching, Autrey later recalled, "I had to make a split decision" (Buckley, 2007). His decision, as his girls looked on in horror, was to leap onto the track, push the man off the rails and into a foot-deep space between them, and lie on top of him. As the train screeched to a halt, five cars traveled just above his head, leaving grease on his knit cap. When Autrey cried out, "I've got two

AP Photo/Newsday, Nick Brooks

Subway hero Wesley Autrey: "I don't feel like I did something spectacular; I just saw someone who needed help."

daughters up there. Let them know their father is okay," the onlookers erupted into applause.

Such selfless goodness made New Yorkers proud to call that city home. Another New York story, four decades earlier, had a different ending. In 1964, a stalker repeatedly stabbed Kitty Genovese, then raped her as she lay dying outside her Queens, New York, apartment at 3:30 A.M. "Oh, my God, he stabbed me!" Genovese screamed into the early morning stillness. "Please help me!" Windows opened and lights went on as neighbors (38, said an initial *New York Times* report, though that number was later disputed) heard her screams. Her attacker fled. Then he returned to stab her eight more times and rape her again. Not until he had fled for good did anyone so much as call the police, at 3:50 A.M.

Bystander Intervention

In an emergency, some people intervene, as Wesley Autrey did, but others, like the Genovese bystanders, fail to offer help. WHY DO SOME PEOPLE BECOME HEROES IN ◄ EMERGENCIES WHILE OTHERS JUST STAND AND WATCH? Social psychologists John Darley and Bibb Latané (1968b) believed three conditions were necessary for bystanders to help (**FIGURE 14.8**). They would have to

- *notice* the incident.
- *interpret* the event as an emergency.
- *assume responsibility* for helping.

At each step, the presence of others can turn people away from the path that leads to helping. Darley and Latané (1968a) reached these conclusions after interpreting the results of a series of experiments. For example, they staged a fake emergency in their laboratory as students participated in a discussion over an intercom. Each student was in a separate cubicle, and only the person whose microphone was switched on could be heard. When his turn came, one student (an accomplice of the experimenters) made sounds as though he were having an epileptic seizure, and he called for help.

How did the other students react? As **FIGURE 14.9** on the next page shows, those who believed only they could hear the victim—and therefore thought they alone had responsibility for helping him—usually went to his aid. Students who thought others also could hear the victim's cries were more likely to react as Kitty Genovese's neighbors had. When more people shared responsibility for helping—when no one person was clearly responsible—each listener was less likely to help.

self-disclosure revealing intimate aspects of ourselves to others.

altruism unselfish concern for the welfare of others.

bystander effect the tendency for any given bystander to be less likely to give aid if other bystanders are present.

Hundreds of additional experiments have confirmed this **bystander effect**. For example, researchers and their assistants took 1497 elevator rides in three cities and "accidentally" dropped coins or pencils in front of 4813 fellow passengers (Latané & Dabbs, 1975). When alone with the person in need, 40 percent helped; in the presence of five other bystanders, only 20 percent helped.

Observations of behavior in thousands of situations—relaying an emergency phone call, aiding a stranded motorist, donating blood, picking up dropped books, contributing money, giving time, and more—show that the *best* odds of our helping someone occur when

- the person appears to need and deserve help.
- the person is in some way similar to us.

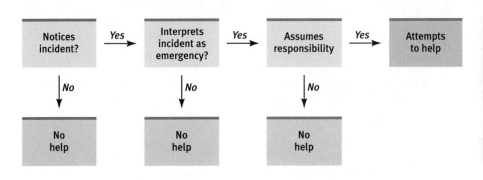

FIGURE 14.8 • **The decision-making process for bystander intervention** Before helping, one must first notice an emergency, then correctly interpret it, and then feel responsible. For Wesley Autrey, the quick answer to each question was *Yes*. (From Darley & Latané, 1968b.)

Notices incident?	→ *Yes*	Interprets incident as emergency?	→ *Yes*	Assumes responsibility	→ *Yes*	Attempts to help
↓ *No*		↓ *No*		↓ *No*		
No help		No help		No help		

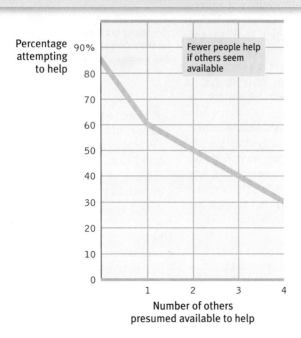

Percentage attempting to help

Fewer people help if others seem available

Number of others presumed available to help

- the person is a woman.
- we have just observed someone else being helpful.
- we are not in a hurry.
- we are in a small town or rural area.
- we are feeling guilty.
- we are focused on others and not preoccupied.
- we are in a good mood.

This last result, that happy people are helpful people, is one of the most consistent findings in all of psychology. As poet Robert Browning (1868) observed, "Oh, make us happy and you make us good!" It doesn't matter how we are cheered. Whether by being made to feel successful and intelligent, by thinking happy thoughts, by finding money, or even by receiving a posthypnotic suggestion, we become more generous and more eager to help (Carlson et al., 1988).

Conflict and Peacemaking

15 What social processes fuel conflict? How can we transform feelings of prejudice and conflict into behaviors that promote peace?

We live in surprising times. With astonishing speed, late-twentieth-century democratic movements swept away to-talitarian rule in Eastern European countries. Hopes for a new world order displaced the Cold War chill. Yet the twenty-first century began with terrorist acts and war. *Every* day the world continues to spend $2 billion for arms and armies—money that could be used for housing, nutrition, education, and health care. Knowing that wars begin in human minds, psychologists have wondered: WHAT IN THE HUMAN MIND CAUSES DE- ◄ STRUCTIVE CONFLICT? HOW MIGHT THE PERCEIVED THREATS OF OUR DIFFERENCES BE REPLACED BY A SPIRIT OF COOPERATION?

To a social psychologist, a **conflict** is the perception that actions, goals, or ideas are incompatible. The elements of conflict are much the same, whether we are speaking of nations at war, cultural groups feuding within a society, or partners sparring in a relationship. In each situation, people become tangled in a destructive process that can produce results no one wants.

Enemy Perceptions

Psychologists have noticed a curious tendency: People in conflict form evil images of one another. These distorted images are so similar that we call them **mirror-image perceptions.** As we see "them"—untrustworthy, with evil intentions—so "they" see us. Each sees a demon in the other.

Mirror-image perceptions can feed a vicious cycle of hostility. In 2001, newly elected President George W. Bush spoke of Saddam Hussein. "Some of today's tyrants are gripped by an implacable hatred of the United States of America. They hate our friends, they hate our values, they hate democracy and freedom and individual liberty. Many care little for the lives of their own people." Hussein mirrored the perception in 2002. The United States, he said, is "an evil tyrant," with Satan as its protector. It lusts for oil and aggressively attacks those who "defend what is right."

The point is not that truth must lie midway between two such views (one may be more accurate). The point is that enemy perceptions often form mirror images. Moreover, as enemies change, so do perceptions. During World War II, Americans viewed the Japanese as "bloodthirsty, cruel, treacherous." Three decades later, American minds and media lauded those same people as our "intelligent, hardworking, self-disciplined, resourceful allies" (Gallup, 1972).

How can we change perceptions and make peace? CAN COOPERATION TRANS-◄ FORM THE ANGER AND FEAR FED BY PREJUDICE AND CONFLICTS INTO ATTITUDES THAT PROMOTE PEACE? Research indicates that, in some cases, it can.

Cooperation

Does it help to put two conflicting parties into close contact? It depends. When contact is free of competition and between parties with equal status, such as fellow store clerks, it typically helps. Initially prejudiced co-workers of different races have, in such circumstances, usually come to accept one another. Across a quarter million people studied in 38 nations, friendly contact with ethnic minorities, the elderly, and those with disabilities has usually led to less prejudice (Pettigrew & Tropp, 2006). This has also been true when heterosexual people knowingly have gay friends (Neidorf & Morin, 2007; Smith et al., 2009). Heterosexuals' attitudes toward gay people are influenced not just by what they know but also by whom they know.

However, mere contact is not always enough. In most desegregated schools, ethnic groups resegregate themselves in the lunchrooms and on the school grounds (Clack et al., 2005; Schofield, 1986). Students in each group often think they would welcome more contact with the other group, but they assume the other group is not interested in more contact with them (Richeson & Shelton, 2007). When these mirror-image untruths are corrected, friendships can form and prejudices melt.

To see if enemies could overcome their differences, researcher Muzafer Sherif (1966) set a conflict in motion. He separated 22 boys into two separate camp areas. Then he had the two groups compete for prizes in a series of activities. Before long, each group became intensely proud of itself and hostile to the other group's "sneaky," "smart-alecky stinkers." Food wars broke out. Cabins were ransacked. Fistfights had to be broken up by camp counselors. Brought together, the two groups avoided each other, except to taunt and threaten. Little did they know that within a few days, they would be friends.

> "You cannot shake hands with a clenched fist."
>
> Indira Gandhi, 1971

Sherif accomplished this by giving them **superordinate goals**—shared goals that could be achieved only through cooperation. When he arranged for the camp water supply to "fail," all 22 boys had to work together to restore water. To rent a movie in those pre-DVD days, they all had to pool their resources. To move a stalled truck, all the boys had to combine their strength, pulling and pushing together. Sherif used shared predicaments and goals to turn enemies into friends. What reduced conflict was not mere contact, but *cooperative* contact.

A shared predicament likewise had a powerfully unifying effect in the weeks after 9/11. Patriotism soared as Americans felt "we" were under attack. Gallup-surveyed approval of "our President" shot up from 51 percent the week before the attack to a highest-ever level of 90 percent just 10 days after (Newport, 2002). In chat groups and everyday speech, even the word *we* (relative to *I*) surged in the immediate aftermath (Pennebaker, 2002).

At such times, cooperation can lead people to define a new, inclusive group that dissolves their former subgroups (Dovidio & Gaertner, 1999). If this were a social psychology experiment, you might seat members of two groups not on opposite sides, but alternately around a table. Give them a new, shared name. Have them work together. Then watch "us" and "them" become "we." After 9/11, one 18-year-old New Jersey man described this shift in his own social identity. "I just thought of myself as Black. But now I feel like I'm an American, more than ever" (Sengupta, 2001).

If cooperative contacts between members of rival groups encourage positive attitudes, might this principle bring people together in multicultural schools? Could interracial friendships replace competitive classroom situations with cooperative ones? Could cooperative learning maintain or even enhance student achievement? Experiments with

Kofi Annan: "Most of us have overlapping identities which unite us with very different groups. We *can* love what we are, without hating what—and who—we are *not*. We can thrive in our own tradition, even as we learn from others" (Nobel lecture, 2001).

conflict a perceived incompatibility of actions, goals, or ideas.

mirror-image perceptions mutual views often held by conflicting people, as when each side sees itself as ethical and peaceful and views the other side as evil and aggressive.

superordinate goals shared goals that override differences among people and require their cooperation.

teens from 11 countries confirm that, in each case, the answer is *Yes* (Roseth et al., 2008). In the classroom as in the sports arena, members of interracial groups who form teams and work together typically come to feel friendly toward one another. Knowing this, thousands of teachers have made interracial cooperative learning part of their classroom experience.

The power of cooperative activity to make friends of former enemies has led psychologists to urge increased international exchange and cooperation (Klineberg, 1984). Let us engage in mutually beneficial trade, working together to protect our common destiny on this fragile planet and becoming more aware that our hopes and fears are shared. By taking such steps, we can change misperceptions that drive us apart and instead join together in a common cause based on common interests. As working toward shared goals reminds us, we are more alike than different.

PRACTICE TEST

THE BASICS

11. When things go wrong, _____ gives us someone to blame.
    a. ingroup bias
    b. creating a scapegoat
    c. an aversive event
    d. the just-world phenomenon

12. If several well-publicized murders are committed by members of a particular group, we tend to react with fear and suspicion toward all members of that group. In other words, we
    a. blame the victim.
    b. overgeneralize from vivid, memorable cases.
    c. create a scapegoat.
    d. rationalize inequality.

13. Evidence of a biological influence on aggression is the finding that
    a. aggressive behavior varies widely from culture to culture.
    b. animals can be bred for aggressiveness.
    c. the brain has a violence center in the frontal lobes.
    d. men who commit violent crimes have low levels of testosterone.

14. A conference of social scientists studying the effects of pornography unanimously agreed that violent pornography
    a. has little effect on most viewers.
    b. is the primary cause of reported and unreported rapes.
    c. leads viewers to be more accepting of coercion in sexual relations.
    d. has no effect, other than short-term arousal and entertainment.

15. The mere exposure effect helps explain why people tend to marry someone
    a. about as attractive as themselves.
    b. who lives or works nearby.
    c. of similar religious or ethnic background.
    d. who has similar attitudes and habits.

16. According to the two-factor theory of emotion, emotions such as passionate love consist of physical arousal plus
    a. a reward.
    b. proximity.
    c. companionate love.
    d. our interpretation of that arousal.

17. Companionate love is described as a deep, affectionate attachment. _____ is (are) vital to the maintenance of such loving relationships.
    a. Equity and self-disclosure
    b. Physical attraction
    c. Intense positive absorption
    d. Passionate love

18. The bystander effect states that a bystander will be less likely to give aid if
    a. the victim is similar to the bystander in appearance.
    b. no one else is present.

    c. other people are present.
    d. the incident occurs in a deserted or rural area.

19. One way of fostering cooperation is by providing groups with superordinate goals, which are
    a. the goals of friendly competition.
    b. shared goals that override differences.
    c. goals for winning at negotiations.
    d. goals for reducing conflict through increased contact.

THE BIG PICTURE

14D. What psychological and biological influences interact to produce aggressive behaviors?

14E. How does being physically attractive influence the way others think about you?

14F. Why didn't anybody help Kitty Genovese? What social psychology principle did this incident illustrate?

14G. Why might an otherwise calm and softhearted person take great joy when her school's archrival team loses? Why do such feelings make conflict resolution more challenging?

IN YOUR EVERYDAY LIFE

▪ What negative attitudes might professors and students have toward each other? What strategies might change those attitudes?

▪ In what ways has your generation been affected by social scripts for aggression? Have TV or video games contributed such scripts?

▪ To what extent have your closest relationships been affected by proximity, physical attractiveness, and similarity?

▪ What could you do to motivate your friends to contribute their time or money to a cause that is important to you?

▪ Think of a conflict between friends and family members. What strategies would you suggest to help them reconcile that relationship?

Answers: 11. b, 12. b, 13. b, 14. c, 15. b, 16. d, 17. a, 18. c, 19. b. Answers to The Big Picture questions can be found in Appendix B at the end of the book.

Terms and Concepts to Remember

social psychology, p. 376

fundamental attribution error, p. 378

attitude, p. 379

foot-in-the-door phenomenon, p. 380

role, p. 380

cognitive dissonance theory, p. 381

conformity, p. 382

social facilitation, p. 386

social loafing, p. 387

deindividuation, p. 388

group polarization, p. 388

groupthink, p. 389

prejudice, p. 390

stereotype, p. 390

discrimination, p. 390

just-world phenomenon, p. 391

ingroup, p. 392

outgroup, p. 392

ingroup bias, p. 392

scapegoat theory, p. 392

other-race effect, p. 393

aggression, p. 393

frustration-aggression principle, p. 394

social script, p. 395

mere exposure effect, p. 397

passionate love, p. 401

companionate love, p. 401

equity, p. 401

self-disclosure, p. 402

altruism, p. 402

bystander effect, p. 403

conflict, p. 404

mirror-image perceptions, p. 404

superordinate goals, p. 405

Multiple-choice **self-tests** and more may be found at www.worthpublishers.com/myers

Social Thinking

1 **What are three main focuses of social psychology? How does the fundamental attribution error describe how we tend to explain others' behavior compared with our own?**

- *Social psychology* focuses on how we think about, influence, and relate to one another.

- We may commit the *fundamental attribution error* when explaining others' behavior (by underestimating the influence of the situation and overestimating the effects of personality).

- When we explain our own behavior, however, we more often recognize the influence of the situation.

2 **What is an attitude, and how do attitudes and actions affect each other?**

- *Attitudes* are feelings, based on beliefs, that predispose us to respond in certain ways.

- Attitudes that are stable, specific, and easily recalled can affect our actions when other influences are minimal.

- Actions also modify our attitudes. This can be seen in the *foot-in-the-door phenomenon* and *role-playing*.

- When our attitudes don't fit with our actions, *cognitive dissonance theory* suggests that we will reduce tension by changing our attitudes to match our actions.

Social Influence

3 **What do experiments on conformity and obedience reveal about the power of social influence?**

- Asch and others have found that we are most likely to *conform* to a group standard when (a) we feel incompetent or insecure, (b) our group has at least three people, (c) everyone else agrees, (d) we admire the group's status, (e) we have not committed to another response, (f) we know we are being observed, and (g) our culture encourages respect for social standards.

- In Milgram's famous experiments, people usually obeyed the experimenter's orders even when they thought they were harming another person. Obedience was highest when (a) the experimenter was nearby and (b) was a legitimate authority figure supported by an important institution, (c) the victim was not nearby, and (d) there were no role models for defiance.

4 **What do the social influence studies teach us about ourselves? How much power do we have as individuals?**

- Strong social influences can exert pressures to conform to falsehoods or give in to cruelty.

- Even a small minority sometimes sways a group, especially when the minority expresses its views consistently.

- Social control (the power of the situation) and personal control (the power of the individual) interact.

5 **How does the presence of others influence our actions, via social facilitation, social loafing, or deindividuation?**

- *Social facilitation:* The presence of others arouses us, improving performance on easy tasks but hindering it on difficult ones.

- *Social loafing:* In a group project, we may feel less responsible and free-ride on others' efforts.

- *Deindividuation:* When the presence of others both arouses us and makes us feel less responsible, we may lose self-awareness and self-restraint.

6 **How can group interaction enable group polarization and groupthink?**

- *Group polarization:* In a group, discussions with like-minded others cause us to feel more strongly about our shared beliefs and attitudes. Internet communication magnifies this effect, for better and for worse.

- *Groupthink:* A desire for harmony within a group can cause its members to overlook important alternatives.

Social Relations

7 **What are the three parts of prejudice, and how has prejudice changed over time?**

- *Prejudice* is an unjustifiable, usually negative attitude toward a group, consisting of (a) beliefs (often *stereotypes*), (b) negative feelings, and (c) predispositions to action *(discrimination)*.
- Open prejudice has decreased, but subtle prejudice and automatic prejudice—occurring without our awareness—continues.

8 **What factors contribute to the social roots of prejudice, and how does scapegoating illustrate the emotional roots of prejudice?**

- Social inequalities and social divisions feed prejudice. Favored social groups often justify their higher status with the *just-world phenomenon*.
- We tend to favor our own group *(ingroup bias)* as we divide ourselves into us (the *ingroup*) and them (the *outgroup*).
- We may use prejudice to protect our emotional well-being, such as when focusing anger on a *scapegoat*.

9 **What cognitive processes help create and maintain prejudice?**

- The cognitive roots of prejudice grow from our natural ways of processing information: forming categories, remembering vivid cases, and believing that the world is just and our culture's way of doing things is the right way.

10 **What biological factors predispose us to be aggressive?**

- Biology influences our threshold for aggressive behaviors at three levels: genetic (inherited traits), neural (activity in key brain areas), and biochemical (such as alcohol or excess testosterone in the bloodstream).
- Aggression is a complex behavior resulting from the interaction of biology and experience.

11 **What psychological factors trigger aggression? How does viewing multimedia violence affect aggressive behavior?**

- Frustration *(frustration-aggression principle)*, rejection, getting rewarded for aggression, and seeing an aggressive role model can all contribute to aggression.
- Viewing sexual violence contributes to greater aggression toward women.
- Exposure to violence on screen provides aggressive *social scripts* for children to follow. Playing violent video games has a stronger effect on aggressive behavior than does viewing violence on TV or in movies.

12 **How do proximity, attractiveness, and similarity influence whom we befriend or fall in love with?**

- Proximity (geographical nearness) increases liking; even repeated *mere exposure* to novel stimuli increases liking of those stimuli.
- Physical attractiveness increases social opportunities and improves the way we are perceived.
- Similarity of attitudes and interests greatly increases liking, especially as relationships develop.

13 **How does physical arousal affect passionate love? What predicts enduring companionate love?**

- Intimate love relationships start with *passionate love*—an intensely aroused state.
- Over time, the strong affection of *companionate love* may develop, especially if enhanced by an *equitable* relationship and by intimate *self-disclosure*.

14 **What is altruism? When are we most—and least—likely to intervene as bystanders?**

- *Altruism* is unselfish regard for the well-being of others.
- We are most likely to help when we (a) notice an incident, (b) interpret it as an emergency, and (c) assume responsibility for helping. Other factors, including our mood and our similarity to the victim, also affect our willingness to help.
- We are least likely to help if other bystanders are present (the *bystander effect*).

15 **What social processes fuel conflict? How can we transform feelings of prejudice and conflict into behaviors that promote peace?**

- *Conflicts* between individuals and cultures are often fed by distorted *mirror-image perceptions*—each party views itself as moral and the other as untrustworthy and evil-intentioned.
- Peace can result when individuals or groups cooperate to achieve *superordinate* (shared) *goals*.

appendix A

PSYCHOLOGY AT WORK

For most of us, to live is to work. Work is life's biggest single waking activity, helping to satisfy several levels of our needs. Work supports us, giving us food, water, and shelter. Work connects us, meeting our social needs. Work defines us, satisfying our self-esteem needs. Work helps us understand someone we've met for the first time. Wondering, "Who are you?" we may instead ask, "So, what do you do?"

The answer, however, may give us only a fleeting snapshot of that person at a particular time and place. On the day we retire from the work force, few of us will look back and say we have followed a predictable career path. We will have changed jobs, some of us often. The trigger for those changes may have been a desire for better pay, happier on-the-job relationships, or more fulfilling work.

Work and Life Satisfaction

> **1 What is *flow*?**

Across various occupations, attitudes toward work tend to fall into one of three categories (Wrzesniewski et al., 1997, 2001). Some people view their work as a *job*, an unfulfilling but necessary way to make money. Others view their work as a *career*. Their present position may not be ideal, but it is at least a rung on a ladder leading to increasingly better options. The third group views their work as a *calling*. For them, work is a fulfilling and socially useful activity. Of all these groups, those who see their work as a calling report the highest satisfaction with their work and their lives.

This finding would not surprise Mihaly Csikszentmihalyi (1990, 1999). He has observed that people's quality of life increases when they are purposefully engaged. Between the anxiety of being overwhelmed and stressed, and the apathy of being underwhelmed and bored, lies **flow**. In this intense, focused state, our skills are totally engaged, and we lose our awareness of self and time. Can you recall being in a zoned-out flow state while playing a video game or text messaging? If so, then perhaps you can sympathize with the two Northwest Airlines pilots who in 2009 were so focused on their laptops that they missed earth-to-pilot messages from their control tower. The pilots flew 150 miles past their Minneapolis destination—and lost their jobs.

Csikszentmihalyi (Chick-SENT-me-hi) came up with the flow concept while studying artists who spent hour after hour wrapped up in a project. After painting or sculpting for hours as if nothing else mattered, they finished and appeared to forget about the project. The

> Sometimes, notes Gene Weingarten (2002), a humor writer knows "when to just get out of the way." Here are some sample job titles from the U.S. Department of Labor *Dictionary of Occupational Titles*: Animal impersonator, human projectile, banana ripening-room supervisor, impregnator, impregnator helper, dope sprayer, finger waver, rug scratcher, egg smeller, bottom buffer, cookie breaker, brain picker, hand pouncer, bosom presser, mother repairer.

Disrupted flow: Internet-related distractions can disrupt flow. It takes time to refocus mental concentration after the distraction of an email or text message.

artists seemed driven less by the external rewards for producing their art—money, praise, promotion—than by the internal rewards for creating the work.

Fascinated, Csikszentmihalyi broadened his observations. He studied dancers, chess players, surgeons, writers, parents, mountain climbers, sailors, and farmers. His research included Australians, North Americans, Koreans, Japanese, and Italians. Participants ranged from the teen years to the golden years. A clear principle emerged. An activity that fully engages our skills leads to a state of flow, which boosts our sense of self-esteem, competence, and well-being. How did researchers discover

> **flow** a completely involved, focused state, with lowered awareness of self and time; results from full engagement of our skills.

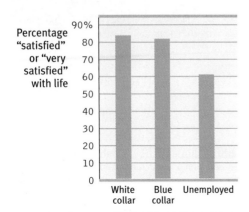

FIGURE A.1 • **Unemployment and life satisfaction** To want work but not have it is to feel less satisfied with life. (Data from 169,776 adults in 16 nations—Inglehart, 1990.)

this? They beeped people at random intervals and asked them to report what they were doing and how much they were enjoying themselves. People reported more positive feelings when beeped while doing something active—work or play that engaged their skills. Those interrupted while passive usually reported little sense of flow and low satisfaction.

Other research supports these findings (Inglehart, 1990). In almost every developed nation, people have reported much lower well-being if unemployed (**FIGURE A.1**). Idleness may sound like bliss, but purposeful work enriches our lives. (For some tips on enriching your own work life, see Close-Up: Finding Your Own Flow.)

Industrial-Organizational Psychology

2 What are the three main subfields of industrial-organizational psychology?

In developed nations, work has been changing, from farming to manufacturing to *knowledge work*. More and more work is *outsourced* to temporary employees. Consultants in remote locations now communicate electronically with the

main office and with one another. (This book and its teaching package are developed and produced by a team of people in a dozen cities, from Alaska to Florida.)

As work changes, will our attitudes toward our work also change? Will our satisfaction with work increase or decrease? What will happen to the *psychological contract*—that two-way feeling of duty between workers and employers? These are among the questions that fascinate those interested in **industrial-organizational (I/O) psychology,** a profession that applies psychology's principles to the workplace.

I/O psychology has three main subfields (see Close-Up: I/O Psychologists on the Job). **Human factors psychology** explores how machines and environments can best be designed to fit human abilities. **Personnel psychology** applies psychology's methods and

principles to selecting, placing, training, and evaluating workers. **Organizational psychology** is the primary focus of this appendix. This subfield considers an organization's goals, work environments, and management styles, and their influence on worker motivation, satisfaction, and productivity.

Motivating Achievement

3 Why is it important to motivate achievement?

Organizational psychologists help motivate employees and keep them engaged. But what motivates any of us to pursue high standards or difficult goals?

Finding Your Own Flow

Want to identify your own path to flow? You can start by pinpointing your strengths and the types of work that may prove satisfying and successful. Marcus Buckingham and Donald Clifton (2001) have suggested asking yourself four questions.

1. What activities give me pleasure? (Bringing order out of chaos? Playing host? Helping others? Challenging sloppy thinking?)
2. What activities leave me wondering, "When can I do this again?" (Rather than "When will this be over?")
3. What sorts of challenges do I relish? (And which do I dread?)
4. What sorts of tasks do I learn easily? (And which do I struggle with?)

There are no "right" answers to these questions, but considering possible answers may lead you to your own zone of flow. You may find your skills engaged and time flying when teaching or selling or writing or cleaning or consoling or creating or repairing. If an activity feels good, if it comes easily, if you look forward to it, then look deeper. You'll see your strengths at work (Buckingham, 2007).

Top performers are "rarely well rounded" (Buckingham & Clifton, 2001, p. 26). Satisfied and successful people devote far less time to correcting their weaknesses than to sharpening their existing skills. Given how stable our traits and temperaments are, this is probably wise. There may be limits to the benefits of assertiveness training if you are shy, or of public speaking courses if you tend to be nervous and soft-spoken. Drawing classes may not help much if you express your artistic side in stick figures.

But identifying your talents can help you recognize the activities you learn quickly and find absorbing. Knowing your strengths, you can develop them further.

As Robert Louis Stevenson said in *Familiar Studies of Men and Books* (1882), "To be what we are, and to become what we are capable of becoming, is the only end of life."

CLOSE-UP

I/O Psychologists on the Job

As scientists, consultants, and management professionals, I/O psychologists are found working in varied areas.

HUMAN FACTORS (ENGINEERING) PSYCHOLOGY

- Designing optimum work environments
- Optimizing person-machine interactions
- Developing systems technologies

PERSONNEL PSYCHOLOGY

Selecting and placing employees

- Developing and testing assessment tools for selecting, placing, and promoting workers
- Analyzing job content
- Optimizing worker placement

Training and developing employees

- Identifying needs
- Designing training programs
- Evaluating training programs

Appraising performance

- Developing guidelines
- Measuring individual performance
- Measuring organizational performance

ORGANIZATIONAL PSYCHOLOGY

Developing organizations

- Analyzing organizational structures
- Increasing worker satisfaction and productivity
- Making organizational change easier

Enhancing quality of work life

- Expanding individual productivity
- Identifying elements of satisfaction
- Redesigning jobs

Adapted from the Society of Industrial and Organizational Psychology (siop.org).

study that followed the lives of 1528 California children. All had scored in the top 1 percent on an intelligence test. Forty years later, researchers compared those who were most and least successful professionally. The most successful were the most highly motivated—they were ambitious, energetic, and persistent. As children, these individuals had enjoyed more active hobbies. As adults, they participated in more groups and preferred *playing* sports over watching sports (Goleman, 1980). Gifted children are able learners. Accomplished adults are determined doers.

Motivation differences also appear in other studies, including those of high school and college students. Self-discipline, not intelligence score, has been the best predictor of school performance, attendance, and graduation honors. Intense, sustained effort predicts success for teachers, too, especially when combined with a positive enthusiasm. Students of these motivated educators make good academic progress (Duckworth et al., 2009).

"Discipline outdoes talent," conclude researchers Angela Duckworth and Martin Seligman (2005, 2006). It also refines talent. By their early twenties, top violinists have fiddled away 10,000 hours of their life practicing. This is double the practice time of other violin students

industrial-organizational (I/O) psychology the application of psychological concepts and methods to human behavior in workplaces.

human factors psychology a subfield of I/O psychology that explores how people and machines interact and how machines and physical environments can be made safe and easy to use.

personnel psychology a subfield of I/O psychology that focuses on employee selection, placement, training, and appraisal.

organizational psychology a subfield of I/O psychology that examines organizational influences on worker satisfaction and productivity and facilitates organizational change.

achievement motivation a desire for significant accomplishment; for mastery of things, people, or ideas; and for attaining a high standard.

Grit

Think of someone you know who seems driven to be the best—to excel at any task where performance can be judged. Now think of someone who is less driven. For psychologist Henry Murray (1938), the difference between these two people is a reflection of their **achievement motivation.** If you score high in achievement motivation, you have a desire for significant accomplishment, for mastering skills or ideas, for control, and for meeting a high standard.

Achievement motivation matters. Just how much it matters can be seen in a

Calum's road: What grit can accomplish: Having spent his life on the Scottish island of Raasay farming a small patch of land, tending its lighthouse, and fishing, Malcolm ("Calum") MacLeod (1911–1988) felt anguished. His local government had refused to build a road that would enable electricity and vehicles to reach his north end of the island. With the once-flourishing population there having dwindled to two—MacLeod and his wife—he responded with heroic determination. One spring morning in 1964, MacLeod, then in his fifties, gathered an ax, a chopper, a shovel, and a wheelbarrow. By hand, he began to transform the existing footpath into a 1.75 mile road (Miers, 2009).

"With a road," a former neighbor explained, "he hoped new generations of people would return to the north end of Raasay," restoring its culture (Hutchinson, 2006). Day after day he worked through rough hillsides, along hazardous cliff-faces, and over peat bogs. Finally, 10 years later, he completed his supreme achievement. The road, which the government has since surfaced, remains a visible example of what vision plus determined grit can accomplish. It bids us each to ponder: What "roads"—what achievements—might we, with sustained effort, build in the years before us?

Calum MacLeod at work on his road; photograph © Campbell Sandilands.

aiming to be teachers (Ericsson et al., 2001, 2006, 2007).

Similarly, a study of outstanding scholars, athletes, and artists found that all were highly motivated and self-disciplined. They dedicated hours every day to the pursuit of their goals (Bloom, 1985). These achievers became superstars through daily discipline, not just natural talent. Great achievement, it seems, mixes a teaspoon of inspiration with a gallon of perspiration.

Duckworth and Seligman have a name for this passionate dedication to an ambitious, long-term goal: *grit*. Intelligence scores and many other physical and psychological traits can be displayed as a *bell-shaped curve*. Most scores cluster around an average, and fewer scores fall at the two far ends of the bell shape. Achievement scores don't follow this pattern. That is why organizational psychologists seek ways to engage and motivate ordinary people to be superstars in their own jobs. And that is why training students in *hardiness*—resilience under stress—leads to better grades (Maddi et al., 2009).

Satisfaction and Engagement

I/O psychologists know that everyone wins when workers are satisfied with their jobs. For employees, satisfaction

with work feeds satisfaction with life. Moreover, lower job stress feeds improved health (Chapter 10).

HOW DO EMPLOYERS BENEFIT FROM◄ WORKER SATISFACTION? Positive moods can translate into greater creativity, persistence, and helpfulness (Brief & Weiss,

2002; Kaplan et al., 2009). The correlation between individual job satisfaction and performance is modest but real (Judge et al., 2001; Ng et al., 2009; Parker et al., 2003). One analysis tracked 4500 employees at 42 British manufacturing companies. The most productive workers tended to be those in satisfying work environments (Patterson et al., 2004). In the United States, the *Fortune* "100 Best Companies to Work For" have also produced much higher-than-average returns for their investors (Dickler, 2007).

The biggest-ever study of worker satisfaction and job performance was an analysis of Gallup data (**TABLE A.1**) from more than 198,000 employees (Harter et al., 2002). These people were employed in nearly 8000 business units of 36 large companies, including some 1100 bank branches, 1200 stores, and 4200 teams or departments. The study focused on links between various measures of organizational success and employee engagement—the extent of workers' involvement, enthusiasm,

TABLE A.1	The Gallup Workplace Audit

Overall satisfaction—On a 5-point scale, where 5 is extremely satisfied and 1 is extremely dissatisfied, how satisfied are you with (name of company) as a place to work? _____

On a scale of 1 to 5, where 1 is strongly disagree and 5 is strongly agree, please indicate your agreement with the following items.

1. I know what is expected from me at work.

2. I have the materials and equipment I need to do my work right.

3. At work, I have the opportunity to do what I do best every day.

4. In the last seven days, I have received recognition or praise for doing good work.

5. My supervisor, or someone at work, seems to care about me as a person.

6. There is someone at work who encourages my development.

7. At work, my opinions seem to count.

8. The mission/purpose of my company makes me feel my job is important.

9. My associates (fellow employees) are committed to doing quality work.

10. I have a best friend at work.

11. In the last six months, someone at work has talked to me about my progress.

12. This last year, I have had opportunities at work to learn and grow.

Note: These statements are proprietary and copyrighted by The Gallup Organization. They may not be printed or reproduced in any manner without the written consent of The Gallup Organization. Reprinted here by permission.

TABLE A.2	Three Types of Employees
Engaged: working with passion and feeling a profound connection to their company or organization.	
Not engaged: putting in the time but investing little passion or energy into their work.	
Actively disengaged: unhappy workers undermining what their colleagues accomplish.	
(*Source:* Adapted from Gallup via Crabtree, 2005.)	

and identification with their organizations (**TABLE A.2**). The researchers found that engaged workers (compared with not-engaged workers who are just putting in time) know what's expected of them, have what they need to do their work, feel fulfilled in their work, have regular opportunities to do what they do best, perceive that they are part of something significant, and have opportunities to learn and develop. They also found that business units with engaged employees have more loyal customers, less turnover, higher productivity, and greater profits. A follow-up analysis compared companies with top-quartile versus below-average employee engagement levels. Over a three-year period, earnings grew 2.6 times faster for the companies with highly engaged workers (Ott, 2007).

Leadership

4 | How can leaders be most effective?

The best leaders want their organization to be successful. They also want the people who work for them and with them to be satisfied, engaged, and productive. To achieve these ends, effective leaders harness people's strengths, set goals, and choose an appropriate leadership style.

Harnessing Strengths

Engaged employees don't just happen. Effective leaders engage their employees' interests and loyalty. They figure out people's natural talents, adjust roles to suit their talents, and develop those talents into great strengths (**FIGURE A.2**). Consider, for example, instructors at a given school. Should they all be expected to teach the same load? To advise the same number of students? To serve on the same number of committees? To take on the same number of additional responsibilities in the department? Or should their job descriptions be tailored to their specific strengths? Would most schools and their students be better served if instructors' tasks were matched to their strengths?

Trying to create talents that are not there can be a waste of time. Leaders who excel spend more time developing and drawing out talents that already exist. Effective managers share certain traits (Tucker, 2002). They

- start by helping people identify and measure their talents.
- match tasks to talents and then give people freedom to do what they do best.
- care how people feel about their work.
- reinforce positive behaviors through recognition and reward.

Good managers also try not to promote people into roles ill-suited to their strengths. Imagine that you're a manager with a limited budget for training. Will you focus on your employees' weaknesses and send them to training seminars to fix those problems? Or will you focus on educating your employees about their strengths and building upon them? Good managers choose the second option. In Gallup surveys, 77 percent of engaged workers strongly agreed that "my supervisor focuses on my strengths or positive characteristics." Only 23 percent of not-engaged workers agreed with that statement (Krueger & Killham, 2005).

Does all this sound familiar? Bringing out the best in people within an organization builds upon a basic principle of

An engaged employee: Mohamed Mamow, left, is joined by his employer in saying the Pledge of Allegiance as he becomes a U.S. citizen. Mamow and his wife met in a Somali refugee camp and now are parents of five children, whom he supports by working as a machine operator. Mindful of his responsibility—"I don't like to lose my job. I have a responsibility for my children and my family"—he arrives for work a half hour early and tends to every detail on his shift. "He is an extremely hard-working employee," noted his employer, and "a reminder to all of us that we are really blessed" (Roelofs, 2010).

Darren Breen, *Grand Rapids Press*, 9/22/2010

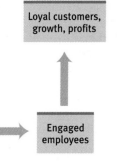

FIGURE **A.2** • **The Gallup Organization path to organizational success** (Adapted from Fleming, 2001.)

Identify strengths → Match to work → Positive managing → Engaged employees → Loyal customers, growth, profits

Positive coaching: Larry Brown has been an adviser to the youth sports organization The Positive Coaching Alliance. He was observed during practices offering his players 4 to 5 positive comments for every negative comment (Insana, 2005). In 2004, he coached his underdog Detroit Pistons to the National Basketball Association championship.

Kirthmon F. Dozier/KRT/Newscom

operant conditioning (Chapter 6). To teach a behavior, catch a person doing something right and reinforce it. It sounds simple, but too many managers act like the parents who focus on the one low score on a child's almost-perfect report card. As a report by the Gallup Organization (2004) observed, "65 percent of Americans received no praise or recognition in their workplace last year."

Setting Specific, Challenging Goals

In study after study, people merely asked to do their best do not do so. Good managers know that a better way to motivate higher achievement is to set specific, challenging goals. For example, you might state your own goal in this course as "Finish studying Appendix A by Friday." Specific goals focus our attention and stimulate us to work hard, persist, and try creative strategies. Such goals are especially effective when workers or team members participate in setting them. Achieving goals that are challenging yet within our reach boosts our self-evaluation (White et al., 1995).

Stated goals are most effective when combined with progress reports (Johnson et al., 2006; Latham & Locke, 2007). Action plans that break large goals into smaller steps (subgoals) and specify when, where, and how to achieve those steps will increase the chances of completing a project on time (Burgess et al., 2004; Fishbach et al., 2006; Koestner et al., 2002). (Before writing this book, my editors, my associates, and I agreed on target dates for completing each chapter draft.) Creating your own action plans can help you become a more effective leader. To motivate high productivity, you can work with people to define goals, make a plan for achieving its subgoals, and provide feedback on progress.

Choosing an Appropriate Leadership Style

WHAT QUALITIES PRODUCE A GREAT ◄ LEADER? Psychologists and others once believed that all great leaders share certain traits. That *great person theory of leadership* now seems overstated (Vroom & Jago, 2007). The same coach may seem great or not great, depending on the team and its competition. But a leader's personality does matter (Zaccaro, 2007). Effective leaders are not overly assertive; that trait can damage social relationships within the group. They are not unassertive, because that trait can limit their ability to lead (Ames & Flynn, 2007). Effective leaders of laboratory groups, work teams, and large corporations tend to be self-confident. They have *charisma*, which seems to have three main ingredients (House & Singh, 1987; Shamir et al., 1993).

- They have a *vision* of some goal.
- They are able to *communicate* that vision clearly and simply.
- They have enough optimism and faith to *inspire* their group to follow them.

Consider a study rating company morale at 50 Dutch firms (de Hoogh et al., 2004). Firms with the highest ratings had chief executives who inspired their colleagues "to transcend their own self-interests for the sake of the collective." This ability to motivate others to commit themselves to a group's mission is *transformational leadership.* Transformational leaders are often natural extraverts. They set their standards high, and they inspire others to share their vision. They pay attention to other people (Bono & Judge, 2004). The frequent result is a work force that is more engaged, trusting, and effective (Turner et al., 2002). (For an impressive example of transformational leadership skills, see Close-Up: Doing Well While Doing Good.)

Women more than men tend to be transformational leaders. This may help explain why companies with women in top management positions recently tended to enjoy superior financial results (Eagly, 2007). That tendency held, even after researchers controlled for variables such as company size.

Leadership styles vary, depending both on the qualities of the leader and the demands of the situation. In some situations (think of a commander leading troops into battle), a *directive* style may be needed (Fiedler, 1981). In other situations, the strategies that work on the battlefield may smother creativity. If developing a comedy show, for example, a leader might get better results using a *democratic* style that welcomes team member creativity.

Leaders differ in the personal qualities they bring to the job. Some excel at **task leadership**—by setting standards, organizing work, and focusing attention on goals. To keep the group centered on its mission, task leaders typically use a directive style. This style can work well if the leader is smart enough to give good orders (Fiedler, 1987).

Other managers excel at **social leadership.** They explain decisions, help group members solve their conflicts, and build teams that work well together (Evans & Dion, 1991). Social leaders often have a democratic style. They share authority and welcome the opinions of team members.

Doing Well While Doing Good—"The Great Experiment"

At the end of the 1700s, the cotton mill at New Lanark, Scotland had more than 1000 workers. Many were children drawn from Glasgow's poorhouses. They worked 13-hour days and lived in grim conditions. Education and sanitation were neglected. Theft and drunkenness were common. Most families occupied just one room.

On a visit to Glasgow, Welsh-born Robert Owen—an idealistic young cotton-mill manager—chanced to meet and fall in love with the mill owner's daughter. After their marriage, Owen, with several partners, purchased the mill. On the first day of the 1800s he took control as its manager. Before long, he began what he said was "the most important experiment for the happiness of the human race that had yet been instituted at any time in any part of the world" (Owen, 1814). The abuse of child and adult labor was, he observed, producing unhappy and inefficient workers. Owen believed that better working and living conditions could pay economic dividends.

Owen showed transformational leadership skills when he bravely began many new practices. He started a nursery for preschool children, and education for older children (with encouragement rather than corporal punishment). Workers had Sundays off. They received health care, paid sick days, and unemployment pay for days when the mill could not operate. He set up a company store, selling goods at reduced prices. When his partners resisted his changes, he bought their shares.

Owen also designed a goals and worker-assessment program, with detailed records of daily productivity and costs. By each employee's workstation, one of four colored boards indicated that person's performance for the previous day. Owen could walk through the mill and at a glance see how individuals were performing. There was, he said, "no beating, no abusive language. . . . I merely looked at the person and then at the color. . . . I could at once see by the expression [which color] was shown."

The financial success of Owen's mill supported a reform movement for better working and living conditions. By 1816, with decades of profits still ahead, Owen believed he had demonstrated "that society may be formed so as to exist without crime, without poverty, with health greatly improved, with little if any misery, and with intelligence and happiness increased a hundredfold." Although that vision has not been fulfilled, Owen's great experiment did lay the groundwork for employment practices that are accepted in much of the world today.

Courtesy of New Lanark World Heritage Site

The great experiment: New Lanark Mills showed that industries could do well while doing good. In its time, Owen's mill was visited by many European royals and reformers who came to observe its vibrant work force and prosperous business. New Lanark today is preserved as a World Heritage Site (www.newlanark.org).

Social leadership is good for morale. We usually feel more satisfied and motivated and perform better when we can participate in decision making (Cawley et al., 1998; Pereira & Osburn, 2007).

Effective managers often exhibit a high degree of *both* task and social leadership. This finding applies in many locations, including coal mines, banks, and government offices in India, Taiwan, and Iran (Smith & Tayeb, 1989). As achievement-minded people, effective managers certainly care about how well people do their work. Yet they are sensitive to their workers' needs. That sensitivity is often repaid by worker loyalty. In one national survey of American workers, those in family-friendly organizations offering flexible hours reported feeling greater loyalty to their employers (Roehling et al., 2001).

Employee participation in decision making is common in Sweden, Japan, the United States, and elsewhere (Cawley et al., 1998; Sundstrom et al., 1990). Giving workers a chance to voice their opinion before a decision is made engages them in the process. They then tend to respond more positively to the final decision (van den Bos & Spruijt, 2002). And, as we noted earlier, positive, engaged employees are a mark of thriving organizations.

task leadership goal-oriented leadership that sets standards, organizes work, and focuses attention on goals.

social leadership group-oriented leadership that builds teamwork, resolves conflict, and offers support.

Harley-Davidson management and employees worked together to drive their company from rags to riches (Teerlink & Ozley, 2000). In 1987, the struggling company began transforming its management process. The aim: "To push decision making, planning, and strategizing from a handful of people at the top, down throughout the organization. We wanted all the employees to think every day about how to improve the company," reported CEO Jeffrey Bleustein (2002). In the mid-1990s, Harley-Davidson signed a cooperative agreement with its unions that included them "in decision making in virtually every aspect of the business." Shared decision making can take longer, Bleustein noted. But "when the decision is made, it gets implemented quickly and the commitment is by the group." Satisfied stockholders agreed. Every $1 of Harley-Davidson stock purchased at the beginning of 1988 was worth $100 by 2010. For Harley-Davidson, an engaged work force was a win-win solution.

PRACTICE TEST

THE BASICS

1. People who report great satisfaction with their work often experience _____, a focused state in which they lose awareness of themselves and of time.
   a. stress
   b. apathy
   c. flow
   d. grit

2. The three main divisions within I/O psychology are _____, _____, and _____ psychology.
   a. motivational; management; small group
   b. human factors; personnel; organizational
   c. motivational; personnel; human factors
   d. personnel; management; small group

3. When people at similar intelligence levels are compared, those with higher achievement motivation tend to
   a. be more successful.
   b. be less successful.
   c. be less satisfied.
   d. have less grit.

4. Which of the following is NOT a quality of an effective leader?
   a. Helping people identify and measure their talents.
   b. Setting specific, challenging goals.
   c. Focusing on people's weaknesses with training to fix the problems.
   d. Reinforcing positive behaviors.

5. Task leadership is goal-oriented, whereas social leadership is group-oriented. Research indicates that effective managers exhibit
   a. mainly task leadership.
   b. mainly social leadership.
   c. both task and social leadership, depending on the situation and the person.
   d. task leadership for building teams and social leadership for setting standards.

THE BIG PICTURE

A-1. What is the value of finding flow in your work?

A-2. What characteristics are important for transformational leaders?

IN YOUR EVERYDAY LIFE

■ How motivated are you to achieve in school? How has this affected your academic success? How could you increase your motivation?

■ Have you ever experienced the zoned-out enjoyment of flow? What were you doing? What could you do to find more flow in your life?

Answers: 1. c, 2. b, 3. a, 4. c, 5. c. Answers to The Big Picture questions can be found in Appendix B at the end of the book.

Terms and Concepts to Remember

flow, p. 411

industrial-organizational (I/O) psychology, p. 412

human factors psychology, p. 412

personnel psychology, p. 412

organizational psychology, p. 412

achievement motivation, p. 413

task leadership, p. 416

social leadership, p. 416

Multiple-choice **self-tests** and more may be found at www.worthpublishers.com/myers

Work and Life Satisfaction

1 **What is *flow*?**

- Having our skills fully engaged; losing awareness of self and time.
- Work may be just a job, a somewhat fulfilling career, or a calling, which produces the highest levels of satisfaction.

Industrial-Organizational Psychology

2 **What are the three main subfields of industrial-organizational psychology?**

- *Human factors psychologists* explore how people and machines interact for optimal safety and effectiveness.
- *Personnel psychologists* use psychology's principles to select, place, train, and evaluate workers.
- *Organizational psychologists* consider an organization's goals, environments, and management styles in an effort to improve worker motivation, satisfaction, and productivity.

Motivating Achievement

3 **Why is it important to motivate achievement?**

- High *achievement motivation* leads to greater success, especially when combined with determined, persistent grit.
- The most satisfied and engaged employees tend to be the most productive and successful.
- Managers motivate most effectively when they make clear what is expected, provide needed materials, allow employees to do what they do best, affirm employees, and ensure opportunities to learn and develop.

Leadership

4 **How can leaders be most effective?**

- Harness strengths, by matching tasks to talents and reinforcing positive behaviors.
- Set specific, challenging goals that stretch employees, but not beyond what they can do.
- Choose an appropriate leadership style for the situation, such as *task leadership* when a more directive style is needed, or *social leadership* when a more democratic style fits best.
- The most effective leaders often combine task and social leadership styles.

appendix B

ANSWERS TO "THE BIG PICTURE" QUESTIONS

CHAPTER 1 Psychology's Roots, Big Ideas, and Critical Thinking Tools

1A. What event defined the start of scientific psychology?
ANSWER: The event that marked the start of scientific psychology was Wilhelm Wundt's opening of the first psychology laboratory in 1879 at a German university. There, he and his students performed psychology's first experiment, an attempt to measure "atoms of the mind."

1B. What are the four big ideas that organize material in this book?
ANSWER: The four big ideas that organize material in this book are (a) critical thinking, (b) the biopsychosocial approach, (c) the two-track mind (dual processing), and (d) exploring human strengths.

1C. What is the scientific attitude, and why is it important for critical thinking?
ANSWER: The scientific attitude combines (a) curiosity, (b) *skeptical* testing of various claims and ideas, and (c) *humility* about one's own unexamined presumptions. Examining assumptions, searching for hidden values, evaluating evidence, and assessing conclusions are essential parts of critical thinking.

1D. Let's say we are testing a new blood pressure drug. Why would we learn more about its effectiveness from giving it to half a group of 1000 people than to all 1000 participants?
ANSWER: To learn whether a drug is medically effective—not just serving as a placebo—we must compare its effect on those randomly assigned to receive it (the experimental group) with those who receive a placebo (the control group). The only difference between the groups is whether they receive the actual drug. So, if blood pressure is lower in the experimental group, then we know that the drug itself has produced this effect, not just the participants' knowledge that they are being treated (placebo effect).

1E. How are human and animal research subjects protected?
ANSWER: Government regulations and guidelines set by professional associations and funding agencies protect the well-being of human and animal subjects. Most colleges and universities have ethics committees that enforce these requirements.

CHAPTER 2 The Biology of Mind and Consciousness

2A. How do neurons communicate with one another?
ANSWER: Neurons communicate with one another by converting an *electrical* impulse into a *chemical* message: A neuron fires when incoming excitatory signals exceed incoming inhibitory signals by a sufficient threshold. The resulting neural impulse travels to the axon's end, where it triggers the release of chemical neurotransmitters. After crossing a tiny gap, these molecules activate receptor sites on neighboring neurons.

2B. How does information flow through your nervous system as you pick up a fork? Can you summarize this process?
ANSWER: Your central nervous system's hungry brain activates and guides the muscles of your arm and hand via your peripheral nervous system's motor neurons. As you pick up the fork, your brain processes the information from your sensory nervous system, enabling it to continue to guide the fork to your mouth. The functional circle starts with sensory input, continues with interneuron processing by the central nervous system, and finishes with motor output.

2C. How are the nervous and endocrine systems alike, and how do they differ?
ANSWER: Both of these communication systems produce chemical molecules that act on the body's receptors to influence our behavior and emotions. The endocrine system, which secretes hormones into the bloodstream, delivers its messages much more slowly than the speedy nervous system, and the effects of the endocrine system's messages tend to linger much longer than those of the nervous system.

2D. In what brain region would damage be most likely to disrupt your ability to skip rope? Your ability to hear and taste? In what brain region would damage perhaps leave you in a coma? Without the very breath and heartbeat of life?
ANSWER: These regions are, respectively, the *cerebellum,* the *thalamus,* the *reticular formation,* and the *medulla.* These questions assess your understanding of the essential functions of the lower-level brain areas.

2E. How is the limbic system involved in fear and anger?
ANSWER: The amygdala, two lima-bean-sized neural clusters, is one of the limbic structures that can trigger

fear and anger. The limbic system's hypothalamus is also involved in emotion regulation—in part through its role in governing the endocrine system. The whole limbic system is associated with emotions and drives.

2F. **Which area of the human brain is most similar to that of primitive animals? Which part of the human brain distinguishes us most from primitive animals?**
ANSWER: The human brainstem is most similar to that of primitive animals. The cerebral cortex is most different.

2G. **How did the split-brain research teach us about the normal functions of our intact brains?**
ANSWER: Split-brain research enabled scientists to isolate and study some of the specific functions of the left and right hemispheres. For example, we've learned more about how the left hemisphere normally processes speech, and that the right hemisphere is usually more involved in perceiving and expressing emotion. This research has also clarified the importance of the intact corpus callosum (fibers connecting the two hemispheres), which normally allows the left and right hemispheres to communicate.

2H. **Would we function better if we were completely aware of all of our thought processes? Why or why not?**
ANSWER: It is actually adaptive that our mind operates at two levels at the same time. With an unconscious mind running largely on autopilot, our conscious thought processes can focus on executive-level, important decisions. While reading this textbook, for example, you don't have to remind yourself to inhale and exhale. Capable "assistants" in your unconscious mind—in this case, your medulla—are handling these tasks. Thanks to selective attention, you can focus consciously on only a fraction of the several billion bits of sensory information your mind processes in any given moment. Without this dual-processing ability, your information-processing system would be completely overwhelmed.

2I. **Most teens in the United States start school early—by 7:30 or 8:00 AM. Critics say that early to rise is not making kids wise, it's making them sleepy. Do you think later start times would remedy the tired-teen problem?**
ANSWER: Chronic sleep deprivation can impair the ability to concentrate, slow reaction times, and decrease creativity and productivity. Teens who used the later start time to get more sleep would benefit. Those who stayed up later would not.

2J. **Do you normally remember your dreams? How do sleep researchers find out what people are dreaming about?**
ANSWER: Many people (37 percent) say they rarely or never have dreams they can remember. However, researchers

using EEGs to track sleep stages have found that 80 percent of people wakened during REM sleep can recall and describe their dreams.

CHAPTER 3 Developing Through the Life Span

3A. **Your friend, who is a regular drinker, hopes to become pregnant soon and has stopped drinking. Why is this a good idea?**
ANSWER: There is no known safe amount of alcohol during pregnancy, so your friend is wise to quit drinking before becoming pregnant. Harmful effects may occur even before a woman knows she is pregnant. The child of a woman who drank alcohol regularly and heavily during her pregnancy may be born with physical or cognitive impairments (such as fetal alcohol syndrome).

3B. **Use Piaget's first three stages of cognitive development to explain why young children are not just miniature adults in the way they think.**
ANSWER: Infants in the *sensorimotor stage* tend to be focused only on their own perceptions of the world and may, for example, be unaware that objects continue to exist when unseen. A *preoperational* child is still egocentric and unable to appreciate simple logic, such as the concept of conservation. A preteen in the *concrete operational stage* is beginning to think logically about concrete events but not about abstract concepts.

3C. **How is our development affected by both nature and nurture?**
ANSWER: Each of us is born with a unique combination of genes (our nature) that lays down our body's basic design. What we experience (our nurture) can build and alter our brain pathways and enhance or impair our body's abilities. Our genetic predispositions can evoke reactions in others and direct us toward certain paths. Nature and nurture *interact* during development.

3D. **In Western cultures, how has the transition from childhood to adulthood changed in the last century or so?**
ANSWER: Over the last 100 years, Western teens have experienced earlier onset of puberty (now around age 11 for girls and 13 for boys) and a delay in becoming an independent adult. The not-yet-settled phase of life from age 18 to the mid-twenties is now often referred to as emerging adulthood.

3E. **How is our development affected by both continuity and stages?**
ANSWER: The idea of stages in development is reflected in the work of Piaget (cognitive development), Kohlberg (moral development), and Erikson (psychosocial

development). Stage theories are challenged by findings that suggest that change is more gradual and less culturally universal than these theorists supposed.

3F. What are some of the most significant challenges and rewards of growing older?
ANSWER: As we age, we do face challenges as muscular strength, reaction times, stamina, sensory keenness, cardiac output, and immune system functioning gradually decline. Social circles become smaller, and income often decreases. But aging is more than a series of losses. For most people, the rapid-processing skills of fluid intelligence will decrease steadily, but the vocabulary and knowledge of crystallized intelligence will increase well into older adulthood. With age, positive feelings tend to grow, negative emotions are less intense, and the risk of depression often decreases.

3G. How is our development affected by both stability and change?
ANSWER: Some traits, such as temperament, are very stable across the life span. Social attitudes and other traits are more likely to change. And chance events introduce change sometimes when we least expect it. In our lives we need both stability (which gives us our identity) and change (which gives us hope and lets us alter what we dislike about ourselves).

CHAPTER 4 Gender and Sexuality

4A. What are gender roles, and what do their variations tell us about our human capacity for learning and adaptation?
ANSWER: *Gender roles* are sets of expected behaviors for females or for males. Gender roles vary widely in different cultures, which is proof that we are very capable of learning and adapting to the social demands of different environments.

4B. What factors affect sexual expression?
ANSWER: Our genes and sex hormones (testosterone and the estrogens) influence our sexual behavior. Psychological stimuli and cultural attitudes and expectations affect the ways we express our sexuality.

4C. Which factors have researchers thus far found to be *unrelated* to the development of our sexual orientation?
ANSWER: Researchers have found no evidence that any environmental factor (parental relationships, childhood sexual experiences, peer relationships, or dating experiences) influences the development of our sexual orientation.

CHAPTER 5 Sensation and Perception

5A. What is the rough distinction between sensation and perception?
ANSWER: *Sensation* is the process by which our sensory receptors and nervous system take in stimulus energies from our environment. *Perception* is the mental process by which our brain organizes and interprets sensory information, transforming it into meaningful objects and events.

5B. What is the rapid sequence of events that occurs when you see and recognize someone you know?
ANSWER: Light waves reflect off the person and travel into your eye, where the rods and cones convert the light waves' energy into neural impulses sent to your brain. Your brain processes the subdimensions of this visual input—including color, depth, movement, and form—separately but simultaneously. It integrates this information (along with previously stored information) into a conscious perception of the person you know.

5C. What do we mean when we say that, in perception, the whole is greater than the sum of its parts?
ANSWER: Gestalt psychologists used this saying to describe our perceptual tendency to organize clusters of sensations into meaningful forms or groups.

5D. What are the basic steps in transforming sound waves into perceived sound?
ANSWER: A simple figure offers a synopsis.

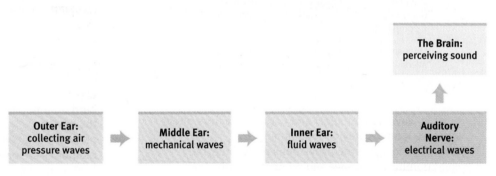

5E. How does our system for sensing smell differ from our sensory systems for vision, touch, and taste?

ANSWER: We have two types of retinal receptors, four basic touch senses, and five taste sensations. But we have no basic smell receptors. Instead, different combinations of odor receptors send messages to the brain, enabling us to recognize some 10,000 different smells.

CHAPTER 6 Learning

6A. As we develop, we learn cues that lead us to expect and prepare for good and bad events. We learn to repeat behaviors that bring rewards. And we learn through language, and by observing events and people. What do psychologists call these three types of learning?

ANSWER: Through *classical conditioning,* we learn cues that lead us to expect and prepare for good and bad events. Through *operant conditioning,* we learn to repeat behaviors that bring rewards. Through *cognitive learning,* we watch others (observational learning), read about their experiences, or otherwise acquire mental information that guides our behavior.

6B. In slasher movies, sexually arousing images of women are sometimes paired with violence against women. Based on classical conditioning principles, what might be an effect of this pairing?

ANSWER: If viewing an attractive nude or semi-nude woman (a US) elicits sexual arousal (a UR), then pairing that US (nude woman) with an NS (violence) could turn the previously neutral stimulus of violence into a conditioned stimulus (CS) that now also elicits sexual arousal, a conditioned response (CR).

6C. Positive reinforcement, negative reinforcement, positive punishment, and negative punishment are tricky concepts for many students. Can you fit the right term in the four boxes in this table?

ANSWER:

Type of Stimulus	Give It	Take It Away
Desired (for example, a compliment):	Positive reinforcement	Negative Punishment
Undesired/ aversive (for example, an insult):	Positive Punishment	Negative reinforcement

6D. In what ways do biological and cognitive factors affect what we learn by way of conditioning?

ANSWER: Biological predispositions place limits on conditioning because we and other organisms come prepared to learn certain tendencies (such as taste aversion) that aid our survival. Despite operant training, animals may revert to biologically predisposed patterns. Our expectations and ways of thinking may override attempts to condition us as well. For example, the effectiveness of treatment for alcohol dependence may be lessened because of patients' awareness that outside the therapist's office, they will not be nauseated by alcoholic drinks because they will not then be taking the drugs that cause nausea. Other evidence of cognition's influence on conditioning includes latent learning and cognitive maps, which demonstrate that rats learn from experience, without being reinforced for learning maze pathways, for example.

6E. Jason's parents and older friends all smoke, but they advise him not to. Juan's parents and friends don't smoke, but they say nothing to discourage him from doing so. Will Jason or Juan be more likely to start smoking?

ANSWER: Although both saying and doing can influence people, experiments suggest that children more often do as others do and say as they say. As children watch, their mirror neurons imitate the behaviors they are observing. Generalizing this finding to smoking, we can expect that Jason will be more likely to start smoking, because his mirror neurons have been practicing that behavior for years.

CHAPTER 7 Memory

7A. What two important new concepts now update the classic three-stage information-processing model of memory?

ANSWER: (a) We form some memories through *unconscious processing,* without our awareness. (b) To stress the active processing that takes place in the middle stage, many psychologists now prefer the term *working memory.*

7B. What would be the most effective strategy to learn and retain a list of names of key historical figures for a week? For a year?

ANSWER: For a week: Make the names personally meaningful. For a year: Overlearn the list and space out rehearsals over the course of several weeks.

7C. Your friend tells you that her father experienced brain damage in an accident. She wonders if psychology can explain why he can still play checkers very well but has a hard time holding a sensible conversation. What can you tell her?

ANSWER: Our consciously recalled *explicit* (declarative) memories are processed in the hippocampus, and our *implicit* (nondeclarative) memories of skills and procedures, such as checkers, are processed in other parts of our brain, including the cerebellum. It seems your friend's father did not suffer damage to the part of his brain that processes implicit memories.

7D. What are three ways we forget, and how does each of these happen?

ANSWER: (a) Encoding failure: Information never entered our memory system because we were not paying attention to it (absent-mindedness), or the information was entered inaccurately due to misattribution or suggestibility. (b) Storage decay: Information fades from our memory (transience). (c) Retrieval failure: We cannot access stored information accurately because of blocking (sometimes due to interference), motivated forgetting, or bias.

7E. What—given the commonality of source amnesia—might life be like if we remembered all our waking experiences and all our dreams?

ANSWER: Real experiences would be confused with those we dreamed. When meeting someone, we might therefore be unsure whether we were reacting to something they previously did or to something we dreamed they did. William Dement (1999, p. 298) thinks this "would put a great burden on your sanity. . . . I truly believe that the wall of memory is a blessed protection."

7F. What are the recommended memory strategies you just read about? (One advised rehearsing to-be-remembered material. What were the others?)

ANSWER: Study repeatedly to boost long-term recall. Schedule spaced (not crammed) study times. Spend more time rehearsing or actively thinking about the material. Make the material personally meaningful, with well-organized and vivid associations. Refresh your memory by returning to contexts and moods to activate retrieval cues. Minimize interference. Plan for a complete night's sleep. Test your own knowledge, both to rehearse it and to help determine what you do not yet know.

CHAPTER 8 Thinking, Language, and Intelligence

8A. The availability heuristic is a quick-and-easy but sometimes misleading guide to judging reality. What is the availability heuristic?

ANSWER: The *availability heuristic* is our tendency to judge the likelihood of an event based on how easily we can recall instances of it. This guide is efficient, but it can mislead, as when we attempt to judge various risks (for example, of plane travel).

8B. If children are not yet speaking, is there any reason to think they would benefit from parents and other caregivers reading to them?

ANSWER: Indeed there is, because well before age 1 children are learning to detect words among the stream of spoken sounds and to discern grammatical rules. Before age 1, they also are babbling with the phonemes of their own language. More than many parents realize, their infants are soaking up language. As researcher Peter Jusczyk reminds us, "Little ears are listening."

8C. What is "mental practice," and how can it help you to prepare for an upcoming event?

ANSWER: Skills improve with practice. Mental practice uses visual imagery to mentally rehearse future behaviors, and it will activate some of the same brain areas that become active during the actual behaviors. Visualizing the details of the process is more effective than visualizing only your end goal.

8D. If your dog barks at a stranger at the front door, does this qualify as language? What if the dog yips in a telltale way to let you know she needs to go out?

ANSWER: These are definitely communications. But if language consists of words and the grammatical rules we use to combine them to communicate meaning, few scientists would label a dog's barking and yipping as language.

8E. Joseph, a Harvard Law School student, has a straight-A average, writes for the *Harvard Law Review,* and will clerk for a Supreme Court justice next year. His grandmother, Judith, is very proud of him, saying he is way more intelligent than she ever was. But Joseph is also very proud of Judith: As a young woman, she was imprisoned by the Nazis. When the war ended, she walked out of Germany, contacted an agency helping refugees, and began a new life in the United States as an assistant chef in her cousin's restaurant. According to the definition of *intelligence* in this chapter, is Joseph the only intelligent person in this story? Why or why not?

ANSWER: Joseph is not the only intelligent person in this story. Intelligence is the ability to learn from experience, solve problems, and use knowledge to adapt to new situations. Judith certainly fits this description, given all that she has accomplished.

8F. What was the purpose of Binet's pioneering intelligence test?

ANSWER: Binet's original test and those built upon it were designed to predict school achievement.

8G. As society succeeds in creating equality of opportunity, it will also increase the heritability of ability. The heritability of intelligence scores will be greater in a society marked

by equal opportunity than in a society of peasants and aristocrats. Why?

ANSWER: Perfect environmental equality would create 100 percent heritability—because genes alone would account for any remaining human differences.

CHAPTER 9 Motivation and Emotion

9A. **While on a long road trip, you suddenly feel very hungry. You see a diner that looks pretty deserted and creepy, but you are *really* hungry, so you stop anyway. What motivational perspective would most easily explain this behavior, and why?**

ANSWER: *Drive-reduction theory*—the idea that physical needs create an aroused state that drives us to reduce the need—helps explain your behavior.

9B. **Sanjay recently adopted the typical college diet high in fat and sugar. He knows he may gain weight, but he figures it's no big deal because he can lose the extra pounds in the future. How would you evaluate Sanjay's plan?**

ANSWER: Sanjay's plan is problematic. Yes, he could someday lose his "college weight" by using more calories than he takes in, but gaining weight now could make future weight loss and maintenance more challenging. With weight gain, his fat cells may increase in number. Even if he tries to lose weight later, those cells will shrink in size but will never be eliminated entirely. Sanjay would be better off to maintain his current, healthy weight by adopting a balanced diet and exercising regularly.

9C. **How might the evolutionary perspective, drive-reduction theory, and arousal theory explain our need to belong?**

ANSWER: *Evolutionary psychologists* have noted that our ancestors found safety in numbers. Social bonds helped keep children close to their caregivers, and adults hunted and survived threats by working together in groups. We, their descendants, are predisposed to live in groups, connected to supportive others. *Drive-reduction theory* might say that being threatened and afraid drives us to find safety in the company of others (thus reducing our aroused state). *Arousal theory* reminds us that we welcome optimal levels of arousal, and that the presence of others is arousing.

9D. **Christine is holding her 8-month-old baby when a fierce dog appears out of nowhere and, with teeth bared, leaps for the baby's face. Christine immediately ducks for cover to protect the baby, screams at the dog, then notices that her heart is banging in her chest and she's broken out in a cold sweat. How would the James-Lange, Cannon-Bard, and two-factor theories explain Christine's emotional reaction?**

ANSWER: The James-Lange theory would say that Christine's emotional reaction consists of her awareness of her physiological responses to the dog attack. The Cannon-Bard theory would say that her fear experience happened simultaneously with her physiological arousal. Schachter-Singer's two-factor theory would presume that her emotional reaction stemmed from her interpreting and labeling the arousal.

9E. **How do the two divisions of the autonomic nervous system help us respond to and recover from a crisis, and why is this relevant to the study of emotions?**

ANSWER: Without our conscious effort, the sympathetic division of our ANS arouses us, pumping out stress hormones and preparing our body for fight or flight. The parasympathetic division of the ANS takes over when the crisis passes, restoring our body to a calm state. Because stress hormones leave the bloodstream gradually, our arousal can spill over from one event to another, influencing our emotional responses.

9F. **Who tends to express more emotion—men or women? How do we know the answer to that question?**

ANSWER: Women tend to surpass men not only as emotion detectors but also at expressing emotions (though men have slightly surpassed women in conveying anger). Researchers study such differences in the laboratory, for example by showing people brief, silent clips of men's and women's faces expressing various emotions and then observing who is most skilled at reading and sending emotions.

9G. **What things do (and do not) predict self-reported happiness?**

ANSWER: Our age, gender, education level, parental status, and physical attractiveness don't seem to be much related to our happiness. Our genes, outlook, personality traits, close relationships, "flow" in work and leisure, spirituality, and sleep and exercise habits do tend to influence our happiness levels.

CHAPTER 10 Stress, Health, and Human Flourishing

10A. **How does our stress response work?**

ANSWER: When alerted to a threat, our sympathetic nervous system arouses us. Heart rate and respiration increase, blood is diverted from digestion to the skeletal muscles, adrenal glands pump stress hormones into the bloodstream, and the body releases sugar and fat. All this prepares us for fight or flight. These responses occur in a three-stage process (alarm, resistance, and exhaustion) known as the general adaptation syndrome.

10B. A Chinese proverb warns, "The fire you kindle for your enemy often burns you more than him." How is this true of Type A individuals?

ANSWER: During their frequent bouts of anger, Type A individuals put themselves greatly at risk for health problems, including heart disease. Their sympathetic nervous system diverts blood away from the liver, leaving fat and cholesterol circulating in the bloodstream for deposit near the heart and other organs. These angry outbursts also correlate with unhealthy habits, such as smoking, drinking, and overeating (leading to obesity).

10C. How do problem-focused coping and emotion-focused coping differ? What are some examples of each?

ANSWER: Problem-focused coping attempts to reduce stress directly, by changing the stressor or the way we interact with it (for example, reducing test anxiety by studying harder, or lowering tension in a relationship by talking things out). Emotion-focused coping attempts to reduce stress by avoiding or ignoring the stressor and attending to the emotional needs related to the stress reaction (for example, reaching out to friends for comfort after escaping from a damaging relationship, or taking up a new hobby to distract attention from an old addiction).

10D. What are some of the tactics we can use to manage stress successfully?

ANSWER: When we cannot avoid stress, we can try to manage it with aerobic exercise, relaxation procedures, meditation, and spirituality.

CHAPTER 11 Personality

11A. What, according to Freud, were some of the important defense mechanisms, and what do they defend against?

ANSWER: Freud believed repression was the basic defense mechanism. Others include regression, reaction formation, projection, rationalization, displacement, and denial. All supposedly function indirectly and unconsciously to reduce anxiety. Current research does not support the idea that defense mechanisms disguise sexual and aggressive impulses. Rather, some self-protective defenses may protect our self-esteem. Freud's idea of *projection* is similar to what is now called the *false consensus effect*, but there is little support for the others.

11B. How does today's psychological science assess Freud's theory?

ANSWER: Current research does not support Freud's view of the unconscious or of repression. It views the unconscious as part of our two-track mind—the many types and instances of information processing that take place outside of our awareness, such as priming and parallel processing of various aspects of vision. Freudian theory does not enable predictions, and it tends to explain things after the fact.

11C. What does it mean to be "empathic"? To be "self-actualized"?

ANSWER: To be *empathic* is to share and mirror another person's feelings. Carl Rogers believed that people nurture growth in others by being empathic. Abraham Maslow viewed *self-actualization*—the motivation to fulfill one's potential—as one of the ultimate psychological needs (the other is self-transcendence).

11D. What are some advantages of assessing personality by using the Big Five Factors?

ANSWER: The Big Five Factors (conscientiousness, agreeableness, neuroticism, openness, and extraversion) have two main advantages as personality assessment traits. They are relatively stable across the life span, and they apply to all cultures in which they have been studied.

11E. How do our personality traits typically interact with the situations in which we find ourselves?

ANSWER: Behavior is influenced by the interaction between the person (personal traits, past learning, and current thinking) and the situation (social context). Our personality traits tend to be consistent, but our specific behaviors may vary with time and across situations.

11F. What is the difference between *defensive self-esteem* and *secure self-esteem,* and which one provides a higher quality of life?

ANSWER: *Defensive self-esteem* is fragile and seeks to protect itself, which means any kind of criticism or failure is considered threatening. This type of self-esteem correlates with aggressive and antisocial behavior. *Secure self-esteem* relies less on other people's evaluations. This healthier self-image allows us to focus beyond ourselves and enjoy a higher quality of life.

11G. How do individualist and collectivist cultures differ?

ANSWER: Individualism gives priority to personal goals over group goals. People in individualist cultures tend to define their identity in terms of their own personal attributes. Collectivism gives priority to group goals over individual goals. People in collectivist cultures tend to define their identity in terms of group identifications. Cultures vary in the extent to which they favor individualism or collectivism.

CHAPTER 12 Psychological Disorders

12A. What is the biopsychosocial perspective, and why is it important in our understanding of psychological disorders?

ANSWER: This contemporary perspective assumes that biological, psychological, and social-cultural influences combine to produce psychological disorders. Genes matter. The brain matters. Inner thoughts and feelings matter. Social and cultural influences matter. To get the whole integrated picture, a biopsychosocial perspective helps.

12B. What is the value, and what are the dangers, of labeling individuals with disorders?

ANSWER: Therapists and others use disorder labels to communicate with one another using a common language, and to share concepts during research. Insurance companies require a diagnosis before they will pay for therapy, and that diagnosis is a label. The danger of labeling people is that labels can create expectations that will change our behavior toward the people we label.

12C. How do generalized anxiety disorder, phobias, obsessive-compulsive disorder, and PTSD differ?

ANSWER: *Generalized anxiety disorder* is unfocused tension, apprehension, and arousal. *Phobias* focus anxiety on specific feared objects or situations. *Obsessive-compulsive disorders* express anxiety through unwanted repetitive thoughts (obsessions) or actions (compulsions). In *post-traumatic stress disorder (PTSD)*, anxiety may be accompanied by recurring memories and nightmares, social withdrawal, and insomnia for periods of four or more weeks after a traumatic event.

12D. The psychoanalytic and learning perspectives agree that DID symptoms are ways of dealing with anxiety. How do their explanations differ?

ANSWER: The psychoanalytic explanation of dissociative identity disorder (DID) symptoms is that they are defenses against anxiety generated by unacceptable urges. The learning perspective attempts to explain these symptoms as behaviors that have been reinforced by relieving anxiety in the past. Others attempt to explain DID symptoms as detachment resulting from horrific experiences, such as childhood abuse.

12E. Is antisocial personality disorder an inherited condition?

ANSWER: *Antisocial personality disorder*—in which a person exhibits a lack of conscience for wrongdoing—seems to have both biological and psychological components. Twin and adoption studies show that biological relatives of people with this disorder are at increased risk for antisocial behavior. Environmental factors, such as childhood abuse, may trigger genetic tendencies. No single gene controls complex behaviors such as crime.

12F. Studies have found that people who begin drinking in the early teens are much more likely to become alcohol dependent than those who begin at age 21 or after. What possible explanations might there be for this correlation between early use and later abuse?

ANSWER: Possible explanations include (a) a biological predisposition to both early use and later abuse, (b) brain changes and taste preferences triggered by early use, and (c) enduring habits, attitudes, activities, and/or peer relationships that foster alcohol abuse.

12G. What factors contribute to the onset and development of schizophrenia?

ANSWER: Schizophrenia may appear suddenly, as a reaction to stress (acute or reactive schizophrenia), or develop gradually (chronic or process schizophrenia). The disorder is found worldwide and typically appears as people mature into young adults—either suddenly as a reaction to significant stress, or gradually after a long history of social inadequacy. It affects both women and men, but it tends to strike men earlier, more severely, and slightly more often. Thin young men who were not breastfed may be at higher risk, as may those whose mothers suffered a virus in the middle of their pregnancy.

CHAPTER 13 Therapy

13A. What is the major distinction between the underlying assumption in psychodynamic therapies and in behavior therapies?

ANSWER: The psychodynamic therapies seek to relieve problems by providing an understanding of their origins. Behavior therapies assume the problem behavior *is* the problem and treat it directly, paying less attention to its origins.

13B. How do the humanistic and cognitive therapies differ?

ANSWER: The humanistic therapies attempt to foster personal growth by helping clients become more self-aware and self-accepting. In a nondirective setting, the therapist tries to reflect the client's feelings. Cognitive therapists guide people toward new ways of explaining good and bad experiences. They try to make clients aware of self-defeating patterns of thinking and help them learn new, more adaptive ways of thinking about themselves and their world.

13C. What is evidence-based clinical decision making, and who benefits from it?

ANSWER: In evidence-based clinical decision making, therapists make decisions about treatment based on research evidence, clinical expertise, and knowledge of the client. Both clients and therapists may benefit from this approach due to increasing effectiveness of the treatment.

13D. How do researchers evaluate the effectiveness of particular drug therapies?

ANSWER: Ideally, researchers assign people to treatment and no-treatment conditions to see if those who receive the drug improve more than those who don't. In double-blind studies, neither the staff members nor the clients know who is receiving the drug and who is receiving the placebo. Any difference between the treated and untreated groups will therefore reflect the treatment's actual effect.

13E. How does the placebo effect bias clients' attitudes about the effectiveness of biomedical therapies?

ANSWER: The *placebo effect* is the healing power of *belief* in a treatment. When patients expect a treatment to be effective, they may believe it was.

13F. What is the difference between preventive mental health and psychotherapy or biomedical therapy?

ANSWER: Psychotherapy and biomedical therapy attempt to relieve people's suffering from psychological disorders. Preventive mental health attempts to prevent suffering by identifying and eliminating the conditions that contribute to the development of disorders.

CHAPTER 14 Social Psychology

14A. Driving to school one snowy day, Marco narrowly misses a car that slides through a red light. "Slow down! What a terrible driver," he thinks to himself. Moments later, Marco himself slips through an intersection and yelps, "Wow! These roads are awful. The city plows need to get out here." What social psychology principle has Marco just demonstrated? Explain.

ANSWER: Marco is explaining the other driver's behavior as an aspect of the driver's personal qualities ("he's a terrible driver"). He's explaining his own behavior as a result of the situation ("these roads are awful"). Marco has made the *fundamental attribution error*.

14B. What are some examples of social situations in which people are more likely to be obedient?

ANSWER: The Milgram studies showed that people were most likely to follow orders when the experimenter was nearby and was a legitimate authority figure; the victim was not nearby; and there were no other models for defiance.

14C. You are organizing a group meeting of fiercely competitive political candidates. To add to the fun, friends have suggested handing out masks of the candidates' faces for supporters to wear. Based on what you read about deindividuation, what do you think might happen if people wear these masks?

ANSWER: The anonymity provided by the masks, combined with the arousal of the fierce competition, might create *deindividuation* (lessened self-awareness and self-restraint).

14D. What psychological and biological influences interact to produce aggressive behaviors?

ANSWER: Our biology (our genes, neural systems, and biochemistry) influences our tendencies to be aggressive. Psychological factors (such as frustration, previous rewards for aggressive acts, and observation of others' aggression) can trigger any aggressive tendencies we may have.

14E. How does being physically attractive influence the ways others think about you?

ANSWER: Physical attractiveness influences first impressions. People tend to assume that attractive people are healthier, happier, and more socially skilled than others are. If we are attractive, we probably will be more successful in the workplace and more popular.

14F. Why didn't anybody help Kitty Genovese? What social psychology principle did this incident illustrate?

ANSWER: The incident illustrated the *bystander effect*. This occurs because, in the presence of others, an individual is less likely to notice a situation, correctly interpret it as an emergency, and then take responsibility for offering help.

14G. Why might an otherwise calm and softhearted person take great joy when her school's archrival team loses? Why do such feelings make conflict resolution more challenging?

ANSWER: Our tendency to form categories and establish our own social identity accordingly is influencing this person's thoughts and emotions (even more so than her enduring personality traits). As a fan of her school's team, this person is a member of an ingroup that sets itself apart from an outgroup (the school's archrival). In such cases, ingroup bias tends to develop, leading to prejudice and the view that the outgroup is worthy of misfortune. So when the archrival loses, this normally softhearted person (and other fans of the school's team) will take pleasure in the loss and view it as justified.

APPENDIX A Psychology at Work

A-1. What is the value of finding flow in your work?

ANSWER: Those who find flow in their work are so completely engaged that they may lose track of time. They tend to view their work as fulfilling and socially useful, and they find their work life very satisfying.

A-2. What characteristics are important for transformational leaders?

ANSWER: Characteristics of a transformational leader include being naturally extraverted, setting high standards, and being able to inspire others to share your vision and to commit themselves to a group's mission. More women than men are transformational leaders.

Glossary

A

absolute threshold the minimum stimulation needed to detect a particular stimulus 50 percent of the time. (p. 124)

achievement motivation a desire for significant accomplishment; for mastery of things, people, or ideas; and for attaining a high standard. (p. 413)

achievement test a test designed to assess what a person has learned. (p. 223)

acquisition (1) in classical conditioning, the initial stage, when we link a neutral stimulus and an unconditioned stimulus so that the neutral stimulus begins triggering the conditioned response. (2) In operant conditioning, the strengthening of a reinforced response. (p. 158)

action potential a nerve impulse. (p. 28)

active listening empathic listening in which the listener echoes, restates, and clarifies. A feature of Rogers' client-centered therapy. (p. 354)

adaptation-level phenomenon our tendency to form judgments (of sounds, of lights, of income) relative to a neutral level defined by our past experiences. (p. 267)

addiction compulsive drug craving and use. (p. 329)

adolescence the transition period from childhood to adulthood, extending from puberty to independence. (p. 81)

adrenal [ah-DREEN-el] **glands** pair of endocrine glands that sit just above the kidneys and secrete hormones (epinephrine and norepinephrine) that help arouse the body in times of stress. (p. 34)

aerobic exercise sustained activity that increases heart and lung fitness; may also reduce depression and anxiety. (p. 285)

aggression any physical or verbal behavior intended to hurt or destroy. (pp. 102, 393)

AIDS (acquired immune deficiency syndrome) a life-threatening, sexually transmitted infection caused by the *human immunodeficiency virus* (HIV). AIDS depletes the immune system, leaving the person vulnerable to infections. (p. 108)

alcohol dependence (popularly known as alcoholism). Alcohol use marked by tolerance, withdrawal if suspended, and a drive to continue use. (p. 330)

algorithm a methodical, logical rule or procedure that guarantees you will solve a particular problem. Contrasts with the usually speedier but also more error-prone use of *heuristics*. (p. 206)

all-or-none response a neuron's reaction of either firing (with a full-strength response) or not firing. (p. 29)

alpha waves relatively slow brain waves of a relaxed, awake state. (p. 51)

altruism unselfish concern for the welfare of others. (p. 402)

amphetamines drugs that stimulate neural activity, causing speeded-up body functions and associated energy and mood changes. (p. 332)

amygdala [uh-MIG-duh-la] two lima-bean–sized neural clusters in the limbic system; linked to emotion. (p. 37)

anorexia nervosa an eating disorder in which a person (usually an adolescent female) maintains a starvation diet despite being significantly (15 percent or more) underweight. (p. 243)

antianxiety drugs drugs used to control anxiety and agitation. (p. 367)

antidepressant drugs drugs used to treat depression and some anxiety disorders. Different types work by altering the availability of various neurotransmitters. (p. 367)

antipsychotic drugs drugs used to treat schizophrenia and other forms of severe thought disorders. (p. 366)

antisocial personality disorder a personality disorder in which the person (usually a man) exhibits a lack of conscience for wrongdoing, even toward friends and family members. May be aggressive and ruthless or a clever con artist. (p. 327)

anxiety disorders psychological disorders characterized by distressing, persistent anxiety or maladaptive behaviors that reduce anxiety. (p. 322)

aptitude test a test designed to predict a person's future performance; *aptitude* is the capacity to learn. (p. 223)

association areas cerebral cortex area involved primarily in higher mental functions, such as learning, remembering, thinking, and speaking. (p. 42)

associative learning learning that certain events occur together. The events may be two stimuli (as in classical conditioning) or a response and its consequences (as in operant conditioning). (p. 156)

attachment an emotional tie with another person; shown in young children by their seeking closeness to the caregiver, and showing distress on separation. (p. 76)

attitude feelings, often based on our beliefs, that predispose us to respond in a particular way to objects, people, and events. (p. 379)

audition the sense or act of hearing. (p. 139)

autism a disorder that appears in childhood and is marked by deficient communication, social interaction, and understanding of others' state of mind. (p. 74)

automatic processing unconscious encoding of everyday information, such as space, time, frequency, and well-learned word meanings. (p. 183)

autonomic [aw-tuh-NAHM-ik] **nervous system** peripheral nervous system division controlling the glands and the muscles of the internal organs (such as the heart). Its sympathetic subdivision arouses; its parasympathetic subdivision calms. (p. 31)

availability heuristic estimating the likelihood of an event based on its availability in memory; if instances come readily to mind (perhaps because of their vividness), we assume such events are common. (p. 207)

aversive conditioning a type of counterconditioning that associates an unpleasant state (such as nausea) with an unwanted behavior (such as drinking alcohol). (p. 357)

axon neuron extension that sends messages to other neurons or cells. (p. 28)

B

babbling stage beginning at about 4 months, the stage of speech development in which the infant spontaneously utters various sounds at first unrelated to the household language. (p. 213)

barbiturates drugs that depress the activity of the central nervous system, reducing anxiety but impairing memory and judgment. (p. 331)

basal metabolic rate the body's resting rate of energy output. (p. 242)

basic trust according to Erik Erikson, a sense that the world is predictable and trustworthy; said to be formed during infancy by appropriate experiences with responsive caregivers. (p. 78)

behavior therapy therapy that applies learning principles to the elimination of unwanted behaviors. (p. 355)

behaviorism the view that psychology (1) should be an objective science that (2) studies behavior without reference to mental processes. Most research psychologists today agree with (1) but not with (2). (pp. 2, 171)

belief perseverance clinging to beliefs and ignoring evidence that proves they are wrong. (p. 210)

binge-eating disorder significant binge-eating, followed by distress, disgust, or guilt, but without the purging, fasting, or excessive exercise that marks bulimia nervosa. (p. 243)

binocular cue a depth cue, such as retinal disparity, that depends on the use of two eyes. (p. 135)

biological psychology a branch of psychology concerned with the links between biology and behavior. (p. 28)

biomedical therapy prescribed medications or procedures that act directly on the person's physiology. (p. 352)

biopsychosocial approach an integrated approach that incorporates different but complementary views from biological, psychological, and social-cultural perspectives. (p. 6)

bipolar disorder a mood disorder in which the person alternates between the hopelessness and lethargy of depression and the overexcited state of mania. (Formerly called *manic-depressive disorder*.) (p. 339)

blind spot the point at which the optic nerve leaves the eye; this part of the retina is "blind" because it has no receptor cells. (p. 130)

brainstem the oldest part and central core of the brain, beginning where the spinal cord swells as it enters the skull; responsible for automatic survival functions. (p. 35)

Broca's area frontal lobe area, usually in the left hemisphere, that directs the muscle movements involved in speech; controls language expression. (p. 44)

bulimia nervosa an eating disorder in which a person alternates binge eating (usually of high-calorie foods) with purging (by vomiting or laxative use), fasting, or excessive exercise. (p. 243)

bystander effect the tendency for any given bystander to be less likely to give aid if other bystanders are present. (p. 403)

C

Cannon-Bard theory the theory that an emotion-arousing stimulus simultaneously triggers (1) physiological responses and (2) the subjective experience of emotion. (p. 253)

case study a descriptive technique in which one person is studied in depth in the hope of revealing universal principles. (p. 12)

catharsis emotional release. The catharsis hypothesis maintains that "releasing" aggressive energy (through action or fantasy) relieves aggressive urges. (p. 263)

central nervous system (CNS) the brain and spinal cord. (p. 31)

cerebellum [sehr-uh-BELL-um] the "little brain" at the rear of the brainstem; functions include processing sensory input and coordinating movement output and balance. (p. 36)

cerebral [seh-REE-bruhl] **cortex** thin layer of interconnected neurons covering the cerebral hemispheres; the body's ultimate control and information-processing center. (p. 40)

chromosomes threadlike structures made of DNA molecules that contain the genes. (p. 64)

circadian [ser-KAY-dee-an] **rhythm** internal biological clock; regular bodily rhythms (for example, of temperature and wakefulness) that occur on a 24-hour cycle. (p. 51)

classical conditioning a type of learning in which we learn to link two or more stimuli and anticipate events. (p. 157)

client-centered therapy a humanistic therapy, developed by Carl Rogers, in which the therapist uses techniques such as active listening within a genuine, accepting, empathic environment to promote clients' growth. (Also called *person-centered therapy*.) (p. 354)

cochlea [KOHK-lee-uh] a coiled, bony, fluid-filled tube in the inner ear; sound waves traveling through the cochlear fluid trigger nerve impulses. (p. 140)

cognition all the mental activities associated with thinking, knowing, remembering, and communicating. (pp. 72, 206)

cognitive dissonance theory the theory that we act to reduce the discomfort (dissonance) we feel when two of our thoughts (cognitions) clash. For example, when we become aware that our attitudes and our actions don't match, we may change our attitudes so that we feel more comfortable. (p. 381)

cognitive learning the acquisition of mental information, whether by observing events, watching others, or through language. (p. 156)

cognitive map a mental image of the layout of one's environment. (p. 171)

cognitive neuroscience the interdisciplinary study of the brain activity linked with mental activity (including perception, thinking, memory, and language). (p. 3)

cognitive therapy therapy that teaches people new, more adaptive ways of thinking, based on the assumption that thoughts intervene between events and our emotional reactions. (p. 358)

cognitive-behavioral therapy a popular integrative therapy that combines cognitive therapy (changing self-defeating thinking) with behavior therapy (changing behavior). (p. 359)

collectivism giving priority to goals of our group (often our extended family or work group) and defining our identity accordingly. (p. 312)

color constancy perceiving familiar objects as having consistent color, even if changing illumination alters the wavelengths reflected by the object. (p. 137)

companionate love the deep affectionate attachment we feel for those with whom our lives are intertwined. (p. 401)

concrete operational stage in Piaget's theory, the stage of cognitive development (from about 6 or 7 to 11 years of age) during which children gain the mental operations that enable them to think logically about concrete events. (p. 74)

conditioned reinforcer (also known as *secondary reinforcer*) an event that gains its reinforcing power through its link with a primary reinforcer. (p. 164)

conditioned response (CR) in classical conditioning, a learned response to a previously neutral (but now conditioned) stimulus (CS). (p. 158)

conditioned stimulus (CS) in classical conditioning, an originally irrelevant stimulus that, after association with an unconditioned stimulus (US), comes to trigger a conditioned response (CR). (p. 158)

cones retinal receptor cells that are concentrated near the center of the retina; in daylight or well-lit conditions, cones detect fine detail and give rise to color sensations. (p. 130)

confirmation bias a tendency to search for information that supports our preconceptions and to ignore or distort evidence that contradicts them. (p. 209)

conflict a perceived incompatibility of actions, goals, or ideas. (p. 404)

conformity adjusting our behavior or thinking to coincide with a group standard. (p. 382)

consciousness our awareness of ourselves and our environment. (p. 49)

conservation the principle (which Piaget believed to be a part of concrete operational reasoning) that properties such as mass, volume, and number remain the same despite changes in shapes. (p. 73)

continuous reinforcement reinforcing a desired response every time it occurs. (p. 164)

control group the group in an experiment that is not exposed to the treatment and therefore serves as a comparison with the experimental group for evaluating the effect of the treatment. (p. 15)

coronary heart disease the clogging of the vessels that nourish the heart muscle; the leading cause of death in North America and many other countries. (p. 279)

corpus callosum [KOR-pus kah-LOW-sum] large band of neural fibers connecting the two brain hemispheres and carrying messages between them. (p. 46)

correlation a measure of the extent to which two events vary together, and thus of how well either one predicts the other. The *correlation coefficient* is the mathematical expression of the relationship, ranging from −1 to +1. (p. 13)

counterconditioning a behavior therapy procedure that uses classical conditioning to evoke new responses to stimuli that are triggering unwanted behaviors; includes *exposure therapies* and *aversive conditioning*. (p. 356)

creativity the ability to produce new and valuable ideas. (p. 221)

critical period a period early in life when exposure to certain stimuli or experiences is needed for proper development. (p. 70)

critical thinking thinking that does not blindly accept arguments and conclusions. Rather, it examines assumptions, uncovers hidden values, weighs evidence, and assesses conclusions. (p. 5)

crystallized intelligence accumulated knowledge and verbal skills; tends to increase with age. (p. 92)

culture the enduring behaviors, ideas, attitudes, and traditions shared by a group of people and transmitted from one generation to the next. (p. 6)

D

defense mechanisms in psychoanalytic theory, the ego's protective methods of reducing anxiety by unconsciously distorting reality. (p. 296)

deindividuation the loss of self-awareness and self-restraint occurring in group situations that foster arousal and anonymity. (p. 388)

déjà vu that eerie sense that "I've experienced this before." Cues from the current situation may unconsciously trigger retrieval of an earlier experience. (p. 191)

delusions false beliefs, often of persecution or grandeur, that may accompany schizophrenia and other disorders. (p. 344)

dendrites neuron extensions that receive messages and conduct them toward the cell body. (p. 28)

dependent variable the outcome factor; the variable that may change in response to manipulations of the independent variable. (p. 16)

depressants drugs (such as alcohol, barbiturates, and opiates) that reduce (depress) neural activity and slow body functions. (p. 330)

depth perception the ability to see objects in three dimensions, although the images that strike the retina are two dimensional; allows us to judge distance. (p. 134)

developmental psychology branch of psychology that studies physical, cognitive, and social change throughout the life span. (p. 64)

difference threshold the minimum difference between two stimuli required for detection 50 percent of the time. We experience the difference threshold as a *just noticeable difference* (or jnd). (p. 125)

discrimination (1) in classical conditioning, the learned ability to distinguish between a conditioned stimulus and other irrelevant stimuli. (2) unjustifiable negative behavior toward a group and its members. (pp. 160, 390)

dissociative disorders disorders in which conscious awareness becomes separated (dissociated) from previous memories, thoughts, and feelings. (p. 326)

dissociative identity disorder (DID) a rare dissociative disorder in which a person exhibits two or more distinct and alternating personalities. Formerly called *multiple personality disorder*. (p. 326)

DNA (deoxyribonucleic acid) a molecule containing the genetic information that makes up the chromosomes. (p. 64)

double-blind procedure a procedure in which participants and research staff are ignorant (blind) about who has received the treatment or a placebo. (p. 16)

dream sequence of images, emotions, and thoughts passing through a sleeping person's mind. (p. 56)

drive an aroused, motivated state often created when the body is deprived of some substance it needs. (p. 238)

drive-reduction theory the idea that a physiological need creates an aroused state (a drive) that motivates us to satisfy the need. (p. 238)

DSM-IV-TR the American Psychiatric Association's *Diagnostic and Statistical Manual of Mental Disorders*, a widely used system for classifying psychological disorders. (p. 320)

dual processing the principle that information is often simultaneously processed on separate conscious and unconscious tracks. (p. 7)

E

eclectic approach an approach to psychotherapy that, depending on the client's problems, uses techniques from various forms of therapy. (p. 352)

Ecstasy (MDMA) a synthetic stimulant and mild hallucinogen. Produces euphoria and social intimacy, but with short-term health risks and longer-term harm to serotonin-producing neurons and to mood and cognition. (p. 333)

EEG (electroencephalograph) device that uses electrodes placed on the scalp to record waves of electrical activity sweeping across the brain's surface. (The tracing of those brain waves is an *electroencephalogram*.) (p. 35)

effortful processing encoding that requires attention and conscious effort. (p. 183)

ego the largely conscious, "executive" part of personality that, according to Freud, balances the demands of the id, superego, and reality. The ego operates on the *reality principle*, satisfying the id's desires in ways that will realistically bring pleasure rather than pain. (p. 295)

egocentrism in Piaget's theory, the preoperational child's difficulty taking another's point of view. (p. 73)

electroconvulsive therapy (ECT) a biomedical therapy for severely depressed patients in which a brief electric current is sent through the brain of an anesthetized patient. (p. 368)

embryo the developing human organism from about 2 weeks after fertilization through the second month. (p. 66)

emerging adulthood a period from about age 18 to the mid-twenties, when many in Western cultures are no longer adolescents but have not yet achieved full independence as adults. (p. 86)

emotion a response of the whole organism, involving (1) bodily arousal, (2) expressive behaviors, and (3) conscious experience. (p. 252)

emotion-focused coping attempting to reduce stress by avoiding or ignoring a stressor and attending to emotional needs related to our stress reaction. (p. 280)

emotional intelligence the ability to perceive, understand, manage, and use emotions. (p. 222)

encoding the process of getting information into the memory system. (p. 182)

endocrine [EN-duh-krin] **system** the body's "slow" chemical communication system; a set of glands that secrete hormones into the bloodstream. (p. 33)

endorphins [en-DOR-fins] "morphine within"—natural, opiatelike neurotransmitters linked to pain control and to pleasure. (p. 30)

environment every external influence, from prenatal nutrition to social support in later life. (p. 65)

equity a condition in which people receive from a relationship in proportion to what they give to it. (p. 401)

estrogens sex hormones secreted in greater amounts by females than by males. In nonhuman female mammals, estrogen levels peak during ovulation, promoting sexual receptivity. (p. 107)

evolutionary psychology the study of how our behavior and mind have changed in adaptive ways over time due to natural selection. (p. 116)

experiment a method in which researchers vary one or more factors (independent variables) to observe the effect on some behavior or mental process (the dependent variable). (p. 15)

experimental group the group in an experiment that is exposed to the treatment, that is, to one version of the independent variable. (p. 15)

explicit memory memories of facts and personal events that you can consciously retrieve. (p. 185)

exposure therapies behavioral techniques, such as *systematic desensitization* and *virtual reality exposure therapy,* that treat anxieties by exposing people (in imagination or actual situations) to the things they fear and avoid. (p. 356)

external locus of control the perception that chance or outside forces beyond our personal control determine our fate. (p. 282)

extinction in classical conditioning, the weakening of a conditioned response when an unconditioned stimulus does not follow a conditioned stimulus. (In operant conditioning, the weakening of a response when it is no longer reinforced.) (p. 159)

extrasensory perception (ESP) the controversial claim that perception can occur apart from sensory input, such as through *telepathy, clairvoyance,* and *precognition.* (p. 150)

extrinsic motivation a desire to perform a behavior to gain a reward or avoid a punishment. (p. 172)

F

facial feedback effect the tendency of facial muscle states to trigger corresponding feelings such as fear, anger, or happiness. (p. 262)

factor a cluster of behavior tendencies that occur together. (p. 303)

family therapy therapy that treats the family as a system. Views an individual's unwanted behaviors as influenced by or directed at other family members. (p. 360)

feature detector nerve cell in the brain that responds to specific features of a stimulus, such as edges, lines, and angles. (p. 132)

feel-good, do-good phenomenon our tendency to be helpful when already in a good mood. (p. 264)

fetal alcohol syndrome (FAS) physical and cognitive abnormalities in children caused by a pregnant woman's heavy drinking. In severe cases, symptoms include noticeable facial misproportions. (p. 66)

fetus the developing human organism from 9 weeks after conception to birth. (p. 66)

fight-or-flight response an emergency response, including activity of the sympathetic nervous system, that mobilizes energy and activity for attacking or escaping a threat. (p. 275)

figure-ground the organization of the visual field into objects (the *figures*) that stand out from their surroundings (the *ground*). (p. 134)

fixation (1) according to Freud, a lingering focus of pleasure-seeking energies at an earlier psychosexual stage, in which conflicts were unresolved. (2) the inability to see a problem from a new perspective; an obstacle to problem solving. (pp. 207, 296)

fixed-interval schedule in operant conditioning, a reinforcement schedule that reinforces a response only after a specified time has elapsed. (p. 165)

fixed-ratio schedule in operant conditioning, a reinforcement schedule that reinforces a response only after a specified number of responses. (p. 165)

flashbulb memory a clear memory of an emotionally significant moment or event. (p. 189)

flow a completely involved, focused state, with lowered awareness of self and time; results from full engagement of our skills. (p. 411)

fluid intelligence ability to reason speedily and abstractly; tends to decrease during late adulthood. (p. 92)

fMRI (functional magnetic resonance imaging) a technique for revealing bloodflow and, therefore, brain activity by comparing successive MRI scans. fMRI scans show brain function. (p. 35)

foot-in-the-door phenomenon the tendency for people who have first agreed to a small request to comply later with a larger request. (p. 380)

formal operational stage in Piaget's theory, the stage of cognitive development (normally beginning about age 12) during which people begin to think logically about abstract concepts. (p. 75)

framing the way an issue is posed; framing can significantly affect decisions and judgments. (p. 209)

fraternal twins twins who develop from separate fertilized eggs. They are genetically no closer than nontwin brothers and sisters, but they share a prenatal environment. (p. 66)

free association   in psychoanalysis, a method of exploring the unconscious in which the person relaxes and says whatever comes to mind, no matter how trivial or embarrassing. (p. 294)

frequency   the number of complete wavelengths that pass a point in a given time (for example, per second). (p. 140)

frontal lobes   portion of the cerebral cortex lying just behind the forehead; involved in speaking and muscle movements and in making plans and judgments. (p. 40)

frustration-aggression principle   the principle that frustration—the blocking of an attempt to achieve some goal—creates anger, which can generate aggression. (p. 394)

fundamental attribution error   the tendency, when analyzing another's behavior, to overestimate the influence of personal traits and underestimate the effects of the situation. (p. 378)

G

gender   in psychology, the biologically and socially influenced characteristics by which members of a culture define *male* and *female*. (p. 102)

gender identity   one's sense of being male or female. (p. 106)

gender role   a set of expected behaviors for males or for females. (p. 105)

gender schema   a culturally learned concept of what it means to be male and female. (p. 106)

gender typing   taking on a traditional masculine or feminine role. (p. 106)

general adaptation syndrome (GAS)   Selye's concept of the body's adaptive response to stress in three stages—alarm, resistance, exhaustion. (p. 275)

general intelligence (*g*)   a general intelligence factor that, according to Spearman and others, underlies specific mental abilities and is therefore measured by every task on an intelligence test. (p. 219)

generalization   in classical conditioning, the tendency, after conditioning, to respond similarly to stimuli that resemble the conditioned stimulus. (p. 160)

generalized anxiety disorder   an anxiety disorder in which a person is continually tense, fearful, and in a state of autonomic nervous system arousal. (p. 322)

genes   the biochemical units of heredity that make up the chromosomes; a segment of DNA. (p. 64)

genome   the complete instructions for making an organism, consisting of all the genetic material in that organism's chromosomes. (p. 64)

gestalt   an organized whole. Gestalt psychologists emphasized our tendency to integrate pieces of information into meaningful wholes. (p. 134)

glucose   the form of sugar that circulates in the blood and provides the major source of energy for body tissues. When its level is low, we feel hunger. (p. 241)

group polarization   strengthening of a group's preexisting attitudes through discussions within the group. (p. 388)

grouping   the perceptual tendency to organize stimuli into meaningful groups. (p. 134)

groupthink   the mode of thinking that occurs when the desire for harmony in a decision-making group overrides a realistic appraisal of alternatives. (p. 389)

H

hallucination   false sensory experience, such as hearing something in the absence of an external auditory stimulus. (p. 42)

hallucinogens   psychedelic ("mind-manifesting") drugs, such as LSD, that distort perceptions and evoke sensory images in the absence of sensory input. (p. 334)

heredity   the genetic transfer of characteristics from parents to offspring. (p. 64)

heritability   the portion of variation among individuals that we can attribute to genes. The heritability of a trait may vary, depending on the population and the environment. (p. 227)

heuristics   simple thinking strategies that often allow us to make judgments and solve problems efficiently; usually speedier but also more error-prone than *algorithms*. (p. 206)

hierarchy of needs   Maslow's pyramid of human needs; at the base are physiological needs that must be satisfied before higher-level safety needs, and then psychological needs, become active. (pp. 238, 301)

hindsight bias   the tendency to believe, after learning an outcome, that we could have predicted it. (Also known as the *I-knew-it-all-along phenomenon.*) (p. 9)

hormones   chemical messengers that are manufactured by the endocrine glands, travel through the bloodstream, and affect other tissues. (p. 33)

hue   the dimension of color that is determined by the wavelength of light; what we know as the color names *blue, green,* and so forth. (p. 130)

human factors psychology   a subfield of I/O psychology that explores how people and machines interact and how machines and physical environments can be made safe and easy to use. (p. 412)

humanistic psychology   emphasized the growth potential of healthy people and the individual's potential for personal growth. (p. 3)

hypnosis   a social interaction in which one person (the hypnotist) suggests to another (the subject) that certain perceptions, feelings, thoughts, or behaviors will spontaneously occur. (p. 144)

hypothalamus [hi-po-THAL-uh-muss]   a neural structure lying below (*hypo*) the thalamus; directs several maintenance activities (eating, drinking, body temperature), helps govern the endocrine system via the pituitary gland, and is linked to emotion. (p. 38)

hypothesis   a testable prediction, often implied by a theory. (p. 11)

I

id   a reservoir of unconscious psychic energy that, according to Freud, strives to satisfy basic sexual and aggressive drives. The id operates on the *pleasure principle,* demanding immediate gratification. (p. 294)

identical twins   twins who develop from a single fertilized egg that splits in two, creating two genetically identical siblings. (p. 66)

identification   the process by which, according to Freud, children incorporate their parents' values into their developing superegos. (p. 296)

identity   our sense of self; according to Erikson, the adolescent's task is to solidify a sense of self by testing and integrating various roles. (p. 84)

illusory correlation   the perception of a relationship where none exists. (p. 15)

imagery   mental pictures; a powerful aid to effortful processing, especially when combined with encoding meaning. (p. 187)

implicit memory   retaining learned skills or conditioning, often without conscious awareness of this learning. (p. 185)

inattentional blindness failure to see visible objects when our attention is directed elsewhere. (p. 49)

incentive a positive or negative environmental stimulus that motivates behavior. (p. 238)

independent variable the experimental factor that is manipulated; the variable whose effect is being studied. (p. 16)

individualism giving priority to our own goals over group goals and defining our identity in terms of personal traits rather than group membership. (p. 312)

industrial-organizational (I/O) psychology the application of psychological concepts and methods to human behavior in workplaces. (p. 412)

ingroup "us"—people with whom we share a common identity. (p. 392)

ingroup bias the tendency to favor our own group. (p. 392)

insight a sudden realization of the solution to a problem; it contrasts with strategy-based solutions. (p. 206)

insomnia recurring problems in falling or staying asleep. (p. 55)

intelligence mental quality consisting of the ability to learn from experience, solve problems, and use knowledge to adapt to new situations. (p. 219)

intelligence quotient (IQ) defined originally as the ratio of mental age (*ma*) to chronological age (*ca*) multiplied by 100 (thus, IQ = *ma* ÷ *ca* × 100). On contemporary intelligence tests, the average performance for a given age is assigned a score of 100. (p. 224)

intelligence test a method for assessing an individual's mental aptitudes and comparing them with those of others, using numerical scores. (p. 223)

intensity the amount of energy in a light wave or sound wave, which we perceive as brightness or loudness, as determined by the wave's amplitude. (p. 130)

interaction the interplay that occurs when the effect of one factor (such as environment) depends on another factor (such as heredity). (p. 65)

interference the blocking of recall as old or new learning disrupts the recall of other memories. (p. 194)

internal locus of control the perception that we control our own fate. (p. 282)

interneuron neuron that processes information between sensory inputs and motor outputs. (p. 31)

interpretation in psychoanalysis, the analyst's noting supposed dream meanings, resistances, and other significant behaviors and events in order to promote insight. (p. 353)

intimacy in Erikson's theory, the ability to form close, loving relationships; a primary developmental task in early adulthood. (p. 85)

intrinsic motivation a desire to perform a behavior for its own sake. (p. 171)

J

James-Lange theory the theory that our experience of emotion is our awareness of our physiological responses to emotion-arousing stimuli. (p. 253)

just-world phenomenon the tendency to believe that the world is just and people therefore get what they deserve and deserve what they get. (p. 391)

K

kinesthesis [kin-ehs-THEE-sehs] the system for sensing the position and movement of individual body parts. (p. 147)

L

language our spoken, written, or signed words and the ways we combine them to communicate meaning. (p. 212)

latent content according to Freud, the underlying meaning of a dream. (p. 57)

latent learning learning that is not apparent until there is an incentive to demonstrate it. (p. 171)

learned helplessness the hopelessness and passive resignation an animal or human learns when unable to avoid repeated aversive events. (p. 281)

learning a relatively permanent behavior change due to experience. (p. 156)

limbic system neural system (including the *hippocampus, amygdala,* and *hypothalamus*) located below the cerebral hemispheres; associated with emotions and drives. (p. 37)

lobotomy a psychosurgical procedure once used to calm uncontrollably emotional or violent patients. The procedure cut the nerves connecting the frontal lobes to the emotion-controlling centers of the inner brain. (p. 370)

long-term memory the relatively permanent and limitless storehouse of the memory system. Includes knowledge, skills, and experiences. (p. 182)

long-term potentiation (LTP) an increase in a synapse's firing potential. Believed to be a neural basis for learning and memory. (p. 188)

LSD a powerful hallucinogenic drug; also known as *acid (lysergic acid diethylamide).* (p. 334)

lymphocytes the two types of white blood cells that are part of the body's immune system: B *lymphocytes* release antibodies that fight bacterial infections; T *lymphocytes* attack cancer cells, viruses, and foreign substances. (p. 277)

M

major depressive disorder a mood disorder in which a person experiences, in the absence of drugs or a medical condition, two or more weeks of significantly depressed moods, feelings of worthlessness, and diminished interest or pleasure in most activities. (p. 338)

mania a mood disorder marked by a hyperactive, wildly optimistic state. (p. 339)

manifest content according to Freud, the remembered story line of a dream. (p. 57)

maturation biological growth processes leading to orderly changes in behavior, independent of experience. (p. 70)

medical model the concept that diseases, in this case psychological disorders, have physical causes that can be diagnosed, treated, and, in most cases, cured, often through treatment in a hospital. (p. 319)

medulla [muh-DUL-uh] the base of the brainstem; controls heartbeat and breathing. (p. 35)

memory trace enduring physical changes in the brain as a memory forms. (p. 194)

memory the persistence of learning over time through the encoding, storage, and retrieval of information. (p. 182)

menarche [meh-NAR-key] the first menstrual period. (p. 81)

menopause the end of menstruation. In everyday use, it can also mean the biological transition a woman experiences from before to after the end of menstruation. (p. 90)

mental age a measure of intelligence test performance devised by Binet; the chronological age that most typically corresponds to a given level of performance. Thus, a child who does as well as the average 8-year-old is said to have a mental age of 8. (p. 223)

mere exposure effect the phenomenon that repeated exposure to novel stimuli increases liking of them. (p. 397)

methamphetamine a powerfully addictive drug that stimulates the central nervous system with speeded-up body functions and associated energy and mood changes; over time, appears to reduce baseline dopamine levels. (p. 333)

mirror neuron neuron that fires when we perform certain actions and when we observe others performing those actions; neural basis for imitation and observational learning. (p. 173)

mirror-image perceptions mutual views often held by conflicting people, as when each side sees itself as ethical and peaceful and views the other side as evil and aggressive. (p. 404)

misinformation effect a memory that has been corrupted by misleading information. (p. 196)

modeling the process of observing and imitating a specific behavior. (p. 172)

monocular cue a depth cue, such as interposition or linear perspective, available to either eye alone. (p. 136)

mood disorders psychological disorders characterized by emotional extremes. See *major depressive disorder, mania,* and *bipolar disorder.* (p. 338)

mood-congruent memory the tendency to recall experiences that are consistent with your current good or bad mood. (p. 191)

motivation a need or desire that energizes and directs behavior. (p. 238)

motor cortex cerebral cortex area at the rear of the frontal lobes; controls voluntary movements. (p. 40)

motor neuron neuron that carries outgoing information from the central nervous system to the muscles and glands. (p. 31)

MRI (magnetic resonance imaging) a technique that uses magnetic fields and radio waves to produce computer-generated images of soft tissue. MRI scans show brain anatomy. (p. 35)

N

narcolepsy sleep disorder in which a person has uncontrollable sleep attacks, sometimes lapsing directly into REM sleep. (p. 55)

natural selection the adaptive process; among the range of inherited trait variations, those that lead to increased reproduction and survival will most likely be passed on to succeeding generations. (p. 116)

naturalistic observation a descriptive technique of observing and recording behavior in naturally occurring situations without trying to change or control the situation. (p. 13)

nature-nurture issue the longstanding controversy over the relative contributions that genes and experience make to the development of psychological traits and behaviors. Today's psychological science sees traits and behaviors arising from the interaction of nature and nurture. (p. 6)

near-death experience an altered state of consciousness reported after a close brush with death (such as through cardiac arrest); often similar to drug-induced hallucinations. (p. 334)

negative reinforcement increases behaviors by stopping or reducing negative stimuli, such as shock. A negative reinforcer is anything that, when *removed* after a response, strengthens the response. (Note: negative reinforcement is *not* punishment.) (p. 163)

nerves bundled axons that form neural "cables" connecting the central nervous system with muscles, glands, and sense organs. (p. 31)

nervous system the body's speedy, electrochemical communication network, consisting of all the nerve cells of the central and peripheral nervous systems. (p. 31)

neurogenesis formation of new neurons. (p. 45)

neuron a nerve cell; the basic building block of the nervous system. (p. 28)

neurotransmitters neuron-produced chemicals that cross synapses to carry messages to other neurons or cells. (p. 29)

neutral stimulus (NS) in classical conditioning, a stimulus that elicits no response before conditioning. (p. 158)

nicotine a stimulating and highly addictive psychoactive drug in tobacco. (p. 332)

normal curve the bell-shaped curve that describes the distribution of many physical and psychological attributes. Most scores fall near the average, and fewer and fewer scores lie near the extremes. (p. 224)

O

object permanence the awareness that things continue to exist even when not perceived. (p. 73)

observational learning learning by observing others. (p. 172)

obsessive-compulsive disorder (OCD) an anxiety disorder characterized by unwanted repetitive thoughts (obsessions) and/or actions (compulsions). (p. 323)

occipital [ahk-SIP-uh-tuhl] **lobes** portion of the cerebral cortex lying at the back of the head; includes areas that receive information from the visual fields. (p. 40)

Oedipus [ED-uh-puss] **complex** according to Freud, a boy's sexual desires toward his mother and feelings of jealousy and hatred for the rival father. (p. 296)

one-word stage the stage in speech development, from about age 1 to 2, during which a child speaks mostly in single words. (p. 213)

operant behavior behavior that operates on the environment, producing consequences. (p. 168)

operant chamber a box (also known as a *Skinner box*) with an attached recording device to track the rate at which an animal presses the box's bar to obtain a reinforcer. Used in operant conditioning research. (p. 162)

operant conditioning a type of learning in which behavior is strengthened if followed by a reinforcer or diminished if followed by a punisher. (p. 162)

operational definition a statement of the procedures (operations) used to define research variables. For example, *human intelligence* may be operationally defined as what an intelligence test measures. (p. 11)

opiates chemicals, such as opium, morphine, and heroin, that depress neural activity, temporarily lessening pain and anxiety. (pp. 30, 331)

optic nerve the nerve that carries neural impulses from the eye to the brain. (p. 130)

optimism the anticipation of positive outcomes. Optimists are people who expect the best and expect their efforts to lead to good things. (p. 283)

organizational psychology   a subfield of I/O psychology that examines organizational influences on worker satisfaction and productivity and facilitates organizational change. (p. 412)

other-race effect   the tendency to recall faces of one's own race more accurately than faces of other races. (p. 393)

outgroup   "them"—those perceived as different or apart from our group. (p. 392)

overconfidence   the tendency to be more confident than correct—to overestimate the accuracy of your beliefs and judgments. (p. 209)

P

panic disorder   an anxiety disorder marked by unpredictable minutes-long episodes of intense dread in which a person experiences terror and accompanying chest pain, choking, or other frightening sensations. (p. 323)

parallel processing   the processing of many aspects of a problem or scene at the same time; the brain's natural mode of information processing for many functions, including vision. (p. 132)

parasympathetic nervous system   autonomic nervous system subdivision that calms the body, conserving its energy. (p. 31)

parietal [puh-RYE-uh-tuhl] **lobes**   portion of the cerebral cortex lying at the top of the head and toward the rear; receives sensory input for touch and body position. (p. 40)

partial (intermittent) reinforcement   reinforcing a response only part of the time; results in slower acquisition but much greater resistance to extinction than does continuous reinforcement. (p. 164)

passionate love   an aroused state of intense positive absorption in another, usually present at the beginning of a love relationship. (p. 401)

perception   the process by which our brain organizes and interprets sensory information, transforming it into meaningful objects and events. (p. 124)

perceptual adaptation   in vision, the ability to adjust to an artificially displaced or even inverted visual field. (p. 138)

perceptual constancy   perceiving objects as unchanging (having consistent color, brightness, shape, and size) even as illumination and retinal images change. (p. 137)

perceptual set   a mental predisposition to perceive one thing and not another. (p. 127)

peripheral nervous system (PNS)   the sensory and motor neurons connecting the central nervous system (CNS) to the rest of the body. (p. 31)

personal control   our sense of controlling our environment rather than feeling helpless. (p. 281)

personality   an individual's characteristic pattern of thinking, feeling, and acting. (p. 292)

personality disorders   psychological disorders characterized by inflexible and enduring behavior patterns that impair social functioning. (p. 327)

personnel psychology   a subfield of I/O psychology that focuses on employee selection, placement, training, and appraisal. (p. 412)

pessimism   the anticipation of negative outcomes. Pessimists are people who expect the worst and doubt that their goals will be achieved. (p. 283)

PET (positron emission tomography) scan   a view of brain activity showing where a radioactive form of glucose goes while the brain performs a given task. (p. 35)

phobia   an anxiety disorder marked by a persistent, irrational fear and avoidance of a specific object or situation. (p. 323)

physical dependence   a physiological need for a drug, marked by unpleasant withdrawal symptoms when the drug is discontinued. (p. 329)

physiological need   a basic bodily requirement. (p. 238)

pitch   a tone's experienced highness or lowness; depends on frequency. (p. 140)

pituitary gland   most influential endocrine gland. Under the influence of the hypothalamus, the pituitary regulates growth and controls other endocrine glands. (p. 34)

placebo [pluh-SEE-bo; Latin for "I shall please"]   an inactive substance or condition that is sometimes given to control group members in place of the treatment given to the experimental group. (p. 16)

placebo effect   results caused by expectations alone. (p. 16)

plasticity   the brain's ability to change, especially during childhood, by reorganizing after damage or by building new pathways based on experience. (p. 45)

polygraph   a machine, commonly used in attempts to detect lies, that measures some bodily responses (such as changes in perspiration, heart rate, and breathing) accompanying emotion. (p. 257)

positive psychology   the scientific study of human functioning, with the goals of discovering and promoting strengths and virtues that help individuals and communities to thrive. (p. 8)

positive reinforcement   increases behaviors by presenting positive stimuli, such as food. A positive reinforcer is anything that, when *presented* after a response, strengthens the response. (p. 163)

post-traumatic stress disorder (PTSD)   an anxiety disorder characterized by haunting memories, nightmares, social withdrawal, jumpy anxiety, and/or insomnia lingering for four weeks or more after a traumatic experience. (p. 324)

prejudice   an unjustifiable and usually negative attitude toward a group and its members. Prejudice generally involves stereotyped beliefs, negative feelings, and a predisposition to discriminatory action. (p. 390)

preoperational stage   in Piaget's theory, the stage (from about 2 to 6 or 7 years of age) in which a child learns to use language but cannot yet perform the mental operations of concrete logic. (p. 73)

primary reinforcer   an event that is innately reinforcing, often by satisfying a biological need. (p. 164)

priming   activating, often unconsciously, associations in our mind, thus setting us up to perceive or remember objects or events in certain ways. (p. 125)

problem-focused coping   attempting to reduce stress directly—by changing the stressor or the way we interact with that stressor. (p. 280)

projective test   a personality test, such as the Rorschach test, that provides an unclear image designed to trigger projection of the test-taker's unconscious thoughts or feelings. (p. 298)

prosocial behavior   positive, constructive, helpful behavior. The opposite of antisocial behavior. (p. 174)

psychoactive drug   a chemical substance that alters perceptions and mood. (p. 329)

psychoanalysis   (1) Freud's theory of personality that attributes thoughts and actions to unconscious motives and conflicts; (2) Freud's therapeutic technique used in treating psychological disorders. Freud believed that the patient's free associations, resistances, dreams, and transferences—and the therapist's interpretations of them—released previously repressed feelings, allowing the patient to gain self-insight. (pp. 294, 352)

psychodynamic theory a Freud-influenced perspective that sees behavior, thinking, and emotions as reflecting unconscious motives. (p. 297)

psychodynamic therapy a Freud-influenced perspective that sees behavior, thinking, and emotions in terms of unconscious motives. (p. 353)

psychological dependence a psychological need to use a drug, such as to relieve negative emotions. (p. 329)

psychological disorder deviant (atypical), distressful, and dysfunctional patterns of thoughts, feelings, or behaviors. (p. 318)

psychology the science of behavior and mental processes. (p. 3)

psychoneuroimmunology the study of how psychological, neural, and endocrine processes combine to affect our immune system and health. (p. 277)

psychosexual stages the childhood stages of development (oral, anal, phallic, latency, genital) during which, according to Freud, the id's pleasure-seeking energies focus on distinct erogenous zones. (p. 295)

psychosurgery surgery that removes or destroys brain tissue in an effort to change behavior. (p. 370)

psychotherapy treatment involving psychological techniques; consists of interactions between a trained therapist and someone seeking to overcome psychological difficulties or achieve personal growth. (p. 352)

puberty the period of sexual maturation, during which a person becomes capable of reproducing. (p. 81)

punishment an event that decreases the behavior it follows. (p. 165)

R

random assignment assigning participants to experimental and control groups by chance, thus minimizing any differences between the groups. (p. 15)

random sample a sample that fairly represents a population because each member has an equal chance of inclusion. (p. 12)

recall memory demonstrated by retrieving information learned earlier, as on a fill-in-the-blank test. (p. 189)

reciprocal determinism the interacting influences of behavior, internal personal factors, and environment. (p. 308)

recognition memory demonstrated by identifying items previously learned, as on a multiple-choice test. (p. 189)

reflex an unlearned, automatic response to a sensory stimulus. (p. 67)

refractory period a resting period after orgasm, during which a man cannot achieve another orgasm. (p. 108)

rehearsal the conscious repetition of information, either to maintain it in consciousness or to encode it for storage. (p. 183)

reinforcement in operant conditioning, any event that *strengthens* the behavior it follows. (p. 162)

reinforcement schedule a pattern that defines how often a desired response will be reinforced. (p. 164)

relative deprivation the perception that we are worse off relative to those with whom we compare ourselves. (p. 267)

relearning memory demonstrated by time saved when learning material a second time. (p. 189)

reliability the extent to which a test yields consistent results, as assessed by the consistency of scores on two halves of the test, on alternate forms of the test, or on retesting. (p. 225)

REM rebound the tendency for REM sleep to increase following REM sleep deprivation. (p. 58)

REM (rapid eye movement) sleep recurring sleep stage during which vivid dreams commonly occur. Also known as *paradoxical sleep,* because the muscles are relaxed (except for minor twitches) but other body systems are active. (p. 51)

repetitive transcranial magnetic stimulation (rTMS) the application of repeated pulses of magnetic energy to the brain; used to stimulate or suppress brain activity. (p. 370)

replication repeating the essence of a research study, usually with different participants in different situations, to see whether the basic finding extends to other participants and circumstances. (p. 11)

repression in psychoanalytic theory, the basic defense mechanism that banishes anxiety-arousing thoughts, feelings, and memories from consciousness. (pp. 195, 296)

resilience the personal strength that helps most people cope with stress and recover from adversity and even trauma. (p. 371)

resistance in psychoanalysis, the blocking from consciousness of anxiety-laden material. (p. 353)

respondent behavior behavior that occurs as an automatic response to some stimulus. (p. 168)

reticular formation nerve network running through the brainstem and thalamus; plays an important role in controlling arousal. (p. 36)

retina the light-sensitive inner surface of the eye; contains the receptor rods and cones plus layers of neurons that begin the processing of visual information. (p. 130)

retinal disparity a binocular cue for perceiving depth. By comparing images from the two eyes, the brain computes distance—the greater the disparity (difference) between the two images, the closer the object. (p. 135)

retrieval the process of getting information out of memory storage. (p. 182)

retrieval cue any stimulus (event, feeling, place, and so on) linked to a specific memory. (p. 190)

rods retinal receptors that detect black, white, and gray; necessary for peripheral and twilight vision, when cones don't respond. (p. 130)

role a set of expectations about a social position, defining how those in the position ought to behave. (pp. 105, 380)

Rorschach inkblot test the most widely used projective test, a set of 10 inkblots, designed by Hermann Rorschach; seeks to identify people's inner feelings by analyzing their interpretations of the blots. (p. 298)

S

savant syndrome a condition in which a person otherwise limited in mental ability has an exceptional specific skill, such as in computation or drawing. (p. 219)

scapegoat theory the theory that prejudice offers an outlet for anger by providing someone to blame. (p. 392)

schema a concept or framework that organizes and interprets information. (p. 72)

schizophrenia a group of severe disorders characterized by disorganized and delusional thinking, disturbed perceptions, and inappropriate emotions and actions. (p. 343)

selective attention focusing conscious awareness on a particular stimulus. (p. 49)

self your image and understanding of who you are; in modern psychology, the idea that this is the center of personality, organizing your thoughts, feelings, and actions. (p. 309)

self-actualization according to Maslow, the psychological need that arises after basic physical and psychological needs are met and self-esteem is achieved; the motivation to fulfill our potential. (p. 301)

self-concept all our thoughts and feelings about ourselves, in answer to the question, "Who am I?" (p. 302)

self-disclosure revealing intimate aspects of ourselves to others. (p. 402)

self-esteem your feelings of high or low self-worth. (p. 310)

self-serving bias our readiness to perceive ourselves favorably. (p. 311)

self-transcendence according to Maslow, the striving for identity, meaning, and purpose beyond the self. (p. 301)

sensation the process by which our sensory receptors and nervous system take in stimulus energies from our environment. (p. 124)

sensorimotor stage in Piaget's theory, the stage (from birth to about 2 years of age) during which infants know the world mostly in terms of their sensory impressions and motor activities. (p. 72)

sensory adaptation reduced sensitivity in response to constant stimulation. (p. 126)

sensory cortex cerebral cortex area at the front of the parietal lobes; registers and processes body touch and movement sensations. (p. 41)

sensory interaction the principle that one sense may influence another, as when the smell of food influences its taste. (p. 146)

sensory memory the immediate, very brief recording of sensory information in the memory system. (p. 182)

sensory neuron neuron that carries incoming information from the sensory receptors to the central nervous system. (p. 31)

serial position effect the tendency to recall best the last and first items in a list. (p. 184)

set point the point at which your "weight thermostat" is supposedly set. When your body falls below this weight, increased hunger and a lowered metabolic rate may combine to restore lost weight. (p. 241)

sexual orientation an enduring sexual attraction toward members of either our own sex (homosexual orientation) or the other sex (heterosexual orientation). (p. 112)

sexual response cycle the four stages of sexual responding described by Masters and Johnson—excitement, plateau, orgasm, and resolution. (p. 108)

shaping an operant conditioning procedure in which reinforcers guide actions closer and closer toward a desired behavior. (p. 162)

short-term memory activated memory that holds a few items briefly (such as the seven digits of a phone number while dialing) before the information is stored or forgotten. (p. 182)

sleep periodic, natural, reversible loss of consciousness—as distinct from unconsciousness resulting from a coma, general anesthesia, or hibernation. (Adapted from Dement, 1999.) (p. 51)

sleep apnea a sleep disorder in which a sleeping person repeatedly stops breathing until blood oxygen is so low it awakens the person just long enough to draw a breath. (p. 55)

social clock the culturally preferred timing of social events such as marriage, parenthood, and retirement. (p. 94)

social facilitation stronger responses on simple or well-learned tasks in the presence of others. (p. 386)

social identity the "we" aspect of our self-concept; the part of our answer to "Who am I?" that comes from our group memberships. (p. 84)

social leadership group-oriented leadership that builds teamwork, resolves conflict, and offers support. (p. 416)

social learning theory the theory that we learn social behavior by observing and imitating and by being rewarded or punished. (p. 106)

social loafing the tendency for people in a group to exert less effort when pooling their efforts toward attaining a common goal than when individually accountable. (p. 387)

social psychology the scientific study of how we think about, influence, and relate to one another. (p. 378)

social script culturally modeled guide for how to act in various situations. (p. 395)

social-cognitive perspective views behavior as influenced by the interaction between persons (and their thinking) and their social context. (p. 307)

somatic nervous system peripheral nervous system division controlling the body's skeletal muscles. Also called the *skeletal nervous system.* (p. 31)

source amnesia faulty memory for how, when, or where information was learned or imagined. (p. 197)

spacing effect the tendency for distributed study or practice to yield better long-term retention than is achieved through massed study or practice. (p. 184)

split brain condition in which the brain's two hemispheres are isolated by cutting the fibers (mainly those of the corpus callosum) connecting them. (p. 46)

spontaneous recovery the reappearance, after a pause, of an extinguished conditioned response. (p. 159)

spotlight effect overestimating others' noticing and evaluating our appearance, performance, and blunders (as if we presume a spotlight shines on us). (p. 310)

SQ3R a study method incorporating five steps: **S**urvey, **Q**uestion, **R**ead, **R**ehearse, **R**eview. (p. 22)

standardization defining scores by comparing them with the performance of a pretested standardization group. (p. 224)

Stanford-Binet the widely used American revision (by Terman at Stanford University) of Binet's original intelligence test. (p. 224)

stereotype a generalized (sometimes accurate but often overgeneralized) belief about a group of people. (p. 390)

stereotype threat a self-confirming concern that we will be evaluated based on a negative stereotype. (p. 232)

stimulants drugs (such as caffeine, nicotine, and the more powerful amphetamines, cocaine, and Ecstasy) that excite neural activity and speed up body functions. (p. 332)

stimulus any event or situation that evokes a response. (p. 156)

storage retaining of encoded information over time. (p. 182)

stranger anxiety the fear of strangers that infants commonly display, beginning by about 8 months of age. (p. 75)

stress the process by which we perceive and respond to certain events, called *stressors,* that we appraise as threatening or challenging. (p. 274)

subjective well-being self-perceived happiness or satisfaction with life. Used along with measures of objective well-being (for example, physical and economic indicators) to evaluate our quality of life. (p. 265)

subliminal below our absolute threshold for conscious awareness. (p. 124)

substance-related disorders a maladaptive pattern of substance use leading to clinically significant impairment or distress. (p. 329)

superego   the part of personality that, according to Freud, represents internalized ideals and provides standards for judgment (the conscience). (p. 295)

superordinate goals   shared goals that override differences among people and require their cooperation. (p. 405)

survey   a descriptive technique for obtaining the self-reported attitudes or behaviors of people, usually by questioning a representative, random sample of a population. (p. 12)

sympathetic nervous system   autonomic nervous system subdivision that arouses the body, mobilizing its energy in stressful situations. (p. 31)

synapse [SIN-aps]   a junction between the axon tip of a sending neuron and the dendrite or cell body of a receiving neuron. (p. 28)

systematic desensitization   a type of exposure therapy that associates a pleasant relaxed state with gradually increasing, anxiety-triggering stimuli. Commonly used to treat phobias. (p. 356)

T

task leadership   goal-oriented leadership that sets standards, organizes work, and focuses attention on goals. (p. 416)

telegraphic speech   early speech stage in which a child speaks like a telegram—"go car"—using mostly nouns and verbs. (p. 213)

temperament   a person's characteristic emotional reactivity and intensity. (p. 68)

temporal lobes   portion of the cerebral cortex lying roughly above the ears; includes areas that receive information from the ears. (p. 40)

tend and befriend   under stress, people (especially women) often provide support to others (*tend*) and bond with and seek support from others (*befriend*). (p. 276)

teratogen   an agent, such as a chemical or virus, that can reach the embryo or fetus during prenatal development and cause harm. (p. 66)

testosterone   the most important male sex hormone. Stimulates the growth of the male sex organs in the fetus and the development of the male sex characteristics during puberty. Females have testosterone, but less of it. (p. 104)

thalamus [THAL-uh-muss]   area at the top of the brainstem; directs sensory messages to the cortex and transmits replies to the cerebellum and medulla. (p. 36)

THC   the major active ingredient in marijuana; triggers a variety of effects, including mild hallucinations. (p. 334)

theory   an explanation using an integrated set of principles that organizes observations and predicts behaviors or events. (p. 11)

theory of mind   people's ideas about their own and others' mental states—about their feelings, perceptions, and thoughts, and the behaviors these might predict. (p. 74)

threshold   level of stimulation required to trigger a neural impulse. (p. 29)

token economy   an operant conditioning procedure in which people earn a token for exhibiting a desired behavior and can later exchange the tokens for privileges or treats. (p. 358)

tolerance   the diminishing effect with regular use of the same dose of a drug, requiring the user to take larger and larger doses before experiencing the drug's effect. (p. 329)

trait   a characteristic pattern of behavior or a tendency to feel and act in a certain way, as assessed by self-reports on a personality test. (p. 303)

transduction   changing one form of energy into another. In sensation, the transforming of stimulus energies, such as sights, sounds, and smells, into neural impulses our brains can interpret. (p. 124)

transference   in psychoanalysis, the patient's transfer to the analyst of emotions linked with other relationships (such as love or hatred for a parent). (p. 353)

two-factor theory   Schachter-Singer's theory that to experience emotion we must (1) be physically aroused and (2) cognitively label the arousal. (p. 253)

two-word stage   beginning about age 2, the stage in speech development during which a child speaks mostly two-word statements. (p. 213)

Type A   Friedman and Rosenman's term for competitive, hard-driving, impatient, verbally aggressive, and anger-prone people. (p. 279)

Type B   Friedman and Rosenman's term for easygoing, relaxed people. (p. 279)

U

unconditional positive regard   a caring, nonjudgmental attitude of total acceptance toward another person, which Carl Rogers believed would help clients develop self-awareness and self-acceptance. (pp. 301, 355)

unconditioned response (UR)   in classical conditioning, an unlearned, naturally occurring response (such as salivation) to an unconditioned stimulus (US) (such as food in the mouth). (p. 158)

unconditioned stimulus (US)   in classical conditioning, a stimulus that unconditionally—naturally and automatically—triggers a response (UR). (p. 158)

unconscious   (1) according to Freud, a reservoir of mostly unacceptable thoughts, wishes, feelings, and memories. (2) According to contemporary psychologists, information processing of which we are unaware. (p. 294)

V

validity   the extent to which a test measures or predicts what it is supposed to. (p. 225)

variable-interval schedule   in operant conditioning, a reinforcement schedule that reinforces a response at unpredictable time intervals. (p. 165)

variable-ratio schedule   in operant conditioning, a reinforcement schedule that reinforces a response after an unpredictable number of responses. (p. 165)

vestibular sense   the sense of body movement and position, including the sense of balance. (p. 148)

virtual reality exposure therapy   an anxiety treatment that progressively exposes people to electronic simulations of their greatest fears, such as airplane flying, spiders, or public speaking. (p. 356)

visual cliff   a laboratory device for testing depth perception in infants and young animals. (p. 135)

W

wavelength   the distance from the peak of one light or sound wave to the peak of the next. (p. 130)

Weber's law   the principle that, to be perceived as different, two stimuli must differ by a constant minimum proportion (rather than a constant amount). (p. 125)

Wechsler Adult Intelligence Scale (WAIS) the WAIS is the most widely used intelligence test; contains verbal and performance (nonverbal) subtests. (p. 224)

Wernicke's area brain area, usually in the left temporal lobe, involved in language comprehension and expression; controls language reception. (p. 44)

withdrawal the discomfort and distress that follow discontinuing the use of an addictive drug. (p. 329)

working memory a view of short-term memory that stresses conscious, active processing of information, whether newly encoded or retrieved from long-term memory. (p. 182)

X

X chromosome the sex chromosome found in both men and women. Females have two X chromosomes; males have one X chromosome and one Y chromosome. (p. 104)

Y

Y chromosome the sex chromosome found only in males. When paired with an X chromosome from the mother, it produces a male child. (p. 104)

Z

zygote the fertilized egg; it enters a 2-week period of rapid cell division and develops into an embryo. (p. 66)

Glosario

absolute threshold/umbral absoluto Estímulo mínimo necesario para detectar un estímulo particular el 50 por ciento del tiempo. (pág. 124)

achievement motivation/motivación de logro Deseo de lograr algo importante, con respecto a cosas, personas o ideas; deseo de lograr un alto estándar. (pág. 413)

achievement test/prueba de rendimiento Prueba diseñada para evaluar lo que una persona ha aprendido. (pág. 223)

acquisition/adquisición (1) Según el condicionamiento clásico, etapa inicial en la que relacionamos un estímulo neutral con uno incondicionado, de tal modo que el estímulo neutral comienza a desencadenar la respuesta condicionada. (2) Según el condicionamiento operante, intensificación de una respuesta reforzada. (pág. 158)

action potential/potencial de acción Impulso nervioso. (pág. 28)

active listening/escucha activa Escucha empática en la que el oyente hace eco, reitera y clarifica. Una característica de la terapia de Rogers centrada en el cliente. (pág. 354)

adaptation-level phenomenon/fenómeno del nivel de adaptación Nuestra tendencia de formar juicios (de sonidos, de luces, de ingreso) relacionado a un nivel neutro definido por nuestra experiencia de antes. (pág. 267)

addiction/adicción Ansia y uso compulsivo de droga. (pág. 329)

adolescence/adolescencia Período de transición de la niñez a la madurez, extendiéndose de la pubertad a la independencia. (pág. 81)

adrenal glands/glándulas suprarrenales Par de glándulas endocrinas ubicadas sobre los riñones que segregan hormonas (epinefrina y norepinefrina) y contribuyen a la estimulación del cuerpo cuando hay estrés. (pág. 34)

aerobic exercise/ejercicios aeróbicos Actividad sostenida que aumenta la salud cardíaca y pulmonar; posiblemente reduce también la depresión y la ansiedad. (pág. 285)

aggression/agresión Comportamiento físico o verbal que tiene la intención de causar daño o destruir. (págs. 102, 393)

AIDS (acquired immune deficiency syndrome)/SIDA (síndrome de inmunodeficiencia adquirida) Infección peligrosa transmitida sexualmente y causada por *el virus de inmunodeficiencia humana* (VIH). El SIDA debilita el sistema de inmunidad y hace que el individuo se torne vulnerable a infecciones. (pág. 108)

alcohol dependence/dependencia alcohólica (conocida comúnmente como alcoholismo) Consumo de bebidas alcohólicas caracterizado por tolerancia, síntomas de abstinencia cuando se interrumpe el consumo y deseo de continuar bebiendo. (pág. 330)

algorithm/algoritmo Regla o procedimiento metódico y lógico que garantiza la resolución de un problema en particular. Contrasta con el empleo de la *heurística,* un método generalmente más rápido pero también más propenso a registrar errores. (pág. 206)

all-or-none response/respuesta de todo o nada Reacción que produce una neurona al activarse (con una respuesta de máxima intensidad) o al no activarse. (pág. 29)

alpha waves/ritmo alfa Ritmo con ondas cerebrales relativamente lentas que corresponden a un estado relajado y de vigilia. (pág. 51)

altruism/altruismo Consideración desinteresada por el bienestar de los demás. (pág. 402)

amphetamines/anfetaminas Drogas que estimulan la actividad neural, causando aceleración de las funciones corporales y de los niveles de energía asociadas con éstas así como cambios de humor. (pág. 332)

amygdala/amígdala Dos conjuntos de fibras nerviosas del tamaño de una haba que se hallan en el sistema límbico e intervienen en las emociones. (pág. 37)

anorexia nervosa/anorexia nerviosa Trastorno alimenticio en el cual una persona (generalmente una muchacha adolescente) se somete a una dieta de hambre a pesar de padecer de delgadez extrema (de un 15 por ciento o menos que el peso normal). (pág. 243)

antianxiety drugs/medicación antiansiedad Medicamentos recetados para aliviar los síntomas de la ansiedad y la agitación. (pág. 367)

antidepressant drugs/medicamentos antidepresivos Medicamentos recetados para tratar la depresión y ciertos trastornos de ansiedad. Los distintos tipos de medicamentos antidepresivos alteran la disponibilidad de diversos neurotransmisores. (pág. 367)

antipsychotic drugs/medicamentos antipsicóticos Medicación recetada para tratar la esquizofrenia y otros tipos de trastornos graves del pensamiento. (pág. 366)

antisocial personality disorder/trastorno antisocial de la personalidad Trastorno de la personalidad que se manifiesta cuando la persona (generalmente un hombre) no exhibe sentimiento de culpa por actuar con maldad, incluso hacia los amigos y miembros de la familia. Puede ser agresivo y cruel o un estafador listo. (pág. 327)

anxiety disorders/trastornos de ansiedad Trastornos psicológicos que se caracterizan por la preocupación y tensión crónicas o comportamientos desadaptados que reducen la ansiedad. (pág. 322)

aptitude test/prueba de aptitud Prueba diseñada para predecir la actuación de una persona en el futuro; la *aptitud* es la capacidad de aprender. (pág. 223)

association areas/áreas de asociación Áreas de la corteza cerebral principalmente relacionadas con las funciones mentales superiores como el aprendizaje, la memoria, el pensamiento y el habla. (pág. 42)

associative learning/aprendizaje asociativo El aprender que ciertos eventos ocurren juntos. Los eventos pueden ser dos estímulos (como en el condicionamiento clásico) o una respuesta y sus consecuencias (como en el condicionamiento operante). (pág. 156)

attachment/apego Vínculo emocional con otra persona; mostrado en niños pequeños quienes buscan cercanía física con la persona que los cuida y muestran angustia cuando se les separa de quien los cuida. (pág. 76)

attitude/actitud Sentimientos, a menudo basados en nuestras creencias que nos predisponen para responder de una manera particular a los objetos, las personas y eventos. (pág. 379)

audition/audición Sentido o acto de oír. (pág. 139)

autism/autismo Trastorno que se manifiesta en la niñez y que está marcado por una comunicación deficiente, falta de interacción social, y una incapacidad para entender el estado de ánimo de los otros. (pág. 74)

automatic processing/procesamiento automático Codificación inconsciente de información corriente, por ejemplo, de espacio, de tiempo, de frecuencia y de significados de palabras bien asimilados. (pág. 183)

autonomic nervous system/sistema nervioso autónomo División del sistema nervioso periférico que controla las glándulas y los músculos de los órganos (tales como el corazón). Su división simpática produce estimulación, y su división parasimpática produce relajación. (pág. 31)

availability heuristic/heurística de disponibilidad Acto de estimar la probabilidad de un evento, basándose en la facilidad con la que es rememorado. Si los casos vienen prontamente a la mente (quizás debido a su intensidad), presumimos que tales eventos son comunes. (pág. 207)

aversive conditioning/condicionamiento aversivo Paradigma de condicionamiento en el cual los efectos aversivos (náusea) son asociados con estímulos externos no deseados (beber alcohol). (pág. 357)

axons/axones Prolongaciones de las neuronas que transmiten impulsos a otras neuronas o células. (pág. 28)

B

babbling stage/fase balbuciente Fase del desarrollo del lenguaje que se da aproximadamente a los 4 meses de edad, y en la cual el infante espontáneamente emite sonidos que al principio no están relacionados con el idioma de la casa. (pág. 213)

barbiturates/barbitúricos Drogas que deprimen la actividad del sistema nervioso central, reduciendo la ansiedad; pero que afectan la memoria y el discernimiento. (pág. 331)

basal metabolic rate/tasa de metabolismo basal Cantidad de energía requerida por el organismo en reposo absoluto. (pág. 242)

basic trust/confianza básica Según Erik Erikson, la percepción de que el mundo es predecible y fidedigno; esta percepción se forma durante la infancia a través de experiencias apropiadas con cuidadores sensibles. (pág. 78)

behavior therapy/terapia del comportamiento Terapia que aplica los principios de aprendizaje para lograr la eliminación de comportamientos no deseados. (pág. 355)

behaviorism/conductismo Posición de que la psicología (1) debe ser una ciencia objetiva que (2) estudia el comportamiento sin referencia a los procesos mentales. La mayoría de los psicólogos en investigación hoy están de acuerdo con (1) pero no con (2). (págs. 2, 171)

belief perseverance/perseverancia en las creencias Empeño en mantener creencias e ignorar las evidencias que las desacreditan. (pág. 210)

binge-eating disorder/trastorno alimentario compulsivo Ingestión excesiva de alimentos, seguida de angustia, disgusto o culpa, pero sin las purgas, el ayuno o los ejercicios físicos excesivos que caracterizan a la bulimia nerviosa. (pág. 243)

binocular cue/clave binocular Señal de profundidad, por ejemplo, la disparidad retiniana, que requieren el uso de los dos ojos. (pág. 135)

biological psychology/psicología biológica Especialidad de la psicología que estudia la relación entre la biología y el comportamiento. (pág. 28)

biomedical therapy/terapia biomédica Medicamentos recetados o procedimientos médicos que actúan directamente sobre la psicología de la persona. (pág. 352)

biopsychosocial approach/enfoque biopsicosocial Enfoque integrado que resulta de la incorporación de diversas ideas complementarias donde se combinan perspectivas biológicas, psicológicas y socioculturales. (pág. 6)

bipolar disorder/trastorno bipolar Trastorno que afecta el estado de ánimo; la persona alterna entre la desesperanza y el letargo de la depresión y el estado eufórico de la manía. (Anteriormente llamado *trastorno maníaco-depresivo*.) (pág. 339)

blind spot/punto ciego Punto en el cual el nervio óptico sale del ojo; esta parte de la retina es "ciega" porque carece de células receptoras. (pág. 130)

brainstem/tronco encefálico Parte más antigua y meollo del cerebro, empezando donde la médula espinal se inflama al entrar en el cráneo; el tronco encefálico es responsable por las funciones automáticas de supervivencia. (pág. 35)

Broca's area/área de Broca Parte del lóbulo frontal del cerebro, generalmente en el hemisferio izquierdo, que dirige los movimientos musculares relacionados con el habla y controla la expresión del lenguaje. (pág. 44)

bulimia nervosa/bulimia nerviosa Trastorno de alimentación que se caracteriza por episodios de ingestión excesiva de alimentos (generalmente de alto contenido calórico) seguidos de purgas (vómito o uso de laxantes), ayuno o ejercicios físicos excesivos. (pág. 243)

bystander effect/efecto espectador Tendencia que tienen las personas a no brindar ayuda si hay otras personas presentes. (pág. 403)

C

Cannon-Bard theory/teoría de Cannon–Bard Teoría de que un estímulo que despierta emociones simultáneamente puede provocar (1) respuestas fisiológicas y (2) la experiencia subjetiva de la emoción. (pág. 253)

case study/caso Técnica de observación en la cual se estudia a una persona a profundidad con la esperanza de revelar principios universales. (pág. 12)

catharsis/catarsis Liberación emocional. La hipótesis de la catarsis sostiene que al "liberar" la energía agresiva (mediante la acción o la fantasía) se alivian los impulsos agresivos. (pág. 263)

central nervous system (CNS)/sistema nervioso central (SNC) El cerebro y la médula espinal. (pág. 31)

cerebellum/cerebelo Es el "cerebro pequeño" y está unido a la parte posterior del tronco cerebral. Sus funciones incluyen el procesamiento de la información sensorial y la coordinación de los movimientos y el equilibrio. (pág. 36)

cerebral cortex/corteza cerebral Capa delgada de neuronas conectadas entre sí, que forman los hemisferios cerebrales; es el principal centro de control y procesamiento de información del organismo. (pág. 40)

chromosomes/cromosomas Estructuras semejantes a hilos conformados de moléculas de ADN que contienen los genes. (pág. 64)

circadian rhythm/ritmo circadiano Reloj biológico; ritmos regulares del cuerpo (por ejemplo, temperatura y estado de vigilia) que ocurren en ciclos de 24 horas. (pág. 51)

classical conditioning/condicionamiento clásico Tipo de aprendizaje en el cual aprendemos a relacionar dos o más estímulos y a anticipar sucesos. (pág. 157)

client-centered therapy/terapia centrada en el cliente Tipo de terapia humanista creada por Carl Rogers, en la cual el terapeuta emplea técnicas tales como escuchar activamente dentro de un entorno genuino, con aceptación y empatía, para facilitar el crecimiento personal del cliente. (También se denomina *terapia centrada en la persona*). (pág. 354)

cochlea/cóclea Estructura tubular en forma de espiral, ósea y rellena de fluido que se halla en el oído interno; las ondas sonoras que pasan por el fluido coclear se convierten en impulsos nerviosos. (pág. 140)

cognition/cognición Todas las actividades mentales asociadas con el pensar, saber, recordar y comunicar. (págs. 72, 206)

cognitive dissonance theory/disonancia cognitiva Teoría según la cual llevamos a cabo una acción con el propósito de reducir la incomodidad (disonancia) que sentimos cuando tenemos dos pensamientos (cogniciones) contradictorios. Por ejemplo, cuando tenemos consciencia de que nuestra actitud y nuestras acciones entran en conflicto, cambiamos nuestra actitud para sentirnos más cómodos. (pág. 381)

cognitive learning/aprendizaje cognitivo Adquisición de información mental, ya sea a partir de la observación de acontecimientos, la observación de otras personas o a través del lenguaje. (pág. 156)

cognitive map/mapa cognitivo Imagen mental del trazado de nuestro entorno. (pág. 171)

cognitive neuroscience/neurociencia cognitiva Estudio interdisciplinario de las conexiones entre la actividad cerebral y los procesos del pensamiento, el saber, la memoria y el lenguaje. (pág. 3)

cognitive therapy/terapia cognitiva Terapia que ayuda a los pacientes a pensar y actuar de un modo más realista y adaptativo. Está basada en el supuesto de que los pensamientos intervienen entre los eventos y nuestras reacciones emocionales. (pág. 358)

cognitive-behavior therapy/terapia cognitivo-conductual Terapia muy difundida e integrada que combina la terapia cognitiva (que cambia los pensamientos contraproducentes) con la terapia conductual (que cambia la conducta). (pág. 359)

collectivism/colectivismo Modo de dar prioridad a las metas del grupo (a menudo de la familia extendida o el grupo de trabajo) y de definir la identidad personal según dicta el grupo. (pág. 312)

color constancy/constancia de color El percibir que las superficies familiares parecen mantener la apariencia cromática incluso bajo condiciones luminosas muy diferentes. (pág. 137)

companionate love/amor compañero Apego afectuoso profundo que sentimos por aquéllos con quienes nuestras vidas se entrelazan. (pág. 401)

concrete operational stage/etapa del pensamiento lógico-concreto En la teoría de Piaget, la fase del desarrollo cognitivo (desde aproximadamente los 6 ó 7 años hasta los 11 años de edad) durante la cual los niños desarrollan las operaciones mentales que les permiten pensar lógicamente sobre eventos concretos. (pág. 74)

conditioned reinforcer/reforzador condicionado (También denominado *reforzador secundario*) (pág. 164)

conditioned response (CR)/respuesta condicionada (RC) En el condicionamiento clásico, la respuesta aprendida a un estímulo previamente neutral (pero ahora condicionado). (pág. 158)

conditioned stimulus (CS)/estímulo condicionado (EC) En el condicionamiento clásico, un estímulo originalmente irrelevante que, después de ser asociado con un estímulo incondicionado (EI) produce una respuesta condicionada. (pág. 158)

cones/conos Células receptoras que se concentran cerca del centro de la retina; con la luz del día o en lugares bien iluminados, los conos detectan detalles finos y producen las sensaciones del color. (pág. 130)

confirmation bias/sesgo confirmatorio Tendencia a buscar información que confirme nuestras ideas preconcebidas e ignorar las evidencias que las contradigan. (pág. 209)

conflict/conflicto Incompatibilidad percibida de acciones, metas o ideas. (pág. 404)

conformity/conformidad Tendencia a ajustar el comportamiento o la forma de pensar hasta hacerlos coincidir con las normas que tiene un grupo. (pág. 382)

consciousness/conciencia Percepción de nosotros mismos y de nuestro ambiente. (pág. 49)

conservation/conservación Principio de que las propiedades de masa, volumen y número no varían a pesar de los cambios en las formas de los objetos. (Piaget era de la opinión que éste formaba parte de la etapa operacional concreta). (pág. 73)

continuous reinforcement/refuerzo continuo El reforzar la respuesta deseada cada vez que ocurre. (pág. 164)

control group/grupo control En un experimento, el grupo de participantes que contrastan con las condiciones experimentales y que sirve de comparación para evaluar el efecto del tratamiento. (pág. 15)

coronary heart disease/enfermedad coronaria Obstrucción de los vasos que nutren el músculo cardíaco; causa principal de muerte en muchos países desarrollados, por ejemplo, en los países de América del Norte. (pág. 279)

corpus callosum/cuerpo calloso Banda grande de fibras neurales que conecta los dos hemisferios del cerebro y lleva mensajes entre ellos. (pág. 46)

correlation/correlación Medida del grado en que dos factores varían juntos y por ende, si es que uno de ellos es capaz de predecir el otro. El *coeficiente de correlación* es la expresión matemática de relación yendo de -1 a 1. (pág. 13)

counterconditioning/contracondicionamiento Técnica de terapia conductual que se basa en el empleo del condicionamiento clásico para provocar respuestas alternativas a estímulos que producen comportamientos no deseados; incluye *las terapias de exposición y el condicionamiento aversivo*. (pág. 356)

creativity/creatividad Capacidad para generar ideas novedosas y valiosas. (pág. 221)

critical period/período crítico Etapa después del nacimiento, en la cual son necesarios ciertos estímulos o experiencias para que se produzca el desarrollo apropiado del organismo. (pág. 70)

critical thinking/pensamiento crítico Forma de pensar en la que no se aceptan razones y conclusiones ciegamente; por el contrario, se examinan las suposiciones, se distinguen los valores escondidos, se evalúa la evidencia y se calculan las conclusiones. (pág. 5)

crystallized intelligence/inteligencia cristalizada Todo el conocimiento y capacidad verbal que hemos acumulado; tiende a aumentar con la edad. (pág. 92)

culture/cultura Ideas, actitudes, tradiciones y comportamientos duraderos que comparte un grupo de personas y que se trasmiten de una generación a otra. (pág. 6)

D

defense mechanisms/mecanismos de defensa En la teoría psicoanalítica, los métodos de protección del ego para reducir la ansiedad distorsionando la realidad inconcientemente. (pág. 296)

deindividuation/desindividualización Pérdida de identidad personal y del sentido de responsabilidad en situaciones de grupo que fomentan la excitación y el anonimato. (pág. 388)

déjà vu/déjà vu Sensación extraña de haber vivido antes una experiencia específica. Señales de la presente situación pueden de manera subconsciente activar la recuperación de una experiencia previa. (pág. 191)

delusions/delirios Creencias falsas, generalmente de persecución o grandeza, que son síntomas de esquizofrenia y otros trastornos psicológicos. (pág. 344)

dendrites/dendritas Prolongaciones de las neuronas que reciben mensajes y envían impulsos hacia el cuerpo neuronal. (pág. 28)

dependent variable/variable dependiente Factor resultante; el factor que puede cambiar en respuesta a cambios en la variable independiente. (pág. 16)

depressants/depresivos Drogas (como el alcohol, barbitúricos y opiatos) que hacen más lenta o reducen la actividad neuronal y física. (pág. 330)

depth perception/percepción de profundidad Habilidad de ver objetos en tres dimensiones aunque las imágenes percibidas por la retina son bidimensionales. Esto nos permite juzgar la distancia. (pág. 134)

developmental psychology/psicología del desarrollo Rama de la psicología que estudia el cambio físico, cognitivo y social a lo largo de la vida. (pág. 64)

difference threshold/umbral diferencial Diferencia mínima que un individuo es capaz de detectar entre dos estímulos la mitad de las veces. El umbral diferencial se experimenta como una *diferencia apenas perceptible (dap)*. (pág. 125)

discrimination/discriminación (1) Según el condicionamiento clásico, capacidad aprendida de distinguir entre un estímulo condicionado y otros estímulos irrelevantes. (2) Conducta negativa injustificada dirigida a un grupo y sus miembros. (págs. 160, 390)

dissociative disorders/trastornos disociativos Trastornos en los que el conocimiento conciente se separa (se disocia) de los recuerdos, pensamientos y sentimientos anteriores. (pág. 326)

dissociative identity disorder (DID)/trastorno de identidad disociativo (TID) Trastorno disociativo poco común, en el cual una persona experimenta dos o más personalidades claramente definidas que se alternan entre sí. También se denomina *trastorno de personalidad múltiple*. (pág. 326)

DNA (deoxyribonucleic acid)/ADN (ácido desoxirribonucleico) Molécula que contiene la información genética de la que se constituyen los cromosomas. (pág. 64)

double-blind procedure/procedimiento doble ciego Procedimiento en el cual tanto los participantes como el personal de investigación ignoran (van a ciegas) quién ha recibido el tratamiento y quién el placebo. (pág. 16)

dream/sueño Sucesión de imágenes, emociones y pensamientos que fluyen en la mente de una persona dormida. (pág. 56)

drive/impulso Estado interno de estimulación y motivación causado a menudo por la privación de una sustancia necesaria. (pág. 238)

drive-reduction theory/teoría de la reducción del impulso Idea que una necesidad fisiológica crea un estado de excitación (un impulso) que motiva al organismo a satisfacer esta necesidad. (pág. 238)

DSM-IV-TR/DSM-IV Manual estadístico y diagnóstico de trastornos mentales, *Cuarta edición*, sistema ampliamente utilizado para clasificar los trastornos psicológicos. (pág. 320)

dual processing/procesamiento dual Principio que sostiene que la información a menudo se procesa simultáneamente en vías separadas concientes e inconcientes. (pág. 7)

E

eclectic approach/aproximación ecléctica Enfoque de la psicoterapia que, dependiendo de los problemas del cliente, utiliza técnicas de distintas formas de terapia. (pág. 352)

Ecstasy (MDMA)/éxtasis (MDMA) Estimulante sintético y alucinógeno leve. Produce euforia e intimidad social, pero tiene riesgos de salud a corto plazo. Además, a largo plazo daña las neuronas que producen la serotonina, y afecta el ánimo y el proceso de cognición. (pág. 333)

EEG (electroencephalogram)/(EEG) electroencefalograma Aparato que emplea electrodos colocados sobre el cuero cabelludo y produce un registro de las ondas de actividad eléctrica que circulan por la superficie del cerebro. (El trazado de dichas ondas cerebrales es un *electroencefalograma*). (pág. 35)

effortful processing/procesamiento con esfuerzo Codificación que requiere atención y esfuerzo concientes. (pág. 183)

ego/ego Parte conciente y ejecutiva de la personalidad que, de acuerdo a Freud, media entre las demandas del id, el superego, y la realidad. El ego opera bajo el *principio de realidad*, satisfaciendo los deseos del id en formas que de manera realista le brindarán placer y no dolor. (pág. 295)

egocentrism/egocentrismo En la teoría de Piaget, la dificultad de los niños en la etapa preoperacional de aceptar el punto de vista ajeno. (pág. 73)

electroconvulsive therapy (ECT)/terapia electroconvulsiva (TEC) Terapia biomédica para pacientes severamente deprimidos en la que una corriente eléctrica de corta duración se envía a través del cerebro de un paciente anestesiado. (pág. 368)

embryo/embrión Etapa de desarrollo en el organismo humano a partir de las dos semanas de fertilización hasta el segundo mes. (pág. 66)

emerging adulthood/adultez emergente Etapa que se extiende desde los 18 hasta alrededor de los 25 años, durante la cual muchos individuos de los países occidentales ya no son adolescentes pero aún no han alcanzado la independencia plena de un adulto. (pág. 86)

emotion/emoción Reacción que involucra a todo el organismo, e incluye (1) excitación fisiológica, (2) comportamientos expresivos y (3) experiencia conciente. (pág. 252)

emotion-focused coping/superación con enfoque en las emociones Medidas para sobrellevar el estrés enfocadas en aliviar o ignorar una situación estresante y atender las necesidades emocionales relacionadas con nuestra reacción al estrés. (pág. 280)

emotional intelligence/inteligencia emocional Habilidad de percibir, entender, administrar y utilizar las emociones. (pág. 222)

encoding/codificación El procesar información al sistema de memoria. (pág. 182)

endocrine system/sistema endocrino Sistema "lento" de comunicación química del cuerpo; un conjunto de glándulas que secretan hormonas al torrente sanguíneo. (pág. 33)

endorphins/endorfinas "Morfina adentro"—neurotransmisores naturales similares a los opiatos que están asociados con el control del dolor y con el placer. (pág. 30)

environment/ambiente Toda influencia externa, desde la alimentación prenatal hasta el apoyo social que se recibe en la vejez. (pág. 65)

equity/equidad Condición en la cual las personas reciben de manera proporcional lo que aportan a una relación. (pág. 401)

estrogens/estrógenos Hormonas sexuales secretadas en mayor cantidad en la mujer que en el hombre. En las hembras de los animales mamíferos, los niveles de estrógeno alcanzan su nivel máximo durante la ovulación, facilitando la receptividad sexual. (pág. 107)

evolutionary psychology/psicología evolutiva   Estudio de la evolución del comportamiento y la mente, que emplea los principios de la selección natural para una adaptación efectiva. (pág. 116)

experiment/experimento   Método de investigación en el cual el investigador manipula uno o más factores (variables independientes) para observar su efecto en un comportamiento o proceso mental (variable dependiente). (pág. 15)

experimental group/grupo experimental   Sujetos de un experimento que están expuestos al tratamiento, o sea, a una versión de la variable independiente. (pág. 15)

explicit memory/memoria explícita   Memoria de hechos y experiencias personales que somos capaces de recuperar conscientemente. (pág. 185)

exposure therapies/terapias de exposición   Técnicas conductuales, como la *desensibilización sistemática*, y la *terapia de exposición a una realidad virtual* para tratar la ansiedad exponiendo a la persona (en situaciones imaginarias o reales) a las cosas que teme o evita. (pág. 356)

external locus of control/locus de control externo   Impresión de que nuestro destino está determinado por el azar o por fuerzas que están más allá de nuestro control. (pág. 282)

extinction/extinción   Según el condicionamiento clásico, disminución de una respuesta condicionada cuando un estímulo incondicionado no sigue a un estímulo condicionado. (En el condicionamiento operante, disminución de una respuesta cuando deja de ser reforzada). (pág. 159)

extrasensory perception (ESP)/percepción extrasensorial (PES)   Idea polémica que propone que la percepción ocurre por una vía distinta de la estimulación de los sentidos, por ejemplo, por *telepatía, clarividencia* y *precognición*. (pág. 150)

extrinsic motivation/motivación extrínseca   Deseo de realizar un comportamiento para obtener una recompensa o evitar un castigo. (pág. 172)

F

facial feedback effect/efecto de reacción facial   Tendencia de los músculos faciales a provocar sentimientos correspondientes como el miedo, el enojo o la felicidad. (pág. 262)

factor/factor   Conjunto de tendencias del comportamiento que ocurren al mismo tiempo. (pág. 303)

family therapy/terapia de familia   Tipo de terapia que trata a la familia como sistema y considera que los comportamientos no deseados del individuo son influenciados por otros miembros de la familia o dirigidos a ellos. (pág. 360)

feature detector/detector específico   Célula nerviosa del cerebro que responde a características específicas de un estímulo, por ejemplo, a bordes, líneas y ángulos. (pág. 132)

feel-good, do-good phenomenon/fenómeno de sentirse bien y hacer el bien   Tendencia a ayudar a los demás cuando estamos de buen humor. (pág. 264)

fetal alcohol syndrome (FAS)/síndrome de alcoholismo fetal (SAF)   Anomalías físicas y cognitivas en los niños causadas por la ingestión de alcohol de las madres durante el embarazo. En casos agudos, los síntomas incluyen desproporciones faciales observables. (pág. 66)

fetus/feto   Organismo humano en vías de desarrollo a partir de las 9 semanas de concepción hasta el nacimiento. (pág. 66)

fight-or-flight/respuesta de lucha o huida   Reacción de emergencia que incluye actividad del sistema nervioso simpático y genera energía y actividad dirigidas a atacar o escapar de una amenaza. (pág. 275)

figure-ground/figura-fondo   Organización del campo visual en objetos (*figuras*) que se distinguen de sus ambientes (*fondos*). (pág. 134)

fixation/fijación   (1) De acuerdo a Freud, un permanente foco de energía en busca de placer en una etapa psicosexual temprana cuando los conflictos todavía no estaban resueltos. (2) Incapacidad de ver un problema desde una perspectiva nueva; un impedimento para resolver problemas. (págs. 207, 296)

fixed-interval schedule/calendario de intervalo fijo   Según el condicionamiento operante, calendario refuerzo que refuerza la respuesta solo después de haber transcurrido un tiempo específico. (pág. 165)

fixed-ratio schedule/calendario de razón fija   Según el condicionamiento operante, calendario refuerzo que refuerza la respuesta solo después de un número específico de respuestas. (pág. 165)

flashbulb memory/memoria de flash   Memoria clara de un momento o evento emocionalmente significativo. (pág. 189)

flow/fluidez   Estado de total participación y concentración, con disminución de la conciencia de uno mismo y del tiempo, que ocurre cuando empleamos nuestras destrezas al máximo. (pág. 411)

fluid intelligence/inteligencia fluida   Capacidad que tenemos de razonar de manera rápida y abstracta; tiende a disminuir en la vejez. (pág. 92)

fMRI (functional magnetic resonance imaging)/(RMNf) imágenes de resonancia magnética funcional   Técnica para observar la circulación de la sangre, y por lo tanto, la actividad cerebral, que consiste en comparar sucesivas imágenes de resonancia magnética. Las imágenes de resonancia magnética funcional muestran el funcionamiento del cerebro. (pág. 35)

foot-in-the-door phenomenon/fenómeno de pie en la puerta   Tendencia de la gente que ha accedido a algo pequeño en primer lugar, a después satisfacer una demanda más grande. (pág. 380)

formal operational stage/período operacional formal   En la teoría de Piaget, el período en el desarrollo cognitivo (normalmente empieza a los 12 años) durante el que la persona empieza a pensar lógicamente sobre conceptos abstractos. (pág. 75)

framing/encuadre   Forma en que se presenta un asunto; el encuadre puede influenciar considerablemente las decisiones y las opiniones. (pág. 209)

fraternal twins/mellizos   Se desarrollan de dos óvulos fecundados distintos. Genéticamente no están más cercanos que los hermanos y hermanas; pero comparten un medio ambiente fetal. (pág. 66)

free association/asociación libre   En psicoanálisis, un método de explorar el inconciente en el que la persona se relaja y dice lo primero que le viene a la mente, no importa cuán trivial o incómodo. (pág. 294)

frequency/frecuencia   Número de ondas completas que pasan un punto en un tiempo dado (por ejemplo, por segundo). (pág. 140)

frontal lobes/lóbulos frontales   Porción de la corteza cerebral que se halla inmediatamente detrás de la frente; se relaciona con el habla y los movimientos musculares y con la planificación y la formación de opiniones. (pág. 40)

frustration-aggression principle/principio de frustración-agresión   Principio de que la frustración—el bloqueo de un intento para lograr alguna meta—crea ira, la cual puede generar agresión. (pág. 394)

fundamental attribution error/error fundamental de la atribución   Tendencia de los observadores, cuando analizan el comportamiento ajeno, a sobrestimar el impacto de las características personales y subestimar el impacto de la situación. (pág. 378)

G

gender/género En psicología, las características biológicas y sociales por las cuales la sociedad define *hombre y mujer*. (pág. 102)

gender identity/identidad de género Sensación personal de ser hombre o mujer. (pág. 106)

gender role/rol de género Expectativas de cómo las mujeres y los hombres deben comportarse. (pág. 105)

gender schema/esquema sexual Concepto culturalmente aprendido de lo que significa ser hombre y mujer. (pág. 106)

gender typing/tipificación sexual o de género Adopción de un papel masculino o femenino tradicional. (pág. 106)

general adaptation syndrome (GAS)/síndrome de adaptación general Término usado por Selye para la respuesta común del cuerpo al estrés que se da en tres etapas: alarma, resistencia, y agotamiento. (pág. 275)

general intelligence (g)/factor g de inteligencia general Factor de inteligencia general que de acuerdo a Spearman y otros subyace habilidades mentales específicas y es por lo tanto cuantificado por cada tarea de las pruebas de inteligencia. (pág. 219)

generalization/generalización Según el condicionamiento clásico, tendencia posterior al condicionamiento, de responder de manera similar a los estímulos que se parecen al estímulo condicionado. (pág. 160)

generalized anxiety disorder/trastorno de ansiedad generalizado Trastorno de ansiedad en el cual el individuo está constantemente tenso, asustado y con el sistema nervioso autónomo activado. (pág. 322)

genes/genes Unidades bioquímicas de la herencia que forman los cromosomas. Segmentos de ADN. (pág. 64)

genome/genoma Instrucciones completas para crear un organismo; consiste de todo el material genético en los cromosomas de ese organismo. (pág. 64)

gestalt/Gestalt Un todo organizado. Los psicólogos de la Gestalt ponen énfasis en nuestra tendencia a integrar segmentos de información en todos significativos. (pág. 134)

glucose/glucosa Forma de azúcar que circula en la sangre y provee de la mayor fuente de energía a los tejidos del cuerpo. Cuando su nivel es bajo, sentimos hambre. (pág. 241)

group polarization/efecto de polarización de grupo Solidificación y fortalecimiento de las posiciones imperantes en un grupo a través de discusiones del grupo. (pág. 388)

grouping/agrupamiento Tendencia de percepción que clasifica los estímulos en grupos que tienen sentido. (pág. 134)

groupthink/pensamiento del grupo Modo de pensar que ocurre cuando el deseo de armonía en un grupo de toma de decisiones anula la evaluación objetiva de las alternativas. (pág. 389)

H

hallucinations/alucinaciones Experiencias sensoriales falsas, por ejemplo, cuando una persona escucha algo sin recibir ningún estímulo auditivo externo. (pág. 42)

hallucinogens/alucinógenos Drogas psicodélicas ("que se manifiestan en la mente"), como el LSD, que distorsionan las percepciones y evocan imágenes sensoriales sin ninguna inducción sensorial. (pág. 334)

heredity/herencia Transferencia genética de características, de los padres a los hijos. (pág. 64)

heritability/heredabilidad Proporción de la variación entre individuos que es posible atribuir a los genes. La heredabilidad de un rasgo puede variar, según el número de poblaciones y ambientes que se estudien. (pág. 227)

heuristics/heurística Simples estrategias de pensamiento que nos permiten formar juicios y resolver problemas de manera eficiente. Normalmente son más rápidas que el utilizar *algoritmos*; pero también pueden conducir a más errores. (pág. 206)

hierarchy of needs/jerarquía de necesidades Pirámide de Maslow de las necesidades humanas. En la base de la pirámide están las necesidades fisiológicas, que deben satisfacerse antes que las necesidades de seguridad personal; las necesidades psicológicas se activan por último, después de satisfacer las anteriores. (págs. 238, 301)

hindsight bias/distorsión retrospectiva Tendencia a creer después de saber un resultado, que uno lo habría previsto. (También conocido como el *fenómeno de "ya yo lo sabía".*) (pág. 9)

hormones/hormonas Mensajeros químicos producidos por las glándulas endocrinas, que circulan por la sangre y tienen efecto en los tejidos del cuerpo. (pág. 33)

hue/tono Dimensión del color determinada por la longitud de onda de luz; lo que conocemos como los nombre de los colores: *azul, verde,* etc. (pág. 130)

human factors psychology/psicología de factores humanos División de la psicología industrial y organizacional que explora la interacción entre las personas y las máquinas y las maneras de hacer que las máquinas y los entornos físicos sean más seguros y fáciles de utilizar. (pág. 412)

humanistic psychology/psicología humanista Perspectiva que enfatiza el potencial de crecimiento de las personas sanas y la capacidad de crecimiento personal del individuo. (pág. 3)

hypnosis/hipnosis Interacción social en la cual una persona (el hipnotizador) sugiere a otra (el sujeto) que ciertas percepciones, sentimientos, pensamientos o comportamientos se producirán espontáneamente. (pág. 144)

hypothalamus/hipotálamo Estructura anterior localizada bajo (*hipo*) el tálamo; regula actividades como el comer, beber, y la temperatura del cuerpo; ayuda a dirigir el sistema endocrino a través de la glándula pituitaria; y está conectado a la emoción. (pág. 38)

hypothesis/hipótesis Predicción comprobable, a menudo implicada por una teoría. (pág. 11)

I

id/id Un depósito de energía psíquica inconciente que, según Freud, se esfuerza por satisfacer los impulsos sexuales y agresivos esenciales. El id opera bajo el *principio de placer,* exigiendo satisfacción inmediata. (pág. 294)

identical twins/gemelos Se desarrollan de un sólo huevo fertilizado que se parte en dos, creando dos organismos genéticamente idénticos. (pág. 66)

identification/identificación Proceso en el que, según Freud, los niños incorporan los valores de sus padres en sus súper-egos en vías de desarrollo. (pág. 296)

identity/identidad Sentido de uno mismo; de acuerdo con Erikson, la tarea del adolescente es de solidificar el sentido de sí mismo probando e integrando una variedad de roles. (pág. 84)

illusory correlation/correlación ilusoria Percepción de una relación donde no hay ninguna. (pág. 15)

imagery/imágenes mentales Imágenes de la mente; ayuda poderosa en el procesamiento esforzado, especialmente cuando se combina con la codificación de significados. (pág. 187)

implicit memory/memoria implícita   Retención de destrezas o condicionamientos aprendidos, que ocurre generalmente sin tener consciencia del aprendizaje. (pág. 185)

inattentional blindness/ceguera por falta de atención   El no ver los objetos visibles cuando nuestra atención se dirige a otra parte. (pág. 49)

incentive/incentivo   Estímulo positivo o negativo medioambiental que motiva el comportamiento. (pág. 238)

independent variable/variable independiente   Factor experimental que se manipula; la variable cuyo efecto es el objeto de estudio. (pág. 16)

individualism/individualismo   Manera de poner las metas personales antes que las metas del grupo y definir la identidad de acuerdo con las cualidades personales y no con la pertenencia al grupo. (pág. 312)

industrial-organizational (I/O) psychology/psicología industrial y organizacional   Aplicación de conceptos y métodos psicológicos al comportamiento humano en ambientes laborales. (pág. 412)

ingroup/endogrupo   "Nosotros"—personas con las que uno comparte una identidad común. (pág. 392)

ingroup bias/estereotipo de grupo propio   Tendencia a favorecer al grupo al que se pertenece. (pág. 392)

insight/agudeza   Entendimiento repentino de cómo se resuelve un problema; contrasta con las soluciones basadas en estrategias. (pág. 206)

insomnia/insomnio   Problemas recurrentes para dormir o quedarse dormido. (pág. 55)

intelligence/inteligencia   Calidad mental que consiste en la habilidad de aprender de la experiencia, resolver problemas y utilizar el conocimiento para adaptarse a nuevas situaciones. (pág. 219)

intelligence quotient (IQ)/coeficiente intelectual (CI)   Número definido originalmente como la edad mental (*em*) dividida entre la edad cronológica (*ec*) y el resultado multiplicado por 100 (por lo tanto, CI = *em/ec* × 100). En las pruebas actuales de inteligencia, el rendimiento promedio para una edad dada recibe un puntaje de 100. (pág. 224)

intelligence test/prueba de inteligencia   Método para evaluar las aptitudes mentales de un individuo y compararlas con las de otros utilizando puntajes numéricos. (pág. 223)

intensity/intensidad   Cantidad de energía en una onda de luz o en una onda sonora que percibimos como brillo o fuerza ,determinada por la amplitud de la onda. (pág. 130)

interaction//interacción   La interacción se produce cuando el efecto de un factor (por ejemplo, el ambiente) depende de otro factor (por ejemplo, la herencia). (pág. 65)

interference/teoría de interferencia   Bloqueo de un recuerdo cuando un aprendizaje anterior o uno nuevo perturba la memoria de otros recuerdos. (pág. 194)

internal locus of control/locus de control interno   Impresión de que controlamos nuestro propio destino. (pág. 282)

interneuron/interneurona   Neurona que procesa información entre la estimulación sensorial y las respuestas motoras. (pág. 31)

interpretation/interpretación   En psicoanálisis, las observaciones del analista con relación al significado de los sueños, las resistencias, y otros comportamientos y eventos significativos, a fin de promover la sagacidad. (pág. 353)

intimacy/intimidad   Según la teoría de Erikson, capacidad de formar relaciones cercanas y afectivas; tarea primordial del desarrollo al comienzo de la vida adulta. (pág. 85)

intrinsic motivation/motivación intrínseca   Deseo de comportarse de una manera por el comportamiento en sí. (pág. 171)

J

James-Lange theory/teoría de James-Lange   Teoría que nuestra experiencia emocional es nuestra conciencia de nuestras respuestas fisiológicas a los estímulos que despiertan nuestras emociones. (pág. 253)

just-world phenomenon/hipótesis del "mundo justo"   Tendencia a creer que el mundo es justo y que las personas consiguen lo que se merecen y se merecen lo que consiguen. (pág. 391)

K

kinesthesis/cinética   Sistema que siente la posición y el movimiento de las partes individuales de cuerpo. (pág. 147)

L

language/lenguaje   Palabras habladas, escritas o en señas y las maneras que se combinan para comunicar significado. (pág. 212)

latent content/contenido latente   Según Freud, significado subyacente de un sueño. (pág. 57)

latent learning/aprendizaje latente   Aprendizaje que no se demuestra hasta que aparece un incentivo para demostrarlo. (pág. 171)

learned helplessness/indefensión aprendida   Desesperación y resignación pasiva que un animal o un ser humano desarrollan cuando son incapaces de evitar repetidos eventos de aversión. (pág. 281)

learning/aprendizaje   Cambio relativamente permanente de comportamiento que resulta de la experiencia. (pág. 156)

limbic system/sistema límbico   Sistema de neuronas (incluye el *hipocampo*, la *amígdala* y el *hipotálamo*), ubicado debajo de los hemisferios cerebrales; se lo asocia con las emociones y los impulsos. (pág. 37)

lobotomy/lobotomía   Procedimiento psico-quirúrgico hoy en día inusual que se utilizó para calmar pacientes emocionalmente incontrolables o violentos. Este procedimiento separaba la conexión entre la corteza pre-frontal y el resto del cerebro. (pág. 370)

long-term memory/memoria a largo plazo   Tipo de memoria relativamente permanente que mantiene grandes cantidades de información. Incluye el conocimiento, habilidades, y experiencias. (pág. 182)

long-term potentiation (LTP)/potenciación a largo plazo   Aumento en la eficacia de una sinapsis para transmitir impulsos. Se considera la base nerviosa del aprendizaje y la memoria. (pág. 188)

LSD/ácido lisérgico   Poderosa droga alucinógena; también se conoce como *ácido* (*ácido lisérgico y dietilamina*). (pág. 334)

lymphocytes/linfocitos   Los dos tipos de glóbulos blancos que forman parte del sistema de inmunidad del organismo: los *linfocitos* B liberan anticuerpos que combaten las infecciones bacterianas; los *linfocitos* T atacan las células cancerosas, los virus y las substancias extrañas al cuerpo. (pág. 277)

M

major depressive disorder/trastorno depresivo mayor   Trastorno del estado de ánimo en el cual una persona —sin una condición médica y sin el uso de drogas— se siente deprimida, inútil y muestra poco interés o placer en la mayoría de las actividades por un período de por lo menos dos semanas. (pág. 338)

mania/manía   Trastorno del estado de ánimo marcado por una condición hiperactiva y desenfrenadamente optimista. (pág. 339)

manifest content/contenido manifiesto Según Freud, argumento del sueño que se recuerda al estar despierto. (pág. 57)

maturation/maduración Procesos de crecimiento biológico que permiten cambios ordenados en el comportamiento y son independientes de la experiencia. (pág. 70)

medical model/modelo médico Concepto que afirma que las enfermedades, en este caso los trastornos psicológicos, tienen causas físicas que se pueden diagnosticar, tratar y, en la mayoría de los casos, curar, generalmente por medio de tratamientos que se llevan a cabo en un hospital. (pág. 319)

medulla/médula Base del bulbo raquídeo; controla el latido del corazón y la respiración. (pág. 35)

memory trace/rastro de memoria Cambios físicos duraderos que ocurren en el cerebro al formarse un recuerdo. (pág. 194)

memory/memoria El aprender de manera persistente a través del tiempo usando almacenaje y recuperación de la información. (pág. 182)

menarche/menarquia Primer período menstrual. (pág. 81)

menopause/menopausia Cesación de la menstruación. En el uso diario, el término se refiere a la transición biológica que experimenta una mujer desde antes hasta después de acabar de menstruar. (pág. 90)

mental age/edad mental Medida de desempeño en pruebas de inteligencia diseñada por Bidet. La edad cronológica normalmente corresponde a un nivel dado de desempeño. Por ende, una criatura que se desempeña como una persona normal de 8 años, tiene una edad mental de 8 años. (pág. 223)

mere exposure effect/efecto de la mera exposición Fenómeno que sostiene que la exposición repetida a estímulos novedosos aumenta su atracción. (pág. 397)

methamphetamine/metanfetamina Droga poderosamente adictiva que estimula el sistema nervioso central con funciones corporales aceleradas y cambios de energía y estado de ánimo. Aparentemente, con el tiempo reduce los niveles mínimos de dopamina. (pág. 333)

mirror neuron/neurona espejo Neurona que se activa cuando se llevan a cabo ciertas acciones o se observa a otras personas realizar una actividad. (pág. 173)

mirror-image perceptions/percepciones idénticas Opiniones mutuas que generalmente sostienen las personas que discrepan o experimentan conflictos entre sí, como cuando cada parte se ve a sí misma como ética y pacifica y a la otra parte como maligna y agresiva. (pág. 404)

misinformation effect/efecto de información errónea Recuerdo que se deforma al recibir información engañosa. (pág. 196)

modeling/modelar Proceso de observar e imitar un comportamiento en particular. (pág. 172)

monocular cue/indicación monocular Señal de profundidad como la interposición y la perspectiva lineal, que puede ser extraídas de las imágenes de cada uno de los ojos. (pág. 136)

mood disorders/trastornos del estado de ánimo Trastornos psicológicos caracterizados por extremos de emociones. Ver *trastorno depresivo mayor, manía y trastorno bipolar*. (pág. 338)

mood-congruent memory/memoria congruente con el estado de ánimo Tendencia a recordar experiencias que concuerdan con el buen o mal estado de ánimo que estamos experimentando. (pág. 191)

motivation/motivación Necesidad o deseo que da energía y dirige el comportamiento. (pág. 238)

motor cortex/corteza motora Parte del cerebro en la parte posterior del lóbulo frontal, que controla los movimientos voluntarios. (pág. 40)

motor neuron/neurona motriz Neurona que lleva la información del sistema nervioso central hacia los músculos y glándulas. (pág. 31)

MRI (magnetic resonance imaging)/(RMN) imágenes de resonancia magnética Técnica que emplea campos magnéticos y ondas de radio para producir imágenes de tejidos blandos generadas por una computadora. Las imágenes de resonancia magnética nos permiten ver la anatomía cerebral. (pág. 35)

N

narcolepsy/narcolepsia Trastorno caracterizado por ataques incontrolables de sueño, en el que a veces el individuo entra directamente en el sueño MOR. (pág. 55)

natural selection/selección natural Proceso de adaptación; entre la variedad de rasgos heredados, aquellos que contribuyen al aumento de la reproducción y la supervivencia tienen mayor probabilidad de pasar a las generaciones futuras. (pág. 116)

naturalistic observation/observación naturalista El observar y registrar la conducta en situaciones reales sin tratar de manipular y controlar la situación. (pág. 13)

nature-nurture issue/debate naturaleza-crianza Antigua controversia acerca del aporte relativo que ejercen los genes y la experiencia en el desarrollo de los rasgos y comportamientos psicológicos. La ciencia psicológica actual opina que los rasgos y comportamientos tienen origen en la interrelación entre la naturaleza y la crianza. (pág. 6)

near-death experience/experiencia al borde de la muerte Estado de alteración experimentado por personas que llegan al borde de la muerte, o que parecen morir pero luego retornan a la vida (por ejemplo, cuando uno sufre un paro cardíaco). Son similares a las alucinaciones inducidas por las drogas. (pág. 334)

negative reinforcement/reforzamiento negativo Aumento en la expresión de comportamientos mediante la interrupción o reducción de estímulos negativos tales como golpes de corriente. Un reforzamiento negativo es cualquier cosa que, *eliminada* después de una respuesta, refuerza la respuesta. (Nota: reforzamiento negativo *no significa* castigo). (pág. 163)

nerves/nervios Haces de axones neuronales que forman "cables" de nervios y conectan el sistema nervioso central con los músculos, las glándulas y los órganos sensoriales. (pág. 31)

nervous system/sistema nervioso Veloz red electroquímica de comunicación del cuerpo que consiste de todas las células nerviosas del sistema periférico y del sistema nervioso central. (pág. 31)

neurogenesis/neurogénesis Formación de neuronas nuevas. (pág. 45)

neuron/neurona Célula nerviosa; el componente básico del sistema nervioso. (pág. 28)

neurotransmitters/neurotransmisores Químicos producidos por las neuronas que atraviesan las sinapsis y transmiten mensajes a otras neuronas o a las células del cuerpo. (pág. 29)

neutral stimulus (NS)/estímulos neutrales (EN) Según el condicionamiento clásico, un estímulo que no produce respuesta antes del condicionamiento. (pág. 158)

nicotine/nicotina Droga estimulante, altamente adictiva y psicoactiva que se halla en el tabaco. (pág. 332)

normal curve/curva normal Curva simétrica y en forma de campana que describe la distribución de muchos atributos físicos y psicológicos. La mayoría de los puntajes están cerca del promedio, disminuyendo en número conforme se acercan a los extremos. (pág. 224)

O

object permanence/permanencia de objeto Conocimiento que las cosas existen aunque no las veamos. (pág. 73)

observational learning/aprendizaje observacional El aprender observando a otros. (pág. 172)

obsessive-compulsive disorder (OCD)/trastorno obsesivo-compulsivo (TOC) Trastorno de ansiedad caracterizado por pensamientos repetitivos no deseados (obsesiones) y/o acciones (compulsiones). (pág. 323)

occipital lobes/lóbulos occipitales Porción de la corteza cerebral ubicada en la parte posterior de la cabeza; incluye las áreas que reciben información de los campos visuales. (pág. 40)

Oedipus complex/complejo de Edipo Según Freud, los deseos sexuales de un muchacho hacia su madre y sentimientos de celos y odio para el padre rival. (pág. 296)

one-word stage/etapa holofrástica Etapa en el desarrollo del habla, entre 1 y 2 años, en la que el niño se expresa principalmente en palabras aisladas. (pág. 213)

operant behavior/comportamiento operante Comportamiento que opera en el ambiente, produciendo consecuencias. (pág. 168)

operant chamber/cámara operante Caja con un aparato de grabación que registra la frecuencia con la que un animal dentro de la misma presiona una barra para obtener un refuerzo. Se emplea en experimentos de condicionamiento operante. (También se conoce como *caja de Skinner*). (pág. 162)

operant conditioning/condicionamiento operante Aprendizaje donde el comportamiento se consolida si está seguido por un refuerzo o se atenúa si está seguido por un castigo. (pág. 162)

operational definition/definición operacional Manifestación de los procedimientos (operaciones) utilizadas para definir las variables de investigación. Por ejemplo, la *inteligencia humana* puede ser operacionalmente definida como lo que mide una prueba de inteligencia. (pág. 11)

opiates/opiáceos El opio y sus derivados, como la morfina y la heroína, que deprimen la actividad neuronal y alivian temporalmente el dolor y la ansiedad. (págs. 30, 331)

optic nerve/nervio óptico Nervio que transporta los impulsos neuronales del ojo al cerebro. (pág. 130)

optimism/optimismo Anticipación de resultados positivos. Son optimistas las personas que esperan lo mejor y creen que sus esfuerzos conducen a obtener buenos resultados. (pág. 283)

organizational psychology/psicología organizacional Subdivisión de la psicología industrial y organizacional que examina las influencias organizacionales en la satisfacción y productividad de los trabajadores, y facilita cambios organizacionales. (pág. 412)

other-race effect/efecto de otras razas Tendencia a recordar caras de la raza de uno mismo con mayor precisión que las caras de otras razas. (pág. 393)

outgroup/grupo ajeno "Ellos", o sea, las personas a las que percibimos como distintas o separadas de nuestro grupo. (pág. 392)

overconfidence/exceso de confianza Tendencia a ser más confiado que acertado, o sea, a sobreestimar las creencias y las opiniones propias. (pág. 209)

P

panic disorder/trastorno de pánico Trastorno de ansiedad marcado por el inicio repentino y recurrente de episodios de aprehensión intensa o terror que pueden durar varios minutos. Incluyen dolor de pecho, sofocamiento, y otras sensaciones atemorizantes. (pág. 323)

parallel processing/procesamiento paralelo Procesamiento de varias partes de un problema o escena a la vez; modo natural del cerebro de procesar la información de varias funciones, incluida la visión. (pág. 132)

parasympathetic nervous system/sistema nervioso autonómico parasimpático División del sistema nervioso autonómico que calma el cuerpo conservando su energía. (pág. 31)

parietal lobes/lóbulos parietales Área de la corteza cerebral en la parte superior y hacia la parte posterior de la cabeza que recibe suministro sensorial para el tacto y la posición del cuerpo. (pág. 40)

partial (intermittent) reinforcement/refuerzo parcial (intermitente) Refuerzo a una respuesta sólo parte del tiempo; tiene como resultado la adquisición más lenta de una respuesta pero mucho más resistente a la extinción que el refuerzo continuo. (pág. 164)

passionate love/amor apasionado Estado excitado de intensa y positiva absorción en otro ser, normalmente presente al comienzo de una relación amorosa. (pág. 401)

perception/percepción Proceso mediante el cual el cerebro organiza e interpreta la información sensorial transformándola en objetos y sucesos que tienen sentido. (pág. 124)

perceptual adaptation/adaptación visual Habilidad de acomodarnos a un campo visual artificialmente desplazado o hasta invertido. (pág. 138)

perceptual constancy/constancia perceptiva Tendencia a percibir objetos como si fueran constantes e inalterables (como si mantuvieran el color, el brillo, la forma y el tamaño), a pesar de los cambios que se produzcan en la iluminación y las imágenes de la retina. (pág. 137)

perceptual set/predisposición perceptiva Predisposición mental para percibir una cosa y no otra. (pág. 127)

peripheral nervous system (PNS)/sistema nervioso periférico (SNP) Neuronas sensoriales y motrices conectando el sistema nervioso central al resto del cuerpo. (pág. 31)

personal control/control personal Nuestro sentido de controlar nuestro ambiente en lugar de sentirnos impotentes. (pág. 281)

personality/personalidad Forma característica de pensar, sentir y actuar de un individuo. (pág. 292)

personality disorders/trastornos de la personalidad Trastornos psicológicos caracterizados por modelos de comportamiento inflexibles y duraderos que impiden el funcionamiento social. (pág. 327)

personnel psychology/psicología de personal Subdivisión de la psicología industrial y organizacional, que se encarga de la selección, ubicación, capacitación y evaluación de los empleados. (pág. 412)

pessimism/pesimismo Anticipación de resultados negativos. Son pesimistas las personas que esperan lo peor y dudan de que sus metas se cumplirán. (pág. 283)

PET (positron emission tomography) scan/(TEP) tomografía por emisión de positrones Muestra visual de la actividad cerebral que detecta por dónde va un tipo de glucosa radiactiva en el momento en que el cerebro realiza una función en particular. (pág. 35)

phobia/fobia Trastorno de ansiedad marcado por un temor persistente e irracional y la evasión de un objeto o situación específicos. (pág. 323)

physical dependence/dependencia física Necesidad fisiológica de una droga, demostrada por un desagradable síndrome de abstinencia cuando se corta el suministro. (pág. 329)

physiological need/necesidad fisiológica Requerimiento básico del cuerpo. (pág. 238)

pitch/tono Propiedad de los sonidos que los caracteriza como agudos o graves, en función de su frecuencia (pág. 140)

pituitary gland/glándula pituitaria Glándula más influyente del sistema endocrino. Bajo la influencia del hipotálamo, la pituitaria regula el crecimiento y controla otras glándulas endocrinas. (pág. 34)

placebo/placebo [En latín significa "yo complaceré"] Substancia o condición inactiva que a veces se suministra a los miembros de un grupo de control en lugar del tratamiento que se da al grupo experimental. (pág. 16)

placebo effect/efecto placebo Resultados producidos únicamente por las expectativas. (pág. 16)

plasticity/plasticidad Capacidad del cerebro de modificarse, especialmente en los niños, reordenándose después de un daño cerebral o formando nuevas vías basadas en la experiencia. (pág. 45)

polygraph/detector de mentiras Máquina que se emplea comúnmente como medio para detectar mentiras y mide varias de las respuestas fisiológicas que acompañan las emociones (tales como los cambios en la transpiración, el ritmo cardíaco y la respiración). (pág. 257)

positive psychology/psicología positiva Estudio científico del funcionamiento humano, que tiene las metas de descubrir y promover la fortaleza y las virtudes que ayudan a los individuos y las comunidades a prosperar. (pág. 8)

positive reinforcement/reforzamiento positivo Aumento en la expresión de comportamientos mediante la presentación de estímulos positivos, por ejemplo, un alimento. Un reforzamiento positivo es cualquier cosa que, *presentada* después de una respuesta, refuerza la respuesta. (pág. 163)

post-traumatic stress disorder (PTSD)/trastorno de estrés post-traumático (TEPT) Trastorno de ansiedad caracterizado por recuerdos obsesionantes, pesadillas, aislamiento social, ansiedad asustadiza, y/o insomnio que dura por cuatro semanas o más después de una experiencia traumática. (pág. 324)

prejudice/prejuicio Actitud injustificable (y normalmente negativa) hacia un grupo y sus miembros. El prejuicio generalmente implica creencias estereotipadas, sentimientos negativos y una predisposición a acción discriminatoria. (pág. 390)

preoperational stage/etapa preoperacional En la teoría de Piaget, la etapa (desde los 2 hasta los 6 ó 7 años) durante la que el niño aprende a utilizar el lenguaje; pero todavía no comprende las operaciones mentales de lógica concreta. (pág. 73)

primary reinforcer/reforzador primario Suceso que es inherentemente reforzador y a menudo satisface una necesidad biológica. (pág. 164)

priming/preparación Activación de asociaciones en nuestra mente, que es a menudo inconsciente y nos dispone a percibir o recordar objetos o sucesos de una manera determinada. (pág. 125)

problem-focused coping/superación con enfoque en los problemas Intento de sobrellevar el estrés de manera directa cambiando ya sea la situación estresante o la forma en que nos relacionamos con dicha situación. (pág. 280)

projective test/prueba de proyección Tipo de prueba de la personalidad, como la prueba de Rorschach, en la cual se proporciona a un individuo una imagen ambigua diseñada para provocar una proyección de pensamientos o sentimientos inconscientes. (pág. 298)

prosocial behavior/comportamiento prosocial Comportamiento positivo, constructivo, útil. Lo contrario del comportamiento antisocial. (pág. 174)

psychoactive drug/droga psicoactiva Sustancia química que altera las percepciones y el humor. (pág. 329)

psychoanalysis/psicoanálisis (1) Teoría de la personalidad de Freud que atribuye los pensamientos y acciones a los motivos y conflictos inconcientes. (2) Técnica terapéutica que utilizó Freud en tratamientos de trastornos psicológicos. Freud creía que las asociaciones libres del paciente, las resistencias, los sueños y la transferencia —y las interpretaciones del terapeuta sobre ellos— liberaban los sentimientos previamente reprimidos, permitiendo al paciente ganar introspección. (págs. 294, 352)

psychodynamic theory/teoría psicodinámica Perspectiva de influencia freudiana que considera que la conducta, el pensamiento y las emociones están basados en motivos inconscientes. (pág. 297)

psychodynamic therapy/terapia psicodinámica Perspectiva de influencia freudiana que considera que la conducta, el pensamiento y las emociones en términos de motivos inconscientes. (pág. 353)

psychological dependence/dependencia psicológica Necesidad psicológica de utilizar una droga, como para aliviar las emociones negativas. (pág. 329)

psychological disorder/trastorno psicológico Pensamientos, sentimientos o comportamientos desviados (anormales), angustiantes y disfuncionales. (pág. 318)

psychology/psicología Estudio científico del comportamiento y de los procesos mentales. (pág. 3)

psychoneuroimmunology (PNI)/psiconeuroinmunología (PNI) Estudio de cómo se combinan en nuestro organismo los procesos psicológicos y las funciones del sistema nervioso y endocrino para influenciar el sistema de inmunidad y la salud en general. (pág. 277)

psychosexual stages/etapas psicosexuales Etapas del desarrollo infantil según Freud (oral, anal, fálica, latente, genital), durante las cuales la energía del id en busca de placer se enfoca en zonas erógenas específicas (pág. 295)

psychosurgery/psicocirugía Cirugía que remueve o destruye tejido cerebral para cambiar el comportamiento. (pág. 370)

psychotherapy/psicoterapia Tratamiento que consiste en la interacción entre un terapeuta calificado y una persona que desea superar dificultades psicológicas o lograr un crecimiento personal, mediante técnicas psicológicas. (pág. 352)

puberty/pubertad Período de maduración sexual durante el cual una persona adquiere la capacidad de reproducirse. (pág. 81)

punishment/castigo Evento que disminuye el comportamiento que le precede. (pág. 165)

R

random assignment/asignación aleatoria Asignación de participantes a grupos de control y experimentales, que se realiza al azar para minimizar las diferencias que hubiere entre los asignados. (pág. 15)

random sample/muestra aleatoria Muestra en la que cada elemento de la población tiene igual oportunidad de ser seleccionado. (pág. 12)

recall/recordación Memoria que se demuestra recuperando información aprendida anteriormente, tal como en las pruebas que consisten en completar espacios en blanco. (pág. 189)

reciprocal determinism/determinismo recíproco Influencias de la interacción entre la conducta, los factores internos de la personalidad y el ambiente. (pág. 308)

recognition/reconocimiento Memoria que se demuestra identificando cosas que se aprendieron anteriormente, tal como en las pruebas de escogencia múltiple. (pág. 189)

reflex/reflejo Respuesta no aprendida y automática a un estímulo sensorial. (pág. 67)

refractory period/período refractario Fase de descanso después del orgasmo, en la que un hombre no es capaz de tener otro orgasmo. (pág. 108)

rehearsal/ensayo Repetición conciente de información ya sea para mantenerla concientemente o para codificarla para almacenamiento. (pág. 183)

reinforcement/reforzamiento Según el condicionamiento operante, todo suceso que *fortalece* el comportamiento al que sigue. (pág. 162)

reinforcement schedule/plan de refuerzo Patrón que define la frecuencia con que se reforzará una respuesta deseada. (pág. 164)

relative deprivation/privación relativa Impresión de que estamos en peor situación que aquellos con quienes nos comparamos. (pág. 267)

relearning/reaprendizaje Memoria que se demuestra por el tiempo que se ahorra cuando se aprende un material por segunda vez. (pág. 189)

reliability/confiabilidad Grado en el que una prueba produce resultados consistentes, comprobados por la consistencia en puntajes en dos mitades de la prueba, en formas alternas de la prueba, o al retomar la prueba. (pág. 225)

REM rebound/rebote de MOR Aumento marcado del sueño REM como consecuencia de la privación del sueño MOR (producida por despertares repetidos durante el sueño MOR). (pág. 58)

REM (rapid eye movement) sleep/sueño MOR (movimiento ocular rápido) Etapa recurrente del sueño en la cual generalmente ocurren sueños vívidos. También se conoce como *sueño paradójico* porque los músculos están relajados (excepto por unos temblores mínimos) pero los demás sistemas del cuerpo están activos. (pág. 51)

repetitive transcranial magnetic stimulation (rTMS)/estimulación magnética transcraneal repetitiva (EMTr) Aplicación repetitiva de pulsos de energía magnética al cerebro; utilizado para estimular o suprimir la actividad cerebral. (pág. 370)

replication/replicación El repetir la esencia de un estudio de investigación, usualmente con diferentes participantes y en diferentes situaciones para ver si las conclusiones básicas se extienden a otros participantes y circunstancias. (pág. 11)

repression/represión En la teoría psicoanalítica, el mecanismo básico de defensa por medio del cual el sujeto elimina de su conciente aquellos pensamientos, emociones o recuerdos que le producen ansiedad. (págs. 195, 296)

resilience/resiliencia Fuerza personal que ayuda a la mayoría de las personas a lidiar con el estrés y recuperarse de la adversidad e inclcuso de un trauma. (pág. 371)

resistance/resistencia En psicoanálisis, el bloquear del conciente aquello que está cargado de ansiedad. (pág. 353)

respondent behavior/comportamiento de respuesta Comportamiento que ocurre como respuesta automática a un estímulo. (pág. 168)

reticular formation/formación reticular Red de nervios en el bulbo raquídeo que juega un papel importante en el control de la excitación. (pág. 36)

retina/retina Superficie sensitiva a la luz en la parte interior del ojo que contiene los receptores de luz llamados bastoncillos y conos además de capas de neuronas que inician el procesamiento de la información visual. (pág. 130)

retinal disparity/disparidad retiniana Clave binocular para la percepción de la profundidad Mediante la comparación de las imágenes que provienen de los dos ojos, el cerebro calcula la distancia. Cuanto mayor sea la disparidad (diferencia) entre dos imágenes, más cerca se verá el objeto. (pág. 135)

retrieval/recuperación Acto de sacar la información que está almacenada en la memoria. (pág. 182)

retrieval cue/clave de recuperación Todo estímulo (suceso, sentimiento, lugar, etc.) relacionado con un recuerdo específico. (pág. 190)

rods/bastoncillos Receptores de la retina que detectan el negro, blanco y gris; necesarios para la visión periférica y en la penumbra cuando los conos no responden. (pág. 130)

role/rol Conjunto de expectativas acerca de una posición social, que definen la forma en que deben comportarse las personas que ocupan esa posición. (págs. 105, 380)

Rorschach inkblot test/test de Rorschach Prueba proyectiva de amplio uso, un conjunto de 10 manchas de tinta, diseñado por Hermann Rorschach; busca identificar los sentimientos internos de las personas analizando sus interpretaciones de las manchas. (pág. 298)

S

savant syndrome/síndrome de savant Condición según la cual una persona de habilidad mental limitada, tiene una destreza excepcional en un campo como la computación o el dibujo. (pág. 219)

scapegoat theory/teoría del chivo expiatorio Teoría de que el prejuicio ofrece un escape para la cólera porque nos brinda a alguien a quien culpar. (pág. 392)

schema/esquema Concepto o principio que organiza e interpreta la información. (pág. 72)

schizophrenia/esquizofrenia Grupo de trastornos severos caracterizados por un pensamiento desorganizado y delirante, percepciones ofuscadas, así como emociones y acciones impropias. (pág. 343)

selective attention/atención selectiva Capacidad de enfocar la consciencia en un estímulo en particular. (pág. 49)

self/yo Imagen que tenemos de nosotros mismos y entendimiento de quiénes somos. Según la psicología moderna, centro de la personalidad, de la organización de los pensamientos, sentimientos y acciones. (pág. 309)

self-actualization/autorrealización Según Maslow, necesidad psicológica que surge después de satisfacer las necesidades físicas y psicológicas y de lograr la autoestima; motivación para realizar nuestro potencial. (pág. 301)

self-concept/concepto de uno mismo Todo lo que pensamos y sentimos acerca de nosotros mismos cuando respondemos a la pregunta: "¿Quién soy?". (pág. 302)

self-disclosure/revelación de uno mismo Revelación a los demás de cosas que consideramos íntimas. (pág. 402)

self-esteem/autoestima Sentimientos de alto o bajo valor con los que nos valoramos a nosotros mismos. (pág. 310)

self-serving bias/parcialidad interesada Disposición para percibirnos a nosotros mismos favorablemente. (pág. 311)

self-transcendence/autotrascendencia Según Maslow, esfuerzo por alcanzar una identidad, un sentido y un propósito que vaya más allá de uno mismo. (pág. 301)

sensation/sensación Proceso mediante el cual los receptores sensoriales y el sistema nervioso reciben las energías de los estímulos de nuestro ambiente. (pág. 124)

sensorimotor stage/etapa sensorio-motriz En la teoría de Piaget, la etapa (0–2 años) durante la que los infantes conocen el mundo principalmente en términos de sus impresiones sensoriales y actividades motoras. (pág. 72)

sensory adaptation/adaptación sensorial Disminución en la sensibilidad como respuesta a la estimulación constante. (pág. 126)

sensory cortex/corteza sensorial Área de la parte frontal de los lóbulos parietales que registra y procesa las sensaciones de tacto y movimiento del cuerpo. (pág. 41)

sensory interaction/interacción sensorial Principio que un sentido puede influir a otro, como cuando el olor de la comida influye en su sabor. (pág. 146)

sensory memory/memoria sensorial Registro breve e inmediato de la información sensorial en el sistema de la memoria. (pág. 182)

sensory neuron/neurona sensorial Neurona que recibe la información relacionada con las sensaciones, de los receptores la transportan al sistema nervioso central. (pág. 31)

serial position effect/efecto de posición serial Tendencia a recordar los elementos del comienzo y el final de una lista con mayor facilidad. (pág. 184)

set point/punto fijo Punto de equilibrio en el "termostato del peso" de un individuo. Cuando el cuerpo llega a un peso debajo de este punto, se produce un aumento en el hambre y una disminución en el índice metabólico, los cuales pueden actuar para restablecer el peso perdido. (pág. 241)

sexual orientation/orientación sexual Atracción sexual duradera hacia miembros de nuestro mismo sexo (orientación homosexual) o del sexo opuesto (orientación heterosexual). (pág. 112)

sexual response cycle/ciclo de respuesta sexual Las cuatro etapas de respuesta sexual descritas por Masters y Johnson—excitación, meseta, orgasmo y resolución. (pág. 108)

shaping/modelamiento Procedimiento del condicionamiento operante en el cual los reforzadores conducen una acción con aproximaciones sucesivas hasta lograr un comportamiento deseado. (pág. 162)

short-term memory/memoria a corto plazo Memoria activada que retiene algunos elementos por un corto tiempo, tales como los siete dígitos de un número telefónico mientras se marca, antes que la información se almacene o se olvide. (pág. 182)

sleep/sueño Pérdida reversible del conocimiento que es periódica y natural. Esto es distinto de la inconsciencia que puede resultar del estado de coma, anestesia general, o hibernación. (Adaptado de Dement, 1999.) (pág. 51)

sleep apnea/apnea del sueño Trastorno del sueño en el que se interrumpe repetidamente la respiración hasta tal punto que el oxígeno en sangre llega a ser tan poco que la persona tiene que despertarse para respirar. (pág. 55)

social clock/reloj social Manera que la sociedad tiene de marcar el tiempo adecuado de los eventos sociales, tales como matrimonio, paternidad y jubilación. (pág. 94)

social facilitation/facilitación social Respuestas más fuertes a las tareas simples o bien aprendidas en la presencia de otros. (pág. 386)

social identity/identidad social Aspecto "nostros" del concepto de nosotros mismos; parte de nuestra respuesta a "¿Quién soy?" que proviene de nuestra pertenencia a grupos. (pág. 84)

social leadership/liderazgo social Liderazgo orientado hacia el grupo que construye trabajo en grupo, media en el conflicto y ofrece apoyo. (pág. 416)

social learning theory/teoría de aprendizaje social Teoría que aprendemos la conducta social observando e imitando y al ser recompensados o castigados. (pág. 106)

social loafing/haraganería social Tendencia de las personas en un grupo de realizar menos esfuerzo cuando juntan sus esfuerzos para lograr una meta común que cuando son responsables individualmente. (pág. 387)

social psychology/psicología social Estudio científico de comó pensamos, influimos y nos relacionamos con los otros. (pág. 378)

social script/guión social Guías modeladas culturalmente acerca de cómo actuar en diversas situaciones. (pág. 395)

social-cognitive perspective/perspectiva socio-cognoscitiva Ve la conducta como influida por la interacción entre los individuos (y sus pensamientos) y su contexto social. (pág. 307)

somatic nervous system/sistema nervioso somático División del sistema nervioso periférico que controla los músculos del esqueleto. También llamado *sistema nervioso del esqueleto*. (pág. 31)

source amnesia/amnesia de la fuente Situación en la que relacionamos una fuente equivocada con un suceso que hemos vivido, leído o imaginado, o del cual nos hemos enterado. (pág. 197)

spacing effect/efecto del aprendizaje espaciado Tendencia a que el estudio o práctica distribuidos logren mejor retención a largo plazo que la que se logra a través de estudio o prácticas masivas. (pág. 184)

split brain/cerebro dividido Condición en la que los dos hemisferios cerebrales se privan de la comunicación mediante el corte de las fibras que los conectan (principalmente las del cuerpo calloso). (pág. 46)

spontaneous recovery/recuperación espontánea Reaparición, después de una pausa, de una respuesta condicionada extinguida. (pág. 159)

spotlight effect/efecto reflector Sobreestimación de lo que los demás advierten y evalúan de nuestra apariencia, desempeño y desatinos (como si estuviéramos apuntados por un reflector). (pág. 310)

SQ3R/inspeccionar, preguntar, leer, recitar, repasar Método de estudio en el que se siguen los pasos de inspeccionar, preguntar, leer, recitar y repasar. (pág. 22)

standardization/estandarización El definir puntajes significativos mediante la comparación del desempeño de un grupo examinado con anterioridad. (pág. 224)

Stanford-Binet/Stanford-Binet Revisión (por Terman en la Universidad de Stanford) de la prueba original de inteligencia de Binet. Esta prueba revisada es usada extensamente. (pág. 224)

stereotype/estereotipo Creencia (a veces acertada; pero frecuentemente demasiado generalizada) sobre las características de un grupo. (pág. 390)

stereotype threat/amenaza de estereotipos Preocupación autoconfirmada de que seremos evaluados en base a un estereotipo negativo. (pág. 232)

stimulants/estimulantes Drogas (como cafeína, nicotina y las anfetaminas más poderosas, cocaína y éxtasis) que excitan la actividad neuronal y aceleran las funciones corporales. (pág. 332)

stimulus/estímulo Todo suceso o situación que provoca una respuesta. (pág. 156)

storage/almacenamiento Retención a través del tiempo de información codificada. (pág. 182)

stranger anxiety/miedo a los extraños Miedo a los extraños que los infantes normalmente expresan a partir de los 8 meses. (pág. 75)

stress/estrés Proceso a través del cual percibimos y respondemos a ciertos eventos llamados *estresores*, los cuales evaluamos como amenazantes o desafiantes. (pág. 274)

subjective well-being/bienestar subjetivo   Felicidad o satisfacción con la vida de uno mismo. Se emplea junto con medidas de bienestar objetivo (por ejemplo, con indicadores físicos y económicos) para evaluar nuestra calidad de vida. (pág. 265)

subliminal/subliminal   Aquello que ocurre por debajo de nuestro umbral absoluto de consciencia. (pág. 124)

substance-related disorders/trastornos causados por el abuso de sustancias adictivas   Patrón desequilibrado de consumo de una sustancia que resulta en aflicciones o daños clínicos significativos. (pág. 329)

superego/superyó   Según Freud, componente de la personalidad que representa ideales internalizados y proporciona parámetros de juicio (el consciente). (pág. 295)

superordinate goals/metas comunes   Metas compartidas que hacen caso omiso de las diferencias entre las personas y que requieren su cooperación. (pág. 405)

survey/encuesta   Técnica para verificar las actitudes o conductas reportadas por las personas; usualmente se pregunta a una muestra aleatoria y representativa. (pág. 12)

sympathetic nervous system/sistema nervioso simpático   División del sistema nervioso autonómico que en situaciones estresantes despierta al cuerpo y moviliza su energía. (pág. 31)

synapse/sinapsis   Intersección entre el extremo del axón de una neurona que envía un mensaje y la dendrita o cuerpo celular de la neurona receptora. (pág. 28)

systematic desensitization/desensibilización sistemática   Tipo de terapia de exposición en la cual se asocia un estado tranquilo y agradable con estímulos que provocan ansiedad y que se aplican de manera gradual y en aumento. Se emplea comúnmente para tratar fobias. (pág. 356)

T

task leadership/liderazgo específico   Liderazgo orientado a metas específicas que establece las normas, organiza el trabajo y centra la atención en metas. (pág. 416)

telegraphic speech/habla telegráfica   Etapa del habla de un niño, que tiene forma de telegrama y está formada mayormente por sustantivos y verbos; por ejemplo, "voy carro". (pág. 213)

temperament/temperamento   Característica de reactividad emocional e intensidad de una persona. (pág. 68)

temporal lobes/lóbulos temporales   Porción de la corteza cerebral ubicada más o menos encima de las orejas; incluye las áreas que reciben información de los oídos. (pág. 40)

tend and befriend/cuidar y amigarse   En situaciones de estrés, las personas (especialmente las mujeres) generalmente proporcionan apoyo y cuidan a los demás (*cuidar*), a la vez que forman vínculos y buscan apoyo de los demás (*amigarse*). (pág. 276)

teratogen/teratógenos   Agentes químicos o virales que pueden afectar al embrión o al feto durante el desarrollo prenatal y causarle daño. (pág. 66)

testosterone/testosterona   Principal hormona sexual masculina. Estimula el crecimiento de los órganos sexuales masculinos en el feto y el desarrollo de las características sexuales masculinas secundarias durante la pubertad. Las mujeres tienen menores cantidades de testosterona. (pág. 104)

thalamus/tálamo   Área ubicada encima del tronco cerebral; dirige mensajes sensoriales a la corteza cerebral y transmite respuestas al cerebelo y la médula oblonga. (pág. 36)

THC/THC   Principal sustancia activa encontrada en la marihuana, produce distintos efectos incluyendo alucinaciones leves. (pág. 334)

theory/teoría   Explicación que emplea un conjunto de principios integrados, organiza observaciones y predice comportamientos o sucesos. (pág. 11)

theory of mind/teoría de la mente   Ideas que tienen las personas acerca de sus propios procesos mentales y los de los demás; es decir, de sus sentimientos, percepciones y pensamientos y los comportamientos que éstos podrían predecir. (pág. 74)

threshold/umbral   Nivel de estímulo requerido para activar un impulso neuronal. (pág. 29)

token economy/economía de fichas   Procedimiento conductual en el cual los individuos ganan una ficha cuando exhiben un comportamiento deseado y luego pueden intercambiar las fichas ganadas por privilegios o para darse algún gusto. (pág. 358)

tolerance/tolerancia   Efecto decreciente de la misma dosis de una droga después de un tiempo de uso, requiriendo que el usuario aumente la dosis para poder experimentar el efecto de la droga. (pág. 329)

trait/rasgo   Patrón de comportamiento característico o disposición a sentirse y actuar de cierta forma, según se evalúa en los autoinformes de una prueba de la personalidad. (pág. 303)

transduction/transducción   Transformación de un tipo de energía en otro. En las sensaciones, transformación de la energía de los estímulos, como las imágenes, los sonidos y los olores, en impulsos nerviosos que el cerebro es capaz de interpretar. (pág. 124)

transference/transferencia   En el psicoanálisis, la transferencia de emociones ligadas a otras relaciones, del paciente al analista (como el amor u odio hacia uno de los padres). (pág. 353)

two-factor theory/teoría de los dos factores   Teoría de Schachter y Singer que propone que para experimentar emociones debemos (1) recibir estimulación física y (2) identificar el estímulo a nivel cognitivo. (pág. 253)

two-word stage/etapa de dos palabras   A partir de los 2 años, etapa del desarrollo del lenguaje durante la cual el niño emite mayormente frases de dos palabras. (pág. 213)

Type A/Tipo A   Término de Friedman y Rosenman para las personas competitivas, compulsivas, impacientes, verbalmente agresivas y con tendencia a enojarse. (pág. 279)

Type B/Tipo B   Término de Friedman y Rosenman para las personas tolerantes y relajadas. (pág. 279)

U

unconditional positive regard/consideración positiva incondicional   Actitud de cuidado, imparcialidad y aceptación total hacia otra persona, que Carl Roger creía que ayudaría a los clientes a desarrollar consciencia y aceptación de uno mismo. (págs. 301, 355)

unconditioned response (UR)/respuesta incondicionada (RI)   En el condicionamiento clásico, la respuesta no aprendida e innata que es producida por el estímulo incondicionado (EI) como la salivación cuando la comida está en la boca. (pág. 158)

unconditioned stimulus (US)/estímulo incondicionado (EI)   En el condicionamiento clásico, estímulo que provoca incondicionalmente una respuesta (RI) de manera natural y automática. (pág. 158)

unconscious/inconciente   (1) Según Freud, un depósito de pensamientos, deseos, sentimiento y memorias en su mayoría inaceptables. (2) Según los psicólogos contemporáneos, el procesamiento de información del cual no estamos alertas. (pág. 294)

V

validity/validez Grado en que una prueba mide o predice lo que se supone debe medir o predecir. (pág. 225)

variable-interval schedule/calendario de intervalo variable Según el condicionamiento operante, calendario de refuerzos que refuerza una respuesta en intervalos de tiempo impredecibles. (pág. 165)

variable-ratio schedule/calendario de razón variable Según el condicionamiento operante, calendario de refuerzos que refuerza una respuesta después de un número de respuestas impredecible. (pág. 165)

vestibular sense/sentido vestibular Sentido de movimiento del cuerpo y posición, incluyendo el sentido de equilibrio. (pág. 148)

virtual reality exposure therapy/terapia de exposición a una realidad virtual Tratamiento de ansiedad que progresivamente expone a las personas a simulaciones electrónicas de sus más grandes miedos, como volar en avión, arañas o hablar en público. (pág. 356)

visual cliff/precipicio visual Dispositivo del laboratorio para examinar la percepción de profundidad en los infantes y animales jóvenes. (pág. 135)

W

wavelength/longitud de onda Distancia entre la cresta de una onda de luz o de sonido y la cresta de la siguiente onda. (pág. 130)

Weber's law/ley de Weber Principio que sostiene que para que dos estímulos se perciban como distintos, éstos deben diferir por una proporción mínima y constante (en vez de una cantidad constante). (pág. 125)

Wechsler Adult Intelligence Scale (WAIS)/escala de la Inteligencia de Wechsler para adultos (EIWA) Prueba de inteligencia más ampliamente utilizada; contiene pruebas verbales y de desempeño (no verbales). (pág. 224)

Wernicke's area/área de Wernicke Parte del cerebro generalmente ubicada en el lóbulo temporal izquierdo, que participa en la comprensión y la expresión del lenguaje, y controla la recepción del mismo. (pág. 44)

withdrawal/síndrome de abstinencia Conjunto de síntomas que afectan a un individuo cuando se ve privado bruscamente de alguna droga adictiva. (pág. 329)

working memory/memoria operativa Entendimiento más reciente de la memoria a corto plazo que supone un procesamiento consciente y activo de la infomación recibida y de información obtenida de la memoria a largo plazo. (pág. 182)

X

X chromosome/cromosoma X Cromosoma sexual que se encuentra en el hombre y la mujer. Las mujeres tienen dos cromosomas X; los hombres tienen un cromosoma X y un cromosoma Y. (pág. 104)

Y

Y chromosome/cromosoma Y Cromosoma del sexo encontrado sólo en los hombres. Cuando se aparea con un cromosoma X de la madre, produce un niño. (pág. 104)

Z

Zygote/cigoto Huevo fertilizado, que atraviesa por un período de dos semanas de división celular rápida y se convierte en un embrión. (pág. 66)

AAS. (2009, April 25). USA suicide: 2006 final data. Prepared for the American Association of Suicidology by J. L. McIntosh (www.suicidology.org). (p. 340)

Abbey, A. (1991). Acquaintance rape and alcohol consumption on college campuses: How are they linked? *Journal of American College Health, 39,* 165–169. (p. 330)

Abrams, D. B., & Wilson, G. T. (1983). Alcohol, sexual arousal, and self-control. *Journal of Personality and Social Psychology, 45,* 188–198. (p. 331)

Abrams, M. (2002, June). Sight unseen—Restoring a blind man's vision is now a real possibility through stem-cell surgery. But even perfect eyes cannot see unless the brain has been taught to use them. *Discover, 23,* 54–60. (p. 138)

Abramson, L. Y., Metalsky, G. I., & Alloy, L. B. (1989). Hopelessness depression: A theory-based subtype. *Psychological Review, 96,* 358–372. (p. 342)

ACHA. (2009). *American College Health Association-National College Health Assessment II: Reference group executive summary Fall 2008.* Baltimore: American College Health association. (p. 338)

Ackerman, D. (2004). *An alchemy of mind: The marvel and mystery of the brain.* New York: Scribner. (p. 28)

Adelmann, P. K., Antonucci, T. C., Crohan, S. F., & Coleman, L. M. (1989). Empty nest, cohort, and employment in the well-being of midlife women. *Sex Roles, 20,* 173–189. (p. 93)

Affleck, G., Tennen, H., Urrows, S., & Higgins, P. (1994). Person and contextual features of daily stress reactivity: Individual differences in relations of undesirable daily events with mood disturbance and chronic pain intensity. *Journal of Personality and Social Psychology, 66,* 329–340. (p. 265)

Ai, A. L., Park, C. L., Huang, B., Rodgers, W., & Tice, T. N. (2007). Psychosocial mediation of religious coping styles: A study of short-term psychological distress following cardiac surgery. *Personality and Social Psychology Bulletin, 33,* 867–882. (p. 288)

Aiello, J. R., Thompson, D. D., & Brodzinsky, D. M. (1983). How funny is crowding anyway? Effects of room size, group size, and the introduction of humor. *Basic and Applied Social Psychology, 4,* 193–207. (p. 387)

Ainsworth, M. D. S. (1973). The development of infant-mother attachment. In B. Caldwell & H. Ricciuti (Eds.), *Review of child development research* (Vol. 3). Chicago: University of Chicago Press. (p. 77)

Ainsworth, M. D. S. (1979). Infant-mother attachment. *American Psychologist, 34,* 932–937. (p. 77)

Ainsworth, M. D. S. (1989). Attachments beyond infancy. *American Psychologist, 44,* 709–716. (p. 77)

Albee, G. W. (1986). Toward a just society: Lessons from observations on the primary prevention of psychopathology. *American Psychologist, 41,* 891–898. (p. 372)

Alcock, J. E. (1981). *Parapsychology: Science or magic?* Oxford: Pergamon. (p. 191)

Aldrich, M. S. (1989). Automobile accidents in patients with sleep disorders. *Sleep, 12,* 487–494. (p. 55)

Aldridge-Morris, R. (1989). *Multiple personality: An exercise in deception.* Hillsdale, NJ: Erlbaum. (p. 326)

Allen, J. R., & Setlow, V. P. (1991). Heterosexual transmission of HIV: A view of the future. *Journal of the American Medical Association, 266,* 1695–1696. (p. 108)

Allen, K. (2003). Are pets a healthy pleasure? The influence of pets on blood pressure. *Current Directions in Psychological Science, 12,* 236–239. (p. 284)

Allen, L. S., & Gorski, R. A. (1992). Sexual orientation and the size of the anterior commisure in the human brain. *Proceedings of the National Academy of Sciences, 89,* 7199–7202. (p. 114)

Allen, M. W., Gupta, R., & Monnier, A. (2008). The interactive effect of cultural symbols and human values on taste evaluation. *Journal of Consumer Research, 35,* 294–308. (p. 146)

Allen, N. B., & Badcock, P. B. T. (2003). The social risk hypothesis of depressed mood: Evolutionary, psychosocial, and neurobiological perspectives. *Psychological Bulletin, 129,* 887–913. (p. 338)

Allport, G. W. (1954). *The nature of prejudice.* New York: Addison-Wesley. (pp. 12, 392)

Altman, L. K. (2004, November 24). Female cases of HIV found rising worldwide. *New York Times* (www.nytimes.com). (p. 278)

Alwin, D. F. (1990). Historical changes in parental orientations to children. In N. Mandell (Ed.), *Sociological studies of child development* (Vol. 3). Greenwich, CT: JAI Press. (p. 79)

AMA. (2010, accessed 13 January). Women medical school applicants (Table 2 of Statistics History). ama-assn.org. (p. 118)

Amabile, T. M. (1983). *The social psychology of creativity.* New York: Springer-Verlag. (p. 310)

Amabile, T. M., & Hennessey, B. A. (1992). The motivation for creativity in children. In A. K. Boggiano & T. S. Pittman (Eds.), *Achievement and motivation: A social-developmental perspective.* New York: Cambridge University Press. (p. 222)

Amabile, T. M., Barsade, S. G., Mueller, J. S., & Staw, B. M. (2005). Affect and creativity at work. *Administrative Science Quarterly, 50,* 367–403. (p. 264)

Amato, P. R., Booth, A., Johnson, D. R., & Rogers, S. J. (2007). *Alone together: How marriage in America is changing.* Cambridge, MA: Harvard University Press. (p. 105)

Ambady, N., & Rosenthal, R. (1992). Thin slices of expressive behavior as predictors of interpersonal consequences: A meta-analysis. *Psychological Bulletin, 111,* 256–274. (p. 308)

Ambady, N., & Rosenthal, R. (1993). Half a minute: Predicting teacher evaluations from thin slices of nonverbal behavior and physical attractiveness. *Journal of Personality and Social Psychology, 64,* 431–441. (p. 308)

Amen, D. G., Stubblefield, M., Carmichael, B., & Thisted, R. (1996). Brain SPECT findings and aggressiveness. *Annals of Clinical Psychiatry, 8,* 129–137. (p. 394)

American Academy of Pediatrics. (2009). Policy statement—media violence. *Pediatrics, 124,* 1495–1503. (p. 177)

American Enterprise. (1992, January/February). Women, men, marriages & ministers. P. 106. (p. 313)

American Psychological Association. (2007). Answers to your questions about sexual orientation and homosexuality (www.apa.org. Accessed December 6, 2007). (p. 112)

Ames, D. R., & Flynn, F. J. (2007). What breaks a leader: The curvilinear relation between assertiveness and leadership. *Journal of Personality and Social Psychology, 92,* 307–324. (p. 416)

Andersen, S. M. (1998). *Service learning: A National Strategy for Youth Development.* A position paper issued by the Task Force on Education Policy. Washington, DC: Institute for Communitarian Policy Studies, George Washington University. (p. 83)

Anderson, B. L. (2002). Biobehavioral outcomes following psychological interventions for cancer patients. *Journal of Consulting and Clinical Psychology, 70,* 590–610. (p. 279)

Anderson, C. A. (2004a). An update on the effects of playing violent video games. *Journal of Adolescence, 27,* 113–122. (p. 396)

Anderson, C. A., & Dill, K. E. (2000). Video games and aggressive thoughts, feelings, and behavior in the laboratory and in life. *Journal of Personality and Social Psychology, 78,* 772–790. (p. 396)

Anderson, C. A., & Gentile, D. A. (2008). Media violence, aggression, and public policy. In E. Borgida & S. Fiske (Eds.), *Beyond common sense: Psychological science in the courtroom.* Malden, MA: Blackwell. (p. 176)

Anderson, C. A., Lindsay, J. J., & Bushman, B. J. (1999). Research in the psychological laboratory: Truth or triviality? *Current Directions in Psychological Science, 8,* 3–9. (p. 18)

Anderson, C. A., Shibuya, A., Ihori, N., Swing, E. L., Bushman, B. J., Sakamoto, A., Rothstein, H. R., & Saleem, M. (2010). Violent video game effects on aggression, empathy, and prosocial behavior in Eastern and Western countries: A meta-analytic review. *Psychological Bulletin, 136,* 151–173. (p. 396)

Anderson, R. C., Pichert, J. W., Goetz, E. T., Schallert, D. L., Stevens, K. V., & Trollip, S. R. (1976). Instantiation of general terms. *Journal of Verbal Learning and Verbal Behavior, 15,* 667–679. (p. 190)

Anderson, S. R. (2004). *Doctor Dolittle's delusion: Animals and the uniqueness of human language.* New Haven: Yale University Press. (p. 218)

Andreasen, N. C. (1997). Linking mind and brain in the study of mental illnesses: A project for a scientific psychopathology. *Science, 275,* 1586–1593. (p. 345)

Andreasen, N. C. (2001). *Brave new brain: Conquering mental illness in the era of the genome.* New York: Oxford University Press. (p. 345)

Andreasen, N. C. (2008, September 16). A conversation with Nancy C. Andreasen, by Claudia Dreifus. *New York Times* (www.nytimes.com). (p. 345)

Andrews, P. W., & Thomson, Jr., J. A. (2009). The bright side of being blue: Depression as an adaptation for analyzing complex problems. *Psychological Review, 116,* 620–654. (p. 338)

Annan, K. A. (2001). We can love what we are, without hating who—and what—we are not. Nobel Peace Prize lecture. (p. 405)

Antoni, M. H., & Lutgendorf, S. (2007). Psychosocial factors and disease progression in cancer. *Current Directions in Psychological Science, 16,* 42–46. (p. 279)

Antony, M. M., Brown, T. A., & Barlow, D. H. (1992). Current perspectives on panic and panic disorder. *Current Directions in Psychological Science, 1,* 79–82. (p. 325)

Antrobus, J. (1991). Dreaming: Cognitive processes during cortical activation and high afferent thresholds. *Psychological Review, 98,* 96–121. (p. 58)

AP. (2007). AP-Ipsos poll of 1,013 U.S. adults taken October 16–18, 2007 and distributed via Associated Press. (p. 149)

AP. (2009, May). mtvU/Associated Press survey by Edison Research. Surveys.ap.org. (p. 272)

APA. (2002). *Ethical principles of psychologists and code of conduct.* Washington, DC: American Psychological Association. (p. 19)

APA. (2009). *Stress in America 2009.* American Psychological Association (apa.org). (p. 275)

APA. (2010, accessed April 28). *Answers to your questions about transgender individuals and gender identity.* American Psychological Association (apa.org). (p. 105)

Archer, J. (2009). Does sexual selection explain human sex differences in aggression? *Behavioral and Brain Sciences, 32,* 249–311. (p. 102)

Arent, S. M., Landers, D. M., & Etnier, J. L. (2000). The effects of exercise on mood in older adults: A meta-analytic review. *Journal of Aging and Physical Activity, 8,* 407–430. (p. 286)

Aries, E. (1987). Gender and communication. In P. Shaver & C. Henrick (Eds.), *Review of Personality and Social Psychology, 7,* 149–176. (p. 102)

Arkowitz, H., & Lilienfeld, S. O. (2006, April/May). Psychotherapy on trial. *Scientific American: Mind,* pp. 42–49. (p. 363)

Armony, J. L., Quirk, G. J., & LeDoux, J. E. (1998). Differential effects of amygdala lesions on early and late plastic components of auditory cortex spike trains during fear conditioning. *Journal of Neuroscience, 18,* 2592–2601. (p. 325)

Arnett, J. J. (2006). Emerging adulthood: Understanding the new way of coming of age. In J. J. Arnett & J. L. Tanner (Eds.), *Emerging adults in America: Coming of age in the 21st century.* Washington, DC: American Psychological Association. (p. 87)

Arnett, J. J. (2007). Socialization in emerging adulthood: From the family to the wider world, from socialization to self-socialization. In J. E. Grusec & P. D. Hastings (Eds.), *Handbook of socialization: Theory and research.* New York: Guilford Press. (p. 87)

Aron, A., Melinat, E., Aron, E. N., Vallone, R. D., & Bator, R. J. (1997). The experimental generation of interpersonal closeness: A procedure and some preliminary findings. *Personality and Social Psychology Bulletin, 23,* 363–377. (p. 402)

Aronson, E. (2001, April 13). Newsworthy violence. E-mail to SPSP discussion list, drawing from *Nobody Left to Hate.* New York: Freeman, 2000. (p. 86)

Artiga, A. I., Viana, J. B., Maldonado, C. R., Chandler-Laney, P. C., Oswald, K. D., & Boggiano, M. M. (2007). Body composition and endocrine status of long-term stress-induced binge-eating rats. *Physiology and Behavior, 91,* 424–431. (p. 242)

ASAPS. (2010). *Despite recession, overall plastic surgery demand drops only 2 percent from last year.* American Society for Aesthetic Plastic Surgery (www.surgery.org). (p. 400)

Asch, S. E. (1955). Opinions and social pressure. *Scientific American, 193,* 31–35. (p. 382)

Aserinsky, E. (1988, January 17). Personal communication. (p. 51)

ASHA. (2003). *STD statistics.* American Social Health Association (www.ashastd.org/stdfaqs/statistics.html). (p. 108)

Askay, S. W., & Patterson, D. R. (2007). Hypnotic analgesia. *Expert Review of Neurotherapeutics, 7,* 1675–1683. (p. 145)

Aspy, C. B., Vesely, S. K., Oman, R. F., Rodine, S., Marshall, L., & McLeroy, K. (2007). Parental communication and youth sexual behaviour. *Journal of Adolescence, 30,* 449–466. (p. 109)

Assanand, S., Pinel, J. P. J., & Lehman, D. R. (1998). Personal theories of hunger and eating. *Journal of Applied Social Psychology, 28,* 998–1015. (p. 242)

Atkinson, R. C., & Schiffrin, R. M. (1968). Human memory: A control system and its control processes. In K. Spence (Ed.), *The psychology of learning and motivation* (Vol. 2). New York: Academic Press. (p. 182)

Atwell, R. H. (1986, July 28). Drugs on campus: A perspective. *Higher Education & National Affairs*, p. 5. (p. 331)

Averill, J. R. (1983). Studies on anger and aggression: Implications for theories of emotion. *American Psychologist, 38*, 1145–1160. (p. 263)

Averill, J. R. (1993). William James's other theory of emotion. In M. E. Donnelly (Ed.), *Reinterpreting the legacy of William James.* Washington, DC: American Psychological Association. (p. 253)

Avery, R. D., & others. (1994, December 13). Mainstream science on intelligence. *Wall Street Journal*, p. A–18. (p. 228)

Ax, A. F. (1953). The physiological differentiation of fear and anger in humans. *Psychosomatic Medicine, 15*, 433–442. (p. 255)

Ayan, S. (2009, April/May). Laughing matters. *Scientific American Mind*, pp. 24–31. (p. 283)

Azar, B. (1998, June). Why can't this man feel whether or not he's standing up? *APA Monitor* (www.apa.org/monitor/jun98/touch.html). (p. 147)

Babyak, M., Blumenthal, J. A., Herman, S., Khatri, P., Doraiswamy, M., Moore, K., Craighead, W. W., Baldewics, T. T., & Krishnan, K. R. (2000). Exercise treatment for major depression: Maintenance of therapeutic benefit at ten months. *Psychosomatic Medicine, 62*, 633–638. (p. 371)

Bachman, J., O'Malley, P. M., Schulenberg, J. E., Johnston, L. D., Freedman-Doan, P., & Messersmith, E. E. (2007). *The education-drug use connection: How successes and failures in school relate to adolescent smoking, drinking, drug use, and delinquency.* Mahwah, NJ: Erlbaum. (p. 337)

Back, M. D., Stopfer, J. M., Vazire, S., Gaddis, S., Schmukle, S. C., Egloff, B., & Gosling, S. D. (2010). Facebook profiles reflect actual personality not self-idealization. *Psychological Science, 21*, 372–274. (p. 251)

Backman, L., & MacDonald, S. W. S. (2006). Death and cognition: Synthesis and outlook. *European Psychologist, 11*, 224–235. (p. 92)

Baddeley, A. D. (1982). *Your memory: A user's guide.* New York: Macmillan. (pp. 183, 184)

Bagemihl, B. (1999). *Biological exuberance: Animal homosexuality and natural diversity.* New York: St. Martins. (p. 113)

Bahrick, H. P. (1984). Semantic memory content in permastore: 50 years of memory for Spanish learned in school. *Journal of Experimental Psychology: General, 111*, 1–29. (p. 193)

Bahrick, H. P., Bahrick, P. O., & Wittlinger, R. P. (1975). Fifty years of memory for names and faces: A cross-sectional approach. *Journal of Experimental Psychology: General, 104*, 54–75. (p. 189)

Bailenson, J. N., Iyengar, S., Yee, N., & Collins, N. (2008). Facial similarity as a voting heuristic. *Public Opinion Quarterly*, in press. (p. 398)

Bailey, J. M., Dunne, M. P., & Martin, N. G. (2000). Genetic and environmental influences on sexual orientation and its correlates in an Australian twin sample. *Journal of Personality and Social Psychology, 78*, 524–536. (p. 117)

Bailey, J. M., Gaulin, S., Agyei, Y., & Gladue, B. A. (1994). Effects of gender and sexual orientation on evolutionary relevant aspects of human mating psychology. *Journal of Personality and Social Psychology, 66*, 1081–1093. (p. 116)

Bailey, J. M., Kirk, K. M., Zhu, G., Dunne, M. P., & Martin, N. G. (2000). Do individual differences in sociosexuality represent genetic or environmentally contingent strategies? Evidence from the Australian twin registry. *Journal of Personality and Social Psychology, 78*, 537–545. (p. 117)

Bailey, R. E., & Gillaspy, J. A., Jr. (2005). Operant psychology goes to the fair: Marian and Keller Breland in the popular press, 1947–1966. *The Behavior Analyst, 28*, 143–159. (p. 154)

Baillargeon, R. (1995). A model of physical reasoning in infancy. In C. Rovee-Collier & L. P. Lipsitt (Eds.), *Advances in infancy research* (Vol. 9). Stamford, CT: Ablex. (p. 73)

Baillargeon, R. (2008). Innate ideas revisited: For a principle of persistence in infants' physical reasoning. *Perspectives in Psychological Science, 3*, 2–13. (p. 73)

Baker, T. B., McFall, R. M., & Shoham, V. (2008). Current status and future prospects of clinical psychology: Toward a scientifically principles approach to mental and behavioral health care. *Psychological Science in the Public Interest, 9*, 67–103. (p. 363)

Baker, T. B., Piper, M. E., McCarthy, D. E., Majeskie, M. R., & Fiore, M. C. (2004). Addiction motivation reformulated: An affective processing model of negative reinforcement. *Psychological Review, 111*, 33–51. (p. 164)

Bakermans-Kranenburg, M. J., van IJzendoorn, M. H., & Juffer, F. (2003). Less is more: Meta-analyses of sensitivity and attachment interventions in early childhood. *Psychological Bulletin, 129*, 195–215. (p. 77)

Bandura, A. (1982). The psychology of chance encounters and life paths. *American Psychologist, 37*, 747–755. (p. 94)

Bandura, A. (1986). *Social foundations of thought and action: A social-cognitive theory.* Englewood Cliffs, NJ: Prentice-Hall. (p. 308)

Bandura, A. (2005). The evolution of social cognitive theory. In K. G. Smith & M. A. Hitt (Eds.), *Great minds in management: The process of theory development.* Oxford: Oxford University Press. (pp. 94, 172)

Bandura, A. (2006). Toward a psychology of human agency. *Perspectives on Psychological Science, 1*, 164–180. (p. 308)

Bandura, A. (2008). An agentic perspective on positive psychology. In S. J. Lopez (Ed.), *The science of human flourishing.* Westport, CT: Praeger. (p. 308)

Bandura, A. (2008). Reconstrual of "free will" from the agentic perspective of social cognitive theory. In J. Baer, J. C. Kaufman, & R. F. Baumeister (Eds.), *Are we free? Psychology and free will.* Oxford: Oxford University Press. (p. 62)

Bandura, A., Ross, D., & Ross, S. A. (1961). Transmission of aggression through imitation of aggressive models. *Journal of Abnormal and Social Psychology, 63*, 575–582. (p. 172)

Bargh, J. A., McKenna, K. Y. A., & Fitzsimons, G. M. (2002). Can you see the real me? Activation and expression of the "true self" on the Internet. *Journal of Social Issues, 58*, 33–48. (p. 398)

Barinaga, M. B. (1997). How exercise works its magic. *Science, 276*, 1325. (p. 285)

Barnes, M. L., & Sternberg, R. J. (1989). Social intelligence and decoding of nonverbal cues. *Intelligence, 13*, 263–287. (p. 260)

Barnett, P. A., & Gotlib, I. H. (1988). Psychosocial functioning and depression: Distinguishing among antecedents, concomitants, and consequences. *Psychological Bulletin, 104*, 97–126. (p. 342)

Barnier, A. J., & McConkey, K. M. (2004). Defining and identifying the highly hypnotizable person. In M. Heap, R. J. Brown, & D. A. Oakley (Eds.), *High hypnotisability: Theoretical, experimental and clinical issues.* London: Brunner-Routledge. (p. 144)

Baron, R. S., Cutrona, C. E., Hicklin, D., Russell, D. W., & Lubaroff, D. M. (1990). Social support and immune function among spouses of cancer patients. *Journal of Personality and Social Psychology, 59*, 344–352. (p. 284)

Barr, R. (2008, February 12). Stores use sonic devices to chase kids. *Associated Press* (news.yahoo.com). (p. 91)

Barrett, L. F. (2006). Are emotions natural kinds? *Perspectives on Psychological Science, 1,* 28–58. (pp. 253, 255)

Barry, D. (1998). *Dave Barry turns 50.* New York: Crown Publishers. (p. 90)

Barry, D. (2002, April 26). *The Dave Barry 2002 Calendar.* Kansas City: Andrews McMeel. (p. 19)

Bashore, T. R., Ridderinkhof, K. R., & van der Molen, M. W. (1997). The decline of cognitive processing speed in old age. *Current Directions in Psychological Science, 6,* 163–169. (p. 91)

Baskind, D. E. (1997, December 14). Personal communication, from Delta College. (p. 357)

Bassett, D. R., Schneider, P. L., & Huntington, G. E. (2004). Physical activity in an Old Order Amish community. *Medicine and Science in Sports and Exercise, 36,* 79–85. (p. 246)

Baum, A., & Posluszny, D. M. (1999). Health psychology: Mapping biobehavioral contributions to health and illness. *Annual Review of Psychology, 50,* 137–163. (p. 278)

Baumeister, H., & Härter, M. (2007). Prevalence of mental disorders based on general population surveys. *Social Psychiatry and Psychiatric Epidemiology, 42,* 537–546. (p. 316)

Baumeister, R. F. (1989). The optimal margin of illusion. *Journal of Social and Clinical Psychology, 8,* 176–189. (p. 209)

Baumeister, R. F. (2000). Gender differences in erotic plasticity: The female sex drive as socially flexible and responsive. *Psychological Bulletin, 126,* 347–374. (p. 113)

Baumeister, R. F. (2001, April). Violent pride: Do people turn violent because of self-hate, or self-love? *Scientific American,* 96–101. (p. 310)

Baumeister, R. F. (2006, August/September). Violent pride. *Scientific American Mind,* pp. 54–59. (p. 310)

Baumeister, R. F., & Bratslavsky, E. (1999). Passion, intimacy, and time: Passionate love as a function of change in intimacy. *Personality and Social Psychology Review, 3,* 49–67. (p. 402)

Baumeister, R. F., & Exline, J. J. (2000). Self-control, morality, and human strength. *Journal of Social and Clinical Psychology, 19,* 29–42. (p. 282)

Baumeister, R. F., & Leary, M. R. (1995). The need to belong: Desire for interpersonal attachments as a fundamental human motivation. *Psychological Bulletin, 117,* 497–529. (p. 248)

Baumeister, R. F., & Tice, D. M. (1986). How adolescence became the struggle for self: A historical transformation of psychological development. In J. Suls & A. G. Greenwald (Eds.), *Psychological perspectives on the self* (Vol. 3). Hillsdale, NJ: Erlbaum. (p. 87)

Baumeister, R. F., & Vohs, K. D. (2002). The pursuit of meaningfulness in life. In C. R. Snyder & S. Lopez (Eds.), *Handbook of positive psychology.* New York: Oxford. (p. 285)

Baumeister, R. F., Campbell, J., Krueger, J. I., & Vohs, K. D. (2003). Does high self-esteem cause better performance, interpersonal success, happiness, or healthier lifestyles? *Psychological Science in the Public Interest, 4*(1), 1–44. (p. 311)

Baumeister, R. F., Catanese, K. R., & Vohs, K. D. (2001). Is there a gender difference in strength of sex drive? Theoretical views, conceptual distinctions, and a review of relevant evidence. *Personality and Social Psychology Review, 5,* 242–273. (p. 116)

Baumeister, R. F., Dale, K., & Sommer, K. L. (1998). Freudian defense mechanisms and empirical findings in modern personality and social psychology: Reaction formation, projection, displacement, undoing, isolation, sublimation, and denial. *Journal of Personality, 66,* 1081–1125. (p. 300)

Baumeister, R. F., DeWall, C. N., & Vohs, K. D. (2009). Social rejection, control, numbness, and emotion: How not to be fooled by Gerber and Wheeler (2009). *Perspectives on Psychological Science, 4,* 489–493. (p. 250)

Baumeister, R. F., Twenge, J. M., & Nuss, C. K. (2002). Effects of social exclusion on cognitive processes: Anticipated aloneness reduces intelligent thought. *Journal of Personality and Social Psychology, 83,* 817–827. (p. 250)

Baumgardner, A. H., Kaufman, C. M., & Levy, P. E. (1989). Regulating affect interpersonally: When low esteem leads to greater enhancement. *Journal of Personality and Social Psychology, 56,* 907–921. (p. 310)

Baumrind, D. (1982). Adolescent sexuality: Comment on Williams' and Silka's comments on Baumrind. *American Psychologist, 37,* 1402–1403. (p. 111)

Baumrind, D. (1996). The discipline controversy revisited. *Family Relations, 45,* 405–414. (p. 79)

Baumrind, D., Larzelere, R. E., & Cowan, P. A. (2002). Ordinary physical punishment: Is it harmful? Comment on Gershoff (2002). *Psychological Bulletin, 128,* 602–611. (p. 166)

Bavelier, D., Newport, E. L., & Supalla, T. (2003). Children need natural languages, signed or spoken. *Cerebrum, 5*(1), 19–32. (p. 214)

BBC. (2008, February 26). Anti-depressants 'of little use.' *BBC News* (www.news.bbc.co.uk). (p. 368)

Beaman, A. L., & Klentz, B. (1983). The supposed physical attractiveness bias against supporters of the women's movement: A meta-analysis. *Personality and Social Psychology Bulletin, 9,* 544–550. (p. 400)

Beardsley, L. M. (1994). Medical diagnosis and treatment across cultures. In W. J. Lonner & R. Malpass (Eds.), *Psychology and culture.* Boston: Allyn & Bacon. (p. 319)

Beardsley, T. (1996, July). Waking up. *Scientific American,* pp. 14, 18. (p. 54)

Beauchamp, G. K. (1987). The human preference for excess salt. *American Scientist, 75,* 27–33. (p. 242)

Beck, A. T., & Steer, R. A. (1989). Clinical predictors of eventual suicide: A 5- to 10-year prospective study of suicide attempters. *Journal of Affective Disorders, 17,* 203–209. (p. 358)

Beck, A. T., Rush, A. J., Shaw, B. F., & Emery, G. (1979). *Cognitive therapy of depression.* New York: Guilford Press. (p. 358)

Beck, H. P., Levinson, S., & Irons, G. (2009). Finding Little Albert: A journey to John B. Watson's infant laboratory. *American Psychologist, 64,* 605–614. (p. 161)

Beck, H. P., Levinson, S., & Irons, G. (2010). The evidence supports Douglas Merritte as Little Albert. *American Psychologist, 65,* 301-303. (p. 161)

Becker, D. V., Kenrick, D. T., Neuberg, S. L., Blackwell, K. C., & Smith, D. M. (2007). The confounded nature of angry men and happy women. *Journal of Personality and Social Psychology, 92,* 179–190. (p. 260, 261)

Becker, S., & Wojtowicz, J. M. (2007). A model of hippocampal neurogenesis in memory and mood disorders. *Trends in Cognitive Sciences, 11,* 70–76. (p. 367)

Becklen, R., & Cervone, D. (1983). Selective looking and the noticing of unexpected events. *Memory and Cognition, 11,* 601–608. (p. 49)

Beckman, M. (2004). Crime, culpability, and the adolescent brain. *Science, 305,* 596–599. (p. 82)

Beeman, M. J., & Chiarello, C. (1998). Complementary right- and left-hemisphere language comprehension. *Current Directions in Psychological Science, 7,* 2–8. (p. 48)

Bell, A. P., Weinberg, M. S., & Hammersmith, S. K. (1981). *Sexual preference: Its development in men and women.* Bloomington: Indiana University Press. (p. 113)

Belot, M., & Francesconi, M. (2006, November). *Can anyone be 'the one'? Evidence on mate selection from speed dating.* London: Centre for Economic Policy Research (www.cepr.org). (p. 399)

Belsher, G., & Costello, C. G. (1988). Relapse after recovery from unipolar depression: A critical review. *Psychological Bulletin, 104,* 84–96. (p. 340)

Bem, D. J. (1984). Quoted in *The Skeptical Inquirer, 8,* 194. (p. 150)

Bem, D. J., & Honorton, C. (1994). Does psi exist? Replicable evidence for an anomalous process of information transfer. *Psychological Bulletin, 115,* 4–18. (p. 150)

Bem, D. J., Palmer, J., & Broughton, R. S. (2001). Updating the Ganzfeld database: A victim of its own success? *Journal of Parapsychology, 65,* 207–218. (p. 150)

Bem, S. L. (1987). Masculinity and femininity exist only in the mind of the perceiver. In J. M. Reinisch, L. A. Rosenblum, & S. A. Sanders (Eds.), *Masculinity/femininity: Basic perspectives.* New York: Oxford University Press. (p. 106)

Bem, S. L. (1993). *The lenses of gender.* New Haven, CT: Yale University Press. (p. 106)

Bennett, W. I. (1995). Beyond overeating. *New England Journal of Medicine, 332,* 673–674. (p. 248)

Ben-Shakhar, G., & Elaad, E. (2003). The validity of psychophysiological detection of information with the guilt knowledge test: A meta-analytic review. *Journal of Applied Psychology, 88,* 131–151. (p. 257)

Benson, H. (1996). *Timeless healing: The power and biology of belief.* New York: Scribner. (p. 286)

Benson, K., & Feinberg, I. (1977). The beneficial effect of sleep in an extended Jenkins and Dallenbach paradigm. *Psychophysiology, 14,* 375–384. (p. 194)

Benson, P. L., Sharma, A. R., & Roehlkepartain, E. C. (1994). *Growing up adopted: A portrait of adolescents and their families.* Minneapolis: Search Institute. (p. 86)

Berger, B. G., & Motl, R. W. (2000). Exercise and mood: A selective review and synthesis of research employing the profile of mood states. *Journal of Applied Sports Psychology, 12,* 69–92. (p. 286)

Bergin, A. E. (1980). Psychotherapy and religious values. *Journal of Consulting and Clinical Psychology, 48,* 95–105. (p. 364)

Bergsholm, P., Larsen, J. L., Rosendahl, K., & Holsten, F. (1989). Electroconvulsive therapy and cerebral computed tomography. *Acta Psychiatrica Scandinavia, 80,* 566–572. (p. 369)

Bering, J. (2010, May/June). The third gender. *Scientific American Mind,* pp. 60–63. (p. 105)

Berk, L. S., Felten, D. L., Tan, S. A., Bittman, B. B., & Westengard, J. (2001). Modulation of neuroimmune parameters during the eustress of humor-associated mirthful laughter. *Alternative Therapies, 7,* 62–76. (p. 283)

Berkel, J., & de Waard, F. (1983). Mortality pattern and life expectancy of Seventh Day Adventists in the Netherlands. *International Journal of Epidemiology, 12,* 455–459. (p. 287)

Berkowitz, L. (1983). Aversively stimulated aggression: Some parallels and differences in research with animals and humans. *American Psychologist, 38,* 1135–1144. (p. 394)

Berkowitz, L. (1989). Frustration-aggression hypothesis: Examination and reformulation. *Psychological Bulletin, 106,* 59–73. (p. 394)

Berndt, T. J. (1992). Friendship and friends' influence in adolescence. *Current Directions in Psychological Science, 1,* 156–159. (p. 103)

Bernstein, D. M., & Loftus, E. F. (2009). The consequences of false memories for food preferences and choices. *Perspectives on Psychological Science, 4,* 135-139. (p. 196)

Berscheid, E. (1981). An overview of the psychological effects of physical attractiveness and some comments upon the psychological effects of knowledge of the effects of physical attractiveness. In G. W. Lucker, K. Ribbens, & J. A. McNamara (Eds.), *Psychological aspects of facial form* (Craniofacial growth series). Ann Arbor: Center for Human Growth and Development, University of Michigan. (p. 399)

Berscheid, E., Gangestad, S. W., & Kulakowski, D. (1984). Emotion in close relationships: Implications for relationship counseling. In S. D. Brown & R. W. Lent (Eds.), *Handbook of counseling psychology.* New York: Wiley. (p. 401)

Bettencourt, B. A., & Kernahan, C. (1997). A meta-analysis of aggression in the presence of violent cues: Effects of gender differences and aversive provocation. *Aggressive Behavior, 23,* 447–457. (p. 102)

Beyerstein, B., & Beyerstein, D. (Eds.) (1992). *The write stuff: Evaluations of graphology.* Buffalo, NY: Prometheus Books. (p. 306)

Bhatt, R. S., Wasserman, E. A., Reynolds, W. F., Jr., & Knauss, K. S. (1988). Conceptual behavior in pigeons: Categorization of both familiar and novel examples from four classes of natural and artificial stimuli. *Journal of Experimental Psychology: Animal Behavior Processes, 14,* 219–234. (p. 163)

Bianchi, S. M., Milkie, M. A., Sayer, L. C., & Robinson, J. P. (2000). Is anyone doing the housework? Trends in the gender division of household labor. *Social Forces, 79,* 191–228. (p. 118)

Bianchi, S. M., Robinson, J. P., & Milkie, M. A. (2006). *Changing rhythms of American family life.* New York: Russell Sage. (p. 118)

Bickman, L. (1999). Practice makes perfect and other myths about mental health services. *American Psychologist, 54,* 965–978. (p. 362)

Birnbaum, G. E., Reis, H. T., Mikulincer, M., Gillath, O., & Orpaz, A. (2006). When sex is more than just sex: Attachment orientations, sexual experience, and relationship quality. *Journal of Personality and Social Psychology, 91,* 929–943. (p. 78)

Birnbaum, S. G., Yuan, P. X., Wang, M., Vijayraghavan, S., Bloom, A. K., Davis, D. J., Gobeski, K. T., Sweatt, J. D., Manhi, H. K., & Arnsten, A. F. T. (2004). Protein kinase C overactivity impairs prefrontal cortical regulation of working memory. *Science, 306,* 882–884. (p. 188)

Bjorklund, D. F., & Green, B. L. (1992). The adaptive nature of cognitive immaturity. *American Psychologist, 47,* 46–54. (p. 75)

Blakemore, S-J., Wolpert, D. M., & Frith, C. D. (1998). Central cancellation of self-produced tickle sensation. *Nature Neuroscience, 1,* 635–640. (p. 142)

Blakeslee, S. (2005, February 8). Focus narrows in search for autism's cause. *New York Times* (www.nytimes.com). (p. 74)

Blakeslee, S. (2006, January 10). Cells that read minds. *New York Times* (www.nytimes.com). (p. 173)

Blanchard, R. (1997). Birth order and sibling sex ratio in homosexual versus heterosexual males and females. *Annual Review of Sex Research, 8,* 27–67. (p. 115)

Blanchard, R. (2008). Review and theory of handedness, birth order, and homosexuality in men. *Laterality, 13,* 51–70. (pp. 114, 115)

Blanchard-Fields, F. (2007). Everyday problem solving and emotion: An adult developmental perspective. *Current Directions in Psychological Science, 16,* 26–31. (p. 92)

Blanton, H., Jaccard, J., Klick, J., Mellers, B., Mitchell, G., & Tetlock, P. E. (2009). Strong claims and weak evidence: Reassessing the predictive validity of the IAT. *Journal of Applied Psychology, 94,* 567–582. (p. 391)

Blanton, H., Jaccard, J., Christie, C., & Gonzales, P. M. (2007). Plausible assumptions, questionable assumptions and post hoc rationalizations: Will the real IAT please stand up? *Journal of Experimental Social Psychology, 43,* 399–409. (p. 391)

Blanton, H., Jaccard, J., Gonzales, P. M., & Christie, C. (2006). Decoding the implicit association test: Implications for criterion prediction. *Journal of Experimental Social Psychology, 42,* 192–212. (p. 391)

Blascovich, J., Seery, M. D., Mugridge, C. A., Norris, R. K., & Weisbuch, M. (2004). Predicting athletic performance from cardiovascular indexes of challenge and threat. *Journal of Experimental Social Psychology, 40,* 683–688. (p. 274)

Blass, T. (1999). The Milgram paradigm after 35 years: Some things we now know about obedience to authority. *Journal of Applied Social Psychology, 29,* 955–978. (p. 384)

Blatt, S. J., Sanislow, C. A., III, Zuroff, D. C., & Pilkonis, P. (1996). Characteristics of effective therapists: Further analyses of data from the National Institute of Mental Health Treatment of Depression Collaborative Research Program. *Journal of Consulting and Clinical Psychology, 64,* 1276–1284. (p. 364)

Bleustein, J. (2002, June 15). Quoted in "Harley retooled," by S. S. Smith, *American Way Magazine.* (p. 418)

Bloom, B. C. (Ed.). (1985). *Developing talent in young people.* New York: Ballantine. (p. 414)

Bloom, P. (2000). *How children learn the meanings of words.* Cambridge, MA: MIT Press. (p. 212)

Boesch-Achermann, H., & Boesch, C. (1993). Tool use in wild chimpanzees: New light from dark forests. *Current Directions in Psychological Science, 2,* 18–21. (p. 216)

Bogaert, A. F. (2003). Number of older brothers and sexual orientation: New texts and the attraction/behavior distinction in two national probability samples. *Journal of Personality and Social Psychology, 84,* 644–652. (p. 115)

Bogaert, A. F. (2006a). Toward a conceptual understanding of asexuality. *Review of General Psychology, 10,* 241–250. (p. 112)

Bogaert, A. F. (2006b). Biological versus nonbiological older brothers and men's sexual orientation. *Proceedings of the National Academy of Sciences, 103,* 10771–10774. (p. 115)

Boggiano, A. K., Harackiewicz, J. M., Bessette, M. M., & Main, D. S. (1985). Increasing children's interest through performance-contingent reward. *Social Cognition, 3,* 400–411. (p. 172)

Boggiano, M. M., Chandler, P. C., Viana, J. B., Oswald, K. D., Maldonado, C. R., & Wauford, P. K. (2005). Combined dieting and stress evoke exaggerated responses to opioids in binge-eating rats. *Behavioral Neuroscience, 119,* 1207–1214. (p. 242)

Bolger, N., DeLongis, A., Kessler, R. C., & Schilling, E. A. (1989). Effects of daily stress on negative mood. *Journal of Personality and Social Psychology, 57,* 808–818. (p. 265)

Bolwig, T. G., & Madsen, T. M. (2007). Electroconvulsive therapy in melancholia: The role of hippocampal neurogenesis. *Acta Psychiatrica Scandinavica, 115,* 130–135. (p. 369)

Bonanno, G. A. (2004). Loss, trauma, and human resilience: Have we underestimated the human capacity to thrive after extremely aversive events? *American Psychologist, 59,* 20–28. (p. 324)

Bonanno, G. A. (2005). Adult resilience to potential trauma. *Current Directions in Psychological Science, 14,* 135–137. (p. 324)

Bonanno, G. A. (2009). *The other side of sadness: What the new science of bereavement tells us about life after loss.* New York: Basic Books. (p. 95)

Bonanno, G. A., & Kaltman, S. (1999). Toward an integrative perspective on bereavement. *Psychological Bulletin, 125,* 760–777. (p. 94)

Bonanno, G. A., Galea, S., Bucciarelli, A., & Vlahov, D. (2006). Psychological resilience after disaster. *Psychological Science, 17,* 181–186. (p. 324)

Bonanno, G. A., Galea, S., Bucciarelli, A., & Vlahov, D. (2007). What predicts psychological resilience after disaster? The role of demographics, resources, and life stress. *Journal of Consulting and Clinical Psychology, 75*(5), 671–682. (p. 371)

Bond, M. H. (1988). Finding universal dimensions of individual variation in multi-cultural studies of values: The Rokeach and Chinese values surveys. *Journal of Personality and Social Psychology, 55,* 1009–1015. (p. 312)

Bond, R., & Smith, P. B. (1996). Culture and conformity: A meta-analysis of studies using Asch's (1952b, 1956) line judgment task. *Psychological Bulletin, 119,* 111–137. (p. 383)

Bono, J. E., & Judge, T. A. (2004). Personality and transformational and transactional leadership: A meta-analysis. *Journal of Applied Psychology, 89,* 901–910. (p. 416)

Boos, H. B. M., Aleman, A., Cahn, W., Hulshoff, H., & Kahn, R. S. (2007). Brain volumes in relatives of patients with schizophrenia. *Archives of General Psychiatry, 64,* 297–304. (p. 345)

Bornstein, M. H., Cote, L. R., Maital, S., Painter, K., Park, S-Y., Pascual, L., Pecheux, M-G., Ruel, J., Venute, P., & Vyt, A. (2004). Cross-linguistic analysis of vocabulary in young children: Spanish, Dutch, French, Hebrew, Italian, Korean, and American English. *Child Development, 75,* 1115–1139. (p. 214)

Bornstein, M. H., Tal, J., Rahn, C., Galperin, C. Z., Pecheux, M-G., Lamour, M., Toda, S., Azuma, H., Ogino, M., & Tamis-LeMonda, C. S. (1992a). Functional analysis of the contents of maternal speech to infants of 5 and 13 months in four cultures: Argentina, France, Japan, and the United States. *Developmental Psychology, 28,* 593–603. (p. 80)

Bornstein, M. H., Tamis-LeMonda, C. S., Tal, J., Ludemann, P., Toda, S., Rahn, C. W., Pecheux, M-G., Azuma, H., & Vardi, D. (1992b). Maternal responsiveness to infants in three societies: The United States, France, and Japan. *Child Development, 63,* 808–821. (p. 80)

Bornstein, R. F. (1989). Exposure and affect: Overview and meta-analysis of research, 1968–1987. *Psychological Bulletin, 106,* 265–289. (p. 397)

Bornstein, R. F. (1999). Source amnesia, misattribution, and the power of unconscious perceptions and memories. *Psychoanalytic Psychology, 16,* 155–178. (p. 397)

Bornstein, R. F., Galley, D. J., Leone, D. R., & Kale, A. R. (1991). The temporal stability of ratings of parents: Test-retest reliability and influence of parental contact. *Journal of Social Behavior and Personality, 6,* 641–649. (p. 191)

Boroditsky, R., Fisher, W., & Sand, M. (1995, July). Teenagers and contraception. Section of The Canadian contraception study. *Journal of the Society of Obstetricians and Gynaecologists of Canada, Special Supplement,* 22–25. (p. 212)

Boscarino, J. A. (1997). Diseases among men 20 years after exposure to severe stress: Implications for clinical research and medical care. *Psychosomatic Medicine, 59,* 605–614. (p. 274)

Bösch, H., Steinkamp, F., & Boller, E. (2006a). Examining psychokinesis: The interaction of human intention with random number generators—A meta-analysis. *Psychological Bulletin, 132,* 497–523. (p. 150)

Bösch, H., Steinkamp, F., & Boller, E. (2006b). In the eye of beholder: Reply to Wilson and Shadish (2006) and Radin, Nelson, Dobyns, and Houtkooper (2006). *Psychological Bulletin, 132,* 533–537. (p. 150)

Bostwick, J. M., & Pankratz, V. S. (2000). Affective disorders and suicide risk: A re-examination. *American Journal of Psychiatry, 157,* 1925–1932. (p. 339)

Bothwell, R. K., Brigham, J. C., & Malpass, R. S. (1989). Cross-racial identification. *Personality and Social Psychology Bulletin, 15,* 19–25. (p. 393)

Bouchard, T. J., Jr. (1995). Longitudinal studies of personality and intelligence: A behavior genetic and evolutionary psychology perspective. In D. H. Saklofske & M. Zeidner (Eds.), *International handbook of personality and intelligence*. New York: Plenum. (p. 227)

Bouchard, T. J., Jr. (1996). Behavior genetic studies of intelligence, yesterday and today: The long journey from plausibility to proof. *Journal of Biosocial Science, 28*, 527–555. (p. 227)

Bouchard, T. J., Jr. (2004). Genetic influence on human psychological traits. *Current Directions in Psychological Science, 13*, 148–151. (p. 68)

Bowden, E. M., & Beeman, M. J. (1998). Getting the right idea: Semantic activation in the right hemisphere may help solve insight problems. *Psychological Science, 9*, 435–440. (p. 48)

Bower, G. H., & Morrow, D. G. (1990). Mental models in narrative comprehension. *Science, 247*, 44–48. (p. 186)

Bower, J. E., Kemeny, M. E., Taylor, S. E., & Fahey, J. L. (1998). Cognitive processing, discovery of meaning, CD4 decline, and AIDS-related mortality among bereaved HIV-seropositive men. *Journal of Consulting and Clinical Psychology, 66*, 979–986. (pp. 278, 285)

Bower, J. M., & Parsons, L. M. (2003, August). Rethinking the "lesser brain." *Scientific American*, 50–57. (p. 36)

Bowers, T. G., & Clum, G. A. (1988). Relative contribution of specific and nonspecific treatment effects: Meta-analysis of placebo-controlled behavior therapy research. *Psychological Bulletin, 103*, 315–323. (p. 362)

Bowles, S., & Kasindorf, M. (2001, March 6). Friends tell of picked-on but 'normal' kid. *USA Today*, 4A. (p. 249)

Boxer, P., Huesmann, L. R., Bushman, B. J., O'Brien, M., & Moceri, D. (2009). The role of violent media preference in cumulative developmental risk for violence and general aggression. *Journal of Youth and Adolescence, 38*,417–428. (p. 176)

Boyatzis, C. J., Matillo, G. M., & Nesbitt, K. M. (1995). Effects of the "Mighty Morphin Power Rangers" on children's aggression with peers. *Child Study Journal, 25*, 45–55. (p. 177)

Braden, J. P. (1994). *Deafness, deprivation, and IQ*. New York: Plenum. (p. 229)

Bradley, D. R., Dumais, S. T., & Petry, H. M. (1976). Reply to Cavonius. *Nature, 261*, 78. (p. 134)

Bradley, R. B., & 15 others. (2008). Influence of child abuse on adult depression: Moderation by the corticotropin-releasing hormone receptor gene. *Archives of General Psychiatry, 65*, 190–200. (p. 78)

Brainerd, C. J. (1996). Piaget: A centennial celebration. *Psychological Science, 7*, 191–195. (p. 71)

Brandon, S., Boakes, J., Glaser, & Green, R. (1998). Recovered memories of childhood sexual abuse: Implications for clinical practice. *British Journal of Psychiatry, 172*, 294–307. (p. 199)

Brannon, L. A., & Brock, T. C. (1994). Perilous underestimation of sex partners' sexual histories in calculating personal AIDS risk. Paper presented to the American Psychological Society convention. (p. 108)

Bransford, J. D., & Johnson, M. K. (1972). Contextual prerequisites for understanding: Some investigations of comprehension and recall. *Journal of Verbal Learning and Verbal Behavior, 11*, 717–726. (p. 186)

Braun, S. (1996). New experiments underscore warnings on maternal drinking. *Science, 273*, 738–739. (p. 66)

Braun, S. (2001, Spring). Seeking insight by prescription. *Cerebrum*, pp. 10–21. (p. 334)

Bray, G. A. (1969). Effect of caloric restriction on energy expenditure in obese patients. *The Lancet, 2*, 397–398. (p. 245)

Breedlove, S. M. (1997). Sex on the brain. *Nature, 389*, 801. (p. 114)

Brehm, S., & Brehm, J. W. (1981). *Psychological reactance: A theory of freedom and control*. New York: Academic Press. (p. 386)

Brewer, W. F. (1977). Memory for the pragmatic implications of sentences. *Memory & Cognition, 5*, 673–678. (p. 186)

Brewin, C. R., Andrews, B., Rose, S., & Kirk, M. (1999). Acute stress disorder and posttraumatic stress disorder in victims of violent crime. *American Journal of Psychiatry, 156*, 360–366. (p. 324)

Brief, A. P., & Weiss, H. M. (2002). Organizational behavior: Affect in the workplace. *Annual Review of Psychology, 53*, 279–307. (p. 414)

Briñol, P., Petty, R. E., & Barden, J. (2007). Happiness versus sadness as a determinant of thought confidence in persuasion: A self-validation analysis. *Journal of Personality and Social Psychology, 93*, 711–727. (p. 264)

Brislin, R. W. (1988). Increasing awareness of class, ethnicity, culture, and race by expanding on students' own experiences. In I. Cohen (Ed.), *The G. Stanley Hall Lecture Series*. Washington, DC: American Psychological Association. (p. 79)

British Psychological Society. (1993). Ethical principles for conducting research with human participants. *The Psychologist: Bulletin of the British Psychological Society, 6*, 33–36. (p. 306)

Brockmann, H., Delhey, J., Welzel, C., & Yuan, H. (2009). The China puzzle: Falling happiness in a rising economy. *Journal of Happiness Studies, 10*, 387–405. (p. 266)

Brody, J. E. (1999, November 30). Yesterday's precocious puberty is norm today. *New York Times* (www.nytimes.com). (p. 81)

Brody, J. E. (2003, September). Addiction: A brain ailment, not a moral lapse. *New York Times* (www.nytimes.com). (p. 334)

Brodzinsky, D. M., & Schechter, M. D. (Eds.) (1990). *The psychology of adoption*. New York: Oxford University Press. (p. 86)

Brooks, D. (2010, January 12). The Tel Aviv cluster. *New York Times* (www.nytimes.com). (p. 230)

Brooks, R., & Meltzoff, A. N. (2005). The development of gaze following and its relation to language. *Developmental Science, 8*, 535–543. (p. 173)

Brown, A. S. (2003). A review of the déjà vu experience. *Psychological Bulletin, 129*, 394–413. (p. 191)

Brown, A. S. (2004). *The déjà vu experience*. East Sussex, England: Psychology Press. (p. 191)

Brown, A. S., Begg, M. D., Gravenstein, S., Schaefer, C. A., Wyatt, R. J., Bresnahan, M., Babulas, V. P., & Susser, E. S. (2004). Serologic evidence of prenatal influenza in the etiology of schizophrenia. *Archives of General Psychiatry, 61*, 774–780. (p. 346)

Brown, A. S., Bracken, E., Zoccoli, S., & Douglas, K. (2004). Generating and remembering passwords. *Applied Cognitive Psychology, 18*, 641–651. (p. 194)

Brown, A. S., Schaefer, C. A., Wyatt, R. J., Goetz, R., Begg, M. D., Gorman, J. M., & Susser, E. S. (2000). Maternal exposure to respiratory infections and adult schizophrenia spectrum disorders: A prospective birth cohort study. *Schizophrenia Bulletin, 26*, 287–295. (p. 346)

Brown, E. L., & Deffenbacher, K. (1979). *Perception and the senses*. New York: Oxford University Press. (p. 141)

Brown, J. D., Steele, J. R., & Walsh-Childers, K. (2002). *Sexual teens, sexual media: Investigating media's influence on adolescent sexuality*. Mahwah, NJ: Erlbaum. (p. 109)

Brown, S. L., Brown, R. M., House, J. S., & Smith, D. M. (2008). Coping with spousal loss: Potential buffering effects of self-reported helping behavior. *Personality and Social Psychology Bulletin, 34*, 849–861. (p. 94)

Brown, S. W., Garry, M., Loftus, E., Silver, B., DuBois, K., & DuBreuil, S. (1996). People's beliefs about memory: Why don't we have better memories? Paper presented at the American Psychological Society convention. (p. 195)

Browning, C. (1992). *Ordinary men: Reserve police battalion 101 and the final solution in Poland.* New York: HarperCollins. (p. 385)

Brownmiller, S. (1975). *Against our will: Men, women, and rape.* New York: Simon & Schuster. (p. 111)

Bruck, M., & Ceci, S. J. (1999). The suggestibility of children's memory. *Annual Review of Psychology, 50,* 419–439. (p. 198)

Bruck, M., & Ceci, S. J. (2004). Forensic developmental psychology: Unveiling four common misconceptions. *Current Directions in Psychological Science, 15,* 229–232. (p. 198)

Bruer, J. T. (1999). *The myth of the first three years: A new understanding of early brain development and lifelong learning.* New York: Free Press. (p. 228)

Bruno, M-A., Pellas, F., & Laureys, S. (2008). Quality of life in locked-in syndrome survivors. In J. L. Vincent (ed.), *2008 yearbook of intensive care and emergency medicine.* New York: Springer. (p. 265)

Brunwasser, S. M., Gillham, J. E., & Kim, E. S. (2009). A meta-analytic review of the Penn Resiliency Program's effect on depressive symptoms. *Journal of Consulting and Clinical Psychology, 77,* 1042–1054. (p. 359)

Bryant, R. A. (2001). Posttraumatic stress disorder and traumatic brain injury: Can they co-exist? *Clinical Psychology Review, 21,* 931–948. (p. 199)

Buchanan, T. W. (2007). Retrieval of emotional memories. *Psychological Bulletin, 133,* 761–779. (p. 189)

Buckingham, M. (2007). *Go put your strengths to work: 6 powerful steps to achieve outstanding performance.* New York: Free Press. (p. 412)

Buckingham, M., & Clifton, D. O. (2001). *Now, discover your strengths.* New York: Free Press. (p. 412)

Buckley, C. (2007, January 3). Man is rescued by stranger on subway tracks. *New York Times* (www.nytimes.com). (p. 402)

Buckley, K. E., & Leary, M. R. (2001). Perceived acceptance as a predictor of social, emotional, and academic outcomes. Paper presented at the Society of Personality and Social Psychology annual convention. (p. 250)

Buehler, R., Griffin, D., & Ross, M. (1994). Exploring the "planning fallacy": Why people underestimate their task completion times. *Journal of Personality and Social Psychology, 67,* 366–381. (p. 209)

Buffardi, L. E., & W. K. Campbell (2008). Narcissism and social networking web sites. *Personality and Social Psychology Bulletin, 34,* 1303–1314. (p. 251)

Buka, S. L., Goldstein, J. M., Seidman, L. J., Zornberg, G., Donatelli, J-A. A., Denny, L. R., & Tsuang, M. T. (1999). Prenatal complications, genetic vulnerability, and schizophrenia: The New England longitudinal studies of schizophrenia. *Psychiatric Annals, 29,* 151–156. (p. 345)

Bullough, V. (1990). The Kinsey scale in historical perspective. In D. P. McWhirter, S. A. Sanders, & J. M. Reinisch (Eds.), *Homosexuality/heterosexuality: Concepts of sexual orientation.* New York: Oxford University Press. (p. 112)

Burcusa, S. L., & Iacono, W. G. (2007). Risk for recurrence in depression. *Clinical Psychology Review, 27,* 959–985. (p. 340)

Bureau of Labor Statistics. (2004, September 14). *American time-user survey summary.* Washington, DC: United States Department of Labor (www.bls.gov). (p. 105)

Bureau of the Census. (2004). *Statistical abstract of the United States 2004.* Washington, DC: U.S. Government Printing Office. (p. 366)

Burger, J. M. (2009). Replicating Milgram: Would people still obey today? *American Psychologist, 64,* 1–11. (pp. 384, 386)

Burgess, M., Enzle, M. E., & Schmaltz, R. (2004). Defeating the potentially deleterious effects of externally imposed deadlines: Practitioners' rules-of-thumb. *Personality and Social Psychology Bulletin, 30,* 868–877. (p. 416)

Buri, J. R., Louiselle, P. A., Misukanis, T. M., & Mueller, R. A. (1988). Effects of parental authoritarianism and authoritativeness on self-esteem. *Personality and Social Psychology Bulletin, 14,* 271–282. (p. 79)

Burish, T. G., & Carey, M. P. (1986). Conditioned aversive responses in cancer chemotherapy patients: Theoretical and developmental analysis. *Journal of Counseling and Clinical Psychology, 54,* 593–600. (p. 161)

Burkholder, R. (2005a, January 11). Chinese far wealthier than a decade ago—but are they happier? *Gallup Poll News Service* (www.gallup.com). (p. 267)

Burkholder, R. (2005b, January 18). China's citizens optimistic, yet not entirely satisfied. *Gallup Poll News Service* (www.gallup.com). (p. 267)

Burns, B. C. (2004). The effects of speed on skilled chess performance. *Psychological Science, 15,* 442–447. (p. 211)

Bushman, B. J. (1993). Human aggression while under the influence of alcohol and other drugs: An integrative research review. *Current Directions in Psychological Science, 2,* 148–152. (p. 394)

Bushman, B. J. (2002). Does venting anger feed or extinguish the flame? Catharsis, rumination, distraction, anger, and aggressive responding. *Personality and Social Psychology Bulletin, 28,* 724–731. (p. 264)

Bushman, B. J., Baumeister, R. F., Thomaes, S., Ryu, E., Begeer, S., & West, S. G. (2009). Looking again, and harder, for a link between low self-esteem and aggression. *Journal of Personality, 77,* 427–446. (p. 310)

Bushman, B. J., Rothstein, H. R., & Anderson, C. A. (2010). Much ado about something: Violent video game effects and a school of red herring: Reply to Ferguson and Kilburn (2010). *Psychological Bulletin, 136,* 182–187. (p. 396)

Buss, A. H. (1989). Personality as traits. *American Psychologist, 44,* 1378–1388. (p. 308)

Buss, D. M. (1994). The strategies of human mating: People worldwide are attracted to the same qualities in the opposite sex. *American Scientist, 82,* 238–249. (p. 116)

Buss, D. M. (1995). Evolutionary psychology: A new paradigm for psychological science. *Psychological Inquiry, 6,* 1–30. (p. 117)

Buss, D. M. (1996). Evolutionary insights into feminism and the "battle of the sexes." In D. M. Buss & N. M. Malamuth (Eds.), *Sex, power, conflict: Evolutionary and feminist perspectives.* New York: Oxford University Press. (p. 117)

Buss, D. M. (2000). *The dangerous passion: Why jealousy is as necessary as love and sex.* New York: Free Press. (p. 117)

Buster, J. E., Kingsberg, S. A., Aguirre, O., Brown, C., Breaux, J. G., Buch, A., Rodenberg, C. A., Wekselman, K., & Casson, P. (2005). Testosterone patch for low sexual desire in surgically menopausal women: A randomized trial. *Obstetrics and Gynecology, 105*(5), 944–952. (p. 107)

Butler, R. A. (1954, February). Curiosity in monkeys. *Scientific American,* pp. 70–75. (p. 238)

Bynum, R. (2004, November 1). Associated Press article. (p. 142)

Byrne, D. (1982). Predicting human sexual behavior. In A. G. Kraut (Ed.), *The G. Stanley Hall Lecture Series* (Vol. 2). Washington, DC: American Psychological Association. (p. 107, 159)

Byrne, J. (2003, September 21). From correspondence reported by Michael Shermer, E-Skeptic for September 21, 2003, from The Skeptics Society. (p. 149)

Byrne, R. W. (1991, May/June). Brute intellect. *The Sciences,* pp. 42–47. (p. 217)

Cacioppo, J. T., & Hawkley, L. C. (2009). Perceived social isolation and cognition. *Trends in Cognitive Sciences, 13,* 447–454. (p. 250)

Cahill, L. (1994). (Beta)-adrenergic activation and memory for emotional events. *Nature, 371,* 702–704. (p. 189)

Cahn, B. R., & Polich, J. (2006). Meditation states and traits: EEG, ERP, and neuroimaging studies. *Psychological Bulletin, 132,* 180–211. (p. 287)

Cale, E. M., & Lilienfeld, S. O. (2002). Sex differences in psychopathy and antisocial personality disorder: A review and integration. *Clinical Psychology Review, 22,* 1179–1207. (p. 328)

Call, K. T., Riedel, A. A., Hein, K., McLoyd, V., Petersen, A., & Kipke, M. (2002). Adolescent health and well-being in the twenty-first century: A global perspective. *Journal of Research on Adolescence, 12,* 69–98. (p. 109)

Callaghan, T., Rochat, P., Lillard, A., Claux, M. L., Odden, H., Itakura, S., Tapanya, S., & Singh, S. (2005). Synchrony in the onset of mental-state reasoning. *Psychological Science, 16,* 378–384. (p. 74)

Calvo-Merino, B., Glaser, D. E., Grèzes, J., Passingham, R. E., & Haggard, P. (2004). Action observation and acquired motor skills: An fMRI study with expert dancers. *Cerebral Cortex, 15,* 1243–1249. (p. 215)

Campbell, D. T. (1975). On the conflicts between biological and social evolution and between psychology and moral tradition. *American Psychologist, 30,* 1103–1126. (p. 267)

Campbell, D. T., & Specht, J. C. (1985). Altruism: Biology, culture, and religion. *Journal of Social and Clinical Psychology, 3*(1), 33–42. (p. 303)

Campbell, S. (1986). *The Loch Ness Monster: The evidence.* Willingborough, Northamptonshire, U.K.: Acquarian Press. (p. 127)

Camper, J. (1990, February 7). Drop pompom squad, U. of I. rape study says. *Chicago Tribune,* p. 1. (p. 330)

Camperio-Ciani, A., Corna, F., & Capiluppi, C. (2004). Evidence for maternally inherited factors favouring male homosexuality and promoting female fecundity. *Proceedings of the Royal Society of London B, 271,* 2217–2221. (p. 114)

Camperio-Ciani, A., Lemmola, F., & Blecher, S. R. (2009). Genetic factors increase fecundity in female maternal relatives of bisexual men as in homosexuals. *Journal of Sexual Medicine, 6,* 449–455. (p. 114)

Canli, T., Desmond, J. E., Zhao, Z., & Gabrieli, J. D. E. (2002). Sex differences in the neural basis of emotional memories. *Proceedings of the National Academy of Sciences, 99,* 10789–10794. (p. 261)

Cannon, W. B. (1929). *Bodily changes in pain, hunger, fear, and rage.* New York: Branford. (p. 275)

Cannon, W. B., & Washburn, A. (1912). An explanation of hunger. *American Journal of Physiology, 29,* 441–454. (p. 240)

Cantor, N., & Kihlstrom, J. F. (1987). *Personality and social intelligence.* Englewood Cliffs, NJ: Prentice-Hall. (p. 222)

Caplan, N., Choy, M. H., & Whitmore, J. K. (1992, February). Indochinese refugee families and academic achievement. *Scientific American,* pp. 36–42. (p. 86)

Carducci, B. J., Cosby, P. C., & Ward, D. D. (1978). Sexual arousal and interpersonal evaluations. *Journal of Experimental Social Psychology, 14,* 449–457. (p. 401)

Carey, B. (2007, September 4). Bipolar illness soars as a diagnosis for the young. *New York Times* (www.nytimes.com). (p. 339)

Carey, B. (2010, February 10). Revising book on disorders of the mind. *New York Times* (www.nytimes.com). (p. 320)

Carey, G. (1990). Genes, fears, phobias, and phobic disorders. *Journal of Counseling and Development, 68,* 628–632. (p. 325)

Carlson, M. (1995, August 29). Quoted by S. Blakeslee, In brain's early growth, timetable may be crucial. *New York Times,* pp. C1, C3. (p. 78)

Carlson, M., Charlin, V., & Miller, N. (1988). Positive mood and helping behavior: A test of six hypotheses. *Journal of Personality and Social Psychology, 55,* 211–229. (p. 404)

Carlson, S. (1985). A double-blind test of astrology. *Nature, 318,* 419–425. (p. 306)

Carnahan, T., & McFarland, S. (2007). Revisiting the Stanford Prison Experiment: Could participant self-selection have led to the cruelty? *Personality and Social Psychology Bulletin, 33,* 603–614. (p. 381)

Carpusor, A., & Loges, W. E. (2006). Rental discrimination and ethnicity in names. *Journal of Applied Social Psychology, 36,* 934–952. (p. 16)

Carrière, G. (2003). Parent and child factors associated with youth obesity. *Statistics Canada, Catalogue 82–003,* Supplement to Health Reports, 2003. (p. 246)

Carroll, J. (2007, August 10). *Most Americans approve of interracial marriages.* Gallup News Services (www.gallup.com). (p. 390)

Carstensen, L. I., & Mikels, J. A. (2005). At the intersection of emotion and cognition: Aging and the positivity effect. *Current Directions in Psychological Science, 14,* 117–121. (pp. 92, 95)

Cartwright, R. D. (1978). *A primer on sleep and dreaming.* Reading, MA: Addison-Wesley. (p. 53)

Carver, C. S., Johnson, S. L., & Joormann, J. (2008). Serotonergic function, two-mode models of self-regulation, and vulnerability to depression: What depression has in common with impulsive aggression. *Psychological Bulletin, 134,* 912–943. (p. 341)

CASA. (2003). *The formative years: Pathways to substance abuse among girls and young women ages 8–22.* New York: National Center on Addiction and Substance Use, Columbia University. (pp. 331, 336)

Cash, T., & Janda, L. H. (1984, December). The eye of the beholder. *Psychology Today,* pp. 46–52. (p. 399)

Caspi, A., Harrington, H., Milne, B., Amell, J. W., Theodore, R. F., & Moffitt, T. E. (2003). Children's behavioral styles at age 3 are linked to their adult personality traits at age 26. *Journal of Personality, 71,* 496–513. (p. 96)

Cassidy, J., & Shaver, P. R. (1999). *Handbook of attachment.* New York: Guilford. (p. 77)

Castillo, R. J. (1997). *Culture and mental illness: A client-centered approach.* Pacific Grove, CA: Brooks/Cole. (p. 319)

Catanese, K. R., & Tice, D. M. (2005). The effect of rejection on anti-social behaviors: Social exclusion produces aggressive behaviors. In K. D. Williams, J. P. Forgas, & W. Von Hippel (Eds.), *The social outcast: Ostracism, social exclusion, rejection, and bullying.* New York: Psychology Press. (p. 395)

Cattell, R. B. (1963). Theory of fluid and crystallized intelligence: A critical experiment. *Journal of Educational Psychology, 54,* 1–22. (p. 92)

Cavalli-Sforza, L., Menozzi, P., & Piazza, A. (1994). *The history and geography of human genes.* Princeton, NJ: Princeton University Press. (p. 229)

Cavigelli, S. A., & McClintock, M. K. (2003). Fear of novelty in infant rats predicts adult corticosterone dynamics and an early death. *Proceedings of the National Academy of Sciences, 100,* 16131–16136. (p. 276)

Cawley, B. D., Keeping, L. M., & Levy, P. E. (1998). Participation in the performance appraisal process and employee reactions: A meta-analytic review of field investigations. *Journal of Applied Psychology, 83,* 615–633. (p. 417)

CDC. (2007, accessed May 31). Basic statistics. www.cdc.gov/hib/topics/surveillance/basic.htm#hivaidsage. (p. 109)

CDC. (2008). Prevalence of sexually transmitted infections and bacterial vaginosis among female adolescents in the United States. Data from the National Health and Nutritional Examination Survey (NHANES) 2003–2004. Presentation at National STD Prevention Conference, March 11–13, 2008, Chicago, IL. (pp. 107, 108)

CDC. (2010, June 4). Youth risk behavior surveillance—United States, 2009. *Morbidity and Mortality Weekly*, 59SS05, 1-142 (by D. K. Eaton & 13 others). (p. 107)

Ceci, S. J. (1993). Cognitive and social factors in children's testimony. Master lecture, American Psychological Association convention. (p. 198)

Ceci, S. J., & Bruck, M. (1993). Child witnesses: Translating research into policy. *Social Policy Report* (Society for Research in Child Development), 7(3), 1–30. (p. 198)

Ceci, S. J., & Bruck, M. (1995). *Jeopardy in the courtroom: A scientific analysis of children's testimony*. Washington, DC: American Psychological Association. (p. 198)

Ceci, S. J., Huffman, M. L. C., Smith, E., & Loftus, E. F. (1994). Repeatedly thinking about a non-event: Source misattributions among preschoolers. *Consciousness and Cognition, 3*, 388–407. (p. 198)

Centers for Disease Control Vietnam Experience Study. (1988). Health status of Vietnam veterans. *Journal of the American Medical Association, 259*, 2701–2709. (p. 324)

Cepeda, N. J., Pashler, H., Vul, E., Wixted, J. T., & Rohrer, D. (2006). Distributed practice in verbal recall tasks: A review and quantitative synthesis. *Psychological Bulletin, 132*, 354–380. (p. 184)

Cepeda, N. J., Vul, E., Rohrer, D., Wixted, J. T., & Pashler, H. (2008). Spacing effects in learning: A temporal ridgelines of optimal retention. *Psychological Science, 19*, 1095–1102. (p. 184)

Cerella, J. (1985). Information processing rates in the elderly. *Psychological Bulletin, 98*, 67–83. (p. 91)

CFI. (2003, July). International developments. Report. Amherst, NY: Center for Inquiry International. (p. 150)

Chamove, A. S. (1980). Nongenetic induction of acquired levels of aggression. *Journal of Abnormal Psychology, 89*, 469–488. (p. 174)

Chance News. (1997, 25 November). More on the frequency of letters in texts. Dart.Chance@Dartmouth.edu. (p. 12)

Chang, E. C. (2001). Cultural influences on optimism and pessimism: Differences in Western and Eastern construals of the self. In E. C. Chang (Ed.), *Optimism and pessimism*. Washington, DC: APA Books. (p. 283)

Chang, P. P., Ford, D. E., Meoni, L. A., Wang, N-Y., & Klag, M. J. (2002). Anger in young men and subsequent premature cardiovascular disease: The precursors study. *Archives of Internal Medicine, 162*, 901–90. (p. 279)

Chaplin, W. F., Phillips, J. B., Brown, J. D., Clanton, N. R., & Stein, J. L. (2000). Handshaking, gender, personality, and first impressions. *Journal of Personality and Social Psychology, 79*, 110–117. (p. 260)

Charles, S. T., Reynolds, C. A., & Gatz, M. (2001). Age-related differences and change in positive and negative affect over 23 years. *Journal of Personality and Social Psychology, 80*, 136–151. (p. 95)

Charpak, G., & Broch, H. (2004). *Debunked! ESP, telekinesis, and other pseudoscience*. Baltimore, MD: Johns Hopkins University Press. (p. 149)

Chartrand, T. L., & Bargh, J. A. (1999). The chameleon effect: The perception-behavior link and social interaction. *Journal of Personality and Social Psychology, 76*, 893–910. (p. 382)

Cheek, J. M., & Melchior, L. A. (1990). Shyness, self-esteem, and self-consciousness. In H. Leitenberg (Ed.), *Handbook of social and evaluation anxiety*. New York: Plenum. (p. 312)

Chen, S-Y., & Fu, Y-C. (2008). Internet use and academic achievement: Gender differences in early adolescence. *Adolescence, 44*, 797–812. (p. 251)

Chen, X., Beydoun, M. A., & Wang, Y. (2008). Is sleep duration associated with childhood obesity? A systematic review and meta-analysis. *Obesity, 16*, 265–274. (p. 55)

Chess, S., & Thomas, A. (1987). *Know your child: An authoritative guide for today's parents*. New York: Basic Books. (pp. 69, 77)

Chida, Y., & Hamer, M. (2008). Chronic psychosocial factors and acute physiological responses to laboratory-induced stress in healthy populations: A quantitative review of 30 years of investigations. *Psychological Bulletin, 134*, 829–885. (p. 279)

Chida, Y., & Steptoe, A. (2009). The association of anger and hostility with future coronary heart disease: A meta-analytic review of prospective evidence. *Journal of the American College of Cardiology, 17*, 936–946. (pp. 279, 287)

Child Trends. (2001, August). Facts at a glance. (www.childtrends.org). (p. 109)

Chisholm, K. (1998). A three year follow-up of attachment and indiscriminate friendliness in children adopted from Romanian orphanages. *Child Development, 69*, 1092–1106. (p. 78)

Chivers, M. L. (2005). A brief review and discussion of sex differences in the specificity of sexual arousal. *Sexual and Relationship Therapy, 20*, 377–390. (p. 113)

Choi, I., & Choi, Y. (2002). Culture and self-concept flexibility. *Personality and Social Psychology Bulletin, 28*, 1508–1517. (p. 312)

Christakis, N. A., & Fowler, J. H. (2007). The spread of obesity in a large social network over 32 years. *New England Journal of Medicine, 357*, 370–379. (p. 247)

Christakis, N. A., & Fowler, J. H. (2009). *Connected: The surprising power of social networks and how they shape our lives*. New York: Little, Brown. (p. 284)

Christensen, A., & Jacobson, N. S. (1994). Who (or what) can do psychotherapy: The status and challenge of nonprofessional therapies. *Psychological Science, 5*, 8–14. (p. 364)

Christophersen, E. R., & Edwards, K. J. (1992). Treatment of elimination disorders: State of the art 1991. *Applied & Preventive Psychology, 1*, 15–22. (p. 355)

Chua, H. F., Boland, J. E., & Nisbett, R. E. (2005). Cultural variation in eye movements during scene perception. *Proceedings of the National Academy of Sciences, 102*, 12629–12633. (p. 378)

Chugani, H. T., & Phelps, M. E. (1986). Maturational changes in cerebral function in infants determined by 18FDG positron emission tomography. *Science, 231*, 840–843. (p. 70)

CIA. (2008). *The world factbook*. Washington, DC: Central Intelligence Agency (cia.gov/library/publications/the-world-factbook/geos/xx.html#People). (p. 91)

Cialdini, R. B. (1993). *Influence: Science and practice* (3rd ed.). New York: HarperCollins. (p. 380)

Cialdini, R. B., & Richardson, K. D. (1980). Two indirect tactics of image management: Basking and blasting. *Journal of Personality and Social Psychology, 39*, 406–415. (p. 392)

Ciarrochi, J., Forgas, J. P., & Mayer, J. D. (2006). *Emotional intelligence in everyday life* (2nd ed.). New York: Psychology Press. (p. 223)

Clack, B., Dixon, J., & Tredoux, C. (2005). Eating together apart: Patterns of segregation in a multi-ethnic cafeteria. *Journal of Community and Applied Social Psychology, 15*, 1–16. (p. 405)

Clancy, S. A. (2005). *Abducted: How people came to believe they were abducted by aliens*. Boston: Harvard University Press. (p. 52)

Clark, A., Seidler, A., & Miller, M. (2001). Inverse association between sense of humor and coronary heart disease. *International Journal of Cardiology, 80,* 87–88. (p. 283)

Cleary, A. M. (2008). Recognition memory, familiarity, and déjà vu experiences. *Current Directions in Psychological Science, 17,* 353–357. (p. 191)

Coan, J. A., Schaefer, H. S., & Davidson, R. J. (2006). Lending a hand: Social regulation of the neural response to threat. *Psychological Science, 17,* 1032–1039. (p. 284)

Coffey, C. E. (Ed.) (1993). *Clinical science of electroconvulsive therapy.* Washington, DC: American Psychiatric Press. (p. 369)

Cohen, D. (1995, June 17). Now we are one, or two, or three. *New Scientist,* pp. 14–15. (p. 326)

Cohen, G. L., Garcia, J., Apfel, N., & Master, A. (2006). Reducing the racial achievement gap: A social-psychological intervention. *Science, 313,* 1307–1310. (p. 232)

Cohen, K. M. (2002). Relationships among childhood sex-atypical behavior, spatial ability, handedness, and sexual orientation in men. *Archives of Sexual Behavior, 31,* 129–143. (p. 115)

Cohen, S. (2004). Social relationships and health. *American Psychologist, 59,* 676–684. (p. 284)

Cohen, S., & Pressman, S. D. (2006). Positive affect and health. *Current Directions in Psychological Science, 15,* 122–125. (p. 277)

Cohen, S., Alper, C. M., Doyle, W. J., Treanor, J. J., & Turner, R. B. (2006). Positive emotional style predicts resistance to illness after experimental exposure to rhinovuros or influenza A virus. *Psychosomatic Medicine, 68,* 809–815. (p. 277)

Cohen, S., Doyle, W. J., & Skoner, D. P. (1999). Psychological stress, cytokine production, and severity of upper respiratory illness. *Psychosomatic Medicine, 61,* 175–180. (p. 278)

Cohen, S., Doyle, W. J., Skoner, D. P., Rabin, B. S., & Gwaltney, J. M., Jr. (1997). Social ties and susceptibility to the common cold. *Journal of the American Medical Association, 277,* 1940–1944. (p. 284)

Cohen, S., Doyle, W. J., Turner, R., Alper, C. M., & Skoner, D. P. (2003). Sociability and susceptibility to the common cold. *Psychological Science, 14,* 389–395. (p. 277)

Cohen, S., Kaplan, J. R., Cunnick, J. E., Manuck, S. B., & Rabin, B. S. (1992). Chronic social stress, affiliation, and cellular immune response in non-human primates. *Psychological Science, 3,* 301–304. (p. 277)

Cohen, S., Tyrrell, D. A. J., & Smith, A. P. (1991). Psychological stress and susceptibility to the common cold. *New England Journal of Medicine, 325,* 606–612. (p. 277)

Colapinto, J. (2000). *As nature made him: The boy who was raised as a girl.* New York: HarperCollins. (p. 104)

Colarelli, S. M., Spranger, J. L., & Hechanova, M. R. (2006). Women, power, and sex composition in small groups: An evolutionary perspective. *Journal of Organizational Behavior, 27,* 163–184. (p. 102)

Colcombe, S. J., Kramer, A. F., Erickson, K. I., Scalf, P., McAuley, E., Cohen, N. J., Webb, A., Jerome, G. J., Marquex, D. X., & Elavsky, S. (2004). Cardiovascular fitness, cortical plasticity, and aging. *Proceedings of the National Academy of Sciences, 101,* 3316–3321. (p. 92)

Coleman, P. D., & Flood, D. G. (1986). Dendritic proliferation in the aging brain as a compensatory repair mechanism. In D. F. Swaab, E. Fliers, M. Mirmiram, W. A. Van Gool, & F. Van Haaren (Eds.), *Progress in brain research* (Vol. 20). New York: Elsevier. (p. 92)

Collins, D. W., & Kimura, D. (1997). A large sex difference on a two-dimensional mental rotation task. *Behavioral Neuroscience, 111,* 845–849. (p. 231)

Collins, F. (2007, February 1). In the cathedral or the laboratory, it's the same God, National Prayer Breakfast told. www.newsweek.washingtonpost.com/onfaith. (p. 65)

Collins, G. (2009, March 9). The rant list. *New York Times* (nytimes.com). (p. 20)

Collins, R. L., Elliott, M. N., Berry, S. H., Danouse, D. E., Kunkel, D., Hunter, S. B., & Miu, A. (2004). Watching sex on television predicts adolescent initiation of sexual behavior. *Pediatrics, 114,* 280–289. (p. 14)

Collinson, S. L., MacKay, C. E., James, A. C., Quested, D. J., Phillips, T., Roberts, N., & Crow, T. J. (2003). Brain volume, asymmetry and intellectual impairment in relation to sex in early-onset schizophrenia. *British Journal of Psychiatry, 183,* 114–120. (p. 345)

Collishaw, S., Pickles, A., Natarajan, L., & Maughan, B. (2007, June). 20-year trends in depression and anxiety in England. Paper presented at the Thirteenth Scientific Meeting on The Brain and the Developing Child, London. (p. 340)

Comer, R. J. (2004). *Abnormal psychology.* New York: Worth Publishers. (p. 318)

Consumer Reports. (1995, November). Does therapy help? Pp. 734–739. (p. 361)

Conway, A. R. A., Skitka, L. J., Hemmerich, J. A., & Kershaw, T. C. (2009). Flashbulb memory for 11 September 2001. *Applied Cognitive Psychology, 23,* 605–623. (p. 189)

Conway, M. A., Wang, Q., Hanyu, K., & Haque, S. (2005). A cross-cultural investigation of autobiographical memory. On the universality and cultural variation of the reminiscence bump. *Journal of Cross-Cultural Psychology, 36,* 739–749. (p. 91)

Cooke, L. J., Wardle, J., & Gibson, E. L. (2003). Relationship between parental report of food neophobia and everyday food consumption in 2–6-year-old children. *Appetite, 41,* 205–206. (p. 145)

Coopersmith, S. (1967). *The antecedents of self-esteem.* San Francisco: Freeman. (p. 79)

Coren, S. (1996). *Sleep thieves: An eye-opening exploration into the science and mysteries of sleep.* New York: Free Press. (pp. 53, 55)

Corey, D. P., & 15 others. (2004). TRPA1 is a candidate for the mechanosensitive transduction channel of vertebrate hair cells. *Nature* (advance online publication, October 13, at www.nature.com). (p. 140)

Corina, D. P. (1998). The processing of sign language: Evidence from aphasia. In B. Stemmer & H. A. Whittaker (Eds.), *Handbook of neurolinguistics.* San Diego: Academic Press. (p. 48)

Corina, D. P., Vaid, J., & Bellugi, U. (1992). The linguistic basis of left hemisphere specialization. *Science, 255,* 1258–1260. (p. 48)

Corkin, S., quoted by R. Adelson (2005, September). Lessons from H. M. *Monitor on Psychology,* p. 59. (p. 180)

Correll, J., Park, B., Judd, C. M., & Wittenbrink, B. (2002). The police officer's dilemma: Using ethnicity to disambiguate potentially threatening individuals. *Journal of Personality and Social Psychology, 83,* 1314–1329. (p. 391)

Correll, J., Park, B., Judd, C. M., Wittenbrink, B., Sadler, M. S., & Keesee, T. (2007). Across the thin blue line: Police officers and racial bias in the decision to shoot. *Journal of Personality and Social Psychology, 92,* 1006–1023. (p. 391)

Costa, P. T., Jr., & McCrae, R. R. (2006). Trait and factor theories. In J. C. Thomas, D. L. Segal, & M. Hersen (Eds.), *Comprehensive handbook of personality and psychopathology: Vol. 1. Personality and everyday functioning.* Hoboken, NJ: Wiley. (p. 305)

Costa, P. T., Jr., Terracciano, A., & McCrae, R. R. (2001). Gender differences in personality traits across cultures: Robust and surprising findings. *Journal of Personality and Social Psychology, 81,* 322–331. (p. 260)

Costa, P. T., Jr., Zonderman, A. B., McCrae, R. R., Cornoni-Huntley, J., Locke, B. Z., & Barbano, H. E. (1987). Longitudinal analyses of psychological well-being in a national sample: Stability of mean levels. *Journal of Gerontology, 42,* 50–55. (p. 95)

Costello, E. J., Compton, S. N., Keeler, G., & Angold, A. (2003). Relationships between poverty and psychopathology: A natural experiment. *Journal of the American Medical Association, 290,* 2023–2029. (p. 14)

Courneya, K. S., & Carron, A. V. (1992). The home advantage in sports competitions: A literature review. *Journal of Sport and Exercise Psychology, 14,* 13–27. (p. 387)

Courtney, J. G., Longnecker, M. P., Theorell, T., & de Verdier, M. G. (1993). Stressful life events and the risk of colorectal cancer. *Epidemiology, 4,* 407–414. (p. 278)

Covin, R., Ouimet, A. J., Seeds, P. M., & Dozois, D. J. A. (2008). A meta-analysis of CBT for pathological worry among clients with GAD. *Journal of Anxiety Disorders, 22,* 108–116. (p. 359)

Cowart, B. J. (1981). Development of taste perception in humans: Sensitivity and preference throughout the life span. *Psychological Bulletin, 90,* 43–73. (p. 145)

Cowart, B. J. (2005). Taste, our body's gustatory gatekeeper. *Cerebrum, 7(2),* 7–22. (p. 146)

Cox, J. J. & 18 others. (2006). An *SCN9A* channelopathy causes congenital inability to experience pain. *Nature, 444,* 894–898. (p. 143)

Crabbe, J. C. (2002). Genetic contributions to addiction. *Annual Review of Psychology, 53,* 435–462. (p. 336)

Crabtree, S. (2005, January 13). Engagement keeps the doctor away. *Gallup Management Journal* (gmj.gallup.com). (p. 415)

Crandall, C. S. (1994). Prejudice against fat people: Ideology and self-interest. *Journal of Personality and Social Psychology, 66,* 882–894. (p. 244)

Crandall, C. S. (1995). Do parents discriminate against their heavyweight daughters? *Personality and Social Psychology Bulletin, 21,* 724–735. (p. 244)

Crary, D. (2009, May 9). 5 years on, gay marriage debate fades in Mass. AP article in *The Guardian* (guardian.co.uk). (p. 117)

Crawford, E. F., Drescher, K. D., & Rosen, C. S. (2009). Predicting mortality in veterans with posttraumatic stress disorder thirty years after Vietnam. *Journal of Nervous and Mental Disease, 197,* 260–265. (p. 324)

Credé, M., & Kuncel, N. R. (2008). Study habits, skills, and attitudes: The third pillar supporting collegiate academic performance. *Perspectives on Psychological Science, 3,* 425–453. (p. 221)

Crews, F., He, J., & Hodge, C. (2007). Adolescent cortical development: A critical period of vulnerability for addiction. *Pharmacology, Biochemistry and Behavior, 86,* 189–199. (p. 330)

Crews, F. T., Mdzinarishvili, A., Kim, D., He, J., & Nixon, K. (2006). Neurogenesis in adolescent brain is potently inhibited by ethanol. *Neuroscience, 137,* 437–445. (p. 330)

Crocker, J., & Major, B. (1989). Social stigma and self-esteem: The self-protective properties of stigma," *Psychological Review, 89,* 608–630. (p. 310)

Crocker, J., & Park, L. E. (2004). The costly pursuit of self-esteem. *Psychological Bulletin, 130,* 392–414. (p. 310)

Crocker, J., Thompson, L. L., McGraw, K. M., & Ingerman, C. (1987). Downward comparison, prejudice, and evaluation of others: Effects of self-esteem and threat. *Journal of Personality and Social Psychology, 52,* 907–916. (p. 392)

Croft, R. J., Klugman, A., Baldeweg, T., & Gruzelier, J. H. (2001). Electro-physiological evidence of serotonergic impairment in long-term MDMA ("Ecstasy") users. *American Journal of Psychiatry, 158,* 1687–1692. (p. 334)

Crook, T. H., & West, R. L. (1990). Name recall performance across the adult life-span. *British Journal of Psychology, 81,* 335–340. (p. 92)

Cross, S., & Markus, H. (1991). Possible selves across the life span. *Human Development, 34,* 230–255. (p. 309)

Cross-National Collaborative Group. (1992). The changing rate of major depression. *Journal of the American Medical Association, 268,* 3098–3105. (p. 340)

Crowell, J. A., & Waters, E. (1994). Bowlby's theory grown up: The role of attachment in adult love relationships. *Psychological Inquiry, 5,* 1–22. (p. 77)

Csikszentmihalyi, M. (1990). *Flow: The psychology of optimal experience.* New York: Harper & Row. (p. 411)

Csikszentmihalyi, M. (1999). If we are so rich, why aren't we happy? *American Psychologist, 54,* 821–827. (p. 411)

Csikszentmihalyi, M., & Hunter, J. (2003). Happiness in everyday life: The uses of experience sampling. *Journal of Happiness Studies, 4,* 185–199. (p. 85)

Culbert, K. M., Burt, S. A., McGue, M., Iacono, W. G., & Klump, K. L. (2009). Puberty and the genetic diathesis of disordered eating attitudes and behaviors. *Journal of Abnormal Psychology, 118,* 788–796. (p. 243)

Cullen, L. T., & Masters, C. (2008, January 28). We just clicked. *Time,* pp. 84–89. (p. 398)

Cullum, J., & Harton, H. C. (2007). Cultural evolution: Interpersonal influence, issue importance, and the development of shared attitudes in college residence halls. *Personality and Social Psychology Bulletin, 33,* 1327–1339. (p. 383)

Cunningham, M. R., & others. (2005) "Their ideas of beauty are, on the whole, the same as ours": Consistency and variability in the cross-cultural perception of female physical attractiveness. *Journal of Personality and Social Psychology, 68,* 261–279. (p. 400)

Cunningham, W. A., Johnson, M. K., Raye, C. L., Gatenby, J. C., Gore, J. C., & Banaji, M. R. (2004). Separable neural components in the processing of Black and White faces. *Psychological Science, 15,* 806–813. (p. 391)

Curtis, G. C., Magee, W. J., Eaton, W. W., Wittchen, H-U., & Kessler, R. C. (1998). Specific fears and phobias: Epidemiology and classification. *British Journal of Psychiatry, 173,* 212–217. (p. 323)

Curtis, R. C., & Miller, K. (1986). Believing another likes or dislikes you: Behaviors making the beliefs come true. *Journal of Personality and Social Psychology, 51,* 284–290. (p. 400)

Cynkar, A. (2007, June). The changing gender composition of psychology. *Monitor on Psychology,* 46–47. (p. 105)

Dabbs, J. M., Jr. (2000). *Heroes, rogues, and lovers: Testosterone and behavior.* New York: McGraw-Hill. (p. 107)

Dabbs, J. M., Jr., Riad, J. K., & Chance, S. E. (2001a). Testosterone and ruthless homicide. *Personality and Individual Differences, 31,* 599–603. (p. 394)

Dabbs, J. M., Jr., Ruback, R. B., & Besch, N. F. (1987). Male saliva testosterone following conversations with male and female partners. Paper presented at the American Psychological Association convention. (p. 107)

Damasio, A. R. (1994). *Descartes error: Emotion, reason, and the human brain.* New York: Grossett/Putnam & Sons. (p. 259)

Damasio, A. R. (2003). *Looking for Spinoza: Joy, sorrow, and the feeling brain.* New York: Harcourt. (pp. 253, 259)

Damasio, H., Grabowski, T., Frank, R., Galaburda, A. M., & Damasio, A. R. (1994). The return of Phineas Gage: Clues about the brain from the skull of a famous patient. *Science, 264,* 1102–1105. (p. 43)

Danner, D. D., Snowdon, D. A., & Friesen, W. V. (2001). Positive emotions in early life and longevity: Findings from the Nun Study. *Journal of Personality and Social Psychology, 80,* 804–813. (p. 283)

Danso, H., & Esses, V. (2001). Black experimenters and the intellectual test performance of white participants: The tables are turned. *Journal of Experimental Social Psychology, 37,* 158–165. (p. 232)

Darley, J., & Alter, A. (in press). Behavioral issues of punishment and deterrence. In E. Shafir (Ed.), *The behavioral foundations of policy.* Princeton, NJ: Princeton University Press and the Russell Sage Foundation. (p. 165)

Darley, J. M., & Latané, B. (1968a). Bystander intervention in emergencies: Diffusion of responsibility. *Journal of Personality and Social Psychology, 8,* 377–383. (pp. 403, 404)

Darley, J. M., & Latané, B. (1968b, December). When will people help in a crisis? *Psychology Today,* pp. 54–57, 70–71. (p. 403)

Darrach, B., & Norris, J. (1984, August). An American tragedy. *Life,* pp. 58–74. (p. 328)

Darwin, C. (1859). *On the origin of species by means of natural selection.* London: John Murray. (p. 117)

Daskalakis, Z. J., Levinson, A. J., & Fitzgerald, P. B. (2008). Repetitive transcranial magnetic stimulation for major depressive disorder: A review. *Canadian Journal of Psychiatry, 53,* 555–564. (p. 370)

Daum, I., & Schugens, M. M. (1996). On the cerebellum and classical conditioning. *Psychological Science, 5,* 58–61. (p. 186)

Davey, G. C. L. (1995). Preparedness and phobias: Specific evolved associations or a generalized expectancy bias? *Behavioral and Brain Sciences, 18,* 289–297. (p. 326)

Davidson, R. J. (2000). Affective style, psychopathology, and resilience: Brain mechanisms and plasticity. *American Psychologist, 55,* 1196–1209. (p. 256)

Davidson, R. J. (2003). Affective neuroscience and psychophysiology: Toward a synthesis. *Psychophysiology, 40,* 655–665. (p. 256)

Davidson, R. J., Kabat-Zinn, J., Schumacher, J., Rosenkranz, M., Muller, D., Santorelli, S. F., Urbanowski, F., Harrington, A., Bonus, K., & Sheridan, J. F. (2003). Alterations in brain and immune function produced by mindfulness meditation. *Psychosomatic Medicine, 65,* 564–570. (p. 287)

Davidson, R. J., Pizzagalli, D., Nitschke, J. B., & Putnam, K. (2002). Depression: Perspectives from affective neuroscience. *Annual Review of Psychology, 53,* 545–574. (p. 341)

Davidson, R. J., Putnam, K. M., & Larson, C. L. (2000). Dysfunction in the neural circuitry of emotion regulation—a possible prelude to violence. *Science, 289,* 591–594. (p. 394)

Davies, P. (1992). *The mind of God: The scientific basis for a rational world.* New York: Simon & Schuster. (p. 119)

Davies, P. (1999). *The fifth miracle: The search for the origin and meaning of life.* New York: Simon & Schuster. (p. 119)

Davies, P. (2004, April 14). Into the 21st century. *Metaviews* (www.metanexus.net). (p. 119)

Davis, J. O., & Phelps, J. A. (1995a). Twins with schizophrenia: Genes or germs? *Schizophrenia Bulletin, 21,* 13–18. (p. 346)

Davis, J. O., Phelps, J. A., & Bracha, H. S. (1995b). Prenatal development of monozygotic twins and concordance for schizophrenia. *Schizophrenia Bulletin, 21,* 357–366. (p. 346)

Davis, S., Rees, M., Ribot, J., Moufarege, A., Rodenberg, C., & Purdie, D. (2003). Efficacy and safety of testosterone patches for the treatment of low sexual desire in surgically menopausal women. Presented to the American Society for Reproductive Medicine, San Antonio, October 11–15. (p. 107)

Dawes, R. M. (1994). *House of cards: Psychology and psychotherapy built on myth.* New York: Free Press. (p. 310)

de Boysson-Bardies, B., Halle, P., Sagart, L., & Durand, C. (1989). A cross linguistic investigation of vowel formats in babbling. *Journal of Child Language, 16,* 1–17. (p. 213)

de Courten-Myers, G. M. (2005, February 4). Personal correspondence (estimating total brain neurons, extrapolating from her carefully estimated 20 to 23 billion cortical neurons). (p. 32)

de Hoogh, A. H. B., den Hartog, D. N., Koopman, P. L., Thierry, H., van den Berg, P. T., van der Weide, J. G., & Wilderom, C. P. M. (2004). Charismatic leadership, environmental dynamism, and performance. *European Journal of Work and Organisational Psychology, 13,* 447–471. (p. 416)

De Koninck, J. (2000). Waking experiences and dreaming. In M. Kryger, T. Roth, & W. Dement (Eds.), *Principles and practice of sleep medicine* (3rd ed.). Philadelphia: Saunders. (p. 57)

de Moraes, L. (2010, March 18). Reality show contestants willing to kill in French experiment. *Washington Post* (www.washingtonpost.com). (p. 384)

Dean, G. A., Kelly, I. W., Saklofske, D. H., & Furnham, A. (1992). Graphology and human judgment. In B. Beyerstein & D. Beyerstein (Eds.), *The write stuff: Evaluations of graphology.* Buffalo, NY: Prometheus Books. (p. 306)

Deary, I. J., Johnson, W., & Houlihan, L. M. (2009). Genetic foundations of human intelligence. *Human Genetics, 126,* 215–232. (p. 227)

Deary, I. J., Thorpe, G., Wilson, V., Starr, J. M., & Whalley, L. J. (2003). Population sex differences in IQ at age 11: The Scottish mental survey 1932. *Intelligence, 31,* 533–541. (p. 230)

Deary, I. J., Whalley, L. J., & Starr, J. M. (2009). *A lifetime of intelligence: Follow-up studies of the Scottish Mental Surveys of 1932 and 1947.* Washington, DC: American Psychological Association. (pp. 227, 230)

Deci, E. L., & Ryan, R. M. (Eds.) (2002). *Handbook of self-determination research.* Rochester, NJ: University of Rochester Press. (p. 249)

Deci, E. L., Koestner, R., & Ryan, R. M. (1999, November). A meta-analytic review of experiments examining the effects of extrinsic rewards on intrinsic motivation. *Psychological Bulletin, 125(6),* 627–668. (p. 171)

DeLamater, J. D., & Sill, M. (2005). Sexual desire in later life. *Journal of Sex Research, 42,* 138–149. (p. 91)

Delaney, H. D., Miller, W. R., & Bisonó, A. M. (2007). Religiosity and spirituality among psychologists: A survey of clinician members of the American Psychological Association. *Professional Psychology: Research and Practice, 38,* 538–546. (p. 364)

DeLoache, J. S., & Brown, A. L. (1987, October–December). Differences in the memory-based searching of delayed and normally developing young children. *Intelligence, 11(4),* 277–289. (p. 73)

DeLoache, J. S., Uttal, D. H., & Rosengren, K. S. (2004). Scale errors offer evidence for a perception-action dissociation early in life. *Science, 304,* 1027–1029. (p. 72)

Dement, W. C. (1978). *Some must watch while some must sleep.* New York: Norton. (pp. 51, 55)

Dement, W. C. (1999). *The promise of sleep.* New York: Delacorte Press. (pp. 51, 52, 54, 55)

Dement, W. C., & Wolpert, E. A. (1958). The relation of eye movements, body mobility, and external stimuli to dream content. *Journal of Experimental Psychology, 55,* 543–553. (p. 57)

Demir, E., & Dickson, B. J. (2005). Fruitless splicing specifies male courtship behavior in Drosophila. *Cell, 121,* 785–794. (p. 114)

DeNeve, K. M., & Cooper, H. (1998). The happy personality: A meta-analysis of 137 personality traits and subjective well-being. *Psychological Bulletin, 124,* 197–229. (p. 268)

Denton, K., & Krebs, D. (1990). From the scene to the crime: The effect of alcohol and social context on moral judgment. *Journal of Personality and Social Psychology, 59,* 242–248. (p. 330)

Dermer, M., Cohen, S. J., Jacobsen, E., & Anderson, E. A. (1979). Evaluative judgments of aspects of life as a function of vicarious exposure to hedonic extremes. *Journal of Personality and Social Psychology, 37,* 247–260. (p. 267)

Dermer, M., & Pyszczynski, T. A. (1978). Effects of erotica upon men's loving and liking responses for women they love. *Journal of Personality and Social Psychology, 36,* 1302–1309. (p. 401)

DeSteno, D., Dasgupta, N., Bartlett, M. Y., & Cajdric, A. (2004). Prejudice from thin air: The effect of emotion on automatic intergroup attitudes. *Psychological Science, 15,* 319–324. (p. 263)

DeSteno, D., Petty, R. E., Wegener, D. T., & Rucker, D. D. (2000). Beyond valence in the perception of likelihood: The role of emotion specificity. *Journal of Personality and Social Psychology, 78,* 397–416. (p. 191)

Deutsch, J. A. (1972, July). Brain reward: ESP and ecstasy. *Psychology Today,* pp. 46–48. (p. 39)

Devilly, G. J., Gist, R., & Cotton, P. (2006). Ready! Fire! Aim! The status of psychological debriefing and therapeutic interventions: In the work place and after disasters. *Review of General Psychology, 10,* 318–345. (p. 324)

Devine, P. G. (1995). Prejudice and outgroup perception. In A. Tesser (Ed.), *Advanced social psychology.* New York: McGraw-Hill. (p. 398)

DeWall, C. N., Baumeister, R. F., Stillman, T. F., & Gaillot, M. T. (2007). Violence restrained: Effects of self-regulation and its depletion on aggression. *Journal of Experimental Social Psychology, 43,* 62–76. (p. 282)

Diamond, J. (1989, May). The great leap forward. *Discover,* pp. 50–60. (p. 212)

Diamond, J. (2001, February). A tale of two reputations: Why we revere Darwin and give Freud a hard time. *Natural History,* pp. 20–24. (p. 117)

Diamond, L. M. (2007). A dynamical systems approach to the development and expression of female same-sex sexuality. *Perspectives on Psychological Science, 2,* 142–161. (p. 113)

Dickens, W. T., & Flynn, J. R. (2006). Black Americans reduce the racial IQ gap: Evidence from standardization samples. *Psychological Science, 17,* 913–920. (p. 228)

Dickler, J. (2007, January 18). *Best employers, great returns.* CNNMoney.com. (p. 414)

Dickson, B. J. (2005, June 3). Quoted in E. Rosenthal, For fruit flies, gene shift tilts sex orientation. *New York Times* (www.nytimes.com). (p. 114)

Diener, E., & Biswas-Diener, R. (2009). *Rethinking happiness: The science of psychological wealth.* Malden, MA: Wiley Blackwell. (p. 266)

Diener, E., Emmons, R. A., & Sandvik, E. (1986). The dual nature of happiness: Independence of positive and negative moods. Unpublished manuscript, University of Illinois. (p. 95)

Diener, E., Ng, W., Harter, J., & Arora, R. (2009). Wealth and happiness across the world: Material prosperity predicts life evaluation, while psychosocial prosperity predicts positive feeling. Unpublished manuscript, University of Illinois and the Gallup Organization. (p. 266)

Diener, E., Nickerson, C., Lucas, R. E., & Sandvik, E. (2002). Dispositional affect and job outcomes. *Social Indicators Research, 59,* 229–259. (p. 264)

Diener, E., & Oishi, S. (2000). Money and happiness: Income and subjective well-being across nations. In E. Diener & E. M. Suh (Eds.), *Subjective well-being across cultures.* Cambridge, MA: MIT Press. (p. 267)

Diener, E., Oishi, S., & Lucas, R. E. (2003). Personality, culture, and subjective well-being: Emotional and cognitive evaluations of life. *Annual Review of Psychology, 54,* 403–425. (p. 268)

Diener, E., Wolsic, B., & Fujita, F. (1995). Physical attractiveness and subjective well-being. *Journal of Personality and Social Psychology, 69,* 120–129. (p. 399)

DiLalla, D. L., Carey, G., Gottesman, I. I., & Bouchard, T. J., Jr. (1996). Heritability of MMPI personality indicators of psychopathology in twins reared apart. *Journal of Abnormal Psychology, 105,* 491–499. (p. 341)

Dimberg, U., Thunberg, M., & Elmehed, K. (2000). Unconscious facial reactions to emotional facial expressions. *Psychological Science, 11,* 86–89. (pp. 174, 258, 263)

Dimberg, U., Thunberg, M., & Grunedal, S. (2002). Facial reactions to emotional stimuli: Automatically controlled emotional responses. *Cognition and Emotion, 16,* 449–472. (p. 174)

Dindia, K., & Allen, M. (1992). Sex differences in self-disclosure: A meta-analysis. *Psychological Bulletin, 112,* 106–124. (p. 103)

Dion, K. K., & Dion, K. L. (1993). Individualistic and collectivistic perspectives on gender and the cultural context of love and intimacy. *Journal of Social Issues, 49,* 53–69. (p. 313)

Dion, K. K., & Dion, K. L. (2001). Gender and cultural adaptation in immigrant families. *Journal of Social Issues, 57,* 511–521. (p. 105)

DiSalvo, D. (2010, January/February). Are social networks messing with your head? *Scientific American Mind,* pp. 48–55. (p. 251)

Di Tella, R., & MacCulloch, R. (2008). Happiness adaptation to income beyond "basic needs." National Bureau of Economic Research, Working Paper 14539. (nber.org/papers/w14539).

Dobbs, D. (2009, April). The post-traumatic stress trap. *Scientific American,* pp. 64–69. (p. 324)

Dodge, K. A. (2009). Mechanisms of gene-environment interaction effects in the development of conduct disorder. *Perspectives on Psychological Science, 4,* 408–414. (p. 328)

Dohrenwend, B. P., Pearlin, L., Clayton, P., Hamburg, B., Dohrenwend, B. P., Riley, M., & Rose, R. (1982). Report on stress and life events. In G. R. Elliott & C. Eisdorfer (Eds.), *Stress and human health: Analysis and implications of research* (A study by the Institute of Medicine/National Academy of Sciences). New York: Springer. (p. 275)

Dohrenwend, B. P., Turner, J. B., Turse, N. A., Adams, B. G., Koenen, K. C., & Marshall, R. (2006). The psychological risks of Vietnam for U.S. veterans: A revisit with new data and methods. *Science, 313,* 979-982. (p. 324)

Dolan, C. M., Kraemer, H., Browner, W., Ensrud, K., & Kelsey, J. L. (2007). Associations between body composition, anthropometry and mortality in women of age 65 and older. *American Journal of Public Health, 97,* 913–918. (p. 244)

Dolezal, H. (1982). *Living in a world transformed.* New York: Academic Press. (p. 139)

Domhoff, G. W. (1996). *Finding meaning in dreams: A quantitative approach.* New York: Plenum. (p. 57)

Domhoff, G. W. (1999). New directions in the study of dream content using the Hall and Van de Castle coding system. *Dreaming, 9,* 115–137. (p. 57)

Domhoff, G. W. (2000). Moving Dream Theory Beyond Freud and Jung. Paper presented to the symposium "Beyond Freud and Jung?" Graduate Theological Union, Berkeley, CA, 9/23/2000. (p. 57)

Domhoff, G. W. (2003a). *The scientific study of dreams: A quantitative approach.* New York: Plenum. (p. 58)

Domhoff, G. W. (2003b). *The scientific study of dreams: Neural networks, cognitive development, and content analysis.* Washington, DC: APA Books. (p. 58)

Domjan, M. (1992). Adult learning and mate choice: Possibilities and experimental evidence. *American Zoologist, 32,* 48–61. (p. 159)

Domjan, M. (1994). Formulation of a behavior system for sexual conditioning. *Psychonomic Bulletin & Review, 1,* 421–428. (p. 159)

Domjan, M. (2005). Pavlovian conditioning: A functional perspective. *Annual Review of Psychology, 56.* (p. 159)

Donnellan, M. B., Trzesniewski, K. H., Robins, R. W., Moffitt, T. E., & Caspi, A. (2005). Low self-esteem is related to aggression, antisocial behavior, and delinquency. *Psychological Science, 16,* 328–335. (pp. 309, 310)

Donnerstein, E. (1998). Why do we have those new ratings on television. Invited address to the National Institute on the Teaching of Psychology. (pp. 175, 177)

Donnerstein, E., Linz, D., & Penrod, S. (1987). *The question of pornography.* New York: Free Press. (p. 177)

Doty, R. L., Shaman, P., Applebaum, S. L., Giberson, R., Siksorski, L., & Rosenberg, L. (1984). Smell identification ability: Changes with age. *Science, 226,* 1441–1443. (p. 91)

Dovidio, J. F., & Gaertner, S. L. (1999). Reducing prejudice: Combating intergroup biases. *Current Directions in Psychological Science, 8,* 101–105. (p. 405)

Doyle, R. (2005, March). Gay and lesbian census. *Scientific American,* p. 28. (p. 116)

Draguns, J. G. (1990a). Normal and abnormal behavior in cross-cultural perspective: Specifying the nature of their relationship. *Nebraska Symposium on Motivation 1989, 37,* 235–277. (p. 316)

Draguns, J. G. (1990b). Applications of cross-cultural psychology in the field of mental health. In R. W. Brislin (Ed.), *Applied cross-cultural psychology.* Newbury Park, CA: Sage. (p. 316)

Draguns, J. G. (1997). Abnormal behavior patterns across cultures: Implications for counseling and psychotherapy. *International Journal of Intercultural Relations, 21,* 213-248. (p. 316)

Druckman, D., & Bjork, R. A. (Eds.) (1994). *Learning, remembering, believing: Enhancing human performance.* Washington, DC: National Academy Press. (p. 144)

Duckworth, A. L., & Seligman, M. E. P. (2005). Discipline outdoes talent: Self-discipline predicts academic performance in adolescents. *Psychological Science, 12,* 939–944. (p. 413)

Duckworth, A. L., & Seligman, M. E. P. (2006). Self-discipline gives girls the edge: Gender in self-discipline, grades, and achievement tests. *Journal of Educational Psychology, 98,* 198–208. (p. 413)

Duckworth, A. L., Quinn, P. D., & Seligman, M. E. P. (2009). Positive predictors of teacher effectiveness. *Journal of Positive Psychology, 4,* 540–547. (pp. 310, 413)

Duclos, S. E., Laird, J. D., Sexter, M., Stern, L., & Van Lighten, O. (1989). Emotion-specific effects of facial expressions and postures on emotional experience. *Journal of Personality and Social Psychology, 57,* 100–108. (p. 262)

Duffy, M. (2003, June 9). Weapons of mass disappearance. *Time,* pp. 28–33. (p. 381)

Duggan, J. P., & Booth, D. A. (1986). Obesity, overeating, and rapid gastric emptying in rats with ventromedial hypothalamic lesions. *Science, 231,* 609–611. (p. 241)

Dumont, K. A., Widom, C. S., & Czaja, S. J. (2007). Predictors of resilience in abused and neglected children grown-up: The role of individual and neighborhood characteristics. *Child Abuse & Neglect, 31,* 255–274. (p. 78)

Duncan, B. L. (1976). Differential social perception and attribution of intergroup violence: Testing the lower limits of stereotyping of blacks. *Journal of Personality and Social Psychology, 34,* 590–598. (p. 390)

Dunn, A. L., Trivedi, M. H., Kampert, J. B., Clark, C. G., & Chambliss, H. O. (2005). Exercise treatment for depression: Efficacy and dose response. *American Journal of Preventive Medicine, 28,* 1–8. (pp. 286, 371)

Dunson, D. B., Colombo, B., & Baird, D. D. (2002). Changes with age in the level and duration of fertility in the menstrual cycle. *Human Reproduction, 17,* 1399–1403. (p. 90)

Durgin, F. H., Evans, L., Dunphy, N., Klostermann, S., & Simmons, K. (2007). Rubber hands feel the touch of light. *Psychological Science, 18,* 152–157. (p. 143)

Dush, C. M. K, Cohan, C. L., & Amato, P. R. (2003). The relationship between cohabitation and marital quality and stability: Change across cohorts? *Journal of Marriage and Family, 65,* 539–549. (p. 93)

Dutton, D. G., & Aron, A. P. (1974). Some evidence for heightened sexual attraction under conditions of high anxiety. *Journal of Personality and Social Psychology, 30,* 510–517. (p. 401)

Dutton, D. G., & Aron, A. P. (1989). Romantic attraction and generalized liking for others who are sources of conflict-based arousal. *Canadian Journal of Behavioural Sciences, 21,* 246–257. (p. 401)

Dye, M. W. G., Green, C. S., & Bavelier, D. (2009). Increasing speed of processing with action video games. *Current Directions in Psychological Science, 18,* 321–326. (p. 396)

Eagly, A. H. (2007). Female leadership advantage and disadvantage: Resolving the contradictions. *Psychology of Women Quarterly, 31,* 1–12. (pp. 102, 103, 416)

Eagly, A. H. (2009). The his and hers of prosocial behavior: An examination of the social psychology of gender. *American Psychologist, 64,* 644–658. (pp. 102, 103)

Eagly, A. H., & Wood, W. (1999). The origins of sex differences in human behavior: Evolved dispositions versus social roles. *American Psychologist, 54,* 408–423. (p. 118)

Eagly, A. H., Ashmore, R. D., Makhijani, M. G., & Kennedy, L. C. (1991). What is beautiful is good, but … : A meta-analytic review of research on the physical attractiveness stereotype. *Psychological Bulletin, 110,* 109–128. (p. 399)

Ebbesen, E. B., Duncan, B., & Konecni, V. J. (1975). Effects of content of verbal aggression on future verbal aggression: A field experiment. *Journal of Experimental Social Psychology, 11,* 192–204. (p. 263)

Ebbinghaus, H. (1885). Über das Gedachtnis. Leipzig: Duncker & Humblot. Cited in R. Klatzky (1980), *Human memory: Structures and processes.* San Francisco: Freeman. (p. 193)

Ebbinghaus, H. (1885/1964). *Memory: A contribution to experimental psychology* (tr. by H. A. Ruger & C. E. Bussenius). New York: Dover. (p. 193)

Eberhardt, J. L. (2005). Imaging race. *American Psychologist, 60,* 181–190. (p. 391)

Eckensberger, L. H. (1994). Moral development and its measurement across cultures. In W. J. Lonner & R. Malpass (Eds.), *Psychology and culture.* Boston: Allyn & Bacon. (p. 83)

Eckert, E. D., Heston, L. L., & Bouchard, T. J., Jr. (1981). MZ twins reared apart: Preliminary findings of psychiatric disturbances and traits. In

L. Gedda, P. Paris, & W. D. Nance (Eds.), *Twin research: Vol. 3. Pt. B. Intelligence, personality, and development*. New York: Alan Liss. (p. 325)

Economist. (2001, December 20). An anthropology of happiness. *The Economist* (www.economist.com/world/asia). (p. 249)

Edelman, S., & Kidman, A. D. (1997). Mind and cancer: Is there a relationship? A review of the evidence. *Australian Psychologist, 32*, 1–7. (p. 278)

Edwards, C. P. (1981). The comparative study of the development of moral judgment and reasoning. In R. H. Munroe, R. L. Munroe, & B. B. Whiting (Eds.), *Handbook of cross-cultural human development*. New York: Garland Press. (p. 82)

Edwards, C. P. (1982). Moral development in comparative cultural perspective. In D. A. Wagner & H. W. Stevenson (Eds.), *Cultural perspectives on child development*. San Francisco: Freeman. (p. 82)

Ehrlichman, H., & Halpern, J. N. (1988). Affect and memory: Effects of pleasant and unpleasant odors on retrieval of happy and unhappy memories. *Journal of Personality and Social Psychology, 55*, 769–779. (p. 147)

Eisenberg, N., & Lennon, R. (1983). Sex differences in empathy and related capacities. *Psychological Bulletin, 94*, 100–131. (p. 260)

Eisenberger, R., & Rhoades, L. (2001). Incremental effects of reward on creativity. *Journal of Personality and Social Psychology, 81*, 728–741. (p. 172)

Ekman, P. (1994). Strong evidence for universals in facial expressions: A reply to Russell's mistaken critique. *Psychological Bulletin, 115*, 268–287. (p. 261)

Ekman, P., & Friesen, W. V. (1975). *Unmasking the face*. Englewood Cliffs, NJ: Prentice-Hall. (p. 261)

Ekman, P., Friesen, W. V., O'Sullivan, M., Chan, A., Diacoyanni-Tarlatzis, I., Heider, K., Krause, R., LeCompte, W. A., Pitcairn, T., Ricci-Bitti, P. E., Scherer, K., Tomita, M., & Tzavaras, A. (1987). Universals and cultural differences in the judgments of facial expressions of emotion. *Journal of Personality and Social Psychology, 53*, 712–717. (p. 261)

Elfenbein, H. A., & Ambady, N. (1999). Does it take one to know one? A meta-analysis of the universality and cultural specificity of emotion recognition. Unpublished manuscript, Harvard University. (p. 261)

Elfenbein, H. A., & Ambady, N. (2002). On the universality and cultural specificity of emotion recognition: A meta-analysis. *Psychological Bulletin, 128*, 203–235. (p. 261)

Elfenbein, H. A., & Ambady, N. (2003a). When familiarity breeds accuracy: Cultural exposure and facial emotion recognition. *Journal of Personality and Social Psychology, 85*, 276–290. (p. 261)

Elfenbein, H. A., & Ambady, N. (2003b). Universals and cultural differences in recognizing emotions. *Current Directions in Psychological Science, 12*, 159–164. (p. 261)

Elkin, I., Shea, T., Watkins, J. T., Imber, S. D., Sotsky, S. M., Collins, J. F., Glass, D. R., Pilkonis, P. A., Leber, W. R., Docherty, J. P., Fiester, S. J., & Parloff, M. B. (1989). National Institute of Mental Health treatment of depression collaborative research program. *Archives of General Psychiatry, 46*, 971–983. (p. 362)

Elkind, D. (1970). The origins of religion in the child. *Review of Religious Research, 12*, 35–42. (p. 82)

Elkind, D. (1978). *The child's reality: Three developmental themes*. Hillsdale, NJ: Erlbaum. (p. 82)

Ellenbogen, J. M., Hu, P. T., Payne, J. D., Titone, D., & Walker, M. P. (2007). Human relational memory requires time and sleep. *Proceedings of the National Academy of Sciences, 104*, 7723–7728. (p. 54)

Elliot, A. J., & Niesta, D. (2008). Romantic red: Red enhances men's attraction to women. *Journal of Personality and Social Psychology, 95*, 1150–1164. (p. 170)

Ellis, A. (1980). Psychotherapy and atheistic values: A response to A. E. Bergin's "Psychotherapy and religious values." *Journal of Consulting and Clinical Psychology, 48*, 635–639. (p. 364)

Ellis, B. J. (2004). Timing of pubertal maturation in girls: An integrated life history approach. *Psychological Bulletin, 130*, 920–958. (p. 87)

Ellis, B. J., Bates, J. E., Dodge, K. A., Fergusson, D. M., John, H. L., Pettit, G. S., & Woodward, L. (2003). Does father absence place daughters at special risk for early sexual activity and teenage pregnancy? *Child Development, 74*, 801–821. (p. 110)

Ellis, L., & Ames, M. A. (1987). Neurohormonal functioning and sexual orientation: A theory of homosexuality-heterosexuality. *Psychological Bulletin, 101*, 233–258. (p. 114)

Else-Quest, N. M., Hyde, J. S., & Linn, M. C. (2010). Cross-national patterns of gender differences in mathematics: A meta-analysis. *Psychological Bulletin, 136*, 103–127. (p. 230)

Elzinga, B. M., Ardon, A. M., Heijnis, M. K., De Ruiter, M. B., Van Dyck, R., & Veltman, D. J. (2007). Neural correlates of enhanced working-memory performance in dissociative disorder: A functional MRI study. *Psychological Medicine, 37*, 235–245. (p. 327)

Emerging Trends. (1997, September). *Teens turn more to parents than friends on whether to attend church*. Princeton, NJ: Princeton Religion Research Center. (p. 87)

Emery, G. (2004). *Psychic predictions 2004*. Committee for the Scientific Investigation of Claims of the Paranormal (www.csicop.org). (p. 149)

Emmons, R. A. (2007). *Thanks! How the new science of gratitude can make you happier*. Boston: Houghton Mifflin. (p. 269)

Emmons, S., Geisler, C., Kaplan, K. J., & Harrow, M. (1997). *Living with schizophrenia*. Muncie, IN: Taylor and Francis (Accelerated Development). (pp. 316, 344)

Endler, N. S. (1982). *Holiday of darkness: A psychologist's personal journey out of his depression*. New York: Wiley. (pp. 342, 369)

Engemann, K. M., & Owyang, M. T. (2005, April). So much for that merit raise: The link between wages and appearance. *Regional Economist* (www.stlouisfed.org). (p. 399)

Engen, T. (1987). Remembering odors and their names. *American Scientist, 75*, 497–503. (p. 147)

Epley, N., Keysar, B., Van Boven, L., & Gilovich, T. (2004). Perspective taking as egocentric anchoring and adjustment. *Journal of Personality and Social Psychology, 87*, 327–339. (p. 74)

EPOCH. (2000). *Legal reforms: Corporal punishment of children in the family*. (www.stophitting.com/laws/legalReform.php). (p. 166)

Epstein, J., Stern, E., & Silbersweig, D. (1998). Mesolimbic activity associated with psychosis in schizophrenia: Symptom-specific PET studies. In J. F. McGinty (Ed.), *Advancing from the ventral striatum to the extended amygdala: Implications for neuropsychiatry and drug use: In honor of Lennart Heimer. Annals of the New York Academy of Sciences, 877*, 562–574. (p. 345)

Epstein, S. (1983a). Aggregation and beyond: Some basic issues on the prediction of behavior. *Journal of Personality, 51*, 360–392. (p. 307)

Epstein, S. (1983b). The stability of behavior across time and situations. In R. Zucker, J. Aronoff, & A. I. Rabin (Eds.), *Personality and the prediction of behavior*. San Diego: Academic Press. (p. 307)

Epstein, S., & Meier, P. (1989). Constructive thinking: A broad coping variable with specific components. *Journal of Personality and Social Psychology, 57*, 332–350. (p. 222)

Erdberg, P. (1990). Rorschach assessment. In G. Goldstein & M. Hersen (Eds.), *Handbook of psychological assessment* (2nd ed.). New York: Pergamon. (p. 298)

Erdelyi, M. H. (1985). *Psychoanalysis: Freud's cognitive psychology.* New York: Freeman. (p. 299)

Erdelyi, M. H. (1988). Repression, reconstruction, and defense: History and integration of the psychoanalytic and experimental frameworks. In J. Singer (Ed.), *Repression: Defense mechanism and cognitive style.* Chicago: University of Chicago Press. (p. 299)

Erdelyi, M. H. (2006). The unified theory of repression. *Behavioral and Brain Sciences, 29,* 499–551. (p. 299)

Erickson, M. F., & Aird, E. G. (2005). *The motherhood study: Fresh insights on mothers' attitudes and concerns.* New York: The Motherhood Project, Institute for American Values. (p. 93)

Ericsson, K. A. (2001). Attaining excellence through deliberate practice: Insights from the study of expert performance. In M. Ferrari (Ed.), *The pursuit of excellence in education.* Hillsdale, NJ: Erlbaum. (p. 414)

Ericsson, K. A. (2002). Attaining excellence through deliberate practice: Insights from the study of expert performance. In C. Desforges & R. Fox (Eds.), *Teaching and learning: The essential readings.* Malden, MA: Blackwell Publishers. (p. 221)

Ericsson, K. A. (2006). The influence of experience and deliberate practice on the development of superior expert performance. In K. A. Ericsson, N. Charness, P. J. Feltovich, & R. R. Hoffman (Eds.), *The Cambridge handbook of expertise and expert performance.* Cambridge: Cambridge University Press. (p. 414)

Ericsson, K. A. (2007). Deliberate practice and the modifiability of body and mind: Toward a science of the structure and acquisition of expert and elite performance. *International Journal of Sport Psychology, 38,* 4–34. (pp. 221, 414)

Ericsson, K. A., Roring, R. W., & Nandagopal, K. (2007). Giftedness and evidence for reproducibly superior performance: An account based on the expert performance framework. *High Ability Studies, 18,* 3–56. (p. 221)

Erikson, E. H. (1963). *Childhood and society.* New York: Norton. (p. 83)

Ertmer, D. J., Young, N. M., & Nathani, S. (2007). Profiles of focal development in young cochlear implant recipients. *Journal of Speech, Language, and Hearing Research, 50,* 393–407. (p. 214)

Escobar-Chaves, S. L., Tortolero, S. R., Markham, C. M., Low, B. J., Eitel, P., & Thickstun, P. (2005). Impact of the media on adolescent sexual attitudes and behaviors. *Pediatrics, 116,* 303–326. (p. 109)

Esser, J. K., & Lindoerfer, J. S. (1989). Groupthink and the space shuttle *Challenger* accident: Toward a quantitative case analysis. *Journal of Behavioral Decision Making, 2,* 167–177. (p. 389)

Esterling, B. A., L'Abate, L., Murray, E. J., & Pennebaker, J. W. (1999). Empirical foundations for writing in prevention and psychotherapy: Mental and physical health outcomes. *Clinical Psychology Review, 19,* 79–96. (p. 285)

Esterson, A. (2001). The mythologizing of psychoanalytic history: Deception and self-deception in Freud's accounts of the seduction theory episode. *History of Psychiatry, 12,* 329–352. (p. 299)

Evans, C. R., & Dion, K. L. (1991). Group cohesion and performance: A meta-analysis. *Small Group Research, 22,* 175–186. (p. 416)

Ewing, R., Schmid, T., Killingsworth, R., Zlot, A., & Raudenbush, S. (2003). Relationship between urban sprawl and physical activity, obesity, and morbidity. *American Journal of Health Promotion, 18,* 47–57. (p. 246)

Exner, J. E. (2003). *The Rorschach: A comprehensive system* (4th ed.). Hoboken, NJ: Wiley. (p. 298)

Eysenck, H. J. (1952). The effects of psychotherapy: An evaluation. *Journal of Consulting Psychology, 16,* 319–324. (p. 362)

Eysenck, H. J. (1990, April 30). An improvement on personality inventory. *Current Contents: Social and Behavioral Sciences, 22*(18), 20. (p. 303)

Eysenck, H. J. (1992). Four ways five factors are *not* basic. *Personality and Individual Differences, 13,* 667–673. (p. 303)

Eysenck, H. J., Wakefield, J. A., Jr., & Friedman, A. F. (1983). Diagnosis and clinical assessment: The DSM-III. *Annual Review of Psychology, 34,* 167–193. (p. 321)

Eysenck, M. W., MacLeod, C., & Mathews, A. (1987). Cognitive functioning and anxiety. *Psychological Research, 49,* 189–195. (p. 308)

Eysenck, S. B. G., & Eysenck, H. J. (1963). The validity of questionnaire and rating assessments of extraversion and neuroticism, and their factorial stability. *British Journal of Psychology, 54,* 51–62. (p. 304)

Fagan, J. F., & Holland, C. R. (2007). Racial equality in intelligence: Predictions from a theory of intelligence as processing. *Intelligence, 35,* 319–334. (p. 230)

Fagan, J. F., III. (1992). Intelligence: A theoretical viewpoint. *Current Directions in Psychological Science, 1,* 82–86. (p. 229)

Farah, M. J., Rabinowitz, C., Quinn, G. E., & Liu, G. T. (2000). Early commitment of neural substrates for face recognition. *Cognitive Neuropsychology, 17,* 117–124. (p. 45)

Farina, A. (1982). The stigma of mental disorders. In A. G. Miller (Ed.), *In the eye of the beholder.* New York: Praeger. (pp. 319, 321)

Farley, M., Baral, I., Kiremire, M., & Sezgin, U. (1998). Prostitution in five countries: Violence and post-traumatic stress disorder. *Feminism and Psychology, 8,* 405–426. (p. 324)

Farrington, D. P. (1991). Antisocial personality from childhood to adulthood. *The Psychologist: Bulletin of the British Psychological Society, 4,* 389–394. (p. 328)

FBI. (2008). Expanded homicide data Table 3. Murder offenders by age, sex, and race. *Uniform Crime Reports.* (p. 102)

Feder, H. H. (1984). Hormones and sexual behavior. *Annual Review of Psychology, 35,* 165–200. (p. 107)

Feeney, J. A., & Noller, P. (1990). Attachment style as a predictor of adult romantic relationships. *Journal of Personality and Social Psychology, 58,* 281–291. (p. 78)

Feingold, A. (1990). Gender differences in effects of physical attractiveness on romantic attraction: A comparison across five research paradigms. *Journal of Personality and Social Psychology, 59,* 981–993. (p. 399)

Feingold, A. (1992). Good-looking people are not what we think. *Psychological Bulletin, 111,* 304–341. (p. 399)

Feingold, A., & Mazzella, R. (1998). Gender differences in body image are increasing. *Psychological Science, 9,* 190–195. (p. 243)

Feng, J., Spence, I., & Pratt, J. (2007). Playing an action video game reduces gender differences in spatial cognition. *Psychological Science, 18,* 850–855. (p. 231)

Fenton, W. S., & McGlashan, T. H. (1991). Natural history of schizophrenia subtypes: II. Positive and negative symptoms and long-term course. *Archives of General Psychiatry, 48,* 978–986. (p. 344)

Fenton, W. S., & McGlashan, T. H. (1994). Antecedents, symptom progression, and long-term outcome of the deficit syndrome in schizophrenia. *American Journal of Psychiatry, 151,* 351–356. (p. 344)

Ferbyhough, C. (2008). Getting Vygotskian about theory of mind: Mediation, dialogue, and the development of social understanding. *Developmental Review, 28,* 225-262. (p. 75)

Ferguson, C. (2009, June 14). Not every child is secretly a genius. *The Chronicle Review* (http://chronicle.com/article/Not-Every-Child-Is-Secretly/48001). (p. 220)

Ferguson, C. J., & Kilburn, J. (2010). Much ado about nothing: The misestimation and overinterpretation of violent video game effects in Eastern and Western nations: Common on Anderson et al. (2010). *Psychological Bulletin, 136,* 174–178. (p. 396)

Ferguson, M. J., & Zayas, V. (2009). Automatic evaluation. *Current Directions in Psychological Science, 18,* 362–366. (p. 125)

Fergusson, D. M., & Woodward, L. G. (2002). Mental health, educational, and social role outcomes of adolescents with depression. *Archives of General Psychiatry, 59,* 225–231. (p. 340)

Fernandez, E., & Turk, D. C. (1989). The utility of cognitive coping strategies for altering pain perception: A meta-analysis. *Pain, 38,* 123–135. (p. 144)

Fernandez-Dols, J-M., & Ruiz-Belda, M-A. (1995). Are smiles a sign of happiness? Gold medal winners at the Olympic Games. *Journal of Personality and Social Psychology, 69,* 1113–1119. (p. 262)

Ferris, C. F. (1996, March). The rage of innocents. *The Sciences,* pp. 22–26. (p. 78)

Feynman, R. (1997). Quoted by E. Hutchings (Ed.), *"Surely you're joking, Mr. Feynman."* New York: Norton. (p. 8)

Fiedler, F. E. (1981). Leadership effectiveness. *American Behavioral Scientist, 24,* 619–632. (p. 416)

Fiedler, F. E. (1987, September). When to lead, when to stand back. *Psychology Today,* pp. 26–27. (p. 416)

Fiedler, K., Nickel, S., Muehlfriedel, T., & Unkelbach, C. (2001). Is mood congruency an effect of genuine memory or response bias? *Journal of Experimental Social Psychology, 37,* 201–214. (p. 191)

Field, A. P. (2006). Is conditioning a useful framework for understanding the development and treatment of phobias? *Clinical Psychology Review, 26,* 857–875. (p. 324)

Field, T., Diego, M., & Hernandez-Reif, M. (2007). Massage therapy research. *Developmental Review, 27,* 75–89. (p. 70)

Field, T., Hernandez-Reif, M., Feijo, L, & Freedman, J. (2006). Prenatal, perinatal and neonatal stimulation: A survey of neonatal nurseries. *Infant Behavior & Development, 29,* 24–31. (p. 70)

Fincham, F. D., & Bradbury, T. N. (1993). Marital satisfaction, depression, and attributions: A longitudinal analysis. *Journal of Personality and Social Psychology, 64,* 442–452. (p. 379)

Fink, M. (2009). *Electroconvulsive therapy: A guide for professionals and their patients.* New York: Oxford University Press. (p. 369)

Finkel, E. J., & Eastwick, P. W. (2008). Speed-dating. *Current Directions in Psychological Science, 17,* 193–197. (p. 399)

Finzi, E., & Wasserman, E. (2006). Treatment of depression with botulinum toxin A: A case series. *Dermatological Surgery, 32,* 645–650. (p. 262)

Fischer, P., & Greitemeyer, T. (2006). Music and aggression: The impact of sexual-aggressive song lyrics on aggression-related thoughts, emotions, and behavior toward the same and the opposite sex. *Personality and Social Psychology Bulletin, 32,* 1165–1176. (p. 395)

Fischhoff, B. (1982). Debiasing. In D. Kahneman, P. Slovic, & A. Tversky (Eds.), *Judgment under uncertainty: Heuristics and biases.* New York: Cambridge University Press. (p. 209)

Fischhoff, B., Slovic, P., & Lichtenstein, S. (1977). Knowing with certainty: The appropriateness of extreme confidence. *Journal of Experimental Psychology: Human Perception and Performance, 3,* 552–564. (p. 209)

Fishbach, A., Dhar, R., & Zhang, Y. (2006). Subgoals as substitutes or complements: The role of goal accessibility. *Journal of Personality and Social Psychology, 91,* 232–242. (p. 416)

Fisher, H. E. (1993, March/April). After all, maybe it's biology. *Psychology Today,* pp. 40–45. (p. 93)

Fisher, H. T. (1984). Little Albert and Little Peter. *Bulletin of the British Psychological Society, 37,* 269. (p. 356)

Fisher, K., Egerton, M., Gershuny, J. I., & Robinson, J. P. (2006). Gender convergence in the American Heritage Time Use Study (AHTUS). *Social Indicators Research, 82,* 1–33. (p. 105)

Fitzgerald, P. B., & Daskalakis, Z. J. (2008). The use of repetitive transcranial magnetic stimulation and vagal nerve stimulation in the treatment of depression. *Current Opinion in Psychiatry, 21,* 25–29. (p. 369)

Flegal, K. M., Carroll, M. D., Ogden, C. L., & Curtin, L. R. (2010). Prevalence and trends in obesity among US adults, 1999–2008. *JAMA, 303,* 235–241. (p. 244)

Fleming, I., Baum, A., & Weiss, L. (1987). Social density and perceived control as mediator of crowding stress in high-density residential neighborhoods. *Journal of Personality and Social Psychology, 52,* 899–906. (p. 281)

Fleming, J. H. (2001, Winter/Spring). Introduction to the special issue on linkage analysis. *The Gallup Research Journal,* pp. i-vi. (p. 415)

Fleming, J. H., & Scott, B. A. (1991). The costs of confession: The Persian Gulf War POW tapes in historical and theoretical perspective. *Contemporary Social Psychology, 15,* 127–138. (p. 261)

Fletcher, G. J. O., Fitness, J., & Blampied, N. M. (1990). The link between attributions and happiness in close relationships: The roles of depression and explanatory style. *Journal of Social and Clinical Psychology, 9,* 243–255. (p. 379)

Flora, S. R. (2004). *The power of reinforcement.* Albany, NJ: SUNY Press. (p. 167)

Flora, S. R., & Bobby, S. E. (2008, September/October). The bipolar bamboozle. *Skeptical Inquirer,* pp. 41–45. (p. 339)

Flynn, J. R. (2003). Movies about intelligence: The limitations of g. *Current Directions in Psychological Science, 12,* 95–99. (p. 227)

Flynn, J. R. (2007). *What is intelligence?* New York: Cambridge University Press. (pp. 227, 229)

Foa, E. B., & Kozak, M. J. (1986). Emotional processing of fear: Exposure to corrective information. *Psychological Bulletin, 99,* 20–35. (p. 356)

Ford, E. S. (2002). Does exercise reduce inflammation? Physical activity and B-reactive protein among U.S. adults. *Epidemiology, 13,* 561–569. (p. 285)

Ford, E. S., Mokdad, A. H., & Giles, W. H. (2003). Trends in waist circumference among U.S. adults. *Obesity Research, 11,* 1223–1231. (p. 246)

Foree, D. D., & LoLordo, V. M. (1973). Attention in the pigeon: Differential effects of food-getting versus shock-avoidance procedures. *Journal of Comparative and Physiological Psychology, 85,* 551–558. (p. 171)

Forgas, J. P. (2008). Affect and cognition. *Perspectives on Psychological Science, 3,* 94–101. (p. 259)

Forgas, J. P., Bower, G. H., & Krantz, S. E. (1984). The influence of mood on perceptions of social interactions. *Journal of Experimental Social Psychology, 20,* 497–513. (p. 191)

Foss, D. J., & Hakes, D. T. (1978). *Psycholinguistics: An introduction to the psychology of language.* Englewood Cliffs, NJ: Prentice-Hall. (p. 299)

Foster, R. G. (2004). Are we trying to banish biological time? *Cerebrum, 6(2),* 7–26. (p. 53)

Foulkes, D. (1999). *Children's dreaming and the development of consciousness.* Cambridge, MA: Harvard University Press. (p. 58)

Fournier, J. A., DeRubeis, J. C., Hollon, S. D., Dimidjian, S., Amsterdam, J. D., Shelton, R. C., & Fawcett, M. D. (2010). Antidepressant drug effects and depression severity. *JAMA, 303,* 47–53. (p. 368)

Fouts, R. S. (1992). Transmission of a human gestural language in a chimpanzee mother-infant relationship. *Friends of Washoe*, 12/13, pp. 2–8. (p. 218)

Fouts, R. S. (1997). *Next of kin: What chimpanzees have taught me about who we are.* New York: Morrow. (p. 218)

Fowler, M. J., Sullivan, M. J., & Ekstrand, B. R. (1973). Sleep and memory. *Science*, 179, 302–304. (p. 194)

Fowles, D. C. (1992). Schizophrenia: Diathesis-stress revisited. *Annual Review of Psychology*, 43, 303–336. (p. 344)

Fowles, D. C., & Dindo, L. (2009). Temperament and psychopathy: A dual-pathway model. *Current Directions in Psychological Science*, 18, 179–183. (p. 328)

Fox, B. H. (1998). Psychosocial factors in cancer incidence and prognosis. In P. M. Cinciripini & others (Eds.), *Psychological and behavioral factors in cancer risk.* New York: Oxford University Press. (p. 278)

Fox, E., Lester, V., Russo, R., Bowles, R. J., Pichler, A., & Dutton, K. (2000). Facial expression of emotion: Are angry faces detected more efficiently? *Cognition and Emotion*, 14, 61–92. (p. 260)

Fox, J. L. (1984). The brain's dynamic way of keeping in touch. *Science*, 225, 820–821. (p. 45)

Fracassini, C. (2000, August 27). Holidaymakers led by the nose in sales quest. *Scotland on Sunday.* (p. 147)

Fraley, R. C. (2002). Attachment stability from infancy to adulthood: Meta-analysis and dynamic modeling of developmental mechanisms. *Personality and Social Psychology Review*, 6, 123–151. (p. 78)

Frank, J. D. (1982). Therapeutic components shared by all psychotherapies. In J. H. Harvey & M. M. Parks (Eds.), *The Master Lecture Series: Vol. 1. Psychotherapy research and behavior change.* Washington, DC: American Psychological Association. (pp. 363, 364)

Frankenburg, W., Dodds, J., Archer, P., Shapiro, H., & Bresnick, B. (1992). The Denver II: A major revision and restandardization of the Denver Developmental Screening Test. *Pediatrics*, 89, 91–97. (p. 71)

Frankl, V. E. (1962). *Man's search for meaning: An introduction to logotherapy.* Boston: Beacon Press. (p. 285)

Frasure-Smith, N., & Lesperance, F. (2005). Depression and coronary heart disease: Complex synergism of mind, body, and environment. *Current Directions in Psychological Science*, 14, 39–43. (p. 280)

Frattaroli, J. (2006). Experimental disclosure and its moderators: A meta-analysis. *Psychological Bulletin*, 132, 823–865. (p. 285)

Fredrickson, B. L. (2006). The broaden-and-build theory of positive emotions. In M. Csikszentmihalyi & I. S. Csikszentmihalyi (Eds.), *A life worth living: Contributions to positive psychology.* New York: Oxford University Press. (p. 264)

Freedman, D. J., Riesenhuber, M., Poggio, T., & Miller, E. K. (2001). Categorical representation of visual stimuli in the primate prefrontal cortex. *Science*, 291, 312–316. (p. 216)

Freedman, J. L. (1988). Television violence and aggression: What the evidence shows. In S. Oskamp (Ed.), *Television as a social issue.* Newbury Park, CA: Sage. (p. 176)

Freedman, J. L., & Perlick, D. (1979). Crowding, contagion, and laughter. *Journal of Experimental Social Psychology*, 15, 295–303. (p. 387)

Freeman, W. J. (1991, February). The physiology of perception. *Scientific American*, pp. 78–85. (p. 140)

Freud, S. (1935; reprinted 1960). *A general introduction to psychoanalysis.* New York: Washington Square Press. (p. 92)

Freyd, J. J., DePrince, A. P., & Gleaves, D. H. (2007). The state of betrayal trauma theory: Reply to McNally—Conceptual issues and future directions. *Memory*, 15, 295–311. (p. 199)

Freyd, J. J., Putnam, F. W., Lyon, T. D., Becker-Blease, K. A., Cheit, R. E., Siegel, N. B., & Pezdek, K. (2005). The science of child sexual abuse. *Science*, 308, 501. (p. 78)

Friedman, M., & Ulmer, D. (1984). *Treating Type A behavior—and your heart.* New York: Knopf. (pp. 279, 286)

Friedrich, O. (1987, December 7). New age harmonies. *Time*, pp. 62–72. (p. 318)

Friend, T. (2004). *Animal talk: Breaking the codes of animal language.* New York: Free Press. (p. 218)

Frith, U., & Frith, C. (2001). The biological basis of social interaction. *Current Directions in Psychological Science*, 10, 151–155. (p. 74)

Fritz, T., Jentschke, S., Gosselin, N., Sammler, D., Peretz, I., Turner, R., Friederici, A., & Koelsch, S. (2009). Universal recognition of three basic emotions in music. *Current Biology*, 19, 573–576. (p. 261)

Fromkin, V., & Rodman, R. (1983). *An introduction to language* (3rd ed.). New York: Holt, Rinehart & Winston. (p. 214)

Fry, A. F., & Hale, S. (1996). Processing speed, working memory, and fluid intelligence: Evidence for a developmental cascade. *Psychological Science*, 7, 237–241. (p. 91)

Fuhriman, A., & Burlingame, G. M. (1994). Group psychotherapy: Research and practice. In A. Fuhriman & G. M. Burlingame (Eds.), *Handbook of group psychotherapy.* New York: Wiley. (p. 359)

Fujita, F., & Diener, E. (2005). Life satisfaction set point: Stability and change. *Journal of Personality and Social Psychology*, 88, 158–164. (p. 268)

Fuller, M. J., & Downs, A. C. (1990). Spermarche is a salient biological marker in men's development. Poster presented at the American Psychological Society convention. (p. 81)

Funder, D. C., & Block, J. (1989). The role of ego-control, ego-resiliency, and IQ in delay of gratification in adolescence. *Journal of Personality and Social Psychology*, 57, 1041–1050. (p. 83)

Furlow, F. B., & Thornhill, R. (1996, January/February). The orgasm wars. *Psychology Today*, pp. 42–46. (p. 108)

Furnham, A. (1982). Explanations for unemployment in Britain. *European Journal of Social Psychology*, 12, 335–352. (p. 379)

Furnham, A., & Baguma, P. (1994). Cross-cultural differences in the evaluation of male and female body shapes. *International Journal of Eating Disorders*, 15, 81–89. (p. 244)

Furr, R. M., & Funder, D. C. (1998). A multimodal analysis of personal negativity. *Journal of Personality and Social Psychology*, 74, 1580–1591. (p. 342)

Gaertner, L., & Iuzzini, J. (2005). Rejection and entitativity: A synergistic model of mass violence. In K. D. Williams, J. P. Forgas, & W. von Hippel (Eds.). *The social outcast: Ostracism, social exclusion, rejection, and bullying.* New York: Psychology Press. (p. 395)

Gaillard, R., Dehaene, S., Adam, C., Clémenceau, S., Hasboun, D., Baulac, M., Cohen, L., & Naccache, L. (2009). Converging intracranial markers of conscious access. *PLoS Biology*, 7(e), e1000061. (p. 49)

Gaillot, M. T., & Baumeister, R. F. (2007). Self-regulation and sexual restraint: Dispositionally and temporarily poor self-regulatory abilities contribute to failures at restraining sexual behavior. *Personality and Social Psychology Bulletin*, 33, 173–186. (p. 282)

Galambos, N. L. (1992). Parent-adolescent relations. *Current Directions in Psychological Science*, 1, 146–149. (p. 85)

Galanter, E. (1962). Contemporary psychophysics. In R. Brown, E. Galanter, E. H. Hess, & G. Mandler (Eds.), *New directions in psychology*. New York: Holt Rinehart & Winston. (p. 124)

Gale, C. R., Batty, G. D., & Deary, I. J. (2008). Locus of control at age 10 years and health outcomes and behaviors at age 30 years: The 1970 British Cohort Study. *Psychosomatic Medicine, 70,* 397–403. (p. 282)

Gallo, W. T., Teng, H. M., Falba, T. A., Kasl, S. V., Krumholz, H. M., & Bradley, E. H. (2006). The impact of late career job loss on myocardial infarction and stroke: A 10 year follow up using the health and retirement survey. *Occupational and Environmental Medicine, 63,* 683–687. (p. 274)

Gallup Brain. (2008, accessed February 20). Woman for president: Question qn2f, March, 2007 wave. Brain.Gallup.com. (p. 390)

Gallup Organization. (2003, July 8). American public opinion about Iraq. *Gallup Poll News Service* (www.gallup.com). (p. 381)

Gallup Organization. (2004, August 16). 65% of Americans receive NO praise or recognition in the workplace. E-mail from Tom Rath: bucketbook Self-recognition. *Science, 167,* 86–87. (p. 416)

Gallup, G., Jr. (2002, April 30). Education and youth. *Gallup Tuesday Briefing* (www.gallup.com/poll/tb/educaYouth/20020430.asp). (p. 175)

Gallup, G. H. (1972). *The Gallup poll: Public opinion 1935–1971* (Vol. 3). New York: Random House. (p. 405)

Gangestad, S. W., & Simpson, J. A. (2000). The evolution of human mating: Trade-offs and strategic pluralism. *Behavioral and Brain Sciences, 23,* 573–587. (p. 117)

Gao, Y., Raine, A., Venables, P. H., Dawson, M. E., & Mednick, S. A. (2010). Association of poor child fear conditioning and adult crime. *American Journal of Psychiatry, 167,* 56–60. (p. 328)

Garcia, J., & Gustavson, A. R. (1997, January). Carl R. Gustavson (1946–1996): Pioneering wildlife psychologist. *APS Observer,* pp. 34–35. (p. 170)

Garcia, J., & Koelling, R. A. (1966). Relation of cue to consequence in avoidance learning. *Psychonomic Science, 4,* 123–124. (p. 170)

Gardner, H. (1983). *Frames of mind: The theory of multiple intelligences.* New York: Basic Books. (p. 219)

Gardner, H. (1998, March 19). An intelligent way to progress. *The Independent* (London), p. E4. (p. 220)

Gardner, H. (1998, November 5). Do parents count? *New York Review of Books* (www.nybooks.com). (p. 87)

Gardner, H. (1999). *Multiple views of multiple intelligence.* New York: Basic Books. (p. 222)

Gardner, H. (1999, February). Who owns intelligence? *Atlantic Monthly,* pp. 67–76. (p. 222)

Gardner, H. (2006). *The development and education of the mind: The selected works of Howard Gardner.* New York: Routledge/Taylor & Francis. (p. 219)

Gardner, J., & Oswald, A. J. (2007). Money and mental well-being: A longitudinal study of medium-sized lottery wins. *Journal of Health Economics, 6,* 49–60. (p. 267)

Gardner, M. (2006, January/February). The memory wars, part one. *Skeptical Inquirer, 30,* 28–31. (p. 199)

Gardner, R. A., & Gardner, B. I. (1969). Teaching sign language to a chimpanzee. *Science, 165,* 664–672. (p. 217)

Gardner, R. M., & Tockerman, Y. R. (1994). A computer-TV video methodology for investigating the influence of somatotype on perceived personality traits. *Journal of Social Behavior and Personality, 9,* 555–563. (p. 244)

Garfield, C. (1986). *Peak performers: The new heroes of American business.* New York: Morrow. (p. 215)

Garon, N., Bryson, S. E., & Smith, I. M. (2008). Executive function in preschoolers: A review using an integrative framework. *Psychological Bulletin, 134,* 31–60. (p. 70)

Garrett, B. L. (2008). Judging innocence. *Columbia Law Review, 108,* 55–142. (p. 197)

Garry, M., Manning, C. G., Loftus, E. F., & Sherman, S. J. (1996). Imagination inflation: Imagining a childhood event inflates confidence that it occurred. *Psychonomic Bulletin & Review, 3,* 208–214. (p. 197)

Gates, W. (1998, July 20). Charity begins when I'm ready (inter-view). *Fortune* (www.pathfinder.com/fortune/1998/980720/bil7.html). (p. 220)

Gawin, F. H. (1991). Cocaine addiction: Psychology and neurophysiology. *Science, 251,* 1580–1586. (p. 333)

Gazzaniga, M. S. (1967, August). The split brain in man. *Scientific American,* pp. 24–29. (p. 46)

Gazzaniga, M. S. (1983). Right hemisphere language following brain bisection: A 20-year perspective. *American Psychologist, 38,* 525–537. (p. 47)

Gazzaniga, M. S. (1988). *Mind matters: How mind and brain interact to create our conscious lives.* Boston: Houghton Mifflin. (p. 47)

Gazzaniga, M. S. (1989). Organization of the human brain. *Science, 245,* 947–952. (p. 47)

Gazzaniga, M. S. (2002, August 22). On "The brain: The final mystery." Broadcast on BBC2. (p. 46)

Geary, D. C. (1995). Sexual selection and sex differences in spatial cognition. *Learning and Individual Differences, 7,* 289–301. (p. 231)

Geary, D. C. (1996). Sexual selection and sex differences in mathematical abilities. *Behavioral and Brain Sciences, 19,* 229–247. (p. 231)

Geary, D. C. (1998). *Male, female: The evolution of human sex differences.* Washington, DC: American Psychological Association. (p. 117)

Geary, D. C., Salthouse, T. A., Chen, G-P., & Fan, L. (1996). Are East Asian versus American differences in arithmetical ability a recent phenomenon? *Developmental Psychology, 32,* 254–262. (p. 230)

Geen, R. G., & Quanty, M. B. (1977). The catharsis of aggression: An evaluation of a hypothesis. In L. Berkowitz (Ed.), *Advances in experimental social psychology* (Vol. 10). New York: Academic Press. (p. 263)

Geen, R. G., & Thomas, S. L. (1986). The immediate effects of media violence on behavior. *Journal of Social Issues, 42*(3), 7–28. (p. 177)

Gehring, W. J., Wimke, J., & Nisenson, L. G. (2000). Action monitoring dysfunction in obsessive-compulsive disorder. *Psychological Science, 11*(1), 1–6. (p. 325)

Genevro, J. L. (2003). *Report on bereavement and grief research.* Washington, DC: Center for the Advancement of Health. (p. 95)

Gentile, D. A., & Gentile, J. R. (2009). Violent video games as exemplary teachers: A conceptual analysis. *Journal of Youth and Adolescence, 37,* 127–141. (p. 396)

Gentile, D. A., Lynch, P. J., Linder, J. R., & Walsh, D. A. (2004). The effects of violent video game habits on adolescent hostility, aggressive behaviors, and school performance. *Journal of Adolescence, 27,* 5–22. (p. 176)

George, L. K., Ellison, C. G., & Larson, D. B. (2002). Explaining the relationships between religious involvement and health. *Psychological Inquiry, 13,* 190–200. (p. 288)

George, L. K., Larson, D. B., Koenig, H. G., & McCullough, M. E. (2000). Spirituality and health: What we know, what we need to know. *Journal of Social and Clinical Psychology, 19,* 102–116. (p. 288)

George, M. S. (2003, September). Stimulating the brain. *Scientific American,* pp. 67–73. (p. 370)

Geraerts, E., Bernstein, D. M., Merckelbach, H., Linders, C., Raymaekers, L., & Loftus, E. F. (2008). Lasting false beliefs and their behavioral consequences. *Psychological Science, 19*, 749–753. (p. 197)

Geraerts, E., Schooler, J. W., Merckelbach, H., Jelicic, M., Hauer, B. J. A., & Ambadar, Z. (2007). The reality of recovered memories: Corroborating continuous and discontinuous memories of childhood sexual abuse. *Psychological Science, 18*, 564–568. (p. 199)

Gerber, J., & Wheeler, L. (2009). On being rejected: A meta-analysis of experimental research on rejection. *Perspectives on Psychological Science, 4*, 468–488. (p. 250)

Gerbner, G. (1990). Stories that hurt: Tobacco, alcohol, and other drugs in the mass media. In H. Resnik (Ed.), *Youth and drugs: Society's mixed messages.* Rockville, MD: Office for Substance Abuse Prevention, U.S. Department of Health and Human Services. (p. 336)

Gerhart, K. A., Koziol-McLain, J., Lowenstein, S. R., & Whiteneck, G. G. (1994). Quality of life following spinal cord injury: Knowledge and attitudes of emergency care providers. *Annals of Emergency Medicine, 23*, 807–812. (p. 265)

Gerrard, M., & Luus, C. A. E. (1995). Judgments of vulnerability to pregnancy: The role of risk factors and individual differences. *Personality and Social Psychology Bulletin, 21*, 160–171. (p. 109)

Gershoff, E. T. (2002). Parental corporal punishment and associated child behaviors and experiences: A meta-analytic and theoretical review. *Psychological Bulletin, 128*, 539–579. (p. 166)

Gibbons, F. X. (1986). Social comparison and depression: Company's effect on misery. *Journal of Personality and Social Psychology, 51*, 140–148. (p. 267)

Gibbons, R. D., Brown, C. H., Hur, K., Marcus, S. M., Bhaumik, D. K., & Mann, J. J. (2007). Relationship between antidepressants and suicide attempts: An analysis of the Veterans Health Administration data sets. *American Journal of Psychiatry, 164*, 1044–1049. (p. 368)

Gibbs, W. W. (2005, June). Obesity: An overblown epidemic? *Scientific American,* pp. 70–77. (p. 244)

Gibson, E. J., & Walk, R. D. (1960, April). The "visual cliff." *Scientific American,* pp. 64–71. (p. 134)

Giesbrecht, T., Lynn, S. J., Lilienfeld, S. O., & Merckelbach, H. (2008). Cognitive processes in dissociation: An analysis of core theoretical assumptions. *Psychological Bulletin, 134*, 617–647. (p. 327)

Giesbrecht, T., Lynn, S. J., Lilienfeld, S. O., & Merckelbach, H. (2010). Cognitive processes, trauma, and dissociation—Misconceptions and misrepresentations: Reply to Bremner (2010). *Psychological Bulletin, 136*, 7–11. (p. 327)

Gigerenzer, G. (2004). Dread risk, September 11, and fatal traffic accidents. *Psychological Science, 15*, 286–287. (p. 208)

Gigerenzer, G. (2006). Out of the frying pan into the fire: Behavioral reactions to terrorist attacks. *Risk Analysis, 26*, 347–351. (p. 208)

Gilbert, D. T. (2006). *Stumbling on happiness.* New York: Knopf. (pp. 93, 196, 256, 311, 338)

Gilbert, D. T., Pinel, E. C., Wilson, T. D., Blumberg, S. J., & Wheatley, T. P. (1998). Immune neglect: A source of durability bias in affective forecasting. *Journal of Personality and Social Psychology, 75*, 617–638. (p. 265)

Gill, A. J., Oberlander, J., & Austin, E. (2006). Rating e-mail personality at zero acquaintance. *Personality and Individual Differences, 40*, 497–507. (p. 308)

Gilligan, C. (1982). *In a different voice: Psychological theory and women's development.* Cambridge, MA: Harvard University Press. (p. 103)

Gilligan, C., Lyons, N. P., & Hanmer, T. J. (Eds.). (1990). *Making connections: The relational worlds of adolescent girls at Emma Willard School.* Cambridge, MA: Harvard University Press. (p. 103)

Gilovich, T. D. (1991). *How we know what isn't so: The fallibility of human reason in everyday life.* New York: Free Press. (p. 15)

Gilovich, T. D. (1996). The spotlight effect: Exaggerated impressions of the self as a social stimulus. Unpublished manuscript, Cornell University. (p. 310)

Gilovich, T. D., & Medvec, V. H. (1995). The experience of regret: What, when, and why. *Psychological Review, 102*, 379–395. (p. 95)

Gilovich, T. D., & Savitsky, K. (1999). The spotlight effect and the illusion of transparency: Egocentric assessments of how we are seen by others. *Current Directions in Psychological Science, 8*, 165–168. (p. 310)

Gingerich, O. (1999, February 6). Is there a role for natural theology today? *The Real Issue* (www.origins.org/real/n9501/natural.html). (p. 119)

Gladue, B. A. (1990). Hormones and neuroendocrine factors in atypical human sexual behavior. In J. R. Feierman (Ed.), *Pedophilia: Biosocial dimensions.* New York: Springer-Verlag. (p. 114)

Gladue, B. A. (1994). The biopsychology of sexual orientation. *Current Directions in Psychological Science, 3*, 150–154. (pp. 114, 115)

Glasman, L. R., & Albarracin, D. (2006). Forming attitudes that predict future behavior: A meta-analysis of the attitude-behavior relation. *Psychological Bulletin, 132*, 778–822. (p. 379)

Glass, R. I. (2004). Perceived threats and real killers. *Science, 304*, 927. (p. 208)

Glass, R. M. (2001). Electroconvulsive therapy: Time to bring it out of the shadows. *Journal of the American Medical Association, 285*, 1346–1348. (p. 369)

Glater, J. D. (2001, March 26). Women are close to being majority of law students. *New York Times* (www.nytimes.com). (p. 105)

Gleaves, D. H. (1996). The sociocognitive model of dissociative identity disorder: A reexamination of the evidence. *Psychological Bulletin, 120*, 42–59. (p. 327)

Glenn, N. D. (1975). Psychological well-being in the postparental stage: Some evidence from national surveys. *Journal of Marriage and the Family, 37*, 105–110. (p. 93)

Godden, D. R., & Baddeley, A. D. (1975). Context-dependent memory in two natural environments: On land and underwater. *British Journal of Psychology, 66*, 325–331. (pp. 190, 191)

Goel, V., & Dolan, R. J. (2001). The functional anatomy of humor: Segregating cognitive and affective components. *Nature Neuroscience, 4*, 237–238. (p. 44)

Goff, D. C., & Simms, C. A. (1993). Has multiple personality disorder remained consistent over time? *Journal of Nervous and Mental Disease, 181*, 595–600. (p. 326)

Gold, M., & Yanof, D. S. (1985). Mothers, daughters, and girlfriends. *Journal of Personality and Social Psychology, 49*, 654–659. (p. 85)

Goldapple, K., Segal, Z., Garson, C., Lau, M., Bieling, P., Kennedy, S., & Mayberg, H. (2004). Modulation of cortical-limbic pathways in major depression. *Archives of General Psychiatry, 61*, 34–41. (p. 367)

Goldberg, J. (2007, accessed May 31). *Quivering bundles that let us hear.* Howard Hughes Medical Institute (www.hhmi.org/senses/c120.html). (p. 140)

Goldfried, M. R., & Padawer, W. (1982). Current status and future directions in psychotherapy. In M. R. Goldfried (Ed.), *Converging themes in psychotherapy: Trends in psychodynamic, humanistic, and behavioral practice.* New York: Springer. (p. 363)

Goldfried, M. R., Raue, P. J., & Castonguay, L. G. (1998). The therapeutic focus in significant sessions of master therapists: A comparison of cognitive-behavioral and psychodynamic-interpersonal interventions. *Journal of Consulting and Clinical Psychology, 66*, 803–810. (p. 363)

Golding, J. M. (1999). Sexual-assault history and the long-term physical health problems: Evidence from clinical and population epidemiology. *Current Directions in Psychological Science, 8,* 191–194. (p. 324)

Goldman, A. L., Pezawas, L., Mattay, V. S., Fischl, B., Verchinski, B. A., Chen, Q., Weinberger, D. R., & Meyer-Lindenberg, A. (2009). Widespread reductions of cortical thickness in schizophrenia and spectrum disorders and evidence of heritability. *Archives of General Psychiatry, 66,* 467–477. (p. 345)

Goldstein, A. P., Glick, B., & Gibbs, J. C. (1998). *Aggression replacement training: A comprehensive intervention for aggressive youth* (rev. ed.). Champaign, IL: Research Press. (p. 395)

Goldstein, I. (2000, August). Male sexual circuitry. *Scientific American,* pp. 70–75. (p. 33)

Goldstein, I., Lue, T. F., Padma-Nathan, H., Rosen, R. C., Steers, W. D., & Wicker, P. A. (1998). Oral sildenafil in the treatment of erectile dysfunction. *New England Journal of Medicine, 338,* 1397–1404. (p. 16)

Goleman, D. (1980, February). 1,528 little geniuses and how they grew. *Psychology Today,* pp. 28–53. (p. 413)

Goleman, D. (1995). *Emotional intelligence.* New York: Bantam. (p. 256)

Goleman, D. (2006). *Social intelligence.* New York: Bantam Books. (p. 222)

Gonsalves, B., Reber, P. J., Gitelman, D. R., Parrish, T. B., Mesulam, M-M., & Paller, K. A. (2004). Neural evidence that vivid imagining can lead to false remembering. *Psychological Science, 15,* 655–659. (p. 197)

Goodale, M. A., & Milner, D. A. (2004). *Sight unseen: An exploration of conscious and unconscious vision.* Oxford: Oxford University Press. (p. 7)

Goodale, M. A., & Milner, D. A. (2006). One brain—two visual systems. *The Psychologist, 19,* 660–663. (p. 7)

Goode, E. (1999, April 13). If things taste bad, 'phantoms' may be at work. *New York Times* (www.nytimes.com). (p. 143)

Goodhart, D. E. (1986). The effects of positive and negative thinking on performance in an achievement situation. *Journal of Personality and Social Psychology, 51,* 117–124. (p. 283)

Goodman, G. S., & Quas, J. A. (2008). Repeated interviews and children's memory. *Current Directions in Psychological Science, 17,* 386–389. (p. 198)

Goodman, G. S., Ghetti, S., Quas, J. A., Edelstein, R. S., Alexander, K. W., Redlich, A. D., Cordon, I. M., & Jones, D. P. H. (2003). A prospective study of memory for child sexual abuse: New findings relevant to the repressed-memory controversy. *Psychological Science, 14,* 113–118. (p. 199)

Goranson, R. E. (1978). The hindsight effect in problem solving. Unpublished manuscript, cited by G. Wood (1984), Research methodology: A decision-making perspective. In A. M. Rogers & C. J. Scheirer (Eds.), *The G. Stanley Hall Lecture Series* (Vol. 4). Washington, DC. (p. 9)

Gore-Felton, C., Koopman, C., Thoresen, C., Arnow, B., Bridges, E., & Spiegel, D. (2000). Psychologists' beliefs and clinical characteristics: Judging the veracity of childhood sexual abuse memories. *Professional Psychology: Research and Practice, 31,* 372–377. (p. 199)

Gortmaker, S. L., Must, A., Perrin, J. M., Sobol, A. M., & Dietz, W. H. (1993). Social and economic consequences of overweight in adolescence and young adulthood. *New England Journal of Medicine, 329,* 1008–1012. (p. 245)

Gosling, S. D. (2008). *Snoop: what your stuff says about you.* New York: Basic Books. (p. 308)

Gosling, S. D., Gladdis, S., & Vazire, S. (2007). Personality impressions based on Facebook profiles. Paper presented to the Society for Personality and Social Psychology meeting. (p. 308)

Gotlib, I. H., & Hammen, C. L. (1992). *Psychological aspects of depression: Toward a cognitive-interpersonal integration.* New York: Wiley. (p. 342)

Gottesman, I. I. (1991). *Schizophrenia genesis: The origins of madness.* New York: Freeman. (p. 347)

Gottesman, I. I. (2001). Psychopathology through a life span—genetic prism. *American Psychologist, 56,* 867–881. (p. 346)

Gottfredson, L. S. (2002a). Where and why g matters: Not a mystery. *Human Performance, 15,* 25–46. (p. 220)

Gottfredson, L. S. (2002b). g: Highly general and highly practical. In R. J. Sternberg & E. L. Grigorenko (Eds.), *The general factor of intelligence: How general is it?* Mahwah, NJ: Erlbaum. (p. 220)

Gottfredson, L. S. (2003a). Dissecting practical intelligence theory: Its claims and evidence. *Intelligence, 31,* 343–397. (p. 220)

Gottfredson, L. S. (2003b). On Sternberg's "Reply to Gottfredson." *Intelligence, 31,* 415–424. (p. 220)

Gould, E. (2007). How widespread is adult neurogenesis in mammals? *Nature Neuroscience, 8,* 481–488. (p. 45)

Gould, S. J. (1997, June 12). Darwinian fundamentalism. *The New York Review of Books, XLIV*(10), 34–37. (p. 118)

Grady, C. L., McIntosh, A. R., Horwitz, B., Maisog, J. M., Ungeleider, L. G., Mentis, M. J., Pietrini, P., Schapiro, M. B., & Haxby, J. V. (1995). Age-related reductions in human recognition memory due to impaired encoding. *Science, 269,* 218–221. (p. 193)

Gray-Little, B., & Burks, N. (1983). Power and satisfaction in marriage: A review and critique. *Psychological Bulletin, 93,* 513–538. (p. 402)

Gray-Little, B., & Hafdahl, A. R. (2000). Factors influencing racial comparisons of self-esteem: A quantitative review. *Psychological Bulletin, 126,* 26–54. (p. 310)

Green, J. D., Sedikides, C., & Gregg, A. P. (2008). Forgotten but not gone: The recall and recognition of self-threatening memories. *Journal of Experimental Social Psychology, 44,* 547–561. (p. 299)

Green, J. T., & Woodruff-Pak, D. S. (2000). Eyeblink classical conditioning: Hippocampal formation is for neutral stimulus associations as cerebellum is for association-response. *Psychological Bulletin, 126,* 138–158. (p. 186)

Greenberg, J. (2008). Understanding the vital human quest for self-esteem. *Perspectives on Psychological Science, 3,* 48–55. (p. 310)

Greenwald, A. G. (1992). Subliminal semantic activation and subliminal snake oil. Paper presented to the American Psychological Association Convention, Washington, DC. (p. 126)

Greenwald, A. G., McGhee, D. E., & Schwartz, J. L. K. (1998). Measuring individual differences in implicit cognition: The implicit association test. *Journal of Personality and Social Psychology, 74,* 1464–1480. (p. 391)

Greenwald, A. G., Oakes, M. A., & Hoffman, H. (2003). Targets of discrimination: Effects of race on responses to weapons holders. *Journal of Experimental Social Psychology, 39,* 399. (p. 391)

Greenwald, A. G., Spangenberg, E. R., Pratkanis, A. R., & Eskenazi, J. (1991). Double-blind tests of subliminal self-help audiotapes. *Psychological Science, 2,* 119–122. (p. 126)

Greenwood, M. R. C. (1989). Sexual dimorphism and obesity. In A. J. Stunkard & A. Baum (Eds.). *Perspectives in behavioral medicine: Eating, sleeping, and sex.* Hillsdale, NJ: Erlbaum. (p. 244)

Greers, A. E. (2004). Speech, language, and reading skills after early cochlear implantation. *Archives of Otolaryngology—Head & Neck Surgery, 130,* 634–638. (p. 214)

Gregory, R. L. (1978). *Eye and brain: The psychology of seeing* (3rd ed.). New York: McGraw-Hill. (p. 138)

Gregory, R. L., & Gombrich, E. H. (Eds.). (1973). *Illusion in nature and art.* New York: Charles Scribner's Sons. (p. 128)

Greif, E. B., & Ulman, K. J. (1982). The psychological impact of menarche on early adolescent females: A review of the literature. *Child Development, 53,* 1413–1430. (p. 81)

Greist, J. H., Jefferson, J. W., & Marks, I. M. (1986). *Anxiety and its treatment: Help is available.* Washington, DC: American Psychiatric Press. (p. 323)

Grèzes, J., & Decety, J. (2001). Function anatomy of execution, mental simulation, observation, and verb generation of actions: A meta-analysis. *Human Brain Mapping, 12,* 1–19. (p. 215)

Grilo, C. M., & Pogue-Geile, M. F. (1991). The nature of environmental influences on weight and obesity: A behavior genetic analysis. *Psychological Bulletin, 110,* 520–537. (p. 246)

Grobstein, C. (1979, June). External human fertilization. *Scientific American,* pp. 57-67. (p. 66)

Gross, A. E., & Crofton, C. (1977). What is good is beautiful. *Sociometry, 40,* 85–90. (p. 400)

Grossman, M., & Wood, W. (1993). Sex differences in intensity of emotional experience: A social role interpretation. *Journal of Personality and Social Psychology, 65,* 1010–1022. (p. 260)

Grunebaum, M. F., Ellis, S. P., Li, S., Oquendo, M. A., Mann, J. J. (2004). Antidepressants and suicide risk in the United States, 1985–1999. *Journal of Clinical Psychiatry, 65,* 1456–1462. (p. 368)

Guerin, B. (1986). Mere presence effects in humans: A review. *Journal of Personality and Social Psychology, 22,* 38–77. (p. 386)

Guerin, B. (2003). Language use as social strategy: A review and an analytic framework for the social sciences. *Review of General Psychology, 7,* 251–298. (p. 212)

Gustavson, C. R., Garcia, J., Hankins, W. G., & Rusiniak, K. W. (1974). Coyote predation control by aversive conditioning. *Science, 184,* 581–583. (p. 170)

Gustavson, C. R., Kelly, D. J., & Sweeney, M. (1976). Prey lithium aversions I: Coyotes and wolves. *Behavioral Biology, 17,* 61–72. (p. 170)

Guttmacher Institute. (1994). *Sex and America's teenagers.* New York: Alan Guttmacher Institute. (pp. 88, 108)

Guttmacher Institute. (2000). *Fulfilling the promise: Public policy and U.S. family planning clinics.* New York: Alan Guttmacher Institute. (p. 88)

H., Sally. (1979, August). *Videotape recording number T–3, Fortunoff Video Archive of Holocaust Testimonies.* New Haven, CT: Yale University Library. (p. 299)

Haber, R. N. (1970, May). How we remember what we see. *Scientific American,* pp. 104–112. (p. 180)

Haidt, J. (2006). *The happiness hypothesis: Finding modern truth in ancient wisdom.* New York: Basic Books. (p. 82)

Hakuta, K., Bialystok, E., & Wiley, E. (2003). Critical evidence: A test of the critical-period hypothesis for second-language acquisition. *Psychological Science, 14,* 31–38. (p. 214)

Halberstadt, J. B., Niedenthal, P. M., & Kushner, J. (1995). Resolution of lexical ambiguity by emotional state. *Psychological Science, 6,* 278–281. (p. 128)

Haldeman, D. C. (1994). The practice and ethics of sexual orientation conversion therapy. *Journal of Consulting and Clinical Psychology, 62,* 221–227. (p. 112)

Haldeman, D. C. (2002). Gay rights, patient rights: The implications of sexual orientation conversion therapy. *Professional Psychology: Research and Practice, 33,* 260–264. (p. 112)

Hall, C. S., & Lindzey, G. (1978). *Theories of personality* (2nd ed.). New York: Wiley. (p. 300)

Hall, C. S., Dornhoff, W., Blick, K. A., & Weesner, K. E. (1982). The dreams of college men and women in 1950 and 1980: A comparison of dream contents and sex differences. *Sleep, 5,* 188–194. (p. 57)

Hall, G. (1997). Context aversion, Pavlovian conditioning, and the psychological side effects of chemotherapy. *European Psychologist, 2,* 118–124. (p. 161)

Hall, J. A. (1984). *Nonverbal sex differences: Communication accuracy and expressive style.* Baltimore: Johns Hopkins University Press. (p. 260)

Hall, J. A. (1987). On explaining gender differences: The case of nonverbal communication. In P. Shaver & C. Hendrick (Eds.), *Review of Personality and Social Psychology, 7,* 177–200. (pp. 102, 260)

Hall, S. S. (2004, May). The good egg. *Discover,* pp. 30-39. (p. 66)

Hall, W. (2006). The mental health risks of adolescent cannabis use. *PloS Medicine, 3*(2), e39. (p. 335)

Halpern, C. T., Joyner, K., Udry, J. R., & Suchindran, C. (2000). Smart teens don't have sex (or kiss much either). *Journal of Adolescent Health, 26*(3), 213–215. (p. 109)

Halpern, D. F. (1991). Cognitive sex differences: Why diversity is a critical research issue. Paper presented to the American Psychological Association convention. (p. 231)

Halpern, D. F. (2000). *Sex-related ability differences: Changing perspectives, changing minds.* Mahwah, NJ: Erlbaum. (pp. 230, 231)

Halpern, D. F., Benbow, C. P., Geary, D. C., Gur, R. C., Hyde, J. S., & Gernsbacher, M. A. (2007). The science of sex differences in science and mathematics. *Psychological Science in the Public Interest, 8,* 1–51. (pp. 230, 231)

Halsey, A., III. (2010). U.S. bans truckers, bus drivers from texting while driving. *Washington Post* (www.washingtonpost.com). (p. 49)

Hamani, C., Mayberg, H., Snyder, B., Giacobbe, P., Kennedy, S., & Lozano, A. M. (2009). Deep brain stimulation of the subcallosal cingulated gyrus for depression: Anatomical location of active contacts in clinical responders and a suggested guideline for targeting. *Journal of Neurosurgery, 111,* 1209–1215. (p. 369)

Hammersmith, S. K. (1982, August). Sexual preference: An empirical study from the Alfred C. Kinsey Institute for Sex Research. Paper presented at the meeting of the American Psychological Association, Washington, DC. (p. 113)

Hampson, R. (2000, April 10). In the end, people just need more room. *USA Today,* p. 19A. (p. 246)

Hankin, B. L., & Abramson, L. Y. (2001). Development of gender differences in depression: An elaborated cognitive vulnerability-transactional stress theory. *Psychological Bulletin, 127,* 773–796. (p. 342)

Hansen, C. H., & Hansen, R. D. (1988). Finding the face-in-the-crowd: An anger superiority effect. *Journal of Personality and Social Psychology, 54,* 917–924. (p. 260)

Hardt, O., Einarsson, E. O., & Nader, K. (2010). A bridge over troubled water: Reconsolidation as a link between cognitive and neuroscientific memory research traditions. *Annual Review of Psychology, 61,* 141–167. (p. 196)

Hare, R. D. (1975). Psychophysiological studies of psychopathy. In D. C. Fowles (Ed.), *Clinical applications of psychophysiology.* New York: Columbia University Press. (p. 328)

Harker, L. A., & Keltner, D. (2001). Expressions of positive emotion in women's college yearbook pictures and their relationship to personality and life outcomes across adulthood. *Journal of Personality and Social Psychology, 80,* 112–124. (p. 264)

Harkins, S. G., & Szymanski, K. (1989). Social loafing and group evaluation. *Journal of Personality and Social Psychology, 56*, 934–941. (p. 388)

Harlow, H. F., Harlow, M. K., & Suomi, S. J. (1971). From thought to therapy: Lessons from a primate laboratory. *American Scientist, 59*, 538–549. (p. 76)

Harmon-Jones, E., Abramson, L. Y., Sigelman, J., Bohlig, A., Hogan, M. E., & Harmon-Jones, C. (2002). Proneness to hypomania/mania symptoms or depression symptoms and asymmetrical frontal cortical responses to an anger-evoking event. *Journal of Personality and Social Psychology, 82*, 610–618. (p. 256)

Harper, C., & McLanahan, S. (2004). Father absence and youth incarceration. *Journal of Research on Adolescence, 14*, 369–397. (p. 395)

Harris, B. (1979). Whatever happened to Little Albert? *American Psychologist, 34*, 151–160. (p. 161)

Harris, J. R. (1998). *The nurture assumption.* New York: Free Press. (pp. 77, 85)

Harris, J. R. (2000). Beyond the nurture assumption: Testing hypotheses about the child's environment. In J. G. Borkowski & S. L. Ramey (Eds.), *Parenting and the child's world: Influences on academic, intellectual, and social-emotional development.* Washington, DC: APA Books. (p. 85)

Harris, J. R. (2007, August 8). Do pals matter more than parents? *The Times* (www.timesonline.co.uk). (p. 85)

Harris, R. J. (1994). The impact of sexually explicit media. In J. Brant & D. Zillmann (Eds.), *Media effects: Advances in theory and research.* Hillsdale, NJ: Erlbaum. (p. 395)

Harrison, Y., & Horne, J. A. (2000). The impact of sleep deprivation on decision making: A review. *Journal of Experimental Psychology: Applied, 6*, 236–249. (p. 54)

Harter, J. K., Schmidt, F. L., & Hayes, T. L. (2002). Business-unit-level relationship between employee satisfaction, employee engagement, and business outcomes: A meta-analysis. *Journal of Applied Psychology, 87*, 268–279. (p. 414)

Hartmann, E. (1981, April). The strangest sleep disorder. *Psychology Today,* pp. 14, 16, 18. (p. 56)

Haselton, M. G., Mortezaie, M., Pillsworth, E. G., Bleske-Rechek, A., & Frederick, D. A. (2006). Ovulatory shifts in human female ornamentation: Near ovulation, Alcoholism and Related Conditions. *Archives of General Psychiatry, 62*, 1097–1106. (p. 107)

Haslam, S. A., & Reicher, S. (2007). Beyond the banality of evil: Three dynamics of an interactionist social psychology of tyranny. *Personality and Social Psychology Bulletin, 33*, 615–622. (p. 381)

Hatfield, E. (1988). Passionate and companionate love. In R. J. Sternberg & M. L. Barnes (Eds.), *The psychology of love.* New Haven, CT: Yale University Press. (p. 401)

Hatfield, E., & Sprecher, S. (1986). *Mirror, mirror . . . The importance of looks in everyday life.* Albany: State University of New York Press. (p. 399)

Haworth, C. M. A. & 17 others. (2009). A twin study of the genetics of high cognitive ability selected from 11,000 twin pairs in sex studies from four countries. *Behavior Genetics, 39*, 359–370. (p. 226)

Haxby, J. V. (2001, July 7). Quoted by B. Bower, Faces of perception. *Science News,* pp. 10–12. See also J. V. Haxby, M. I. Gobbini, M. L. Furey, A. Ishai, J. L. Schouten & P. Pietrini, Distributed and overlapping representations of faces and objects in ventral temporal cortex. *Science, 293*, 2425–2430. (p. 132)

Headey, B., Schupp, J., Tucci, I., & Wagner, G. G. (2010). Authentic happiness theory supported by impact of religion on life satisfaction: A longitudinal analysis with data for Germany. *Journal of Positive Psychology,* in press. (p. 268)

Heatherton, T. F., & Sargent, J. D. (2009). Does watching smoking in movies promote teenage smoking? *Current Directions in Psychological Science, 18*, 63–67. (p. 337)

Hebl, M. R., & Mannix, L. M. (2003). The weight of obesity in evaluating others: A mere proximity effect. *Personality and Social Psychology Bulletin, 29*, 28–38. (p. 245)

Hedges, L. V., & Nowell, A. (1995). Sex differences in mental test scores, variability, and numbers of high-scoring individuals. *Science, 269*, 41–45. (p. 230)

Heider, F. (1958). *The psychology of interpersonal relations.* New York: Wiley. (p. 378)

Heiman, J. R. (1975, April). The physiology of erotica: Women's sexual arousal. *Psychology Today,* pp. 90–94. (p. 110)

Heine, S. J., & Hamamura, T. (2007). In search of East Asian self-enhancement. *Personality and Social Psychology Review, 11*, 4–27. (p. 311)

Helmreich, W. B. (1992). *Against all odds: Holocaust survivors and the successful lives they made in America.* New York: Simon & Schuster. (p. 299)

Helmreich, W. B. (1994). Personal correspondence. Department of Sociology, City University of New York. (p. 299)

Helms, J. E., Jernigan, M., & Mascher, J. (2005). The meaning of race in psychology and how to change it: A methodological perspective. *American Psychologist, 60*, 27–36. (p. 229)

Helmuth, L. (2001). Boosting brain activity from the outside in. *Science, 292*, 1284–1286. (p. 370)

Henderlong, J., & Lepper, M. R. (2002). The effects of praise on children's intrinsic motivation: A review and synthesis. *Psychological Bulletin, 128*, 774–795. (p. 172)

Henkel, L. A., Franklin, N., & Johnson, M. K. (2000, March). Cross-modal source monitoring confusions between perceived and imagined events. *Journal of Experimental Psychology: Learning, Memory, & Cognition, 26*, 321–335. (p. 197)

Herman, C. P., & Polivy, J. (1980). Restrained eating. In A. J. Stunkard (Ed.), *Obesity.* Philadelphia: Saunders. (pp. 242, 248)

Hernandez, A. E., & Li, P. (2007). Age of acquisition: Its neural and computational mechanisms. *Psychological Bulletin, 133*, 638–650. (p. 214)

Herrmann, E., Call, J., Hernández-Lloreda, M. V., Hare, B., & Tomasello, M. (2007). Humans have evolved specialized skills of social cognition: The cultural intelligence hypothesis. *Science, 317*, 1360–1365. (p. 173)

Herrnstein, R. J., & Loveland, D. H. (1964). Complex visual concept in the pigeon. *Science, 146*, 549–551. (p. 163)

Herrnstein, R. J., & Murray, C. A. (1994). *The bell curve: Intelligence and class structure in American life.* New York: Free Press. (p. 228)

Hertenstein, M. J., Hansel, C., Butts, S., Hile, S. (2009). Smile intensity in photographs predicts divorce later in life. *Motivation & Emotion, 33*, 99–105. (p. 96)

Hertenstein, M. J., Verkamp, J. M., Kerestes, A. M., & Holmes, R. M. (2006). The communicative functions of touch in humans, nonhumans primates, and rats: A review and synthesis of the empirical research. *Genetic, Social, and General Psychology Monographs, 132*, 5–94. (p. 76)

Hertzog, C., Kramer, A. F., Wilson, R. S., & Lindenberger, U. (2008). Enrichment effects on adult cognitive development: Can the functional capacity of older adults be preserved and enhanced? *Psychological Science in the Public Interest, 9*(1), 1–65. (p. 92)

Herz, R. S. (2001). Ah sweet skunk! Why we like or dislike what we smell. *Cerebrum, 3*(4), 31–47. (p. 147)

Hess, E. H. (1956, July). Space perception in the chick. *Scientific American,* pp. 71–80. (p. 139)

Hettema, J. M., Neale, M. C., & Kendler, K. S. (2001). A review and meta-analysis of the genetic epidemiology of anxiety disorders. *American Journal of Psychiatry, 158,* 1568–1578. (p. 325)

Hewlett, B. S. (1991). *Intimate fathers: The nature and context of Aka Pygmy.* Ann Arbor: University of Michigan Press. (p. 77)

Hickok, G., Bellugi, U., & Klima, E. S. (2001, June). Sign language in the brain. *Scientific American,* pp. 58–65. (p. 48)

Hilgard, E. R. (1986). *Divided consciousness: Multiple controls in human thought and action.* New York: Wiley. (p. 145)

Hilgard, E. R. (1992). Dissociation and theories of hypnosis. In E. Fromm & M. R. Nash (Eds.), *Contemporary hypnosis research.* New York: Guilford. (p. 145)

Hill, C. E., & Nakayama, E. Y. (2000). Client-centered therapy: Where has it been and where is it going? A comment on Hathaway. *Journal of Clinical Psychology, 56,* 961–875. (p. 354)

Hines, M. (2004). *Brain gender.* New York: Oxford University Press. (p. 104)

Hingson, R. W., Heeren, T., & Winter M. R. (2006). Age at drinking onset and alcohol dependence. *Archives of Pediatrics & Adolescent Medicine, 160,* 739–746. (pp. 331, 337)

Hingson, R. W., Heeren, T., Zakocs, R. C., Kopstein, A., & Wechsler, H. (2002). Magnitude of alcohol-related mortality and morbidity among U.S. college students ages 18–24. *Journal of Studies on Alcohol, 63,* 136–144. (p. 330)

Hinz, L. D., & Williamson, D. A. (1987). Bulimia and depression: A review of the affective variant hypothesis. *Psychological Bulletin, 102,* 150–158. (p. 243)

Hirsch, J. (2003). Obesity: Matter over mind? *Cerebrum, 5*(1), 7–18. (p. 246)

HMHL. (2007, February). Electroconvulsive therapy. *Harvard Mental Health Letter,* Harvard Medical School, pp. 1–4. (p. 369)

Hobson, J. A. (2003). *Dreaming: An introduction to the science of sleep.* New York: Oxford. (p. 58)

Hobson, J. A. (2004). *13 dreams Freud never had: The new mind science.* New York: Pi Press. (p. 58)

Hoebel, B. G., & Teitelbaum, P. (1966). Effects of forcefeeding and starvation on food intake and body weight in a rat with ventromedial hypothalamic lesions. *Journal of Comparative and Physiological Psychology, 61,* 189–193. (p. 241)

Hoffman, C., & Hurst, N. (1990). Gender stereotypes: Perception or rationalization? *Journal of Personality and Social Psychology, 58,* 197–208. (p. 392)

Hoffman, D. D. (1998). *Visual intelligence: How we create what we see.* New York: Norton. (p. 132)

Hoffman, H. G. (2004, August). Virtual-reality therapy. *Scientific American,* pp. 58–65. (pp. 144, 357)

Hogan, R. (1998). Reinventing personality. *Journal of Social and Clinical Psychology, 17,* 1–10. (p. 308)

Hoge, C. W., & Castro, C. A. (2006). Post-traumatic stress disorder in UK and U.S. forces deployed to Iraq. *The Lancet, 368,* 837. (p. 324)

Hoge, C. W., Castro, C. A., Messer, S. C., McGurk, D., Cotting, D. I., & Koffman, R. L. (2004). Combat duty in Iraq and Afghanistan, mental health problems, and barriers to care. *New England Journal of Medicine, 351,* 13–22. (p. 324)

Hoge, C. W., Terhakopian, A., Castro, C. A., Messer, S. C., & Engel, C. C. (2007). Association of posttraumatic stress disorder with somatic symptoms, health care visits, and absenteeism among Iraq War veterans. *American Journal of Psychiatry, 164,* 150–153. (p. 324)

Hogg, M. A. (1996). Intragroup processes, group structure and social identity. In W. P. Robinson (Ed.), *Social groups and identities: Developing the legacy of Henri Tajfel.* Oxford: Butterworth Heinemann. (p. 392)

Hohmann, G. W. (1966). Some effects of spinal cord lesions on experienced emotional feelings. *Psychophysiology, 3,* 143–156. (p. 253)

Hokanson, J. E., & Edelman, R. (1966). Effects of three social responses on vascular processes. *Journal of Personality and Social Psychology, 3,* 442–447. (p. 263)

Holden, C. (1993). Wake-up call for sleep research. *Science, 259,* 305. (p. 54)

Holden, C. (2008). Poles apart. *Science, 321,* 193–195. (p. 65)

Holden, C. (2009). Behavioral geneticist celebrates twins, scorns PC science. *Science, 325,* 27. (p. 68)

Hollis, K. L. (1997). Contemporary research on Pavlovian conditioning: A "new" functional analysis. *American Psychologist, 52,* 956–965. (p. 159)

Hollon, S. D., Thase, M. E., & Markowitz, J. C. (2002). Treatment and prevention of depression. *Psychological Science in the Public Interest, 3,* 39–77. (p. 367)

Holstege, G., Georgiadis, J. R., Paans, A. M. J., Meiners, L. C., van der Graaf, F. H. C. E., & Reinders, A. A. T. S. (2003a). Brain activation during male ejaculation. *Journal of Neuroscience, 23,* 9185–9193. (p. 108)

Holstege, G., Reinders, A. A. T., Paans, A. M. J., Meiners, L. C., Pruim, J., & Georgiadis, J. R. (2003b). *Brain activation during female sexual orgasm. Program No. 727.7.* Washington, DC: Society for Neuroscience. (p. 108)

Hooper, J., & Teresi, D. (1986). *The three-pound universe.* New York: Macmillan. (p. 39)

Horn, J. L. (1982). The aging of human abilities. In J. Wolman (Ed.), *Handbook of developmental psychology.* Englewood Cliffs, NJ: Prentice-Hall. (p. 92)

Horner, V., Whiten, A., Flynn, E., & de Waal, F. B. M. (2006). Faithful replication of foraging techniques along cultural transmission chains by chimpanzees and children. *Proceedings of the National Academy of Sciences, 103,* 13878–13883. (p. 216)

Horrey, W. J., & Wickens, C. D. (2006). Examining the impact of cell phone conversations on driving using meta-analytic techniques. *Human Factors and Ergonomics Society, 48,* 196–205. (p. 49)

Horwood, L. J., & Fergusson, D. M. (1998). Breastfeeding and later cognitive and academic outcomes. *Pediatrics, 101*(1). (p. 14)

House, R. J., & Singh, J. V. (1987). Organizational behavior: Some new directions for I/O psychology. *Annual Review of Psychology, 38,* 669–718. (p. 416)

Houts, A. C., Berman, J. S., & Abramson, H. (1994). Effectiveness of psychological and pharmacological treatments for nocturnal enuresis. *Journal of Consulting and Clinical Psychology, 62,* 737–745. (p. 355)

Howell, R. T., & Howell, C. J. (2008). The relation of economic status to subjective well-being in developing countries: A meta-analysis. *Psychological Bulletin, 134,* 536–560. (p. 266)

Hu, F. B., Li, T. Y., Colditz, G. A., Willett, W. C., & Manson, J. E. (2003). Television watching and other sedentary behaviors in relation to risk of obesity and type 2 diabetes mellitus in women. *Journal of the American Medical Association, 289,* 1785–1791. (p. 246)

Hubel, D. H., & Wiesel, T. N. (1979, September). Brian mechanisms of vision. *Scientific American,* pp. 150–162. (p. 132)

Hublin, C., Kaprio, J., Partinen, M., Heikkila, K., & Koskenvuo, M. (1997). Prevalence and genetics of sleepwalking—A population-based twin study. *Neurology, 48,* 177–181. (p. 55)

Hublin, C., Kaprio, J., Partinen, M., & Koskenvuo, M. (1998). Sleeptalking in twins: Epidemiology and psychiatric comorbidity. *Behavior Genetics, 28,* 289–298. (p. 55)

Hucker, S. J., & Bain, J. (1990). Androgenic hormones and sexual assault. In W. Marshall, R. Law, & H. Barbaree (Eds.), *The handbook on sexual assault.* New York: Plenum. (p. 108)

Hudson, J. I., Hiripi, E., Pope, H. G., & Kessler, R. C. (2007). The prevalence and correlates of eating disorders in the National Comorbidity Survey Replication. *Biological Psychiatry, 61,* 348–358. (p. 243)

Huey, E. D., Krueger, F., & Grafman, J. (2006). Representations in the human prefrontal cortex. *Current Directions in Psychological Science, 15,* 167–171. (p. 43)

Hughes, H. C. (1999). *Sensory exotica: A world beyond human experience.* Cambridge, MA: MIT Press. (p. 124)

Hughes, J. R., Peters, E. N., & Naud, S. (2008). Relapse to smoking after 1 year of abstinence: A meta-analysis. *Addictive Behaviors, 33,* 1516–1520. (p. 333)

Hugick, L. (1989, July). Women play the leading role in keeping modern families close. *Gallup Report, No. 286,* p. 27–34. (p. 103)

Hull, J. M. (1990). *Touching the rock: An experience of blindness.* New York: Vintage Books. (pp. 190, 399)

Hummer, R. A., Rogers, R. G., Nam, C. B., & Ellison, C. G. (1999). Religious involvement and U.S. adult mortality. *Demography, 36,* 273–285. (pp. 287, 288)

Humphrey, S. E., Nahrgang, J. D., & Morgeson, F. P. (2007). Integrating motivational, social, and contextual work design features: A meta-analytic summary and theoretical extension of the work design literature. *Journal of Applied Psychology, 92,* 1332–1356. (p. 281)

Hunsley, J., & Di Giulio, G. (2002). Dodo bird, phoenix, or urban legend? The question of psychotherapy equivalence. *Scientific Review of Mental Health Practice, 1,* 11–22. (p. 362)

Hunt, C., Slade, T., & Andrews, G. (2004). Generalized anxiety disorder and major depressive disorder comorbidity in the National Survey of Mental Health and Well-Being. *Depression and Anxiety, 20,* 23–31. (p. 322)

Hunt, E., & Carlson, J. (2007). Considerations relating to the study of group differences in intelligence. *Perspectives on Psychological Science, 2,* 194–213. (p. 231)

Hunt, J. M. (1982). Toward equalizing the developmental opportunities of infants and preschool children. *Journal of Social Issues, 38*(4), 163–191. (p. 228)

Hunt, M. (1974). *Sexual behavior in the 1970s.* Chicago: Playboy Press. (p. 111)

Hunt, M. (1990). *The compassionate beast: What science is discovering about the humane side of humankind.* New York: William Morrow. (p. 4)

Hunt, M. (1993). *The story of psychology.* New York: Doubleday. (p. 2)

Huston, A. C., Donnerstein, E., Fairchild, H., Feshbach, N. D., Katz, P. A., & Murray, J. P. (1992). *Big world, small screen: The role of television in American society.* Lincoln: University of Nebraska Press. (p. 175)

Hutchinson, R. (2006). *Calum's road.* Edinburgh: Burlinn Limited. (p. 414)

Hyde, J. S. (1983, November). Bem's gender schema theory. Paper presented at GLCA Women's Studies Conference, Rochester, IN. (p. 196)

Hyde, J. S., & Mertz, J. E. (2009). Gender, culture, and mathematics performance. *Proceedings of the National Academy of Sciences, 106,* 8801–8807. (p. 230)

Hyde, J. S., Mezulis, A. H., & Abramson, L. Y. (2008). The ABCs of depression: Integrating affective, biological, and cognitive models to explain the emergence of the gender difference in depression. *Psychological Review, 115,* 291–313. (p. 340)

Hyman, I. E., Jr., Boss, S. M., Wise, B. M., McKenzie, K. E., & Caggiano, J. M. (2010). Did you see the unicycling clown? Inattentional blindness while walking and talking on a cell phone. *Applied Cognitive Psychology, 24,* 597–607. (p. 49)

Hyman, R. (1981). Cold reading: How to convince strangers that you know all about them. In K. Frazier (Ed.), *Paranormal borderlands of science.* Buffalo, NY: Prometheus. (p. 306)

Iacoboni, M. (2009). Imitation, empathy, and mirror neurons. *Annual Review of Psychology, 60,* 653–670. (p. 173)

Ickes, W., Snyder, M., & Garcia, S. (1997). Personality influences on the choice of situations. In R. Hogan, J. Johnson, & S. Briggs (Eds.). *Handbook of personality psychology.* San Diego, CA: Academic Press. (p. 308)

Idson, L. C., & Mischel, W. (2001). The personality of familiar and significant people: The lay perceiver as a social-cognitive theorist. *Journal of Personality and Social Psychology, 80,* 585–596. (p. 378)

Ikonomidou, C. C. Bittigau, P. Ishimaru, M. J., Wozniak, D. F., Koch, C., Genz, K., Price, M. T., Stefovska, V., Hoerster, F., Tenkova, T., Dikranian, K., & Olney, J. W. (2000). Ethanol-induced apoptotic neurodegeneration and fetal alcohol syndrome. *Science, 287,* 1056–1060. (p. 66)

Ilardi, S. S. (2009). *The depression cure: The six-step program to beat depression without drugs.* Cambridge, MA: De Capo Lifelong Books. (pp. 341, 371)

Ingham, A. G., Levinger, G., Graves, J., & Peckham, V. (1974). The Ringelmann effect: Studies of group size and group performance. *Journal of Experimental Social Psychology, 10,* 371–384. (p. 387)

Inglehart, R. (1990). *Culture shift in advanced industrial society.* Princeton, NJ: Princeton University Press. (pp. 95, 96, 249, 412)

Inglehart, R. (2009). Cultural change and democracy in Latin America, in F. Hagopian (Ed.), *Contemporary Catholicism, religious pluralism and democracy in Latin America.* South Bend: Notre Dame University Press. (p. 266)

Inglehart, R., Foa, R., Peterson, C., & Welzel, C. (2008). Development, freedom, and rising happiness: A global perspective (1981–2007). *Perspectives on Psychological Science, 3,* 264–285. (p. 282)

Insana, R. (2005, February 21). Coach says honey gets better results than vinegar (interview with Larry Brown). *USA Today,* p. 4B. (p. 416)

International Schizophrenia Consortium (2009). Common polygenic variation contributes to risk of schizophrenia and bipolar disorder. *Nature, 460,* 748–752. (p. 347)

Inzlicht, M., & Ben-Zeev, T. (2000). A threatening intellectual environment: Why females are susceptible to experiencing problem-solving deficits in the presence of males. *Psychological Science, 11,* 365–371. (p. 232)

IPU. (2010). Women in national parliaments: Situation as of 30 November 2009. International Parliamentary Union (www.ipu.org). (p. 102)

Irwin, M., Mascovich, A., Gillin, J. C., Willoughby, R., Pike, J., & Smith, T. L. (1994). Partial sleep deprivation reduces natural killer cell activity in humans. *Psychosomatic Medicine, 56,* 493–498. (p. 54)

Isaacson, W. (2009, Spring). Einstein's final quest. In Character. http://incharacter.org/features/einsteins-final-quest. (p. 221)

Iso, H., Simoda, S., & Matsuyama, T. (2007). Environmental change during postnatal development alters behaviour. *Behavioural Brain Research, 179,* 90–98. (p. 45)

Ito, T. A., Miller, N., & Pollock, V. E. (1996). Alcohol and aggression: A meta-analysis on the moderating effects of inhibitory cues, triggering events, and self-focused attention. *Psychological Bulletin, 120,* 60–82. (p. 394)

ITU. (2010). The world in 2009: ICT facts and figures. International Telecommunication Union (www.itu.int/ict). (p. 250)

Iversen, L. L. (2000). *The science of marijuana*. New York: Oxford. (p. 335)

Iyengar, S. S., & Lepper, M. R. (2000). When choice is demotivating: Can one desire too much of a good thing? *Journal of Personality and Social Psychology, 79*, 995–1006. (p. 282)

Izard, C. E. (1977). *Human emotions*. New York: Plenum Press. (pp. 261, 263)

Izard, C. E. (1994). Innate and universal facial expressions: Evidence from developmental and cross-cultural research. *Psychological Bulletin, 114*, 288–299. (p. 261)

Jablensky, A. (1999). Schizophrenia: Epidemiology. *Current Opinion in Psychiatry, 12*, 19–28. (p. 345)

Jackson, J. M., & Williams, K. D. (1988). Social loafing: A review and theoretical analysis. Unpublished manuscript, Fordham University. (p. 387)

Jackson, S. W. (1992). The listening healer in the history of psychological healing. *American Journal Psychiatry, 149*, 1623–1632. (p. 364)

Jacobs, B. L. (1987). How hallucinogenic drugs work. *American Scientist, 75*, 386–392. (p. 334)

Jacobs, B. L. (1994). Serotonin, motor activity, and depression-related disorders. *American Scientist, 82*, 456–463. (p. 341)

Jacobs, B. L. (2004). Depression: The brain finally gets into the act. *Current Directions in Psychological Science, 13*, 103–106. (p. 367)

Jacques, C., & Rossion, B. (2006). The speed of individual face categorization. *Psychological Science, 17*, 485–492. (p. 124)

Jaffe, E. (2004, October). Peace in the Middle East may be impossible: Lee D. Ross on naive realism and conflict resolution. *APS Observer*, pp. 9–11. (p. 128)

James, W. (1890). *The principles of psychology* (Vol. 2). New York: Holt. (pp. 142, 200)

James, W. (1902; reprinted 1958). *Varieties of religious experience*. New York: Mentor Books. (p. 253)

Jameson, D. (1985). Opponent-colors theory in light of physiological findings. In D. Ottoson & S. Zeki (Eds.), *Central and peripheral mechanisms of color vision*. New York: Macmillan. (p. 137)

Jamison, K. R. (1993). Touched with fire: Manic-depressive illness and the artistic temperament. New York: Free Press. (p. 339)

Jamison, K. R. (1995). *An unquiet mind*. New York: Knopf. (pp. 339, 350, 368)

Janis, I. L. (1982). *Groupthink: Psychological studies of policy decisions and fiascoes*. Boston: Houghton Mifflin. (p. 388)

Janis, I. L. (1986). Problems of international crisis management in the nuclear age. *Journal of Social Issues, 42*(2), 201–220. (p. 207)

Jenkins, J. G., & Dallenbach, K. M. (1924). Obliviscence during sleep and waking. *American Journal of Psychology, 35*, 605–612. (p. 194)

Jenkins, J. M., & Astington, J. W. (1996). Cognitive factors and family structure associated with theory of mind development in young children. *Developmental Psychology, 32*, 70–78. (p. 74)

Jensen, J. P., & Bergin, A. E. (1988). Mental health values of professional therapists: A national interdisciplinary survey. *Professional Psychology: Research and Practice, 19*, 290–297. (p. 364)

Ji, D., & Wilson, M.A. (2007). Coordinated memory replay in the visual cortex and hippocampus during sleep. *Nature Neuroscience, 10*, 100–107. (p. 185)

Job, D. E., Whalley, H. C., McIntosh, A. M., Owens, D. G. C., Johnstone, E. C., & Lawrie, S. M. (2006). Grey matter changes can improve the prediction of schizophrenia in subjects at high risk. *BMC Medicine, 4*, 29. (p. 345)

John, O. P., & Srivastava, S. (1999). The Big Five trait taxonomy: History, measurement, and theoretical perspectives. In L. A. Pervin & O. P. John (Eds.), *Handbook of personality: Theory and research*. New York: Guilford. (p. 305)

John Paul II. (1995). Address of His Holiness Pope John Paul II to the Fiftieth General Assembly of the United Nations Organization. Available from: http://www.vatican.va/holy_father/john_paul_ii/speeches/1995/october/documents/hf_jp-ii_spe_05101995_address-to-uno_en.html.

Johnson, D. L., Wiebe, J. S., Gold, S. M., Andreasen, N. C., Hichwa, R. D., Watkins, G. L., & Ponto, L. L. B. (1999). Cerebral blood flow and personality: A positron emission tomography study. *American Journal of Psychiatry, 156*, 252–257. (p. 304)

Johnson, E., with Novak, W. (1993). *My life*. New York: Random House. (p. 284)

Johnson, E. J., & Goldstein, D. (2003). Do defaults save lives? *Science, 302*, 1338–1339. (p. 210)

Johnson, J. A. (2007, June 26). Not so situational. Commentary on the SPSP listserv (spsp-discuss@stolaf.edu). (p. 386)

Johnson, J. G., Cohen, P., Kotler, L., Kasen, S., & Brook, J. S. (2002). Psychiatric disorders associated with risk for the development of eating disorders during adolescence and early adulthood. *Journal of Consulting and Clinical Psychology, 70*, 1119–1128. (p. 243)

Johnson, J. S., & Newport, E. L. (1991). Critical period affects on universal properties of language: The status of subjacency in the acquisition of a second language. *Cognition, 39*, 215–258. (p. 214)

Johnson, M. H., & Morton, J. (1991). *Biology and cognitive development: The case of face recognition*. Oxford: Blackwell Publishing. (p. 69)

Johnson, R. E., Chang, C-H., & Lord, R. G. (2006). Moving from cognition to behavior: What the research says. *Psychological Bulletin, 132*, 381–415. (p. 416)

Johnson, W., Carothers, A., & Deary, I. J. (2009). A role for the X chromosome in sex differences in variability in general intelligence? *Perspectives on PsychologicalScience, 4*, 598–611. (pp. 68, 231)

Johnson, W., te Nijenhuis, Jl, & Bouchard, Jr., T. J. (2008). Still just 1 *g*: Consistent results from five test batteries. *Intelligence, 36*, 81–95. (p. 220)

Johnston, L. D., O'Malley, P. M., Bachman, J. G., & Schulenberg, J. E. (2007). *Monitoring the Future: National results on adolescent drug use: Overview of key findings, 2006*. Bethesda, MD: National Institute on Drug Abuse. (pp. 336, 337)

Johnston, L. D., O'Malley, P. M., Bachman, J. G., & Schulenberg, J. E. (2010). *Monitoring the future: National results on adolescent drug use: Overview of key findings, 2009*. Bethesda, MD: National Institute on Drug Abuse. (pp. 333, 336)

Joiner, T. (2006). *Why people die by suicide*. Cambridge, MA: Harvard University Press. (p. 339)

Jolly, A. (2007). The social origin of mind. *Science, 317*, 1326. (p. 216)

Jones, J. M. (2003, February 12). Fear of terrorism increases amidst latest warning. *Gallup News Service* (www.gallup.com/releases/pr030212.asp). (p. 322)

Jones, J. M. (2007, July 25). Latest Gallup update shows cigarette smoking near historical lows. *Gallup Poll News Service* (poll.gallup.com). (p. 332)

Jones, J. M., & Moore, D. W. (2003, June 17). Generational differences in support for a woman president. The Gallup Organization (www.gallup.com). (p. 390)

Jones, J. T., Pelham, B. W., Carvallo, M., & Mirenberg, M. C. (2004). How do I love thee? Let me count the Js: Implicit egotism and interpersonal attraction. *Journal of Personality and Social Psychology, 87*, 665–683. (p. 397)

Jones, M. C. (1924). A laboratory study of fear: The case of Peter. *Journal of Genetic Psychology, 31*, 308–315. (p. 356)

Jones, M. V., Paull, G. C., & Erskine, J. (2002). The impact of a team's aggressive reputation on the decisions of association football referees. *Journal of Sports Sciences, 20*, 991–1000. (p. 128)

Jones, S. S. (2007). Imitation in infancy: The development of mimicry. *Psychological Science, 18*, 593–599. (p. 173)

Jones, S. S., Collins, K., & Hong, H-W. (1991). An audience effect on smile production in 10–month-old infants. *Psychological Science, 2*, 45–49. (p. 261)

Jost, J. T., Kay, A. C., & Thorisdottir, H. (eds.) (2009). *Social and psychological bases of ideology and system justification.* New York: Oxford University Press. (p. 393)

Judge, T. A., Thoresen, C. J., Bono, J. E., & Patton, G. K. (2001). The job satisfaction/job performance relationship: A qualitative and quantitative review. *Psychological Bulletin, 127*, 376–407. (p. 414)

Jung-Beeman, M., Bowden, E. M., Haberman, J., Frymiare, J. L., Arambel-Liu, S., Greenblatt, R., Reber, P. J., & Kounios, J. (2004). Neural activity when people solve verbal problems with insight. *PloS Biology 2*(4), e111. (p. 206)

Kagan, J. (1976). Emergent themes in human development. *American Scientist, 64*, 186–196. (p. 78)

Kagan, J. (1984). *The nature of the child.* New York: Basic Books. (p. 76)

Kagan, J. (1995). On attachment. *Harvard Review of Psychiatry, 3*, 104–106. (p. 77)

Kagan, J. (1998). *Three seductive ideas.* Cambridge, MA: Harvard University Press. (p. 96)

Kagan, J., & Snidman, N. (2004). *The long shadow of temperament.* Cambridge, MA: Belknap Press. (p. 69)

Kagan, J., Lapidus, D. R., & Moore, M. (December, 1978). Infant antecedents of cognitive functioning: A longitudinal study. *Child Development, 49*(4), 1005–1023. (p. 96)

Kahneman, D. (1999). Assessments of objective happiness: A bottom-up approach. In D. Kahneman, E. Diener, & N. Schwartz (Eds.), *Understanding well-being: Scientific perspectives on enjoyment and suffering.* New York: Russell Sage Foundation. (p. 144)

Kahneman, D. (2005, January 13). What were they thinking? Q&A with Daniel Kahneman. *Gallup Management Journal* (gmj.gallup.com). (p. 207)

Kahneman, D. (2005, February 10). Are you happy now? *Gallup Management Journal* interview (www.gmj.gallup.com). (p. 265)

Kahneman, D., Fredrickson, B. L., Schreiber, C. A., & Redelmeier, D. A. (1993). When more pain is preferred to less: Adding a better end. *Psychological Science, 4*, 401–405. (p. 144)

Kahneman, D., Krueger, A. B., Schkade, D. A., Schwarz, N., & Stone, A. A. (2004). A survey method for characterizing daily life experience: The day reconstruction method. *Science, 306*, 1776–1780. (p. 265)

Kail, R. (1991). Developmental change in speed of processing during childhood and adolescence. *Psychological Bulletin, 109*, 490–501. (p. 91)

Kaiser Family Foundation. (2003, October 28). New study finds children age zero to six spend as much time with TV, computers and video games as playing outside. www.kff.org/entmedia/entmedia102803nr.cfm. (p. 14)

Kaiser Family Foundation. (2010, January). *Generation M^2: Media in the lives of 8- to 18-year-olds* (by V. J. Rideout, U. G. Foeher, & D. F. Roberts). Menlo Park, CA: Henry J. Kaiser Family Foundation. (pp. 250, 251)

Kamarck, T., & Jennings, J. R. (1991). Biobehavioral factors in sudden cardiac death. *Psychological Bulletin, 109*, 42–75. (p. 279)

Kaminski, J., Cali, J., & Fischer, J. (2004). Word learning in a domestic dog: Evidence for "fast mapping." *Science, 304*, 1682–1683. (p. 217)

Kandel, E. R., & Schwartz, J. H. (1982). Molecular biology of learning: Modulation of transmitter release. *Science, 218*, 433–443. (p. 188)

Kaplan, H. I., & Saddock, B. J. (Eds.). (1989). *Comprehensive textbook of psychiatry, V.* Baltimore, MD: Williams and Wilkins. (p. 366)

Kaplan, R. M., & Kronick, R. G. (2006). Marital status and longevity in the United States population. *Journal of Epidemiology and Community Health, 60*, 760–765. (p. 284)

Kaplan, S., Bradley, J. C., Luchman, J. N., & Haynes, D. (2009). On the role of positive and negative affectivity in job performance: A meta-analytic investigation. *Journal of Applied Psychology, 94*, 162–176. (p. 414)

Kaprio, J., Koskenvuo, M., & Rita, H. (1987). Mortality after bereavement: A prospective study of 95,647 widowed persons. *American Journal of Public Health, 77*, 283–287. (p. 275)

Karacan, I., Goodenough, D. R., Shapiro, A., & Starker, S. (1966). Erection cycle during sleep in relation to dream anxiety. *Archives of General Psychiatry, 15*, 183–189. (p. 52)

Karau, S. J., & Williams, K. D. (1993). Social loafing: A meta-analytic review and theoretical integration. *Journal of Personality and Social Psychology, 65*, 681–706. (p. 387)

Karberg, J. C., & James, D. J. (2005, July). Substance dependence, abuse, and treatment of jail inmates, 2002. *Bureau of Justice Statistics Special Report, U.S. Department of Justice* (NCJ 209588). (p. 394)

Kark, J. D., Shemi, G., Friedlander, Y., Martin, O., Manor, O., & Blondheim, S. H. (1996). Does religious observance promote health? Mortality in secular vs. religious kibbutzim in Israel. *American Journal of Public Health, 86*, 341–346. (p. 287)

Kaufman, J. C., & Baer, J. (2002). I bask in dreams of suicide: Mental illness, poetry, and women. *Review of General Psychology, 6*, 271–286. (p. 339)

Kaufman, L., & Kaufman, J. H. (2000). Explaining the moon illusion. *Proceedings of the National Academy of Sciences, 97*, 500–505. (p. 137)

Kay, A. C., Baucher, D., Peach, J. M., Laurin, K., Friesen, J., Zanna, M. P., & Spencer, S. J. (2009). Inequality, discrimination, and the power of the status quo: Direct evidence for a motivation to see the way things are as the way they should be. *Journal of Personality and social Psychology, 97*, 421–434. (p. 393)

Kazdin, A. E., & Benjet, C. (2003). Spanking children: Evidence and issues. *Current Directions in Psychological Science, 12*, 99–103. (p. 166)

Keesey, R. E., & Corbett, S. W. (1983). Metabolic defense of the body weight set-point. In A. J. Stunkard & E. Stellar (Eds.), *Eating and its disorders.* New York: Raven Press. (p. 241)

Keith, S. W., & 19 others. (2006). Putative contributors to the secular increase in obesity: Exploring the roads less traveled. *International Journal of Obesity, 30*, 1585–1594. (p. 246)

Keller, M. B., McCullough, J. P., Klein, D. N., Arnow, B., Dunner, D. L., Gelenberg, A. J., Markowitz, J. C., Nemeroff, C. B., Russell, J. M., Thase, M. E., Trivedi, M. H., & Zajecka J. (2000). A comparison of nefazodone, the cognitive behavioral-analysis system of psychotherapy, and their combination for the treatment of chronic depression. *New England Journal of Medicine, 342*, 1462–1470. (p. 367)

Kellerman, J., Lewis, J., & Laird, J. D. (1989). Looking and loving: The effects of mutual gaze on feelings of romantic love. *Journal of Research in Personality, 23*, 145–161. (p. 260)

Kellermann, A. L. (1997). Comment: Gunsmoke—changing public attitudes toward smoking and firearms. *American Journal of Public Health, 87*, 910–913. (p. 393)

Kellermann, A. L., Rivara, F. P., Rushforth, N. B., Banton, H. G., Feay, D. T., Francisco, J. T., Locci, A. B., Prodzinski, J., Hackman, B. B., & Somes, G. (1993). Gun ownership as a risk factor for homicide in the home. *New England Journal of Medicine, 329,* 1084–1091. (p. 393)

Kellermann, A. L., Somes, G. Rivara, F. P., Lee, R. K., & Banton, J. G. (1998). Injuries and deaths due to firearms in the home. *Journal of Trauma, 45,* 263-267. (p. 393)

Kelley, J., & De Graaf, N. D. (1997). National context, parental socialization, and religious belief: Results from 15 nations. *American Sociological Review, 62,* 639–659. (p. 86)

Kelling, S. T., & Halpern, B. P. (1983). Taste flashes: Reaction times, intensity, and quality. *Science, 219,* 412–414. (p. 145)

Kellner, C. H., & 15 others. (2005). Relief of expressed suicidal intent by ECT: A consortium for research in ECT study. *American Journal of Psychiatry, 162,* 977–982. (p. 369)

Kellner, C. H. & 16 others. (2006). Continuation electroconvulsive therapy vs. pharmacotherapy for relapse prevention in major depression: A multisite study from the Consortium for Research in Electroconvulsive Therapy (CORE). *Archives of General Psychiatry, 63,* 1337–1344. (p. 369)

Kelly, A. E. (2000). Helping construct desirable identities: A self-presentational view of psychotherapy. *Psychological Bulletin, 126,* 475–494. (p. 358)

Kelly, D. J., Quinn, P. C., Slater, A. M., Lee, K., Ge, L., & Pascalis, O. (2007). The other-race effect develops during infancy: Evidence of perceptual narrowing. *Psychological Science, 18,* 1084–1089. (p. 393)

Kelly, I. W. (1997). Modern astrology: A critique. *Psychological Reports, 81,* 1035–1066. (p. 306)

Kelly, I. W. (1998). Why astrology doesn't work. *Psychological Reports, 82,* 527–546. (p. 306)

Kelly, T. A. (1990). The role of values in psychotherapy: A critical review of process and outcome effects. *Clinical Psychology Review, 10,* 171–186. (p. 364)

Kempermann, G., Kuhn, H. G., & Gage, F. H. (May, 1998). Experience-induced neurogenesis in the senescent dentate gyrus. *Journal of Neuroscience, 18*(9), 3206–3212. (p. 92)

Kendall-Tackett, K. A. (Ed.) (2004). *Health consequences of abuse in the family: A clinical guide for evidence-based practice.* Washington, DC: American Psychological Association. (p. 78)

Kendall-Tackett, K. A., Williams, L. M., & Finkelhor, D. (1993). Impact of sexual abuse on children: A review and synthesis of recent empirical studies. *Psychological Bulletin, 113,* 164–180. (pp. 78, 199)

Kendler, K. S. (1997). Social support: A genetic-epidemiologic analysis. *American Journal of Psychiatry, 154,* 1398–1404. (p. 309)

Kendler, K. S. (1998, January). Major depression and the environment: A psychiatric genetic perspective. *Pharmacopsychiatry, 31*(1), 5–9. (p. 340)

Kendler, K. S., Jacobson, K. C., Myers, J., & Prescott, C. A. (2002a). Sex differences in genetic and environmental risk factors for irrational fears and phobias. *Psychological Medicine, 32,* 209–217. (p. 325)

Kendler, K. S., Karkowski, L. M., & Prescott, C. A. (1999). Fears and phobias: Reliability and heritability. *Psychological Medicine, 29,* 539–553. (p. 325)

Kendler, K. S., Myers, J., & Prescott, C. A. (2002b). The etiology of phobias: An evaluation of the stress-diathesis model. *Archives of General Psychiatry, 59,* 242–248. (p. 325)

Kendler, K. S., Neale, M. C., Kessler, R. C., Heath, A. C., & Eaves, L. J. (1992). Generalized anxiety disorder in women: A population-based twin study. *Archives of General Psychiatry, 49,* 267–272. (p. 325)

Kendler, K. S., Neale, M. C., Thornton, L. M. Aggen, S. H., Gilman, S. E., & Kessler, R. C. (2002). Cannabis use in the last year in a U.S. national sample of twin and sibling pairs. *Psychological Medicine, 32,* 551–554. (p. 336)

Kendler, K. S., Thornton, L. M., & Gardner, C. O. (2001). Genetic risk, number of previous depressive episodes, and stressful life events in predicting onset of major depression. *American Journal of Psychiatry, 158,* 582–586. (p. 340)

Kennedy, S., & Over, R. (1990). Psychophysiological assessment of male sexual arousal following spinal cord injury. *Archives of Sexual Behavior, 19,* 15–27. (p. 33)

Kenrick, D. T., & Gutierres, S. E. (1980). Contrast effects and judgments of physical attractiveness: When beauty becomes a social problem. *Journal of Personality and Social Psychology, 38,* 131–140. (p. 111)

Kenrick, D. T., Gutierres, S. E., & Goldberg, L. L. (1989). Influence of popular erotica on judgments of strangers and mates. *Journal of Experimental Social Psychology, 25,* 159–167. (p. 111)

Kenrick, D. T., Nieuweboer, S., & Bunnk, A. P. (2009). Universal mechanisms and cultural diversity: Replacing the blank slate with a coloring book. In M. Schaller, S. Heine, A. Norenzayan, T. Yamagishi, & T. Kameda (Eds.), *Evolution, culture, and the human mind.* Mahwah, NJ: Erlbaum. (p. 116)

Keough, K. A., Zimbardo, P. G., & Boyd, J. N. (1999). Who's smoking, drinking, and using drugs? Time perspective as a predictor of substance use. *Basic and Applied Social Psychology, 2,* 149–164. (p. 294)

Kerr, N. L., & Bruun, S. E. (1983). Dispensability of member effort and group motivation losses: Free-rider effects. *Journal of Personality and Social Psychology, 44,* 78–94. (p. 388)

Kessler, M., & Albee, G. (1975). Primary prevention. *Annual Review of Psychology, 26,* 557–591. (p. 373)

Kessler, R. C. (2000). Posttraumatic stress disorder: The burden to the individual and to society. *Journal of Clinical Psychiatry, 61*(suppl. 5), 4–12. (p. 324)

Kessler, R. C. (2001). Epidemiology of women and depression. *Journal of Affective Disorders, 74,* 5–1. (p. 342)

Kessler, R. C., Berglund, P., Demler, O., Jin, R., Merikangos, K. R., & Walters, E. E. (2005). Lifetime prevalence and age-of-onset distributions of DSM-IV disorders in the National Comorbidity Survey Replication. *Archives of General Psychiatry, 62,* 593–602. (p. 321)

Kessler, R. C., Foster, C., Joseph, J., Ostrow, D., Wortman, C., Phair, J., & Chmiel, J. (1991). Stressful life events and symptom onset in HIV infection. *American Journal of Psychiatry, 148,* 733–738. (p. 279)

Keynes, M. (1980, December 20/27). Handel's illnesses. *The Lancet,* pp. 1354–1355. (p. 339)

Keys, A., Brozek, J., Henschel, A., Mickelsen, O., & Taylor, H. L. (1950). *The biology of human starvation.* Minneapolis: University of Minnesota Press. (p. 240)

Khan, A., Warner, H. A., & Brown, W. A. (2000). Symptom reduction and suicide risk inpatients treated with placebo in antidepressant clinical trials. *Archives of General Psychiatry, 57,* 311–317. (p. 368)

Kiecolt-Glaser, J. K. (2009). Psychoneuroimmunology: Psychology's gateway to the biomedical future. *Perspectives on Psychological Science, 4,* 367–369. (p. 277)

Kiecolt-Glaser, J. K., & Glaser, R. (1995). Psychoneuoriimmunology and health consequences: Data and shared mechanisms. *Psychosomatic Medicine, 57,* 269–274. (p. 278)

Kiecolt-Glaser, J. K., Loving, T. J., Stowell, J. R., Malarkey, W. B., Lemeshow, S., Dickinson, S. L., & Glaser, R. (2005). Hostile marital interactions, proinflammatory cytokine production, and wound healing. *Archives of General Psychiatry, 62,* 1377–1384. (p. 277)

Kiecolt-Glaser, J. K., Page, G. G., Marucha, P. T., MacCallum, R. C., & Glaser, R. (1998). Psychological influences on surgical recovery: Perspectives from psychoneuroimmunology. *American Psychologist, 53,* 1209–1218. (p. 277)

Kihlstrom, J. F. (1990). Awareness, the psychological unconscious, and the self. Address to the American Psychological Association convention. (p. 299)

Kihlstrom, J. F. (2005). Dissociative disorders. *Annual Review of Clinical Psychology, 1,* 227–253. (p. 327)

Kihlstrom, J. F. (2006). Repression: A unified theory of a will-o'-the-wisp. *Behavioral and Brain Sciences, 29,* 523. (p. 299)

Kim, B. S. K., Ng, G. F., & Ahn, A. J. (2005). Effects of client expectation for counseling success, client-counselor worldview match, and client adherence to Asian and European American cultural values on counseling process with Asian Americans. *Journal of Counseling Psychology, 52,* 67–76. (p. 364)

Kimata, H. (2001). Effect of humor on allergen-induced wheal reactions. *Journal of the American Medical Association, 285,* 737. (p. 283)

King, R. N., & Koehler, D. J. (2000). Illusory correlations in graphological interference. *Journal of Experimental Psychology: Applied, 6,* 336–348. (p. 306)

Kingston, D. W., Malamuth, N. M., Fedoroff, N. M., & Marshall, W. L. (2009). The importance of individual differences in pornography use: Theoretical perspectives and implications for treating sexual offenders. *Journal of Sex Research, 46,* 216–232. (p. 395)

Kinnier, R. T., & Metha, A. T. (1989). Regrets and priorities at three stages of life. *Counseling and Values, 33,* 182–193. (p. 95)

Kinsey, A. C., Pomeroy, W., & Martin, C. (1948). *Sexual behavior in the human male.* Philadelphia: Saunders. (p. 107)

Kinsey, A. C., Pomeroy, W., Martin, C., & Gebhard, P. (1953). *Sexual behavior in the human female.* Philadelphia: Saunders. (p. 107)

Kinzler, K. D., Shutts, K., Dejesus, J., & Spelke, E. S. (2009). Accent trumps race in guiding children's social preferences. *Social Cognition, 27,* 623–634. (p. 392)

Kirby, D. (2002). Effective approaches to reducing adolescent unprotected sex, pregnancy, and childbearing. *Journal of Sex Research, 39,* 51–57. (p. 110)

Kirsch, I., & Sapirstein, G. (1998). Listening to Prozac but hearing placebo: A meta-analysis of antidepressant medication. *Prevention and Treatment, 1,* posted June 26 at (journals.apa.org/prevention/volume1). (pp. 16, 368)

Kirsch, I., Deacon, B. J., Huedo-Medina, T. B., Scoboria, A., Moore, T. J., & Johnson, B. T. (2008). Initial severity and antidepressant benefits: A meta-analysis of data submitted to the Food and Drug Administration. *Public Library of Science Medicine, 5,* e45. (p. 368)

Kirsch, I., Moore, T. J., Scoboria, A., & Nicholls, S. S. (2002, July 15). New study finds little difference between effects of antidepressants and placebo. *Prevention and Treatment* (journals.apa.org/prevention). (p. 368)

Klayman, J., & Ha, Y-W. (1987). Confirmation, disconfirmation, and information in hypothesis testing. *Psychological Review, 94,* 211–228. (p. 209)

Klein, D. N., & 16 others. (2003). Therapeutic alliance in depression treatment: Controlling for prior change and patient characteristics. *Journal of Consulting and Clinical Psychology, 71,* 997–1006. (p. 364)

Klein, S. B., & Kihlstrom, J. F. (1998). On bridging the gap between social-personality psychology and neuropsychology. *Personality and Social Psychology Review, 2,* 228–242. (p. 74)

Kleinfeld, J. (1998). *The myth that schools shortchange girls: Social science in the service of deception.* Washington, DC: Women's Freedom Network. Available from ERIC, Document ED423210, and via www.uaf.edu/northern/schools/myth.html. (p. 231)

Kleinke, C. L. (1986). Gaze and eye contact: A research review. *Psychological Bulletin, 1000,* 78–100. (p. 260)

Kleinmuntz, B., & Szucko, J. J. (1984). A field study of the fallibility of polygraph lie detection. *Nature, 308,* 449–450. (p. 257)

Kleitman, N. (1960, November). Patterns of dreaming. *Scientific American,* pp. 82–88. (p. 51)

Klemm, W. R. (1990). Historical and introductory perspectives on brainstem-mediated behaviors. In W. R. Klemm & R. P. Vertes (Eds.), *Brainstem mechanisms of behavior.* New York: Wiley. (p. 35)

Kline, D., & Schieber, F. (1985). Vision and aging. In J. E. Birren & K. W. Schaie (Eds.), *Handbook of the psychology of aging.* New York: Van Nostrand Reinhold. (p. 90)

Kline, G. H., Stanley, S. M., Markman, J. H., Olmos-Gallo, P. A., St. Peters, M., Whitton, S. W., & Prado, L. M. (2004). Timing is everything: Preengagement cohabitation and increased risk for poor marital outcomes. *Journal of Family Psychology, 18,* 311–318. (p. 93)

Kline, N. S. (1974). *From sad to glad.* New York: Ballantine Books. (p. 343)

Klineberg, O. (1984). Public opinion and nuclear war. *American Psychologist, 39,* 1245–1253. (p. 406)

Kluft, R. P. (1991). Multiple personality disorder. In A. Tasman & S. M. Goldfinger (Eds.), *Review of Psychiatry* (Vol. 10). Washington, DC: American Psychiatric Press. (p. 326)

Klump, K. L., Suisman, J. L., Burt, S. A., McGue, M., & Iacono, W. G. (2009). Genetic and environmental influences on disordered eating: An adoption study. *Journal of Abnormal Psychology, 118,* 797–805. (p. 243)

Klüver, H., & Bucy, P. C. (1939). Preliminary analysis of functions of the temporal lobes in monkeys. *Archives of Neurology and Psychiatry, 42,* 979–1000. (p. 38)

Knapp, S., & VandeCreek, L. (2000, August). Recovered memories of childhood abuse: Is there an underlying professional consensus? *Professional Psychology: Research and Practice, 31,* 365–371. (p. 199)

Knickmeyer, E. (2001, August 7). In Africa, big is definitely better. *Associated Press (Seattle Times,* p. A7). (p. 243)

Knight, W. (2004, August 2). *Animated face helps deaf with phone chat.* NewScientist.com. (p. 146)

Knutson, K. L., Spiegel, K., Penev, P., & Van Cauter, E. (2007). The metabolic consequences of sleep deprivation. *Sleep Medicine Reviews, 11,* 163–178. (p. 55)

Koenig, L. B., & Vaillant, G. E. (2009). A prospective study of church attendance and health over the lifespan. *Health Psychology, 28,* 117–124. (p. 287)

Koenig, L. B., McGue, M., Krueger, R. F., & Bouchard, T. J., Jr. (2005). Genetic and environmental influences on religiousness: Findings for retrospective and current religiousness ratings. *Journal of Personality, 73,* 471–488. (p. 86)

Koenigs, M., Young, L., Adolphs, R., Tranel, D., Cushman, F., Hauser, M., & Damasio, A. (2007). Damage to the prefrontal cortex increases utilitarian moral judgements. Nature, 446, 908–911. (p. 43)

Koestner, R., Lekes, N., Powers, T. A., & Chicoine, E. (2002). Attaining personal goals: Self-concordance plus implementation intentions equals success. *Journal of Personality and Social Psychology, 83,* 231–244. (p. 416)

Kohlberg, L. (1981). *The philosophy of moral development: Essays on moral development* (Vol. I). San Francisco: Harper & Row. (p. 82)

Kohlberg, L. (1984). *The psychology of moral development: Essays on moral development* (Vol. II). San Francisco: Harper & Row. (p. 82)

Kohler, I. (1962, May). Experiments with goggles. *Scientific American*, pp. 62–72. (p. 139)

Köhler, W. (1925; reprinted 1957). *The mentality of apes*. London: Pelican. (p. 216)

Kolata, G. (1987). Metabolic catch-22 of exercise regimens. *Science, 236*, 146–147. (p. 248)

Kolata, G. (2010, January 21). I.O.C. panel calls for treatment in sex ambiguity cases. *New York Times* (www.nytimes.com). (p. 104)

Kolb, B. (1989). Brain development, plasticity, and behavior. *American Psychologist, 44*, 1203–1212. (p. 45)

Kolb, B., & Whishaw, I. Q. (1998). Brain plasticity and behavior. *Annual Review of Psychology, 49*, 43–64. (p. 70)

Kolker, K. (2002, December 8). Video violence disturbs some: Others scoff at influence. *Grand Rapids Press*, pp. A1, A12. (p. 396)

Kolodziej, M. E., & Johnson, B. T. (1996). Interpersonal contact and acceptance of persons with psychiatric disorders: A research synthesis. *Journal of Consulting and Clinical Psychology, 64*, 1387–1396. (p. 321)

Koltko-Rivera, M. E. (2006). Rediscovering the later version of Maslow's hierarchy of needs: Self-transcendence and opportunities for theory, research, and unification. *Review of General Psychology, 10*, 302–317. (p. 239)

Kopta, S. M., Lueger, R. J., Saunders, S. M., & Howard, K. I. (1999). Individual psychotherapy outcome and process research: Challenges leading to greater turmoil or a positive transition? *Annual Review of Psychology, 30*, 441–469. (p. 362)

Kornell, N., & Bjork, R. A. (2008). Learning concepts and categories: Is spacing the "enemy of induction"? *Psychological Science, 19*, 585–592. (p. 184)

Kosslyn, S. M. (2005). Reflective thinking and mental imagery: A perspective on the development of posttraumatic stress disorder. *Development and Psychopathology, 17*, 851–863. (p. 324)

Kosslyn, S. M., & Koenig, O. (1992). *Wet mind: The new cognitive neuroscience*. New York: Free Press. (p. 32)

Kotchick, B. A., Shaffer, A., & Forehand, R. (2001). Adolescent sexual risk behavior: A multi-system perspective. *Clinical Psychology Review, 21*, 493–519. (p. 109)

Kotkin, M., Daviet, C., & Gurin, J. (1996). The Consumer Reports mental health survey. *American Psychologist, 51*, 1080–1082. (p. 361)

Kounios, J., & Beeman, M. (2009). The Aha! moment: The cognitive neuroscience of insight. *Current Directions in Psychological Science, 18*, 210–215. (p. 206)

Kraft, R. N. (2002). *Memory perceived: Recalling the Holocaust*. Westport, CT: Praeger. (p. 199)

Kramer, A. F., & Erickson, K. I. (2007). Capitalizing on cortical plasticity: Influence of physical activity on cognition and brain function. *Trends in Cognitive Sciences, 11*, 342–348. (p. 286)

Kramer, M. S., & 17 others. (2008). Breastfeeding and child cognitive development: New evidence from a large randomized trial. *Archives of General Psychiatry, 65*, 578–584. (pp. 15, 16)

Kranz, F., & Ishai, A. (2006). Face perception is modulated by sexual preference. *Current Biology, 16*, 63–68. (p. 114)

Kraus, N., Malmfors, T., & Slovic, P. (1992). Intuitive toxicology: Expert and lay judgments of chemical risks. *Risk Analysis, 12*, 215–232. (p. 210)

Kraut, R. E., & Johnston, R. E. (1979). Social and emotional messages of smiling: An ethological approach. *Journal of Personality and Social Psychology, 37*, 1539–1553. (p. 261)

Kraut, R. E., Patterson, M., Lundmark, V., Kiesler, S., Mukopadhyay, T., & Scherlis, W. (1998). Internet paradox: A social technology that reduces social involvement and psychological well being? *American Psychologist, 53*, 1017–1031. (p. 250)

KRC Research & Consulting. (2001, August 7). Memory isn't quite what it used to be (survey for General Nutrition Centers). *USA Today*, p. D1. (p. 92)

Krijn, M., Emmelkamp, P. M. G., Olafsson, R. P., & Biemond, R. (2004). Virtual reality exposure therapy of anxiety disorders: A review. *Clinical Psychology Review, 24*, 259–281. (p. 357)

Kring, A. M., & Gordon, A. H. (1998). Sex differences in emotion: Expression, experience, and physiology. *Journal of Personality and Social Psychology, 74*, 686–703. (p. 261)

Kroll, R., Danis, S., Moreau, M., Waldbaum, A., Shifren, J., & Wekselman, K. (2004, October). Testosterone transdermal patch (TPP) significantly improved sexual function in naturally menopausal women in a large Phase III study. Paper presented to the American Society of Reproductive Medicine annual meeting, Philadelphia. (p. 107)

Krosnick, J. A., Betz, A. L., Jussim, L. J., & Lynn, A. R. (1992). Subliminal conditioning of attitudes. *Personality and Social Psychology Bulletin, 18*, 152–162. (p. 125)

Krueger, A. (2007, November/December). What makes a terrorist. *The American* (www.american.com). (p. 394)

Krueger, A. B., & Malečková, J. (2009). Attitudes and action: Public opinion and the occurrence of international terrorism. *Science, 325*, 1534–1536. (p. 379)

Krueger, J., & Killham, E. (2005, December 8). At work, feeling good matters. *Gallup Management Journal* (www.gmj.gallup.com). (p. 415)

Krueger, J., & Killham, E. (2006, March 9). Why Dilbert is right. Uncomfortable work environments make for disgruntled employees—just like the cartoon says. *Gallup Management Journal* (www.gmj.gallup.com). (p. 281)

Kruger J., Epley, N., Parker, J., & Ng, Z-W. (2005). Egocentrism over e-mail: Can we communicate as well as we think? *Journal of Personality and Social Psychology, 89*, 925–936. (p. 74)

Krützen, M., Mann, J., Heithaus, M. R., Connor, R. C., Bejder, L., & Sherwin, W. B. (2005). Cultural transmission of tool use in bottlenose dolphins. *Proceedings of the National Academy of Sciences, 102*, 8939–8943. (p. 216)

Kubey, R., & Csikszentmihalyi, M. (2002, February). Television addiction is no mere metaphor. *Scientific American*, pp. 74–80. (p. 175)

Kübler, A., Winter, S., Ludolph, A. C., Hautzinger, M., & Birbaumer, N. (2005). Severity of depressive symptoms and quality of life in patients with amyotrophic lateral sclerosis. *Neurorehabilitation and Neural Repair, 19*(3), 182–193. (p. 265)

Kuhl, P. K., & Meltzoff, A. N. (1982). The bimodal perception of speech in infancy. *Science, 218*, 1138–1141. (p. 213)

Kuncel, N. R., Nezlett, S. A., & Ones, D. S. (2004). Academic performance, career potential, creativity, and job performance: Can one construct predict them all? *Journal of Personality and Social Psychology, 86*, 148–161. (p. 220)

Kunkel, D. (2001, February 4). *Sex on TV*. Menlo Park, CA: Henry J. Kaiser Family Foundation (www.kff.org). (p. 109)

Kunkel, D., Cope-Farrar, K., Biely, E., Farinola, W. J. M., & Donnerstein, E. (2001). *Sex on TV (2): A biennial report to the Kaiser Family Foundation*. Menlo Park, CA: Kaiser Family Foundation. (p. 395)

Kutas, M. (1990). Event-related brain potential (ERP) studies of cognition during sleep: Is it more than a dream? In R. R. Bootzin, J. F. Kihlstrom, & D. Schacter (Eds.), *Sleep and cognition*. Washington, DC: American Psychological Association. (p. 52)

Kvavilashvili, L., Mirani, J., Schlagman, S., Foley, K., & Kornbrot, D. E. (2009). Consistency of flashbulb memories of September 11 over long delays: Implications for consolidation and wrong time slice hypotheses. *Journal of Memory and Language, 61,* 556–572. (p. 189)

Lacayo, R. (1995, June 12). Violent reaction. *Time Magazine,* pp. 25–39. (p. 12)

Lacey, H. P., Smith, D. M., & Ubel, P. A. (2006). Hope I die before I get old: Mispredicting happiness across the lifespan. *Journal of Happiness Studies, 7,* 167–182. (p. 95)

Lachman, M. E., Rocke, C., Rosnick, C., & Ryff, C. D. (2008, September). Realism and illusion in Americans' temporal views of their life satisfaction: Age differences in reconstructing the past and anticipating the future. *Psychological Science, 19,* 889–897. (p. 95)

Laird, J. D. (1974). Self-attribution of emotion: The effects of expressive behavior on the quality of emotional experience. *Journal of Personality and Social Psychology, 29,* 475–486. (p. 262)

Laird, J. D. (1984). The real role of facial response in the experience of emotion: A reply to Tourangeau and Ellsworth, and others. *Journal of Personality and Social Psychology, 47,* 909–917. (p. 262)

Laird, J. D., Cuniff, M., Sheehan, K., Shulman, D., & Strum, G. (1989). Emotion specific effects of facial expressions on memory for life events. *Journal of Social Behavior and Personality, 4,* 87–98. (p. 262)

Lambird, K. H., & Mann, T. (2006). When do ego threats lead to self-regulation failure? Negative consequences of defensive high self-esteem. *Personality and Social Psychology Bulletin, 32,* 1177–1187. (p. 310)

Lampinen, J. M. (2002). What exactly is déjà vu? *Scientific American* (scieam.com/askexpert/biology/biology63). (p. 191)

Landauer, T. K. (2001, September). Quoted by R. Herbert, You must remember this. *APS Observer,* p. 11. (p. 200)

Landauer, T. K., & Whiting, J. W. M. (1979). Correlates and consequences of stress in infancy. In R. Munroe, B. Munroe & B. Whiting (Eds.), *Handbook of Cross-Cultural Human Development.* New York: Garland. (p. 274)

Landry, M. J. (2002). MDMA: A review of epidemiologic data. *Journal of Psychoactive Drugs, 34,* 163–169. (p. 334)

Langer, E. J. (1983). *The psychology of control.* Beverly Hills, CA: Sage. (p. 281)

Langer, E. J., & Abelson, R. P. (1974). A patient by any other name . . .: Clinician group differences in labeling bias. *Journal of Consulting and Clinical Psychology, 42,* 4–9. (p. 321)

Langer, E. J., & Imber, L. (1980). The role of mindlessness in the perception of deviance. *Journal of Personality and Social Psychology, 39,* 360–367. (p. 321)

Langleben, D. D., & Dattilio, F. M. (2008). Commentary: The future of forensic functional brain imaging. *Journal of the American Academy of Psychiatry and the Law, 36,* 502-504. (p. 257)

Langlois, J. H., Kalakanis, L., Rubenstein, A. J., Larson, A., Hallam, M., & Smoot, M. (2000). Maxims or myths of beauty? A meta-analytic and theoretical review. *Psychological Bulletin, 126,* 390–423. (pp. 399, 400)

Langlois, J. H., Roggman, L. A., Casey, R. J., Ritter, J. M., Rieser-Danner, L. A., & Jenkins, V. Y. (1987). Infant preferences for attractive faces: Rudiments of a stereotype? *Developmental Psychology, 23,* 363–369. (p. 399)

Lankford, A. (2009). Promoting aggression and violence at Abu Ghraib: The U.S. military's transformation of ordinary people into torturers. *Aggression and Violent Behavior, 14,* 388–395. (p. 386)

Larkin, K., Resko, J. A., Stormshak, F., Stellflug, J. N., & Roselli, C. E. (2002). Neuroanatomical correlates of sex and sexual partner preference in sheep. Paper presented at Society for Neuroscience convention. (p. 114)

Larson, R. W., & Verma, S. (1999). How children and adolescents spend time across the world: Work, play, and developmental opportunities. *Psychological Bulletin, 125,* 701–736. (p. 230)

Larzelere, R. E. (2000). Child outcomes of non-abusive and customary physical punishment by parents: An updated literature review. *Clinical Child and Family Psychology Review, 3,* 199–221. (p. 166)

Larzelere, R. E., & Kuhn, B. R. (2005). Comparing child outcomes of physical punishment and alternative disciplinary tactics: A meta-analysis. *Clinical Child and Family Psychology Review, 8,* 1–37. (p. 166)

Larzelere, R. E., Kuhn, B. R., & Johnson, B. (2004). The intervention selection bias: An underrecognized confound in intervention research. *Psychological Bulletin, 130,* 289–303. (p. 166)

Lassiter, G. D., & Irvine, A. A. (1986). Video-taped confessions: The impact of camera point of view on judgments of coercion. *Journal of Personality and Social Psychology, 16,* 268–276. (p. 378)

Latané, B. (1981). The psychology of social impact. *American Psychologist, 36,* 343–356. (p. 387)

Latané, B., & Dabbs, J. M., Jr. (1975). Sex, group size and helping in three cities. *Sociometry, 38,* 180–194. (p. 403)

Latham, G. P., & Locke, E. A. (2007). New developments in and directions for goal-setting research. *European Psychologist, 12,* 290–300. (p. 416)

Laumann, E. O., Gagnon, J. H., Michael, R. T., & Michaels, S. (1994). *The social organization of sexuality: Sexual practices in the United States.* Chicago: University of Chicago Press. (p. 117)

Laws, K. R., & Kokkalis, J. (2007). Ecstasy (MDMA) and memory function: A meta-analytic update. *Human Psychopharmacology: Clinical and Experimental, 22,* 381–388. (p. 334)

Lazarus, R. S. (1990). Theory-based stress measurement. *Psychological Inquiry, 1,* 3–13. (p. 275)

Lazarus, R. S. (1991). Progress on a cognitive-motivational-relational theory of emotion. *American Psychologist, 46,* 352–367. (p. 259)

Lazarus, R. S. (1998). *Fifty years of the research and theory of R. S. Lazarus: An analysis of historical and perennial issues.* Mahwah, NJ: Erlbaum. (pp. 259, 274)

Lea, S. E. G. (2000). Towards an ethical use of animals. *The Psychologist, 13,* 556–557. (p. 19)

Leaper, C., & Ayres, M. M. (2007). A meta-analytic review of gender variations in adults' language use: Talkativeness, affiliative speech, and assertive speech. *Personality and Social Psychology Review, 11,* 328–363. (p. 102)

Leary, M. R. (1999). The social and psychological importance of self-esteem. In R. M. Kowalski & M. R. Leary (Eds.), *The social psychology of emotional and behavioral problems.* Washington, DC: APA Books. (p. 310)

Leary, M. R., Haupt, A. L., Strausser, K. S., & Chokel, J. T. (1998). Calibrating the sociometer: The relationship between interpersonal appraisals and state self-esteem. *Journal of Personality and Social Psychology, 74,* 1290–1299. (p. 249)

Leary, W. E. (1998, September 28). Older people enjoy sex, survey says. *New York Times* (www.nytimes.com). (p. 91)

LeDoux, J. (1996). *The emotional brain: The mysterious underpinnings of emotional life.* New York: Simon & Schuster. (p. 185)

LeDoux, J. (2009, July/August). Quoted by K. McGowan, Out of the past. *Discover,* pp. 28–37. (p. 196)

LeDoux, J. E. (2002). *The synaptic self.* London: Macmillan. (p. 258)

LeDoux, J. E., & Armony, J. (1999). Can neurobiology tell us anything about human feelings? In D. Kahneman, E. Diener, & N. Schwartz (Eds.), *Well-being: The foundations of hedonic psychology.* New York: Sage. (p. 259)

Lee, L., Frederick, S., & Ariely, D. (2006). Try it, you'll like it: The influence of expectation, consumption, and revelation on preferences for beer. *Psychological Science, 17,* 1054–1058. (p. 127)

Lefcourt, H. M. (1982). *Locus of control: Current trends in theory and research.* Hillsdale, NJ: Erlbaum. (p. 282)

Legrand, L. N., Iacono, W. G., & McGue, M. (2005). Predicting addiction. *American Scientist, 93,* 140–147. (p. 337)

Lehman, A. F., Steinwachs, D. M., Dixon, L. B., Goldman, H. H., Osher, F., Postrado, L., Scott, J. E., Thompson, J. W., Fahey, M., Fischer, P., Kasper, J. A., Lyles, A., Skinner, E. A., Buchanan, R., Carpenter, W. T., Jr., Levine, J., McGlynn, E. A., Rosenheck, R., & Zito, J. (1998). Translating research into practice: The schizophrenic patient outcomes research team (PORT) treatment recommendations. *Schizophrenia Bulletin, 24,* 1–10. (p. 366)

Lehman, D. R., Wortman, C. B., & Williams, A. F. (1987). Long-term effects of losing a spouse or child in a motor vehicle crash. *Journal of Personality and Social Psychology, 52,* 218–231. (p. 94)

Leichsenring, F., & Rabung, S. (2008). Effectiveness of long-term psychodynamic psychotherapy: A meta-analysis. *JAMA, 300,* 1551–1565. (p. 362)

Leigh, B. C. (1989). In search of the seven dwarves: Issues of measurement and meaning in alcohol expectancy research. *Psychological Bulletin, 105,* 361–373. (p. 331)

Leitenberg, H., & Henning, K. (1995). Sexual fantasy. *Psychological Bulletin, 117,* 469–496. (pp. 108, 111)

Lemonick, M. D. (2002, June 3). Lean and hungrier. *Time,* p. 54. (p. 241)

Lenhart, A. (2010, April 20). *Teens, cell phones and texting.* Pew Internet and American Life Project. Pew Research Center (www.pewresearch.org). (p. 250)

Lenhart, A., Purcell, K., Smith, A., & Zickuhr, K. (2010). *Social media and mobile Internet use among teens and young adults.* Pew Internet and American Life Project. Pew Research Center (www.pewresearch.org). (p. 250)

Lennox, B. R., Bert, S., Park, G., Jones, P. B., & Morris, P. G. (1999). Spatial and temporal mapping of neural activity associated with auditory hallucinations. *Lancet, 353,* 644. (p. 42)

Lenzenweger, M. F., Dworkin, R. H., & Wethington, E. (1989). Models of positive and negative symptoms in schizophrenia: An empirical evaluation of latent structures. *Journal of Abnormal Psychology, 98,* 62–70. (p. 366)

Leserman, J., Jackson, E. D., Petitto, J. M., Golden, R. N., Silva, S. G., Perkins, D. O., Cai, J., Folds, J. D., & Evans, D. L. (1999). Progression to AIDS: The effects of stress, depressive symptoms, and social support. *Psychosomatic Medicine, 61,* 397–406. (p. 278)

Leucht, S., Barnes, T. R. E., Kissling, W., Engel, R. R., Correll, C., & Kane, J. M. (2003). Relapse prevention in schizophrenia with new-generation antipsychotics: A systematic review and exploratory meta-analysis of randomized, controlled trials. *American Journal of Psychiatry, 160,* 1209–1222. (p. 367)

LeVay, S. (1991). A difference in hypothalamic structure between heterosexual and homosexual men. *Science, 253,* 1034–1037. (p. 114)

LeVay, S. (1994, March). Quoted in D. Nimmons, Sex and the brain. *Discover,* p. 64–71. (p. 114)

LeVay, S. (2010). *Gay, straight, and the reason why: The science of sexual orientation.* New York: Oxford University Press. (p. 115)

Levenson, R. W. (1992). Autonomic nervous system differences among emotions. *Psychological Science, 3,* 23–27. (p. 255)

Levin, I. P., & Gaeth, G. J. (1988). How consumers are affected by the framing of attribute information before and after consuming the product. *Journal of Consumer Research, 15,* 374–378. (p. 210)

Levine, R., Sato, S., Hashimoto, T., & Verma, J. (1995). Love and marriage in eleven cultures. *Journal of Cross-Cultural Psychology, 26,* 554–571. (p. 401)

Lewandowski, G. W., Jr., Aron, A., & Gee, J. (2007). Personality goes a long way: The malleability of opposite-sex physical attractiveness. *Personality Relationships, 14,* 571–585. (p. 400)

Lewinsohn, P. M., & Rosenbaum, M. (1987). Recall of parental behavior by acute depressives, remitted depressives, and nondepressives. *Journal of Personality and Social Psychology, 52,* 611–619. (p. 191)

Lewinsohn, P. M., Hoberman, H., Teri, L., & Hautziner, M. (1985). An integrative theory of depression. In S. Reiss & R. Bootzin (Eds.), *Theoretical issues in behavior therapy.* Orlando, FL: Academic Press. (p. 340)

Lewinsohn, P. M., Petit, J., Joiner, T. E., Jr., & Seeley, J. R. (2003). The symptomatic expression of major depressive disorder in adolescents and young adults. *Journal of Abnormal Psychology, 112,* 244–252. (p. 340)

Lewinsohn, P. M., Rohde, P., & Seeley, J. R. (1998). Major depressive disorder in older adolescents: Prevalence, risk factors, and clinical implications. *Clinical Psychology Review, 18,* 765–794. (p. 340)

Lewis, D. O., Yeager, C. A., Swica, Y., Pincus, J. H., & Lewis, M. (1997). Objective documentation of child abuse and dissociation in 12 murderers with dissociative identity disorder. *American Journal of Psychiatry, 154,* 1703–1710. (p. 327)

Lewis, M. (1992). Commentary. *Human Development, 35,* 44–51. (p. 191)

Lewontin, R. (1976). Race and intelligence. In N. J. Block & G. Dworkin (Eds.), *The IQ controversy: Critical readings.* New York: Pantheon. (p. 229)

Lewontin, R. (1982). *Human diversity.* New York: Scientific American Library. (p. 229)

Li, J., Laursen, T. M., Precht, D. H., Olsen, J., & Mortensen, P. B. (2005). Hospitalization for mental illness among parents after the death of a child. *New England Journal of Medicine, 352,* 1190–1196. (p. 94)

Lieberman, J. A. (2006). Comparative effectiveness of antipsychotic drugs. *Archives of General Psychiatry, 63,* 1069–1072. (p. 367)

Lieberman, J. A., & 11 others. (2005). Effectiveness of antipsychotic drugs in patients with chronic schizophrenia. *New England Journal of Medicine, 353,* 1209–1223. (p. 367)

Lilienfeld, S. O. (2009, Winter). Tips for spotting psychological pseudoscience: A student-friendly guide. *Eye of Psi Chi,* pp. 23–26. (p. 149)

Lilienfeld, S. O., Lynn, S. J., Kirsch, I., Chaves, J. F., Sarbin, T. R., Ganaway, G. K., & Powell, R. A. (1999). Dissociative identity disorder and the sociocognitive model: Recalling the lessons of the past. *Psychological Bulletin, 125,* 507–523. (p. 327)

Linville, P. W., Fischer, G. W., & Fischhoff, B. (1992). AIDS risk perceptions and decision biases. In J. B. Pryor & G. D. Reeder (Eds.), *The social psychology of HIV infection.* Hillsdale, NJ: Erlbaum. (p. 210)

Lippa, R. A. (2007a). The relation between sex drive and sexual attraction to men and women: A cross-national study of heterosexual, bisexual, and homosexual men and women. *Archives of Sexual Behavior, 36,* 209–222. (pp. 115, 399)

Lippa, R. A. (2007b). The preferred traits of mates in a cross-national study of heterosexual and homosexual men and women: An examination of biological and cultural influences. *Archives of Sexual Behavior, 36,* 193–208. (p. 115)

Lippa, R. A. (2008). Sex differences and sexual orientation differences in personality: Findings from the BBC Internet survey. *Archives of Sexual Behavior, Special Issue: Biological research on sex-dimorphic behavior and sexual orientation, 37*(1), 173–187. (p. 115)

Lippa, R. A. (2009). Sex differences in sex drive, sociosexuality, and height across 53 nations: Testing evolutionary and social structural theories. *Archives of Sexual Behavior, 38,* 631–651. (p. 116)

Livesley, W. J., & Jang, K. L. (2008). The behavioral genetics of personality disorder. *Annual Review of Clinical Psychology, 4,* 247–274. (p. 328)

Livingstone, M., & Hubel, D. (1988). Segregation of form, color, movement, and depth: Anatomy, physiology, and perception. *Science, 240,* 740–749. (p. 132)

LoBue, V., & DeLoache, J. S. (2008). Detecting the snake in the grass: Attention to fear-relevant stimuli by adults and young children. *Psychological Science, 19,* 284–289. (p. 326)

Loehlin, J. C., & Nichols, R. C. (1976). *Heredity, environment, and personality.* Austin: University of Texas Press. (p. 68)

Loehlin, J. C., McCrae, R. R., & Costa, P. T., Jr. (1998). Heritabilities of common and measure-specific components of the Big Five personality factors. *Journal of Research in Personality, 32,* 431–453. (p. 305)

Loewenstein, G., & Furstenberg, F. (1991). Is teenage sexual behavior rational? *Journal of Applied Social Psychology, 21,* 957–986. (p. 164)

Loftus, E. (1979). The malleability of human memory. *American Scientist, 67,* 313–320. (p. 196)

Loftus, E. (1995, March/April). Remembering dangerously. *Skeptical Inquirer,* pp. 20–29. (p. 299)

Loftus, E. F. (1979). The malleability of human memory. *American Scientist, 67,* 313–320. (p. 196)

Loftus, E. F. (2001, November). Imagining the past. *The Psychologist, 14,* 584–587. (p. 197)

Loftus, E. F., & Loftus, G. R. (1980). On the permanence of stored information in the human brain. *American Psychologist, 35,* 409–420. (p. 188)

Loftus, E. F., & Palmer, J. C. (October, 1974). Reconstruction of automobile destruction: An example of the interaction between language and memory. *Journal of Verbal Learning & Verbal Behavior, 13*(5), 585–589. (p. 196)

Logan, T. K., Walker, R., Cole, J., & Leukefeld, C. (2002). Victimization and substance abuse among women: Contributing factors, interventions, and implications. *Review of General Psychology, 6,* 325–397. (p. 336)

Logue, A. W. (1998a). Laboratory research on self-control: Applications to administration. *Review of General Psychology, 2,* 221–238. (p. 164)

Logue, A. W. (1998b). Self-control. In W. T. O'Donohue (Ed.), *Learning and behavior therapy.* Boston, MA: Allyn & Bacon. (p. 164)

London, P. (1970). The rescuers: Motivational hypotheses about Christians who saved Jews from the Nazis. In J. Macaulay & L. Berkowitz (Eds.), *Altruism and helping behavior.* New York: Academic Press. (p. 174)

Looy, H. (2001). Sex differences: Evolved, constructed, and designed. *Journal of Psychology and Theology, 29,* 301–313. (p. 118)

Lopes, P. N., Brackett, M. A., Nezlek, J. B., Schutz, A., Sellin, II, & Salovey, P. (2004). Emotional intelligence and social interaction. *Personality and Social Psychology Bulletin, 30,* 1018–1034. (p. 223)

López-Ibor, J. J., López-Ibor, M-I., & Pastrana, J. I. (2008). Transcranial magnetic stimulation. *Current Opinion in Psychiatry, 21,* 640–644. (p. 370)

Lord, C. G., Lepper, M. R., & Preston, E. (1984). Considering the opposite: A corrective strategy for social judgment. *Journal of Personality and Social Psychology, 47,* 1231–1247. (p. 210)

Lord, C. G., Ross, L., & Lepper, M. (1979). Biased assimilation and attitude polarization: The effects of prior theories on subsequently considered evidence. *Journal of Personality and Social Psychology, 37,* 2098–2109. (p. 210)

Louie, K., & Wilson, M. A. (2001). Temporally structured replay of awake hippocampal ensemble activity during rapid eye movement sleep. *Neuron, 29,* 145–156. (p. 57)

Lourenco, O., & Machado, A. (1996). In defense of Piaget's theory: A reply to 10 common criticisms. *Psychological Review, 103,* 143–164. (p. 75)

Lovaas, O. I. (1987). Behavioral treatment and normal educational and intellectual functioning in young autistic children. *Journal of Consulting and Clinical Psychology, 55,* 3–9. (p. 357)

Lozano, A., Mayberg, H., Giacobbe, P., Hami, C., Craddock, R., & Kennedy, S. (2008). Subcallosal cingulated gyrus deep brain stimulation for treatment-resistant depression. *Biological Psychiatry, 64,* 461–467. (p. 369)

Lubinski, D. (2009). Cognitive epidemiology: With emphasis on untangling cognitive ability and socioeconomic status. *Intelligence, 37,*625–633. (p. 220)

Lubinski, D., & Benbow, C. P. (1992). Gender differences in abilities and preferences among the gifted: Implications for the math-science pipeline. *Current Directions in Psychological Science, 1,* 61–66. (p. 230)

Luborsky, L., Rosenthal, R., Diguer, L., Andrusyna, T. P., Berman, J. S., Levitt, J. T., Seligman, D. A., & Krause, E. D. (2002). The dodo bird verdict is alive and well—mostly. *Clinical Psychology: Science and Practice, 9,* 2–34. (p. 362)

Lucas, A., Morley, R., Cole, T. J., Lister, G., & Leeson-Payne, C. (1992). Breast milk and subsequent intelligence quotient in children born preterm. *Lancet, 339,* 261–264. (p. 15)

Lucas, R. E. (2007a). Adaptation and the set-point model of subjective well-being. *Current Directions in Psychological Science, 16,* 75–79. (p. 265)

Lucas, R. E. (2007b). Long-term disability is associated with lasting changes in subjective well-being: Evidence from two nationally representative longitudinal studies. *Journal of Personality and Social Psychology, 92,* 717–730. (p. 265)

Lucas, R. E., & Schimmack, U. (2009). Income and well-being: How big is the gap between the rich and the poor? *Journal of Research in Personality, 43,* 75–78. (p. 266)

Lucas, R. E., Clark, A. E., Georgellis, Y., & Diener, E. (2003). Re-examining adaptation and the setpoint model of happiness: Reactions to changes in marital status. *Journal of Personality and Social Psychology, 84,* 527–539. (p. 95)

Lucas, R. E., Clark, A. E., Georgellis, Y., & Diener, E. (2004). Unemployment alters the set point for life satisfaction. *Psychological Science, 15,* 8–13. (p. 268)

Lucero, S. M., Kusner, K. G., & Speace, E. A. (2008, May 24). Religiousness and adolescent sexual behavior: A meta-analytic review. Paper presented at Association for Psychological Science Convention. (p. 110)

Ludwig, A. M. (1995). *The price of greatness: Resolving the creativity and madness controversy.* New York: Guilford Press. (p. 339)

Luria, A. M. (1968). In L. Solotaroff (Trans.), *The mind of a mnemonist.* New York: Basic Books. (p. 180)

Lustig, C., & Buckner, R. L. (2004). Preserved neural correlates of priming in old age and dementia. *Neuron, 42,* 865–875. (p. 185)

Lyall, S. (2005, November 29). What's the buzz? Rowdy teenagers don't want to hear it. *New York Times* (www.nytimes.com). (p. 91)

Lykken, D. T. (1991). Science, lies, and controversy: An epitaph for the polygraph. Invited address upon receipt of the Senior Career Award for Distinguished Contribution to Psychology in the Public Interest, American Psychological Association convention. (p. 257)

Lykken, D. T. (1995). *The antisocial personalities.* Hillsdale, NJ: Erlbaum. (p. 394)

Lykken, D. T. (1999). *Happiness*. New York: Golden Books. (p. 226)

Lykken, D. T., & Tellegen, A. (1993). Is human mating adventitious or the result of lawful choice? A twin study of mate selection. *Journal of Personality and Social Psychology, 65*, 56–68. (p. 94)

Lykken, D. T., & Tellegen, A. (1996). Happiness is a stochastic phenomenon. *Psychological Science, 7*, 186–189. (p. 268)

Lynch, G. (2002). Memory enhancement: The search for mechanism-based drugs. *Nature Neuroscience, 5* (suppl.), 1035–1038. (p. 188)

Lynch, G., & Staubli, U. (1991). Possible contributions of long-term potentiation to the encoding and organization of memory. *Brain Research Reviews, 16*, 204–206. (p. 188)

Lynn, M. (1988). The effects of alcohol consumption on restaurant tipping. *Personality and Social Psychology Bulletin, 14*, 87–91. (p. 330)

Lynn, R. (2008). *The global bell curve: Race, IQ and inequality worldwide*. Augusta, GA: Washington Summit Publishers. (p. 228)

Lynn, S. J., Rhue, J. W., & Weekes, J. R. (1990). Hypnotic involuntariness: A social cognitive analysis. *Psychological Review, 97*, 169–184. (p. 145)

Lyons, L. (2005, January 4). Teens stay true to parents' political perspectives. *Gallup Poll News Service* (www.gallup.com). (p. 87)

Lytton, H., & Romney, D. M. (1991). Parents' differential socialization of boys and girls: A meta-analysis. *Psychological Bulletin, 109*, 267–296. (p. 106)

Lyubomirsky, S. (2001). Why are some people happier than others? The role of cognitive and motivational processes in well-being. *American Psychologist, 56*, 239–249. (p. 267)

Lyubomirsky, S., King, L., & Diener, E. (2005). The benefits of frequent positive affect: Does happiness lead to success? *Psychological Bulletin, 131*, 803–855. (p. 264)

Maas, J. B. (1999). *Power sleep. The revolutionary program that prepares your mind and body for peak performance*. New York: HarperCollins. (p. 54)

Maccoby, E. E. (1990). Gender and relationships: A developmental account. *American Psychologist, 45*, 513–520. (p. 103)

Maccoby, E. E. (1995). Divorce and custody: The rights, needs, and obligations of mothers, fathers, and children. *Nebraska Symposium on Motivation, 42*, 135–172. (p. 105)

Maccoby, E. E. (1998). *The paradox of gender*. Cambridge, MA: Harvard University Press. (p. 103)

MacDonald, T. K., Zanna, M. P., & Fong, G. T. (1995). Decision making in altered states: Effects of alcohol on attitudes toward drinking and driving. *Journal of Personality and Social Psychology, 68*, 973–985. (p. 330)

MacFarlane, A. (1978, February). What a baby knows. *Human Nature*, pp. 74–81. (p. 67)

Machin, S., & Pekkarinen, T. (2008). Global sex differences in test score variability. *Science, 322*, 1331–1332. (p. 231)

MacKinnon, D. W., & Hall, W. B. (1972). Intelligence and creativity. In *Proceedings, XVIIth International Congress of Applied Psychology* (Vol. 2). Brussels: Editest. (p. 221)

MacLeod, C., & Campbell, L. (1992). Memory accessibility and probability judgments: An experimental evaluation of the availability heuristic. *Journal of Personality and Social Psychology, 63*, 890–902. (p. 207)

Maddi, S. R., Harvey, R. H., Khoshaba, D. M., Fazel, M., & Resurreccion, N. (2009). Hardiness training facilitates performance in college. *Journal of Positive Psychology, 4*, 566–577. (p. 414)

Madrian, B. C., & Shea, D. F. (2001). The power of suggestion: Inertia in 401(k) participation and savings behavior. *Quarterly Journal of Economics, 116*, 1149–1187. (p. 210)

Maes, H. H. M., Neale, M. C., & Eaves, L. J. (1997). Genetic and environmental factors in relative body weight and human adiposity. *Behavior Genetics, 27*, 325–351. (p. 246)

Maestripieri, D. (2003). Similarities in affiliation and aggression between cross-fostered rhesus macaque females and their biological mothers. *Developmental Psychobiology, 43*, 321–327. (p. 68)

Magnusson, D. (1990). Personality research—challenges for the future. *European Journal of Personality, 4*, 1–17. (p. 328)

Maier, S. F., Watkins, L. R., & Fleshner, M. (1994). Psychoneuroimmunology: The interface between behavior, brain, and immunity. *American Psychologist, 49*, 1004–1017. (pp. 277, 278)

Major, B., Carrington, P. I., & Carnevale, P. J. D. (1984). Physical attractiveness and self-esteem: Attribution for praise from an other-sex evaluator. *Personality and Social Psychology Bulletin, 10*, 43–50. (p. 399)

Malamuth, N. M., & Check, J. V. P. (1981). The effects of media exposure on acceptance of violence against women: A field experiment. *Journal of Research in Personality, 15*, 436–446. (p. 111)

Malloy, E. A. (1994, June 7). Report of the Commission on Substance Abuse at Colleges and Universities, reported by *Associated Press*. (p. 331)

Malmquist, C. P. (1986). Children who witness parental murder: Post-traumatic aspects. *Journal of the American Academy of Child Psychiatry, 25*, 320–325. (p. 299)

Malnic, B., Hirono, J., Sato, T., & Buck, L. B. (1999). Combinatorial receptor codes for odors. *Cell, 96*, 713–723. (p. 146)

Mandel, D. (1983, March 13). One man's holocaust: Part II. The story of David Mandel's journey through hell as told to David Kagan. *Wonderland Magazine* (*Grand Rapids Press*), pp. 2–7. (p. 240)

Mann, T., Tomiyama, A. J., Westling, E., Lew, A-M., Samuels, B., & Chatman, J. (2007). Medicare's search for effective obesity treatments: Diets are not the answer. *American Psychologist, 62*, 220–233. (p. 247)

Manson, J. E. (2002). Walking compared with vigorous exercise for the prevention of cardiovascular events in women. *New England Journal of Medicine, 347*, 716–725. (p. 285)

Maquet, P. (2001). The role of sleep in learning and memory. *Science, 294*, 1048–1052. (p. 57)

Marangell, L. B., Martinez, M., Jurdi, R. A., & Zboyan, H. (2007). Neurostimulation therapies in depression: A review of new modalities. *Acta Psychiatrica Scandinavica, 116*, 174–181. (p. 369)

Marcus, B., Machilek, F., & Schütz, A. (2006). Personality in cyberspace: Personal web sites as media for personality expressions and impressions. *Journal of Personality and Social Psychology, 90*, 1014–1031. (p. 308)

Margolis, M. L. (2000). Brahms' lullaby revisited: Did the composer have obstructive sleep apnea? *Chest, 118*, 210–213. (p. 56)

Marinak, B. A., & Gambrell, L. B. (2008). Intrinsic motivation and rewards: What sustains young children's engagement with text? *Literacy Research and Instruction, 47*, 9–26. (p. 171)

Markus, H. R., & Kitayama, S. (1991). Culture and the self: Implications for cognition, emotion, and motivation. *Psychological Review, 98*, 224–253. (p. 312)

Markus, H. R., & Nurius, P. (1986). Possible selves. *American Psychologist, 41*, 954–969. (p. 309)

Marlatt, G. A. (1991). Substance abuse: Etiology, prevention, and treatment issues. Master lecture, American Psychological Association convention. (p. 331)

Marschark, M., Richman, C. L., Yuille, J. C., & Hunt, R. R. (1987). The role of imagery in memory: On shared and distinctive information. *Psychological Bulletin, 102*, 28–41. (p. 187)

Marshall, M. J. (2002). *Why spanking doesn't work*. Springville, UT: Bonneville Books. (p. 166)

Marteau, T. M. (1989). Framing of information: Its influences upon decisions of doctors and patients. *British Journal of Social Psychology, 28*, 89–94. (p. 210)

Martin, C. L., & Ruble, D. (2004). Children's search for gender cues. *Current Directions in Psychological Science, 13*, 67–70. (p. 106)

Martin, C. L., Ruble, D. N., & Szkrybalo, J. (2002). Cognitive theories of early gender development. *Psychological Bulletin, 128*, 903–933. (p. 106)

Martin, R. J., White, B. D., & Hulsey, M. G. (1991). The regulation of body weight. *American Scientist, 79*, 528–541. (p. 242)

Martino, S. C., Collins, R. L., Kanouse, D. E., Elliott, M., & Berry, S. H. (2005). Social cognitive processes mediating the relationship between exposure to television's sexual content and adolescents' sexual behavior. *Journal of Personality and Social Psychology, 89*, 914–924. (p. 109)

Martins, Y., Preti, G., Crabtree, C. R., & Wysocki, C. J. (2005). Preference for human body odors is influenced by gender and sexual orientation. *Psychological Science, 16*, 694–701. (p. 114)

Maslow, A. H. (1970). *Motivation and personality* (2nd ed.). New York: Harper & Row. (pp. 238, 239, 301)

Maslow, A. H. (1971). *The farther reaches of human nature*. New York: Viking Press. (p. 239)

Mason, C., & Kandel, E. R. (1991). Central visual pathways. In E. R. Kandel, J. H. Schwartz, & T. M. Jessell (Eds.), *Principles of neural science* (3rd ed.). New York: Elsevier. (p. 31)

Mason, H. (2003, March 25). Wake up, sleepy teen. *Gallup Poll Tuesday Briefing* (www.gallup.com). (p. 54)

Mason, H. (2003, September 2). Americans, Britons at odds on animal testing. *Gallup Poll News Service* (www.gallup.com). (p. 19)

Mason, H. (2005, January 25). Who dreams, perchance to sleep? *Gallup Poll News Service* (www.gallup.com). (p. 54)

Mason, R. A., & Just, M. A. (2004). How the brain processes causal inferences in text. *Psychological Science, 15*, 1–7. (p. 48)

Masse, L. C., & Tremblay, R. E. (1997). Behavior of boys in kindergarten and the onset of substance use during adolescence. *Archives of General Psychiatry, 54*, 62–68. (p. 336)

Massimini, M., Ferrarelli, F., Huber, R., Esser, S. K., Singh, H., & Tononi, G. (2005). Breakdown of cortical effective connectivity during sleep. *Science, 309*, 2228–2232. (p. 51)

Masters, W. H., & Johnson, V. E. (1966). *Human sexual response*. Boston: Little, Brown. (p. 107)

Mastroianni, G. R. (2002). Milgram and the Holocaust: A reexamination. *Journal of Theoretical and Philosophical Psychology, 22*, 158–173. (p. 385)

Mastroianni, G. R., & Reed, G. (2006). Apples, barrels, and Abu Ghraib. *Sociological Focus, 39*, 239–250. (p. 381)

Masuda, T., & Kitayama, S. (2004). Perceiver-induced constraint and attitude attribution in Japan and the US: A case for the cultural dependence of the correspondence bias. *Journal of Experimental Social Psychology, 40*, 409–416. (p. 378)

Mataix-Cols, D., Rosario-Campos, M. C., & Leckman, J. F. (2005). A multidimensional model of obsessive-compulsive disorder. *American Journal of Psychiatry, 162*, 228–238. (p. 325)

Mataix-Cols, D., Wooderson, S., Lawrence, N., Brammer, M. J., Speckens, A., & Phillips, M. L. (2004). Distinct neural correlates of washing, checking, and hoarding symptom dimensions in obsessive-compulsive disorder. *Archives of General Psychiatry, 61*, 564–576. (p. 325)

Mather, M., Canli, T., English, T., Whitfield, S., Wais, P., Ochsner, K., Gabrieli, J. D. E., & Carstensen, L. L. (2004). Amygdala responses to emotionally valenced stimuli in older and younger adults. *Psychological Science, 15*, 259–263. (p. 95)

Matsumoto, D., & Ekman, P. (1989). American-Japanese cultural differences in intensity ratings of facial expressions of emotion. *Motivation and Emotion, 13*, 143–157. (p. 262)

Matsumoto, D., & Willingham, B. (2006). The thrill of victory and the agony of defeat: Spontaneous expressions of medal winners of the 2004 Athens Olympic Games. *Journal of Personality and Social Psychology, 91*, 568–581. (p. 262)

Matsumoto, D., & Willingham, B. (2009). Spontaneous facial expressions of emotion of congenitally and noncongenitally blind individuals. *Journal of Personality and Social Psychology, 96*, 1–10. (p. 262)

Matthews, R. N., Domjan, M., Ramsey, M., & Crews, D. (2007). Learning effects on sperm competition and reproductive fitness. *Psychological Science, 18*, 758–762. (p. 159)

Maurer, D., & Maurer, C. (1988). *The world of the newborn*. New York: Basic Books. (p. 67)

May, C., & Hasher, L. (1998). Synchrony effects in inhibitory control over thought and action. *Journal of Experimental Psychology: Human Perception and Performance, 24*, 363–380. (p. 51)

May, P. A., & Gossage, J. P. (2001). Estimating the prevalence of fetal alcohol syndrome: A summary. *Alcohol Research and Health, 25*, 159–167. (p. 66)

Mayberg, H. S., Lozano, A. M., Voon, V., McNeely, H. E., Seminowicz, D., Hamani, C., Schwalb, J. M., & Kennedy, S. H. (2005). Deep brain stimulation for treatment-resistant depression. *Neuron, 45*, 651–660. (p. 369)

Mayberry, R. I., Lock, E., & Kazmi, H. (2002). Linguistic ability and early language exposure. *Nature, 417*, 38. (p. 215)

Mayer, J. D. Salovey, P., & Caruso, D. (2002). *The Mayer-Salovey-Caruso emotional intelligence test (MSCEIT)*. Toronto: Multi-Health Systems, Inc. (p. 222)

Mazure, C., Keita, G., & Blehar, M. (2002). *Summit on women and depression: Proceedings and recommendations*. Washington, DC: American Psychological Association (www.apa.org/pi/wpo/women&depression.pdf). (p. 342)

Mazzoni, G., & Memon, A. (2003). Imagination can create false autobiographical memories. *Psychological Science, 14*, 186–188. (p. 197)

McAneny, L. (1996, September). Large majority think government conceals information about UFO's. *Gallup Poll Monthly*, pp. 23–26. (p. 191)

McBurney, D. H. (1996). *How to think like a psychologist: Critical thinking in psychology*. Upper Saddle River, NJ: Prentice-Hall. (p. 43)

McBurney, D. H., & Gent, J. F. (1979). On the nature of taste qualities. *Psychological Bulletin, 86*, 151–167. (p. 145)

McCann, I. L., & Holmes, D. S. (1984). Influence of aerobic exercise on depression. *Journal of Personality and Social Psychology, 46*, 1142–1147. (pp. 285, 286)

McCann, U. D., Eligulashvili, V., & Ricaurte, G. A. (2001). (+-)3,4-Methylenedioxymethamphetamine ('Ecstasy')-induced serotonin neurotoxicity: Clinical studies. *Neuropsychobiology, 42*, 11–16. (p. 334)

McCarthy, P. (1986, July). Scent: The tie that binds? *Psychology Today*, pp. 6, 10. (p. 146)

McCaul, K. D., & Malott, J. M. (1984). Distraction and coping with pain. *Psychological Bulletin, 95*, 516–533. (p. 144)

McCauley, C. R. (2002). Psychological issues in understanding terrorism and the response to terrorism. In C. E. Stout (Ed.), *The psychology of terrorism* (Vol. 3). Westport, CT: Praeger/Greenwood. (p. 388)

McCauley, C. R., & Segal, M. E. (1987). Social psychology of terrorist groups. In C. Hendrick (Ed.), *Group processes and intergroup relations*. Beverly Hills, CA: Sage. (p. 388)

McClendon, B. T., & Prentice-Dunn, S. (2001). Reducing skin cancer risk: An intervention based on protection motivation theory. *Journal of Health Psychology, 6*, 321–328. (p. 379)

McClure, E. B. (2000). A meta-analytic review of sex differences in facial expression processing and their development in infants, children, and adolescents. *Psychological Bulletin, 126*, 424–453. (p. 230)

McConnell, R. A. (1991). National Academy of Sciences opinion on parapsychology. *Journal of the American Society for Psychical Research, 85*, 333–365. (p. 149)

McCool, G. (1999, October 26). Mirror-gazing Venezuelans top of vanity stakes. *Toronto Star* (via web.lexis-nexis.com). (p. 399)

McCormick, C. M., & Witelson, S. F. (1991). A cognitive profile of homosexual men compared to heterosexual men and women. *Psychoneuroendocrinology, 16*, 459–473. (p. 115)

McCrae, R. R., & Costa, P. T., Jr. (1986). Clinical assessment can benefit from recent advances in personality psychology. *American Psychologist, 41*, 1001–1003. (p. 305)

McCrae, R. R., & Costa, P. T., Jr. (1994). The stability of personality: Observations and evaluations. *Current Directions in Psychological Science, 3*, 173–175. (p. 96)

McCrae, R. R., Costa, P. T., Jr., de Lirna, M. P., Simoes, A., Ostendorf, F., Angleitner, A., Marusic, I., Bratko, D., Caprara, G. V., Barbaranelli, C., Chae, J-H., & Piedmont, R. L. (1999). Age differences in personality across the adult life span: Parallels in five cultures. *Developmental Psychology, 35*, 466–477. (p. 305)

McCrae, R. R., Costa, P. T., Jr., Ostendorf, F., Angleitner, A., Hrebickova, M., Avia, M. D., Sanz, J., Sanchez-Bernardos, M. L., Kusdil, M. E., Woodfield, R., Saunders, P. R., & Smith, P. B. (2000). Nature over nurture: Temperament, personality, and life span development. *Journal of Personality and Social Psychology, 78*, 173–186. (p. 69)

McCrae, R. R., Terracciano, A., & 78 others. (2005). Universal features of personality traits from the observer's perspective: Data from 50 cultures. *Journal of Personality and Social Psychology, 88*, 547–561. (p. 305)

McCrae, R. R., Terracciano, A., & Khoury, B. (2007). Dolce far niente: The positive psychology of personality stability and invariance. In A. D. Ong & M. H. Van Dulmen (Eds.), *Oxford handbook of methods in positive psychology*. New York: Oxford University Press. (p. 69)

McCullough, M. E., & Laurenceau, J-P. (2005). Religiousness and the trajectory of self-rated health across adulthood. *Personality and Social Psychology Bulletin, 31*, 560–573. (p. 287)

McCullough, M. E., Hoyt, W. T., Larson, D. B., Koenig, H. G., & Thoresen, C. (2000). Religious involvement and mortality: A meta-analytic review. *Health Psychology, 19*, 211–222. (p. 287)

McDaniel, M. A., Howard, D. C., & Einstein, G. O. (2009). The read-recite-review study strategy: Effective and portable. *Psychological Science, 20*, 516–522. (p. 22)

McDermott, T. (2005). *Perfect soldiers: The 9/11 hijackers: Who they were, why they did it.* New York: HarperCollins. (p. 395)

McGaugh, J. L. (1994). Quoted by B. Bower, Stress hormones hike emotional memories. *Science News, 146*, 262. (p. 189)

McGaugh, J. L. (2003). *Memory and emotion: The making of lasting memories.* New York: Columbia University Press. (p. 189)

McGhee, P. E. (June, 1976). Children's appreciation of humor: A test of the cognitive congruency principle. *Child Development, 47*(2), 420–426. (p. 75)

McGrath, J. J., & Welham, J. L. (1999). Season of birth and schizophrenia: A systematic review and meta-analysis of data from the Southern hemisphere. *Schizophrenia Research, 35*, 237–242. (p. 345)

McGrath, J., Welham, J., & Pemberton, M. (1995). Month of birth, hemisphere of birth and schizophrenia. *British Journal of Psychiatry, 167*, 783–785. (p. 345)

McGue, M., & Bouchard, T. J., Jr. (1998). Genetic and environmental influences on human behavioral differences. *Annual Review of Neuroscience, 21*, 1–24. (p. 68)

McGue, M., Bouchard, T. J., Jr., Iacono, W. G., & Lykken, D. T. (1993). Behavioral genetics of cognitive ability: A life-span perspective. In R. Plomin & G. E. McClearn (Eds.), *Nature, nurture and psychology*. Washington, DC: American Psychological Association. (pp. 226, 227)

McGuire, W. J. (1986). The myth of massive media impact: Savings and salvagings. In G. Comstock (Ed.), *Public communication and behavior*. Orlando, FL: Academic Press. (p. 176)

McGurk, H., & MacDonald, J. (1976). Hearing lips and seeing voices. *Nature, 264*, 746–748. (p. 146)

McHugh, P. R. (1995). Witches, multiple personalities, and other psychiatric artifacts. *Nature Medicine, 1*(2), 110–114. (p. 326)

McKenna, K. Y. A., & Bargh, J. A. (1998). Coming out in the age of the Internet: Identity "demarginalization" through virtual group participation. *Journal of Personality and Social Psychology, 75*, 681–694. (p. 398)

McKenna, K. Y. A., & Bargh, J. A. (2000). Plan 9 from cyberspace: The implications of the Internet for personality and social psychology. *Personality and Social Psychology Review, 4*, 57–75. (p. 398)

McLaughlin, C. S., Chen, C., Greenberger, E., & Biermeier, C. (1997). Family, peer, and individual correlates of sexual experience among Caucasian and Asian American late adolescents. *Journal of Personality and Social Psychology: Journal of Research on Adolescence, 7*, 33–53. (p. 107)

McMurray, B. (2007). Defusing the childhood vocabulary explosion. *Science, 317*, 631. (p. 212)

McMurray, C. (2004, January 13). U.S., Canada, Britain: Who's getting in shape? *Gallup Poll Tuesday Briefing* (www.gallup.com). (p. 285)

McMurray, J. (2006, August 28). *Cause of deadly Comair crash probed.* Associated Press release. (p. 208)

McNally, R. J. (2003a). Progress and controversy in the study of posttraumatic stress disorder. *Annual Review of Psychology, 54*, 229–252. (p. 324)

McNally, R. J. (2003b). *Remembering trauma.* Cambridge, MA: Harvard University Press. (p. 199)

McNally, R. J. (2007). Betrayal trauma theory: A critical appraisal. *Memory, 15*, 280–294. (p. 199)

McNally, R. J., & Geraerts, E. (2009). A new solution to the recovered memory debate. *Perspectives on Psychological Science, 4*, 126–134. (p. 199)

McNally, R. J., Bryant, R. A., & Ehlers, A. (2003). Does early psychological intervention promote recovery from posttraumatic stress? *Psychological Science in the Public Interest, 4*, 45–79. (p. 324)

McNeil, B. J., Pauker, S. G., & Tversky, A. (1988). On the framing of medical decisions. In D. E. Bell, H. Raiffa, & A. Tversky (Eds.), *Decision making: Descriptive, normative, and prescriptive interactions*. New York: Cambridge University Press. (p. 210)

Meador, B. D., & Rogers, C. R. (1984). Person-centered therapy. In R. J. Corsini (Ed.), *Current psychotherapies* (3rd ed.). Itasca, IL: Peacock. (p. 355)

Medical Institute for Sexual Health. (1994, April). Condoms ineffective against human papilloma virus. *Sexual Health Update*, p. 2. (p. 108)

Mednick, S. A., Huttunen, M. O., & Machon, R. A. (1994). Prenatal influenza infections and adult schizophrenia. *Schizophrenia Bulletin, 20*, 263–267. (p. 345)

Mehl, M. R., & Pennebaker, J. W. (2003). The sounds of social life: A psychometric analysis of students' daily social environments and natural conversations. *Journal of Personality and Social Psychology, 84*, 857–870. (p. 13)

Mehl, M. R., Gosling, S. D., & Pennebaker, J. W. (2006). Personality in its natural habitat: Manifestations and implicit folk theories of personality in daily life. *Journal of Personality and Social Psychology, 90*, 862–877. (p. 307)

Mehl, M. R., Vazire, S., Holleran, S. E., & Clark, C. S. (2010). Eavesdropping on happiness: Well-being is related to having less small talk and more substantive conversations. *Psychological Science, 21*, 539–541. (p. 402)

Mehta, M. R. (2007). Cortico-hippocampal interaction during up-down states and memory consolidation. *Nature Neuroscience, 10*, 13–15. (p. 185)

Meichenbaum, D. (1977). *Cognitive-behavior modification: An integrative approach*. New York: Plenum Press. (p. 359)

Meichenbaum, D. (1985). *Stress inoculation training*. New York: Pergamon. (p. 359)

Meltzoff, A. N., & Moore, M. K. (1997). Explaining facial imitation: A theoretical model. *Early Development and Parenting, 6*, 179–192. (p. 173)

Melzack, R. (1992, April). Phantom limbs. *Scientific American*, pp. 120–126. (p. 143)

Melzack, R. (1993). Distinguished contribution series. *Canadian Journal of Experimental Psychology, 47*, 615–629. (p. 143)

Melzack, R. (1998, February). Quoted in Phantom limbs. *Discover*, p. 20. (p. 143)

Mendes, E. (2009, May 26). In U.S., nearly half exercise less than three days a week. www.gallup.com. (p. 285)

Merari, A. (2002). Explaining suicidal terrorism: Theories versus empirical evidence. Invited address to the American Psychological Association. (p. 388)

Merskey, H. (1992). The manufacture of personalities: The production of multiple personality disorder. *British Journal of Psychiatry, 160*, 327–340. (p. 327)

Merton, R. K., & Kitt, A. S. (1950). Contributions to the theory of reference group behavior. In R. K. Merton & P. F. Lazarsfeld (Eds.), *Continuities in social research: Studies in the scope and method of the American soldier*. Glencoe, IL: Free Press. (p. 267)

Mesch, G. (2001). Social relationships and Internet use among adolescents in Israel. *Social Science Quarterly, 82*, 329–340. (p. 250)

Mestel, R. (1997, April 26). Get real, Siggi. *New Scientist* (www.newscientist.com/ns/970426/siggi.html). (p. 58)

Meyer-Bahlburg, H. F. L. (1995). Psychoneuroendocrinology and sexual pleasure: The aspect of sexual orientation. In P. R. Abramson & S. D. Pinkerton (Eds.), *Sexual nature/sexual culture*. Chicago: University of Chicago Press. (p. 114)

Mezulis, A. M., Abramson, L. Y., Hyde, J. S., & Hankin, B. L. (2004). Is there a universal positivity bias in attributions? A meta-analytic review of individual, developmental, and cultural differences in the self-serving attributional bias. *Psychological Bulletin, 130*, 711–747. (p. 311)

Middlebrooks, J. C., & Green, D. M. (1991). Sound localization by human listeners. *Annual Review of Psychology, 42*, 135–159. (p. 141)

Miers, R. (2009, Spring). Calum's road. *Scottish Life*, pp. 36–39, 75. (p. 414)

Mikulincer, M., & Shaver, P. R. (2001). Attachment theory and intergroup bias: Evidence that priming the secure base schema attenuates negative reactions to out-groups. *Journal of Personality and Social Psychology, 81*, 97–115. (p. 392)

Milan, R. J., Jr., & Kilmann, P. R. (1987). Interpersonal factors in premarital contraception. *Journal of Sex Research, 23*, 289–321. (p. 109)

Miles, D. R., & Carey, G. (1997). Genetic and environmental architecture of human aggression. *Journal of Personality and Social Psychology, 72*, 207–217. (p. 393)

Milgram, S. (1963). Behavioral study of obedience. *Journal of Abnormal & Social Psychology, 67*(4), 371–378. (p. 383)

Milgram, S. (1974). *Obedience to authority*. New York: Harper & Row. (pp. 383, 385, 386)

Miller, E. J., Smith, J. E., & Trembath, D. L. (2000). The "skinny" on body size requests in personal ads. *Sex Roles, 43*, 129–141. (p. 245)

Miller, G. (2004). Axel, Buck share award for deciphering how the nose knows. *Science, 306*, 207. (p. 146)

Miller, G., & Holden, C. (2010). Proposed revisions to psychiatry's canon unveiled. *Science, 327*, 770–771. (p. 320)

Miller, G., Tybur, J. M., & Jordan, B. D. (2007). Ovulatory cycle effects on tip earnings by lap dancers: Economic evidence for human estrus? *Evolution and Human Behavior, 28*, 375–381. (p. 107)

Miller, G. A. (1956). The magical number seven, plus or minus two: Some limits on our capacity for processing information. *Psychological Review, 63*, 81–97. (p. 187)

Miller, J. G., & Bersoff, D. M. (1995). Development in the context of everyday family relationships: Culture, interpersonal morality and adaptation. In M. Killen & D. Hart (Eds.), *Morality in everyday life: A developmental perspective*. New York: Cambridge University Press. (p. 83)

Miller, L. (2005, January 4). U.S. airlines have 34 deaths in 3 years. *Associated Press*. (p. 208)

Miller, L. K. (1999). The Savant Syndrome: Intellectual impairment and exceptional skill. *Psychological Bulletin, 125*, 31–46. (p. 219)

Miller, S. L., & Maner, J. K. (2010). Scent of a woman: Men's testosterone responses to olfactory ovulation cues. *Psychological Science, 21*, 276–283. (p. 107)

Mills, M., & Melhuish, E. (1974). Recognition of mother's voice in early infancy. *Nature, 252*, 123–124. (p. 69)

Milton, J., & Wiseman, R. (2002). A response to Storm and Ertel (2002). *Journal of Parapsychology, 66*, 183–185. (p. 150)

Mineka, S. (1985). The frightful complexity of the origins of fears. In F. R. Brush & J. B. Overmier (Eds.), *Affect, conditioning and cognition: Essays on the determinants of behavior*. Hillsdale, NJ: Erlbaum. (p. 325)

Mineka, S., & Zinbarg, R. (1996). Conditioning and ethological models of anxiety disorders: Stress-in-dynamic-context anxiety models. In D. Hope (Ed.), *Perspectives on anxiety, panic, and fear* (Nebraska Symposium on Motivation). Lincoln: University of Nebraska Press. (pp. 326, 372)

Mineka, S., & Zinbarg, R. (2006). A contemporary learning theory perspective on the etiology of anxiety disorders: It's not what you thought it was. *American Psychologist, 61*, 10–26. (p. 324)

Miner-Rubino, K., & Winter, D. G., & Stewart, A. J. (2004). Gender, social class, and the subjective experience of aging: Self-perceived personality change from early adulthood to late midlife. *Personality and Social Psychology Bulletin, 30*, 1599–1610. (p. 95)

Mischel, W. (1968). *Personality and assessment.* New York: Wiley. (p. 307)

Mischel, W. (1984). Convergences and challenges in the search for consistency. *American Psychologist, 39,* 351–364. (p. 307)

Mischel, W. (2004). Toward an integrative science of the person. *Annual Review of Psychology, 55,* 1–22. (p. 307)

Mischel, W., Shoda, Y., & Peake, P. K. (1988). The nature of adolescent competencies predicted by preschool delay of gratification. *Journal of Personality and Social Psychology, 54,* 687–696. (p. 83)

Mischel, W., Shoda, Y., & Rodriguez, M. L. (1989). Delay of gratification in children. *Science, 244,* 933–938. (p. 83)

Mita, T. H., Dermer, M., & Knight, J. (1977). Reversed facial images and the mere-exposure hypothesis. *Journal of Personality and Social Psychology, 35,* 597–601. (p. 397)

Mitte, K. (2008). Memory bias for threatening information in anxiety and anxiety disorders: A meta-analytic review. *Psychological Bulletin, 134,* 886–911. (p. 322)

Moffitt, T. E., Caspi, A., Harrington, H., & Milne, B. J. (2002). Males on the life-course-persistent and adolescence-limited antisocial pathways: Follow-up at age 26 years. *Development and Psychopathology, 14,* 179–207. (p. 96)

Moffitt, T. E., Caspi, A., Harrington, H., Milne, B. J., Melchior, M., Goldberg, D., & Poulton, R. (2007a). Generalized anxiety disorder and depression: Childhood risk factors in a birth cohort followed to age 32. *Psychological Medicine, 37,* 441–452. (p. 322)

Moffitt, T. E., Harrington, H., Caspi, A., Kim-Cohen, J., Goldberg, D., Gregory, A. M., & Poulton, R. (2007b). Depression and generalized anxiety disorder: Cumulative and sequential comorbidity in a birth cohort followed prospectively to age 32 years. *Archives of General Psychiatry, 64,* 651–660. (p. 322)

Moghaddam, F. M. (2005). The staircase to terrorism: A psychological exploration. *American Psychologist, 60,* 161–169. (p. 388)

Mondloch, C. J., Lewis, T. L., Budreau, D. R., Maurer, D., Dannemiller, J. L., Stephens, B. R., & Kleiner-Gathercoal, K. A. (1999). Face perception during early infancy. *Psychological Science, 10,* 419–422. (p. 69)

Money, J. (1987). Sin, sickness, or status? Homosexual gender identity and psychoneuroendocrinology. *American Psychologist, 42,* 384–399. (p. 114)

Money, J., Berlin, F. S., Falck, A., & Stein, M. (1983). *Antiandrogenic and counseling treatment of sex offenders.* Baltimore: Department of Psychiatry and Behavioral Sciences, The Johns Hopkins University School of Medicine. (p. 108)

Moody, R. (1976). *Life after life.* Harrisburg, PA: Stackpole Books. (p. 334)

Mook, D. G. (1983). In defense of external invalidity. *American Psychologist, 38,* 379–387. (p. 18)

Moorcroft, W. H. (2003). *Understanding sleep and dreaming.* New York: Kluwer/Plenum. (p. 53)

Moore, D. W. (2004, December 17). Sweet dreams go with a good night's sleep. *Gallup News Service* (www.gallup.com). (p. 53)

Moore, D. W. (2005, June 16). Three in four Americans believe in paranormal. *Gallup New Service* (www.gallup.com). (p. 149)

Moore, D. W. (2006, March 10). Close to 6 in 10 Americans want to lose weight. *Gallup News Service* (poll.gallup.com). (p. 247)

Moreira, M. T., Smith, L. A., & Foxcroft, D. (2009). Social norms interventions to reduce alcohol misuse in university or college students. *Cochrane Database of Systematic Reviews.* 2009, Issue 3., Art. No. C06748. (p. 337)

Moreland, R. L., & Beach, S. R. (1992). Exposure effects in the classroom: The development of affinity among students. *Journal of Experimental Social Psychology, 28,* 255–276. (p. 398)

Moreland, R. L., & Zajonc, R. B. (1982). Exposure effects in person perception: Familiarity, similarity, and attraction. *Journal of Experimental Social Psychology, 18,* 395–415. (p. 397)

Morell, V. (1995). Zeroing in on how hormones affect the immune system. *Science, 269,* 773–775. (pp. 108, 227)

Morell, V. (2008, March). Minds of their own: Animals are smarter than you think. *National Geographic,* pp. 37–61. (p. 216)

Morelli, G. A., Rogoff, B., Oppenheim, D., & Goldsmith, D. (1992). Cultural variation in infants' sleeping arrangements: Questions of independence. *Developmental Psychology, 26,* 604–613. (p. 79)

Moreno, C., Laje, G., Blanco, C., Jiang, H., Schmidt, A. B., & Olfson, M. (2007). National trends in the outpatient diagnosis and treatment of bipolar disorder in youth. *Archives of General Psychiatry, 64,* 1032–1039. (p. 339)

Morey, R. A., Inan, S., Mitchell, T. V., Perkins, D. O., Lieberman, J. A., & Belger, A. (2005). Imaging frontostriatal function in ultra-high-risk, early, and chronic schizophrenia during executive processing. *Archives of General Psychiatry, 62,* 254–262. (p. 345)

Morgan, A. B., & Lilienfeld, S. O. (2000). A meta-analytic review of the relation between antisocial behavior and neuropsychological measures of executive function. *Clinical Psychology Review, 20,* 113–136. (p. 328)

Mori, K., & Mori, H. (2009). Another test of the passive facial feedback hypothesis: When you face smiles, you feel happy. *Perceptual and Motor Skills, 109,* 1–3. (p. 262)

Morrison, A. R. (2003). The brain on night shift. *Cerebrum, 5*(3), 23–36. (p. 53)

Mortensen, P. B. (1999). Effects of family history and place and season of birth on the risk of schizophrenia. *New England Journal of Medicine, 340,* 603–608. (p. 345)

Moruzzi, G., & Magoun, H. W. (1949). Brain stem reticular formation and activation of the EEG. *Electroencephalography and Clinical Neurophysiology, 1,* 455–473. (p. 36)

Moscovici, S. (1985). Social influence and conformity. In G. Lindzey & E. Aronson (Eds.), *The handbook of social psychology* (3rd ed). Hillsdale, N.J.: Erlbaum. (p. 386)

Mosher, D. L., & Anderson, R. D. (1986). Macho personality, sexual aggression, and reactions to guided imagery of realistic rape. *Journal of Research in Personality, 20,* 77–94. (p. 330)

Mosher, W. D., Chandra, A., & Jones, J. (2005, September 15). Sexual behavior and selected health measures: Men and women 15–44 years of age, United States, 2002. *Advance Data from Vital and Health Statistics, No. 362,* National Center for Health Statistics, Centers for Disease Control and Prevention, U.S. Department of Health and Human Services. (p. 112)

Moss, H. A., & Susman, E. J. (1980). Longitudinal study of personality development. In O. G. Brim, Jr., & J. Kagan (Eds.), *Constancy and change in human development.* Cambridge, MA: Harvard University Press. (p. 96)

Moulton, S. T., & Kosslyn, S. M. (2008). Using neuroimaging to resolve the psi debate. *Journal of Cognitive Neuroscience, 20,* 182–192. (p. 150)

Moyer, K. E. (1983). The physiology of motivation: Aggression as a model. In C. J. Scheier & A. M. Rogers (Eds.), *G. Stanley Hall Lecture Series* (Vol. 3). Washington, DC: American Psychological Association. (p. 393)

Mroczek, D. K. (2001). Age and emotion in adulthood. *Current Directions in Psychological Science, 10,* 87–90. (p. 95)

Mroczek, D. K., & Spiro, A., III (2005). Change in life satisfaction during adulthood: Findings from the Veterans Affairs normative aging study. *Journal of Personality and Social Psychology, 88,* 189–202. (p. 268)

Muller, J. E., & Verrier, R. L. (1996). Triggering of sudden death—Lessons from an earthquake. *New England Journal of Medicine, 334,* 461. (p. 275)

Mullin, C. R., & Linz, D. (1995). Desensitization and resensitization to violence against women: Effects of exposure to sexually violent films on judgments of domestic violence victims. *Journal of Personality and Social Psychology, 69,* 449–459. (p. 177)

Murray, C. A., & Herrnstein, R. J. (1994, October 31). Race, genes and I.Q.—An apologia. *New Republic,* pp. 27–37. (p. 228)

Murray, H. (1938). *Explorations in personality.* New York: Oxford University Press. (p. 413)

Murray, H. A., & Wheeler, D. R. (1937). A note on the possible clairvoyance of dreams. *Journal of Psychology, 3,* 309–313. (p. 149)

Murray, R., Jones, P., O'Callaghan, E., Takei, N., & Sham, P. (1992). Genes, viruses, and neurodevelopmental schizophrenia. *Journal of Psychiatric Research, 26,* 225–235. (p. 345)

Murray, R. M., Morrison, P. D., Henquet, C., & Di Forti, M. (2007). Cannabis, the mind and society: The hash realities. *Nature Reviews: Neuroscience, 8,* 885–895. (p. 335)

Murray, S. L., Bellavia, G. M., Rose, P., & Griffin, D. W. (2003). Once hurt, twice hurtful: How perceived regard regulates daily marital interactions. *Journal of Personality and Social Psychology, 84,* 126–147. (p. 128)

Musick, M. A., Herzog, A. R., & House, J. S. (1999). Volunteering and mortality among older adults: Findings from a national sample. *Journals of Gerontology, 54B,* 173–180. (p. 288)

Mustanski, B. S., & Bailey, J. M. (2003). A therapist's guide to the genetics of human sexual orientation. *Sexual and Relationship Therapy, 18,* 1468–1479. (p. 114)

Myers, D. G. (1993). *The pursuit of happiness.* New York: Avon Books. (p. 268)

Myers, D. G. (2000). *The American paradox: Spiritual hunger in an age of plenty.* New Haven, CT: Yale University Press. (pp. 268, 395)

Myers, D. G. (2001, December). Do we fear the right things? *American Psychological Society Observer,* p. 3. (p. 208)

Myers, D. G. (2010). *Social psychology,* 10th edition. New York: McGraw-Hill. (p. 311)

Myers, D. G., & Bishop, G. D. (1970). Discussion effects on racial attitudes. *Science, 169,* 778–779. (p. 388)

Myers, D. G., & Diener, E. (1995). Who is happy? *Psychological Science, 6,* 10–19. (p. 268)

Myers, D. G., & Diener, E. (1996, May). The pursuit of happiness. *Scientific American,* pp. 54–56. (p. 268)

Myers, D. G., & Scanzoni, L. D. (2005). *What God has joined together?* San Francisco: HarperSanFrancisco. (pp. 93, 112)

Myers, T. A., & Crowther, J. H. (2009). Social comparison as a predictor of body dissatisfaction: A meta-analytic review. *Journal of Abnormal Psychology, 118,* 683–698. (p. 243)

Mykletun, A., Bjerkeset, O., Øverland, S., & Prince, M. (2009). Levels of anxiety and depression as predictors of mortality: The HUNT study. *British Journal of Psychiatry, 195,* 118–125 (p. 280)

Napolitan, D. A., & Goethals, G. R. (1979). The attribution of friendliness. *Journal of Experimental Social Psychology, 15,* 105–113. (p. 378)

National Academy of Sciences. (2001). *Exploring the biological contributions to human health: Does sex matter?* Washington, DC: Institute of Medicine, National Academy Press. (p. 104)

National Center for Health Statistics. (1990). *Health, United States, 1989.* Washington, DC: U.S. Department of Health and Human Services. (p. 91)

National Center for Health Statistics. (2004, December 15). Marital status and health: United States, 1999–2002 (by Charlotte A. Schoenborn). *Advance Data from Vital and Human Statistics, number 351.* Centers for Disease Control and Prevention. (p. 284)

National Institute of Mental Health. (2008). The numbers count: Mental disorders in America. (nimh.nih.gov). (pp. 316, 318, 321)

National Safety Council (2010). Attributable risk estimate model. www.nsc.org. (p. 208)

National Safety Council. (2010, January 12). NSC estimates 1.6 million crashes caused by cell phone use and texting. www.nsc.org. (p. 49)

Naumann, L. P., Vazire, S., Rentfrow, P. J., & Gosling, S. D. (2009). Personality judgments based on physical appearance. *Personality and Social Psychology Bulletin, 35,* 1661–1671. (p. 308)

Nazimek, J. (2009). Active body, healthy mind. *The Psychologist, 22,* 206–208. (p. 92)

NCHS. (1970). Skinfolds, body girths, biacromial diameter, and selected anthropometric indices of adults, United States, 1960-1962. *Vital and Health Statistics,* Series 11, Number 35. (p. 246)

NCHS. (2007). *Health, United States, 2007.* Hyattsville, MD: National Center for Health Statistics. (p. 244)

Neese, R. M. (1991, November/December). What good is feeling bad? The evolutionary benefits of psychic pain. *The Sciences,* pp. 30–37. (pp. 143, 170)

Neidorf, S., & Morin, R. (2007, May 23). Four-in-ten Americans have close friends or relatives who are gay. *Pew Research Center Publications* (pewresearch.org). (p. 405)

Neisser, U. (1979). The control of information pickup in selective looking. In A. D. Pick (Ed.), *Perception and its development: A tribute to Eleanor J. Gibson.* Hillsdale, NJ: Erlbaum. (p. 49)

Neisser, U., Boodoo, G., Bouchard, T. J., Jr., Boykin, A. W., Brody, N., Ceci, S. J., Halpern, D. F., Loehlin, J. C., Perloff, R., Sternberg, R. J., & Urbina, S. (1996). Intelligence: Knowns and unknowns. *American Psychologist, 51,* 77–101. (p. 231)

Nelson, C. A., III, Furtado, E. Z., Fox, N. A., & Zeanah, Jr., C. H. (2009). The deprived human brain. *American Scientist, 97,* 222–229. (p. 78)

Nelson, M. D., Saykin, A. J., Flashman, L. A., & Riordan, H. J. (1998). Hippocampal volume reduction in schizophrenia as assessed by magnetic resonance imaging. *Archives of General Psychiatry, 55,* 433–440. (p. 345)

Nesca, M., & Koulack, D. (1994). Recognition memory, sleep and circadian rhythms. *Canadian Journal of Experimental Psychology, 48,* 359–379. (p. 194)

Nestoriuc, Y., Rief, W., & Martin, A. (2008). Meta-analysis of biofeedback for tension-type headache: Efficacy, specificity, and treatment moderators. *Journal of Consulting and Clinical Psychology, 76,* 379–396. (p. 286)

Neumann, R., & Strack, F. (2000). "Mood contagion": The automatic transfer of mood between persons. *Journal of Personality and Social Psychology, 79,* 211–223. (p. 263)

Newberg, A., & D'Aquili, E. (2001). *Why God won't go away: Brain science and the biology of belief.* New York: Simon & Schuster. (p. 287)

Newcomb, M. D., & Harlow, L. L. (1986). Life events and substance use among adolescents: Mediating effects of perceived loss of control and meaninglessness in life. *Journal of Personality and Social Psychology, 51,* 564–577. (p. 336)

Newman, A. J., Bavelier, D., Corina, D., Jezzard, P., & Neville, H. J. (2002). A critical period for right hemisphere recruitment in American Sign Language processing. *Nature Neuroscience, 5,* 76–80. (p. 215)

Newport, E. L. (1990). Maturational constraints on language learning. *Cognitive Science, 14,* 11–28. (p. 215)

Newport, F. (2001, February). Americans see women as emotional and affectionate, men as more aggressive. *The Gallup Poll Monthly*, pp. 34–38. (p. 260)

Newport, F. (2002, July 29). Bush job approval update. *Gallup News Service* (www.gallup.com/poll/releases/pr020729.asp). (p. 405)

Newport, F. (2007, May 11). The age factor: Older Americans most negative about Iraq war. (www.galluppoll.com). (p. 102)

Newport, F., & Pelham, B. (2009, December 14). Don't worry, be 80: Worry and stress decline with age. www.gallup.com. (pp. 272, 275)

Newport, F., Moore, D. W., Jones, J. M., & Saad, L. (2003, March 21). Special release: American opinion on the war. *Gallup Poll Tuesday Briefing* (www.gallup.com). (p. 381)

Neylan, T. C., Metzler, T. J., Best, S. R., Weiss, D. S., Fagan, J. A., Liberman, A., Rogers, C., Vedantham, K., Brunet, A., Lipsey, T. L., & Marmar, C. R. (2002). Critical incident exposure and sleep quality in police officers. *Psychosomatic Medicine, 64*, 345–352. (p. 56)

Nezlek, J. B. (2001). Daily psychological adjustment and the planfulness of day-to-day behavior. *Journal of Social and Clinical Psychology, 20*, 452–475. (p. 282)

Ng, T. W. H., Sorensen, K. L., & Eby, L. T. (2006). Locus of control at work: A meta-analysis. *Journal of Organizational Behavior, 27*, 1057–1087. (p. 282)

Ng, T. W. H., Sorensen, K. L., & Yim, F. H. K. (2009). Does the job satisfaction—job performance relationship vary across cultures? *Journal of Cross-Cultural Psychology, 40*, 761–796. (p. 414)

Nguyen, H-H. D., & Ryan, A. M. (2008). Does stereotype threat affect test performance of minorities and women? A meta-analysis of experimental evidence. *Journal of Applied Psychology, 93*, 1314–1334. (p. 232)

Nickell, J. (Ed.) (1994). *Psychic sleuths: ESP and sensational cases.* Buffalo, New York: Prometheus Books. (p. 149)

Nickell, J. (2005, July/August). The case of the psychic detectives. *Skeptical Inquirer* (skeptically.org/skepticism/id10.html). (p. 149)

NIDA. (2002). Methamphetamine abuse and addiction. *Research Report Series.* National Institute on Drug Abuse, NIH Publication Number 02–4210. (p. 332)

NIDA. (2005, May). Methamphetamine. *NIDA Info Facts.* National Institute on Drug Abuse. (p. 332)

Nie, N. H. (2001). Sociability, interpersonal relations and the Internet: Reconciling conflicting findings. *American Behavioral Scientist, 45*, 420–435. (p. 250)

NIH. (2001, July 20). *Work shop summary: Scientific evidence on condom effectiveness for sexually transmitted disease (STD) prevention.* Bethesda: National Institute of Allergy and Infectious Diseases, National Institutes of Health. (p. 108)

Nisbett, R. E. (2003). *The geography of thought: How Asians and Westerners think differently...and why.* New York: Free Press. (p. 378)

Nisbett, R. E. (2009). *Intelligence and how to get it: Why schools and culture count.* New York: Norton. (p. 230)

Nixon, G. M., Thompson, J. M. D., Han, D. Y., Becroft, D. M., Clark, P. M., Robinson, E., Waldie, K E., Wild, C. J., Black, P. N., & Mitchell, E. A. (2008). Short sleep duration in middle childhood: Risk factors and consequences. *Sleep, 31*, 71–78. (p. 55)

Noel, J. G., Forsyth, D. R., & Kelley, K. N. (1987). Improving the performance of failing students by overcoming their self-serving attributional biases. *Basic and Applied Social Psychology, 8*, 151–162. (p. 283)

Nolen-Hoeksema, S. (2001). Gender differences in depression. *Current Directions in Psychological Science, 10*, 173–176. (p. 342)

Nolen-Hoeksema, S. (2003). *Women who think too much: How to break free of overthinking and reclaim your life.* New York: Holt. (p. 342)

Nolen-Hoeksema, S., & Davis, C. G. (2002). Positive responses to loss: Perceiving benefits and growth. In C.R. Snyder & S. Lopez (eds.), *Handbook of positive psychology.* New York: Oxford. (p. 285)

Nolen-Hoeksema, S., & Larson, J. (1999). *Coping with loss.* Mahwah, NJ: Erlbaum. (p. 95)

NORC. (2007). National Opinion Research Center (University of Chicago) General Social Survey data, 1972 through 2004, accessed via sda.berkeley.edu. (p. 249)

Norem, J. K. (2001). *The positive power of negative thinking: Using defensive pessimism to harness anxiety and perform at your peak.* New York: Basic Books. (p. 283)

Nosek, B. A. & 24 others. (2009). National differences in gender-science stereotypes predict national sex differences in science and math achievement. *Proceedings of the National Academy of Sciences, 106*, 10593–10597. (p. 230)

Nowak, R. (1994). Nicotine scrutinized as FDA seeks to regulate cigarettes. *Science, 263*, 1555–1556. (p. 332)

NPR. (2009, July 11). Afraid to fly? Try living on a plane. www.npr.org. (p. 161)

Nunes, A., & Kramer, A. F. (2009). Experience-based mitigation of age-related performance declines: Evidence from air traffic control. *Journal of Experimental Psychology: Applied, 15*, 12–24. (p. 92)

Nuttin, J. M., Jr. (1987). Affective consequences of mere ownership: The name letter effect in twelve European languages. *European Journal of Social Psychology, 17*, 381–402. (p. 397)

Oaten, M., & Cheng, K. (2006a). Longitudinal gains in self-regulation from regular physical exercise. *British Journal of Health Psychology, 11*, 717–733. (p. 282)

Oaten, M., & Cheng, K. (2006b). Improved self-control: The benefits of a regular program of academic study. *Basic and Applied Social Psychology, 28*, 1–16. (p. 282)

Oberlander, J., & Gill, A. J. (2006). Language with character: A stratified corpus comparison of individual differences in e-mail communication. *Discourse Processes, 42*, 239–270. (p. 308)

O'Connor, P., & Brown, G. W. (1984). Supportive relationships: Fact or fancy? *Journal of Social and Personal Relationships, 1*, 159–175. (p. 364)

O'Donnell, L., Stueve, A., O'Donnell, C., Duran, R., San Doval, A., Wilson, R. F., Haber, D., Perry, E., & Pleck, J. H. (2002). Long-term reduction in sexual initiation and sexual activity among urban middle schoolers in the reach for health service learning program. *Journal of Adolescent Health, 31*, 93–100. (p. 110)

Oettingen, G., & Seligman, M. E. P. (1990). Pessimism and behavioural signs of depression in East versus West Berlin. *European Journal of Social Psychology, 20*, 207–220. (p. 282)

Offer, D., Ostrov, E., Howard, K. I., & Atkinson, R. (1988). *The teenage world: Adolescents' self-image in ten countries.* New York: Plenum. (p. 85)

Öhman, A. (1986). Face the beast and fear the face: Animal and social fears as prototypes for evolutionary analyses of emotion. *Psychophysiology, 23*, 123–145. (p. 326)

Öhman, A., Lundqvist, D., & Esteves, F. (2001). The face in the crowd revisited: A threat advantage with schematic stimuli. *Journal of Personality and Social Psychology, 80*, 381–396. (p. 260)

Oishi, S., Diener, E. F., Lucas, R. E., & Suh, E. M. (1999). Cross-cultural variations in predictors of life satisfaction: Perspectives from needs and values. *Personality and Social Psychology Bulletin, 25*, 980–990. (p. 239)

Olds, J. (1975). Mapping the mind onto the brain. In F. G. Worden, J. P. Swazey, & G. Adelman (Eds.), *The neurosciences: Paths of discovery.* Cambridge, MA: MIT Press. (p. 38)

Olds, J., & Milner, P. (1954). Positive reinforcement produced by electrical stimulation of the septal area and other regions of rat brain. *Journal of Comparative and Physiological Psychology, 47,* 419–427. (p. 38)

Olff, M., Langeland, W., Draijer, N., & Gersons, B. P. R. (2007). Gender differences in posttraumatic stress disorder. *Psychological Bulletin, 135,* 183–204. (p. 324)

Olfson, M., & Marcus, S. C. (2009). National patterns in antidepressant medication treatment. *Archives of General Psychiatry, 66,* 848–856. (pp. 366, 368)

Oliner, S. P., & Oliner, P. M. (1988). *The altruistic personality: Rescuers of Jews in Nazi Europe.* New York: Free Press. (p. 174)

Olshansky, S. J., Passaro, D. J., Hershow, R. C., Layden, J., Carnes, B. A., Brody, J., Hayflick, L., Butler, R. N., Allison, D. B., & Ludwig, D. S. (2005). A potential decline in life expectancy in the United States in the 21st century. *New England Journal of Medicine, 352,* 1138–1145. (p. 244)

Olsson, A., & Phelps, E. A. (2004). Learned fear of "unseen" faces after Pavlovian, observational, and instructed fear. *Psychological Science, 15,* 822–828. (p. 325)

Orth, U., Robins, R. W., & Roberts, B. W. (2008). Low self-esteem prospectively predicts depression in adolescence and young adulthood. *Journal of Personality and Social Psychology, 95,* 695–708. (p. 310)

Orth, U., Robins, R. W., Trzesniewski, K. H., Maes, J., & Schmitt, M. (2009). Low self-esteem is a risk factor for depressive symptoms from young adulthood to old age. *Journal of Abnormal Psychology, 118,* 472–478. (p. 310)

Osborne, J. W. (1997). Race and academic disidentification. *Journal of Educational Psychology, 89,* 728–735. (p. 232)

Osborne, L. (1999, October 27). A linguistic big bang. *New York Times Magazine* (www.nytimes.com). (p. 214)

Ost, L. G., & Hugdahl, K. (1981). Acquisition of phobias and anxiety response patterns in clinical patients. *Behaviour Research and Therapy, 16,* 439–447. (p. 325)

Ostfeld, A. M., Kasl, S. V., D'Atri, D. A., & Fitzgerald, E. F. (1987). *Stress, crowding, and blood pressure in prison.* Hillsdale, NJ: Erlbaum. (p. 281)

Ott, B. (2007, June 14). Investors, take note: Engagement boosts earnings. *Gallup Management Journal* (gmj.gallup.com). (p. 415)

Ott, C. H., Lueger, R. J., Kelber, S. T., & Prigerson, H. G. (2007). Spousal bereavement in older adults: Common, resilient, and chronic grief with defining characteristics. *Journal of Nervous and Mental Disease, 195,* 332–341. (p. 95)

Owen, A. M., Coleman, M. R., Boly, M., Davis, M. H., Laureys, S., & Pickard, J. D. (2006). Detecting awareness in the vegetative state. *Science, 313,* 1402. (p. 34)

Owen, R. (1814). First essay in *New view of society or the formation of character.* Quoted in *The story of New Lanark Mills,* Lanark, Scotland: New Lanark Conservation Trust, 1993. (p. 417)

Oxfam. (2005, March 26). Three months on: New figures show tsunami may have killed up to four times as many women as men. *Oxfam Press Release* (www.oxfam.org.uk). (p. 105)

Ozer, E. J., & Weiss, D. S. (2004). Who develops posttraumatic stress disorder. *Current Directions in Psychological Science, 13,* 169–172. (p. 324)

Ozer, E. J., Best, S. R., Lipsey, T. L., & Weiss, D. S. (2003). Predictors of posttraumatic stress disorder and symptoms in adults: A meta-analysis. *Psychological Bulletin, 129,* 52–73. (p. 324)

Pacifici, R., Zuccaro, P., Farre, M., Pichini, S., Di Carlo, S., Roset, P. N., Ortuno, J., Pujadus, M., Bacosi, A., Menoyo, E., Segura, J., & de la Torre, R. (2001). Effects of repeated doses of MDMA ("Ecstasy") on cell-mediated immune response in humans. *Life Sciences, 69,* 2931–2941. (p. 334)

Padgett, V. R. (1989). Predicting organizational violence: An application of 11 powerful principles of obedience. Paper presented to the American Psychological Association convention. (p. 384)

Paivio, A. (1986). *Mental representations: A dual coding approach.* New York: Oxford University Press. (p. 187)

Palace, E. M. (1995). Modification of dysfunctional patterns of sexual response through autonomic arousal and false physiological feedback. *Journal of Consulting and Clinical Psychology, 63,* 604–615. (p. 256)

Pallier, C., Colomé, A., & Sebastián-Gallés, N. (2001). The influence of native-language phonology on lexical access: Exemplar-based versus abstract lexical entries. *Psychological Science, 12,* 445–448. (p. 213)

Pandey, J., Sinha, Y., Prakash, A., & Tripathi, R. C. (1982). Right-left political ideologies and attribution of the causes of poverty. *European Journal of Social Psychology, 12,* 327–331. (p. 379)

Panksepp, J. (2007). Neurologizing the psychology of affects: How appraisal-based constructivism and basic emotion theory can coexist. *Perspectives on Psychological Science, 2,* 281–295. (p. 256)

Panzarella, C., Alloy, L. B., & Whitehouse, W. G. (2006). Expanded hopelessness theory of depression: On the mechanisms by which social support protects against depression. *Cognitive Theory and Research, 30,* 307–333. (p. 342)

Park, C. L. (2007). Religiousness/spirituality and health: A meaning systems perspective. *Journal of Behavioral Medicine, 30,* 319–328. (p. 287)

Park, D. C., Lautenschlager, G., Hedden, T., Davidson, N. S., Smith, A. D., & Smith, P. K. (2002). Models of visuospatial and verbal memory across the adult life span. *Psychology and Aging, 17,* 299–320. (p. 92)

Park, R. L. (1999). Liars never break a sweat. *New York Times,* July 12, 1999 (www.nytimes.com). (p. 257)

Parker, C. P., Baltes, B. B., Young, S. A., Huff, J. W., Altmann, R. A., LaCost, H. A., & Roberts, J. E. (2003). Relationships between psychological climate perceptions and work outcomes: A meta-analytic review. *Journal of Organizational Behavior, 24,* 389–416. (p. 414)

Parker, E. S., Cahill, L., & McGaugh, J. L. (2006). A case of unusual autobiographical remembering. *Neurocase, 12,* 35–49. (p. 192)

Parsons, T. D., & Rizzo, A. A. (2008). Affective outcomes of virtual reality exposure therapy for anxiety and specific phobias: A meta-analysis. *Journal of Behavior Therapy and Experimental Psychiatry, 39,* 250–261. (p. 356)

Pascoe, E. A., & Richman, L. S. (2009). Perceived discrimination and health: A meta-analytic review. *Psychological Bulletin, 135,* 531–554. (p. 275)

Patel, S. R., Malhotra, A., White, D. P., Gottlieb, D. J., & Hu, F. B. (2006). Association between reduced sleep and weight gain in women. *American Journal of Epidemiology, 164,* 947–954. (p. 55)

Patrick, H., Knee, C. R., Canevello, A., & Lonsbary, C. (2007). The role of need fulfillment in relationship functioning and well-being: A self-determination theory perspective. *Journal of Personality and Social Psychology, 92,* 434–457. (p. 249)

Patterson, D. R. (2004). Treating pain with hypnosis. *Current Directions in Psychological Science, 13,* 252–255. (p. 144)

Patterson, D. R., & Jensen, M. (2003). Hypnosis for clinical pain control. *Psychological Bulletin, 129,* 495–521. (p. 145)

Patterson, F. (1978, October). Conversations with a gorilla. *National Geographic,* pp. 438–465. (p. 217)

Patterson, G. R., Chamberlain, P., & Reid, J. B. (1982). A comparative evaluation of parent training procedures. *Behavior Therapy, 13,* 638–650. (pp. 166, 395)

Patterson, G. R., Reid, J. B., & Dishion, T. J. (1992). *Antisocial boys.* Eugene, OR: Castalia. (p. 395)

Patterson, M., Warr, P., & West, M. (2004). Organizational climate and company productivity: The role of employee affect and employee level. *Journal of Occupational and Organizational Psychology, 77,* 193–216. (p. 414)

Patterson, P. H. (2007). Maternal effects on schizophrenia risk. *Science, 318,* 576–577. (p. 345)

Patton, G. C., Coffey, C., Carlin, J. B., Degenhardt, L., Lynskey, M., & Hall, W. (2002). Cannabis use and mental health of young people: Cohort study. *British Medical Journal, 325,* 1195–1198. (p. 335)

Paulos, J. A. (1995). *A mathematician reads the newspaper.* New York: Basic Books. (p. 368)

Paus, T., Zijdenbos, A., Worsley, K., Collins, D. L., Blumenthal, J., Giedd, J. N., Rapoport, J. L., & Evans, A. C. (1999). Structural maturation of neural pathways in children and adolescents: In vivo study. *Science, 283,* 1908–1911. (p. 70)

Pavlov, I. (1927). *Conditioned reflexes: An investigation of the physiological activity of the cerebral cortex.* Oxford: Oxford University Press. (p. 157)

Payne, B. K., & Corrigan, E. (2007). Emotional constraints on intentional forgetting. *Journal of Experimental Social Psychology, 43,* 780–786. (p. 195)

Pekkanen, J. (1982, June). Why do we sleep? *Science, 82,* 86. (p. 54)

Pelham, B. W. (1993). On the highly positive thoughts of the highly depressed. In R. F. Baumeister (Ed.), *Self-esteem: The puzzle of low self-regard.* New York: Plenum. (p. 310)

Pelham, B. W. (2009, October 22). About one in six Americans report history of depression. www.gallup.com. (p. 340)

Pendick, D. (1994, January/February). The mind of violence. *Brain Work: The Neuroscience Newsletter,* pp. 1–3, 5. (p. 394)

Pennebaker, J. W. (1990). *Opening up: The healing power of confiding in others.* New York: William Morrow. (pp. 285, 299)

Pennebaker, J. W. (2002, January 28). Personal communication. (p. 405)

Pennebaker, J. W., & O'Heeron, R. C. (1984). Confiding in others and illness rate among spouses of suicide and accidental death victims. *Journal of Abnormal Psychology, 93,* 473–476. (p. 285)

Pennebaker, J. W., & Stone, L. D. (2003). Words of wisdom: Language use over the life span. *Journal of Personality and Social Psychology, 85,* 291–301. (p. 95)

Pennebaker, J. W., Barger, S. D., & Tiebout, J. (1989). Disclosure of traumas and health among Holocaust survivors. *Psychosomatic Medicine, 51,* 577–589. (p. 285)

Peplau, L. A., & Fingerhut, A. W. (2007). The close relationships of lesbians and gay men. *Annual Review of Psychology, 58,* 405–424. (pp. 93, 117)

Peplau, L. A., & Garnets, L. D. (2000). A new paradigm for understanding women's sexuality and sexual orientation. *Journal of Social Issues, 56,* 329–350. (p. 113)

Peppard, P. E., Szklo-Coxe, M., Hia, K. M., & Young, T. (2006). Longitudinal association of sleep-related breathing disorder and depression. *Archives of Internal Medicine, 166,* 1709–1715. (p. 55)

Pepperberg, I. M. (2006). Grey parrot numerical competence: A review. *Animal Cognition, 9,* 377–391. (p. 216)

Pereira, A. C., Huddleston, D. E., Brickman, A. M., Sosunov, A. A., Hen, R., McKhann, G. M., Sloan, R., Gage, F. H., Brown, T. R., & Small, S. A. (2007).

An *in vivo* correlate of exercise-induced neurogenesis in the adult dentate gyrus. Proceedings of the National Academic of Sciences, 104, 5638–5643. (pp. 45, 92)

Pereira, G. M., & Osburn, H. G. (2007). Effects of participation in decision making on performance and employee attitudes: A quality circles meta-analysis. *Journal of Business Psychology, 22,* 145–153. (p. 417)

Perkins, A., & Fitzgerald, J. A. (1997). Sexual orientation in domestic rams: Some biological and social correlates. In L. Ellis & L. Ebertz (Eds.), *Sexual orientation: Toward biological understanding.* Westport, CT: Praeger Publishers. (p. 113)

Perls, T., & Silver, M. H., with Lauerman, J. F. (1999). *Living to 100: Lessons in living to your maximum potential.* Thorndike, ME: Thorndike Press. (p. 280)

Person, C., Tracy, M., & Galea, S. (2006). Risk factors for depression after a disaster. *Journal of Nervous and Mental Disease, 194,* 659–666. (p. 372)

Pert, C. B., & Snyder, S. H. (1973). Opiate receptor: Demonstration in nervous tissue. *Science, 179,* 1011–1014. (p. 30)

Peschel, E. R., & Peschel, R. E. (1987). Medical insights into the castrati in opera. *American Scientist, 75,* 578–583. (p. 108)

Peters, T. J., & Waterman, R. H., Jr. (1982). *In search of excellence: Lessons from America's best-run companies.* New York: Harper & Row. (p. 168)

Petersen, J. L., & Hyde, J. S. (2009) A meta-analytic review of research on gender differences in sexuality, 1993–2007. *Psychological Bulletin, 136,* 21–38. (p. 116)

Peterson, C., & Barrett, L. C. (1987). Explanatory style and academic performance among university freshmen. *Journal of Personality and Social Psychology, 53,* 603–607. (p. 283)

Peterson, C., Peterson, J., & Skevington, S. (1986). Heated argument and adolescent development. *Journal of Social and Personal Relationships, 3,* 229–240. (p. 82)

Peterson, L. R., & Peterson, M. J. (1959). Short-term retention of individual verbal items. *Journal of Experimental Psychology, 58,* 193–198. (p. 187)

Petitto, L. A., & Marentette, P. F. (1991). Babbling in the manual mode: Evidence for the ontogeny of language. *Science, 251,* 1493–1496. (p. 213)

Pettegrew, J. W., Keshavan, M. S., & Minshew, N. J. (1993). 31P nuclear magnetic resonance spectroscopy: Neurodevelopment and schizophrenia. *Schizophrenia Bulletin, 19,* 35–53. (p. 345)

Petticrew, C., Bell, R., & Hunter, D. (2002). Influence of psychological coping on survival and recurrence in people with cancer: Systematic review. *British Medical Journal, 325,* 1066. (p. 278)

Petticrew, M., Fraser, J. M., & Regan, M. F. (1999). Adverse life events and risk of breast cancer: A meta-analysis. *British Journal of Health Psychology, 4,* 1–17. (p. 278)

Pettigrew, T. F., & Tropp, L. R. (2006). A meta-analytic test of intergroup contact theory. *Journal of Personality and Social Psychology, 90,* 751–783. (p. 405)

Pew Research Center. (2003). Views of a changing world 2003. The Pew Global Attitudes Project. Washington, DC: Pew Research Center for the People and the Press. (http://people-press.org/reports/pdf/185.pdf). (p. 105)

Pew Research Center. (2006). Remembering 9/11. Pew Research Center. (www.pewresearch.org). (p. 189)

Pew Research Center. (2006, November 14). Attitudes toward homosexuality in African countries (www.pewresearch.org). (p. 112)

Pew Research Center. (2007, July 18). Modern marriage: "I like hugs. I like kisses. But what I really love is help with the dishes." Pew Research Center. (www.pewresearch.org). (p. 402)

Pew Research Center. (2009, November 16). Teens and distracted driving. Internet & American Life Project, Pew Research Center. (www.pewinternet.org). (p. 49)

Pew Research Center. (2009, November 4). Social isolation and new technology: How the Internet and mobile phones impact Americans' social networks. Pew Research Center. (www.pewresearch.org). (p. 250)

Pew Research Center. (2010, February 1). Almost all millennials accept interracial dating and marriage. Pew Research Center. (www.pewresearch.org). (p. 391)

Phelps, J. A., Davis J. O., & Schartz, K. M. (1997). Nature, nurture, and twin research strategies. *Current Directions in Psychological Science, 6,* 117–120. (p. 346)

Philip Morris Companies, Inc. (1999, October 13). Referenced in Myron Levin, Philip Morris' new campaign echoes medical experts, *Los Angeles Times.* (p. 332)

Piaget, J. (1930). *The child's conception of physical causality.* London: Routledge & Kegan Paul. (p. 71)

Piaget, J. (1932). *The moral judgment of the child.* New York: Harcourt, Brace & World. (p. 82)

Picchioni, M. M., & Murray, R. M. (2007). Schizophrenia. *British Medical Journal, 335,* 91–95. (p. 344)

Pido-Lopez, J., Imami, N., & Aspinall, R. (2001). Both age and gender affect thymic output: More recent thymic migrants in females than males as they age. *Clinical and Experimental Immunology, 125,* 409–413. (p. 277)

Piliavin, J. A. (2003). Doing well by doing good: Benefits for the benefactor. In C. L. M. Keyes & J. Haidt (Eds.), *Flourishing: Positive psychology and the life well-lived.* Washington, DC: American Psychological Association. (p. 83)

Pillemer, D. G. (1998). *Momentous events, vivid memories.* Cambridge, MA: Harvard University Press. (p. 91)

Pillsworth, E. G., & Haselton, M. G. (2006). Male sexual attractiveness predicts differential ovulatory shifts in female extra-pair attraction and male mate retention. *Evolution and Human Behavior, 27,* 247–258. (p. 107)

Pillsworth, E. G., Haselton, M. G., & Buss, D. M. (2004). Ovulatory shifts in female desire. *Journal of Sex Research, 41,* 55–65. (p. 107)

Pincus, H. A. (1997). Commentary: Spirituality, religion, and health: Expanding, and using the knowledge base. *Mind/Body Medicine, 2,* 49. (p. 288)

Pingitore, R., Dugoni, B. L., Tindale, R. S., & Spring, B. (1994). Bias against overweight job applicants in a simulated employment interview. *Journal of Applied Psychology, 79,* 909–917. (p. 245)

Pinker, S. (1995). The language instinct. *The General Psychologist, 31,* 63–65. (p. 218)

Pinker, S. (1998). Words and rules. *Lingua, 106,* 219–242. (p. 212)

Pinkerton, S. D., & Abramson, P. R. (1997). Condoms and the prevention of AIDS. *American Scientist, 85,* 364–373. (p. 108)

Pinstrup-Andersen, P., & Cheng, F. (2007). Still hungry. *Scientific American, 297,* 96–103. (p. 246)

Pipe, M-E., Lamb, M. E., Orbach, Y., & Esplin, P. W. (2004). Recent research on children's testimony about experienced and witnessed events. *Developmental Review, 24,* 440–468. (p. 198)

Pipher, M. (2002). *The middle of everywhere: The world's refugees come to our town.* New York: Harcourt Brace. (p. 249)

Pitman, R. K., & Delahanty, D. L. (2005). Conceptually driven pharmacologic approaches to acute trauma. *CNS Spectrums, 10*(2), 99–106. (p. 189)

Pitman, R. K., Sanders, K. M., Zusman, R. M., Healy, A. R., Cheema, F., Lasko, N. B., Cahill, L., & Orr, S. P. (2002). Pilot study of secondary prevention of posttraumatic stress disorder with propranolol. *Biological Psychiatry, 51,* 189–192. (p. 189)

Place, S. S., Todd, P. M., Penke, L., & Asendorph, J. B. (2009). The ability to judge the romantic interest of others. *Psychological Science, 20,* 22–26. (p. 260)

Plassmann, H., O'Doherty, J., Shiv, B., & Rangel, A. (2008). Marketing actions can modulate neural representations of experienced pleasantness. *Proceedings of the National Academy of Sciences, 105,* 1050–1054. (p. 146)

Plomin, R., & Daniels, D. (1987). Why are children in the same family so different from one another? *Behavioral and Brain Sciences, 10,* 1–60. (p. 86)

Plomin, R., & DeFries, J. C. (1998, May). The genetics of cognitive abilities and disabilities. *Scientific American,* pp. 62–69. (p. 227)

Plomin, R., & McGuffin, P. (2003). Psychopathology in the postgenomic era. *Annual Review of Psychology, 54,* 205–228. (p. 341)

Plomin, R., Corley, R., Caspi, A., Fulker, D. W., & DeFries, J. (1998). Adoption results for self-reported personality: Evidence for nonadditive genetic effects? *Journal of Personality and Social Psychology, 75,* 211–219. (p. 68)

Plomin, R., DeFries, J. C., McClearn, G. E., & Rutter, M. (1997). *Behavioral genetics.* New York: Freeman. (pp. 227, 346)

Plomin, R., Fulker, D. W., Corley, R., & DeFries, J. C. (1997). Nature, nurture and cognitive development from 1 to 16 years: A parent-offspring adoption study. *Psychological Science, 8,* 442–447. (p. 246)

Plotkin, H. (1994). *Darwin machines and the nature of knowledge.* Cambridge, MA: Harvard University Press. (p. 341)

Plous, S., & Herzog, H. A. (2000). Poll shows researchers favor lab animal protection. *Science, 290,* 711. (p. 19)

Poldrack, R. A., Halchenko, Y. O., & Hanson, S. J. (2009). Decoding the large-scale structure of brain function by classifying mental states across individuals. *Psychological Science, 20,* 1364–1372. (p. 35)

Polivy, J., & Herman, C. P. (1985). Dieting and binging: A causal analysis. *American Psychologist, 40,* 193–201. (p. 248)

Polivy, J., & Herman, C. P. (1987). Diagnosis and treatment of normal eating. *Journal of Personality and Social Psychology, 55,* 635–644. (p. 248)

Polivy, J., & Herman, C. P. (2002). Causes of eating disorders. *Annual Review of Psychology, 53,* 187–213. (p. 243)

Pollak, S., Cicchetti, D., & Klorman, R. (1998). Stress, memory, and emotion: Developmental considerations from the study of child maltreatment. *Developmental Psychopathology, 10,* 811–828. (p. 160)

Polusny, M. A., & Follette, V. M. (1995). Long-term correlates of child sexual abuse: Theory and review of the empirical literature. *Applied & Preventive Psychology, 4,* 143–166. (p. 78)

Poon, L. W. (1987). Myths and truisms: Beyond extant analyses of speed of behavior and age. Address to the Eastern Psychological Association convention. (p. 91)

Pope, H. G., & Yurgelun-Todd, D. (1996). The residual cognitive effects of heavy marijuana use in college students. *Journal of the American Medical Association, 275,* 521–527. (p. 335)

Popenoe, D. (1993). The evolution of marriage and the problem of stepfamilies: A biosocial perspective. Paper presented at the National Symposium on Stepfamilies, Pennsylvania State University. (p. 313)

Popenoe, D., & Whitehead, B. D. (2002). *Should we live together?* (2nd ed.). New Brunswick, NJ: The National Marriage Project, Rutgers University. (p. 93)

Popkin, B. M. (2007, September). The world is fat. *Scientific American,* pp. 88–95. (p. 246)

Porter, S., & Peace, K. A. (2007). The scars of memory: A prospective, longitudinal investigation of the consistency of traumatic and positive emotional memories in adulthood. *Psychological Science, 18,* 435–441. (p. 199)

Porter, S., Birt, A. R., Yuille, J. C., & Lehman, D. R. (2000, November). Negotiating false memories: Interviewer and rememberer characteristics relate to memory distortion. *Psychological Science, 11,* 507–510. (p. 197)

Posavac, H. D., Posavac, S. S., & Posavac, E. J. (1998). Exposure to media images of female attractiveness and concern with body weight among young women. *Sex Roles, 38,* 187–201. (p. 243)

Posner, M. I., & Carr, T. H. (1992). Lexical access and the brain: Anatomical constraints on cognitive models of word recognition. *American Journal of Psychology, 105,* 1–26. (p. 44)

Powell, K. E., Thompson, P. D., Caspersen, C. J., & Kendrick, J. S. (1987). Physical activity and the incidence of coronary heart disease. *Annual Review of Public Health, 8,* 253–287. (p. 285)

Powell, L. H., Schahabi, L., & Thoresen, C. E. (2003). Religion and spirituality: Linkages to physical health. *American Psychologist, 58,* 36–52. (p. 288)

Powell, R. A., & Boer, D. P. (1994). Did Freud mislead patients to confabulate memories of abuse? *Psychological Reports, 74,* 1283–1298. (p. 299)

Prentice, D. A., & Miller, D. T. (1993). Pluralistic ignorance and alcohol use on campus: Some consequences of misperceiving the social norm. *Journal of Personality and Social Psychology, 64,* 243–256. (p. 337)

Presley, C. A., Meilman, P. W., & Lyerla, R. (1997). *Alcohol and drugs on American college campuses: Issues of violence and harrassment.* Carbondale: Core Institute, Southern Illinois University. (p. 330)

Price, G. M., Uauq, R., Breeze, E., Bulpitt, C. J., & Fletcher, A. E. (2006). Weight, shape, and mortality risk in older persons: Elevated waist-hip ratio, not high body mass index, is associated with a greater risk of death. *American Journal of Clinical Nutrition, 84,* 449–460. (p. 244)

Prince Charles. (2000). BBC Reith Lecture. (p. 8)

Prioleau, L., Murdock, M., & Brody, N. (1983). An analysis of psychotherapy versus placebo studies. *The Behavioral and Brain Sciences, 6,* 275–310. (p. 363)

Pritchard, R. M. (1961, June). Stabilized images on the retina. *Scientific American,* pp. 72–78. (p. 126)

Pronin, E. (2007). Perception and misperception of bias in human judgment. *Trends in Cognitive Sciences, 11,* 37–43. (p. 311)

Pronin, E., & Ross, L. (2006). Temporal differences in trait self-ascription: When the self is seen as an other. *Journal of Personality and Social Psychology, 90,* 197–209. (p. 378)

Pronin, E., Berger, J., & Molouki, S. (2007). Alone in a crowd of sheep: Asymmetric perceptions of conformity and their roots in an introspection illusion. *Journal of Personality and Social Psychology, 92,* 585–595. (p. 383)

Pryor, J. H., Hurtado, S., DeAngelo, L., Blake, L. P., & Tran, S. (2010). *The American Freshman: National Norms Fall 2009; Expanded edition.* Higher Education Research Institute, UCLA. (p. 231)

Pryor, J. H., Hurtado, S., Saenz, V. B., Korn, J. S., Santos, J. L., & Korn, W. S. (2006). *The American freshman: National norms for fall 2006.* Los Angeles: UCLA Higher Education Research Institute. (p. 342)

Pryor, J. H., Hurtado, S., Saenz, V. B., Lindholm, J. A., Korn, W. S., & Mahoney, K. M. (2005). *The American freshman: National norms for Fall 2005.* Los Angeles: Higher Education Research Institute, UCLA. (p. 117)

Pryor, J. H., Hurtado, S., Sharkness, J., & Korn, W. S. (2007). *The American freshman: National norms for Fall 2007.* Los Angeles, UCLA Higher Education Research Institute. (p. 103)

Psychologist (2003, April). Who's the greatest? *The Psychologist, 16,* 17. (p. 75)

Puetz, T. W., O'Connor, P. J., & Dishman, R. K. (2006). Effects of chronic exercise on feelings of energy and fatigue: A quantitative synthesis. *Psychological Bulletin, 132,* 866-876. (p. 285)

Putnam, F. W. (1991). Recent research on multiple personality disorder. *Psychiatric Clinics of North America, 14,* 489–502. (p. 327)

Putnam, F. W. (1995). Rebuttal of Paul McHugh. *Journal of the American Academy of Child and Adolescent Psychiatry, 34,* 963. (p. 327)

Pyszczynski, T. A., Solomon, S., & Greenberg, J. (2002). *In the wake of 9/11: The psychology of terror.* Washington, DC: American Psychological Association. (p. 392)

Qirko, H. N. (2004) "Fictive kin" and suicide terrorism. *Science, 304,* 49–50. (p. 388)

Quinn, P. C., Bhatt, R. S., Brush, D., Grimes, A., & Sharpnack, H. (2002). Development of form similarity as a Gestalt grouping principle in infancy. *Psychological Science, 13,* 320–328. (p. 134)

Rabins, P., & 18 others. (2009). Scientific and ethical issues related to deep brain stimulation for disorders of mood, behavior, and thought. *Archives of General Psychiatry, 66,* 931–937. (p. 369)

Radin, D., Nelson, R., Dobyns, Y., & Houtkooper, J. (2006). Reexamining psychokinesis: Comment on Bösch, Steinkamp, and Boller (2006). *Psychological Bulletin, 132,* 529–532. (p. 150)

Rahman, Q., & Wilson, G. D. (2003). Born gay? The psychobiology of human sexual orientation. *Personality and Individual Differences, 34,* 1337–1382. (pp. 114, 115)

Raine, A. (1999). Murderous minds: Can we see the mark of Cain? *Cerebrum: The Dana Forum on Brain Science 1(1),* 15–29. (pp. 328, 394)

Raine, A. (2005). The interaction of biological and social measures in the explanation of antisocial and violent behavior. In D. M. Stoff & E. J. Susman (Eds.) *Developmental psychobiology of aggression.* New York: Cambridge University Press. (pp. 328, 394)

Raine, A., Lencz, T., Bihrle, S., LaCasse, L., & Colletti, P. (2000). Reduced prefrontal gray matter volume and reduced autonomic activity in antisocial personality disorder. *Archives of General Psychiatry, 57,* 119–127. (p. 328)

Ralston, A. (2004). Enough rope. Interview for ABC TV, Australia, by Andrew Denton (www.abc.net.au/enoughrope/stories/s1227885.htm). (p. 236)

Ramachandran, V. S., & Blakeslee, S. (1998). *Phantoms in the brain: Probing the mysteries of the human mind.* New York: Morrow. (pp. 32, 45)

Ramachandran, V. S., & Oberman, L. M. (2006, November). Broken mirrors: A theory of autism. *Scientific American,* pp. 63–69. (p. 174)

Ramirez, J. M., Bonniot-Cabanac, M-C., & Cabanac, M. (2005). Can aggression provide pleasure? *European Psychologist, 10,* 136–145. (p. 264)

Randi, J. (1999, February 4). 2000 club mailing list e-mail letter. (p. 150)

Rapoport, J. L. (1989, March). The biology of obsessions and compulsions. *Scientific American,* pp. 83–89. (p. 326)

Räsänen, S., Pakaslahti, A., Syvalahti, E., Jones, P. B., & Isohanni, M. (2000). Sex differences in schizophrenia: A review. *Nordic Journal of Psychiatry, 54,* 37–45. (p. 344)

Ray, J. (2005, April 12). U.S. teens walk away from anger: Boys and girls manage anger differently. *The Gallup Organization* (www.gallup.com). (p. 263)

Ray, O., & Ksir, C. (1990). *Drugs, society, and human behavior* (5th ed.). St. Louis: Times Mirror/Mosby. (p. 333)

Raynor, H. A., & Epstein, L. H. (2001). Dietary variety, energy regulation, and obesity. *Psychological Bulletin, 127,* 325–341. (p. 242)

Reason, J. (1987). The Chernobyl errors. *Bulletin of the British Psychological Society, 40,* 201–206. (p. 389)

Reason, J., & Mycielska, K. (1982). *Absent-minded? The psychology of mental lapses and everyday errors.* Englewood Cliffs, NJ: Prentice-Hall. (p. 127)

Reed, P. (2000). Serial position effects in recognition memory for odors. *Journal of Experimental Psychology: Learning, Memory, and Cognition, 26,* 411–422. (p. 184)

Reiner, W. G., & Gearhart, J. P. (2004). Discordant sexual identity in some genetic males with cloacal exstrophy assigned to female sex at birth. *New England Journal of Medicine, 350,* 333–341. (p. 104)

Reis, H. T., & Aron, A. (2008). Love: What is it, why does it matter, and how does it operate? *Perspectives on Psychological Science, 3,* 80–86. (p. 401)

Reisenzein, R. (1983). The Schachter theory of emotion: Two decades later. *Psychological Bulletin, 94,* 239–264. (p. 256)

Reiser, M. (1982). *Police psychology.* Los Angeles: LEHI. (p. 149)

Remley, A. (1988, October). From obedience to independence. *Psychology Today,* pp. 56–59. (p. 79)

Renner, M. J. (1992). Curiosity and exploration. In L. R. Squire (Ed.), *Encyclopedia of Learning and Memory.* New York: Macmillan. (p. 238)

Renner, M. J., & Renner, C. H. (1993). Expert and novice intuitive judgments about animal behavior. *Bulletin of the Psychonomic Society, 31,* 551–552. (p. 70)

Renner, M. J., & Rosenzweig, M. R. (1987). *Enriched and impoverished environments: Effects on brain and behavior.* New York: Springer-Verlag. (pp. 70, 71)

Rentfrow, P. J., & Gosling, S. D. (2003). The Do Re Mi's of everyday life: The structure and personality correlates of music preferences. *Journal of Personality and Social Psychology, 84,* 1236–1256. (p. 308)

Repetti, R. L., Taylor, S. E., & Seeman, T. E. (2002). Risky families: Family social environments and the mental and physical health of offspring. *Psychological Bulletin, 128,* 330–366. (p. 274)

Resnick, M. D., Bearman, P. S., Blum, R. W., Bauman, K. E., Harris, K. M., Jones, J., Tabor, J., Beuhring, T., Sieving, R., Shew, M., Bearinger, L. H., & Udry, J. R. (1997). Protecting adolescents from harm: Findings from the National Longitudinal Study on Adolescent Health. *Journal of the American Medical Association, 278,* 823–832. (pp. 14, 85)

Resnick, R. A., O'Regan, J. K., & Clark, J. J. (1997). To see or not to see: The need for attention to perceive changes in scenes. *Psychological Science, 8,* 368–373. (p. 50)

Resnick, S. M. (1992). Positron emission tomography in psychiatric illness. *Current Directions in Psychological Science, 1,* 92–98. (p. 345)

Reuters. (2000, July 5). Many teens regret decision to have sex (National Campaign to Prevent Teen Pregnancy survey). www.washingtonpost.com. (p. 109)

Reyna, V. F., & Farley, F. (2006). Risk and rationality in adolescent decision making: Implications for theory, practice, and public policy. *Psychological Science in the Public Interest, 7*(1), 1–44. (p. 82)

Rhoades, G. K., Stanley, S. M., & Markman, H. J. (2009). The pre-engagement cohabitation effect: A replication and extension of previous findings. *Journal of Family Psychology, 23,* 107–111. (p. 93)

Rhodes, S. R. (1983). Age-related differences in work attitudes and behavior: A review and conceptual analysis. *Psychological Bulletin, 93,* 328–367. (p. 91)

Rholes, W. S., Simpson, J. A., & Friedman, M. (2006). Avoidant attachment and the experience of parenting. *Personality and Social Psychology Bulletin, 32,* 275–285. (p. 78)

Richeson, J. A., & Shelton, J. N. (2007). Negotiating interracial interactions. *Current Directions in Psychological Science, 16,* 316–320. (p. 405)

Rieff, P. (1979). *Freud: The mind of a moralist* (3rd ed.). Chicago: University of Chicago Press. (p. 300)

Rieger, G., Chivers, M. L., & Bailey, J. M. (2005). Sexual arousal patterns of bisexual men. *Psychological Science, 16,* 579–584. (p. 112)

Riis, J., Loewenstein, G., Baron, J., Jepson, C., Fagerlin, A., & Ubel, P. A. (2005). Ignorance of hedonic adaptation to hemodialysis: A study using ecological momentary assessment. *Journal of Experimental Psychology: General, 134,* 3–9. (p. 265)

Riley, L. D., & Bowen, C. (2005). The sandwich generation: Challenges and coping strategies of multigenerational families. *The Family Journal, 13,* 52–58. (p. 87)

Rindermann, H., & Ceci, S. J. (2009). Educational policy and country outcomes in international cognitive competence studies. *Perspectives on Psychological Science, 4,* 551–577. (p. 230)

Ring, K. (1980). *Life at death: A scientific investigation of the near-death experience.* New York: Coward, McCann & Geoghegan. (p. 334)

Riskind, J. H., Beck, A. T., Berchick, R. J., Brown, G., & Steer, R. A. (1987). Reliability of DSM-III diagnoses for major depression and generalized anxiety disorder using the structured clinical interview for DSM-III. *Archives of General Psychiatry, 44,* 817–820. (p. 320)

Rizzolatti, G., Fadiga, L., Fogassi, L., & Gallese, V. (2002). From mirror neurons to imitation: Facts and speculations. In A. N. Meltzoff & W. Prinz (Eds.), *The imitative mind: Development, evolution, and brain bases.* Cambridge: Cambridge University Press, 2002. (p. 173)

Rizzolatti, G., Fogassi, L., & Gallese, V. (2006, November). Mirrors in the mind. *Scientific American,* pp. 54–61. (p. 173)

Roberts, B. W., Caspi, A., & Moffitt, T. E. (2001). The kids are alright: Growth and stability in personality development from adolescence to adulthood. *Journal of Personality and Social Psychology, 81,* 670–683. (p. 96)

Roberts, B. W., Caspi, A., & Moffitt, T. E. (2003). Work experiences and personality development in young adulthood. *Journal of Personality and Social Psychology, 84,* 582–593. (p. 96)

Roberts, B. W., Kuncel, N. R., Shiner, R., Caspi, A., & Goldberg, L. R. (2007). The power of personality: The comparative validity of personality traits, socioeconomic status, and cognitive ability for predicting important life outcomes. *Perspectives on Psychological Science, 2,* 313–345. (p. 308)

Roberts, B. W., Walton, K. E., & Viechtbauer, W. (2006). Patterns of mean-level change in personality traits across the life course: A meta-analysis of longitudinal studies. *Psychological Bulletin, 132,* 1–25. (p. 96)

Roberts, L. (1988). Beyond Noah's ark: What do we need to know? *Science, 242,* 1247. (p. 281)

Roberts, T.-A. (1991). Determinants of gender differences in responsiveness to others' evaluations. *Dissertation Abstracts International, 51*(8-B). (p. 103)

Robins, R. W., & Trzesniewski, K. H. (2005). Self-esteem development across the lifespan. *Current Directions in Psychological Science, 14*(3), 158–162. (p. 95)

Robins, R. W., Trzesniewski, K. H., Tracy, J. L., Gosling, S. D., & Potter, J. (2002). Global self-esteem across the lifespan. *Psychology and Aging, 17,* 423–434. (p. 85)

Robinson, F. P. (1970). *Effective study.* New York: Harper & Row. (p. 22)

Robinson, T. N. (1999). Reducing children's television viewing to prevent obesity. *Journal of the American Medical Association, 282,* 1561–1567. (p. 247)

Robinson, T. N., Borzekowski, D. L. G., Matheson, D. M., & Kraemer, H. C. (2007). Effects of fast food branding on young children's taste preferences. *Archives of Pediatric and Adolescent Medicine, 161,* 792–797. (p. 127)

Robinson, V. M. (1983). Humor and health. In P. E. McGhee & J. H. Goldstein (Eds.), *Handbook of humor research: Vol. II. Applied studies.* New York: Springer-Verlag. (p. 283)

Rochat, F. (1993). How did they resist authority? Protecting refugees in Le Chambon during World War II. Paper presented at the American Psychological Association convention. (p. 385)

Rock, I., & Palmer, S. (1990, December). The legacy of Gestalt psychology. *Scientific American,* pp. 84–90. (p. 134)

Rodin, J. (1986). Aging and health: Effects of the sense of control. *Science, 233,* 1271–1276. (p. 281)

Rodin, J. (1986). Aging and health: Effects of the sense of control. *Science, 233,* 1271–1276. (p. 281)

Roediger, H. L., III, & Karpicke, J. D. (2006). Test-enhanced learning: Taking memory tests improves long-term retention. *Psychological Science, 17,* 249–255., 184

Roediger, H. L., III, Wheeler, M. A., & Rajaram, S. (1993). Remembering, knowing, and reconstructing the past. In D. L. Medin (Ed.), *The psychology of learning and motivation: Advances in research and theory* (Vol. 30). Orlando, FL: Academic Press. (p. 196)

Roehling, M. V. (1999). Weight-based discrimination in employment: Psychological and legal aspects. *Personnel Psychology, 52,* 969–1016. (p. 245)

Roehling, M. V., Roehling, P. V., & Pichler, S. (2007). The relationship between body weight and perceived weight-related employment discrimination: The role of sex and race. *Journal of Vocational Behavior, 71,* 300–318. (p. 245)

Roehling, P. V., Roehling, M. V., & Moen, P. (2001). The relationship between work-life policies and practices and employee loyalty: A life course perspective. *Journal of Family and Economic Issues, 22,* 141–170. (p. 417)

Roelofs, T. (2010, September 22). Somali refugee takes oath of U.S. citizenship year after his brother. *Grand Rapids Press* (www.mlive.com). (p. 415)

Roenneberg, T., Kuehnle, T., Pramstaller, P. P., Ricken, J., Havel, M., Guth, A., & Merrow, M. (2004). A marker for the end of adolescence. *Current Biology, 14,* R1038–R1039. (p. 51)

Roese, N. J., & Summerville, A. (2005). What we regret most . . . and why. *Personality and Social Psychology Bulletin, 31,* 1273-1285. (p. 95)

Roesser, R. (1998). What you should know about hearing conservation. *Better Hearing Institute* (www.betterhearing.org). (p. 140)

Rogers, C. R. (1958). Reinhold Niebuhr's *The self and the dramas of history: A criticism. Pastoral Psychology, 9,* 15–17. (p. 311)

Rogers, C. R. (1961). *On becoming a person: A therapist's view of psychotherapy.* Boston: Houghton Mifflin. (p. 354)

Rogers, C. R. (1980). *A way of being.* Boston: Houghton Mifflin. (pp. 301, 302, 354)

Rohan, M. J., & Zanna, M. P. (1996). Value transmission in families. In C. Seligman, J. M. Olson, & M. P. Zanna (Eds.), *The psychology of values: The Ontario Symposium* (Vol. 8). Mahwah, NJ: Erlbaum. (p. 86)

Rohner, R. P. (1986). *The warmth dimension: Foundations of parental acceptance-rejection theory.* Newbury Park, CA: Sage. (p. 80)

Rohner, R. P., & Veneziano, R. A. (2001). The importance of father love: History and contemporary evidence. *Review of General Psychology, 5,* 382–405. (p. 77)

Roiser, J. P., Cook, L. J., Cooper, J. D., Rubinsztein, D. C., & Sahakian, B. J. (2005). Association of a functional polymorphism in the serotonin transporter gene with abnormal emotional processing in Ecstasy users. *American Journal of Psychiatry, 162,* 609–612. (p. 334)

Rosa-Alcázar, A. I., Sáncez-Meca, J., Gómez-Conesa, A., & Marín-Martínez, F. (2008). Psychological treatment of obsessive-compulsive disorder: A meta-analysis. *Clinical Psychology Review, 28,* 1310–1325. (p. 356)

Rose, A. J., & Rudolph, K. D. (2006). A review of sex differences in peer relationship processes: Potential trade-offs for the emotional and behavioral development of girls and boys. *Psychological Bulletin, 132,* 98–131. (p. 103)

Rose, J. S., Chassin, L., Presson, C. C., & Sherman, S. J. (1999). Peer influences on adolescent cigarette smoking: A prospective sibling analysis. *Merrill-Palmer Quarterly, 45,* 62–84. (p. 85)

Rose, R. J., Viken, R. J., Dick, D. M., Bates, J. E., Pulkkinen, L., & Kaprio, J. (2003). It *does* take a village: Nonfamiliar environments and children's behavior. *Psychological Science, 14,* 273–277. (p. 85)

Rose, S., Bisson, J., & Wessely, S. (2003). A systematic review of single-session psychological interventions ('debriefing') following trauma. *Psychotherapy and Psychosomatics, 72,* 176–184. (p. 324)

Roselli, C. E., Larkin, K., Schrunk, J. M., & Stormshak, F. (2004). Sexual partner preference, hypothalamic morphology and aromatase in rams. *Physiology and Behavior, 83,* 233–245. (p. 114)

Roselli, C. E., Resko, J. A., & Stormshak, F. (2002). Hormonal influences on sexual partner preference in rams. *Archives of Sexual Behavior, 31,* 43–49. (p. 114)

Rosenhan, D. L. (1973). On being sane in insane places. *Science, 179,* 250–258. (p. 321)

Rosenthal, R., Hall, J. A., Archer, D., DiMatteo, M. R., & Rogers, P. L. (1979). The PONS test: Measuring sensitivity to nonverbal cues. In S. Weitz (Ed.), *Nonverbal communication* (2nd ed.). New York: Oxford University Press. (pp. 230, 260)

Rosenzweig, M. R. (1984). Experience, memory, and the brain. *American Psychologist, 39,* 365–376. (pp. 70, 71)

Roseth, C. J., Johnson, D. W., & Johnson, R. T. (2008). Promoting early adolescents' achievement and peer relationships: The effects of cooperative, competitive, and individualistic goal structures. *Psychological Bulletin, 134,* 223–246. (p. 406)

Rossi, P. J. (1968). Adaptation and negative after effect to lateral optical displacement in newly hatched chicks. *Science, 160,* 430–432. (p. 139)

Rothbart, M. K. (2007). Temperament, development, and personality. *Current Directions in Psychological Science, 16,* 207–212. (p. 69)

Rothbart, M., Fulero, S., Jensen, C., Howard, J., & Birrell, P. (1978). From individual to group impressions: Availability heuristics in stereotype formation. *Journal of Experimental Social Psychology, 14,* 237–255. (p. 393)

Rothblum, E. D. (2007). Same-sex couples in legalized relationships: I do, or do I? Unpublished manuscript, Women's Studies Department, San Diego State University. (p. 117)

Rothman, A. J., & Salovey, P. (1997). Shaping perceptions to motivate healthy behavior: The role of message framing. *Psychological Bulletin, 121,* 3–19. (p. 210)

Rovee-Collier, C. (1989). The joy of kicking: Memories, motives, and mobiles. In P. R. Solomon, G. R. Goethals, C. M. Kelley, & B. R. Stephens (Eds.), *Memory: Interdisciplinary approaches.* New York: Springer-Verlag. (p. 71)

Rovee-Collier, C. (1999). The development of infant memory. *Current Directions in Psychological Science, 8,* 80–85. (p. 71)

Rowe, D. C. (1990). As the twig is bent? The myth of child-rearing influences on personality development. *Journal of Counseling and Development, 68,* 606–611. (p. 68)

Rowe, D. C. (2005). Under the skin: On the impartial treatment of genetic and environmental hypotheses of racial differences. *American Psychologist, 60*, 60–70. (p. 229)

Rowe, D. C., Almeida, D. M., & Jacobson, K. C. (1999). School context and genetic influences on aggression in adolescence. *Psychological Science, 10*, 277–280. (p. 393)

Rowe, D. C., Jacobson, K. C., & Van den Oord, E. J. C. G. (1999). Genetic and environmental influences on vocabulary IQ: Parental education level as moderator. *Child Development, 70*(5), 1151–1162. (p. 227)

Rozin, P., Dow, S., Mosovitch, M., & Rajaram, S. (1998). What causes humans to begin and end a meal? A role for memory for what has been eaten, as evidenced by a study of multiple meal eating in amnesic patients. *Psychological Science, 9*, 392–396. (p. 242)

Ruback, R. B., Carr, T. S., & Hopper, C. H. (1986). Perceived control in prison: Its relation to reported crowding, stress, and symptoms. *Journal of Applied Social Psychology, 16*, 375–386. (p. 281)

Rubenstein, J. S., Meyer, D. E., & Evans, J. E. (2001). Executive control of cognitive processes in task switching. *Journal of Experimental Psychology: Human Perception and Performance, 27*, 763–797. (p. 49)

Rubin, D. C., Rahhal, T. A., & Poon, L. W. (1998). Things learned in early adulthood are remembered best. *Memory and Cognition, 26*, 3–19. (p. 91)

Rubin, L. B. (1985). *Just friends: The role of friendship in our lives.* New York: Harper & Row. (p. 103)

Rubin, Z. (1970). Measurement of romantic love. *Journal of Personality and Social Psychology, 16*, 265–273. (p. 260)

Rubio, G., & López-Ibor, J. J. (2007). Generalized anxiety disorder: A 40-year follow-up study. *Acta Psychiatrica Scandinavica, 115*, 372–379. (p. 322)

Ruchlis, H. (1990). *Clear thinking: A practical introduction.* Buffalo, NY: Prometheus Books. (p. 206)

Ruffin, C. L. (1993). Stress and health—little hassles vs. major life events. *Australian Psychologist, 28*, 201–208. (p. 275)

Rule, B. G., & Ferguson, T. J. (1986). The effects of media violence on attitudes, emotions, and cognitions. *Journal of Social Issues, 42*(3), 29–50. (p. 177)

Rumbaugh, D. M. (1977). *Language learning by a chimpanzee: The Lana project.* New York: Academic Press. (p. 217)

Rumbaugh, D. M., & Savage-Rumbaugh, S. (1994, January/February). Language and apes. *Psychology Teacher Network*, pp. 2–5, 9. (p. 218)

Rumbaugh, D. M., & Washburn, D. A. (2003). *Intelligence of apes and other rational beings.* New Haven, CT: Yale University Press. (p. 218)

Rushton, J. P., & Jensen, A. R. (2010). Race and IQ: A theory-based review of the research in Richard Nisbett's *Intelligence and how to get it.* *The Open Psychology Journal, 3*, 9–35. (p. 228)

Ryan, R. M., & Deci, E. L. (2004). Avoiding death or engaging life as accounts of meaning and culture: Comment on Pyszczynski et al. (2004). *Psychological Bulletin, 130*, 473–477. (p. 310)

Ryckman, R. M., Robbins, M. A., Kaczor, L. M., & Gold J. A. (1989). Male and female raters' stereotyping of male and female physiques. *Personality and Social Psychology Bulletin, 15*, 244–251. (p. 244)

Saad, L. (2002, November 21). Most smokers wish they could quit. *Gallup News Service* (www.gallup.com). (p. 332)

Sabbagh, M. A., Xu, F., Carlson, S. M., Moses, L. J., & Lee, K. (2006). The development of executive functioning and theory of mind: A comparison of Chinese and U.S. preschoolers. *Psychological Science, 17*, 74–81. (p. 74)

Sabini, J. (1986). Stanley Milgram (1933–1984). *American Psychologist, 41*, 1378–1379. (p. 384)

Sachdev, P., & Sachdev, J. (1997). Sixty years of psychosurgery: Its present status and its future. *Australian and New Zealand Journal of Psychiatry, 31*, 457–464. (p. 370)

Sacks, O. (1985). *The man who mistook his wife for a hat.* New York: Summit Books. (pp. 147, 184)

Salmon, P. (2001). Effects of physical exercise on anxiety, depression, and sensitivity to stress: A unifying theory. *Clinical Psychology Review, 21*, 33–61. (p. 371)

Salovey, P. (1990, January/February). Interview. *American Scientist*, pp. 25–29. (p. 264)

Salovey, P., & Grewal, D. (2005). The science of emotional intelligence. *Current Directions in Psychological Science, 14*, 281–285. (p. 222)

Salthouse, T. A. (2004). What and when of cognitive aging. *Current Directions in Psychological Science, 13*, 140–144. (p. 92)

Sampson, E. E. (2000). Reinterpreting individualism and collectivism: Their religious roots and monologic versus dialogic person–other relationship. *American Psychologist, 55*, 1425–1432. (p. 312)

Sanders, G., & Wright, M. (1997). Sexual orientation differences in cerebral asymmetry and in the performance of sexually dimorphic cognitive and motor tasks. *Archives of Sexual Behavior, 26*, 463–479. (p. 115)

Sandfort, T. G. M., de Graaf, R., Bijl, R., & Schnabel, P. (2001). Same-sex sexual behavior and psychiatric disorders. *Archives of General Psychiatry, 58*, 85–91. (p. 112)

Sandkühler, S., & Bhattacharya, J. (2008). Deconstructing insight: EEG correlates of insightful problem solving. *PloS ONE, 3*, e1459 (www.plosone.org). (p. 206)

Sandler, W., Meir, I., Padden, C., & Aronoff, M. (2005). The emergence of grammar: Systematic structure in a new language. *Proceedings of the National Academy of Sciences, 102*, 2261–2265. (p. 214)

Sanford, A. J., Fray, N., Stewart, A., & Moxey, L. (2002). Perspective in statements of quantity, with implications for consumer psychology. *Psychological Science, 13*, 130–134. (p. 210)

Sanz, C., Blicher, A., Dalke, K., Gratton-Fabri, L., McClure-Richards, T., & Fouts, R. (1998, Winter-Spring). Enrichment object use: Five chimpanzees' use of temporary and semi-permanent enrichment objects. *Friends of Washoe, 19*(1,2), 9–14. (p. 217)

Sanz, C., Morgan, D., & Gulick, S. (2004). New insights into chimpanzees, tools, and termites from the Congo Basin. *American Naturalist, 164*, 567–581. (p. 216)

Sapadin, L. A. (1988). Friendship and gender: Perspectives of professional men and women. *Journal of Social and Personal Relationships, 5*, 387–403. (p. 103)

Sapolsky, B. S., & Tabarlet, J. O. (1991). Sex in primetime television: 1979 versus 1989. *Journal of Broadcasting and Electronic Media, 35*, 505–516. (p. 395)

Sapolsky, R. (2005). The influence of social hierarchy on primate health. *Science, 308*, 648–652. (p. 281)

Saulny, S. (2006, June 21). A legacy of the storm: Depression and suicide. *New York Times* (www.nytimes.com). (p. 274)

Savage-Rumbaugh, E. S., Murphy, J., Sevcik, R. A., Brakke, K. E., Williams, S. L., & Rumbaugh, D. M., with commentary by Bates, E. (1993). Language comprehension in ape and child. *Monographs of the Society for Research in Child Development, 58* (no. 233), 1–254. (p. 218)

Savage-Rumbaugh, S., Rumbaugh, D., & Fields, W. M. (2009). Empirical Kanzi: The ape language controversy revisited. *The Skeptic, 15*(1), 25–33. (p. 218)

Savic, I., Berglund, H., & Lindstrom, P. (2005). Brain response to putative pheromones in homosexual men. *Proceedings of the National Academy of Sciences, 102,* 7356–7361. (p. 114)

Savitsky, K., & Gilovich, T. (2003). The illusion of transparency and the alleviation of speech anxiety. *Journal of Experimental Social Psychology, 39,* 618–625. (p. 310)

Savitsky, K., Epley, N., & Gilovich, T. (2001). Do others judge us as harshly as we think? Overestimating the impact of our failures, shortcomings, and mishaps. *Journal of Personality and Social Psychology, 81,* 44–56. (p. 310)

Savoy, C., & Beitel, P. (1996). Mental imagery for basketball. *International Journal of Sport Psychology, 27,* 454–462. (p. 215)

Scarr, S. (1984, May). What's a parent to do? A conversation with E. Hall. *Psychology Today,* pp. 58–63. (p. 228)

Scarr, S. (1989). Protecting general intelligence: Constructs and consequences for interventions. In R. J. Linn (Ed.), *Intelligence: Measurement, theory, and public policy.* Champaign: University of Illinois Press. (p. 220)

Scarr, S. (1993, May/June). Quoted by *Psychology Today,* Nature's thumbprint: So long, superparents, p. 16. (p. 86)

Schab, F. R. (1991). Odor memory: Taking stock. *Psychological Bulletin, 109,* 242–251. (p. 147)

Schachter, S., & Singer, J. E. (1962). Cognitive, social and physiological determinants of emotional state. *Psychological Review, 69,* 379–399. (pp. 253, 256)

Schacter, D. L. (1992). Understanding implicit memory: A cognitive neuroscience approach. *American Psychologist, 47,* 559–569. (p. 185)

Schacter, D. L. (1996). *Searching for memory: The brain, the mind, and the past.* New York: Basic Books. (pp. 91, 185, 198, 299)

Schall, T., & Smith, G. (2000, Fall). Career trajectories in baseball. *Chance,* pp. 35–38. (p. 90)

Scheier, M. F., & Carver, C. S. (1992). Effects of optimism on psychological and physical well-being: Theoretical overview and empirical update. *Cognitive Therapy and Research, 16,* 201–228. (p. 283)

Schein, E. H. (1956). The Chinese indoctrination program for prisoners of war: A study of attempted brainwashing. *Psychiatry, 19,* 149–172. (p. 380)

Scherer, K. R., Banse, R., & Wallbott, H. G. (2001). Emotion inferences from vocal expression correlate across languages and cultures. *Journal of Cross-Cultural Psychology, 32,* 76–92. (p. 260)

Schiffenbauer, A., & Schiavo, R. S. (1976). Physical distance and attraction: An intensification effect. *Journal of Experimental Social Psychology, 12,* 274–282. (p. 387)

Schilt, T., de Win, M. M. L, Koeter, M., Jager, G., Korf, D. J., van den Brink, W., & Schmand, B. (2007). Cognition in novice ecstasy users with minimal exposure to other drugs. *Archives of General Psychiatry, 64,* 728–736. (p. 334)

Schimel, J., Arndt, J., Pyszczynski, T., & Greenberg, J. (2001). Being accepted for who we are: Evidence that social validation of the intrinsic self reduces general defensiveness. *Journal of Personality and Social Psychology, 80,* 35–52. (p. 303)

Schkade, D., Sunstein, C. R., & Hastie, R. (2006). *What happened on deliberation day?* (University of Chicago Law and Economics, Olin Working Paper No. 298.) (p. 388)

Schloss, J. (2009). Totally, for a Martian. Essay for "Does evolution explain human nature," Templeton Foundation, http://www.templeton.org/evolution. (p. 116)

Schmitt, D. P. (2005). Sociosexuality from Argentina to Zimbabwe: A 48-nation study of sex, culture, and strategies of human mating. *Behavioral and Brain Sciences, 28,* 247–311. (p. 116)

Schmitt, D. P., & Allik, J. (2005). Simultaneous administration of the Rosenberg Self-esteem Scale in 53 nations: Exploring the universal and culture-specific features of global self-esteem. *Journal of Personality and Social Psychology, 89,* 623–642. (p. 311)

Schmitt, D. P., Allik, J., McCrae, R. R., & Benet-Martínez, V., with many others. (2007). The geographic distribution of Big Five personality traits: Patterns and profiles of human self-description across 56 nations. *Journal of Cross-Cultural Psychology, 38,* 173–212. (p. 305)

Schnall, E., Wassertheil-Smnoller, S., Swencionis, C., Zemon, V., Tinker, L., O'Sullivan, M. J., Van Horn, L., & Goodwin, M. (2010). The relationship between religion and cardiovascular outcomes and all-cause mortality in the women's health initiative observational study. *Psychology and Health, 25,* 249–263. (p. 287)

Schnaper, N. (1980). Comments germane to the paper entitled "The reality of death experiences" by Ernst Rodin. *Journal of Nervous and Mental Disease, 168,* 268–270. (p. 334)

Schneider, S. L. (2001). In search of realistic optimism: Meaning, knowledge, and warm fuzziness. *American Psychologist, 56,* 250–263. (p. 283)

Schneiderman, N. (1999). Behavioral medicine and the management of HIV/AIDS. *International Journal of Behavioral Medicine, 6,* 3–12. (p. 278)

Schneier, B. (2007, May 17). Virginia Tech lesson: Rare risks breed irrational responses. *Wired* (www.wired.com). (p. 208)

Schoenborn, C. A., & Adams, P. F. (2008). Sleep duration as a correlate of smoking, alcohol use, leisure-time physical inactivity, and obesity among adults: United States, 2004–2006. *Centers for Disease Control and Prevention.* (www.cdc.gov/nchs). (p. 55)

Schoeneman, T. J. (1994). Individualism. In V. S. Ramachandran (Ed.), *Encyclopedia of human behavior.* San Diego: Academic Press. (p. 312)

Schofield, J. W. (1986). Black-White contact in desegregated schools. In M. Hewstone & R. Brown (Eds.), *Contact and conflict in intergroup encounters.* Oxford: Basil Blackwell. (p. 405)

Schonfield, D., & Robertson, B. A. (1966). Memory storage and aging. *Canadian Journal of Psychology, 20,* 228–236. (p. 92)

Schooler, J. W., Gerhard, D., & Loftus, E. F. (1986). Qualities of the unreal. *Journal of Experimental Psychology: Learning, Memory, and Cognition, 12,* 171–181. (p. 196)

Schuman, H., & Scott, J. (June, 1989). Generations and collective memories. *American Sociological Review, 54*(3), 359–381. (p. 91)

Schwartz, B. (1984). *Psychology of learning and behavior* (2nd ed.). New York: Norton. (p. 325)

Schwartz, B. (2000). Self-determination: The tyranny of freedom. *American Psychologist, 55,* 79–88. (p. 282)

Schwartz, B. (2004). *The paradox of choice: Why more is less.* New York: Ecco/HarperCollins. (p. 282)

Schwartz, B., & Rubel, T. (2005). Sex differences in value priorities: Cross-cultural and multimethod studies. *Journal of Personality and Social Psychology, 89,* 1010–1028. (p. 102)

Schwartz, J. M., Stoessel, P. W., Baxter, L. R., Jr., Martin, K. M., & Phelps, M. E. (1996). Systematic changes in cerebral glucose metabolic rate after successful behavior modification treatment of obsessive-compulsive disorder. *Archives of General Psychiatry, 53,* 109–113. (pp. 359, 371)

Schwartz, J., & Estrin, J. (2004, November 7). Living for today, locked in a paralyzed body. *New York Times* (www.nytimes.com). (p. 265)

Schwartz, S. H., & Rugel-Lifschitz, T. (2009). Cross-national variation in the size of sex differences in values: Effects of gender equality. *Journal of Personality and Social Psychology, 97,* 171–185. (p. 103)

Schwarz, N., Strack, F., Kommer, D., & Wagner, D. (1987). Soccer, rooms, and the quality of your life: Mood effects on judgments of satisfaction with life in general and with specific domains. *European Journal of Social Psychology, 17,* 69–79. (p. 191)

Sclafani, A. (1995). How food preferences are learned: Laboratory animal models. *Proceedings of the Nutrition Society, 54,* 419–427. (p. 243)

Scott, D. J., & others. (2004, November 9). U-M team reports evidence that smoking affects human brain's natural "feel good" chemical system (press release by Kara Gavin). *University of Michigan Medical School.* (www.med.umich.edu). (p. 332)

Scott, W. A., Scott, R., & McCabe, M. (1991). Family relationships and children's personality: A cross-cultural, cross-source comparison. *British Journal of Social Psychology, 30,* 1–20. (p. 80)

Sdorow, L. M. (2005). The people behind psychology. In B. Perlman, L. McCann, & W. Buskist (Eds.), *Voices of experience: Memorable talks from the National Institute on the Teaching of Psychology.* Washington, DC: American Psychological Society. (p. 298)

Seal, K. H., Bertenthal, D., Miner, C. R., Sen, S., & Marmar, C. (2007). Bringing the war back home: Mental health disorders among 103,788 U.S. veterans returning from Iraq and Afghanistan seen at Department of Veterans Affairs facilities. *Archives of Internal Medicine, 167,* 467–482. (p. 324)

Sechrest, L., Stickle, T. R., & Stewart, M. (1998). The role of assessment in clinical psychology. In A. Bellack, M. Hersen (series eds.), & C. R. Reynolds (vol. ed.), *Comprehensive clinical psychology: Vol. 4. Assessment.* New York: Pergamon. (p. 298)

Seeman, P. (2007). Dopamine and schizophrenia. *Scholarpedia, 2*(10), 3634 (www.scholarpedia.org). (p. 345)

Seeman, P., Guan, H-C., & Van Tol, H. H. M. (1993). Dopamine D4 receptors elevated in schizophrenia. *Nature, 365,* 441–445. (p. 345)

Segall, M. H., Dasen, P. R., Berry, J. W., & Poortinga, Y. H. (1990). *Human behavior in global perspective: An introduction to cross-cultural psychology.* New York: Pergamon. (p. 75)

Segerstrom, S. C., Taylor, S. E., Kemeny, M. E., & Fahey, J. L. (1998). Optimism is associated with mood, coping, and immune change in response to stress. *Journal of Personality and Social Psychology, 74,* 1646–1655. (p. 283)

Seidlitz, L., & Diener, E. (1998). Sex differences in the recall of affective experiences. *Journal of Personality and Social Psychology, 74,* 262–271. (p. 342)

Self, C. E. (1994). *Moral culture and victimization in residence halls.* Dissertation: Thesis (M.A.). Bowling Green University. (p. 337)

Seligman, M. E. P. (1975). *Helplessness: On depression, development and death.* San Francisco: Freeman. (p. 281)

Seligman, M. E. P. (1991). *Learned optimism.* New York: Knopf. (pp. 281, 342)

Seligman, M. E. P. (1994). *What you can change and what you can't.* New York: Knopf. (pp. 285, 300, 310)

Seligman, M. E. P. (1995). The effectiveness of psychotherapy: The Consumer Reports study. *American Psychologist, 50,* 965–974. (pp. 361, 362)

Seligman, M. E. P. (2002). *Authentic happiness: Using the new positive psychology to realize your potential for lasting fulfillment.* New York: Free Press. (pp. 8, 310)

Seligman, M. E. P., & Yellen, A. (1987). What is a dream? *Behavior Research and Therapy, 25,* 1–24. (p. 51)

Seligman, M. E. P., Steen, T. A., Park, N., & Peterson, C. (2005). Positive psychology progress: Empirical validation of interventions. *American Psychologist, 60,* 410–421. (pp. 8, 269)

Sellers, H. (2010). *You don't look like anyone I know.* New York: Riverhead Books. (p. 122)

Selye, H. (1936). A syndrome produced by diverse nocuous agents. *Nature, 138,* 32. (p. 275)

Selye, H. (1976). *The stress of life.* New York: McGraw-Hill. (p. 275)

Senate Intelligence Committee (2004, July 9). *Report of the select committee on intelligence on the U.S. intelligence community's prewar intelligence assessments on Iraq.* Washington, DC: Author. (pp. 209, 389)

Senghas, A., & Coppola, M. (2001). Children creating language: How Nicaraguan Sign Language acquired a spatial grammar. *Psychological Science, 12,* 323–328. (p. 214)

Sengupta, S. (2001, October 10). Sept. 11 attack narrows the racial divide. *New York Times* (www.nytimes.com). (p. 405)

Senju, A., Maeda, M., Kikuchi, Y., Hasegawa, T., Tojo, Y., & Osanai, H. (2007). Absence of contagious yawning in children with autism spectrum disorder. *Biology Letters, 3,* 706–708. (p. 174)

Serdula, M. K., Mokdad, A., Williamson, D. F., Galuska, D. A., Mendlein, J. M., & Heath, G. W. (1999). Prevalence of attempting weight loss and strategies for controlling weight. *Journal of the American Medical Association, 282,* 1353–1358. (p. 248)

Service, R. F. (1994). Will a new type of drug make memory-making easier? *Science, 266,* 218–219. (p. 188)

Shadish, W. R., & Baldwin, S. A. (2005). Effects of behavioral marital therapy: A meta-analysis of randomized controlled trials. *Journal of Consulting and Clinical Psychology, 73,* 6–14. (p. 362)

Shadish, W. R., Matt, G. E., Navarro, A. M., & Phillips, G. (2000). The effects of psychological therapies under clinically representative conditions: A meta-analysis. *Psychological Bulletin, 126,* 512–529. (p. 362)

Shafir, E., & LeBoeuf, R. A. (2002). Rationality. *Annual Review of Psychology, 53,* 491–517. (p. 210)

Shamir, B., House, R. J., & Arthur, M. B. (1993). The motivational effects of charismatic leadership: A self-concept based theory. *Organizational Science, 4*(4), 577–594. (p. 416)

Shamir, B., House, R. J., & Arthur, M. B. (1993). The motivational effects of charismatic leadership: A self-concept based theory. *Organizational Science, 4*(4), 577–594. (p. 416)

Shanahan, L., McHale, S. M., Osgood, D. W., & Crouter, A. C. (2007). Conflict frequency with mothers and fathers from middle childhood to late adolescence: Within- and between-families comparisons. *Developmental Psychology, 43,* 539–550. (p. 85)

Shapiro, D. (1999). *Psychotherapy of neurotic character.* New York: Basic Books. (p. 353)

Sharma, A. R., McGue, M. K., & Benson, P. L. (1998). The psychological adjustment of United States adopted adolescents and their nonadopted siblings. *Child Development, 69,* 791–802. (p. 86)

Shaver, P. R., & Mikulincer, M. (2007). Adult attachment strategies and the regulation of emotion. In J. J. Gross (Ed.), *Handbook of emotion regulation.* New York: Guilford Press. (p. 78)

Sheehan, S. (1982). *Is there no place on earth for me?* Boston: Houghton Mifflin. (p. 344)

Sheldon, K. M., & Niemiec, C. P. (2006). It's not just the amount that counts: Balanced need satisfaction also affects well-being. *Journal of Personality and Social Psychology, 91,* 331–341. (p. 249)

Shenton, M. E. (1992). Abnormalities of the left temporal lobe and thought disorder in schizophrenia: A quantitative magnetic resonance imaging study. *New England Journal of Medicine, 327,* 604–612. (p. 345)

Shepard, R. N. (1990). *Mind sights.* New York: Freeman. (p. 20)

Shepherd, C. (1999, June). News of the weird. *Funny Times*, p. 21. (p. 246)

Sherif, M. (1966). *In common predicament: Social psychology of intergroup conflict and cooperation*. Boston: Houghton Mifflin. (p. 405)

Sherman, P. W., & Flaxman, S. M. (2001). Protecting ourselves from food. *American Scientist, 89*, 142–151. (p. 244)

Sherry, S. B., & Hall, P. A. (2009). The perfectionism model of binge eating: Tests of an integrative model. *Journal of Personality and Social Psychology, 96*, 690–709. (p. 243)

Shettleworth, S. J. (1973). Food reinforcement and the organization of behavior in golden hamsters. In R. A. Hinde & J. Stevenson-Hinde (Eds.), *Constraints on learning*. London: Academic Press. (p. 171)

Shettleworth, S. J. (1993). Where is the comparison in comparative cognition? Alternative research programs. *Psychological Science, 4*, 179–184. (p. 188)

Showers, C. (1992). The motivational and emotional consequences of considering positive or negative possibilities for an upcoming event. *Journal of Personality and Social Psychology, 63*, 474–484. (p. 283)

Siegel, J. M. (2003, November). Why we sleep. *Scientific American*, pp. 92–97. (p. 54)

Siegel, R. K. (1977, October). Hallucinations. *Scientific American*, pp. 132–140. (p. 334)

Siegel, R. K. (1980). The psychology of life after death. *American Psychologist, 35*, 911–931. (p. 334)

Siegel, R. K. (1982, October). Quoted by J. Hooper, Mind tripping. *Omni*, pp. 72–82, 159–160. (p. 334)

Siegel, R. K. (1984, March 15). Personal communication. (p. 334)

Siegel, R. K. (1990). *Intoxication*. New York: Pocket Books. (pp. 333, 334)

Siegel, S. (2005). Drug tolerance, drug addiction, and drug anticipation. *Current Directions in Psychological Science, 14*, 296–300. (p. 156)

Siegler, R. S., & Ellis, S. (1996). Piaget on childhood. *Psychological Science, 7*, 211–215. (p. 72)

Silbersweig, D. A., Stern, E., Frith, C., Cahill, C., Holmes, A., Grootoonk, S., Seaward, J., McKenna, P., Chua, S. E., Schnorr, L., Jones, T., & Frackowiak, R. S. J. (1995). A functional neuroanatomy of hallucinations in schizophrenia. *Nature, 378*, 176–179. (p. 345)

Silva, A. J., Stevens, C. F., Tonegawa, S., & Wang, Y. (1992). Deficient hippocampal long-term potentiation in alpha-calcium-calmodulin kinase II mutant mice. *Science, 257*, 201–206. (p. 188)

Silva, C. E., & Kirsch, I. (1992). Interpretive sets, expectancy, fantasy proneness, and dissociation as predictors of hypnotic response. *Journal of Personality and Social Psychology, 63*, 847–856. (p. 144)

Silver, M., & Geller, D. (1978). On the irrelevance of evil: The organization and individual action. *Journal of Social Issues, 34*, 125–136. (p. 386)

Silver, N. (2009, December 27). The odds of airborne terror. www.fivethirtyeight.com. (p. 208)

Silverman, J. (2008, September 8). (2008, September 8). Quoted by A. Zaharov-Reutt, Skype: The "wow" started 5 years ago. www.itwire.com. (p. 248)

Silverman, K., Evans, S. M., Strain, E. C., & Griffiths, R. R. (1992). Withdrawal syndrome after the double-blind cessation of caffeine consumption. *New England Journal of Medicine, 327*, 1109–1114. (p. 332)

Simon, G. E., & Savarino, J. (2007). Suicide attempts among patients starting depression treatment with medications or psychotherapy. *American Journal of Psychiatry, 164*, 1029–1034. (p. 368)

Simon, H. (2001, February). Quoted by A. M. Hayashi, "When to trust your gut." *Harvard Business Review*, pp. 59–65. (p. 211)

Simons, D. J. (1996). In sight, out of mind: When object representations fail. *Psychological Science, 7*, 301–305. (p. 50)

Simons, D. J., & Ambinder, M. S. (2005). Change blindness: Theory and consequences. *Current Directions in Psychological Science, 14*, 44–48. (p. 50)

Simons, D. J., & Chabris, C. F. (1999). Gorillas in our midst: Sustained inattentional blindness for dynamic events. *Perception, 28*, 1059–1074. (p. 49)

Simonton, D. K. (1988). Age and outstanding achievement: What do we know after a century of research? *Psychological Bulletin, 104*, 251–267. (p. 92)

Simonton, D. K. (1990). Creativity in the later years: Optimistic prospects for achievement. *The Gerontologist, 30*, 626–631. (p. 92)

Simonton, D. K. (1992). The social context of career success and course for 2,026 scientists and inventors. *Personality and Social Psychology Bulletin, 18*, 452–463. (p. 222)

Simonton, D. K. (2000). Creativity: Cognitive, personal, developmental, and social aspects. *American Psychologist, 55*, 151–158. (p. 221)

Sin, N. L., & Lyubomirsky, S. (2009). Enhancing well-being and alleviating depressive symptoms with positive psychology interventions: A practice-friendly meta-analysis. *Journal of Clinical Psychology: In session, 65*, 467–487. (p. 268)

Sinclair, R. C., Hoffman, C., Mark, M. M., Martin, L. L., & Pickering, T. L. (1994). Construct accessibility and the misattribution of arousal: Schachter and Singer revisited. *Psychological Science, 5*, 15–18. (p. 256)

Singelis, T. M., & Sharkey, W. F. (1995). Culture, self-construal, and embarrassability. *Cross-Cultural Psychology, 26*, 622–644. (p. 312)

Singelis, T. M., Bond, M. H., Sharkey, W. F., & Lai, C. S. Y. (1999). Unpackaging culture's influence on self-esteem and embarrassability: The role of self-construals. *Journal of Cross-Cultural Psychology, 30*, 315–341. (p. 312)

Singer, T., Seymour, B., O'Doherty, J., Kaube, H., Dolan, R. J., & Frith, C. (2004). Empathy for pain involves the affective but not sensory components of pain. *Science, 303*, 1157–1162. (p. 174)

Singh, D. (1995). Female health, attractiveness, and desirability for relationships: Role of breast asymmetry and waist-to-hip ratio. *Ethology and Sociobiology, 16*, 465–481. (p. 117)

Singh, S. (1997). *Fermat's enigma: The epic quest to solve the world's greatest mathematical problem*. New York: Bantam Books. (p. 221)

Singh, S., & Riber, K. A. (1997, November). Fermat's last stand. *Scientific American*, pp. 68–73. (p. 222)

Sipski, M. L., & Alexander, C. J. (1999). Sexual response in women with spinal cord injuries: Implications for our understanding of the able bodied. *Journal of Sex and Marital Therapy, 25*, 11–22. (p. 33)

Sjöstrum, L. (1980). Fat cells and body weight. In A. J. Stunkard (Ed.), *Obesity*. Philadelphia: Saunders. (p. 246)

Skinner, B. F. (1953). *Science and human behavior*. New York: Macmillan. (p. 164)

Skinner, B. F. (1956). A case history in scientific method. *American Psychologist, 11*, 221–233. (p. 165)

Skinner, B. F. (1961, November). Teaching machines. *Scientific American*, pp. 91–102. (p. 164)

Skinner, B. F. (1983, September). Origins of a behaviorist. *Psychology Today*, pp. 22–33. (p. 167)

Skinner, B. F. (1986). What is wrong with daily life in the Western world? *American Psychologist, 41*, 568–574. (p. 167)

Skinner, B. F. (1988). The school of the future. Address to the American Psychological Association convention. (p. 167)

Skinner, B. F. (1989). Teaching machines. *Science, 243*, 1535. (p. 167)

Skitka, L. J., Bauman, C. W., & Mullen, E. (2004). Political tolerance and coming to psychological closure following the September 11, 2001, terrorist attacks: An integrative approach. *Personality and Social Psychology Bulletin, 30,* 743–756. (p. 263)

Sklar, L. S., & Anisman, H. (1981). Stress and cancer. *Psychological Bulletin, 89,* 369–406. (p. 278)

Skov, R. B., & Sherman, S. J. (1986). Information-gathering processes: Diagnosticity, hypothesis-confirmatory strategies, and perceived hypothesis confirmation. *Journal of Experimental Social Psychology, 22,* 93–121. (p. 209)

Sloan, R. P. (2005). *Field analysis of the literature on religion, spirituality, and health.* Columbia University (available at www.metanexus.net/tarp). (p. 287)

Sloan, R. P., & Bagiela E. (2002). Claims about religious involvement and health outcomes. *Annals of Behavioral Medicine, 24,* 14–21. (p. 287)

Sloan, R. P., Bagiella, E., & Powell, T. (1999). Religion, spirituality, and medicine. *Lancet, 353,* 664–667. (p. 287)

Sloan, R. P., Bagiella, E., VandeCreek, L., & Poulos, P. (2000). Should physicians prescribe religious activities? *New England Journal of Medicine, 342,* 1913–1917. (p. 287)

Slutske, W. S. (2005). Alcohol use disorders among U.S. college students and their non-college-attending peers. *Archives of General Psychiatry, 62,* 321–327. (p. 331)

Small, M. F. (1997). Making connections. *American Scientist, 85,* 502–504. (p. 80)

Small, M. F. (2002, July). What you can learn from drunk monkeys. *Discover,* pp. 40–45. (p. 336)

Smedley, A., & Smedley, B. D. (2005). Race as biology is fiction, racism as a social problem is real: Anthropological and historical perspectives on the social construction of race. *American Psychologist, 60,* 16–26. (p. 229)

Smelser, N. J., & Mitchell, F. (Eds.) (2002). *Terrorism: Perspectives from the behavioral and social sciences.* Washington, DC: National Research Council, National Academies Press. (p. 393)

Smith, A. (1983). Personal correspondence. (p. 345)

Smith, D. M., Loewenstein, G., Jankovic, A., & Ubel, P. A. (2009). Happily hopeless: Adaptation to a permanent, but not to a temporary, disability. *Health Psychology, 28,* 787–791. (p. 265)

Smith, E., & Delargy, M. (2005). Locked-in syndrome. *British Medical Journal, 330,* 406–409. (p. 265)

Smith, J. E., Waldorf, V. A., & Trembath, D. L. (1990). "Single white male looking for thin, very attractive . . ." *Sex Roles, 23,* 675–685. (p. 245)

Smith, M. B. (1978). Psychology and values. *Journal of Social Issues, 34,* 181–199. (p. 303)

Smith, M. L., & Glass, G. V. (1977). Meta-analysis of psychotherapy outcome studies. *American Psychologist, 32,* 752–760. (p. 362)

Smith, M. L., Glass, G. V., & Miller, R. L. (1980). *The benefits of psychotherapy.* Baltimore: Johns Hopkins Press. (p. 362)

Smith, P. B., & Tayeb, M. (1989). Organizational structure and processes. In M. Bond (Ed.), *The cross-cultural challenge to social psychology.* Newbury Park, CA: Sage. (p. 417)

Smith, P. F. (1995). Cannabis and the brain. *New Zealand Journal of Psychology, 24,* 5–12. (p. 335)

Smith, S. J., Axelton, A. M., & Saucier, D. A. (2009). The effects of contact on sexual prejudice: A meta-analysis. *Sex Roles, 61,* 178–191. (p. 405)

Smith, T. B., Bartz, J., & Richards, P. S. (2007). Outcomes of religious and spiritual adaptations to psychotherapy: A meta-analytic review. *Psychotherapy Research, 17,* 643–655. (p. 364)

Smith, T. W. (1998, December). *American sexual behavior: Trends, sociodemographic differences, and risk behavior.* (National Opinion Research Center GSS Topical Report No. 25). (pp. 107, 113)

Smith, T. W. (2006). Personality as risk and resilience in physical health. *Current Directions in Psychological Science, 15,* 227–231. (p. 279)

Smoreda, Z., & Licoppe, C. (2000). Gender-specific use of the domestic telephone. *Social Psychology Quarterly, 63,* 238–252. (p. 103)

Snarey, J. R. (1985). Cross-cultural universality of social-moral development: A critical review of Kohlbergian research. *Psychological Bulletin, 97,* 202–233. (p. 82)

Snarey, J. R. (1987, June). A question of morality. *Psychology Today,* pp. 6–7. (p. 82)

Snedeker, J., Geren, J., & Shafto, C. L. (2007). Starting over: International adoption as a natural experiment in language development. *Psychological Science, 18,* 79–86. (p. 214)

Snodgrass, S. E., Higgins, J. G., & Todisco, L. (1986). The effects of walking behavior on mood. Paper presented at the American Psychological Association convention. (p. 263)

Snyder, F., & Scott, J. (1972). The psychophysiology of sleep. In N. S. Greenfield & R. A. Sterbach (Eds.), *Handbook of psychophysiology.* New York: Holt, Rinehart & Winston. (p. 54)

Snyder, M. (1984). When belief creates reality. In L. Berkowitz (Ed.), *Advances in experimental social psychology* (Vol. 18). New York: Academic Press. (p. 321)

Snyder, S. H. (1984). Neurosciences: An integrative discipline. *Science, 225,* 1255–1257. (p. 28)

Snyder, S. H. (1986). *Drugs and the brain.* New York: Scientific American Library. (p. 368)

Solomon, D. A., Keitner, G. I., Miller, I. W., Shea, M. T., & Keller, M. B. (1995). Course of illness and maintenance treatments for patients with bipolar disorder. *Journal of Clinical Psychiatry, 56,* 5–13. (p. 368)

Solomon, J. (1996, May 20). Breaking the silence. *Newsweek,* pp. 20–22. (p. 321)

Solomon, M. (1987, December). Standard issue. *Psychology Today,* pp. 30–31. (p. 399)

Søndergård, L., Kvist, K., Andersen, P. K., & Kessing, L. V. (2006a). Do antidepressants precipitate youth suicide? A nationwide pharmacoepidemiological study. *European Journal of Adolescent Psychiatry, 15,* 232–240. (p. 368)

Søndergård, L., Kvist, K., Andersen, P. K., & Kessing, L. V. (2006b). Do antidepressants prevent suicide? *International Clinical Psychopharmacology, 21,* 211–218. (p. 368)

Søndergård, L., Kvist, K., Lopez, A. G., Andersen, P. K., & Kessing, L. V. (2006). Temporal changes in suicide rates for persons treated and not treated with antidepressants in Denmark during 1995–1999. *Acta Psychiatrica Scandinavica, 114,* 168–176. (p. 368)

Song, S. (2006, March 27). Mind over medicine. *Time,* p. 47. (p. 145)

Sørensen, H. J., Mortensen, E. L., Reinisch, J. M., & Mednick, S. A. (2005). Breastfeeding and risk of schizophrenia in the Copenhagen Perinatal Cohort. *Acta Psychiatrica Scandinavica, 112,* 26–29. (p. 344)

Sørensen, H. J., Mortensen, E. L., Reinisch, J. M., & Mednick, S. A. (2006). Height, weight, and body mass index in early adulthood and risk of schizophrenia. *Acta Psychiatrica Scandinavica, 114,* 49–54. (p. 344)

Spanos, N. P., & Coe, W. C. (1992). A social-psychological approach to hypnosis. In E. Fromm & M. R. Nash (Eds.), *Contemporary hypnosis research.* New York: Guilford. (p. 145)

Spencer, S. J., Steele, C. M., & Quinn, D. M. (1999). Stereotype threat and women's math performance. *Journal of Experimental Social Psychology, 3,* 4–28. (p. 232)

Sperling, G. (1960). The information available in brief visual presentations. *Psychological Monographs, 74* (Whole No. 498). (p. 187)

Sperry, R. W. (1964). Problems outstanding in the evolution of brain function. James Arthur Lecture, American Museum of Natural History, New York. Cited by R. Ornstein (1977), *The psychology of consciousness* (2nd ed.). New York: Harcourt Brace Jovanovich. (p. 47)

Speulda, N., & McIntosh, M. (2004, May 13). Global gender gaps. Pew Global Attitudes Project. Pew Research Center (pewglobal.org). (p. 107)

Spiegel, D. (2008, January 31). Coming apart: Trauma and the fragmentation of the self. *Dana Foundation* (www.dana.org). (p. 327)

Spiegel, K., Leproult, R., & Van Cauter, E. (1999). Impact of sleep debt on metabolic and endrocrine function. *Lancet, 354,* 1435–1439. (p. 54)

Spiegel, K., Leproult, R., L'Hermite-Balériaux, M., Copinschi, G., Penev, P. D., & Van Cauter, E. (2004). Leptin levels are dependent on sleep duration: Relationships with sympathovagal balance, carbohydrate regulation, cortisol, and thyrotropin. *Journal of Clinical Endocrinology and Metabolism, 89,* 5762–5771. (p. 55)

Spielberger, C., & London, P. (1982). Rage boomerangs. *American Health, 1,* 52–56. (p. 280)

Sprecher, S. (1989). The importance to males and females of physical attractiveness, earning potential, and expressiveness in initial attraction. *Sex Roles, 21,* 591–607. (p. 399)

Sprecher, S., & Sedikides, C. (1993). Gender differences in perceptions of emotionality: The case of close heterosexual relationships. *Sex Roles, 28,* 511–530. (p. 260)

Spring, B., Pingitore, R., Bourgeois, M., Kessler, K. H., & Bruckner, E. (1992). The effects and non-effects of skipping breakfast: Results of three studies. Paper presented at the American Psychological Association convention. (p. 248)

Srivastava, S., John, O. P., Gosling, S. D., & Potter, J. (2003). Development of personality in early and middle adulthood: Set like plaster or persistent change? *Journal of Personality & Social Psychology, 84,* 1041–1053. (pp. 96, 305)

St. Clair, D., Xu, M., Wang, P., Yu, Y., Fang, Y., Zhang, F., Zheng, X., Gu, N., Feng, G., Sham, P., & He, L. (2005). Rates of adult schizophrenia following prenatal exposure to the Chinese famine of 1959–1961. *Journal of the American Medical Association, 294,* 557–562. (p. 345)

Stager, C. L., & Werker, J. F. (1997). Infants listen for more phonetic detail in speech perception than in word-learning tasks. *Nature, 388,* 381–382. (p. 213)

Stanford University Center for Narcolepsy. (2002). Narcolepsy is a serious medical disorder and a key to understanding other sleep disorders. (www.med.stanford.edu/school/Psychiatry/narcolepsy). (p. 55)

Stanovich, K. (1996). *How to think straight about psychology.* New York: HarperCollins. (p. 294)

Stathopoulou, G., Powers, M. B., Berry, A. C., Smiths, J. A. J., & Otto, M. W. (2006). Exercise interventions for mental health: A quantitative and qualitative review. *Clinical Psychology: Science and Practice, 13,* 179–193. (p. 371)

Statistics Canada. (2008). Table 9. Homicide victims and accused persons, by sex, Canada , 1998 to 2008. (p. 102)

Staub, E. (1989). *The roots of evil: The psychological and cultural sources of genocide.* New York: Cambridge University Press. (p. 381)

Staub, E., & Vollhardt, J. (2008). Altruism born of suffering: The roots of caring and helping after experiences of personal and political victimization. *American Journal of Orthopsychiatry, 78,* 276–280. (p. 372)

Steel, P., Schmidt, J., & Schultz, J. (2008). Refining the relationship between personality and subject well-being. *Psychological Bulletin, 134,* 138–161. (p. 268)

Steele, C. M. (1990, May). A conversation with Claude Steele. *APS Observer,* pp. 11–17. (p. 228)

Steele, C. M. (1995, August 31). Black students live down to expectations. *New York Times.* (p. 232)

Steele, C. M. (1997). A threat in the air: How stereotypes shape intellectual identity and performance. *American Psychologist, 52,* 613–629. (p. 232)

Steele, C. M., Spencer, S. J., & Aronson, J. (2002). Contending with group image: The psychology of stereotype and social identity threat. *Advances in Experimental Social Psychology, 34,* 379–440. (p. 232)

Stein, S. (2009, August 20). New poll: 77 percent support "choice" of public option. *Huffington Post* (huffingtonpost.com). (p. 12)

Steinberg, L. (1987, September). Bound to bicker. *Psychology Today,* pp. 36–39. (p. 85)

Steinberg, L. (2007). Risk taking in adolescence: New perspectives from brain and behavioral science. *Current Directions in Psychological Science, 16,* 55–59. (p. 82)

Steinberg, L., & Morris, A. S. (2001). Adolescent development. *Annual Review of Psychology, 52,* 83–110. (pp. 85, 86)

Steinberg, L., & Scott, E. S. (2003). Less guilty by reason of adolescence: Developmental immaturity, diminished responsibility, and the juvenile death penalty. *American Psychologist, 58,* 1009–1018. (p. 82)

Steinberg, L., Cauffman, E., Woolard, J., Graham, S., & Banich, M. (2009). Are adolescents less mature than adults? Minors' access to abortion, the juvenile death penalty, and the alleged APA "flip-flop." *American Psychologist, 64,* 583–594. (p. 82)

Steinberg, N. (1993, February). Astonishing love stories (from an earlier United Press International report). *Games,* p. 47. (p. 398)

Steinhauer, J., & Holson, L. M. (2008, September 20). As text messages fly, danger lurks. *New York Times* (www.nytimes.com). (p. 86)

Stern, S. L., Dhanda, R., & Hazuda, H. P. (2001). Hopelessness predicts mortality in older Mexican and European Americans. *Psychosomatic Medicine, 63,* 344–351. (p. 283)

Sternberg, R. J. (1988). Applying cognitive theory to the testing and teaching of intelligence. *Applied Cognitive Psychology, 2,* 231–255. (p. 221)

Sternberg, R. J. (2003). *Wisdom, intelligence, and creativity synthesized.* New York: Cambridge University Press. (p. 221)

Sternberg, R. J. (2006). The Rainbow Project: Enhance the SAT through assessments of analytical, practical, and creative skills. *Intelligence, 34,* 321–350. (p. 222)

Sternberg, R. J., & Grajek, S. (1984). The nature of love. *Journal of Personality and Social Psychology, 47,* 312–329. (p. 402)

Sternberg, R. J., & Kaufman, J. C. (1998). Human abilities. *Annual Review of Psychology, 49,* 479–502. (p. 219)

Sternberg, R. J., Grigorenko, E. L., & Kidd, K. K. (2005). Intelligence, race, and genetics. *American Psychologist, 60,* 46–59. (p. 229)

Stetter, F., & Kupper, S. (2002). Autogenic training: A meta-analysis of clinical outcome studies. *Applied Psychophysiology and Biofeedback, 27,* 45–98. (p. 286)

Stevenson, H. W. (1992, December). Learning from Asian schools. *Scientific American,* pp. 70–76. (p. 230)

Stewart, B. (2002, April 6). Recall of the wild. *New York Times* (www.nytimes.com). (p. 19)

Stewart, R. E., & Chambless, D. L. (2009). Cognitive-behavioral therapy for adult anxiety disorders in clinical practice: A meta-analysis of effectiveness studies. *Journal of Consulting and Clinical Psychology, 77,* 595–606. (p. 363)

Stice, E., & Shaw, H. E. (1994). Adverse effects of the media portrayed thin-ideal on women and linkages to bulimic symptomatology. *Journal of Social and Clinical Psychology, 13,* 288–308. (p. 243)

Stice, E., Shaw, H., Bohon, C., Marti, C. N., & Rohde, P. (2009). A meta-analytic review of depression prevention programs for children and adolescents: Factors that predict magnitude of intervention effects. *Journal of Consulting and Clinical Psychology, 77,* 486–503. (p. 359)

Stice, E., Spangler, D., & Agras, W. S. (2001). Exposure to media-portrayed thin-ideal images adversely affects vulnerable girls: A longitudinal experiment. *Journal of Social and Clinical Psychology, 20,* 270–288. (p. 243)

Stickgold, R., Hobson, J. A., Fosse, R., & Fosse, M. (2001). Sleep, learning, and dreams: Off-line memory processing. *Science, 294,* 1052–1057. (p. 57)

Stickgold, R., James, L., & Hobson, J. A. (2000). Visual discrimination learning requires sleep after training. *Nature Neuroscience, 3,* 1237–1238. (p. 57)

Stith, S. M., Rosen, K. H., Middleton, K. A., Busch, A. L., Lunderberg, K., & Carlton, R. P. (2000). The intergenerational transmission of spouse abuse: A meta-analysis. *Journal of Marriage and the Family, 62,* 640–654. (p. 174)

Stockton, M. C., & Murnen, S. K. (1992). *Gender and sexual arousal in response to sexual stimuli: A meta-analytic review.* Paper presented at the American Psychological Society convention. (p. 110)

Stone, A. A., & Neale, J. M. (1984). Effects of severe daily events on mood. *Journal of Personality and Social Psychology, 46,* 137–144. (p. 265)

stophitting.com, 2009. (p. 166)

Stoppard, J. M., & Gruchy, C. D. G. (1993). Gender, context, and expression of positive emotion. *Personality and Social Psychology Bulletin, 19,* 143–150. (p. 260)

Storbeck, J., Robinson, M. D., & McCourt, M. E. (2006). Semantic processing precedes affect retrieval: The neurological case for cognitive primary in visual processing. *Review of General Psychology, 10,* 41–55. (p. 259)

Storm, L. (2000). Research note: Replicable evidence of psi: A revision of Milton's (1999) meta-analysis of the ganzfeld data bases. *Journal of Parapsychology, 64,* 411–416. (p. 150)

Storm, L. (2003). Remote viewing by committee: RV using a multiple agent/multiple percipient design. *Journal of Parapsychology, 67,* 325–342. (p. 150)

Storms, M. D. (1973). Videotape and the attribution process: Reversing actors' and observers' points of view. *Journal of Personality and Social Psychology, 27,* 165–175. (p. 378)

Storms, M. D., & Thomas, G. C. (1977). Reactions to physical closeness. *Journal of Personality and Social Psychology, 35,* 412–418. (p. 387)

Strack, F., Martin, L., & Stepper, S. (1988). Inhibiting and facilitating conditions of the human smile: A nonobtrusive test of the facial feedback hypothesis. *Journal of Personality and Social Psychology, 54,* 768–777. (p. 262)

Stranahan, A. M., Khalil, D., & Gould, E. (2006). Social isolation delays the positive effects of running on adult neurogenesis. *Nature Neuroscience, 9,* 526–533. (p. 45)

Strand, S., Deary, I. J., & Smith, P. (2006). Sex differences in cognitive abilities test scores: A UK national picture. *British Journal of Educational Psychology, 76,* 463–480. (p. 231)

Strange, B. A., & Dolan, R. J. (2004). b-Adrenergic modulation of emotional memory-evoked human amygdala and hippocampal responses. *Proceedings of the National Academy of Sciences, 101,* 11454–11458. (p. 188)

Stratton, G. M. (1896). Some preliminary experiments on vision without inversion of the retinal image. *Psychological Review, 3,* 611–617. (p. 139)

Straub, R. O., Seidenberg, M. S., Bever, T. G., & Terrace, H. S. (1979). Serial learning in the pigeon. *Journal of the Experimental Analysis of Behavior, 32,* 137–148. (p. 218)

Straus, M. A. (2008). Dominance and symmetry in partner violence by male and female university students in 32 nations. *Children and Youth Services Review, 30,* 252–275. (p. 102)

Straus, M. A., Sugarman, D. B., & Giles-Sims, J. (1997). Spanking by parents and subsequent antisocial behavior of children. *Archives of Pediatric Adolescent Medicine, 151,* 761–767. (p. 166)

Strawbridge, W. J., Shema, S. J., Cohen, R. D., & Kaplan, G. A. (2001). Religious attendance increases survival by improving and maintaining good health behaviors, mental health, and social relationships. *Annals of Behavioral Medicine, 23,* 68–74. (p. 287)

Strayer, D. L., & Drews, F. A. (2007). Cell-phone-induced driver distraction. *Current Directions in Psychological Science, 16,* 128–131. (p. 49)

Strayer, D. L., Drews, F. A., & Johnston, W. A. (2003). Cell phone-induced failures of visual attention during simulated driving. *Journal of Experimental Psychology: Applied, 9,* 23–32. (p. 49)

Stroebe, M., Stroebe, W., & Schut, H. (2001). Gender differences in adjustment to bereavement: An empirical and theoretical review. *Review of General Psychology, 5,* 62–83. (p. 95)

Stroebe, M., Stroebe, W., Schut, H., Zech, E., & van den Bout, J. (2002). Does disclosure of emotions facilitate recovery from bereavement? Evidence from two prospective studies. *Journal of Consulting and Clinical Psychology, 70,* 169–178. (p. 95)

Stroebe, W., Schut, H., & Stroebe, M. S. (2005). Grief work, disclosure and counseling: Do they help the bereaved? *Clinical Psychology Review, 25,* 395–414. (p. 95)

Strully, K. W. (2009). Job loss and health in the U.S. labor market. *Demography, 46,* 221–246. (p. 275)

Strupp, H. H. (1986). Psychotherapy: Research, practice, and public policy (How to avoid dead ends). *American Psychologist, 41,* 120–130. (p. 363)

Stumpf, H., & Jackson, D. N. (1994). Gender-related differences in cognitive abilities: Evidence from a medical school admissions testing program. *Personality and Individual Differences, 17,* 335–344. (p. 230)

Stunkard, A. J., Harris, J. R., Pedersen, N. L., & McClearn, G. E. (1990). A separated twin study of the body mass index. *New England Journal of Medicine, 322,* 1483–1487. (p. 246)

Su, R., Rounds, J., & Armstrong, P. I. (2009). Men and things, women and people: A meta-analysis of sex differences in interests. *Psychological Bulletin, 135,* 859–884. (p. 103)

Subrahmanyam, K., & Greenfield, P. (2008). Online communication and adolescent relationships. *The Future of Children, 18,* 119–146. (p. 86)

Suddath, R. L., Christison, G. W., Torrey, E. F., Casanova, M. F., & Weinberger, D. R. (1990). Anatomical abnormalities in the brains of monozygotic twins discordant for schizophrenia. *New England Journal of Medicine, 322,* 789–794. (p. 346)

Sue, S. (2006). Research to address racial and ethnic disparities in mental health: Some lessons learned. In S. I. Donaldson, D. E. Berger, & K. Pezdek (Eds.), *Applied psychology: New frontiers and rewarding careers.* Mahwah, NJ: Erlbaum. (p. 364)

Suedfeld, P. (1998). Homo invictus: The indomitable species. *Canadian Psychology, 38,* 164–173. (p. 372)

Suedfeld, P. (2000). Reverberations of the Holocaust fifty years later: Psychology's contributions to understanding persecution and genocide. *Canadian Psychology, 41,* 1–9. (p. 372)

Suedfeld, P., & Mocellin, J. S. P. (1987). The "sensed presence" in unusual environments. *Environment and Behavior, 19,* 33–52. (p. 334)

Suinn, R. M. (1997). Mental practice in sports psychology: Where have we been, where do we go? *Clinical Psychology: Science and Practice, 4,* 189-207. (p. 215)

Sullivan, D., & von Wachter, T. (2009). Job displacement and mortality: An analysis using administrative data. *Quarterly Journal of Economics, 124,* 1265–1306. (p. 274)

Sullivan, P. F., Neale, M. C., & Kendler, K. S. (2000). Genetic epidemiology of major depression: Review and meta-analysis. *American Journal of Psychiatry, 157,* 1552–1562. (p. 341)

Sullivan/Anderson, A. (2009, March 30). How to end the war over sex ed. *Time,* pp. 40–43. (p. 109)

Summers, M. (1996, December 9). Mister clean. *People Weekly,* pp. 139–142. (p. 316)

Sundstrom, E., De Meuse, K. P., & Futrell, D. (1990). Work teams: Applications and effectiveness. *American Psychologist, 45,* 120–133. (p. 417)

Suomi, S. J. (1986). Anxiety-like disorders in young nonhuman primates. In R. Gettleman (Ed.), *Anxiety disorders of childhood.* New York: Guilford Press. (p. 325)

Surgeon General. (1986). *The Surgeon General's workshop on pornography and public health,* June 22–24. Report prepared by E. P. Mulvey & J. L. Haugaard and released by Office of the Surgeon General on August 4, 1986. (p. 396)

Susser, E., Neugenbauer, R., Hoek, H. W., Brown, A. S., Lin, S., Labovitz, D., & Gorman, J. M. (1996). Schizophrenia after prenatal famine. *Archives of General Psychiatry, 53(1),* 25–31. (p. 345)

Sutherland, A. (2006a). *Bitten and scratched: Life and lessons at the premier school for exotic animal trainers.* New York: Viking. (p. 154)

Sutherland, A. (2006b, June 25). What Shamu taught me about a happy marriage. *New York Times* (www.nytimes.com). (p. 154)

Swami, V., & 60 others. (2010). The attractive female body weight and female body dissatisfaction in 26 countries across 10 world regions: Results of the international body project I. *Personality and Social Psychology Bulletin, 36,* 309–325. (p. 243)

Swann, W. B., Jr., Chang-Schneider, C., & McClarty, K. L. (2007). Do people's self-views matter: Self-concept and self-esteem in everyday life. *American Psychologist, 62,* 84–94. (p. 310)

Sweat, J. A., & Durm, M. W. (1993). Psychics: Do police departments really use them? *Skeptical Inquirer, 17,* 148–158. (p. 149)

Swerdlow, N. R., & Koob, G. F. (1987). Dopamine, schizophrenia, mania, and depression: Toward a unified hypothesis of cortico-stiato-pallido-thalamic function (with commentary). *Behavioral and Brain Sciences, 10,* 197–246. (p. 345)

TADS. (Treatment for Adolescents with Depression Study Team). (2004). Fluoxetine, cognitive-behavioral therapy, and their combination for adolescents with depression: Treatment for adolescents with depression study (TADS) randomized controlled trial. *Journal of the American Medical Association, 292,* 807–820. (p. 367)

Taheri, S. (2004a, 20 December). Does the lack of sleep make you fat? *University of Bristol Research News.* (www.bristol.ac.uk). (pp. 54, 246)

Taheri, S. (2004b). The genetics of sleep disorders. *Minerva Medica, 95,* 203–212. (p. 246)

Tajfel, H. (Ed.). (1982). *Social identity and intergroup relations.* New York: Cambridge University Press. (p. 392)

Talarico, J. M., & Rubin, D. C. (2003). Confidence, not consistency, characterizes flashbulb memories. *Psychological Science, 14,* 455–461. (p. 189)

Tang, S-H., & Hall, V. C. (1995). The overjustification effect: A meta-analysis. *Applied Cognitive Psychology, 9,* 365–404. (p. 171)

Tangney, J. P., Baumeister, R. F., & Boone, A. L. (2004). High self-control predicts good adjustment, less pathology, better grades, and interpersonal success. *Journal of Personality, 72,* 271–324. (p. 282)

Tannen, D. (1990). *You just don't understand: Women and men in conversation.* New York: Morrow. (p. 103)

Tannenbaum, P. (2002, February). Quoted by R. Kubey & M. Csikszentmihalyi, Television addiction is no mere metaphor. *Scientific American,* pp. 74–80. (p. 127)

Tanner, J. M. (1978). *Fetus into man: Physical growth from conception to maturity.* Cambridge, MA: Harvard University Press. (p. 81)

Tardif, T., Fletcher, P., Liang, W., Zhang, Z., Kaciroti, N., & Marchman, V. A. (2008). Baby's first 10 words. *Developmental Psychology, 44,* 929–938. (p. 213)

Taubes, G. (2001). The soft science of dietary fat. *Science, 291,* 2536–2545. (p. 248)

Taubes, G. (2002, July 7). What if it's all been a big fat lie? *New York Times.* (www.nytimes.com). (p. 248)

Taylor, S., Kuch, K., Koch, W. J., Crockett, D. J., & Passey, G. (1998). The structure of posttraumatic stress symptoms. *Journal of Abnormal Psychology, 107,* 154–160. (p. 324)

Taylor, S. E. (1983). Adjustment to threatening events: A theory of cognitive adaptation. *American Psychologist, 38,* 1161–1173. (p. 285)

Taylor, S. E. (1989). *Positive illusions.* New York: Basic Books. (p. 209)

Taylor, S. E. (2006). Tend and befriend: Biobehavioral bases of affiliation under stress. *Current Directions in Psychological Science, 15,* 273–277. (p. 276)

Taylor, S. E., Cousino, L. K., Lewis, B. P., Gruenewald, T. L., Gurung, R. A. R., & Updegraff, J. A. (2000). Biobehavioral responses to stress in females: Tend-and-befriend, not fight-or-flight. *Psychological Review, 107,* 411–430. (p. 276)

Taylor, S. E., Pham, L. B., Rivkin, I. D., & Armor, D. A. (1998). Harnessing the imagination: Mental simulation, self-regulation, and coping. *American Psychologist, 53,* 429–439. (p. 215)

Taylor, S. E., Way, B. M., Welch, W. T., Hilmert, C. J., Lehman, B. J., & Eisenberger, N. I. (2006). Early family environment, current adversity, the serotonin transporter promoter polymorphism, and depressive symptomatology. *Biological Psychiatry, 60,* 671–676. (p. 276)

Taylor, S. P., & Chermack, S. T. (1993). Alcohol, drugs and human physical aggression. *Journal of Studies on Alcohol,* Supplement No. 11, 78–88. (p. 394)

Tedeschi, R. G., & Calhoun, L. G. (2004). Posttraumatic growth: Conceptual foundations and empirical evidence. *Psychological Inquiry, 15,* 1–18. (p. 372)

Teerlink, R., & Ozley, L. (2000). *More than a motorcycle: The leadership journey at Harley-Davidson.* Cambridge, MA: Harvard Business School Press. (p. 418)

Teghtsoonian, R. (1971). On the exponents in Stevens' law and the constant in Ekinan's law. *Psychological Review, 78,* 71–80 (p. 126)

Teran-Santos, J., Jimenez-Gomez, A., & Cordero-Guevara, J. (1999). The association between sleep apnea and the risk of traffic accidents. *New England Journal of Medicine, 340,* 847–851. (p. 55)

Terracciano, A., Costa, Jr., P. T., & McCrae, R. R. (2006). Personality plasticity after age 30. *Personality and Social Psychology Bulletin, 32,* 999–1009. (p. 96)

Terrace, H. S. (1979, November). How Nim Chimpsky changed my mind. *Psychology Today*, pp. 65–76. (p. 218)

Tesser, A., Forehand, R., Brody, G., & Long, N. (1989). Conflict: The role of calm and angry parent-child discussion in adolescent development. *Journal of Social and Clinical Psychology, 8*, 317–330. (p. 85)

Thaler, R. H., & Sunstein, C. R. (2008). *Nudge: Improving decisions about health, wealth, and happiness*. New Haven, CT: Yale University Press. (p. 210)

Thatcher, R. W., Walker, R. A., & Giudice, S. (1987). Human cerebral hemispheres develop at different rates and ages. *Science, 236*, 1110–1113. (pp. 70, 88)

Thiel, A., Hadedank, B., Herholz, K., Kessler, J., Winhuisen, L., Haupt, W. F., & Heiss, W-D. (2006). From the left to the right: How the brain compensates progressive loss of language function. *Brain and Language, 98*, 57–65. (p. 45)

Thiele, T. E., Marsh, D. J., Ste. Marie, L., Bernstein, I. L., & Palmiter, R. D. (1998). Ethanol consumption and resistance are inversely related to neuropeptide Y levels. *Nature, 396*, 366–369. (p. 336)

Thomas, A., & Chess, S. (1986). The New York Longitudinal Study: From infancy to early adult life. In R. Plomin & J. Dunn (Eds.), *The study of temperament: Changes, continuities, and challenges*. Hillsdale, NJ: Erlbaum. (p. 96)

Thomas, L. (1992). *The fragile species*. New York: Scribner's. (pp. 214, 362)

Thompson, J. K., Jarvie, G. J., Lahey, B. B., & Cureton, K. J. (1982). Exercise and obesity: Etiology, physiology, and intervention. *Psychological Bulletin, 91*, 55–79. (p. 248)

Thompson, P. M., Giedd, J. N., Woods, R. P., MacDonald, D., Evans, A. C., & Toga, A. W. (2000). Growth patterns in the developing brain detected by using continuum mechanical tensor maps. *Nature, 404*, 190–193. (p. 70)

Thompson, R., Emmorey, K., & Gollan, T. H. (2005). "Tip of the fingers" experiences by Deaf signers. *Psychological Science, 16*, 856–860. (p. 194)

Thompson-Schill, S. L., Ramscar, M., & Chrysikou, E. G. (2009). Cognition without control: When a little frontal lobe goes a long way. *Current Directions in Psychological Science, 18*, 259–263. (p. 70)

Thorndike, A. L., & Hagen, E. P. (1977). *Measurement and evaluation in psychology and education*. New York: Macmillan. (p. 224)

Thorne, J., with Larry Rothstein. (1993). *You are not alone: Words of experience and hope for the journey through depression*. New York: HarperPerennial. (p. 316)

Thornton, B., & Moore, S. (1993). Physical attractiveness contrast effect: Implications for self-esteem and evaluations of the social self. *Personality and Social Psychology Bulletin, 19*, 474–480. (p. 399)

Thorpe, W. H. (1974). *Animal nature and human nature*. London: Metheun. (p. 218)

Tiedens, L. Z. (2001). Anger and advancement versus sadness and subjugation: The effect of negative emotion expressions on social status conferral. *Journal of Personality and Social Psychology, 80*, 86–94. (p. 264)

Tiihonen J., Lönnqvist J, Wahlbeck K, Klaukka T, Niskanen L, Tanskanen A, Haukka J. (2009). 11-year follow-up of mortality in patients with schizophrenia: a population-based cohort study (FIN11 study). *Lancet, 374*, 260–267. (p. 367)

Time. (1997, December 22). Greeting card association data, p. 19. (p. 103)

Time/CNN Survey. (1994, December 19). Vox pop: Happy holidays, *Time*. (p. 338)

Timmerman, T. A. (2007) "It was a thought pitch": Personal, situational, and target influences on hit-by-pitch events across time. *Journal of Applied Psychology, 92*, 876–884. (p. 394)

Tirrell, M. E. (1990). Personal communication. (p. 159)

Toews, P. (2004, December 30). Dirk Willems: A heart undivided. *Mennonite Brethren Historical Commission*. (www.nbhistory.org/profiles/dirk.en.html). (p. 376)

Tondo, L., Jamison, K. R., & Baldessarini, R. J. (1997). Effect of lithium maintenance on suicidal behavior in major mood disorders. In D. M. Stoff & J. J. Mann (Eds.), *The neurobiology of suicide: From the bench to the clinic*. New York: New York Academy of Sciences. (p. 368)

Torrey, E. F. (1986). *Witchdoctors and psychiatrists*. New York: Harper & Row. (p. 364)

Torrey, E. F., & Miller, J. (2002). *The invisible plague: The rise of mental illness from 1750 to the present*. New Brunswick, NJ: Rutgers University Press. (p. 345)

Torrey, E. F., Miller, J., Rawlings, R., & Yolken, R. H. (1997). Seasonality of births in schizophrenia and bipolar disorder: A review of the literature. *Schizophrenia Research, 28*, 1–38. (p. 345)

Totterdell, P., Kellett, S., Briner, R. B., & Teuchmann, K. (1998). Evidence of mood linkage in work groups. *Journal of Personality and Social Psychology, 74*, 1504–1515. (p. 382)

Tovee, M. J., Mason, S. M., Emery, J. L., McCluskey, S. E., & Cohen-Tovee, E. M. (1997). Supermodels: Stick insects or hourglasses? *The Lancet, 350*, 1474–1475. (p. 243)

Treffert, D. A., & Christensen, D. D. (2005, December). Inside the mind of a savant. *Scientific American*, pp. 108–113. (p. 219)

Treffert, D. A., & Wallace, G. L. (2002). Island of genius—The artistic brilliance and dazzling memory that sometimes accompany autism and other disorders hint at how all brains work. *Scientific American, 286*, 76–86. (p. 219)

Treisman, A. (1987). Properties, parts, and objects. In K. R. Boff, L. Kaufman, & J. P. Thomas (Eds.), *Handbook of perception and human performance*. New York: Wiley. (p. 134)

Triandis, H. C. (1994). *Culture and social behavior*. New York: McGraw-Hill. (pp. 312, 395)

Triandis, H. C., Bontempo, R., Villareal, M. J., Asai, M., & Lucca, N. (1988). Individualism and collectivism: Cross-cultural perspectives on self-ingroup relationships. *Journal of Personality and Social Psychology, 54*, 323–338. (p. 313)

Trickett, P. K., & McBride-Chang, C. (1995). The developmental impact of different forms of child abuse and neglect. *Developmental Review, 15*, 311–337. (p. 78)

Trillin, C. (2006, March 27). Alice off the page. *The New Yorker*, p. 44. (p. 302)

Trimble, J. E. (1994). Cultural variations in the use of alcohol and drugs. In W. J. Lonner & R. Malpass (Eds.), *Psychology and culture*. Boston: Allyn & Bacon. (p. 337)

Triplett, N. (1898). The dynamogenic factors in pacemaking and competition. *American Journal of Psychology, 9*, 507–533. (p. 386)

Trolier, T. K., & Hamilton, D. L. (1986). Variables influencing judgments of correlational relations. *Journal of Personality and Social Psychology, 50*, 879–888. (p. 15)

Tsang, Y. C. (1938). Hunger motivation in gastrectomized rats. *Journal of Comparative Psychology, 26*, 1–17. (p. 240)

Tse, D., Langston, R. F., Kakeyama, M., Bethus, I., Spooner P. A., Wood, E. R., Witter, M. P., & Morris, R. G. M. (2007). Schemas and memory consolidation. *Science, 316*, 76–82. (p. 185)

Tsien, J. Z. (2007, July). The memory code. *Scientific American*, pp. 52–59. (p. 188)

Tsuang, M. T., & Faraone, S. V. (1990). *The genetics of mood disorders*. Baltimore, MD: Johns Hopkins University Press. (p. 341)

Tuber, D. S., Miller, D. D., Caris, K. A., Halter, R., Linden, F., & Hennessy, M. B. (1999). Dogs in animal shelters: Problems, suggestions, and needed expertise. *Psychological Science, 10,* 379–386. (p. 20)

Tucker, K. A. (2002). I believe you can fly. *Gallup Management Journal.* (www.gallupjournal.com/CA/st/20020520.asp). (p. 415)

Turner, J. C. (1987). *Rediscovering the social group: A self-categorization theory.* New York: Basil Blackwell. (p. 392)

Turner, N., Barling, J., & Zacharatos, A. (2002). Positive psychology at work. In C. R. Snyder & S. J. Lopez (Eds.), *The handbook of positive psychology.* New York: Oxford University Press. (p. 416)

Tversky, A. (1985, June). Quoted in K. McKean, Decisions, decisions. *Discover,* pp. 22–31. (p. 207)

Tversky, A., & Kahneman, D. (1974). Judgment under uncertainty: Heuristics and biases. *Science, 185,* 1124–1131. (p. 207)

Twenge, J. M. (1997). Changes in masculine and feminine traits over time: A meta-analysis. *Sex Roles 36*(5–6), 305–325. (p. 100)

Twenge, J. M. (2000). The age of anxiety? Birth cohort change in anxiety and neuroticism, 1952–1993. *Journal of Personality and Social Psychology, 79,* 1007–1021. (p. 326)

Twenge, J. M. (2006). *Generation me.* New York: Free Press. (p. 107)

Twenge, J. M., & Campbell, W. K. (2001). Age and birth cohort differences in self-esteem: A cross-temporal meta-analysis. *Personality and Social Psychology Review, 5,* 321–344. (p. 85)

Twenge, J. M., & Crocker, J. (2002). Race and self-esteem: Meta-analyses comparing Whites, Blacks, Hispanics, Asians, and American Indians and comment on Gray-Little and Hafdahl (2000). *Psychological Bulletin, 128,* 371–408. (p. 310)

Twenge, J. M., & Nolen-Hoeksema, S. (2002). Age, gender, race, socioeconomic status, and birth cohort differences on the children's depression inventory: A meta-analysis. *Journal of Abnormal Psychology, 111,* 578–588. (p. 85)

Twenge, J. M., Baumeister, R. F., DeWall, C. N., Ciarocco, N. J., & Bartels, J. M. (2007). Social exclusion decreases prosocial behavior. *Journal of Personality and Social Psychology, 92,* 56–66. (p. 250)

Twenge, J. M., Baumeister, R. F., Tice, D. M., & Stucke, T. S. (2001). If you can't join them, beat them: Effects of social exclusion on aggressive behavior. *Journal of Personality and Social Psychology, 81,* 1058–1069. (pp. 250, 395)

Twenge, J. M., Catanese, K. R., & Baumeister, R. F. (2002). Social exclusion causes self-defeating behavior. *Journal of Personality and Social Psychology, 83,* 606–615. (pp. 250, 395)

Twenge, J. M., Catanese, K. R., & Baumeister, R. F. (2003). Social exclusion and the deconstructed state: Time perception, meaninglessness, lethargy, lack of emotion, and self-awareness. *Journal of Personality and Social Psychology, 85,* 409–423. (p. 395)

Twenge, J. M., Freeman, E. C., & Campbell, W. K. (2010, April 15). The effect of social networking websites on narcissistic personality traits: An experimental investigation. Keynote address to the Undergraduate Research and Discovery Symposium, University of Alaska, Anchorage. (p. 251)

Tyler, K. A. (2002). Social and emotional outcomes of childhood sexual abuse: A review of recent research. *Aggression and Violent Behavior, 7,* 567–589. (p. 78)

Uchino, B. N. (2009). Understanding the links between social support and physical health. *Perspectives on Psychological Science, 4,* 236–255. (p. 284)

Uchino, B. N., Cacioppo, J. T., & Kiecolt-Glaser, J. K. (1996). The relationship between social support and physiological processes: A review with emphasis on underlying mechanisms and implications for health. *Psychological Bulletin, 119,* 488–531. (p. 284)

Uchino, B. N., Uno, D., & Holt-Lunstad, J. (1999). Social support, physiological processes, and health. *Current Directions in Psychological Science, 8,* 145–148. (p. 284)

UK ECT Review Group. (2003). Efficacy and safety of electroconvulsive therapy in depressive disorders: A systematic review and meta-analysis. *Lancet, 361,* 799–808. (p. 369)

Ulrich, R. E. (1991). Animal rights, animal wrongs and the question of balance. *Psychological Science, 2,* 197–201. (p. 19)

UNAIDS. (2010). *UNAIDS report on the global AIDS epidemic 2010.* www.unaids.org. (p. 109)

UNICEF. (2006). *The state of the world's children 2007.* New York: UNICEF. (p. 105)

Urbany, J. E., Bearden, W. O., & Weilbaker, D. C. (1988). The effect of plausible and exaggerated reference prices on consumer perceptions and price search. *Journal of Consumer Research, 15,* 95–110. (p. 210)

Urry, H. L., Nitschke, J. B., Dolski, I., Jackson, D. C., Dalton, K. M., Mueller, C. J., Rosenkranz, M. A., Ryff, C. D., Singer, B. H., & Davidson, R. J. (2004). Making a life worth living: Neural correlates of well-being. *Psychological Science, 15,* 367–372. (p. 256)

USAID. (2004, January). *The ABCs of HIV prevention.* www.usaid.gov. (p. 278)

Vaidya, J. G., Gray, E. K., Haig, J., & Watson, D. (2002). On the temporal stability of personality: Evidence for differential stability and the role of life experiences. *Journal of Personality and Social Psychology, 83,* 1469–1484. (p. 305)

Vaillant, G. E. (2002). *Aging well: Surprising guideposts to a happier life from the landmark Harvard study of adult development.* Boston: Little, Brown. (p. 284)

Vaillant, G. E. (2009). Quoted by J. W. Shenk, What makes us happy? *The Atlantic* (www.theatlantic.com). (p. 250)

Valenstein, E. S. (1986). *Great and desperate cures: The rise and decline of psychosurgery.* New York: Basic Books. (p. 370)

Valkenburg, P. M., & Peter, J. (2009). Social consequences of the Internet for adolescents: A decade of research. *Current Directions in Psychological Science, 18,* 1–5. (pp. 86, 251)

Vallone, R. P., Griffin, D. W., Lin, S., & Ross, L. (1990). Overconfident prediction of future actions and outcomes by self and others. *Journal of Personality and Social Psychology, 58,* 582–592. (p. 10)

van Anders, S. M., & Dunn, E. J. (2009). Are gonadal steroids linked with orgasm perceptions and sexual assertiveness in women and men? *Journal of Sexual Medicine, 6,* 739–751. (p. 107)

Van Cauter, E., Holmback, U., Knutson, K., Leproult, R., Miller, A., Nedeltcheva, A., Pannain, S., Penev, P., Tasali, E., & Spiegel, K. (2007). Impact of sleep and sleep loss on neuroendocrine and metabolic function. *Hormone Research, 67*(1), 2–9. (p. 55)

van den Boom, D. C. (1990). Preventive intervention and the quality of mother-infant interaction and infant exploration in irritable infants. In W. Koops, H. J. G. Soppe, J. L. van der Linden, P. C. M. Molenaar, & J. J. F. Schroots (Eds.), *Developmental psychology research in The Netherlands.* The Netherlands: Uitgeverij Eburon. Cited by C. Hazan & P. R. Shaver (1994). Deeper into attachment theory. *Psychological Inquiry, 5,* 68–79. (p. 77)

van den Boom, D. C. (1995). Do first-year intervention effects endure? Follow-up during toddlerhood of a sample of Dutch irritable infants. *Child Development, 66,* 1798–1816. (p. 77)

van den Bos, K., & Spruijt, N. (2002). Appropriateness of decisions as a moderator of the psychology of voice. *European Journal of Social Psychology, 32,* 57–72. (p. 417)

Van Dyke, C., & Byck, R. (1982, March). Cocaine. *Scientific American,* pp. 128–141. (p. 333)

van Goozen, S. H. M., Fairchild, G., Snoek, H., & Harold, G. T. (2007). The evidence for a neurobiological model of childhood antisocial behavior. *Psychological Bulletin, 133,* 149–182. (p. 328)

van IJzendoorn, M. H., & Juffer, F. (2005). Adoption is a successful natural intervention enhancing adopted children's IQ and school performance. *Current Directions in Psychological Science, 14,* 326-330. (p. 226)

van IJzendoorn, M. H., & Juffer, F. (2006). The Emanual Miller Memorial Lecture 2006: Adoption as intervention. Meta-analytic evidence for massive catch-up and plasticity in physical, socio-emotional, and cognitive development. *Journal of Child Psychology and Psychiatry, 47,* 1228–1245. (p. 226)

van IJzendoorn M. H., & Kroonenberg, P. M. (1988). Cross-cultural patterns of attachment: A meta-analysis of the strange situation. *Child Development, 59,* 147–156. (p. 77)

Van Leeuwen, M. S. (1978). A cross-cultural examination of psychological differentiation in males and females. *International Journal of Psychology, 13,* 87–122. (p. 105)

Van Rooy, D. L., & Viswesvaran, C. (2004). Emotional intelligence: A meta-analytic investigation of predictive validity and nomological net. *Journal of Vocational Behavior, 65,* 71–95. (p. 223)

van Schaik, C. P., Ancrenaz, M., Borgen, G., Galdikas, B., Knott, C. D., Singleton, I., Suzuki, A., Utami, S. S., & Merrill, M. (2003). Orangutan cultures and the evolution of material culture. *Science, 299,* 102–105. (p. 216)

Van Yperen, N. W., & Buunk, B. P. (1990). A longitudinal study of equity and satisfaction in intimate relationships. *European Journal of Social Psychology, 20,* 287–309. (p. 402)

Van Zeijl, J., Mesman, J., van IJzendoorn, M. H., Bakermans-Kranenburg, M. J., Juffer, F., Stolk, M. N., Koot, H. M., & Alink, L. R. A. (2006). Attachment-based intervention for enhancing sensitive discipline in mothers of 1- to 3-year-old children at risk for externalizing behavior problems: A randomized controlled trial. *Journal of Consulting and Clinical Psychology, 74,* 994–1005. (p. 77)

Vance, E. B., & Wagner, N. N. (1976). Written descriptions of orgasm: A study of sex differences. *Archives of Sexual Behavior, 5,* 87–98. (p. 108)

Vandenberg, S. G., & Kuse, A. R. (1978). Mental rotations: A group test of three-dimensional spatial visualization. *Perceptual and Motor Skills, 47,* 599–604. (p. 231)

Vanman, E. J., Saltz, J. L., Nathan, L. R., & Warren, J. A. (2004). Racial discrimination by low-prejudiced Whites. *Psychological Science, 15,* 711–714. (p. 391)

Vaughn, K. B., & Lanzetta, J. T. (1981). The effect of modification of expressive displays on vicarious emotional arousal. *Journal of Experimental Social Psychology, 17,* 16–30. (p. 263)

Vecera, S. P., Vogel, E. K., & Woodman, G. F. (2002). Lower region: A new cue for figure-ground assignment. *Journal of Experimental Psychology: General, 13,* 194–205. (p. 136)

Velliste, M., Perel, S., Spalding, M. C., Whitford, A. S., & Schwartz, A. B. (2008). Cortical control of a prosthetic arm for self-feeding. *Nature, 453,* 1098–1101. (p. 42)

Verhaeghen, P., & Salthouse, T. A. (1997). Meta-analyses of age-cognition relations in adulthood: Estimates of linear and nonlinear age effects and structural models. *Psychological Bulletin, 122,* 231–249. (p. 91)

Vigil, J. M. (2009). A socio-relational framework of sex differences in the expression of emotion. *Behavioral and Brain Sciences, 32,* 375–428. (p. 261)

Vigliocco, G., & Hartsuiker, R. J. (2002). The interplay of meaning, sound, and syntax in sentence production. *Psychological Bulletin, 128,* 442–472. (p. 212)

Visich, P. S., & Fletcher, E. (2009). Myocardial infarction. In J. K. Ehrman, P. M. Gordon, P. S. Visich, & S. J. Keleyian (Eds.). *Clinical exercise physiology, 2nd Edition.* Champaign, IL: Human Kinetics. (p. 285)

Vitello, P. (2006, June 12). A ring tone meant to fall on deaf ears. *New York Times* (www.nytimes.com). (p. 91)

Vittengl, J. R., Clark, L. A., Dunn, T. W., & Jarrett, R. B. (2007). Reducing relapse and recurrence in unipolar depression: A comparative meta-analysis of cognitive-behavioral therapy's effects. *Journal of Consulting and Clinical Psychology, 75,* 475–488. (p. 367)

von Hippel, W. (2007). Aging, executive functioning, and social control. *Current Directions in Psychological Science, 16,* 240–244. (p. 91)

von Senden, M. (1932). *The perception of space and shape in the congenitally blind before and after operation.* Glencoe, IL: Free Press. (p. 138)

Vroom, V. H., & Jago, A. G. (2007). The role of the situation in leadership. *American Psychologist, 62,* 17–24. (p. 416)

VTTI. (2009, September). *Driver distraction in commercial vehicle operations.* Virginia Tech Transportation Institute and U.S. Department of Transportation. (p. 49)

Wade, K. A., Garry, M., Read, J. D., & Lindsay, D. S. (2002). A picture is worth a thousand lies: Using false photographs to create false childhood memories. *Psychonomic Bulletin & Review, 9,* 597–603. (p. 197)

Wade, N. G., Worthington, E. L., Jr., & Vogel, D. L. (2007). Effectiveness of religiously tailored interventions in Christian therapy. *Psychotherapy Research, 17,* 91–105. (p. 364)

Wagner, U., Gais, S., Haider, H., Verleger, R., & Born, J. (2004). Sleep inspires insight. *Nature, 427,* 352–355. (p. 54)

Wagstaff, G. (1982). Attitudes to rape: The "just world" strikes again? *Bulletin of the British Psychological Society, 13,* 275–283. (p. 379)

Wahlberg, D. (2001, October 11). We're more depressed, patriotic, poll finds. *Grand Rapids Press,* p. A15. (p. 274)

Wakefield, J. C., & Spitzer, R. L. (2002). Lowered estimates—but of what? *Archives of General Psychiatry, 59,* 129–130. (p. 324)

Walker, M. P., & Stickgold, R. (2006). Sleep, memory, and plasticity. *Annual Review of Psychology, 57,* 139–166. (p. 54)

Walker, W. R., Skowronski, J. J., & Thompson, C. P. (2003). Life is pleasant—and memory helps to keep it that way! *Review of General Psychology, 7,* 203–210. (p. 95)

Wall, B. (2002, August 24–25). Profit matures along with baby boomers. *International Herald Tribune,* p. 13. (p. 400)

Wallach, M. A., & Wallach, L. (1983). *Psychology's sanction for selfishness: The error of egoism in theory and therapy.* New York: Freeman. (p. 303)

Wallach, M. A., & Wallach, L. (1985, February). How psychology sanctions the cult of the self. *Washington Monthly,* pp. 46–56. (p. 303)

Wallis, C. (1983, June 6). Stress: Can we cope? *Time,* pp. 48–54. (p. 275)

Walster (Hatfield), E., Aronson, V., Abrahams, D., & Rottman, L. (1966). Importance of physical attractiveness in dating behavior. *Journal of Personality and Social Psychology, 4,* 508–516. (p. 399)

Walton, G. M., & Spencer, S. J. (2009). Latent ability: Grades and test scores systematically underestimate the intellectual ability of negatively stereotyped students. *Psychological Science, 20,* 1132–1139. (p. 232)

Wampold, B. E. (2001). *The great psychotherapy debate: Models, methods, and findings.* Mahwah, NJ: Erlbaum. (pp. 363, 364)

Wampold, B. E. (2007). Psychotherapy: The humanistic (and effective) treatment. *American Psychologist, 62,* 857–873. (pp. 362, 363)

Wansink, B. (2007). *Mindless eating: Why we eat more than we think.* New York: Bantam Dell. (p. 242)

Ward, A., & Mann, T. (2000). Don't mind if I do: Disinhibited eating under cognitive load. *Journal of Personality and Social Psychology, 78,* 753–763. (p. 248)

Ward, C. (1994). Culture and altered states of consciousness. In W. J. Lonner & R. Malpass (Eds.), *Psychology and culture.* Boston: Allyn & Bacon. (pp. 329, 330)

Ward, K. D., Klesges, R. C., & Halpern, M. T. (1997). Predictors of smoking cessation and state-of-the-art smoking interventions. *Journal of Social Issues, 53,* 129–145. (p. 333)

Ward, L. M., & Friedman, K. (2006). Using TV as a guide: Associations between television viewing and adolescents' sexual attitudes and behavior. *Journal of Research on Adolescence, 16,* 133–156. (p. 109)

Wardle, J., Cooke, L. J., Gibson, L., Sapochnik, M., Sheiham, A., & Lawson, M. (2003). Increasing children's acceptance of vegetables: A randomized trial of parent-led exposure. *Appetite, 40,* 155–162. (pp. 145, 201)

Wargo, E. (2007, December). Understanding the have-knots. *APS Observer,* pp. 18–21. (p. 286)

Warner, J., McKeown, E., Johnson, K., Ramsay, A., Cort, C., & King, M. (2004). Rates and predictors of mental illness in gay men, lesbians and bisexual men and women. *British Journal of Psychiatry, 185,* 479–485. (p. 112)

Wason, P. C. (1960). On the failure to eliminate hypotheses in a conceptual task. *Quarterly Journal of Experimental Psychology, 12,* 129–140. (p. 209)

Wason, P. C. (1981). The importance of cognitive illusions. *The Behavioral and Brain Sciences, 4,* 356. (p. 209)

Wasserman, E. A. (1993). Comparative cognition: Toward a general understanding of cognition in behavior. *Psychological Science, 4,* 156–161. (p. 163)

Wasserman, E. A. (1995). The conceptual abilities of pigeons. *American Scientist, 83,* 246–255. (p. 216)

Watson, D. (2000). *Mood and temperament.* New York: Guilford Press. (p. 265)

Watson, J. B. (1913). Psychology as the behaviorist views it. *Psychological Review, 20,* 158–177. (pp. 161, 171)

Watson, J. B. (1924). The unverbalized in human behavior. *Psychological Review, 31,* 339–347. (p. 171)

Watson, J. B., & Rayner, R. (1920). Conditioned emotional reactions. *Journal of Experimental Psychology, 3,* 1–14. (p. 161)

Watson, R. I., Jr. (1973). Investigation into deindividuation using a cross-cultural survey technique. *Journal of Personality and Social Psychology, 25,* 342–345. (p. 388)

Watson, S. J., Benson, J. A., Jr., & Joy, J. E. (2000). NEWS AND VIEWS—Marijuana and medicine: Assessing the science base: A summary of the 1999 Institute of Medicine report. *Archives of General Psychiatry, 57,* 547–553. (p. 335)

Watters, E. (2010). *Crazy like us: The globalization of the American psyche.* New York: Free Press. (p. 319)

Wayment, H. A., & Peplau, L. A. (1995). Social support and well-being among lesbian and heterosexual women: A structural modeling approach. *Personality and Social Psychology Bulletin, 21,* 1189–1199. (p. 93)

Weaver, J. B., Masland, J. L., & Zillmann, D. (1984). Effect of erotica on young men's aesthetic perception of their female sexual partners. *Perceptual and Motor Skills, 58,* 929–930. (p. 111)

Webb, W. B. (1992). *Sleep: The gentle tyrant.* Bolton, MA: Anker Publishing. (pp. 53, 55)

Webb, W. B., & Campbell, S. S. (1983). Relationships in sleep characteristics of identical and fraternal twins. *Archives of General Psychiatry, 40,* 1093–1095. (p. 53)

Wechsler, H., Davenport, A., Dowdall, G., Moeykens, B., & Castillo, S. (1994). Health and behavioral consequences of binge drinking in college. *Journal of the American Medical Association, 272,* 1672–1677. (p. 330)

Wechsler, H., Lee, J. E., Kuo, M., Seibring, M., Nelson, T. F., & Lee, H. (2002). Trends in college binge drinking during a period of increased prevention efforts. *Journal of American College Health, 50,* 203–217. (p. 330)

Weinberger, D. R. (2001, March 10). A brain too young for good judgment. *New York Times* (www.nytimes.com). (p. 82)

Weingarten, G. (2002, March 10). Below the beltway. *Washington Post,* p. W03. (p. 411)

Weinstein, N. D. (1980). Unrealistic optimism about future life events. *Journal of Personality and Social Psychology, 39,* 806–820. (p. 283)

Weinstein, N. D. (1982). Unrealistic optimism about susceptibility to health problems. *Journal of Behavioral Medicine, 5,* 441–460. (p. 283)

Weinstein, N. D. (1996, October 4). 1996 optimistic bias bibliography. (weinstein_c@aesop.rutgers.edu). (p. 283)

Weisbuch, M., Ivcevic, Z., & Ambady, N. (2009). On being liked on the web and in the "real world": Consistency in first impressions across personal webpages and spontaneous behavior. *Journal of Experimental Social Psychology, 45,* 573-576. (p. 251)

Weissman, M. M., Bland, R. C., Canino, G. J., Faravelli, C., Greenwald, S., Hwu, H-G., Joyce, P. R., Karam, E. G., Lee, C-K., Lellouch, J., Lepine, J-P., Newman, S. C., Rubio-Stepic, M., Wells, J. E., Wickramaratne, P. J., Wittchen, H-U., & Yeh, E-K. (1996). Cross-national epidemiology of major depression and bipolar disorder. *Journal of the American Medical Association, 276,* 293–299. (p. 341)

Welch, W. W. (2005, February 28). Trauma of Iraq war haunting thousands returning home. *USA Today* (www.usatoday.com). (p. 324)

Wellings, K., Collumbien, M., Slaymaker, E., Singh, S., Hodges, Z., Patel, D., & Bajos, N. (2006). Sexual behaviour in context: A global perspective. *Lancet, 368,* 1706–1728. (p. 107)

Wellman, H. M., & Gelman, S. A. (1992). Cognitive development: Foundational theories of core domains. *Annual Review of Psychology, 43,* 337–375. (p. 73)

Wells, G. L. (1981). Lay analyses of causal forces on behavior. In J. Harvey (Ed.), *Cognition, social behavior and the environment.* Hillsdale, NJ: Erlbaum. (p. 156)

Wender, P. H., Kety, S. S., Rosenthal, D., Schulsinger, F., Ortmann, J., & Lunde, I. (1986). Psychiatric disorders in the biological and adoptive families of adopted individuals with affective disorders. *Archives of General Psychiatry, 43,* 923–929. (p. 341)

Wener, R., Frazier, W., & Farbstein, J. (1987, June). Building better jails. *Psychology Today,* pp. 40–49. (p. 281)

Westen, D. (1996). Is Freud really dead? Teaching psychodynamic theory to introductory psychology. Presentation to the Annual Institute on the Teaching of Psychology, St. Petersburg Beach, FL. (p. 297)

Westen, D. (1998). The scientific legacy of Sigmund Freud: Toward a psychodynamically informed psychological science. *Psychological Bulletin, 124,* 333–371. (p. 299)

Westen, D. (2007). *The political brain: The role of emotion in deciding the fate of the nation.* New York: PublicAffairs. (p. 259)

Whalen, P. J., Kagan, J., Cook, R. G., Davis, F. C., Kim, H., Polis, S., McLaren, D. G., Somerville, L. H., McLean, A. A., Maxwell, J. S., & Johnstone, T. (2004). Human amygdala responsibility to masked fearful eye whites. *Science, 302,* 2061. (pp. 258, 259)

White, G. L., & Kight, T. D. (1984). Misattribution of arousal and attraction: Effects of salience of explanations for arousal. *Journal of Experimental Social Psychology, 20,* 55–64. (p. 401)

White, H. R., Brick, J., & Hansell, S. (1993). A longitudinal investigation of alcohol use and aggression in adolescence. *Journal of Studies on Alcohol,* Supplement No. 11, 62–77. (p. 394)

White, L., & Edwards, J. (1990). Emptying the nest and parental well-being: An analysis of national panel data. *American Sociological Review, 55,* 235–242. (p. 93)

White, P. H., Kjelgaard, M. M., & Harkins, S. G. (1995). Testing the contribution of self-evaluation to goal-setting effects. *Journal of Personality and Social Psychology, 69,* 69–79. (p. 416)

Whitehead, B. D., & Popenoe, D. (2001). *The state of our unions 2001: The social health of marriage in America.* Rutgers University: The National Marriage Project. (p. 93)

Whiten, A., & Boesch, C. (2001, January). Cultures of chimpanzees. *Scientific American,* pp. 60–67. (p. 216)

Whiting, B. B., & Edwards, C. P. (1988). *Children of different worlds: The formation of social behavior.* Cambridge, MA: Harvard University Press. (p. 79)

Whitlock, J. R., Heynen, A. L., Shuler, M. G., & Bear, M. F. (2006). Learning induces long-term potentiation in the hippocampus. *Science, 313,* 1093–1097. (p. 188)

WHO. (1979). *Schizophrenia: An international followup study.* Chicester, England: Wiley. (p. 344)

WHO. (2001). *The World Health report 2001. Mental health: New understanding, new hope.* Geneva: World Health Organization. (www.who.int). (p. 339)

WHO. (2004). *Women, girls, HIV, and AIDS.* World Health Organization, Western Pacific Regional Office. (p. 108)

WHO. (2007, accessed December 11). *Obesity and overweight.* http://www.who.int/dietphysicalactivity/publications/facts/obesity/en/. (p. 244)

WHO. (2008a). *Mental health (nearly 1 million annual suicide deaths).* Geneva: World Health Organization. (www.who.int/mental_health/en). (p. 339)

WHO. (2008b). *Schizophrenia.* Geneva: World Health Organization. (www.who.int). (pp. 316, 344)

WHO. (2008c). *WHO report on the global tobacco epidemic, 2008.* Geneva: World Health Organization. (www.who.int). (p. 332)

Wickelgren, I. (2005). Autistic brains out of sync? *Science, 308,* 1856–1858. (p. 74)

Wickelgren, W. A. (1977). *Learning and memory.* Englewood Cliffs, NJ: Prentice-Hall. (p. 187)

Widom, C. S. (1989a). Does violence beget violence? A critical examination of the literature. *Psychological Bulletin, 106,* 3–28. (p. 78)

Widom, C. S. (1989b). The cycle of violence. *Science, 244,* 160–166. (p. 78)

Wiens, A. N., & Menustik, C. E. (1983). Treatment outcome and patient characteristics in an aversion therapy program for alcoholism. *American Psychologist, 38,* 1089–1096. (p. 357)

Wierson, M., & Forehand, R. (1994). Parent behavioral training for child noncompliance: Rationale, concepts, and effectiveness. *Current Directions in Psychological Science, 3,* 146–149. (p. 168)

Wierzbicki, M. (1993). Psychological adjustment of adoptees: A meta-analysis. *Journal of Clinical Child Psychology, 22,* 447–454. (p. 86)

Wiesel, T. N. (1982). Postnatal development of the visual cortex and the influence of environment. *Nature, 299,* 583–591 (p. 138)

Wigdor, A. K., & Garner, W. R. (1982). *Ability testing: Uses, consequences, and controversies.* Washington, DC: National Academy Press. (p. 231)

Wilcox, A. J., Baird, D. D., Dunson, D. B., McConnaughey, D. R., Kesner, J. S., & Weinberg, C. R. (2004). On the frequency of intercourse around ovulation: Evidence for biological influences. *Human Reproduction, 19,* 1539–1543. (p. 107)

Wilder, D. A. (1981). Perceiving persons as a group: Categorization and intergroup relations. In D. L. Hamilton (Ed.), *Cognitive processes in stereotyping and intergroup behavior.* Hillsdale, NJ: Erlbaum. (p. 392)

Williams, J. E., & Best, D. L. (1990). *Measuring sex stereotypes: A multination study.* Newbury Park, CA: Sage. (p. 102)

Williams, J. E., Paton, C. C., Siegler, I. C., Eigenbrodt, M. L., Nieto, F. J., & Tyroler, H. A. (2000). Anger proneness predicts coronary heart disease risk: Prospective analysis from the artherosclerosis risk in communities (ARIC) study. *Circulation, 101*(17), 2034–2040. (p. 279)

Williams, J. H. G., Waister, G. D., Gilchrist, A., Perrett, D. I., Murray, A. D., & Whiten, A. (2006). Neural mechanisms of imitation and 'mirror neuron' functioning in autistic spectrum disorder. *Neuropsychogia, 44,* 610–621. (p. 174)

Williams, K. D. (2007). Ostracism. *Annual Review of Psychology, 58,* 425–452. (p. 249)

Williams, K. D. (2009). Ostracism: A temporal need-threat model. *Advances in Experimental Social Psychology, 41,* 275–313. (p. 249)

Williams, K. D., & Zadro, L. (2001). Ostracism: On being ignored, excluded and rejected. In M. Leary (Ed.), *Rejection.* New York: Oxford University Press. (p. 250)

Williams, L. E., & Bargh, J. A. (2008). Experiencing physical warmth promotes interpersonal warmth. *Science, 322,* 606–607. (p. 146)

Williams, L. M., Brown, K. J., Palmer, D., Liddell, B. J., Kemp, A. H., Olivieri, G., Peduto, A., & Gordon, E. (2006). The mellow years? Neural basis of improving emotional stability over age. *Journal of Neuroscience, 26,* 6422–6430. (p. 95)

Williams, R. (1993). *Anger kills.* New York: Times Books. (p. 279)

Williams, S. L. (1987). Self-efficacy and mastery-oriented treatment for severe phobias. Paper presented to the American Psychological Association convention. (p. 356)

Willingham, D. T. (2010, Summer). Have technology and multitasking rewired how students learn? *American Educator, 42,* 23–28. (p. 252)

Willmuth, M. E. (1987). Sexuality after spinal cord injury: A critical review. *Clinical Psychology Review, 7,* 389–412. (p. 111)

Wilson, A. E., & Ross, M. (2001). From chump to champ: People's appraisals of their earlier and present selves. *Journal of Personality and Social Psychology, 80,* 572–584. (p. 311)

Wilson, C. M., & Oswald, A. J. (2002). How does marriage affect physical and psychological health? A survey of the longitudinal evidence. Working paper, University of York and Warwick University. (p. 284)

Wilson, D. B., & Shadish, W. R. (2006). On blowing trumpets to the tulips: To prove or not to prove the null hypothesis—Comment on Bösch, Steinkamp, and Boller (2006). *Psychological Bulletin, 132,* 524–528. (p. 150)

Wilson, R. S. (1979). Analysis of longitudinal twin data: Basic model and applications to physical growth measures. *Acta Geneticae medicae et Gemellologiae, 28,* 93–105. (p. 71)

Wilson, R. S., Beck, T. L., Bienias, J. L., & Bennett, D. A. (2007). Terminal cognitive decline: Accelerated loss of cognition in the last years of life. *Psychosomatic Medicine, 69,* 131–137. (p. 92)

Wilson, T. D. (2006). The power of social psychological interventions. *Science, 313,* 1251–1252. (p. 232)

Windholz, G. (1989, April-June). The discovery of the principles of reinforcement, extinction, generalization, and differentiation of conditional reflexes in Pavlov's laboratories. *Pavlovian Journal of Biological Science, 26,* 64–74. (p. 160)

Windholz, G. (1997). Ivan P. Pavlov: An overview of his life and psychological work. *American Psychologist, 52,* 941–946. (p. 158)

Wiseman, R. (2002). *Laugh Lab—final results.* University of Hertfordshire (www.laughlab.co.uk). (p. 206)

Witvliet, C. V. O., & Vrana, S. R. (1995). Psychophysiological responses as indices of affective dimensions. *Psychophysiology, 32,* 436–443. (p. 256)

Witvliet, C. V. O., Ludwig, T., & Vander Laan, K. (2001). Granting forgiveness or harboring grudges: Implications for emotions, physiology, and health. *Psychological Science, 12,* 117–123. (p. 264)

Wixted, J. T., & Ebbesen, E. B. (1991). On the form of forgetting. *Psychological Science, 2,* 409–415. (p. 193)

Wolfson, A. R., & Carskadon, M. A. (1998). Sleep schedules and daytime functioning in adolescents. *Child Development, 69,* 875–887. (p. 57)

Wolitzky-Taylor, K. B., Horowitz, J. D., Powers, M. B., & Telch, M. J. (2008). Psychological approaches in the treatment of specific phobias: A meta-analysis. *Clinical Psychology Review, 28,* 1021–1037. (p. 356)

Woll, S. (1986). So many to choose from: Decision strategies in videodating. *Journal of Social and Personal Relationships, 3,* 43–52. (p. 399)

Wolpe, J. (1958). *Psychotherapy by reciprocal inhibition.* Stanford, CA: Stanford University Press. (p. 356)

Wolpe, J., & Plaud, J. J. (1997). Pavlov's contributions to behavior therapy: The obvious and the not so obvious. *American Psychologist, 52,* 966–972. (p. 356)

Wong, D. F., Wagner, H. N., Tune, L. E., Dannals, R. F., & others. (1986). Positron emission tomography reveals elevated D2 dopamine receptors in drug-naive schizophrenics. *Science, 234,* 1588–1593. (p. 345)

Wong, M. M., & Csikszentmihalyi, M. (1991). Affiliation motivation and daily experience: Some issues on gender differences. *Journal of Personality and Social Psychology, 60,* 154–164. (p. 103)

Wood, J. M. (2003, May 19). Quoted by R. Mestel, Rorschach tested: Blot out the famous method? Some experts say it has no place in psychiatry. *Los Angeles Times* (www.latimes.com). (p. 298)

Wood, J. M., Bootzin, R. R., Kihlstrom, J. F., & Schacter, D. L. (1992). Implicit and explicit memory for verbal information presented during sleep. *Psychological Science, 3,* 236–239. (p. 194)

Wood, J. M., Nezworski, M. T., Garb, H. N., & Lilienfeld, S. O. (2006). The controversy over the Exner Comprehensive System and the Society for Personality Assessment's white paper on the Rorschach. *Independent Practitioner,* pp. 26. (p. 298)

Wood, J. N., Glynn, D. D., Phillips, B. C., & Hauser, M. C. (2007). The perception of rational, goal-directed action in nonhuman primates. *Science, 317,* 1402–1405. (p. 217)

Wood, W. (1987). Meta-analytic review of sex differences in group performance. *Psychological Bulletin, 102,* 53–71. (p. 102)

Wood, W., & Eagly, A. (2002). A cross-cultural analysis of the behavior of women and men: Implications for the origins of sex differences. *Psychological Bulletin, 128,* 699–727. (pp. 100, 102, 118)

Wood, W., & Eagly, A. H. (2007). Social structural origins of sex differences in human mating. In S. W. Gagestad & J. A. Simpson (Eds.), *The evolution of mind: Fundamental questions and controversies.* New York: Guilford Press. (p. 102)

Wood, W., & Neal, D. T. (2007, October). A new look at habits and the habit-goal interface. *Psychological Review, 114,* 843–863. (p. 156)

Wood, W., Lundgren, S., Ouellette, J. A., Busceme, S., & Blackstone, T. (1994). Minority influence: A meta-analytic review of social influence processes. *Psychological Bulletin, 115,* 323–345. (p. 386)

Woods, N. F., Dery, G. K., & Most, A. (1983). Recollections of menarche, current menstrual attitudes, and premenstrual symptoms. In S. Golub (Ed.), *Menarche: The transition from girl to woman.* Lexington, MA: Lexington Books. (p. 81)

World Health Organization. (2000). *Global strategy for infant and young child feeding.* Geneva: WHO. (p. 16)

Wortham, J. (2010, May 13). Cellphones now used more for data than for calls. *New York Times* (www.nytimes.com). (p. 250)

Worthington, E. L., Jr. (1989). Religious faith across the life span: Implications for counseling and research. *The Counseling Psychologist, 17,* 555–612. (p. 82)

Worthington, E. L., Jr., Kurusu, T. A., McCullogh, M. E., & Sandage, S. J. (1996). Empirical research on religion and psychotherapeutic processes and outcomes: A 10-year review and research prospectus. *Psychological Bulletin, 119,* 448–487. (p. 364)

Wortman, C. B., & Silver, R. C. (1989). The myths of coping with loss. *Journal of Consulting and Clinical Psychology, 57,* 349–357. (p. 94)

Wren, C. S. (1999, April 8). Drug survey of children finds middle school a pivotal time. *New York Times* (www.nytimes.com). (p. 337)

Wright, I. C., Rabe-Hesketh, S., Woodruff, P. W. R., David, A. S., Murray, R. M., & Bullmore, E. T. (2000). Meta-analysis of regional brain volumes in schizophrenia. *American Journal of Psychiatry, 157,* 16–25. (p. 345)

Wright, P., Takei, N., Rifkin, L., & Murray, R. M. (1995). Maternal influenza, obstetric complications, and schizophrenia. *American Journal of Psychiatry, 152,* 1714–1720. (p. 345)

Wrosch, C., & Miller, G. E. (2009). Depressive symptoms can be useful: Self-regulatory and emotional benefits of dysphoric mood in adolescence. *Journal of Personality and Social Psychology, 96,* 1181–1190. (p. 338)

Wrzesniewski, A., & Dutton, J. E. (2001). Crafting a job: Revisioning employees as active crafters of their work. *Academy of Management Review, 26,* 179–201. (p. 411)

Wrzesniewski, A., McCauley, C. R., Rozin, P., & Schwartz, B. (1997). Jobs, careers, and callings: People's relations to their work. *Journal of Research in Personality, 31,* 21–33. (p. 411)

Wuethrich, B. (2001, March). Features—GETTING STUPID—Surprising new neurological behavioral research reveals that teenagers who drink too much may permanently damage their brains and seriously compromise their ability to learn. *Discover, 56,* 56–64. (p. 331)

Wulsin, L. R., Vaillant, G. E., & Wells, V. E. (1999). A systematic review of the mortality of depression. *Psychosomatic Medicine, 61,* 6–17. (p. 280)

Wyatt, J. K., & Bootzin, R. R. (1994). Cognitive processing and sleep: Implications for enhancing job performance. *Human Performance, 7,* 119–139. (p. 194)

Wynne, C. (2008). Aping language: A skeptical analysis of the evidence for nonhuman primate language. *Skeptic, 13*(4), 10–13. (p. 217)

Wynne, C. D. L. (2004). *Do animals think?* Princeton, NJ: Princeton University Press. (p. 217)

Xu, Y., & Corkin, S. (2001). H.M. revisits the Tower of Hanoi puzzle. *Neuropsychology, 15,* 69–79. (p. 185)

Yamagata, S., & 11 others. (2006). Is the genetic structure of human personality universal? A cross-cultural twin study from North America, Europe, and Asia. *Journal of Personality and Social Psychology, 90,* 987–998. (p. 305)

Yang, S., Markoczy, L., & Qi, M. (2006). Unrealistic optimism in consumer credit card adoption. *Journal of Economic Psychology, 28,* 170–185. (p. 284)

Yarnell, P. R., & Lynch, S. (1970, April 25). Retrograde memory immediately after concussion. *Lancet,* 863–865. (p. 188)

Ybarra, O. (1999). Misanthropic person memory when the need to self-enhance is absent. *Personality and Social Psychology Bulletin, 25,* 261–269. (p. 310)

Yirmiya, N., Erel, O., Shaken, M., & Solomonica-Levi, D. (1998). Meta-analyses comparing theory of mind abilities of individuals with autism, individuals with mental retardation, and normally developing individuals. *Psychological Bulletin, 124,* 283–307. (p. 74)

Youngentob, S. L., Kent, P. F., Scheehe, P. R., Molina, J. C., Spear, N. E., & Youngentob, L. M. (2007). Experience-induced fetal plasticity: The effect of gestational ethanol exposure on the behavioral and neurophysiologic olfactory response to ethanol odor in early postnatal and adult rats. *Behavioral Neuroscience, 121,* 1293–1305. (p. 66)

Zaccaro, S. J. (2007). Triat-based perspectives of leadership. *American Psychologist, 62,* 6–16. (p. 416)

Zajonc, R. B. (1965). Social facilitation. *Science, 149,* 269–274. (p. 386)

Zajonc, R. B. (1980). Feeling and thinking: Preferences need no inferences. *American Psychologist, 35,* 151–175. (p. 258)

Zajonc, R. B. (1984a). On the primacy of affect. *American Psychologist, 39,* 117–123. (p. 258)

Zajonc, R. B. (1984b, July 22). Quoted by D. Goleman, Rethinking IQ tests and their value. *The New York Times,* p. D22. (p. 225)

Zajonc, R. B. (1998). Emotions. In D. Gilbert, S. T. Fiske, & G. Lindzey (Eds.), *Handbook of social psychology* (4th ed.). New York: McGraw-Hill. (p. 398)

Zajonc, R. B. (2001). Mere exposure: A gateway to the subliminal. *Current Directions in Psychological Science, 10,* 224–228. (p. 397)

Zammit, S., Rasmussen, F., Farahmand, B., Gunnell, D., Lewis, G., Tynelius, P., & Brobert, G. P. (2007). Height and body mass index in young adulthood and risk of schizophrenia: A longitudinal study of 1,347,520 Swedish men. *Acta Psychiatrica Scandinavica, 116,* 378–385. (p. 344)

Zauberman, G., & Lynch, J. G., Jr. (2005). Resource slack and propensity to discount delayed investments of time versus money. *Journal of Experimental Psychology: General, 134,* 23–37. (p. 209)

Zeidner, M. (1990). Perceptions of ethnic group modal intelligence: Reflections of cultural stereotypes or intelligence test scores? *Journal of Cross-Cultural Psychology, 21,* 214–231. (p. 228)

Zhong, C. B., & Leonardelli, G. J. (2008). Cold and lonely: Does social exclusion literally feel cold? *Psychological Science, 19,* 838–842. (p. 146)

Zietsch, B. P., Morley, K. I., Shekar, S. N., Verweij, K. J. H., Keller, M. C., Macgregor, S., Wright, M. J., Bailey, J. M., & Martin, N. G. (2008). Genetic factors predisposing to homosexuality may increase mating success in heterosexuals. *Evolution and Human Behavior, 29,* 424–433. (p. 114)

Zilbergeld, B. (1983). *The shrinking of America: Myths of psychological change.* Boston: Little, Brown. (p. 361)

Zillmann, D. (1986). Effects of prolonged consumption of pornography. Background paper for *The surgeon general's workshop on pornography and public health,* June 22–24. Report prepared by E. P. Mulvey & J. L. Haugaard and released by Office of the Surgeon General on August 4, 1986. (p. 256)

Zillmann, D. (1989). Effects of prolonged consumption of pornography. In D. Zillmann & J. Bryant (Eds.), *Pornography: Research advances and policy considerations.* Hillsdale, NJ: Erlbaum. (pp. 111, 395)

Zillmann, D., & Bryant, J. (1984). Effects of massive exposure to pornography. In N. Malamuth & E. Donnerstein (Eds.), *Pornography and sexual aggression.* Orlando, FL: Academic Press. (p. 396)

Zimbardo, P. G. (1970). The human choice: Individuation, reason, and order versus deindividuation, impulse, and chaos. In W. J. Arnold & D. Levine (Eds.), *Nebraska Symposium on Motivation, 1969.* Lincoln, NE: University of Nebraska Press. (p. 388)

Zimbardo, P. G. (1972, April). Pathology of imprisonment. *Transaction/Society,* pp. 4–8. (p. 380)

Zimbardo, P. G. (2001, September 16). Fighting terrorism by understanding man's capacity for evil. Op-ed essay distributed by spsp-discuss@stolaf.edu. (p. 392)

Zimbardo, P. G. (2004, May 25). Journalist interview re: Abu Ghraib prison abuses: Eleven answers to eleven questions. Unpublished manuscript, Stanford University. (p. 380)

Zimbardo, P. G. (2007, September). Person x situation x system dynamics. *The Observer* (Association for Psychological Science), p. 43. (pp. 380, 381)

Zimmer-Gembeck, M. J., & Helfand, M. (2008). Ten years of longitudinal research on U.S. adolescent sexual behavior: Developmental correlates of sexual intercourse, and the importance of age, gender and ethnic background. *Developmental Review, 28,* 153–224. (p. 109)

Zogby, J. (2006, March). Survey of teens and adults about the use of personal electronic devices and head phones. *Zogby International.* (p. 140)

Zornberg, G. L., Buka, S. L., & Tsuang, M. T. (2000). At issue: The problem of obstetrical complications and schizophrenia. *Schizophrenia Bulletin, 26,* 249–256. (p. 345)

Zou, Z., & Buck, L. B. (2006, Mar.). Combinatorial effects of odorant mixes in olfactory cortex. *Science, 311,* 1477-1481. (p. 146)

Zubieta, J-K., Heitzeg, M. M., Smith, Y. R., Bueller, J. A., Xu, K., Xu, Y., Koeppe, R. A., Stohler, C. S., & Goldman, D. (2003). COMT val158met genotype affects μ-opioid neurotransmitter responses to a pain stressor. *Science, 299,* 1240–1243. (p. 143)

Zucker, G. S., & Weiner, B. (1993). Conservatism and perceptions of poverty: An attributional analysis. *Journal of Applied Social Psychology, 23,* 925–943. (p. 379)

Zuckerman, M. (1979). *Sensation seeking: Beyond the optimal level of arousal.* Hillsdale, NJ: Erlbaum. (p. 238)

Zvolensky, M. J., & Bernstein, A. (2005). Cigarette smoking and panic psychopathology. *Current Directions in Psychological Science, 14,* 301–305. (p. 323)

A

Absent-mindedness, forgetting and, 193
Absolute thresholds, 124–125
Abu Ghraib prison, 380
Acetylcholine (ACh), 30
Achievement, 223
Achievement motivation, 413
Acquired immunodeficiency syndrome (AIDS),
    stress and, 278
Acquisition, in classical conditioning, 158–159,
    160
Action(s)
    affecting attitudes, 379–381
    attitudes affecting, 379
    moral, 83
    prejudice and, 390
Action potentials, 28
Activation-synthesis theory of dreaming, 58
Active listening, 354–355
Acute schizophrenia, 344
Adaptation, sensory, 126–127
Adaptation-level phenomenon, 267
Addiction, 329
ADHD (attention-deficit hyperactivity
    disorder), 318
Adolescence, 81–88
    cognitive development in, 82–83
    continuity and stages and, 87–88
    emerging adulthood and, 87
    physical development in, 81–82
    pregnancy in, 109–110
    social development in, 83–87
Adoption studies, 68
    of intelligence, 226–227
    of parenting effects on children's successes,
        86
Adrenal glands, 34
Adrenaline, 34
Adulthood, 89–96
    cognitive development in, 91–92
    commitments of, 92–94
    emerging, 87
    late, 90–91
    middle, 90
    physical development in, 89–91

social development in, 92–96
    young, 89
Aerobic exercise,
    cognitive function and aging and, 92
    depression and, 367
    happiness levels and, 268, 269
    obesity and, 246
    for stress management, 285–286
    in therapeutic life-style change, 371, 372
    for weight control, 248
Age. *See also* Adolescence; Adulthood;
    Infancy and childhood
    mental, 223
Aggression, 393–397
    biology of, 393–394
    gender and, 102
    media violence and, 176–177
    psychology of, 394–397
    video games and, 396
Aggression-replacement program, 395
Aging
    intelligence and, 92
    memory and, 91–92
Agoraphobia, 323
AIDS, stress and, 278
Alcohol, 330–331
    aggression and, 394
    dependence on, 330–331
    effects of, 330, 335
    sleep and, 55
    teen sexual behavior and, 109
    teratogenic effects of, 66
Algorithms, 206, 211
All-or-none response, 29
Alpha waves, 51
Altruism, 402–404
    bystander intervention and, 403–404
American Psychological Association (APA), 2
    on death penalty for adolescents, 82
    ethics code of, 20
Amphetamines, 332
Amplitude
    of light waves, 130
    of sound waves, 140
Amygdala, 37–38

Anal stage, 296
Analysis, levels of, 6
Anger, 263–264
Angular gyrus, 44
The Animal Mind (Washburn), 2
Animals
    language in, 217–218
    research using, 19–20
    same-sex attraction in, 113
    thinking in, 216–217
Anorexia nervosa, 243, 319
ANS (autonomic nervous system), 31–32
    emotion and, 254–255
Antianxiety drugs, 367
Antidepressant drugs, 367–368
Antipsychotic drugs, 366–367
Antisocial behavior, observational learning
    and, 175–176
Antisocial personality disorder, 327–328
Anxiety
    free-floating, 322
    stranger, 75–76
Anxiety disorders, 322–326
    biological perspective on, 325–326
    generalized anxiety disorder, 322
    learning perspective on, 324–325
    obsessive-compulsive disorder, 323–324
    panic disorder, 323
    phobias, 323
    post-traumatic stress disorder (PTSD), 324
    treatment of, 367
APA. *See* American Psychological Association
    (APA)
Appetite. *See* Hunger
Aptitude, 223
Arousal theory, 238
Association areas, 42–43
Associative learning, 156. *See also* Classical
    conditioning; Conditioning; Operant
    conditioning
Astrology, 306
Attachment, 76–78
    deprivation of, 78
    differences in, 77
    styles of, later relationships and, 77–78

Continued from inside front cover.

Why can't we remember learning to talk and walk? **p. 199**

Which sounds more tempting, a hamburger that is "75 percent lean" or "25 percent fat"? **p. 210**

Can we use mental rehearsal to help reach our academic goals? **p. 215**

How many teen cell-phone users were texting in 2009? **p. 250**

Can our outward expressions and movements affect our inner feelings and emotions? **p. 262**

Do lonely people use social networks to fill their social void? Do online relationships divert time from existing "real-world" relationships? **p. 250**

Should children be told to "vent" angry feelings? **p. 263**

Could reducing stress help control AIDS? **p. 278**

Who really copes better with stress—optimists or pessimists? **p. 283**

Do men and women think alike? **p. 230**

Are there gender differences in empathy? **p. 260**

Are intelligence tests biased for or against some people? **p. 231**

Do facial expressions have different meanings in different cultures? **p. 261**